ASIA'S NEW GIANT

HUGH PATRICK AND HENRY ROSOVSKY

Editors

WITHDRAWN
ASIA'S NEW GIANT
How the Japanese Economy Works

HUGH PATRICK AND HENRY ROSOVSKY

EDWARD F. DENISON AND WILLIAM K. CHUNG

GARDNER ACKLEY AND HIROMITSU ISHI

HENRY C. WALLICH AND MABLE I. WALLICH

JOSEPH A. PECHMAN AND KEIMEI KAIZUKA

LAWRENCE B. KRAUSE AND SUEO SEKIGUCHI

RICHARD E. CAVES WITH THE COLLABORATION OF MASU UEKUSA

MERTON J. PECK WITH THE COLLABORATION OF SHŪJI TAMURA

WALTER GALENSON WITH THE COLLABORATION OF KONOSUKE ODAKA

EDWIN S. MILLS AND KATSUTOSHI OHTA

PHILIP H. TREZISE WITH THE COLLABORATION OF YUKIO SUZUKI

NATHAN GLAZER

THE BROOKINGS INSTITUTION
Washington, D.C.

Library of Congress Cataloging in Publication Data:

Main entry under title:
Asia's new giant.
Includes bibliographical references and index.
1. Japan—Economic policy—1945–
2. Japan—Economic conditions—1945–
3. Japan—Social conditions—1945–
I. Patrick, Hugh T.
II. Rosovsky, Henry.
HC462.9.A84   330.9′52′04   75-42304
ISBN 0-8157-6934-2
ISBN 0-8157-6933-4 pbk.

1 2 3 4 5 6 7 8 9

THE BROOKINGS INSTITUTION is an independent organization devoted to nonpartisan research, education, and publication in economics, government, foreign policy, and the social sciences generally. Its principal purposes are to aid in the development of sound public policies and to promote public understanding of issues of national importance.

The Institution was founded on December 8, 1927, to merge the activities of the Institute for Government Research, founded in 1916, the Institute of Economics, founded in 1922, and the Robert Brookings Graduate School of Economics and Government, founded in 1924.

The Board of Trustees is responsible for the general administration of the Institution, while the immediate direction of the policies, program, and staff is vested in the President, assisted by an advisory committee of the officers and staff. The by-laws of the Institution state: "It is the function of the Trustees to make possible the conduct of scientific research, and publication, under the most favorable conditions, and to safeguard the independence of the research staff in the pursuit of their studies and in the publication of the results of such studies. It is not a part of their function to determine, control, or influence the conduct of particular investigations or the conclusions reached."

The President bears final responsibility for the decision to publish a manuscript as a Brookings book. In reaching his judgment on the competence, accuracy, and objectivity of each study, the President is advised by the director of the appropriate research program and weighs the views of a panel of expert outside readers who report to him in confidence on the quality of the work. Publication of a work signifies that it is deemed a competent treatment worthy of public consideration but does not imply endorsement of conclusions or recommendations.

The Institution maintains its position of neutrality on issues of public policy in order to safeguard the intellectual freedom of the staff. Hence interpretations or conclusions in Brookings publications should be understood to be solely those of the authors and should not be attributed to the Institution, to its trustees, officers, or other staff members, or to the organizations that support its research.

Foreword

IMAGES of one country usually change very slowly in the mind of another. Thus it is remarkable that in a span of a decade or so, the popular image of Japan has changed from that of a struggling country requiring U.S. economic help and protection to that of the leading challenger of American economic prowess and competitive strength. Furthermore, the reality of change was even more dramatic than the perception. Japan emerged from the widespread destruction of the Second World War to become the world's third largest industrial country in less than twenty-five years. In a span of only five years, from 1965 to 1970, Japan actually doubled its industrial capital stock—a feat never before accomplished by an advanced industrial country. In international trade, Japan shifted from being mainly a provider of labor-intensive products, such as textiles, pottery, and Christmas tree ornaments, to being the world's leading exporter of steel, ships, optical equipment, and consumer electronics and a leading contender in heavy machinery and sophisticated business machines. Similarly, Japan changed from being a country with a weak international balance of payments to being one with the strongest, from a borrower in international money markets to a considerable lender to other countries.

The Japanese miracle clearly invites detailed economic analysis. Though the studies leading to the publication of this book began in 1972, the Institution's interest in the subject can be traced back to a 1969 visit to Japan by one of its senior economists to attend a conference and his astonishment at what he found about him. Vast and detailed literature on the Japanese economy does exist, but it is in the Japanese language and well-nigh inaccessible to the Western world. Consequently, Americans, Europeans, and others interested in understanding one of the most significant developments in postwar economic history have had to rely on translations (often of poor quality), the writings of a few Western specialists, and sketchy newspaper and magazine coverage.

This book helps to fill the gap. It adds to the literature on the Japanese economy accessible to readers of English by explaining how the Japanese have managed their economy during the last twenty years and assessing Japan's present and future economic prospects. Its main purpose is to contribute to better informed policymaking toward Japan in both the public and the private sectors.

This book is in some ways similar to an earlier Brookings study published in 1968, *Britain's Economic Prospects,* by Richard E. Caves and ten associates. In that project, as in this, a group of leading U.S. social analysts was assembled to make an intensive study, each in his own field of expertise, of recent developments in a single nation and to evaluate that nation's performance. Unlike Caves and his associates, however, the group that prepared the present volume includes members not previously familiar with the country in question. Although the project directors, Hugh Patrick of Yale University and Henry Rosovsky of Harvard University, are noted experts on the Japanese economy, the other American authors were without earlier exposure to Japan or specialized knowledge of the structure and behavior of its economy. The impossibility of assembling in the United States a group consisting entirely of experts on Japanese economic affairs of a stature matching that of the project directors is evidence of the lag between Japanese economic accomplishment and Western understanding.

The project was organized with the cooperation of a Japanese Advisory Committee comprising Dr. Saburo Okita, then president and now chairman of the board of the Japan Economic Research Center, Professor Kazushi Ohkawa of Hitotsubashi University, and Professor Tsunehiko Watanabe of Osaka University. Also, with three exceptions, each U.S. author was paired with a younger Japanese scholar to encourage cooperative research and to enable the American partners to overcome obstacles, such as the language barrier, associated with working in an unfamiliar cultural setting. Each U.S. author made at least one extensive research trip to Japan, and several of the Japanese scholars visited their collaborators in the United States.

Apart from the contribution to knowledge represented by the publication of this study, the project has added eleven American scholars to the roster of those well acquainted with Japan. This diffusion of expertise among U.S. economists constitutes a by-product of the project whose value will increase as time passes.

The Brookings Institution and the authors express their appreciation to the Japan Economic Research Center for its cooperation throughout the project. The Center was host to the U.S. authors during their visits to Japan, helped select and organize the Japanese collaborators, and assisted in arranging interviews for the authors with knowledgeable Japanese government officials and private citizens. The authors' research benefited greatly from the close association between Brookings and the Center.

The authors also acknowledge with gratitude the cooperation they received from various organizations and from many persons in government, business, labor unions, and the universities. (Individual acknowledgements appear in each chapter.) Without such assistance, the authors could not have carried out their tasks.

The book was edited by Ellen A. Ash, with the assistance of other members of the Brookings publications staff. The risk of factual error was reduced by Genevieve B. Wimsatt, who verified source data and references. The indexes were prepared by Florence Robinson.

The project was supported by a grant from the Andrew W. Mellon Foundation. Funds were also provided by the Bureau of Economic Analysis of the U.S. Department of Commerce for preparing the estimates of the sources of Japanese economic growth presented in Chapter 2.

The views expressed in this book are those of its contributors, and should not be ascribed to the staff members, officers, or trustees of the Brookings Institution, to the Andrew W. Mellon Foundation, or to the Bureau of Economic Analysis.

KERMIT GORDON
President

December 1975
Washington, D.C.

Contents

ASIA'S NEW GIANT

CHAPTER ONE

Japan's Economic Performance: An Overview

Hugh Patrick, Yale University
and
Henry Rosovsky, Harvard University

1

Tables

Figure

JAPAN'S SURGE over the past quarter-century, seemingly from nowhere, to join the vanguard of the world's economies has been an unprecedented, exciting, and at times disruptive event. By any economic criteria Japan is now an immense, rich nation. Since the mid-1960s it has ranked third in total gross national product (GNP), still substantially behind the United States and Russia, but somewhat ahead of West Germany, France, and all other nations; in 1973 its GNP was about $400 billion. This output was produced and used by some 108 million Japanese citizens, a figure that is about double the population of major European nations. Thus, by 1973 GNP per capita was about $3,700, more than that of Italy and the United Kingdom, though still somewhat less than that of West Germany and France, and only three-fifths that of the United States level.[1] Living standards were relatively lower in Japan, where a smaller proportion of production is devoted to private consumption and to the provision of public services, yet certainly in most respects they are comparable to those in Western Europe.

In a historical perspective, wealth and economic strength have been achieved rapidly indeed. The Japanese postwar rate of growth is unprecedented, though the economic performance during the 1960s of such developing countries as South Korea, Taiwan, and Brazil suggests that the Japanese rate may not be unique. Nonetheless, between 1951 and 1973 the Japanese economy grew at an average annual rate of 10 percent in real terms, which represents a seven-and-a-half-fold increase in the size of real GNP. What makes this economic performance even more impressive is that it has occurred in a nation geographically small relative to its population,[2] and with very limited natural resources. Data comparing Japan's overall economic performance with that of Western Europe and the United States appear in Table 1-1.[3]

Note. We have benefited from the research assistance of Robert Feldman, especially in the preparation of the tables.

1. Computed at an exchange rate of ¥280 = $1. Direct comparisons are difficult owing to differences in purchasing power and spender preferences. The rapid changes in relative prices that began in 1973 also obstruct international comparisons. See *International Economic Report of the President, February 1974*, p. 91.

2. Japan's area, 377,420 square kilometers, is about 10 percent smaller than California and two-thirds the size of France; it is, however, one and a half times the size of the United Kingdom or West Germany. For a good introductory geography, see Toshio Noh and Douglas H. Gordon (eds.), *Modern Japan: Land and Man* (Tokyo: Teikoku-Shoin, 1974).

3. It should be noted that problems in international comparability arise in the defini-

3

Table 1-1. *International Comparisons of Economic Performance, Japan and Major Western Industrialized Countries*[a]

Item	Japan	United States	West Germany	United Kingdom	France	Italy
(1) Population, 1972 (millions)	107.0	208.8	61.7	55.9	51.7	54.3
(2) Gross national product (billions of current dollars)						
1952[b]	16.3	348.2	31.9	44.3	40.4	17.1
1972[c]	299.2	1,159.3	260.2	153.0	197.7	117.6
(3) Gross national product per capita (current dollars)						
1952	188	2,181	643	870	947	359
1972	2,823	5,551	4,218	2,472	3,823	2,164
(4) Gross domestic investment as percent of gross national product						
1952[d]	27.2	17.1	22.8	10.6	18.9	19.5
1971[e]	36.3	17.4	27.5	18.1	28.0	20.4
(5) Government current expenditure as percent of gross national product						
1952[f]	10.9	20.1	16.2	19.1	15.9	12.1
1971[g]	14.4	24.7	22.0	34.2	21.1	25.1
(6) Exports and imports[h] as percent of gross national product						
1952	26.6	9.0	31.5	45.1	29.8	25.0
1971[i]	21.2	11.7	41.8	44.4	32.9	38.0
(7) Share of world trade (percent)[j]						
1952	2.2	17.1	5.2	11.0	5.4	2.5
1972[k]	6.2	12.5	10.2	6.2	6.3	4.5
(8) Percent of labor force in agriculture						
Early 1950s[l]	41.7	12.2	23.2	5.1	27.7	32.8
1972[m]	19.1	4.2	8.2	3.1	12.3	17.5

(9) *Average annual rate of price change (percent)*[n]

1953–62: Wholesale price index	−0.1	0.9	0.9[o]	0.1[o]	3.4	0.2
Consumer price index	2.8	1.3	1.9	3.0	4.1	2.4
1963–72: Wholesale price index	1.3	2.6	1.6	3.7	3.2	2.7
Consumer price index	5.2	3.5	3.3	5.2	4.3	3.9
1972–73: Wholesale price index	14.8	12.2	8.0	6.7	13.1	15.4
Consumer price index	11.1	6.0	6.7	8.8	7.1	10.2
July 1973–July 1974: Wholesale price index	34.2	20.4	15.3	25.0	32.5	41.8
Consumer price index	25.2	11.8	6.9	17.1	14.4	16.8

Sources: Item (1): Organisation for Economic Co-operation and Development, *OECD Observer*, no. 68 (February 1974). Item (2): United Nations, *Yearbook of National Accounts Statistics, 1957*; UN, *Statistical Yearbook, 1957*, p. 494, and *1973*, table 183. Item (3): GNP data same as for item (2); population data from UN, *Statistical Yearbook, 1957*, table 1, and *1973*, table 183. Item (4): UN, *Yearbook of National Accounts Statistics, 1957 and 1972*. Item (5): ibid. Item (6): ibid. Item (7): UN, *Yearbook of International Trade Statistics, 1954*, table A, pp. 12–19, and *1972–73*, table A, pp. 14–21. Item (8): International Labour Office, *Year Book of Labour Statistics, 1957*, table 4, and *1973*, table 2. Item (9): UN, *Statistical Yearbook, 1962*, tables 161, 168, and *1973*, tables 172, 173; OECD, *Main Economic Indicators*, September 1974, pp. 144–48.

a. It should be noted that not all economic indicators are internationally comparable; for example, the United States classifies as government current expenditures certain items included in gross domestic investment by other nations.
b. Currencies converted into dollars at official exchange rates.
c. Gross domestic product in purchasers' values.
d. Ratio of gross domestic capital formation to gross national product.
e. Ratio of gross domestic capital formation to gross domestic product in purchasers' values.
f. Ratio of general government consumption expenditure to gross national product.
g. For all countries except Japan, ratio of current disbursements of central, state, and local governments to gross domestic product; for Japan, disbursements of general government only.
h. Exports and imports of goods and services.
i. Ratio of exports and imports to gross domestic product.
j. Share of world trade = (import + export)/(world import + world export) × 100.
k. World trade in U.S. dollars: imports are $427.5 billion; exports are $412.4 billion. Excludes trade among China, Mongolia, North Korea, North Vietnam, and the two Germanys.
l. Data are for 1950 for the United States and West Germany, 1951 for the United Kingdom and Italy, 1954 for France, and 1955 for Japan.
m. Data are for 1966 for the United Kingdom, 1970 for Japan, 1971 for West Germany, and 1972 for the remainder.
n. Compound annual rate of growth for the periods indicated.
o. 1954–62.

To many observers, Americans and others, this economic performance has appeared virtually miraculous. Some have sought to locate the source of this "miracle" in allegedly unique Japanese features—government policy or leadership, labor-management practices and institutions, or more vaguely defined cultural attributes. We gently suggest that Japanese growth was not miraculous: it can be reasonably well understood and explained by ordinary economic causes. Part of the problem for the foreign observer has been that most of us have been ignorant of Japan, which makes us particularly susceptible to the use of stereotypes and ideal-types, both as applied to Japan and in making comparisons with other countries.

This book attempts to cut through simplistic stereotypes in order to provide interpretations of major specific aspects of the Japanese economy, as seen through American eyes. In this introductory chapter we provide a broad overview, without attempting to summarize the major points or conclusions of the succeeding chapters. We begin with a brief historical summary, which then is amplified in sections on the postwar domestic economic performance, the evolving role of the government, and Japan's expanding presence in the world economy.[4]

Historical Summary

Although the purpose of this volume is to provide an overview of the contemporary Japanese economy and its remarkable growth since World War II, a few paragraphs must be devoted to describing historical developments up to that time. Although in doing so we cannot avoid superficiality, it is necessary to remind ourselves that Japan's modern economic history did not begin with the end of the war. By the end of World War II, Japan had experienced nearly a century of modernization, and even one hundred years ago it was not a typical underdeveloped country.

tion and measurement of these economic indicators. There are also minor differences between some data used here and those used in other chapters in this volume, depending on their purposes and sources.

4. For a more detailed treatment in historical perspective see Kazushi Ohkawa and Henry Rosovsky, *Japanese Economic Growth: Trend Acceleration in the Twentieth Century* (Stanford University Press, 1973). Certain of the approaches taken in this chapter were foreshadowed in Hugh Patrick, "The Phoenix Risen from the Ashes: Postwar Japan," in James B. Crowley (ed.), *Modern East Asia: Essays in Interpretation* (Harcourt Brace and World, Inc., 1970). Good contemporary surveys of the Japanese economy, published annually, include Economic Planning Agency, *Economic Survey of Japan* (Tokyo: The Japan Times), and Organisation for Economic Co-operation and Development, *Economic Surveys: Japan* (Paris: OECD).

Tokugawa Japan

From the early seventeenth century until 1868, Japan was under the feudal rule of the Tokugawa family. During that period, the economy can certainly be described as traditional. Approximately three-quarters of the working population was engaged in peasant agriculture. This group paid a heavy annual harvest tax that supported a hereditary warrior class, the samurai. Western technology was nearly entirely unknown; indeed, with a few insignificant exceptions, all contacts with foreigners were strictly forbidden and the Japanese themselves were not allowed to go abroad. Non-agricultural economic activity consisted of the usual crafts and services, all employing typical labor-intensive methods. Population growth was very slow: in 1600 there may have been 25 million Japanese; by 1868 there were perhaps 30 million.

Some other features of Tokugawa Japan deserve mention. Japan at that time was a *country*, almost in the contemporary sense of that word: it possessed functioning local and central governments that had preserved peace for about two hundred years, a system of courts, and other administrative services. By the standards of the time it was also relatively urbanized, containing three of the largest cities in the world: Edo (now Tokyo), Kyoto, and Osaka. The educational levels of its citizens were also unusual, in that some formal schooling was available to about half the male population. This leads to an important conclusion: "In Tokugawa Japan the gap between economic and 'other' backwardness was unusually large, and this made the prospect of modern economic growth all the more promising. This gap between the technology actually applied and the capability of borrowing and absorbing more advanced methods based on a well-functioning sociopolitical infrastructure deserves particular stress because it has been a fundamental factor in Japan's success."[5]

Modern Economic Growth

In 1868, under a variety of internal and external pressures, the Tokugawa regime yielded power to the restored imperial dynasty; the Meiji restoration was to see a series of revolutionary changes. The old social and economic order was discarded, frontiers were opened to foreign commerce and know-how, and the new rulers set themselves the task of building a modern country on the basis of an industrialized economy. Japan became

5. Ohkawa and Rosovsky, *Japanese Economic Growth*, p. 8.

the first Asian nation, by a margin of at least seventy-five years, to succeed in this difficult endeavor.

The years between 1868 and World War II fall into a number of distinct phases of growth. During the initial phase—essentially the last third of the nineteenth century—Japan exploited its traditional agricultural resources in order to generate exports and revenues for the government. These funds were used to build up such items of social overhead capital as railroads and ports and to import technology for the establishment of industries such as cotton textiles and the manufacture of items related to military needs. By 1900, the share of agricultural employment had fallen to 66 percent, capital formation was 13 percent of GNP, and modern factory output accounted for 6 percent of the domestic product. This was a good beginning at modernization, good enough at least to administer a defeat to the Russian empire in 1905.

The next phase of growth lasted from the beginning of this century until the Great Depression, and included the great development boom of World War I and the years of difficult adjustment during the 1920s. On average, the economy continued to expand rapidly at a real annual rate of about 3.5 percent of GNP. Cotton textiles became the most important industry, and by World War I finished textile products made in Japan were competitive throughout the world, especially in Asia and Africa. By 1931, less than half the labor force remained in agriculture, the investment ratio had reached 17.7 percent during the World War I boom, and factory output had risen to 19 percent of domestic product.

During the 1930s—the final prewar phase—Japan, unlike many other countries, experienced rapid growth: GNP was expanding at over 5 percent a year. This was the period when, in response to the militarist ambitions of the government, chemicals, metals and machinery, and large industrial units came to dominate the economic scene. Activities associated with heavy industry were thus added to the existing textile base. Politically, this was a most tumultuous period; Japan became embroiled in a series of expansionist adventures that culminated in war with China and the United States. But by the time of Pearl Harbor it was a relatively advanced economic power. The labor force in agriculture had declined to nearly 40 percent, capital formation had topped 20 percent, and factory output had achieved 30 percent of domestic product.

The entire prewar period of modern economic growth, from 1868 to 1940, can be summarized as follows. First, the prewar rate of growth was substantial—around 3 percent a year for GNP, with the population expanding at only 1 percent—and before World War II Japan was already one of the most rapidly growing economies in the world. Second, despite this notable expansion based largely on the introduction of imported industries, the economy retained its "dual" character: modern and traditional services, large modern factories and small craft establishments, continued to exist side by side. Third, the internationalization of the economy increased throughout the period, and by the 1930s Japan was both a major exporter of manufactured products and a major importer of raw materials.

The Occupation

Japan's postwar history starts in August of 1945 in the wake of its surrender to the Allies. World War II—or the Pacific War as it is known in Japan—had inflicted enormous costs: 2.8 million dead, cities destroyed, and an empire lost. The home islands were initially occupied by the Americans on an open-ended basis, in that no one knew how long the foreigners would remain. It has been estimated that approximately 40 percent of Japan's capital stock was destroyed during the war, and provision had to be made for over 6 million Japanese who returned home from previous overseas possessions. Japan presented a bleak picture indeed in 1945: food was scarce, lodgings were in a state of disrepair, the standard of living had declined to pre–World War I levels (to the extent that such a comparison has any meaning), and major cities were devastated. The Japanese had fought bravely in a hard and bitter conflict, and the final surrender must have been greeted with a mixture of relief and incredulity: that the war was already lost in August 1945 was obvious; that the country would surrender few had believed possible.

It is all the more astonishing, therefore, to note that the occupiers were greeted with calm, and that the Japanese proved extremely cooperative with the new authorities. There was no resistance and there were no violent incidents. Everyone joined in the effort to bring things back to a state of normalcy as quickly as possible. Initially it had been the intention of the United States to impose a harsh settlement on Japan. The notion was to adopt a modified "Morgenthau Plan" that would permit only very limited industrialization so as to prevent a rebuilding of Japan's war machine. But Japan's dense population relative to arable land as well as world events— specifically the outbreak of the cold war—underlined the impracticality of that policy. Instead the United States participated wholeheartedly in the effort to reconstruct and rehabilitate Japan in all respects—economic, political, and social. Given the devastated base, increases in economic output were largely due (as was the rate of inflation) to the elimination of war-caused bottlenecks and excess capacity. Germany and other devastated European countries had a similar experience.

The American-dominated occupation embodied perhaps one of the most ambitious attempts at social engineering the world has seen. The major goal was to achieve in Japan the ideology, institutions, and distribution of power thought to be required for the creation of a stable, peaceful, parliamentary democracy. The economic reforms aimed to establish a competitive market economy with a more egalitarian distribution of income and wealth. Ownership of land farmed by tenants, some 45 percent of the total, was redistributed to the tenants. The labor union movement was initially strongly encouraged, and unionism spread like wildfire; however, the evolution into both enterprise unionism and an active political role for the unions at the national level was unanticipated. (See Chapters 9 and 11 for a discussion of labor unions.) Reduction of the concentration of business power and the establishment of more competitive markets involved a variety of actions: dissolution of family-owned *zaibatsu* conglomerates; elimination of cartels and monopolies; breakup of a few extremely large firms; and establishment of the Fair Trade Commission to monitor and enforce the new rules of competition in business. Most efforts at economic reform occurred in the first two years of the occupation. Thereafter the policy emphasis shifted to economic recovery, in response to the cold war, the failure of American policy in China, and the American desire to reduce the burden of aid to Japan on American taxpayers.

While no overall appraisal of occupation policies and their degree of success has yet been made, in many respects they—together with the catastrophic defeat in the war—profoundly affected all aspects of Japanese society. The degree of success of specific reforms has depended much upon their appeal to Japanese leaders and the general public. Land reform worked well because landlord-tenant problems had long been severe, and changes had already been planned by the Japanese bureaucracy before World War II. On the other hand, few Japanese came to accept the traditional Anglo-American belief that the self-oriented, profit-maximizing behavior of firms and optimizing behavior of individuals would, through competition, automatically create the maximum output and lowest prices for the benefit of consumers. Rather, many Japanese, especially in the government bureaucracy, have noted the deviations in practice from the competitive model: the existence of oligopolistic markets, the efficiency of large-scale economies, lumpiness of large investment requirements in certain industries and consequent problems of excess capacity, and situations of market failure—all of which allegedly compel direct government intervention. And, as is discussed in Chapter 7, not only did the occupation reforms directed at the concentration of business power not go very far, but rapid growth has substantially influenced further the conditions of industrial organization.[6]

An unexpected boost to Japan's economy was provided by the Korean War, which began in June 1950. This conflict lasted for roughly three years and caused a great American military buildup in East Asia. Japan became the focal point of that effort—in effect, a giant supply base serving the American war effort. The first postwar boomlet thus developed: vast sums of money were poured into Japan; vehicles and armaments were made and repaired by the Japanese; and the traffic in soldiers was large. The war also tied Japan and the United States even more closely together politically. The Korean War reinforced Washington's perception of the threat of communist aggression in the area and its recognition that a revitalized and independent Japan would be a valuable ally.

Independence

The Allied occupation of Japan came to a formal end on April 28, 1952, and Japan once again became an independent nation. In overwhelming contrast to its situation today, Japan was then poor and weak. Per capita GNP in 1952 was only $188,[7] below that of Brazil, Malaysia, and Chile among other less developed countries. Reconstruction, in terms of average output and living standards, from the devastation of World War II was not achieved until the mid-1950s; the war thus cost Japan some seventeen to eighteen years of lost growth and decline in output.

Japan in the early 1950s combined a mixture of characteristics of less developed countries and of economically advanced countries. Thus while its income was low, and never had been high, its potential for growth was substantial. Like other low-income countries, Japan had a high proportion (about 40 percent) of its labor force in agriculture, a relatively small capital stock, a technology level that in most industries lagged far behind the West, and low labor productivity. However, it also possessed three features that

6. See also Kozo Yamamura, *Economic Policy in Postwar Japan: Growth versus Economic Democracy* (University of California Press, 1967); and idem, "Structure Is Behavior: An Appraisal of Japanese Economic Policy," in Isaiah Frank (ed.), *The Japanese Economy in International Perspective* (The Johns Hopkins University Press, 1975), pp. 67–100.

7. In 1965 constant prices Japan's GNP per capita was $342 in 1952, compared with $1,709 in 1972 (at an exchange rate of ¥360 = $1). Computed from Economic Planning Agency, *Annual Report on National Income Statistics, 1974*, p. 185; and Bureau of Statistics, Office of the Prime Minister, *Japan Statistical Yearbook, 1973–74*, p. 11.

differentiated it from other poor countries and indicated that it had already moved far along in the development process. These features, which were to be important ingredients in subsequent rapid growth, were: (1) a highly educated and skilled labor force—in a sense overeducated relative to the static needs of the economy; (2) widespread dualism in labor use, in that there existed great differentials in productivity and wages in various sectors, with labor productivity especially low in agriculture, many services, and small-scale manufacturing enterprises; and (3) substantial managerial, organizational, scientific, and engineering skills capable of rapidly absorbing and adapting the best foreign technology. As already noted, these conditions reflected the disequilibrium between the actual performance of the economy, as demonstrated in the substantial, diversified industrial base Japan had developed before the war, and its potential capability; the capital and technology required to close this gap were to be forthcoming.

At the time of renewed independence, and for some years to come, both Japanese and Western experts were rather gloomy about the future: the traditional markets in Asia were gone and the inefficient level of domestic industry offered little hope for future prosperity. Early economic plans of the Japanese government that projected aggregate growth rates in the neighborhood of 5 percent were considered to be extremely optimistic.

The aura of uncertainty prevailed until 1958–59, when, following the Suez crisis and a severe but brief recession, the Japanese economy started to show the first clear signs of its postwar growth potential. By 1959 people were speaking of the "Jimmu Boom" to refer to the greatest expansion since the reign of Japan's first, and mythical, emperor. In 1961, Prime Minister Ikeda announced his "Doubling National Income Plan." It envisaged accomplishment of this task over a decade, projecting an annual GNP growth rate of 7.2 percent. Though there were many skeptics at home and abroad, the fact is that from 1959 until the early 1970s the Japanese economy grew at an annual average rate of 10.8 percent. And, despite the 1974 recession, the expectation is that Japan will continue to grow relatively rapidly, though at more moderate rates. (This expectation is considered in more detail in Chapter 13.)

In the period from the early 1950s to the late 1960s there was substantial unity regarding policy objectives. These were the years during which growth reigned supreme in fact and in the minds of the policymakers, albeit with some emphasis on "stable growth" (that is, reduced cyclical instability and only moderate price rises). There also developed a definite pattern of industrial growth and evolution. Priority was given to the development of certain basic industries such as steel, electric power, chemicals, and coal, which received extensive government support. Newer industries also began to grow rapidly: optics, consumer electronics, machinery, and, somewhat later, automobiles and computers. Initially, the products of these industries served as substitutes for imports in the large and growing domestic market; by the 1960s many had become large exporters. During the entire period, exports grew at least twice as rapidly as world trade, making Japan once again an increasingly weighty factor in the world economy.

Before the Jimmu Boom began Japan had too small an economy and was too far away to arouse much interest in the West. But by the second half of the 1960s storm clouds brewed by Japanese economic growth began to appear in any number of directions. The rapid growth of Japanese exports created unhappiness among producers in the importing countries, and accusations of unfair competition and dumping became frequent. American textile and steel producers took the lead in this and were soon followed by a host of others. This situation was exacerbated by what was widely viewed as an undervalued yen and by Japan's own protected domestic market. The storm clouds were not confined to the United States; they became especially black in those parts of Asia where Japan made its economic presence most felt in the exploitation of raw materials, direct investment, and selling products.

As rapid growth continued without interruption in the 1960s, there gradually occurred a significant change in Japan's balance-of-payments position. Instead of facing periodic payments crises, the economy started to build surpluses around 1968, and it is estimated that the official and hidden surpluses approached $30 billion by 1972. All of a sudden, in the early 1970s, Japan was seen as a destabilizing factor in the world economy: a very large economy exporting vast quantities of manufactured products, importing primarily raw materials, and growing much more rapidly than the rest of the world. Concern was perhaps greatest in the United States, which was Japan's leading market. The United States was suffering from an increasingly overvalued dollar combined with the large foreign currency obligations imposed by its role as "leader of the free world." In addition, many American industries were severely affected by Japanese competition. The rigidity of the Bretton Woods arrangements prevented easy and rapid adjustments, and bilateral negotiations with Japan to force an appreciation of the yen were not making much progress. It seemed to some observers at the beginning of the seventies as if Japan did not fully understand that, from the international perspective, a large and rising surplus is as bad as a large and rising deficit. The Japanese economy continued to grow as before, expanding into new markets, and there was little disposition to change course.

This situation culminated in the Nixon "economic shock" of August 1971, following hard on the Nixon "China shock." Initially the United States devalued the dollar and applied temporary import restrictions; these eventually led to a system of world-wide controlled floating exchange rates that caused the yen to fluctuate between 280 and 300 to the dollar. It is difficult to evaluate the effects of these measures on Japanese growth because they are entangled with those of the oil crisis that hit the major industrialized countries in October 1973. A few facts stand out clearly, however. The Japanese economy continued to grow rapidly until late 1973, and the effects of the currency appreciation were much milder than anticipated. But beginning in late 1972 the economy became the victim of severe inflation: until then wholesale prices had risen only very slowly while consumer prices increased at an average rate of 5 to 6 percent. Now, both prices were rising more rapidly, and following the oil crisis the consumer price index (CPI) moved upward by about 25 percent a year.

By the summer of 1974 Japan was in the grip of a severe inflationary spiral: wage increases that spring averaged about 30 percent in large firms. At the same time it was in the midst of its most severe postwar recession. The government implemented a very restrictive fiscal-monetary policy to break the inflationary spiral, with increasing success. The very moderate wage increases of about 14 percent in the spring of 1975 are expected to break the back of excessive inflation; it is anticipated that the rise in consumer prices will gradually wind down. The cost in terms of economic output forgone was nonetheless substantial: in 1974 GNP declined by 1.8 percent.[8] By the end of 1974 actual production was about 20 percent below capacity potential. In the spring of 1975 the recession appeared to be bottoming out, but recovery has proceeded slowly in Japan as elsewhere.

Japan's Economic Performance

This book is concerned predominantly with various aspects of the performance of the contemporary Japanese economy. Here we evaluate the long-run, overall performance of the postwar Japanese economy by standard macroeconomic criteria: growth and the evolving structure of production; maintenance of full employment; the degree of price stability; and, ultimately most important, the improvement in the economic welfare of the Japanese people, including distribution of income and wealth.

8. Statistics Department, Bank of Japan, *Economic Statistics Monthly* (February 1975), p. 157. The base year for constant price calculations was revised from 1965 to 1970, a standard and ongoing procedure.

Growth and the Structure of Production

The dominant feature of the Japanese economy since postwar reconstruction has been very rapid and sustained growth. Aggregate productive capacity, measured by the quantity and quality of the capital stock, the labor force, and the level of technology, has increased dramatically, while aggregate demand has been sufficient to maintain high rates of capacity utilization. We do not analyze these aggregate supply and demand forces in detail here; they are treated fully in Chapters 2, 3, 8, and 9. Moreover, in Chapter 2 Denison and Chung provide detailed estimates and analyses of Japanese economic growth and its sources; while their approach and data differ in some respects from ours, the general conclusions are the same.

We have already noted Japan's economic potential in the early 1950s, which was based on the existing stock of a well-educated labor force together with a large supply of managerial and technical skills. This base, plus further increments in labor quantity and quality, combined with high rates of investment and rapid technological improvement to constitute the basic force in rapid growth. While each ingredient was important in itself, their synergistic interactions meant more growth than the marginal contribution of any single ingredient. We can trace the story of postwar growth in its broad outlines by focusing on four major strands: the labor force—its quantity, quality, and allocation; the growth of the capital stock through high and increasing rates of saving and investment; the absorption and effective utilization of technology, mostly of foreign origin; and government growth-related policies.

THE LABOR FORCE. One of the most important factors in its economic growth is that Japan has had an ample supply of well-trained, well-motivated, hard-working labor, much of it initially employed in relatively low productivity activities from which it could be deployed effectively. While conditions of labor use and labor relations are discussed in more detail by Galenson and Odaka in Chapter 9, the following overview summarizes labor's contribution to growth performance.

In 1950 Japan had a labor force comparable to that of Western Europe in quality (measured in average years of workers' education) but with a much lower productivity due to lack of capital and advanced technology. Japan was not far behind the United States in average years of schooling for males (8.15 versus 9.68 in 1950) and for females (7.22 versus 10.01).[9] This high educational level is one reason why the contribution of further increases in education to productivity improvement is less important in Japan

9. See Chapter 2, table 15, for Japanese data, and Edward F. Denison, *Why Growth Rates Differ* (Brookings Institution, 1967), p. 107, for U.S. data.

than in many industrialized countries. Indeed, despite continued rapid expansion of education such that now roughly four-fifths of students finish senior high school and one-quarter go on to college, the stock of educated persons is sufficiently large that it takes time for the increased flow to affect it greatly. However, it may mean also that there still remains a younger portion of the labor force overeducated relative to its present economic use, which serves as an ongoing potential contribution to continued rapid economic growth.

Japan underwent a major demographic transformation in the decade following the end of the war. After an initial postwar baby boom, birth rates dropped sharply. Japanese came to regard the optimal number of children as about two, and legalized abortion and dissemination of birth control techniques made family planning highly efficient. The death rate also declined substantially. Since the mid-1950s Japan has had low crude birth (about seventeen to nineteen per thousand) and death (seven to eight per thousand) rates that yield a population growth rate of about 1.1 percent. During most of the postwar period the labor force increased somewhat more rapidly, at about 1.5 percent annually, despite increased numbers of young people in school; the effect of lower birth rates on the labor force was not felt until the late 1960s.

More important than absolute increases in the labor force was the high proportion of labor in low-productivity uses. Workers have moved readily into more productive, higher paying jobs as they became available; the aggregate reallocation of labor among sectors of the economy has been phenomenal, as is shown in Table 1-2. To a considerable extent this reallocation has been caused by new workers entering sectors and occupations different from those of the older generation. In particular, a high proportion of the children of farmers have entered nonagricultural occupations.

In the early 1960s, the large reservoir of labor supply began to decrease significantly as workers were ever more rapidly absorbed by the demand generated by rapid growth, and by the late 1960s the supply of labor was increasingly tight relative to demand. As discussed by Galenson and Odaka in Chapter 9, the appearance of a labor shortage is in part a consequence of such institutional practices as early retirement and the tendency of large organizations to hire predominantly new school graduates. These practices are changing in response to changing labor market conditions, but labor still appears to be in less short supply than in Western Europe.

With rapid growth and a tightening labor market, industrial wage rates have increased rapidly in both money terms and real terms after adjustments for increases in the cost of living. The cash earnings of regular employees rose seven times between 1952 and 1972, with annual increases reaching 15 percent or more by the late 1960s. Adjusted for the cost of living, real

Table 1-2. *Japan's Gross Domestic Product and Labor Force, by Sector, 1956 and 1971*

Percent, at current market prices

Sector	1956		1971		Average annual growth[a]	
	Gross domestic product	Labor force	Gross domestic product	Labor force	Nominal sectoral output	Sectoral labor force
Primary	17.4	41.9	5.8	17.4	6.8	−4.2
Agriculture	12.5	39.3	4.0	15.9	6.6	−4.3
Forestry	3.2	1.0	0.7	0.4	3.7	−4.3
Fishing	1.7	1.6	1.1	1.0	12.0	−1.5
Secondary	34.5	23.9	41.1	35.5	15.3	4.3
Mining	2.2	1.5	0.7	0.4	6.2	−6.8
Manufacturing	27.8	17.7	33.3	27.2	15.3	4.6
Construction	4.5	4.7	7.1	7.9	17.6	5.2
Tertiary	48.1	34.1	53.2	47.2	15.9	3.8
Electricity, gas, water	2.1	0.7	1.9	0.6	13.8	0.4
Wholesale and retail trade	16.5	13.7	17.1	19.2	16.1	3.9
Transport and communication	8.5	4.6	7.1	6.4	13.4	3.9
Banking and insurance	3.8	} 1.7	4.8	} 3.0	16.6	} 5.8
Real estate	3.8		6.0		18.1	
Services	9.8	10.7	13.0	14.7	16.9	3.8
Public administration	3.7	2.7	3.3	3.3	14.2	3.0

Sources: Gross domestic product, Economic Planning Agency, *Annual Report on National Income Statistics, 1972*, pp. 282–83. Labor force, Bureau of Statistics, Office of the Prime Minister, *1956 Employment Status Survey Summary*, p. 26, table I-3; and ibid., *1971*, pp. 142–45.
a. Estimated from beginning- and end-year data.

wages tripled in the twenty-year period. Because of even more rapid productivity increases, wage increases did not cause a significant rise in industrial prices. As inflation accelerated sharply in 1973 and early 1974, wages rose in response, though with some lag. The ability of firms to provide large wage increases because of rapidly rising productivity and their willingness to do so, coupled with union reasonableness, has resulted in relatively peaceful labor-management relations. Strikes have been few, brief, and symbolic. Far fewer labor days have been lost and far less output forgone through strikes in Japan than in the United States or in most European countries.

CAPITAL STOCK. The growth of labor productivity, and the absorption of workers into higher productivity jobs, would not have been possible without a very high rate of investment in plant and equipment and other directly productive capacity. Japan's level of labor productivity, even after recovery from World War II, was low largely because the capital stock per worker was small. Capital has grown much more rapidly than the labor force—at over

9 percent a year, or more than twice the average rate for the Western industrialized countries.

Japan achieved this by a high and rising investment rate. Real gross domestic investment, private and public, increased by an average of 12.9 percent a year between 1952 and 1973, and private business plant and equipment investment increased by 14.4 percent. This meant that in real terms gross investment, about 20 percent of GNP in the early 1950s, has composed close to 40 percent of GNP since the mid-1960s, and the share of business plant and equipment investment has increased from about 10 percent of GNP to more than 20 percent. This is the most impressive investment performance ever achieved in any peacetime, democratic, market economy; no other such industrialized nation has voluntarily plowed back such a high share of output into further expansion.

One important cause of this investment performance has been widespread business and managerial optimism about the growth of the economy, along with a perception of the profit opportunities in rapid growth and technological improvement, and the very aggressive attempts by large firms to increase market share. While Japanese corporate investment strategy could lead to devastatingly excess capacity for a single firm or industry if it were out of line with overall demand, such behavior was so widespread that sufficient additional demand was generated for virtually all products, with only temporary periods of excess capacity. Business optimism was thus self-fulfilling.

Although subject to substantial cyclical swings, the rates of return on new investment have generally been high, greater than the interest rate on borrowed funds. Since (as discussed in Chapters 4 and 5) Japanese firms are highly leveraged—that is, they rely predominantly upon borrowed funds—the return on net worth has been substantially greater than on total capital employed. The high capital return is due to a variety of factors: rapid growth of demand, extraordinary rates of improvement in labor (and total factor) productivity, stability of the wage share in value added, and oligopolistic market structure in some industries (see Chapter 7). Large firms appear to be interested more in long-run than short-run profit maximization; they also apparently regard sales growth maximization and profit growth maximization as consistent and mutually reinforcing over the long run.

The other important cause of Japan's rapid investment rate has been its high and rising saving rates. In aggregate, all of Japan's domestic investment has been financed by domestic saving, though of course some individual firms borrow from abroad. Not surprisingly, the corporate sector plows back the major share of its after-tax profits—about 85 percent for the corporate sector as a whole. Even so, firms have to rely heavily on external finance

Table 1-3. *Gross Saving in Japan, by Components, 1952–54 and 1970–72*

	1952–54[a]		1970–72[a]		
Component	Percent of gross national product	Percent of saving	Percent of gross national product	Percent of saving	Percent of increase in saving rate
Depreciation	8.1	33.3	14.2	35.8	35.9
Corporate retained earnings	3.3	13.5	5.7	14.4	14.4
Personal	6.0	24.6	13.1	33.0	33.5
Government	5.7	23.4	7.4	18.7	18.4
Statistical discrepancy	1.3	5.2	−0.7	−1.9	−2.3
Gross saving	24.3	100.0	39.6	100.0	100.0

Sources: Computed from Economic Planning Agency, *Revised Report on National Income Statistics, 1951–67*, pp. 3, 11; EPA, *Annual Report on National Income Statistics, 1974*, pp. 2, 10.
a. Arithmetic average of three years.

because of their high investment demand. Individual saving rates in Japan, which were low in the early 1950s, have risen tremendously; for example, urban workers now save about 20 percent of their disposable income—about triple the rate of American workers. This frugality has many sources, but much of it can be explained by institutional factors and by the rapid growth of income (see Chapter 4).

Personal saving accounts for only about a third of gross domestic saving and of the increase in saving rates, as shown in Table 1-3. Business depreciation allowances have been equally important. This is primarily due to the business investment boom and the use of the standard declining balance method of depreciation. (Japanese depreciation schedules are similar to American ones, with slightly shorter lives for machinery; on this, see Chapter 5.) Despite high retention rates, corporate profits account for less than a sixth of gross saving. The government too is a substantial saver, mainly for investment in government buildings, social overhead, and the like.

TECHNOLOGY. A major reason why Japan's high investment rate, and the labor it required, could be so productive is that it incorporated new and better technology. Most advanced industrial technology utilized in Japan has been imported from other industrialized nations, though some has been developed by Japan's own research and development efforts, as in shipbuilding, optics, and agriculture.[10] In some instances industrial technology

10. The main exception in agricultural technology has been chemical inputs, especially insecticides and pesticides. See Yujiro Hayami and others, *Sources of Agricultural Growth in Modern Japan* (University of Minnesota Press and University of Tokyo Press, 1975).

was imported in the form of highly sophisticated machinery. A substantial component of foreign technology has been readily available in technical and professional journals, in American graduate schools that Japanese have attended, and similar "costless" sources of information. Much has also come through technology license arrangements between Japanese and foreign firms, as discussed in Chapter 8. Japanese firms have been extremely efficient in learning, commercializing, and improving upon foreign technology. Most Japanese R&D is carried out and financed by private firms, and much is complementary to the foreign technology they have purchased. Japan's R&D expenditures as a percentage of GNP are only now reaching the ratios of European nations; most is still in adaptation and complementary activities rather than in basic science and technology, in which Japan has remained relatively weak. The economy has obtained large productivity benefits from its R&D expenditures, which have been mainly in civilian industries with an emphasis on cutting costs and increasing efficiency rather than for military purposes.

GOVERNMENT POLICIES. The main impetus to growth has come from the private sector, both in business initiative and in private demand. The government's role has been supportive, mainly by providing an environment well suited to economic growth. We consider the government's role in a later section of this chapter. Relevant aspects of government policy are considered throughout this book, especially in Chapters 3, 5, and 11.

STRUCTURAL CHANGE. Economic growth and the transformation of the structure and location of production and labor force use have gone hand in hand. Table 1-2 makes clear the major changes in the sectoral composition of production. The primary sector, predominantly agriculture, is now a small component of output; its economically inefficient level of production is reflected in its much higher share of the labor force than of output. Substantial increases in the relative share of production and employment occurred in manufacturing, construction, and a variety of services. The implication of these changes for economic growth are discussed in Chapter 2.

The structure of production and of labor force use changed substantially within the manufacturing sector. The share of labor-intensive light industries, notably processed foods and beverages and textiles, declined sharply. In contrast, electrical machinery (especially consumer electronics) and transport and equipment (especially ships and automobiles) grew particularly rapidly. It must be kept in mind that these changes in the relative importance of industries occurred within the context of overall rapid growth. Even industries in relative decline grew absolutely, in fact rapidly in comparison with other industrial nations. In virtually no major industry has there yet been any absolute decline in output; coal mining and cotton textiles are the main exceptions.

The geographical distribution of population, labor force, and production has changed dramatically in response to rapid industrial growth. Industry has concentrated in urban areas, and, accordingly, so has population. (See Chapter 10 for a discussion of urban conditions and problems.) According to the 1970 population census, 75 million of Japan's population of 104 million lived in cities, most (55.5 million) in densely populated areas of more than 10,000 persons per square mile. The fifteen cities with a population over 500,000 contained 25 million residents. Most (78.7 percent) of the population and economic activity (84.1 percent of net domestic product in 1971) is on the main island of Honshu, including twelve of the fifteen largest cities.

Economic activity has increasingly become centered in three metropolitan areas: Tokyo-Yokohama, Osaka-Kyoto-Kobe, and Nagoya, with the latter still a distinct third. There are other substantial industrial centers, including several now growing rapidly, but they are still of relatively less importance. Almost half of the national labor force (51 percent in the tertiary sector and 41 percent in the secondary sector) and three-fifths of the net domestic product is located in the three major metropolitan areas; production and income per capita there are substantially above national averages. Osaka was the historical center of commerce and industry, but Tokyo has come to take the leading position, especially since World War II. Tokyo in many ways now dominates Japan just as Paris dominates France. It is the seat of government, location of head offices of most major corporations, and the center of university, publishing, intellectual, and cultural activities. Yet it is important to remember that four-fifths of Japan's population and seven-tenths of its domestic production are outside the Tokyo metropolitan area; it is almost as simplistic to judge Japan by Tokyo as it is to judge the United States by New York.

A major feature of the structure of production, both historically and to a lesser degree even now, is economic dualism—that is, substantial differences in output per worker by sector or by firm size within the same industry, differences greater than can be explained by differences in the quality of labor. The sectoral differences in labor productivity have been greatest between agriculture or traditional services and modern industry. The aggregate data in Table 1-2 show that in 1971 average output per worker in manufacturing was almost five times that in agriculture at current prices, despite the relative increase in the prices of agricultural products. It must be admitted that this comparison is not entirely just, since farmers do not have the same characteristics as factory workers. Nonetheless, and especially so when labor was most abundant, the traditional sectors, mainly agriculture, contained large numbers of workers whose productivity and income were substantially lower than those of workers of comparable age, sex, and education in manufacturing. The gap between labor productivity in agriculture and small manufacturing firms has not been as great, but it widens considerably as the size of the firms being used for comparison increases. For this reason considerations of scale dominate the discussion of economic dualism. Even so, the main shifts in growth rates stemming from the reallocation of labor to higher productivity uses have been from sector to sector—notably away from agriculture—rather than from smaller to larger firm within the industrial sector.

A common but mistaken impression is that in Japan giant corporations predominate in production and labor force use. For the private sector as a whole, almost 70 percent of the labor force works in small-scale units of fewer than 100 workers.[11] Large enterprises, those with 1,000 or more employees, employ only one-sixth of the total. Almost all workers in agriculture, more than three-quarters of the workers in construction, wholesale and retail trade, and personal services, and half the workers in manufacturing are in small production units.

This employment pattern understates the production importance of large-scale enterprises, however, because labor productivity is considerably higher in large enterprises than in small ones. Unfortunately sales and value-added data are not available by size of enterprise for sectors other than manufacturing. Census of Manufactures data indicate that in 1970 the 866 largest manufacturing firms (those with 1,000 or more employees) employed 28.2 percent of the manufacturing labor force and produced 42.9 of the gross value added in manufactures.[12] This suggests that large firms produced slightly more than one-third of gross value added by the private sector as a whole, and small units about one-half.

The substantial, monotonic increases in labor productivity by size of firm up to those with 1,000 employees are associated with similar differences in capital per worker and average wages per worker. Although the gap has narrowed substantially over time, for all manufacturing in 1970 the gross value added per worker in firms with 50 to 99 employees was only 52.1 per-

    11. Bureau of Statistics, *1971 Employment Status Survey Summary* (1973), tables 5, 7, 11. A more extended discussion of small business and labor use appears in Chapters 7 and 9.
    12. Bureau of Statistics, *Japan Statistical Yearbook, 1973–74,* p. 190.

cent that in firms with 1,000 or more employees, tangible fixed assets per worker 34.2 percent, and wages per worker 65.1 percent.[13] Not all these differences are attributable to firm size, since "all manufacturing" is an aggregation of heterogeneous industries with varying characteristics of size, capital intensity, and labor requirements. Nonetheless, for all manufacturing the differentials in output and wages in Japan remain substantially greater than in the United States.

This economic dualism became significant early in the twentieth century; its existence and extent are related in a complex way to the long-run process of economic development. Large firms more than small ones have taken advantage of relatively capital-intensive modern technologies. Both capital and labor markets have been characterized by substantial market imperfections (as is discussed in Chapters 4, 7, and 9). Large firms have preferential access to credit, and at lower interest rates (8 to 10 percent on the average) than for small firms (which typically pay interest rates of 12 to 15 percent). Various explanations have been given as to why large firms have paid substantially higher wages than small ones, though the issue has not been fully resolved. Large firms have had greater financial resources because of their higher labor productivity; they have preferred to select the best new employees and to retain those who have developed skills on the job; and perhaps unions (organized predominantly in large firms) were effective in the early postwar period in bargaining for higher wages. In addition, it has been suggested that the management of large firms has been willing to share to some extent the profits of market power with the workers, perhaps in part to compensate for the lower degree of personal involvement between managers and workers than exists in small enterprises.

Under the pressure of burgeoning labor demand, wage rate differentials by firm size have narrowed much more rapidly than differentials in capital or output, especially for younger employees. One might well ask, then, why small firms continue to exist and apparently even to thrive under such wage-cost pressure. Much depends on the market conditions they face.

Some small firms produce final goods, and especially services, for local markets, where transport costs and service features give them a competitive edge, particularly in industries in which there are no great economies of scale. Others produce specialty products with small production runs, for example such consumer luxury goods as kimono cloth or high technology machinery.[14] Or, as is stereotypic of subcontracting, some small firms still

13. Ibid.
14. The recent development of R&D and skill-intensive small firms is of increasing significance in any assessment of small enterprise in Japan.

operate in segmented labor and capital markets where they combine low-wage labor with high-cost capital using relatively simple technology, and with greater flexibility in changing specific product lines. Where local markets are protected and where consumer demand is rising rapidly (as with luxury goods), small producers have been able to raise prices substantially. In subcontract manufacturing, however, large firms have placed great pressure on their small suppliers to reduce prices, not to increase them. Successful small firms have responded by vigorous investment programs to substitute capital for labor and to incorporate better technologies into production processes. And at times firms have responded with lower quality products.

On the whole, small business in Japan has done very well, despite its problems, because rapid growth has provided many opportunities. As in other industrial countries, the variance of profits is greater for small firms, both over time and among firms. Subcontractors bear much of the brunt of recessions; large firms produce more components themselves and delay payment for goods received from subcontractors. The rates both of establishing new small firms and of bankruptcy are high, though failure rates are about the same as in the United States. Most of the reasons given for bankruptcy lie in managerial ignorance, inflexibility, and inefficiency, which are exacerbated in periods of recessions or particularly tight credit. The enterpreneurial drive for ownership and control of one's own business is widespread and strong among Japanese. Many small firms have succeeded in becoming large ones in the past twenty-five years, even to being ranked among the top 500 industrial firms in Japan.

Full Employment and Price Stability

One of the impressive features of the postwar Japanese economy is that overt unemployment has never been a serious, or even minor, problem. Despite definitional differences, unemployment rates were between 1 and 1.8 percent between 1960 and 1974, and at 2 to 2.5 percent in the 1950s—constituting no more than frictional unemployment; in other words, most unemployed persons had either just entered the job market, were between jobs, or were involved in similar temporary lags and dislocations at little social or personal cost. Unemployment rates are thus not very useful indicators of the tightness or ease of labor markets. Instead the ratio of job offers by hiring companies to job seekers at government employment exchanges has come to be used; since the early 1960s the ratio has been greater than 1, though with considerable fluctuation.

The achievement of full employment has been due to rapid growth, mild and brief recessions, institutional labor practices of large firms, and economic dualism. Obviously the fundamental cause is rapid growth itself, which has generated such strong demand for labor. Recessions typically have meant only slowdowns of economic growth, not actual declines; moreover they have lasted only about twelve months on average. (For a discussion of the business cycle and anticyclical policies see Chapter 3.) Large firms and the government typically employ workers permanently until retirement at age fifty-five to sixty. While not a legal commitment, this practice has strong moral force and constitutes a basic plank of union policy. The commitment has been tested by real adversity only in 1974–75, and it seems to have been substantially honored. Large firms have usually been concerned about possible labor shortages, so they have hired new school graduates even during recessions in order to be assured of sufficient labor in the anticipated next boom. That unemployment did not become a serious social problem in the 1974–75 recession attests to the strength of the system. At the same time it made unions and workers more aware of the primacy of job security, even at the expense of rapid wage increases. The shock of the recession, and less optimistic views of the future by management, may lead to changed employment arrangements in the future.

Perhaps most important of all has been the persistence of the dual structure in production and in labor markets. Small enterprises have constituted an elastic absorber of new entrants and others seeking work at relatively low wages; the legal minimum wage rates in Japan are so low as to be operationally unimportant. In effect, small enterprises serve as a residual market for labor, so that all job seekers find some employment. A substantial part of the reason lies in the relatively high continuing proportion of self-employed and unpaid family workers, constituting a third of the total labor force. This group comprises almost all agricultural workers, 37.5 percent of workers in wholesale and retail trade (especially in the latter), 32.3 percent of workers in services, and 14.9 percent of workers even in manufacturing.[15] The widespread opportunity of working in a family enterprise undoubtedly is a major factor in the elastic labor-absorptive capacity of Japanese small business.

The one aspect of Japan's macroeconomic performance which has been less satisfactory is inflation. Figure 1-1 shows the average annual rates of change in the indexes of consumer prices, wholesale prices, GNP implicit deflator, exports, and imports. Several patterns are apparent: a general rising

15. Bureau of Statistics, *1971 Employment Status Survey Summary* (1973), tables 5, 7, 11.

Figure 1-1. *Average Annual Rates of Change in Selected Japanese Price Indexes, 1953–74*[a]

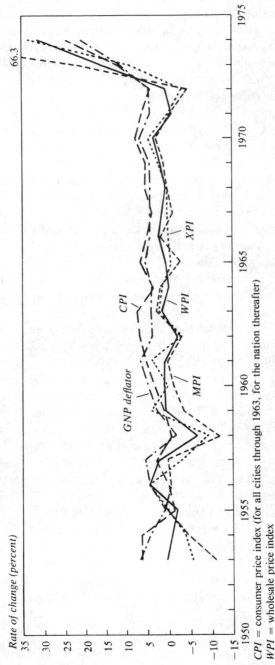

CPI = consumer price index (for all cities through 1963, for the nation thereafter)
WPI = wholesale price index
GNP deflator = the implicit price deflator for gross national product
XPI = export price index
MPI = import price index

Sources: WPI, Bank of Japan, *Economic Statistics Annual, 1967*, p. 205; *1972*, p. 263; *1974*, p. 265. GNP, for 1953–67, Economic Planning Agency, *Revised Report on National Income Statistics, 1951–67* (September 1969), pp. 86–87; for 1968–74, calculated from *Economic Statistics Annual, 1974*, pp. 301–04, and BOJ, *Economic Statistics Monthly* (June 1975), p. 167. CPI, for 1953–63 (for all cities), calculated from *Economic Statistics of Japan, 1962*, p. 303, and 1965, p. 279; for 1964–74 (for nation), *Economic Statistics Annual, 1972*, p. 273, and *1974*, p. 279. XPI and MPI, for 1953–63, calculated from *Economic Statistics of Japan, 1965*, pp. 305–06; for 1964–74, *Economic Statistics Annual, 1972*, p. 272, and *1974*, p. 270.
a. The underlying respective indexes have been linked; the base-year weights for calculation have shifted over time from 1960 to 1965 to 1970.

trend in consumer prices of 5 to 6 percent annually from the early 1960s through 1972; a substantial divergence over the same period between the CPI and the wholesale and export price indexes, with the latter rather stable; and a highly inflationary rise in all price indexes that began in 1973, spiraling upward even more rapidly in 1974, with wholesale price increases temporarily outstripping consumer price rises. In the latter part of 1974 and the first half of 1975 the rate of inflation slowed substantially as recession, tight fiscal-monetary policy, and leveling world prices all had their impact. (The general inflationary trend is discussed in detail in Chapter 3.)

Japanese have been willing to accept a higher rate of rising consumer prices than Americans. The terms of the tradeoff have been different in Japan, however; 5 to 6 percent inflation was tolerable in the context of real growth at a rate twice as fast, with rapidly rising nominal and real wages and incomes. Moreover the adverse welfare effects were minimal for most Japanese since almost everybody was working. The 1973–74 inflationary surge is another story, however; inflation climbed to socially intolerable rates, real wages did not keep up, those on welfare and retired persons were hard hit, and a demand-pull, cost-push spiral emerged as various interest groups scrambled not to fall behind.

The longer-run divergence between the performance of consumer prices and wholesale and export prices, wider than in other industrial societies, is noteworthy. The statistical explanation is that the different indexes embody different components, having different weights. In particular the consumer price index places substantially greater weight on services and agricultural products than does the wholesale price index. Underlying this statistical explanation are changes in economic structure and relative prices. Relative price changes occur as various sectors have different growths in demand for their output, have different rates of productivity increase, and respond with different supply elasticities to changing wages of labor and prices of other inputs. In Japan the rates of productivity change have differed greatly, a manifestation of rapid growth: in many services and in agriculture increases in labor productivity, though often substantial, have lagged behind the outstanding industrial productivity performance, a phenomenon common to most growing economies. Since in competitive labor markets wage divergences are smaller (and in situations of perfect competition equal for homogeneous labor, regardless of sector), changes in relative prices are inevitable.

In Japan the continuing decrease in the degree of economic dualism has enhanced the degree of change in relative prices. This has been one manifestation of Japan's evolution from a labor-abundant, less developed country to a relatively labor-scarce, advanced industrial economy. Put simply, once abundant, unskilled, low-wage labor has been absorbed into more productive uses, not only have wages risen absolutely but wage differentials have narrowed substantially. This process has included a narrowing of unskilled wage differentials among sectors and by size of firm; thus economic dualism has decreased. Employers who once relied on low-wage workers under the dual structure increasingly are unable to do so. This has put even further cost pressures on such enterprises, pressures that spill over into higher prices when they cannot be compensated for by productivity improvements. In some sectors rising demand as income grows has offset adverse relative price movements enough that adjustment burdens have not been severe. In others government policy has abetted higher relative prices and eased adjustment; agricultural price supports with restrictions on imports, and restrictions on large-scale competition against "Mom-and-Pop" retail establishments are prime examples. And, as already noted, most of the price increases in manufactured goods have been for the output of small firms, since their productivity increases have not been as great as that of large firms. Thus both wholesale and consumer prices of small firm products have increased more rapidly than for large firms.[16] While it is not clear whether the output of large firms constitutes a larger component of the wholesale price index than of the consumer price index, it is certainly the case for exports. Large firms, especially in high productivity, price-competitive industries, dominate export production; the share of small firms in exports has been substantially lower than in all manufacturing during most of the postwar period.[17]

In 1973–75 the historical patterns of divergence among various price indexes were overwhelmed by the forces contributing to the high rate of inflation and its subsequent slowdown. While some divergence will persist in the future, we expect its degree to be smaller than in the past as wage differentials become smaller.

The Welfare Effects of Growth

Much of the discussion of Japan's outstanding economic performance focuses on production, with an implicit assumption that increasing output has brought about an improvement in the people's economic welfare. Increasing public concern over the past several years with problems of urban-

16. EPA, *Economic Survey of Japan, 1972–1973*, pp. 140–41. Statistics Department, Bank of Japan, *Price Indexes Annual, 1974*, p. 100.

17. William V. Rapp, "Firm Size and Japan's Export Structure: A Micro-view of Japan's Changing Export Competitiveness Since Meiji," in Hugh Patrick (ed.), *Japanese Industrialization and Its Social Consequences* (University of California Press, forthcoming).

ization and of environmental pollution has brought this assumption into question.[18] Evaluation of economic welfare, and more broadly of the quality of life, is at best difficult and rather subjective. In the case of Japan appraisal is made even more difficult by the striking inbalances and contrasts that exist —an expanding supply of most private consumption goods and services, but concomitantly an urban housing shortage, inadequate public amenities and services, and substantial deterioration of the living environment. (Certain of these themes are treated in Chapters 9 and 10.) To many Americans Japan, especially the 72 percent that is urban, seems an affluent, expensive, crime-free, pollution-ridden, poorly housed, congested nation of happy, industrious people.

In historical perspective, it is incontrovertible that the objective economic conditions of almost all Japanese have improved immensely over the past twenty years as a consequence of rapid industrial growth. The terrible trage-dies of Minamata disease, of respiratory disease in air-polluted Yokkaichis, and of high death rates in traffic accidents cannot be denied; but such ex-treme cases of the ill effects of industrialization are relatively few in com-parison to Japan's total population. (This does not mean, of course, that they should be tolerated or accepted as an inevitable by-product of growth, though in fact they have been by many Japanese until recently.) Nor does the lag-ging supply of housing or most public services mean an absolute worsening of the quality of life, but simply that improvements have not kept up with the rising demand for them. The more subtle and difficult tradeoff is between certain absolutely worsening conditions—such as increases in urban com-muting time and increasingly polluted air and water—and the more wide-spread improvements in the quantity and quality of consumption. In retro-spect, Japan's pattern of rapid growth, in which public services and housing lagged relatively and the environment worsened absolutely, was not optimal in terms of social welfare; nonetheless, the quality of life of the average Japanese has improved significantly, in many respects dramatically, during the past quarter century of this kind of growth.

In Japan as elsewhere it has come to be recognized that conventional per capita measures of economic activity—GNP, national income, personal dis-posable income, private consumption, public current expenditures—indicate only certain aspects of changes even in a rather narrowly defined concept of economic welfare. Using the methodology developed by Nordhaus and

18. For a discussion focusing on the social costs of Japanese postwar industrializa-tion, see John W. Bennett and Solomon B. Levine, "Industrialization and Social Depriva-tion: Welfare, Environment, and the Post-Industrial Society in Japan," in Patrick (ed.), *Japanese Industrialization*.

Tobin,[19] the Economic Planning Agency has made preliminary estimates of the net national welfare (NNW) of Japan between 1955 and 1970.[20] While the methodology is crude and the data are considerably cruder, the estimates suggest that Japanese economic welfare as measured by NNW has increased quite rapidly, though less so than the relevant GNP output measure. A major increase in welfare has come from the greatly expanded holdings of consumer durable goods. In contrast to the situation two decades ago, Japanese families have an abundance of color TV sets, kitchen equipment, and the like; they lag behind European levels only in housing and automobile ownership. On the other hand, leisure has not increased, mainly because thus far the number of hours worked per year has not declined significantly despite the large increases in personal income. Japan remains a country of hard workers, with a long work week and vacations that are few and brief. Perhaps most striking has been the sharp decrease in welfare in the form of environmental pollution. The NNW measure includes a negative valuation for the absolute worsening of environmental conditions compared to 1955 levels.

The aggregate figures on net national welfare are a pale reflection of what have been major transformations of lifestyles for most Japanese. Almost everyone is so much better off that the range of options available to the individual has expanded substantially. Life is much more urban; even those living in more rural areas have better transport facilities to nearby towns, travel more, have a wide range of consumer goods available for purchase, and are influenced by urban taste patterns. The share of family household income spent on necessities has sharply declined; more income is available for discretionary uses. The proportion of income spent on food and beverages (the Engel coefficient) decreased to 32.7 percent in 1972; more important, the quality of food consumption has been substantially upgraded.[21] The typical Japanese diet now contains much more fish and meat, dairy products, and vegetables and fruit, and much less grain; generational differences are perhaps most pronounced in such food preferences. Japanese, long avid readers, have also become avid television watchers.[22] A considerable portion

19. William Nordhaus and James Tobin, "Economic Growth," in National Bureau of Economic Research, *Economic Research: Retrospect and Prospect*, vol. 5 (Columbia University Press, 1972).

20. Economic Council of Japan, NNW Measurement Committee, *Measuring Net National Welfare of Japan* (1973).

21. See Economic Planning Agency, *Whitepaper on National Life, 1973*, pt. 1, chap. 1.

22. Television watching is the single most important leisure activity in Japan, for both males and females. For an interesting discussion and data on leisure, see EPA, *Whitepaper on National Life, 1972*, pt. 2, chap. 4; pt. 2 is published in English as *The Japanese and Their Society: Part II of the Report on National Life, 1972*.

of leisure time is also spent outside the house, at restaurants, theaters, bars, sports activities, *pachinko* (a type of pinball) parlors, and in travel. Japanese frequently point out that this is due to inadequate housing facilities; housing indeed remains a substantial problem, especially in urban areas, since despite absolute improvements demands are far from satisfied (see Chapter 10 on this point).

Economic measures by no means capture the full range of changes in material welfare that are usually associated with economic growth. A much broader approach lies in "social indicators" that incorporate physical measures of health, safety, the natural environment, residential conditions, work conditions, educational, cultural, and leisure activities, and the like. While informative, this approach presents serious problems of determining which indicators are relevant, and especially how they should be weighted to obtain an aggregate welfare index. Moreover, causal relationships among economic and noneconomic variables in the process of growth have yet to be well specified and measured.[23]

In the last few years considerable government and private research on social indicators has been undertaken.[24] Table 1-4 provides time series data on a representative set of such indicators. Almost all measures indicate absolute improvement, though at substantially different rates. The main exceptions are the increase in total traffic accidents and the worsening air pollution caused by carbon monoxide, mainly from automobile exhausts. Air and water pollution measures are probably deficient in that they cover only a few of the largest urban areas, while pollution has probably worsened on a much wider scale nationally.

Earlier we stressed that Japan's productive activities in per capita terms had reached Western European levels. Consumption lags somewhat behind production, since a higher proportion of GNP is devoted to investment. Nonetheless, in general, production comparisons apply also to consumption and economic welfare and also to major social indicators. Table 1-5 provides comparative data for Japan, Western European nations, and the United States.[25] Japan ranks relatively high in life expectancy, newspaper usage, and

23. For an interesting preliminary effort at econometric model-building involving the interrelationships among economic and noneconomic variables, see Kimio Uno, "The Limits of Japanese Growth: An Econometric Study" (Ph.D. dissertation, University of Illinois, 1973).

24. For a useful discussion, see Naomi Maruo, "A Measure of Welfare Standards of the Japanese People," *The Annual of the Institute of Economic Research*, vol. 3 (Chuo University, 1972), pp. 101–34.

25. As noted earlier, such comparative data, while appearing in standard international sources and often used, should not be accepted uncritically because of differences

Table 1-4. Social Indicators, Japan, 1960–71[a]

Indicator	1960	1961	1962	1963	1964	1965	1966	1967	1968	1969	1970	1971
Subsistence												
1. Engel coefficient[b]	40.6 (100.0)	40.3 (103.2)	39.0 (106.7)	38.5 (108.1)	37.9 (109.1)	38.1 (109.2)	37.1 (112.1)	36.6 (113.7)	35.6 (116.9)	34.6 (120.2)	34.2 (121.6)	n.a.
Safety												
2. Tuberculosis mortality rate per 100,000 persons	34.2 (100.0)	29.6 (115.5)	29.3 (116.7)	24.2 (141.3)	23.6 (144.9)	22.8 (150.0)	20.3 (168.5)	17.8 (192.1)	16.7 (204.8)	16.1 (212.4)	15.5 (220.6)	12.9 (265.1)
3. Infant mortality rate per 1,000 births	30.7 (100.0)	28.6 (107.3)	26.4 (116.3)	23.2 (132.3)	20.4 (150.5)	18.5 (165.9)	19.3 (159.1)	14.9 (206.0)	15.1 (203.3)	14.2 (216.2)	13.1 (234.4)	12.4 (247.6)
4. Maternal mortality rate per 100,000 births	131.0 (100.0)	120.0 (100.2)	n.a.	102.0 (128.4)	n.a.	88.0 (148.9)	93.0 (140.9)	71.0 (184.5)	68.0 (192.6)	58.0 (225.9)	52.0 (251.9)	45.0 (291.9)
5. Traffic accident mortality rate per 100,000 persons	12.9 (100.0)	13.6 (91.9)	12.0 (107.5)	12.8 (100.8)	13.7 (94.2)	12.7 (101.6)	14.0 (92.1)	13.6 (94.9)	14.1 (91.5)	15.9 (81.1)	16.2 (79.6)	15.5 (83.2)
6. Homicide rate per 100,000 persons	2.8 (100.0)	2.8 (101.8)	2.5 (114.6)	2.4 (119.4)	2.4 (116.9)	2.3 (121.5)	2.3 (127.5)	2.2 (134.8)	2.2 (130.4)	2.1 (138.0)	1.9 (148.2)	1.9 (153.0)
7. Life expectancy (average for one-year-old male and female)	67.8 (100.0)	68.4 (100.9)	69.2 (102.1)	69.8 (102.9)	70.2 (103.5)	70.8 (104.4)	71.0 (104.7)	71.5 (105.5)	71.7 (105.8)	71.9 (106.2)	72.0 (106.2)	72.9 (107.5)
Average index	100.0	104.4	...	119.9	...	130.6	130.6	151.2	152.9	161.3	164.4	...
Health												
8. Doctors per 100,000 persons	110.4 (100.0)	110.6 (100.2)	110.8 (100.4)	110.7 (100.3)	111.2 (100.7)	111.3 (100.8)	111.8 (101.3)	111.4 (100.9)	112.1 (101.5)	113.0 (102.4)	114.7 (103.9)	n.a.
9. Nurses per 100,000 persons	198.7 (100.0)	206.4 (103.9)	215.4 (108.4)	224.0 (112.7)	236.4 (119.0)	249.5 (125.6)	267.6 (134.7)	228.1 (114.8)	235.7 (118.6)	248.1 (124.9)	263.8 (132.8)	n.a.
10. Hospital beds per 100,000 persons	735.0 (100.0)	759.0 (103.3)	791.0 (107.6)	821.0 (112.4)	858.0 (116.7)	889.0 (121.0)	927.0 (126.1)	961.0 (130.7)	950.0 (134.7)	1,007.0 (137.0)	1,025.0 (139.5)	n.a.
Average index	100.0	102.5	105.5	108.5	112.1	115.8	120.7	115.5	118.3	121.4	125.4	...
Environmental pollution												
11. Air pollution												
Sulfa-oxide levels in Tokyo (parts per million)	n.a.	n.a.	0.053 (100.0)	0.042 (126.2)	0.049 (108.2)	0.059 (80.8)	0.074 (71.0)	0.068 (77.9)	0.074 (71.6)	0.068 (77.4)	0.053 (100.0)	n.a.
Carbon monoxide levels in Tokyo (parts per million)	n.a.	n.a.	n.a.	n.a.	n.a.	4.1 (100.0)	4.4 (93.2)	4.9 (83.7)	5.1 (80.4)	6.4 (64.1)	5.0 (80.0)	n.a.
Dust fall per month (tons per square kilometer)	n.a.	19.7 (100.0)	19.1 (103.1)	18.5 (106.4)	15.4 (127.9)	17.0 (115.9)	16.8 (117.3)	16.2 (121.6)	16.0 (123.1)	15.8 (124.7)	n.a.	n.a.
12. Water pollution: biological oxygen demand (parts per million)	n.a.	22.4 (100.0)	14.0 (100.0)	40.9 (54.8)	21.8 (102.8)	16.7 (134.1)	15.1 (148.3)	17.0 (131.8)	16.3 (137.4)	18.9 (118.5)	n.a.	n.a.

Residential environment

	1	2	3	4	5	6	7	8	9	10	11	12
13. Average house space per person (1 unit = 1.6 square meters)	4.3 (100.0)	n.a.	n.a.	4.9 (114.0)	n.a.	5.1 (118.6)	n.a.	n.a.	5.6 (130.2)	n.a.	6.1 (141.9)	n.a.
14. Sewerage (percent of houses connected to public system)	n.a.	19.3 (100.0)	19.6 (101.6)	20.8 (108.7)	23.6 (122.3)	23.8 (123.3)	24.7 (128.0)	27.0 (139.9)	28.6 (148.2)	28.7 (148.7)	26.4 (136.8)	n.a.
15. Park area per one inhabitant, Tokyo (square meters)	0.46 (100.0)	0.51 (110.9)	0.57 (123.9)	0.63 (137.0)	0.69 (150.0)	0.76 (165.2)	0.83 (180.9)	0.89 (193.5)	0.99 (215.2)	1.07 (232.6)	1.20 (260.9)	n.a.
Average index	100.0	...	...	119.6	...	135.7	...	...	164.5	...	179.9	...

Work and social welfare

	1	2	3	4	5	6	7	8	9	10	11	12
16. Mortality rate for work-related accidents per 100,000 workers	17.4 (100.0)	17.4 (100.0)	15.5 (112.3)	13.8 (126.1)	13.5 (128.9)	12.4 (140.3)	12.5 (139.2)	11.8 (147.5)	13.5 (128.9)	12.7 (137.0)	11.3 (154.0)	10.0 (174.0)
17. Workdays lost by labor disputes per trade union member	0.6526 (100.0)	0.7542 (86.7)	0.6148 (106.3)	0.2989 (218.7)	0.3279 (199.3)	0.5630 (116.1)	0.2660 (245.7)	0.1747 (374.1)	0.2637 (247.9)	0.2363 (276.6)	0.3410 (191.7)	0.5160 (126.7)
18. Average hours worked per month	202.7 (100.0)	201.0 (110.8)	197.8 (102.5)	196.6 (103.1)	195.7 (103.6)	192.9 (105.1)	193.2 (104.9)	193.0 (105.0)	192.7 (105.2)	199.0 (106.7)	187.7 (108.0)	185.7 (109.2)
19. Social workers per 1,000 persons	1.42 (100.0)	1.42 (100.0)	1.46 (102.8)	1.45 (102.1)	1.46 (102.8)	1.46 (102.8)	1.46 (102.8)	1.44 (101.4)	1.43 (100.7)	1.27 (89.4)	n.a.	n.a.
20. Social welfare facilities per 100,000 persons	4.2 (100.0)	4.5 (106.7)	4.6 (108.6)	4.7 (111.7)	5.1 (120.2)	5.4 (127.4)	5.8 (137.6)	6.1 (145.7)	8.2 (194.8)	8.8 (209.8)	9.5 (225.2)	9.9 (236.2)
Average index	100.0	98.8	106.5	132.3	131.0	118.3	146.0	174.7	155.5	163.9	...	...

Education and culture

	1	2	3	4	5	6	7	8	9	10	11	12
21. University and college students (percent of age group)	17.2 (100.0)	17.9 (104.1)	19.3 (112.2)	20.9 (121.5)	23.4 (136.0)	25.4 (147.7)	24.5 (142.4)	23.7 (137.8)	23.1 (134.3)	23.1 (134.3)	24.2 (140.7)	26.8 (155.8)
22. Senior high school pupils (percent of age group)	57.7 (100.0)	62.3 (108.0)	64.0 (110.9)	66.8 (115.8)	69.3 (120.1)	70.7 (122.5)	72.3 (125.3)	74.5 (129.1)	76.8 (133.1)	79.4 (137.6)	82.1 (142.3)	85.0 (147.3)
23. Pupils per teacher — Elementary schools	35.0 (100.0)	34.0 (99.8)	32.0 (106.5)	31.0 (110.2)	29.0 (118.4)	28.0 (122.9)	28.0 (125.6)	27.0 (130.7)	26.0 (136.4)	26.0 (136.4)	26.0 (136.4)	25.0 (139.1)
Secondary schools	29.0 (100.0)	28.0 (102.9)	28.0 (100.4)	27.0 (107.4)	25.0 (120.7)	28.0 (125.0)	28.0 (125.0)	27.0 (120.6)	26.0 (134.6)	26.0 (134.6)	26.0 (134.6)	25.0 (140.0)
24. Daily newspaper copies per day per 100 persons	26.0 (100.0)	27.0 (103.8)	27.0 (103.6)	29.0 (111.5)	30.0 (116.0)	31.0 (120.8)	32.0 (126.1)	33.0 (131.8)	34.0 (130.8)	34.0 (138.1)	36.0 (138.5)	37.0 (142.3)
25. Television sets per 100 families	33.2 (100.0)	49.5 (149.1)	64.8 (195.2)	75.9 (228.6)	83.0 (250.0)	75.6 (227.7)	79.8 (240.4)	84.2 (253.6)	88.1 (265.4)	91.7 (276.2)	94.8 (285.5)	96.7 (291.3)
26. Telephones per 100 persons	0.5 (100.0)	0.6 (120.0)	0.8 (160.0)	1.1 (220.0)	1.4 (280.0)	2.0 (400.0)	2.7 (540.0)	3.6 (720.0)	4.8 (960.0)	6.1 (1220.0)	n.a.	n.a.
Average index	100.0	110.6	125.2	141.0	157.1	157.6	133.5	219.9	254.1	288.5	...	...

Table 1-4 (continued)

Indicator	1960	1961	1962	1963	1964	1965	1966	1967	1968	1969	1970	1971
Leisure												
27. Average leisure hours in a year per person	2,022.8 (100.0)	n.a.	n.a.	n.a.	n.a.	2,359.1 (116.6)	n.a.	n.a.	n.a.	n.a.	2,348.8 (116.1)	n.a.
28. Travel												
Travelers making trips of more than one night per 100,000 persons	32.0 (100.0)	37.0 (115.6)	n.a.	n.a.	47.0 (146.9)	n.a.	n.a.	60.0 (187.5)	65.0 (203.1)	71.0 (221.9)	n.a.	n.a.
Travelers abroad per 100,000 persons	127.9 (100.0)	152.1 (119.3)	153.1 (119.7)	193.8 (151.5)	227.7 (178.0)	270.3 (211.3)	344.5 (269.4)	427.0 (333.9)	534.2 (417.7)	693.7 (542.4)	902.6 (713.5)	1,203.0 (940.6)
29. Leisure consumption coefficient[c]	n.a.	n.a.	n.a.	18.2 (100.0)	18.5 (101.6)	18.5 (101.6)	19.4 (106.6)	20.2 (111.0)	21.4 (117.6)	22.4 (123.1)	23.3 (128.0)	23.4 (128.6)
Alienation												
30. Suicide rate per 100,000 persons	21.6 (100.1)	19.6 (110.2)	17.6 (112.7)	16.1 (134.2)	15.1 (143.0)	14.7 (146.9)	15.2 (142.1)	12.2 (152.1)	14.5 (149.0)	14.5 (149.0)	15.3 (141.2)	15.6 (138.5)

Source: Naomi Maruo, "A Measure of Welfare Standards of the Japanese People," *The Annual of the Institute of Economic Research*, vol. 3 (Chuo University, 1972), table 5.

n.a. Not available.

a. The numbers in parentheses are indexes.

b. Ratio of expenditures on food, beverages, and tobacco to final private consumption expenditure.

c. Ratio of expenditures on entertainment activities and travel to total consumption expenditures.

lack of homicides, but low in housing and environmental pollution. Aggregate welfare index measures based on these data suggest that Japan in 1970 ranked somewhat below the other nations in the sample, though admittedly the estimates are quite arbitrary.[26]

Income and Wealth Distribution

Thus far we have focused on the improvements in aggregate or average per capita welfare. Rapid growth has indeed caused a major improvement in general standards of living; almost everyone has benefited absolutely in higher real incomes and wealth. But the benefits of growth have not been distributed evenly. Income and wealth distribution by individual or family unit has not yet attracted wide attention or systematic sudy in Japan, in part, perhaps, because this issue has been overshadowed by the general absolute improvements as well as by the emerging general problems of urbanization and environmental pollution.[27] Furthermore, comprehensive data on the distribution of income, and particularly of wealth, are lacking.

Several broad conclusions can nonetheless be stated about income distribution—when capital gains are excluded from the definition of income. First, war destruction, occupation policies, and early postwar inflation resulted in a substantially more even distribution of income in the early 1950s compared with the prewar period. Second, income has become somewhat more evenly distributed since then.[28] Third, income distribution is probably about as even in Japan as in the United States.[29]

The evolving pattern of wealth distribution is much less clear. The early

---

in definitions, measurement techniques, coverage, and the like. For example, good data are not available for international comparisons of pollution levels, and the number of hours worked per week in Japan appears to be seriously underestimated here. (On this, see Chapter 2.)

26. Maruo, "A Measure of Welfare Standards," pp. 120–21. The ranking of countries on a particular category were determined by their relation either to the highest and lowest values or to the mean and standard deviation. The individual indicators were weighted equally in the aggregate index in two of the three methods. The rank orders were Sweden, the United Kingdom, the United States (all close together), West Germany and France, and Italy and Japan.

27. See, however, Economic Planning Agency, *Economic Survey of Japan, 1971–1972*, chap. 4.

28. See Chapter 5, and Akira Ono and Tsunehiko Watanabe, "Changes in Income Inequality in the Japanese Economy," in Patrick (ed.), *Japanese Industrialization*.

29. Data in EPA, *Economic Survey of Japan, 1971–1972*, pp. 132–38, suggest that wage income is more evenly distributed in Japan than in the United States but that total income of wage earners less so. Unfortunately, comparable data for all income using the same definitions and measures are not available.

Table 1-5. Social Indicators, Japan and Selected Western Industrialized Countries

Indicator	Japan	United States	United Kingdom	West Germany	France	Italy	Sweden
Subsistence							
1. Engel coefficient,[a] 1971	33.75	18.22	32.53	28.82	32.63	41.73	28.87
Safety							
2. Motor vehicle mortality rate per 100,000 persons[b]	20.2	25.4	17.3[e]	31.9	23.5	24.3	17.1
3. Maternal mortality rate per 100,000 births, 1968	68.1	24.8	24.4	51.0	29.0	75.0	8.7
4. Infant mortality rate[d] per 100,000 live births, 1971	12.4	19.2[e]	17.5[e]	23.3	17.1	28.3[e]	11.1
5. Purposeful homicide rate per 100,000 persons, 1971	1.0	2.9[f]	0.6	1.3	1.2	0.8	1.0
6. Life expectancy at birth, 1975–80	74.1	70.9	73.1	71.6	74.3	73.5	73.3
Health							
7. Doctors per 100,000 persons, 1970	11.3	15.8	12.2[e]	17.2	13.4	18.1	13.6
8. Nurses per 100,000 persons, 1970	41.5	53.4	32.7	29.0	27.1	21.4	50.8
9. Hospital beds per 100,000 persons, 1970	126.9	78.9	91.8	111.0	77.2	106.9	149.5
Environmental pollution[g]							
10. Sulfurous gas (parts per million)	0.051	0.103	0.070	0.080	n.a.	n.a.	n.a.
11. Mercury content in hair (parts per million)	6.50	0.50	1.50	1.10	n.a.	n.a.	n.a.
Residential environment							
12. Rooms per capita[h]	0.97	1.43	1.43	1.11	1.11	n.a.	n.a.
13. Residential construction as percent of gross domestic product, 1971	7.15[i]	4.13	2.93	5.88	6.68	5.95	4.74
14. Sewerage (percent of dwellings with flush toilets)[j]	17.1	83.8	98.9	94.2	51.8	n.a.	90.1
15. Roads							
Paved roads as percent of total, 1973	25.2	79.8[k]	100.0	85.0	84.3[l]	93.0	50.0
Road density (kilometers of roads per square kilometers of land), 1973	2.82	0.65	1.48	1.85	1.44	0.96	0.24
16. Park area per capita in selected urban areas (square meters)[m]	1.15	19.2	22.8	20.3	7.4	10.4	n.a.

Work environment

17. Mortality rate for work-related accidents per 1,000 workers, 1970	0.04	0.04	0.04	0.17	0.10	0.13	0.05
18. Workdays lost to strikes per 1,000 workers, average 1970–72[n]	96	544	633	57	152	960	97
19. Hours worked per person in manufacturing							
Per week, 1972	42.3	40.6	44.1	42.7	44.0	n.a.	n.a.
Per year, 1969	2,280	1,952[o]	1,997[o]	1,870	1,988	n.a.	1,800
Education and culture							
20. University and college students as percent of age group, 1970[p]	18.7	44.4	14.1	12.3	15.6	n.a.	n.a.
21. Newspaper circulation per 1,000 persons, 1972	519	297	528	319[i]	237[q]	133	534[i]
22. Television sets per 1,000 persons, 1971	291	388	593	781	397	154	958
23. Telephones per 100 persons, 1972	31.5	62.8	31.5	26.8	19.9	20.6	57.6
24. Films attended per capita, 1971	2.0	5.0[i]	3.2	3.0	3.5	10.0	3.3
Alienation							
25. Suicide rate per 100,000 persons[r]	15.6	11.1	8.1[r]	21.2	15.4	5.8	22.3

Sources: Row (1): United Nations, *Yearbook of National Accounts Statistics, 1972*, pp. 645, 636–37, 587, 392, 359–60, 589–90, 468–69. Row (2): UN, *Demographic Yearbook, 1972*, pp. 582–97. Row (3): Maruo, "A Measure of Welfare Standards of the Japanese People," table 5. Row (4): UN, *Demographic Yearbook, 1972*, pp. 503–07. Row (5): ibid., pp. 582–97. Row (6): UN Statistical Office, *Monthly Bulletin of Statistics*, April 1971, pp. xxx–xxxiii. Row (7): WHO, *World Health Statistics Annual, 1970, 1971*. Row (8): ibid., vol. III, pp. 54–55. Row (9): ibid., pp. 222–25. Row (10): Maruo, "A Measure of Welfare Standards," table 5. Row (11): ibid. Row (12): Ministry of Construction, *Kensetsu hakusho* [White-paper on Construction] (1972), p. 5. Row (13): UN, *Yearbook of National Accounts Statistics, 1972*, vol. 1, pp. 640, 648, 384, 394, 352, 363, 580, 593; vol. 2, pp. 629, 640, 576, 591, 453, 473. Row (14): UN, *Statistical Yearbook, 1974*, pp. 786–819. Row (15): International Road Federation, *World Road Statistics, 1969–73* (1974), pp. 12–21. Row (16): Ministry of Construction, *Whitepaper on Construction, 1972*, pp. 5, 76; Maruo, "A Measure of Welfare Standards," table 5. Row (17): ibid. Row (18): calculated from International Labour Office, *Yearbook of Labour Statistics, 1973*, pp. 8–41, 750–58; *1972*, pp. 9–42; *1971*, pp. 10–43. Row (19): UN Statistical Office, *Monthly Bulletin of Statistics*, June 1974, p. 16; Maruo, "A Measure of Welfare Standards," table 5. Row (20): Ministry of Education, *Daigaku shiryō* [Research Materials on Universities], no. 50 (1974), p. 51. Row (21): UN, *Statistical Yearbook, 1973*, pp. 805–07. Row (22): UNESCO, *Statistical Yearbook, 1972*, pp. 872–75. Row (23): UN, *Statistical Yearbook, 1973*, pp. 495–98. Row (24): UNESCO, *Statistical Yearbook, 1972*, pp. 826–30. Row (25): UN, *Demographic Yearbook, 1972*, pp. 582–97.

a. Ratio of expenditures on food, beverages, and tobacco to final private consumption expenditure.
b. Data are for 1971 for Japan, the United States, and the United Kingdom; for 1970 for the remainder.
c. England and Wales only.
d. Deaths of infants under one year old.
e. Provisional figure.

Footnotes continued on page 38

Table 1-5 (*continued*)

f. 1969.
g. Data are for 1966 for Japan, 1965 and 1969 for the United States, 1968 for the United Kingdom, and 1967 and 1968 for West Germany.
h. Data are for 1968 for Japan, 1961 for the United Kingdom, and 1960 for the remainder.
i. 1970.
j. Data are for 1968 for Japan and France, 1970 for the United States and Sweden, 1971 for the United Kingdom, and 1972 for West Germany.
k. 1972.
l. Calculated from information given in the source.
m. Data are for Tokyo (1971), New York City (1967), London (1967), Munich (1968), Paris (1965), and Rome (no date).
n. Workers in the total labor force, that is, the economically active population. Figures used were rough ones.
o. 1968.
p. Age group consists of persons eighteen to twenty-one for Japan and the United States, eighteen to twenty for the United Kingdom, nineteen to twenty-two for West Germany, and eighteen to twenty-two for France.
q. 1971.
r. Data are for 1971 for Japan, the United States, and the United Kingdom; for 1970 for the remainder.

postwar distribution of wealth was no doubt substantially less uneven than that before the war. However, since then the value of real reproducible capital and of land, especially in and near urban areas, has risen rapidly, and the owners of these assets have thus had major increments in their wealth, both absolutely and relative to persons holding financial assets and those without substantial assets (such as renters of dwellings). Between 1952 and 1973 the price of urban land went up by 58.0 times, while in current prices GNP increased by 17.7 times, average money wages increased by 8.6 times, and the Dow Jones stock index average rose 19.4 times. Not all owners of real assets have benefited, however; it has not been so lucrative to own submarginal farm land far from urban areas or other land without rapidly rising opportunity costs in alternative uses, or to own inefficient small (or large) businesses facing cost pressures greater than increases in demand for their products. To the extent that land ownership has been widely dispersed among farmers and urban home owners, the price rises have made these large groups of people moderately wealthy. One suspects, however, that as in other countries the ownership of land, and particularly of equity claims on real assets, is rather concentrated; the sharp absolute and relative increase in their value has probably tended to concentrate wealth, despite high saving rates among most families.

While there are obviously substantial numbers of very well-to-do Japanese families, major fortunes are not well publicized. Certain well-known prewar families of immense wealth—the Mitsuis, the Iwasakis, the Yasudas—no longer have such wealth or prominence. Even where families control and manage large and well-known firms, their stock ownership is frequently of a surprisingly small proportion. Management in large firms are well rewarded, especially in perquisites, but typically do not amass substantial fortunes. (See the discussion in Chapter 5 on managerial incentives.) The owners of the many successful small- and medium-size enterprises have built modest fortunes. Who really owns Japan's real wealth is something of a mystery once the veils of institutional holdings are stripped away. Unfortunately, no data are available on the distribution of wealth by size when the all-important real assets are included.

These evolving patterns of income and wealth distribution have been caused by much the same forces. The occupation authorities changed the tax structure to place major emphasis on direct taxes on personal and corporate income with progressive rates (see Chapter 5). The farmland and *zaibatsu* dissolution reforms were not confiscatory in principle since previous owners were compensated in nontransferable long-term bonds, but they were so in practice because of inflation. Aside, perhaps, from wartime destruction itself, rampant inflation between 1945 and 1949 turned out to be by far the most important force, if an erratic one, in the early postwar equalization of income and wealth. It wiped out the value of public and private debt.

Over the past twenty years the most important factor affecting income and wealth distribution has been rapid growth itself, with government policy also of some importance. Growth-induced demand for labor has caused not only a major increase in wages but also substantial narrowing of virtually all wage differentials—by age, education, sex, size of firm, occupation, and even degree of skill (see Chapter 9). This has substantially reduced income differentials. Chūbachi and Taira go so far as to argue that there no longer is an urban poor class, as defined by a distinctive life-style and substantial income differential; the poor are joining the middle class.[30]

The net effect of the government tax policy on income distribution is minimal, since progressive rates are offset by preferential treatment of dividend and interest income and since realized capital gains are taxed only in the case of land (see Chapter 5). However, government protection and subsidization of agriculture, and to a lesser extent of small business, has had a substantial equalizing impact on both income and wealth distribution. Historically, most farmers have been at the lower end of the income and wealth scale. Now farm family income is at parity with that of urban worker families. This is partly attributable to the growth-induced increase in nearby nonfarm job opportunities; approximately three-fifths of farm family income is now derived from family members working elsewhere. Heavy protection and high prices for agricultural products—notably for rice, which still comprises two-fifths of farm output—has been an effective means of income redistribution from consumers and taxpayers to farmers. While the motivation of this policy has been heavily political—farmers have been among the strongest supporters of the reigning Liberal-Democratic party in a gerrymandered district system (on which see Chapter 11)—its effect has been to promote greater equalization of income and wealth. Higher prices for agricultural products are rapidly translated into higher land values, even in those areas of more limited alternative land uses.

The Japanese government does not substantially redistribute income through social security and related transfer payments, unlike most Western European nations (though not so different from the United States). Such social insurance transfer payments—pensions, unemployment compensation, assistance to unemployable households, and the like—have constituted 5 to 6

30. Masao Chūbachi and Kōji Taira, "Poverty in Japanese Development," in Patrick (ed.), *Japanese Industrialization.*

percent of GNP in Japan, about one-third the European ratios.[31] Government retirement benefits for other than government employees are very limited. Perhaps the main redistributive component of government expenditures, aside from agricultural price supports, lies in the national health program, which provides universal coverage.

The rapidly increasing wealth values of land and equities are also directly attributable to growth. Land has become relatively much more scarce as the labor supply, and particularly the stock of capital, has risen. Price increases have been exacerbated in urban areas by the inflow of people, and by lagging adjustments and continuing inefficiency in land use. The rising value of the stock of real assets, and especially of equities, is attributable to the increasing size of the capital stock itself, the higher valuation placed on it (reflected in the rising price-earnings ratios of equities), and the extensive use of debt to finance asset acquisition. Postwar inflation, especially in 1973–74, has also had a substantial impact on wealth distribution, probably more so than directly on income distribution. The general rise in consumer prices has been reflected in upward movements in the nominal prices of real assets as well; on the other hand, the price of most financial assets (including time deposits, the major saving vehicle of most Japanese) did not rise, thereby worsening the relative position of those holding them.

All this is not to assert that there are no distributional problems in Japan. There are, but they often are seen not so much in terms of size distribution as in conflicts among different groups—farmers versus consumers, landowners versus urban renters who desire residential lots but cannot afford the high prices, large versus small business, workers versus capitalists, young versus old.

One age-related issue is the degree to which wages increase with age and seniority. Another problem now emerging concerns the aged. With the early formal retirement age between fifty-five and sixty and the poor public and private retirement benefits, most retirees continue to work, but at substantially lower wages.[32] In times of stress employment opportunities may diminish and unemployment rise among this age group. The increase in life expectancy to higher than American levels, the rising proportion of aged in the population (10.6 percent of the population in 1970), and the prevalence of the nuclear family in urban settings are bringing forth a host of distributional and social issues.

The distribution of income by factor share, notably the proportion of na-

31. EPA, *Economic Survey of Japan, 1971–1972*, pp. 138–44.
32. Economic Planning Agency, *Whitepaper on National Life, 1973*, pp. 64–81.

tional income accruing to labor, has attracted considerable attention in Japan as elsewhere (see Chapter 9). While the share of wages in national income has risen, so also has the share of wage-earning employees in the total labor force. (The still relatively large proportion of self-employed and family workers makes estimation of total labor income more difficult.) In aggregate the worker share of income is about 70 percent, below that in Western European countries and the United States.[33] Within manufacturing, the labor share in gross value added has also been relatively low, more so for large firms than small, and is not substantially changing. The relatively large income share going to owners of capital and land, and the presumed uneven distribution of ownership, suggest that the standard income distribution data overstate the degree of equality.

Regional disparities in productivity and income distribution have also narrowed somewhat but remain substantial. In 1960 the ratio of average personal income in the highest prefecture (Tokyo) to the lowest (Kagoshima) was 2.58; by 1970 the ratio had declined to 2.24. Most new high-income, high-productivity job opportunities have arisen in urban metropolitan areas. The great labor migration has been primarily by young, unmarried persons. The consequent dearth of youths in rural villages has come to be considered something of a social problem.

In sum, while life opportunities have improved absolutely for almost all Japanese, some groups continue to be discriminated against. Employees in smaller firms still receive lower wages and fringe benefits than those in larger firms, though the gap is narrowing and undoubtedly some of what remains reflects differences in education, skill, and native ability. More pronounced is discrimination against female workers. While young women may begin at the same wages as men, they are excluded from many well-paying occupations, have fewer opportunities for promotion, receive lower seniority increments and fewer fringe benefits, and are forced into retirement earlier. While Japan has by no means the problems of minority-group discrimination that the United States does, nonetheless Japanese outcastes (*burakumin*)[34] and Korean residents (most of whom were born in Japan but are unable to obtain

33. Worker share is defined as employee compensation divided by the sum of employee compensation, private income from property, and corporate income; see Maruo, "A Measure of Welfare Standards," pp. 129–30. Ohkawa and Rosovsky (*Japanese Economic Growth*, pp. 268–69) estimate that in the early 1960s Japan's aggregate labor share was several percentage points below that in the West.

34. The *burakumin* constitute about 2 percent of the population, and have a distinctive life-style and mode of speech. See George DeVos and Hiroshi Wagatsuma, *Japan's Invisible Race* (University of California Press, 1966), p. 13.

citizenship) face discriminatory employment conditions, and tend to congregate in the lower end of the income and wealth distribution scale.

The Government and the Economy

No economy operates in a vacuum. Economic behavior, incentives, and performance are shaped by legal structures and other institutional arrangements, by the political system, government policy goals and means of implementation, and ultimately by individual and societal values and ideologies. We thus regard it as important that readers have the broader perspective on the Japanese economy provided in the papers by Trezise and Suzuki on the relation of the political system to the economy (Chapter 11) and Glazer on selected social characteristics (Chapter 12) to complement the more specialized examinations of various aspects of the economy. As elsewhere in this chapter we do not attempt to summarize our coauthors' conclusions and confine ourselves to making a few general points.

Japan: A Business-Oriented Society

The domestic environment has in most respects been supportive of a market-oriented, private enterprise economic system. Japanese are industrious and strongly motivated by materialistic desires. Political stability has been the norm. A rather conservative probusiness and proagriculture political party (since 1955 the Liberal Democratic party) has been in power continuously for more than two decades. Economic policy has been effectively administered (and often formulated) by an able, purposeful, highly motivated, elite career bureaucracy of the central government. Certainly Japan has never been more business oriented than in the 1960s, when success based on private business had come to be broadly accepted as a goal and before pollution and congestion problems became important issues.

A persistent feature of postwar Japan has been the high priority given to economic goals among social objectives, and especially to growth. The loss of World War II with all its destruction initially caused the Japanese government to focus its priorities and efforts on economic reconstruction. The political, social, and economic reforms of the Allied occupation aimed at establishing a democratic Japan generated a new vitality and a widespread sense of participation. In a period when great sacrifices were required, the solution of individual inequities and the provision of public services could be deferred. By the late 1950s political leaders came to recognize that rapid economic growth solved many problems; the 1961 ten-year income-doubling plan epitomized the era of what was regarded as "virtuous growth." Growth provided the wherewithal for virtually all groups in society to lead better lives: it created jobs, and good jobs; it made the adjustment process much easier for declining industries, and alternative jobs more readily available; and it enhanced Japan's international power and prestige. Japanese have contrasted their great focus on economic growth with the different economic priorities of other industrial nations, particularly the policies of the United States government that have allocated men, skills, R&D, and capital to aerospace, defense, and the Vietnam War. The problems created by growth, though foreshadowed in the popular concerns about the rise in consumer prices starting in the early 1960s, came to be widely perceived only at the end of the decade, when both the rising costs of pollution and environmental disruption and the increasing striking imbalance between affluence in private consumption and poverty of public services and welfare activities could no longer be ignored.

Government Economic Policies

Japanese economic policy may be characterized as a mixture of active intervention and benign neglect. At the macro level, the government allowed private business the first claim on investible resources, in a secular context in which private demand was so strong that an expansive aggregate demand policy was not required. The government accordingly held down the public sector's tax and expenditure share to less than a quarter of GNP until the early 1970s, considerably below that in Western Europe and the United States. Government social overhead investment in roads, sewage systems, water supplies, and public housing was relatively neglected, as were welfare and social insurance programs, and defense expenditures were kept below 1 percent of GNP.

Japan's defense policy deserves brief attention. Article 9 of the constitution, pacifist sentiment, and political realities have dictated a minimal and essentially defensive capability. Security against external threat has been obtained by alliance with the United States, now primarily in the form of the "nuclear umbrella," that is, the promise of U.S. retaliation against any nuclear attack on Japan. Japan's defense expenditures, while low relative to GNP, maintain a sophisticated conventional force of about 250,000 men, modern interceptor jet fighters, and a small navy. A significant increase in the percentage of Japan's GNP allocated to defense could realistically be spent only for a nuclear weapons system, and such a policy would make little strategic sense for either Japan or its allies.

The low level of defense expenditures is only one factor, and certainly not a dominant one, in the explanation of Japan's rapid growth. Even if as much as 6 or 7 percent of GNP has been allocated to defense, it would have reduced the growth rate by at most only two percentage points,[35] even assuming no beneficial spillover effects of defense expenditures. Thus Japan's growth rate would still have averaged in excess of 8 percent annually. Nonetheless, the combination of circumstance and sensible Japanese policy have resulted in an allocation of resources to uses more beneficial to the economy than defense.

Despite the small share of the public sector in GNP, the government has persistently taken an active role in the economy through a variety of measures, as is amply demonstrated in the other chapters of this book. Particularly significant has been an interrelated set of policies on balance of payments, foreign trade, and industrial development (see Chapters 6, 7, and 11). Balance-of-payments deficits were the operative constraint on growth until the late 1960s. Throughout the 1950s and 1960s, despite some liberalization in the early 1960s, the government maintained the wartime and occupation policy of import restriction and provided a variety of export incentives, though on the whole they were not great.

It is not correct to say that the government developed export industries; rather it provided export incentives for industries that were sufficiently well developed domestically to begin to compete in foreign markets. The government did pursue an import-competing industrialization policy until the late 1960s, implemented with quotas and tariffs. The policy was a mixture of key-sector and infant industry approaches. Designation as a key industry brought favorable tax and depreciation treatment, loans on favorable terms, duty-free equipment imports, and protection from import competition. As the economy grew and evolved, the key industries of the occupation period—steel, shipbuilding, electric power, coal, and fertilizer—needed and received relatively less help, and were superseded by new key industries such as petrochemicals, automobiles, and computers.

As the economy grew and its capabilities and structure evolved, the government bureaucracy envisaged a shift of emphasis from labor-intensive,

35. This estimate is based on the assumption that all defense expenditures would be at the expense of investment rather than consumption and that the average incremental capital-output ratio would prevail. A reduction in the annual growth rate by two percentage points from 10 to 8 percent during 1954–74 would have reduced the size of the 1974 economy by about 30 percent.

technologically unsophisticated industries, such as cotton textiles, into more technologically advanced industries for which demand would be large and labor productivity high, such as cars, television, and computers. These were infant industries in which costs were initially high; protection of the home market from imports enabled them to cut costs through learning by doing, economies of ever-larger scales of production, and further technological innovations. As noted earlier, government policies on technology importation facilitated this process. In many instances such infant industries were designated key industries, qualifying for special help. In many other cases, notably consumer durables, industries developed in response to private demand without significant government help.

However, what governments envisage and what they do are not always identical. The Japanese government has never taken the lead in directly encouraging the transfer of resources away from inefficient uses; rather, this has occurred through the operations of the marketplace. High-growth, high-productivity industries have provided greater opportunities for profitable investment and high wages, and capital and labor have flowed there in response. As Trezise and Suzuki stress in Chapter 11, the government's response to the problem of inefficient and declining industries has been a mixture of protection from low-priced imports, other forms of direct and indirect subsidy, and, almost as a last resort, adjustment assistance in helping labor and capital move out. For example, from the late 1950s coal was no longer competitive with cheap imported oil; whether it once again becomes competitive depends on the future price of oil. After a period of trying unsuccessfully to protect coal, the government subsidized the closing of inefficient mines, the transfer and retraining of redundant workers, and the enhanced productivity of remaining facilities. In coal mining the labor force has been reduced by more than 90 percent, and new equipment has made the remaining labor much more productive.

Agriculture is by far the largest and most conspicuous sector of economic inefficiency in Japan. The transfer of labor out of agriculture has indeed been rapid, and the workers that remain are older and more difficult to absorb into industrial activity. For both social welfare and political reasons the Japanese government, as in the case of Western Europe, has heavily protected agriculture from import competition, enabling farmers to sell their output at high and rising prices. Government policy has, if anything, served to keep resources in agriculture rather than assisting directly in the long-run process of shifting these resources to more efficient uses elsewhere.

In general, government economic policy has operated through the private economy rather than by trying to replace it. Fiscal and monetary measures have been used to restructure profit incentives into favored activities. The public sector as owner and producer of goods and services has been limited in size and scope to traditional or standard areas of economic activity. Table 1-2 shows that public administration per se comprises less than 3.5 percent of GNP and the labor force. This figure does not fully reflect the range of government activities, which have an important economic impact in transportation, communications, and services—mainly educational, health, and medical. Some 8 percent of the total labor force is employed by the public sector, of which about 45 percent works for the central government. The government-owned Japan National Railways, which provides most railroad services except for regional private commuter lines servicing the major cities, employs 442,000 workers alone. The government provides postal services and also communications services through the Japan Telephone and Telegraph Public Corporation. Of the close to 1.5 million teachers, almost three-quarters are public employees, predominantly at local-government levels for the elementary and high school systems. Although the government employs some 200,000 persons in the provision of medical services, more than three-quarters of the workers in this field are private. The only significant manufacturing activity of the government is in the production of cigarettes and other tobacco products, traditionally a government monopoly for revenue purposes, with about 40,000 employees.[36]

Government and Economic Growth

One of the great issues in any analysis of Japan's postwar economic history is the evaluation of the contribution of government policy to rapid economic growth. How important has the government been? How effective its policies? Has the government role been unique? These themes underlie much of the discussion in the subsequent chapters of this book. Our view is that, while the government has certainly provided a favorable environment, the main impetus to growth has been private—business investment demand, private saving, and industrious and skilled labor operating in a market-oriented environment of relative prices. Government intervention generally has tended (and intended) to accelerate trends already put in motion by private market forces—the development of infant industries, the structural adjustment of declining industries, and the like. Protection was certainly important, as has been typical of the economic history of all industrializing countries (other than England). Careful examination of Japan's postwar trade and industrial

36. The employment figures in this paragraph are from Bureau of Statistics, *1969 Establishment Census of Japan*, vol. 1, table 5.

development in comparison with general world performance indicates that
the Japanese pattern was not unique at all; thus, while government policy
may have been important, its impact on economic performance was not
"uniquely·Japanese."[37] Indeed, the nature and extent of the government-
business relationship is in many respects similar to that in France, West
Germany, and other continental European nations; the United States is
perhaps the atypical case.

Who Governs?

A further issue of importance and interest is one of political economy:
who determines government policy? What immediately springs to mind in
this connection is the close and generally harmonious relation between government and business. While the interaction between the political system
and the economy is explored in detail in Chapter 11, the issue is of sufficient importance to be noted here.

Two elitist interpretations—equally simplistic, extreme, and, in our view,
incorrect—have been propounded: the one that government controls business (the "Japan, Inc." thesis), the other that big business controls the government (the "monopoly capitalism" or "America, Inc." thesis[38]). Such
analyses focus on three groups—the Liberal Democratic party (LDP), the
central government administrative bureaucracy, and big business. The argument is that these are the major power nodes, each is monolithic, and one
group somehow controls the others. A broader, vaguer interpretation is that
the distinctions between big business and the government (both the LDP
and the bureaucracy) are so blurred that the two form a homogeneous unity;
there is then no issue of control, since all are working for the common goal
of national betterment. This view is open to the same criticism as "Japan,
Inc." and "monopoly capitalism."

"Japan, Inc." implies central government leadership of a highly cooperative big business sector so as to constitute a homogeneous, unified, undif-
ferentiated force that purposefully, vigorously, and effectively pursues the
national interest. One definition draws an analogy to a great multidivisional
company: "The Japanese government corresponds to corporate headquarters, responsible for planning and coordination, formation of long-term
policies and major investment decisions. The large corporations of Japan

37. For a more detailed analysis, see Hugh Patrick and Gary Saxonhouse, *Japan in
the World Economy: From the 1950s to the 1980s* (prepared for the Twentieth Century
Fund, forthcoming).
38. Morton Mintz and Jerry S. Cohen, *America, Inc.: Who Owns and Operates the
United States* (Dial Press, 1971).

are akin to corporate divisions, with a good deal of operating autonomy within the overall policy framework laid down by corporate headquarters, free to compete with each other within broad limits, and charged with direct operating responsibility."[39]

This image of the government as monolithic and united is contrary to the facts. First, there are substantial differences between the LDP and the central government administrative bureaucracy. The LDP itself is far from monolithic, consisting as it does of a number of competitive factions vying for power. Government ministries have a tradition of considerable autonomy and independence of views, and they jealously guard their powers. Consensus among ministries on the "national interest" is only at a high level of generality, and hence not very operative. Each ministry in fact has its own special constituency and its own perception of the "national interest."

Not surprisingly, ministries are often at loggerheads, as is evidenced in almost any policy debate. The Ministry of Agriculture and Forestry focuses on improvement of agricultural incomes by expansion of production, restriction of imports, and higher prices for farm products. The Bank of Japan places priority on price stability and balance-of-payments equilibrium. The Ministry of Finance seeks a balanced budget and adequate aggregate demand. The Ministry of International Trade and Industry (MITI) is the champion of industrial production and productivity improvement, and the Economic Planning Agency is concerned with stable growth, efficient resource allocation, and, recently, social welfare. The MITI has been perhaps the most actively interventionist (other than the Ministry of Agriculture) and the most articulate in espousing and taking credit for an industrial development policy.

On most matters businesses have gone along with the policy prescriptions of the government, usually because they serve business interests. There are, nonetheless, numerous instances in which the big business community, specific industries, specific groups, or even individual firms have strongly resisted policies not in their interests. Recent examples include business's success in weakening the antipollution legislation proposed in 1971, the textile industry's 1971 fight against Prime Minister Sato's agreement with President Nixon on textile export quotas, and the refusal of Toyo Kogyo, Honda, Mitsubishi, and other automobile producers to merge into large firms despite pressure from the MITI.[40] The government is far from omnipotent.

39. James C. Abegglen (ed.), *Business Strategies for Japan* (Tokyo: Sophia University, 1970), p. 71.

40. For case studies of the steel, automobile, and computer industries, see Eugene J. Kaplan, *Japan: The Government-Business Relationship, A Guide for the American Businessman* (U.S. Department of Commerce, February 1972).

The case for monolithic big business control of government is only slightly more persuasive, and ultimately must also be rejected. The persuasiveness of the model lies in the recognition that the Japanese government has helped create an economic environment very favorable to Japanese business, not only in a general way but in specific measures creating new opportunities and enhancing economic incentives. However, big business can develop substantial consensus only on very broad issues; on specific issues conflicts of interest, a high degree of competitiveness, and factionalism predominate. Even the presumed apex of big business elitism, the *zaikai,* are neither that representative nor that powerful.[41] Business, even big business, cannot be characterized as monolithic on specific issues.

Other authors, notably Caves and Uekusa in Chapter 7, have noted rather different mixes and manifestations of cooperation and competition in the Japanese economy as compared with the West. All too often foreign observers miss the competitive, factionalist spirit that permeates the Japanese economy, in both big organizations and small. Large firms, and groups of affiliated firms, fight hard to increase their market share and industry (or group) ranking—especially those firms not quite in the top position that keep trying harder. The high degree of competitiveness is reflected in considerable price fluctuation, in changes in industry ranking, and in movement of certain large firms from one industrial group to another. That competition predominates does not preclude rival firms or groups from cooperating at times with each other under circumstances of mutual benefit—for instance in dealing with other industries, the government, or foreign competitors domestically or abroad.

Deep conflicts of interest among different industries also make it difficult to achieve any comprehensive big business unity. Many of these cleavages have become obvious in the early 1970s as the Japanese government and big business sought means to counter the excessive balance-of-payments surplus. Industries, such as petrochemicals, that use imports benefited from revaluation; export industries, especially those with large foreign balances such as shipbuilding, were hurt. The textile industry and other efficient exporters fought direct controls limiting exports; industries competing with imports fought import liberalization. Clean industries (and those producing antipollution equipment) favor pollution controls; dirty industries oppose them. These conflicts of interest are inherent in any industrial society.

Even if big business were unified and monolithic, could it control the

41. Gerald L. Curtis, "Big Business and Political Influence," in Ezra F. Vogel (ed.), *Modern Japanese Organization and Decision-Making* (University of California Press, 1975), pp. 33–70.

government? Probably not. It certainly does not appear that bureaucrats can be directly controlled to any substantial degree by business. In general they cannot be bought off by bribes, lavish entertainment, or high posts upon retirement. Nor can they readily be threatened; their autonomy and status are too great. Yet there is an on-going, generally positive but subtle and complex relationship between businessmen and the government bureaucrats responsible for the problems of their industry; often bureaucrats appear to identify as the national interest the interests of the specific industry with which they deal.

Business control over government policy can best be exercised through the Liberal Democratic party. Yet, as we have noted, the LDP is pluralistic rather than monolithic. In addition to their past heavy contributions to the LDP and its central fund-raising organization, many big enterprises maintain special relationships by making contributions to selected factions or individual leaders. Competition among LDP factions spills over and reinforces competition among firms, groups, and industries—and vice versa.

Yet the LDP cannot afford to be a captive of big business. While much of its financing comes from large business contributions, it must seek elsewhere for the votes needed to keep it in power. Thus, it has to shape policies so as at least to ameliorate conditions for farmers, small businessmen, white-collar workers, professionals, and workers (particularly those not members of militant leftist unions). Moreover, to retain control of the parliament the LDP has to provide reasonable alternatives to the policy positions of the opposition parties. Popular opinion, especially as reflected in election returns, thus constitutes an important power that can undermine the objectives of business.

So we must conclude that a pluralist interpretation of the distribution of power in economic decision making—an interpretation that takes into account the competition among big business, small business, farmers, labor, the government bureaucracy, the media, consumers, urban residents, environmentalists—is more useful in understanding Japan's contemporary political economy. The group-oriented and highly competitive behavior of Japanese, together with conflicts of interest on concrete issues, is reflected in the multitude of factions and interest groups within the government bureaucracy, big business, and the LDP, and expressed in the dealings of each group with the others. Pluralism is reinforced by the power of outside interest groups to influence and shape certain government policy decisions. Furthermore, alliances of interest are not static: various interest groups compete in some areas, on some problems, under some circumstances, and cooperate on others.

Pluralism is not unique to Japan; indeed it is an important feature of the democracies of the United States and Western Europe. The power of various groups to influence policy differs in different countries, of course. Compared with the United States, in Japan farmers are considerably more powerful, organized labor substantially less so, small business certainly more organized and cohesive and probably more powerful. The use of the pluralist model for description and prediction does not necessarily mean that this system is the most desirable. One might ask whether the diffusion of economic (and political) power among interest groups is sufficient, whether the bias in favor of producers and against consumers is desirable, whether the flow of power and influence from money is excessive—for Japan, for the United States, or for any other country.

Government and Big Business

Despite all these qualifications, it can be said that in Japan big business has had a close, friendly relationship with a supportive government. Whether this support is greater in Japan than in the United States, or France, or West Germany, or England, we really do not know, both because we do not know a great deal about the actual state of government-business relations in any country and because we do not have good techniques of comparison.

There are a number of reasons, of varying importance, for this close government-business relationship in Japan. Relatively less important are the following. First, the LDP has been continuously in power as a probusiness party since its formation in 1955; over time, ways of working together have naturally developed. Second, the strong, able government bureaucracy is respected by businessmen and politicians alike; it is taken as an important source of initiative in the definition of national interest and in policy formulation. Third, aggressive price and market-share competition among large firms has meant that the largest firms at times have welcomed government interference to restrict "excessive" competition.

Two much more important factors have underlain the government-business relationship: consensus on economic goals and on means of attaining them, and common ideology or values. From soon after the war until about 1970 the LDP politicians, the government bureaucracy, and big business leaders were in substantial agreement on three matters: the high priority of economic objectives in societal goals; the high priority of relatively rapid growth in economic objectives; and the belief that the way to achieve economic growth was through the expansion of the capacity, capabilities, and output of private business, especially big business. The government's main role was thus to be of help to private growth wherever possible. This consensus meant that the goals of business and government overlapped significantly and were seldom in conflict.

In the early 1970s, as the imbalance between the growth of private production and the lack of public facilities increased and pollution and other environmental degradation became worse, the consensus eroded substantially. From the mid-1960s the LDP increasingly lost political control of the major cities, with the opposition parties rallying to antipollution, antiinflation, consumer welfare, and related issues. If the LDP expects to remain in power, it must restructure government policy to give greater priority to social welfare improvement. Awareness of these needs had developed earlier in some elements of the bureaucracy, but it did not prevail until the political climate changed. Nonetheless, by 1972 a senior MITI official could say, and mean, that "the time had come to shift from mothering to fathering industry," to stop coddling and nurturing business and start being strict with it on issues of pollution control, consumer protection, and the like. These new goals of the LDP and the bureaucracy conflict with the goals of business, making consensus both more difficult to achieve and more tenuous. The implications of the new policies for business are not just acceptance of governmental controls over pollution; they include also a reallocation of government resources into social welfare and related areas, paid for in part by higher business taxes and less money available for loan to the private sector. Government-business relations in Japan in the 1970s will certainly be less to the advantage of business than in the 1950s and 1960s.

Japan's historical experience and value system have resulted in an economic ideology supportive of close and harmonious government-business relations. One thinks immediately of emphasis on group rather than individual, on cooperation and conciliation aimed at harmony, on national rather than personal welfare. The right of the government to lead, and to interfere where necessary, has substantial basis in ideology as well as in historical experience. This ethos contrasts with the traditional Anglo-American economic ideology of the "invisible hand" of perfect competition, whereby individualistic maximizaton of one's own benefits results in the greatest social welfare, with government interference limited to maintaining the conditions of perfect competition.

Ideology is a means of establishing norms of economic behavior and of legitimizing economic institutions and practices, yet we must be careful not to attach too much importance to it. In Japan at least, the ideology is not well articulated and its role in directly shaping the economic system is not large; the focus is pragmatic—on what succeeds in achieving desired goals.

Moreover, ideology, in both Japan and the United States, is to a considerable extent a facade masking actual economic conditions and practices. Large firms and oligopolistic market structures characterize all advanced industrial market economies, and the degree of oligopoly is similar among them. Such large enterprises both compete and cooperate with one another, depending upon circumstances. This reality is substantially different from the stereotype of monolithic, harmonious cooperation with one another and with the government in Japanese ideology, and equally different from the ideal of perfectly competitive relationships with one another and the non-involvement of government in American ideology.

Japan's Expanding Presence in the World Economy[42]

We have already noted Japan's poverty and domestic economic weakness in the early 1950s. Internationally its position was even more fragile and insignificant. The world environment was not yet particularly hospitable to a defeated and ravaged Japan. Most countries were struggling through post-war reconstruction and adjustment themselves. The cold war was in full force. Currency convertibility and a multilateral, nondiscriminatory trade and payments system were goals, but had yet to be established. The "dollar shortage" was a serious problem. The United States was preeminent—economically, politically, militarily. It took the lead in successfully building a liberal world economic system. The improvement in the world economic environment and the attendant rapid growth of world trade in the 1950s and 1960s were of particular benefit to Japan.

U.S.–Japan Alliance

The 1951 peace treaty did not mean that Japan was immediately or automatically reaccepted into the community of nations. Most other nations were hostile, or at best indifferent, to Japan. The regional opportunities for Japan to make economic and political friends were minimal, unlike the European situation; most other Asian nations still regarded Japan with considerable suspicion. Japan was alone, defenseless, in need of a patron in international affairs.

Alliance with the United States was clearly in Japan's self-interest, for economic, political, and security reasons; Robert Scalapino has appropriately

42. This section owes much to Patrick and Saxonhouse, *Japan in the World Economy*. For more detailed analysis in this book, see especially Chapter 6, and also Chapters 3, 7, and 11.

described it as a low-risk, high-returns policy.[43] After all, the United States was the world's strongest power economically and militarily; it exercised the political leadership of the noncommunist world; it had just completed a generally successful and friendly occupation of Japan; it was by far Japan's largest trading partner (eight times greater than any other country). In the early 1950s Japan's leaders were eager to enter into alliance with America as a very junior partner in the relationship.

This alliance was also much in the interests of the United States. The initial premises of postwar American policy toward East Asia had proven grievously incorrect: China did not become a friendly, unified democracy under Nationalist rule; Russia did not cooperate amicably in reaching satisfactory agreements on East Asian issues; and the process of decolonialization in South and Southeast Asia was not quick or easy, nor did stable democratic political systems emerge. The Korean War reinforced the American decision to rely upon Japan as the bastion of stable democracy and industrial strength in Asia. And Japan, as a member of the American-oriented bloc, could be expected to provide military bases for Asian security, support the United States on most political issues in the United Nations, and so forth.[44]

The benefits to Japan have been immense. Security from external threat has been assured by the United States–Japan Security Treaty.[45] Economic relations with the United States have prospered. Japan had the patron it needed for much of its international activities, including entry into the International Monetary Fund, the World Bank, the General Agreement on Tariffs and Trade (GATT), and the Organisation for Economic Co-operation and Development. The benefits have also been great for the United States.

Japan's Postwar Role

Japan's role in the postwar world economy was initially small, if not insignificant. Its share of world commodity exports in 1953 was 1.7 percent, ranking it thirteenth, far below the United States and most European countries.[46] Capital flows in or out were insignificant. Japanese leaders perceived their economy as having very little impact on the world, notably on the American economic situation, while it was very vulnerable to what hap-

43. *American-Japanese Relations in a Changing Era* (The Library Press, 1972).
44. Ibid., pp. 56–57.
45. For detailed treatment, see Martin E. Weinstein, *Japan's Postwar Defense Policy, 1947–1968* (Columbia University Press, 1971).
46. In 1953 the United States' share of world exports was 21.3 percent, the United Kingdom's 9.8 percent, West Germany's 6.0 percent, France's 5.1 percent, and Italy's 2.1 percent. See United Nations, *Yearbook of International Trade Statistics, 1954*, pp. 13–17.

pened abroad, especially in the American economy. (Japanese were quick
to apply to themselves the then-common phrase "when the United States
sneezes, the rest of the world catches pneumonia.") Thus, Japanese policymakers felt they could ignore the possibility of substantial feedback effects
from other economies stemming from their own actions. This position was
generally accepted in the 1950s (and later) by American policymakers, who
shared the perception of Japan as relatively unimportant to the world and
American economies.

Other countries—notably those in Western Europe, Southeast Asia, and
Oceania—were not so sanguine. The Western European attitude at that
time might be characterized as one of negatively ignoring Japan. While trade
with Japan was then insignificant, Western European countries feared
Japan's potential competitive strength in textiles and other labor-intensive
manufactured consumer goods, the older and relatively less efficient industries in Europe. On Japan's accession to the GATT they (and others, together accounting for a third of the value of world trade) invoked Article 35,
the provision enabling them to maintain special restrictions on imports from
Japan. Australia, and particularly Southeast Asian nations, feared that
Japanese competition would stifle their own nascent industrial efforts. Japanese policymakers tended to regard these restrictions as arbitrarily imposed
by the other nations rather than as a consequence of their own policies. An
important component of their economic diplomacy has thus been to eliminate
or reduce any special discrimination against Japan.

Foreign trade has been and will be vital for a prosperous Japan, though
not so much so in macro demand-supply terms. Japan's natural resource base
is so overwhelmingly deficient that almost all industrial raw materials must
be imported; and the land-man ratio in agriculture is so unfavorable that a
high degree of food self-sufficiency is not just economically inefficient, but
virtually impossible. Imported raw materials—the dominant portion of
Japan's import bill—thus have been and will be essential for the growth of
production. Exports have been essential to earn the foreign exchange to pay
for imports; but export-led growth, in terms of the effects of increased foreign
demand on Japanese aggregate demand or terms of trade, has not been a
major cause of Japan's growth performance (see Chapter 6). Exports have
been chiefly of manufactured goods.

Yet over time exports and imports of goods and services in current prices
have each constituted only about one-tenth of GNP—ratios that did not
change significantly from the early 1950s until 1974, when skyrocketing
import and export prices increased shares to about 15 percent of GNP. The
somewhat lower share of trade in the GNP of Japan than of Europe (though

considerably higher than in the United States) is due mainly to Japan's distance from major world markets, with its implications of high costs of transportation, lack of knowledge, and communications barriers. Japan does not share the advantage of European countries in each being close to the burgeoning markets of the others.[47] The rise in the real share of exports and imports in Japan's GNP has been masked by relative price movements. As shown in Figure 1-1, prior to 1974 the GNP deflator increased more rapidly than export and import price indexes; moreover, the commodity terms of trade moved in Japan's favor until 1973, so that fewer exports were needed to pay the import bill.

As Chapters 3 and 6 document in detail, the balance of payments was the dominant immediate constraint upon Japanese economic growth throughout the 1950s, and indeed until the late 1960s. In the circumstances of the fifties, exports plus special dollar earnings from U.S. military-related "special procurement" were barely sufficient to pay for Japan's imports of essential industrial raw materials, foodstuffs, and sophisticated machinery. Japan, like most other countries then, relied heavily on restrictions on imports, foreign exchange, and capital outflows to keep balance-of-payments difficulties within manageable range. Reducing the balance-of-payments constraint on growth was the major objective of Japanese foreign economic policy, and economics dominated Japanese foreign policy generally.

Rapid domestic growth has been intertwined with rapid growth in foreign trade. Between 1953 and 1973, imports of goods and services increased at an average annual rate of 13.2 percent (12.7 percent in 1965 constant prices) and exports at 13.7 percent (12.7 percent in constant prices).[48] This trade performance was more impressive than that of most other major nations; as a consequence Japan's share of world trade increased. Between 1955 and 1972, commodity exports as a share of world exports rose from 2.4 percent to 6.9 percent;[49] the comparable figures for imports are 2.5 percent and 6.1 percent. Japan's rank among trading nations in share of world ex-

47. A simulation test in which it was assumed that Japan was located at the same distance as West Germany from world markets but was otherwise unchanged raised Japan's commodity exports in 1965 from 9.4 percent of GNP to 19.7 percent; West Germany's actual commodity exports that year were 16.3 percent of its GNP. See Patrick and Saxonhouse, *Japan in the World Economy,* chap. 3.

48. Compounded continuously, based on data from Economic Planning Agency, *Revised Report on National Income Statistics, 1951–1967* (1969), pp. 60, 82; Statistics Department, Bank of Japan, *Economic Statistics Monthly* (September 1974), p. 157. These growth rates are influenced somewhat by the initial year selected.

49. The comparable figures for 1955 and 1972, respectively, were: the United States, 18.6 percent and 11.9 percent; the United Kingdom, 9.8 percent and 6.8 percent; West Germany, 7.4 percent and 11.2 percent; France, 5.9 percent and 6.3 percent; and Italy,

ports increased commensurately, from ninth in 1955 to seventh in the early 1960s, and to fourth by the late 1960s.

An extremely important factor was the secular tendency for Japanese exports to outstrip imports, causing in the late 1960s a trade and current account surplus in the balance of payments. The cyclical pattern of growth and trade, the natural proclivity of policymakers in Japan as elsewhere to be concerned primarily with relatively short-run economic policy, and difficulty in predicting future events all masked this long-run trend. Moreover, the evolving potential current surplus was used more or less continuously to shift upward the import schedule. As good export performance enabled Japan to import more, the balance-of-payments constraint on growth eased, and growth became even more rapid. In addition, imports were also somewhat liberalized, most notably in the early 1960s. Thus, large and continuing surpluses on current account did not manifest themselves until the late 1960s.

The rapid growth of GNP and trade between the early 1950s and late 1960s transformed Japan's position in the world economy, qualitatively even more than quantitatively. Most of major premises on which Japanese foreign economic policy had been based, and the policies of the United States and other countries toward Japan as well, had become increasingly invalid. The era in which the balance of payments was the major constraint on Japanese growth, and in which Japan's international economic role was sufficiently small that feedback reactions by other major nations could safely be ignored, had come to an end.

Japan and the World Crisis

The dating of economic eras is rather arbitrary; the process of long-run change is in fact continuous and usually gradual. One symbolic date for Japan, and indeed for the entire world, is August 15, 1971, when President Nixon shocked the world by announcing the unilateral New Economic Program. By then, however, the deficiencies of the Bretton Woods system of fixed exchange rates were obvious: it could not provide a satisfactory mechanism of adjustment for persistent U.S. balance-of-payments deficits, persistent West German surpluses, and the new but rapidly increasing Japanese surpluses. Nor were major European countries willing to hold more reserves in dollars.

2.2 percent and 4.5 percent. Calculated from UN, *Yearbook of International Trade Statistics, 1957*, vol. 2, p. 13, and *1972*, p. 15. Interestingly, between 1953 and 1972 the increase in share of world exports was the same for Japan and West Germany (5.2 percentage points).

By hindsight we can date the ending of the era for Japan at about 1969. (Krause and Sekiguchi come to a similar conclusion in Chapter 6.) But Japanese policymakers were slow to recognize the fundamental change in the country's balance-of-payments position—which, indeed, was hidden in part by cyclical phenomena—or to understand its implications. They thus were slow to react in 1970 and even in 1971. They persisted in viewing Japan as small and poor, while Japan's suddenly increasing trade surplus, current account surplus, and foreign exchange reserves were putting intolerable pressure on the world trade and payments system, and especially on the United States. Perception of Japan's new position in the world economy came considerably more rapidly in the United States and Europe than in Japan. Americans talked increasingly of Japan taking on the "responsibilities" of the "equal partnership" the Japanese leadership desired. Europeans talked of Japanese "unfair competition" and suggested a united front with the United States against Japan. At the same time tensions were increasing beween the United States and Europe.

Japanese surpluses in 1971, and even in 1972, were both a catalyst and a partial cause of the ending of the fixed exchange rate system. While the policy approach of all nations to this system was supposedly global, or at least trilateral (the United States–Europe–Japan), much of the initial American thinking was bilateral, focused on Japan. The United States had the most pronounced balance-of-payments deficit and Japan the most pronounced surplus. It was tempting to make Japan a scapegoat for America's balance-of-payments problems, though in fact the American deficit had more fundamental causes—it might well have diminished but certainly would not have disappeared even if Japan did not exist, or had not had a surplus.[50] After all, it was a world of general, not bilateral, equilibria or disequilibria. And the fundamental problems were systemic, not simply caused by Japanese surpluses or deficits. Certain features of the international monetary system— fixed exchange rates, the fixed dollar-gold relationship, the emphasis in practice on devaluation rather than revaluation for adjustment of fundamental balance-of-payments disequilibria, the fact that as other economies recovered

50. See Chapter 6. There has been a spate of books and articles on the bilateral economic relationship that developed between 1970 and 1972. See, for example, Henry Rosovsky (ed.), *Discord in the Pacific: Challenges to the Japanese-American Alliance* (Columbia Books, 1972); Jerome B. Cohen (ed.), *Pacific Partnership: United States– Japan Trade* (D. C. Heath, 1972); and Allen Taylor (ed.), *Perspectives on United States–Japan Economic Relations* (Ballinger, 1973). See also Hugh Patrick, "Problems in United States–Japanese Economic Relations," *Asia Research Bulletin*, vol. 1 (March 1972), pp. 691–95; and Gary Saxonhouse, "A Review of Recent United States–Japanese Economic Relations," *Asian Survey*, vol. 12 (September 1972), pp. 726–52.

from war devastation they would gain strength relative to the United States—
all these led inevitably to an overvalued dollar with little the United States
could do about it within the constraints of the system.

In retrospect, 1971–73 was a period of dramatic swings in Japan's international economic position: massive current account surpluses; speculative
capital inflows; an increase in foreign exchange reserves—official and "hidden"—from $4 billion to almost $30 billion; remarkable changes in Japanese foreign economic policy and use of policy instruments; then in 1973 an
abrupt reverse in the current account position and loss of foreign exchange
reserves; worldwide inflation; and the oil crisis. The process of ending surpluses and restoring balance-of-payments equilibrium brought about fundamental changes in Japanese attitudes toward trade liberalization, direct investment abroad, and exchange rate adjustment. With great trepidation and
initial slowness Japanese policymakers came to accept a managed floating
exchange rate system. Between 1971 and 1973, Japan carried out a major
trade liberalization, moving from being one of the most restrictive to being
among the more liberal of the advanced industrial nations. By mid-1974, the
tension of 1971–72 between the United States and Japan on economic issues
had evaporated; there appeared to most policymakers to be no serious bilateral economic problems.

Both countries have joined Europe, and indeed all the world, in facing a
host of new global economic problems. The Middle East war of October 1973
and the attendant oil crisis brought home to Japan once again its extreme
vulnerability to world events. Japan relies more heavily than other major
industrial nations on oil (for three-quarters of its total energy), and 99 percent of its oil is imported—85 percent from the Middle East and North
Africa. The threats of reduced oil supplies from the OAPEC nations (Organization of Arab Petroleum Exporting Countries), and fears of diversion to the United States and Europe of other oil destined for Japan,
panicked the Japanese at first. They became highly conscious of Arab political pressures, and rushed to offer immense aid projects to placate the Arab
nations, while intensifying their already close relations with Iran and Indonesia. Once the immediate political crisis was over and supply curtailments
ended, the more serious problem of price emerged. Japan found itself facing
a serious deterioration in its terms of trade in 1974 and possibly thereafter.
Moreover, as a resource-deficient nation, it was particularly concerned that
the unspent oil-dollar revenues of Saudi Arabia and other surplus oil nations
be recycled in such a way that Japan have full access to those capital inflows.

The quadrupling of the world price of oil in late 1973 exacerbated what
were already virulent inflationary pressures in Japan, even more virulent

than elsewhere in the industrial world. The annual price data shown in Figure 1-1 do not reflect fully the acceleration of the inflation rate between the late summer of 1973 and the summer of 1974, to about 25 percent for the CPI and 35 percent for the WPI—rates that were socially intolerable for Japan. Restrictive monetary and fiscal measures were taken. The initial effect was to slow the rate of inflation substantially but also to induce Japan's most severe postwar recession, with the first absolute decline in annual output. At the same time the United States and Europe were pursuing similar antiinflationary policies. The interactions of international economic constriction, trade and capital flows, exchange rates, and national policies for domestic and balance-of-payments equilibrium were putting severe pressure on the world economy.

In Sum

How can we sum up Japan's current economic position, domestically and internationally? Japan is now among the few top major economic powers; it stands alone in Asia in that respect. The standard of living, while still substantially below America's, is close to average European levels. Negotiations on the international economic order can by no means exclude Japan or consideration of Japan's interests. At the same time Japan is eager to cooperate internationally, though thus far often without innovative substantive proposals to achieve their objectives. The economy, made confident by a long period of extremely rapid, self-sustaining growth and newly achieved affluence, has been chastened by the oil crisis and by the difficulty in combating inflation without depression, and perhaps even by pollution. But Japan's problems are indeed the problems of all affluent, highly industrialized nations. In the concluding chapter in this book we discuss, in broad terms, the future prospects for the Japanese economy domestically and internationally.

CHAPTER TWO

Economic Growth
and Its Sources

Edward F. Denison, Brookings Institution
and
William K. Chung, U.S. Department of Commerce

Tables

JAPAN has emerged from the poverty that crushes most of the world's peoples and joined the small group of affluent developed nations. Long before World War II Japan had become a world power, and productivity and living standards had risen above levels prevalent outside Europe, the United States, and the British dominions. But economic gains have been far greater in the postwar period. From 1953, when Japanese output had regained its prewar peak, to 1973 total national income multiplied 5.43 times and national income per person employed 4.06 times.[1] This growth performance is unmatched in any other country, free market or socialist—at least this is so if one excepts such special cases as the oil states and Israel.

Population grew 1.1 percent a year from 1953 to 1973. Though above rates in most European countries and only moderately below the Japanese rate of 1.3 percent from 1900 to 1953, postwar Japanese population growth was much below that of most of the rest of the world, and of Asia. As the number of deaths dwindled, a concurrent fall in the birthrate resulting from birth control and easy and legal access to abortion prevented a postwar population explosion. With the drop in the proportion of children in the population, per capita output multiplied 4.35 times, even more than output per worker.

Output Level Compared with Other Countries

A recent study by Kravis, Kenessey, Heston, and Summers, which was sponsored by the Statistical Office of the United Nations, permits compari-

Note. The authors are greatly indebted to the Economic Planning Agency of Japan, which provided office facilities and cooperation in securing information during our visit to Japan in the summer of 1973. Takeo Takahashi, Tadashi Kusuda, Naohiro Yashiro, and many other members of the agency's staff made us welcome, cheerfully answered inquiries about the Japanese economy and statistics, and provided or arranged for us to secure unpublished data. Guidance provided by Shōzō Ichino, Hisao Kanamori, Tsutomu Noda, Kazushi Ohkawa, Miyohei Shinohara, and Tsunehiko Watanabe was invaluable. The Center for Econometric Data Development and Research made available unpublished estimates of employment by detailed industry prepared by Ichino and of capital stock by industry prepared by Kusuda. Gardner Ackley, Jack Alterman, Henry Rosovsky, and Hugh Patrick provided useful comments on preliminary drafts of this manuscript. Finally, we acknowledge the important contributions to the project of Erna S. Tracy, senior secretary, and Genevieve B. Wimsatt, research assistant.

1. Based on national income measured in 1965 prices and computed by U.S. deflation techniques, as explained later. Data for 1952 through 1971 are shown in Table 2-3, column 2. The preliminary estimate for 1973 is ¥55,184 billion when Okinawa is excluded, as it is in earlier years.

Table 2-1. *International Comparisons of Gross Domestic Product and Consumption, Various Measures, 1970*

Percentages of U.S. values

Measure	Price weights	United States	Japan	France	West Germany	United Kingdom	Italy
GDP per person employed	United States	100.0	55.2	79.1	73.3	60.4	61.6
	Other country	100.0	44.3	65.6	61.5	51.2	49.2
	Ideal index	100.0	49.5	72.1	67.2	55.6	55.1
	International	100.0	49.9	72.6	68.2	53.7	52.8
GDP per capita	United States	100.0	68.1	81.8	80.3	67.9	53.5
	Other country	100.0	54.6	67.8	67.3	57.5	42.7
	Ideal index	100.0	61.0	74.5	73.6	62.5	47.8
	International	100.0	61.5	75.0	74.7	60.3	45.8
Consumption per capita	United States	100.0	56.4	76.7	67.5	70.0	55.0
	Other country	100.0	39.9	60.5	56.0	57.9	42.0
	Ideal index	100.0	47.4	68.1	61.5	63.6	48.1
	International	100.0	48.3	67.9	61.2	62.2	46.0
Total GDP	United States	100.0	34.4	20.3	23.9	18.6	14.2
	Other country	100.0	27.6	16.8	20.0	15.7	11.4
	Ideal index	100.0	30.8	18.5	21.9	17.1	12.7
	International	100.0	31.1	18.6	22.2	16.5	12.2

Sources: Derived from GDP per capita, consumption per capita, and population data in Irving B. Kravis and others, *A System of International Comparisons of Gross Product and Purchasing Power*, United Nations International Comparison Project: Phase One (Johns Hopkins University Press for the World Bank, 1975), pp. 6, 171–78, and from employment figures in Organisation for Economic Co-operation and Development, *Labour Force Statistics, 1961–1972* (Paris: OECD, 1974), tables 1 and 2 for individual countries.

sons of 1970 output and consumption in the six largest developed free market economies.[2] The study was made with care and provides information of exceptional quality. Output data refer to gross domestic product at market prices. Gross domestic product differs from our preferred output measure, national income, in that it is gross of capital consumption, excludes net receipts of property income from abroad, and uses market prices rather than factor costs as weights. But international comparisons are not ordinarily affected greatly by the difference between these measures.

Output per Person Employed

Table 2-1 compares four measures of output and consumption in the five other countries with the corresponding measure in the United States. The first is gross domestic product (GDP) per person employed, a crude measure of productivity.

Comparisons based on four sets of price weights are provided. (1) Outputs of the United States and the other country in 1970 are valued in U.S. prices. GDP per person employed is then found to be 55.2 percent as high

2. Irving B. Kravis, Zoltan Kenessey, Alan Heston, and Robert Summers, *A System of International Comparisons of Gross Product and Purchasing Power*, United Nations International Comparison Project: Phase One (Johns Hopkins University Press for the World Bank, 1975).

in Japan as in the United States. (2) Outputs of the United States and the other country are valued in the prices of the other country. Based on Japanese prices, GDP per person employed is only 44.3 percent as high in Japan as in the United States. (3) Because there is no inherent reason to choose between price weights of one country and the other in general purpose comparisons, the geometric mean of the first two measures, Irving Fisher's "ideal" index, is often used. Japanese GDP per person employed is then 49.5 percent of that of the United States. (4) The authors of the UN report developed an "international" system based on linking comparisons between countries at adjacent levels of development. It meets circular tests, such that if country A's output, for example, is twice that of B, and B's three times that of C, A's must always be six times that of C. Japanese GDP per person employed is 49.9 percent of that of the United States by this measure. In all comparisons in Table 2-1, the international and ideal indexes yield fairly similar results.

By 1970 GDP per person employed in Japan had approached the lower limit of the range observed in developed Western countries. The gaps between the Japanese figures and those for Italy and the United Kingdom were of only moderate size at all price weights. Other countries of northern Europe and North America still stood well above Japan. This was true not only of the countries listed in the table but also of the Scandinavian and Benelux countries, Switzerland, Canada, and probably others. By the international price weight comparisons, the United States exceeded Japan in GDP per person employed by 100 percent, France by 45 percent, West Germany by 37 percent, the United Kingdom by 8 percent, and Italy by 6 percent.[3]

Hours of work are unusually long in Japan, and output per man-hour compares less favorably with other countries than output per person employed. On the other hand, Japan compares more favorably in nonagricultural industries than in the whole economy. Its position would also be elevated by allowance for the rather low proportion of males in the prime working ages in the Japanese labor force.

Output per Capita

Japan ranks considerably higher in GDP per capita than in GDP per person employed. Of the countries listed in Table 2-1 Japan had much the highest percentage of the population employed in 1970—49.2 percent as against 44.9 percent in the United Kingdom, 43.7 in West Germany,

3. Data in this chapter for West Germany cover the Federal Republic (including the Saar) and West Berlin.

41.3 in France, 39.9 in the United States, and 34.7 in Italy. (However, the Japanese percentage exceeded only slightly the highest in Western countries—47.9 in both Denmark and Sweden).[4] With Japan and Italy at opposite extremes in the percentage working, Japan was far above Italy in GDP per capita of the whole population—34 percent according to the international price weight measure. It was approximately equal to the United Kingdom. According to the international measure the United States was 63 percent above Japan, France 22 percent above, and West Germany 21 percent.

Consumption per Capita

Japanese per capita consumption compared much less favorably with the other countries despite the low proportion of Japanese output devoted to national defense. This is because of the very high proportion devoted to gross capital formation. By the international price weight measure, per capita consumption in all the countries shown in Table 2-1 except Italy exceeded that in Japan by at least 27 percent. The Japanese advantage over Italy was only 5 percent whereas its per capita GDP was 34 percent higher.[5]

Total Gross Domestic Product

The Japanese economy is the third largest, after those of the United States and the Soviet Union, of all countries. The margin between Japan and the second and fourth countries is considerable. Abram Bergson put the GNP of the USSR in 1965 at 57.5 percent of that of the United States when valued in dollars and 35.0 percent when measured in rubles.[6] These estimates com-

---

4. These comparisons are computed from Organisation for Economic Co-operation and Development, *Labour Force Statistics, 1961–1972* (Paris: OECD, 1974).

5. The per capita consumption comparison is based on the International Comparison Project classification. To improve international comparability, each category of current expenditures is allocated either to consumption or to government purchases in all countries regardless of whether it is actually paid by private or public expenditure in any particular country. For example, all current expenditures for housing, health, education, and recreation are classified as consumption even though parts of these expenditures are government purchases and so classified in the national accounts of the countries.

6. Soviet estimates, according to Zoltan Kenessey, imply a moderately higher relative position for the USSR in 1968, 62.8 percent, based on national income measured in dollars. For these comparisons, see Abram Bergson, "The Comparative National Income of the USSR and the United States," in D. J. Daly (ed.), *International Comparisons of Prices and Output,* Studies in Income and Wealth, vol. 37, Conference on Research in Income and Wealth (Columbia University Press for National Bureau of Economic Research, 1972), p. 182, and comment by Zoltan Kenessey, p. 196 of the same publication.

pare with 34.4 and 27.6 as the 1970 Japanese percentages of U.S. GDP based on comparisons in dollar and yen prices, respectively. The GDP of West Germany, the fourth largest country, in 1970 was only 23.9 percent of that of the United States based on comparisons in dollars and 20.0 percent in marks. Depending on the price weights used, Japanese GDP exceeded that of West Germany by 38 to 44 percent.

Similar comparisons for earlier years are not available. But it appears that Japan has been the third largest of the world's economies and the second largest market economy since about 1965.[7] This ranking is unlikely to change soon.

It is also apparent that output per worker in Japan was far below that in countries of Northern and Western Europe and North America throughout the period of rapid Japanese growth examined in this chapter, even well below that of Italy in most of the period. This must be borne in mind in interpreting the postwar experience.

Japanese output has fluctuated sharply since 1970, so updated comparisons would depend substantially on the year chosen. But it is clear that the relative Japanese position has continued to improve, at least if the effects of short-term business fluctuations are eliminated.

Some inkling of the immensity of the Japanese economic achievement in moving from Asian to Western productivity standards during the past century is suggested by data for India, also taken from the UN study by Kravis and associates. Based on international price weights, the per capita GDP of Japan in 1970 was $2,952; this compares with $342 for India, the second most populous of the Asian nations (after China). The gap dwarfs the percentage difference between Japan and even the richest of other large nations, France at $3,599 and the United States at $4,801.

The Record of Growth

The long-term background to postwar economic growth was sketched by Patrick and Rosovsky in Chapter 1. Here we note only that the growth rate from around 1890, or even earlier, to World War II was one of the world's highest; that the rate was generally rising, though marked by alternating "long swings" of faster and slower growth; that acceleration of prewar rates

7. This statement is based on extrapolation of the 1970 gross domestic product of each country in international prices (from Table 2-1) by its gross domestic product in its own constant prices. This calculation shows that Japan passed France in 1960, the United Kingdom in 1962, and West Germany temporarily in 1964 and again in 1966.

in the postwar years characterized all advanced countries, not just Japan; but that the acceleration was greater in Japan and, being superimposed on a high prewar base, resulted in a postwar Japanese growth rate much above rates in other countries.[8]

War and Recovery

World War II deprived the Japanese empire of nearly half its 1930 land area, that in Taiwan, Korea, and southern Sakhalin. According to Tsuru's estimates, it also cost the domestic economy more than nine-tenths of its merchant marine, one-fourth of its housing, and one-fifth of its industrial plant, machinery, equipment, and other durables. In all, Tsuru judges, one-fourth of the national wealth vanished during 1941–45. In the wake of this massive destruction, repatriation of 5 million military and civilian personnel stationed overseas intensified the acute shortages of food, clothing, housing, and other daily necessities; together with natural increase, repatriation had raised the population by some 8 million, or 11 percent, by the end of 1948.[9]

Agricultural production, down disastrously in 1945, was recovering sharply by the following year but did not regain the 1933–35 average until 1950. Even then it was well below the level of 1936–40 and insufficient to meet the needs of the expanded population. American food shipments helped Japan through the period of tight food supplies. Industrial output recovered much less quickly; in fact, from 1945 to 1946 it dropped by more than one-half to a level only one-fifth of the 1939–44 average and less than one-quarter of even the 1934–36 average. The Japanese government extended rounds of credit to firms in basic industries to help them attract idle resources and expand production. But credit expansion was followed by soaring prices rather than the hoped-for rehabilitation and recovery. Large government deficits contributed to the inflation. The year-to-year increase in the wholesale price index was 364 percent in 1946, 196 percent in 1947, 166 percent in 1948, and still as much as 63 percent in 1949.[10] Gains in

8. See Kazushi Ohkawa and Henry Rosovsky, *Japanese Economic Growth: Trend Acceleration in the Twentieth Century* (Stanford University Press, 1973), for the timing and an interpretation of Japanese growth rate changes.

9. Economic conditions during the immediate postwar years are presented in detail in Shigeto Tsuru, *Essays on Japanese Economy* (Tokyo: Kinokuniya Bookstore Co., 1958), part 1; Hugh T. Patrick, "The Phoenix Risen from the Ashes: Postwar Japan," in James B. Crowley (ed.), *Modern East Asia: Essays in Interpretation* (Harcourt Brace Jovanovich, 1970); and Kozo Yamamura, *Economic Policy in Postwar Japan* (University of California Press, 1967).

10. Wartime price controls lapsed at the end of the war. The Ministry of Finance instituted controls on selected major items in March 1946 but this did not halt the price rises, as the percentages cited indicate.

industrial production, though substantial if expressed as percentage changes from the prior year, were meager compared to the previous decline; even in 1949 output was only two-fifths of the 1939–44 level.

By the end of 1948, however, the occupation authorities (the Supreme Commander of the Allied Powers, or SCAP) had become determined to see Japan converted from a liability to an economic asset for the free world. Soon thereafter a set of economic stabilization policies, popularly known as the Dodge Line for Joseph Dodge, financial adviser to SCAP, was introduced and implemented. Government budgets were forcefully brought into surplus, and credit expansion and bank lending were slashed. Prices and wages began to stabilize as the fiscal and monetary restrictions took effect.

The Dodge Line, like the currency reform in West Germany, marked the end of economic disorder and laid a solid foundation for recovery and growth. When conflict flared up in Korea in the summer of 1950, the Japanese economy was ready to take effective advantage of the special demand situation created by U.S. needs for military procurement in the area. By mid-1951 the country had become the major workshop and arsenal for the UN troops in Korea. By 1952, when the World War II peace treaty went into effect, the Japanese economy had evolved from the stage of rehabilitation and reconstruction into an era of normalcy. Price levels had stabilized, industrial production was 15 percent above the 1934–36 average (though it was not to exceed the wartime high until 1955), and the market mechanism had resumed its ordinary functions of guiding production and distribution.

Industrial Production

Though postwar Japanese growth was broadly based, it featured the rapid growth of manufacturing output—as had growth in the 1920s, when textiles and other light manufacturing industries spearheaded economic development, and in the 1930s, when the pressure of military requirements resulting from the movement of Japanese armies into Manchuria and northern China caused steel, machinery, chemicals, and other heavy industries, along with electric power, to dominate industrial expansion. The tempo of these industries increased until the outbreak of war in the Pacific in December 1941. By the time Japan recovered its independence in 1952, the heavy industries were ready to resume a leading role in industrialization.

Table 2-2 indicates the magnitude of the production expansion in manufacturing as a whole and in various manufacturing industries. The growth rate of manufacturing output from 1953 to 1971, 14.0 percent, surpassed the rate of national income growth of 8.8 percent (or 9.2 percent, depend-

Table 2-2. *Production Indexes of Selected Manufacturing Industries, 1953, 1961, 1966, and 1971, and Growth Rates, 1953–71*

Industry	Indexes (1953 = 100)			Growth rate, 1953–71 (percent)
	1961	1966	1971	
Iron and steel	337.2	549.2	1,060.0	14.0
Machinery[a]	516.0	923.2	2,489.6	19.6
Chemicals	302.7	625.0	1,200.5	14.8
Petroleum and coal products	404.4	840.7	1,926.9	17.9
Rubber	315.8	424.7	743.2	11.8
Paper and pulp	275.6	413.2	665.0	11.1
Textiles	210.7	316.4	463.5	8.9
All manufacturing	311.4	521.8	1,056.9	14.0

Sources: Computed from Ministry of Foreign Affairs, *Statistical Survey of Japan's Economy* (1972), p. 19, except that indexes for petroleum and coal products, paper and pulp, and rubber were secured from Bank of Japan, *Economic Statistics Annual, 1963*, pp. 217–18, and the 1972 edition of the same publication, pp. 213–14, and for rubber in the years 1963–71 from Economic Planning Agency, *Keizai yōran* [Economic Statistics in Brief] (1973), p. 128.

a. The machinery industry is composed of general machinery, electrical machinery, transportation equipment, and precision instruments.

ing on the method of deflation) in the whole economy, and even the rate of 11.1 percent in the nonagricultural nonresidential business sector as a whole.[11]

Within manufacturing, the growth rate was highest in the important machinery group, and if any portion of the economy can be said to be the "leading sector," this was it in postwar Japan. The machinery industries consist of electrical and nonelectrical machinery, transportation equipment (including automobiles), and precision instruments. Then small, they were themselves almost wholly equipped with new capital facilities in the 1950s. Sales of their products benefited from the long boom in capital expenditures by Japanese business generally, from foreign purchases (especially of ships), and from swelling demand for motorcycles, household durables, and eventually automobiles. We shall sketch the development of some of these industries.

The government has heavily protected and subsidized shipbuilding since the turn of the century. By 1935 Japan was the third largest shipbuilder, with 11 percent of the world's total.[12] After the postwar hiatus in activity, successive credit injections by the Japan Development Bank, starting in 1951, set the shipbuilding industry on a course of swift recovery, and long-term growth soon resumed. Japanese shipbuilders, benefiting from cheap

11. National income growth rates are shown in Table 2-5 below.
12. Ichirō Yano (ed.), *Nihon kokusei zue* [A Graphic Survey of Japan] (1967), p. 342.

labor and technological innovations, were in a supreme position in international competition when the closing of the Suez Canal in 1956 created a booming demand for supertankers, and again as the supertanker gave way first to the giant tanker in the late 1950s and then to the mammoth tanker of 80,000 to 100,000 gross tons during the 1960s. In the early 1970s they were building monster tankers of 470,000 gross tons and expanding facilities so as to be able to construct ships of 1,000,000 gross tons. Japan became the world's leading shipbuilder in the 1950s, but even in 1960 produced only one-fifth of the world's tonnage. By 1971 Japan's production was almost seven times its 1960 production and equaled almost half the world's tonnage; it had increased from 0.5 million gross tons in 1955 to 12.0 million in 1971.[13]

In the 1950s, when automobile ownership was still a symbol of affluence, motorcycles won acceptance as the most popular means of daily transportation. Motorcycle production jumped from 2,600 units in 1950 to 195,500 in 1955, 1,368,000 in 1960, and 2,447,000 in 1966. Though it then tapered off for a time, it rose again to reach 3,565,000 in 1972.[14] Japan displaced France as the largest motorcycle manufacturer. One of every twelve Japanese owned a motorcycle in 1966.

The automotive industry joined the group of growth industries later. Even though domestic markets were completely closed to imports of passenger cars, progress was slow during the 1950s for two reasons: highway systems and other infrastructures related to automobile traffic were not sufficiently developed, and household incomes were too low to permit the general use of cars. The domestic market did not grow to sufficient size in the 1950s to enable manufacturers of passenger cars to reach production volumes corresponding to break-even points.

In the early 1960s the situation changed completely. The government stepped up spending for highways and related facilities. Use of advancing technology enabled Japanese automobile producers to cut prices while consumer incomes were rising sharply, and car ownership came within the reach of many people. Although trade restrictions on foreign cars were somewhat liberalized in the mid-1960s, tariffs on imported cars remained very high. Moreover, the Japanese automotive industry was by then so well established that foreign car manufacturers would have found the Japanese market hard to penetrate even in the absence of protection. Indeed, with their competitive

13. Data in this paragraph exclude ships of less than 100 gross tons. World totals exclude the USSR and China. Data are from Yano, *A Graphic Survey of Japan,* 1967 edition, p. 342; 1971 edition, p. 349; and 1973 edition, pp. 340–42.

14. Data in this and the several following paragraphs are from Yano, *A Graphic Survey of Japan,* 1973 edition, chap. 37, unless otherwise indicated.

position sharpened by cheap labor, technical competence, and economies of large-scale production, the Japanese car manufacturers wedged into markets abroad.

Passenger car production in Japan grew more than 155-fold from 1955 to 1970, truck production 46-fold, and bus production about 9-fold. Since 1967 Japan has ranked as the second largest producer in the world, second only to the United States. In 1972 annual production exceeded 4 million passenger cars, more than one-seventh of total world production.

Equipping a nation of 100 million with modern household appliances for the first time, when accomplished in two decades or less, creates a huge market. This happened in Japan. In the mid-1950s, hardly anyone owned electric cleaners, electric washers, electric refrigerators, or television sets; in the 1970s, nearly everyone did. The speed with which domestic markets for these products moved from original equipment toward dependence on replacement is indicated by the fact that from 1964 to 1971 alone the percentage of households with electric washers jumped from 61 to 94, with electric refrigerators from 38 to 91, and with electric cleaners from 27 to 74.[15] The percentage with television sets had passed 90 by the mid-1960s. From 1955 to 1972 production of electric washers went from 461,000 to 4,204,000, of electric refrigerators from 31,000 to 3,454,000, of electric cleaners from 51,000 to 3,972,000, and of television sets from 137,000 to 13,035,000. Growth of transistor radios, cameras, sewing machines, and watches was no less outstanding. By 1967 Japan was the world's largest producer of television sets, radios, cameras, and sewing machines, and held or was approaching second place in washers, refrigerators, cleaners, and watches.

The enormous growth of the sales of these products stemmed from the increasing affluence of the Japanese and the cost saving and consequent price reductions made possible by sharply rising volume. Sales promotion through the mass media, patterned closely on American techniques, had a bandwagon effect, helping to shift consumption patterns toward consumer durables. With so favorable a home market as a base and aided by low wages at prevailing exchange rates, producers were able to reinforce growth by penetrating foreign markets, especially for television sets.

Such examples illustrate the breadth as well as the almost incredible tempo of growth in the machinery industries. We need add only that private purchases of producers' durables and nonresidential construction, which con-

15. National Life Research Institution, *Kokumin seikatsu tōkei nenpō* [Annual Statistical Report on National Standards of Living] (1970), pp. 120–21, and 1973 edition, pp. 98–99.

sist in important part of products of other branches of the machinery industries, jumped, when measured in 1965 prices, from 1.1 billion yen in 1953 to 5.1 billion in 1965 and 14.0 billion in 1972.[16]

Since the machinery industries are large users of steel, and such other steel-using industries as construction were also booming, swiftly rising demand for steel was assured. It was met by domestic production despite Japan's poor endowment of iron ore, coke, and, initially, scrap. Technological innovations so improved the competitive position of Japanese steel mills that they not only precluded foreign steel from Japanese markets but even made large inroads into foreign markets. Continuous improvements in marine transport facilities reduced transportation costs, and raw materials were brought from such distant sources as India, Malaysia, Chile, Canada, and the United States.[17] Steel ingot production leaped from 7.7 million tons in 1953—just equal to the previous peak in 1943—to 16 million in 1959, 28 million in 1961, 62 million in 1967, and 97 million in 1972. Since 1964 Japan has been the third largest manufacturer (after the United States and the USSR).

Petroleum refining is another large and fast-growing industry that is almost entirely dependent on imported raw material and in which Japan has stood third to the United States and the Soviet Union since 1964 (though with a far wider gap than in steel). Some 99.6 percent of the crude oil consumed in Japan in 1971 was imported; this compares with 79.1 percent in 1935, 82.5 percent in 1950, and 99.1 percent in 1965.[18] Thriving on the growing demand for them for industrial use, electric power generation, house heating, and motorists' needs, petroleum and coal products grew at an annual rate of 17.9 percent from 1953 to 1971 (see Table 2-2).

As in other countries, chemicals developed into a leading growth industry. Heavy industries greatly increased their consumption of basic chemical compounds such as sulphuric acid, caustic soda, soda ash, and dyes. Organic chemical products, especially petroleum chemicals, have been gradually replacing the nonorganic chemicals in importance.

---

16. These estimates are from the Economic Planning Agency's national income statistics. Production data for a wide variety of types of industrial and electrical machinery are also available. Scanning series for even a brief period (the years 1966 through 1970 are shown in Bureau of Statistics, Office of the Prime Minister, *Japan Statistical Yearbook, 1971* [1972], pp. 200–07) conveys an impression of extremely quick and general expansion.

17. In 1971 imports represented 98 percent of total domestic consumption of iron ore, 7 percent of scrap, and 81 percent of coke. See Yano, *A Graphic Survey of Japan, 1973* edition, p. 277.

18. Yano, *A Graphic Survey of Japan, 1973* edition, p. 299.

The textile, paper and pulp, and rubber industries grew less than the average for all manufacturing. But by standards in other parts of the world the growth rates of 9 to almost 12 percent in these industries are high.

Other Industries

Nonmanufacturing industries have of course shared in growth; indeed, most seem to have expanded output at a high rate. The volume of goods handled by retailers increased by perhaps 10.5 percent a year from 1954 to 1970, and wholesale trade by over 11 percent.[19] The general pattern in construction, electric power, and most branches of transportation, communication, finance, and service industries was one of buoyant expansion. Exceptions were the primary industries—agriculture, lumbering and forestry, fisheries, and mining—in which growth of output was slow after the initial recovery from immediate postwar disruption. Output of all but fisheries seems actually to have turned downward in the late 1960s.

Growth in the Economy as a Whole

The main concern of this chapter is the growth of output in the economy as a whole—specifically, of national income—and the changes that produced this growth. National income, which is also called "the net national product valued at factor cost," is a measure of the net output of goods and services produced by the nation's economy. It differs from "net national product valued at market prices" in that each component of output is valued by the factor cost of producing it rather than by its market price. This procedure is more appropriate for the analysis of productivity, but in practice the difference is slight.[20]

19. The rates cited are growth rates of retail and wholesale sales deflated by the implicit deflator for household expenditures, exclusive of "fuel and light" and "housing." (Sales data are from Census of Wholesale and Retail Trade as reported in Bureau of Statistics, *Japan Statistical Yearbook, 1961*, p. 229, and *1972*, p. 284; the implicit deflator is computed from Economic Planning Agency estimates of consumption in current and constant prices.) Wholesale sales increased more than retail sales, as would be expected since other GNP commodity components grew more than consumption. EPA estimates of "value added" in commerce, measured in 1965 prices, grew even more— 13 percent a year.

20. In many time periods it matters more whether net output in current prices is obtained statistically by adding incomes (the basis for both the Economic Planning Agency's and our series for Japanese national income) or by adding expenditures (the statistical basis for the EPA's series for GNP at market prices). The difference is the statistical discrepancy in the national accounts.

Table 2-3. *National Income in Constant Prices, by Sector and Industrial Branch, 1952–71*

Billions of 1965 yen

	National income originating in								
	Total national income		General government, households, institutions, and foreign governments				Nonresidential business		
Calendar year	Japanese deflation procedures (1)	U.S. deflation procedures^a (2)	Japanese deflation procedures (3)	U.S. deflation procedures^a (4)	Services of dwellings (5)	International assets (6)	Total (7)	Agriculture (8)	Nonagricultural industries (9)
1952	8,907	9,446	1,594	2,133	636	−1	6,678	1,400	5,278
1953	9,667	10,170	1,638	2,141	672	−7	7,364	1,497	5,867
1954	10,372	10,855	1,680	2,163	720	−12	7,984	1,714	6,270
1955	11,210	11,705	1,713	2,208	742	−12	8,767	2,150	6,617
1956	11,838	12,313	1,718	2,193	760	−11	9,371	1,962	7,409
1957	13,083	13,533	1,720	2,170	801	−14	10,576	2,026	8,550
1958	13,780	14,136	1,764	2,120	879	−13	11,150	2,116	9,034
1959	14,912	15,233	1,825	2,146	982	−13	12,118	2,327	9,791
1960	16,989	17,305	1,879	2,195	1,023	−12	14,099	2,242	11,857
1961	18,770	19,007	2,037	2,274	1,125	−16	15,624	2,210	13,414
1962	20,418	20,617	2,193	2,392	1,163	−33	17,095	2,208	14,887
1963	22,234	22,370	2,377	2,513	1,192	−41	18,706	2,060	16,646
1964	24,340	24,434	2,549	2,643	1,235	−68	20,624	2,102	18,522
1965	25,613	25,613	2,734	2,734	1,300	−68	21,647	2,115	19,532
1966	28,009	27,900	2,908	2,799	1,367	−65	23,799	2,185	21,614
1967	31,798	31,607	3,050	2,859	1,451	−63	27,360	2,455	24,905
1968	36,141	35,840	3,217	2,916	1,575	−89	31,438	2,502	28,936
1969	40,030	39,596	3,409	2,975	1,674	−98	35,045	2,375	32,670
1970	44,424	43,848	3,605	3,029	1,774	−72	39,117	2,216	36,901
1971	46,907	46,193	3,798	3,084	1,926	−21	41,204	1,987	39,217

Sources: The principal sources of the authors' estimates were Economic Planning Agency, *Annual Report on National Income Statistics, 1973* (1973), *Revised Report on National Income Statistics, 1951–1967* (1969), *Shōwa 40-nen. Kaitei kokumin shotoku tōkei (Suikei shiryōshū)* [Sourcebook of Revised National Income Statistics, Base Year 1965] (1970), and EPA worksheets; Bureau of Statistics, *Japan Statistical Yearbook* (various years) and *Comparison of Employed Persons by Industry in the Population Censuses, 1920 through 1970* (1973). Sources and procedures are fully described in Edward F. Denison and William K. Chung, *How Japan's Economy Grew So Fast* (Brookings Institution, forthcoming).

a. U.S. deflation procedures differ from Japanese only in general government, households, institutions, and foreign governments. For each component of this sector, 1965 national income in current prices was extrapolated by employment.

Table 2-3 shows our estimates of national income, measured in constant prices of 1965. For analyzing growth, it is useful to isolate national income originating in three relatively small sectors in which output changes can be directly ascribed to changes in a single type of input. Data for these sectors and for the rest of the economy, which we call nonresidential business, are shown in the table, as is a division of the latter sector into agriculture and nonagricultural industries.

General government, private households, nonprofit institutions serving mainly individuals, and foreign governments (which together make up the first small sector) not only buy output from business but also purchase labor directly from their own employees. In current prices the value of the output of these employees is measured by their compensation. In constant prices output is measured by different methods than elsewhere. Japanese national income investigators use deflation methods whose net effect is the assumption that output per worker rises over time. In contrast, in the U.S. national accounts the output of each category of employee in this sector is assumed to move like full-time equivalent employment, so that output per full-time employee does not change. Most other countries use this or a similar technique. Table 2-3 shows national income in the sector as estimated by both techniques, and the estimates of total national income that each yields. The series based on U.S. deflation procedures will be emphasized not because we prefer them in all respects—we do not—but because we wish to compare Japanese growth and its sources with experience in other countries.

Isolating this sector permits one to state immediately the amount of the increase in total national income, measured by either procedure, that was created by the addition to labor employed by general governments, households, institutions, and foreign governments. From 1961 to 1971, for example, such labor contributed ¥810 billion, or 3 percent, of the ¥27,186 billion increase in national income in 1965 prices that is obtained by U.S. deflation procedures.

Dwellings represent a large fraction of the capital stock. They contribute to the value of output by providing services to their occupants. National income originating in the "services of dwellings" sector measures the net contribution that the stock of dwellings makes to the national income. It consists of the gross rental value of occupied dwellings minus all expenses (including depreciation) except property income. When measured in 1965 prices this series provides a direct measure of the contribution to the increase in total national income in constant prices that was made by residential capital and land. From 1961 to 1971 this contribution was ¥801 billion, or 3 percent of the total increase. The third small sector, labeled "international assets," consists of the excess of the deflated value of receipts of property income from abroad over payments of property income to foreigners, a series that has been persistently negative.[21] From 1961 to 1971 it declined by ¥5 billion, −0.02 percent of the total change in constant price national income.

The rest of national income originates in the "nonresidential business" sector, which consists almost entirely of enterprises whose output is measured

21. Unlike the EPA series for receipts and payments of investment income, our series for property income received and paid by Japan do not include patent royalties, film rentals, and the like.

by market transactions since they buy and sell for a price. It accounted for 89 percent of 1971 national income measured in 1965 prices, and for 94 percent of the increase in national income from 1961 to 1971. The main task of growth analysis is to distribute the growth of output in this sector among its sources.

In Table 2-3 national income originating in nonresidential business is divided between agriculture and nonagricultural industries. Forestry (except general government activities) and fisheries, industries of some importance in Japan, are classified as nonagricultural industries.

Table 2-4 shows our estimates of employment, classified by sector and also by class of worker. Together Tables 2-3 and 2-4 permit the calculation of national income per person employed.

In this chapter we shall focus on growth from 1953 to 1971 and in the subperiods 1953–61 and 1961–71.[22] It was probably in 1953 that national income first exceeded the prewar peak. The decade for which the Ikeda administration announced the target of doubling national income started in 1961, and that year subdivides the postwar period as well as any other, though perhaps no better than 1960. We end with 1971 because it was the last year for which detailed national accounting information could be obtained when we undertook the project. Use of 1970, 1972, or 1973 as the terminal year would yield growth rates that are slightly higher because 1971 was a year of moderate recession.

Table 2-5 shows the principal growth rates for these periods computed from Tables 2-3 and 2-4. We are chiefly concerned with explaining the high rates for total national income growth in the whole economy based on U.S. deflation procedures—8.8 percent over the whole period, 8.1 percent in 1953–61, and 9.3 percent in 1961–71—and with the even higher rates for total national income originating in the nonresidential business sector, which approximate 10 percent in all these periods.[23]

The estimates of national income in constant prices were prepared by the authors but are based largely on the national accounts of the Economic

22. Estimates for 1952 are shown in all annual tables, although they are less reliable than those for later years.
23. Growth rates for the whole economy are lower than those usually quoted; the latter are based on GNP measured from the expenditure side of the accounts and deflated according to Japanese procedures. The growth rate of GNP, as published in the Japanese national accounts, was 10.15 percent from 1961 to 1971. In this particular period estimates from the income side of the accounts yield a still higher rate for GNP, 10.46 percent. (The direction of difference between the growth rates of these two series varies with the particular years compared.) This rate is lowered to 9.74 percent by deducting depreciation, to 9.59 percent by using factor cost weighting, and finally to 9.29 percent by substituting U.S. for Japanese deflation procedures.

Table 2-4. *Employment by Sector, Industrial Branch, and Class*
of Worker, 1952–71

Thousands

Calen-dar year	Total employ-ment (1)	General government, households, institutions, and foreign governments (2)	Nonresidential business					Addendum: nonagri-cultural wage and salary workers[a] (8)
					Nonagricultural industries			
							Self-employed and family workers (7)	
						Wage and salary workers (6)		
			Total (3)	Agri-culture (4)	Total (5)			
1952	37,199	3,033	34,166	13,394	20,772	12,739	8,033	15,772
1953	39,376	3,068	36,308	14,035	22,273	13,411	8,862	16,479
1954	39,862	3,120	36,742	13,695	23,047	13,798	9,249	16,918
1955	41,047	3,196	37,851	14,046	23,805	14,392	9,413	17,588
1956	41,715	3,180	38,535	13,615	24,920	15,553	9,367	18,733
1957	42,778	3,152	39,626	13,160	26,466	16,925	9,541	20,077
1958	43,000	3,078	39,922	12,709	27,213	18,059	9,154	21,137
1959	43,273	3,112	40,161	12,072	28,089	18,947	9,142	22,059
1960	44,345	3,175	41,170	11,959	29,211	20,053	9,158	23,228
1961	44,640	3,266	41,374	11,630	29,744	20,848	8,896	24,114
1962	45,381	3,407	41,974	11,337	30,637	22,035	8,602	25,442
1963	45,824	3,547	42,277	10,720	31,557	22,808	8,749	26,355
1964	46,517	3,695	42,822	10,312	32,510	23,669	8,841	27,364
1965	47,453	3,795	43,658	9,900	33,758	24,883	8,875	28,678
1966	48,528	3,889	44,639	9,544	35,095	26,101	8,994	29,990
1967	49,545	3,966	45,579	9,290	36,289	26,889	9,400	30,855
1968	50,365	4,041	46,324	9,077	37,247	27,639	9,608	31,680
1969	50,757	4,118	46,639	8,787	37,852	28,104	9,748	32,222
1970	51,289	4,183	47,106	8,242	38,864	29,121	9,743	33,304
1971	51,421	4,253	47,168	7,509	39,659	29,998	9,661	34,251

Sources: The principal sources used for the authors' estimates were Bureau of Statistics, *Rōdō-ryōku chōsa hokoku* [Report on the Labor Force Survey] (various annual editions), *Rōdōryōku chōsa kaisan kekka hōkoku* [Report on the Revised Figures of the Labor Force Survey for the Period January 1953 to September 1961], and *Comparison of Employed Persons, 1920 through 1970;* Ministry of Labor, *Shōwa 44-nen rōdō keizai no bunseki* [An Economic Study of the 1969 Labor Market] (1970); Economic Planning Agency, *Annual Report on National Income Statistics, 1973* and *Revised Report on National Income Statistics, 1951–1967.* Sources and procedures are fully described in Denison and Chung, *How Japan's Economy Grew So Fast.*

a. Sum of columns 2 and 6.

Planning Agency. The EPA provides GNP in constant prices but national income only in current prices. The employment series is based primarily on EPA estimates for nonagricultural wage and salary workers and on the Labor Force Survey conducted by the Bureau of Statistics for other groups. Gaps were filled from other sources, and estimates were adjusted by the authors where necessary for continuity or consistency. The derivation of these series and those shown in subsequent tables cannot be described here; we provide a full explanation in a forthcoming publication, *How Japan's Economy Grew So Fast.*

Estimates of the Sources of Growth

The size of any nation's output is governed by many determinants, and changes in these determinants cause its output to change. Analysis of the sources of growth seeks to measure the size of the contribution to the growth rate of national income made by changes in each determinant. Techniques for preparing such estimates were developed by one of us in three studies of Western nations, and previously applied by the other to Japanese experience.[24] The estimates presented here for Japan are wholly new.[25] In derivation and presentation they follow very closely those provided for the United States in *Accounting for United States Economic Growth.*

Several tables that will be used to analyze the Japanese experience are introduced here. Some are needed for estimates of the sources of growth, others provide the estimates themselves, and the remainder compare the sources of growth in Japan and other countries.

24. Edward F. Denison, *The Sources of Economic Growth in the United States and the Alternatives Before Us,* CED Supplementary Paper 13 (Committee for Economic Development, 1962); *Why Growth Rates Differ: Postwar Experience in Nine Western Countries* (Brookings Institution, 1967); and *Accounting for United States Economic Growth, 1929–1969* (Brookings Institution, 1974). William K. Chung, "Study of Economic Growth in Postwar Japan for the Period of 1952–1967: An Application of Total Productivity Analysis" (Ph.D. dissertation, New School for Social Research, New York, 1971).

25. Previous investigations were of course consulted. Especially worthy of mention are detailed estimates of the contributions of inputs, and of output per unit of input as a whole, by Hisao Kanamori ("What Accounts for Japan's High Rate of Growth?" *Review of Income and Wealth,* Series 18 [June 1972], pp. 155–71, and unpublished supplementary "Explanation of Estimation"); estimates of growth sources in manufacturing and the whole economy by Tsunehiko Watanabe and F. Egaizu ("Gijutsu shinpo to keizai seichō" [Technological Advance and Economic Growth], in Motoo Kaji (ed.), *Keizai seichō to shigen bunpai* [Economic Growth and Resource Allocation] [Iwanami Shoten, 1967], pp. 121–51, especially p. 130); estimates of the contribution of labor input by Watanabe ("Improvement of Labor Quality and Economic Growth: Japan's Postwar Experience," in *Economic Development and Cultural Change,* vol. 21 [October 1972], pp. 33–53; estimates by Watanabe and Egaizu from the Japanese language *Economic Studies Quarterly* of March 1968 are included); and analysis by Kazushi Ohkawa and Henry Rosovsky (*Japanese Economic Growth*), much of which is along similar lines though results are not presented in the form of sources of growth tables. Our main results and those of these writers seem to be broadly consistent where we estimate the contributions of the same determinants.

Table 2-5. *Selected Growth Rates, 1953–71*
Percent per year

Item	Total national income			Employment			National income per person employed		
	1953–71	1953–61	1961–71	1953–71	1953–61	1961–71	1953–71	1953–61	1961–71
Japanese deflation procedures									
Whole economy	9.17	8.65	9.59	1.49	1.58	1.42	7.56	6.96	8.05
United States deflation procedures									
Whole economy	8.77	8.13	9.29	1.49	1.58	1.42	7.17	6.45	7.75
Nonresidential business	10.04	9.86	10.18	1.46	1.65	1.32	8.45	8.08	8.75
Agriculture	1.59	4.99	–1.06	–3.42	–2.32	–4.28	5.18	7.49	3.37
Nonagricultural industries	11.13	10.89	11.32	3.26	3.68	2.92	7.63	6.95	8.17
Wage and salary workers	...	...	...	4.57	5.67	3.71	...	...	...
Self-employed and unpaid family workers	...	...	...	0.48	0.05	0.83	...	...	...

Source: Computed from Tables 2-3 and 2-4.

Income Shares

Table 2-6 gives our estimates of the percentage distribution of national income originating in nonresidential business by type of earnings. After smoothing to eliminate the effects of business fluctuations, these data provide weights that are used to combine labor, two types of capital, and land in order to obtain a series measuring total factor input in nonresidential business. This choice of weights is based on the proposition that, if a small percentage increase in the number of units of all of the factors would raise the sector's output by x, the same percentage increase in the number of units of any one factor would raise output by x times the share of that factor in total

Table 2-6. *Percentage Distribution of National Income Originating in Nonresidential Business, by Income Share, 1952–71*

Calendar year	National income[a] (1)	Labor (2)	Nonresidential structures and equipment (3)	Inventories (4)	Land (5)
1952	100.00	79.11	10.08	5.39	5.42
1953	100.00	79.47	10.53	5.77	4.23
1954	100.00	78.02	11.12	6.05	4.81
1955	100.00	79.39	9.66	5.13	5.82
1956	100.00	79.09	10.47	5.66	4.78
1957	100.00	74.88	13.38	7.41	4.33
1958	100.00	76.31	12.44	6.72	4.53
1959	100.00	76.06	12.64	6.71	4.59
1960	100.00	72.08	15.44	8.15	4.33
1961	100.00	71.48	15.95	8.36	4.21
1962	100.00	72.86	15.00	7.74	4.40
1963	100.00	74.33	14.07	7.17	4.43
1964	100.00	74.44	14.04	7.03	4.49
1965	100.00	76.33	12.80	6.29	4.58
1966	100.00	75.52	13.08	6.71	4.69
1967	100.00	73.80	13.44	7.62	5.14
1968	100.00	72.44	14.40	7.92	5.24
1969	100.00	72.07	14.43	8.33	5.17
1970	100.00	71.28	14.82	8.82	5.08
1971	100.00	73.13	13.96	8.32	4.59

Sources: Estimated from Economic Planning Agency, *Annual Report on National Income Statistics, 1973, Revised Report on National Income Statistics, 1951–1967,* and *Estimation of Gross Fixed Capital Stock of Private Enterprises, 1952–1964* (1967); Bureau of Statistics, *Japan Statistical Yearbook, 1971* (1972), input-output table, corporation enterprise survey, establishment census data, census of commerce for 1968, and national wealth survey; unpublished estimates of corporate GNP for 1952–64 by Tsutomu Noda.

a. Excludes corporate transfers to households and private nonprofit institutions.

earnings. The reasoning is as follows. Total earnings of each factor are the product of the number of units of the factor and its price, or earnings, per unit, while the marginal product of each factor is the extra output that would be added by one additional unit of that factor when the quantities of the other factors are held constant. To minimize costs, enterprises must combine factors in such proportions that the marginal products per unit of the several factors are proportional to their prices, or earnings, per unit; this condition is presumed to be satisfied.

The United States is the only other country for which estimates for non-residential business have been prepared. In two periods the shares compare as follows:

	1952–59		1960–68	
	Japan	United States	Japan	United States
Nonresidential				
business national income	100.0	100.0	100.0	100.0
Labor	77.8	81.2	73.7	80.2
Nonresidential struc-tures and equipment	11.3	11.1	14.3	11.9
Inventories	6.1	4.2	7.4	4.0
Nonresidential land	4.8	3.5	4.6	3.9

Table 2-7 compares the share of labor earnings in the whole economy of eleven countries in two time periods. (Neither period is the same for all the countries; in most countries the first ends in 1959, the second in 1964.) In the 1950s Japan had one of the highest labor shares; since 1960 its labor share has been one of the lowest. Up to the time the data stop, at least, Japan is the only country in which the labor share dropped appreciably.

The data for Japan are necessarily crude, if only because of the impor-tance of proprietors' income, a mixed share that must be allocated between labor and property. Our results nevertheless support the general belief that since 1960 the labor share has been lower than in most other countries. The shares of inventories (especially), of dwellings, and of nonresidential land are relatively high in Japan; that of nonresidential structures and equipment is not exceptional.

Of course, the most striking feature of Table 2-7 is the broad similarity of shares in all countries and both time periods despite large differences in factor proportions and other conditions.[26]

26. Because Table 2-7 refers to the whole economy rather than just nonresidential business, labor shares are considerably affected by the size of the three special sectors, each of which consists entirely of either labor or nonlabor income.

Table 2-7. *Labor Earnings as a Percentage of National Income for the Whole Economy, by Country, Various Periods, 1950–71*[a]

Country	Period	Labor share	Period	Labor share
Japan	1952–59	77.6	1960–71	72.7
Belgium	1950–59	72.6	1960–64	74.9
Canada	1950–62	77.3	1963–67	78.4
Denmark	1950–59	75.2	1960–62	75.5
France	1950–59	76.8	1960–64	78.6
Germany	1950–59	73.5	1960–64	74.0
Italy	1950–59	72.0	1960–62	72.0
Netherlands	1950–59	73.8	1960–64	76.1
Norway	1950–59	72.7	1960–64	78.3
United Kingdom	1950–59	77.6	1960–64	78.4
United States	1950–59	79.9	1960–68	79.3

Sources: For Japan, computed from estimates of national income by sector in current prices and from Table 2-6; corporate transfers to households and private nonprofit organizations are excluded from national income. For Canada, Dorothy Walters, *Canadian Growth Revisited, 1950–1967*, Staff Study 28 (Economic Council of Canada, 1970), p. 59. For the United States, computed from data underlying Denison, *Accounting for United States Economic Growth*, tables 3-1 and J-1, pp. 18 and 260. For other countries, computed from data underlying Denison, *Why Growth Rates Differ*, table 4-2, p. 42.

a. Figures given are averages of percentages for the years in the periods shown.

Indexes of Input and Output per Unit of Input

Only the barest description of the remaining tables will be provided now; amplification is deferred until our substantive discussion of sources of growth.

Table 2-8 shows indexes of labor input in nonresidential business and the component series that were multiplied to obtain it. Employment, average hours, and total hours worked are shown in the first three columns. They are the starting point, but only that, for measuring labor input. Hours worked by persons in different demographic groups (five age groups are distinguished for each sex) or who have received differing amounts of education (ten levels for each sex) are not considered to represent the same amount of labor input and consequently cannot simply be added. Rather, the labor input embodied in an average hour worked by different demographic or education groups is considered to be proportional to the average hourly earnings of the people in the groups. Changes in the average labor input content of an hour worked resulting from changes in the demographic and educational composition of total hours worked are measured by the indexes in columns 4 and 7, respectively.

Other columns refer to the effects on output of changes in average hours. We consider that a change in average hours yields a proportional change in

Table 2-8. *Indexes of Sector Labor Input for Nonresidential Business, 1952–71*

1965 = 100

Calendar year	Employment (1)	Average weekly hours (2)	Total weekly hours (3)	Age-sex composition of total hours (4)	Intragroup changes (5)	Specified intergroup shifts (6)	Amount of education (7)	Labor input (8)
						Efficiency of an hour's work as affected by changes in hours due to		
1952	78.26	99.49	77.86	98.11	97.22	98.81	93.31	68.47
1953	83.16	98.88	82.24	98.24	96.97	98.68	93.81	72.52
1954	84.16	100.46	84.55	98.44	96.29	98.25	94.31	74.26
1955	86.70	99.34	86.12	97.84	96.22	98.25	94.82	75.53
1956	88.27	101.11	89.26	98.18	95.39	98.30	95.33	78.34
1957	90.76	102.63	93.16	98.48	95.28	98.55	95.84	82.56
1958	91.44	102.99	94.18	98.21	95.54	98.69	96.36	84.04
1959	91.99	103.36	95.09	98.44	95.70	98.95	96.88	85.88
1960	94.30	103.68	97.78	99.04	95.62	99.04	97.40	89.33
1961	94.77	103.51	98.10	99.18	96.11	99.87	97.91	91.44
1962	96.14	101.88	97.97	99.07	98.16	99.97	98.43	93.75
1963	96.84	100.90	97.72	99.31	98.94	99.97	98.95	94.98
1964	98.09	101.01	99.07	99.73	99.32	99.98	99.47	97.59
1965	100.00	100.00	100.00	100.00	100.00	100.00	100.00	100.00
1966	102.25	100.19	102.44	100.12	100.02	100.01	100.53	103.14
1967	104.40	101.11	105.57	100.26	99.56	99.77	101.06	106.25
1968	106.11	100.37	106.51	100.61	100.71	99.76	101.59	109.37
1969	106.83	100.43	107.30	101.24	100.93	99.83	102.13	111.78
1970	107.90	99.91	107.82	101.64	101.41	99.87	102.67	113.95
1971	108.04	99.36	107.36	102.12	101.81	99.98	103.22	115.19

Sources: Column 1 is computed from column 3 of Table 2-4 and column 8 is the product of columns 3 through 7. The principal sources for the authors' estimates of hours, age-sex composition, efficiency of an hour's work, and education indexes were Bureau of Statistics, *Report on the Revised Figures of the Labor Force Survey* (1957), *Report on the Labor Force Survey* (1970 and 1972), and *Census of Population* (1950, 1960, and 1970); Ministry of Labor, *Basic Survey of the Wage Structure* (1967, 1970, and 1971); Ministry of Education, *Japan's Growth and Education: Educational Development in Relation to Socio-Economic Growth* (1963). Sources and procedures are fully described in Denison and Chung, *How Japan's Economy Grew So Fast.*

labor input when it results from shifting proportions of part-time or female workers or from a change in average part-time hours, but not if it is a consequence of two other types of change. First, reductions in the average hours of a homogeneous group of full-time workers tend to raise output per hour, preventing total work done from declining in proportion to the decline in hours; when full-time hours are extremely long, as in most activities in Japan during most of the period covered, the offset may be complete. Column 5 implements these assumptions, which are the same as those used in the analysis of U.S. growth.[27] Second, column 6 offsets changes in the average hours worked in nonresidential business that result from shifts in the distribution of full-time workers of each sex among nonagricultural wage and salary employment, agricultural employment, and nonagricultural self-employment. Even though their average hours differ, we consider that full-time workers in the three groups provide the same amount of labor input if they work the average number of hours for their group and their other characteristics are similar.

Table 2-9 supplements the index of labor input used by nonresidential business with indexes of the sector's inputs (holdings) of inventories, fixed capital (the index is a weighted average of gross and net stock, with gross stock given three-fourths of the weight), and land.[28] The inventory and gross fixed capital stock series are from the Economic Planning Agency. The quantity of land available for use is estimated not to have changed. Total factor input is a weighted index (based on income share weights, with weights changed in each pair of years) of the series for labor, capital, and land. The table also shows the index of sector national income per unit of input.

In Table 2-10 this last index is shown as the product of indexes of the effects of nine separate determinants of output per unit of input. These indexes are all measured on a scale such that a difference of, say, 1 percent in the value of an index in any year would change total national income in

27. Full-time workers in nonresidential business were divided among agricultural workers, nonagricultural self-employed and unpaid family workers, and nonagricultural wage and salary workers, and each of these three groups was further divided by sex to secure six full-time groups in all. So long as average weekly hours (as shortened by inclusion of vacation and holiday weeks) exceeded 52.7 for any male group and 49.0 for any female group, changes in average full-time hours were assumed not to affect output per worker. The assumption covered all cases except nonagricultural wage and salary workers after 1967 and, for females only, in two earlier years. Between these levels and levels of 42.7 for males and 39.0 for females, changes in average hours are assumed to be partially offset by changes in work done per hour—almost entirely offset at the upper end of the range, which is all that is observed in Japan, and to only a small extent at the lower end.

28. Inventories and fixed capital held by government enterprises are deliberately omitted. With the capital stock of government enterprises increasing less than the stock of private firms, and their earnings close to zero, omission of their stock is necessary to avoid understating the contribution of capital to the growth rate. The situation in Japan is nearly the same as that in the United Staes (where earnings of governmen enterprises are simply omitted from national income); the problem is discussed in Denison, *Accounting for United States Economic Growth*, pp. 273–74.

Table 2-9. *Indexes of Sector National Income, Inputs, and National Income per Unit of Total Factor Input for Nonresidential Business, 1952–71*
1965 = 100

Calendar year	Sector national income in 1965 prices (1)	Labor (2)	Inventories (3)	Nonresidential structures and equipment (4)	All reproducible capital (5)	Land (6)	Total factor input (7)	Sector national income per unit of input (8)
				Indexes of inputs				
1952	30.85	68.47	25.87	38.66	33.49	100.00	59.83	51.56
1953	34.02	72.52	28.31	39.92	35.30	100.00	63.14	53.88
1954	36.88	74.26	29.52	41.52	36.75	100.00	64.74	56.97
1955	40.50	75.53	31.72	43.20	38.68	100.00	66.18	61.20
1956	43.29	78.34	35.78	44.88	41.39	100.00	68.90	62.83
1957	48.86	82.56	41.59	47.37	45.24	100.00	72.91	67.01
1958	51.51	84.04	46.41	50.58	49.07	100.00	75.07	68.62
1959	55.98	85.88	49.72	54.13	52.54	100.00	77.40	72.33
1960	65.13	89.33	54.52	58.72	57.20	100.00	81.18	80.23
1961	72.18	91.44	64.52	65.00	64.82	100.00	84.98	84.94
1962	78.97	93.75	74.00	72.86	73.24	100.00	89.02	88.71
1963	86.41	94.98	80.97	81.60	81.38	100.00	92.07	93.85
1964	95.27	97.59	91.21	90.67	90.85	100.00	96.22	99.01
1965	100.00	100.00	100.00	100.00	100.00	100.00	100.00	100.00
1966	109.94	103.14	107.66	109.38	108.79	100.00	104.15	105.56
1967	126.39	106.25	121.85	120.26	120.83	100.00	108.78	116.19
1968	145.23	109.37	142.08	134.30	137.06	100.00	114.16	127.22
1969	161.89	111.78	162.87	151.52	155.53	100.00	119.40	135.59
1970	180.70	113.95	189.01	172.46	178.29	100.00	125.03	144.52
1971	190.35	115.19	213.74	195.48	201.92	100.00	129.80	146.65

Sources: Column 1 is computed from column 7, Table 2-3; column 2 is column 8, Table 2-8; column 5 is the weighted combination of columns 3 and 4; column 7 is the weighted product of columns 2, 3, 4, and 6; column 8 is column 1 divided by column 7. Primary sources for the authors' estimates of inventories and nonresidential structures and equipment were Economic Planning Agency, *Revised Report on National Income Statistics, 1951–1967, Annual Report on National Income Statistics, 1973,* "Minkan kigyō sōshihon sutokku no suikei" ["Estimates of Gross Capital Stock of Private Enterprises: Quarterly Data for the Period June 1952–September 1972"] (February 1973; processed), and EPA worksheets. Sources and procedures are fully described in Denison and Chung, *How Japan's Economy Grew So Fast.*

nonresidential business by an estimated 1 percent. The meaning of the individual series, insofar as it is not self-evident, will be explained later.[29]

29. The derivation of these series is briefly explained where they are discussed, but full description will appear in Denison and Chung, *How Japan's Economy Grew So Fast.* It may be noted here that Table 2-10 corresponds to Table 6-1 in Denison, *Accounting for United States Economic Growth,* and that columns 2, 3, 5, and 6 were obtained by

Sources of Growth in Japan

Table 2-11 provides estimates of the sources of growth of national income in the nonresidential business sector and in the economy as a whole. Using growth rates and the contribution of each determinant to the growth rate to present results in such tables has a number of advantages, one of which is the possibility of comparing periods of different lengths. The contribution of each determinant is the estimated amount by which the growth rate would have been lowered if there had been no change in that determinant while all others changed as they did.[30]

The estimates for nonresidential business in Table 2-11 are obtained by dividing the growth rate of output (from Table 2-5) between total factor input and total output per unit of input in proportion to their growth rates (calculated from Table 2-9); dividing the contribution of total output per unit of input among its determinants in proportion to the growth rates of the nine individual component indexes (calculated from Table 2-10); dividing the contribution of total factor input among labor, inventories, nonresidential structures and equipment, and land in proportion to their contributions to the growth rate of total factor input (roughly, the product of their growth rates, calculable from Table 2-9), and their weights, which are derived from Table 2-6); and, finally, dividing the contribution of labor among its com-

procedures similar to those followed for the corresponding series in the U.S. estimates. Column 9, which has no U.S. counterpart, was secured by a procedure similar to that for European countries described in Denison, *Why Growth Rates Differ*, pp. 243–45. The derivation of column 8 has elements of the methodology from both of these previous studies. Column 4 is a judgmental series; additional explanation is provided below. Columns 7 and 10 require special comment. There are notable swings in output per unit of input as a result of changes in the intensity of use of employed resources stemming from fluctuations in the intensity of demand. In the case of the U.S. estimates, an index for the effects of such fluctuations (corresponding definitionally to column 7 of Table 2-10) was independently estimated. The index of the effects of the incorporation of advances in knowledge into production together with those of miscellaneous unmeasured determinants (corresponding definitionally to column 10 of Table 2-10) was obtained by division of output per unit of input by all the other components (that is, as the residual). For Japan, an index for the joint effects of the determinants covered by columns 7 and 10 was secured by dividing column 1 by columns 2–6, 8, and 9. After studying its behavior, we assumed (1) that the average value of the demand-intensity index (column 7) was the same in three pairs of years: 1952–53, 1962–63, and 1970–71; and (2) that the index for advances in knowledge and n.e.c. grew at a constant rate, equal to the rate from 1952–53 to 1962–63, from the beginning of 1952 to the end of 1962, and thereafter at a constant rate equal to the rate from 1962–63 to 1970–71. These assumptions permitted calculation of column 10, and column 7 was obtained by division.

30. Estimates are computed to two decimal points to avoid rounding discrepancies in further calculations. This practice, of course, has no implications as to accuracy.

Table 2-10. *Indexes of Sector Output per Unit of Input, Nonresidential Business, 1952–71*

1965 = 100

| Calendar year | Output per unit of input (1) | Gains from reallocation of resources from | | Effects of irregular factors | | Changes in intensity of utilization of employed resources resulting from | | Economies of scale | | Advances in knowledge and n.e.c.[a] (10) |
		Farming (2)	Nonfarm self-employment (3)	Reduction of international trade barriers (4)	Effect of weather on farm output (5)	Work stoppages (6)	Fluctuations in intensity of demand (7)	With output measured in U.S. prices (8)	Associated with income elasticities (9)	
1952	51.56	89.95	94.81	99.97	99.99	99.97	104.68	86.30	86.36	77.55
1953	53.88	90.59	94.49	99.97	98.87	100.00	105.04	87.27	88.04	78.91
1954	56.97	91.13	94.44	99.97	99.94	100.00	105.36	88.17	88.82	80.30
1955	61.20	91.49	94.76	99.97	103.62	100.00	104.79	89.33	89.10	81.70
1956	62.83	92.61	95.57	99.97	99.97	100.00	105.05	89.99	90.37	83.14
1957	67.01	93.75	96.12	99.97	99.47	100.00	105.81	91.43	91.37	84.60
1958	68.62	94.61	97.04	99.97	100.15	100.00	101.53	91.89	92.94	86.09
1959	72.33	95.79	97.47	99.97	101.51	100.00	100.46	92.93	93.34	87.60

1960	80.23	96.32	97.99	99.97	100.46	100.00	105.29	94.73	95.19	89.14
1961	84.94	96.75	98.45	99.97	100.31	100.00	105.72	95.92	96.66	90.72
1962	88.71	97.33	99.11	99.97	100.57	100.00	104.77	97.05	97.45	92.32
1963	93.85	98.36	99.27	99.98	99.89	100.01	105.01	98.09	98.88	94.48
1964	99.01	99.13	99.51	99.99	100.16	100.00	103.68	99.29	100.16	97.20
1965	100.00	100.00	100.00	100.00	100.00	100.00	100.00	100.00	100.00	100.00
1966	105.56	100.67	100.31	100.01	99.95	100.01	99.62	101.25	100.77	102.87
1967	116.19	101.16	100.07	100.02	100.79	100.01	102.06	103.11	102.22	105.83
1968	127.22	101.71	99.94	100.03	100.81	100.01	105.25	105.11	103.04	108.86
1969	135.59	102.04	99.94	100.06	100.51	100.00	106.32	106.60	104.16	111.99
1970	144.52	102.76	100.20	100.09	100.26	100.00	106.72	108.14	105.21	115.20
1971	146.65	103.67	100.58	100.12	99.90	100.00	103.03	108.86	105.80	118.50

Sources: Column 1 is column 8 from Table 2-9. The authors have drawn upon various materials from sources listed in earlier tables in constructing the indexes in columns 2 through 10. Sources and procedures are fully described in Denison and Chung, *How Japan's Economy Grew So Fast*.

a. Not elsewhere classified.

Table 2-11. *Sources of Growth of Actual National Income, Nonresidential Business and Whole Economy, 1953–71*
Percentage points

Item	Nonresidential business			Whole economy[a]		
	1953–71 (1)	1953–61 (2)	1961–71 (3)	1953–71 (4)	1953–61 (5)	1961–71 (6)
National income	**10.04**	**9.86**	**10.18**	**8.77**	**8.13**	**9.29**
Total factor input	**4.18**	**3.88**	**4.43**	**3.95**	**3.53**	**4.35**
Labor	1.99	2.30	1.75	1.85	1.91	1.78
Employment	1.14	1.30	0.99	1.14	1.14	1.09
Hours	0.27	0.48	0.14	0.21	0.38	0.11
Average hours	0.02	0.45	−0.31	0.01	0.35	−0.27
Efficiency offset	0.21	−0.09	0.44	0.18	−0.06	0.38
Intergroup shift offset	0.04	0.12	0.01	0.02	0.09	0.00
Age-sex composition	0.17	0.09	0.22	0.14	0.07	0.19
Education	0.41	0.43	0.40	0.34	0.33	0.35
Unallocated	...	...	...	0.02	−0.01	0.04
Capital	2.19	1.58	2.68	2.10	1.62	2.57
Inventories	0.89	0.75	1.00	0.73	0.57	0.86
Nonresidential structures and equipment	1.30	0.83	1.68	1.07	0.64	1.44
Dwellings	...	...	...	0.30	0.42	0.27
International assets	...	...	...	0.00	−0.01	0.00
Land	0.00	0.00	0.00	0.00	0.00	0.00
Output per unit of input	**5.86**	**5.98**	**5.75**	**4.82**	**4.60**	**4.94**
Advances in knowledge and n.e.c.[b]	2.39	1.84	2.83	1.97	1.42	2.43
Improved resource allocation	1.15	1.40	0.95	0.95	1.08	0.82
Contraction of agricultural inputs	0.78	0.87	0.72	0.64	0.67	0.62
Contraction of nonagricultural self-employment	0.36	0.53	0.22	0.30	0.41	0.19
Reduction in international trade barriers	0.01	0.00	0.01	0.01	0.00	0.01
Economies of scale	2.36	2.47	2.28	1.94	1.90	1.96
Measured in U.S. prices	1.29	1.25	1.33	1.06	0.96	1.14
Income elasticities	1.07	1.22	0.95	0.88	0.94	0.82
Irregular factors	−0.04	0.27	−0.31	−0.04	0.20	−0.27
Effect of weather on farming	0.06	0.19	−0.04	0.05	0.14	−0.04
Labor disputes	0.00	0.00	0.00	0.00	0.00	0.00
Intensity of demand	−0.10	0.08	−0.27	−0.09	0.06	−0.23

Sources: Derived from Tables 2-3, 2-6, 2-8, 2-9, and 2-10.
a. Growth rates based on U.S. deflation procedures. See Table 2-5 for rates based on Japanese deflation procedures.
b. Not elsewhere classified.

ponents in proportion to the growth rates of the individual indexes in Table 2-8.[31]

Estimates of the sources of growth of national income in the whole economy are easily calculated from those for nonresidential business and the estimates of constant-price national income by sector in Table 2-3. Changes in output in sectors other than nonresidential business can be ascribed to a single factor: in general government, households, institutions, and foreign governments, to labor; in the services of dwellings, to capital (the stock of dwellings); and in international assets (the net flow of property income from abroad), also to capital (international assets).[32] The change in total national income that arises in nonresidential business is allocated among determinants in proportion to their contributions to the growth rate in nonresidential business. Table 2-11 is the most important of our tables, and the main product of our growth investigation.

Sources of Growth in Eleven Countries

We have available for comparison estimates of the sources of growth of total national income in a postwar period of at least twelve years' duration, computed on a substantially comparable basis, for two North American and eight Western European countries. To improve and simplify the comparisons, Table 2-12 introduces several adjustments to the growth rates of Japan and the other countries to eliminate, insofar as possible, irrelevant influences from comparisons of growth sources. Thus not only Japan but also Belgium and France adopt deflation procedures that are not followed in the remaining countries and that raise the growth rate; the effects are eliminated in row 2. An adjustment of the Canadian series to allow for a different treatment of the statistical discrepancy is also included here. Rows 3 and 4 eliminate the effects of irregular factors on the growth rates of output per unit of input.

The remaining adjustments were made because the analysis of European growth rates begins with 1950 and in the early 1950s—perhaps up to about

31. The estimate for each component is slightly higher than would be obtained without the allocation procedure: that is, by measuring the contribution of total input, total output per unit of input, and each component of output per unit of input as the growth rate of its index, and each component of input as the product of the growth rate of its index and its average weight (using the labor weight for all labor input components).

32. In the first of these sectors, changes in output (measured by U.S. deflation procedures) that would have occurred if output had changed in proportion to employment in the sector as a whole are ascribed to employment; the small remainder, which results statistically from changes in mix, to unallocated factors.

Table 2-12. Derivation of Standardized Growth Rates of Total National Income

Growth rates and contributions to growth rates in percentage points

Item	Japan, 1953–71	United States, 1948–69	Canada, 1950–67	Belgium, 1950–62	Denmark, 1950–62	France, 1950–62	West Germany, 1950–62	Italy, 1950–62	Netherlands, 1950–62	Norway, 1950–62	United Kingdom, 1950–62
1. National income	9.17	3.85	5.15	3.20	3.51	4.92	7.26	5.96	4.73	3.45	2.29
2. Differences from U.S. in deflation procedures[a]	0.40	...	0.33	0.17	...	0.23	...	...	...	...	...
3. Effect of weather on farming[b]	0.05	−0.01	−0.03	0.00	−0.07	−0.01	0.00	0.01	0.02	−0.02	0.00
4. Intensity of demand[b]	−0.09	−0.14	−0.10	0.00	0.22	0.00	0.00	0.00	0.19	0.00	−0.09
5. Capital adjustments (pre-1955)[c]	...	...	...	...	0.04	...	0.30	...	...	0.04	...
6. Other special pre-1955 adjustments[d]	...	...	...	...	−0.31	...	0.69	0.35	0.45	...	...
7. National income, standardized rate[e]	8.81	4.00	4.95	3.03	3.63	4.70	6.27	5.60	4.07	3.43	2.38

Sources: Japan, Tables 2-5 and 2-11; United States, Denison, *Accounting for United States Economic Growth*, p. 127; Canada, Walters, *Canadian Growth Revisited*, p. 37 (weighted average of 1950–62 and 1962–67 periods); European countries, Denison, *Why Growth Rates Differ*, pp. 302–16.

a. Differences are in deflation of employee compensation in general government, households, institutions, and foreign governments, and in construction. For Canada, includes half the statistical discrepancy between output series.

b. Only the effect on output per unit of input is measured here. The effect of a third irregular factor, labor disputes, was zero in the only countries in which it was explicitly estimated.

c. Includes "balancing of the capital stock" in West Germany and "reduction in the age of capital" in Denmark, West Germany, and Norway.

d. Difference between 1950–62 and 1955–62 contributions of advances in knowledge and its application, general efficiency, and errors and omissions.

e. Row 1 minus rows 2–6.

1953—output changes in certain European countries were greatly affected by factors directly related to World War II. To eliminate some of the effects, unusual gains in West Germany from balancing the capital stock after wartime destruction and division of the country, and in three countries from modernizing the stock after the war, are eliminated in row 5.

The adjustments in line 6 are perhaps more speculative. For the European countries separate estimates of growth sources are available for 1950–55 and 1955–62, and the 1950–55 residual estimates of the contributions of advances in knowledge and n.e.c. in Germany and Italy, the defeated Western powers, are large. We believe this simply reflects the restoration of a functioning economy and balanced production during the period from 1950 to 1952 or 1953. For the comparisons here, we have adjusted the German and Italian growth rates for 1950–62 downward by the amounts of the difference between the 1950–62 and 1955–62 residuals.[33] The 1950–55 residual was also especially large in the Netherlands and unusually small in Denmark. We have similarly substituted 1955–62 for 1950–62 residuals for these countries in the belief that the unusual 1950–55 figures, if not related to the war, probably result from imperfections of the data.[34]

Table 2-13 shows the sources of growth of the standardized growth rates derived for each country in Table 2-12. Table 2-14, derived from Table 2-13, shows the amount by which the standardized growth rate of Japan in 1953–71 exceeds the standardized rate of each of the other countries in the period specified (row 18), and the amount by which the contribution of each determinant fell below its contribution to Japanese growth in 1953–71.

Data from these tables should not be used to judge the relative growth of countries in a common time period. Growth rates of national income from 1953 to 1971, the period for which Japanese growth is analyzed, are not readily available for the other countries, but estimated 1953–71 growth rates for net national product can be provided (without adjustment for differences in deflation procedures or special or irregular factors). They are: Japan, 9.3 percent (or 8.9 percent based on U.S. deflation procedures); the United States, 3.4 percent; Canada, 4.9 percent; Belgium, 4.2 percent; Denmark, 4.1 percent; France, 5.5 percent; West Germany, 5.5 percent; Italy, 5.3 percent; the Netherlands, 5.0 percent; Norway, 4.0 percent; and the United Kingdom, 2.6 percent.

33. Correspondingly, in Table 2-13 the 1955–62 estimate for "advances in knowledge and n.e.c." is substituted for the 1950–62 estimate.

34. Some of these adjustments should logically be accompanied by further adjustments to the European estimates for the contributions of economies of scale. They have not been made, but would be too small to affect any interpretation of Japanese growth.

Table 2-13. Sources of Growth of Standardized Growth Rate of National Income, Whole Economy, Various Countries and Time Periods

Percentage points

Item	Japan, 1953–71	United States, 1948–69	Canada, 1950–67a	Belgium, 1950–62	Denmark, 1950–62	France, 1950–62	West Germany, 1950–62	Italy, 1950–62	Netherlands, 1950–62	Norway, 1950–62	United Kingdom, 1950–62
Standardized growth rate	**8.81**	**4.00**	**4.95**	**3.03**	**3.63**	**4.70**	**6.27**	**5.60**	**4.07**	**3.43**	**2.38**
Total factor input	**3.95**	**2.09**b	**3.02**	**1.17**	**1.55**	**1.24**	**2.78**	**1.66**	**1.91**	**1.04**	**1.11**
Labor	1.85	1.30	1.85	0.76	0.59	0.45	1.37	0.96	0.87	0.15	0.60
Employment	1.14	1.17	1.82	0.40	0.70	0.08	1.49	0.42	0.78	0.13	0.50
Hours of work	0.21	−0.21	−0.20	−0.15	−0.18	−0.02	−0.27	0.05	−0.16	−0.15	−0.15
Age-sex composition	0.14	−0.10	−0.13	0.08	−0.07	0.10	0.04	0.09	0.01	−0.07	−0.04
Education	0.34	0.41	0.36	0.43	0.14	0.29	0.11	0.40	0.24	0.24	0.29
Unallocated	0.02	0.03	0.00	0.00	0.00	0.00	0.00	0.00	0.00	0.00	0.00
Capital	2.10	0.79b	1.14	0.41	0.96	0.79	1.41	0.70	1.04	0.89	0.51
Inventories	0.73	0.12	0.10	0.06	0.15	0.19	0.33	0.12	0.22	0.13	0.09
Nonresidential structures and equipment	1.07	0.36	0.87	0.39	0.66	0.56	1.02	0.54	0.66	0.79	0.43
Dwellings	0.30	0.28b	0.30	0.02	0.13	0.02	0.14	0.07	0.06	0.04	0.04
International assets	0.00	0.03	−0.12	−0.06	0.02	0.02	−0.08	−0.03	0.10	−0.07	−0.05

Land										
0.00	0.00	0.00	0.00	0.00	0.00	0.00	0.00	0.00	0.00	0.00
Output per unit of input, standardized										
4.86	**1.91**[b]	**1.96**	**1.86**	**2.08**	**3.46**	**3.49**	**3.94**	**2.16**	**2.39**	**1.27**
Advances in knowledge and n.e.c.[c]										
1.97	1.19	0.66	0.84	0.75[d]	1.51	0.87[d]	1.30[d]	0.75[d]	0.90	0.79
Improved resource allocation										
0.95	0.30	0.64	0.51	0.68	0.95	1.01	1.42	0.63	0.92	0.12
Contraction of agricultural inputs										
0.64	0.23	0.54	0.20	0.41	0.65	0.77	1.04	0.21	0.54	0.06
Contraction of nonagricultural self-employment										
0.30	0.07	0.10	0.15	0.18	0.23	0.14	0.22	0.26	0.23	0.04
Reduction of international trade barriers										
0.01	0.00	0.00	0.16	0.09	0.07	0.10	0.16	0.16	0.15	0.02
Economies of scale										
1.94	0.42	0.66	0.51	0.65	1.00	1.61	1.22	0.78	0.57	0.36
Measured in U.S. prices										
1.06	0.42	0.63	0.40	0.42	0.51	0.70	0.62	0.55	0.45	0.27
Income elasticities										
0.88	...	0.03	0.11	0.23	0.49	0.91	0.60	0.23	0.12	0.09

Sources: Same as Table 2-12.
a. Details may not add to totals because of rounding.
b. The −0.01 percentage point contribution of the "dwellings occupancy ratio" is included in the contribution of "dwellings" for comparability with other countries.
c. Not elsewhere classified.
d. Estimate for 1955–62 period.

Table 2-14. *Contributions of the Sources to Growth of Standardized Total National Income, Shortfalls from Japan in 1953–71*

Percentage points

Source of growth	United States, 1948–69	Canada, 1950–67[a]	Belgium, 1950–62	Denmark, 1950–62	France, 1950–62	West Germany, 1950–62	Italy, 1950–62	Netherlands, 1950–62	Norway, 1950–62	United Kingdom, 1950–62
1. Employment	−0.03	−0.68	0.74	0.44	1.06	−0.35	0.72	0.36	1.01	0.64
2. Hours of work	0.42	0.41	0.36	0.39	0.23	0.48	0.16	0.37	0.36	0.36
3. Age-sex composition	0.24	0.27	0.06	0.21	0.04	0.10	0.05	0.13	0.21	0.18
4. Education	−0.07	−0.02	−0.09	0.20	0.05	0.23	−0.06	0.10	0.10	0.05
5. Unallocated labor input	−0.01	0.02	0.02	0.02	0.02	0.02	0.02	0.02	0.02	0.02
6. Inventories	0.61	0.63	0.67	0.58	0.54	0.40	0.61	0.51	0.60	0.64
7. Nonresidential structures and equipment	0.71	0.20	0.68	0.41	0.51	0.05	0.53	0.41	0.28	0.64
8. Dwellings	0.02	0.00	0.28	0.17	0.28	0.16	0.23	0.24	0.26	0.26
9. International assets	−0.03	0.12	0.06	−0.02	−0.02	0.08	0.03	−0.10	0.07	0.05
10. Total factor input, lines 1 to 9	1.86	0.95	2.78	2.40	2.71	1.17	2.29	2.04	2.91	2.84
11. Advances in knowledge and n.e.c.[b]	0.78	1.31	1.13	1.22	0.46	1.10	0.67	1.22	1.07	1.18
12. Contraction of agricultural inputs	0.41	0.10	0.44	0.23	−0.01	−0.13	−0.40	0.43	0.10	0.58
13. Contraction of nonagricultural self-employment	0.23	0.20	0.15	0.12	0.07	0.16	0.08	0.04	0.07	0.26
14. Reduction of international trade barriers	0.01	0.01	−0.15	−0.08	−0.06	−0.09	−0.15	−0.15	−0.14	−0.01
15. Total, lines 10 to 14	3.29	2.57	4.35	3.89	3.17	2.21	2.49	3.58	4.01	4.85
16. Economies of scale: growth of market measured in U.S. prices	0.64	0.43	0.66	0.64	0.55	0.36	0.44	0.51	0.61	0.79
17. Economies of scale: income elasticities	0.88	0.85	0.77	0.65	0.39	−0.03	0.28	0.65	0.76	0.79
18. Standardized growth rate	4.81	3.86	5.78	5.18	4.11	2.54	3.21	4.74	5.38	6.43

Source: Computed from Table 2-13.
a. Details may not add to totals because of rounding.
b. Not elsewhere classified.

How Japan Grew So Fast: An Overview

How did Japan obtain a postwar growth rate far above that experienced by any other advanced country? According to our results, the answer is not to be found in any single determinant of output. Rather, changes in almost all important determinants were highly favorable in comparison with other countries, and in none was the change particularly unfavorable.

We base this conclusion on our analysis of the sources of growth in Japan from 1953 to 1971 and the comparison with similar analyses for ten other advanced countries. These analyses are not for the same time periods as that for Japan; for eight European countries they cover 1950–62, for Canada 1950–67, and for the United States 1948–69. The lack of more recent data for Europe is inconvenient but not a serious handicap. We make international comparisons to learn what is unusual about Japanese growth; for this purpose a sample of ten other countries, including all the large, advanced, free enterprise economies, is highly satisfactory even though the time periods differ.

For a preliminary summary, the contributions of groups of determinants to Japanese growth from 1953 to 1971 may be compared with the simple average of their contributions in the other ten countries.

After adjustments of growth rates to improve statistical comparability, to eliminate the effects of irregular factors on output per unit of input, and to screen out the effects of some early postwar recovery elements in certain European countries (Table 2-12), the Japanese growth rate (8.8 percent a year) exceeded the average of the other ten (4.2 percent) by 4.6 percentage points. Of this difference 0.9 percentage points are accounted for by an above-average contribution from changes in employment, hours of work, and the distribution by age and sex of total hours worked, 1.2 percentage points by a greater contribution from capital, 1.0 percentage point by a greater contribution from the application of new knowledge to production, and 0.3 percentage points by greater than average contributions from the reallocation of resources away from agriculture and from nonagricultural self-employment. The contributions of these determinants (as well as of others that do not contribute to exceptional growth in Japan) are computed as if countries operate under conditions of constant returns to scale, which is by no means the case; we believe that economies of scale are important. Markets were growing much faster in Japan than the average for the other countries as a result of the growth sources already enumerated. Chiefly for this reason, economies of scale contributed 1.2 percentage points more to growth in Japan than to the average growth rate of the other ten countries.

The pervasiveness of the Japanese advantage is striking. *All* of the five groups of sources enumerated in the preceding paragraph made a larger contribution to growth in Japan in 1953–71 than to growth in *any* of the other ten countries in the periods analyzed, with the sole exception that Italy (1950–62) is estimated to have gained more from the reallocation of resources away from agriculture and nonfarm self-employment.

It may be noted that Japan gained only about an average amount from one of the principal remaining growth sources, increased education of the labor force, and a lower than average amount from another, the relaxation of barriers to international trade. Four countries gained more than Japan from education and eight gained more from the reduction of trade barriers. But the margins are not large.

Not only did Japan stand first in the contributions from most of the important growth sources; other countries tended not to stand high or low in all major determinants but rather to have a mixed ranking. The latter feature helps explain why the Japanese growth rate exceeded others by so wide a margin.

The table below features the relative contributions of the sources to the growth of Japanese national income, a subject of interest quite apart from international comparisons. Summarized from Table 2-11, it provides estimates for growth during our two subperiods. The contributions of irregular factors are eliminated first so as to secure the growth rate of standardized national income.[35] Remaining determinants are consolidated into seven groups. These are ranked by the size of their contributions over the 1953–71 period as a whole (which happens to be the same as the 1961–71 ranking).

The growth rate was higher by one-fifth in 1961–71 than it had been in 1953–61 once the effect of irregular determinants has been eliminated. Capital and advances in knowledge account for the acceleration. The contribution of capital increased greatly, by six-tenths, and that of advances in knowledge even more, by seven-tenths.[36] The increase in labor input (except

---

35. The standardized series is not a potential output series. Unlike potential output series, it eliminates the effects on productivity of weather in agriculture and of labor disputes (in addition to those of fluctuations in demand, which are eliminated from both types of series). On the other hand, it does not eliminate the effect on total output of differences between actual and potential labor input. We think there is no great difference in Japan between growth rates of standardized and potential national income in these periods. In the United States the difference in 1948–69 is only 0.02 percentage points. (In *Accounting for United States Economic Growth,* p. 124, the growth rate of potential national income is given as 4.02.)

36. These statements assume that the net contribution of miscellaneous determinants, which is combined with that of advances in knowledge, did not change much.

Growth rate or contribution

Output measure or source of growth	Percentage points		Percent of standardized growth rate	
	1953–61	*1961–71*	*1953–61*	*1961–71*
National income (U.S. deflation procedures)	8.13	9.29	...	...
Irregular factors	0.20	−0.27	...	...
Standardized national income	7.93	9.56	100.0	100.0
More capital	1.62	2.57	20.4	26.9
Advances in knowledge and miscellaneous determinants	1.42	2.43	17.9	25.4
Economies of scale	1.90	1.96	24.0	20.5
More work done, with account taken of workers' character- istics except education	1.58	1.43	19.9	15.0
Less labor misallocated to agriculture and nonagri- cultural self-employment	1.08	0.81	13.6	8.5
Increased education per worker	0.33	0.35	4.2	3.7
Reduced international trade barriers	0.00	0.01	0.0	0.1

education) and the reallocation of labor contributed less in the second period than in the first, but the differences were much smaller.

In subsequent sections of this chapter we will discuss each determinant. Here we anticipate certain findings.

The largest contribution to growth was made by capital. The main components of the capital stock increased at extraordinary rates; over the whole 1953–71 period the gross stock of private nonresidential structures and equipment grew at an average annual rate of 9.2 percent, the stock of inventories at 11.9 percent. This achievement required similarly large increases in annual gross investment, which were made possible by the combination of three developments, all big in size. These were the increase in total annual national income (or output), which is to say in the resources available for division between saving and consumption; a rise in the proportion of income saved; and a decline in the price of capital goods (including inventories) relative to the price of other components of the national product, presumably reflecting a decline in the relative production cost of capital goods.

The next largest contribution was made by advances in knowledge and miscellaneous determinants. This combination includes all growth sources, positive or negative, not separately estimated. Comparison of the estimates for Japan with estimates for other countries strongly suggests that the world's stock of knowledge was not advancing fast enough to contribute as much to growth as we estimate Japan secured from advances in knowledge and miscellaneous determinants. The probable explanation is that the average state of technology, business organization, and management practice—which has been not only well below (or behind) the efficiency permitted by the world's stock of knowledge concerning how to produce at low cost but also below average actual practice in the industrialized West—was moving closer to the technological and managerial frontier. There was, in other words, a major element of "catching up" in the contribution of this source. In making this statement we do not mean to distinguish sharply between the dissemination of knowledge and the elimination of other sources of inefficiency as ways of narrowing the productivity differential between Japan and Western countries.

Economies of scale made possible by expanding markets were the third largest source of growth. According to our estimates there were two reasons for their large size. First, the growth of total output, and therefore of the size of the market for the average commodity (whether the market was local, regional, national, or international), was very rapid. Second, among consumer goods the expansion of markets was especially large for commodities such as consumer durables that offered especially big opportunities for gains from scale economies.

Because all components of labor input except education are closely interrelated, they are combined in the preceding text table. This combination makes up the fourth largest growth source. Total man-hours worked in the whole economy increased at the high annual rate of 1.5 percent from 1953 to 1971. Average hours scarcely changed in this period; the growth rate of employment was also 1.5. The growth rate of total hours worked was much higher in 1953–61, 2.2 percent, than in 1961–71, when it fell to 1.0 percent. Other components (in addition to education) raised labor input further in both periods.

The allocation of resources was substantially improved by reducing the proportion of the total labor supply that is inefficiently used in agriculture or consists of self-employed and unpaid family workers in nonfarm enterprises too small for efficiency. Agricultural employment fell from 35.6 percent of all employment in Japan in 1953 to 14.6 percent in 1971, while self-employed and family workers in nonagricultural industries slipped from 22.5 to 18.8 percent.[37] Because of this reallocation, nonagricultural wage

37. Numbers in this paragraph were calculated from Table 2-4.

and salary employment—the type of employment most closely related to the increase in the value of output—increased far more than total employment: by 108 percent from 1953 to 1971 as compared with 31 percent. The situation was not as favorable to growth as if total employment had risen by 108 percent with no change in allocation because the additional agricultural and self-employed workers who would then have been present in 1971 would have contributed something to 1971 output. But this lost contribution was much less than that actually made by the extra nonfarm wage and salary workers in their actual employment, so the gain from reallocation was large. We estimate that, by the grouping in the preceding text table, it was the fifth largest source of growth.

Educational background is a very important determinant of the quality of labor, and the increase in the education of the labor force was a significant source of growth of national income. However, its contribution was dwarfed by those of the five preceding groups of output determinants. The last source listed in the text table is the gain from the reduction of barriers to international trade. This gain was trivial because changes in trade barriers had little effect on trade in 1953–71.

Because most sources shared responsibility for the very high rate of Japanese growth, none contributed an unusually large percentage of the standardized growth rate in comparison with other countries. Indeed, the percentage distribution of growth by source in Japan was not so very different from that in the United States, where the growth rate was far lower. The chief differences in the United States in the 1948–69 period were that economies of scale contributed a smaller percentage (10.7) than in Japan and education a larger percentage (10.4).[38]

Labor Input

We now examine the separate sources of growth. In this section the components of labor input are considered.

Employment

Employment, shown in Table 2-4, rose almost 31 percent from 1953 to 1971, equivalent to the high annual rate of 1.49 percent (1.58 percent in 1953–61 and 1.42 percent in 1961–71). Without changes in working hours or in the demographic composition or educational background of employed

38. See *Accounting for United States Economic Growth,* p. 128, table 9-5, column 3.

persons (all of which will be examined separately), an increase in employment of the size observed would have contributed an estimated 1.14 percentage points to the 1953–71 growth rate (Table 2-11). This is much more than in seven of the ten other countries, a trifle less than in the United States (1948–69), and considerably less than in West Germany (1950–62) and, especially, Canada (1950–67), where the employment contribution was 1.82 percentage points (Tables 2-13 and 2-14).

The Japanese employment increase from 39.4 million in 1953 to 51.4 million in 1971 is more than accounted for by the increase in the working-age population. Only 0.1 million of the 12.0 million increase in employment is ascribable to reduced unemployment; the rest is the consequence of a larger labor force. But the labor force increased much less than the adult population, especially after 1961. It equaled 70.0 percent of the population fifteen and older in 1953, 69.1 percent in 1961, and 65.0 percent in 1971— still a high figure by international standards. Corresponding percentages for males were 86.8, 84.9, and 82.2; for females, 54.3, 54.3, and 48.8. If the participation rate had not changed, the employment increase from 1953 to 1971 would have been 17.2 million instead of 12.0 million. Changes in the age distribution of the adult population may have affected the overall participation rate, but the main reasons for the decline were extension of schooling and the decreasing importance of agriculture, which tended to lower the rates for teenagers and females.

The growth rate of employment in the United States was 1.55 percent from 1948 to 1969. This exceeds the 1953–71 rate of 1.49 in Japan, but it was achieved only by a very large increase in the employment of adult women, many available only for part-time work, and by a huge increase in the number of students holding part-time jobs. Such workers added a much lower than average amount to output; remaining components of labor input bring their special characteristics into the calculation.

Hours of Work

Japan and Italy (1950–62) were the only countries examined in which changes in working hours made a *positive* contribution to the growth rate. In Japan it amounted to 0.21 percentage points in 1953–71. (It was 0.38 points in 1953–61 and still as much as 0.11 points in 1961–71.) In most countries changes in hours subtracted appreciably from growth. As a result, the Japanese advantage was substantial: 0.36 to 0.48 percentage points in comparisons with all countries except France (0.23 points) and Italy (0.16 points).

Diminution of part-time employment, which served to raise average hours per person employed, was a main element in the favorable Japanese experience. In the business sector (including agriculture) full-time employment rose from 77.0 percent of total employment in 1953 to 82.5 percent in 1961 and 85.3 percent in 1971. The reduction of more than one-third in the part-time proportion resulted from the rapidly expanding demand for labor that made full-time jobs available to persons previously able to find only part-time work. The rise in the percentage of full-time employment in Japan is the reverse of the decline in the United States—from 88.9 percent of business employment in 1948 to 83.9 in 1969—which resulted from the increasing number of persons not previously in the labor force who desired only part-time work.

Reductions in full-time hours in Japan were only moderate, especially since they are much longer than in other advanced countries. Moreover, the hours of full-time workers, including even nonagricultural wage and salary workers, were so long that the assumptions underlying the estimates for all the countries imply that the reductions that did take place were almost entirely offset by higher output per hour—the consequence of reduced fatigue and related effects.[39]

Weekly hours per person employed are shown in the table below for Japanese full-time workers in the business sector at the initial and terminal dates of the periods, and in the United States in the nearest years for which data are available.[40] The workweek (even as shortened by the inclusion of vacation and holiday weeks) has been long. For nonagricultural wage and salary workers it averaged 8.7 hours longer in Japan in 1971 than in the United States in 1969 for males, and 9.5 hours longer for females.

39. Estimates of the effects of changes in hours in nonresidential business are constructed in three parts which sometimes, as in Table 2-11, are shown separately. "Average hours" show what the effect would be if changes in average hours altered labor input proportionally. The "efficiency offset" to intragroup changes cancels the portion of this estimate that results from changes in average hours within six groups of full-time workers to the extent, nearly complete in Japan, that offsetting efficiency gains are assumed to occur. The "intergroup shift offset" cancels the effect on average hours of changes in the employment weights of the six groups of full-time workers. For further explanation of the procedures, see *Accounting for United States Economic Growth*, pp. 24–26, 31–33, 35–43, 47–48, 105–06, and 125, or our forthcoming publication, *How Japan's Economy Grew So Fast*.

40. Our basic data appear with overlapping time series for different periods. For this table we have linked so as to adjust all years to conform to the levels for the latest year shown.

The 1953 estimate of 56.1 hours for female nonagricultural self-employed and unpaid family workers in Japan is erratically low. Estimates for 1952 and 1954 are 58.4 and 59.6, respectively.

Average weekly hours worked

	Japan			United States		
	1953	*1961*	*1971*	*1953*	*1961*	*1969*
Nonagricultural wage and salary workers						
Male	54.2	54.2	51.1	42.6	42.8	42.4
Female	52.7	51.7	47.5	39.5	39.0	38.0
Nonagricultural self-employed and unpaid family workers						
Male	61.1	61.7	57.5	53.1	53.9	53.1
Female	56.1	59.3	55.0	53.3	52.5	50.9
Agricultural workers						
Male	55.0	55.7	53.4	55.8	53.9	55.5
Female	52.5	54.0	52.5	48.5	47.9	48.8

Composition of Labor by Age and Sex

Average hourly earnings (which include bonus payments) vary by age and sex in much the same pattern as in other countries; by far the highest earnings accrue to males in the middle age ranges.[41] The earnings of females average around half of the earnings of males, only moderately less than in the United States.

However, postwar changes in the composition of total hours worked in the business sector in Japan were unusual. The percentage worked by females, after an initial increase from 38.0 in 1953 to 39.1 in 1955, dwindled steadily, falling to 38.5 in 1961 and 35.9 in 1971.[42] Probably because of extension of education, the percentages worked by teenagers, both males and females, dropped sharply, especially after 1967. Over the four-year period from 1967 to 1971 alone, the percentage of total hours worked by teenagers dropped by nearly two-fifths, from 8.2 percent to 5.1 percent. The proportion of hours worked by males in the prime working ages increased steadily. These compositional shifts toward the age-sex groups with the highest earnings, and presumptively the highest marginal products, are estimated to have

41. When expressed as percentages of the average hourly earnings of all age-sex groups combined, average earnings of eight of the ten age-sex groups we distinguish are almost the same in Japan and the United States. The Japanese percentages are above the American for two groups, males fifteen to nineteen years old (54 percent as against 36 percent) and males thirty-five to fifty-nine (145 percent as against 128 percent).

42. Data cited in this paragraph have been adjusted to provide comparable series over time.

contributed 0.14 percentage points to the 1953–71 growth rate, the largest figure among the eleven countries. The contribution rose from 0.07 points in 1953–61 to 0.19 points in 1961–71.

In the United States, in contrast, the dominant change was an increase in the proportion of total hours worked by females. In the business sector this proportion had already risen from 16.6 percent in 1929 to 22.3 percent in 1948. It was 24.3 percent in 1953, 26.1 percent in 1961, and 29.7 percent in 1969. (Despite the convergence of the Japanese and American percentages, it will be noted that the Japanese percentage remained much the highest.) With the contribution made to growth by changes in age-sex composition negative in the United States, this determinant contributed 0.24 percentage points to the difference between Japanese and U.S. growth rates.

Education of Employed Persons

Educational background exerts a decisive influence on the types of work an individual can perform and his proficiency in any particular occupation. The Japanese labor force has received as much education as the labor forces of northwest Europe and Canada, or perhaps a bit more, a little less than that of the United States, and considerably more than that of Italy. In the 1950s it had had much more education than was typical in countries at Japan's economic level at that time.

The increase in the education of employed persons during the postwar period was of intermediate size in comparison with other advanced countries, as was the contribution of this change to the growth rate of national income. At 0.34 percentage points, this contribution exceeded that in six of the other countries (by as much as 0.23 percentage points) and fell short of that in four (but at most by only 0.09 points).

Table 2-15 shows percentage distribution of employed persons of each sex (excluding those still in school) among ten educational levels in 1950, 1960, and 1970 (columns 3 to 8). It also shows the estimated average number of years of education of persons in each education category (column 1) and the weight assigned to persons in each education category in constructing a labor input index (column 2). The weights are intended to represent the relative hourly earnings of persons employed in the business sector who differ only in amount of education. The basic earnings data distinguish only four educational levels, so considerable estimation was required to obtain additional detail. Despite the formality and rigidity of the wage structure in large Japanese firms, these differences, like differences

Table 2-15. *Distribution of Employed Persons Not in School by Amount of Education, and Related Data, 1950, 1960, and 1970*

Education	Average years of education (1)	Weight (8 years = 100) (2)	Percentage distribution of employed persons					
			Males			Females		
			1950 (3)	1960 (4)	1970 (5)	1950 (6)	1960 (7)	1970 (8)
No school	0	70	1.57	0.55	0.24	4.78	1.52	0.55
Elementary, junior high, youth training								
1–3 years	2	80	1.99	0.69	0.31	3.13	0.99	0.36
4 years	4	86	5.34	3.27	0.85	6.30	2.85	0.70
5–6 years	5.8	91	15.15	7.32	5.21	24.03	14.83	11.26
7–8 years	7.5	97	41.35	34.04	25.06	33.12	27.84	21.70
9 years	9	107	7.93	21.28	22.93	7.78	26.80	29.38
Middle school (old)[a]	10.7	117	16.29	13.43	10.16	16.75	11.80	9.28
Senior high school	12	122	3.79	9.92	21.41	2.37	11.04	21.37
Junior college and college preparatory school (old)[a]	14	147	3.91	4.05	4.04	1.64	1.90	4.08
University and postgraduate	17	172	2.68	5.45	9.79	0.10	0.43	1.32
Total	...	...	100.00	100.00	100.00	100.00	100.00	100.00
Average years of education	...	...	8.15	9.16	10.17	7.22	8.42	9.31
Average weight (8 years = 100)	...	...	103.71	109.34	115.52	98.66	104.29	109.20
Indexes (1950 = 100)								
Average years of education	...	...	100.00	112.39	124.79	100.00	116.62	128.95
Average weight	...	...	100.00	105.44	111.39	100.00	105.71	110.69

Sources: The primary sources for the authors' estimates were Bureau of Statistics, *Census of Population* (1950, 1960, and 1970), and Ministry of Labor, *Basic Survey on Wage Structure* (1967, 1970, and 1971).
a. Refers to types of schools eliminated by the 1947 reorganization of the school structure.

among broad demographic groups, are much like those in the United States and other countries.

At the bottom of Table 2-15 are estimates of average years of education (which do not enter into the calculation of sources of growth estimates) and the average weight implied by each distribution.

The upward movement in the distributions by amount of education is pronounced. By careful selection of breaking points, it can even be made to sound sensational. For example, the percentage of males with zero to six years of education plummeted from 24.0 in 1950 to 6.6 in 1970, and the corresponding percentage for females from 38.2 to 12.9. Males with twelve or more years of education jumped from 10.4 percent in 1950 to 35.2 percent in 1970, females from 4.1 percent to 26.8 percent. This mode of expression may give an exaggerated impression of changes, but increases in the average number of years of education are more representative and these amounted to 25 percent and 29 percent for males and females, respectively—quite considerable increases. Years of education, however, do not give a satisfactory indication of the economic significance of the change. The index of "educational quality" of labor, based on the use of relative earnings rather than years of school to compare groups, is the appropriate measure for growth analysis. It rose 11.4 percent for males and 10.7 percent for females over the same period.[43]

The upward movement in the education distributions results from the greater education of persons entering the labor force than had been attained by those who left it. Persons leaving the labor force in the early 1950s had received their education many years before. Changes in education back to the late nineteenth century would have to be described in detail for a full explanation of the postwar upward shift; here we can only sketch them.

Three partially related types of development account for the shift. The first is compulsory education. Although a modern school system was promulgated in 1872 and a four-year requirement for compulsory education was established in 1886, enrollment data show clearly that enforcement of the four-year requirement was only gradually introduced and the nation did not approach full compliance before 1909. At about that time (1908) the requirement was raised from four years to six. In 1947 it went to the current nine years. Second, the school system has been reorganized from time to time in such a way that students reaching what might be regarded as a certain point in the educational ladder obtained more years of education. One major reorganization was the introduction in 1947 of the American school system; among other changes, junior high school required three years, one more than the previous "upper elementary" school—both after six years of ordinary elementary school. Third, voluntary continuation of education after completing compulsory schooling has increased, the joint effect of growing desire and financial ability to continue schooling on the part of students and parents and of expansion of the educational establishment. Continuation on a massive scale is a new development of the postwar period; in this respect Japanese experience resembles that of the United Kingdom and some other countries of Western Europe.

Unallocated Labor Input

Contributions of the labor input components described so far, except employment, stem from changes within the business sector only. In general government, households, institutions, and foreign governments, changes in output are measured by changes in employment (according to U.S. deflation

43. Estimates for some countries, including the United States, allow for an increase in the number of days attended per year of education. No such allowance has been made for Japan except insofar as reduction in absenteeism may have reduced the years elapsed before a particular certificate or degree is obtained. Historical data on attendance are sparse, but it seems unlikely that more than a minor adjustment could be justified.

techniques) so that other labor characteristics do not affect measured output. However, within this nonbusiness sector the change in output in each individual segment is measured by the change in employment in that segment, so that changes in the relative importance of segments that have different base-year values of output per worker may affect the growth rate. The "unallocated" component of labor input, calculated separately only for Japan and the United States, measures this effect. The amounts are too small to require discussion.

Capital Input

The increase in the stock of private capital contributed an estimated 2.10 percentage points to the growth rate of national income from 1953 to 1971. The contribution was much larger in 1961–71, at 2.57 percentage points, than in 1953–61, when it was 1.62 points. We first discuss the capital stock of firms—including inventories as well as structures and equipment—and offer some general comments on investment and saving. We conclude with additional remarks about dwellings and international assets.

Growth of Private Nonresidential Business Capital

The stock of private nonresidential business capital increased at a pace quite outside the range observed in other advanced countries.[44] The growth rate of the gross stock of nonresidential structures and equipment was 9.2 percent and that of inventories was 11.9 percent. The highest rates among the other ten countries listed in Tables 2-12 to 2-14, those for West Germany in 1950–62, were 5.5 percent for the gross stock of nonresidential structures and equipment and 7.0 percent for inventories. Rates in West Germany, in turn, were well above those in the remaining countries. Rates in the United States in 1948–69 were 3.5 percent both for gross stock of fixed capital and for inventories. Even in a short boom period such as 1964–69 these rates reached only 4.5 and 5.2 percent.[45]

44. We must except Israel, where both gross and net stock of nonresidential structures and equipment in the private economy grew at an annual rate of 12.5 percent from 1950 to 1965, according to A. L. Gaathon, *Economic Productivity in Israel,* Praeger Special Studies in International Economics and Development (Praeger Publishers in cooperation with the Bank of Israel, 1971), p. 42. Israel, however, is a quite special case.
45. Computed from *Accounting for United States Economic Growth,* p. 54, table 5-2, columns 1 and 3.

Growth rates of private nonresidential business capital in postwar Japan were not only high but also rising. The following table provides growth rates of the gross stock of fixed capital and the stock of inventories in our two main subperiods and in four shorter periods:[46]

	Growth rates (percent)	
Period (calendar years)	Fixed capital (gross stock)	Inventories
1953–61	6.0	10.8
1961–71	11.8	12.7
1953–56	3.8	8.1
1956–60	6.7	11.1
1960–67	10.8	12.2
1967–71	13.1	15.1

Nonresidential business capital receives at least as much weight in total input in Japan as in the other countries, so these high growth rates resulted in a contribution to growth in Japan that was much greater than elsewhere (Table 2-14). This was also true of the separate components, fixed capital and inventories. (The bigger difference is in the contribution of inventories, partly because they receive especially great weight in Japan.) The acceleration of capital stock growth rates combined with the previously noted increase in earnings weights to yield a 90 percent increase from 1953–61 to 1961–71 in the contribution of these two types of capital.

Rise in Annual Gross Investment by Private Business

To achieve the capital stock growth rates recorded, truly enormous increases were required in annual gross investment, measured in constant (1965) prices, and one may well ask how it was possible for Japan to expand investment so much. An increase in output available for division between consumption and saving, a higher saving rate, and a falling relative price for investment goods all *could* contribute to an increase in investment; for any particular type of investment, so could an increase in its share of total investment. To examine what actually happened to the quantity of any type of investment, its index can be regarded as the product of indexes of these four quantities or ratios that govern its behavior.

46. Dividing points between the shorter periods were selected to match jumps in the annual percentage increases in fixed capital. They are clearly delineated except that 1961 might be substituted for 1960.

Table 2-16. *Analysis of Indexes of Fixed Nonresidential Business Investment*

Description[a]	1960/53[b]	1971/60[b]	1971/53[b]
1. GNP (constant prices)	176.3	298.4	526.2
2. GPI/GNP (current prices)	152.2	106.0	161.4
3. FNBI/GPI (current prices)	104.3	88.1	91.9
4. Price ratio, GNP/FNBI	100.2	143.2	143.4
5. FNBI (constant prices)	280.3	399.5	1,119.8

Sources: Economic Planning Agency, *Annual Report on National Income Statistics, 1973*, and *Revised Report on National Income Statistics, 1951–1967*.

a. GNP, gross national product at market prices; GPI, gross private investment; FNBI, fixed nonresidential business investment.

b. Percentages, based on fiscal year data.

Table 2-16 provides such indexes for the largest component of gross private investment, fixed nonresidential investment by private business.[47] As shown in row 5, such investment, valued in 1965 prices, reached 280.3 percent of its 1953 level in 1960. In 1971 it reached 399.5 percent of its 1960 level and 1,119.8 percent of its 1953 level.

In this table, gross private investment is defined to include inventory accumulation by private business, private residential construction, and net foreign investment, in addition to gross fixed nonresidential investment by private business. Gross private investment is conceptually identical to gross national saving—private saving plus government saving—when government saving is defined as the government surplus on income and product account —that is, as the excess of government receipts over expenditures. As explained below, expenditures include investment by government enterprises.

We start with the change from 1953 to 1960. Row 1 shows that in 1960 gross national product in constant prices was 176.3 percent of 1953. This would have been the index of total gross private investment (of all types) valued in constant prices if there had been no change either in the proportion of the nation's gross output saved and invested or in relative prices. Actually, gross national saving (gross private investment) jumped from 18.05 percent of GNP in 1953 to 27.47 percent in 1960, an index of 152.2 as shown in row 2. This would have been the index of total gross private investment of all types valued in constant prices if there had been no change in the nation's gross output or in relative prices. As is customary in the calculation of saving rates, these percentages are based on current-price data because decisions about how much to save from income are presumed to be

47. Here we divide the 1953–71 period at 1960 rather than 1961 because some 1961 relationships were abnormal. Data in this section are based on the national accounts as reported by the EPA, and refer to fiscal years ending March 31 following the year named.

based on prevailing price relationships rather than on the relative prices of consumption goods and investment goods operative in some past or (as in this case) future base year. Next, as shown in row 3, the percentage of total gross private investment (in current prices) that was allocated to private fixed nonresidential business increased moderately, from 68.29 percent to 71.23 percent, or to an index of 104.3. Finally, as shown in row 4, the ratio of the average price of all output (GNP) to the price of fixed nonresidential business investment rose slightly, to an index of 100.2. Consequently, the quantity (constant-price value) of this type of investment would have risen slightly even if there had been no change in constant-price GNP, in the saving rate, or in the share of saving allocated to this type of investment.

Only the first two of the four indexes changed much, so that by this way of looking at the matter the rise from 1953 to 1960 in fixed nonresidential business investment was due mainly to the increase in GNP and the rise in the national saving (or total gross private investment) rate. Both changes were big.

The further rise in fixed nonresidential business investment after 1960 must be explained differently. With 1960 equal to 100, the 1971 index was 399.5. The increase in real GNP—to an index of 298.4—was again the biggest factor. But the further rise in the gross saving rate was small—from 27.47 to 29.13 percent, an index of 106.0. The share of nonresidential fixed investment in total investment actually dropped; the index was only 88.1. Although the annual share is somewhat erratic because of the volatility of two of the other components (inventory accumulation and net foreign investment), the 1960–71 drop was fairly representative of the downward trend, which resulted from the swelling importance of residential construction.

The fourth index, the ratio of the implicit price deflator for GNP to the deflator for fixed nonresidential business investment, was 143.2 in 1971 (with 1960 equaling 100). This means that real fixed nonresidential business investment was 43 percent bigger in 1971 than it would have been if its relative price had not changed, provided that real GNP and the proportion of current dollar GNP devoted to such investment are considered to be unaffected by the change in relative prices. The drop in the relative price of fixed nonresidential business investment was persistent, and began even before 1960. A sizable drop occurred every year from 1957 to 1971. The decreasing relative price of investment goods was thus a major factor facilitating the sharp rise in real investment. This was not an international development, at least on any such scale. The 1960–71 index corresponding to the Japanese figure of 143.2 was only 102.7 in the United States.

When the whole period from 1953 to 1971 is considered, increases in three of the four series—real GNP, the gross saving rate, and the ratio of the price deflator for GNP to that for fixed nonresidential business investment—are all found to have contributed greatly to the rise in this type of investment. The decline in the share of total private investment devoted to fixed nonresidential business investment provided a moderate offset.

It is unnecessary to repeat all these calculations for investment in inventories, which fluctuates widely on an annual basis. Suffice it to note that the first two indexes in Table 2-16 apply also to inventory investment, and that the price of goods held in private business inventories fell even more, relative to the GNP deflator, than did the price of fixed nonresidential business investment. In the case of inventories the drop was important in both periods. The index of the ratio of GNP prices to prices of goods held in private inventories was 124.5 in 1960 with 1953 taken as 100, 147.5 in 1971 with 1960 as 100, and 183.6 in 1971 with 1953 as 100.

Consideration of inventories thus strengthens the conclusion that the increase in real investment by business enterprises was facilitated enormously by the decline in the relative price of investment goods.[48]

Distribution of Investment and Saving

Important as was the change in relative prices, the rates of saving and investment command the most attention. Table 2-17 shows private gross investment and gross saving as percentages of GNP, together with details to indicate the groups doing the investment and saving. Definitions and classification correspond approximately to those of the U.S. national income and product accounts.[49] Data shown are averages of the annual percentages for the fiscal years in each period.

Gross private investment rose from an average of 17.2 percent of GNP in 1952–54 to 30.5 percent of a vastly increased GNP in 1970–71. With one exception, the increase was continuous between the periods shown in the table. From 1967 through 1971 roughly two-thirds of private investment, equal to 20 percent of GNP, was made by private corporations; this includes

48. However, this conclusion does not extend to the price index for residential construction, which rose a trifle more than the GNP deflator until 1965, and much more thereafter.

49. The Japanese national accounts put total investment, total saving, and government saving higher by the amounts of government expenditures that are classified as gross government investment. Table 3-7 in the chapter by Ackley and Ishi follows this practice. Gross government investment ranged from 7.0 to 9.4 percent of GNP in the periods shown in Table 2-17.

Table 2-17. *Gross Investment and Saving as Percentages
of Gross National Product*

Annual averages

| Fiscal years | Gross private investment | | | | Gross private saving | | | Government surplus on income and product account | | | Statistical discrepancy |
	Total (1)	Corporate rate[a] (2)	Non-corporate rate[a] (3)	Net foreign (4)	Total (5)	Corporate rate[b] (6)	Non-corporate rate (7)	Total (8)	General government[c] (9)	Government enterprises[d] (10)	(11)
1952–54	17.2	11.1	6.4	−0.3	16.5	7.4	9.1	−0.6	0.6	−1.1	1.3
1955–57	21.8	15.9	6.3	−0.4	22.8	9.2	13.5	−0.6	1.3	−1.9	−0.4
1958–60	24.3	17.3	6.5	0.5	24.9	11.0	13.9	−0.5	1.1	−1.6	−0.1
1961–63	27.2	21.6	6.7	−1.1	27.2	12.6	14.6	−0.1	2.0	−2.1	0.2
1964–66	25.5	16.6	8.2	0.7	26.6	12.5	14.1	−2.3	0.7	−2.9	1.2
1967–69	29.9	20.2	9.0	0.6	30.6	14.9	15.8	−1.1	1.8	−2.9	0.4
1970–71	30.5	19.7	8.9	1.9	31.9	15.6	16.3	−0.5	1.7	−2.2	−0.9

Sources: Derived from Economic Planning Agency, *Revised Report on National Income Statistics, 1951–1967*, pp. 10–11, 18–19, 20–21, 238–39, 258–59, and *Annual Report on National Income Statistics, 1973*, pp. 14–15, 20–21, 24–25, 222–23, 240–41.

a. The small "balancing item" appearing in tables for fixed investment by legal form of organization was allocated in proportion to other fixed investment.

b. Includes "damage of fixed capital by accident."

c. Equals "saving of general government" in the Japanese national accounts minus profit of government enterprises and gross fixed capital formation by general government.

d. Equals profit and depreciation of government enterprises less gross fixed capital formation and increase in stocks by government enterprises.

their fixed investment and additions to their inventories. Similar investment by unincorporated firms was only one-sixth as big, at about 3.5 percent of GNP, despite these firms' importance in production and employment. Although, as shown in Table 2-17, about 9.0 percent of GNP was devoted to private noncorporate investment in 1967–71, dwellings acquired by households and nonprofit organizations accounted for about 5.5 points of this total. The remaining investment component, net foreign investment, having been negative in three of the first four periods shown, turned positive in the last three.[50] In 1970–71 it averaged as much as 1.9 percent of GNP and over 6 percent of gross private investment.

Gross private investment is, by definition, equal to the sum of gross private saving and government saving when the latter is construed as the value of the government surplus on income and product account. This equality is missing in the actual data because the series for saving are statistically inconsistent with those for investment. The statistical discrepancy in the national income accounts must be added to saving or subtracted from investment to secure equality. Consequently, in Table 2-17 column 1 equals the sum of columns 5, 8, and 11.

50. This item is termed "net lending to the rest of the world" in the Japanese national accounts.

If they were consistently measured, private saving would have exceeded private investment in all periods because part of private saving was absorbed by a government deficit, as shown in Table 2-17, column 8.[51] The nature of this deficit is brought out in columns 9 and 10. Receipts of general government exceeded general government expenditures (including outlays for construction and equipment), but the excess (column 9) was insufficient to finance fully the excess of capital outlays by government enterprises (including their inventory accumulation) over their depreciation charges and profits (column 10). The government deficit was usually modest, averaging only 0.82 percent of GNP from 1952 to 1971.[52] Hence nearly all private saving was available to finance private investment.

Gross private saving has behaved quite differently in the United States and Japan. In the United States it has been stable at around 16 percent of GNP throughout the postwar period, and indeed much longer if one excepts major wars and depressions. In Japan it started at about the same level, 16.5 percent, in 1952–54 but then rose sharply, reaching 31.9 percent in 1970–71. From 1961 through 1971 it averaged 28.8 percent (as against 15.8 percent in the United States). Both the level of and increase in the Japanese gross private saving rate are extraordinary; the former exceeds the rate in any other major country.[53] Moreover, even though good comparable data are lacking for capital consumption, it is clear that the big excess of the gross saving rate in Japan over that in other major countries results from more net saving, not from more capital consumption.

Both corporations and households contributed to the high rate of private saving. Columns 6 and 7 of Table 2-17 show that in recent years corpora-

51. In a few individual years government had a surplus on income and product account.

52. This percentage was larger than in the United States, where the deficit averaged 0.53 percent of GNP during the same period. However, investment by government enterprises was bigger in Japan, and such enterprises financed most of their investment from external sources.

53. Note that the figures cited are for the gross *private* saving rate. National saving rates of 30 percent or thereabouts are sometimes cited for a few Western countries but these include not only private saving and the government surplus on income and product account (i.e., gross private investment), but also expenditures for construction and durable equipment by both general government and government enterprises and sometimes (as in the Economic Planning Agency's national accounts for Japan) inventory accumulation by government enterprises. In Japan such government outlays averaged 9.0 percent of GNP in 1970–71. Adding them to gross private investment would bring the 1970–71 national saving or investment ratio up to 39.5 percent of GNP (or 40.5 percent when measured as the sum of the components of saving). Their balancing addition to the surplus on income and product account yields gross government saving equal to 8.5 percent of GNP.

tions have contributed nearly half of gross private saving and households (including owners of unincorporated enterprises) a little more than half. Earlier the corporate share was smaller. Worth mentioning are other familiar saving rates besides the percentages of GNP shown in the table. From 1967 to 1971 net corporate saving averaged no less than 85 percent of corporate profits after tax and net personal saving averaged an equally remarkable 19.6 percent of disposable personal income.[54] Despite payment of only 15 percent of profits as dividends, corporate saving fell short of corporate investment by 4 or 5 percent of GNP in 1964–71 (column 2 less column 6). Earlier the gap was even larger. The deficiency (as well as the excess of government expenditures over receipts) was of course made good by the excess of noncorporate saving over noncorporate investment, including investment in owner-occupied houses. The transfer was largely effectuated by bank intermediation; new equity investment in corporations by individuals was small.

Corporate and personal saving freed resources for investment on the huge scale observed, and in Chapter 4 the Wallichs explore the conditions responsible for high saving rates. To understand the Japanese investment experience one also needs to know why business wished to undertake so much investment. We have already touched upon aspects of this question and will now approach it more systematically.

The Demand for Business Investment

Why was business investment demand so strong? Why did the rapid increase in capital stock resulting from so enormous a flood of investment fail to drive the rate of return so low that further investment would be discouraged, if not choked off? The following circumstances seem ample to explain sustained high investment in Japan, given the availability of saving.

1. A booming, fast-growing economy creates a strong demand for capital, and the Japanese economy grew faster than any other. The main reason investment grew so much is the obvious one: the demand for investment was derived from the expanding demand for end products, which, in turn, stemmed from the rise in income created by the increase in production.

The expansion of investment, big as it was, sufficed only to increase total capital input in the nonresidential business sector about as fast as the output

54. The corporate percentage is 85 whether the inventory valuation adjustment is included or omitted. The capital consumption allowances deducted by the Economic Planning Agency to calculate profits (and hence net corporate saving) appear to be generous estimates in this period.

of the sector from 1953 to 1971. The increase was somewhat less than that
of output before, and more after, 1961 and over the whole period somewhat
less for fixed capital and somewhat more for inventories. Growth rates compare as follows:

	Nonresidential business national income	Input of reproducible capital		
		Total	Nonresidential structures and equipment	Inventories
1953–71	10.0	10.2	9.2	11.9
1953–61	9.9	7.9	6.3	10.8
1961–71	10.2	12.0	11.7	12.7

We are not suggesting merely that a spiral was under way in which increased investment raised output and higher output induced more investment. According to Table 2-11, output determinants *other* than capital were
responsible for some 78 percent of the 1953–71 growth of output in nonresidential business, and 71 percent even if a proportional share of the gains
from economies of scale is transferred to capital. Had other determinants
not been so extraordinarily favorable to output growth, capital would have
increased less and it too would have contributed less to growth. For, with a
smaller expansion of national income, the derived demand for capital would
have been smaller. (Also, to revert to the determinants of saving, with lower
GNP the saving to finance so much investment would not have been forthcoming.)

2. Japanese business has sought to duplicate production conditions, including the use of capital, of efficient Western firms, particularly those in the
United States. The effort to raise output per worker by adopting American
practices, including the amount of capital used per worker, appears to have
been pursued more consciously and energetically than in other countries.
The ratio of capital input to labor input in the nonresidential business sector
in fact rose greatly: it was 3.61 times as high in 1971 as in 1953 (Table 2-9,
columns 2 and 5), which is equivalent to a growth rate of 7.4 percent.[55]
The point to be stressed, however, is that the capital–labor ratio was very
low in 1953 and the burst of investment has by no means brought the ratio
of capital to labor into unexplored territory; other countries have higher
ratios.

That this is so for fixed capital can be inferred from investment data

55. The change in the ratio of capital to labor used *effectively* was somewhat less
because the proportion of labor misallocated to agriculture and self-employment was
curtailed. But even on this basis the increase was huge.

Table 2-18. *International Comparisons of Gross Fixed Investment by Nonresidential Business, 1970 and 1960–71*

Percentages of U.S. values

Measure	Price weights	United States	Japan	France	West Germany	United Kingdom	Italy
Gross investment during 1970	United States	100.0	90.8	119.3	114.3	53.4	59.0
per civilian employed in 1970	Other country	100.0	78.3	106.5	97.2	49.0	50.8
Gross investment from 1960	United States	100.0	64.3	103.0	102.8	54.6	57.2
through 1971 per civilian employed in 1971	Other country	100.0	55.5	91.9	87.5	50.1	49.3

Sources: Gross investment in 1970 prices of the United States and the other countries from Kravis and others, *A System of International Comparisons*, table I-3; gross investment in 1963 prices of the respective countries from Organisation for Economic Co-operation and Development, *National Accounts of OECD Countries, 1960–1971* (Paris: OECD, 1973), table 2; civilian employment from same organization, *Labour Force Statistics, 1961–1972*, table 2.

obtained from the United Nations study by Kravis and associates.[56] The top two rows of Table 2-18 compare gross fixed investment in four European countries and Japan in 1970 with gross investment in the United States. The United States is compared with each of the other countries by the use of both U.S. and the other country's price weights. To approximate investment by nonresidential business, residential construction and construction performed primarily for general government and nonprofit organizations are omitted.

The comparisons in the table are based on investment per civilian worker. The gross amount invested during 1970, per employed civilian, was much less in Japan than in France or West Germany and less also than in the United States. Moreover, it is obvious that Japan's capital stock position in any recent year has compared less favorably with other countries than its investment position, because capital stock depends on previous investment and investment has been rising fastest in Japan. A rough international comparison of cumulative investment from 1960 to 1971 was made by multiplying 1970 investment in each country by the ratio of 1960–71 to 1970 investment obtained from data valued in the country's own constant prices. The results, per civilian employed in 1971, are shown in the two bottom rows of the table. They give a rough indication of the position of the countries with respect to fixed nonresidential business capital per civilian worker at the end of 1971, even though allowance must be made for a wide margin of error if they are so interpreted. When measured in U.S. prices, cumulative investment from 1960 through 1971 per civilian worker was a bit higher in France and West Germany than in the United States. Japan was 36 percent

56. Kravis and others, *A System of International Comparisons of Gross Product and Purchasing Power*.

below the United States, though above the United Kingdom and Italy. All the countries compare less favorably with the United States when calculations are based on their prices: cumulative investment per worker in France and West Germany fell below the United States on this basis and Japan 44 percent below the United States.

To judge relative capital intensities it would be better to divide net stock, or investment, in the nonresidential business sector by employment in that sector rather than by total civilian employment. When this is done for three countries, the following indexes are obtained for 1960–71 gross fixed investment by nonresidential business per person employed in that sector in 1971:

Percentages of U.S. values

Price weights	United States	West Germany	Japan
United States	100	91	51
Other country	100	77	44

The change drops Japan relative to both the United States and West Germany, and West Germany relative to the United States. Although satisfactory data for business employment in other countries shown in Table 2-18 are lacking, we think it probable that the percentage of civilian employment allocated to the business sector is smallest in the United States and biggest in Japan. If so, use of business employment would lower Japanese investment per worker relative to all the other countries, and investment per worker in all the other countries relative to the United States.

In any case, it is evident even from Table 2-18 that at the end of 1971 Japan was far from a world leader in capital per worker.

3. Labor was becoming much more expensive relative to capital. Hence the incentive to increase the use of capital was great. In the nonresidential business sector, current-price earnings of labor, per unit of labor input, were 6.3 times as large in 1971 as in 1953 while the comparable ratio for capital was 2.6.[57] Prices of capital goods themselves rose little. Whereas the price of GNP was 2.08 times as high in 1971 as in 1953, the price of private nonresidential fixed investment (which determines depreciation costs) was only 1.44 times as high, and for goods held in private inventories the price ratio was only 1.14.[58]

57. The index of each factor's estimated total earnings in current prices (net of depreciation, in the case of capital) was divided by the index of the quantity of its input to secure these ratios. Total earnings are the yen values underlying Table 2-6. The input indexes are from Table 2-9. Capital earnings, as estimated, include "pure" profit, so the comparison is only an approximation.

58. Ratios quoted in this sentence are based on the Economic Planning Agency's deflators for its national product series.

4. General economic conditions and the political system were favorable, or at least not unfavorable, to investment. Stabilization policy was generally successful during the period considered, as explained by Ackley and Ishi in Chapter 3. Prices were stable enough for efficient planning and operation, and recessions were mild and brief enough to keep production near capacity most of the time. Taxes, including those on corporate profits and upper bracket personal incomes, were not onerous and tax rates were repeatedly reduced; the absence of defense expenditures and a swiftly rising tax base helped to make this comfortable policy possible (see Pechman and Kaizuka, Chapter 5).[59] Fairly low interest rates were maintained except in brief periods of overexpansion (see the Wallichs, Chapter 4). This was especially important for business investment, which in Japan is financed heavily by bank loans. Capital goods could be imported as freely as the nation's foreign exchange earnings allowed, and investment shared with raw materials the first claim to whatever exchange was available. Relations between business and the governing Liberal Democratic party were amicable; this is discussed by Trezise and Suzuki in Chapter 11. Threats of nationalization or other punitive attacks on business that could jeopardize the safety of investment were confined to the opposition Marxist parties, which were always in a minority position. Foreign governments restricted Japanese exports, to be sure, but on balance restrictions were not increasing and only a small percentage of the national product was affected. In short, business operated in an atmosphere of confidence in its own and the nation's future. The Economic Planning Agency as well as private organizations repeatedly issued optimistic projections, these were surpassed, and the next projections were both higher and accepted even more confidently by business.

Dwellings

In measuring the contribution made to the growth rate by increases in the services of dwellings, we seek to establish the amount contributed to the increase in the actual output measure, based on the methods of measurement actually used. In the case of Japan, this contribution to 1953–71 growth is estimated to be 0.30 percentage points. This is about the same as the contribution in Canada (1950–67) and the United States (1948–69) but much above the contributions in Europe (Table 2-13).

Housing has been persistently insufficient and inadequate in Japan, so the

59. By U.S. bookkeeping methods there may have been government deficits, but the current account budget for general government was in surplus, and this was considered the budget appropriate to tax policy.

strong demand for dwelling space, and hence for new construction, is not difficult to explain. The rise in real income was so rapid as to virtually guarantee that housing demand would rise faster than the capital stock of dwellings could be improved and increased. This would have been so even if there had been no shortage at the conclusion of World War II, which was of course far from the case. The rise in residential construction, relative even to total investment, has already been noted.

There is little doubt that the increase in national income earned in the provision of housing services was especially large in Japan, but it must be admitted that international differences for this component depend almost as much on estimating methods in different countries as on changes in the stock of housing. In most countries there is little correspondence between changes in gross rents of dwellings (the starting point for estimates of national income originating in this sector) and changes in the gross stock of dwellings, both expressed in constant prices. Japan is no exception; the annual rent on dwellings, measured as a component of personal consumption expenditures in 1965 prices, rose 7.6 percent a year from 1953 to 1971 and 8.3 percent from 1961 to 1971. This is far more than estimates of the gross capital stock of dwellings, also measured in 1965 prices. Estimates for the United States display a similar difference.

International Assets

The net inflow of property income from abroad has remained just slightly negative at all dates. (Table 2-3, column 6, shows the constant price estimates.) Consequently the contribution to growth has been approximately zero. This is partly because net foreign investment has not usually been a large part of GNP (Table 2-17) and partly because it took the form mainly of changes in international financial assets yielding no, or little, return. (However, some direct investment has been undertaken; see Krause and Sekiguchi, Chapter 6.)

In the other ten countries the contribution of international assets ranged from −0.12 percentage points in Canada (1950–67) to 0.10 points in the Netherlands (1950–62).

Land

Land is scarce and expensive in Japan, and during the postwar years its price has increased many times over. Availability and ownership of land obviously condition the composition and distribution of output. But in the absence of changes in the quantity of land available for use in production, the contribution of land to the growth rate of total output is necessarily zero. This is the case in all countries.

Advances in Knowledge

Advances in knowledge of how to produce at low cost are responsible for most productivity growth in the very long run. The concept of "knowledge" relevant to production, it must be noted, is comprehensive; it includes managerial and organizational as well as technological knowledge.

Estimates of the contribution of advances in knowledge refer to the effects of adopting advances in production practice. Because of the way output is measured, the scope of these estimates is limited in two respects. First, incorporation of new knowledge into the productive process can raise output per unit of input, as it is actually measured, only in nonresidential business. Second, even within this sector a contribution to measured growth is made only by those advances that reduce the labor, capital, and land used to produce a unit of final product of existing types, as distinguished from advances that result in the introduction of new or improved final products (that is, in "unmeasured" or "noneconomic" quality change).[60]

The contribution made by the incorporation of new knowledge into production can be estimated only as a residual, secured by eliminating from the growth rate of national income the contributions of all other growth sources which are considered significant and reasonably ascertainable. Consequently, it is combined with the effects of miscellaneous determinants that are not estimated.[61] (It also includes the net error in the total contribution of series that are estimated.)

A résumé of estimates for other countries is required to permit interpretation of results for Japan. The growth rate of the residual index for the contribution of advances in knowledge and miscellaneous determinants to growth of output in the U.S. nonresidential business sector was 1.43 percent

60. Growth rates of nonresidential business and the contribution of advances in knowledge do reflect reductions in the unit costs of obtaining final products that result from improvements in *intermediate* products, including capital goods. Hence, they include the contribution of what is sometimes called technical progress "embodied" in capital.

61. Miscellaneous determinants included in the U.S. estimates are listed and discussed in *Accounting for United States Economic Growth*, pp. 76–79, and citations provided there. They (the "n.e.c." portion of "advances in knowledge and n.e.c.") are the same in the Japanese estimates.

a year from 1948 to 1969. Aside from a small dip of dubious significance during the middle years, this rate was stable throughout the period. It was judged that the miscellaneous determinants were probably of little importance so that 1.43 percentage points approximated the contribution of the incorporation of advances of knowledge into production. Morever, it seems unlikely that in the U.S. economy, the most productive and largest in the world, the rate at which advances were incorporated departed much from the worldwide rate of new advances; that is to say, it is unlikely that average practice moved closer to or further from the frontier of best practice enough to affect the growth rate very much. The rate of 1.43 percent in 1948–69 was almost double the rate of 0.72 percent in 1929–48. Although comparable data are not available for prior years, it is highly unlikely that the postwar rate was matched in any earlier period.[62]

The contribution to the growth rate of U.S. national income in the whole economy, including sectors where no contribution was made to measured growth, was of course lower: 1.19 percentage points in 1948–69 (and 0.62 points in 1929–48).[63] We have similar estimates of the contributions of advances in knowledge and miscellaneous determinants to growth in eight European countries during each of two rather short time periods. The estimates from 1955 to 1962 for Belgium, Denmark, West Germany, the Netherlands, Norway, and the United Kingdom were in the narrow range of 0.75 to 0.97 percentage points; for Italy the estimate was 1.30 points and for France, 1.51 points. Belgium, France, Norway, and the United Kingdom had rates in 1950–55 that were close to their 1955–62 rates. Three of the other European countries (West Germany, 2.55 percentage points; Italy, 2.12; the Netherlands, 1.79) in 1950–55 had particularly high residual rates and one (Denmark, 0.05 points) a low one. These four residuals were thought likely to have resulted either from the elimination of immediate postwar imbalances or from errors of estimate. With both periods considered, only the data for France suggested any significant "catching-up" with the United States in technique, and even the difference between France and the United States was moderate.[64] Finally, the estimate of the contribution in Canada is 0.66 percentage points over the 1950–67 period.[65] The statistical

62. *Accounting for United States Economic Growth*, pp. 79–83.
63. Ibid., p. 127.
64. Data for Europe are from *Why Growth Rates Differ*, pp. 283–84. When that study was made, the estimate for the United States was 0.76 percentage points in 1950–62 (and in both subperiods). It was subsequently revised upward to 1.15 points, which strengthens the original conclusion that there was little catch-up in Europe. See *Accounting for United States Economic Growth*, p. 345.
65. See Table 2-13 above.

discrepancy between two series for Canadian output is rather large, and an alternative procedure would yield a residual of nearly 1.0 percentage point.

These previous investigations suggest two conclusions. First, it is hardly likely that—with the ratio of actual to best practice held constant—the postwar advance of the world's knowledge has been sufficient to raise output per unit of input in the nonresidential business sector of advanced economies much, if any, faster than the 1.43 percent annual rate observed in the United States from 1948 to 1969. This implies a rate for whole economies which is lower by an amount that depends on the weight of other sectors in a particular country and period. Second, although one might expect it to be easy for modern economies like those of Western Europe and Canada to reduce the efficiency gap between themselves and the most advanced country, the United States, such evidence as we have indicates that they usually have not done so.[66]

Against this background the Japanese performance is impressive. Within nonresidential business the index of the contribution of the adoption of advances in knowledge and miscellaneous determinants (Table 2-10) grew at an annual rate of 2.30 percent over the whole period from 1953 to 1971 as compared with 1.43 percent in the United States from 1948 to 1969. If the U.S. rate measures the rate of advance in new knowledge, this leaves 0.87 points in Japan for narrowing the gap between actual and best practice. Moreover, the Japanese rate was higher in the latter part of the period. We estimate that it was 1.76 percent until the end of 1962 and 2.91 percent thereafter. Difficulties of eliminating cyclical influences make it hard to be sure just when to date the acceleration; a later date would also be tenable. Its use would yield an even higher growth rate for the later period.

The contribution to the growth rate of total national income made by the incorporation of knowledge into production, together with miscellaneous determinants, was 1.97 percentage points in 1953–71. This exceeded the contributions to growth of standardized national income in all of the other ten countries—by amounts ranging from 0.46 percentage points in the case of France (1950–62) to as much as 1.07 to 1.31 points for Norway, West Germany, Belgium, the United Kingdom, Denmark, the Netherlands (all 1950–62), and Canada (1950–67). The contribution to Japanese growth was even higher in 1961–71, 2.43 percentage points.

The gap between the United States and Japan in output per worker, shown for 1970 in Table 2-1, is big—sufficiently so to leave no doubt that Japan was also decidedly below the United States in output per unit of input,

66. We do not have estimates for Europe after 1962. A detailed investigation would be required to test whether the situation there has changed.

even after eliminating the effects of all the determinants that are measured separately in our growth analysis (labor, capital, and land input per worker, irregular factors, resource allocation, and economies of scale). Comparisons of this type showed that in 1960 what was termed "residual efficiency" was 28 percent lower in Northwest Europe than in the United States when output was measured in U.S. prices. Individual countries ranged from 23 percent lower in France to 34 percent lower in the United Kingdom in 1960.[67] Crude estimates prepared in this study show that on a comparable basis Japan was 30 percent below the United States in 1970.

The study from which the European estimates are drawn put residual efficiency in Western Europe in 1960 much below that in the United States in 1925. It expressed the opinion that the difference between the United States in 1925 and the United States in 1960 is ascribable to new knowledge developed in the interim but that the larger difference between Western Europe in 1960 and the United States in 1960 could not reasonably be laid to differences in the knowledge available to the two areas.[68] Knowledge is a worldwide commodity. Lags in its availability are at most a few years, not several decades. Especially is this so when the leading country is the United States, where nearly all knowledge circulates freely and where productivity teams sent from other countries for the express purpose of observing American practices have been not only welcomed but sponsored. What applies to the gap between the United States and Europe applies also to the gap between the United States and Japan.[69]

One would like to know what the determinants of international differences in residual productivity are, how they arise, and, most of all, how it is possible for them to persist for long periods. Only then could one hope to explore successfully why Japan was better able to cut into the gap in residual efficiency than were other countries in the periods for which we have estimates. For Japan's success is less surprising than the inability of other countries to do as well.

Attitudes and practices that *may* have helped Japan can be suggested. The Japanese people are reputed to be unusually attracted by and receptive to new and foreign ideas. The search for useful information from abroad,

67. *Why Growth Rates Differ,* p. 289, table 20-2, column 1.
68. Ibid., p. 335.
69. Japan's payments for foreign (mostly American) technology do not qualify this discussion materially. They were largely confined to late developments in high-technology manufacturing industries, for the most part were required only because foreign firms were barred from direct entry to Japan, and at their peak scarcely exceeded one-fourth of 1 percent of the Japanese national income.

and its application in Japan, has been favored and supported by the Japanese government since the Meiji restoration. When Japanese accept practices found effective in America or elsewhere, they seem more willing than Europeans to adopt them without incurring more than a minimum of delay and expense in an effort to improve upon them before adoption. (This, of course, implies no lack of interest in improvement of a practice once established.) Workers' resistance to the introduction of labor-saving procedures seems rarer than in most if not all Western countries; with management determined to reduce costs by innovation, this can be an important advantage. This advantage is a perhaps inseparable part of a labor relations package that includes guaranteed employment to the age of fifty-five or so for permanent employees of large firms, differentials in compensation based more on seniority and education and less on duties and performance than is customary elsewhere, paying employees much of their compensation as semiannual bonuses that may vary with a firm's success, an unusual degree of paternalism and of employee identification with the enterprise, and unions that are organized on a company- rather than on a craft- or industry-wide basis. Some of these conditions, viewed separately, seem more likely to reduce than to raise efficiency, but they may not affect the growth rate unless they change in strength.

Management is a key element in efficiency. Our measures of labor input include proprietors and hired managers as well as all other workers, but there is no way to bring into the measures the special talents of management people, procedures for selecting them, or the effects of competition or its absence on managerial performance. Changes in managerial performance necessarily are reflected largely in the residual. A characteristic feature of management in large Japanese firms is decisionmaking by consensus. Whether this leads to better decisions we cannot judge. Although it may delay decisions, good or bad, it is said to facilitate wholehearted implementation by all concerned.

Other possibly pertinent conditions may be mentioned. Competition, both among Japanese firms and, in international markets, from foreign firms, may have become stronger and intensified pressure to reduce costs, but we do not know whether this has been of real importance. Nor do we attempt to make independent judgments either of the impact of government planning and detailed intervention in business (which Trezise and Suzuki examine in Chapter 11) or about whether there is any significance to the observation that the largest residuals (suggesting the highest rate of catch-up in efficiency) appear for Japan and France, two countries with developed systems of indicative planning.

One cannot be sure how closely the high rate for the residual in Japan, which exceeds residuals observed anywhere else, corresponds to the effects of incorporating new knowledge into production as distinguished from the effects of miscellaneous unmeasured determinants, or, consequently, just how much catching-up with best knowledge is implied. But the large residual is certainly consistent with the common belief that Japan has been closing the gap with the United States, and we believe this to be the case.

Later chapters deal with topics that are or may be related to the catch-up, among them Galenson and Odaka on the labor market in Chapter 9, Caves and Uekusa on industrial organization in Chapter 7, and Peck and Tamura on the purchase and introduction of technology in Chapter 8.

Reallocation of Resources

For an advanced country, Japan allocates an unusually large percentage of employment to agriculture. Within nonagricultural employment, the percentage of self-employed and unpaid family workers is high. Both percentages are well above those that would maximize national income. They are also well above those in Western countries, except Italy. In 1970 the employment distribution, like output per worker, was about the same in Japan and Italy.

From 1953 to 1971 both agricultural employment and self-employment declined substantially relative to total employment. The adverse effects on total output of declines in these employment categories were small relative to the increments added by the labor released to nonagricultural wage and salary employment. We estimate that these shifts of labor contributed some 0.94 percentage points to the growth rate of national income. Relaxation of international trade barriers brought to 0.95 points the total contribution of improved resource allocation—or, more precisely, of the aspects of resource allocation that we attempt to estimate.

Agriculture

Some 35.6 percent of all employed persons were primarily engaged in agriculture in 1953. This may have been a little above a "trend" percentage; immediately after the war farm employment was swollen by the disruption of the nonfarm economy and the repatriation of Japanese from abroad, and in absolute numbers it did not clearly recede until after 1955. The percentage, however, dropped every year from at least 1952, touching 26.1 percent in 1961 and 14.6 percent in 1971.[70]

A decline of nearly three-fifths in eighteen years in the agricultural percentage is not really exceptional; it is only a bit above the average of the advanced countries examined. Moreover, the decline in the agricultural percentage in Japan was facilitated by a particularly large increase in total employment. The actual reduction in agricultural employment was 46 percent, from 14,035,000 in 1953 to 7,509,000 in 1971.

What is unusual about the Japanese situation is that agriculture was so important that the decline in the agricultural percentage represented an especially large proportion (21 percent) of the total labor force. This was matched only in Italy, though the employment shift was also big in some other countries.

To estimate gains from reallocation we relate agriculture to totals for nonresidential business rather than for the whole economy.[71] Agriculture's percentages of key nonresidential business aggregates in the boundary years of our periods are as follows:

	1953	1961	1971
Employment	38.66	28.11	15.92
Labor input	32.64	22.85	12.51
National income in 1965 prices	20.33	14.14	4.82

With technical progress and mechanization there was a steady decline in the proportions of employment and labor input whose allocation to agriculture would have maximized national income. The actual proportions, though

70. These percentages, computed from Table 2-4, are based on the agricultural component of the labor force employment series, which is much smaller than the agricultural employment series used in earlier appraisals of gains from reallocation. The level for all postwar years of the labor force series for agriculture was much higher until it was revised following the introduction in 1967 of a new form for interviews. Estimates even larger than the old labor force series were sometimes used; unlike the labor force concept, they counted agricultural workers who worked only part of the year as employed all year and counted in agriculture persons with secondary jobs in agriculture whose primary jobs were in nonagricultural industries. Also, forestry and fisheries were usually combined with agriculture in measuring gains from reallocation. We have not done this because earnings in these industries do not appear to be low enough to give any clear indication of industrial misallocation. (The self-employed in these industries, however, are counted in estimating gains from the reduction in importance of nonagricultural self-employment.)

71. Because we use labor input instead of employment and our agricultural employment estimates themselves are lower, our estimates of the proportion of labor devoted to agriculture are considerably smaller than those that have customarily been made. This leads to lower estimates of the reduction in misallocation and hence of the contribution to growth.

also falling, were always much above the optimum for the same date. Our estimates of the gains from reallocation are based on the percentages of labor input rather than of employment. The labor input percentages are lower because there is a bigger percentage of part-time workers in agriculture than in nonagricultural industries, fewer males, and a less educated labor force.[72]

The percentage by which national income in constant prices originating in the nonresidential business sector would have been raised each year if labor input had been distributed in the following year's proportion is calculated on the basis of two estimates. The first is that if labor input had been 1 percent smaller in farming in any year agricultural national income would have been smaller by one-fourth as much, or 0.25 percent. The ratio of one-quarter is placed much below the labor share of agricultural national income (two-thirds to three-fourths) because the farm employment eliminated, which was mainly excess labor on small farms, was that with the least output.[73] This ratio is not firmly based, but it could be changed considerably without altering our final estimates much because national income per unit of input is much smaller in agriculture than in nonagricultural industries.[74] The second estimate is that if in nonagricultural nonresidential business labor input had been 1 percent larger output would have been larger by a fraction of 1 percent equal to the labor share in that subsector (0.72 to 0.82 percent, depending on the year). A chain index of annual percentage gains (Table 2-10, column 2) is used to calculate contributions to the growth rate of nonresidential business output (Table 2-11, columns 1 to 3); these are reduced appropriately to arrive at contributions to the growth rate of total national income (Table 2-11, columns 4 to 6). The amount is 0.64 percentage points in 1953–71.

72. The distribution by age in agriculture is often presumed to be adverse too, but on the basis of our weighting structure this is not so; a paucity of teenagers offsets an above-average proportion of elderly people. Differences between agriculture and non-agriculture in hours of full-time workers of the same sex are not considered a difference in labor input.

73. There were no really large farms. Even in 1940 there were few large farms and land reform under the occupation limited farm size to three hectares (twelve in Hokkaido). Land reform also nearly eliminated tenancy. As there are hardly any hired farm workers, farm labor consists almost entirely of farm owners and members of their families.

74. Our assumption lies between assumptions implicit in procedures that handle reallocation gains as gains from shifts in industry weights and those often implied by two-sector models that divide an economy into a growing modern sector and a dwindling traditional sector. The former procedures assume that agricultural output is reduced by the same proportion as agricultural employment (or by the product of this percentage and the labor share), whereas two-sector models often imply that agricultural output is not reduced at all if employment is cut.

The contribution, it should be noted, is affected not only by the amount of labor diverted from agriculture and the relationships between percentage changes in labor input and output in farm and nonfarm business, but also by the ratio of national income in 1965 prices per unit of labor input in agriculture to the corresponding figure in nonagricultural industries. In 1953 and 1965 the ratio was 0.53; in 1971, it dropped to 0.35. The lower the ratio, the greater is the gain in constant price national income from the transfer of labor. Substantial government support for agriculture, especially rice, helped to make the 1965 ratio higher than it would otherwise have been and hence to minimize the gain in constant price national income from labor reallocation. Partly because this ratio was higher in Japan, the contribution to Japanese growth from 1953 to 1971 was 0.40 percentage points less than the contribution to growth in Italy from 1950 to 1962, and less by much smaller amounts than the contribution to French and German growth from 1950 to 1962. (It probably was not smaller than in France or Germany in 1953–71.) The Japanese advantage over the United States (1948–69) and over Belgium, the Netherlands, and the United Kingdom (all 1950–62) was a sizable 0.41 to 0.58 percentage points.

Nonagricultural Self-Employment

In Japan and Italy an extraordinarily large proportion of civilian nonagricultural employment has consisted of self-employed and unpaid family workers. In 1964, for example, the proportion in these two countries was 24 to 25 percent as compared with 12 to 16 percent in the other continental European countries listed in Table 2-13, 11 percent in the United States, and 7 percent in the United Kingdom. In all these countries the percentage has been declining. In all, too, there are independent professionals and proprietors of large establishments whose labor is in no sense misallocated, but also many own-account and family workers who operate firms too small to occupy their time fully or to permit efficient operation. With no cash payroll, or almost none, to meet, they can continue in business despite low earnings. Among this group are many who could earn more in paid employment but stick stubbornly to the independence of self-employment, often until death or retirement arrives and their children decide not to take their places.

We believe the decline in the percentage of self-employed and unpaid family workers is concentrated among those least efficiently utilized—usually in businesses with no paid employees—and with the lowest value of output. The effect of their disappearance on output could be made good by an increase in the output of the remaining self-employed or family workers or by a much smaller increase in wage-salary employment. Specifically, we assume that to perform the same work an increase of only one nonagricultural wage and salary worker—or, more exactly, of one unit of labor input— was required to offset the loss of four units of the labor previously performed by self-employed and unpaid family workers.[75]

Expressed as a percentage of total nonagricultural employment in nonresidential business, self-employed and unpaid family workers dropped from 39.8 in 1953 to 29.9 in 1961 and 24.4 in 1971. The corresponding percentages for labor input were 34.6, 25.7, and 21.3. These are sharp declines. They were achieved not by an absolute drop in the number of self-employed but by a huge increase in the number of wage and salary workers. The percentage gain in output per unit of input in nonresidential business from the reduction in misallocation is the same either way, of course, but the general increase in employment made it much easier to achieve.

Reduction of the overallocation of labor to self-employment is estimated to have contributed 0.30 percentage points to the growth of the total national income in 1953–71. This exceeds the contributions in all the other countries. The Japanese advantage was greatest (0.20 to 0.26 points) over Canada, the United States, and the United Kingdom.

It is possible that the distribution of wage and salary workers among enterprises of different sizes approached the optimal distribution more closely or diverged further from it. We have attempted no estimate of the contribution, positive or negative, of such a change but believe it cannot be large relative to the effects of reallocation from agriculture and self-employment.

Reduction in International Trade Barriers

Artificial barriers to international trade prevent the most efficient international division of labor and restrict the size of markets and hence economies of scale. Reduction of barriers to both imports and exports contributed appreciably to the growth of some European countries. This was not so in Japan, where there was little change in trade barriers. Throughout the period we examine, imports of both raw materials and machinery were unrestricted or restrained only by the availability of foreign exchange. The market for rice was consistently reserved for domestic farmers. Imports of manufactured consumer products were forbidden, or subjected to prohibitive tariffs, throughout the period. Restrictions on Japanese exports also seem on balance to have changed little relative to the size of the Japanese economy.

75. See *Why Growth Rates Differ,* chap. 16, for Western data and further discussion.

These statements must be modified to note that some slight easing of restraints on both sides, including increased access to the Japanese market for foods other than rice, is observable in the 1960s, especially after 1968, but this easing had little effect on trade until after the period we consider. Estimates cited in Chapter 6 by Krause and Sekiguchi credit Japanese import liberalization with only 2.7 percent of the growth of Japanese imports and foreign import liberalization with only 6.2 percent of the growth of Japanese exports even from 1961 to 1971. These increases amount to 0.36 percent and 0.58 percent, respectively, of Japanese GNP in 1971.

To give quantitative expression to our qualitative impression of how trade barriers may have affected the growth rate of output per unit of input, we introduced the index in Table 2-10, column 4. We held the index constant until 1962, then raised it by 0.01 percent a year until 1968, and by 0.03 percent a year thereafter. This pattern implies that in nonresidential business in 1971 output, and hence output per unit of input, was 0.15 percent larger than it would have been if there had been no change in trade barriers. This in turn implies the gain was almost one-sixth of the total induced increase in trade turnover (exports plus imports).

The implied contribution to growth of total national income from 1953 to 1971 comes to only 0.01 percentage points. In other countries amounts ranged from nothing in the United States and Canada up to 0.16 points during 1950–62 in Belgium, Italy, and the Netherlands.

Economies of Scale

Growth of an economy automatically means growth in the average size of the local, regional, and national markets that business serves. Growth of markets brings opportunities for greater specialization—both among and within industries, firms, and establishments—and opportunities for establishments and firms to become larger without impairing the competitive pressure that stimulates efficiency. Longer production runs for individual products become possible as, in almost all industries including wholesale and retail trade, do larger transactions in buying, selling, and shipping. Expanded regional and local markets permit greater geographic specialization and less transporting of products. The opportunities for greater specialization, bigger units, longer runs, and larger transactions provide clear reason to expect increasing returns in the production and distribution of many products, and examples of increasing returns are plentiful.

In our judgment, gains from economies of scale are important in all modern economies. Moreover, as markets and output grow, knowledge of technology and business organization develops about, and adapts to, the new situation resulting from enlarged markets, and opportunities for scale economies are constantly replenished. We classify gains from economies of scale as a separate source of growth. They magnify substantially the difference that would have existed between growth rates in Japan and elsewhere if constant returns to scale had prevailed.

Derivation of Estimates

To estimate the size of the gains from this source we followed procedures very similar to those used previously for European countries.[76] The estimates were made in two parts.

1. In the appraisal of U.S. growth it was estimated that each increase of 1 percent in total input in the nonresidential business sector, or gains from advances in knowledge, reallocation of resources, or any other change that would have raised national income by 1 percent under constant returns to scale, actually raised the output of the sector by 15 percent more than this, or by 1.15 percent.[77] (No such gains occur in other sectors.) In the appraisal of European growth it was judged that, if price relationships among commodities and the composition of output had been the same in Europe as in the United States, the European percentage would have been larger because the European economies were smaller than that of the United States—but it would not have been much larger. We make a similar judgment for Japan, and use 16 percent for Japan to correspond to 15 percent in the United States. This implies that when output is valued in U.S. prices 13.79 percent (16/116) of the growth rate of Japanese output in nonresidential business is due to economies of scale. To compute an index of Japanese output in U.S. prices, the index of nonresidential business national income valued in 1965 Japanese prices (Table 2-9, column 1) was divided by the index of gains from economies of scale associated with income elasticities (Table 2-10, column 9), the series to be described next. The resulting estimates are identified as economies of scale with output "measured in U.S. prices."[78]

76. See *Why Growth Rates Differ,* chap. 17. The chief modification is that the estimates "in U.S. prices" were derived by reference to growth in the nonresidential business sector (as in *Accounting for United States Economic Growth,* pp. 71–76 and 314–17) rather than to growth in the whole economy.

77. The estimate was based on correlation analysis described in *Accounting for United States Economic Growth,* pp. 71–76 and 314–17.

78. Estimates of this item shown here for the European countries and Canada include a small allowance for independent growth of local markets brought about by population shifts and increased automobile use. The estimates for the United States and Japan, for which the procedure differs a little from that used for the other countries, are assumed to include this item.

2. Actually neither price relationships among individual consumer goods and services nor the distribution of consumption among individual goods and services were the same in Europe or Japan as in the United States, and the differences were systematic.

Differences in consumption patterns between eight European countries and the United States reflect chiefly differences in levels of per capita income and consumption. Although per capita consumption of nearly every product was lower in Europe than in the United States in 1950 (the year for which data are most abundant), the gap was wider the greater the income elasticity of demand for the product. Also, chiefly because of economies of scale, the higher the income elasticity and the lower the consumption of a commodity in a European country relative to the United States, the higher was the ratio of the European to the American price. Consequently, the lower the level of per capita consumption in a European country, the more consumption patterns and relative prices diverged from those in the United States.

Where per capita consumption in Europe has risen markedly toward the U.S. level during the postwar period, the increase in consumption has been heavily concentrated in products for which demand is income-elastic and European prices are high. In France, for example, per capita consumption of product groups for which the ratio of French to U.S. prices was above average by more than half increased by 74 or 79 percent (depending on the weights applied) from 1950 to 1962. In contrast, there was only a 19 percent increase in product groups for which the ratio of French to U.S. prices was below average by more than half. The former groups include products, such as consumer durables and utilities, that offered especially good opportunities for achieving economies of scale by adopting methods and techniques that were already in use in the United States but could not have been used in Europe until a sufficiently large market came into existence. They are given a much higher weight, and the latter a much lower weight, when French price weights are used to measure changes in consumption than when U.S. price weights are used. European experience indicates that the greater is the rise in per capita consumption and the lower its initial level, the larger is the amount by which the rise in consumption in each country measured in its own constant prices exceeds the rise measured in U.S. constant prices.

The difference between the growth rate of national product when the components of consumption are weighted by U.S. prices and the rate when they are weighted by national prices reflects the concentration of consumption increases in products where potential gains from economies of scale are particularly large. For this reason it is classified as a gain from economies of scale, labeled as "associated with income elasticities."

The actual estimating procedure is indirect. It rests on the systematic relationship between the ratios of European to U.S. per capita consumption by the alternative sets of price weights. Use of the regression line expressing this relationship and of time series data for each country based on its own prices permits estimation of the change in per capita consumption in European countries based on U.S. price weights, and hence of the difference between series based on U.S. and those based on national price weights.

The situation in Japan paralleled that in Europe. Moreover, when the ratio of Japanese to U.S. per capita consumption in 1967 is calculated in both U.S. and Japanese prices, the relation between the two falls close to the regression line established from European data. The same procedure was therefore adopted in preparing estimates for Japan.[79]

Importance in Growth

Both components of economies of scale made large contributions to growth. Together they contributed 1.94 percentage points to the growth rate of total national income in 1953–71 (1.90 points in 1953–61 and 1.96 points in 1961–71). They raised the growth rate of standardized national income in 1953–71 28 percent above what it would have been without scale economies.

Gains from economies of scale were greater than in any other country and much greater than in most; the difference ranged from 0.33 to 1.58 percentage points. The chief reason is that both markets in general and per capita consumption were expanding faster in Japan; the separate significance of per capita consumption is that, starting from a very low level, its fast advance caused a particularly large shift in consumption patterns.[80]

79. Japanese per capita consumption in 1967 was 47.5 percent of per capita consumption in the United States based on U.S. prices, and 32.6 percent based on Japanese prices, according to the study by Kravis and others, *A System of International Comparisons*. These figures refer to consumption as defined in the standardized system of national accounts. Estimates for 1967 were preferred to those for 1970 (the only other year available) because of their chronological proximity to 1965, the base year of the Japanese time series.

80. The statement about consumption patterns cannot be confirmed directly because the Japanese national accounts show little detail for consumption. It is, however, supported by production data.

The contribution of economies of scale associated with income elasticities is smaller than would otherwise be the case because the ratio of consumption to output has been both low and falling in Japan, and because the base year for deflation in Japan (1965) is later than in the output series used for the other countries (1954 or 1958). The contribution in most European countries after 1962 was probably smaller than in the period covered.

Can the Growth Rate Be Sustained?

In the 1950s Japanese frequently credited fast growth to highly temporary factors, especially recovery from disruptions caused by war and defeat. Many regarded much slower growth as imminent. By late 1960 confidence had so increased that the government announced its plan to double national income in ten years. But even this target required a growth rate of only 7.2 percent, a large drop from the rate then prevailing. By 1970 popular projections extended the growth rate of real GNP in the 1960s, which exceeded 11 percent by Japanese deflation procedures, into the indefinite future. Japan was expected to lead the world in output per person by the late 1980s and in total output not so very much later. In 1971 even the careful Japan Economic Research Center, in analyzing the future, was assuming a 10 percent growth rate in real GNP from 1970 to 1985. Achievement of this rate, which took into account expected costs of controlling pollution, would make GNP 4.2 times as large in 1985 as in 1970.

By 1973 growth anticipations were receding. Premier Kakuei Tanaka was promising a new initiative sacrificing growth for other welfare purposes, especially dispersion of population and industry. In 1974 expectations were further dampened in some quarters by the high price of oil, almost all imported, and a recession—brought on by credit tightening to check the 1972–73 inflation as well as by recession abroad—which, unlike earlier recessions, brought an absolute drop in output in Japan. At the end of 1974 anticipations were diverse.

Insofar as there is continuity between the past and the future, examination of the postwar sources of growth can bring perspective to the outlook and that is our purpose here. We do not discuss the special events of 1973 and 1974.

We first divide the contribution made by each determinant to the 1961–71 growth rate into two parts (see Table 2-19, columns 1 to 3). One part, which we call the "transitional" component, is the amount that was possible only because Japan was a late comer to economic development or, closely related, was eliminating a cause of chronic inefficiency. Some random developments which could not continue may also be included. The remainder of the contribution is the "sustainable" portion. The sustainable components will not necessarily contribute the same amounts in the future as in the past but there is no apparent reason they cannot do so, and changes are unlikely to be big.

The 1961–71 standardized growth rate of national income, based on

Table 2-19. *Sustainable and Transitional Contributions to the Standardized Growth Rate of National Income, 1961–71, and Year Transitional Contribution Expires*

| Rate or source | Contribution in percentage points, 1961–71 | | | Year transitional contribution expires[a] |
	Total (1)	Sustainable (2)	Transitional (3)	(4)
Standardized growth rate	9.56	3.24	6.32	b
Labor	1.78	0.68	1.10	b
Employment	1.09	0.33	0.76	1973
Hours	0.11	−0.15	0.26	1974
Age-sex composition	0.19	0.11	0.08	1977
Education	0.35	0.35	0.00	b
Unallocated	0.04	0.04	0.00	b
Capital	2.57	0.86	1.71	b
Inventories	0.86	0.21	0.65	1976
Nonresidential structures and equipment	1.44	0.38	1.06	1976
Dwellings	0.27	0.27	0.00	b
International assets	0.00	0.00	0.00	b
Land	0.00	0.00	0.00	b
Advances in knowledge and n.e.c.[c]	2.43	1.28	1.15	2002
Contraction of agricultural inputs	0.62	0.00	0.62	1982
Contraction of nonagricultural self-employment	0.19	0.00	0.19	1990
Reduction in international trade barriers	0.01	0.00	0.01	2002
Economies of scale				
Measured in U.S. prices	1.14	0.42	0.72	d
Income elasticities	0.82	0.00	0.82	1995

Source: For column 1, Table 2-11, column 6.
a. Assumes contribution continues at 1961–71 size until expiration.
b. Not applicable.
c. Not elsewhere classified.
d. The distribution among years, in percentage points, is: 1973, 0.10; 1974, 0.03; 1976, 0.22; 1977, 0.01; 1982, 0.08; 1990, 0.02; 1995, 0.11; 2002, 0.15.

U.S. deflation procedures, was 9.56 percent a year. Of this amount, it is estimated, sustainable sources contributed 3.24 percentage points and transitional sources, 6.32 points. We hasten to stress that the purpose of this section is not to arrive at this result; anyone familiar with long-term growth in a number of countries could probably guess that a figure in the neighborhood of 3 percent or so would be arrived at in such an examination of any advanced nation. Rather, the purpose is to identify transitional growth sources, quantify their separate importance, and appraise the prospects for continuance of their contributions. In each case, we ask, how much of a backlog remains? To put the estimates in a common framework, column 4 of Table 2-19 shows the last year in which the transitional component of the contribution of each growth source would be obtained if the possibilities for gains were used up fast enough to maintain the contribution at its 1961–71 size. We would not actually expect so abrupt a cessation in most cases; it is more likely that the contribution would start to decline before the specified year and a reduced contribution would be obtained for a time thereafter.

The transitional component of the Japanese growth rate is exceptionally big, but it should be understood that probably all countries have a transitional component. The United States, for example, secured a contribution to its 1948–69 growth rate from the contraction of agricultural employment and nonfarm self-employment that is estimated at 0.30 percentage points, and a small contribution from increasing labor force participation by students and adult women.

The glitter is in no way removed from the Japanese achievement by the finding that it was made possible only by initial economic backwardness. The existence of possibilities to secure rapid growth from transitional sources, which we shall now detail, by no means ensured that they would be seized and rapid growth actually attained.

We shall now review the individual growth sources. It facilitates explanation to examine most components of output per unit of input before considering the input components. As stated, our base is the period from 1961 to 1971 and we refer to standardized national income.

Advances in Knowledge and Miscellaneous Determinants

In Japan the 1961–71 growth rate of the nonresidential business sector index for the incorporation of new knowledge into production, together with the effects of miscellaneous determinants, was 2.71. We suggested earlier that, on the basis of American and other Western experience, the worldwide advance of knowledge has been sufficient to raise national income originating in nonresidential business by about 1.43 percent a year, or 52.8 percent as much. It thus appears that of the contribution of 2.43 percentage points made by advances in knowledge and n.e.c. to the growth rate of national income in the *whole* economy only 52.8 percent, or 1.28 percentage points, represented the contribution that would have been made if new knowledge had been incorporated at the rate at which it appeared. The remaining 1.15 points resulted from narrowing the gap between average Japanese practice and best practice. Only the portion associated with the appearance of new knowledge can continue indefinitely.[81]

We estimate that after the effects of all measurable sources of difference in output are eliminated residual efficiency was 30 percent lower in Japan than in the United States in 1970. This implies that a contribution of the 1961–71 size could be obtained from this source through 2001—or 2002 if allowance is made for a probable increase in the weight of nonresidential business—before average practice in Japan was as close to best practice as it was in the United States in 1970. This seems a realistic criterion for our estimate of the exhaustion of transitional gains even though Japan conceivably could approach the technological frontier still more closely.

Reallocation of Labor from Agriculture

From 1961 to 1971 agricultural employment dropped from 26.1 percent of total employment to 14.6 percent, or by 1.15 percentage points a year, and this shift in the use of labor contributed 0.62 percentage points, all classified as transitional, to the growth rate. Suppose productivity gains continue until the agricultural percentage drops another 10.6 points, to 4.0. It seems unlikely to go lower, or even this low, although it has already done so in the United States and the United Kingdom. As a first approximation, one might calculate that a contribution of 0.62 points could be secured for nine years (10.6 divided by 1.15) after 1971. Provided the base year for deflation remains 1965, this can be stretched a little, because it is likely that the ratio of farm to nonfarm national income measured in 1965 prices will be lower than it was in 1961–71 and that the labor share will be bigger. We use 1982 as the date by which continuation of a contribution of the previous size would exhaust this source. Of course, we expect a more gradual decline.[82]

81. Obviously, the rate at which new knowledge appears, and becomes available to all countries, may be higher or lower in the future than in the past.

82. Continuation of a drop of 1.15 percentage points a year in the agricultural share of employment would require that the decline in farm employment each year be bigger in the future than in 1961–71 in absolute terms (because total employment will increase less) and far bigger in percentage terms (because farm employment will be smaller). Even so, the agricultural percentage may drop quite rapidly. The Japan Economic Research Center projected only 8 percent of employment in all primary industries in 1985, which implies only about 6 percent in agriculture. Japan Economic Research Center, "Japan's Economy in 1985: The Outlook for a Trillion Dollar Economy" (abridged translation, processed; 1971), p. 3.

Reallocation of Labor from Nonagricultural Self-Employment

As a percentage of nonagricultural business employment, nonagricultural self-employment (including unpaid family workers) declined from 29.9 percent in 1961 to 24.4 percent in 1971, which was still much higher than in Western countries except Italy. The drop of 0.55 points per year in this percentage was responsible for a contribution of 0.19 percentage points, all transitional in character, to the growth rate of national income in the whole economy.

The percentage that would eliminate misallocation may be higher than in the West because cramped living quarters and custom encourage eating out and (though decreasingly so) purchases of commercial amusements and personal services, activities adapted to small enterprises. Estimates that labor and capital earn only moderately less in noncorporate firms as a group (outside agriculture) than in corporate firms reinforce this suspicion. But even if we consider the percentage required for efficiency to be as high as 15, which is much above present percentages in major Western countries except Italy, a contribution to the growth rate of nonagricultural nonresidential business as large as in 1961–71 could continue for seventeen years after 1971. Because of the probability that the weight of this sector in national income and the labor share will both be higher, the period can be extended through 1990.

The annual gain from this source in the near future could easily surpass 0.19 points, and the total remaining potential gain may be greater than we imply because the 15 percent figure we selected may be too big.

Reduction in International Trade Barriers

The contribution from this source could surely continue at the 1961–71 amount of 0.01 percentage points until at least 2002, the last year for any other determinant. This is so if Japanese and foreign trade barriers reduced national income by as little as 0.3 percent in 1971. In view of the small size of the contribution, greater precision is unnecessary.

Economies of Scale Associated with Income Elasticities

Like gains from improved resource allocation, economies of scale associated with income elasticities are entirely transitional. When and if per capita consumption reaches the U.S. level, it will be found to do so whether Japanese or U.S. price weights are used in the comparison, because consumption patterns and price ratios will converge in the two countries; at least, this is the implication of our estimates. This source will then disappear. The gap between Japanese and American per capita consumption, and hence the amount by which the size of the gap differs when different price weights are used, is still big. A contribution of 0.82 percentage points, the 1961–71 amount, could continue through 1995 before the growth possibilities are exhausted.

Employment

The annual growth rate of 1.07 percent in total population from 1961 to 1971 was made up of rates of −0.95 percent for people less than fifteen years old, 1.84 for those fifteen to sixty-four, and 2.52 for those sixty-five and over. The fast growth of the population of working age resulted from the earlier era, continuing into World War II, during which birthrates were at or near their peak, combined with the long and continuing decline in death rates. Unless augmented by immigration, such fast growth of the working-age population was rare in advanced Western nations during the 1960s and will be rarer in the future. Japan's own rate already has dropped abruptly.

Labor force and employment grew 1.40 and 1.42 percent a year, respectively, from 1961 to 1971—less than the working-age population because the age of leaving school rose and the decline of agriculture reduced the female labor force participation rate. These influences, of which the second, and perhaps both, should be considered transitional, offset part of the employment increase from population change.

Projections to 1985 by the Japan Economic Research Center help us to appraise future changes in labor input. In Table 2-20 the projections by five-year periods are shown, as are the Center's estimates of actual changes from 1960 to 1970 and the most nearly corresponding estimates from our own study for 1961–71 and (to provide an overlap) 1960–70.

From 1970 to 1985 the population aged fifteen to sixty-four will grow at a rate about one full percentage point less than in 1961–71, and employment will do so after 1975. The projected rates for the working-age population are above the median for Western Europe in recent years but not greatly so. The employment projection assumes that, unlike the United States in the 1960s but like a majority of Western countries, Japan will not experience a

Table 2-20. *Population and Labor Input, Selected Growth Rates*

Item	Estimates from this study		Estimates from Japan Economic Research Center			
	1961–71 (1)	*1960–70* (2)	*1960–70* (3)	*1970–75*[a] (4)	*1975–80*[a] (5)	*1980–85*[a] (6)
Population						
Total	1.07	1.05	1.06	1.19	1.11	0.87
Aged 15–64	1.84	1.81	1.81	0.85	0.75	0.85
Employment	1.42	1.49	1.46[b]	0.76[b]	0.46[b]	0.39[b]
Hours	0.18[c,d]	0.30[c,d]	n.a.	n.a.	n.a.	n.a.
Average hours	−0.41[c]	−0.37[c]	−0.55	−1.0	−0.7	−0.4
Efficiency offset	0.58[c]	0.59[c]	n.a.	n.a.	n.a.	n.a.
Intergroup shift offset	0.01[c]	0.08[c]	n.a.	n.a.	n.a.	n.a.
Age-sex composition	0.29[c]	0.26[c]	0.3	0.3	0.2	0.1
Education	0.53[c]	0.53[c]	0.3	0.4	0.3	0.3

Sources: Columns 1 and 2 computed from Tables 2-4 and 2-8, except that population figures were obtained from the Bureau of Statistics. Other columns from (or computed from) Japan Economic Research Center, "Japan's Economy in 1985: The Outlook for a Trillion Dollar Economy" (abridged translation, processed; 1971), pp. 2, 20, 24.
n.a. Not available.
a. Projections.
b. Labor force.
c. Estimates refer to the nonresidential business sector.
d. Refers to the product of the three component indexes.

substantial increase in the labor force participation rate for women outside agriculture (which already is high).[83]

We shall suppose that in the absence of transitional factors the 1961–71 growth rate of employment would have been 0.42 percent instead of 1.42 percent. Of the contribution of employment to the growth rate, which was 1.09 percentage points, we first calculate that only 0.32 points (1.09 times 0.42 divided by 1.42) were sustainable. Although we judge that the share of labor in national income would have been greater if Japan had not been in a transitional state, our adjustment raises the figure only to 0.33, leaving 0.76 points as the transitional component of the employment contribution. Table 2-20 implies that the transitional component is about exhausted. To secure an employment contribution at the 1961–71 rate after 1971 would

83. Where such an increase has occurred, much of the employment expansion has been in part-time work. If we were to assume it would occur in Japan, the effect on the employment entries in Table 2-20 would be partially offset in the entries for hours and age-sex composition.

have used up the margin in the projected 1970–75 growth rate of employment by 1973, and after 1975 there is no margin. Numbers for the actual labor force after 1970 show only small increases.

Hours

Two circumstances introduced a large transitional element into the contribution of hours in 1961–71. The less important was the last phase of the absorption into full-time employment of persons who had been able to secure only part-time work during the previous period of labor surplus. The more important was that hours of full-time workers were so long that their reduction, we estimate, had almost no effect on the work done in a week or a year. If part-time employment had not diminished and if the reductions in full-time hours had been from the levels prevalent in the United States, changes in hours would have contributed about −0.23 percentage points to the 1961–71 growth rate of total national income on the basis of the actual labor share, or −0.24 points when the share is adjusted upward. However, a typical figure for the contribution of hours in an advanced Western country not experiencing a rising female share of employment would be perhaps −0.15 points, and we use this as the sustainable component, leaving 0.26 points as the transitional component.

Absorption of involuntary part-time employment was completed by 1971, but full-time hours still were very long. Both male and female full-time wage and salary workers in nonagricultural business worked about two more hours a week in Japan in 1971 than in the United States in 1929. This means the efficiency offset to reductions in hours of such workers was still big, but it is likely to mean also that workers will demand large reductions so as to approach Western standards. "Backwardness" in the retention of long hours will become a handicap to future growth when the efficiency offset dwindles while hours are reduced rapidly. This is likely to happen in the 1980s at the latest.

Suppose that in the future the percentages of part-time employment and average part-time hours do not change; that average full-time hours in agriculture and nonagricultural self-employment either do not change or are fully offset by greater output per hour; that average full-time hours of nonagricultural wage and salary workers drop smoothly to the 1969 U.S. level by 1985; and that our assumed relationship between hours and output of those workers applies. Under these conditions, and with a small allowance for a probable increase in the share of nonresidential business labor, the contribution of hours to the 1970–85 growth rate would be −0.26 percentage points (as against 0.11 points in 1961–71). The figure would start in 1972 as a small negative and steadily increase, hitting −0.15 points, the sustainable rate, about 1975. Thereafter, the transitional component would be negative because of the fast drop in full-time hours we have assumed. Even in 1971–75 the transitional component is less than in 1961–71, so under our assumptions the former contribution could not be maintained until 1975. We enter 1974 in Table 2-19.

Age-Sex Composition of Hours Worked

A reduction in young workers as young people remain in school longer is normal for an advanced society. But a declining female component of the labor force is not; in Japan it is the consequence of dwindling agricultural employment. Two-fifths of the advance in the age-sex composition index from 1961 to 1971 resulted from a reduction in the percentage of hours worked by females. We therefore regard as transitional two-fifths, or 0.08 percentage points, of the 0.19 points contributed to the growth rate by changes in age-sex composition of hours worked. The sustainable contribution was then 0.11 points.

Based on the relation between estimates for past and future growth shown by the Japan Economic Research Center series (Table 2-20), changes in age-sex composition will contribute about 0.20 percentage points to the growth rate of national income in 1970–75, 0.13 points in 1975–80, and 0.07 points in 1980–85. If the contribution continued at the 1961–71 level until the opportunity for a transitional contribution were exhausted, this would occur six years after 1971, or in 1977.

Education and Unallocated Labor Input

Education of the labor force in Japan is comparable to that in Western countries, it can increase at the 1961–71 rate for a long time (many decades), and we classify its entire contribution as sustainable. We do so even though education cannot continue to increase forever. If there is any transitional element in the small "unallocated" component, we disregard it.

Capital

Two transitional conditions were responsible for the big increase in investment and consequently for most of the contribution of capital to the growth of output. One was the sharp drop in the relative price of capital goods; the other, the high growth rate of real output which resulted from transitional elements in many growth sources.

Measured as the sum of expenditures, in 1965 prices, and by Japanese deflation techniques, growth rates from 1961 to 1971 were 10.2 percent for GNP and 12.5 percent for gross private investment (business, residential, and net foreign). The difference was due to the falling relative price of investment goods; the current-price ratio of national saving or investment to GNP did not change much.[84] When judged by American price relationships, the ratio of capital goods prices to prices of consumption (or of all GNP) in the 1950s apparently was high in Japan, as it was in Europe. Estimates by Kravis and associates in *A System of International Comparisons* show that even in 1970, after the long decline, relative prices of producers' durables and nonresidential structures were considerably higher in Japan than in the United States. We consider the decline to be transitional—in part, especially in the case of inventories, it may have been random. We assume that in its absence gross private investment would have grown at about the same rate as GNP when both are measured in constant prices.

To estimate the sustainable portion of the growth rate of output, we must anticipate the results for components not yet estimated, including capital itself. We conclude that a little over 3 percentage points out of the 9.5 percent growth rate of adjusted national income resulted from sustainable contributions. In the absence of transitional contributions the figure for the GNP series used in the previous paragraph would have been around 3⅓ percent, and we assume that the growth rate of gross investment in constant prices would also have been 3⅓ percent. The fact that the average level of the saving rate was higher in 1961–71 than it had been earlier would have meant a growth rate of capital stock above that of investment, but the consequences of this change in the saving rate are themselves transitional. Hence we use 3⅓ percent as the sustainable growth rate of capital stock as well as of gross investment.

If inputs of nonresidential structures and equipment and of inventories had each grown only 3⅓ percent a year instead of at their actual rates, the contribution of the former would have been cut from 1.44 percentage points to 0.41 points and that of inventories from 0.86 points to 0.23 points. Allowance for the probability that the appropriate weights of these inputs would have been smaller under conditions prevalent in more advanced economies reduces our estimates of the sustainable portions of their contributions a bit further, to 0.38 and 0.21 percentage points. The entire contributions of

---

84. In 1971 the ratio was actually a bit lower than in 1961 but, as shown in Table 2-16, a little above 1960. Table 2-17 suggests some uptrend.

dwellings and international assets are entered as sustainable, partly because the actual figures seem only remotely related to the growth of capital stock.

How long could transitional contributions of the 1961–71 size be obtained from nonresidential fixed capital and inventories? A possible reference point for the end of transitional gains is provided by capital stock per worker in the United States. We estimate that, per person employed in the whole economy, the stock of private nonresidential business structures and equipment was 69 percent greater in the United States than in Japan in 1970 and the stock of inventories 79 percent greater.[85] To provide as large a transitional contribution to growth as in 1961–71, the stock of nonresidential structures and equipment and of inventories would have to increase so fast that both would attain the then prevailing U.S. level per person employed soon after the end of 1976.[86]

Capital per worker in Japan may, of course, rise above the U.S. amount and break new ground. If it does so, the additional growth would hardly be regarded as transitional.[87]

Economies of Scale, U.S. Prices

The contribution of this source to growth in 1961–71 was allocated between sustainable and transitional components in the same proportion as the sum of all other growth sources (except economies of scale associated with income elasticities). Of the total of 1.14 percentage points, 0.42 points result from growth of the market attributable to contributions from sustainable sources and 0.72 points from growth attributable to contributions from

85. Use of U.S. price weights is implied. The first estimate is derived from the finding in Table 2-18 that gross fixed nonresidential business investment from 1960 through 1971, per civilian employed in 1971, was 61.7 percent as large in Japan as in the United States and the assumption that in 1971 the percentage per worker was the same for capital stock of this type. The inventory estimate for 1970 is a compromise between results of a direct comparison and the assumption that the ratio of private inventories to national income originating in nonresidential business was the same in the two countries.

86. These results are obtained without allowance for lower capital shares in the future. The effect of lower shares is offset by the fact that nonresidential business is a bigger part of the economy in Japan than in the United States, so the ratio of capital to total labor can be higher before the capital–labor ratio in nonresidential business, the relevant ratio, becomes higher.

87. We have chosen to regard no part of the contribution of dwellings as transitional but note that, if U.S. housing is used as a standard for comparison, it would in any case take a long time to eliminate the transitional element. The estimates of Kravis and his associates in *A System of International Comparisons* imply that in 1970 the quantity of housing per worker in the United States was 315 percent of the quantity in Japan. (The per capita quantity, perhaps more pertinent for this component, was 256 percent.)

transitional sources. The period for which transitional gains could continue at the 1961–71 rate depends on continuation of gains from other transitional sources. Transitional gains from economies of scale, measured in U.S. prices, were therefore allocated among expiration dates like the transitional contributions from the sources that make them possible.

The Combined Estimates

When summarized, our estimates imply that sources we deemed sustainable contributed 3.24 percentage points to the 9.56 percent growth rate of standardized national income from 1961 to 1971 and sources we deemed transitional contributed 6.32 points. For the most part, contributions from transitional sources were possible only because Japan was a late comer to growth, but this circumstance did not make growth at the high rate achieved inevitable, or even probable if we judge from the experience of other nations.

From Table 2-19 it can be easily computed that if the transitional contribution of each source continued at its 1961–71 level until the potential for a further contribution was exhausted, if sustainable sources continued indefinitely to contribute the same amount as in 1961–71, and if no new sources appeared, the growth rate would be as follows:

Actual			Implied	
1961–71	9.56		1971–73	9.56
			1973–74	8.70
			1974–76	8.41
			1976–77	6.48
			1977–82	6.39
			1982–90	5.69
			1990–95	5.48
			1995–2002	4.55
			2002–	3.24

The assumptions stated are not necessarily those one would wish to introduce if he were preparing an actual projection, but they do bring past experience to bear upon the future.

All rates calculated for periods after 1973 are down from the 1961–71 rate. The calculated 1977–82 rate is down by one-third and the 1982–90 rate by two-fifths. All transitional elements will be gone by 2002. We would, of course, expect the exhaustion of individual transitional sources to cut into the standardized growth rate less abruptly than assumed in the table above, but this pattern gives approximate timing.

The rate implied for standardized national income is 7.1 percent from

1971 to 1985, 6.5 percent from 1971 to 1995, and 6.2 percent from 1971 to 2000. Rates based on Japanese deflation procedures would be a little higher throughout.

The costs of conforming to regulations for environmental protection will adversely affect the future growth rate, but by an amount that is likely to be small. Government actions intended to shift priorities away from growth are also unlikely, in our view, to have much effect on growth. The outlook for the price of oil is too uncertain for us to venture any appraisal of its possible influence.

Irregular factors may cause actual growth rates in any period to depart widely from standardized rates. Indeed, they have already done so in the period from 1971 to 1974, which is included in the calculation above. Irregular factors that we have attempted to isolate in the past, and especially changes in output per unit of input that result from fluctuations in intensity of utilization, can be very important quantitatively. Employment and working hours have not previously been sensitive to changes in business activity but may become more so in the future. If they do, this will provide additional scope for actual output to diverge from standardized output. National income was depressed in the years 1971 and 1974 and is likely to be low in 1975 too. The low initial level will elevate rates computed with these years as a base.

For all these reasons the calculated growth rates are not forecasts of the future course of actual national income. Our intention is to confine the scope of our study to a description of past growth and the implications of this description for future growth prospects.

CHAPTER THREE

Fiscal, Monetary, and Related Policies

Gardner Ackley, University of Michigan
with the collaboration of
Hiromitsu Ishi, Hitotsubashi University

IN ALMOST ALL of the relatively free-market, developed economies of the world, including Japan's, the instruments of governmental fiscal and monetary policy have been used quite deliberately since World War II to promote achievement of objectives related to the economy's overall performance. Clearly, neither in Japan nor elsewhere has the record of monetary, fiscal, and related policies been faultless. But given the spectacular success of Japan's postwar economy, it seems appropriate to attempt to determine the extent to which the use of these particular policy tools by the Japanese government has contributed to the overall success, and whether there are lessons that can be learned from this experience.

The Role and Goals of Macroeconomic Policy

Monetary, fiscal, and related macroeconomic policies each affect the economy in very different ways; but all such policies are to be distinguished from other—that is, microeconomic—governmental economic policies in that their impact is designed to affect such global quantities as total national production or incomes, employment and unemployment, the price level, and balance-of-payments totals, rather than the composition of total output (as among particular firms, industries, products, or geographical areas) or the distribution of income among occupations or income classes. To a large extent macroeconomic policies operate through affecting buyers' demands for goods and services; hence they are often referred to as instruments of "demand management." Still, either through their impact on demand or in other ways, they also have potentially significant effects on the growth of the economy's total supply capabilities, or "potential output." They operate mainly as indirect controls, through affecting the incentives or opportunities

Note. Many Japanese economists, businessmen, and government officials contributed generously both to the general education of the American author and to the clarification of many detailed problems of fact and analysis. Among them, the following—all of whom read and commented on drafts of this study—deserve particular thanks: Isamu Miyazaki, Director-General, Research Bureau, Economic Planning Agency, and several of his associates; Sadao Ishida, Economic Adviser, Bank of Japan; Professors Ryuichiro Tachi, Ryutaro Komiya, Mikio Sumiya, and Tadao Uchida (Tokyo); Tsunehiko Watanabe, Masahiro Tatemoto, Hisao Kumagai, and Susumu Koizumi (Osaka); Yūichi Shionoya (Hitotsubashi); Miyohei Shinohara (Seikei); and Kazushi Ohkawa (Hitotsubashi and Yale). A number of our coauthors made extremely helpful comments on earlier drafts; but special thanks are due Hugh Patrick and Joseph A. Pechman. Radcliffe Edmunds, Jr., served as a most willing and efficient research assistant.

for voluntary private action; but political guidance or suasion is rarely entirely absent—particularly in Japan. And governmental policies principally designed and usually used mainly for microeconomic purposes may also be deliberately adjusted to have some macroeconomic impact.[1]

Macroeconomic policies can only be evaluated in terms of how they have modified what would otherwise have occurred; thus, some understanding of Japan's economic structure is necessary to the analysis of policies. And because the character of Japan's social, political, and economic history and institutions frequently gives rise to significant differences between the nature and use of macroeconomic policies there and elsewhere, some reference to these special characteristics is also necessary for an assessment of Japanese performance. Many of these aspects of Japan's economic structure and social arrangements, important for understanding its macroeconomic policies, have either already been described in earlier chapters of this study or will be discussed in later ones; others will need some elaboration in this chapter.

Although Japan's special economic and social characteristics are important for understanding and evaluating its particular use of macroeconomic policy, there are many similarities between Japanese problems in the use of macroeconomic policy and those encountered by other countries, including the United States—and the similarities are surely more important than the differences. Discovering these similarities, often in an unfamiliar institutional setting, can occasionally advance somewhat a foreign observer's understanding of how economic policy operates in his own country. It also may occasionally suggest possible improvements in the design or use of macroeconomic policy in another country and even contribute at least marginally to the resolution of current controversies in economic theory.

Gross National Product, Potential Output, and the Current Account Balance

As already noted, monetary, fiscal, and related policies operate primarily through affecting the aggregate demand for output, and thus the level of production and the incomes earned by those participating in that production. In a market economy, goods and services are produced only when, and to the

1. As this suggests, the distinction between macroeconomic and microeconomic policies is not precise, inasmuch as many policies serve both sectoral and economywide purposes, and most purely sectoral policies have clear macroeconomic implications. Thus, many policies discussed in other chapters of this study—for example, those related to technology, education, international economic matters, or taxation—could also be described as macroeconomic. References in this chapter to the term "macroeconomic policies" represent only a shorthand way of saying "monetary, fiscal, and related macroeconomic policies," and what policies are considered "related" is rather arbitrarily determined.

extent that, buyers stand ready to take them. Apart from any temporary involuntary accumulation of unwanted inventories (or temporary unintended
reductions of inventories below desired levels) as a result of a misjudgment
of market demand, total domestic production, or gross national product
(GNP), can be identified as the sum of all purchases of current output by
domestic consumers, by domestic businesses (to increase or maintain their
stocks of capital goods and of desired inventories), by domestic governmental units, and by foreign buyers. But from the sum of these purchases
must be subtracted all purchases made from foreign suppliers. Monetary and
fiscal policies can directly or indirectly affect the volume of each of these
five categories of purchases and thus of GNP, which is their algebraic sum.

Actual production (GNP) is usually contrasted with potential output,
which represents the maximum feasible production currently permitted by
the existing quantity and quality of capital and labor resources. Although it
is sometimes useful to represent an economy's potential output (as of any
particular date) by a specific number, the concept is inherently somewhat
ambiguous, and it is more realistic to consider potential output as a range or
band, not a number, and to think of any point-estimate of potential output
as representing the lower boundary of this range. Actual GNP then can exceed potential output at least somewhat; but if it does it brings about an overheated economy and will generate an inflation whose extent depends both on
the amount and the duration of the excess. On the other hand, GNP can also
fall considerably short of potential output: in most countries it often does,
sometimes for considerable periods. Shortfalls of GNP below potential output represent an unnecessary loss of production and incomes, most of which
can never be made up. Thus, it is not surprising that a principal assignment
of monetary and fiscal policy in all countries is to sustain aggregate demand
at a level that keeps production close to potential output.

At any one time potential output imposes a clear limit on GNP; but of
course this limit does not remain fixed over time—especially not in Japan.
Japanese potential output has expanded rapidly as supplies of productive
inputs—mainly capital and labor—have increased, as well as through the
increased average productivity or efficiency of these inputs, reflecting improved technology; the improving skills, energy, and knowledge of the labor
force; more effective management; and a changing distribution of the available inputs among various products and industries in which their efficiency
differs.[2]

Growth of potential output has little significance, however, except to the
extent that the growth of aggregate demand causes that growth of potential

2. See Chapter 2 in this volume for details and for estimates of the relative importance of each factor.

to be realized in growing GNP and incomes. Indeed, unless demand grows more or less in line with potential, the widening margin of unused potential is almost certain to depress its further growth. Macroeconomic policies that maintain steady but not excessive pressure of aggregate demand and GNP against potential output tend to speed up the growth of potential, whereas frequent or prolonged shortfalls of GNP are almost certain to reduce its growth. In postwar Japan, where so many of the ingredients for growth of potential output were at hand, the contribution of growth of demand to growth of potential was great.

Not only the level but also the composition of aggregate demand can be affected by macroeconomic policies; and composition of demand has important implications for the growth of potential, especially the relative importance of investment expenditures in the total. Investment increases the flow of the productive inputs of capital, is usually necessary to incorporate the newest technology, and is almost always required to accommodate a shift of production (and of labor) from lower to higher productivity employments.

On the other hand, if aggregate demand is allowed to press too hard against potential output, the economy will overheat, resulting in inflation and possibly serious misallocation of production and investment. Moreover, at least under a regime of fixed or semifixed exchange rates, such pressure can also produce a diversion of exports to satisfy domestic demand and a rapid growth of demand for imports. To the extent that inflation occurs and is irreversible, there may be a more or less permanent loss of exports and increase in demand for imports. Thus, a demand-management policy that permits overheating can—depending on what is happening abroad—have serious consequences not only for the domestic economy but also for the balance of payments. Even at levels of GNP short of potential output, imports and exports, and the relation between them, may create problems for demand-management policy. Rapid growth of production and incomes requires massive increases in imports of raw materials and foodstuffs and stimulates imports of all kinds of finished and international products—especially in a country that lacks significant mineral resources and large areas of arable land (relative to population). Unless exports grow with equal rapidity, or unless capital imports expand, balance-of-payments problems may become serious.

The Goals of Policy in Postwar Japan

The directions of a nation's macroeconomic policies are not always formally stated; and, where formally stated, they are not always an accurate representation of the true objectives of governmental action. In Japan the institution of economic planning and the role of the economic staff of the Economic Planning Agency in the reporting of macroeconomic events, forecasts, and policies tend to produce a verbalization of policy goals and a quantification of expectations not often found in other countries. Such rather fully articulated targets appear in the several Japanese multiyear plans of the postwar period, in annual statements on "outlook and basic policy for the national economy" now adopted by the cabinet each January, and in the annual "white paper" on the economy presented each July or August by the Economic Planning Agency.

The first multiyear plan drawn up by the Japanese government following the end of the occupation appeared in 1955. The goals of Japan's postwar economic policy, clearly enunciated in that plan, centered around the interlocking triad of "growth, investment, and exports." A rapid growth of output and employment in the modern, high-income, industrial sectors of the economy was seen as needed to absorb into these sectors the large numbers of underemployed workers in agriculture and small enterprises whose weight created the dual structure of incomes. A rapid growth of the modern, capital-intensive sectors and a relative if not absolute shrinkage of the traditional sector obviously required massive investments and thus a high level of national saving. It also required rapidly expanding markets for the products of the modern sectors, a significant part of which would need to be found abroad, both because expanding output of these industries could not be fully absorbed domestically and as a means to pay for the vast expansion of imports of raw materials and finished products that a rapid growth of domestic production and incomes would generate.

Indeed, in the absence of either massive economic aid or special procurement from the United States, a rapid growth of Japanese exports seemed needed merely to pay for the imports required at then existing levels of output and incomes; and this would be especially difficult as the exporting capacity of Europe was restored. This recognition was clear in the very title of the 1955 plan: "The Five-Year Plan for Economic Independence." Contemporary expert opinion, both at home and abroad, saw Japan's need for expanded exports as a matter simply of independent national survival. The notion that a resource-poor Japan, denied the opportunity for an overseas empire, could export enough to permit not merely survival but growth—and certainly rapid growth—seemed rather fatuous. Only by the standards of a later date would the initial numerical expression of the goals of the 1955 plan appear modest: a 5.0 percent average annual growth of real GNP, average annual growth of 8.8 percent in exports and 7.4 percent in imports (based on an assumed average annual growth of total world trade of 4.5 percent).

It is interesting for students of Western economies to note that full employment was not among the explicit goals of Japan's postwar economic policy. The main reason was that the still substantial sector of family-organized production in Japanese agriculture, services, and even manufacturing, together with the generally stable long-term job commitment made by large enterprises to their workers, made (and still make) overt unemployment a relatively unimportant social problem in Japan. What in other countries would emerge as outright unemployment—either long term or short term—in postwar Japan took the form mainly of underemployment—sometimes referred to as "disguised unemployment" or "dual structure" employment. The policy goals of a rapid growth of potential output and the full utilization of that potential were thus expressed in terms of the elimination of dual structure or of underemployment—that is, the shifting of workers to better-paid and more productive jobs. They were not expressed in terms of the securing or maintenance of full employment, which in a superficial sense was already assured by Japan's institutional structure. Not unrelated to the absence of an explicit full-employment goal was the absence of any explicit concern with the stability of the rate of industrial expansion. To the extent that there existed a tradeoff between stability of growth rate and extent of cumulative growth, stability was readily sacrificed.

This, of course, is not to say that Japanese policymakers would at any time have been undisturbed by the emergence of any appreciable volume of overt unemployment. Moreover, the government also undertook to help support incomes depressed by underemployment in agriculture and small business through high price supports for rice and many special tax and financial measures favoring small firms.

The goals of Japanese policy as seen in 1955 had many implications for a wide variety of governmental policies, both microeconomic and macroeconomic.[3] Many of their implications for microeconomic policies—import protection, export subsidy, financial aid and guidance to favored lines of production and investment, massive imports of technology, and so on—are discussed elsewhere in this book. But the implications of the goals for general macroeconomic policy were also clear and well understood. They included the following:

—Governmental tax and expenditure policies that would encourage saving, investment, and exports, including heavy governmental investment in productive (but not in social) capital.

3. For an excellent review of the goals of policy and their implications as seen in 1955, see Saburo Okita and Takeo Takahashi, "International Aspects of Planning in Japan," in Japan Economic Research Center, *Economic Planning and Macroeconomic Policy: Papers and Proceedings of a Conference Held by the Japan Economic Research Center,* vol. 2 (1971), pp. 442–65.

—A monetary policy involving low interest rates and easy credit designed to stimulate highly capital-intensive private investment (but not housing or consumer durables) and to provide an indirect form of export subsidy.

—A significant role for the government as financial intermediary to ensure that adequate amounts of both personal and governmental savings flowed to the favored kinds of investments.

—The encouragement of a rapid growth of aggregate demand so long as the current account of the balance of payments remained positive and export prices did not rise; but a readiness to check expansion of demand whenever the continuation of either of these conditions was threatened; yet a willingness to tolerate rising domestic prices, especially if they supported import-competing domestic production or did not significantly encourage imports of consumer goods.

—Although never made explicit, the ready sacrifice of stability to growth.

The growth-investment-exports triad of goals reflected an essentially intellectual analysis of Japan's economic situation, problems, and needs. Yet the analysis did not remain the property of an elite group of leaders. Rather, it was preached and popularized to Japan's literate public by politicians, businessmen, and press. It came to be embodied in such popular slogans as "prosperity through exports and stability through savings." Policies to promote the government's goals succeeded not only because they were well designed to harness the incentives of private self-interest, but perhaps also in part through a widely shared identification of self-interest with national interest.

As experience during the 1950s and 1960s indicated that higher rates of growth of exports, output, incomes, and investment were feasible, the numerical targets were raised repeatedly, but little or no revision was made in the priorities. Whereas the goals had been set initially in a context of survival, their achievement—or overachievement—had come to represent a source of national pride and fulfillment. Growth of the modern sector seemed no less important even as underemployment in the traditional sector and the dual structure of incomes essentially disappeared. Investment for growth to permit more investment for even faster growth appeared to acquire a value of its own, somewhat independent of the advantages derivable from higher incomes and consumption. Fear of potential balance-of-payments deficits apparently remained as pressing when Japan became one of the world's most successful exporters (and began to accumulate substantial international reserves) as when growing exports were needed merely to maintain a 1930s standard of living. Artificially low interest rates, initially valued as an investment stimulus and indirect export subsidy, maintained a strong attraction even after investment and exports ceased to need special encouragement. And artificial supports to agriculture and small business were maintained even as incomes in these sectors approached parity.

By around 1965 the original postwar macroeconomic policy goals began to lose their original justification. Policies based upon them began to come into question, not only among intellectuals—including many prominent economists—but even among some government and business leaders. As the economic problems reflected in the earlier goals were resolved, important new problems could be perceived. Yet there was a significant social lag: only in the 1970s did the old goals begin to be replaced by a new set (described by Patrick and Rosovsky in Chapter 1). Thus, most of this chapter is devoted to understanding how the several major instruments of macroeconomic policy were used to help in the pursuit—and achievement—of the earlier goals. Only at the end of the chapter are there some tentative comments on how these policies may need to be adapted to the pursuit of the newer goals.

Aggregate Demand and the Limits on Output, 1955 to 1970

Japanese economic growth since World War II has been exceedingly rapid—but also quite irregular. Expansion has been interrupted by a series of seven recognized recessions, each lasting roughly a year.[4] Once or twice, these involved an actual decline of GNP for a quarter or two; all others involved sharp slowdowns in the growth of aggregate output, as well as actual declines in one or more categories of investment. The business cycles marked off by these recessions are intimately involved with several aspects of the macroeconomic policies that are the subject of this chapter. However, several significant aspects of economic development and of the policies related to it can be best discussed in relation to the postwar macroeconomic history of Japan as a whole and without detailed specific reference to business cycles. The present section considers these aspects, while the section following concentrates on the cyclical features.

The Strength of Aggregate Demand

Western economists who study the postwar Japanese economy (especially, perhaps, those from the United States or Britain) cannot fail to be struck by what they may describe as the great secular vigor or buoyancy of aggre-

4. An eighth recession began in late 1973, but at this writing had not been officially dated.

gate demand in Japan, seemingly very unlike the usual situation of their own economies. As will be demonstrated later, each postwar Japanese recession appears to have resulted from a deliberate tightening of monetary policy, not from a weakening of private demand; nor did policy restraint seem to trip off a significantly self-reinforcing downward spiral of incomes and output; and, with debatable exceptions, no special stimulus has been needed for demand and output growth to resume prerecession rates of expansion—once the special monetary restraint was lifted, demand and output quickly bounced upward.

Over this same period, aggregate demand has seemed adequate, without special stimulus, to maintain reasonably full realization of potential output in the United States or the United Kingdom during an occasional period of economic boom. But this condition has usually appeared unsustainable. Frequent recessions occurred, even in the absence of special restraint; these ordinarily developed a life of their own, which often required considerable policy stimulus—and time—to reverse. And in the absence of continuing stimulus, GNP frequently stagnated or expanded insufficiently fast to utilize the economy's growing potential output, even though the growth of that potential was relatively slow.

Of course, if macroeconomic policies operated perfectly, the difference in actual results might not be very great: whether in Japan or in the United States or Britain, GNP might remain steadily close to potential output. If demand management was less than perfect (as in fact was the case in each country), aggregate demand might be (and sometimes was) either excessive or deficient both in Japan and in the West. Still, even though demand management in many Western countries has been reasonably flexible and sophisticated, taking the postwar period as a whole, unwanted gaps between actual and potential output in other major countries have probably been larger and more persistent than in Japan. And when, in Japan, monetary policy was used to depress the level of demand, policymakers apparently needed only an "on-off" switch—special monetary restraint "on" and demand waned; special restraint "off" and demand quickly bounced up. Little or no active stimulus was required; nor did much fine tuning of restraint appear necessary. The unusual buoyancy of aggregate demand seemingly gave Japan's policymakers a considerably easier task to perform; on the whole, therefore, they appear to have achieved better results.[5]

5. Comparisons like those in the text cannot avoid being impressionistic rather than rigorously scientific. To be sure, quantitative estimates of potential output are available both for Japan and for many other countries; and attempts can be made to compare the extent of cumulative shortfalls of GNP from potential output. Such results, however,

INVESTMENT: THE PRIMARY SOURCE OF DEMAND BUOYANCY. An examination and comparison of the components of aggregate demand in Japan and in the West quickly reveals the particular source of the different buoyancy of demand. It does not lie in consumer demand, which in Japan, as elsewhere, tends to respond passively to changes in aggregate disposable income. Indeed, in postwar Japan consumer spending is far lower relative to disposable income than in any major Western country.[6] The growth of consumer demand for durable goods has, of course, played an important role in the Japanese productive explosion. Modern consumer durable goods were largely missing from Japanese households at the beginning of the period, so that there was a large initial stock to be provided; and the demand for such goods in Japan, as in most other countries, is highly elastic to income growth.[7] Nevertheless, the extremely high rate of personal savings in Japan suggests that, however emotionally intense, the demand for consumer goods—relative to income and to the growth of income—was not unusually strong.

Still, the expansion of consumer durable goods had several significant indirect impacts on Japanese postwar industrial growth. The fact that automobiles and appliances are effectively produced only by highly capital-intensive technologies meant that the shift of consumption to these products from more traditional ones contributed significantly to investment demand. And once these industries were well established domestically, they could and did contribute notably to export growth.

The source of the demand buoyancy certainly does not lie in government purchases. Government spending is an unusually low fraction of GNP in Japan, and Japan may be the only major country in which government spending has expanded less rapidly than GNP during the postwar period. Nor do

cannot be conclusive: for, by whatever technique potential output is estimated, its level (as opposed to its rate of growth) must be determined either judgmentally (by some concept of "full"—that is, "desirable"—employment), mechanically (to minimize the aggregate of deviations—or of squared deviations—between GNP and potential), or in some other equally arbitrary way. Reference will be made below to two studies that estimate Japan's potential output: one, an unpublished study by the EPA for the period beginning in 1955; the other, by the Organisation for Economic Co-operation and Development, beginning with 1959 ("The Measurement of Domestic Cyclical Fluctuations," *OECD Economic Outlook: Occasional Studies* [July 1973], pp. 20–22). Given their methods of construction, neither would be at all useful for evaluating the conclusions in the text.

6. For reasons explored in Chapter 4.

7. Popular slogans reflect the importance of durable goods to the Japanese consumer. Between 1955 and 1962 all who were able sought to acquire "the three sacred treasures": refrigerator, electric washing machine, and vacuum cleaner. From 1963 to 1970 the objective was "the three C's": car, color television, and cooler (air conditioner). In the early 1970s "the three V's"—villa, visa, and visit—became the goal.

imports—purchases that subtract from GNP—play a qualitatively different role: as elsewhere, Japan's imports respond, largely passively, to changes in domestic output and incomes.

The source of the unusual strength and buoyancy of demand in postwar Japan instead lies basically in private investment in plant, equipment, and inventories and to a lesser but still appreciable extent in exports. In Chapter 6, Krause and Sekiguchi evaluate the hypothesis that the growth of Japan's postwar output was export led, and they explain the sources of the rapid although somewhat erratic expansion of postwar Japanese exports, at a rate considerably faster than the growth of world trade as a whole. Thus, the principal question that needs to be addressed here is why investment demand has been both so strong and so buoyant.

A number of reasons can be suggested for the buoyancy of investment, although it is impossible to assign the relative importance of each. One source, which did not exist at the beginning of the postwar period, became increasingly important as the years went by: past experience with strongly growing aggregate demand—which made yesterday's investments so successful—bred confidence in the continuing growth of markets for the products of today's investments. This confidence apparently was not impaired by the frequent interruptions of expansion brought about by restrictive monetary policy; these were apparently well understood to be temporary and easily reversible. By the mid-1960s, the confidence factor was surely significant, and a series of unsuccessful episodes would have been required for such confidence to be shaken.

Yet the confidence could not have developed in the absence of whatever more basic factors assured the past success, and it could not have survived if other, more fundamental, factors had failed to assure continuing success. Thus, it is necessary to look behind the fact of investor confidence for relevant structural factors or policies that account for its origin and continuance. Three categories of reasons are here suggested: governmental policies favoring investment; the fact that capital facilities rather than labor supply were the main factor limiting production and its growth; and the rapid growth of aggregate demand.

GOVERNMENTAL POLICIES SUPPORTING INVESTMENT. Governmental policies surely supply part of the explanation. First, Japanese tax policies have been highly favorable to investment, both in their general structure and through abundant special provisions (as Pechman and Kaizuka explain in Chapter 5). Second, in a number of relevant ways Japan's government has underwritten—or at least has given its major industrial and financial corporations the feeling that it underwrites—the risks assumed by large firms whose investments support the nation's economic objectives: through its administration of government loans and foreign exchange; the approval or even encouragement of recession cartels and of mergers to avoid what is considered destructive competition; and a multitude of other special arrangements made for the protection and growth of large firms in important industries. Third, and perhaps most important, governmental monetary and interest-rate policies have made abundant investment funds freely available (except during the recurrent periods of tight money) and at relatively low and stable rates of interest. The nature of this system is described in detail later in this chapter.

CAPITAL AS THE LIMIT ON OUTPUT. Quite apart from governmental policies, the strategic importance of capital facilities as the usual primary short-run limit on aggregate output—a significant aspect of Japan's postwar economic structure—may help to explain the strength of its investment demand. In the United States or other Western countries there is a meaningful sense in which it can be said that the strategic factor limiting aggregate output is normally the full employment of the labor force: indeed, the concept of potential output usually goes by that name. In every economy, of course, growth of potential output normally requires more capital as well as more labor. But at any given time in the more mature Western economies there exist few unexploited opportunities dramatically to increase output through massive investments directed either toward introduction of radically different technologies than those currently in use or toward fundamental changes in the mix of products produced. Even though saving and investment rates are relatively low in the West, capital facilities appropriate to the current best technology and market structure are relatively abundant. Most firms have some margin of spare plant and equipment most of the time; and although labor supply does not ordinarily limit the output of any single firm or industry, it has ordinarily provided the effective limit on aggregate output.[8]

In postwar Japan the situation was otherwise. Any effective short-run limit on expansion of aggregate output was set essentially by the size and technological quality of the existing capital facilities, not by the supply of qualified labor. At first this was partly the result of massive wartime destruction of structures and equipment, along with a significant increase in the labor supply through repatriation. But much of the surviving capital stock was not adapted to the best available technologies. Given the domestic and international structure of prices, new productive facilities, which permitted

8. The possibility that aggregate U.S. output was limited in 1973 by significant capital bottlenecks rather than by labor supply may be the partial exception that, in a sense, proves the rule.

incorporation of more advanced technology, provided highly profitable investment opportunities for Japanese firms. Equally important, the distribution of capital and labor as between labor-intensive and capital-intensive products and industries could very profitably be shifted in the direction of the latter—but only as rapidly as new productive facilities could be put in place. For one thing, in relatively low-income Japan increments of consumer income would be directed in substantial proportion toward consumer durable goods that are capable of efficient production mainly by highly capital-intensive methods. Worldwide trends in consumption were moving in the same direction.

To take advantage of these opportunities, of course, firms needed more qualified workers, as well as new capital facilities. But the supply of labor to the modern, capital-intensive sectors of Japan's economy was no problem. It was highly elastic, at real wage rates only moderately above the average incomes that could be earned in family enterprises in agriculture, services, or small-scale industry.

Reference was earlier made to the spectacular increase in Japanese exports, as an element in the buoyancy of aggregate demand. Such export growth also contributed significantly to the demand for capital goods. The expansion of exports of many major industrial products was as often effectively limited by Japanese supply as by foreign demand: by, on the one hand, capital facilities available for the manufacture of such products, and, on the other, the rapidly expanding domestic demand for these products. Once again, this meant that the limit to output was expressed in terms of pressure on capital facilities rather than of a shortage of labor to operate such facilities. Investment in further such facilities thus remained attractive.[9]

RAPID GROWTH OF AGGREGATE DEMAND. Japan's stock of capital facilities may have grown rapidly as a result of exceedingly high rates of investment, but the growth of the total demand for the output of such facilities was equally rapid, in significant part as the result of the rapid growth of investment demand itself; thus, the new facilities, once completed, could almost immediately be fully and profitably utilized. As a consequence, the initial backlog of attractive investment opportunities could—and did—shrink only slowly, if at all. The rapid growth of aggregate demand thus constitutes a

---

9. The substance of the three preceding paragraphs seems generally consistent with views expressed in Kazushi Ohkawa and Henry Rosovsky, *Japanese Economic Growth: Trend Acceleration in the Twentieth Century* (Stanford University Press, 1973). Ohkawa and Rosovsky indeed suggest the foregoing as crucial elements in each of the "long swings" in Japanese economic growth of the past century. For a summary, see ibid., pp. 200–04.

third general reason why investment demand was so buoyant in postwar Japan. The rapid growth of investment, sparking a rapid growth of total demand, maintained strong pressures on the growing productive facilities which that investment provided, helping to assure that further rapid investment growth would be profitable. This is, of course, a circular relation, but not for that reason invalid. Economists call this relation the "acceleration principle." In highly simplified theoretical models based on this principle (usually called Harrod-Domar models after their earliest exponents), the strong and steady growth of investment demand is, in effect, self-generating. Such simplified models have been occasionally directly applied by both Japanese and Western economists to the case of postwar Japan. And although any such direct application seems far-fetched, the more basic acceleration principle is clearly one relevant component of the strength of investment demand. To be sure, economic analysis clearly demonstrates that, though the acceleration principle can strongly reinforce investment incentives, it can also be a source of violent instability. It was not so in Japan, presumably because the growth of demand came to be seen by Japanese entrepreneurs in longer-run terms, and because in these terms capacity never fully caught up with demand.

HIGHLY LEVERED CAPITAL STRUCTURE. In Chapter 5 of this book Pechman and Kaizuka refer to comparative data on the profitability of investment in postwar Japan and in the United States. They note that, as a rate of return on owner's equity, the profit rate was almost twice as high in Japan, mainly because of the exceedingly low percentage (by American standards) of total capital supplied by owners and the extremely high percentages supplied (at relatively low interest rates) by the banking system. This high degree of leverage can be considered another important structural reason for the high profitability and therefore the buoyancy of investment; equally well, perhaps, it can be considered an aspect of governmental policy, which permits—and indeed encourages—such a highly levered capital structure. Further discussion of this characteristic of Japan's industrial system will be found in Chapters 4 and 7.

The above explanations for the strong incentives to invest, even if broadly correct, raise about as many questions as they answer. High rates of investment are not automatically profitable in capital-poor, labor-abundant, and technologically backward economies. Most underdeveloped countries are both capital poor and technologically backward yet remain underdeveloped because investment fails to occur. Other governments also have provided special incentives to investment without generating explosive growth. Was it different in Japan because entrepreneurs were more alert and imaginative in sensing the opportunities for profit—and if so, why? Or was it that governmental policies in Japan (but not elsewhere) encouraged firms to expand in those sectors in which demand was most sensitively responsive to the growth of the domestic and the world economy? Was postwar Japanese entrepreneurship made more imaginative and aggressive as the result of a new, more competitive order created by the postwar social and economic reforms? Did the strong demand for Japanese exports, and thus for investment to produce exports, perhaps reflect a postwar structure of exchange rates that undervalued the yen? But the yen became visibly undervalued only because—and long after—Japanese firms learned more effectively than their competitors in other countries to find potentially profitable export opportunities.

Thus, it seems impossible to isolate any single basic explanation for the strength of Japanese aggregate demand, to rate the relative importance of the many possible explanations, or even to be sure that some crucial element of the total explanation has not been omitted. Undoubtedly, a whole constellation of circumstances—some historical, some structural, some socio-psychological, some policy related, some accidental—explains the strength of investment in Japan and the secular vigor of aggregate demand. But whatever the source of this vigor, it seems exceedingly important for understanding the operation of Japan's postwar macroeconomic policies.

Balance of Payments as a Limit on Expansion

The possibility was noted briefly earlier that, even at levels of GNP short of potential output, imports and exports and the relation between them might create problems for demand-management policy—at least under a regime of fixed exchange rates. Thus, the possibility must be considered that the effective limit on Japan's postwar GNP and its growth may have been set not always or even ordinarily by potential output, but rather by balance-of-payments considerations deriving from either Japan's economic structure or its economic policies—or both. Economists sometimes argue (or merely assume) that any limit on aggregate output that relates to the balance of payments is necessarily only another form, or a special dimension, of the limits summarized in the concept of potential output. But this is true only under rather special and not necessarily realistic assumptions—including highly flexible individual and average prices and wages and the existence of few obstacles to the rapid shift of resources between production of domestically and internationally traded goods and services.

Because Japan possesses few mineral resources and little arable land relative to its population, rapid growth of its industrial production requires a formidable expansion of imports of fuels and industrial materials, and rapid growth of consumer incomes calls for substantial enlargement of food and other resource-related imports. Given the initial absence of international reserve assets in postwar Japan, given the government's commitment (as a badge of international respectability) to the value of the yen established in 1949, given the policy decision (for reasons historical, ideological, and reflective of powerful economic interests) not to admit significant direct investment and a Japanese (and foreign) prejudice against appreciable long-term Japanese borrowing abroad, Japan's economic expansion could well have been limited, even short of potential output, by the extent to which its exports could expand (or its imports could be restrained).

As already noted, Japan's exports expanded with great speed. Yet (as will be described in some detail in the later discussion of business cycles), there was a persistent tendency in boom periods for imports to expand even faster; this was followed almost invariably by a restrictive use of monetary policy designed to slow the expansion of aggregate demand, GNP, and imports; and usually the imposition of such a restrictive policy was followed by a recession. It is thus an interesting and possibly important question, both of economic analysis and historical description, to determine under what fundamental circumstances, and why, restrictive policies became necessary. Was it always, sometimes, or never because expansion of total output was running into limits set by potential output (or seemed about to do so), thus threatening an inflationary overheating of the economy? Or was it simply because expansion was generating a negative balance on current account (or was expected to), leading to an unacceptable or unsustainable loss of reserve assets? These questions are relevant for an understanding and evaluation of Japan's demand-management policies, of its balance-of-payments policies, and also of its price-level movements and problems with inflation.

The contention here—to be supported in later argument—is that, first, until the mid- or late 1960s intermittently restrictive monetary policies often had to be applied and were applied primarily for reasons related to the current account balance alone, which did not necessarily involve actual or imminent general overheating of the economy; and that, second, they were removed primarily when and because the balance of payments improved, not because a potential inflation due to overheating had been controlled or averted.

This is not to contend that before 1968 the rate of expansion could have been appreciably faster during boom periods than it was, without running into the limits set by potential output. Most of the time the capital facilities provided by private and public investment in plant, equipment, and social capital related to production were rather fully utilized during booms; much faster rates of output growth might well have caused overheating, even if the balance of payments were no problem. Perhaps more important, even though the supply of labor may have been ample, there were limits on the speed with which it could be transferred to the modern sectors, and these limits might have prevented significantly faster overall growth during booms. Nevertheless, at least some of the slowdown of output growth and the reductions of investment during policy-created recessions might have been avoided had the need to restrain expansions of imports for balance-of-payments reasons been eliminated by other factors: by, for example, different circumstances in the world economy, different attitudes or policies toward balance-of-payments deficits, a greater ability to speed the transfer of resources into export production, or more effective direct restraint on imports. Thus, the average rate of growth of GNP—taking periods of both expansion and recession— might even have been somewhat faster, at least until the mid-1960s.

Changes in Expansion Limits and Strength of Demand

Beginning in the late 1960s changes began to be evident in the nature of the limits on the expansion of Japan's aggregate output. Improvements in Japan's international competitiveness and the growing U.S. military involvement in Vietnam essentially removed (at least for a time) the rate of growth of exports as an effective limit on the expansion of aggregate output. (The nature and effects of these and other changes is described in Chapter 6.) Far less suddenly, the labor supply began during the 1960s to become a more significant limit on the expansion of output—as the pool of underemployed labor in agriculture and smaller enterprises was progressively drained and as per capita incomes in those sectors rose toward, and then to equality with, incomes in the modern industrial sectors. As reviewed in more detail by Galenson and Odaka in Chapter 9, some of the slack began to disappear from labor markets. Measures of the balance between the aggregate supply and demand for labor showed a growing tightness, especially after about 1965. This is most evident in the ratio of job offers to applicants (other than new graduates), which first reached unity in 1967 and rose almost to 1.5 at the end of 1969, before the 1970 recession brought it back to 1.0 at the end of 1971. Thereafter it spurted to 1.9 in late 1973. On the other hand, average hours per week declined steadily after about 1960, and, more significantly, overtime hours fell sharply. Perhaps the safest generalization is that the substantial slack of earlier years was gone. But there was yet no certain evidence of labor shortage.

These two major changes, occurring during roughly the same period, may suggest that, although balance-of-payments constraints may often have limited the expansion of output prior to the mid-1960s, labor shortage thereafter became the principal limiting factor.[10] If this generalization has validity, it might be supposed that a change in the strength or buoyancy of aggregate demand should also have occurred: to the extent that the buoyancy reflected a scarcity of capital relative to labor, this relative scarcity should have progressively weakened as high rates of investment and relatively low rates of labor force growth and the cumulative absorption of the underemployed shifted the balance of factor availability. Real wage rates should have risen and real profit rates declined as labor shortages began to replace capital shortages as the limiting factor on output.

Moreover, other reasons might suggest that a weakening should have occurred in the buoyancy of aggregate demand as the postwar period lengthened. First, the most profitable of the available technological opportunities presumably were the first to be exploited, the most profitable sectoral shifts of production the first to be achieved. Second, as Table 3-1 indicates, private saving (and each major element thereof) increased rather steadily and strongly relative to GNP over the period—from 9.9 percent of GNP in 1952–54 to 19.3 percent in 1970–72. Unless fully offset by increases in private investment, or in the excess of government investment over government saving, such an increase in private saving constitutes a weakening of private demand for goods and services.

Many observers have actually postulated a progressive weakening of aggregate demand relative to potential output. As will be indicated below, the business cycle expansion of 1963–64 was both shorter than earlier ones and drew less of its strength from private investment; the recession that followed was widely believed to be more serious than earlier ones. Moreover, the next Japanese recession, that of 1970–71, was the longest to date since the war. Following each of these two recessions, recovery initially seemed weaker than usual; each time it was concluded that a stimulative fiscal policy, not merely the removal of monetary restraint, was necessary to initiate and sustain recovery.

But the unprecedented length and strength of the boom from 1966 to 1970 hardly support the thesis of progressively weakening demand; and a special explanation is available for the longer duration of the recession of 1970–71 and the initially hesitant recovery. Taking account of all the evidence (including some to be presented later), the most reasonable hypothesis

10. In various publications, Miyohei Shinohara has advanced this hypothesis and illustrated it with an interesting diagram. See, for example, his "Causes and Patterns of Postwar Growth," *The Developing Economies* (December 1970), p. 360.

Table 3-1. *Saving as a Percent of the Gross National Product in Japan, 1952–72*

Period	Total gross saving	Private saving (net)			Capital consumption allowances[a]	Government saving	Statistical discrepancy
		Total	House-hold	Corpo-rate			
		Annual percentages					
1952	26.4	10.2	7.5	2.6	7.8	7.9	0.6
1953	22.9	8.6	5.6	3.0	7.8	5.7	0.8
1954	23.2	10.8	7.0	3.8	9.0	4.7	−1.3
1955	25.6	12.5	9.9	2.6	9.2	4.4	−0.4
1956	28.6	12.6	9.8	2.8	9.6	5.2	1.3
1957	31.3	16.0	11.0	5.0	9.4	6.7	−0.9
1958	28.5	14.7	10.8	3.8	9.8	5.4	−1.3
1959	30.8	15.7	12.0	3.7	10.1	5.9	−0.8
1960	34.1	18.2	12.0	6.2	10.3	7.1	−1.4
1961	38.7	18.1	12.6	5.5	10.7	8.1	1.9
1962	35.7	17.3	12.7	4.6	11.4	8.2	−1.1
1963	34.7	16.1	12.4	3.7	11.7	7.6	−0.7
1964	35.7	14.9	10.9	4.0	12.1	6.7	1.9
1965	34.0	14.9	11.9	3.0	12.6	6.1	0.5
1966	34.8	15.7	11.8	3.9	12.9	5.7	0.5
1967	37.2	17.9	12.7	5.3	12.6	6.0	0.6
1968	38.8	19.4	13.1	6.3	12.9	6.3	−0.2
1969	39.7	18.8	12.6	6.2	13.4	7.1	0.4
1970	40.5	20.0	13.3	6.7	13.5	7.7	−0.7
1971	39.2	18.8	13.2	5.6	13.5	7.5	−0.6
1972	38.8	19.1	13.8	5.2	15.0	6.9	−2.2
		Averages of annual percentages					
1952–54	24.2	9.9	6.7	3.1	8.2	6.1	*
1955–59	29.0	14.3	10.7	3.6	9.6	5.5	−0.4
1960–64	35.8	16.9	12.1	4.8	11.2	7.6	0.1
1965–69	36.9	17.4	12.4	4.9	12.9	6.2	0.3
1970–72	39.5	19.3	13.4	5.8	14.0	7.4	−1.2

Sources: Economic Planning Agency, *Research Report on National Income Statistics, 1951–67* (1968), pp. 61, 69; EPA, *Annual Report on National Income 1972*, pp. 37, 45; *1974*, pp. 32, 33, 40, 41.

* Less than 0.05.

a. Capital consumption allowances include only a small component (less than 10 percent) of allowances for consumption of government capital; the remainder is private.

appears to be that, although the buoyancy of aggregate demand was not of the same intensity throughout the period, and that the years 1962 through 1966 may have been a period of relative weakness, there was no clear trend over the postwar period as a whole toward any weakening of aggregate demand relative to potential output.

Table 3-1 is of interest not only for its indication of the strong upward trend in the saving ratio, but also (and equally) for the exceedingly high levels of saving rates it reports for the Japanese economy—surely the highest among the major countries of the world.[11] As will be shown later, government saving in Japan typically exceeds government investment; nevertheless, private investment was so strong and buoyant and rose sufficiently rapidly relative to GNP that only occasionally did Japan experience a significant unwanted deficiency of aggregate demand relative to potential output.

Aggregate Demand and Inflation

One of the paradoxes of Japanese postwar development is that its economy can correctly be described either as having, from about 1953 to the end of 1972, the most stable price level of any of the major free enterprise countries; or as one of the two major countries with the highest rates of postwar inflation. The first description is correct relative to export prices or wholesale industrial prices, the second, relative to the consumer price index or the GNP deflator (France being the only major Western country with a worse record on both of the latter indexes during the period 1955–70).[12]

The basic facts about price level changes in Japan during this period (and subsequently) are shown in Table 3-2, as well as in Table 1-1 and Figure 1-1 in Chapter 1. Wholesale and export prices were essentially stable over the entire period 1955–72, except for a small rise during 1965–70. (Annual figures for this period show that roughly half of the 1965–70 wholesale price increase and nearly all of the export price increase occurred in 1969 and 1970.) From 1970 through 1972, during part of which time the economy was in recession, wholesale prices again were stable, and export prices actually declined. Consumer prices rose relatively slowly during 1955–60, but thereafter rose at a fairly steady rate of 5 or 6 percent a year, a rate that showed no tendency to accelerate. The pattern of the GNP deflator, of which consumer prices are a major component, was roughly the same. Between 1960 and 1972, the deflator rose at a rather steady 4.5 to 5 percent a year pace—with,

11. Comparisons using OECD data for fourteen countries show that in 1969 Japan's rate of private net saving (19.4 percent, as against 18.8 shown in Table 3-1) was about one-third higher than the next highest for that year (Italy, 15.0 percent and the Netherlands, 14.9 percent), and more than three times that of the United States (5.9 percent). Comparisons for the same year of total gross saving rates, private plus public (which, of course, also means total gross investment as percentages of GNP) show that Japan's rate (39.9 percent) was one-third higher than the next highest (Finland, 29.6 percent), more than 40 percent higher than the highest among the major countries (Germany, 27.9 percent), and more than twice that of the United States (18.1 percent). See OECD, *National Accounts of OECD Countries 1953–1969* (Paris: OECD, 1971), tables 1, 10.

12. See Gardner Ackley, *Stemming World Inflation* (Atlantic Institute, 1971), pp. 12, 13.

Table 3-2. *Changes in Major Price Indexes in Japan,*
Various Periods, 1955–74[a]

Percent

Period	Consumer price index	GNP deflator	Wholesale price index	Export price index
1955–60	1.9	3.2	0.5	−0.8
1960–65	6.2	4.9	0.4	−0.8
1965–70	5.5	4.7	2.2	1.7
1970–72	5.5	4.8	0.0	−1.1
1955–72	4.6	4.4	0.9	−0.1
1960–72	5.8	4.8	1.1	0.2
1972–73	11.8	12.3	15.9	9.0
1973–74	22.6[b]	n.a.	31.3	33.4

Sources: 1955–73—for CPI, GNP deflator, and WPI, Federal Reserve Bank of St. Louis' *Rates of Change in Economic Data for Ten Industrial Countries, Annual Data 1954–1973* (October 1974), pp. F-1, F-2; for EPI (1955–72), Economic Planning Agency, *Annual Report on Business Cycle Indicators* (May 1973), p. 192. 1973–March 1974—Bank of Japan, *Economic Statistics Monthly* (March 1974), p. 151. April–December 1974—BOJ, *Economic Indicators* (February 1975).

n.a. Not available.

a. Changes are calculated from annual averages.

b. Tokyo only.

again, no acceleration. But after 1972, of course, all four indexes rose explosively.

The divergent behavior of the four indexes reflects the divergent patterns of movement of the prices of the goods and services included in the several indexes. As Patrick and Rosovsky have explained in Chapter 1, the basic divergence was between rising prices for most of the products of what is often called the traditional sector (agriculture, consumer services, much of trade, and small-firm manufacturing), whereas prices of the products of the modern sector (essentially large-scale industrial firms) were stable or declining. The latter products constitute the bulk of wholesale and export sales. Traditional products are, however, very important in consumer expenditures; and consumer purchases constitute roughly half of GNP and are thus heavily represented in the GNP deflator.

Given these patterns of price change, was Japan experiencing inflation prior to 1973? Inasmuch as the GNP deflator is the broadest measure of price change and the consumer price index the one most relevant to every individual's perceptions and behavior, it can probably be said that, from 1960 to 1972, Japan was experiencing a rather steady and (for that period) relatively high rate of creeping inflation.

THE NATURE OF JAPANESE INFLATION. But what kind of inflation was it —"demand-pull," "cost-push," "imported," "demand-shift," or some unique Japanese phenomenon? Patrick and Rosovsky have provided an explanation for the different price behaviors in the traditional and modern sectors, which it is unnecessary to repeat. This difference in movement might have occurred, however, through stable prices in the traditional sector and falling prices in the modern one or through prices rising—or falling—in both sectors, but at different rates. Why was the average of wholesale prices and export prices essentially stable over the entire period 1955–72, requiring that the average of other prices—and thus of all prices—should be rising? This is a far more difficult question than that of different movement, and one on which there is less agreement.[13]

Any hypothesis that inflation was imported can be rejected at least in the simplest sense that prices of imported goods were rising. The movement of import prices over the entire period 1955–72 was strikingly parallel with that of export prices and showed essentially no net change over the period as a whole.

It also seems difficult to sustain a convincing argument that cost-push forces were of major importance with respect either to prices or wages, especially in the sectors in which the price increases were concentrated. Postwar Japanese prices have proved quite as capable of declining as of rising, and many individual prices fell appreciably over the entire period. The products of large industrial firms, which might have been capable of maintaining rigid prices when demand or costs fell and of pushing prices upward at other times, are heavily represented in the wholesale and export price indexes. These indexes show not only no net increase over the whole period, but also a decline during each of the postwar recessions prior to 1973–74; the GNP deflator also declined in the recessions of 1954 and 1957, and its rate of increase was sharply reduced in the recession of 1961–62. The consumer price index, to be sure, showed practically no cyclical sensitivity; but this index includes the heaviest representation of traditional products. The absence of cost push by large industrial corporations is at least suggested by the further fact that corporate profits as a share of national income show no trend over the period and declined as a share of corporate sales.

Although wage rates rose very rapidly, there is no clear evidence that their movement reflected any significant cost-push element.[14] For example, their

13. Unless it is answered, it seems idle to describe Japan's inflation before 1973 as "productivity differential inflation"—the term used by the Economic Planning Agency in *Summary of Economic Survey of Japan, 1973–1974* (Aug. 9, 1974).

14. Some Japanese economists point to substantial differences in wage rates between profitable and unprofitable firms as evidence of cost push and of the strengths of unions. No one can deny the importance of many institutional elements in wage determination, particularly in explaining wage differentials. But the idea of "wage cost push" usually implies institutional elements that exert a significant upward pressure on unit labor costs and thus on prices. This is difficult to establish in the Japanese case.

rate of increase was highly sensitive to the business cycle, even though variations in unemployment rates were exceedingly small. Certainly, the rate of wage increase not only was high by international standards but also accelerated over the postwar period, especially after about 1970. A rather sharp and discontinuous acceleration in 1961 brought the annual rate of increase (in regular wages to regular workers) from a rate of roughly 5 percent a year or less in the previous five years to one of roughly 10 percent a year through 1968, followed by another increase to roughly 15 percent a year through 1972. But each of these successive plateaus was subject to substantial cyclical variation. Because rates of productivity increase also accelerated, unit labor costs rose only slightly over the period.[15] In the absence of cost push, either domestic or imported, it would appear necessary to put the major explanation for price movements in familiar supply and demand terms.

This is essentially the interpretation given by the Price, Incomes, and Productivity Committee that was appointed in 1970 by the Economic Council (the advisory body for the Economic Planning Agency, responsible for proposing the broad macroeconomic objectives of Japanese economic plans) to study the problem of inflation and possible remedies. The committee's report, submitted in May 1972, reviewed possible sources of cost-push inflation; although it found much evidence of institutional or administered elements in wage and price determination and did not rule out all possibility of influence from cost-push forces, its conclusion was that—at least prior to 1970—the Japanese price level was basically demand determined. The rise of wages at a rate too fast to permit stability of the consumer price index was essentially charged to "the tightening situation of labor force which has been in progress since the beginning of the 1960s."[16]

Was Japanese inflation, then, the result of "demand pull"? At least before the late 1960s, there seems little evidence for such a presumption, in any meaningful sense of the term "demand pull." Aggregate demand was exceedingly buoyant; it surely grew very rapidly; but what is relevant for demand-pull inflation is the level and growth of aggregate demand relative to the level

15. A small rise of unit labor costs in manufacturing from 1965 to 1970 just about explains the modest rise in wholesale prices of manufactured products (and presumably the rise in the total wholesale price index and in the export price index shown in Table 3-2 for that period).

16. The quotation is from a mimeographed English translation of the "unauthorized Japanese summary" of the Committee's report. The chairman of the committee was Professor Mikio Sumiya. An earlier commission with a similar mandate, chaired by Professor Hisao Kumagai, had given greater emphasis to cost-push elements in Japanese inflation and, as a result, was considerably more sympathetic to incomes-policy approaches. A third commission has recently been appointed to consider the same questions, this one headed by Professor Keinosuke Baba.

and growth of potential output. And, in general, demand and GNP were not pressing strongly against potential. If and when they did so press, the result was evident mainly in an increased tendency for the current account balance to deteriorate and in increased order backlogs and delivery delays for capital goods; but not in a competitive bidding up of wage rates or other domestic incomes.

More detailed attention is given later to the question of whether any significant overheating occurred even at the peaks of the recurrent cyclical booms. It is concluded that, before the late 1960s, there is, at best, an inconclusive presumption that overheating may have occurred or was threatened at the peaks of two or three of the booms. Instead, the typical and more basic reason why restrictive policy was invoked to cut off the booms was as a defense of Japan's balance-of-payments position. On the other hand, when in the late 1960s there was no longer a need to restrict the growth of output for balance-of-payments reasons while it was still short of potential—and when at about the same time labor supply became a more significant factor limiting total output—Japan's economy did become considerably more exposed to the possibility of demand-pull inflation. It will be argued later that this was a relevant factor in 1968–69 and a major element in the 1973–74 experience.

INTERNATIONAL TRADE AND INFLATION. In light of the above analysis, what explanation and characterization can be applied to the relatively high and steady creeping inflation that was evident in consumer prices and the GNP deflator between 1955 and 1972? If neither cost-push nor demand-pull forces were ordinarily operating and inflation was not imported, why did it occur? The key may lie in the fixation of Japanese economic policymakers, first, on the importance of export expansion as a constraint on rapid domestic growth, and, second, on the importance of export price levels for export expansion. (This fixation of Japanese policy seems conclusively demonstrated by the trauma involved in Japan's acceptance of dollar devaluation in 1971 and of subsequent yen revaluations.)

In those foreign markets into which Japan had to enter in order to achieve its export objectives, competitive prices for the average of Japanese export products were roughly stable or rising only slightly—at least until the late 1960s. Thus, there was no requirement that average Japanese export prices should fall; on the other hand, it seemed essential that they not be allowed to rise appreciably. The stability of export prices in yen—which in a fixed exchange rate system meant their stability in other currencies—thus became, if not a policy objective in itself, at least a prime symbol of policy success: the success not only of exports but also of the entire growth strategy. Although there was little or no resistance to rapid wage increases as long as they did not require higher prices in major export industries, increases that exceeded average productivity gains in export industries clearly threatened achievement of the national goals.

Whenever export prices did rise or the current account moved toward deficit, monetary policy was invariably made restrictive. The conventional explanation of the effects of such tightening on the price level is that this reduced the rate of growth of aggregate demand for goods and services and thus the growth of demand for labor—sufficiently so that the rate of wage increase again slowed down to a rate that did not require higher export prices. A somewhat more institutional explanation suggests that tighter monetary policies reduced profits (or the rate of growth of profits), mainly through a reduced rate of plant use (and thus higher unit overhead costs). Lower profits or slower growth of profits reduced employers' willingness to grant large wage increases and weakened labor's argument that equity demanded them.

On the other hand, wage rates in export industries rose only about as rapidly as productivity in years in which policy was not restrictive; and several of the occasions when policy did become restrictive were not preceded by a rise of export prices. It is our hypothesis that the full explanation for the stability of export prices may lie not only in the above market responses to governmental policy changes, but also in the direct discipline of an accepted national goal of export expansion, and in a generally held belief (at least by employers and possibly even by workers) about the consequences of excessive wage increases for the achievement of that goal.

During this period, stability of consumer goods prices or of the GNP deflator would have been possible only if there had been periodic revaluations of the yen, forcing export prices in yen to decline and requiring that wage increases (in yen) be smaller. It is hardly surprising that this course was not adopted—or probably even seriously advanced. In this rather remote and probably inappropriate sense, it could be said that Japan's inflation in the 1970s was imported. But it seems equally inappropriate to label Japanese inflation in the 1960s as the result of excessive aggregate demand—demand pull—or to describe it as cost push in character.[17]

17. Some have argued that consumer prices were forced upward by a cost push originating in the wage leadership of the industrial sectors, but this also seems to be a forced and inappropriate usage of that term. For a detailed and sophisticated analysis of Japan's postwar inflation, see Yūichi Shionoya, *Gendai no bukka* [The Recent Inflation] (Nihon Keizai Shinbunsha, 1973). A short version appears in his "The Current Inflation in Japan" (paper prepared for the Conference Board Conference on U.S.–Japan Economic Policy, April 1974; processed). The argument in the text reflects several

Increased world demand for Japanese products late in the 1960s, in part
the result of inflation in other countries, began to produce export levels adequate not merely to pay for Japan's imports but also to generate considerable
balance-of-payments surpluses. This high export demand probably contributed to the modest acceleration of domestic inflation in 1968 and 1969.
(This is still another kind of imported inflation.) Much more significant,
however, were the accelerating political pressures from Japan's trading partners that were produced by the payment surpluses. These pressures appeared
to force Japan's policymakers, ultimately, to choose among, first, an accelerated, unilateral liberalization of imports and promotion of capital exports;
second, still faster domestic inflation; and, third, yen revaluation. In the effort to avoid the second or third, they chose the first; and when that proved
inadequate, they accepted (and some seemed rather deliberately to embrace)
the second. In the end, they were forced to accept the third as well. As a by-
product of the indecision and delay in accepting revaluation and of the inter-
vening massive inflow of funds from abroad, Japan experienced in 1973 a
substantial inflation that clearly involved highly excessive domestic demand
—that is, a true demand pull. (The monetary consequences of this fund
inflow constitute a final sense in which inflation may be imported.) The
mechanics of the 1973 inflation are discussed later.

Postwar Business Cycles

Before World War II the Japanese economy, like that of other industrial
and industrializing nations, was subject to frequent and rather severe cyclical
fluctuations. There is clearly some continuity between these fluctuations and
those of the postwar period; and a full understanding of the latter can no
doubt be aided by a study of the earlier experience. Concern here, however,
is with those fluctuations which occurred since 1951,[18] ignoring both prewar
cycles and immediate postwar fluctuations.

---

of Shionoya's points and in general seems not to be basically inconsistent with his
treatment.

18. For a brief but useful summary of Japan's prewar business cycles and an extensive analysis of the postwar cyclical experience up to 1962, see Hugh Patrick, "Cyclical
Instability and Fiscal-Monetary Policy in Postwar Japan," in William W. Lockwood
(ed.), *The State and Economic Enterprise in Japan: Essays in the Political Economy of
Growth* (Princeton University Press, 1965), pp. 555–618; and the references therein to
other studies. A great deal of useful information and analysis appears in a paper by
Miyohei Shinohara, "Postwar Business Cycles in Japan," in Martin Bronfenbrenner
(ed.), *Is the Business Cycle Obsolete?* A Conference of the Social Science Research
Council Committee on Economic Stability (Wiley, 1969).

The Cyclical Record, 1951 to 1973

Most economic analysts accept the dating of postwar business cycles proposed by the Economic Planning Agency (EPA), reproduced in Table 3-3. The duration of expansions varied from two years to almost five, whereas recessions or contractions typically lasted a year or less. Although the EPA has not yet provided an official date for it, another business cycle peak was undoubtedly reached in the fourth quarter of 1973. The expansion terminating then would thus have been of about two years' duration.

What is most remarkable about these cycles is that total real output continued to increase during every contraction except those of 1954 and 1974; only the speed of expansion was reduced. In aggregate terms, true cycles occurred mainly in the rate of expansion. The data in Table 3-4 summarize the record of the movement of GNP in constant prices (and of its main components) during the phases marked off by calendar quarters corresponding to the monthly dates of peaks and troughs given in Table 3-3, beginning with the November 1954 trough and including the expansion that began at the end of 1971 and is assumed to have terminated in the fourth quarter of 1973. During the four contractions shown in Table 3-4, real GNP expanded at annual rates that would have been considered relatively satisfactory for expansion periods in the United States. During the five expansions, on the other hand, real GNP grew at average rates of 10.3, 12.9, 12.9, 12.7, and 9.7 percent. Both the size and the similarity of these rates is surely remarkable.

Unlike total GNP, private expenditures for new plant, equipment, and related durable productive facilities actually decreased during each recession phase except one, that of 1970–71; inventory investment also decreased dur-

Table 3-3. *Dates and Durations of Japanese Business Cycles, 1951–71*

		Duration (in months) of	
Business cycle peak	Business cycle trough	Expansions ending at peak dates	Contractions ending at trough dates
June 1951	October 1951	. . .	4
January 1954	November 1954	27	10
June 1957	June 1958	31	12
December 1961	October 1962	42	10
October 1964	October 1965	24	12
July 1970	December 1971	57	17

Source: Economic Planning Agency, *Japanese Economic Indicators* (April 1974), inside back cover.

Table 3-4. *Changes in Japan's Gross National Product and Its Components during Expansions and Contractions, in Constant 1965 Prices, 1954–73*[a]

Expansion or contraction	Gross national product	Business gross fixed investment	Private residential con- struction	Change in private inven- tories	Net exports of goods and servces	Consumer expendi- tures	Govern- ment purchases[b]
Expansion of 1954:4–1957:2							
Amount (billions of yen)	3,246	949	115	894	−430	1,575	143
Percent[c]	10.3	19.2	10.3	...	...	7.9	1.3
Contraction of 1957:2–1958:2							
Amount (billions of yen)	661	−206	66	−753	475	733	347
Percent[c]	4.4	−10.2	12.4	...	...	8.0	13.1
Expansion of 1958:2–1961:4							
Amount (billions of yen)	8,266	2,601	336	1,649	−646	3,290	1,037
Percent[c]	12.9	29.0	13.6	...	...	8.6	8.9
Contraction of 1961:4–1962:4							
Amount (billions of yen)	576	−109	120	−1,871	474	1,255	708
Percent[c]	2.4	−2.5	12.8	...	...	9.5	17.6
Expansion of 1962:4–1964:4							
Amount (billions of yen)	6,723	1,291	592	736	106	3,213	785
Percent[c]	12.9	13.6	25.0	...	...	10.6	8.0
Contraction of 1964:4–1965:4							
Amount (billions of yen)	1,241	−721	246	108	118	863	626
Percent[c]	4.0	−12.9	14.9	...	...	4.9	11.4
Expansion of 1965:4–1970:3							
Amount (billions of yen)	24,929	8,169	1,490	2,562	57	9,956	2,696
Percent[c]	12.7	23.0	12.5	...	...	9.5	8.0
Contraction of 1970:3–1971:4							
Amount (billions of yen)	3,845	76	230	−1,514	1,302	2,187	1,564
Percent[c]	5.3	0.5	5.4	...	...	6.1	13.9
Expansion of 1971:4–1973:4							
Amount (billions of yen)	12,429	4,896	1,243	359	−1,624	6,072	1,483
Percent[c]	9.7	17.2	15.9	...	...	9.5	6.9

Sources: Economic Planning Agency, *Annual Report on National Income Statistics* (1970 and 1974), table 4; for 1973:4, EPA, *Japanese Economic Indicators* (April 1974), p. 42.

a. All data are seasonally adjusted; yen data are at annual rates.

b. Government purchases represent the sum of "general government consumption expenditure," "gross fixed capital formation by government," and "increase in stocks, government enterprises."

c. Percent change at annual rate.

ing each contraction except that of 1965.[19] Declines of inventory investment typically were larger in absolute amount than declines in fixed investment. But expansions of fixed investment were larger than those of inventory investment—usually far larger. In three of the expansions the rise of business fixed investment exceeded 30 percent of the rise in GNP; and in two, the increment of business fixed investment plus inventory investment exceeded 50 percent of the total rise. Clearly, postwar Japanese business cycles have been basically cycles in private investment: each expansion reflected a boom in fixed investment and, to a lesser extent, in inventory investment; contractions reflected a collapse in inventory investment and, typically, major reductions in fixed investment.

Private residential construction expanded during every cyclical phase, both

19. Even the latter exception is only apparent, however; inventory investment declined sharply in connection with the 1965 recession, but its timing was substantially out of phase.

expansion and recession. Moreover, its expansion rate was sometimes faster during contractions than expansions. As is the case in the United States, the cyclical role of residential construction was irregular, and sometimes countercyclical.

Fluctuations in Japan's net exports of goods and services played a significant and regular role in cycles: declining from a substantial positive to a substantial negative figure during each expansion until that of 1963 and increasing sharply during every contraction.[20] During the three latest expansions—those of 1963–64, 1965–70, and 1972–73—net exports not only remained positive but increased slightly, at least when measured from trough to peak. But as can be seen in Figure 3-1 below, they did decline steadily and sharply, from positive to negative figures, during at least some portion of each of these expansions.

Purchases by Japanese consumers expanded during every postwar cyclical phase. They showed some procyclical pattern, however, in the sense that they expanded somewhat more rapidly during each expansion than during the preceding contraction. Basically, though, they exerted a moderating influence on cyclical movements: during expansions they rose less rapidly than GNP and during contractions more rapidly.

Government purchases of current output—consumption and investment, including that of government enterprises and public corporations, both of fixed capital and in inventories—have played a regular and significant countercyclical role beginning with the 1955–57 expansion. Although government purchases expanded in every cycle phase (except the contraction of 1954, not shown in Table 3-4), their rate of expansion was appreciably faster during each contraction than during the previous expansion.

The foregoing interpretive paragraphs stress the rather impressive regularities in the cyclical pattern, but certain peculiar features of two of the cycles are also revealed in the table. The cycle of 1962:4–1965:4 was the shortest of the postwar cycles, and business fixed investment advanced more slowly than usual during the expansion and fell more sharply during the contraction. The cycle in inventory investment reached both peak and trough well ahead of the general movement. Because of the sharp decline in inventory investment during 1964, the expansion of total output was unusually slow during that last year of expansion. Although fixed investment was relatively weak and the expansion short, the recession itself does not appear unusual either in severity or duration—despite the fact that it was so regarded at the time. And although much publicity was given to the use of fiscal policy

20. Although not shown in Table 3-4, this also occurred in the cycle of 1951–54.

as a means of moderating and shortening the recession, the table reveals no unusual role for government purchases during the recession period.

The cycle of 1965:4–1971:4, on the other hand, is notable for the very long duration of its expansion (fifty-seven months), followed by a somewhat longer contraction than usual. Actually, it was thought in Japan that recovery had begun in the spring or summer of 1971, which would have been consistent with the usual duration of a contraction; but apparently it was deferred by the psychological trauma of those unexpected international monetary and trade events following August 1971 which have become known as "the Nixon shock." Many activities that had turned upward in the spring or early summer turned downward again after August, reaching new lows around the turn of the year. Unusual aspects of the 1972–73 expansion are considered later.

Examination of data other than national product data—including the usual monthly business cycle indicators—adds little to the generalized description in the preceding paragraphs. Cyclical variations in employment, unemployment, and profits appear narrow by U.S. standards; variation in hours worked and overtime hours, however, are pronounced. Interestingly, despite the fact that aggregate production has not declined during recent business cycle contractions in Japan, strong cycles appear in the rate of capacity utilization, resulting from wide swings in fixed investment and in the rate of expansion of output.

As noted earlier, although consumer prices showed no cyclical sensitivity, wholesale and export prices declined in each contraction period, as did the GNP deflator in the contractions of 1954 and 1957–58.

The Cyclical Mechanism and the Role of Policy

Postwar Japanese business cycles have been essentially policy generated: their distinctive profile emerged as restrictive monetary policy drastically slowed the expansion of demand—producing the contraction, or recession—and then the subsequent removal of restrictive policy allowed expansion to resume. This is not to say that cycles might not have occurred in the absence of macroeconomic policies; almost surely they would have. But such cycles have not been observed, their mechanism cannot be described, and in the present context there is little point in attempting to imagine the nature or causes of such hypothetical cycles.

Although post hoc–propter hoc reasoning is never adequate, the schematic presentation of Figure 3-1 immediately suggests the critical role of policy. It shows that:

—Every postwar recession was preceded by a period of policy restraint.

Figure 3-1. *Relation of Phases in Japan's Monetary Policy and Business Cycles, 1953–73*

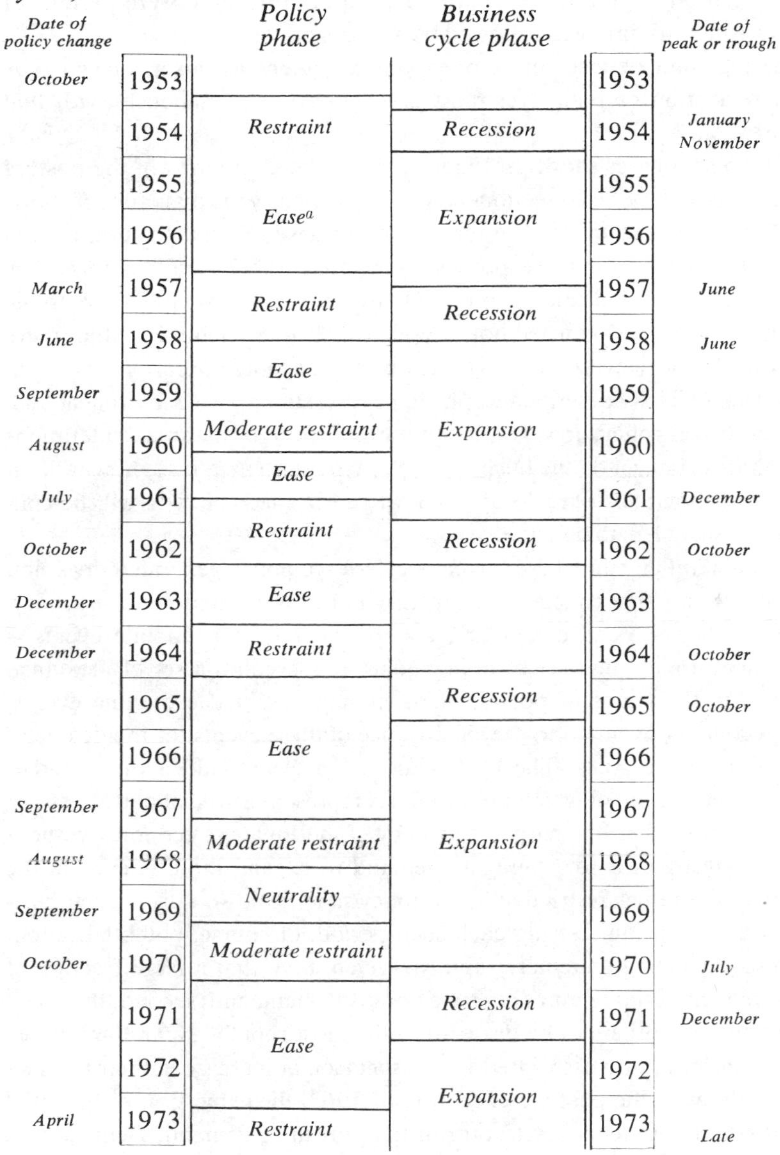

Date of policy change		Policy phase	Business cycle phase		Date of peak or trough
October	1953			1953	
	1954	Restraint	Recession	1954	January November
	1955			1955	
	1956	Ease[a]	Expansion	1956	
March	1957	Restraint	Recession	1957	June
June	1958			1958	June
September	1959	Ease		1959	
August	1960	Moderate restraint	Expansion	1960	
July	1961	Ease		1961	December
October	1962	Restraint	Recession	1962	October
December	1963	Ease		1963	
December	1964	Restraint		1964	October
	1965		Recession	1965	October
	1966	Ease		1966	
September	1967			1967	
August	1968	Moderate restraint	Expansion	1968	
September	1969	Neutrality		1969	
October	1970	Moderate restraint		1970	July
	1971		Recession	1971	December
	1972	Ease		1972	
April	1973	Restraint	Expansion	1973	Late

Sources: Policy data—OECD, *Monetary Policy in Japan* (December 1972), pp. 87–91; Bank of Japan, Economic Research Department, *The Bank of Japan: Its Organization and Monetary Policies* (1973), pp. 31–44; Economic Planning Agency, *Economic Survey of Japan* (various issues). Business cycle data—Table 3-3, above.

a. The shift to ease in 1954–55 is impossible to date because it was not marked by any overt action.

—Each period of restraint except two (and both of these were periods of moderate restraint) was followed by a recession.

—The beginning of each period of expansion either was closely preceded by the relaxation of policy restraint or occurred simultaneously with that relaxation.

The policy phases shown in Figure 3-1 are dated in terms of the posture of monetary policy, because monetary policy is clearly the main tool of short-run demand management. The terms used to describe this posture, as well as the dates given for these phases, come from official publications. The terms immediately indicate the on-off character of monetary policy. With the exception of one period when policy was described as "neutral," either there was restraint or there was ease (no restraint). Japanese fiscal policy has at times been officially described as playing a discretionary role in cyclical fluctuations. Fiscal policy, however, is heavily influenced by many considerations other than its impact on the business cycle. Whether (and, if so, how well) it has been deliberately used to affect short-run business activity will be considered at some length below.

To maintain that Japanese business cycles are policy generated does not, of course, imply that changes in monetary policy were random or arbitrary. Rather, policy responded regularly and predictably to economic events—given, first, a particular set of policy goals and, second, a set of presumed relations in the minds of policymakers among observed economic events, future economic events, and the significance of these events for the degree of realization of the goals. The cycle thus has a clear—and actually rather stable—mechanism, of which policy effects represent a crucial part.

As argued earlier, the natural tendency of the Japanese economy without monetary restraint is for aggregate demand to expand rapidly, even in the presence of a rather restrictive fiscal policy; and it did so during each business cycle expansion. During each such period, of course, potential output was also expanding extremely rapidly—given, first, that a large fraction of the increment of total output consisted of investment, and, second, the ready availability of workers to be drawn into the most rapidly expanding sectors (their transfer in turn associated with a spectacular increase in their productivity). Yet with the possible exception of 1964, the expansion of potential output showed no tendency to outrun the growth of demand. Demand was creating its own supply; and the growth of supply was helping to create the added demand to use it. Nor was there any clear tendency for the expansion of demand to outrun the growth of potential output. Why, then, did the expansions have to be terminated? Why did restraining policy have to slow down the economy? The answer, until the late 1960s, lies mainly in the balance of payments.

Table 3-5. *Percentage Change (at Annual Rate) of Exports and Imports during Business Cycle Expansions and Contractions, 1965 Prices*
Percent

	Annual rate of change	
Expansion or contraction	Exports[a]	Imports[b]
Expansion of 1951:4–1954:1	1.61	38.27
Contraction of 1954:1–1954:4	19.12	−30.96
Expansion of 1954:4–1957:2	13.38	35.63
Contraction of 1957:2–1958:2	7.49	−26.42
Expansion of 1958:2–1961:4	11.93	25.67
Contraction of 1961:4–1962:4	15.24	−7.16
Expansion of 1962:4–1964:4	19.00	17.88
Contraction of 1964:4–1965:4	9.88	6.72
Expansion of 1965:4–1970:3	16.78	17.89
Contraction of 1970:3–1971:4	13.47	−0.22
Expansion of 1971:4–1973:4	12.27	21.38

Sources: Same as Table 3-4.
a. "Exports of goods and services and factor incomes from abroad."
b. "Imports of goods and services and factor incomes paid abroad."

BALANCE OF PAYMENTS AND THE BUSINESS CYCLE. As indicated earlier, each business cycle expansion except those of 1963–64 and 1966–70—and even during at least the first five or six quarters of each of these—was associated with a sharp and steady decline in net exports, from a significant positive to a significant negative figure. Propelled by strong world demand, effective export promotion efforts, and relatively low and stable export prices, Japanese gross exports expanded strongly—in real terms, even more rapidly than GNP—throughout both boom and recession. But except during periods of business cycle contraction, imports increased even faster.

These patterns are clearly shown in Table 3-5, which uses national income and product account data and definitions of exports and imports. Although the growth of exports certainly tended, other things being equal, to accelerate somewhat during recessions (as a lessened rate of growth of demand in the home market freed up supplies for shipment abroad), this effect was apparently swamped by noncyclical factors affecting the growth of exports, for it fails to show up systematically in the table. On the other hand, the table shows that very wide and cyclically systematic swings occurred in imports: from exceedingly rapid growth during expansions to appreciable decline during every contraction except one.[21] During booms, their annual rate of in-

21. During the latter part of the 1964 expansion and early part of the 1965 contraction imports actually fell sharply, probably reflecting the out-of-phase decline of inventory investment. But from peak to trough, imports did rise.

Figure 3-2. *Relation of Net Exports and Export Prices to Changes in Japanese Monetary Policy and Business Cycle Phases, 1951–74*[a]

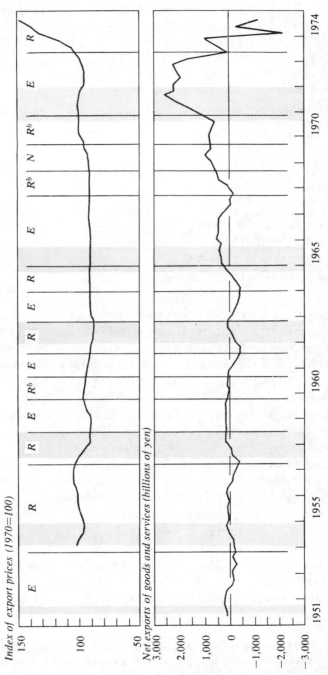

Sources: Export price index, same as Table 3-2. Net exports: 1951–1973:1, EPA, *Annual Report on National Income Statistics* (annual issues); 1973:2, 3, 4, *Japanese Economic Journal* (June 11, Sept. 10, Dec. 10, 1973).
a. Shaded areas represent recessions.
R, E, N = periods of restrictive, easy, and neutral monetary policy, respectively.
b. Period of moderately restrictive policy.

crease ranged between 17.9 and 38.3 percent; the simple average of these rates is 28.1 percent.

During each contraction, the slowing of the growth of consumer incomes and purchases also slowed the expansion of consumer goods imports; to the substantial extent that foreign sellers were the residual source of supply, and given the continued growth of domestic capacity, imports of consumer goods might actually decline even though domestic consumption did not. Imports of capital goods typically declined during contractions, both because imports were a residual source and because total business investment actually declined during almost every contraction period. And because inventory investment declined sharply in every recession, this component of import demand was highly sensitive to the business cycle. These effects were compounded by the fact that the import component of the several categories of GNP varies widely and is highest for those components which are most cyclically sensitive.

Thus, each policy-induced recession—actually, each period of monetary restraint—caused net exports to rise sharply, a tendency clearly visible in Figure 3-2, in which net exports are shown at current prices. But once restraint was removed and expansion began again, the accelerating rise of imports soon surpassed the more steady but also very rapid rise of exports. Sooner or later in each expansion net exports not only declined but turned negative. Because neither substantial or long-term foreign borrowing nor the admission of foreign direct investment was regarded as a desirable means of financing an import surplus, a continuing excess of imports threatened to exhaust the limited available stock of international reserve assets. Before long the brakes had to be applied once more.[22]

A more complete explanation of policy shifts will take account not only of the sign and direction of movement of net exports, but also of the movement of export prices and perhaps of prices more generally. Although there is no clear pattern of export prices rising during expansions, Figure 3-2 shows that export prices rose appreciably over periods of a year or more on several occasions: throughout 1955 and 1956; from late 1958 to the end of 1959; from the end of 1962 until mid-1964; and from early 1969 to mid-1970. Each of these periods of rising export prices coincided with a period

22. For an elegant business cycle model embodying essentially the same hypothesis as presented in the text, see Masao Fukuoka, "The Balance of Payments and a Model of Cyclical Growth," in Ryūtarō Komiya (ed.), *Postwar Economic Growth in Japan* (University of California Press, 1966), pp. 99–103. Support for the argument that the current account balances dominated other objectives of monetary policy, at least through 1963, is found in Keimei Kaizuka, "Objectives of a Stabilization Policy and Monetary Policy" (1967), reprinted in Kaizuka (ed.), *Kin'yu seisaku* [Monetary Policy] (Nihon Keizai Shinbunsha, 1972), pp. 353–73.

of falling net exports and undoubtedly contributed to the restraining policy subsequently adopted.[23] And the decline of export prices in each contraction surely contributed to each decision to terminate restraint.

Obviously, there were important influences on Japan's net export position other than its internal business cycle, including cyclical patterns in the economies of its principal trading partners and such international events as the Korean War, the Suez crisis, and the Vietnam War. All such events that improved Japan's balance of payments permitted expansions to be extended; those which worsened it tended to shorten the period before policy restraint had to be imposed to cut the rate of expansion. After the middle 1960s changes both abroad and in Japan eliminated altogether the need to cut off a boom for balance-of-payments reasons. Thus, somewhat different explanations, discussed below, are required for the ending of the long 1965–70 and the shorter 1972–73 expansions.

DOMESTIC OVERHEATING AND THE BUSINESS CYCLE. This view of the matter rejects alternative interpretations of Japan's business cycles, which insist on finding (or assuming) some evidence of imbalance or distortion during the latter part of each boom. Although some accounts imply that expansions had to end because investment began to outrun the need for additional capacity, most imply the opposite: that demand became excessive relative to potential output, causing the economy to overheat. Such an interpretation of the need for restraint was almost invariably given by the Bank of Japan and other government spokesmen, and is reflected in business and general press accounts. Most analysts argue that the imbalances or distortions or overheating of the boom would inevitably have brought it to an end whether or not policy intervened to do so.

One way to discover whether booms had to terminate because the economy had become overheated—in some sense a more fundamental measure than that net exports had turned negative—is to ask such questions as: "Could the boom have been extended had there been an autonomous spurt in the growth of foreign demand for Japan's exports? Could it have been extended had the Japanese government at that time loosened its restraints on the import of foreign capital?" If the answer to either question is "yes"— and it seems to be—it is difficult to maintain that the boom had to end because the economy became overheated.

A more direct test of whether booms had to be terminated because aggregate demand ran up against potential output would appear to be possible as the result of recent econometric studies that estimate potential output and

23. In many cases, however, rising export prices coincided with rising import prices, part of a general fluctuation of prices of internationally traded goods.

thereby permit measurement of changes over time in the gap between actual and potential. Unfortunately, however, the available estimates of potential do not appear to be sufficiently reliable to permit very precise judgments of changing pressures of demand on productive capacity. Figure 3-3 shows three such measurements: two made by the Economic Planning Agency (for the total economy and for the manufacturing sector) and a third for the whole economy by the Organisation for Economic Co-operation and Development.[24]

The semiannual OECD gap estimates show three periods when the gap was unusually small: late 1955 and early 1956, not close in time to any known period of monetary restriction; from late 1960 through early 1962, corresponding to the restraint period from July 1961 to October 1962; and from 1968 through the first half of 1970, during which time monetary policy moved to moderate restraint in September 1967, to neutral in August 1968, and back to moderate restraint from September 1969 to October 1970. On the other hand, periods of restraint that began in March 1957, September 1959, and December 1963 occurred at times when the OECD index suggests no unusual pressures on capacity.

The message of the quarterly EPA estimates is rather different on several crucial occasions. For example, according to the EPA estimates the restraint decision of July 1961 came a full year and a half after the maximum pressure on capacity; likewise, the movement of the EPA indexes (especially that for manufacturing) is very different from OECD's throughout 1968. EPA's overall index shows the gap to have been at a maximum at the end of 1962; OECD's largest gap was at the end of 1965, and it was nearly as large in 1972. But all three series show the gap to have been unusually large during the period 1962 through 1966 and suggest that the business cycle expansion of 1963–64 did not bring the economy at all close to full utilization of potential output.

A different kind of test of whether monetary restriction was necessitated by pressures on potential output involves a careful examination of the month-

24. The EPA estimates and a description of their methodology were supplied to the author directly. An earlier version, without much detail, appears in S. Shishido, N. Jinsenji, and A. Kohno, *Capital Planning and Capacity Production in Japan* (EPA, 1969). The OECD estimates and an explanation of their basis appear in "The Measurement of Domestic Cyclical Fluctuations." Both essentially first estimate an aggregate production function fitted to actual data for employment, hours worked, capital stock and its rate of utilization, a vintage index measuring the proportion of the capital stock that is new, and a time trend. To obtain the estimates of potential output, hypothetical "high-employment" (or maximum) levels of employment, hours, and (in the EPA measurement) the rate of capital use are inserted into this production function.

Figure 3-3. *Three Measures of the Gap in Japan's Gross National Product during Periods of Restraint and Ease in Monetary Policy, 1955–74*[a]

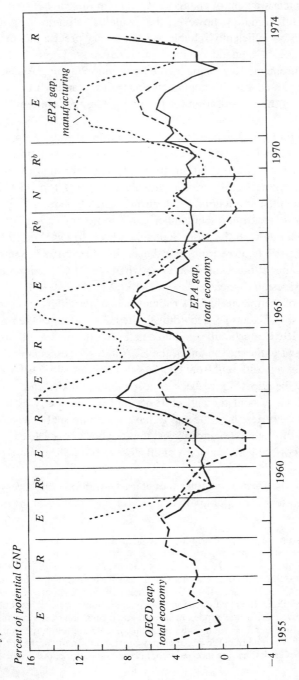

Percent of potential GNP

OECD gap,
total economy

EPA gap,
total economy

EPA gap,
manufacturing

Sources: Organisation for Economic Co-operation and Development (OECD) data, "The Measurement of Domestic Cyclical Fluctuations," *OECD Economic Outlook: Occasional Studies* (July 1973), p. 22; Economic Planning Agency (EPA) data, unpublished materials from the Research Bureau of the EPA.

a. *R, E, N* = periods of restrictive, easy, and neutral monetary policy, respectively.
b. Period of moderately restrictive policy.

by-month movement of a number of monthly time series—which might provide evidence of overheating—during the nine months immediately before each period of monetary restraint. The indicators used, not all of which were available for the entire period, were wholesale prices, all commodities; wholesale prices, manufacturing; overtime in manufacturing; unfilled orders for machinery; the ratio of job offers to applicants (except new graduates) in all industries; the ratio of producers' inventories to shipments, finished goods, mining and manufacturing; and the operating rate in manufacturing. The results of the review may be summarized as follows: First, at each date when monetary policy switched to restraint, the behavior of at least some of these indicators is inconsistent with the overheating hypothesis: its level fails to suggest pressure on resources, its movement is in the wrong direction to suggest overheating, or its movement in the direction suggesting overheating is modest (or not long sustained) or is decelerating (that is, moving less rapidly immediately before the decision than earlier). Thus, there is in each case some ambiguity. Second, in at least two cases—the decisions of December 1963 and September 1967—the preponderance of the evidence seems distinctly counter to the overheating hypothesis. Third, in perhaps three cases —March 1957, September 1959, and September 1969—the preponderance of the evidence might be judged consistent with an expectation of overheating. These findings are thus only in part consistent with those based on general measurements of potential output.

In contrast with the ambiguity of signals of overheating, however, a sharply declining and usually negative current account balance, accompanied on several occasions by rising export prices, gave clear and unambiguous signals for policy tightening on balance-of-payments grounds—in each case before September 1969. But neither the statistics of trade and export prices nor the public discussion of policy issues in the summer and fall of 1969 indicate that balance-of-payments considerations played any significant part in the decision to tighten policy in September, though both the statistics and the contemporary discussion reveal grounds for appreciable concern about inflation. (It was noted earlier that a large part of the entire net increase in the wholesale price index between 1955 and 1970 occurred in 1969 and 1970.) Clearly, this decision in favor of restraint was based on considerations quite different from the earlier ones.

MONETARY POLICY AND THE ECONOMY. There is need only to sketch the mechanism through which restrictive policy brought each business cycle expansion to an end and through which the release of restrictive policy generated a takeoff into renewed rapid expansion. The direct impact of restrictive monetary policy on inventory investment occurred almost immediately through announcement effects and, perhaps secondarily, and with some lag, through financial effects. Announcement effects involve a simple change in expectations: Japanese businessmen are likely to believe that a policy decision to slow down the economy will in fact slow it down, and they may begin to act on the basis of that announcement without waiting for a demonstration that the economy has in fact slowed down. Because business action to reduce the rate of inventory accumulation can be taken almost immediately —through reducing the level (or rate of increase) of production and purchases—restrictive effects begin to be felt almost at once. Similar effects, both announcement and financial, are felt on business fixed investment; but because of the considerable lag between investment decisions and production of capital goods, effects on the rate of increase of output occur more slowly through this channel.

A mere slowing down of the rate of expansion of output can easily cumulate, through accelerator effects, into a greater slowdown or even an actual downturn in either inventory investment or fixed investment. A slowing down of the rate of increase of output together with a continued rapid increase in industrial capacity as a result of past investment decisions reduces the rate of capacity use (creates excess capacity), which in turn leads to a further slowing down of the increase (or even a reduction of the level) of new fixed investment and thus of the production of capital goods. Lower rates of production expansion in their turn slow the growth of consumer incomes and thus of consumer purchases, further strengthening the accelerator-effect repercussions on investment both in plant and inventories. On the other hand, net exports quickly began to recover; residential construction is little affected (or is possibly affected favorably by the easier availability of construction labor and materials as a result of reduced industrial construction); and government spending continues to rise and its increase even accelerates (see Table 3-4). Given the strength of these latter components of demand and the confidence that strong expansion would soon be renewed, Japanese recessions normally took the form of a sharp slowdown of expansion but not a contraction of total output.

The mechanism of the "lower turning point"—the revival of rapid expansion—is not necessarily exactly the reverse of the mechanism which operates at the peak. Once begun, the cumulative interactions of the recessionary process take some time to work themselves out, and the removal of restraint may have come before this point is reached. Even when it is reached, strong revival, especially of fixed capital investment, may not occur immediately, since the recession almost surely has created a substantial volume of temporarily excess capacity. A faster rate of fixed investment, or even of inventory investment, is not immediately urgent, even though businesses may be fully confident that the boom will soon revive once restraint has been lifted. Moreover, because there is some lag between investment decisions and production of capital goods, it may take a while for the process of expansion to pick up steam. Conceivably, some external nudge may even have been needed to get the expansion under way—as was believed to have been the case in both 1965 and 1972.

Monetary Policy[25]

Direct management of Japanese monetary policy is vested in the Bank of Japan (BOJ). Although the BOJ has nominal independence, its actions in all fundamental policy matters are fully consistent with governmental policy, in which the powerful Ministry of Finance (MOF) usually calls the tune. (The MOF also carries operational responsibilities for all fiscal affairs, including preparation of the budget, and plays the primary role in international monetary and domestic financial affairs.) The other major power center in economic matters is the Ministry of International Trade and Industry (MITI), which has major operating responsibilities in microeconomic and international economic affairs and close ties to the centers of private economic power (as a result of which it is reputed to have a more expansionary policy bias than the MOF and the BOJ). As in any parliamentary system, all major policy decisions in principle are made by the cabinet, which is chaired by the prime minister and responsible to the Diet. But unless the prime minister is actively interested and especially knowledgeable in macroeconomic affairs, the minister of finance usually plays a dominant role in monetary (as in fiscal) policy decisions.

In addition to the ministries, there is the Economic Planning Agency, which is headed by a director general of cabinet rank and is responsible to a committee chaired by the prime minister. The EPA's large and well-qualified

25. Useful and up-to-date descriptions in English of Japan's monetary policy arrangements can be found in two publications of the Bank of Japan, Economic Research Department: *The Japanese Financial System* (1972), and *The Bank of Japan: Its Organization and Monetary Policies* (1973). A more analytical account is found in OECD, "Monetary Policy in Japan," *OECD Monetary Studies Series* (December 1972). A more extensive work is L. S. Pressnell (ed.), *Money and Banking in Japan,* Bank of Japan, Economic Research Department, trans. S. Nishimura (London: Macmillan, 1973). A Japanese discussion of the workings of monetary policy, which is believed to be generally consistent with the account given here, appears in a symposium on monetary policy by Ryūichirō Tachi, Shōzaburo Fujino, Yoichi Shinkai, and Yoshio Suzuki, *Tōyō keizai* [The Oriental Economist] (February 1974), pp. 10–29.

economic staff supplies the secretariat for Japanese economic planning and has important responsibilities and capabilities in monitoring, analysis, reporting, and forecasting all aspects of economic developments and policies.

Although there are many formal similarities between monetary policy in Japan and elsewhere, the use of a common terminology often conceals wide differences of substance. The essential purpose of monetary policy in Japan, as elsewhere, is to influence—mainly through alterations in the availability of credit—the rate of expansion of business activity through affecting the volume of business fixed and inventory investment and residential construction.

No understanding of Japan's monetary policy is possible without reference to the structure of its financial arrangements, which are described in some detail in Chapter 4 of this volume. Unlike the situation in the United States and some other developed industrial countries, banks in Japan are by far the largest source of finance for private business. Corporate equity is quite narrow by international standards and industrial bonds essentially just a special form of bank loan. For reasons explained in Chapter 4, very little new capital is raised by stock issues, and there is, in effect, almost no open market in long- or medium-term debt securities, governmental or private. Thus, little investment is financed other than through bank loans or trade credit; and individual savers hold little of their financial wealth other than in the form either of currency or of demand, time, or saving deposits. Oversimplifying, there are two major forms of assets, money (and near moneys) and real goods, and two forms of private financial liability, the loan liability of businesses to banks and the deposit liability of banks to individuals and businesses. Government securities, the total amount of which is modest, are held mainly by the Central Bank and private financial institutions; and the latter hold most of the relatively small volume of local government securities, government-guaranteed securities of public companies, industrial bonds, and the debentures issued by a special class of banks (long-term credit banks). Because the yields on these securities are maintained artificially low, banks and other financial institutions hold these securities unwillingly. (Yields can be artificially low because almost all of these securities are, in effect, forced upon the banks.) The relevance of these characteristics of financial markets will become clear as the operations of monetary policy are discussed.

Policy Instruments

For the banking system to be able to expand the total of its loans to private business, it must receive either an increment in its reserve balances with the Bank of Japan or a reduction in the ratio of legally required reserves to deposits (since Japanese banks apparently never hold reserves significantly in excess of minimum legal requirements). One way in which the volume of bank reserves is altered originates on the initiative of particular banks. Some of these (particularly the larger ones) are allowed to borrow from the BOJ, on the collateral of selected bank assets, at an interest (or discount) rate whose variation is regarded as indicating the basic posture of current monetary policy.

DISCOUNT POLICY. Although variations in the discount rate are of great symbolic significance, their practical importance ordinarily is slight. The discount rate—for example, that applicable against government securities[26]— varied during the 1960s between a low of 5.84 percent and a high of 7.67 percent; most of the variation was between 6.21 percent and 6.94 percent. Variation during the 1970s has been considerably wider: after reaching a low of 4.25 percent in 1972, it was successively raised to a high of 9.00 percent in December 1973.[27] By agreement, the banks adjust their basic, or prime, rate of business lending by a formula that reflects a part of the variation in the discount rate. Clearly, the resulting changes in the cost of credit to business have normally been meaningless in encouraging or deterring business borrowing.[28] But the signal of a discount rate increase—or several such increases within a few months—represents a very clear announcement that the government has decided to slow down the economy.

Banks that borrow from the BOJ (and that wish to do so in the future) become thereby subject to a very real oversight of their business by the BOJ,

26. In the past, different discount rates on various kinds of bank collateral—for example, bills originating in export trade or in imports, domestic bills, and government securities—have been used as a special means of encouraging or discouraging banks to lend in specified directions. Since the existence and variation of these differences reflect microeconomic or balance-of-payments objectives, the complications which these different rates would otherwise add to this simple description of discount policy are ignored here. These differences have now been eliminated.

27. See Bank of Japan, *Economic Statistics Annual, 1973*, table 10, pp. 23–24.

28. Between 1955 and 1973 the annual average of the lending rates of major banks was never lower than 6.8 percent nor higher than 8.1 percent. See ibid., table 23, pp. 61–62. (In January 1975, however, it stood at 9.48 percent.) It is possible that changes in the percentage of compensating balances required by banks to be held on deposit by borrowers may somewhat reinforce interest rate variation. Available evidence suggests, however, that the importance of this effect is rather minimal. See, for example, OECD, *Monetary Policy in Japan* (1972), p. 37 and note. Clearly, greater effective variation of average recorded interest rates could have been obtained, not only through larger changes in the basic rate but also through more substantial reclassification of borrowers as between those entitled to the lowest, or basic, rate and all others. Frequency distributions published by the BOJ show an extremely wide range of variation in the interest rates charged to individual borrowers (quite consistent with other data cited by Caves and Uekusa in Chapter 7 in this book).

for borrowing from the BOJ is a privilege, not a right. If BOJ personnel believe that a bank is abusing its privilege either in the quantity and continuity of its borrowing or in the nature of its lending, it can be turned down the next time it applies or have uncomfortable conditions imposed. To be sure, most banks eligible to borrow were heavily in debt to the BOJ throughout most of the postwar period—and they needed to be, because for many years this was the major channel through which reserves were supplied to the banks to support the fantastic increase in credit and deposits required by postwar economic growth.[29] Thus, it was difficult for anyone to be sure what was or should be considered a proper or an excessive use of BOJ credit. To give more content to this notion, various forms of quantitative ceilings were established during the postwar period on the amounts individual banks could borrow, defined in terms of penalty rates applicable to borrowing above set amounts.[30] Although the aggregates of these ceilings are now essentially fixed, the total of bank borrowing outstanding can and does fluctuate (at the initiative of the banks), from very small amounts up to the limit set by the aggregate of ceilings, and with the BOJ showing increasing concern about each bank's operations the closer it approaches its own ceiling.

OPEN-MARKET OPERATIONS. The second way in which the reserves of the banking system fluctuate is through what are called open-market operations by the Bank of Japan. In the United States, the Federal Reserve System buys and sells government securities in the open market that exists for such securities—from any holder who may wish to sell or to any person or institution who may wish to buy. The intervention of the Federal Reserve as buyer or seller directly affects the prices of such securities (and thus the market rate of interest) either appreciably or little, depending on the magnitude of its transactions and on the effects of the resulting price (that is, interest rate) changes on the willingness or desire of the private holders or prospective purchasers to own securities. Sellers to the Federal Reserve may include banks, whose reserves increase when the Fed pays for the securities; however, sellers other than banks deposit their payments from the Fed in their banks, which simi-

---

29. For a discussion of this overloan, see Chapter 4.

30. These individual ceilings, of course, are adjusted frequently to reflect the growth of individual banks' resources other than from the BOJ. Once the system of open-market operations (described below) became in the late 1960s the major means by which reserves were supplied to the system, the aggregate amount of the individual banks' discount ceilings was essentially stabilized—even though the ceilings of individual banks continue to vary on the basis of a formula that is designed to measure the growth of its own resources but inevitably is arbitrary. There remains a penalty rate (now an extra 4 percent) for above-ceiling borrowing; but ceilings apparently are no longer ever exceeded (other than over the year's end, when the penalty rate does not apply).

larly adds to aggregate bank reserves. Sales by the Fed withdraw reserves in parallel fashion. But which banks gain and lose reserves by open market operations is not determined by—nor is it of interest to—the Federal Reserve.

In Japan, however, there is effectively no open market for government (or government-guaranteed) bonds, and only modest amounts of such securities are held outside the financial system. Thus, when the BOJ engages in open-market purchases, the amount of such purchases is allocated among specific banks in specified amounts. This allocation is administratively determined, although the individual quotas are calculated by formulas that attempt to provide reasonable equity among competing institutions. Banks are always happy enough to give up some of their bonds on a call from the BOJ, because such bonds had been acquired in the first instance under duress, through their compulsory participation (also in accordance with specific quotas) in the underwriting of government securities. BOJ purchases are made at the (largely nominal) prices previously ruling in the (thin) open market, and do not affect that price. Although these so-called open-market operations in bonds preserve the form and fiction of voluntary transactions (on the side of the private sector), they can be thought of as, in effect, compensated compulsory changes either in the reserves or the reserve ratios of particular institutions.[31]

CONTROL OF RESERVE-RATIO. In addition to the above methods, through which banks seek and acquire additional reserves at their own initiative (discounts at, and borrowing from, the Bank of Japan) or by which reserves are

31. As a means of smoothing seasonal variations in reserves, short-term sales and purchases to and from the banks have recently been introduced under repurchase agreements under which the repurchase price is fixed at the price of the initial purchase. During the period between purchase and repurchase interest is paid or received based on the call-money rate in effect on the date of original purchase. Other means have been developed even more recently for the BOJ to supply to or recapture reserves from the banking system—namely, through buying and selling of bills: beginning in 1966 the sale to call-loan dealers of short-term government securities, which until then had been held only by the BOJ; beginning in 1971 the sale of Bank of Japan bills (of three-month maturity or less) to call dealers and banks; and, beginning in 1972 (and of by far the greatest importance) the sale to, and purchase from, dealers and banks of selected commercial bills of three-month maturity or less. These transactions are made either directly or through the new discount market that came into being in 1971 as an adjunct to the call-money market (see below). The BOJ buys and sells at rates that obviously make the market, that vary somewhat more frequently than the discount rate, and that generally range from 1.25 to 2 percent above the discount rate. By the end of 1973 the purchase of such bills had become the single largest means through which the BOJ was providing reserves to the banking system (bills bought were 4.03 billion yen, government securities [bonds], 2.25 billion; loans and discounts, 2.37 billion; and foreign exchange, 3.73 billion). See BOJ, *Economic Statistics Annual, 1973*, table 12, pp. 27–28.

provided or withdrawn at the initiative of the BOJ (open-market operations), a third tool of monetary policy lies in the authority of the BOJ to vary the required ratios of reserves against deposits within a wide range permitted by the basic law.[32] To date, however, these ratios have been set at very low levels: during the 1960s the ratio of required reserves against time deposits varied only between 0.50 percent and 1.00 percent for the largest banks, and for the smallest banks and other financial institutions subject to reserve requirements it was at 0.25 percent throughout. Against other deposits the required ratio ranged from a minimum of 1 percent to a maximum of 3 percent for the largest banks and was usually lower for others.[33] Changes were infrequent: on only six occasions during the 1960s was there a change in the level of any reserve ratio, and several of the changes affected only one or a few types of deposits or groups of institutions. During 1973 and early 1974, however, the ratios were raised five times, and by July 1974 they ranged up to 4.25 percent.

Low reserve ratios mean that small changes in them can have very large effects on the volume of deposits. With the same volume of reserves, a reduction of reserve requirements from 0.75 to 0.50 percent or from 3.00 to 2.00 percent would permit a 50 percent expansion in the total volume of deposits. More significantly, low ratios mean that—with a fixed reserve ratio —small changes in the volume of reserves can permit very large changes in deposits.

The volume of reserves does change, of course, not only through the exercise of monetary policy, but also as the result of factors unassociated with short-run monetary policy. Unless fully offset by deliberate policy actions, reserves increase when there is a balance-of-payments surplus and decrease with a deficit; they increase when the BOJ lends to the government and the government spends the proceeds, and decrease when a government surplus is used to retire debt to the BOJ or to increase the government's deposit balance with the BOJ; they decrease when currency is withdrawn by the public, and increase when currency flows back into the banking system; they increase or decrease as the float of uncleared checks increases or decreases; and they change for still other reasons. Monetary policy either offsets or reinforces such changes in bank reserves—through the operations just re-

32. Under present law the BOJ is permitted to set required reserve ratios at any level up to 10 percent; an increase to a 20 percent maximum is under discussion.

33. See BOJ, *Economic Statistics Annual, 1973,* table 11, pp. 25–26. By contrast, the ratio against time and savings deposits in the United States in the 1960s ranged between 3 and 6 percent, and against demand deposits, between 12 and 17 percent. See Board of Governors of the Federal Reserve System, *Federal Reserve Bulletin.*

viewed—to achieve that particular growth of reserves deemed appropriate to the economic situation.

RESERVE MANAGEMENT AND THE CALL MARKET. The various means through which reserves are provided or withdrawn obviously are closely interrelated. If sufficient reserves were supplied through open-market operations or a balance-of-payments surplus, no bank would ever need to borrow; whereas if reserve policy were sufficiently restrictive all banks would be borrowing or discounting up to their individual ceilings. Because the BOJ only occasionally wishes the growth of reserves to approach either such limit, a substantial, though varying, volume of BOJ loans and discounts is usually outstanding. Within these limits, the discount mechanism provides banks some flexibility in what would otherwise be the rigid constraints imposed by the Japanese methods for supplying reserves: on the one hand, the rigid quotas on open-market sales or purchases and on the other, the individual bank ceilings on borrowing. When money is tight, however, and all or most banks are at their ceilings, it is difficult for them to increase their net lending —no matter how urgent the needs of their customers.

To be sure, *individual banks* have means of acquiring added reserves, though at a price: they can borrow in the call market or sell bills through the new discount market. These markets essentially correspond in function to the federal funds market in the United States. Smaller banks and other nonbank financial institutions typically lend in the call market on short term (from a half day to a month) or purchase in the bill market, using any excess reserves or otherwise temporarily unneeded funds, and at what may be a good rate of return. Such institutions are likely to receive deposits substantially in excess of the loan demand directed to them; and since there is no genuine securities market (as, for example, in U.S. Treasury bills) in which such funds can be placed, they usually have (in the aggregate) rather substantial assets in call loans and purchased bills. The borrowers in these markets are almost entirely large banks (the so-called city banks), which need extra funds (given their customers' demands for loans) to meet their reserve requirements without borrowing (or borrowing excessively) from the BOJ. Thus, the call and bill markets provide a means through which every bank— regardless of the loan demand of its own customers—can avoid idle reserves or acquire needed reserves on short notice and through which all of the outstanding reserves are mobilized to support the maximum volume of bank credit which that volume of reserves (and the required reserve ratios) will permit.

Call-market rates are rather more flexible than other Japanese interest rates: during periods of tight money in the 1950s and early 1960s the rate on the principal type of call money several times briefly exceeded 11 percent and once exceeded 20 percent; in periods of easy money it fell as low as 3.65 percent. But between 1965 and 1973 the call rate never exceeded 8.75 percent, which, given the several tight money periods during this interval, might seem rather surprising.[34] As noted earlier, the BOJ can use the call market as a means of supplying reserve funds, although it has not ordinarily made extensive use of this method. (Now, of course, the closely related bill market has become a major means of supplying reserves.) Whether in these ways, however, or through its reputed occasional direct guidance to call-market participants, or through the use of its other policy instruments, the BOJ obviously kept the call rate within fairly narrow limits, at least between 1965 and 1973. If the call rate or bill rate were to fluctuate sharply, it might have a significant effect on the marginal cost of banks' lending and thereby generate fluctuations in banks' loan rates that might help to equate the supply and demand for loans. But the past fluctuations in call rates do not appear wide enough to have any such effect—and, as already noted, the interest rate on bank loans is exceedingly stable, and is tied by formula to the discount rate.

WINDOW GUIDANCE.[35] The final instrument of monetary policy, a specific quantitative ceiling on the aggregate lending of each bank, is used only during periods of tight money; and at other times it remains essentially in abeyance. Originally confined to major banks, this control now extends to banks of all sizes, as well as to some nonbank financial institutions. In the 1960s it usually was applied on a quarterly basis, but more recently it has been sharpened to be applicable monthly. In many ways this is the single most significant instrument of Japanese monetary policy. More accurately, perhaps, it might be described as the sharp cutting edge of monetary policy, its precision permitting restrictive policy to be applied far more rigorously than would otherwise be possible.

There are probably several major reasons why it was judged necessary to resort to this detailed direct control. First, given the very low reserve ratios applicable in Japan, small variation in the volume of reserves could, as noted, permit exceedingly wide variation in credit expansion. Very precise control of reserve volume would thus be necessary if control of this volume were to

34. BOJ, *Economic Statistics Annual, 1973,* table 27, pp. 65–66.
35. This control is called "guidance" because the BOJ asserts that it provides only suggestions that banks can take or leave. It is called "window guidance" because these suggestions are made to banks as they come to the BOJ's "discount window." There is, of course, no window, and the guidance is invariably accepted.

be the principal method of monetary restraint. But this control can never be precise because of unexpected and uncontrollable changes in the flow of international payments, the rate of absorption of currency, changes in float, and so on. During easy-money periods this causes no great problem, because the discount mechanism and the call market can cushion short-run fluctuations in reserve volume, as well as in the needs and resources of individual banks. But when money is tight the cushion of flexibility supplied by the discount mechanism disappears, because all banks then approach their borrowing limits. At these times, moreover, the adjustment of reserves through open-market operations is very difficult (or certainly was difficult before development of the bills market), because of the personalized and essentially arbitrary character of its quota system.

Administration of an exceedingly tight reserve position under these circumstances would throw an enormous burden of adjustment on the call (and now the bills) market. Call rates not only would rise to very high levels but also would be subject to violent fluctuation. Under such circumstances banks actually might be tempted—or occasionally even forced—to try to liquidate some of their bond holdings by dumping them on the very thin open securities market. But this market cannot absorb more than trivial amounts of bonds without having prices fall to extremely low levels. The Japanese government, like most others, does not relish having the prices of its bonds falling to such levels. Moreover, even very wide swings in call-market or bond interest rates—given the facts that ordinary enterprises do not borrow in these markets nor ordinary holders of wealth participate in them—would do little or nothing either to curtail business investment or to draw extra liquidity into the banking system from the nonbank sector.[36] Thus, it must have seemed far more sensible—indeed, almost necessary—not to attempt to exert the maximum of restraint on bank lending through pressure on reserve volume, but instead to use quantitative ceilings on each bank's lending, through window guidance as the cutting edge of restrictive policy.

Administrative limitation on the volume of loans that each bank can make of course forces each bank to impose some form of rationing on its loan customers, who therefore will be required in some way to share any shortage of loanable funds. The basis for each bank's allocations to its individual customers will presumably reflect the extent and nature of traditional ties be-

36. To be sure, high call rates might require higher bank loan rates, which would somewhat deter investment. However, all the evidence suggests that Japanese banks are not strict profit maximizers in the short run; thus, it is unlikely that bank loan rates would reflect the true marginal cost of funds to the banks.

tween bank and borrower, as well as consideration of the bank's long-term business strategy.[37] The administered sharing of a shortage of funds by a form of rationing removes or reduces any role for the price of credit in rationing its use. Consequently, the supply of resources to the banks can be kept less stringent than would otherwise be necessary, the price of funds (interest rates) in the call market and elsewhere can remain lower (as well as more stable) than otherwise, yet the supply of bank lending can be effectively restricted. In short, reliance on window guidance supports the maintenance of Japan's policy of low and stable interest rates.

The use of rationing devices at various points in the machinery of monetary policy—quotas for the conduct of open-market operation, ceilings on each bank's discounts, and direct limits on each bank's lendings—can be and is in each case explained and defended as required by the absence of effective securities markets. Banks have no reason to hold secondary reserves in the form of government securities if there is no bond market in which they can be liquidated. A bond market cannot exist in the face of a strong preference of savers to hold their wealth in the form of deposit balances rather than fixed income securities. But these circumstances, which require the use of rationing, are never going to change as long as the low interest rate policy is maintained and rationing remains the central weapon of monetary restraint. Businesses might very well prefer to issue bonds to fund their indebtedness, even if the bond rate were as high or higher on the average than the cost of bank loans. (Naturally, with the bond rate maintained artificially low, they would prefer to issue bonds, but are unable to do so except in limited amounts and to banks that can be persuaded to acquire them as part of some kind of package deal.) But in compensation for their inability to borrow long term at contractually assured interest rates, at least the larger and more powerful firms have reasonable assurance of a supply of loans, even in periods of tight money, from the bank or banks with which they have traditional relations, in a volume large enough at least to roll over current outstanding indebtedness and at an interest cost at most only moderately higher than normal. They may be unable to borrow all they would like at such

37. Window guidance has been described in the past as unconcerned with the type or distribution of a bank's lending but only with its aggregate amount. There is unofficial evidence, however, that banks were also given informal instruction—or chose to follow certain signals—that indicated that preference should be given to particular types of customers or of loans. In 1973 banks were officially instructed to discriminate against loans for "speculative purchases of commodities and land," and in January 1974 the discrimination was broadened to include wholesale and retail establishments, trading companies, loans for villas and luxury housing, and so on; a preferential list was also provided.

times; but they are in no danger of ever having to refinance their bank indebtedness at some frightful interest rate. Thus, the larger enterprises, at least, have no powerful stake in changing the system.[38]

The tools of monetary policy, the structure of financial markets, and the low interest rate policy therefore are all part of a single system. In this system, monetary policy—in many of its aspects and for a considerable part of the time—takes essentially the form of a direct control that involves essentially arbitrary quantitative quotas or ceilings at several points. Instead of allowing impersonal market forces to decide which banks will grow faster or slower, which bank customers will be served or denied, it is all decided (at least during periods of tight money) by various forms of rationing. There is little doubt that the system works in controlling aggregate investment—and rather effectively. And although there is clearly some economic cost in terms of efficiency when arbitrary and personalized decisions are substituted for the impersonal direction of a competitive market, it is only an article of faith on the part of liberal economists, rather than a demonstrated fact, that this cost is high.[39] And to whatever extent that rationing provides preferred financing for favored industries, it further serves as a tool of microeconomic policy.

Obviously, the use of rationing instead of price during periods of restriction—which has been in effect during about 40 percent of the time over the past twenty years—means that the average rate of interest could be kept considerably lower than it would otherwise have been. Low interest rates raise the present value of the yield from real investments in plant, equipment, and inventories relative to the cost of those investments. Yet the volume of such investments is restricted (by credit rationing) from expanding to the point at which investment yields would be bid down—or costs bid up—sufficiently to reduce the profits of entrepreneurship to equal the minimum supply price of entrepreneurship. This actually may be the most fundamental reason for the buoyancy of investment demand in Japan.

38. In describing this system and its effects, Tsunehiko Watanabe argues that the really powerful firms are taken care of otherwise—presumably through government loans—and that *ordinary* borrowers, who must depend on the banks, bear the brunt of rationing. See his "National Planning and Economic Development: A Critical Review of the Japanese Experience," *Economics of Planning,* vol. 10 (1970), pp. 45–46.

39. Undoubtedly there are administrative difficulties, which use up real resources, in connection with such a system. For example, there is reputed to be a considerable amount of secret—that is, illegal—lending, presumably concealed behind some kind of window dressing. A newspaper report in 1973 estimated the amount of secret lending at ¥800 billion, or about 1.5 percent of total bank lending. Neither private nor official sources apparently challenge this estimate, but they do suggest that tighter administrative procedures had (in 1974) reduced it somewhat.

Moreover, interest rates have been progressively lowered during the postwar period. The basic discount rate, which for this purpose adequately represents the movement of other interest rates, stood at 7.67 percent in the easy-money period of 1956–57, reached 7.30 percent in that of 1958–59, 6.94 percent in 1960–61, 6.21 percent in 1962–63, 5.84 percent in 1965–67, and was progressively reduced to 4.25 percent in 1971–72. A roughly similar downward progression of interest rates describes successive periods of tight money—until, that is, that of 1973–74.[40]

Monetary Policy Tools in Combination

The execution of monetary policy in Japan has generally not involved choices among the four tools described above but the more or less simultaneous adjustment of all four. The on-off character of monetary policy during alternating periods described as "severe (or moderate) restraint" and "ease" ordinarily has involved sharp, discontinuous changes in the use of all four tools.

During periods of easy money, reserves are provided to banks in essentially whatever amount they need to meet the loan needs of their customers and at essentially stable interest rates. The movement from easy to tight money may be foreshadowed by some reduction in the rate at which open-market operations provide additional reserves to the banks or perhaps by a less accommodating attitude toward discount requests. Some evidence of these appears in a tendency for interest rates on call money to begin to edge up a few months prior to the onset of most tight-money periods. During this time BOJ officials usually make public statements referring to the dangers of overheating, and warning about overextension of credit. But when tight money is invoked, all major guns in the BOJ arsenal are fired almost simultaneously. Within a few months—sometimes within a single month—one or more of these steps is usually taken: the discount rate is raised; reserve ratios are increased; and window guidance is formally resumed. With the first of these steps, usually an increase in the discount rate, tight money has formally arrived. If reserve ratios are increased, some immediate provision of reserves through open-market operations may be required; and, in any case, the action is likely to force a number of banks into (or deeper into) debt to the BOJ through discount operations. But, clearly, the BOJ is not playing games: reserve positions and loan rationing are indeed tightened, and the growth of bank lending rather quickly begins to be curtailed.

40. BOJ, *Economic Statistics Annual, 1973*, pp. 55, 57.

These initial steps have usually been followed by others over a period of some months: the discount rate may be raised a second or third time; related steps may be taken to limit further the access of banks to funds from abroad; and adjustments in the structure of discount rates or in the exchange control system may be made to discourage imports.

The transition from tight money back to easy usually is not as sharply delineated. But the first step, typically a cut in the discount rate, is seen to mark the official end of the tight-money policy. By that time, the growth of bank reserves will already have gotten under way, and the call-money rate will probably have begun to soften. Over the subsequent six months or more a series of further actions will be taken, reversing all of the earlier tightening measures.

As noted earlier, two periods of "moderate restraint" failed to generate a recession—even one of the Japanese variety. But in every case restraint has slowed down the rate of increase of bank lending and the growth either of inventory investment or business fixed investment or both. And in every case—until 1969—it has caused or been accompanied by a reversal in the direction of movement of net exports and often of export prices.

Recent Monetary Policy

The fact that one period, in 1968 and 1969, has been officially labeled as one of "neutral money" might suggest that the on-off character of monetary policy has begun to evolve toward one of more continuous fine tuning, which may have been the intention at the time.[41] But whatever the intention, the subsequent episode of restraint in 1969–70, again labeled "moderate," was followed at first by a period in which money was aggressively made more easy than at any time in the past, and then by one of record tightness in restraint. This episode merits closer attention, both because of its inherent interest and to illustrate more concretely the use of the tools described earlier.

The monetary restraint begun in September 1969 took hold about as usual and precipitated a peak in business activity in July 1970. Within a few months, the wholesale price index had stabilized, the increase in consumer prices was normal, and the only problem with the balance of payments was the embarrassingly large surplus. In October 1970, therefore, the shift to

41. Objectively, however, it is difficult to see how this period differed from earlier "easy-money" periods other than, first, in the continuation of something called "liquidity condition guidance" to major banks when window guidance was terminated, and, second, in the fact that the discount rate was reduced to a level somewhat higher than in the preceding easy-money period of 1965–67.

ease began, with a reduction of the discount rate from 6.25 to 6 percent. (There had been no increase in the reserve ratio during the preceding period of moderate restraint, so there was no occasion to reduce it.)

Despite the shift to ease, recession continued throughout 1971, prolonged by the adverse psychological effects of the dollar devaluation and import surcharge that accompanied the imposition of wage and price controls in the United States in August. Throughout 1971 policy moved progressively toward extreme ease, with further successive 0.25 percentage point reductions of the discount rate in January, May, and July, and a 0.5 percentage point reduction in December. Simultaneously the massive inflow of foreign exchange that was swelling bank reserves was only partly offset by a reduction of the BOJ's open-market position and by a remarkable drop in bank borrowing and discounting. For almost the first time in the postwar period, Japanese banks were practically out of debt to the Bank of Japan.[42]

With money easy and interest rates falling steadily, businesses increased their borrowing sharply, even though they were cutting back both fixed and inventory investment. Thus, business firms as well as banks became highly liquid, with large reductions in trade credit and the accumulation of large deposit balances. During 1971 fiscal policy also moved in a stimulative direction. By the year's end, with the Smithsonian agreement (on a new set of exchange rates for major currencies) having restored some measure of confidence, investment began to turn up, and December is officially recorded as marking the end of the unusually long recession.

Although recovery became apparent in the spring of 1972, it was at first regarded as slow and inadequate. Moreover, a large balance-of-payments surplus continued to embarrass the authorities, and there were increasing international pressures on Japan further to revalue the yen. Thus, monetary and fiscal policy continued highly stimulative throughout almost all of 1972, including a further 0.5 percentage point reduction of the discount rate in June, to 4.25 percent. Although the net inflow of foreign exchange was greatly reduced, the banks resumed moderate borrowing from, and discounting with, the BOJ, which also made substantial purchases of bills, more than offsetting some further decline in its holdings of government securities. Business borrowing from banks expanded by 26 percent during 1972, and at an annual rate of 33 percent in the second half. Thus, the large reserves of business liquidity were little impaired, even though private fixed and inventory investment was now expanding sharply.

Although both domestic and foreign observers were impressed, even after

42. This also occurred for a few months in late 1956 and early 1957.

midyear, with the weakness of recovery and the prevalence of excess capacity,[43] tightness in the labor market became very evident: the ratio of job offers to applicants (except new graduates) rose steadily throughout 1972, reaching 1.4 in the fourth quarter, an all-time peak in this ratio; and capacity utilization in manufacturing increased dramatically after midyear. In September wholesale prices of manufactured goods began to rise sharply, led by construction materials, although no acceleration of consumer prices or export prices was noticeable before the year's end.[44] Late in the year the BOJ began to put some pressure on money markets and requested banks to moderate their increase in lending. But—as will be reported in some detail below—fiscal policy continued stimulative, with an expansionary supplementary budget in the fall.

Monetary policy began to move toward restraint in January 1973 and continued in that direction throughout the year. Reserve ratios were raised in January, March, June, and September, for a total rise in the most representative ratio from 1.5 to 3.75 percent, reaching 4.25 percent on January 1, 1974. The discount rate was raised by 0.75 percentage point in April, by 0.5 in May and again in June, by 1.0 in August, and by 2.0 in December, moving in all from 4.25 to 9 percent. Window guidance was reintroduced in January, and was progressively tightened throughout the year. Of course, substantial reserves had to be provided to the banking system, mainly through massive purchases of bills; but the growth of bank lending (by "all banks") to business slowed to 18 percent during 1973 (from 34 percent in the second half of 1973), and the gap between the demand for loans by business and the permitted expansion of supply obviously became very large. However, business liquidity—the residue of aggressively easy money in 1971 and 1972— had been so substantial that private fixed and inventory investment was able to increase by 43 percent during 1973. The ratio of job offers to applicants (except new graduates) reached 1.9 in November.[45]

Even before the increase in oil prices in October, a virulent inflation was evident. Wage rates were rising at a rate of 16.5 percent, consumer prices at

43. EPA's Economic White Paper, issued in August, describes the upswing as "limp" in comparison with previous recoveries and refers repeatedly to "excess capacity." The *OECD Economic Survey of Japan* (June 1972) describes an "overhang" of excess capacity; and even in December the *OECD Economic Outlook* continued to describe business investment as weak, referred to sizable overcapacity, and described the growth of GNP during 1972 as "insufficient to reduce the margin of slack." Clearly, these diagnoses were far off the mark.

44. See EPA, *Annual Report on Business Cycle Indicators* (May 1973), pp. 68, 177, 183; and EPA, *Japanese Economic Indicators* (April–May 1973), pp. 48, 77–79.

45. EPA, *Economic Statistics Monthly* (March 1974), pp. 15, 16, 21–24, 159–60; EPA, *Japanese Economic Indicators* (April 1974), p. 73.

18 percent, and wholesale prices at 26 percent. Obviously, a major error in monetary policy had been made—and, as the next section will show, fiscal policy must share some of the blame.[46]

Fiscal Policy

Japan's unitary system of government blurs the distinction, so clear in a federal system, between the functions and finances of the central and local governments. Nevertheless, Japan's national income and product accounts permit the subdivision of most major categories of revenues and outlays among the central government, local governments, and the social insurance system. By making arbitrary allocations of the remaining items it is possible to reach some rough conclusions about the relative importance of these three systems.[47] This is done in Table 3-6, insofar as general government revenue and outlays are concerned. ("General government" excludes government enterprises.) The data suggest that, although the central government levies, collects, and disposes of more than half of all general government revenues, local governments and social insurance funds make most of the outlays. In 1972 the central government's current and capital outlays constituted between 22 and 33.5 percent of all general government outlays (depending on how certain expenditures described as "transferred to local governments" are classified).

Nevertheless, it is the central government which is responsible for the overall character of Japan's fiscal policy—including, to a large extent, that of local governments. The Budget Bureau of the Ministry of Finance (MOF) each year receives and reviews the expenditure recommendations of all central government ministries and agencies, on the basis of which it prepares a proposed expenditure budget. At the same time, the MOF's Tax Bureau prepares recommended changes in the tax schedule (rates, exemptions, deductions, and so on) and forecasts government revenues based on those changes. The MOF also prepares plans for bond issues and other borrowing, the budgets of "government-affiliated agencies" (mostly public corporations), and a Fiscal Investment and Loan Program (FILP). This entire package is

46. EPA, *Japanese Economic Indicators* (April 1974), pp. 13, 14, 22.
47. Treating social insurance funds separately is consistent with official Japanese budgets, which do not include social insurance contributions as government revenues, and which include in government outlays only the government's own contributions to the social insurance funds.

Table 3-6. *General Government Expenditure and Revenue in National Income Accounts, Fiscal 1971*

Billions of yen

Item	Central government	Local governments	Social insurance funds	Total general government
Expenditure				
Government consumption	2,552.6	4,603.5	...	7,156.1
Government investment	2,003.5	3,001.2	...	5,004.7
Subsidies plus transfers to rest of world[a]	957.5		...	957.5
Transfers to households[b]			3,613.5	3,613.5
Interest on public debt	278.5	248.7		527.2
Total outlays	5,792.1	7,853.4	3,613.5	17,259.0
Total outlays, adjusted for central government transfers to local governments[c]	3,799.6	9,845.9	3,613.5	17,259.0
Revenue				
Direct taxes and charges on households	2,856.2	1,077.6	...	3,933.7
Direct taxes and charges on corporations	3,029.5	429.3	...	3,458.7
Indirect taxes	2,838.8	2,970.8	...	5,809.6
Social insurance contributions			3,173.7	3,173.7
Other current transfers from households and rest of world	139.3	722.4	...	861.6
Income from property and entrepreneurship	440.7	148.0	166.1	754.8
Total income	9,303.1	5,348.1	3,339.8	17,992.1

Source: Economic Planning Agency, *Annual Report on National Income Statistics, 1973*, pp. 13, 223, 235, 237. (Similar detail is not available in the corresponding volume for 1974.)

a. Division not recorded; the total was arbitrarily assigned to central government.

b. Division not recorded; the total was arbitrarily assigned to social insurance funds.

c. Included in adjustment are ¥802.5 billion included in central government's consumption expenditure but listed as "current grants to local [governments] for specific services," and ¥1,190.0 billion included in central government fixed capital formation, but not in "central government's executed projects, etc.," and instead described as "capital transfers to local [governments]."

submitted to, and must secure the approval of, the cabinet and then the Diet.[48] Almost every year one or more supplementary budgets are also submitted and approved late in the fiscal year. (Usually these include pay increases for government workers.) Supplementary budgets occasionally involve substantial changes from the original budget—especially in FILP.

48. The Diet's approval provides the equivalent of authorization and appropriation action in the U.S. system. Before 1973 the Diet's formal approval was not required for the larger part of FILP.

Only once in recent years (in 1971) has such a budget included any change in taxation.

Several basic principles appear to have guided Japanese budgetary policy throughout most of the postwar period. First, there is the principle that tax schedules (including rates, brackets, exemptions, deductions, and so forth) should be adjusted frequently (in practice, annually), predominantly downward, in order to keep total tax revenues (national and local) at or near 20 percent of national income. Second, based on recommendations of the Dodge Mission of 1949, the U.S. occupation authorities established a balanced-budget rule. The precise content of such a principle can be debated, but it came to mean that the central government should not borrow (other than temporarily) from the Bank of Japan nor issue marketable bonds. This rule was strictly maintained long after the occupation, until it was dramatically revoked in 1965 as part of the strategy for recovery from the recession of that year. Subsequently bonds have been issued in each year, in amounts that declined steadily, from 16.9 percent of "general account" expenditures in fiscal 1966 to 4.5 percent in 1971, then rebounded to 17.0 percent in fiscal 1972 and 16.4 percent in 1973.[49] In addition, there is direct borrowing by a few of the "special accounts" in the budget, as well as by a number of the "government-affiliated agencies" (often with a government guarantee). Local governments also borrow directly.

After 1965 the balanced-budget "rule of sound finance" was replaced by alternative rules: that government bond issues never exceed the amount spent on construction, and that bond issues meet the "test of market acceptance" —that is, they could never be sold directly to the Bank of Japan. Despite their obviously mythical status as rules of sound finance (especially given Japanese financial markets and practices), these principles are annually and solemnly attested to.

In addition to these fairly specific rules, Japanese budgets are declared to reflect the principle that the budget should "harmonize the internal and external equilibrium of the economy."[50] This presumably means that fiscal policy—like monetary policy—should at appropriate times either stimulate or restrain aggregate demand: in the interest of balance-of-payments equilibrium, high but not excessive rates of use of productive capacity and price stability should prevail. The main purpose of this section is to evaluate whether or to what extent this principle is in fact put into practice.

49. Ministry of Finance, Budget Bureau, *The Budget in Brief, Japan 1973*, p. 13.
50. These words come from the preface to the budget for fiscal 1973, but similar expressions are found in all recent government documents referring to budgetary policy.

The Restraining Force of the Budget

Japan's postwar fiscal policy has been frequently described as consistently and strongly restrictive of aggregate demand. Whether this is the case depends on the definition of those budgetary elements which it is appropriate to consider in reaching this judgment: regular government expenditure, tax and other revenue sources, government investment, government-enterprise investment, and private investment financed by government loans. These elements will be considered in roughly this order.

International comparisons show that, relative both to the size of the economy and to government revenues, government expenditure in postwar Japan has been smaller than in any other major developed country. An OECD study of comparative public expenditures during the years 1955–65 shows that total government expenditure in Japan in 1965 was 21.5 percent of gross national product, lower than in any other of the fifteen OECD member countries for which these data were available.[51] (The next lowest percentages were 27.6 in Greece and 27.7 in the United States; the highest percentages were 40.5 in Sweden and 40.1 in the Netherlands.) Even if defense expenditure is omitted, Japan ranked about even with the United States and still well below all other principal countries. Fixed investment expenditure represented a far higher percentage of total government expenditures in Japan than in any other major country, and transfers to households a relatively low percentage.

To be sure, government expenditure was growing in 1955–65 considerably more rapidly in Japan than in any other country covered by the study, except Greece, and more than twice as rapidly as in the United States. Nevertheless, Japan was the only OECD country in which government expenditure grew less rapidly in that period than GNP. Other data show that government spending in Japan continued to grow less rapidly than GNP into the early 1970s. So far as expenditure is concerned, fiscal policy has clearly been restraining.

But government's net influence on aggregate demand is measured not by the size of government expenditure alone nor by its size relative to GNP, but in some sense by its size relative to government revenue. On this basis as well, Japanese fiscal policy appears to have been restrictive. "General government" has typically spent far less on current purchases, transfer payments,

51. Mary Garin-Painter, "Public Expenditure Trends," *OECD Economic Outlook: Occasional Studies* (July 1970), pp. 43–55. Expenditure is at all levels of government; basically, it excludes only investments by government enterprises.

Table 3-7. *General Government Saving and Investment,*
All Units of Government, 1955–72

| | General government saving[a] | | | | Excess of saving over investment | | |
| | | Percent | | General government fixed investment (billions of yen) | | Percent | |
Fiscal year	Amount (billions of yen)	Of government revenue	Of gross national product		Amount (billions of yen)	Of government revenues	Of gross national product
1955	358	21.7	4.0	346	12	0.7	0.1
1956	581	30.2	5.8	368	213	11.1	2.1
1957	759	33.6	6.7	451	308	13.7	2.7
1958	627	27.2	5.3	518	109	4.7	0.9
1959	843	31.9	6.2	631	212	8.0	1.6
1960	1,249	37.3	7.7	756	493	14.7	3.0
1961	1,697	40.5	8.5	957	740	17.7	3.7
1962	1,769	37.9	8.2	1,233	536	11.7	2.5
1963	1,930	35.9	7.5	1,359	571	10.6	2.2
1964	1,999	32.9	6.7	1,569	430	7.1	1.4
1965	1,956	29.3	6.0	1,775	181	2.7	0.6
1966	2,140	28.1	5.6	2,062	78	1.0	0.2
1967	2,819	31.0	6.2	2,279	540	5.9	1.2
1968	3,641	33.6	6.8	2,681	960	8.9	1.8
1969	4,731	36.1	7.5	3,141	1,590	12.1	2.5
1970	5,799	36.5	7.9	3,912	1,887	11.9	2.6
1971	5,888	32.5	7.2	4,989	899	5.0	1.1
1972	6,825	31.5	7.1	6,222	603	2.8	0.6

Source: Same as Table 3-4.
a. General government revenue includes (a small amount) of "income from property and entrepreneurship"—that is, interest and dividends—which some economists (but not the authors) find inappropriate.

and subsidies (but excluding investment) than it has received in taxes, social insurance contributions, transfers, and property or entrepreneurial income. The difference in these amounts is typically described as "government saving"; and the extent of such saving is one widely used measure of the extent of fiscal restraint on aggregate demand. The data in Table 3-7 show that general government saving has ranged between 21 and 41 percent of total government current revenue, and between 4 and 8.5 percent of GNP. From Table 3-6, it can be judged that all or the larger part of this saving can be identified with the central government and social insurance funds.

But government in Japan is also a large investor. Like private investment, government investment plays a dual economic role: it constitutes an element of aggregate demand for current output, and it adds to the stock of productive capital and thus contributes to the future growth of potential output. In the postwar period general government has in most years undertaken between 13 and 18 percent of the economy's total gross domestic investment, in the form of public buildings, roads, flood-control works, harbors, airports, and the like. Although the amount of such investment is large, it has been regularly exceeded by the amount of government saving (Table 3-7). This excess—which can be considered a second measure of fiscal restraint—has reached as much as 17.7 percent of government revenue and 3.7 percent of GNP. Although no fully satisfactory comparative studies exist, it is almost certain that Japan's postwar fiscal policy—measured either by government saving or by its excess over general government investment—has been consistently more restrictive than that of other major countries.[52] At the same time that the budget has restrained current aggregate demand, government investment has contributed substantially to the growth of potential output, thereby making room for expansion of *future* aggregate demand and output.

There is a widespread impression that not only did abandonment of the balanced-budget rule after 1965 permit the budget to be used as an instrument of expansionary fiscal policy, but also that fiscal policy thereafter was in fact both less restrictive and often positively expansionary. The two measures of fiscal restraint analyzed above show considerable year-to-year variation in the extent of restraint, but on the average (as will be seen in Figure 3-4) policy remained about as restrictive after 1965 as before. This may seem surprising if it is assumed that the only purpose of bond issues is to permit an excess of government expenditure over current government revenue and that the bond issues constitute the only way to finance such an excess. In fact, however, the amount of a government's bond issues bears only indirect relation to any such excess.

Government expenditure and revenue, as defined in the national income and product accounts, include only those items which directly affect current production and income; the above measures of the restraining (or stimulating) effect of the budget reflect (as they should) these definitions. But government units in Japan are involved in many other kinds of transactions with the rest of the domestic (and international) economy, including loans and loan repayments, the acceptance of deposits and insurance premiums, and the purchase and sale of various financial assets, land, and other assets not currently produced—none of which directly affects production and incomes.

52. OECD data show that in 1969 government saving was higher in Japan, as a percentage of GNP, than in any other of the fourteen countries for which such data are available, except Sweden and Finland. See OECD, *National Accounts of OECD Countries, 1953–69*, tables 1, 10.

Moreover, there can be and are substantial changes in government holdings of deposits and currency; and the central government's public bond issues are only one of the numerous forms of borrowing engaged in by central and local governments and their special accounts. It would be surprising to find any close correlation between the amount of the central government's public bond issues and the difference between total general government expenditure and revenue on national income and product account.

Budgetary Financing of Investment by Government and Private Enterprises

Perhaps the most important of the expenditure transactions that appear in the government's financial budget but are not reflected in the national income accounts for general government are the loans made to help finance the investments of both government enterprises and selected private enterprises. Government enterprises are activities that are organized and to some degree controlled by government and that produce goods or services for sale at prices approximating or exceeding their cost of production. In socialist economies most enterprises are of this character. These goods and services might have been produced privately, and in many countries some of them are. Such enterprises are usually organized and operated as semi-independent corporations, and Japan has a large number and variety of them.[53] General government not only contributes some part of the financing of the investments of these enterprises, but also may provide them with direct or indirect subsidies —including the lower interest rates paid on funds borrowed from government sources (or the greater risk assumed by the lender) than would be available in private borrowing, as well as the provision of equity capital at a lower expected return than private investors would require (or even at a negative rate of return).

In the aggregate, the capital investment of Japanese government enterprises from 1955 to 1971 constituted about one-tenth of Japan's total domestic investment. Although in most respects similar to private investment, the amount and timing of these investments can, of course, be altered as an element in the government's demand-management program. This does not require equivalent changes in the amount of government lending—the enterprises also borrow from private sources and use internally generated funds

53. They include, at the national level, such large undertakings as the National Railways, Japan Telegraph and Telephone Corporation, Metropolitan Subway Corporation, Japan Airlines, various expressway companies, and one or more public housing enterprises; at the local level, they include many power, transportation, water and sewer, housing, and similar enterprises.

—nor does a change in government lending necessarily alter the volume of government-enterprise investment. There is likely to be some considerable correspondence, however, between changes in the two magnitudes.

Most central government funds that finance government-enterprise investments are accounted for in the annual Fiscal Investment and Loan Program. This program provides financing not only for the investments of government enterprises (including some by local governments), but also for selected categories of private business that are regarded as having special social importance or that often have trouble finding adequate private financing. However financed, the investments made by the private borrowers are, of course, always (and properly) regarded as private investment. Most government loans, either to government or private enterprises, are administered through a variety of special banks or finance corporations.[54]

To the substantial extent that Japanese general government is a net lender —that is, uses the excess of its own saving over its own investments to finance investments by government and private enterprises—it restrains aggregate demand. This can be seen clearly by an alternative situation, in which the government reduces its lending and its taxes by equal amounts, and the enterprises finance the same investments instead by greater direct borrowing.

Because the total of government loans to (or equity investment in) government and private enterprises usually is substantially greater than the excess of government saving over general government investment, the difference (together with any net increase in government deposits and other financial assets) must be financed. The principal sources of such financing are, first, the substantial net receipts of the government's postal saving and postal insurance systems (and other government insurance activities); and, second, government borrowing, since 1965 mainly in the form of bond issues. Through such financing the Japanese government operates like any other financial intermediary: it issues one set of financial liabilities (securities, passbooks, or insurance policies) to the public and uses the proceeds to acquire a different set of financial liabilities—in this case, those of certain government and private enterprises. The net effect of the double transaction is still not necessarily to alter the magnitude of aggregate demand, but mainly to change its composition.[55] Thus, the existence of substantial government

54. The largest of these many lending agencies are the Housing Loan Corporation, the Small Business Finance Corporation, the Japan Development Bank, and the Export-Import Bank of Japan.

55. This alteration in the composition of demand is probably most important during periods of tight money, when government lending assures government enterprises and the eligible private enterprises of a more generous availability of funds than private sources, mainly banks, might be able to provide.

bond issues, accompanied by an even larger amount of government lending, does not necessarily require significant modification of earlier conclusions about the strongly restrictive character of Japan's fiscal policy.[56]

Aggregate demand will be increased by government lending to the extent that the easier availability (or lower cost) of the government loans causes the borrowing enterprises to make larger investments than these or other enterprises would have made had they all been private enterprises—or, although public, had they been required to borrow directly from those who instead loaned to the government. Although the net effect on aggregate demand is surely positive, its amount is difficult to estimate. Nevertheless, since government financing of investment by government and private enterprises may cause the total amount of such investment to be larger than it would otherwise have been, some economists prefer to use, as a measure of the restrictive impact of the budget, a third accounting, which subtracts from government saving not only government investment but also government-enterprise investment.[57] Because this measure (which is also shown in Figure 3-4) tends to be in deficit in the case of Japan, those who believe that the impact of government financing on aggregate spending is large can maintain that Japan's fiscal policy has not been highly restrictive.

The Short-Run Role of Fiscal Policy

Japanese economic policymakers sometimes talk a great deal about how fiscal policy not only should be but in fact is varied in the short run as a means of contributing to healthy performance of the economy. Attention in such statements is usually directed toward variations in planned expenditure, particularly that financed by the FILP, although mention is occasionally made of tax policy as well. A number of economists, both Japanese and foreign, have attempted—with varying conclusions—to measure and assess the significance of variations on both sides of the budget for purposes of short-run demand management. The present analysis finds that alterations of fiscal policy have been of minor importance as a tool of short-run demand man-

56. The fact that public bond issues were nonexistent before 1965, but were substantial thereafter, may suggest either that government was financing a relatively larger amount of government enterprise and private investments after that date than before, or that it had previously been borrowing more in ways other than bonds. But to establish the relative importance of these (or of other possible) explanations would require considerable research.

57. Some American economists seem to believe that the appropriate subtraction also includes the total amount of government loans to private enterprises or households and of capital raised through government-guaranteed borrowing. Such a definition seems to us entirely indefensible.

agement, and have sometimes contributed to an unhealthy economic performance.

Economists analyzing Japanese fiscal policy (as well as that of other countries) almost invariably seek to discover whether and to what extent it has acted in a stabilizing direction—that is, has operated to counter or dampen booms and recessions—with the implication that an affirmative finding merits approval for the policy. This may be the natural way to direct such an analysis given the assumption that recessions and booms occur only by mistake or accident and are always unwelcome. If so, it is reasonable to hope and expect that policies might either prevent recessions or at least moderate their amplitude and duration. Our contention, however, has been that Japanese recessions have been the direct and deliberate result of monetary policy actions taken to slow down a rate of growth considered too fast because (usually) it had created or threatened to create balance-of-payments problems. When a recession had sufficiently redressed the payments imbalance (and perhaps the level or direction of movement of export prices), monetary policy was shifted toward ease, encouraging growth to resume at its own pace until the need for restriction again became clear. If this description is essentially correct, it implies that Japanese fiscal policies should merit approval only if it were found that—working in tandem with monetary policy—they had helped, not to counter, but rather to bring about recessions; and had helped to end them only when they had done their job. The present discussion therefore focuses less on whether fiscal policy has been stabilizing in the sense of countering recessions, than on its conformity with monetary policy. This is not meant to imply that changes in monetary policy were always optimally timed, when judged according to some purely economic criterion. Rather, it reflects an assumption that changes in monetary policy accurately reflected the government's view of whether and when stimulus or restraint was needed, and that it ordinarily moved in that direction at the earliest time when such a change was feasible—given lags of recognition and analysis, as well as the political climate and level of public understanding.

Most contemporary discussions of short-run fiscal policy also invoke a questionable distinction between discretionary and automatic (or built-in) changes in aggregate tax revenue and expenditure. Automatic, or built-in, variation in revenue or expenditure is usually defined as that which occurs in response to changes in the economy, without alteration of basic tax schedules or expenditure programs, whereas discretionary variation reflects changes in such schedules or programs.

Almost all changes in expenditure are clearly discretionary in this sense, as are also the revenue changes that result from Japan's appreciable annual tax reductions. Most studies, however, regard as discretionary tax changes only that part of any revenue change which results directly from tax schedule changes—and regard as automatic any remaining revenue change from one year to the next. This view appears particularly strange in the case of Japan. Prospective revenues are systematically reviewed each year, and their amount (after tax cut) is forecast in the light of the prospective economic situation. If the tax reduction eliminates only a part of the growth of revenue, and decisionmakers thus permit—and expect—another part to occur, the amount of the remaining change expected to occur would seem to be as much the product of a deliberate, discretionary decision as is the amount of the reduction. (Whether the discretionary decision was correct on the basis of some criterion or other is a different question; but, with a rapidly growing budget such as Japan's, it would be strange if some substantial increment of revenue would not in most years also be regarded as appropriate.) Only that change in revenue which resulted from an unexpected change of gross national product would seem properly to be regarded as automatic rather than discretionary.

Calculating what automatic changes in revenues would have occurred if tax schedules had not been altered—as, for example, Pechman and Kaizuka do in Chapter 5—may be of considerable interest, especially for the purpose of comparative analysis of tax structures. Here, however, no distinction between automatic and discretionary tax changes seems appropriate: rather, the aggregate amount of tax revenue will simply be treated as determined by an annual policy decision.[58]

Economists have made several rather sophisticated studies of the short-run impact of Japanese fiscal policy. Unfortunately, not only have most of these studies devoted the bulk of their analysis to the questionable distinction between discretionary and automatic changes, but also all except one of these have used annual data. Because Japan's recessions, like its periods of monetary restraint, have usually lasted a year or less (and begun in differing seasons), studies based on annual data are not really useful in answering most of the important questions about the adequacy of short-run Japanese fiscal policy.[59]

58. In countries in which tax schedule changes are made only rarely and in which the assignment of fiscal policy is conceived in terms of occasional interventions to meet some specific threat to stability, the discretionary-automatic distinction may be useful in analyzing and evaluating policy. It would seem, however, that it is not only in Japan that the absence of change in tax schedules should be treated as an act of discretion.

59. Several of these studies attempt to apply to Japan a methodology first developed by Bent Hansen in his *Fiscal Policy in Seven Countries, 1955–65* (Paris: OECD, 1969). Japan was not one of Hansen's seven countries. At least four other studies, however,

Most of the studies using annual data attempt not only to distinguish between changes in revenues and expenditures resulting from discretionary action and those which occurred automatically, but also to reflect a different relative economic importance for changes in each of several categories of taxes and of expenditure. Although economic theory supports this latter procedure, so many drastically simplifying assumptions and crude statistical procedures are involved in applying it that a real question can be raised about whether it contributes any significant information beyond that provided by the simple concept of net surplus or deficit, the measure used here.[60]

In contrast with the usual practice, Hiromitsu Ishi[61] has used not only monthly and quarterly data for the analysis of short-run policy, but also data that directly represent net government surplus or deficit. Two of Ishi's series consist of monthly data based on MOF and BOJ receipts and payments;[62] his third series, based on quarterly national income and product account data, will also be used here.

---

have now explicitly applied the Hansen methodology to Japan: Sei Fujita, *Nihon zaiseiron* [Fiscal Policy in Japan] (Keiso Press, 1972); Wayne Snyder and Tsutomu Tanaka, "Budget Policy and Economic Stability in Japan," *International Economic Review,* vol. 13 (February 1972), pp. 85–110; an unpublished staff paper of the Japanese Ministry of Finance, 1970; and an unpublished staff paper of the International Monetary Fund, 1973. An earlier study—Keimei Kaizuka, "The Stabilization Effect of Fiscal Policy," in Ryūtarō Komiya (ed.), *Postwar Economic Growth in Japan* (University of California Press, 1969), pp. 210–26 (with "Comment" by Sei Fujita)— essentially anticipated the Hansen methodology. All these studies use annual data and stress the automatic-discretionary distinction.

60. A far more promising approach to a sophisticated economic analysis of the impact of budgetary changes involves simulations, using complete econometric models, of results with and without the policy change. The EPA has in recent years been assessing the impact of actual and proposed budgetary changes in this way, although it has apparently not published any time series showing the impact of each year's budgetary changes. There are, moreover, difficult and unsettled questions about the baseline for such estimates, as well as about the adequacy of the EPA model's representation of the impacts of fiscal policy, especially on investment.

61. Hiromitsu Ishi, "Cyclical Behavior of Government Receipts and Expenditures: A Case Study of Postwar Japan," *Hitotsubashi Journal of Economics,* vol. 14 (June 1973), pp. 56–83.

62. Use of monthly data not only introduces considerable random variation, but probably is unnecessary to reflect short-run policy changes adequately. Moreover, the available monthly series raise conceptual problems. One of Ishi's monthly series consists of MOF data on the net balance between the receipts and disbursements of the central government's general account; the second is a BOJ series on the net balance of cash receipts and disbursements of general and special accounts and government-affiliated agencies. These seem conceptually somewhat inappropriate, since (among other things) they include financial as well as income transactions (for example, deposits and loans), intermediate as well as final purchases and sales, and even surplus receipts of the previous year as current revenue, whereas they exclude social insurance.

Earlier, the high levels of government saving and of the excess of government saving over general government investment were used as evidence of
the highly restrictive impact of postwar Japanese budgets over the postwar
period as a whole. Short-run changes in these same measures can also furnish
at least a crude indication of the use of fiscal policy for short-run purposes
(if it is accepted that changes in actual tax collections are basically policy
determined rather than partly discretionary and partly automatic). Moreover, since government can influence the timing of government-enterprise
investment, both directly and through its lending, it is appropriate to consider also variations in the difference between government saving and the
sum of government and government-enterprise investment—the series Ishi
used. Because government policymakers stress variations in the FILP as the
principal instrument of discretionary short-run fiscal policy, and because
most of such variation is not reflected in the national income account measures of general government saving and investment, this third series may best
reflect the effects of discretionary government policy.[63]

Quarterly movement of the three series is shown in Figure 3-4. The shaded
areas in the figure represent periods of recession, and the areas marked
R, E, and N indicate periods of restraint, ease, or neutrality, respectively,
in monetary policy. An upward movement of any of the measures implies that fiscal policy was becoming more restrictive, according to that
measure; a downward movement implies that policy was moving toward
fiscal stimulus.

Several conclusions are immediately clear. First, all three measures show
essentially the same time pattern of variation, one at least partly related to
the business cycle. Second, fiscal policy became steadily more stimulative
during each recession, according to at least two or all three of the measures.
Third, fiscal policy became more restrictive during three of the five completed
expansions shown, but more stimulative during two: those of 1952–53 and
1963–64. Given the relative weakness of the expansion of private fixed and
inventory investment during the latter period, this pattern was undoubtedly
appropriate. The unusual continuation—and intensification—of fiscal ease
in late 1965 and early 1966, even after the end of the recession, shows up

---

63. Although the quarterly data needed to derive these three measures are all available in the national income and product accounts, neither government revenues nor expenditures (other than purchases of goods and services) are provided on a seasonally
adjusted basis. Because these components exhibit strong patterns of seasonal variation
—patterns that appear to change over time—it is not possible to reach any significant
conclusions about the timing of policy actions from these data.   Fortunately, Professor
Ishi had calculated seasonally adjusted data for these components (using the EPA
method) and an extension of his calculations through 1972 is used here.

extremely clearly in two of the three measures, and especially strongly in the third. It is at least arguable that this stimulus was an essential element, if not in ending the recession, at least in getting the long boom of 1966–70 off to a strong beginning. Insofar as the 1972–73 expansion is concerned, data are available only through the first quarter of 1973; they show no clear tendency to that time for policy to move toward either restriction or ease. According to the first measure (government saving), the level of policy in this period seems relatively restraining; according to the other two measures its level was relatively stimulative. This period is considered in more detail below.

Thus, insofar as the business cycle is concerned, fiscal policy tended to act in a generally stabilizing way, usually dampening aggregate demand during booms (except when weak) and sustaining demand during recessions.

Yet if fiscal policy is evaluated in terms of its coordination with monetary policy, which it has been argued here is the more appropriate criterion, the two policy tools appear to have been working at cross-purposes much of the time. On one or two occasions fiscal policy began to move toward expansion just at the time when monetary policy shifted toward restraint—for example, in late 1961. In 1953 and 1964 fiscal policy had already been moving toward ease before monetary restraint was implemented; if anything, the pace of the move toward ease accelerated thereafter. On occasion the reverse occurred: for example, in mid-1958 fiscal policy had been moving toward ease well before monetary policy turned toward ease; but once monetary policy turned easy, fiscal policy stopped moving in that direction. On most occasions there appears to be little association between shifts in monetary policy and the degree of fiscal restraint or ease. Only during the period 1969–72 do fiscal and monetary policy appear to have been reasonably well coordinated. When monetary policy turned restraining in the summer of 1969, fiscal policy remained restraining, even into the early stages of the recession; it switched sharply toward ease only when monetary policy also became easy.

It might be argued, of course, that there is nothing wrong with a policy mix in which the several elements appear at times to work at cross-purposes, so long as at least one set of policymakers knows what the other is doing and adjusts its action to take account of the effects of the other tool. It can be assumed that the MOF was at all times aware of—if indeed it did not largely dictate—the character of both monetary and fiscal policy. The criticism implied by the cross-purposes comment applies only to the claim made in some public statements that each policy tool (and, in particular, fiscal policy) was being used in support of a single policy objective.

It must be emphasized that the above tentative conclusions do not take

Figure 3-4. *Relation of Three Measures of Fiscal Restraint (as Percentages of Gross National Product) to Japanese Monetary Policy and the Business Cycle, 1951–73*[a]

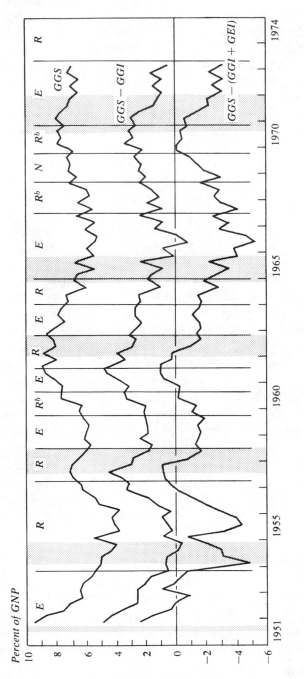

Percent of GNP

Sources: Economic Planning Agency, *Revised Report on National Income Statistics, 1951–1967* (1969), pp. 114–21; idem, *Annual Report on National Income Statistics, 1974* (1974), pp. 120–27.

a. Shaded areas represent recessions.

R, E, N = periods of restrictive, easy, and neutral monetary policy, respectively.

GGS = general government saving; GGI = general government investment; GEI = government-enterprise investment.

b. Period of moderately restrictive policy.

into account what are probably substantial lags in the effects of policy changes—and, in particular, the possibility of different lags in fiscal and monetary effects. But not enough is known about these to permit useful judgments, and it is doubtful whether the makers of policy have any better or more precise ideas about these lags than do others.

Before attempting a final evaluation of this record, it is useful to look at the behavior of taxes and expenditure separately, both in order to ascertain whether the overall pattern primarily reflects one rather than the other side of the budget, and because it is at least possible that appropriate variations on one side of the budget have sometimes been offset by inappropriate variations on the other side.

Tax Flexibility

The revenue impact of Japan's large annual changes in tax schedules is tabulated and described in some detail in the chapter by Pechman and Kaizuka. It seems clear that only on rare occasions have tax changes been deliberately used as an instrument of short-run demand management. Rather, the principle of adjusting tax schedules annually to keep tax revenues close to 20 percent of national income (NI) was clearly designed as a means of discouraging pressures for too sharply rising public expenditure.[64] But such a rule, if maintained in continuous effect, also has considerable implications (however unintended) for the short-run impact of tax policy. Holding revenue at a constant percentage of the forecast level of NI (or GNP) at least tends to prevent what might otherwise be inappropriate and destabilizing effects of tax changes.[65] Moreover, if tax schedules are set at the beginning of each fiscal year to provide revenue proportional to the forecast of GNP and the forecast turns out to be mistaken, revenue will rise as a percentage of GNP if GNP is unexpectedly high or fall if GNP is unexpectedly low, thus introducing a stabilizing element.

Many Japanese observers believe that there has been a deliberate government policy of underestimating GNP growth and therefore also the natural increase of tax revenues. The purposes are said to have been further to dis-

64. Although annual tax reductions and keeping tax revenues near 20 percent of NI had been a common practice long before 1960, the policy achieved semiofficial status in that year when endorsed by the MOF's Tax Commission. A decade later, the Tax Commission recognized as inevitable some gradual rise in the ratio of taxes to NI to meet expanding needs for social services and public investments.

65. Compare this policy, for example, with making tax reductions only once every five or ten years or even with a policy of attempting to keep revenue increasing at some constant percentage rate (for example, equal to the trend growth of GNP).

courage increases in government spending, especially for nongrowth-promoting purposes, and also to keep the budget consistently even more restrictive than otherwise.[66] Less worthy motives are said to have been to provide a "kitty" of unbudgeted revenue that can be used in a supplementary budget to reward political friends. An equally plausible interpretation for the underestimate is merely the traditional conservatism of MOF officials. In any case, so long as a policy of deliberate underestimate of GNP growth is consistently applied, it would not appear to make much difference in the short-run impact of tax policy. And the fact that the ratio of actual taxes to actual GNP appears, in Figure 3-5, to have remained close to 20 percent suggests that any consistent underestimate cannot be large.[67]

The varying of tax schedules to maintain revenues proportional to GNP therefore may not be an entirely inappropriate principle, even from the standpoint of short-run demand management; at the very least, it prevents taxes from becoming a source of major short-run instability. Clearly, a far superior procedure from the standpoint of demand management would be to vary the target percentage in accordance with the short-term situation: increasing or decreasing it when additional restraint or stimulus, respectively, appeared needed. There is no evidence that this has ever been deliberately done. Tax revenue has not remained an absolutely constant percentage of GNP, however, and it is possible to get some impression about whether changes in this ratio (whether deliberate or accidental) seem to have been appropriate or inappropriate. The material in Figure 3-5 shows that, although quarterly tax revenue has indeed stayed rather close to 20 percent of GNP, there has been not only a gradual upward drift in the percentage, but also considerable short-run fluctuation.[68]

66. Watanabe, in "National Planning and Economic Development," argues that the EPA deliberately has underestimated the expected growth of GNP and the Tax Bureau has estimated revenue (correctly?) on the basis of the underestimate, while the MOF has stressed the need for a balanced budget, in opposition to pressures for higher investment in social overhead. Normally, a surplus then appeared, which was used to reduce the next year's taxes. The argument implies that, were it not for this deception, investment in social overhead would have been considerably larger. But if there really were public support for investment in social overhead, the surplus resulting from each year's overestimate could have been allocated for this purpose rather than for tax reduction.

67. Of course, the "rule" is stated in terms of national income, which is somewhat smaller than GNP; on the other hand, taxes in Figure 3-5 include social insurance contributions, which the MOF's rule presumably ignores.

68. Quarterly tax data used for this figure were the aggregate of all central and local government direct and indirect taxes and charges, social insurance contributions, and "other current transfers from households," from the national income accounts, with seasonal movements crudely smoothed by the authors (by the method of four-quarter centered moving average), expressed as a percentage of seasonally adjusted quarterly GNP.

Beginning with fiscal 1954 the figure also shows a second measure of tax variation: the MOF's estimate of the net revenue impact of each fiscal year's tax-schedule changes (excluding, however, social insurance contributions), also expressed as percentages of the fiscal year's GNP. In general, the two measures of tax variation appear reasonably consistent. The most striking apparent inconsistency relates to fiscal 1962, when the ratio of taxes to GNP rose sharply despite an estimated large net tax reduction.

The figure conveys a clear impression that taxes rose as a percentage of GNP during each recession, a movement that might be described as "desta-bilizing," in the usual sense of that term.[69] But the relation of changes in the tax percentage to the restraint-ease chronology of monetary policy is of greater interest than their relation to the chronology of the business cycle. On this basis, the larger-than-average tax reductions of fiscal 1958, 1966, and 1971, which occurred when monetary policy had recently shifted to ease, seem reasonably appropriate.[70] On the other hand, the rather large tax reduc-tions of fiscal 1957, 1964, 1970, and 1973, each occurring in a period of monetary restraint and before the start of recession, seem badly coordinated with monetary policy. And the massive tax reduction of fiscal 1974 appears to have been highly inconsistent with monetary policy, and indeed, very diffi-cult to justify in any economic terms—at a time when every effort should have been made to combat a virulent inflation.[71] It is more difficult to judge the appropriateness of the large tax reduction of fiscal 1962, which occurred relatively early in the recession and well before monetary policy had been eased. (As noted, however, there appears to be a data problem in 1962, since the quarterly series shows a sharply rising ratio of taxes to GNP.) It appears that, on balance, variation in taxes as a percentage of GNP has been in the wrong direction more often than not from the standpoint of short-run demand management.

Variations in the amount of annual tax reduction presumably are almost entirely reflections of factors other than demand-management policy—the approach of elections, the need to make structural changes for reasons unre-lated to the business cycle (for example, growth considerations or tax equity) and the awkwardness of spreading such changes evenly over time, adminis-trative convenience, and the like. Sometimes changes desirable for other rea-

69. No simple explanation suggests itself as to why such a rise would occur. If the recessions were unanticipated when rates were adjusted, the high elasticity of the tax system (see Chapter 5) should have caused the percentage to fall.

70. The figures for 1971 include a second substantial tax reduction, made as part of that year's supplementary budget. This unusual step was prompted by the setback to economic recovery which followed the "Nixon shock."

71. This reduction—in an election year—kept a political commitment made a year earlier.

Figure 3-5. *Relation of Total Taxes and Tax Changes (as Percentages of Gross National Product) to the Business Cycle and Phases of Monetary Policy, Japan, 1951–74*[a]

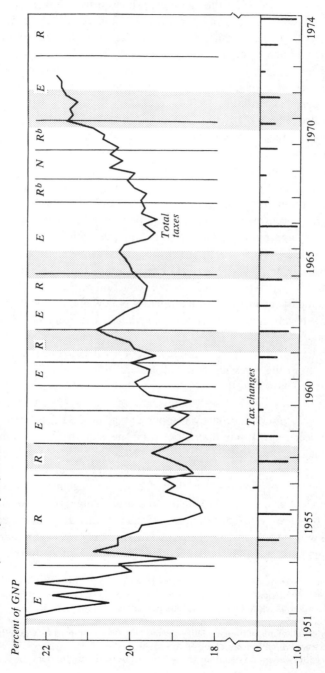

Sources: Total taxes, same as Figure 3-4. Tax changes, Table 5-3 in Chapter 5 of this volume.
a. Shaded areas represent recessions.
R, E, N = periods of restrictive, easy, and neutral monetary policy, respectively.
b. Period of moderately restrictive policy.

sons might be conveniently coordinated with short-run demand management, and perhaps occasionally they may have been; usually they apparently could not be—or at least were not. If otherwise desirable tax reductions could be saved up for several years, to be made all at once at times appropriate for short-run macroeconomic policy, tax variation could be an extremely powerful instrument, as Pechman and Kaizuka well argue. But if enough other policy tools are available for short-run policy purposes, a long-term policy of tax reduction directed toward maintaining a desired relative importance for the public sector can reasonably be accomplished through annual changes that vary somewhat randomly with respect to the business cycle or to monetary policy—but that also serve some political or administrative convenience. It should be possible, however, to avoid major tax changes that are clearly inconsistent with the appropriate posture for monetary policy.

Expenditure Variation

The earlier description of Japanese business cycles reported (based on Table 3-4) that total government purchases of goods and services in constant prices, including the investments of government enterprises, played a consistently countercyclical role in all business cycles after that of 1951–54, in that they expanded more rapidly between each peak and trough than during either the previous or subsequent trough-to-peak period. Examination of the various components of this total—that is, government consumption, general government investment, and government-enterprise investment—suggests that this pattern generally holds for each component separately. This suggests that government expenditures have been stabilizing at least with respect to the business cycle.

But peak-trough-peak comparisons are not adequate for evaluating the timing of expenditure policy. A careful examination was therefore made of the quarter-by-quarter rate of change in the aggregate of government and government-enterprise purchases of goods and services (seasonally adjusted and in constant prices) over the period 1956–71.

Several conclusions of this examination can be summarized. First, the rate of increase of total government purchases accelerated right from the start of each recession—usually beginning, in fact, one quarter in advance of the business peak. Second, dates of shifts toward monetary restraint were usually either preceded or followed by from one to three quarters of somewhat slower growth in expenditures—or even expenditure decline—but never by one that extended up to or into a recession. Third, the dates of shifts to monetary ease were usually either preceded or followed (or both) by accelerated growth of expenditure, but especially so if these dates occurred during a period of recession.

In short, expenditure policy was indeed systematically countercyclical in the usual sense. To some lesser extent, it was also supportive of monetary policy, but never did this stand in the way of an accelerated increase of expenditure in a period of actual or impending recession—even though monetary policy was actively attempting to bring about or sustain that recession.

Recent Fiscal Policy

Reference has already been made to the apparent impropriety of the moderate tax reduction of fiscal 1973 and surely of the massive tax reduction of fiscal 1974. The expenditure side of recent fiscal policy is equally subject to criticism.

The very substantially stimulative budget for fiscal 1972 was clearly appropriate, planned as it was with the economy still in recession, prices stable, and monetary policy already turned to ease. It involved a 22 percent increase in general account expenditure and a 32 percent increase in the FILP above the original budgets for fiscal 1971. In May 1972 the timing of the public works portion of the budget was sharply accelerated; in August the FILP was further expanded; and in October a large supplementary budget was proposed. Enacted in November, it involved additional spending estimated as equivalent to 1.4 percent of gross national product.[72]

Given the widespread fear that recovery would be inadequate to avoid substantial excess capacity and the desire to avoid revaluation of the yen even (if necessary) at the cost of some extra inflation, an aggressive fiscal policy stimulus could well be justified—surely in the first half of 1972. But the ominous evidence of a growing labor market tightness and the spurt in prices in the fall should have induced caution. As noted earlier, this price rise was led by construction materials, for which the sharp acceleration of public work programs and the FILP is given considerable blame.

Although monetary policy began to back away from extreme ease even before the end of 1972, expenditure policy continued stimulative. The fiscal 1973 budget, passed in April, included a general account expenditure equal to 13 percent of GNP (compared with 12 percent in the fiscal 1972 budget) and an FILP equal to 6.3 percent (compared with 6.0 percent). Only in May, with inflation accelerating sharply, was the first move taken toward restricting expenditures, with a slight stretchout of public works programs that was further extended in July and again in August. Even so, there was a supple-

72. EPA, *Economic Survey of Japan, 1972–1973*, p. 38.

mentary budget in October 1973 that was larger in real terms than the large and intentionally stimulative supplementary budget of 1972. The fiscal 1974 budget, prepared in January, was indeed highly restrictive, with general account spending reported up only 20 percent and FILP up only 14.5 percent. Given the fact that wholesale prices in February were 37 percent higher than a year earlier and that the GNP deflator for the first quarter was up 26 percent over the year, real spending was clearly reduced. But it was at least a year too late—and, moreover, its restrictive impact may have been more than offset by the giant tax reduction that became effective in April.[73]

Evaluation

The section on policy in each of the recent Japanese economic white papers has usually described a fine tuning of fiscal policy, always sensitively coordinated with a flexible monetary policy, the two together achieving a management of aggregate demand appropriate to the short-run situation and problems of the economy. As reviewed here, the record does not fully support these descriptions, which may more accurately characterize intentions than performance. Tax policy until recently can best be described as somewhat random, rather than systematically stabilizing or destabilizing; short-run expenditure policy seemed primarily directed toward offsetting recessions —even when these were being deliberately initiated and sustained by restrictive monetary policy.

The main complaint would perhaps have to be of false advertising. For the tools of monetary policy usually appeared quite adequate to achieve whatever short-run objective the government wished to accomplish, even without fiscal policy pulling in tandem. The role of fiscal policy in Japan— perhaps appropriately and surely quite effectively—was largely confined to the achievement of other macroeconomic (and social) objectives: maintaining a secularly high degree of restraint on an otherwise excessive aggregate demand; promoting investment generally, and particularly productive, as opposed to social welfare, government investments; helping to assure the financing of investment by public corporations and local authorities, and preferred categories of private investment; and keeping the budget small (by international standards) relative to GNP.

But the apparently major fiscal policy mistakes of 1973 and 1974 require a harsher judgment. Their full explanation is not easy. It probably involved, among other things, the confusions entailed in attempting to adjust policy simultaneously to the yen's sudden emergence (or suddenly appreciated

73. Ibid., pp. 38–39; Ministry of Finance, *The Budget in Brief, Japan 1973*, p. 12; *OECD Economic Outlook*, no. 15 (July 1974), p. 84.

emergence) into the status of undervaluation; to the sudden recognition that the international growth race had long since been won; and to the attempt to shift too quickly to a welfare society, one concerned with promoting better living conditions, a fairer distribution of income, and a more adequate provision of public services and with arresting the rapid deterioration of Japan's natural environment. But new claims on the budget do not automatically displace older ones. And the economy's structure, as well as the habitual modes of response within and by business and government, remained geared to expanding exports and to massive investment.

Other Macroeconomic Policies

The difficulty of sustaining any precise distinction between macroeconomic and microeconomic policies was noted at the beginning of this chapter. This difficulty may be especially great in the case of Japan—because, among other reasons, of the rather long Japanese tradition of centralized guidance or direction of the economy in the interest of the nation's total economic development. This tradition differs appreciably from the Western (especially the American) tradition, which places less emphasis on national economic achievement and more on providing *opportunities* for individual economic achievement. Not only has there tended to be a greater amount of government involvement in economic decisions in Japan, but such involvement also seems guided by a far more sharply focused view of a desirable path and pattern of overall economic evolution than is held in the United States and most other Western countries. That is, macroeconomic considerations may play a larger role in Japanese than in Western governmental economic policy-making—even in the making of microeconomic policy.

If this hypothesis is correct, the reader may be able to find evidence to support it in the discussions of international, industrial, labor, tax, technological, and other policies elsewhere in this volume; but in any case, the thesis cannot be specifically defended here. Rather, this discussion of other policies is confined to two further specific instruments through which government policy attempts to affect aggregate economic performance.

Economic Planning

The term "economic planning," even when restricted to *government* economic planning, can have many meanings. In its most inclusive sense it encompasses all governmental economic policy. Its more technical sense, the one used here, restricts it to the organized, formal, and quantitative specification of a desired and desirable level and growth rate of total output (typically measured as GNP) over a period of future years (often five or ten), together with a distribution of the desired output in each year among its various uses (that is, private investment, public investment, private and public consumption, and net exports), its distribution among industrial sources (the production of steel, automobiles, motion pictures, armaments, personal services, and so forth), and—in most plans—a distribution of the resulting incomes among categories of recipients. The distributions among uses, products, and recipients are supposed, first, to accord with certain socially determined objectives or priorities, second, to be mutually consistent and feasible, and, third, to be necessary for attainment of the planned levels and rates of change of GNP. Japan is one of the relatively small number of major free-market countries that practices economic planning in this sense. The phrase "indicative planning" is often used to distinguish the practices of such countries from the mandatory planning used in nonfree-market economies.

Because it will be contended that economic planning has made only minor contributions to Japan's economic success, and because many descriptions of Japanese planning are available in English, there is no need to go into detail regarding planning methods, organization, or procedures.[74] Moreover, a number of aspects of planning are discussed rather fully in Chapter 11 below. We note only that, between December 1955 and February 1973, a period of just over seventeen years, there were six different National Economic Plans in effect. Of these, four were intended to cover five-year periods, one six years, and one ten years. The arithmetic shows that, on the average, each plan was superseded by another before it had reached its intended half-life. A seventh five-year plan, published in February 1973, is reported at this writing to be approaching replacement.

Without further description, we move directly to a summary evaluation of the arguments made about the contribution that indicative planning might have made to the success of Japan's economic development.

• It has been argued that a plan with ambitious overall targets can raise a country's rate of economic growth above what it would otherwise be merely

74. Among the numerous treatments of Japanese economic planning in English, the following include a range of descriptive and evaluative treatments (mostly critical): Shigeto Tsuru, "Rapid Growth with Formal Planning Divorced from Action," in Everett E. Hagen (ed.), *Planning Economic Development* (R. D. Irwin, 1963); Tsunehiko Watanabe, "National Planning and Economic Growth in Japan," in Bert G. Hickman (ed.), *Quantitative Planning of Economic Policy* (Brookings Institution, 1965), pp. 233–51; Japan Economic Research Center, *Economic Planning and Macroeconomic Policy,* especially papers by Kazushi Ohkawa, Tadao Uchida and Masao Baba, and Miyohei Shinohara; and Ryūtarō Komiya, "Economic Planning in Japan" (processed, 1974).

by demonstrating that resources are available to meet those targets and by inducing the belief that most other economic entities (including the government) will be expanding their inputs and outputs more or less in accordance with the plan—and this in a way that makes such expansion by each entity, more or less in accordance with the plan, both possible and profitable. Variously described as "uncertainty reducing" or "confidence building," these effects tend to make any feasible plan self-executing, primarily by inducing firms to undertake the fixed investments contemplated by the plan.

Although it can be argued that the early plans may have had some such effects, most Japanese and foreign economists who have studied the Japanese experience doubt that their contributions in this way were of major importance for investment and growth—and certainly not after about 1960. The primary reason for this conclusion is that, without exception, rates of growth necessary to achieve plan targets were regularly exceeded by actual growth —which was a major reason why each plan was replaced within a brief period by the next.

• A plan sets targets not only for overall growth but also for all major sectors and industries. By showing the quite different implications of an overall growth rate for the expansion of particular sectors and industries, the plan is said to contribute to the avoidance of bottlenecks and shortages in some areas and overinvestment in others, which not only would prevent the overall targets from being achieved, but might contribute as well to inflation and income disparities. This is presumably achieved both by putting individual firms on notice as to the opportunities available to them, and by guiding government actions in support of private firms—in lending, subsidies, import licenses, exchange controls, tax incentives, and so on—in ways that contribute to realizing the pattern of detailed developments necessary for achieving the overall targets.

Undoubtedly, the plans made some contribution in these respects. But it was probably modest, given, first, that the plans quickly became obsolete; second, that at least some Japanese entrepreneurs appear to have been quick to visualize and exploit emerging opportunities, whether or not contemplated in the plan; and, third, that the administrators of special aid and assistance (mainly in the Ministries of International Trade and Industry and of Finance), able to rely on continuous and intimate feedback from their clients, did not require the particular numerical projections of the plan in order successfully to support the plan's broad goals both through their administration of government assistance and through guidance of private actions.

• The plans were also potentially important in guiding the investment by government itself—by general government in productive infrastructure and in the plant and equipment of government enterprises and corporations—as well as governmental policies relating to manpower training, international trade and investment, natural resource management, and all other related government activities. Again, some importance must be attached to the plans as guides for the government's own operations; but they are not generally held to have made a major contribution in this respect—for the reason, among others, that many government ministries have paid little attention to the plans in their own operations.

The point that the government itself has failed to follow the plan is, indeed, sometimes emphasized by the defenders of planning—who may freely concede that Japanese planning has not made a major contribution to Japanese performance. But it could have, they suggest, if only the government had been guided by it, instead of ignoring it. Some even argue that the government itself should have used all its powers and influence to see to it that each of the apparently underambitious plans was fully carried out. Then the plans would not have become so quickly obsolete, which provided the excuse for both the private sector and the ministries to ignore them.

Although not often stated so baldly, this line of argument at least hovers in the background of some defenses of planning. It might have some validity were it not for the fact that each plan became obsolete in large part because it underestimated the rate of growth of which the economy was capable. If a plan underestimates the improvement in productivity that domestic resources will achieve, should production nevertheless be held down to that projected in the plan? If the plan underestimates the growth of foreign demand for Japanese output and therefore limits the planned expansion of domestic production and income in order to avoid an excessive burden on the balance of payments, should domestic production, incomes, and imports be restricted to the plan levels when exports grow more rapidly? Despite the obvious sophistication and dedication of the econometricians and others responsible for producing the plans, economic science is probably still unable satisfactorily to project the inherent growth prospects and the detailed structural interrelations of an economy as dynamic as Japan's has been.[75]

75. Tsunehiko Watanabe, whose rather conspiratorial interpretations of both monetary and fiscal policy have been referred to earlier, extends a similar interpretation to the errors of the plan. He argues that planned growth of GNP was deliberately underestimated by the use of artificially low values for exogenous variables in the econometric models used; he shows, by simulations for the years 1966 and 1967, that most of the error of the projected GNP growth rate was the result of underestimate of exogenous variables, many of which are policy variables. The purpose, again, is said to be to generate low targets for the expansion of investment in social overhead. Thus, he does not

The major benefits of Japanese planning may come not from the plans themselves, but from their preparation. One such benefit is simply the extensive interaction of hundreds of bureaucrats from a broad range of ministries with one another and with thousands of business leaders in a setting that encourages rational thinking about existing and potential problems—a setting that provides, as a minimum, the opportunity to examine and perhaps discard inherited dogmas, and sometimes also the means to reach logically or empirically valid conclusions about the nature of economic problems or even about their solutions. All participants, and particularly those from the private sector, acquire highly useful information that they might not otherwise obtain. And the opportunity for each to learn the thinking and understand the motives and problems of the others builds at least toward a mutual tolerance, and at best toward a consensus, of values and objectives.

In addition to benefits derived from the process of plan preparation, the main advantage of the plans themselves probably lies not in their specific content nor in the chance that they might be carried out in whole or part, but rather in forcing leaders in and out of government to have before them a fairly specific view about the future, which is inevitably compared with actual developments; and forcing, when they diverge, a prompt recognition that those assumptions which underlie present action need to be revised and the present course of action therefore reconsidered. The frequent American refusal—at least in the federal government—to publish more than one-year projections (and perhaps the refusal even to formulate them explicitly for fear of their unauthorized publication) allows policymakers to be fuzzy about those expectations which provide an important basis for present action and fails to force them immediately to reexamine the premises of current policy whenever the best estimate of future developments changes. If medium-term or long-term planning had no other purpose or result than to compel continuing examination of present policy in the light of the best view of the future, all of its complicated apparatus and organization might be worthwhile.

Administrative Guidance

The term "administrative guidance" refers to a method, not a policy. It is a method widely used by the Japanese government to support or reinforce many sorts of policies, both microeconomic and macroeconomic.

Essentially, administrative guidance involves the use of influence, advice,

---

argue that growth of production should have been restricted to the plan, but that the plans were deliberately decorative. See his "National Planning and Economic Development," especially pp. 30–43.

and persuasion to cause firms or individuals to behave in particular ways that the government believes are desirable. The persuasion of course is exerted and the advice given by public officials who may have the power to provide—or withhold—loans, grants, subsidies, licenses, tax concessions, government contracts, permissions to import, foreign exchange, approval of cartel arrangements, and other desirable (or undesirable) outcomes, both now and over the indefinite future. But it is inaccurate to think of administrative guidance exclusively in terms of manipulation of carrot and stick. Rather, the Japanese tradition of private acceptance of government leadership and the widespread recognition that government officials have knowledge, experience, and information superior to that available to the ordinary firm, as well as the sharing of values, beliefs, and political preferences by government officials and business leaders, all contribute to the success of the method.

The Bank of Japan's window guidance is a characteristic use of this method. Official publications blandly note that the BOJ provides only advice, which individual banks are free to accept or ignore as they wish. Administrative guidance is also one important tool through which national economic plans are supposed to be made effective. The particular further uses of administrative guidance to be briefly discussed here are its use to control investment as a supplementary tool of demand management and its use for the direct control of prices.

During the boom and inflation of 1973–74, the MITI, with the advice of its top advisory committee, the Industrial Structure Council, directly controlled through administrative guidance the volume of plant and equipment investments made by approximately 1,700 firms in twelve major industries, including power, steel, petrochemicals, automobiles, and aluminum—industries that account for a substantial proportion of Japan's total investment.[76] Unlike the MITI's longstanding (although less extensive and less continuous) administrative guidance of investment by firms in these industries for such purposes as rationalization, industrial balance, avoiding overinvestment, or assuring adequate capacity for export or domestic needs, the recent guidance was explicit used as a means of controlling an important segment of aggregate demand; thus it constitutes a major supplement to window guidance and other instruments of monetary policy. In effect, guidance is no longer

76. In case there is doubt that this control was actually thought of as an instrument of demand management, the Economic Planning Agency, in *Summary of Economic Survey of Japan, 1973–1974* (1974), states that "restrictive demand management policies" included "direct controls . . . enforced on private machinery and equipment investments" (p. 11).

extended merely to the banks, which lend to finance investments, but beyond the banks to the individual investing firms.[77] There is every indication that the control has been highly effective in achieving the levels of investment specified by the MITI (although there have also been complaints that it perpetuated bottlenecks in some industries). Whether the system would work quite as effectively in reverse—namely, to increase investment in order to strengthen aggregate demand—is difficult to judge. Thus far there have probably been few occasions when such use might have seemed appropriate in Japan.

Price control through administrative guidance is another important phenomenon of the current inflationary period, although surely export prices have at times reflected such guidance in earlier years. In early December 1973 the government drew up legislation—"Emergency Measure Law on Stabilizing People's Living," which the Diet shortly thereafter approved—providing explicit legal authority for price controls. At the time this legislation was being drafted, a newspaper reported as follows:

The Government has repeatedly said that it would try to stay away as much as possible from mobilizing strong controls under the livelihood stabilization and price controls laws, involving a complete price freeze, setting of standard prices and levying surcharges from violators.

Such a stance may be likened to an "undrawn sword" made by a master swordsmith; the sword need not be drawn because everybody knows that it cuts well.

Using this metaphor, International Trade & Industry Minister Yasuhiro Nakasone said that whether the laws are called into action or not, their mere existence will make the Government's administrative guidance "cut better."

According to informants, invoking of the livelihood stabilization law and the price control ordinance actually will be extremely difficult technically, regardless of the Government's intention.[78]

And, indeed, the price freeze that followed[79] made use of the specific legislative authority only for the price controls on propane, kerosene, and toilet paper. All other prices were controlled simply through administrative guidance. (At retail, this was apparently confined to department stores.) Price controls for many of these commodities continued into the fall of 1974, with adjustments permitted in specific cases to reflect higher costs or to permit wider margins. Although there must have been violations of the guidance, it

77. Press reports, especially in the summer of 1973, had referred to extensive discussions among MOF and BOJ personnel of schemes to regulate the detailed structure of investment, industry by industry, through the mechanism of window guidance. Apparently, it was decided that such investment should be regulated directly through administrative guidance by the MITI.

78. *Japan Economic Journal,* Dec. 11, 1973.

79. In December controls were imposed on prices of petroleum products and in March 1974 on prices of some 50 to 60 other basic commodities at wholesale and 148 at retail.

seems probable that major producers of such basic materials as steel and aluminum or of final products such as automobiles adhered closely both to the letter and the spirit of the guidance.[80]

The extensive and perhaps increasing use of administrative guidance in Japan for a wide variety of purposes has given rise to increasing criticism: partly in terms that stress the absence of specific legal authority and (in Anglo-Saxon terminology) of the protections of due process; partly in terms that stress the unhealthy political aspects of a system in which vital decisions are made more or less in secret by a small coterie of bureaucrats and business leaders (many of them retired bureaucrats) who reflect a narrow range of political, economic, and educational backgrounds and interests.[81] At the same time, the MITI has continued to defend the method as one which avoids red tape, complex legal procedures, and an atmosphere of confrontation between business and government. Anyone with experience in administering price controls (in a regime of confrontation and legalistic red tape) can understand how much easier, more effective, and possibly even more equitable price controls could be if the controllers were able to negotiate a simple agreement with a seller of automobiles or steel that his prices might appropriately rise by 3.72 percent on the average and then be confident that the seller's free and unsupervised adjustment of his myriad particular prices, extra charges, credit and delivery terms, and so on, would indeed add to his unit sales revenue something very close to 3.72 percent.

If Japan should explicitly embrace the method of incomes policy to control inflation, it seems clear that—at least on the side of the prices of major industrial products—the use of informal and quasi-voluntary methods of administrative guidance (the Japanese equivalent of jawboning, arm twisting, and finger pointing) might be expected to be rather more successful than such methods have been in the United States.

Evaluation and Prospects

Previous sections, which have treated separately monetary policy, fiscal policy, and economic planning and administrative guidance, have made some attempt to evaluate the separate use of each particular instrument. This con-

80. For some details, see Takao Akabane, "Is the Soft-Landing on 'The New Price Structure' Imminent?" *Technocrat* (July 1974), pp. 56–59, and ibid. (August 1974), pp. 56–59.

81. Japan's Fair Trade Commission actually began legal action (for conspiring to set prices) against petroleum companies that claimed only to have followed the MITI's guidance.

cluding section briefly considers some issues that properly relate to the strategy employed in the combined use of these (and other) macroeconomic policies, and to the success of the results thereby achieved. This is followed by some extremely tentative reflections on possible implications of the analysis for the future use of these policies.

The Combined Impact of Macroeconomic Policies

Government policymakers in postwar Japan appear to have been able to exercise a more precise—and, on the whole, more effective—management of overall economic developments than have their counterparts in most other major free-market countries. On the whole, the makers of macroeconomic policy achieved what they sought to achieve. The following paragraphs attempt to explain and support this judgment.

• An outstanding feature of Japanese macroeconomic policy has been its unique division of labor between fiscal and monetary policies. Fiscal policy has been basically restraining throughout: the size of the budget has been kept small relative to gross national product, and the budget usually has been heavily in surplus. Although there has been some variation in the extent of budgetary restraint, such variation has not ordinarily played any significant role in short-term policy. The large budgetary surplus, augmented by borrowings and deposits from the private sector, has been used to provide credit on easy terms to productive activities deemed essential to the grand strategy of investment, growth, and exports.

• Monetary policy instead played the major short-term role. Basically, Japanese monetary policy has been highly stimulative. During booms the banking system has been permitted—indeed, assisted and encouraged—to supply whatever volume of money and credit was demanded at low and stable interest rates (rates set progressively lower in each period of easy money). During intermittent periods of restraint, interest rates rose only slightly; instead, credit was effectively rationed. Through this mechanism, the incentive to invest was consistently stimulated, but the ability to invest effectively restrained whenever, and as much as, it needed to be to carry out the government's balance-of-payments and anti-inflationary objectives. It was a strategy that maximized the speed with which Japan was able to move both its potential and its actual output steadily closer to the levels of production and productivity permitted by Japan's abundant, energetic, and educated labor force and by the world's stock of advanced technology.

• Japan has never considered stability of the rate of economic expansion an important policy objective; and its policymakers and public opinion have accepted considerable instability. Even though stop-go policies, creating instability in the expansion rate, have not produced appreciable cyclical unemployment, there are still costs of recessions: in loss of income (mostly overtime pay and bonuses), production, and investment. Thus, the question must be raised as to whether Japan might have been better advised to have sought a sustainable rate of expansion, tempering its booms and perhaps thereby avoiding or minimizing its recessions. Had it been possible to have known in advance what the maximum sustainable rate of expansion might be (whether for the maintenance of a desired balance-of-payments position or the avoidance of overheating), a strategy aimed at achieving precisely that rate would perhaps have been superior. But the evidence from the successive national plans is clear that policymakers would have invariably underestimated the sustainable rate of expansion. And the fact that policies were maintaining an expansion rate slower than the maximum sustainable one would not necessarily have become clearly evident. Investment and thus the growth of productive capacity and the speed of introduction of new technology would have been less; the transfer of labor from less productive to more productive employments would have occurred more slowly; and a slower growth of incomes would have produced lower private saving. No clear signal that expansion was falling short of what it might have been would have been apparent—unless, perhaps, it was a surplus of exports. But with less pressure placed upon exporters (and perhaps less restraint on imports), even the trade balance might not have given an unmistakable signal that opportunities for growth of output, incomes, and welfare were being needlessly sacrificed.

• During most of the period under review, the primary objective of Japanese economic policy was rapid growth of output and real incomes. The basic concern was not with whether existing resources were being used at a steady and socially acceptable rate, but with enhancing the volume and productivity of those resources; it was not with the full realization of potential output, but with the fastest possible growth of potential and then of actual output. Given that the quantity and, especially, the quality of Japan's labor force was not a significantly limiting factor, potential output was potentially capable of growing exceedingly fast—faster than almost anyone imagined—through high rates of saving and investment, rapid technological and managerial improvement, and dramatic shifts in industrial structure. Given its inherited economic structure and the goals of the society, Japan's policy of all-out expansion in booms, followed by restraint only when it became clear that it was needed, was probably close to optimal.

• Certainly, it can well be argued that the economic goals of, and the political constraints on, Japanese policy were less than optimal—that rapid growth as a symbol of national fulfillment and international prestige blinded Japanese for too long to some of its associated costs. Perhaps policy paid too much respect to the preservation of a particular exchange value of the yen, or to the maintenance of national control of large enterprises in key industries, or to similar matters. But given Japanese perceptions of the national interest, macroeconomic policy was, on the whole, skillfully and successfully employed to support its realization.

• One reason for the greater precision and effectiveness of macroeconomic policies in Japan has been the willingness and ability of its policymakers to exert—and of the private sector to accept—a more detailed influence on private decisions than occurs elsewhere. Macroeconomic management is carried closer than in most other free-market economies to the "micro" level, through such processes as credit rationing, other forms of administrative guidance, government financial intermediation, special tax provisions, and economic planning.

• An important contribution to this greater precision of macroeconomic control may arise, however, simply from the inherent buoyancy of aggregate private demand in Japan: it is undoubtedly easier to imprint a desired pattern on economic developments through the exercise of restraint than through stimulus. This buoyancy—a tendency for private demand to float quickly and predictably upward against whatever limits are placed upon it—was partly the result of the historical accident of Japan's inherited structure of productive resources and sociopsychological attitudes and of the circumstances of its place in the postwar world; and partly the result simply of a confidence born of success (however accidental that success may initially have been). But it was also partly the product of governmental policies which provided strong stimulus at the level of the firm—through easy money and low interest rates, plus a wide variety of special supports and inducements.

• Despite Japan's basically successful record in the use of macroeconomic policy, there have also been some serious mistakes, especially in the period from 1971 through 1973. But no country can claim to have avoided policy mistakes.

• Although Japan's overall rate of inflation has consistently been close to the highest among industrial countries, inflation has surely been less of a problem in Japan than elsewhere—until 1973. The foremost reason, perhaps, is that the extremely large and widely shared gains in real income, which were the product of spectacular productivity growth, have meant that even those who were relative losers from inflation still achieved large (and unexpectedly growing) gains in real income. The relative redistributions of income and wealth brought about by inflation surely constitute a far more serious problem for a society in which the average annual gain in real income is negligible. Second, because of the stability of Japan's export prices and the inflationary trend in the rest of the world, inflation created no balance-of-payments problems for Japan. Third, unlike the situation in most other countries, inflation showed no tendency to accelerate in the late 1950s and in the 1960s. Possible reasons were that, because unemployment was not a significant problem in Japan (given its institutional structure), political pressures to "risk a little more inflation" in order to minimize the human and social costs of unemployment were negligible; moreover, throughout most of the period the existence of large labor reserves in agriculture and other traditional sectors helped to protect from excessive demand-pull pressures the average unit labor cost, which, in modern economies, serves essentially as the basic standard of value.

Prospective Problems in Macroeconomic Policy

We look, finally, to the future, sparing the "probably's," "possibly's," and "perhaps's" that should dot every sentence, and referring first to the more technical and conventional issues of macroeconomic policy. It is clear that the priorities of Japan's policy have now switched from growth, investment, and exports to improving the quality of life for the average citizen through dealing more effectively with pollution and other unwanted transformations of the natural environment and providing better housing, greater protection for individual livelihoods, expanded availability of urban and social amenities, and the like. The increased production of these new "goods" will require far less private investment than did the earlier product mix; and it is sure to generate a slower growth of measured (or even measurable) productivity and incomes.

A smooth transition from the older pattern of production and investment to the new poses difficult problems for demand management. It will be necessary to avoid, on the one hand, too massive an investment in, and diversion of consumption toward, the new priorities without adequately limiting the use of resources for the older ones (as apparently occurred in 1972–73). On the other hand, too sudden an attempted shift to the new lines of production could generate an unexpected collapse of private investment in the older lines. A slower growth of incomes might well reduce drastically personal or business saving, but it is impossible to be sure in advance whether and how much. In the meantime, private aggregate demand might easily be miscalculated.

With private investment a substantially smaller element in aggregate demand, monetary policy would seem to lose its ability singlehandedly to offset undesired, or to create desired, fluctuations in aggregate demand. The banking system can easily enough turn from lending to business for the finance of private investment to lending to government to finance public investment or enlarged public consumption.[82] But if total demand threatens to be too large or too small, these latter components are not subject to effective control through monetary policy, not even window guidance. To be sure, monetary policy can still influence the smaller volume of private investment in plant and inventories. Moreover, if adequate institutional arrangements are created, there is no reason why the expected larger share of GNP devoted to residential construction cannot be privately financed, and its volume influenced by monetary policy for demand management purposes. But there is no reason why private investment—and not private or public consumption—should do all of the adjusting. Fiscal policy will inevitably become more important, both as a source of potential instability if badly managed and as a tool of stabilization if well managed. There is no reason why it cannot be well managed.

In any case, to return to a concept that recurs throughout this chapter, it would seem likely that the buoyancy of private aggregate demand cannot fail to be reduced in the new welfare society. Thus, short-run policy will need something more than the single tool, that of a monetary policy equipped only with an on-off switch. A flexible short-run fiscal policy can provide various degrees not only of restraint but stimulus; and in a consumption-oriented society, fiscal policy, especially tax policy, may be considerably more effective than monetary policy.

Developing and administering an effective and flexible fiscal policy will not be easy. Perhaps the extensive forecasting and analytical capabilities of Japan's skilled economists, many of them in the Economic Planning Agency, can be used for this purpose more effectively than in the past. But a fiscal policy that will not again have to be accused of serious mistakes—or even

82. Much Japanese discussion, private and governmental, at least through 1972 seemed to take for granted that the new social programs will be financed largely by government bond issues rather than by increased taxation. It can be assumed that many of the resources needed for the new programs will appropriately be released from private investment and net exports, but it would be a serious error to assume a one-to-one substitution. Moreover, there could be a significant increase in private consumption relative to income. The old rules of sound finance—a balanced budget and no direct borrowing from the Bank of Japan—were essentially harmless in their time. But a new rule—that borrowing for social programs is fine—could be very dangerous.

false advertising—will impose even more difficult challenges for political leadership than for economic analysis.

Even more intractable demands on political leadership will arise in connection with the problem of rising prices. For it seems undeniable that inflation has become and will remain a far more serious problem than in the past for Japan (as for all countries), and that it is progressively less amenable to control by traditional methods of demand management. As in all countries, inflation becomes a more serious problem simply because of the greater recent experience with it, of the expectations (and memories) which that experience arouses, and because of faster inflation abroad. Also, perhaps, Japan is or will be exposed to the same social, political, and organizational trends as are other advanced countries, many of which seem to increase the bias toward inflation.[83]

Changes in Japan's balance of resource availability (that is, the increasing labor shortage) and a lesser need (under a regime of more flexible exchange rates) for booms to be slowed down for balance-of-payments reasons are likely from time to time to expose the basic wage level to greater pressure of excess demand than was felt in the past. More serious, however, is the prospect of severe new cost-push pressures. It can by hypothesized that cost-push wage pressures were minimized in the 1950s and first half of the 1960s not only by the relative weakness of labor's bargaining power in a regime of labor surplus, but also throughout the period by the facts that real wage income was rising rapidly and that its rise was always—and always unexpectedly—accelerating. Before workers could become thoroughly accustomed to, and convinced that they were forever entitled to, one rate of income increase, they were pleasantly surprised to find themselves given one even higher.

On the assumption that the rate of growth of Japan's productivity and thus of real wage income must now decline, workers may find it considerably harder to accept (unexpected) declines in the growth of real income than it was to accept (unexpected) increments in that growth. At least four aspects of Japanese labor institutions might worsen the problem.

Although the American economist may think that powerful national unions—and a strong national federation—are essential to the existence of wage cost-push inflation, the highly decentralized structure of Japanese or-

83. For the views of one of the authors on what may be some of these trends, see Gardner Ackley, "Roles and Limits of Incomes Policies," *The Oriental Economist* (April 1974), pp. 18–24, especially p. 21; also published in Japanese in a special issue of the weekly *Tōyō keizai* (April 1974).

ganization may be equally favorable to cost-push. First, the tradition of life-time employment and the absence of an effective labor market for experi-enced workers may make it very difficult for the Japanese employer to resist the wage demands of his enterprise union. Second, the tradition of resolving competing interests through conciliation and consensus—and ultimately agreement—would seem to make it more likely than elsewhere that disputes over wages would be compromised (always upward), with employers pass-ing along the cost of maintaining peace in their own households to their more impersonal markets. Third, the apparent importance in some segments of the Japanese labor movement of Marxist ideology, with its central concepts of exploitation and class struggle, recalls in many respects the Italian situation, in which ideology remained below the surface only so long as the rate of improvement in workers' economic positions accelerated. Fourth, although the leadership of a national union—and especially of a federation of national unions—can recognize (or be led to the recognition) that wage increases steadily and everywhere in excess of productivity growth are not in the eco-nomic interests of members of the larger group (because extra wage gains will inevitably be eroded by higher prices), this calculus is meaningless to an organization confined to a single enterprise.

If it is correct that cost-push forces are otherwise likely to perpetuate and possibly even to accelerate recent rates of inflation, the primary additional defense might appear to lie in an incomes policy, and this is under intense discussion and study in Japan. It was suggested earlier that Japan's economy is probably well adapted to an effective quasi-voluntary control of most in-dustrial prices. But the essence of the problem of incomes policy lies in the control of wage costs. In addition to problems already mentioned, the na-tional politics of Japan seem badly adapted to success in such an enterprise. Wage restraint might conceivably be unilaterally imposed through govern-ment pressures on employers, which might even be moderately effective, at least for a time. But the fact that the political party that controls the govern-ment is so exclusively identified with the economic interest of employers (and farmers) and the major political opposition is so largely identified with labor would almost surely tend to translate an issue of economic management into an acutely political confrontation. The opposition parties would have every reason to seek to use the size of the annually recommended wage increase as a prime electoral weapon; and Marxists would treat the issue as a clear illustration of the doctrines of exploitation and class struggle. If national politics were not thus to be poisoned by the issue of wage restraint, it would seem necessary to attempt directly and formally to involve the leadership of the labor movement in the making of national wage policy. Whether the possible economic gains would be seen by the leadership of labor as exceeding the costs of losing a highly effective political weapon is impossible for an outsider to judge. If they were not, sober leaders of the majority party might well opt for a somewhat higher rate of inflation—perhaps in the belief (of problematic validity) that greater experience with inflation might induce a greater willingness on the part of labor to cooperate in solving a serious national problem.

To end on so pessimistic a note seems inappropriate. This review of the macroeconomic policies of postwar Japan has revealed at every turn a remarkable energy, inventiveness, and flexibility of leadership and an unusual ability of citizens to identify personal with national interest. These suggest that the economic and social progress of the Japanese nation is not likely to founder, however novel and difficult the problems encountered.

CHAPTER FOUR

Banking and Finance

Henry C. Wallich, Federal Reserve Board
and
Mable I. Wallich

Tables

JOHN STUART MILL once said that, so long as its proper functioning was assured, there could be no less important thing than money. In the same spirit he might have extended his remarks to the entire financial system. The structure of the financial markets, instruments, and institutions that make up the financial system does not supply real resources but only transfers and transforms them. In the common phrase, it mobilizes resources. If it performed this function without friction and other imperfections, the result would be what economists, with considerable understatement, refer to as a "perfect capital market"—one in which every participant can both lend and borrow any amount he wants to at the same rate.

Measured by this standard, the financial system of Japan falls far short of perfection. Discrimination among lenders and among borrowers, rationing, and subsidies have been the rule. Along with many other features these defects measure the distance between the financial system of Japan and a perfect capital market.

The contribution of the financial system to economic growth can also be "measured," however, by the amount of external financing obtained by spending units in Japan. External financing (funds raised by private domestic nonfinancial sectors) in 1972 amounted to more than 90 percent of gross private domestic investment and 26 percent of gross national product (GNP).[1] This compares not unfavorably with conditions in the United States, where the respective ratios in 1972 were 81.5 percent and 12.6 percent.

A third way of assessing the contribution of the financial system to economic growth is to focus on the value added by it to the GNP. The national accounts of Japan show that the value added by the financial sector, comprising banking and insurance, was equal to 5 percent of GNP in 1972. The amount is small relative to the volume of financial resources allocated through the financial system. To the extent that this allocation is determined not by the supply and demand originating from the real sectors, but through allocative decisions made by or through the financial system, one may say that the importance of the financial sector in the economy exceeds its contribution to GNP. In Japan the importance of the financial system in this regard is considerable.

Note. We are indebted to Shōichi Rōyama of Osaka University for numerous helpful suggestions. Responsibility for the contents is entirely our own.
    1. Bank of Japan, Economic Research Department, *Flow of Funds of the Japanese Economy in 1973*, Special Paper 51 (1974), p. 2; and Economic Planning Agency, *Annual Report on National Income Statistics, 1974*, p. 33.

Characteristics of the Financial System

Financial technology, like any other, is similar around the world. The activity of transferring financial resources, just like the activity of making steel, is governed by technological factors that are the same in Japan as elsewhere. Financial techniques for the most part are internationally homogenized, moreover, thanks to the international character of the banking industry, which had one of its principal origins in the financing of trade among nations. The vast local variety of legal dispositions governing the relationship between creditors and debtors, determined historically, must not be allowed to obscure this fundamental fact.

The flow of funds through these institutional channels nevertheless is quite different in Japan from that in many other national economies. Historically, the technically easy forms of credit—short-term financing of trade and loans to well-established borrowers—have preceded the more sophisticated forms —long-term financing, borrowers without collateral, and high-risk economic activities. Progress in financial technology has consisted of making bankable the previously unbankable. In Japan this development is still in its early stages, but it is well under way.

Stocks and flows of financial assets, moreover, in contrast to tangible assets, are fungible—short-term debt can be funded, all kinds of debt can be converted into equity, and flows of funds can shift from one channel to another. A flow of funds table lacks the stability that an input-output table derives from near-fixed technological coefficients. In Japan this flexibility of finance is only beginning to become apparent.

Public policy also has contributed to shaping the financial patterns of Japan. It has helped to divert funds to weak sectors, such as agriculture and small business. But in good part public policy has simply reinforced the preferences of the market: large enterprises, which in any event enjoy priority in financial markets, have been given additional advantages in borrowing.

Finally, the risk factor has had much to do with financial structures in Japan. It governs in particular the structure of bank assets, the structure of corporate liabilities, and the asset choices of households. In Japan financial risk, which is largely private risk, has been controlled and manipulated by public and private action to a high degree. As a result, risk exposures that are almost inconceivable elsewhere have prevailed in Japanese business finance without adverse consequences so far, except with respect to inflation losses accompanied by what looks like extreme risk aversion on the part of household savers.

Special Problems of Japan

In examining the financial system of Japan, one needs to maintain a fine balance between two competing approaches. On the one hand, it is obvious that the system differs greatly from Western systems in both its structure and its behavior. Thus tracing these differences must be a principal objective of a study such as this. In doing so, however, it is tempting to stress differences and to find that Japan is indeed unique. On the other hand, since a study of this kind depends on concepts and analytical tools derived from the body of general economic theory, it is tempting as well to show that economics works in Japan as it does elsewhere. To some extent the merit of the analysis will be reflected by how successfully this is done. But this exposes one to the danger of trying to squeeze phenomena into a framework they really do not fit. A triumphant finding that the laws of economics do apply to Japan and that, economically speaking, Japan after all is not very different may be misleading.

For instance, it is not clear that the theoretical concept of money loses usefulness in Japan because of ambiguities affecting the empirical counterpart of money. In Western economies money finds its counterpart in the statistical concept of "currency and demand deposits." In Japan, however, there are several kinds of demand deposits, some paying interest. Likewise, the habit of interpreting the behavior of corporations according to how they maximize stockholders' profits or present worth, which even in the West often is severely strained, may be especially misleading in Japan. There, the stockholder is a subordinate creditor and management's long-run goals often sacrifice short-run profits. An effort to interpret the behavior of Japan's financial markets on the basis of the price system may be misleading because prices are not always allowed to clear markets and allocate resources.

Striking an appropriate balance between these two approaches may well depend on the period of Japan's postwar history that is the focus of study. Japan's financial system has been undergoing a process of rapid transition. It is becoming westernized in the sense that its markets are beginning to function more like Western markets, even though many of its institutions and behavior patterns retain their historical character. Things that have seemed different in Japan may not seem so a few years hence.

Such a shift would not necessarily imply a move from an inferior to a superior financial technology but may represent an adjustment to changing conditions. What many Western observers have regarded as deficiencies—such as the tight control of interest rates, the absence of a bond market, and the discriminatory allocation of resources in favor of a big manufacturing industry—were not the result of ignorance of, or inability to apply, different methods. In the pre–World War II period, Japan's interest rates moved more flexibly, and the government tried to spread credit widely. The policy decision to depart temporarily from these practices was at least partly motivated by the exigencies of the postwar period. These exigencies having been met, a shift toward more market-oriented techniques has become increasingly appropriate.

An Eclectic Approach

A study of a financial system can be directed toward various interests and points of view. One viewpoint is that of the market participant who is interested in a particular market and in the price of the financial asset bought and sold there. Typically, this is the businessman's and the investor's approach to financial analysis. A second point of view is that of the flow-of-funds accountant whose world is divided into sectors, each with its balance sheets and annual flows, such as corporations, households, government, and financial intermediaries. This kind of analysis cuts across the range of assets and markets in which a sector operates and also across the functional activities in which the sector engages. Another viewpoint is that of the macroeconomist or national income accountant who focuses on functional income and expenditure categories, such as investment, saving, consumption, government expenditures, and exports and imports. In Japan there is reason to think that these "real sector" variables have been particularly important in explaining the high rate of growth.

The procedure here will be eclectic. It will begin with an examination of the sources of savings and the use of these savings for investment. This is essentially a GNP approach. It is needed because the massive flow of investible funds into productive investment, no matter from what sources and through what channels and instruments, has been one of the principal factors in Japan's extraordinary growth. Next will come a look at the financing of this capital formation. It will focus on the liabilities of business borrowers and on the assets of savers, these being the most interesting of the numerous flow-of-funds categories. The third step will be an examination of financial intermediaries. Japan's banking system falls somewhere between the unit banking system of the United States and the highly concentrated systems of most other developed countries. The government's very positive and deliberate policies with regard to banking structure are of special interest. Finally, attention will be turned to some of the principal financial assets and their markets—stocks and bonds for the most part. Their behavior is an important part of the financial system and provides a bridge to problems of monetary policy.

The Role of Money

The chapter will be concerned mainly with credit—the asset side of the balance sheet. Only a small part of the investigation will deal with the liabilities side and in particular with money. The resulting imbalance in the treatment of the traditional dualism of money and credit, however, does not seem inappropriate in the case of Japan.

Theory and research concerning the behavior and role of money have not had the same vogue in Japan as in the United States. As far as Japan is concerned, monetarism is still in the future, if anywhere. Various institutional facts help to account for this.

Japan's economy is less "monetary" than that of other industrial countries. The use of checks and giro transfers, characteristic of modern payments systems, has never fully taken hold in Japan, where the bulk of household and small business payments still is being made in currency. Given Japanese technological capabilities, it seems quite possible that monetary habits may move directly from the currency stage to the electronic transfer stage.

The concrete embodiment of the theoretical concept "money" is harder to determine in Japan than elsewhere. Several kinds of demand deposits exist, all with slightly different degrees of liquidity and interest rates. Any definition of money is bound to be rather arbitrary.

Monetary research has been hampered by these and related institutional peculiarities. Not only the definition of money, but also the specification of interest rates, the principal variable determining the demand for money, presents problems. Interest rates are severely controlled. The banks in turn circumvent the controls to some extent by such devices as compensating balances, advertising, and the practice of treating all aspects of the relation between a bank and its customer as part of a package. All this interferes with the measurement of behavioral relationships.

The difficulties of monetary analysis are evident in the Bank of Japan econometric model, which does not contain a demand-for-money equation. The model contains equations for several components of the total money supply but treats what may be the critical component—corporate holdings of demand deposits—as a residual. In the bank's interpretation, this feature serves to indicate that the bank regards corporate balances as essentially determined by credit rationing rather than by variables endogenous to the system.

Japanese monetary authorities have focused their attention specifically on the control of credit rather than of money. Credit is the lever by which the Bank of Japan in the past has very effectively steered the economy. Money is a variable that the bank has watched but has not used as a long-run target or short-run indicator of monetary policy.

None of this implies that the monetary sector does not exhibit some notable regularities that would lend themselves to a systematic interpretation. The velocity of money and the composition of the money supply broadly defined (including time deposits) have shown considerable stability since the early 1950s. While the United States experienced major shifts in velocity, in ownership of deposits, and in the proportion of time and demand deposits, Japan experienced very little of this. In part, the stability of some of Japan's monetary relationships probably reflects the fact that Japan eliminated the monetary overhang created by the war through high inflation and thereafter did not have to "grow into" its money supply as did the United States.

Nor does a downgrading of the role of money imply the same for monetary policy. Monetary policy, as shown by Ackley and Ishi in Chapter 3, has been extremely effective. Some of the factors we will discuss—the heavy dependence of business on credit and the lack of flexible markets for money substitutes—are precisely those that have contributed to the effectiveness of monetary policy. The point to be made here is that the great power exerted by monetary policy in Japan must be rooted in an understanding of credit rather than of money.

Capital Formation

Japan's high rate of growth, interrupted perhaps only temporarily by the oil crisis, is closely linked to Japan's high saving rate. Each probably is both cause and effect of the other. In this section, the effect of growth on saving will receive more attention than the inverse relation.

The high saving rate—approximately 40 percent of GNP in 1972—represents the joint contribution of households, corporations, and government. Each sector engages in what must be considered a very high rate of saving if judged by international standards or compared with the United States, which has a low saving rate. Table 4-1 shows average savings, both gross and net (after deduction of capital consumption allowances) for the years 1970–72.

Personal Savings

Personal savings in Japan probably are the highest of any major country (see Table 4-2). In 1968–72 they amounted to about 20 percent of disposable income; the average personal saving rate in the United States was about

Table 4-1. *Comparison of Average Annual Savings in Japan and the United States, 1970–72*

	Saving in Japan		Saving in the United States	
Category	Amount (billions of yen)	As a percentage of GNP	Amount (billions of dollars)	As a percentage of GNP
Households[a]				
Net saving	10,831	13.5	56.4	5.3
Depreciation	2,646[b]	3.3	33.7	3.2
Corporations				
Net saving[c]	4,649	5.8	16.4	1.5
Depreciation	6,879[b]	8.6	60.9	5.7
Total private				
Net saving[c]	15,480	19.3	72.8	6.8
Depreciation	9,525[b]	11.9	94.6	8.9
Government[d]				
Net saving	5,893	7.3	6.3[e]	0.6
Depreciation	805[b]	1.0	19.6	1.8
Statistical discrepancy	−983	−1.2	−4.0	−0.4
Total gross saving	30,721	38.2	189.3	17.8
Total net saving[c]	20,391	25.4	75.1	7.1

Sources: Economic Planning Agency, *Annual Report on National Income Statistics, 1974*, pp. 41, 157; and U.S. Department of Commerce, Bureau of Economic Analysis, *Survey of Current Business* (July 1974), p. 34.

a. Includes households, private unincorporated businesses, and private nonprofit institutions.
b. Excludes damage to fixed capital by accident.
c. Includes inventory valuation adjustment.
d. Government and government enterprises. Japanese government savings in this table differ from those in Table 2-17 because Denison and Chung do not treat such government investment expenditures as a form of saving. See also note 53, Chapter 2.
e. Excludes inventories and military investment.

Table 4-2. *Household Savings as a Percentage of Disposable Income, for Selected Industrial Countries and Years*[a]

Country	1960	1965	1970	1971	1972
Japan	19.2[b]	17.5	20.7	20.2	21.0
Germany	15.0	15.9	16.7	15.0	15.1
France	9.7	11.1	12.7	12.3	12.1
United States	4.9	6.0	9.0	9.0	7.2
United Kingdom	4.7	6.1	5.2	4.9	5.0

Source: Organisation for Economic Co-operation and Development, *National Accounts of OECD Countries, 1960–1972* (Paris: OECD, 1974).

a. Definitions differ from those given in sources of national statistics; ratios, therefore, will not be the same as those derived from national sources. Disposable income includes households and private nonprofit institutions serving households.
b. 1961.

7 percent during this period. There is, of course, no compelling reason to postulate some external set of circumstances as the cause of high personal saving in Japan. The average household's preference for future rather than present income would suffice to produce the observed behavior. Yet many observers of the Japanese scene have advanced a number of intuitive explanations for the high saving rate, all of them plausible.[2] The hypotheses examined here for the most part do help explain high saving, but their adequacy remains uncertain. The principal hypotheses and findings are as follows:

1. Rapid growth itself may have induced high consumer saving. This could have come about through:

a. A lag in the adjustment of consumption to higher levels of disposable personal income.[3]

b. Saving decisions based on consumers' perceptions of their "permanent" income, which under conditions of rapid growth they might systematically underestimate. The econometric evidence is less persuasive, however, than the simple lag hypothesis.

c. A desired fixed relationship between present and future income that under conditions of rapid growth would require a rapid building up of financial and other assets. The evidence is that for most households stocks of assets are very modest,[4] suggesting that provision for the future is inadequate, but that households may well be trying hard to make it less so.

2. In addition to other sources given in this section, see Miyohei Shinohara, *Growth and Cycles in the Japanese Economy,* The Institute of Economic Research, Hitotsubashi University (Tokyo: Kinokuniya Bookstore Co., 1962); idem, "Savings Behavior of the Farm Household," *Structural Changes in Japan's Economic Development,* Economic Research Series 11, The Institute of Economic Research, Hitotsubashi University (Tokyo: Kinokuniya Bookstore Co., 1970), pp. 79–106; idem, "Causes and Patterns in the Postwar Growth," *The Developing Economies,* vol. 8 (December 1970), pp. 349–68; Toshiyuki Mizoguchi, "High Personal Saving Rate and Changes in the Consumption Pattern in Postwar Japan," *The Developing Economies,* vol. 8 (December 1970), pp. 407–26; idem, *Personal Savings and Consumption in Postwar Japan,* Economic Research Series 12, The Institute of Economic Research, Hitotsubashi University (Tokyo: Kinokuniya Bookstore Co., 1970); Tuvia Blumenthal, "A Note on the Life-Cycle Pattern of Saving in Japan," *Hitotsubashi Journal of Economics,* vol. 9 (February 1969), pp. 61–67; idem, "Nihon keizai no seichō yōin" [Growth Factors of Japanese Economy], *Nihon keizai shinbunsha,* 1972; and Tsutomu Noda, as cited in Kazushi Ohkawa, *Nihon keizai no kōzō-rekishiteki shiten kara* [Structure of Japanese Economy from a Historical Viewpoint] (Keiso Shodo, 1974). We are indebted to Professor Ohkawa for drawing our attention to these data.

3. Kunio Yoshihara, "The Growth Rate as a Determinant of the Saving Ratio," *Hitotsubashi Journal of Economics,* vol. 12 (February 1972), pp. 60–72.

4. Bureau of Statistics, Office of the Prime Minister, *1969 National Survey of Family Incomes and Expenditures,* vol. 7 (1970), p. 122, as cited in Raymond Goldsmith, "The Financial Development of Japan, 1868–1970," pt. 2 (manuscript, 1972), table VI-24, p. 114.

d. Constraint of consumer spending by the pattern of Japan's growth, with purchases of automobiles and space-consuming home goods being discouraged by the lag in road building and in the construction of spacious homes.

All told, the growth hypothesis undoubtedly helps explain high household saving. As Odaka found, however, growth alone is unlikely to account fully for the superiority of Japan's saving performance over that of the United States, Canada, and the United Kingdom.[5]

2. A high degree of inequality of income may have been responsible for high personal saving. The distribution of income in Japan, however, appears to be no more uneven than in the United States.[6]

3. A large proportion of self-employed could be the cause of a high propensity to save.[7] The evidence indicates, however, that the behavior of the self-employed—farmers, professionals, and owners of unincorporated businesses—partly because of a declining share in disposable income, has at best contributed only marginally to the high personal saving ratio.[8]

4. Institutional factors may have contributed to a high saving rate.

a. Semiannual bonuses, which are an important part of labor income, may be saved in part, although the permanent income hypothesis of saving suggests that, since bonuses are largely anticipated, workers would spend the same proportion of the bonuses as of regular wages and salaries.[9]

b. Limited availability of consumer and housing credit may induce higher saving.

c. The low level of social security benefits calls for a greater individual saving effort.

5. The life-cycle hypothesis of saving could be relied on for an explanation of high saving if the groups that do most of the saving—the young and particularly the middle-aged—were unusually numerous relative to the group that consumes savings—the aged. The social practices of Japan,

5. Kōnosuke Odaka, "An Analysis of the Personal Consumption Expenditure in Japan, 1892–1967" (paper presented at the Japan Economic Seminar, New Haven, Conn., April 27, 1974).

6. See Chapter 5 in this volume.

7. Miyohei Shinohara, "The Structure of Saving and the Consumption Function in Postwar Japan," *Journal of Political Economy*, vol. 67 (December 1959), pp. 589–603.

8. Ryūtarō Komiya, "Supply of Personal Savings," in Ryūtarō Komiya (ed.), *Postwar Economic Growth in Japan* (University of California Press, 1966), pp. 157–81; and Tsutomu Noda, "Savings of Farm Households," in Kazushi Ohkawa, Bruce F. Johnston, and Hiromitsu Kaneda (eds.), *Agriculture and Economic Growth: Japan's Experience* (Princeton University Press, 1969).

9. Komiya, "Supply of Personal Savings"; and Shinohara, "The Structure of Saving and Consumption."

however, cast doubt on the applicability of such an explanation, and empirical work shows the relation of saving to age to be unstable when other factors, such as the size of the household, the number of income earners, and the level of income are taken into account.

THE INFLUENCE OF THE FINANCIAL SYSTEM ON PERSONAL SAVING. Personal saving may be affected positively or negatively by the institutions and policies of the financial system. There is little discussion of this subject in the Japanese literature, presumably because there are few hypotheses that would invite discussion. Some positive as well as negative effects on savings can be assumed to have operated, however. Among the positive are:

—The large number of banking offices, amounting to about one for every 10,500 Japanese; approximately 7,000 offices of credit associations and credit cooperatives; an almost equal number of labor, agricultural, and fishery cooperatives; and the facilities of the postal savings system, with some 22,000 offices, whose interest rates are broadly competitive with private facilities.

—Direct promotion of saving by banks through various forms of nonprice competition, such as gifts to depositors, door-to-door solicitation, facilities for special purpose saving, and of late, the revival of the old system of lottery deposits. The costs of this nonprice competition are not in any direct sense a tradeoff against interest rate competition, since interest rates are tightly controlled.

—The subdivision of what in the United States would be demand deposits into three categories—ordinary deposits, notice deposits, and current deposits, of which the first two bear interest. Comments on the possible effects are made below.

—Corporate promotion of saving through payroll saving plans at rates substantially above the controlled rates paid by banks and other intermediaries.

—Governmental policies designed to keep the banking system safe through supervision, deposit insurance (since 1971), and the imposition of ceilings—in practice amounting to rate setting—on deposit rates.

On the negative side, adversely affecting savings, must be counted principally the limited investment choices offered to the saver, especially the very modest role assigned to bonds, which reflects mainly the government's low interest rate policy and the resultant weakness and low liquidity of the bond market.[10]

The direct effect of the low interest rate policy on saving is hard to

10. See Chapter 3 for a discussion of some of the means by which the low interest rate policy was implemented.

Table 4-3. *Selected Interest Rates and Yields on Savings, 1960–74*
Percent

End of year	Banks: time deposits			Trust banks: 5 years or more	Postal savings		Average yield for year		
	Ordinary deposits	3 months	1 year		Ordinary savings	2½ years or more	Stocks	Government bonds	Industrial bonds
1960	2.56	4.30	6.00	7.80	3.96	6.00ᵃ	3.93	...	8.16
1961	2.19	4.00	5.50	7.37	3.60	5.50ᵃ	3.24	...	8.26
1962	2.19	4.00	5.50	7.37	3.60	5.50ᵃ	3.86	...	9.03
1963	2.19	4.00	5.50	7.37	3.60	5.50ᵃ	4.24	...	...
1964	2.19	4.00	5.50	7.37	3.60	5.50ᵃ	5.69	...	...
1965	2.19	4.00	5.50	7.37	3.60	5.50ᵃ	5.92	...	...
1966	2.19	4.00	5.50	7.22	3.60	5.50ᵃ	4.44	6.86	7.46
1967	2.19	4.00	5.50	7.22	3.60	5.50ᵃ	4.74	6.91	7.59
1968	2.19	4.00	5.50	7.27	3.60	5.50ᵃ	4.36	7.03	8.13
1969	2.19	4.00	5.50	7.27	3.60	5.50ᵃ	3.34	7.09	8.51
1970	2.25	4.00	5.75	7.47	3.60	5.75ᵃ	3.47	7.19	8.74
1971	2.25	4.00	5.75	7.27	3.60	6.00	3.41	7.28	7.76
1972	2.00	3.75	5.25	6.82	3.36	5.50	2.24	6.69	6.74
1973	2.50	4.25	6.75ᵇ	8.52	3.84	6.75ᶜ	2.09	7.26	7.87
1974	3.00	5.50	8.00ᵇ	9.02	4.32	8.00ᶜ	2.51	9.26	10.18

Source: Bank of Japan, *Economic Statistics Annual, 1973* and *1974*.
a. On certificates of two years or more.
b. Two years or more.
c. Beginning July 1, 1973, on certificates of three years or more.

assess. The interest rate reflects the price of future income. Whether a person saves more or saves less in response to a higher interest rate (lower price of future income) depends on the elasticity of his demand for future income. Research in the United States suggests that the interest rate has little effect on consumer saving; that is, that the demand for future income has approximately unit elasticity. If that should also be the case in Japan, the government's low interest rate policy, which will be examined in greater detail later, could be regarded as neutral in its impact on consumer saving, although not directly favorable to the welfare of the saver, of course.

The same can be said of the government's policy of tolerating a rate of inflation that during the ten years ending in 1972 caused the cost of living to advance by about 5 percent per year. Inflation, in fact, was a more significant determinant of the real return to saving than was the low interest rate policy, which could hardly have kept rates on savings below their equilibrium level by as much as 5 percentage points. (See Table 4-3.) The effect, if any, that prolonged stable inflation—to say nothing of the much faster inflation beginning in 1973—has on saving behavior is a moot point.

Corporate Savings

The spectacular performance of the personal saver and the intriguing analytical problems it raises seem to have distracted attention from the like-wise impressive saving performance of corporations. Over the years corporations have supplied gross savings equal to approximately one-third of total gross savings, and something over 35 percent in 1972. Their share in total investment, of course, has been substantially higher, financed mostly with the surpluses of the households. The high volume of corporate saving has its roots principally in the comparatively high level of corporate profits since 1968 and a moderate rate of taxation, as well as in substantial depreciation accrued. The dividend policy of large corporations does not appear to have been particularly restrictive, but for the entire corporate sector, a large part of which consists of closely held corporations, dividend payout has been low and retentions consequently have contributed importantly to corporate saving.

The composition of corporate savings in Japan and the United States, together with their respective GNP ratios, appears in Table 4-4. A subgroup of the corporate sector is also shown, representing the principal enterprises that are surveyed twice annually by the Bank of Japan. The profits before taxes of these principal enterprises account for slightly more than one-fifth of the entire corporate sector.

The high rate of corporate saving in Japan becomes immediately apparent from the data. Depreciation plus retained profits averaged about 15

Table 4-4. *Composition of Corporate Savings in Japan and the United States, Annual Average, 1970–72*

Item	Japan (billions of yen)		U.S. corporate sector (billions of dollars)	Percentage of gross operating income		Percentage of GNP[a]	
	Principal enterprises	Corporate sector		Japanese principal enterprises	U.S. corporate sector	Japanese corporate sector	U.S. corporate sector
Gross operating income	6,124.1	n.a.	158.5	100.0	100.0	n.a.	14.9
Less depreciation	1,995.7	6,879.3	60.9	32.6	38.4	8.6	5.7
Net operating income	4,128.4	n.a.	97.6	67.4	61.6	n.a.	9.2
Less interest	2,186.8	n.a.	16.9[b]	35.7	10.7	n.a.	1.6
Profits before taxes	1,941.6	9,134.5[c]	80.7	31.7	50.9	11.4	7.6
Less taxes	675.6	3,543.6	37.9	11.0	23.9	4.4	3.6
Less corporate transfers to households and private nonprofit institutions	...	107.1	...	...	...	1.3	...
Profits after taxes	1,266.1	5,483.8	42.7	20.7	26.9	6.8	4.0
Less dividends	547.6	835.3	22.9	8.9	14.4	1.0	2.2
Retained profits	718.5	4,648.5	19.8	11.7	12.5	5.8	1.9
Cash flow, including dividends	3,261.8	12,363.1	103.6	53.2	65.4	15.4	9.7
Cash flow, excluding dividends	2,714.2	11,527.8	80.7	44.3	50.9	14.3	7.6

Sources: Bank of Japan, *Financial Statements of Principal Enterprises in Japan* (1970, 1971, and 1972); Economic Planning Agency, *Annual Report on National Income Statistics, 1974*, pp. 35, 47, 157; and U.S. Department of Commerce, Bureau of Economic Analysis, *Survey of Current Business* (July 1974), p. 18. Figures are rounded.

n.a. Not available.

a. Average GNP in Japan = ¥80,336.1 billion; average GNP in the United States = $1,063.3 billion.

b. Nonfinancial corporations only.

c. After inventory valuation adjustment.

percent of GNP during the three-year period 1970–72. This high saving
rate was achieved even though a substantial part of the total return to
capital employed by corporations is paid out in the form of interest. For
the principal enterprises, interest amounted to over one-third of gross operating income (income before depreciation, interest, and taxes), slightly exceeding profits before taxes. The direct tax burden was only slightly more
than one-third of pretax profits for all corporations. The dividend payout
ratio was markedly different for the principal enterprises and for the
corporate sector as a whole, equaling 43 percent for the former and 15
percent for the latter. The main reason for this difference probably is that
large corporations are publicly owned and must satisfy the dividend requirements of their stockholders. In part, however, the difference between
the principal enterprises and the entire corporate sector may be attributable
also to the important role of intercorporate stock ownership and dividend
payments, which reduce net dividends paid to noncorporate stockholders.

Comparison with U.S. corporate data provides striking insights into the
difference between the Japanese and the U.S. growth potential. Corporate
depreciation allowances in Japan have exceeded those in the United States
by one-half, measured in relation to GNP. This has occurred despite the
fact that rapid growth and the relative newness of much of the capital stock
would probably hold down depreciation in relation to other corporate magnitudes were it not for the effects of rapid depreciation schedules in Japan.

Corporate profits before taxes in Japan likewise have exceeded those in
the United States by approximately one-half, again measured in relation to
GNP. Corporate profits after taxes have been somewhat less than twice their
U.S. counterpart in relation to GNP. Dividends have been only half those
in the United States; retained profits have been about three times as large.
These results were attained, it must be remembered, despite an interest
burden far heavier than that of U.S. corporations. In short, Japan has
offered its corporations a higher return on capital,[11] has taxed them more
lightly while nevertheless obtaining more revenue, and has experienced
high rates of saving, investment, and growth in the corporate sector and
the entire economy.

Public Sector Savings

The public sector, consisting of the government of Japan, the local
authorities, and public nonfinancial corporations, has also contributed

11. As indicated by the relatively low price/earnings ratios prevailing until 1972.
See p. 269.

importantly to total saving by collecting more taxes than it spends on public consumption. Unlike the United States, Japan distinguishes in its national income accounts between public consumption and public investment outlays. A deficit of the public sector, or of the central government alone, is not inconsistent with positive saving if it results from an excess of public investment over public saving. During the period 1970–72 public sector savings amounted to 8.3 percent of GNP on a gross basis and 7.3 percent on a net basis—equal to approximately 22 percent of total gross saving and 29 percent of total net saving. This result was achieved despite frequent tax reductions.

Investment

From the point of view of the financial system, the annual flow and the accumulated stock of real investment are important in two contexts. One context deals with sectoral surpluses and deficits that the system must finance. The other relates to the properties of the financial system that influence the direction of financial flows toward particular types of investment. In Japan the financial system has contributed to the large investment in business plant and equipment and inventory accumulation. Parts of it have favored big business at the expense of small business, but the latter as well as the farm sector has benefited from specialized institutions, some government sponsored, that have countered that tendency. Housing credit and consumer credit have been stepchildren, although this condition has begun to change. The financial system has done all this by facilitating massive surpluses in the personal sector and transferring them principally to the corporate sector.[12] The sectoral surpluses and deficits will be briefly examined here.

SECTORAL BALANCES. Each of the three principal sectors—personal, corporate, and public—shown in Table 4-1 does some investing, which may fall short of or exceed the amount of its saving. The difference, positive or negative, represents the sector's surplus or deficit; the surplus is lent out to other sectors, while the deficit must be covered by borrowing from the other sectors. The magnitude of these intersectoral transfers can be viewed as an index of the performance of the financial system, as well as of the demands that the income and savings structure makes upon the ability of the financial system to transfer funds among sectors. In Japan these transfers are high relative to those in the United States, as shown in Table 4-5, thus demonstrating the ability of the financial system to effect major intersectoral transfers.

12. See Chapter 2 for details concerning the allocation of investible funds.

Table 4-5. *Sectoral Surpluses and Deficits in Japan and the United States, 1973*

	Japan[a]				United States			
	Surplus		Deficit		Surplus		Deficit	
Sector	Amount (trillions of yen)	As a percentage of GNP	Amount (trillions of yen)	As a percentage of GNP	Amount (billions of dollars)	As a percentage of GNP	Amount (billions of dollars)	As a percentage of GNP
Personal	9.9	8.8	...	...	74.4	5.7	...	...
Business	...	...	6.9[b]	6.1	...	...	72.9	5.6
Government	1.5	1.3	...	...	} 3.5	0.3	...	...
Public corporations and local authorities	...	...	4.6	4.1		...	...	...
Rest of the world	...	...	[c]	0.0	...	...	0.1[d]	0.0
Statistical discrepancy							5.0	0.4
Total	11.4	10.1	11.5	10.2	77.9	6.0	78.0	6.0

Sources: Bank of Japan, Economic Research Department, *Flow of Funds of the Japanese Economy in 1973*, Special Paper 51 (July 1974), p. 1; and U.S. Department of Commerce, Bureau of Economic Analysis, *Survey of Current Business*, July 1974, p. 12.
 a. Nonfinancial sector.
 b. Corporate sector only.
 c. Less than 0.05.
 d. Excess of transfers.

Nevertheless, in Japan the sectoral surplus or deficit accounts for only the smaller part of the savings to be disposed of in the personal sector and of the investment to be financed in the corporate sector. Internal investment in Japan's personal sector and internal financing in the corporate sector exceed intersectoral transfers. The public sector has moved back and forth between surplus and deficit, with a deficit the rule since the early 1960s. The "rest of the world" sector, which represents the current account surplus (net foreign borrowing from Japan) or the current account deficit (net foreign lending to Japan) of the balance of payments, has also swung back and forth until recent years by small amounts.

Intersectoral balances understate the total volume of transfers of savings, and hence the performance of the financial system, by netting out intra-sectoral borrowing and lending. Trade credit in the corporate sector, as well as housing, consumer, unincorporated business, and farm credit in the personal sector, thus is excluded.

FACTORS INFLUENCING INVESTMENT. The investment associated with the internal absorption and external flows of savings described in the foregoing section has been guided both by government policy and market forces.[13] A discussion of the allocation process is relevant here only insofar as it relates to government policy implemented through the financial system. Planning decisions, in the main, have not been made by the government agencies that control the financial system, primarily the Ministry of Finance

13. See Chapter 2 for a discussion of capital inputs.

acting directly or through the Bank of Japan. But control of financing has been an important device for implementing plans and policies.

The government has been able to guide a significant part of total investment directly through its control of government financial institutions. The principal instrument has been the Trust Funds Bureau—employing mainly the deposits of the Postal Savings and Transfer System. Others have been the Industrial Investment Special Account, the Japan Development Bank, and the Export-Import Bank of Japan. Funds raised by government units amounted to 14.2 percent of total funds raised by domestic nonfinancial sectors in 1971, 21.5 percent in 1972, and 18.1 percent in 1973.[14] Another important channel of influence has been acquired through the creation and continuous guidance of private specialized credit institutions serving small businesses, farmers, and workers. Influence over the banking system and skillful use of the system's institutional propensities have given the authorities a third means of guiding the allocation of resources to preferred industries.

The government's choice to rely on administrative control more than on market forces has reflected a traditional pattern. It may have presented some special advantages under postwar conditions of recovery and rapid growth, and it has fitted in with the government's preference for low interest rates. The desire to control allocation while keeping interest rates down made it advisable in turn for the authorities to keep funds flowing through institutions that can be controlled or that, like mutual banks and credit associations and cooperatives, will channel it to a known group of borrowers.

Market factors other than interest rates nevertheless influenced the flow of investible funds. The principal market factor guiding the disposal of savings was the dominant position of large firms as debtors. These firms represented the best risks; they had the closest relation to the large banks and were their best depositors. Thus to the extent that the city banks had funds—and this depended importantly on the will of the authorities—large firms were likely to have preferred access to financing.

In a flexible capital market, free from rigidities and compartmentalization, allocation techniques such as those practiced in Japan may not be particularly effective in increasing the supply of funds to the "favored" sector. As the government pushes funds into a sector, interest rates in that sector are likely to drop. This may cause suppliers to reallocate their funds to other sectors. In Japan there has not been much scope for such a mechanism until perhaps very recently. It seems reasonable to assume that

14. Bank of Japan, *Flow of Funds of the Japanese Economy in 1973*, p. 2.

because of rigidities, compartmentalization, and inflexibility of interest rates, governmentally sponsored allocation largely achieved its objective of increasing the supply of funds to the designated sector during most of the postwar period.

Borrowers' Liabilities

Corporations are by far the biggest borrowers in the nonfinancial sector. In 1973 they accounted for 73 percent of total loans outstanding to non-financial borrowers and 84 percent of total trade credit; the U.S. ratios were 32 percent and 76 percent, respectively. Corporate finance dominates Japan's financial scene far more than does its U.S. counterpart.

As elsewhere, corporations in Japan have a choice among external forms of financing, between debt and equity, and within debt, between short- and long-term financing and negotiable and nonnegotiable liabilities. Among the principal characteristics of Japan's corporate finance are a heavy reliance on debt—referred to in Japan as "overborrowing"—a low proportion of bond financing and a correspondingly high level of bank financing, and a heavy reliance on trade credit. The sample of principal enterprises shows a ratio of equity to total capitalization in 1972 of about 18 percent, compared with 51 percent of all manufacturing and utilities in the United States.

In Japan concern is voiced, particularly by official sources, about two aspects of this unorthodox capital structure. One is the low equity ratio, which is believed to carry substantial risks. In the recession of 1965, the highly leveraged capital structure, together with the "tenure" commitment that prevented large firms from laying off workers, gave rise to concern. The other source of concern is the low proportion of bond financing and the correspondingly high proportion of bank borrowing. The latter is said to lead to excessive intimacy between corporations and their bankers and to push the banks in turn into a position of "overloan," which is widely believed to have adverse consequences (see discussion of overloan later in this chapter).

Three main reasons have been cited for this seemingly lopsided financial structure:

—The low equity ratio reflects Japan's extraordinarily rapid growth, which has kept firms from accumulating proportionate amounts of capital from internal sources.

—As in the United States, the tax law favors debt financing by making interest deductible.

—Equity financing in Japan is regarded as very expensive, quite aside from the tax factor, partly because of the Japanese practice, which is still widely followed, of issuing new stock at par value instead of at or near its market price.

That rapid growth makes it difficult to accumulate equity capital out of earnings in proportion to rising sales is plausible. When the rate of growth of sales and assets exceeds the rate of return on capital, even full retention of profits would not keep the ratio of equity capital to sales constant. It would probably have been possible, however, for at least large corporations to do more of their financing in the form of stock and less through borrowing. Alternatively, it might have been possible to accumulate capital by holding down dividends, even though this might have restricted the salability of new stock. The customary payout ratio of 40–50 percent for the principal enterprises is somewhat lower than the U.S. average. But, particularly in view of the rapid increase in aggregate dividend payments, stockholders of Japan's publicly held corporations seem to have been treated not ungenerously. Rapid growth, therefore, offers only a partial explanation of the low equity ratio.

Tax deductibility of interest unquestionably biases corporate financing toward debt. In Japan the tax system seeks to counteract this bias by placing a lower levy on corporate income distributed in dividends. For large corporations and for the years 1973 and 1974, the difference has amounted to about 10–11 percentage points on the tax rate. A total tax rate of about 45 percent in 1973 and 49 percent in 1974 emerges if one assumes a payout of 30 percent of pretax income and adds the local corporate income taxes while allowing for their tax deductibility.[15] The resultant tax saving, on this 30 percent payout basis, comes to about 3 percentage points on pretax profits. Clearly this compensates for the tax bias only in small part. Even so, however, the strength of the bias in favor of debt is not fully explained, since in other countries roughly comparable tax burdens have not led to a comparable corporate financing decision.

The belief that equity financing is expensive correctly reflects the situation, but the argument is not always stated effectively. Frequently it is said that this cost derives from the sale of new stock at par instead of at a price close to the market, which usually is well above par. If new stock is sold cheaply and a greater number of shares must therefore be sold in order to raise a given sum, the total cost in terms of dividends increases, assuming the dividend rate is left unchanged.

15. See Chapter 5.

Matters are different, however, from the viewpoint of the existing stock-holders. They must ask themselves how they can finance a proposed expansion of their company in the most economical way. The value of the subscription rights then enters into their calculation. Stockholders ordinarily have preemptive rights on new issues at a price more than 15 percent below the market. For such below-market issues, subscription rights are received by stockholders that are valuable in proportion to the difference between the market price and the subscription price. Whether the rights are exercised or sold, the result is the same: the stockholders "gain" what the company "loses." Thus from the stockholders' point of view, it makes no difference at what price the company sells new stock, ignoring for the moment the income tax consequences and the commissions incurred in transactions such as selling rights and buying or selling stock. If the company were to disregard this fact and were to treat the apparent cost of capital obtained through a par value issue as the measure of the required return on new projects, its capital budgeting would become badly distorted.

In Japan it is argued persuasively, nevertheless, that any identification of stockholders with enterprise is unrealistic. It is said that since the dissolution of the old *zaibatsu* (large family-owned holding companies), management and ownership have been substantially separated. Stockholders essentially are subordinated creditors from whom the enterprise, an entity responsible only to itself, in effect "borrows" equity capital. In that case, the valuable rights given to stockholders under a par value financing are simply another cost to the firm analogous to dividends. Par value financing then becomes very expensive.

It is important not to let the plausibility of the sociological argument lead one into error about the financial facts. One might even take issue with the argument itself. Management may be separated from the bulk of the stockholders. But it is not separated from the small core of stockholders that usually forms part of the group to which most major enterprises belong. This, however, is not the true issue.

Equity financing has been made truly expensive in Japan, quite apart from the consequences, if any, of par issue, by the high rate of growth of corporate profits in combination with moderate price/earnings ratios (before 1972). A firm selling new stock is turning over to stockholders a fixed share of a rapidly growing earnings stream. The same money raised by sale of debt would cost a rapidly diminishing fraction of future profits. This is so whether the firm sells to old or new stockholders, or whether it identifies with its old shareholders or thinks of them as subordinated creditors. And so long as price/earnings ratios remained low—they rose sharply beginning in 1972—the share of the earnings stream turned over to the new stockholders had to be relatively high. This is the fundamental reason why equity financing in Japan has been expensive.

The ability of Japanese corporations to benefit from increasing their financial leverage can be interpreted in the light of the financial doctrine that has become popular in the United States under the name of the Modigliani-Miller theorem. This theorem fundamentally asserts that, except for the effects of taxes, the degree of leverage of a corporation has no influence on the market value of its total capitalization. To increase the debt component of the capitalization increases the risk borne by the equity holders and depresses the price of the equity. A corollary of the theorem is that because leverage does not reduce the cost of capital in the absence of taxes, it will clearly reduce the cost of capital if there is a corporate income tax. The fact that Japanese firms engage in extreme leverage suggests that implicitly they accept the theorem, while U.S. firms, by rejecting high leverage, also implicitly seem to be rejecting the theorem. In considering this interpretation, however, it should be noted that empirical evidence from data before 1965 suggests that in Japan price/earnings ratios are uncorrelated with debt/equity ratios.[16]

CORPORATE DEBT. The financial structure of the principal enterprises in 1972 is presented in Table 4-6. The volume of bonds shown in the table would not seem particularly low by U.S. standards if long-term loans from financial institutions were treated as private placements and so combined with bonded debt. The total of such indebtedness would then amount to about 26 percent of total capitalization. In fact, bonds differ from loans, not so much in their only slightly longer typical term to maturity, but in their historically lower interest rate. This rate is determined by government policy. Until recently, therefore, bonds could not be sold to the general public in any volume and usually had to be placed with financial institutions by agreement and on grounds other than yield, sometimes under pressure exerted by the authorities. In 1972 the role of individual buyers began to increase sharply, while market rates temporarily declined. Access to the bond market is limited for corporate borrowers, however, to the amounts and the order of priorities set by a capital issues committee. Further details on the bond market appear later in this study.

The interest rate on term loans has been unregulated in principle but

16. Ryūei Shimizu, "The Calculating Process of the Discount Rate and Capital Cost," *Mita shōgaku kenkyū*, vol. 6, no. 1, cited in the same author's "A Study of the Capital Costs in the Japanese Enterprises for Long-Range Planning," *Keio Business Review*, no. 4 (1965), pp. 177–208.

Table 4-6. *Financial Structure of Principal Enterprises, End of Fiscal 1972*

Category	Percent
Current liabilities	51.3
Trade credit	21.0
Notes and bills payable	13.2
Accounts payable	7.7
Other current liabilities	13.4
Short-term loans from financial institutions	16.8
Long-term liabilities	31.2
Loans from financial institutions	21.0
Bonds	5.3
Other fixed liabilities	5.0
Equity	17.5
Total	100.0

Source: Bank of Japan, *Financial Statements of Principal Enterprises in Japan, 1972* (1973), p. 1. Figures are rounded.

sticky in practice. During most of the 1960s it remained within the 7.5–9.0 percent range. It has followed the prime long-term rate set by the long-term-credit banks and has been largely invariant within a maturity range of from one to as many as fifteen years. Like that on short-term loans, the effective level of the interest rate is increased by a compensating-balance requirement, which for term loans, however, typically has amounted to only 10 percent, in contrast to 30 or even 40 percent on short-term loans.

The supply of long-term loans is increased in some instances by an implicit or explicit agreement to renew a short-term loan. According to a Ministry of Finance survey, the proportion of short-term loans whose de facto maturity exceeded one year was approximately equal to that of loans with contractual maturities in excess of one year for both city banks and local banks.[17]

Short-term (less than one year) bank loans, representing about 17 percent of capitalization in 1972, have for the most part been a relatively low-cost component of total indebtedness, despite the high compensating-balance practice and, before 1973, the practice of collecting interest in advance and of double counting terminal and initial days on ninety-day loan renewals. The principal reasons have been that maximum rates fixed by the authorities have been moderate, averaging below 6 percent in late 1972, although upped to about 9.5 percent in mid-1974, and that compensating balances usually take the form of time rather than demand deposits.

17. Committee on Financial System Research, *Report on Recommended Changes in Working of Private Financial Systems* (1970), pp. 54, 125.

Trade credit, representing some 20 percent of total capitalization, is more difficult to evaluate. Its very high ratio becomes understandable in light of the fact that, for the sample of principal enterprises, trade credit, broadly defined as notes and bills payable and accounts receivable, constituted approximately one-fourth of total assets.[18] The cost of trade credit likewise is difficult to assess. Some discount is given by suppliers for cash payment. On long-term trade credit, explicit rates in the neighborhood of 10 percent have been charged. Some observers, on the other hand, seem to regard trade credit as effectively costless.[19]

The overall cost of capital for a typical corporation during the early 1960s has been computed in the range of 7.7–8.7 percent.[20] The dispersion, however, was wide, owing to the heavy use of trade credit by the big trading companies on one side and the rapid growth of particular enterprises on the other. Rapidly growing firms inevitably have a higher cost of equity capital, if that cost is properly computed, unless they maintain a substandard equity ratio. Consequently the cost of capital was found to be high for innovative industries such as chemical, automobile, and electric equipment firms.[21]

RISK AND ITS CONTROL. The structure of corporate financing in Japan conveys the impression of extreme risk exposure. Official statements concerning the need to improve the corporate structure confirm this. A look at the liquidity position of corporate business in terms of the current ratio (current assets/current liabilities) does not improve the picture. The ratio for the principal enterprises has been approximately 1.1/1, in contrast to the roughly 2/1 that U.S. bankers like to see.[22] Interest charges for the principal enterprises were earned barely 1.9 times in 1973.[23] Such coverage would be regarded as highly unsatisfactory for U.S. manufacturing firms.

Some measures of liquidity and solvency preferred in Japan do make the situation look somewhat better. For instance, the ratio of fixed assets to long-term debt and net worth, which measures the long-term funding of a firm's least liquid assets, stood at 88.1 percent in Japan in 1967 compared with 63.3 percent in the United States and 79.9 percent in West Germany.[24] But the

---

18. Bank of Japan, *Economic Statistics Annual, 1973* (1974), p. 244.
19. Shimizu, "A Study of Capital Costs," p. 202; and CFSR, *Recommended Changes,* p. 101.
20. Shimizu, "A Study of Capital Costs," p. 202.
21. Ibid., pp. 196–202.
22. Bank of Japan, *Economic Statistics Annual, 1974* (1975), p. 243.
23. Ibid.
24. CFSR, *Recommended Changes,* p. 119.

principal factors that reduce the apparent high risk in the Japanese financial structure to its proper proportion lie elsewhere.

For one thing, valuation of equity at current book value as practiced in some of the foregoing analysis considerably understates the value of this protective cushion in the market. The book value of the shares listed on all Japanese stock exchanges, based on stated capital and excluding accumulated surplus, amounted to roughly one-half of market value during the mid-1960s. With accumulated surplus and other equity-type capital accounts approximately equal to stated capital, market value during this period approximated the book value of capital accounts.[25] During the latter part of the 1960s, however, the rising stock market, reflecting among other factors the appreciated real estate holdings of business, lifted market value far above book value. By 1972 market value stood at about six times stated capital, or about three times stated total capital accounts. The equity/total capitalization ratio, recomputed on this more realistic basis, amounted to approximately 40 percent instead of 18 percent (see Table 4-5).

A further intangible improvement in the capital structure of large firms results from the special relation of many such firms to their main bank. The "groups" to which many Japanese firms belong often are headed by banks. Even where this relationship does not prevail, one of the usually numerous banks from which large corporations borrow is ordinarily regarded as the main bank. Facts about amounts and terms of borrowing implicit in these relationships must be made public by corporations in their semiannual securities reports filed with the Ministry of Finance. It is taken for granted that the main bank assumes a special responsibility with respect to the borrower. In an emergency other creditors therefore can expect their claims to effectively though not legally outrank those of the main bank. The share borrowed from the main bank in any one firm's total borrowing varies widely. For the entire membership of each of the six principal groups headed by banks it typically falls in the range of 13–18 percent.[26] If a creditor is prepared to view the main bank as a subordinated creditor, the ratio of subordinated credit plus equity to total capitalization approached 50 percent in 1972.

A different kind of boost to the solvency of debt-burdened corporations derives from growth and inflation. Rapid growth reduced the weight of past debt in relation to present sales. It eased the consequences of some kinds of mistakes of corporate judgment. If a firm had overexpanded, it did not need

25. Japan Securities Research Institute, *Securities Market in Japan, 1973* (1973), p. 36.
26. Goldsmith, "The Financial Development of Japan," pt. 2, p. 96.

to wait long for demand to catch up. Inflation, in turn, reduced the weight of old debt. Whether or not a firm became a beneficiary of inflation through this mechanism depended, of course, on whether its sales prices advanced with the general movement of prices. In Japan the long period of stable wholesale prices before 1973 in the face of rising consumer prices denied debt relief to many corporate borrowers.

Growth and inflation, on the other hand, while they may help solvency, pose a threat to corporate liquidity. Large additions to corporate funds are needed constantly. A firm may quickly find itself in a liquidity squeeze. In Japan, however, liquidity and solvency seem to be less clearly separated than elsewhere. It would be an overstatement to say, as some have, that liquidity is no problem in Japan. Successive periods of monetary tightness imposed by the Bank of Japan testify to the contrary. It is more appropriate to say that, given the close network of financial and other relationships in which large Japanese corporations operate, the lack of liquidity is unlikely to become a fatal problem so long as there is solvency and hence borrowing capacity.

This network of corporate relations is another of the factors that enable Japanese firms to carry what seem to be disproportionate financial risks. In case of need, a firm that is a member of a group can expect help from other members through many channels. The lead bank will help directly, and it can also help indirectly by arranging loans from other banks. Firms that are customers or suppliers within the group can help by paying their bills more promptly or by postponing their own demands for payment, possibly by discriminatory pricing—more likely by channeling orders—or even by management assistance. This does not apply to the same extent to small firms that are only marginally attached to a group or are fending entirely for themselves.

Finally, there is the government. Japan is largely free from the belief that business failures constitute a desirable process because they eliminate the inefficient, at least among large firms. In Japan a large firm is regarded as a national asset. The government views itself as having something of a paternalistic responsibility. Perhaps because in Japan the initial impulses to economic development come in good part from government, business generally regards government as a wise and well-intentioned guide rather than an adversary. In an emergency, government will do what it can to help a large firm in difficulty, and its instruments of action are many.

The unbalanced financial structure of Japan's corporations, however, cannot be viewed with equanimity. There are risks. They are increased, moreover, by a form of fixed costs not known outside Japan—the tenure obligations toward labor that make it difficult to lay off employees. Japan's firms also must consider the possibility that growth may slow permanently. That would end the easy bailout from mistakes due to overoptimism.

The universal call for an improvement in corporate financial structure, therefore, is by no means unrealistic. But while it has lasted and has remained workable, the structure has contributed enormously to the growth of the Japanese economy. One need only think back to the days of World War II in the United States when defense firms had a guaranteed market and un-limited cheap financing. "What can be produced can be financed" was one of the slogans of the planners of those days. Many Japanese firms during the 1950s and 1960s were in a somewhat similar condition. Limitations on ex-pansion have been essentially limitations of resources, that is, limitations of production. Often they may have appeared to individual enterprises as limi-tations of finance. In fact, finance has been stretched to the limits of what could be produced. It has been employed also to guide production into the areas that facilitated further expansion, that is, into investment. Japan's growth probably would not have been possible without the overborrowing that has been the centerpiece of enterprise finance.

LIABILITIES OF THE PERSONAL SECTOR. The outstanding fact about bor-rowing by households is that it has been almost negligible.[27] A substantial part of the liabilities of the personal sector are the obligations of unincorpo-rated businesses. The remainder, which is accounted for by home mortgages, consumer credit, security credit, and minor forms of personal credit, amounted roughly to between 25 and 30 percent of disposable income in 1972. In the United States, on the other hand, consumer credit was equal to nearly 20 percent of disposable income and mortgage credit extended on homes to slightly over 40 percent, or a total of about 60 percent of disposable income.

These figures, inadequate as they are, tell a good deal about Japanese finance. They show that only a minute proportion of the country's enormous flow of savings has been available through credit markets to homeowners and household borrowers. Together with similar data indicative of the extremely modest borrowing propensity of the public sector, they illustrate the intense concentration of financial resources in the corporate sector. Since consumer credit contributes less to the measured growth of GNP than does business investment, and housing also quite possibly contributes less, this allocation obviously has been powerfully growth oriented.[28] As a result, the average

27. Data on liabilities of the personal sector are drawn from ibid., pp. 108–10.
28. See Chapter 2.

Japanese homeowner has been compelled to finance a much higher proportion of the value of his home out of his own resources than has his counterpart in the United States. In a country where housing occupies a larger share of the average household budget than in the United States, the price paid for underfinancing of housing has been high.

GOVERNMENT BORROWING. Japan, for all practical purposes, is unburdened by public debt. The debt created in World War II was largely wiped out by postwar inflation. The strict policy of budget balancing pursued during most of the postwar period precluded government securities issues before the recession of 1965. (Ackley and Ishi discuss the public debt and related matters in Chapter 3.)

The government is a big intermediary, absorbing savings through the postal savings and insurance systems and creating savings of its own in the central government budget to be used mainly to finance local authorities. As part of this process, securities are issued by the central government, by public corporations, and by local authorities. Thus at the end of 1973 some ¥11.7 trillion of national government debt was outstanding (exclusive of postal savings liabilities), equal to 10 percent of GNP, and ¥12.8 trillion of bonded debt of public corporations and local authorities.[29] Combined with the near absence of defense expenditures, the minuteness of the public-debt service has unburdened the budget and helped to account for the low share of tax revenues in the GNP. Very likely this has made some contribution to economic growth, although it should be borne in mind that interest on the public debt is only an income transfer that does not absorb real resources. Its effect on saving and growth depends on the progressiveness of the tax system and on the distribution of interest payments.

The virtual absence of a public debt, nevertheless, has not been an unmixed blessing. It has deprived Japan of a natural way of creating a large central money market in which surplus funds can find employment. It has deprived savers of an investment medium. This shortcoming has been the more perceptible because of a dearth of other kinds of bonds, a condition that is also a result of government policy.

At the same time, even the very modest interest burden seems to have biased the government's attitude toward interest rates. The low interest rate policy of the postwar period seems to have reflected in part the government's desire to hold down its own interest costs and avoid the adverse appearance of being compelled to pay a high rate, even though the main rationale of this policy was investment stimulation. In this way the public debt, small

29. Bank of Japan, *Flow of Funds of the Japanese Economy in 1973*, p. 17.

as it was, seems to have contributed to a policy that on the one hand distorted the financial markets but on the other channeled funds into accelerated growth.

Financial Assets of Savers

The composition of the liabilities of borrowers and the assets of savers is determined by their respective preferences, by the preferences and legal limitations of intermediaries, and by government policy. The financial assets of personal savers, as the ultimate wealth owners, at the end of 1973 are shown in Table 4-7.

The data bring out the predominance of time deposits and the low levels of bond holdings and equities. To the extent that this structure reflects the preferences of savers, one may interpret it as evidence of a high degree of risk aversion, at least with respect to capital risk. Income risk seems to matter less. It should be noted that because real estate is a nonfinancial asset, it is excluded from the table. The value of real estate holdings in Japan is unknown, and the price has appreciated rapidly over time.

With their large holdings of time deposits, many of them fairly liquid, Japan's savers finance loans, both long- and short-term, that banks make to

Table 4-7. *Personal Financial Assets, Japan and the United States, December 31, 1973*

	Japanese personal financial assets		U.S. personal financial assets	
Type of asset	Amount (trillions of yen)	Percentage of total	Amount (billions of dollars)	Percentage of total
Currency and demand deposits	24.5	19.1	170.2	7.4
Time deposits	58.1	45.2	635.6	27.6
Trust fund deposits	6.8	5.3	...	...
Bonds and short-term government securities	7.9	6.1	212.6	9.2
Insurance	15.2	11.8	458.1[a]	19.9[a]
Stocks at market value	13.1[b]	10.2	744.4	32.3
Mutual funds and equities other than stocks	3.0	2.3	81.4	3.5
Total	128.6	100.0	2,302.3	100.0

Sources: Bank of Japan, Economic Research Department, *Flow of Funds in the Japanese Economy in 1973*, Special Paper 51 (July 1974) p. 17; and U.S. Federal Reserve System, *Federal Reserve Bulletin*, vol. 60 (October 1974), p. A59.14. Figures are rounded.
a. Includes pension fund reserves.
b. Book value equals ¥4.4 trillion.

corporations. Banks, moreover, together with other financial institutions own more stock at book value than do individual savers (¥6.4 trillion against ¥4.4 trillion, as of December 31, 1973). Thus intermediation in Japan not only reduces the maturity of debts but also transforms equity into debt. In both cases, the effect is to reduce risk for the saver. Before examining matters pertaining to such assets as equities and bonds, attention needs to be given, therefore, to the main institutions that intermediate between savers and borrowers.

The Banking System

The evolution of Japan's banking system is the history of a continuing struggle between the government, which has a propensity to regulate by imposing various kinds of specialization, and institutions bent on an expansionary drive to broaden their markets and functions. Interestingly enough, in a country where government policy approaches the status of law, the forces of the market have had their share of successes, as well as some setbacks, when the authorities felt it necessary to take a firm stand.

The Principle of Specialization

Specialization in finance takes many forms.[30] One form separates different types of financial operations, particularly the lending business, the business of underwriting and trading in securities, and the trust business. The main purpose, aside from greater ease of control for the regulators, is to reduce risk and conflict of interest.

A second form of specialization separates short- and long-term finance. Here, risk reduction for the intermediary and its creditors is sought by the matching of maturities. It is achieved, however, at some sacrifice in the usefulness of the intermediary to its customers, since intermediation then does not perform its potential function of transforming maturities.

Other forms of specialization involve concentration on size of customer, such as large versus small firms; on some particular form of lending or raising funds, such as making loans versus purchasing securities, or soliciting deposits versus issuing securities; or on some particular area of the economy, for example, farming, home finance, or exports. These types of specialization

---

30. For a historical review of the subject, see T. F. M. Adams and Iwao Hoshii, *A Financial History of the New Japan* (Palo Alto, Calif., and Tokyo: Kodansha International, 1972), sec. 2.

have in common the tendency to increase risk by limiting diversification and to compartmentalize credit markets. They may thereby cause interest rate differentials among markets and create captive sources of or outlets for funds —possibly resulting in discriminatory misallocation. Japan's banking system exhibits most of these forms of specialization.

SPECIALIZATION IN PRACTICE. The basic concepts governing banking laid down originally in the Banking Law of 1927 aimed at establishing a commercial banking system of the British type, specializing in short-term loans.[31] This was in accord with the "real bills" doctrine of central banking then still in vogue. The legislation reflected the experience of the banking crises of 1920 and 1927, when neglect of what were then regarded as sound principles of banking had led to a series of bankruptcies. Long-term credit, other than funds supplied by the stock market and by a bond market that at that time was fairly active, was to be handled by specialized institutions.

This conception did not meet the credit needs of the Japanese economy then, nor does it today. The arm's-length, competitive principles of Anglo-Saxon-style banking did not mesh with the habits of Japan's clannish, cooperative business society. Before World War II the style of the major *zaibatsu* called for banks that were closely associated with them and were capable of supporting the complicated maneuvers of holding-company operations. After the war the largest banks replaced the *zaibatsu* holding companies in their function as leaders of "groups," a role that also called for a variety of capabilities not ordinarily associated with the concept of commercial banking. The banks therefore sought and found ways of living with the law while doing what, given their purpose, the situation called for.

But while the plan for separating short- and long-term finance has been largely defeated, another form of specialization has proved enforceable thus far: the segregation of commercial banking from the securities business. The effort of the occupation authorities to reshape Japanese banking in the U.S. image commended itself to the Japanese authorities because of its orderliness and economic logic. Since the application of the law quickly created powerful vested interests in the form of the securities companies, the vigorous efforts of the commercial banks have thus far been able to make only minor inroads against it. It is evident that in an economy where the banks maintain far more intimate contact with their customers than is the case in the United States, the inability to meet customers' needs in the matter of securities issues, except as buyers of their stocks and bonds, causes real inconvenience.

31. H. D. Schultze-Kimmle, *Japans Banken, Das Kreditwesen eines Industriegiganten*, Bankwirtschaftliche Studien, Folge 1, Physica Verlag (Wuerzburg: Rudolf Liebing KG, 1968).

The attempt to separate short- and long-term lending nevertheless has left some important traces—the trust banks (seven institutions) and the long-term-credit banks (three institutions). The trust banks are essentially savings banks making principally medium-term equipment loans to large enterprises. They finance themselves largely with "loan trusts," that is, savings certificates of medium-term maturity. In addition they carry on a regular commercial banking business. The three long-term-credit banks' principal source of funds derives from the commercial banks, which buy the bulk of their financial debentures and a lesser share of the one-year discount notes partly to facilitate lending by long-term-credit banks to the commercial banks' own customers.

Foreign exchange banking provided for in the legal framework is another instance of seemingly dysfunctional specialization. This arrangement in the past served to facilitate, among other things, the control of international payments but is being phased out.

Specialization by size is almost inevitable wherever large and small banks coexist. Among Japan's commercial banks, however, the distinction between city banks (thirteen institutions) and local banks (sixty-three institutions) is more highly structured and regulated than elsewhere. City banks must be large enough to meet the needs of the large enterprises with which they usually are closely allied, all the more so after the Ministry of Finance initiated a policy in 1974 of reducing the size of loans to single borrowers relative to each bank's capital. Hence they are allowed to have nationwide branch systems, although the Ministry of Finance has at times restricted the establishment of branches. Some 60 percent of their deposits are corporate. The plans of the Ministry of Finance for improving the structure of the banking system focus mainly but by no means exclusively on the city banks.

Local banks engage in regional specialization, being limited by and large to a single prefecture within which they may have numerous branches; however, this restraint has been weakening in recent years. Accordingly the Bank of Japan has recently substituted the term "regional," as being more descriptive for these banks than "local," although in the present study "local" continues to be used in order to preserve continuity with previous literature. While a few of these banks exceed the size of the smaller city banks, most are moderate-sized institutions and thus deal principally but not exclusively with small and medium-sized businesses. About half of their loans are to enterprises whose capital does not exceed ¥10 million. Half of their deposits are personal deposits, three-quarters of which are time deposits. Before 1973 only the larger local banks, about one-third of the total, had access to the Bank of Japan's discount window and were subject to window guidance.

Recently, window facilities and guidance have been extended to other local banks in a moderate form.

Specialization of city and local banks resulting in the former concentrating on big business and the latter on other business, however, is far from complete. For more than ten years city banks have been trying to develop a consumer credit business. This trend in Japan, unlike that in the United States, has not reflected an excess of funds seeking outlets but the reverse. Faced with a shrinkage in their share of total funds (see Table 4-8), the city banks have tried to cultivate the consumer as an important source of time deposits. Moreover, in recent years city banks have occasionally approached smaller firms and have also encouraged housing loans.

Local banks, too, do not specialize exclusively in serving medium and small businesses. Particularly in periods of tightness, some of them have been sought out by large firms whose credit needs were partly unmet by city banks. This is only one of the channels of communication between the two markets; another is the call money market, which will be examined shortly.

Specialization in dealing with small business and agriculture is carried one step further by several groups of institutions that are, or in the past were, mutual in character. These are mutual loan and savings banks (72 institu-

Table 4-8. *Assets and Asset Shares of Private Financial Institutions,*[a] *1953, 1963, and 1973*

Institution	Assets in 1953[b]		Assets in 1963[b]		Assets in 1973[b]	
	Amount (billions of yen)	Per-cent of total	Amount (billions of yen)	Per-cent of total	Amount (billions of yen)	Per-cent of total
City banks	2,640.6	50.5	14,416.1	41.8	64,917.3	36.1
Local ("regional") banks	1,065.1	20.4	6,361.3	18.4	30,828.2	17.1
Trust banks (banking accounts)	97.1	1.9	754.1	2.2	5,561.7	3.1
Long-term-credit banks	250.2	4.8	2,060.8	6.0	12,213.7	6.8
Mutual loan and savings banks	342.0	6.5	2,648.0	7.7	14,608.1	8.1
Credit associations	242.5	4.6	2,667.3	7.7	18,110.9	10.1
Credit cooperatives[e]	19.6	0.4	518.9	1.5	3,757.0	2.1
Labor credit associations[e]	10.2[d]	0.2	87.9	0.2	789.9	0.4
Agricultural cooperatives[e]	347.1	6.6	1,846.8	5.3	12,852.4	7.1
Fishery cooperatives[e]	23.8[d]	0.5	130.6	0.4	876.1	0.5
Subtotal	5,038.2	96.4	31,491.8	91.2	164,515.3	91.4
Trust accounts of all banks	188.9	3.6	3,028.5	8.8	15,485.8	8.6
Total[e]	5,227.1	100.0	34,520.3	100.0	180,001.1	100.0

Source: Bank of Japan, *Economic Statistics Annual, 1954, 1963,* and *1973.* Figures are rounded.

a. An institution is associated with each of the groups serving small business, agriculture, and fisheries that in greater or lesser degree acts as a central bank, accepting surplus funds and lending them out to members or investing them in other forms. While there are specialized credit facilities serving each of the major producers' groups—the degree of specialization varies considerably—there are no institutions specifically designed to serve the consumer in his role as homeowner or personal borrower. Some amount of credit is available to households, of course, through the commercial banking system and the banks serving principally small business.

b. End of calendar year.

c. Assets = sum of liabilities (deposits plus capital and borrowings).

d. Data for 1954.

e. Does not include government-financed institutions or the funds of the central institutions of credit associations and cooperatives that are partly derived from deposits by their member institutions.

tions at the end of 1973), credit associations (484 at the end of 1973), credit cooperatives (499 at the end of 1973), labor credit associations (47), and financing institutions for agriculture, forestry, and fisheries (approximately 7,000 as of March 1972), as well as a small number of special lending institutions operating in the same functional areas.

The mutual loan and savings banks conduct a consumer-financing business, together with providing regular banking services for small business, on a regional basis. In small measure they fill the great void left in the structure of credit facilities by the near absence of financing institutions for large installment purchases familiar in the United States and elsewhere. They evolved through conversion in 1951 from their original status as mutual nonprofit organizations to corporate institutions. Since such conversions are being discussed in the United States with respect to mutual savings and loan associations, the Japanese experience is of special interest. In particular, the troublesome problem of what to do with the surplus accumulated from the past contributions of many savers who had ceased to be members has found a very simple solution in Japan. The matter, in effect, was ignored; the surplus was allocated to the existing depositors who thereby became stockholders and received a windfall. Mutual loan and savings banks have held their share of total funds roughly constant during the years 1953–73; recently they have been subject to the same form of window guidance as local banks.

The group of credit associations is likewise oriented toward small business, performing general banking functions but still in mutual form. Their lending is limited to members that, if businesses, must not have capital exceeding ¥200 million (before 1973, ¥100 million) or a labor force exceeding 300. They can accept deposits from nonmembers and can pay interest rates exceeding those paid by banks by 0.1 percentage point for each maturity of deposits on time deposits and by 0.25 percentage point on other kinds of deposits (such as ordinary deposits and deposit at notice). These modest margins have been a main factor in enabling the credit associations to double their share in total deposits during the years 1953–73. Their experience seems to indicate a high degree of interest sensitivity on the part of Japanese savers, since about two-thirds of their deposits are savings deposits. It contrasts with the view widely held in the United States that the advantage of "one-stop banking," which commercial banks have over savings banks and savings and loan associations, is worth from one-half to three-quarters of 1 percentage point in deposit rates. The comparison, however, is not precise, because U.S. thrift institutions do not render a general banking service and the Japanese institutions do. The Japanese credit associations, moreover, have been aided, relative to their competitors, by a more generous licensing policy for opening new branch offices. Large associations have been subject to a mild form of window guidance.

A third source of funds directed exclusively toward small business is the group of credit cooperatives. They differ from the credit associations in that they do not offer third-party payment services. Their activities are more closely focused on their membership, the element of cooperation is stressed, and supervision and regulation are held to a minimum. Deposit rates enjoy margins of 0.1–0.25 percent over bank rates, depending on the type of deposit. They are perhaps most nearly comparable to U.S. credit unions. Like the latter, their share of total funds has increased rapidly from a modest base.

A different set of cooperative institutions serves agriculture and the fishing industry, which together help keep down Japan's dependence on food imports, along with forestry, which is important in a country that is two-thirds woodland. As in many other countries, commercial banks have proved an inadequate source of farm credit. In Japan the typical lender's distaste for farm loans is enhanced by the exceptionally high seasonality of much of this credit and by the need for long-term financing of irrigation for the rice crop. As in the United States, government or government-sponsored credit plays a role in farm financing. Nevertheless, the farm, forestry, and fishery cooperatives finance two-thirds of the total credit extended in these fields. Owing to the favorable financial condition of the farm sector and of rural households, about half of their deposits is available for uses other than lending to members, through central institutions and other forms of investment. These cooperatives have increased their share in total funds moderately over the past twenty years, despite the decline in the agricultural labor force and in the share of farm output in the GNP.

The tendency of financial institutions to break out of the rigid framework of specialization imposed by law has been operative in the small business and farm sectors as well as among the commercial and long-term-credit banks. The government, whose powers of control are enhanced, even though by no means made absolute, by the rigid framework, has nevertheless recognized the need for change and has permitted various regroupings. The shift of the mutual loan and savings banks away from mutual status is an instance. So, too, is the shift of the credit associations away from the more limited functions of credit cooperatives.

The commercial and long-term-credit banks have seen no major legislative changes recently. But pressures on this group of intermediaries have been even more severe. The most spectacular and, in the literature, most frequently examined and excoriated phenomenon of Japan's commercial banking has been the "overloan" condition of the city banks. While part of the problem was removed by the flood of liquidity stemming from the payments surpluses of the early 1970s, this may well turn out to have been an isolated development. For that reason and even more so because overloan illustrates so vividly some of the nature of the banking process in Japan, a review of the subject is worthwhile.

Overloan

The city banks, as the principal lenders to large enterprises, have been confronted during much of the postwar period with a demand for funds that they have not been able to satisfy from their deposits. They have had recourse, therefore, to (1) the discount window of the Bank of Japan and (2) the call money market in which other financial institutions place their surplus funds. The term "overloan" has been applied to condition (1) as well as to (1) and (2) combined (Table 4-9). The latter will be the usage employed in this chapter. A situation in which the city banks are in debt to the call money market but not to the Bank of Japan is unlikely to arise so long as the Bank of Japan, through its credit policy, keeps the call rate above the discount rate, as it has generally done.

Occasionally the term "overloan" is extended to cover the low equity/ total capitalization ratio characteristic of Japanese corporations. Ordinarily, however, this condition is referred to as "overborrowing." It is related only indirectly to the banks' overloan, in the sense that an increase in debt finance, unless channeled through the bond market, must increase the demand for bank credit. Both overloan and overborrowing can exist or vanish independently of each other.

It is certainly understandable that the monetary authorities view with some misgivings a banking picture characterized by imbalances, such as a minimal liquid asset/deposits ratio and a very modest capital/deposits ratio. Such a system is vulnerable both on the liquidity and the solvency side. If these imbalances are intensified by heavy recourse to nondeposit sources of funds, such as central bank borrowing and call money, one could speak of a risk created by overloan. Even then one would have to note that the imbalances are not primarily due to overloan. They would be reduced only in moderate proportion by eliminating nondeposit sources of funds and the corresponding assets. Adequate liquidity and capital requirements would be much more effective remedies. The need for higher liquidity and solvency ratios, moreover, must be gauged in terms of the peculiar risk conditions prevailing in Japan. A Western standard is not meaningful.

It is not only considerations of bank risk that seem to make overloan a major problem for the Japanese authorities. The concern that has been ex-

Table 4-9. *Indicators of the Overloaned Position of Japanese Banks, 1955–73*

End of year	Loan ratio[a]		Rediscount ratio[b]		Borrowed funds ratio[c]	
	All banks	*City banks*	*All banks*	*City banks*	*All banks*	*City banks*
1955	89	91	1	1	3	7
1956	92	94	3	4	6	10
1957	100	107	10	15	12	19
1958	96	101	5	9	9	14
1959	93	98	4	7	8	14
1960	93	98	5	8	8	14
1961	96	103	11	18	13	22
1962	96	105	9	16	12	22
1963	96	102	7	12	10	19
1964	96	104	5	9	12	21
1965	93	99	5	9	10	19
1966	92	97	6	10	9	17
1967	93	99	4	8	8	16
1968	91	96	4	8	7	15
1969	91	97	5	8	8	16
1970	92	99	5	9	9	18
1971	90	93	1	2	3	8
1972	90	93	3	5	4	8
1973	93	99	3	5	4	8

Sources: Bank of Japan, Economic Research Department, *The Japanese Financial System, 1972* (1972), p. 21; Bank of Japan, *Economic Statistical Annual, 1973* (1974), pp. 67–70; and Bank of Japan, *Economic Statistics Monthly* (June 1974), pp. 43–46.

a. Ratio of loans to liabilities. Liabilities are defined as deposits (excluding checks, bills, and government agency deposits before 1964) plus bank debentures.

b. Ratio of rediscounts to liabilities plus rediscounts.

c. Ratio of total borrowing plus net call money to liabilities plus total borrowing and net call money.

pressed by the Bank of Japan, the Ministry of Finance, and the National Planning Agency goes further.[32] Concern expressed by critics of the government's economic policies go much further.[33] Some of these comments have already been noted. Their principal points may be summarized under the following generalizations:

—Overloan causes monetary overexpansion and inflation.

—The Bank of Japan becomes too deeply involved with the borrowing banks. In a crunch it cannot really enforce tightness.

—Overloan prevents the development of a bond market—since firms and

32. See Bank of Japan, Economic Research Department, *The Japanese Financial System, 1972* (1972), p. 22; and Economic Planning Agency, *Economic Survey of Japan, 1968–69*, p. 181.

33. Kenneth Kurihara, *The Growth Potential of the Japanese Economy* (Johns Hopkins Press, 1971), p. 77.

banks prefer bank financing to bond financing—and this impedes the development of open market operations.

—Corporations become too closely involved with banks. The allocation of resources suffers, and risks are not properly weighed.

—Overloan is both the cause and the vehicle for excessive business investment.

In broadest terms, overloan seems to have become a symbol of what critics believe has been wrong with Japan's economic and social policies—a connotation that is far beyond its economic rationale. To some, overloan stands for the policy that has favored big business above everybody else and that has promoted economic growth at the expense of social objectives, such as housing, clean water, and clean air. The emotional response that overloan arouses is comparable to the heat generated in the United States by such symbols as high interest rates and capital gains. The breadth of the charges makes it worthwhile to examine overloan even at the risk of arriving at conclusions that may be at odds with prevailing Japanese views.

Overloan may indeed lead to overexpansion and inflation, but so will bank credit expansion in other forms if the central bank does not keep it to a noninflationary rate. It is a central bank's job to control money supply and bank credit, and it can do this regardless of overloan.

If a central bank wants to keep money and credit growing at a noninflationary rate, it must see to it that the monetary base (central bank liabilities) grows appropriately. In Japan most of the monetary base supplied is absorbed into currency. Until the end of 1972 bank reserves in the form of deposits with the Bank of Japan were negligible; thereafter they approximately quadrupled their share in the bank's total liabilities. In the absence of a balance-of-payments surplus, the Bank of Japan can supply this base by buying securities or by lending to the banking system. It would probably not have been altogether impossible in the past to supply the required monetary base through open market purchases, even though the supply of government bonds has been limited. The effect of the purchases in increasing the monetary base is the same no matter who the seller is. If the bank decided not to purchase on the open market, the only way of supplying the necessary amount of monetary base was via rediscounts. Under these circumstances, overloan was the inevitable consequence of maintaining the desired growth of the money supply.[34]

As for the risks of continuous intimate contact between the central bank and commercial banks that result from rediscounting, the Bank of Japan may

---

34. For a discussion of the processes of money supply and monetary control, see Chapter 3.

find that this relationship exposes it to some pressure. But in fact the Bank of Japan has far more power over the commercial banks when they are in its debt than when they are not. Strong restraint may indeed pose the danger of crisis. But that risk results from the lack of a liquidity cushion in the banking system rather than from the particular form in which reserves are supplied.

The suggestion that overloan impeded the development of a bond market and thus prevented the growth of open market operations seems to reverse what is the more plausible cause-effect sequence. It was the low interest rate policy that held back the bond market and thus forced corporations to turn to the banks. It is true that both corporations and banks may have preferred this. But if bond issues had been possible on a larger scale, the Bank of Japan could have kept a tighter reign on bank credit, thus compelling corporations to borrow outside the banks.

That overloan tended to make corporations more deeply involved with banks seems to be true. If, however, all the lending made possible by overloan had taken place outside the banks, the average city bank's lending would have been perhaps only 10 percent lower. If, on the other hand, overloan had been eliminated by replacing discounts with open market purchases, bank loans in the aggregate would not have had to be reduced. The distribution of loans among banks might have been different, however, depending on which banks held the reserves created by the open market purchases.

Finally, to consider overloan responsible for the pattern of investment that came about seems a vast exaggeration. Technically, overloan was neither a necessary nor a sufficient condition. The pattern of investment financed with the help of overloan could have been financed without it if the government had chosen alternative arrangements. The pattern of investment that emerged, moreover, was in good part determined by a combination of government decision and market forces in the real sector and the availability of funds through the city banks. At most, overloan has influenced investment only marginally, and it was not necessary for investment. Hence evidence of the unimportance of overloan will not satisfy those who object to the growth policies of Japan. Nevertheless, it is useful to present this evidence.

Overloan, as it is used here in its broader sense, involves two imbalances. One is the maldistribution of deposits and loan demands within the banking system. The city banks have more demand for loans than deposits; the local banks and others have more deposits than demand for loans. The second imbalance is the insufficiency of the unborrowed monetary base for meeting the demand for currency (the demand for reserves on the part of the banks is small), which leads to borrowing from the Bank of Japan.

The imbalance between city banks and other banks is not a particularly startling phenomenon. It exists elsewhere—for instance, in the United States. The New York and Chicago banks typically are borrowers in the federal funds market, while country banks and some other reserve city banks are typically lenders. Big banks in the United States, however, have many ways of curing a deficiency of deposits by flexible liabilities management. Their use of the federal funds market, as long as it does not become excessive, need not be regarded as a major structural defect of the banking system.

In Japan the role of the federal funds market is taken over by the call money market. Because the city banks are deprived of some other means of flexible liabilities management, such as the issuance of certificates of deposit, this market attracts considerable attention. But there are other ways in which the imbalance—now bridged by the call money market—could be cured if the necessary facilities were offered or if reforms were introduced. Certain possibilities of doing so will be outlined shortly.

The imbalance that compels the banking system to borrow from the Bank of Japan reflects the continuing need for an increase in the monetary base. In the United States and many other countries this need is supplied routinely by open market operations. In countries with important balance-of-payments surpluses the necessary growth of the monetary base—and often more—is supplied through the monetization of these surpluses. In Japan part of the monetary base has been supplied through rediscounts, although to a diminished extent during years of payments surpluses. The exact level of borrowing from the central bank is determined by various peculiarities of the Japanese system. These features that affect the magnitude of the rediscount component of overloan are as follows:

• The Japanese household sector carries almost all of its transactions balances in the form of currency because of the virtual nonuse of checks and giro payments. This affects the monetary system by reducing the liabilities of the banks and increasing those of the Bank of Japan. Thus the Bank of Japan has a larger role in the allocation of credit than it would have otherwise. The effect is to increase overloan.

• The foregoing effect is offset in some measure by the near-absence of reserve requirements against deposits. Reserve requirements transfer assets from the banking system to the central bank. The Bank of Japan leaves these funds and the power to allocate them to the banking system, thus reducing overloan.

• The Bank of Japan has relied heavily, though in diminishing degree, on rediscounts as a means of supplying the monetary base. The bank has experimented with a wide variety of techniques for supplying the base, including bilateral securities purchases with selected financial institutions, dealings in nongovernment securities, and repurchase agreements. The limitations of the securities markets, as serious as they have been, do not seem to have been an absolutely compelling reason why, before 1967, securities purchases by the Bank of Japan did not become a larger source of the base than rediscounts. But the bank apparently has never been willing to accept the high rates on securities that reliance on true open market operations would have brought about during periods of severe restraint. Hence, during periods when an increase in the base was needed, including seasonally, it has been unwilling to buy freely securities it could not sell later to absorb an excess in the base.

The call market component of overloan, too, is a result of institutional peculiarities and rigidities that, conceptually, at least, could have been altered. Institutional and political obstacles, of course, might well prove insuperable. Several considerations are relevant.

First, had the government permitted the bond market to function as it did before the war, corporations probably would have drawn their financial resources from a much larger range of lenders. This, to be sure, would not have increased the total supply of savings. In many cases bond purchases by household savers would have disintermediated the deposits of city banks. But overall, the position of city banks would have been eased, and their need to resort to the call money market would have lessened.

Second, city banks have not been permitted to issue certificates of deposit. In the United States, the introduction of certificates of deposit in the early 1960s enabled the banking system as a whole—and to a lesser extent the New York and Chicago banks—to halt the shrinkage in their share of the total resources of financial intermediaries. In Japan the effect would be less dramatic because banks issue time deposits for periods of up to eighteen months. But if certificates of deposit had adequate interest rates and were limited to large denominations to forestall disintermediation, they would nevertheless enable the city banks to attract funds that so far they have had to obtain via the call money market and more recently the discount market. In its 1970 report, the Committee on Financial System Research (CFSR) recognized the role of the certificate of deposit in the United States but judged that its use in Japan would be premature. On the lesser issue of permitting medium-term savings deposits, which would also alleviate the position of the city banks, the CFSR was split. The opposition of the banks that might lose deposits presumably has played a role.

Third, the deposit deficiency of the city banks might be eased if they were allowed to establish branches more freely. Since the bulk of deposits outside the financial centers are savings deposits, most branches do not lend enough to absorb all of their deposits. Thus they become powerful means of attracting funds to head offices. Until very recently the policy of the Ministry of Finance has been adverse to branch expansion by city banks.

Finally, the deposit deficiency of the city banks might also be eased if mergers were permitted with local banks. This, however, has been precisely the type of merger that the Ministry of Finance has been least willing to accept for reasons of structural policy. Branching and merger policies are discussed in a subsequent section.

In sum, overloan is just one of many factors influencing the allocation of resources in a system in which numerous institutional rigidities operate. Whether large enterprises would have borrowed less in a system free of rigidities and uninfluenced by a low interest policy is uncertain. They would have been able to borrow all they could profitably use, given the level of interest rates, but interest rates probably would have been higher. Overloan could have been eliminated by a variety of changes either in the practices of the Bank of Japan or in the structure of the banking system, no matter how much or how little the corporate sector was allowed to borrow. In that sense, overloan must be regarded as a superficial rather than a fundamental phenomenon.

Structural Policy

The evolution of Japan's banking system is characterized by a clearly defined structural policy on the part of the government. The policy of stimulating and maintaining specialization among financial institutions, which has already been discussed, is one instance of this structural policy. Other policies relate to the number of large banks, their branch systems, and the competitive relationship among different groups of banks. In pursuit of its structural aims, the Ministry of Finance has been very deliberate in authorizing and even stimulating bank mergers, and in controlling branching, types of liabilities, and any other means by which intermediaries might affect their relative position.

For years the CFSR has intensively reviewed the banking system. This group, consisting of academicians, experts, and practitioners, is appointed by and attached to the Ministry of Finance, which also provides the research backup for it. It is in effect a continuing analogue of the U.S. Commission on Money and Credit and its successor, the Commission on Financial Structure and Regulation (Hunt Commission). Originally established in December 1945 to study the problems of Japan's monetary system, the CFSR was reestablished in 1956. In a succession of reports it has examined such problems as reconstruction finance, the reform of the Bank of Japan Law (on which the CFSR did not submit agreed proposals), the computerization of banking, the credit problems of small enterprises, and private financial institutions. In the securities industry a similar review process has been carried out by the Securities and Exchange Council, an analogous institution. This intensive and continuing effort to improve the structure of the financial system contrasts with past U.S. attempts at reform that typically were sporadic and that on the whole produced little except when stimulated by a recent crisis. The Japanese and U.S. systems also differ in that the Ministry of Finance exerts more control over the CFSR than the U.S. government has exerted over the Commission on Money and Credit and the Hunt Commission.

OBJECTIVES OF STRUCTURAL POLICY. The objectives of the Ministry of Finance have been both defensive and positive. Defensively, the policymaker has been concerned with the need to protect both the system and the depositor against failure. In contrast to U.S. practice, the maintenance of competition has played a secondary role until quite recently. During World War II the government carried out a ruthless concentration policy that drastically reduced the number of banking institutions. Some further concentration has taken place subsequently, although the number of banks has increased. Concern over excessive competition has been a frequent theme. In the late 1960s a policy shift toward greater emphasis on competition was induced by the realization that, as the CFSR observed, "Government controls on operations of financial institutions heretofore . . . tended to give excessive protection to interests of institutions rather than to those of the public, mostly because of institutional difficulties in separating protection of the depositors from protection of financial institutions."[35] Among the positive objectives have been the supply of credit to particular parts of the economy, the exploitation of economies of scale, the ability of the Japanese banking system to meet international competition, and—less explicitly—a high amenability to monetary control.

The core of Japan's banking system, although a shrinking one, consists of the thirteen city banks. Thus Japan is some distance away from the point reached by industrial countries other than the United States who have their "Big Three," "Big Four," or "Big Five." On the other hand, Japan, with its 63 local banks, 7 trust banks, and 3 long-term-credit banks, is even further away from the structure of the U.S. banking system with its 14,000 commercial banks. The large number of very small credit associations and cooperatives does not essentially change this picture. The process of concen-

35. CFSR, *Recommended Changes*, p. 11.

tration, which in other major industrial countries has stopped just short of total concentration and which in the United States was blocked almost at the start by national and state government policy, has reached an intermediate stage in Japan. The resulting impression of a deliberate structural policy on the part of the Japanese authorities is well justified.

Structural policies aiming at an adequate supply of credit have found expression in measures favoring the development of credit facilities for the small business sector. This is not to say that these facilities have become adequate, given the great predominance of small business in the Japanese economy. But concern for small business was the evident rationale of the policy of first preventing and later severely restricting the establishment of new branches of city banks and of favoring the reduction in the number of local banks to approximately one bank per prefecture. The increase in the asset share of the credit associations, credit cooperatives, and agricultural financial institutions and the shrinkage in the share of city banks from about one-half to about one-third over the past twenty years bears this out. This does not alter the strong impression that the distribution of credit, measured against needs, has remained lopsided.

The desirability of further concentration through mergers has been examined in considerable detail in studies of the economies of scale in banking. The four largest city banks were found to have an advantage in the ratio of interest on deposits and all other deposit-related expenses to the total of deposits of 0.42 of a percentage point over the seven smallest city banks. Excluding interest expense, the advantage was 0.38 of a percentage point. The CFSR employed these findings as a basis for the recommendation for further mergers. It has stressed the advantages of mergers among institutions in the same geographic area, which in U.S. antitrust philosophy would be considered especially anticompetitive. A warning is added concerning the dangers of excessive concentration. Concern regarding the latter may be allayed, in some areas at least, by a 1697 survey that showed that in the area of highest concentration in Tokyo the city banks alone had thirty-eight offices within a radius of 500 meters, while the total number of offices reached seventy-eight. The principal causes of economies of scale appear to be relatively low head-office expenditures, economies of mass-processing, and mechanization and computerization.

Control of deposit rates has been an important device for controlling the structure of banking. As pointed out earlier, the modest advantage conceded to several types of institutions catering to small businesses has contributed to a substantial increase in their deposit share. Controls over the maturity of deposits have been used also to guide the competitive relationship among city banks, long-term-credit banks, and trust banks. Even advertising and the various types of nonprice competition to which interest rate control gives rise are regulated in minute detail.

Equipping the banking system to meet international competition has been a frequently emphasized policy objective. The authorities have been looking toward the entry of foreign banks and corporations into Japan as well as the expansion of Japanese banks into the rest of the world. Many of the actions taken concern the financing of foreign trade and the representation of Japanese banks abroad, both tightly regulated. Domestically, the main common denominator of policy has been a greater stress on ability and willingness to compete. Along with other measures an effort has been made to make banks more profit-oriented by easing the dividend restrictions under which they have been operated. One incidental effect of this appears to have been a massive increase in the stock market quotations of the major banks' stocks.

The policy of the Japanese authorities toward the structure of the banking system can be summarized as follows:

—Japanese structural policy has been a great deal more deliberate than U.S. policy and is developed more systematically and with greater continuity.

—Japanese structural policy is oriented toward particular concrete objectives rather than toward achieving maximum competition and leaving the results to the workings of the free market.

—With regard to the number of banks, Japanese policy seems to aim at an intermediary position between the large number of banks characteristic of the United States and the very high concentration typical of most other industrial countries. Some further concentration among city banks seems to be in prospect, but presumably would stop well short of a "Big Three" or a "Big Five."

The Formation of Groups

The commercial banks of Japan have played an important role since World War II as leaders of the so-called groups that are characteristic of Japan's business structure. Organizationally and functionally, the subject of groups falls under the general heading of "industrial structure."[36] Here the subject will be examined only insofar as it relates to the banking business.

"Banker control" has always had a bad connotation in the United States. It has been equated with hyperconservatism and with a form of management

36. See Chapter 7.

294 HENRY WALLICH AND MABLE WALLICH

that puts the interests of the financier ahead of those of the enterprise. Banker control, in other words, would be presumed to be adverse to rapid growth. The experience of Japanese banks as the heads of groups analogous in many respects to conglomerates is therefore of particular interest.

MOTIVES OF GROUP FORMATION. Of the groups that today are prominent in Japan, several go back in their composition, if not in their method of operation, to the *zaibatsu* of the pre–World War II era. In their day these holding companies, whose diversified interests were controlled by wealthy families, reflected tendencies of an entrepreneurial system that could be observed also in continental Europe.

In the *zaibatsu,* banks played only a subordinate role. A group of enterprises under common control often will find it convenient to form a group bank that takes in the funds of the group members and redistributes them as loans. A more efficient use of available funds is one of the obvious advantages of conglomeration, particularly when the supply of funds is limited or when capital markets are otherwise imperfect. But the *zaibatsu* banks were not in control.

The holding companies and the controlling interests largely disappeared in Japan as a result of postwar reforms. But the largest of these groups— Mitsubishi, Mitsui, and Sumitomo—were in good part reconstituted under the leadership of the banks previously associated with these groups. Other banks have assembled new groups around them. Some groups, however, have been formed that do not rely on the leadership of a bank.

The principal conclusion to be drawn from this diversity of group styles is that whether one regards the Mitsubishis, Mitsuis, and Sumitomos as mere revivals of the old *zaibatsu* or as *keiretsu,* a less tightly structured type of association, the group principle has reasserted itself in Japan. Since the phenomenon appears to repeat itself frequently under very different circumstances, one is bound to conclude that in the Japanese environment the group principle offers important advantages.

Some of these advantages do not seem to be related particularly to control by banks—for example, advantages reflecting financial arrangements, such as the reduction of financial risk through mutual support and the control of stock voting power through ownership within the group. Nonfinancial arrangements might include joint sale and purchase arrangements—for instance through a trading company—vertical integration, assured markets and sources of supply, technological affinity, combined research, and cooperative planning. The focus here will be on benefits from group membership that derive from the leading role played in a number of groups by a bank.

A need for credit undoubtedly has been the principal motive inducing firms to attach themselves to particular banks and their groups. Group membership means both more and less than does a bank line of credit in the United States. It means a commitment by the bank to protect the enterprise in all but the direst circumstances by lending or otherwise finding money for it. Nevertheless, group membership does not guarantee credit in the way a formal credit line does in the United States. If the Bank of Japan orders a cutback or a slowdown in credit expansion, the group bank must cut credit or slow it down. Firm credit lines of the U.S. variety do not exist in Japan.

Loans from the group bank have the effect of improving the lopsided capital structure of Japanese enterprises. Within reason, as noted earlier, the indebtedness of a firm to its group bank can be regarded as subordinated debt. This improves the quality of all other debt. In return for the greater exposure it implicitly assumes, the group bank reportedly generally receives a better grade of collateral than other lenders.

THE BANK AS GROUP LEADER. The activities of a bank as leader of a group differ widely with respect to particular group members and also with respect to particular banks. Members cluster around the bank in concentric circles. The influence of the banks, probably rarely absolute, diminishes toward the periphery. If an enterprise gets into trouble, the bank might replace the management with delegates from its own senior staff, possibly by coordination with the rest of the group. Banks also use the senior management positions of group members as a means of rewarding and retiring its own top executives, just as these enterprises in turn use firms further down the line.

INTRAGROUP AND INTERGROUP FINANCE. For the group bank, its members represent both a source of deposits and an outlet for loan funds. There is no exclusiveness, however. Banks lend margins of, and often major parts of, their resources to nongroup members, and most members obtain much the largest part of their loans from banks other than the group bank. The shrinking share of total financial assets held by city banks has compelled their group members to rely increasingly on other sources. Group banks, however, do not seem to have increased the share of their lending going to their membership. The result is a better diversification of risk from the point of view of the banks than the structure of groups would suggest. The process of deconcentration of lending is likely to continue under the influence of limitations on bank lending to a single borrower that are in the process of implementation. Introduced by the Ministry of Finance in 1974, these limitations are expected to become increasingly severe until they reach their full effective level in 1980. There appears to be little expectation, however, that these measures, taken as a means of controlling bank risk in line with the worldwide movement toward tighter bank supervision that began in 1974, will seriously interfere with the group structure.

PORTFOLIO SELECTION. Changes in membership happen only occasionally. Thus it may be an exaggeration to speak of the formation of a group through the attraction or creation of new members and the occasional departure of others as a process of portfolio selection. Nevertheless, the principles of assembling a group have some of the aspects of portfolio policy. To the extent that the group bank can control or influence this process, it is in the position of a portfolio manager who must be concerned with the optimum composition of the group.

Principles of group formation do not seem to be spelled out very explicitly. In the days of the prewar *zaibatsu,* when powerful entrepreneurs confronted one another, it was not unreasonable for each of them to want what the other had. This led to the "one-set" principle, which implies that a group should be represented to the same degree in each important industry. This principle is still referred to sometimes as a guiding rule for present-day groups. Given a sufficient number of groups, the effect may be to increase the number of firms in an industry beyond the number that would exist in the absence of groups. In that case, group formation combined with the one-set principle would seem to reduce concentration and presumably enhance competition.[37] It has been observed that because some of the new, highly technological industries require substantial amounts of capital, the one-set principle may be damaging and should be replaced by combinations of firms belonging to different groups.

A more logical principle of group formation is vertical integration. Ownership by a single firm of sources of raw materials, processing facilities, and a distribution network has, of course, certain anticompetitive implications, but these are not vigorously attacked even in the United States. Within a more loosely organized group, the effects should be no more serious. In a country where the supply of raw materials is crucial, as it is in Japan, this form of group structure has clear-cut advantages. Combined with a trading company that handles imports and—where appropriate—exports, the arrangement may be highly efficient.

Diversification of risk is the classical portfolio principle. One could visualize it being applied to the selection of firms for membership in a group. Negative covariance of profits may be too much to ask for—in a cyclical economy everything tends to go up and down together. Nevertheless, there may be a

37. See Chapter 7 for findings concerning market shares of the three leading groups.

degree of independence between the earnings of a firm oriented to the domestic market and one oriented to the foreign market, of a trading company and a manufacturer, and of a capital goods producer and a consumer goods producer. There may be negative covariance in other regards, such as in the seasonal cash needs of members. Such diversification facilitates financing and helps all members of the group. Covariance of profit, however, raises the ultimate question to be asked of any group: Who benefits?

MAXIMIZATION. In the case of a holding company, the benefits of diversification, synergism, and other properties of a group ultimately redound to the advantage of the owners of that company. In the case of a group, properties that enhance efficiency benefit chiefly the group members. The benefits of diversification, on the other hand, cannot be shared unless each group member supports the others. This leaves two questions unanswered: On whose behalf does maximization take place, if indeed it does take place? What is maximized?

One possibility is that maximization takes place in the interest of the group bank, since it leads the group. But in that case the maximized profits would have to come to the bank in the form of high interest rates on loans and low interest rates on deposits, since its shareholdings are not a decisive factor in earnings. The earnings of banks, however, although substantial, are not of a kind to suggest that all the gains from group formation have been channeled in their direction. Indeed the rate of return for city banks is lower than that for local banks, mutual banks, and credit associations.[38]

That leaves as the most plausible beneficiaries the companies constituting the membership. Given the traditional role of the small stockholder in Japan as a kind of subordinated creditor, one may assume that maximization is not carried on in his interest. Conceivably it could be conducted in the interests of each firm's management, although the Japanese code of ethics, which is reported to take a dim view of self-seeking within a group, makes that unlikely. Or conceivably the gains from group formation could be shared by all the potential claimants—workers, customers, and suppliers—to the economic benefits that a firm can bestow. Alternatively, the member firms as stockholders in other member firms may be the main beneficiaries.[39]

38. See Chapter 7 for an alternative interpretation of the allocation of gains from group operation.

39. Caves and Uekusa (Chapter 7) have made the important finding that group firms pay higher interest rates than independent firms. This suggests that at least some of the benefits of group formation go to the group banks. On the other hand, the bulk of the interest paid by group firms reflects borrowing from banks other than the group bank. It is not impossible, therefore, that group firms pay higher interest rates because they are charged more by these other banks.

Uncertainty also prevails with respect to the object of maximization. The present value of stock seems to mean little to major stockholders in Japan. Corporations are not valued on the basis of their daily stock market quotation. For the same reason it is unlikely that short-term profit is the objective. Japanese firms are quite willing to take short-term losses in the interest of long-term gains. Group membership helps them to survive temporary periods of low earnings while new projects are being readied. In the Japanese environment, the presumption sometimes expressed in the United States that sales rather than profits are the true object of maximization gains plausibility. Sales must be maintained on a steep growth path in order to benefit from rising productivity. Slow sales result in a loss of competitiveness as well as market share. Thus the alternative goals of sales and long-term profits become even harder to distinguish in Japan, not only for the outside observer but also for management, than they are elsewhere. This is one of the reasons why a question was raised at the beginning of this chapter about the applicability of profit maximization as an analytical tool in the Japanese economy.

The ability of a Japanese bank to attract a group of other enterprises in order to broaden its activities is beginning to be paralleled in the United States by the bank holding company device. In fact a group can do vastly more than a bank holding company, which is limited by statute to affiliates engaging in "bank related activities." There is one activity, however, in which even a Japanese group cannot engage: the securities business. Under Article 65 of the Securities and Exchange Law of 1948, patterned on the Glass-Steagall Act of 1933, the securities business is the preserve of a separate type of firm.

Securities Markets

Given the degree of risk a firm is prepared to accept, its continuing choice between short- and long-term financing is governed mainly by the structure of its assets. The choice between equity and debt, given the cost of these long-run financing options, is governed mainly by the firm's degree of risk aversion. Finally, the choice between financing in negotiable or nonnegotiable long-term debt—that is, by selling bonds to the market or by selling a similar instrument to an investor who will not ordinarily resell—depends mainly on considerations of cost and of control. Together, these three choices are decisive in shaping the structure of business liabilities and of investors' assets. They determine also the potential role of financial markets in the transfer of these assets.

In Japan financing choices have been weighted heavily in favor of debt rather than equity, and of nonnegotiable debt rather than negotiable debt. The reasons for these choices have already been stated. Briefly, the cost of equity financing is high, primarily owing to the rapid growth of earnings. The practice of issuing equities at par, now apparently fading, probably has also contributed to management's perception of a high cost of equity. Debt financing, especially through banks, is further encouraged because close relationships between a firm and its principal bank make heavy indebtedness and high leverage less of a threat in Japan than elsewhere.

The reasons why debt financing in nonnegotiable form—through bank borrowing—has far outweighed the issuance of negotiable debt instruments —financing in the open markets—have likewise become apparent in the course of this chapter. At the short-term end of the maturity spectrum, open market financing so far has been largely precluded by the absence of a well-developed market along U.S. lines for commercial paper or similar instruments. For longer maturities, which in Japan are only medium term by U.S. standards, the principal obstacle to financing in negotiable form—through the bond market—has been the government's low interest rate policy. The government in effect has severely restricted access to the bond market for corporate borrowers by generally fixing rates on new issues at levels below those prevailing in the secondary market and by preempting for itself, state and local governments, and public corporations a large part of the supply of funds "available" at these artificially low rates.

There are additional circumstances that may have weighed on the side of bank financing. For the banks this form of financing has meant a strengthening of ties with the borrower. For the government, in addition to helping to implement the low interest rate policy, it may have meant a higher degree of control over the allocation of resources because of the government's influence over the banks, although the government also can influence priorities in the bond market. For the borrower, bank ownership of his debt may frequently have represented a desirable degree of flexibility in contrast with the immutability of a bond indenture. During periods of tight credit restraint, however, when banks were cutting down on loans, the opposite may have been the case.

The predominance of "indirect" over "direct" financing seems to have given rise to the view that the Japanese financial system is in some sense less sophisticated or less developed than systems possessing a bond market with large numbers of individual investors. This view deserves to be questioned. Intermediation, with its opportunities for risk diversification, may frequently be more efficient than direct financing. Further economies may result from indirect financing. Underwriting fees and disclosure requirements are costly. An intermediary, of course, can acquire debt that is negotiable. But he derives less benefit from this feature than does the individual investor, because the intermediary can obtain liquidity by means other than the sale of debt instruments from his portfolio. Whether negotiable debt is actually liquid, moreover, may be questionable for intermediaries holding large blocks of particular issues. For these reasons a bond market in which a large number of individual investors participate is unnecessary for efficient financing and allocation of resources.

Such a market, on the other hand, may contribute significantly to the utility of investors. Usually bonds offer a higher rate of return than do time deposits. The investor obtains this higher yield at the cost of a market risk and possibly a greater credit risk than is inherent in time deposits. Under these conditions one may suppose that a supply of bonds at market clearing prices would attract some Japanese investors. But there is no reason to assume that a strong preference for bonds over deposits would be in evidence.

These general observations explain why both the stock market and the bond market in Japan are less fully developed than they are, for instance, in the United States. The locus of the deficiency, however, differs between the two markets. Within the bond market, the primary market is well developed, to the extent required by its limited volume. But the secondary market is weak, owing to the gap between the controlled new issue price and what would be the market clearing price if trading were active. For equities, the situation is reversed. The secondary market is broad and active, but the primary market performs only a limited function.

The Equities Market

In Japan as elsewhere, the equities market performs more than one function. It raises capital for enterprises, allocates resources by establishing the cost of capital for particular firms, broadens options by supplying savers and investors with an additional investment medium, and helps to distribute ownership and equalize distribution of wealth and income.

RAISING FUNDS. The Japanese stock market has not been a great fund raiser for Japan's business sector. External funds, to be sure, account for a large part of the total funds raised, averaging well above 50 percent during the period 1959–72. Equities, however, have represented only a small fraction, ranging from 5 percent to 20 percent of total external financing, with the lower end of the range prevailing in 1971–72. Of the companies listed on the first and second section of the Tokyo Stock Exchange, about 20 percent raised a total of ¥870 billion in 1973. But the raising of new capital does not seem to have been the principal reason for many of these issues.

New issues are not, of course, the sole source from which corporations derive their equity. Retained profits are considerably more important, amounting to 12 percent of total funds raised and 27 percent of internal funds raised in calendar year 1965 and 15 percent and 38 percent, respectively, in calendar year 1972. The conversion of convertible bonds, minimal in the early seventies because convertible bonds began to come into fashion only around 1970, also contributes to equity. But the combined effect of these flows of equity funds has not raised the share of equity in the overall capitalization of Japan's corporations above about 18 percent.

In addition to raising funds, new equity issues serve the function of giving valuable subscription rights to stockholders when these issues are offered at par, as was the dominant practice until the late 1960s. In 1971, 38 percent of the new equity financings on the Tokyo Stock Exchange were "public offerings," that is, not at par. By 1973 the percentage had increased to 54 percent. As pointed out before, a subscription price of par, even though the stock may be selling at a multiple thereof, does not affect the cost of capital to the enterprise in an economic sense so long as the management identifies the interests of the firm with those of the stockholders. In that case the high cost of the funds raised, in terms of dividends, is offset by the benefit to the stockholders from the sale or exercise of the rights.

Nevertheless, the popularity of the par value stock subscription method raises doubts about how both management and the stockholders interpret their roles. It suggests that the stockholder regards himself as somehow enriched by the distribution of rights, even though the stock is marked down when it goes "ex-rights." In an economic sense the stockholder owns the corporation and the corporation therefore cannot give him anything that he does not already have. In order to believe that the stockholder is enriched by rights, stock dividends, and splits, a different interpretation is required—one in which the corporation is an entity with a life of its own and the stockholder is a kind of subordinated creditor. This interpretation is not irrational so long as it places the corporation and the old stockholders in juxtaposition with the new stockholders from whom funds are to be obtained. To view old stockholders in that way raises the fundamental question of what, if anything, the corporation maximizes and on whose behalf.

It is worth noting, however, that until quite recently at least some continental European attitudes toward corporations and their stockholders seem to have reflected a similar philosophy. This philosophy has been expressed, among other ways, in legislation that taxes stock dividends and splits as income to the stockholder. In the United States the tax treatment of dividends —sometimes referred to as "double taxation of dividends"—is a vestigial remnant of this interpretation. In Japan the greater prevalence of this philosophy may have influenced the way management looks at the cost of equity capital and may have contributed to holding down the amount of equity financing.

The increasingly common practice of issuing stock at a price close to the market has been met with mixed reactions. Stockholder response in many cases appears to have been adverse, owing to the greatly reduced value of subscription rights under this type of financing. Other more rational complaints have been based on the fact already noted that an issue price less than 15 percent below the market does not require preemptive rights for stockholders. Reportedly this practice has led to the allocation of parts of new issues to favored stockholders to the detriment of the rest. Since 1973 heavy losses on new shares, an experience almost completely new to Japanese stockholders, has further contributed to disenchantment with the new techniques.

In the light of the evidence, it seems fair to conclude that equity financing often has as much to do with stockholder relations as with the raising of funds. One aspect of rights issues used as a means of satisfying stockholders has been the policy of paying a dividend that is stable in amount per share over considerable periods and keeping the payout ratio roughly constant by repeatedly issuing new stock at par. The effect of this policy has been to keep the price of the stock roughly constant over time.

The demand for valuable rights supports the view that an important segment of Japanese investors leans toward dividend orientation rather than growth orientation. Orientation toward dividends, moreover, would be a logical response to the difficulties encountered by security analysts. If present and future earnings are hard to evaluate, dividends may become the focus of analysis. Such an orientation might in turn be reflected by the dividend policies of Japanese corporations, along with their emphasis on relatively frequent rights. These policies, oriented as they are toward stable and frequent payouts, no doubt seek to be responsive to what the Japanese corporation perceives to be investor preference.

It should be noted that the small volume of new capital raised through the stock market does not necessarily reduce the stock market's role in allocating capital. A firm maximizing profits on behalf of its stockholders will also use the cost of capital established by the market as a guide in capital budgeting decisions in which internal funds are used. If a firm cannot find investment projects with a rate of return exceeding the cost of capital, the proper course of action is to return the funds to the stockholder rather than to invest them at a return lower than the stockholder could get elsewhere. Careful work on the cost of capital by Ryûei Shimizu[40] suggests that Japanese management is conscious of the cost of capital.

VALUATION OF EQUITIES AND ACCOUNTING PRACTICES. In recent years a good deal of analytical work has been done on the behavior of Japan's equity market. Much of this analysis reflects theoretical developments in the United States and is beginning to appear in Japanese stock market literature. Even though aimed at a popular audience, the material often is written at a technical level that many users of Wall Street brokerage reports would find demanding. This is also true of some Japanese government publications that in terms of sophistication often are superior to their U.S. counterparts. Tabular material, chart work, and the ready use of regression analysis and other statistical techniques bear out this observation.

For the purpose of analyzing particular securities, however, the advantages of high technical capabilities are to some extent outweighed by the problems presented by Japanese corporate accounting and disclosure rules. Resembling European corporate practice, upon which it is modeled, the policy of Japanese enterprises has been to tell the investor a good deal less than the Securities and Exchange Commisson requires U.S. enterprises to tell him. Some of the main issues center on the treatment of subsidiaries and corporate reserves. The accounting profession, too, has not achieved the degree of independence that it possesses in the United States. Internal audits have been the rule; the use of outside accountants is only gradually being generalized. On the other hand, Japanese corporate accounting has had the virtue of minimizing the frequency with which facts reported to the stockholder differ from those reported to the tax collector.

In the treatment of subsidiaries the principal difficulty has been the frequent lack of consolidation of parent and subsidiary accounts. Under these conditions only dividends received by the parent, not the subsidiary's earnings, enter into the parent's profit and loss statement. Only the book value of the parent's investment in the subsidiary—not its market value, let alone total assets and liabilities—enter into the parent's balance sheet. Recognition that such accounting can be misleading has prompted legislative moves toward consolidation as a legal requirement. Concern about tax revenue losses

40. Shimizu, "A Study of Capital Costs."

that would result from consolidating loss returns with returns showing profits has slowed down the consummation of the legislation.

Charges against gross income to establish diverse reserves, and the possibility of subsequent transfers back to earnings, also obscure the profits picture. These transfers to and from reserve accounts are not allowed without limitation since they affect tax liabilities. Some of the reserves, however, can be kept out of earnings and thus remain untaxed indefinitely. The creation and subsequent dissolution of reserves can be used to report a smoother trend of earnings than that actually realized. Permanent reserves understate earnings permanently.

Earnings reported for taxes, in Japan as in the United States, often are lower than those reported to stockholders. But while in the United States "book" earnings in typical years have exceeded "tax" earnings by approximately 35 percent, in Japan the difference is small because capitalized expenses and timing differences between book and tax are rare, deferred taxes are unknown, and intangible assets—when they exist—are rapidly expensed as a general rule.[41] On the other hand, rapidly rising real estate values may cause book values to understate the market value of assets, as indicated, for instance, by the excess of market valuation of shares over book value (see Table 4-7). The predominant effect of these accounting practices, as well as the frequent failure to consolidate parents and subsidiaries, is to report earnings that are lower than they would be if reported according to U.S. practice.

Analytical Findings

Accurate data are an important prerequisite if the stock market is to do a good job in valuing equities and thereby in allocating capital. It can be argued, in line with the efficient market doctrine, that the market sees through the veil of accounting techniques and defeats efforts to overstate or understate profits. This consideration reduces, although it does not remove, concern about the quality of the data. Much of the theoretical and empirical analysis of the behavior of equities in any event does not derive from corporate statements but focuses instead on the behavior of stocks in the market.

THE RATE OF RETURN. In a recent study, Fumiko Konya supplied data on the annual rate of return for stocks listed on the Tokyo Stock Exchange.[42]

41. See M. Edgar Barrett, Lee N. Price, and Judith Ann Gehrke, "Japan: Some Background for Security Analysts," *Financial Analysts Journal* (January–February 1974), pp. 33–44, and (March–April 1974), pp. 60–67.

42. Fumiko Konya, *Rates of Return on Common Stocks: An Empirical Analysis of the Tokyo Stock Exchange,* Technical Paper 31 of the Division of Economics and Econometrics, Japan Securities Research Institute (JSRI, March 1974).

For the period 1952–72 a compound annual return of 18.1 percent is reported. Rates of return for single years naturally fluctuate widely, although there are few years with negative returns. Over long periods the rates converge rapidly. For instance, for overlapping ten-year periods within the twenty-year span of the data, rates range from a maximum of 22.8 percent for the years 1952–62 to a minimum of 9.5 percent for the years 1961–71. These figures indicate that despite wide fluctuations, which cut the Tokyo Stock Exchange index for the first section by over one-third in the early 1960s and trebled it during the early 1970s, risk in the Japanese stock market has been relatively low for the long-term investor. This is the result, of course, of Japan's high rate of growth.

THE PRICING OF STOCKS. Considerable effort has been invested in determining whether the Japanese stock market prices securities in accordance with the predictions derived from the capital asset pricing model, an analytical technique described below. Findings to that effect would help in evaluating the risk and, under given conditions, also the market prospects of individual securities. In U.S. brokerage literature the key feature of the model has become known as the "beta factor"—the regression coefficient obtained in regressing the return of a particular security on a market index.

The capital asset pricing model starts with the premise that if income has diminishing marginal utility, investors will be risk averse, that is, they will require higher risks to be rewarded by higher returns. Stock market risks can be separated into those that result from market movements and therefore are unavoidable ("systematic risk") and those that reflect fluctuations of particular securities independently of the market ("own risk"), which in a large market can be virtually avoided by full diversification. In a risk-averse market, securities with a greater systematic risk will have a higher rate of return, but not securities with a greater own risk.

Empirical findings concerning the applicability of the capital asset pricing model to the stock market of Japan (usually the Tokyo Stock Exchange) differ. Junko Maru and Shōichi Rōyama, covering the years 1952–71, found that pricing on the Tokyo Stock Exchange differs significantly from what the model predicts.[43] Hiroshi Okada, using data for 1961–73, found that the model in its simplest form does not adequately describe the risk-return relationship in the Japanese capital market.[44] A U.S. study, however, concluded

43. Junko Maru and Shōichi Rōyama, *Rates of Return in Relation to Risk: An Empirical Analysis of the Tokyo Stock Exchange,* Technical Paper 29, Japan Securities Research Institute (JSRI, January 1974).
44. Hiroshi Okada, "Shisan kakaku kettei moderu no ōyō" [Application of the Capital Asset Pricing Model], *Zaikai kansoku* [The Business Review] (February 1974), pp. 48–59.

that the Tokyo Stock Exchange did price securities in accordance with the model during the five-year period October 1964–September 1969.[45]

The studies of valuation of stocks on the Tokyo Stock Exchange permit various comparisons to be made with exchanges in the United States. The rate of return of 18.1 percent found by Konya for the years 1952–72 may be compared with the well-known long-term rate of 9 percent found by Fisher and Lorie for the stocks listed on the New York Stock Exchange over the period 1926–60.[46] The rate of convergence of annual returns is bound to be much slower in the United States than in Japan, given the relatively slow growth of U.S. stock prices and the wide fluctuations that occurred during the period studied by Fisher and Lorie.

The relatively low long-term risk, in terms of the speed of convergence to the average rate of return and the high level of that rate, would suggest that, by U.S. standards, Japanese stocks should sell at a high price/earnings ratio. Before 1972 the opposite was the case, with Japanese price/earnings ratios typically averaging about 12; the average was 15 or more in the United States during most of the 1960s. This difference must be evaluated in light of the fact that Japanese earnings, by U.S. accounting standards, are probably significantly understated, which would overstate the price/earnings ratio. An alternative interpretation might be that for the short-term investor risk is high and would depress the price/earnings ratio, owing to wide short-run fluctuations, and that such investors dominate the market. The rapid rise of the Japanese market beginning in 1972, which more than doubled the index by early 1973, has of course altered these relationships for the time being but may itself be regarded as a recognition by the market of some of the facts stated here. Finally, as noted in the earlier discussion of the Modigliani-Miller theorem, high corporate leveraging in Japan suggests that, given the existence of a corporate income tax, corporations behave as if they accepted a strong form of the theorem.

STOCK OWNERSHIP AND INVESTMENT QUALITY. An important function of the stock market is to help diffuse ownership and equalize the distribution of income and wealth. Ownership of publicly held stocks in Japan is widely distributed. After eliminating duplication from the sometimes cited Tokyo Stock Exchange figure of 17 million stockholders, there nevertheless remain an estimated 6 million stockholders, or about 6 percent of the population, a rate of ownership that falls short of the U.S. rate of about 14 percent.

45. Sheila C. Lau, Stuart R. Quay, and Carl M. Ramsey, "The Tokyo Stock Exchange and the Capital Asset Pricing Model," *Journal of Finance*, vol. 29 (May 1974), pp. 507–13.
46. Lawrence Fisher and James H. Lorie, "Rates of Return on Investments in Common Stock: Year by Year Record 1926–1965," *Journal of Business*, vol. 41 (July 1968), pp. 291–316.

The wide distribution of stock ownership in Japan is at least in part the result of the dissolution of the closely held *zaibatsu* after World War II. Personal ownership is very uneven, however. On the basis of 17 million holders, the data imply that, in 1972, 21 percent of the stockholders held fewer than 500 shares each, with a par value usually of ¥50, or less than 20 cents, representing less than half of 1 percent of the total number of listed stocks. Some 55 percent of the stockholders had 1,000–5,000 shares each, representing 13 percent of listed shares. About 69 percent of the total number of listed shares were in the hands of only one-half of 1 percent of the holders.

In addition to the highly unequal distribution of ownership, it is important to note that the share of individual holdings in the total number of listed shares has declined steadily from 49 percent in 1958 to 33 percent in 1972. Shares held by investment trusts and presumably representing household-sector investment fell from a peak of close to 10 percent in 1963 to 1 percent in 1972. The main gains have been registered by financial institutions, which advanced from 22 percent in 1958 to 34 percent in 1972, and by "other domestic corporations," which advanced from 16 percent in 1958 to 27 percent in 1972. In fiscal year 1973 equities at market value amounted to 16.6 percent of personal financial assets in Japan while other securities accounted for 7.3 percent, compared with 40.1 percent for equities and 8.0 percent for other securities in the United States as of December 31, 1972.

Given a wide distribution of ownership, the investment attributes of stocks become an important addition to the savers' options and welfare. It has been pointed out already that while market fluctuations have been wide and short-term risks therefore high, long-term risk as measured by the speed of convergence to the long-term average rate of return has been relatively low. Return, it was likewise pointed out, has been relatively high. Given risk and return, one measure of the efficiency of the stock market as an investment medium is its predictability.

A market that is predictable, in the sense that it permits participants to earn an above-average rate of return after allowance for risk, may be the kind of market in which many participants would like to be operating and may even believe themselves to be operating. It is nonetheless not an efficient market because it has not at any one time fully incorporated in its prices all the information that is available. The availability of unexploited information is what enables some participants in such a market to do systematically—rather than randomly—better than average. These considerations make it important to examine whether a market is a "random walk," in which case it would be an efficient market, having incorporated all available information.

Two studies of the Tokyo Stock Exchange arrive at the conclusion that this market is not a completely random walk. Kunio Saitō, employing a probability approach, found some systematic behavior in the market that caused him to reject a random walk hypothesis. He recognized, however, that the nature of the available tests makes his results somewhat uncertain.[47]

Hiroaki Yamada likewise found evidence against the validity of the random walk hypothesis for the Tokyo Stock Exchange.[48] At the same time he found that the slight but significant negative correlation of successive daily movements that he discovered was too unstable to be exploited effectively by investors. On these grounds Yamada concluded that the Tokyo Stock Exchange could nevertheless be regarded as an efficient market.

It should be noted that these tests are addressed only to the narrow question of whether past price movements in the Tokyo market contain information that would permit successful forecasting. The findings, in other words, are principally addressed to chartists and users of other technical approaches. A more fundamental question is whether some portfolio managers have been able to generate above-average results, with due allowance for risk, systematically enough to disavow the random character of the market. This important question, which in the United States has repeatedly been examined with the help of data on the performance of mutual funds, appears to be as yet unanswered in Japan.

THE STOCK MARKET AND PUBLIC POLICY. Japan's securities industry, and principally the stock market, is governed by legislation passed after World War II and patterned on the U.S. Securities Act of 1933 and the Securities Exchange Act of 1934. The legislation has been revised repeatedly in ways that appear to bring it more in line with the Japanese style of public administration. Examples are the integration of an originally independent Securities and Exchange Commission with the Ministry of Finance, the licensing —in lieu of simple registration—of securities companies with functions regulated according to capitalization, and the establishment of a permanent body, the Securities Counselling Commission, as the Ministry's chosen instrument to stimulate continuing discussion and reform of legal and administrative arrangements.

As in the United States, commercial banking is separated from the securities business. This separation, effected after World War II, has given rise to the institutional form known as the securities company. This enterprise com-

47. Kunio Saitō, "A Study on the Behaviour of Stock Prices: An Examination of the Random Walk Hypothesis Using Data from the Toyko Stock Exchange" (master's thesis, University of Edinburgh, September 1971).
48. Hiroaki Yamada, "Random Walk Theory and Submartingale: Empirical Test on the Japanese Stock Market" (manuscript, December 27, 1973).

bines the functions of an underwriter, security dealer, and broker according to its capital, which determines the license it can hold. The commercial banks, like those in the United States, are pressing in on the margins of the securities business, while the securities companies are strongly defending their position. The reported goals of the Ministry of Finance are greater tightness of regulation, more adequate underwriting capital, and in general a more competitive and less protected industry.

The Bond Market

In Japan, as in the United States, the bond market raises a substantially larger annual volume of funds than the stock market. During 1973 net bond issues, including those of both the central and local governments, amounted to ¥6.4 trillion against ¥1.4 trillion of new stock issues. The net amount issued annually does not reflect the relationship between the cumulative volume outstanding of the two types of assets, since the value of equities in the market is influenced more by profit retention than by new issues. At the end of 1973, the face value of bonds outstanding was ¥36.4 trillion, while the market value of stocks listed on all stock exchanges at the end of 1973 was ¥40.0 trillion.

From the point of view of the borrower there is only a marginal difference between the relative advantages of a long-term debt that is negotiable and one that is not, provided the cost of capital is the same in both cases. These pros and cons are likely to hinge on the respective cost of placement, on various nonprice terms of the debt, and on the debtor's sensitivity to public quotation of his liabilities. From the point of view of a household lender the difference is substantial, owing to the superior liquidity of negotiable debt. For an institutional lender, however, this difference largely disappears because large blocks of debt may have only limited liquidity and because large lenders can obtain liquidity by means other than selling or borrowing on negotiable securities from their portfolio.

The modest role of bonds in the financial structure of Japan reflects these considerations in part. If institutional lenders predominate, and if they have only limited demand for negotiable long-term debt, a bond market appealing to household lenders will be slow to develop. Long-term lending will in the main be in nonnegotiable form. Since World War II, however, the development of Japan's bond market has been set back also by the government's low interest rate policy. In the bond market the low interest rate policy has meant keeping the rate on news issues below the market clearing level, and thus limiting the volume of bonds that could be floated.

BORROWERS. Long-term-credit banks represent the largest single group of private borrowers in the bond market; at the end of 1973 they accounted for one-fifth of total bonds outstanding. These intermediaries distribute the proceeds on their bond sales in the form of loans. A large part of the limited supply of bond money therefore does not reach the ultimate borrower in that form. There is no equivalent in the United States, although there is in Europe, to the bonds issued by long-term-credit banks, with the possible exception of the commercial banks' capital notes. Public corporations represented one-fourth of total bonds outstanding at the end of 1973. The sum of government bonds and municipal obligations accounted for almost one-third.

With priority given to central and local government and to government corporations, private borrowers have had only modest access to the relatively cheap financing offered by the bond market. They have had indirect access, on probably somewhat less favorable terms, through loans from the long-term-credit banks.

LENDERS. Among the holders of bonds, financial institutions (48 percent at the end of 1973) and especially banks (26 percent) predominate. For banks, bonds listed on the Tokyo Stock Exchange have special advantages: they can be pledged for loans with, and at times sold to, the Bank of Japan, and they are not included by the Bank of Japan under the window guidance ceiling on total bank credit. Banks seem to treat their holdings of bonds issued by their corporate customers as part of their overall financing relationship, much as they treat holdings of stock.

The Finance Ministry's Trust Fund Bureau, which accumulates the inflows of funds to the Postal Savings System, holds almost one-fifth of the total bonds outstanding. It serves the Bank of Japan as a noninflationary outlet for bonds that the Bank has acquired in the secondary market. Households account for approximately another quarter of total bond holdings. With regard to household as well as bank investment in bonds, it should be noted that tax-exempt bonds, which represent a dominant share of commercial bank and household holdings in the United States, play no role in Japan.

THE SECONDARY MARKET. The arbitrary fixing of rates on new issues below the market has created a hiatus between the primary and the secondary market and has impeded the development of the latter. Only during periods of cyclical ease and low interest rates have the rate structures in the two markets coalesced, as they did from 1971 through early 1973. Bonds thus have been deprived of some of their liquidity and have lost some of their attractiveness as an investment medium. This condition, although of the government's own making, has been a matter of official concern. Such was the case especially during the period of large balance-of-payments surpluses, when Japanese authorities as well as underwriters and bankers were becoming increasingly conscious of their country's potential as an international financial center. Public borrowing needs arising out of prospective large environmental expenditures likewise seem to call for improvement in the bond market. Consolidation, along with internationalization, has therefore been an important policy objective.

Part of the move toward consolidation has taken the form of liberalization of interest rates on new issues. Without allowing rates to be determined freely by the market, they have nevertheless been adjusted to follow swings in the secondary market. These swings have at times been wide, as indicated by the rate on telephone bonds, the only issue enjoying a secondary market of some breadth and continuity.[49]

A fairly close relation has been observed between bond rates and call market rates, swings in call rates being wider than those in bond rates. Term-structure studies of the kind popular in the United States, designed to test alternative determinants of term structure such as expectations, liquidity preference, and compartmentalization, have been attempted in Japan but, given the nature of the market, have remained inconclusive. Certain regularities have been found in the lag characterizing the adjustment of long-term rates to short-term rates.[50]

As part of a liberalizing move a new rating system more closely resembling that of the United States was introduced in 1971. The older system of five corporate bond classes based on the size of the issuer's capitalization was replaced by one emphasizing corporate profitability and assets. The spread between bonds with different ratings, however, as well as the general level of rates, continued to be fixed by the Conference on Government Bond Issues and the Bond Issue Council. Precise calculations of interest coverage, asset protection, and the like, as practiced by U.S. bond analysts and embodied in diverse state laws defining eligibility of bonds for trusts and savings banks, has held little promise in Japan because of the lack of consolidated statements and other accounting problems. Until very recently all corporate bonds were secured by mortgages. The use of unsecured bonds has been increasing very gradually. Bonds convertible into stock, on the other hand, have been gaining popularity quite rapidly. All these instances—a more flexible new-issue price, the consolidation of primary and secondary market-price struc-

49. The purchase of such bonds, which subscribers frequently sell upon receipt, is a prerequisite for obtaining telephone service.
50. Shunsaku Nishikawa and Keza Ishiki, "Kinri no sōgokankei to sono henka" [Some Interrelations between Interest Rates and Their Changes: A Statistical Approach], *Mita shōgaku kenkyū* [Mita Journal of Business and Commerce], vol. 11 (October 1968).

ture, ratings, the use of unsecured bonds, and convertible bonds—signify the Japanese bond market's ongoing adaptation of Western, and especially U.S., techniques.

The Money Market

It is indicative of the generally modest state of development of monetary —as contrasted with credit—arrangements in Japan that the financial sector during the postwar period has had to operate with the aid of rather rudimentary markets for money and liquid financial instruments. The wide range of liquid instruments familiar in the United States and in many other industrial countries is not well represented: short-term government issues, commercial paper, certificates of deposit, and, until 1972, bank-endorsed customer's paper have for the most part been lacking. By U.S. standards, in the existing markets—the call money market and more recently the discount market and the market for interbank deposits—the number and range of participants as well as the amounts of transactions have been limited.

Various explanatory factors can be cited. Except for occasional periods of high liquidity, business has been straining to find funds and has been heavily in debt to banks. Adjustments in liquidity positions, therefore, have often been made by changing the level of this indebtedness. Moreover, a modest interest rate, on the order of 2 to 3 percent since 1951, has been paid on some types of demand deposits, reducing the demand for liquid instruments. High compensating balances also have injected some temporary flexibility into cash management. The government, concerned with its low interest rate policy and with keeping control of the allocation of credit, has seen no reason to provide liquid paper tradable at freely fluctuating rates.

One of the consequences of the dearth of liquid instruments capable of functioning as money substitutes has been a high degree of effectiveness of monetary policy. A further consequence, once the economy managed to acquire liquidity through its balance-of-payments surpluses, has been the stock market boom of 1972–73 engendered by the placement of idle corporate funds that could find no other outlet. Still another consequence has been the sharp reduction in the effectiveness of monetary control under these conditions of inadequately absorbed excess liquidity.

CALL MONEY MARKET. The call money market, along with the stock market, has been Japan's outstanding example of a relatively free financial market. The predominant participants in the market are financial intermediaries, including securities companies and life and nonlife insurance companies.

The volume of operations has been modest; the average annual balance outstanding reached a peak level of ¥2 trillion in 1971.

The principal feature of the call money market has been the continuing deficit position of the city banks and their consequent role as the largest borrowers by far. As a result the call money market has not been primarily a means for adjustment of random or seasonal financial surpluses or deficits. Instead it has been a conduit through which the continuing liquidity deficit of the city banks has been financed by the only slightly less persistent surpluses of the local banks, trust banks, credit associations, and financial institutions for agriculture and forestry. It reflects an imbalance among intermediaries in their sources and uses of funds. It is the Japanese analogue, as already noted, of the federal funds market in the United States.

The interest rate in the call money market is on the whole a market-clearing rate. It has fluctuated with the business cycle and with shifts in monetary policy. During the postwar period, its three categories—overnight money, demand loans, and over-month-end money—have experienced monthly average rates as high as 23.7 percent (1961) and as low as 0.37 percent (1956). Since 1972 effectively all call money has been in the form of demand loans.

Despite wide fluctuations the call money market and its rates have not been entirely without control. Particularly since the 1965–66 period the Bank of Japan has operated both on the lending and on the borrowing side of the market in order to limit rate movements. Its policy in general has been to keep the call rate above the discount rate. The bank also keeps in continuing touch with the six dealers operating in the market who consult with it concerning rates.

The call money rate, as the most prominent of the relatively uncontrolled rates, has received considerable analytical attention. It has commonly been viewed as an indicator of financial pressure and therefore of Bank of Japan policy. It was the focal point in the well-known study by Yoshio Suzuki, who concluded that the modus operandi of Japanese monetary policy can be explained in terms of profit maximization and of a market-clearing mechanism.[51]

DISCOUNT MARKET. In 1971 the Bank of Japan in effect split the call money

51. Yoshio Suzuki, "The Effect of Monetary Policy on Bank Credit in Japan: A Theory and Measurements of Bank Behavior" (Tokyo: Bank of Japan, August 1967; processed). For a differing interpretation, see Hugh Patrick, "An Interpretation of the Bank of Japan's Mechanism of Monetary Policy" (paper presented to the Japan Economic Seminar, Cambridge, Mass., February 20, 1971).

market and broadened the scope of short-term money markets by terminating the "over-month-end" category and replacing it with a newly created discount market for short-term bills.[52] There are fewer types of participants in the discount market than in the call money market; the former is limited to commercial banks and six broker-dealers. The definition of eligible paper is tightly drawn, resembling perhaps most closely the U.S. concept of bankers' acceptances. The Bank of Japan's main purpose seems to have been to provide a separate channel for somewhat longer-term money market operations, and at the same time a convenient vehicle for its own open market operations, both of which are designed more particularly to influence bank liquidity than to keep down the range of rate fluctuations. The average monthly level of discount operations reached ¥5 trillion during the summer months of 1974. Bank of Japan operations in this market increased continuously until August 1974, when the central bank's holdings of bills amounted to almost ¥5 trillion. Since that time, although market balances have remained at the ¥4 trillion–¥5 trillion level, the bank has reduced its holdings. By mid-1975 bank holdings were at the ¥3 trillion level.

THE INTERBANK DEPOSIT MARKET. The high liquidity of the year 1972 brought about the apparently spontaneous development of a market for interbank deposits. In contrast to interbank balances in the United States, interbank deposits in Japan seem to have had the character primarily of a placement of funds for fixed periods at rates more profitable than those prevailing in the other parts of the money market, rather than of a means of compensation for services rendered to the smaller banks by their city correspondents. As long as the Bank of Japan does not act to control or influence the interbank deposit market, that market offers to the city banks a means of acquiring funds that are not directly under the control of the Bank of Japan.

Conclusions

The principal conclusions to emerge from this analysis of the financial system of Japan are:

• The system is a disequilibrium system in which institutional controls, including rationing, have taken away from interest rates some of the function of allocating resources. Interest rates, however, do play an important allocative role within each of the sharply segmented areas of the capital market.

---

52. This and the following section draw heavily on Wilbur F. Monroe, *Japan: Financial Markets and the World Economy* (Praeger, 1973). See also Chapter 3 for a discussion of the bill (discount) market.

• These deviations from equilibrium usually have pushed the economy in the direction of faster growth. For the most part this has reflected a deliberate government policy.

• The costs of this disequilibrium system are borne, aside from the disadvantaged credit-seeking sectors, mainly by household savers. These in turn have received some compensation through the effects of faster growth on their future income.

• The manipulation and control of risk plays an important role in the system. Risk appears high, but in fact it is held within acceptable limits by a variety of private and public techniques.

• The structure of financial markets and institutions is strongly influenced by positive public policy. Often, although not always, policy moves the system in the direction in which market forces would cause it to evolve, but moves it faster.

• The virtual absence of familiar channels of financing, such as a broadly based bond market, does not seem to have interfered materially with the effectiveness of the system. The essential financial fact has been the massive flow of savings, which have found their way into investment despite institutional inadequacies.

• Familiar analytical concepts, such as maximization of profit, are of much more doubtful applicability in Japan than in Western countries. In such instances it is fair to say that "Japan is different," even though the basic regularities of economics do apply in Japan as elsewhere.

• The financial system of Japan is in a process of rapid transition, not only under the influence of growing international competition and integration (internationalization), but also under the influence of the rapid progress, at least until the oil crisis, of the economy itself. In its original form, the system may have been particularly effective in helping Japan move from poor-country to rich-country status. In the absence of substantial liberalization, it might be less effective in meeting the needs of a wealthy country.

CHAPTER FIVE

Taxation

Joseph A. Pechman, Brookings Institution
and
Keimei Kaizuka, Tokyo University

317

JAPAN'S TAX SYSTEM resembles that of the United States more than those of the Western European countries. Revenues at the national level are derived primarily from individual and corporate income taxes; the prefectures and local governments rely on the property tax as well as on income taxes. The payroll tax is used to finance social security benefits and the national health insurance system. There is no general sales or value-added tax in Japan, but substantial revenues are raised from selected excise and sumptuary taxes at all levels of government. Death and gift taxes are minor sources of revenue.

In 1972, individual and corporate income taxes together accounted for 50 percent of total tax revenues in Japan; taxes on commodities and services for 24 percent, payroll taxes, 19 percent, the property tax 5 percent, and death and gift taxes, 2 percent (see Table 5-1). The United States raised about the same proportion of total revenues from payroll and death and gift

Table 5-1. *Distribution of Tax Revenues*[a] *in Japan and Six Other Countries, by Source, 1972*

Percent

Tax source	Japan	United States	United Kingdom	France	Germany	Italy	Sweden
Income	50	45	39	17	33	20	46
Individual	26	34	32	11	28	13	42
Corporate	24[b]	11	7	6	5	7	4
Payroll	19	20	18	41	34	39	23
Goods and services[c]	24[b]	19	30	40	30	39	30
Property	5	13	11	1	2	1	1
Death and gift	2	2	2	1	*	1	*
Total	100	100	100	100	100	100	100

Source: Organisation for Economic Co-operation and Development, *Revenue Statistics of OECD Member Countries, 1965–1972* (Paris: OECD, 1975). Data are for the calendar year except for the United States (fiscal year ends June 30, 1972). Figures may not add to totals because of rounding.

* Less than 0.5 percent.

a. Includes national and local taxes.

b. The Japanese enterprise tax levied by prefectural governments is included in the corporate income tax and excluded from the tax on goods and services.

c. Includes sales, value-added, and excise taxes, taxes on imports, exports, and transfers of property and securities, and other transactions taxes paid by enterprises.

Note. The authors wish to acknowledge with gratitude the comments and suggestions on an earlier draft made by Gardner Ackley, Richard M. Bird, Yukihiro Fukuda, Carl S. Shoup, and Stanley S. Surrey. They are particularly grateful to the Staff of the Tax Bureau, Ministry of Finance, who provided much of the data used in this chapter and helped explain the intricacies of the Japanese tax laws.

taxes as Japan, but much more from the individual income tax and property tax and much less from corporate income and commodity taxes. Most European countries rely more heavily on consumption and payroll taxes.

Despite these and other superficial similarities between the Japanese and U.S. tax systems, there are striking differences not only between the structures of particular taxes in the two countries, but also between their respective attitudes and policies toward the use of taxation to promote national objectives. In the first place, the Japanese have virtually a unitary fiscal system, with limited delegation of fiscal responsibilities and powers to the local governments. Second, largely because of the high rate of economic growth, Japanese tax revenues at constant rates and exemptions have greatly exceeded the revenues needed to pay for the relatively low rate of public expenditure. This fiscal dividend has been used to augment national savings and to provide tax reductions virtually every year. Third, the Japanese income taxes are riddled with special provisions that are designed to encourage particular types of consumer and business behavior. The Japanese tax system is probably slightly progressive on balance, but—like the U.S. system—its effect on income distribution is not great.

Outlines of the Tax System

Before World War II Japan derived about two-thirds of its revenue from indirect taxes, mainly on liquor and tobacco; during and since the war income taxation has become the major source. Although the predominance of income taxes is relatively recent, Japan was one of the pioneer countries of the world in their use. The tax on individual income dates back to 1887 and on corporate profits to 1899; but these taxes took their modern form only in 1940, when separate taxes were enacted for individual and corporate incomes. The individual income tax was a schedular tax, under which different rates applied to different sources of income; it was supplemented by a graduated global tax that applied to the individual's combined income above a specific minimum. The corporate tax was levied in the form of an excess profits tax that applied at progressive rates depending on rates of return.

In 1947, under the influence of the American occupation authorities, the schedular individual income tax was replaced by a unified tax with progressive rates, and the excess profits tax was replaced by a regular corporate income tax. Tax rates during the occupation were very high, reaching a maximum of 85 percent on individual incomes above ¥5 million (about $14,000) and 52.5 percent on corporate profits. In addition, a turnover tax (paid each time a commodity "turns over" from one firm to another) was enacted to raise needed revenues.

In 1949 a commission headed by Carl S. Shoup, Professor of Economics at Columbia University, was organized to help reform the tax system and moderate the high tax rates, which had become extremely burdensome as a result of the rapid rise in prices immediately after World War II. The Shoup Mission recommended a complete overhaul of the system, including repeal of the turnover tax, a comprehensive individual income tax (with full taxation of capital gains and full deduction for capital losses), a dividend credit at the individual income tax level, a surcharge on accumulated corporate earnings, a net worth tax, an accessions tax, a local government value-added tax, and a strengthened local property tax.[1]

Many of the taxes contained in major Shoup proposals were repealed or modified soon after enactment; they had proved too far-reaching for the relatively conservative and business-oriented government.[2] The turnover tax was not restored, and the supremacy of the income tax was maintained. The net worth and the accessions taxes were repealed in 1953; the enactment of the value-added tax was postponed several times, and the tax was later repealed without ever having gone into effect. In addition, most capital gains were removed from the individual income tax base, interest and dividends were made taxable at separate low rates, and the surcharge on retained corporate profits was eliminated.[3] Comprehensive income taxation has long since been replaced by an elaborate system of tax preferences—allegedly to improve equity among taxpayer groups and to provide incentives for saving and investment. The major legacies of the Shoup proposals have been to make income taxation acceptable as the basic source of revenue in Japan, to raise the level of tax sophistication, and to improve tax administration.

The tax on individual income, which is used by the national, prefectural, and municipal governments, is a hybrid of a global tax and a schedular tax. This system developed as a result of the modifications of the global income tax approach proposed by the Shoup Mission. Most incomes are aggregated and taxed at progressive rates, but some incomes either are not taxed at all

1. General Headquarters, Supreme Commander for the Allied Powers, *Report on Japanese Taxation by the Shoup Mission*, vols. 1–4 (Tokyo, 1949).
2. The official explanation is that ". . . their intentions seemed somewhat too idealistic to fit in with the reality of the Japanese economy and standard of living of the Japanese people." Tax Bureau, Ministry of Finance, *An Outline of Japanese Taxes, 1974* (Tokyo, 1974), pp. 7–8.
3. For a detailed review of the modifications as of 1956, see Martin Bronfenbrenner and Kiichiro Kogiku, "The Aftermath of the Shoup Tax Reforms, Parts I and II," *National Tax Journal,* vol. 10 (1957), pp. 236–54 and 345–60.

or are taxed at special flat rates. Generous deductions are provided for employment incomes (currently, 40 percent for most wage earners), and the exemptions are relatively high by U.S. standards. The combined national and local income tax rates range from 14 to 93 percent, but the effective rate of tax is limited to a maximum of 80 percent.

The corporate income tax is a split-rate system similar to that used in West Germany and other European countries. Between 1970 and 1973 the combined rates for all levels of government were 48 percent on undistributed profits and 37 percent on distributed profits; in 1974 the rates were raised to 53 percent and 42 percent, respectively. The profits of small corporations are taxed at lower rates.

The tax on transfer of wealth at death is a combination of inheritance and estate taxes. The estate is divided among the heirs according to percentages prescribed by the succession law, and the tax rates are applied to each share with varying exemptions given to the spouse, children, and other heirs. The total tax then is distributed among the heirs in proportion to the amounts they have received. The gift tax, which is levied on gifts cumulated for a period of three years, is also paid by the recipients. Tax rates on both bequests and gifts range from 10 percent to 70 percent, but exemptions are high and only a small proportion of the total wealth transferred between generations is actually subject to tax.

There is no general consumption, or sales, tax in Japan, but selective excise taxes are levied on liquor, tobacco, gasoline, consumer durable goods, energy, and admissions. On the whole, the tax rates are moderate: the taxes on small automobiles and household appliances, for example, are less than 10 percent of the retailers' prices, including tax (see Table 5-17).

Payroll taxes are similar to those levied in the United States and other countries to finance social security and related programs. Several different programs apply to the public and private sectors, however, so the tax rates vary greatly. For employees in large enterprises the combined tax rates paid by employers and employees can reach 14.6 percent on a substantial portion of the employees' earnings.

The property tax is used only at the local level. The prefectures levy a real estate transfer tax of 3 percent but have no annual real estate tax. The standard real estate tax rate at the municipal level is 1.4 percent of assessed valuation; this can be raised by the municipalities to a maximum of 2.1 percent. As in all countries, valuations for property tax purposes represent gross understatements of true value.[4]

4. A more detailed description of the present tax system is given in the appendix to this chapter.

Special Features of the Tax System

The special character of Japan's tax system cannot be conveyed by a brief description of the major taxes. Some of its particular features seem strange to a visitor from a country in which economic conditions and social attitudes are quite different. Japan's high rate of growth and moderate government expenditures (when compared with other developed countries) permit the Japanese to adopt tax policies that can well be envied elsewhere. On the other hand, there is a strong bias toward consensus and gradualism in the development of national policies. This bias does not prevent frequent changes in tax rates and personal exemptions, but it forestalls abrupt changes in the tax structure and perpetuates—and sometimes aggravates—certain tax practices that are acknowledged by experts to be less than optimal.

Those features of the system which are of particular interest to the outsider are the annual tax reductions; the tax process; the special tax measures; executive compensation and expense accounts; administrative practices; and strict control of local taxes by the national government.

Annual Tax Reductions

In an economy in which money gross national product has risen by an average of 15 percent a year or better, the annual growth in revenue is at least 15 percent, even if the elasticity of the tax system is only 1.0 (that is, if revenues grow at the same rate as total income). Since Japan relies heavily on income taxes, the elasticity of the central government's revenues is much greater than 1.0—probably in the neighborhood of 1.3.[5] This means that at recent rates of income growth, the growth of the government's fiscal resources without tax reductions has been in excess of 20 percent a year.

The Japanese government has not used this tremendous revenue growth to increase the size of the public sector relative to the rest of the economy. To the contrary, it has adhered to a calculated policy of restraining the rate of growth of public expenditure relative to the rate of growth of the economy as a whole, so that the ratio of taxes to national income has crept rather than raced upward over the past two decades. As shown in Table 5-2, tax revenues of the national and local governments (not including social security taxes) amounted to 18.1 percent of the national income in fiscal 1955, 19.2

5. Estimates of the elasticity of the major taxes and of the tax system as a whole are given below, in the section "Income Elasticity of the Tax Structure."

Table 5-2. *Tax Revenue as a Percent of National Income in Japan, by Level of Government, Selected Fiscal Years, 1955–74*[a]

Fiscal year	Level of government		Total
	National	Local[b]	
1955	12.8	5.3	18.1
1960	13.6	5.6	19.2
1965	12.6	5.9	18.5
1966	12.0	5.8	17.8
1967	12.1	5.9	18.0
1968	12.4	6.0	18.4
1969	12.9	6.2	19.1
1970	13.1	6.3	19.5
1971	12.9	6.5	19.3
1972	13.7	6.6	20.2
1973[c]	14.1	6.6	20.7
1974[d]	13.3	6.6	19.9

Sources: 1955, data from the Tax Bureau; 1960–74, Research and Planning Division, Minister's Secretariat, Ministry of Finance, *Quarterly Bulletin of Financial Statistics, 1st and 2nd Quarters, 1974 Fiscal Year* (Tokyo, September 1974), p. 63. Figures may not add to totals because of rounding.
a. Social security contributions are excluded.
b. Includes prefectural and municipal governments.
c. Preliminary.
d. Estimated on the basis of budget data.

percent in 1960, 19.5 percent in 1970, and 19.9 percent in 1974.[6] This policy has provided the elbow room for the unique practice of annual tax reductions that is so popular with the Japanese people and the object of envy by taxpayers and political leaders in other countries.

The Tax Bureau has kept a detailed record of the annual tax reductions since 1950; its estimates are available for fiscal years 1950–53 combined and, beginning in fiscal 1954, annually (see Table 5-3). Between 1954 and 1974, individual income tax exemptions were increased in every year but three; the rates were reduced eleven times and increased but once. Corporate income tax rates were reduced six times and increased twice. The special tax measures, which apply to both individuals and corporations, were modified in some respect practically every year, more often than not bringing about a loss in revenue. Some indirect taxes were increased almost every year—be-

6. Although Table 5-2 excludes social security contributions (which are not treated as part of the general budget in Japan), the trend has been roughly the same as that shown in the table when social security contributions are included. See Organisation for Economic Co-operation and Development, *Revenue Statistics of OECD Member Countries, 1965–1972* (Paris: OECD, 1975), table 3, p. 74.

TAXATION 325

Table 5-3. *Estimated Annual Tax Changes in Japan, by Type of Change, Fiscal Years 1950–74*[a]

Billions of yen

| | National taxes | | | | | | | | | | |
| | Individual income | | | | Corporate income | | | Other direct taxes | In-direct taxes | Local taxes[b] | Total |
Fiscal year	Total	Exemptions	Rates	Special tax measures	Total	Rates	Special tax measures				
1950–53	−386	−272	−86	−28	−25	31	−56	16	−138	−46	−580
1954	−31	−29	0	−2	−3	0	−3	−3	20	−26	−43
1955	−53	−23	−13	−18	−12	−14	2	0	−1	−7	−73
1956	−23	−23	0	0	14	0	14	0	7	12	11
1957	−110	−40	−85	15	22	−2	24	0	20	−12	−81
1958	−6	0	0	−6	−22	−20	−2	−3	−6	−20	−57
1959	−23	−28	−12	17	−4	0	−4	0	20	−8	−16
1960	0	0	0	0	0	0	0	0	7	−12	−5
1961	−56	−38	−23	5	−40	0	−40	0	19	−13	−90
1962	−50	−25	−23	−2	−1	0	−1	−2	−62	−40	−156
1963	−67	−32	0	−35	13	0	13	0	4	−18	−68
1964	−75	−66	0	−8	−59	−5	−54	−5	19	−56	−174
1965	−65	−92	0	26	−57	−28	−28	−1	7	−9	−124
1966	−158	−101	−53	−4	−99	−50	−49	−15	−39	−53	−364
1967	−93	−142	11	38	−30	0	−30	−3	32	−19	−113
1968	−125	−135	−11	*	*	0	*	0	57	−21	−89
1969	−183	−142	−41	*	2	0	2	0	*	−95	−276
1970	−289	−173	−131	15	75	97	−22	0	8	−97	−302
1971	−415	−286	−107	−22	12	0	12	−7	93	−87	−403
1972	−32	0	0	−32	31	0	31	−12	9	−98	−103
1973	−375	−335	0	−40	27	0	27	−40	10	−146	−524
1974	−1,783	−1,467	−260	−56	352	424	−72	0	316	−113	−1,228

Source: Research and Planning Division, Minister's Secretariat, Ministry of Finance, *Quarterly Bulletin of Financial Statistics, 1st and 2nd Quarters, 1973 and 1974 Fiscal Years,* (Tokyo, September 1973 and 1974), pp. 68–69. Figures may not add to totals because of rounding.
* Reduction of ¥500 million or less.
a. These estimates of the effect of the tax actions are based on the official economic projections included in the annual national budget. This effect is estimated on the assumption that the tax revision had been enacted at the beginning of the year. The 1971 figures include the effect of tax changes in the budget at the beginning of the fiscal year and of a supplementary tax cut enacted in October 1971.
b. Includes prefectural and municipal governments.

cause many of them are on a specific basis and do not automatically increase as the price of the product rises—but the revenue gains from indirect tax increases were small relative to the income tax reductions. Despite all the reductions in tax rates and increases in exemptions and deductions, tax collections increased at a slightly faster rate than the rate of growth of the national income.

The Tax Process

To assist in the formulation of tax policy, the Japanese developed an institution that illustrates their penchant for consensus in government policy. A Tax Advisory Commission was established by the government in 1955 to assist in the formulation of long-range policy on the structure of the tax system, as well as to review and recommend year-to-year changes; it has played a significant role in the tax process ever since.[7]

The thirty or so members of the Tax Advisory Commission, appointed by the prime minister, come from different walks of life, including academic experts in public finance, journalists, former officials of the ministries of finance and home affairs, former mayors, and representatives of labor unions and of large and small business and agriculture. This diversity of membership was specified deliberately so the commission could act as arbiter among the interest groups that influence tax policy.

The secretariat of the commission consists of high-level Tax Bureau staff of the Ministry of Finance. None of the commission members is a government official, but the government has much influence on its recommendations, both because many of its members formerly were associated with the government and because the commission relies primarily on data and analyses prepared by the Tax Bureau. Outside specialists, usually academic economists and lawyers, are recruited to assist the commission, but they have a significant influence only on long-term policy.

The role of the Tax Bureau in tax policy is typical of the role of the bureaucracy in decisionmaking within the Japanese government. Though they have no independent political influence, the high-level staff members of the bureau (an unusually able group of career officials) are of major importance in the tax process. The interest groups concerned with tax legislation generally exercise their influence through negotiation and accommodation with the Tax Bureau as well as the Tax Advisory Commission.

The annual budget, which contains the government's tax proposals, is submitted early in the calendar year and is acted on by the Diet by April 1. The tax process begins with a presentation of alternative tax proposals by the Tax Bureau to the Tax Advisory Commission sometime in the fall before the budget is to be submitted. The alternatives are discussed by the commission and a set of recommendations is prepared. The tax committee of the ruling political party also makes tax recommendations, but these are usually similar to those of the Tax Bureau. The commission's recommendations are transmitted to the prime minister in time to be used in the budget decisions, which usually are made around the end of the calendar year. The final decisions are made by the cabinet on the basis of the recommendations of the Tax Advisory Commission and the tax committee of the ruling party.

7. The official description of the tax system by the Tax Bureau states that "since then [1955], the succeeding tax reforms of each year have been mainly based on the reports submitted by this Tax Commission." *An Outline of Japanese Taxes, 1974*, p. 9.

In general, the Tax Advisory Commission's recommendations have been adopted virtually intact, although changes occasionally are made by the government. The government's tax proposals are usually approved by the Diet, but in recent years the influential tax committee of the Liberal Democratic party has occasionally succeeded in modifying the proposals significantly.

The government and the Tax Advisory Commission have consistently pursued a number of major objectives. First, until 1968 strong sentiment prevailed that the national and local tax burdens should not increase as the revenue potential of the economy increased. To realize this objective, about one-fifth of the increased revenues generated by economic growth was used every year for tax reduction. This policy has since been changed in response to the need for new public programs and facilities to improve the quality of life in Japan.

Second, the commission believes that it is important to maintain over the years the relative weights of the individual income tax, corporate income tax, and indirect taxes in roughly equal proportions. Because indirect taxes accounted for about half the revenue of the central government in 1955, this balance was not approached until 1970; since then, although an exact balance has not been achieved, the distribution of revenues has not been allowed to deviate too much from this norm (see Table 5-4). Corporate income tax revenues slipped below 30 percent of the total in 1972, but the 1974 tax increase restored them to an estimated 34 percent. Because personal taxation is the major tax source and is highly elastic with respect to income growth, most of the tax adjustments (mainly downward) are made in the individual income tax (see Table 5-3).

Third, at the request of the government, the Tax Advisory Commission is constantly examining individual structural details of the tax system to promote efficient allocation of resources, increase built-in flexibility, and improve tax equity. In recommending tax changes to achieve these objectives, the commission diligently studies practices abroad (often by sending subcommittees to other countries) and seeks to adapt them to Japan's needs. Such major structural features as the dual-rate corporate income tax, the hybrid estate and inheritance tax, and accelerated depreciation have been devised by the commission. These policies are thoroughly discussed with the Ministry of Finance and other agencies before recommendations are actually made by the commission; but the commission is not a rubber stamp, and in some instances, the government's views have been altered as a result of discussions with its members. In the end, a consensus is reached in the commission—which signifies that the government will accept it—thus smoothing the way for the enactment of the following year's tax changes.

Table 5-4. *Distribution of Revenues of the Japanese Central Government, by Major Tax Sources, Selected Fiscal Years, 1955–74*[a]
Percent

	Tax source			
Fiscal year	Individual income	Corporate income	Indirect[b]	Death and gift
1955	27.8	19.6	52.0	0.6
1960	21.7	31.9	45.7	0.7
1965	29.6	28.3	40.8	1.3
1966	29.6	28.2	40.7	1.5
1967	29.3	29.8	39.4	1.5
1968	30.3	29.9	38.3	1.5
1969	31.1	31.1	36.2	1.6
1970	31.2	33.0	34.0	1.8
1971	34.2	30.3	33.0	2.5
1972	35.8	28.8	32.3	3.1
1973	36.2	32.1	28.8	2.9
1974[c]	32.9	34.0	30.1	3.0

Source: Tax Bureau, Ministry of Finance, *An Outline of Japanese Taxes, 1965* (Tokyo, 1965), pp. 252, 253, and *1974*, pp. 273, 277.
  a. Taxes exclude social security contributions.
  b. Includes customs duties.
  c. Estimated on basis of budget data.

Special Tax Measures

There is wide agreement in Japanese government and business circles that the tax system should be actively used to promote economic growth. Hence, numerous measures have been adopted to stimulate private investment and activities that have high national economic priority. Such measures—which include special tax-free reserves, accelerated depreciation, and the like—are contained in the Special Tax Measures Law, which is a catalog of most, though not all, of the incentive provisions applying to the individual and corporate income taxes.[8]

A significant role in the development of the special tax measures is played by the Ministry of International Trade and Industry (MITI). The legislative

8. The distinction between those tax provisions which are regarded as special and those which are not is unclear to an outside observer, since the ordinary income tax laws contain numerous provisions that are preferential in nature. Special tax measures are usually—but not always—adopted with a termination date. Hereafter, the term "special tax measure" is used to refer to the provisions of the Special Tax Measures Law, and "tax preferences" to refer to the preferential provisions in the ordinary income tax laws as well as in the Special Tax Measures Law.

process in the MITI begins in May of each year, when the director for industrial policy sends to his commodity and industry bureaus general guidelines of policy for the coming budget and, in some cases, solicits comments on specific proposals. During the summer the bureau chiefs receive suggestions from representatives of the business federations and trade associations and obtain comments on the proposals developed in the MITI and other government agencies. These views are evaluated and a set of proposals is drawn up for transmission to the Tax Bureau by the end of August. The rest of the calendar year is devoted to negotiation between the two agencies and the Tax Advisory Commission on the details of any reform proposals to be included in the budget.

Although the MITI has no seat on the Tax Advisory Commission, it maintains contact with the commission through the members who represent industry and commerce. The special tax measures proposed by the MITI are relayed to the Tax Commission by the secretariat or by the industrial members of the commission. Thus, the annual negotiations on specific proposals are at least a three-cornered affair involving the MITI, the Tax Bureau, and the Tax Advisory Commission. Other government agencies also participate when their interests are involved.

During the 1960s the major objectives of the special tax measures were technological advancement, industrial rationalization to minimize costs, and promotion of exports. Since May 1971, when the Industrial Structure Council recommended significant changes in economic policy for the 1970s, the MITI's objectives in the tax field have been altered.[9] Promotion of exports has been replaced by international economic cooperation; and industrial rationalization, by improvement of the environment and the quality of life. Promotion of technological progress remains on the agenda. As a result of this shift in emphasis, other ministries such as those of welfare and of construction are expected to influence tax policy more than in past years. But whether these new objectives will be pursued as actively as the former ones remains to be seen.

The impetus for special tax measures appears to come mainly from industry and government. A majority of the Tax Advisory Commission supports this policy, but a minority—including former tax officials, experts from academic life, and representatives of labor—is either uncomfortable about this policy or openly hostile to it. As early as 1964 the Tax Advisory Com-

---

9. The Industrial Structure Council was established in 1964 to advise the MITI on short- and long-range economic policy. The council is made up of 130 individuals from all walks of life who are named by the prime minister for two-year terms.

mission stated officially that the special measures should be curtailed and ultimately abolished,[10] but progress toward this end has been slow. Partly as a result of the less pressing need to stimulate growth and partly in response to the pressures from the labor movement and the political left, more movement in this direction is expected in the future.

Employee Compensation and Expense Accounts

The Japanese tax system has been thoroughly adapted to the system of employee compensation that has been developed since World War II. Cash wages and salaries, including year-end bonuses, are taxable; other ingredients of the compensation package—for the wage earner as well as for the executive—are either not taxable at all or are taxable only after the deduction of unusually generous allowances.

For the wage earner, the most significant preferences are the exclusion of the value of subsidized housing from taxable income and the virtual exemption of company payments on retirement. Most of the large industrial and commercial firms provide housing to some of their employees, either rent free or at rents that are far below market prices for comparable facilities. The subsidized portion of such rents is not taxable. No study of the value of these subsidies has been made, but they probably amount to about 10 percent of cash wages and bonuses. About 10 percent of all wage earners in Japan live in subsidized housing and thus benefit from this tax preference.[11]

Most Japanese firms do not have funded pension plans; instead, they ordinarily make lump-sum payments to their employees on retirement, commonly one or two months' wages in the last year of employment (not including the semiannual bonuses) for every year of employment with the firm. If a worker had been employed for thirty-five years, for example, he would be eligible for a retirement payment equal to three times his last annual wage. Partly to avoid the problem of averaging, such retirement payments (for thirty-five years of service) are taxable only after they exceed ¥10 million (more than $30,000 at 1974 exchange rates), thus effectively removing from the tax base the payments received by all but the highest salaried executives.

Aside from these two major preferences, wage earners also benefit from tax-free recreational and other welfare benefits provided by Japanese firms. Many of the large firms have vacation facilities that are available to their

---

10. *An Outline of Japanese Taxes, 1974*, p. 11.

11. This figure is based on interviews with a number of Japanese government officials. As indicated in Chapter 9, 9 percent of Tokyo households occupied company housing in 1968.

employees and their families for long weekends without cost. In addition, the Japanese are traveling more as incomes have grown, and firms are beginning to subsidize employee tours to Taiwan, Hawaii, and even more distant places such as the continental United States and Europe. These benefits are not nearly as valuable as the housing subsidies and retirement payments, but they are growing in importance as foreign travel becomes both more attractive and more available to the average Japanese family.

For the business executive, the compensation package consists of several other tax-free elements. The corporate executive does not own large blocs of stock in his corporation, primarily because there are virtually no employee stock purchase or stock option plans in Japan. Instead, the executive is given a car and chauffeur, an expense account, and either a large, subsidized residence or a subsidized loan to purchase his own residence.

The expense account is perhaps the most distinctive of these benefits. Most executives spend several nights a week in town on business.[12] A usual procedure is to take one's guests to an expensive restaurant, geisha house, or club. The cost of an evening may run to $100 or more a person, all of which is charged to the host's firm.[13] Firms, however, are permitted to deduct only 25 percent of entertainment expenses in excess of the sum of ¥4 million plus 0.1 percent of capital. For large firms, the amount disallowed averages about 55 percent of the total expenditures for entertainment expenses.[14] Nevertheless, there seems to be no evidence that this restriction has reduced these expenditures. According to the official national income accounts, entertainment expenses in the private sector (which are classified as business consumption expenditures) amounted in calendar 1965 to 2.4 percent of the gross national product and 9 percent of corporate profits plus income of unincorporated enterprises.[15]

As corporate executives move up the management scale, they tend to leave the subsidized housing provided by their firms and to purchase their own

12. Executives in government agencies and academic and nonprofit institutions also have entertainment expense accounts, but they are more limited than those provided by private companies.

13. Usually, the host leaves his calling card and the cost is charged directly to the firm. A sizable portion of these accounts is never paid, and unpaid accounts receivable in restaurants are large.

14. Tax Bureau, Ministry of Finance, *Zeisei shuyō sankō shiryōshū* [Principal Reference Data for the Tax System, 1973] (Tokyo, 1973), p. 131.

15. Economic Planning Agency, *Annual Report on National Income Statistics, 1974* (Tokyo, 1974), pp. 32, 34, and 142. Total business consumption expenditures, which include welfare and travel expenses and other employee outlays, amounted to 6 percent of the gross national product. Data for later years have not been published in Japan, nor are similar estimates available for other countries.

residences. To enable them to do so, many companies give their executives loans that are repayable over ten or more years at no or very low interest. This interest subsidy is not taxable. The availability of such credit and the easy payment terms permit the executive to purchase a home that, given the recent trends of land and housing prices, becomes extremely valuable by the time he retires.

The fact that he has a valuable asset does not ordinarily permit an executive to withdraw from the labor force when he retires from his lifetime career —age fifty-five or sixty for middle managers, sixty or sixty-five for top managers. The final payment he receives upon retirement usually is not large enough to permit him to stop working. To supplement his income, a retired executive usually moves to a subsidiary of his own enterprise or to another firm and works for another ten years or so as an adviser, inspector, or active executive.

Administrative Practices

The Shoup Mission found in 1949 that Japan's system of tax administration was archaic. Because tax rates were stiff, taxpayer morale was at a low ebb, and underreporting was more the rule than the exception. To collect necessary revenues, income tax administrators had developed a system under which each tax office was assigned a quota of collections. This quota was often met by imposing arbitrary assessments of reported tax liabilities, whether the taxpayers' reports were honest or not. In some instances such reassessments actually exceeded the total income of the taxpayer, and several of these cases received wide publicity in the press.[16]

To improve taxpayer morale, the Shoup Mission recommended reduction of the high marginal tax rates, elimination of the goal system, simplification of tax returns for small taxpayers, public disclosure of high-income tax returns, and the elimination of anonymous accounts. Except for the anonymous accounts, the Shoup recommendations were accepted, and the quality of administration improved almost overnight. Japan's tax system is administered today at a cost only moderately higher than that of the U.S. system.[17] Some

---

16. *Report on Japanese Taxation by the Shoup Mission,* vol. 2, pp. 212–13; and Bronfenbrenner and Kogiku, "The Aftermath of the Shoup Tax Reforms, Part I," pp. 237–38.

17. In fiscal 1972 administrative costs amounted to 1.4 percent of national revenues in Japan, compared with 0.7 percent for the cost of administering the federal revenue system in the United States. (National Tax Administration Agency, *An Outline of Japanese Tax Administration, 1972* [Tokyo, 1972] pp. 6, 22; and *The Budget of the United States Government, Fiscal Year 1974* [1973], pp. 268 and 341.) Much of the difference in cost is probably attributable to differences in scale.

of the more interesting practices and remaining administrative problems are discussed in the following paragraphs.

BLUE RETURNS. The Tax Administration Agency regards the "blue return" as the cornerstone of efficient tax administration in Japan. Use of the blue return, designed to encourage small- and medium-size businesses to keep at least a minimum set of accounting records, offers certain significant advantages to individuals and corporations conforming with the accounting standards of the tax offices. The primary advantage is that the enterprise will not be subject to reassessment unless errors are found in accounting books and records. In addition, taxpayers filing a blue return are allowed to deduct reasonable amounts for wages of family members working in the same business; to accumulate reserves for bad debts, losses due to price fluctuations, and employees' retirement allowances; to carry back losses against income in the preceding year and forward against income in the following three years (five years in the case of corporations); to take advantage of special depreciation allowances, deductions for overseas transactions of technical services, and depletion allowances; and to deduct the cost of preparing the return (up to a maximum of ¥100,000). In the early 1970s, about 80 percent of all individual and corporation income taxpayers engaged in a business other than agriculture filed blue returns.[18] But as in other countries, farmers seriously understate their incomes for tax purposes. Most of them do not file blue returns, and tax collection offices estimate their income on the basis of their crops.

PUBLICIZING HIGH-INCOME TAXPAYERS. Beginning in 1947 the public was allowed access to all tax returns to encourage informers to reveal to tax authorities the names of individuals and corporations filing dishonest returns. The Shoup Mission urged that the informer system be abolished and recommended that the information contained on all but the highest tax returns be kept confidential. The recommendation to post high-income and large-inheritance tax returns was adopted in 1950, and the informer system was abolished in 1954.[19] Lists of individuals and corporations are posted on bulletin boards of district tax offices, and the top names usually are widely reported in the press and on radio and television. For calendar 1972 the posted lists included about 126,000 individuals, 14,000 corporations, and 30,000 returns for estates of decedents.

18. *An Outline of Japanese Tax Administration, 1972,* p. 26.
19. The minimum amount to be posted has increased over time: it started at ¥500,000 for individual returns and ¥1 million for returns of corporations and of decedents. Since 1971 the minimum amounts have been ¥10 million for individuals, ¥40 million for corporations, and ¥40 million of taxable value (¥100 million of total value) for decedents.

Japanese tax officials seem to be lukewarm about this practice. The lists are published privately in "who's-who" types of compilation that are used for commercial and social purposes and for the solicitation of campaign contributions. Some people with incomes below the minimum required for posting deliberately inflate their income to appear on the lists, and later they file refund claims; others purposely delay filing their returns to avoid having their names posted. On the other hand, the corporate tax data are useful for research purposes by government and private agencies; and the lists of individuals may help to promote voluntary compliance on the part of the wealthy groups in the population. No serious economic or statistical analysis of the posted returns has ever been made. The major concern of the tax authorities seems to be that the posting requirement imposes heavy administrative costs on the tax offices.

ANONYMOUS ACCOUNTS. A continuing problem in tax administration is the use of anonymous accounts to conceal investment income. This usage was banned administratively in 1950, but the ban was lifted in response to pressure by banking interests. Anonymous and fictitious accounts are commonplace in Japan and apparently are difficult to control. Business as well as individual depositors use seals rather than names and signatures for opening accounts and withdrawing deposits, and the banks make no effort to verify the identification on the seals. The government's bank examiners have attempted unsuccessfully to obtain legislation to prohibit the use of such accounts. Revenue agents may investigate anonymous and fictitious accounts when they suspect tax fraud, but these cases are unusual.

Anonymous and fictitious accounts are obviously subject to abuse by wealthy persons, who can create numerous such accounts, each with small deposits, that are not subject to tax under the Special Tax Measures Law. A study by the National Tax Administration of 105 corporate and individual income tax evasion cases in 1968 revealed that 36 percent of total deposits were held in anonymous accounts, 31 percent were in accounts with fictitious identification, and only 33 percent were in accounts with correct identification.[20]

The exemption of interest on small deposits and separate taxation of interest and dividends are justified in part on the ground that more taxpayers would use anonymous accounts if interest and dividends were taxable in full under the progressive rates. In effect, the inability to close the leakage through anonymous and fictitious accounts acts as a deterrent to evenhanded tax administration and to the improvement of the income tax structure.

20. This information is based on data presented by the Tax Bureau to the Finance Committee of the Diet in 1970.

TAX TREATMENT OF PROPRIETORS AND FAMILY EMPLOYEES. Japanese tax laws reflect the broad influence of small business in the nation's politics. Throughout the postwar period tax authorities have been seeking a means of fair tax treatment for small proprietors and unpaid family members. Tax evasion by the self-employed and unincorporated businesses is known to be widespread, but the magnitude of the evasion is unknown. Since 1952 taxpayers filing blue returns have been permitted to deduct salaries of family employees as a business expense—up to a limit. This treatment was justified on the ground that blue return taxpayers keep proper books and records and therefore are able to distinguish business from household expenses. The limit was increased several times and ultimately abolished in 1968. In 1961 the privilege of deducting salaries of family employees was extended to taxpayers who did not file blue returns, but the allowable deduction remains subject to a limit (currently ¥300,000 for each family employer). Finally, in 1973 taxpayers filing blue returns were allowed to elect to be treated as quasi-corporations for tax purposes. This permits business proprietors to deduct their own salaries as well as the salaries of family employees as expenses of doing business. In addition, the net income of the enterprise remaining after the deduction of these salaries is considered corporate income and taxed at the rate applicable to dividend distributions. Such distributions are taxed together with the imputed salary of the proprietor under the individual income tax, allowing also for the special deduction available to wage and salary income and for the tax credit that is provided for dividends at the individual level.

VALUATION OF PROPERTY FOR TAX PURPOSES. The Japanese have had at least as much difficulty as other countries with keeping property tax assessments in line with the growth in market values. Officials of the Ministry of Home Affairs, which prescribes the standards to be followed by local assessors, are aware of the problem, but their hands are tied by law from raising assessment ratios too rapidly.[21] The same problem applies to valuations for inheritance tax purposes. As might be expected, wealthy people invest heavily in real estate to obtain the benefit of low valuations: because property values have skyrocketed, the amount of property subject to inheritance taxes is only a small fraction of the true value of property that passes from one generation to the next. There is no evidence that this practice will be altered in the foreseeable future.

TAXATION OF WAGE EARNERS. An employer is in a position to discharge the full income tax liability of most of his employees through withholding, because small amounts of the employees' property income are legally disre-

21. For details, see the appendix to this chapter.

garded for tax purposes, whereas larger amounts are subject to separate taxation.[22] Consequently, the mass of wage and salary workers are not required to file tax returns. This arrangement is taken as an article of faith by tax policy officials and tax administrators. The advantage of the system is obvious: almost three-quarters of the individual income tax is withheld at the source and this amount is collected at little direct cost to the government. But this advantage is purchased at the cost of a system of deductions and exclusions from the income tax base that can hardly be justified on grounds of social equity. Until the tax officials are persuaded that the mass of wage earners can file tax returns, it will be impossible to replace the present fractionated system by a unified income tax.

The Local Tax System

There are two types of local government units in Japan: the prefectures, which are large regional units, and the municipalities, which consist of a variety of cities, towns, and villages. There are 47 prefectures and about 3,300 municipalities. The operations of the local governments are subject to substantially more control by the national government in Japan than they are in the United States. The Shoup Mission recommended a greater local autonomy than was traditional in Japan, but this advice was virtually disregarded.

The expenditures of local governments are financed out of three sources: local tax and nontax revenues, grants-in-aid from the national government, and bond issues. The estimated distribution of receipts among these sources for fiscal 1974 was as follows:[23]

Source	Percentage distribution
Local tax and nontax revenues	48.3
Taxes	41.4
Charges, fees, and other nontax revenue sources	6.9
Grants-in-aid	45.8
National subsidies (categorical grants)	26.1
Local allocations (general purpose grants)	19.7
Bond proceeds	5.9
Total	100.0

Practically all of the revenue sources are subject to control by the central government so that local taxes will "not impede trade among local public

22. For details, see the appendix to this chapter.
23. Data derived from *An Outline of Japanese Taxes, 1974*, p. 174.

entities."[24] The tax base and rates of most of the taxes are legislated by the Diet, on the recommendation of the Ministries of Home Affairs and Finance. Local governments are permitted to change tax rates within limits, but this discretion is rarely used for fear of an unfavorable reaction from the central government bureaucracy. Grants-in-aid are, of course, unilaterally provided by the central government. As in most countries—not including the United States—bond issues must be approved by the Ministries of Home Affairs and Finance before they are floated. Local bond issues are purchased by the Trust Fund Bureau of the national government (which buys them with postal savings and pension reserve funds), private banking organizations, and the public.

More than half of all local tax revenues comes from the individual and corporate income taxes. The structural features of these taxes, which are used by both prefectures and municipalities, are dictated by the central government; they are revised annually, concurrently with revisions in the nationwide taxes. Despite the uniformity imposed by the central government, taxpayers are required to pay income taxes directly to the prefectures and municipalities rather than combining them with payments made to the central government. A margin is available to the local governments to raise their income tax rates beyond the standard rates prescribed by the central government, but the flexibility is limited. The standard municipal individual income tax rates, for example, can be raised up to 50 percent, and the municipal corporate tax rate can be raised up to 20 percent.

The property tax, which is levied only by the municipal governments, accounts for a relatively small portion of local tax revenues—16 percent in fiscal 1974. Most municipalities tax real estate at the standard rate of 1.4 percent of assessed value, but they are permitted to go as high as 2.1 percent.

The grants from the central government to the local governments consist of national subsidies and local allocations. The national subsidies are categorical grants for particular purposes, while the local allocations are general purpose grants which are provided on a no-strings-attached basis.

The national subsidies are grants to maintain minimal standards for services provided by local governments. The largest of the subsidies is the payment by the central government of half the salaries of public school teachers. Other national subsidies provide funds for public works and other activities.

The local allocations program, a unique feature of intergovernmental relations, is designed to finance the regular activities of local governments and to provide some equalization on the basis of need. The funds allocated to this

24. Ibid.

program are fixed at 32 percent of the national government's revenue from the individual and corporate income taxes and the liquor tax. The grant to any municipality is equal to the difference between financial need and the basic financial revenue as determined by the Ministry of Home Affairs. Financial need is computed for each local government by aggregating the expenditure requirements for each area of government activity (education, police and fire protection, highways, and so on).[25] The basic financial revenue is 80 percent of prefectural tax revenues as estimated on the basis of the standard rates and 75 percent for municipalities.[26]

The local allocations program is similar in many respects to—but much larger than—the general revenue-sharing program recently enacted in the United States. The Japanese attempt to allocate these funds on the basis of detailed estimates of need, whereas the United States allocations are based primarily on population, per capita income, and revenue effort. Notwithstanding these differences in the method of allocation, both types of grants may be used by the local governments with little or no direction by the national government. No study has yet been made of the relative merits of the two methods of allocation.

Tax Burdens

Perhaps the most significant feature of the Japanese tax system is the relatively light load that it imposes on the taxpayer. Compared with Australia and thirteen other countries in Western Europe and North America, Japan's tax burden in 1972 was the lowest (see Table 5-5). Except for the corporate income tax, all the major taxes were much lower relative to the gross national product in Japan than in most other countries. Individual income tax revenues were only 5.4 percent of the gross national product in Japan, but they averaged 9.8 percent in the other countries; payroll taxes, 4.1 percent in Japan, averaged 10.2 percent in the other countries; and taxes on goods and service, 5.1 percent in Japan, averaged 11.8 percent in the other countries.[27] Surprisingly, the corporate income tax appears to be much heavier in Japan than in most of the other countries—5.1 percent of the gross national product

25. The amount of need in any one activity is calculated by multiplying the units of need by the standard expenditure per unit as determined on the basis of the expenditures of a hypothetical standard municipality that is used as a yardstick.

26. Because the basic financial revenue is an estimate, the amount allocated to each municipality is adjusted two years later for substantial errors in the corporate tax estimates. Other errors in revenue estimates are ignored.

27. The averages for the other countries are based on the median.

Table 5-5. *Tax Revenues as a Percent of Gross National Product,*
by Source, Selected Countries, 1972[a]

				Tax source			
Country	Individual income	Corporate income	Payroll	Goods and services[b]	Property	Death and gift	Total
Norway	12.5	1.1	12.4	18.7	0.9	0.1	45.7
Denmark	21.4	0.9	3.5	16.8	2.0[c]	0.2	44.8
Sweden	18.5	1.7	9.9	13.4	0.3[c]	0.1	43.9
Netherlands	11.7	2.8	14.7	11.7	0.8[c]	0.2	41.8
Austria	8.4	1.6	12.1	14.2	0.7	0.1	37.0
Germany	10.1	1.7	12.4	10.8	0.9	0.1	36.0
France	4.0	2.1	14.8	14.3	0.5	0.2	35.8
Belgium	9.6	2.6	10.6	12.0	0.0	0.3	35.2
United Kingdom	11.1	2.5	6.1	10.3	3.9	0.8	34.7
Canada	11.6	3.6	3.0	11.5	3.5	0.2	33.5
Italy	4.0	2.3	12.1	12.2	0.3	0.2	31.1
United States	9.4	3.1	5.7	5.5	3.7	0.6	28.1
Australia	9.3	3.8	1.0	8.2	1.4	0.5	24.3
Switzerland	8.1	1.9	5.6	6.8	1.4[c]	0.3	24.1
Japan	5.4	5.1[d]	4.1	5.1[d]	1.0	0.4	21.1

Source: Organisation for Economic Co-operation and Development, *Revenue Statistics o OECD Member Countries, 1965–1972* (Paris: OECD, 1975). Data are for the calendar year except for Denmark and Canada (fiscal year ends March 31, 1972) and the United States and Australia (ends June 30, 1972). Figures may not add to totals because of rounding.

a. Includes national and local taxes.

b. Includes sales, value-added, and excise taxes, taxes on imports, exports, and transfers of property and securities, and other transactions taxes paid by enterprises.

c. Includes net worth taxes.

d. The Japanese enterprise tax levied by the prefectural governments is included in the corporate income tax and excluded from the tax on goods and services.

compared with an average of 2.2 percent in the others—but this is in large measure the consequence of the high ratio of corporate profits to GNP in Japan;[28] effective corporate tax rates probably are no higher in Japan than in most other countries.

Individual Income Tax

Although Japanese individual income tax rates are not low by comparison with those of other countries (see Table 5-16), the actual tax paid by taxpayers at various income levels is quite moderate by international standards. This

28. Comparable figures are not available for all the countries shown in Table 5-5, but the following are the calendar year 1969 ratios of corporate profits to the gross national product for the five that are available: Japan, 11.9 percent; United States, 9.1 percent; Switzerland, 9.2 percent; France, 7.4 percent; and Belgium, 6.6 percent. *National Accounts of OECD Countries, 1953–69* (Paris: OECD, 1971).

Table 5-6. *Steps in the Derivation of the Individual Income Tax Base, Japan and the United States, 1970*

	Japan		United States	
Reconciliation item and steps	Amount (trillions of yen)	Percent of total	Amount (billions of dollars)	Percent of total
Tax concept of income	50.1	100.0	677.4	100.0
Less nonreported income	12.6	25.1	45.7	6.7
Equals: income reported on individual returns	37.5ᵃ	74.9	631.7	93.3
Less income on nontaxable returns	3.6ᵇ	7.2	21.4	3.2
Equals: income on taxable returns	33.9	67.7	610.3	90.1
Less exemptions and deductions	17.4	34.7	209.6	30.9
Equals: taxable income, or tax base	16.4	32.7	400.7ᶜ	59.2

Sources: For Japan, estimated by Keimei Kaizuka on the basis of techniques explained in "Tax Base of the Income Tax," in T. Hayashi and K. Kaizuka (eds.), *Nihon no zaisei* [Fiscal System in Japanese Economy] (Tokyo: Tokyo University Press, 1973). For the United States, worksheets of the Bureau of Economic Analysis, U.S. Department of Commerce, and Joseph A. Pechman, *Federal Tax Policy* (rev. ed., Brookings Institution, 1971), table B-4, p. 275. Figures may not add to totals because of rounding.
a. Includes income of employees subject to withholding but not filing tax returns.
b. Earnings of nontaxable employees whose incomes are reported to the government.
c. Does not include $0.8 billion of taxable income of nontaxable individuals.

is explained by major structural features of the tax: the relatively high exemptions, the generous deductions for employment income and family-owned businesses, and the preferential rates for property income.

A comparison of the major steps in the derivation of the individual income tax base from aggregate income is shown for Japan and the United States for 1970 in Table 5-6. Because the exemptions and deductions were so high, 32 percent of the total income (as defined for income tax purposes) was not reported on tax returns in Japan or was reported by persons who were not taxable;[29] the corresponding figure for the United States was 10 percent. Similarly, exemptions and deductions accounted for 35 percent of the income on taxable returns in Japan and 31 percent in the United States. As a result, the tax base amounted to only 33 percent of total income in Japan, as compared with 59 percent in the United States.

Actual tax burdens cannot be compared by income classes in the two countries because consolidated data are not available in Japan for those wage earners who pay their tax entirely through withholding and for those who are required to file returns. But in Table 5-7, which may help to put the matter

29. For purposes of this calculation, wages subject to withholding are considered to be reported on tax returns whether a tax return is actually filed by the wage earner or not.

Table 5-7. *Effective Rates of Individual Income Tax Paid by Families of Four to All Levels of Government, by Various Multiples of Average Family Income, Japan and the United States, 1974*

Multiple of average family income[a]	Percent of income paid in income taxes	
	Japan[b]	United States[c]
0.8	2.0	11.7
1.0	3.6	14.3
1.5	7.0	19.5
2.0	10.1	23.9
2.5	12.6	27.9
3.0	15.3	31.5
4.0	19.9	37.6
5.0	23.9	42.3
7.5	32.0	50.0
10.0	37.5	55.0

Source: Calculations based on exemptions and tax rates applying to incomes in calendar 1974. Taxable income for local tax purposes was assumed to be equal to taxable income for national tax purposes.

a. Average family income was assumed to be ¥2.4 million in Japan and $13,000 in the United States. All income is assumed to be earned.

b. The taxpayer is assumed to have personal deductions amounting to 5 percent of his income, in addition to the employment income deduction.

c. The taxpayer is assumed to reside in New York State (outside of New York City) and to have deductions amounting to 15 percent of income.

in perspective, 1974 income taxes payable to all levels of government are calculated for a family of four at various multiples of the average family income in the two countries.[30] The calculations assume that the families receive only incomes from employment, that the Japanese taxpayer is subject to the standard prefectural and local government tax rates, and that the U.S. taxpayer pays the New York State (but not the New York City) income tax. On this basis, the average family of four paid an income tax of 3.6 percent of its earnings in Japan and of 14.3 percent in the United States. The difference narrowed as incomes rose, but the Japanese family still paid about one-third less than the U.S. family even when earnings reached ten times the average income. And in practice, because the typical family in Japan also receives some property income that is either not taxable or is taxable at very low rates, the figures in Table 5-7 probably overstate the relative tax liabilities of the Japanese families.

For other reasons as well, the income tax load on the highest income

30. Average family incomes in 1974 were assumed to be ¥2.4 million in Japan and $13,000 in the United States. These assumptions were based on projections of average incomes reported for 1972 in the annual Household Survey of Japan and the annual Consumer Population Survey of the United States.

classes in Japan must be significantly lower than in the United States. First, capital gains on the sale of securities generally are not subject to tax in Japan, and gains on land held for more than five years are subject to a maximum rate of 20 percent; all capital gains are subject to tax in the United States, at a maximum rate of 36.5 percent. Second, Japanese taxpayers may elect to be taxed separately on their interest and dividends at a rate of 25 percent; in the United States interest and dividends are fully taxable at marginal rates up to 70 percent. Third, a credit of at least 5 percent of dividends received (10 percent for taxpayers with incomes below ¥10 million) is allowed against the final tax in Japan; in the United States, a deduction of only $100 ($200 on joint returns) is allowed. Because property income accounts for the major fraction of total income in the highest income classes, the tax burden in these classes may well be less than half as much in Japan as in the United States.[31]

Corporate Income Tax

The nominal tax rates applying to corporate profits in Japan are of the same order of magnitude as the rates in other countries, particularly when taxes paid to local governments—which are important in Japan—are taken into account. In 1974, the national corporate income tax was 40 percent on undistributed profits and 30 percent on distributed profits; the prefectural and local inhabitants taxes raised the total to 53 percent and 42 percent, respectively. In the United States, the top federal rate was 48 percent on all corporate earnings—whether distributed or not—and the state taxes added an average of 3 percentage points, making a total of 51 percent.[32] The United Kingdom, France, and Canada levied taxes of 52, 50, and 49 percent, respectively, on corporate profits, but they gave substantial credits for dividends received at the individual income tax level (and Canada, in addition, has

31. For example, suppose a married taxpayer with four exemptions receives $100,000 of interest, $100,000 of dividends, and $200,000 of capital gains on the sale of securities held for more than six months, and reports deductions amounting to 20 percent of his adjusted gross income. The U.S. tax on this $400,000 of income would be $133,492, whereas the Japanese tax would be no more than $50,000. (The latter figure is calculated on the assumption that the taxpayer is allowed no deductions or exemptions in computing his tax liability, since he would elect to be taxed at the maximum rate of 25 percent on his interest and dividends.)

32. Forty-five of the fifty states levy corporate income taxes at rates ranging from 2 to 12 percent; the median rate is 6 percent. (Advisory Commission on Intergovernmental Relations, *Federal-State-Local Finances: Significant Features of Fiscal Federalism* [1973–74], table 148, pp. 286–89.) Because the state taxes are deductible in computing the federal tax, the net burden is roughly half the nominal rates.

Table 5-8. *Effective and Nominal Rates of Corporate Income Taxes on Gross Profits, Japan and the United States, 1965–72*[a]

Percent

	Japan[b]		United States	
Year	Top nominal rate[c]	Effective rate	Top nominal rate[d]	Effective rate
1965	48	22.4	50	28.2
1966	47	19.6	50	28.5
1967	47	20.7	50	27.9
1968	47	20.1	55	30.6
1969	47	20.2	55	30.3
1970	48	22.5	52	27.8
1971	48	21.7	51	26.8
1972	48	20.1	51	27.1

Sources: For Japan, Economic Planning Agency, *Annual Report on National Income Statistics, 1974*, pp. 4–5, 144–45, 156–57. For the United States, U.S. Department of Commerce, *Survey of Current Business* (July 1973), table 1.14, p. 23, and prior annual July issues.

a. Based on data in the official national income accounts. Gross profits are net profits before tax plus capital consumption allowances. Taxes include central and local government taxes.

b. Data are for fiscal years ending on March 31 of year indicated in first column.

c. Rates apply to undistributed profits only and include local enterprise and inhabitants taxes.

d. Assumes state taxes add 2 percentage points to effective rates from 1959 to 1969 and 3 percentage points thereafter.

provincial corporate income taxes that raise the total rate for many corporations). Germany used the split-rate system, with a rate of 51 percent on undistributed profits and 15 percent on distributed profits.

As is well known, however, nominal rates are not representative of relative tax burdens on business incomes, because all countries have adopted a wide variety of accelerated depreciation deductions, investment tax credits or allowances, tax-free reserves, and other devices to encourage private investment or to promote other objectives. Japan actually may have gone much farther in this direction than most other countries.[33] One measure of the effect of the special provisions on the corporate tax base is the effective rate of tax paid by corporations on gross profits: that is, profits before the deduction of depreciation allowances. A comparison of the nominal tax rates (including local taxes) with the effective tax rates on gross profits of all corporations in Japan and the United States is given in Table 5-8 for the period 1965–72.

In both countries, the effective rates are substantially lower than the nom-

33. See the discussion of the special tax measures, below, in the section entitled "Tax Incentives."

inal rates, with the U.S. rates running over 50 percent and the Japanese about 40 percent of the nominal rates. In 1965 the effective rates in Japan were almost 6 percentage points lower than those in the United States; and in 1972 the effective rate was still only 20.1 percent in Japan as compared with 27.1 percent in the United States. However, in 1974 the nominal corporate tax rates were increased by an average of more than 4 percentage points in Japan.[34] In the future, therefore, the average effective tax rate on gross corporate profits probably will be only fractionally lower in Japan than in the United States.

The effective tax rates are close enough in the two countries to suggest that the relative profitability of corporate investment depends on the rates of return before tax. A study by the Industrial Bank of Japan placed the income statements and balance sheets for 1,070 U.S. and 1,000 Japanese industrial corporations on a comparable accounting basis and computed average annual gross rates of return before taxes for each firm on total invested capital and on stockholders' equity for the period 1967–71.[35]

The major conclusion of the study was that both the average and distributions of gross rates of return on all assets—that is, gross profits before taxes plus interest as a percent of borrowed plus equity capital—were roughly the same in Japan and in the United States. The average Japanese equity ratio, however, was roughly half of the U.S. average: 28.7 percent of total assets as compared with 55.5 percent. Thus, the gross rate of return on stockholders' equity was almost twice as high in Japan as in the United States. For the period 1967–71, the average gross rate of return on equity was 46.4 percent for the Japanese companies and 24.9 percent for the U.S. companies.[36] Clearly, the use of relatively large amounts of borrowed capital is a much more important factor than taxation in explaining the high rates of return on equity investment in Japan.[37]

---

34. The central government rates were increased by 3.25 percentage points on undistributed profits and 4 percentage points on distributed profits; and the municipal inhabitants surtax was increased from 9.1 to 12.1 percent.

35. Industrial Bank of Japan, *Differences in Accounting Practices and Returns on Investment between the United States and Japan: 1,000 Industrial Companies, 1967–1971* (Tokyo: IBJ, 1973; available from Standard and Poor's Corporation). The companies were selected from the listings on the major stock exchanges in the two countries; some large unlisted Japanese companies were also included. The major adjustments were to correct gross returns and assets of Japanese firms to account for additions to special tax-free reserves.

36. These conclusions held for most industry groups, except that chemical firms reported a higher gross rate of return on total assets in the United States, and iron and steel companies reported a higher rate of return in Japan.

37. For additional discussion of business borrowing, see Chapters 4 and 7.

Inheritance and Gift Taxes

Like the other direct taxes, the inheritance and gift taxes are not onerous in Japan. Tax rates are not adjusted often, but exemptions have been increased frequently (most recently, in 1966, 1971, and 1973). In 1970 only 3.4 percent of the decedents left estates with any taxable value, and in that year the inheritance tax amounted to 19.1 percent of the value of all taxable property transferred by bequest. For estates with taxable property of ¥100 million or more, the inheritance tax averaged 38.8 percent of taxable value.[38] Even these moderate percentages exaggerate the burden of the inheritance tax, because land and closely held businesses are greatly undervalued for purposes of inheritance taxes. Because the gift tax is cumulative for a period of only three years, it is hardly an effective mechanism for preventing tax avoidance through gifts from one living person to another. Unfortunately, virtually nothing is known about the methods by which wealthy persons in Japan arrange to transfer their wealth to the next generation, but it is safe to assume that the transfer taxes have not been a great impediment.

Other Taxes

As Table 5-1 indicates, half the total Japanese tax burden is accounted for by consumption, payroll, and property taxes. None of these taxes is high by international standards. Japan has been able to avoid a general tax on consumption, and the selective excise taxes it employs are not unusually burdensome.[39] The payroll taxes can run as high as 14.6 percent on the earnings of an industrial employee, but the entire array of payroll taxes applies to only a minority of workers. Even at 14.6 percent, the payroll tax rates are lower than those levied in most countries of Western Europe and are only slightly higher than the combined social security and unemployment compensation taxes in the United States. As in most countries, the property tax is a weak tax for the usual reason: underassessment of property values.

In brief, Japan's taxes are moderate or low when examined either tax by tax or in the aggregate. This fortunate circumstance can be explained in part by the absence of a defense program in the budget, but it also reflects reluctance on the part of the Japanese government—at least in the past—to permit the public sector to expand in relation to the rest of the economy. With the rising demand for a more adequate social security system, however,

38. See *Principal Reference Data for the Tax System, 1973.*
39. See Table 5-17 for some illustrative excise tax rates.

and for a greater variety of public services and facilities, Japan may find it difficult to maintain the ratio of taxes to the gross national product at its recent low level.

Income Elasticity of the Tax Structure

The most prominent feature of Japanese tax policy during the past two decades has been the annual tax reduction. These reductions were designed to keep a roughly constant ratio of government expenditure to national income as the economy grew. Because the progressive individual income tax accounts for about a third of the central government's receipts, frequent tax reductions were needed to prevent the highly elastic individual income tax from generating too much revenue. Although rate reductions were made periodically, most of the reductions came from increases in exemptions, which helped to keep the elasticity of the tax at a high level.[40] Because revenue growth is large in any rapidly growing economy, the ability of the Japanese to reduce taxes annually without reducing the size of the government sector is not surprising. The real question is whether there are any novel features in the Japanese tax structure that make its revenues particularly responsive to income growth.

Responsiveness of the Tax System to Income Growth

Although annual estimates of the tax reductions are available, the Japanese government does not publish estimates of the revenues of an unchanged tax structure over a period of years. Several analysts have made such estimates from time to time on the basis of the annual figures.[41] These estimates show a high degree of variability from year to year, because annual data reflect temporary as well as long-run factors. It is possible, however, to infer the long-run elasticities by averaging the annual figures or, as will be noted below, by computing long-run elasticities retrospectively.

Tables 5-9 and 5-10 provide measures of year-to-year elasticities of the central and local government tax systems, respectively, to changes in income

40. By maintaining the tax rates for relatively long periods, the Japanese in effect safeguarded the additional revenues generated by rate graduation as incomes grew rapidly.

41. See, for example, Wayne Snyder and Tsutomu Tanaka, "Budget Policy and Economic Stability in Postwar Japan," *International Economic Review,* vol. 13 (February 1972), pp. 85–110. The same type of estimates were made independently by Sei Fujita in *Nihon zaiseiron* [Fiscal Policy in Japan] (Keiso Press, 1972).

Table 5-9. *Year-to-Year Elasticity of the Central Government Tax System in Japan, by Type of Tax, 1955–71*

		Elasticity[a]			
Fiscal year	All taxes	Individual income tax	Corporate income tax	Inheri- tance tax	Other taxes
1955	0.35	0.75	−0.12	2.27	0.28
1956	1.37	1.28	2.42	2.18	0.96
1957	1.49	1.28	2.84	1.19	0.94
1958	0.12	1.06	−2.48	0.50	1.33
1959	1.24	1.25	1.36	1.16	0.83
1960	1.64	2.12	2.45	1.27	0.99
1961	1.31	2.14	1.27	1.37	0.95
1962	1.06	2.97	1.02	3.48	0.09
1963	0.92	1.66	0.54	2.00	0.76
1964	1.22	1.98	1.05	1.07	0.89
1965	0.60	2.13	−0.23	2.85	0.19
1966	1.01	1.52	0.92	1.57	0.66
1967	1.28	1.56	1.53	0.89	0.91
1968	1.33	1.91	1.22	1.11	0.99
1969	1.34	1.90	1.45	1.83	0.81
1970	1.44	2.07	1.51	2.14	0.80
1971	1.01	2.43	−0.05	4.78	0.52
Average, 1955–71	1.22[b]	1.77	0.98	1.86	0.76

Source: Computed on basis of data from the annual issues of Tax Bureau, Ministry of Finance, *An Outline of Japanese Taxes*, and *Zeisei shuyō sankō shiryōshū* [Principal Reference Data for the Tax System].

a. Elasticity is the ratio of the percentage change in tax liabilities to the percentage change in gross national product. The calculations are based on estimated tax receipts before the annual tax reductions.

b. Weighted average based on yields of various taxes in fiscal 1971.

for the period 1955–71.[42] The responsiveness of Japanese tax revenues to income growth both at the central and local government levels clearly is primarily the result of the individual income tax. Over the period 1955–71 the elasticity of the individual income tax averaged 1.8 for the central government and 1.6 for the local governments. By contrast, the yield of the corporate income tax is roughly proportional to income over the long run, while the consumption taxes rise more slowly than income. The inheritance tax is somewhat more responsive to income than the national individual income tax—its elasticity averaged 1.9 from 1955 to 1971—but it contributes very

42. Elasticity is the ratio of the percentage change in tax receipts to the percentage change in an income aggregate, such as national income, personal income, or gross national product. The calculations in Tables 5-9 and 5-10 are based on estimated tax receipts before the annual tax reductions.

Table 5-10. *Year-to-Year Elasticity of the Local Tax System in Japan, by Type of Tax, 1955–71*

		Elasticity[a]			
Fiscal year	All taxes	Individual income tax	Enterprise tax	Property tax	Other taxes
1955	0.41	0.78	−0.07	1.00	0.43
1956	1.47	1.28	1.65	0.54	2.68
1957	1.47	1.90	2.18	0.44	1.53
1958	1.08	1.40	−1.56	2.27	2.02
1959	0.79	0.79	1.09	0.50	0.84
1960	1.26	1.72	2.10	0.43	0.95
1961	0.99	1.24	1.23	0.56	0.90
1962	1.99	4.13	1.14	1.23	1.42
1963	0.88	1.35	0.65	0.62	0.79
1964	1.09	1.53	0.62	0.74	1.28
1965	1.17	1.79	0.09	0.97	1.51
1966	0.99	1.31	1.00	0.62	0.88
1967	1.27	1.46	1.54	0.62	1.24
1968	1.34	1.58	1.46	0.84	1.26
1969	1.27	1.42	1.41	1.09	1.12
1970	1.28	1.47	1.50	0.94	1.10
1971	1.24	1.92	0.03	1.95	1.26
Average, 1955–71	1.22[b]	1.59	0.91	0.90	1.25

Source: Computed on basis of data from the annual issues of Tax Bureau, Ministry of Finance, *An Outline of Japanese Taxes*, and *Chihō zeisei sankō shiryōshū* [Principal Reference Data for Local Tax System].

a. Elasticity is the ratio of the percentage change in tax liabilities to the percentage change in gross national product. The calculations are based on estimated tax receipts before the annual tax reductions.

b. Weighted average based on yields of various taxes in fiscal 1971.

little to total revenues. Revenues from the property tax, which is levied exclusively by local governments, have risen less proportionally than incomes, even though the growth of property values greatly exceeds the growth in income.

Another set of estimates of the elasticity of the Japanese tax system is given in Table 5-11. In this table, the elasticities of various taxes are computed for five-year periods to remove the effect of temporary factors. The basic assumption used to prepare these estimates is that the elasticity of the revenues from the tax reductions is the same as the elasticity of the tax that remained.[43]

43. Because the annual tax reductions are small relative to the total tax yield, the error resulting from this approximation must be small. For a five-year period, the elas-

Table 5-11. *Elasticity of Japanese Taxes by Five-Year Periods, 1955–72*[a]

| Fiscal years | National taxes | | | | | All local taxes |
	All taxes	Individual income tax	Corporate income tax	Inheritance tax	Other taxes	
1955–60	1.33	1.50	1.86	2.07	0.84	1.26
1956–61	1.33	1.59	1.65	1.86	0.93	1.21
1957–62	1.34	1.80	1.40	2.41	0.87	1.27
1958–63	1.32	1.87	1.50	1.86	0.82	1.21
1959–64	1.30	1.96	1.30	1.93	0.90	1.20
1960–65	1.15	1.97	0.89	2.27	0.68	1.18
1961–66	1.19	2.03	0.85	2.94	0.61	1.24
1962–67	1.18	1.85	0.99	2.41	0.71	1.13
1963–68	1.21	1.82	1.12	2.17	0.70	1.14
1964–69	1.28	1.89	1.22	2.24	0.74	1.21
1965–70	1.39	1.85	1.43	2.03	0.81	1.26
1966–71	1.30	2.00	1.18	1.95	0.54	1.29
1967–72	1.29	2.04	0.97	2.59	0.59	n.a.

Source: Calculations based on formula given in the text, using official figures of the Ministry of Finance.

n.a. Not available.

a. Elasticity is the ratio of the percentage change in tax liabilities to the percentage change in gross national product.

On the whole, the figures in Table 5-11 confirm the estimates made from the annual data in Table 5-9. When the erratic fluctuations of the annual data are removed, the elasticity of the individual income tax appears to have risen from about 1.5 for 1955–60 to about 2.0 beginning in 1960, and thereafter fluctuated between 1.8 and 2.0. The elasticity of the inheritance tax has been much higher than that of the individual income tax in recent years: 2.6 as compared to 2.0 for 1967–72. The corporate income tax continues to be erratic, reflecting largely the effect of the rate of growth of profits relative to total incomes. The elasticity of the consumption taxes seems to have declined from about 0.8 or 0.9 in the late 1950s to about 0.6 for the period 1967–72. Despite these changes, the elasticity of taxes at the beginning and end of the period was about 1.3 for the central and local governments.

These elasticities were much higher than those for the United States. The

ticities were computed by trial and error (with the use of a computer) from the following formula:

$$T_0(1-eg_{0-5})^5 = T_5 + R_5 + R_4(1+eg_{4-5})^1 + R_3(1+eg_{3-5})^2 + R_2(1+eg_{2-5})^3 + R_1(1+eg_{1-5})^4,$$

where T is tax liabilities; e is elasticity; g is average annual growth rates of gross national product; and R is annual tax reductions during the period. The subscripts refer to years within the period. The subscripts for g show the period over which g is computed.

elasticity of the U.S. federal individual income tax alone was in the neighborhood of 1.43 in the period 1967–72,[44] and the elasticity of the entire federal tax system (including payroll taxes) was probably about 1.10.[45] The differences between the U.S. and Japanese elasticities was attributable entirely to the performance of the Japanese individual income tax. If the elasticity of its individual income tax were only 1.43 instead of 2.0, Japan's national government would also have had a tax system with an elasticity of about 1.10.[46]

Simulation of U.S. Income Tax with Japanese Structural Features

To identify the reasons for the large difference in the elasticities of the two individual income taxes, the behavior of the U.S. tax was simulated for income growth rates similar to those experienced in Japan in recent years on the basis of a file of U.S. individual income tax returns for 1970.[47] These simulations assumed that the relative distribution of income is not altered as incomes increase. Tax liabilities were projected, first, for the years 1970–73 on the basis of the increases in U.S. incomes that occurred during that period and, then, to 1974 on the basis of annual income growth rates varying from 5 to 20 percent a year.

As might be expected, the elasticity of the U.S. income tax increases as income growth increases. The elasticity of the tax in 1974 begins at 1.52 for a 5 percent growth in money income and rises to 1.60 for 10 percent growth, 1.62 for 15 percent growth, and 1.65 for 20 percent growth (see Table 5-12). Even at the 15–20 percent annual growth rates experienced in Japan, however, the elasticity of the U.S. tax is significantly lower than 2.0. Using a per capita exemption that more nearly approximates the 1974 Japanese exemptions relative to their average income—$1,060 instead of $750 per capita[48]

44. Joseph A. Pechman, "Responsiveness of the Federal Individual Income Tax to Changes in Income," *Brookings Papers on Economic Activity* (2:1973), p. 393.

45. This assumes that the elasticity of the corporate income tax was 1.0 and that of all other federal taxes 0.8. The weights for each tax were assumed to be in proportion to receipts in fiscal 1972. It should be emphasized that the elasticity of the U.S. federal tax system has grown tremendously since 1967–72 as a result of the unusually large growth in money incomes. See ibid., pp. 398–402.

46. Based on weights for fiscal 1972, assuming the elasticities of the period 1967–72.

47. For a description of the file and the other assumptions used in the simulations, see Pechman, "Responsiveness of the Federal Individual Income Tax to Changes in Income."

48. In 1974 the minimum taxable level for a family of four in Japan was ¥1.02 million (including the minimum deduction of ¥160,000 for wage earners), or 42.5 percent of estimated family income of ¥2.4 million. The minimum taxable level in the United States was $4,300 (including the low-income allowance of $1,300), or 33.1 percent of estimated family income of $13,000. Thus, the Japanese minimum taxable level was

Table 5-12. *Elasticity of the U.S. Federal Individual Income Tax*
with per Capita Exemptions of $750 and $1,060, and with and
without Income Splitting, at Selected Income Growth Rates, 1974

Annual income growth rate (*percent*)	Exemptions of $750 per capita, with income splitting	Exemptions of $1,060 per capita, with income splitting	Exemptions of $1,060 per capita, without income splitting
	Elasticity[a]		
5	1.52	1.61	1.67
10	1.60	1.70	1.77
15	1.62	1.74	1.82
20	1.65	1.77	1.86

Source: Based on simulations from the 1970 U.S. Internal Revenue Service individual income tax file.
a. Elasticity is the ratio of the percentage change in tax liabilities to the percentage change in personal income less transfer payments.

—the same simulations give elasticities that are closer to those of the Japanese tax. The elasticity of the U.S. tax becomes 1.74 for an annual growth rate of 15 percent and 1.77 percent for an annual growth rate of 20 percent. Finally, to make the rate structures more comparable, the tax rate advantages of the U.S. income-splitting provisions were removed.[49] This raised the elasticity of the U.S. individual income tax to 1.82 for an annual growth rate of 15 percent and 1.86 for an annual growth rate of 20 percent.[50] The relatively small difference between these elasticities and an elasticity of 2.0 is attributable to all other features of the Japanese income tax and the differences in the distribution of income between the two countries.

These results indicate that the Japanese have not discovered a new formula for a high-elasticity income tax. It is only necessary to combine high rates of growth of money income with relatively high exemption levels and moderately progressive rates to achieve an elasticity as high as 2.0. With an elasticity of 2.0 and annual growth of 15 percent in money income, the

28.5 percent higher relative to the average income for a family of four. The $4,300 U.S. minimum taxable level becomes $5,526 when increased by 28.5 percent; deducting the low-income allowance of $1,300 gives a total exemption for the family of four of $4,226, or $1,060 per capita (rounding from $1,056). It was not necessary to change tax rates because the range of rates in Japan is roughly similar to the range in the United States.

49. This means that single persons, heads of households, and married couples filing separate returns would all use the rate schedule now applying to married couples filing separate returns.

50. Higher exemptions reduce the average rate of tax on personal income but do not change the marginal rate significantly. Because elasticity is the ratio of the marginal to the average tax rate, it rises if the average rate falls more than the marginal rate.

yield of the tax doubles in less than three years. Such a yield offers ample room for financing increased public expenditures as well as for reducing taxes.

Tax Incentives

Although most of the tax incentives under the Japanese income taxes are enumerated in the Special Tax Measures Law, a number of significant tax benefits are also contained in the ordinary income tax law. Accordingly, there is no compilation for Japan that is comparable to the comprehensive list of "tax expenditures" that is published annually in the President's budget.[51] The Tax Bureau in Japan does, however, keep a careful record of the revenue cost of the provisions included in the Special Tax Measures Law. This discussion of tax incentives will be concerned chiefly with what the Tax Bureau calls "special measures," but it will also cover the provisions of the ordinary income tax that may have significant economic effects.

Development of Special Measures

The special tax measures were brought together in one statute when the Temporal Tax Measures Law was enacted in 1938. During World War II these measures were substantially expanded to promote tax incentives for the war effort. Just before the end of the war, the number of special measures was over forty. After the war, the Temporal Tax Measures Law was repealed and a new Special Tax Measures Law, containing about twenty provisions, was substituted. This shorter list was curtailed even further when the tax reform recommended by the Shoup Mission was carried out in 1950. The measures that survived the Shoup tax reform consisted of tax exemptions for specified types of interest income, a reduced withholding rate for dividend income, and a tax-free reserve for bad debts.

The list of special tax measures was again considerably expanded from 1951 to 1956. During this period special attention was paid to the promotion of economic growth through tax devices; as a result, the character of the

51. According to the official definition, tax expenditures are exceptions to the "normal" structure of the individual and corporate income tax. To emphasize the close relation between tax benefits and outright subsidies, the estimates are broken down by the functional categories used in the federal budget. These estimates are required by the Congressional Budget and Impoundment Control Act of 1974. For the most recent list of tax expenditures, see "Tax Expenditures," *Special Analysis, Budget of the United States Government, Fiscal Year 1976,* pp. 101–17.

Japanese tax system was changed in a distinctive way. By 1956 the total number of special tax measures exceeded fifty, of which about thirty may be regarded as economically significant. These included accelerated depreciation for important industrial equipment (1951) and for newly built rental housing (1952); additional initial depreciation for important industries (1952); a special deduction for income from exports (1953) and a tax-free reserve for losses from export transactions (1953); reduced tax rates on interest and dividends (1953 and 1954); and complete tax exemption for interest income (1955 and 1956).

The proliferation of special tax measures is a result of the process of accommodation and compromise that plays so vital a role in Japanese decision-making. Once the decision was made to use a particular incentive, people with similar needs who did not benefit from the provision demanded similar tax treatment. To avoid controversy, a new provision was adopted to placate these other groups. The new provision provoked additional demands by other groups; they were also given special treatment; and the cycle was repeated. For example, strong pressure for the reduction or elimination of the tax on interest income came initially from the banking interests. Representatives of industry supported them in the belief that the financial costs of their investments would be reduced if interest were to receive favorable treatment. Once the interest provisions were adopted, securities dealers and representatives of investment companies demanded favorable treatment for dividend income in order to maintain their competitive position relative to the banking industry. An attempt was made to distribute the tax benefits more or less equally among industries and interest groups, although the results could never be perfectly equitable, and the costs in terms of revenue forgone were relatively large.

In 1956 the Tax Advisory Commission changed its attitude toward the special tax measures and recommended that they be substantially curtailed. A few of the commission's proposals were adopted, but most of the special measures survived. In 1957 the tax exemption for interest income was abolished and the maximum amounts allowed for various tax-free reserves were lowered. At the same time accelerated depreciation for important industries was liberalized, and the special deduction for export income was increased.

Since 1957 the record has been spotty. In 1959 the tax-free reserve for losses from export transactions was abolished. In 1963 accelerated depreciation was granted to small- and medium-size enterprises, and interest income from small deposits was made tax exempt. In 1967 the initial depreciation for machinery and equipment used for the prevention of environmental pollution was increased, and tax credits were adopted for savings for housing and for increases in research and development expenditures. In 1968 interest income from small holdings of government bonds was exempted from tax. On the other hand, in 1969, capital gains on the sale of land and buildings held for less than five years was made subject to a heavy tax rate. In 1972 the accelerated depreciation provisions for export industries were abolished, the special deduction for income from exports was sharply curtailed, a new tax credit for the acquisition of a house used as a dwelling unit was adopted, and a special deduction was provided for taxpayers who file blue returns. In 1973 the increased initial depreciation for important industries was reduced and scheduled for elimination in 1976, and a heavier tax rate was applied to capital gains of corporations made from the sale of land. On the whole, the recent trend seems to have been to reduce the range of tax preferences, but there is no more reluctance now than in the past to use tax devices to promote new national objectives.

Inventory of Tax Incentives

According to the Tax Bureau, the Special Tax Measures Law contains more than a hundred provisions. About half of these provisions apply to narrow areas and involve negligible losses of revenue. This inventory will be confined to the most important provisions.

The Tax Bureau classifies the special tax measures into six different categories,[52] but this classification is ambiguous and not useful for economic analysis. As a substitute, the measures are here classified into four categories: promotion of personal saving and housing investment; promotion of business saving and investment; promotion of exports and foreign investments; and miscellaneous.

PROMOTION OF PERSONAL SAVING AND HOUSING INVESTMENT. The basic incentive device used to promote personal saving is the exemption of small amounts of property income from tax and the taxation of other property income at low rates. Interest income from savings deposits, government bonds, and postal savings with principal value up to ¥3 million is not subject to tax. In addition, interest from workers' savings designated as Savings for the For-

---

52. Until 1974 the official classification had the following categories: promotion of savings; promotion of environmental quality and regional development; promotion of development of natural resources; promotion of technological development and modernization of industrial equipment; strengthening the financial position of firms; and miscellaneous. Beginning in 1974, the special taxation measures were rearranged and the number of categories increased to eight.

mation of Employees Assets are not taxable up to a principal value of ¥5 million. Beyond the actual exemption of modest amounts of interest income in these ways, the law also permits taxpayers to elect to be taxed separately on their interest and dividends at a rate of 25 percent.

As in most countries, capital gains from the sale of securities are completely exempt, except where an individual is regarded as being engaged in continuous trading, defined as more than fifty transactions per year that involve a total of more than 200,000 shares. Capital gains from the sale of land or buildings are taxed separately at a 20 percent rate if held for more than five years and 40 percent if held for five years or less. An ordinary deduction of ¥1 million is allowed for all long-term capital gains, or alternative deductions varying from ¥2.5 million to ¥20 million are allowed for specific types of gains. The most important additional deductions are ¥17 million for capital gains on the sale of a taxpayer's house, ¥10 million for capital gains on the sale of land under government land development or relocation programs, and ¥2.5 million for capital gains on the sale of farmland under the government's programs for the rationalization of the use of farmland.

Two modest tax credits have been enacted in recent years to promote homeownership. Taxpayers having specific contracts with financial institutions for savings for housing are given an annual credit of 4 percent of the annual amount saved, up to a maximum of ¥20,000. In addition, taxpayers who start to build or purchase a home are entitled to a tax credit amounting to 1 percent of the standard acquisition cost of the home (¥100,000 per 3.3 square meters of floor space), up to a maximum of ¥30,000 per year.

There are also deductions for premiums for life insurance, up to a maximum of ¥50,000 per year, and for fire and casualty insurance, up to a maximum of ¥15,000 per year.

PROMOTION OF BUSINESS SAVING AND INVESTMENT. The devices to promote business saving and investment include accelerated depreciation, increased initial depreciation, tax-free reserves, and tax credits. These devices are used freely to promote investment in particular industries or activities, and in many instances two or more devices are used to promote the same objective. For example, tax-free reserves and either increased initial depreciation or accelerated depreciation are often provided simultaneously. Total depreciation is always limited to the cost of the asset.

Accelerated depreciation is allowed for plant and equipment of small- and medium-size enterprises and of firms with at least 30 percent of their employees handicapped, for housing newly built for rental, for facilities for storage of grain and crude petroleum, and for truck terminals and fireproof warehouses. The acceleration varies from 33 to 200 percent of the regular depreciation allowances over a five-year period. Depreciation may be taken over a shorter period than the statutory useful lives for depreciable assets of registered hotels. Increased initial depreciation of one-tenth to one-half of acquisition cost is provided for numerous types of plant and equipment.[53]

Taxpayers are allowed to accumulate two types of tax-free reserves. The first represents reserves that are recognized for purposes of business accounting; the second is to encourage involvement in risky activities.[54] The size of the tax-free reserves and the amounts allowed annually are subject to specific limits, but in all cases the limits are generous in relation to the potential risks.

The tax credit device is used to encourage research and development. If a firm's outlays for research and development in any year exceed its outlays in any previous year, 25 percent of the excess is allowed as a tax credit. The credit is raised to 50 percent for the portion of the excess above 15 percent of the amount spent in the previous peak year. The credit is limited, however, to 10 percent of the corporation income tax.

In addition to these measures, special treatment is given to three industries. In mining, a depletion allowance of 15 percent of the proceeds from the sale of minerals is deductible as a current expense (up to a maximum of 50 percent of income from mining), but this amount must be credited to a special reserve and ultimately used for mineral exploration. Timber income is taxed separately from other income, and a standard deduction of ¥400,000

53. This includes plant and equipment used by medium and small enterprises and by industries classified as "important"; equipment produced for the first time in Japan; equipment used for regional development or in large cities (for example, underground electric transmission lines, gas supply equipment, and equipment of privately owned railroads) for the prevention of environmental pollution, or for the conversion of technological ideas into commercial products; buildings for stores and shops operated by retailers; steel vessels used by ocean transportation companies; aircraft used by air transportation companies; shafts and lifts for mining use; and water-supply equipment that is constructed in lieu of wells for industrial use. Increased initial depreciation is also given in the first three years of mergers that are approved by the government.

54. The tax-free accounting reserves include reserves for bad debts, accounts receivable, bonuses payable to employees, and employee retirement allowances. The special inducements include tax-free reserves for losses in market prices of inventories or securities; losses incurred in the development of natural resources, structural improvement projects for small- and medium-size enterprises, railway construction in certain large cities and suburban areas, and construction of atomic power plants, forestation, and pollution control; losses by security companies from stock transactions and defaults or embezzlements in a commodity or securities exchange; losses of hydroelectric corporations resulting from drought; unusual losses of casualty insurance companies; and losses caused by the repurchases of computers and by guarantees of the quality of computer programs.

is allowed for expenses. Farm income from newly cultivated farmland also is exempt from tax.

PROMOTION OF EXPORTS AND FOREIGN INVESTMENTS. At one time promotion of exports was a major consideration in tax policy. From 1953 to 1965 producers of exported goods were permitted to deduct 3 percent of their gross sales abroad, up to 80 percent of their net operating income from exports. This provision was finally eliminated because it was in direct violation of the rules of the General Agreement on Tariffs and Trade, which prohibit export subsidies. From 1961 to 1972 firms were allowed accelerated depreciation for their equipment if they raised the proportion of their business from exports over the previous year's level.

Today, the remaining provisions for exports are minor. A special deduction is allowed for transactions involving the provision of technical services overseas. A tax-free reserve for overseas market development may be accumulated by a corporation that has capital of not more than ¥1 billion and that derives income from exports, from the processing of goods for an exporter, or from large-scale repairing of ships paid for in foreign currencies. Tax-free reserves may also be accumulated for losses from overseas investments. One-fifth of the amount credited to both types of reserves must be added back successively, after five years, to the income in five successive years.

MISCELLANEOUS PROVISIONS. To offset the low levels at which their fees were set under the social insurance system, physicians may deduct 72 percent of their fees for medical care provided. Taxpayers filing a blue return may deduct ¥100,000 a year. Finally, corporations are allowed social and entertainment expenses up to ¥4 million plus 0.1 percent of paid-in capital plus 25 percent of any excess.

Use of the Tax Incentives

As might be expected, large corporations derive greater benefit from the special tax measures than small ones, even though they do not make as much use of the measures to which they are entitled. In fiscal 1970 small corporations—those with paid-in capital of less than ¥1 million—used almost all of the legally permitted deductions under the special tax measures, whereas the largest corporations—those with paid-in capital of ¥10 billion or more —used only about two-thirds (see Table 5-13). On the other hand, special depreciation accounted for only 3.5 percent of the depreciation reported by the small corporations and 16.5 percent of the depreciation reported by the

358   JOSEPH PECHMAN AND KEIMEI KAIZUKA

Table 5-13. *Use of the Special Tax Measures by Japanese Corporations,*
by Size of Corporation and Type of Industry, Fiscal 1970
Percent

Size of corporation and type of industry	Legally permitted deductions under the special tax measures actually used	Total depreciation accounted for by special tax measures
Size of corporation, in millions of yen of paid-in capital		
Less than 1	96.7	3.5
1–5	94.1	5.5
5–10	92.3	7.1
10–50	88.4	7.2
50–100	90.4	9.5
100–1,000	78.2	6.6
1,000–5,000	61.9	9.1
5,000–10,000	43.2	10.1
10,000 and over	61.6	16.5
Type of industry		
Agriculture	78.8	3.5
Mining	56.0	4.2
Construction	92.3	29.1
Textiles	75.7	16.5
Chemicals	74.5	8.4
Steel and metals	69.4	22.0
Machinery	91.3	18.8
Foods	93.0	6.2
Printing	94.4	12.5
Other manufacturing	92.6	12.1
Wholesale trade	90.1	3.6
Retail trade	95.2	1.0
Restaurants	78.1	0.6
Financial	99.1	3.0
Real estate	84.2	5.9
Public utilities	35.7	8.8
Services	97.1	1.9
Cooperatives	99.0	⎫
Mutual companies	100.0	⎬ 4.2
Medical	52.8	⎭
All corporations	66.8	10.4

Source: National Tax Administration Agency, *Hōjin kigyō no jittai* [Sample Survey of Corporate Business] (1972).

largest corporations. The industries that benefited most from the special depreciation measures were construction, steel and metals, machinery, and textiles. Special depreciation accounted for 29.1, 22.0, 18.8, and 16.5 percent, respectively, of total depreciation reported in these industries.

Significance of the Tax Incentives

It is not possible to estimate the revenue loss from all of the tax incentives used by the Japanese. The only estimates that are available cover the particular provisions that are included by the Tax Bureau in its annual compilation of special tax measures. According to these estimates, the revenue loss resulting from the special tax measures varied between 11 and 13 percent of income tax revenues in the late 1950s, declined to 8 percent in 1961, rose to 13 percent in 1965, and then declined to 9 percent in 1971 (see Table 5-14).

Because the special tax measures for the promotion of exports have been curtailed in recent years, revenue losses from these measures are declining relative to total income tax revenues. Special measures to promote business saving and investment declined sharply between 1956 and 1970, but they

Table 5-14. *Comparison of Estimated Revenue Loss from Japanese Special Tax Measures and Total Individual and Corporate Income Tax Revenue, Fiscal Years 1956–72*

| | | Revenue losses from special tax measures[a] | |
Fiscal year	Total individual and corporate income tax revenue (billions of yen)	Amount (billions of yen)	Percent of income tax revenue
1956	565	67	12
1957	616	67	11
1958	568	71	13
1959	669	82	12
1960	964	98	10
1961	1,210	101	8
1962	1,360	126	9
1963	1,554	162	10
1964	1,813	225	12
1965	1,898	250	13
1966	2,116	273	13
1967	2,598	284	11
1968	3,205	322	10
1969	4,014	401	10
1970	4,995	501	10
1971	5,446	498	9
1972	6,718	613	9

Sources: Individual and corporate tax revenues, from Tax Bureau, Ministry of Finance, *An Outline of Japanese Taxes, 1974* (Tokyo, 1974), p. 273; revenue loss from special tax measures, from unpublished data presented to the Tax Advisory Commission by the Tax Bureau of the Ministry of Finance.

a. Includes only the items listed as special tax measures by the Tax Bureau. Excludes revenue gains from the curtailment of large corporate social and entertainment expenses.

Table 5-15. *Percentage Distribution of the Estimated Revenue Loss from Japanese Special Tax Measures, by Type of Incentive, Fiscal Years 1956–72*[a]

Fiscal year	Promotion of individual saving and investment	Promotion of business saving and investment	Promotion of exports and foreign investment	Other
1956	46	38	7	8
1957	45	36	12	7
1958	43	31	19	7
1959	45	36	12	7
1960	45	38	12	6
1961	48	36	11	6
1962	47	27	16	10
1963	57	19	14	9
1964	52	20	12	15
1965	51	22	11	16
1966	53	22	10	15
1967	53	22	10	14
1968	50	21	12	18
1969	45	21	13	21
1970	37	20	16	27
1971	44	32	5	20
1972	40	34	3	23

Source: Unpublished data presented to the Tax Advisory Commission by the Tax Bureau of the Ministry of Finance. Figures may not add to totals because of rounding.

a. Includes only the items listed as special tax measures by the Tax Bureau. Excludes revenue gains from the curtailment of large corporate social and entertainment expenses.

have regained importance largely as a result of the special depreciation provisions for antipollution equipment and for small- and medium-size enterprises. In 1972 the special measures to promote individual saving and investment accounted for 40 percent of the revenue loss, business saving and investment for 34 percent, exports and foreign investment for 3 percent, and other measures (mainly the deduction for physicians' fees) for 23 percent (see Table 5-15).

These official figures understate the significance of the whole gamut of tax incentive measures by a considerable margin. In the first place, the preferential provisions for capital gains, interest, and dividends are part of the basic income tax law and are therefore not counted as a special tax measure by the Tax Bureau. Second, the fractionation of the individual income tax into separate classified taxes[55] loses a great deal of revenue and greatly reduces the

55. For employment income, business income, interest, dividends, capital gains, real estate income, retirement income, timber income, occasional income, and miscellaneous income.

progressivity of the nominal rate structure, particularly in the top brackets. Third, a number of major business tax preferences are also not regarded as special tax measures. These include relatively short useful lives for purposes of depreciation accounting and deductions for part of social and entertainment expenses.[56] Fourth, housing subsidies provided by business firms to their employees and loans to executives at low interest rates are not regarded as special tax measures. Fifth, the official estimates are based on the economic projections included in the budget each year; these projections tend to understate economic growth and thereby the revenue significance of the special tax measures as well. The revenue loss from all the additional preferential provisions greatly exceeds the revenue loss from the official special measures, but there is little basis for making even an approximate estimate of the total. It is clear, however, that Japan sacrifices a great deal of revenue and is forced to maintain much higher nominal rates than otherwise would be needed in order to maintain its complicated set of tax incentives.

Studies of the impact of the special tax measures on Japanese economic growth are, for the most part, inconclusive. On the one hand, many of the special tax measures were used by industries that were not regarded as strategic from the standpoint of growth. For example, the textile industry received very favorable treatment under the special tax measures for the promotion of exports, yet this was an industry that grew relatively slowly. Moreover, there is virtually no relation between the special tax measures to promote household saving and the rate of private saving.[57] On the other hand, initial depreciation allowances were used widely for expansion and modernization in such strategic industries as steel and machinery. Therefore, except for the stimulus in these industries, the special tax measures did not have a substantial effect on investment and growth.

Economic Effects of the Tax System

In the last two decades Japanese governments have placed great stress on taxation as an instrument of economic policy. Some part of the tax system is modified every year, often to a significant extent. Task forces of the Tax

56. In fact, because standard accounting practice permits deductions for such expenses, the revenue gain from the portion of social and entertainment expenses that is disallowed for tax purposes is entered by the Tax Bureau as an offset against the revenue losses from the other special tax measures. This offset has been eliminated in Tables 5-14 and 5-15.

57. Fujita, *Fiscal Policy in Japan,* and Ryūtarō Komiya, "Japan," in *Foreign Tax Policies and Economic Growth* (Columbia University Press, 1966), pp. 39–96.

362   JOSEPH PECHMAN AND KEIMEI KAIZUKA

Advisory Commission are continuously studying new approaches to taxation in the interest of promoting economic growth as well as of improving tax equity; some new special tax measures are being introduced as others are being phased out. Despite all this activity, few empirical studies have been made of the impact of the tax system on economic activity, and the articles on the subject have been inconclusive.[58] The discussion in this section therefore must be largely speculative.

A tax system affects economic activity in several ways. First, it may improve or impair business and managerial incentives. Second, it may increase or decrease the stability of the economy. Third, it may encourage or discourage saving and investment and thereby raise or lower the growth potential of the economy. The effect of Japanese tax policy on each of these matters will be discussed in turn.[59]

Business and Managerial Incentives

The Japanese have opted for an individual income tax with a narrow base and relatively high marginal rates. Because exemptions and the employment income deductions are relatively high, a substantial fraction of the labor force —more than 40 percent—is not subject to income tax. But beyond the taxable income level, the marginal rates run up rather steeply. For example, the combined national and local income tax rate for a married person with two children is 19 percent at the ¥1 million taxable income level, 27 percent at ¥2 million, 40 percent at ¥5 million, and 52 percent at ¥8 million (see Table 5-16). Thus, although the marginal rates on cash earnings are relatively moderate for the mass of wage earners, they are fairly steep on the earnings of individuals in the managerial and professional classes and of successful self-employed persons.[60]

58. See, for example, Sei Fujita, "Tax Policy," in Ryūtarō Komiya (ed.), *Postwar Economic Growth in Japan* (University of California Press, 1966), pp. 32–59; and Komiya, "Japan." The references in these articles suggest that the literature in Japanese is equally inconclusive.

59. Revenues from the tax system also provide the financing for social overhead capital, which may be as important as, or more important than, private investment. Some knowledgeable Japanese believe that public investment in facilities to improve the quality of life has been unnecessarily neglected in recent years. Whether this neglect will show up in a reduced rate of measured growth as an attempt is made to remedy the deficiency is unclear; the question is beyond the scope of this study.

60. A salaried person who is married and has two children and a taxable income of ¥8 million probably has earnings of about ¥12 million. At current exchange rates (¥300 to the dollar), this is equivalent to roughly $40,000. Such incomes are earned in Japan only by corporate executives and the most successful doctors, lawyers, and other professional people.

There is no evidence that these relatively high marginal rates have any effect on the working habits of persons who are subject to them. Anybody who observes business life in Japan cannot fail to be impressed by the tempo of hard work that seems to be characteristic of virtually all members of the economic community. As indicated earlier, corporate executives and managers do not receive large supplements to their cash salaries, except for loans to purchase a residence and lavish expense accounts that do not add to their permanent wealth; nor are their retirement benefits large by U.S. standards. Unlike their counterparts in the United States, most corporate managers do not accumulate a personal stake, through stock purchase or stock option plans, in the firms to which they are attached throughout their working careers. The loyalty of the average Japanese worker to his organization seems to provide the major incentive to continue to work hard even though the rate of his cash earnings after tax seems to increase only moderately as he rises in the corporate hierarchy with advancing age.[61]

Even though the typical salaried employee does not receive unusually large economic rewards for his hard work, Japan is not exactly an egalitarian society. There are many wealthy people in Japan; practically all of this wealth must have been accumulated since the end of World War II, and much of it is in corporate form. It seems that there are very large rewards to the business innovator and risk taker. These rewards are scarcely touched by the tax system, which permits the tax-free accumulation of capital gains (a characteristic of all other tax systems) and requires only modest tax payments on other property incomes. Moreover, once an entrepreneur has demonstrated his capacity to operate a business successfully, he is given access to large amounts of borrowed capital through the banking system. This ability to borrow permits him to expand the scale of his operations rapidly and to enjoy a correspondingly high rate of growth in economic power as well as in business assets.

Thus, the tax system uses no unusual technique to help maintain business and management incentives in Japan. The typical middle-level executive seems to derive satisfaction from the prestige of his job, his expense account, access to a company car, and other noncash emoluments, as well as from his cash earnings. Access to credit is much more important to the business innovator than preferential tax treatment, at least in the initial stages of his work. Later the implicit tax exemption for unrealized capital gains derived from undistributed corporate earnings permits him to accumulate a large

61. For an analysis of the vertical nature of Japanese society and its effect on employees' attitudes toward their own business organizations, see Chie Nakane, *Japanese Society* (University of California Press, 1972).

amount of corporate wealth. This type of tax incentive—available as well in other countries—helps to explain how individuals have been able to amass large fortunes in a single lifetime. Because rates of economic growth differ widely among countries, this particular incentive cannot be regarded as a major determinant of relative economic performance.

Effects on Economic Stability

Because Japan relies heavily on income taxes, the tax system acts automatically to moderate changes in the rate of growth of private demand. As incomes rise or fall, income tax revenues rise or fall proportionately more than incomes and thus reduce fluctuations in private disposable income. Private demand becomes more stable to the extent that it depends on disposable income. And because consumer demand depends more on current disposable income than does investment demand, the individual income tax is probably a more effective economic stabilizer than the corporate income tax.[62]

The importance of the individual income tax as a built-in stabilizer may be illustrated by the following figures. According to Table 5-5, the ratio of the individual income revenues of the central and local governments to the gross national product in 1972 was 0.054. Because the elasticity of the individual income tax is about 2 (see Table 5-11), the built-in flexibility of the tax—that is, the ratio of the change in tax to a change in gross national product—is 0.108 (2×0.054). Thus, the individual income tax alone reduces the growth of money income by about 11 percent. For the tax system as a whole, which has an elasticity of 1.3 and is roughly 21 percent of the gross national product, the same type of calculations suggest that built-in flexibility is on the order of 27 percent. In other words, the individual income tax accounts for about 40 percent of the built-in flexibility of the entire tax system.

The decision of the Japanese government to permit the government sector to grow only at the same rate as the rest of the economy gives it a great deal of fiscal flexibility. Without tax reduction and assuming annual growth in money incomes of 20 percent, tax revenues would grow roughly 1.0 percent relative to gross national product each year. If half this revenue increase were

---

62. Corporate taxes absorb a major share of declining corporate earnings during a downswing and of rising earnings during an upswing. This permits corporations to maintain dividends at a stable rate during a business cycle. But because dividends are a relatively small proportion of after-tax corporate incomes in Japan, the effect of more stable dividends on consumer incomes must be relatively small. Investment demand depends only to a limited extent on current incomes, so the moderating effect on private investment of the type of corporate income tax used in Japan and other countries must be small.

saved during boom times and then given away in tax reductions in periods of slow growth, the potential for countercyclical fiscal policy would be substantial. For example, if booms lasted three years, the buildup of tax revenues would amount to 1.5 percent of the gross national product; in addition to exercising a desirable restraint during the expansion, such a backlog would provide an effective means of combating recessions.[63]

In fact, however, the Japanese rarely permit the built-in flexibility of the tax system to exercise its full stabilizing effect. Tax reductions continue to be made annually regardless of the stage of the business cycle, and there is little evidence that the magnitude of the reductions is manipulated in a counter-cyclical manner.[64] Several studies of the timing of tax changes in Japan have concluded that discretionary tax policy has been, on balance, destabilizing in the short run.[65] Potentially, the built-in flexibility of the Japanese tax system is a powerful tool to promote stable growth, but the government has relied primarily on monetary policy for purposes of short-run stabilization.[66]

Effects on Saving and Investment

The major thrust of Japanese growth policies has been to raise the rate of national saving and investment. Gross saving increased from about 25 percent of the gross national product in the mid-1950s to about 40 percent in the early 1970s.[67] Increasing the stock of capital is important for growth because it raises productivity directly and also permits the adoption of newer and more efficient technologies. Two facets of Japanese tax policy were im-

63. Translated into U.S. figures, a 1.5 percent reserve would amount to over $20 billion at the 1974 gross national product level of about $1,400 billion.

64. Gardner Ackley and Hiromitsu Ishi conclude that, in the last twenty years, the variations in the annual amounts of tax reduction have been in the wrong direction about half the time in relation to the business cycle (see Chapter 3). The 1974 tax reductions, the largest in history in absolute amount (though not relative to national income), came at a time when Japan was suffering the largest inflation since the one immediately after World War II.

65. See, for example, Keimei Kaizuka, "The Stabilization Effect of Fiscal Policy," in *Postwar Economic Growth in Japan*, p. 224; and Snyder and Tanaka, "Budget Policy and Economic Stability in Postwar Japan." On the other hand, Hiromitsu Ishi finds that the government surplus and deficit correspond rather well to the peaks and troughs of the Japanese business cycles; see his "Cyclical Behavior of Government Receipts and Expenditures: A Case Study of Postwar Japan," *Hitotsubashi Journal of Economics,* vol. 14 (June 1973), pp. 56–83. Ishi notes, however, that most of the countercyclical movement of the tax system is attributable to the corporate tax, which is much less effective as an automatic stabilizer than the individual income tax.

66. For a discussion of the roles of monetary and fiscal policy in short-run stabilization policy, see Chapter 3.

67. See Table 3-1, Chapter 3.

portant in this strategy. First, the national budget was set to produce surpluses that added to national saving and helped to provide the margin of resources needed for the production of a large and growing volume of investment goods.[68] Second, numerous structural measures were introduced into the tax system to encourage private saving and investment.

GOVERNMENT SAVING. As a practical matter it is generally difficult to maintain a budget surplus to help stabilize the economy or to promote growth. Taxpayers are always demanding tax relief, and legislatures find it hard to resist these demands when government revenues are more than sufficient to cover essential expenditures. As a consequence, government budgets are rarely allowed to generate significant surpluses, and are in balance usually only at or near high employment. With government saving close to zero or negative most of the time, reliance must be placed almost entirely on private saving to provide the margin of resources needed for public as well as for private investment. In Japan the government has been able to keep the demands for tax reduction sufficiently in check so that it was able to generate a significant amount of government saving during the past two decades. The government succeeded in this policy by systematically underestimating tax receipts. The annual tax reductions were usually estimated to exhaust all, or most, of the prospective surpluses in the general accounts of the national government, yet retrospectively the budget usually turned out to be in surplus.[69]

The degree of success of this policy may be seen in the record of private and government saving since the mid-1950s. General government saving was sufficient to finance all of the government's fixed investment throughout the period, with a margin averaging over 1.5 percent of the gross national product.[70] Moreover, government saving averaged about 40 percent of private saving—a remarkable record for a country with low taxes.[71]

At the same time that government saving was kept at such a high level,

68. National saving is the difference between national output and consumption; investment is the portion of the national output that is not consumed. Thus, saving is equal to investment for the economy as a whole. By saving, a nation in effect sets aside resources that are used for investment purposes; otherwise, the resources would be used for consumption purposes.

69. Ishi, "Cyclical Behavior of Government Receipts and Expenditures," pp. 60–61.

70. See Table 3-7, Chapter 3.

71. In the United States, government saving has contributed little to national saving in the last forty-five years. It is difficult to compare Japan with the United States because public investment expenditures are not segregated from other current outlays in the U.S. national income accounts. If government saving in the United States were equal to the Japanese figure of about 7 percent of the gross national product, it would amount to over $95 billion at current levels. This is more than three times public construction outlays and probably is about that much higher than total net capital formation in the public sector.

total demand was allowed to grow rapidly—primarily by keeping interest rates at artificially low levels—so that the resources made available through saving would not remain idle. When the economy became overheated, the chief instrument of stabilization policy was monetary and credit restraint and not additional fiscal restraint. Thus, although long-run strategy was to maintain a high rate of saving, short-run policy was often destabilizing in the interest of maintaining a sufficiently high rate of growth of demand.[72]

PRIVATE SAVING AND INVESTMENT. The most striking feature of the special tax measures—aside from their complexity—is that the revenue losses are significant in relation to saving and investment aggregates. In fiscal 1970 the revenue cost of the special tax measures for property income alone equaled about 2 percent of the saving of the entire household sector (including nonprofit organizations). If the cost of all the favorable tax provisions for property income (see Tables 5-14 and 5-15) were included in the numerator and saving not directly affected by the tax laws were excluded from the denominator, the percentage would be several times larger. The increase in the balances of tax-free reserves amounted to a third or more of total corporate saving in the 1950s; in recent years, they have aggregated perhaps 10 percent of corporate saving. The special depreciation provisions (that is, accelerated depreciation and additional initial depreciation) have accounted for about 10 percent of total corporate capital consumption allowances in recent years (see Table 5-13).

Unfortunately, it is impossible to estimate the effects of these large tax benefits on saving and investment. What can be observed is a doubling of the rate of private saving and investment relative to the gross national product between 1952 and 1970.[73] What cannot be measured, however, is how much of this spectacular increase is attributable to tax policy and how much to other factors. The high rate of household saving has been explained by the rapid growth in personal disposable income, the inadequacy of the social security system, the large share of income going to the self-employed (who are generally large savers), and the rudimentary nature of the consumer finance system.[74] As for private investment, two econometric studies suggest

72. See Komiya, "Japan," in *Foreign Tax Policies and Economic Growth*, p. 49; and Snyder and Tanaka, "Budget Policy and Economic Stability in Postwar Japan," pp. 102–04.
73. See Table 3-1, Chapter 3.
74. Ryūtarō Komiya, "The Supply of Personal Savings," in *Postwar Economic Growth in Japan*, pp. 157–81; Miyohei Shinohara, *Structural Changes in Japan's Economic Development* (Tokyo: Kinokuniya, 1970), pp. 40–97; and Toshiyuki Mizoguchi, *Personal Savings and Consumption in Postwar Japan* (Tokyo: Kinokuniya, 1970). See also Chapter 4 in this volume.

that the special tax measures have been fairly effective in raising the level of investment.[75] Both studies, however, use an investment function that tends to make tax incentives appear to be much more effective than do other investment functions.[76] In our view, the access of growing firms to abundant amounts of borrowed capital through the banking system is at least as important as the special tax measures. This is particularly true in Japan because the various policy instruments are coordinated to an unusual degree in the interest of promoting private investment. Komiya reports that "Japanese bankers say that they are more willing to make loans on investment for which accelerated depreciation applies. . . ."[77] Similarly, loans to exporters and manufacturers for export were given to the same firms that were given the special tax preferences for the export industry. Such a combination of loan assistance and tax benefits provides an extremely effective set of incentives.

Many independent Japanese fiscal experts outside the government and some members of the Tax Advisory Commission are skeptical of the effectiveness of the special tax measures.[78] They believe that any desirable effects of the special tax measures have been purchased at the price of complexity in the tax laws, substantial inequity among taxpayers, and excessive economic instability. Many of them also point out that the special tax measures greatly moderate the effect of the nominal tax rates as they apply to particular firms and individuals and wonder whether a tax structure with a broader base and lower rates would not be equally, or even more, effective. Finally,

75. Ratcliffe estimated that for the period 1956–67 gross investment in manufacturing was raised about 5 percent by the special depreciation provision and about 1 percent by the special tax-free reserves and other special deductions. See C. T. Ratcliffe, "Tax Policy and Investment Behavior in Postwar Japan" (Ph.D. thesis, University of California, Berkeley, n.d.). Kinoshita estimated that accelerated depreciation increased net investment in 1955–57 by from 10 to 20 percent in four major industries (iron and steel, general machinery, electrical machinery, and transport equipment), but the effect tapered off to from 3 to 8 percent in 1959–61. He also estimated that the reduction in useful lives for depreciation purposes increased net investment by from 1 to 8 percent in 1961 and 1963, and that the 1958 corporate tax cut increased net investment by from 3 to 9 percent in 1958–60. The latter calculations included food, textiles, and pulp, as well as the four industry groups covered by the accelerated depreciation calculations. See Soshichi Kinoshita, "Investment Behavior and Postwar Tax Policy," *Gendai keizai* [Contemporary Economics], vol. 5 (June 1972), pp. 180–98.

76. The functions used are similar to those originated by Dale Jorgenson of Harvard University. For a comparison of results based on these and other approaches to the measurement of the impact of tax incentives on investment in the United States, see Gary Fromm (ed.), *Tax Incentives for Capital Spending* (Brookings Institution, 1971).

77. The reason given is that ". . . they can recover the loans within a shorter period and with more certainty." Komiya, "Japan," in *Foreign Tax Policies and Economic Growth*, p. 83.

78. See, for example, Fujita, "Tax Policy," in *Postwar Economic Growth in Japan*, pp. 56–59, and Komiya, "Japan," pp. 89–90.

the fact that the tax burden is unusually low by the standards of other developed countries (see Table 5-5) may alone be a significant factor in the explanation of the high rate of private saving and investment in Japan.

Effects of Taxation on Distribution of Income and Wealth

Data on the distribution of income in Japan suffer from the usual deficiencies of underreporting and lack of comprehensiveness, with respect to both population coverage and the definition of income. The few analyses that have been made suggest that the distribution of income before taxes in Japan is about as even as it is in the United States and the United Kingdom and is somewhat more even than in most Western European countries.[79] The available data also suggest that the Japanese distribution became more even from the period of the occupation to about 1953, became slightly less even between 1953 and 1961, and has become slightly more even since 1961. But on balance, the net change over the last twenty years has been small.[80]

The information on the distribution of income after taxes is even less satisfactory than the information on a before-tax basis. Kaizuka and Niida calculated the effect of the most important direct tax payments by individuals—individual income taxes, property taxes, and social security taxes—on the incomes of families of wage and salary workers for each year in the period 1953–61. On balance, this set of taxes had an equalizing effect on the distribution of income, but the effect was small and declined somewhat during the period.[81]

79. For a summary of recent data, see Montek S. Ahluwalia, "Income Inequality: Some Dimensions of the Problem," in Hollis Chenery and others (eds.), *Redistribution with Growth* (London: Oxford University Press, 1974), table I.1, p. 9; and Felix Paukert, "Income Distribution at Different Levels of Development: A Survey of the Evidence," *International Labour Review,* vol. 108 (August–September 1973), pp. 97–125.

80. These estimates are based on data from the annual household survey, which covers only households headed by a wage or salary earner. See Tadao Ishizaki, "Income Distribution, Social Welfare, and Education," in Shūji Inaba and others (eds.), *Kokumin keizai to seikatsu* [National Economy and Livelihood] (Tokyo: Nihon Hyōronsha, 1965); Keimei Kaizuka and Hiroshi Niida, "Taxation and Income Distribution," in Ryūtarō Tachi and Tsunehiko Watanabe (eds.), *Keizai seichō to zaiseikin'yū seisaku* [Economic Growth and Fiscal and Monetary Policy] (Tokyo: Inwanamai, 1964); and Hiromitsu Ishi, "Taxation and Income Distribution in Japan," *Tōyō keizai* [The Oriental Economist], Oct. 4, 1973, pp. 136–43.

81. As measured by the Gini coefficient, disposable income was distributed more evenly than before-tax income by 8.1 percent in 1953 and by 5.5 percent in 1961. See Kaizuka and Niida, "Taxation and Income Distribution." The Gini coefficient is the ratio of the area between the Lorenz curve and the line of equal distribution to the entire area below the line of equal distribution.

Similar calculations have been made by Kaizuka from more comprehensive income distributions based on field surveys made by the Ministry of Welfare for the years 1962, 1967, and 1972. These surveys covered families of the self-employed and of those relying on property income, as well as those of wage and salary earners; and the income concept included earnings from employment and self-employment and all property incomes except capital gains. According to these calculations, income before taxes tended to become more evenly distributed between 1962 and 1967 and between 1967 and 1972; but the net equalizing effect of individual income, property, and payroll taxes was small in all three years (3.8 percent in 1962, 3.3 percent in 1967, and 4.4 percent in 1972).[82]

The taxes that were not distributed among household units in these calculations include regressive as well as progressive taxes. Consumption taxes are regressive, while corporate income and inheritance taxes are progressive.[83] Receipts from consumption taxes accounted for 24 percent of total government tax revenues in 1972, while receipts from the corporate income and inheritance taxes accounted for 26 percent (see Table 5-1). Thus, the effects of these taxes on progressivity tend to offset one another. Whether the offset is exact or not, it is fairly clear that the distributional effect of the entire Japanese tax system is small.

The distribution of wealth is even more of a mystery in Japan than the distribution of income. Prewar fortunes were broken up or taxed away during and immediately after the war, and the distribution of wealth—to the extent that there was any—must have been relatively even when the occupation ended in 1951. Since then, wealth has increased rapidly as the country has prospered. Because taxes on property incomes or on the accumulation of wealth have been light, it is virtually certain that inequality in the distribution of wealth also has been increasing. Moreover, the inheritance tax is not a great deterrent to the transmission of wealth to future generations, so there is likely to be even greater concentration of wealth with the passage of time.

82. The before-tax and after-tax distributions are so close that they can barely be distinguished on a Lorenz curve diagram. The Gini coefficients are as follows:

	1962	1967	1972
Distribution before taxes	0.3894	0.3743	0.3538
Distribution after taxes	0.3747	0.3618	0.3384

These estimates were based on data in Ministry of Welfare, *Income Redistribution Survey* (1964, 1969, and 1974).

83. The corporate income tax is progressive on the assumption that the tax is borne by corporate stockholders or by owners of capital in general. Some economists believe that part of the corporate income tax is shifted forward to consumers in the form of higher prices. If this is the case, part of the corporate tax is distributed in the same way as a consumption tax.

Summary and Conclusions

Japan began its postwar recovery with a blueprint by the Shoup Mission that would have made its tax system a model for the rest of the world. But the Shoup blueprint was quickly discarded, and a Japanese brand of taxation was substituted. Thereafter tax policy was oriented toward growth, but there is little evidence that the tax structure contributed significantly to the remarkable economic record of the 1950s and 1960s.

Like the United States, Japan places heavy reliance on the individual and corporate income taxes and eschews a general consumption tax, but the similarity between the two tax systems ends there. The major characteristic of the Japanese tax system is the low effective tax burden that results from a bewildering variety of tax preferences that makes the U.S. tax system look like a model of tax neutrality. In addition, the Japanese are skillful tax planners: they rely heavily on annual tax reductions and reforms to balance the pressures for tax concessions and to make the tax system acceptable to the public. Little of this experience is transferable—or should be transferred—elsewhere; its viability depends on the particular character of the Japanese people and their political system.

The key to Japanese tax policy has been a determination to keep a lid on the growth of the public sector. With its spending on defense at the lowest level among the developed industrial countries, Japan is able to maintain the lowest tax rates among the developed countries. Because the income taxes are highly responsive to economic growth, and because growth was spectacular, Japan also can indulge in the luxury of reducing taxes every year, thus permitting private demand to grow rapidly. At the same time, tax receipts have been high enough to generate a level of public saving sufficient to finance government capital formation with a minimum of borrowing from the private sector. For reasons that are still not fully understood, private saving also has been at a high level and has grown rapidly, so that total national saving has kept pace with the extraordinarily heavy demands for investment. The productive capacity of the economy also grew rapidly because investment grew rapidly; and actual output grew rapidly because demand was permitted to rise with the growth of capacity (but not without some instability).

The structural features of the Japanese tax system that are of particular interest to outside observers are, first, the tremendous elasticity of the individual income tax and, second, the use of special tax measures under the individual and corporate income taxes to promote national economic objectives. The elasticity feature is not unusual for a progressive income tax in a

country with a high rate of economic growth. Tax preferences are not unusual in most countries, but the heavy emphasis that Japan places on special
tax measures to promote national objectives is unusual.

The elasticity of the Japanese individual income tax was on the order of
2.0 during the 1960s, as compared with about 1.4 for the U.S. individual income tax. The major reason for the difference is that the rate of growth of
money incomes was much higher in Japan than in the United States. With
personal exemptions at the same relative levels as those in Japan and the
higher progressivity that would be achieved without income splitting for married couples, the elasticity of the U.S. individual income tax would approach
that of the Japanese individual income tax—assuming the same rates of
growth of money income.

The built-in flexibility of the Japanese tax system could have been used
to good advantage to promote more stable growth. But this would have required forgoing or moderating tax reductions during boom periods to build
up reserves for larger tax reductions during recessions. There is little in the
record to suggest that the Japanese were interested in improving the countercyclical effectiveness of their tax policy in this way.

The special tax measures and other tax preferences illustrate the strong
orientation of the Japanese toward growth in their economic planning and
their faith in tax incentives as a method of stimulating desirable business
activity. In total, the erosion of the tax base through such preferences is much
larger in Japan than it is in the United States and most other developed countries (even though some of the special measures have been abolished in recent years). The few studies that have been made have concluded that the
tax preferences promoted modernization of plant and equipment in the steel
and machinery industries but had little influence either on savings of households or on investment in other industries. On the basis of the evidence, the
Japanese would probably be better off with a broader tax base and lower
nominal tax rates.

The Japanese are skillful administrators as well as tax planners. They administer their tax system at relatively low cost, partly because they are willing to accept inequities in the interest of simplification. Withholding is applied to a much greater variety of income receipts than in most countries,
and most property incomes are subject to flat rates that are not integrated
with the progressive rates on earned incomes. The law exempts the property
incomes of the vast majority of wage earners, who thus are able to discharge
their full liabilities through withholding and are not required to file returns.
The tax preferences do complicate the tax laws and sometimes raise difficult
administrative and compliance problems, but this burden is cheerfully ac-

cepted by the corporations and individuals who benefit from the tax preferences.

The inequality of the distribution of income before taxes is roughly the
same in Japan as it is in the United States and the United Kingdom. The tax
system is only mildly progressive and therefore has little effect on the relative
distribution of income. Data on wealth distribution do not exist, but the
death taxes are relatively ineffective (as they are in most countries) and
therefore do little to prevent an increasing concentration of wealth and economic power as the nation grows. The effect of this policy has not yet become evident to the Japanese people, but it may produce great social and
political strains if continued for long.

Appendix: Description of the Japanese Tax System

This appendix presents a brief description of the Japanese tax system as
it existed in 1974. For further details, the reader is referred to the excellent
annual volumes entitled *An Outline of Japanese Taxes,* published by the Tax
Bureau of the Ministry of Finance.

The Individual Income Tax

The income tax population is divided into two groups: wage and salary
workers with earnings of less than ¥8 million, and all other income recipients. Members of the first group, which includes the large majority of wage
and salary workers, do not file tax returns; instead, their taxes are withheld
during the year from their paychecks, and employers are required to make
any adjustments between withheld amounts and final tax liabilities in the last
paychecks of the year. All other taxpayers file tax returns within two and
one-half months following the end of the year and compute their tax due (or
refund) in a manner similar to that used in the United States. For incomes
earned in fiscal 1972, 26,370,000 wage earners discharged their tax liabilities
through their employers and only 4,900,000 other income recipients filed tax
returns.

The key to this relatively simple structure of tax payment is the virtual
exemption of small amounts of interest and dividends and the application of
a separate flat rate of tax on larger interest and dividend receipts. Interest
income from bank deposits, government bonds, and similar assets with principal value of less than ¥3 million is exempt from tax. Taxpayers may elect
to be taxed at a flat rate of 25 percent on their taxable interest receipts and

dividends or to add these receipts to their other income and be taxed at the regular individual income tax rates.

Special provisions apply to a number of income sources in addition to interest and dividends. Wage and salary workers receive a special deduction in order to put them on a more equal tax basis with proprietors, who are able to deduct personal expenses in the guise of business expenses. The deduction is 40 percent of the first ¥1.5 million, 30 percent of the next ¥1.5 million, 20 percent of the next ¥3 million, and 10 percent for amounts in excess of ¥6 million.

Capital gains on the sale of securities involving no more than fifty transactions of up to 200,000 shares a year are exempt from tax. Gains on real estate sales are taxed at a 20 percent rate if the property was held for more than five years and 40 percent if held for five years or less. However, gains on real estate held less than five years are subject to a tax of 110 percent of the tax computed by including the gain in taxable income if the tax so computed exceeds 40 percent. There is an ordinary deduction of ¥1 million for all taxable long-term capital gains. This deduction is increased substantially under certain circumstances: for example, to ¥17 million for long-term gains on the sale of a residence and ¥20 million for gains on property expropriated by a governmental unit.

Timber income and retirement income are taxed separately under the progressive rates, also after allowance for special deductions. For timber, the deduction is 20 percent of gross receipts (but not more than 50 percent of net income). For retirement income, the deduction is ¥4 million plus ¥400,000 a year for years of employment in excess of twenty. Only 50 percent of retirement income in excess of the special deduction is taxable.

There is a dividend credit of 10 percent if the dividends plus other income are less than ¥10 million, and the credit is reduced to 5 percent to the extent that the dividends and other income exceed ¥10 million.

Business income is taxable after allowance is made for all necessary expenses, but standard deductions are allowed in lieu of actual expenses for particular types of enterprises, varying up to 72 percent for the fees of physicians and dentists received through the health insurance system.[84] Wages paid to family employees are deductible as necessary business expenses unless they are unreasonably large. In addition, proprietors may elect to be taxed as quasi-corporations, in which case the proprietor may deduct his own remuneration, to which the special deduction for wage and salary income then applies.

84. The high standard deduction for physicians and dentists was introduced because the health insurance fees were fixed at what were considered to be unusually low levels.

Withholding applies to a much larger number of income sources than in the United States. In addition to wages, salaries, and employee bonuses, tax is withheld (at varying rates) from interest, dividends, professional fees, taxable prizes, and retirement income. Persons receiving income not subject to withholding pay about two-thirds of their estimated tax on July 31 and November 30 of the taxable year. Year-end payments are made when the final returns are filed.

To compute his final tax liability, the individual adds up his income from all taxable sources and then subtracts certain allowable deductions and personal exemptions to arrive at the amount of income that is subject to tax. The deductions include the special allowance for wages and salaries, medical expenses that exceed the lesser of 5 percent of income or ¥100,000, casualty losses that exceed 10 percent of income, social insurance premiums, life insurance and fire and casualty insurance premiums, and charitable contributions that exceed ¥10,000. The deductions are limited, however, to a maximum of ¥1 million for medical expenses, ¥50,000 for life insurance premiums, ¥3,000 for fire and casualty insurance premiums if the period of insurance is less than ten years and ¥15,000 if the period is ten years or more, and 25 percent of income for charitable contributions.

In 1974 the personal exemptions for the central government income tax were a flat ¥240,000 each for the individual, his or her spouse, and other dependents. The exemptions under the prefectural and municipal income taxes were ¥180,000 each for the taxpayer and spouse and ¥140,000 each for dependents. Exemptions are allowed under the national taxes only for a spouse whose income is not more than ¥200,000 from employment and retirement income, not more than ¥100,000 if it is income from assets, and not more than ¥100,000 if the income is from employment and assets. The corresponding limits for the local taxes are ¥150,000, ¥100,000, and ¥100,000, respectively. For a family of four, exemptions for national taxes were on the order of 40 percent of average family income, compared with 23 percent in the United States (assuming that average family income in 1974 was ¥2.4 million in Japan and $13,000 in the United States.) Including the special deduction for wages and salaries, the minimum taxable level was about 63 percent of average family income, compared to only 33 percent in the United States (assuming that the U.S. taxpayer uses the low-income allowance of $1,300 rather than itemizing deductions).

The central government's income tax rates begin at 10 percent on taxable incomes up to ¥600,000 and rise to a maximum of 75 percent above ¥80 million. The rates for the prefectural tax are 2 percent on the first ¥1.5 million of taxable income and 4 percent above that. The standard municipal tax

376   JOSEPH PECHMAN AND KEIMEI KAIZUKA

rates rise from 2 percent on the first ¥300,000 of taxable income to 14 percent above ¥50 million. These taxes are not deductible from the tax base of
any other, so that the top combined marginal rate on taxable incomes above
¥80 million is 93 percent (see Table 5-16)—but the total amount of income
tax paid cannot exceed 80 percent of taxable income. In cases in which this
limit applies, the adjustment must be made in the prefectural and municipal
taxes.

Table 5-16. *Tax Rates under the Japanese Individual Income Tax,
by Taxable Income Level, 1974*

Taxable income[a] (millions of yen)	Tax rates (percent)			
	Central government	Prefectural government	Municipal government	Total
Under 0.30	10	2	2	14
0.30–0.50	10	2	3	15
0.50–0.60	10	2	4	16
0.60–0.80	12	2	4	18
0.80–1.1	12	2	5	19
1.1–1.2	12	2	6	20
1.2–1.5	14	2	6	22
1.5–1.8	14	4	7	25
1.8–2.4	16	4	7	27
2.4–2.5	18	4	7	29
2.5–3.0	18	4	8	30
3.0–4.0	21	4	8	33
4.0–5.0	24	4	9	37
5.0–6.0	27	4	9	40
6.0–7.0	30	4	10	44
7.0–8.0	34	4	10	48
8.0–10.0	38	4	10	52
10.0–12.0	42	4	11	57
12.0–15.0	46	4	11	61
15.0–20.0	50	4	11	65
20.0–30.0	55	4	12	71
30.0–40.0	60	4	13	77
40.0–50.0	65	4	13	82
50.0–60.0	65	4	14	83
60.0–80.0	70	4	14	88
80.0 and over	75	4	14	93

Source: Tax Bureau, Ministry of Finance, *An Outline of Japanese Taxes, 1974* (Tokyo, 1974),
pp. 245, 259, 265–67.

a. Exemptions for the central government tax are not the same as the exemptions for the
prefectural and municipal taxes (see text). Hence, the taxable income for any particular individual
is not precisely the same under all three taxes. The effective rate of taxes paid to all levels of
government is limited to a maximum of 80 percent.

Prefectural and municipal income tax rates are uniform throughout the country. In addition to the tax based on the progressive rates, a per capita tax of ¥100 is levied by the prefectural governments. The standard per capita taxes levied by municipal governments are ¥600 for cities with a population of 500,000 or more, ¥400 for populations of 50,000 to 500,000, and ¥200 for other municipalities. These amounts can be increased by ¥200, ¥150, and ¥100, respectively, by the municipal governments.

The Corporate Income Tax

During the 1950s the corporate income tax was treated as if it were an advance payment on the shareholders' income taxes. Corporations were subject to a flat tax on their net profits (though since 1955 a reduced rate has applied to the profits of small corporations); and the shareholder-taxpayer was allowed a flat percentage of any dividends he received as a credit against his individual income tax. In keeping with this philosophy, intercorporate dividends were exempted from the corporate income tax. In 1961 the split-rate system used in Germany was substituted. Under this system, the tax rate on distributed earnings was reduced by approximately 25 percent and the dividend credit was lowered.

For 1974 the corporate income tax was levied by the central government at rates of 40 percent on undistributed profits and 30 percent on distributed profits. For corporations with capital of not more than ¥100 million, the tax rates on profits up to ¥7 million were 28 percent on undistributed profits and 22 percent on distributed profits. For accounting periods ending within two years on or after March 31, 1974, a 10 percent surtax is levied on the amount of corporate income that exceeds ¥500 million or 20 percent of paid-in capital, whichever is larger. Prefectures levied an enterprise tax of 12 percent of the net income of corporations (with reduced rates for small corporations). In addition, prefectures and municipalities levied a surtax, known as the inhabitants tax, on corporations; the standard surtax was 5.2 percent of the central government corporation income tax for prefectures and 12.1 percent for municipalities. Corporations with capital of more than ¥10 million also pay prefectural and municipal per capita taxes totaling ¥5,000; smaller corporations pay taxes of ¥3,000. The enterprise tax is allowed as a deduction for the purpose of computing the corporation income tax, but the inhabitants taxes are not.

Corporations are allowed to deduct the usual expenses that are incurred in conducting their business activities. Capital gains of corporations are subject to taxation in full. Inventories may be valued at cost or market value, whichever is lower, by any of a variety of cost methods, including first-in–first-out, last-in–first-out, most recent purchase, or the retail method. Depreciation, which is based on acquisition cost and relatively short useful lives, can be computed according to the declining-balance method or the straight-line method. To stimulate particular types of investments, accelerated depreciation, increased initial depreciation, and special tax-free reserves are allowed.

Aside from business costs, corporations are allowed to deduct contributions to governmental units and to public, scientific, and educational organizations approved by the Ministry of Finance. Contributions to other scientific, educational, and cultural organizations, as well as political and religious organizations, are deductible up to the total of 1.25 percent of profits and 0.125 percent of paid-in capital.

Expense accounts of employees for social and entertainment expenses—many of which are lavish—are deductible by business firms up to ¥4 million plus 0.1 percent of paid-in capital, if the deduction is supported by vouchers. Beyond this limit, only 25 percent of the expense accounts can be deducted.

Corporations file returns within two months after the end of their accounting period. Interim returns and tax payments are required for the first six months within eight months after the beginning of the period; the remaining tax is due when the final return is filed.

Taxes on Consumption

Few of the basic necessities of life are subject to sales or excise taxes in Japan. Food and clothing are completely free of tax, both at the national and local levels. Electricity and gas consumption are taxed at 6 percent and 5 percent rates, respectively, by local governments. Otherwise, the average person pays indirect taxes when he consumes alcoholic beverages or tobacco, when he purchases an automobile, furniture, or other consumer durables, and when he travels or goes to the theater.

Like most countries, Japan imposes specific taxes on alcoholic beverages, gasoline and aviation fuel, and playing cards. It also levies taxes on manufacturers' sales of automobiles, boats, and consumer durables; retailers' sales of precious stones and metals, pearls, fur products, and carpets; passenger travel on trains, buses, ships, and aircraft; restaurant meals and hotel bills; and admissions to motion picture theaters and sports events. Tobacco products, which are sold through a government corporation, are subject to a special municipal retail tax. Motor vehicles are taxed on the basis of their weight. There is also a wide variety of registration and license taxes, stamp taxes on

Table 5-17. *Illustrative Tax Rates Paid on Various Consumer Items in Japan, 1974*

Item	Percent of retail price including tax
Tobacco (Shinsei brand)	51.3
Beer	47.9
Whiskey (second class)	27.9
Sake (second class)	24.1
Small passenger automobile	9.9[a]
Small television set	8.7
Camera	8.7
Small refrigerator	8.5
Theater admission	4.8[b]

Source: Tax Bureau, Ministry of Finance, *An Outline of Japanese Taxes, 1973* (Tokyo, 1973), p. 267, and *1974* (1974), pp. 131, 145.
a. Not including local registration taxes.
b. For admissions of not more than ¥1,000.

documents for transfers of assets, and securities transactions taxes. Imports are subject to the commodity taxes, and exports are exempt. Commodities used for study or research also are exempt. Table 5-17 illustrates the range of excise taxes paid on various commodities and services.

Inheritance and Gift Taxes

The estate tax, first levied in Japan in 1905, was continued until 1950, when the accessions tax proposed by the Shoup Mission was adopted. The latter was repealed in 1953, and an inheritance and a gift tax were substituted. Under this system heirs and donees paid tax on the basis of the value of property they received. This meant that different distributions among the same number of heirs could cause substantial differences in tax, a situation that was regarded as undesirable.[85] The present system, which was adopted in 1958, combines elements of both the estate tax and the inheritance tax. The purpose of the revision was to equalize the tax on estates of the same size with the same number and types of heirs, regardless of how the estate was distributed among the heirs. A separate gift tax was retained when this revision was made.

The death tax is still paid by the heirs, but there is only a loose relation between the amounts they receive and their tax liabilities. The tax is com-

85. The official description of the Japanese tax system states that "In some cases, distribution was made only in an attempt to avoid tax." *An Outline of Japanese Taxes, 1974*, p. 107. No explanation is given of why this type of tax avoidance, which is the natural outcome of an inheritance tax, is contrary to public policy.

puted as follows: the estate is divided among the statutory heirs in accordance with percentages prescribed in the Civil Code. If an estate is divided between the spouse and lineal descendents, for example, the spouse receives one-third and the descendents two-thirds. If it is divided between the spouse and lineal ascendents, the estate is divided equally between the spouse and the ascendents. If it is divided between the spouse and brothers and sisters, the spouse receives two-thirds and the brothers and sisters one-third. The tax rates are then applied to each share computed in this way. The total tax on all the shares then is distributed among the heirs in proportion to the amounts they actually receive.

Since 1973 the inheritance tax has applied to estates with taxable values of more than ¥6 million plus ¥1.2 million for each statutory heir. An additional exemption of up to ¥6 million is allowed for a spouse who was married to the deceased for more than ten years, at a rate of ¥600,000 for each year of marriage beyond ten. Furthermore, the inheritance tax of such a spouse is limited to the ratio of the excess of the amount of property received over the inheritance prescribed by the Civil Code for such a spouse (at least ¥10 million plus ¥2 million for each year of marriage beyond ten years, up to a ¥30 million maximum). If an heir is under twenty years of age, his inheritance tax is reduced by ¥10,000 for each year under twenty. The inheritance tax is increased by 20 percent for heirs other than spouses, children, and parents.

The gift tax is imposed on the donee, with a basic exemption of ¥400,000 a year. In addition, a life-time allowance of ¥5.6 million is provided for gifts of residential property to a spouse who has been married to the donor for more than twenty years. If the donee receives taxable gifts of more than ¥200,000 from the same person within a period of three years, the gift tax is calculated by aggregating the annual gifts in excess of ¥200,000 within the three-year period, and the tax paid in the previous two years is credited against the cumulative tax.

The inheritance tax applies to all property acquired through inheritance, with the exception of life insurance and personal accident insurance acquired by an heir (up to a maximum of ¥1.5 million for each statutory heir) and retirement allowances received because of the death of the decedent (up to a maximum of ¥800,000 for each heir). Bequests and gifts to religious, charitable, educational, and scientific organizations are not subject to inheritance or gift taxes.

Inheritance and gift tax rates begin at 10 percent and rise to a maximum of 70 percent, but progression under the gift tax is much steeper than under the inheritance tax. The tax reaches 70 percent at ¥30 million under the gift

Table 5-18. *Inheritance and Gift Tax Rates in Japan, 1974*

Taxable inheritance (millions of yen)	Taxable gift (millions of yen)	Tax rates (percent)
Under 0.60	Under 0.30	10
0.60–1.50	0.30–0.50	15
1.50–3.0	0.50–0.70	20
3.0–5.0	0.70–1.0	25
5.0–8.0	1.0–1.40	30
8.0–12.0	1.40–2.0	35
12.0–18.0	2.0–3.0	40
18.0–30.0	3.0–4.0	45
30.0–50.0	4.0–7.0	50
50.0–75.0	7.0–10.0	55
75.0–100.0	10.0–15.0	60
100.0–150.0	15.0–30.0	65
150.0 and over	30.0 and over	70

Source: Tax Bureau, Ministry of Finance, *An Outline of Japanese Taxes, 1974* (Tokyo, 1974), pp. 110, 112.

tax and at ¥150 million under the inheritance tax (see Table 5-18). The steeper progression on gifts was adopted in lieu of a cumulative accessions tax that would have applied at a single set of rates to all gifts and bequests received by any individual during his life.

The Payroll Tax

Japan has a full complement of social security programs, including health insurance, old-age and disability pensions, survivors' benefits, unemployment compensation, and workmen's compensation.[86] Most of the programs, which are operated by the national government, are financed by equal contributions from employers and employees and by government subsidies. The contributions are in the form of taxes on the earnings of each employee up to a prescribed maximum. Because of the multiplicity and diversity of programs, the payroll taxes are not uniform among employees in different industries and even among employees in different firms in the same industry. As a partial substitute for the government plans, employers of 1,000 or more workers may establish their own wage-related pension plans if approved by a majority of the employees, the trade union, and the Ministry of Health and Welfare.

86. The benefits under these programs are not nearly as generous as those in other industrial countries. For a detailed description of the various plans and the methods of financing, see Social Insurance Agency, *Outline of Social Insurance in Japan* (Tokyo, 1972).

Such plans are also financed by employer-employee contributions and by a government subsidy. Payrolls of these firms are reduced by about 50 percent for purposes of payroll taxation, and their employees receive a flat government pension on retirement.

In 1973 the tax rate on the taxable earnings of workers employed in large enterprises was 2.87 percent for health insurance, 3.2 percent for males and 2.4 percent for females covered by employee pension insurance, and 0.65 percent for unemployment compensation. Employees pay the same tax rates, except for the health insurance contribution, which is 4.03 percent. Thus, the combined tax rate paid by employees and employers can run as high as 14.6 percent on a substantial portion of the earnings of an industrial employee.

The Property Tax

The property tax is reserved for use by the municipal governments, and it seems to be as badly administered as in most countries.[87] Valuations of land are supposed to be based on market value and those of buildings and equipment on replacement cost less depreciation. In practice, assessments are only a fraction of these values. The standard tax rate is 1.4 percent, but municipalities may raise their rates to a maximum of 2.1 percent. In 1964 municipalities were required to adopt valuation methods prescribed by the Ministry of Home Affairs, but transition provisions were adopted to avoid abrupt increases in assessed valuations.[88] These provisions are still in effect, and assessments still lag well behind the growth in values. Agricultural land is now assessed at no more than one-third of its market value, while urban real estate is assessed at no more than two-thirds of its market value.

87. The prefectures levy real estate transfer taxes of 3 percent of assessed values, but they have no annual real estate tax.

88. The assessment on agricultural land cannot exceed the assessment for fiscal 1963. The annual increases in the assessments on urban land are limited to specific percentages of the 1963 values: for example, 20 percent for land that is from three to eight times more valuable now than in 1963. The maximum annual percentage increase in assessments is 40 percent, but this applies to urban land that is twenty-five times more valuable than in 1963.

CHAPTER SIX

Japan and the World Economy

Lawrence B. Krause, Brookings Institution
and
Sueo Sekiguchi, Japan Economic Research Center

Tables

Figure

BECAUSE INTERNATIONAL trade and finance have played a central role in the evolution of the Japanese economy, an examination of these issues can shed considerable light on the workings of the economy as a whole. This chapter begins with a discussion of some characteristics of the Japanese experience that bear on Japan's economic relations with other countries.

The Japanese Economy: Some Traits

The history of Japan records many different crises that brought forth societal responses with certain similarities. Among these were the complete isolation of the Tokugawa period (beginning in 1603), the reopening of Japan with the Meiji Restoration (1868), the intensive stimuli of the Sino-Japanese War (1894–95), the Russo-Japanese War (1904–05) and World War I, and, finally, the period of military expansion and the mass destruction of World War II. Each of these challenges called for and permitted the government to take a central role in the direction and control of the economy, for massive resources were required that could not be assembled without government participation. Furthermore, the traditional insecurity of the Japanese people and their fear of dealing with foreigners could be assuaged only by the strong hand of the government. The period following World War II conforms to this pattern: it was up to the government then to take steps to bring order out of chaos. Within this historical context, the intervention of the government in the private economy, many instances of which still survive, should not be considered unusual. Whether the oil crisis that began in 1973 is another such challenge remains to be seen, but some form of government participation in the adjustment process would not be out of character.

The many-faceted participation of the government in the operations of the Japanese economy presents a difficult analytical problem. In a sense, the economic model is overdetermined: almost every economic event could be attributed to one or more governmental policies, yet other policies could be cited that seem to have an opposite thrust. More important, there would seem to be little left to be explained by private initiative and changes in exogenous economic conditions, but even casual observation confirms that a vigorous private economy does exist and that it does respond to the usual

Note. The authors wish to acknowledge especially the assistance of Hisao Kanamori, Ryūtarō Komiya, Masaya Miyoshi, Nobuyoshi Namiki, Yoshiro Kurisaka, and Kōichi Hosono.

385

Table 6-1. *Japanese Imports of Selected Raw Materials in Relation to Domestic Consumption and to Total OECD Imports, 1971*

Product	Japanese imports as a share of domestic consumption (percent)	Japanese imports as a share of total OECD imports (percent)	Ranking of Japan among OECD countries as an importer
Crude petroleum	99.7	15.9	1
Coal	58.4	41.0	1
Iron ore	99.3	42.3	1
Manganese ore	84.4	32.3	1
Copper ore	94.2	77.1	1
Zinc ore	78.5	31.2	1
Lead ore	100.0	26.4	1
Bauxite	100.0	12.3	3
Wool	100.0	22.6	1
Cotton	100.0	35.5	1
Rubber	27.4[a]	15.4	2

Sources: Bureau of Statistics, Office of the Prime Minister, *Monthly Statistics of Japan*, no. 143 (May 1973); OECD, *Trade by Commodities*, series C, vol. 1 (January–December 1971).
a. Imports of natural rubber as a percent of consumption of natural plus synthetic rubber.

economic forces. The steel industry, for example, was the object of numerous governmental policies to expand and rationalize production, yet there were private actions in the industry that went counter to government advice and direction.[1] To what, then, can one attribute the success of the Japanese steel industry? How can the effects of government actions be evaluated separately from those of the private sector? This analytical problem means that in any investigation, much must be left to the judgment of the observer.

The most striking characteristic of Japan that influences its economic relations with other countries is its almost total lack of domestic sources of raw materials. The natural resources such as petroleum, iron ore, coal, and nonferrous ores required for a modern economy must be imported. As Table 6-1 shows, Japan is almost totally dependent on imports for these and many other materials as well. Furthermore, with only limited arable land relative to its population, Japan also imports a substantial proportion of its foodstuffs, as shown in Table 6-2. While it is self-sufficient in rice, the staple of the Japanese diet, many other foods, particularly protein foods that are favored at higher income levels, must be imported either directly or indirectly through feed.

1. Eugene J. Kaplan, *Japan: The Government-Business Relationship* (U.S. Department of Commerce, 1972), pp. 138–50.

Table 6-2. *Ratio of Domestic Production to Consumption of Agricultural Products in Japan, Fiscal 1963, 1969, and 1972*

Percent

Agricultural product	Fiscal year		
	1963	1969	1972
Rice	99.3	117.0	90.7[a]
Wheat	38.2	14.5	5.3
Barley	87.3	47.5	14.6
Soybeans	21.0	4.7	3.6
Vegetables	100.1	99.4	98.8
Fruits	100.6	84.7	81.6
Dairy products	82.2	91.4	87.1
Meats (except whale)	94.6	82.9	80.7
Eggs	100.8	98.0	98.0
Sugar and sugar products	45.6	45.0	46.1
Fish	108.0	100.4	102.9
Other cereals (mainly feed)	11.9	1.7	1.0

Sources: For 1963 and 1969, Harry E. English and Keith A. J. Hay (eds.), *Obstacles to Trade in the Pacific Area*, Proceedings of the Fourth Pacific Trade and Development Conference (Ottawa: 1972), p. 60; for 1972, Ministry of Agriculture and Forestry, *Abstract of Statistics on Agriculture, Forestry, and Fisheries* (1973), p. 48.

a. In addition to current production, 12.7 percent of consumption was drawn out of existing stocks.

Dependence on foreigners for the necessities of life is the economic basis for a pervasive sense of national insecurity at all levels of Japanese society, even though the ratio of imports to gross national product is not as high as in many other countries. Occasional interruptions of supply by the deliberate actions of foreign countries, such as was recently the case with soybeans, steel scrap, and petroleum, reinforce this feeling. Before 1965, at cyclical peaks, as in 1953, 1957, and 1961, import dependence also was a constraint on economic growth, as export expansion was insufficient to pay for growing imports. This dependence of the whole economy on imports is so ingrained in the Japanese consciousness that there is a constant awareness of the foreign trade implications of both private and public actions. Furthermore, the society seems to be willing to protect providers of domestic resources, such as farmers, at an inordinate cost in high prices for foods, and to give special social recognition to successful exporters who earn the foreign exchange to pay for imports. Dependence on imported natural resources seems to provide a kind of unifying national challenge to the Japanese.

The impact of Japan's dependence on imports can also be quite strong in other countries. As shown in Table 6-1, Japan is one of the largest purchasers of raw materials in world markets, and for some products in Asian markets,

Japan is by far the largest buyer. For example, Japan bought about 60 percent of Burmese rubber exports and 90 percent of Philippine copper ore exports in 1971. Japanese traders thus have particularly great influence in setting world prices of commodities. This was demonstrated during 1972–73 in the world wool market, for instance, where speculative Japanese purchases were crucial.[2]

Supplying countries, many of which are small relative to Japan, also feel insecure because of their export dependence on Japan. Indeed, the many dimensions of their economic dependence on Japan makes some of these countries fear becoming "client states." Because of the special character of natural resources—whether nonreplaceable ones such as ores or slowly replaceable ones like timber—Japanese purchases can cause nationalistic reactions and even hostility in the supplying countries, particularly because Japan has tended to purchase raw materials at a lower stage of processing than have other developed countries.[3] While these sentiments are not necessarily rational, they lead to tensions in Japan's relations with these countries.

Economic performance in Japan also depends on the quality of its people. Japan has a long history of universal education. Its excellent primary and secondary school system has created a totally literate population and one that is well disciplined and ideally suited for modern industrial activity. The entrepreneurial skills of the Japanese have developed over many decades and have allowed them to organize and adopt modern technology with extraordinary facility. It is human skills that have enabled Japan to overcome its natural resources deficiency and to reach its present high stage of economic development.

Japanese participation in international trade reflects an interplay between these two basic characteristics: Japan's need to import natural resources and Japan's ability to export the product of human resources. The welfare gains that Japan obtains from international commerce over time reflect in part the terms of trade between natural and human resources. While short-term movements have at times favored natural resources, the longer-run trends have been toward human resources, to the benefit of Japan.

---

2. It is estimated that the Japanese textile industry could absorb 2.3 million bales of wool a year, but Japanese traders purchased over 3 million bales during the first half of 1973. Chase Manhattan Bank, *Business in Brief,* no. 112 (October 1973), p. 2.

3. For example, Japan imported $769 million worth of copper in 1971, of which 58.6 percent was in the crudest form of ores and concentrates, 40.6 percent in intermediate products, and only 0.8 percent in worked copper and copper alloys. In contrast, of the $754 million worth of copper imported by Germany in 1971, only 5.0 percent was in crude form, while 79.9 percent was in intermediates and 15.1 percent in advanced forms. Similarly, for France the percentages in 1971 were 0.2 percent in crude, 85.5 percent in intermediate, and 14.3 percent in advanced forms.

General Trading Companies

The Japanese general trading company (*sōgō shōsha*) epitomizes Japan's unique ability to use its entrepreneurial skills to promote the extraordinary growth of the postwar period. The origin of Japanese general trading companies goes back to the early Meiji period when the government, in an attempt to avoid foreign economic domination of the kind that befell China, encouraged Japanese companies to replace the foreign firms then controlling Japanese trade.[4] The need for specialized trading companies grew out of the ignorance of the Japanese of foreign markets, their lack of knowledge of foreign languages, and their desire to become a participant in the world economy. Some of these trading firms grew into the large family-controlled business groups called *zaibatsu*. Although *zaibatsu* were dissolved during the U.S. occupation following World War II, the trading companies as a whole prospered and grew, partially through mergers, and new firms entered the field. While there may be as many as 6,000 trading companies today, ten major firms dominate the field.

Functions

A distinctive characteristic of the general trading company is the number of products that it handles—as many as 20,000 individual items—and the major function it performs is marketing and distributing these products. The trading firms maintain resident offices in the principal cities around the world, and the largest have nearly one hundred foreign locations.[5] These offices gather business information of all kinds and indeed operate a kind of internal intelligence network. Since there is clearly an economy of scale in intelligence gathering, the general trading company has certain advantages over individual manufacturers marketing their own products. Recognizing that their success rests on the quality of their employees, the trading firm is often willing to make large investments in training them. New college graduates are trained at home and abroad in business subjects, foreign languages, and other skills. It may well be a number of years before a new employee begins to make a significant contribution to the firm.

This training is put to use in seeking out sources of supply of raw materials, food, and specialized machinery needed in Japan and, more recently, of

4. Japan External Trade Organization, *Using Trading Companies in Exporting to Japan*, JETRO Marketing Series no. 2, p. 6.

5. Morihisa Emori, "Japanese General Trading Companies: Their Functions and Roles," in Pierre Uri (ed.), *Trade and Investment Policies for the Seventies: New Challenges for the Atlantic Area and Japan* (Praeger, 1971), pp. 111–24.

consumer products either not available or excessively priced by Japanese producers. The trading companies also seek new outlets abroad for the manufactured products made in Japan. Another rapidly expanding part of their business encompasses third country trade—that is, the promotion of trade between two countries other than Japan—an activity that has constituted about 10 percent of total sales in recent years. Illustrations of third country trade include the marketing of Indonesian timber in Western Europe and of U.S. machines in Malaysia and Romania.[6] In addition to marketing, the trading companies arrange for the transportation, insurance, and warehousing (a particularly difficult problem in land-scarce Japan) of the products they handle. The trading company thus performs a comprehensive service for its customers.

The general trading company also functions as a financial intermediary: it borrows big and lends small. Much of the strength of the trading company comes from its banking connections through which it borrows large amounts of money. Each of the ten leading trading companies is closely associated with one or more of the thirteen large city banks. Using its borrowing power to obtain money at relatively low interest rates, the trading company lends money to the small businesses with which it deals. The trading company has knowledge of the creditworthiness of the small firms and thus is in a position to provide small loans at low cost, which banks find it difficult to do. The loans are generally tied to specific uses and often take the form of providing imported raw materials on credit, financing new equipment or even buildings on a long-term basis, or prepayment on export sales before delivery to the foreign buyer. The trading firm might also endorse the note of a small business to enable it to obtain bank credit. When money is tight, the trading firm is in a secure position because it is a valued customer of the bank and thus can cushion credit stringency for small firms. Nevertheless, small firms can be put in a severe financial squeeze, and trading firms often come to their rescue through the purchase of equity shares of their businesses. If bankruptcy should occur, the trading company may take part of the equity in a reorganization and recapitalization of the firm. Trading companies may also buy equity shares of large firms, but generally in small amounts and only to solidify business ties.[7]

Closely related to their financing function is the ability of trading firms

---

6. Alexander K. Young, "Internationalization of the Japanese General Trading Companies," *Columbia Journal of World Business* (Spring 1974), pp. 78–86.

7. The six largest trading companies together own 2 to 3 percent of the equity shares of the corporations listed on the first section of the Tokyo stock exchange, according to a study of the Foreign Trade Council and reported in the *Japan Times,* July 4, 1974.

to absorb foreign exchange risks for their customers. For instance, they can make commitments to buy products from a Japanese producer in yen even though the export sales contract is in dollars. They are able to do this because they handle both import and export transactions and can thus internally off-set exchange losses with gains. Absorbing exchange rate risk is a valuable service, particularly since the change to the new international system of exchange rates, in which the rates are managed by monetary authorities but float in response to market forces and there are continuous movements in the spot rate. This is especially important in Japan, where exchange controls instituted by the Bank of Japan limit participation in exchange markets in a way that has inhibited the development of the forward market and thus made it difficult to hedge against foreign exchange risks. Since the trading companies, on balance, import more than they export, they are more exposed when the yen weakens than when it strengthens. Of course, since they are at the center of both import and export transactions the trading firms can speculate in exchange markets, which their international intelligence network may make it profitable to do, even though exchange controls supposedly limit such speculation. Theoretically the trading firms also could cover their net foreign exchange risk in the forward market, but in practice this is impossible because of the many currencies in which they deal and the various timings of payments and receipts. Thus, the trading company can hardly avoid being a speculator in foreign exchange; the only question is the degree and the aggressiveness of such speculation.

Trading companies are also described as having an organizing function. While this function falls primarily within the domestic economy, such as encouraging production of new products for internal consumption, trading firms also provide technical advice to help small- or medium-size firms produce new products, all or part of which are exported. An unusual characteristic of the Japanese economy that can be attributed to the presence of trading companies is the existence of small manufacturing firms specializing in exporting. In Japan, as elsewhere, however, large firms on average export a larger share of their output than small ones and thus produce most exports and, over time, an increasing share of exports.[8]

The trading firms have a business strategy that is based on the very long view, in part because many of the giants of the industry have been in continuous operation for over one hundred years. Thus they are prepared to make

8. William V. Rapp, "Firm Size and Japan's Export Structure: A Micro-View of Japan's Changing Export Competitiveness since Meiji" (paper prepared for a conference on Industrialization and Its Consequences for Modern Japan, June 1974; processed).

substantial investments in investigating the prospects for new products and even new industries that are emerging in other countries. Since the government through the Ministry of International Trade and Industry (MITI) has been interested in introducing advanced industries into Japan and has provided much information to this end, a symbiotic relationship has developed between the government and the large trading companies.

Finally, general trading companies have an important role in the direct foreign investment activities of Japanese companies and in investment by foreigners in Japan. Because of their access to information and their business connections in other countries, the trading companies are in a good position to ferret out profitable investment possibilities for Japanese firms and arrange joint ventures with local participants. Small firms in particular depend on the trading companies to assist them in setting up investments abroad. The trading companies are not of great help to large manufacturers of sophisticated products, however, who generally are able to invest abroad by themselves. Foreign investment in Japan has also been promoted by the trading companies; the combination of participation in Japanese distribution channels and knowledge of Japanese firms allows the trading companies to participate in joint ventures with foreign partners.

Importance in Foreign Trade

The significance of the general trading companies in the Japanese economy is reflected in the large share of international trade that they handle. As

Table 6-3. *Share of Total Japanese Exports and Imports of the Ten Largest Japanese Trading Companies,*[a] *1963–72*
Percent

Year	Exports	Imports
1963	50	62
1964	52	64
1965	52	64
1966	52	64
1967	51	65
1968	51	64
1969	47	63
1970	48	65
1971	51	62
1972	51	63

Source: Research Department, Mitsui and Co., as cited in Alexander K. Young, "Internationalization of the Japanese General Trading Companies," *Columbia Journal of World Business* (Spring 1974), p. 81.

a. The ten largest firms are Mitsubishi, Mitsui, Marubeni, C. Itoh, Sumitomo Shōji, Nisshō Iwai, Tōyō Menka, Kanematsu Goshō, Ataka, and Nichimen Jitsugyō.

Table 6-3 shows, the share of the ten largest trading firms in Japanese trade was about 50 percent of exports and over 60 percent of imports. These shares have remained relatively stable over the period 1963–72, during which Japanese trade expanded fourfold. This should not be interpreted to mean that no change has taken place in the way Japanese goods are exported. In fact, manufacturers increased their direct sales from 22 percent of exports in 1963 to 30 percent in 1972, but the gain of manufacturers was at the expense of smaller trading firms and specialized wholesalers rather than the largest general trading companies. At 1973 levels of trade, these shares imply that the ten largest trading firms did $19 billion in export and $25 billion in import business. When one adds the approximately $8 billion in third country trade of these companies, the total exceeds the amount of international trade of most countries in the world.

These aggregate figures do not reveal the concentration by the largest trading firms in certain commodity classifications. Between 1963 and 1972, as shown in Table 6-4, these firms were quite active in the export of metals and metal products and textiles and chemicals, but were minor participants in the export of food and tobacco and other items. It is on the import side, however, where the concentration is more extreme. The largest firms have a commanding position in each category of raw materials, and they justify their existence by providing the raw materials needed by Japan at reasonable prices. If one were to use a finer product breakdown, no doubt one would find that certain raw materials are handled exclusively by these firms; for instance, they import 90 percent of all soybeans. Even the large manufacturers, who, as noted

Table 6-4. *Share of Exports and Imports of the Ten Largest Japanese Trading Companies,*[a] *by Commodity, Fiscal 1971*
Percent

Commodity	Exports	Imports
Food and tobacco	45.9	58.7
Textiles and textile materials	56.1	60.5
Wood, pulp, and paper	38.6	69.8
Animal and plant products	43.6	59.4
Coal, petroleum	31.3	41.8
Chemical products	51.1	34.1
Ferrous metals, metal products, and ores	68.0	81.0
Nonferrous metals and ores	26.5	44.3
Machinery	42.8	39.2
Other	11.0	50.9

Source: Ministry of International Trade and Industry, *Bōeki gyōtai tōkeihyō* [Statistics on Foreign Trade by Categories of Firms], edition for fiscal 1971.
a. The original data are classified by value of trade and coincide approximately with the ten largest trading companies.

394   LAWRENCE KRAUSE AND SUEO SEKIGUCHI

above, took a greater role in exporting their own products, have been content to rely on trading firms for imported raw materials.

Gains and Risks for Japan

There is little doubt that the large general trading companies have captured the economies of scale in international commerce and thereby perform a valuable, indeed a critical, service for Japan, since the country is dependent on imported raw materials to sustain a high standard of living. Furthermore, the service must have been performed rather well or Japanese producers would have found an alternative to dealing with the large firms. The trading companies have provided a flexible business organization to meet the evolving opportunities and challenges in international commerce. They were not able to protect the society from the oil crisis or the soybean embargo in the short run, but they no doubt will have a hand in working out longer-run solutions.

The risks to Japan of relying so heavily on a few companies to handle its international commerce lie in the lack of competitors and its implications for the quality of competition in the market. One must ask whether the oligopolistic nature of the market provides enough effective competition to protect society. Insufficient competition might be manifested in unexplained (perhaps even contrived) shortages, price instability, and excessive profits. Another area of concern might be the degree of power that these companies have over small businesses and in society in general. Even without evidence of abuse of power, these risks are real ones.

There is some assurance, however, that gross abuses could not be longlasting. First, there are literally thousands of trading firms, and entry is rather easy for new firms. Second, manufacturers and large retailers do have the option of dealing directly in international commerce rather than utilizing a trading company. The large trading companies have obtained their dominant positions by exploiting economies of scale, and if they did not share the benefits with their customers other firms would have entered the market and become viable competitors. Nevertheless, critics have claimed that the large firms have taken unfair advantage of such emergency situations as the oil crisis, and there has been enough concern to initiate an investigation by the Diet and some official condemnation.

The evidence of the effect of the large trading firms on the prices of internationally traded goods is anecdotal in nature and thus only suggestive at best. On the export side, the trading firms claim that generally they do not make pricing decisions but only set commission fees, and that competition among firms keeps these fees from being excessive. However, the trading companies no doubt advise producers on an appropriate selling price, advice that could lead to widespread price cuts on exports at times of business weakness in Japan. With respect to the importation of raw materials, most products are standardized and prices are set in world markets; but Japanese purchases loom so large in world trade that the behavior of the trading companies can have an effect on world prices. It has been noted that one trading firm tends to emulate another in follow-the-leader fashion. For example, if one company, thinking a product is in short supply, makes anticipatory purchases, the others will follow suit, causing an excess of quantity requirements, rapid escalation of prices, and market instability; ultimately the excess must be sold back into the market, causing a collapse of the price. In this way world market price instability can be exaggerated by the inventory policy of these ten Japanese firms. (It should also be noted that, as in other kinds of speculation, the leader in the market makes profits at the expense of the followers.)

The question of whether the major trading firms are making excessive profits is a difficult one because there is no obvious standard of comparison. Table 6-5 shows some profit comparisons. If current profits in relation to total assets are taken as the appropriate measure of rate of return, the trad-

Table 6-5. *Profit Rates of Japanese General Trading Companies, Manu-facturers, and All Industries, 1962–71*
Percent

	Profit/total asset rates[a]			Profit/owned capital rates[b]		
Year	Trading companies	Manu-facturers	All industries	Trading companies	Manu-facturers	All industries
1962	1.15	4.70	3.93	16.84	15.06	13.92
1963	1.27	5.35	4.40	18.76	17.94	16.32
1964	0.72	4.68	3.96	16.76	16.93	15.68
1965	0.98	3.41	3.10	17.69	13.02	12.82
1966	0.89	4.86	4.05	17.82	19.14	17.41
1967	0.96	5.90	4.68	21.48	24.38	21.24
1968	0.90	5.63	4.58	22.66	24.84	22.06
1969	1.01	6.24	5.04	25.12	26.94	24.52
1970	1.00	5.34	4.34	25.20	23.45	21.82
1971	1.10	3.26	2.92	29.10	14.88	15.44

Source: MITI, *Wagakuni kigyō no keiei bunseki* [Analysis of Financial Statements of Japanese Main Enterprises], various issues.

a. Current profits before tax divided by total assets.

b. Current profits before tax divided by the sum of retained earnings reserved plus paid-in capital plus net profit after tax before dividends. Annual figure is an arithmetic average of semi-annual reports.

ing companies' average rate of about 1 percent is much lower than that of manufacturing firms and than the average rate for all industries. It must be recognized, however, that a much larger proportion of trading company assets is invested in short-term uses such as inventories, accounts receivable, and so forth, than is true for other kinds of firms. As a result, trading companies normally borrow against a much larger share of their total assets than even the highly leveraged manufacturing firms. If the rate of return is measured against owned capital, the trading companies appear to be quite profitable and in line with manufacturers and all industry totals. Not surprisingly, there is some tendency for trading firm profits to be less cyclically sensitive than manufacturers' profits. All three categories tend to show some rise in profit rates over the period 1962 to 1971. Since the trading companies do not stand out in this comparison as being unusually profitable, one cannot conclude that they were making excessive profits.[9]

The source of some of the power of the trading companies in society at large, and particularly with respect to small business, is in their dual role as buyers and sellers of products and also as financiers. One remedy for excessive power would be to separate these functions. This would require an elaboration of the Japanese capital market to improve credit and mortgage facilities for small businesses that would necessitate a much larger number of independent banks than now operate in Japan. The fact that there is little criticism of the trading companies by small business suggests that the potential problem has not in fact materialized. Furthermore, that there is little pressure for capital market reform may indicate that the government does not consider the problem of excessive power to be very serious.

Why Are Trading Companies Unique to Japan?

It is striking that trading companies have prospered and reached a commanding position only in Japan and not in other countries. Some countries such as Canada and Mexico have studied the trading company, and Mexico even asked Japan to provide technical assistance in their development, but trading firms have not yet attained elsewhere the power they have in Japan. The explanation seems to be that the combination of factors required for trading companies to be successful is found in Japan and not in other countries. While Japan has taken major steps in forging ties with the rest of the world, it is still a rather isolated country with a lingering distrust of foreigners. Geographically, Japan, itself a series of islands, is remote from other

---

9. It may well be, however, that the 1973–74 period will show unusual profits, as some critics claim. Also it is assumed that discretionary reserve accumulations do not bias these comparisons.

major countries and its language bears no close relationship to others (except written Chinese). This means that knowledge of foreign markets is still quite difficult to obtain in Japan, although foreign commerce is necessary to sustain the economy, and similarly it is difficult for foreigners to obtain knowledge of the Japanese market. In contrast, in most other countries information is easily available, particularly in European and Latin American countries that are part of a large land mass. Furthermore, most countries have cultural ties with at least a few others, while Japan has weak ties only with China, which date from such an early period as to have little commercial significance today. Thus the need for trading companies is greater in Japan than elsewhere.

Second, Japanese entrepreneurial talents are well developed, a requirement for the successful running of the intricate business of these multifaceted companies. In some other countries that might profit from domestic trading firms, the entrepreneurial skills are lacking, and those that exist are used to better effect in domestic production. In such countries merchandising and distribution in foreign markets are often left to the many foreign firms willing to undertake them. The great organizational capacity of the Japanese comes in part from extensive training, but also may be due to cultural traits developed as a response to the necessity of living a disciplined and organized life on a crowded island.

Third, it appears that the Japanese, more than other peoples, concentrate on the promotion of economic efficiency and are willing to sacrifice other social goals such as income distribution and protection of the natural environment in its interest. As long as the major companies that prosper under this policy do not exploit their position of power, society benefits from their activities. The Japanese on the one hand have faith in the superiority of privately owned business in organizing economic activity, and on the other hand they believe that the government bureaucracy is capable of providing corrective measures if these companies should begin to get out of hand. In most other countries, a need for the functions performed by the very large and powerful Japanese trading companies would be filled by the government itself and not left to private initiative. Thus it is unlikely that an exact replica of the Japanese *sōgō shōsha* will prosper in other environments that are less hospitable to the concentration of power in private hands.

Japanese Growth and the International Economy

Four pertinent questions arise with respect to the relation between Japanese economic growth and the international economy:

• Has Japanese growth been export led?

- How has Japan's real welfare been affected by the commodity terms of trade?
- How can balance-of-payments equilibrium be maintained in view of Japan's growth relative to the rest of the world?
- How has growth affected the structure of Japan's comparative advantage in international trade?

Export-Led Growth?

The relation between the economic growth of Japan and international trade is a complicated one. Foreign trade has played a strategic and possibly critical role in economic growth, but not the role sometimes portrayed, in which large Japanese firms produce highly manufactured products entirely or principally for foreign markets. In a Japan heavily dependent on imported raw materials, economic growth could not proceed without increases in imports, and exports are needed to pay for them. Furthermore, export competitiveness became a goal of government policy and private investment behavior. Since the industries that are able to export are also the ones with the highest rates of productivity increase, economic growth has been generated in practice through structural shifts toward industries that export a sizable portion of their output. In addition, although foreign demand at times of cyclical recoveries has been of great importance in encouraging output, most of the time Japanese growth has been stimulated by domestic demand.

A full discussion of the sources of Japanese growth is found in Chapter 2, but the export-led growth hypothesis, as applied to some European countries, is important in the context of this chapter. The concept of export-led growth has been used in economic literature in three different ways: first as a descriptive concept; second as a positive or analytical concept; and third as a normative concept and policy prescription.

In purely descriptive terms, Japanese growth has been export led in that exports grew faster than the gross national product (GNP), particularly in recent years. Between 1961 and 1970, when real GNP was growing at a 9.5 percent compound annual rate, real exports were growing at a 14.7 percent rate. As can be seen in Table 6-6, exports of goods and services in current prices in relation to current-priced GNP stayed fairly stable at about 10 to 11 percent from 1955 to 1972. This level is rather low compared to Japan's prewar rate of about 20 percent, although higher than the U.S. rate, which averaged 7.2 percent in 1972–73. The picture changes, however, when the differential trend in prices is recognized: the GNP price deflator has risen more than the export price deflator. By the constant price measure shown in

Table 6-6. *Japanese Exports in Relation to Gross National Product, 1955–73*

Year	Exports of goods and services as percent of gross national product		Balance on current account as percent of GNP (current prices)	Indexes of exports of manufactures relative to manufacturing production (1970 = 100)
	Current prices	1965 prices		
1955	12.8	7.6	1.6	83.0
1960	11.4	9.1	0.4	74.0
1961	9.7	8.4	−1.8	67.2
1962	10.1	9.3	0.0	73.3
1963	9.6	9.0	−1.1	76.4
1964	10.0	9.6	−0.5	81.9
1965	11.2	11.2	1.1	101.7
1966	11.3	11.7	1.4	105.1
1967	10.2	11.0	0.0	91.4
1968	10.7	11.8	0.9	98.4
1969	11.3	12.6	1.4	99.4
1970	11.6	13.2	1.1	100.0
1971	12.5	14.6	2.6	117.5
1972	11.4	14.4	2.4	117.4
1973	10.8	13.9	0.0	104.8

Sources: Statistics Department, Bank of Japan, *Economic Statistics of Japan, 1965* (March 1966); idem, *Economic Statistics Annual,* various issues; Economic Planning Agency, *Annual Report on National Income Statistics, 1970.*

the table, the export share of GNP has risen noticeably. The increases occurred in a cyclical pattern, rising during periods of domestic slowdown.

There is also evidence of export-led growth in the relation of manufactured exports to output (see Table 6-6). Exports of manufactures have risen relative to production, particularly in recent years. A cyclical pattern emerges, with the export share falling, then rising, then falling again. There was a pronounced trend toward increase between 1967 and 1972, when exports rose in periods of both rapid and slower growth. But in the same descriptive sense that Japanese growth can be said to be export led, it has also been led by business fixed investment, government investment, housing investment, and even imports, since these components of GNP also grew more rapidly than the average. Clearly the concept has little value in its purely descriptive form.

Export-led growth as a positive or analytical concept is of much greater interest.[10] In this sense, the concept relates economic growth to an exogenous disturbance in the export sector such as the wheat boom in Canada in 1901–

10. As used, for instance, by Richard E. Caves, "Export-Led Growth and the New Economic History," in Jagdish N. Bhagwati and others (eds.), *Trade, Balance of Payments and Growth* (North Holland, 1971), pp. 403–42.

11 or the oil boom in Ecuador beginning in 1973. Such a disturbance leads to a rise in economic rent and in real income that is quite distinct from that caused by higher productivity in domestic production resulting from larger investments in human or physical capital. For this concept to be applicable there must be an identifiable source of external disturbance and a Japanese response mechanism to translate the disturbance into domestic growth. There is little question that Japan had the response mechanism, but identifying the external disturbance is another matter. Caves suggested a simple test to distinguish an external from a domestic disturbance: if the disturbance arises predominantly from external demand, then price and export quantity changes should be positively correlated; if the disturbance arises from shifts in domestic supply, the correlation would be negative. By this test Japanese growth was clearly *not* export led for most of the 1960s since the price index for exports was 92.0 in 1961 and remained virtually unchanged through 1968, when it was 92.9 despite the massive increase in export volume of 232 percent (see Table 6-7).[11] From 1968 through 1971 there was a distinct change. Not only did Japanese export volume *and* prices rise, but a balance-of-payments surplus developed. This was the period of price inflation in the United States caused by the Vietnam War, and Japan's growth might well be described as export led in this short period since exports to the United States grew unusually rapidly.

Export-led growth as a normative concept has been endorsed by Nicholas Kaldor as an element of British policy.[12] According to this prescription, a country such as Great Britain can best raise its growth rate by stimulating exports through subsidizing them or simply undervaluing the exchange rate. Japanese experience is instructive in this regard. While Japan has had many policies that in one way or another promoted exports or inhibited imports, these policies were operative throughout the entire postwar period and were if anything being moderated when the period of export-led growth started in 1969. The closest that Japan came to a policy stance in favor of export-led growth was actually the result of a negative policy—the refusal to revalue the yen when it became undervalued, an issue that is discussed at length below. As a result of this refusal, Japan's economic and political relations with its economic partners suffered, and in general it became a very unhappy time for Japanese foreign relations. What this suggests is that a large industrial

---

11. The Caves test would not pick up those instances of export-led growth triggered by discovery of an exportable commodity such as oil, but the omission is not relevant for Japan.

12. "Conflicts in National Economic Objectives," *Economic Journal*, vol. 81 (March 1971), pp. 1–16.

Table 6-7. *Indexes of Japanese Export, Import, and Manufacturing Prices,*
1955–74

1970 = 100

Year	Export price index (1)	Import price index (2)	Commodity terms of trade (1) ÷ (2) (3)	Wholesale price index for manu-factures (4)	Gross processing margin (4) ÷ (2) (5)	Manufacturing[a] Input prices	Output prices
1955	99.8	111.1	89.8	91.1	82.0	n.a.	n.a.
1960	95.9	94.0	102.0	92.0	97.9	n.a.	n.a.
1961	92.0	94.3	97.6	92.1	97.7	n.a.	n.a.
1962	89.1	91.5	97.4	90.2	98.6	n.a.	n.a.
1963	91.3	94.1	97.0	91.2	96.9	n.a.	n.a.
1964	92.6	95.6	96.9	91.2	95.4	n.a.	n.a.
1965	92.0	93.2	98.7	91.2	97.9	n.a.	n.a.
1966	92.1	95.1	96.8	92.8	97.6	n.a.	n.a.
1967	92.5	94.2	98.2	93.9	99.7	100.0	100.0
1968	92.9	94.6	98.2	94.2	99.6	98.2	100.1
1969	95.4	96.8	98.6	95.9	99.1	100.2	102.0
1970	100.0	100.0	100.0	100.0	100.0	105.0	106.1
1971	100.7	100.0	100.7	98.9	98.9	101.3	105.1
1972	97.8	95.7	102.2	99.8	104.2	102.0	106.5
1973	106.6	115.8	92.1	114.8	99.1	125.3	124.0
1974[b]	141.6	192.4	73.6	144.4	[75.0]	...	...

Sources: Statistics Department, Bank of Japan, *Economic Statistics of Japan, 1965* (March 1966); idem, *Economic Statistics Annual, 1972,* p. 72, and *1973,* pp. 267, 271, 274; idem, *Economic Statistics Monthly* (June 1974), p. 151; Bureau of Statistics, Office of the Prime Minister, *Japan Statistical Yearbook, 1967,* p. 372.

n.a. Not available.

a. 1967 = 100. Input covers purchasing transactions of currently consumed raw materials, fuels, and energy; output covers selling transactions of produced goods (including semifinished goods).

b. Data are through June, except for col. (4), which is through May.

country such as Japan or Great Britain cannot promote export-led growth without destabilizing the international system of which it is a part, although the same might not be true for a less developed country whose impact on the world economy would be much less.

Even though Japanese growth in the main has not been export led in the analytical sense, it does not mean that exports were unimportant to growth. Export expansion has been of strategic importance principally because it has financed the growing imports of raw materials and capital goods that embody new technology.[13] A further effect of export growth was to permit greater expansion of certain industries that could capture larger economies of scale, but

13. Tuvia Blumenthal, "Exports and Economic Growth: The Case of Postwar Japan," *Quarterly Journal of Economics,* vol. 86 (November 1972), pp. 617–31.

domestic sales were much the greater part of total output of these industries, so the stimulus to growth was mainly domestic in origin. Masahiro Tatemoto has suggested that exports cannot be distinguished from domestic sources of growth such as plant and equipment expenditures since both contribute to business profits that perpetuate the growth process.[14] The Japanese government was obviously aware of the strategic nature of exports and devised policies that could be described as export capturing, if not export leading.

Another way in which exports are related to growth can be seen in the current account balance relative to GNP, as shown in Table 6-6. It is possible that a rise in net exports provided a Keynesian stimulus to domestic growth, but little evidence of this can be found. A trend toward external stimulation developed after 1967, but the magnitude was small relative to the growth of the economy and, therefore, little weight can be assigned to it.

Commodity Terms of Trade, Welfare, and Economic Growth

A great deal of attention has been paid in economic literature to the consequences of an adverse trend in the commodity terms of trade of a country—that is, its export prices divided by its import prices. The issue was first raised by Hans W. Singer, and he argued in 1949 that less developed countries were suffering in international trade because the prices of the raw materials they produce (and export) decline relative to the prices of industrial products they import.[15] The issue is particularly relevant to Japan since it imports primarily raw materials and exports almost exclusively manufactured products.

A distinction must be drawn between the price changes caused by domestic forces and those triggered externally. If a deterioration in the commodity terms of trade occurs because of a domestic development such as an increase in the domestic supply curve, domestic welfare may not deteriorate and domestic growth may not be inhibited. In contrast, if the deterioration occurs

---

14. "Stabilization Policy in Japan and Its Relations to Economic Instability in the World" (paper presented at the International Seminar in Public Economics, Williamstown, Mass., June 10, 1974; processed).

15. "The Distribution of Gains between Investing and Borrowing Countries," *American Economic Review*, vol. 40 (May 1950, *Papers and Proceedings*, 1949), pp. 473–85. Recent developments in the literature are discussed in Richard E. Caves and Ronald W. Jones, *World Trade and Payments: An Introduction* (Little, Brown, 1973). For a theoretical and empirical study related to Japan, see Ken'ichi Inada, Sueo Sekiguchi, and Yasutoyo Shōda, *Keizai hatten no mechanism: sono riron to jisshō* [The Mechanism of Economic Development: A Theory and Its Empirical Test] (Tokyo: Sobunsha, 1972). For a theoretical elaboration in a dynamic model, see Ken'ichi Inada, "Development in Monocultural Economies," *International Economic Review*, vol. 12 (June 1971), pp. 161–85.

because of a foreign development such as a fall in a foreign demand curve, then both welfare and growth will be adversely affected. Similarly, domestic welfare and growth are stimulated if the commodity terms of trade rise because of developments abroad.

As shown in Table 6-7, the commodity terms of trade improved for Japan between 1955 and 1960, and economic welfare was probably enhanced by it, particularly because the change was caused in great measure by declines in import prices. Since the balance of payments acted as a constraint on growth during this period, the improvement in the terms of trade also permitted Japan to grow faster.[16] After a downward adjustment in 1960, the terms of trade remained stable for the rest of the decade (with some slight improvement after 1966) despite the dramatic increases in domestic supply curves during those years. A deterioration would not have hurt either welfare or growth, so stability can be considered a very favorable sign—it indicates that world markets easily absorbed increases in Japanese exports. From 1969 through 1972, the terms of trade improved even further under the influence of the yen revaluations.

The connection between terms of trade and welfare is seen most clearly in a comparison of the import price index and the wholesale price index (WPI) for manufactures (see Table 6-7). While the WPI was quite stable for manufactures, particularly as compared to other countries, it still rose more than import prices, indicating that the gross processing margins between imported inputs and manufactured outputs rose. This improvement in the gross processing margin no doubt helped to boost profits and was thus a stimulus to greater investment, and it also permitted some wage increases without adding to price pressures. The improvement is also reflected in the indexes of manufacturing input and output prices—a more accurate measure, though unfortunately available only since 1967—as shown in Table 6-7. The input prices include those from both domestic and import sources, and still the gross processing margin improved. One can conclude from all this that Japanese welfare seems to have been aided by world price developments over the entire period from 1955 through 1972.

The quantitative significance of the improvement in welfare, however, is questionable. Some simple illustrations might clarify the situation. Suppose that Japanese import prices in 1972 were such that they maintained the same terms of trade as existed in 1955. They would then have been 13.8 percent higher than they in actuality were, and ¥809 billion more in exports of goods

16. Hisao Kanamori, "Economic Growth and Exports," in Lawrence Klein and Kazushi Ohkawa (eds.), *Economic Growth: The Japanese Experience since the Meiji Era* (Richard D. Irwin, 1968), pp. 303–25, attached some importance to this point.

would have been required to maintain the same volume of imports. Such a figure represents 0.9 percent of Japanese GNP in 1972. If the entire adjustment were borne by consumption, then 1.7 percent of consumption was involved, or, alternatively, 2.6 percent of gross investment. These magnitudes do not seem very large. They also significantly exaggerate the adjustment burden since some substitution for high-priced imports would have occurred over time unless the price increase occurred quite suddenly.

In 1973 and 1974 Japan was faced with a sudden and rapid rise in import prices as a result of the worldwide commodity boom and oil crisis. The Japanese import price index doubled between January 1972 and June 1974. This created a substantial adjustment problem for the economy. The most immediate response to higher import prices was an increase in wholesale prices and thus in export prices. The Japanese export price index increased by over 40 percent from January 1972 to June 1974, but the terms of trade still deteriorated by close to 30 percent over this short period. The direct price response was by no means completed by mid-1974. The transmission chain of wholesale prices to retail prices to wages led to an average 30 percent rise in wages during the spring of 1974. Such a wage hike cannot be absorbed by gains in productivity, so further price increases can be expected. How much of the import price increase ultimately will be matched by an export price rise is still unknown—possibly most but clearly not all of it. It may well be that the 13.8 percent deterioration in the terms of trade given as a hypothetical illustration above is an approximation of the real burden to be absorbed by the economy. The absolute burden will grow over time as the volume of imports rises, but the relative burden should be reduced as some internal adjustments to the use of more expensive raw materials are accomplished. Therefore it seems unlikely that the adjustment burden from the deterioration in the terms of trade will seriously undermine the prosperity of the country, and it need not by itself greatly reduce Japan's rate of growth.

Growth and Balance-of-Payments Equilibrium

Japan's economic growth rate during most of the postwar period has been almost twice as fast as the average rate of other industrial countries. Such a situation could easily lead to deficits in the balance of payments if, as conventional trade models suggest, demand conditions are dominant in determining both imports and exports. Japanese economists were at first afraid that Japan's more rapid growth would necessarily cause balance-of-payments deficits and thus constrain growth. Such a fear was reflected in the New Long

Range Economic Plan (1957)[17] and captured in a theoretical model by Masao Fakuoka.[18] That growth was not in fact constrained was attributed by Kanamori to a number of factors, of which the most important was the heavy investment in manufacturing industries that permitted improvements in international competitiveness through productivity gains and favorable shifts in the structure of exports.

Nobuyoshi Namiki elaborated the Kanamori analysis and has carried the argument one step further, arguing that rapid economic growth may lead to balance-of-payments surpluses through its effects on the competitive power of Japanese exports.[19] Namiki argues that the greater amount of Japanese investment in manufacturing equipment relative to that of other industrial countries permits Japan's labor productivity to advance faster than that in other countries; this in turn leads to lower export prices and greater export values.

The relation between growth and the balance of payments has also been explored in some econometric works by Masahiro Tatemoto.[20] In some interesting long-run simulations of the Denken model, Tatemoto was able to demonstrate that the current account balance was particularly sensitive to the structure of Japanese growth. In one simulation in which the driving force in the economy was private plant and equipment expenditures, a trend toward surpluses in the current accounts appeared. But in another simulation, in which government purchases of goods and services plus government investments were the driving force, a trend toward deficits in the current account was indicated. Thus the balance of trade depends on the structure, not on the amount, of growth. The overall rate of real growth of the economy did not differ markedly in the two simulations.

In an insightful theoretical article, Ryūtarō Komiya shows that neither

17. Economic Planning Agency, *Shinchōki keizai ni kansuru keizai shingikai tōshin* (Nov. 25, 1957), quoted in Hisao Kanamori, "Economic Growth and the Balance of Payments," in Ryūtarō Komiya (ed.), *Postwar Economic Growth in Japan*, trans. Robert Ozaki (University of California Press, 1966), pp. 79–94.

18. "The Balance of Payments and a Model of Cyclical Growth," in Komiya (ed.), *Postwar Economic Growth in Japan*, pp. 99–103.

19. "Growth of Japanese Exports," *The Developing Economies*, vol. 8 (December 1970), pp. 475–96.

20. "Zaisei shyudogata no keizai seichō" [Government Expenditure-Led Economic Growth for Medium Term], in Masahiro Tatemoto and Tsunehiko Watanabe (eds.), *Gendai no keizaigaku* [Contemporary Economics], vol. 5 (Nihon Keizai Shinbunsha, 1972), pp. 63–71. The Denken model was built by Mitsuho Uchida and Masahiro Tatemoto and has been used as the Japanese country model in Project Link, the international effort to link national econometric models. A version of the Denken model was published in *Denryoku keizai kenkyū*, no. 1 (1972).

deficits nor surpluses are inevitable despite the greater economic growth of Japan.[21] In a three-sector model that contains goods, bonds, and money, he demonstrates that offsetting forces are at work between growth and the balance of payments. In the absence of an autonomous increase of the money supply, growth in output tends to improve the balance of trade and the overall balance, as Kanamori and Namiki found, while reducing the balance of capital account. With increases in the money supply or in autonomous domestic expenditures, on the other hand, the balance of payments deteriorates mainly through the trade balance. Thus deficits or surpluses are possible, but equilibrium can also be achieved if governments carry out judicious monetary and fiscal policies.

Nevertheless some real problems of balance-of-payments maladjustments and market disruption have accompanied the rapid growth of Japan. From 1965 through 1972, as noted below, Japanese imports did not rise as much as exports, causing substantial balance-of-payments surpluses. Since this was a period of rapid economic growth in Japan, the two phenomena could have been causally related, as suggested by Namiki. The seriousness of the problem was increased by the international monetary complications that accompanied it.

In addition to and quite distinct from the balance-of-payments problem, Japan's rapid economic growth, which involved tremendous increases in export potential and import needs, caused difficulties for other countries through market disruption. Japan's share of the exports of manufactures of industrial countries rose markedly during the entire postwar period, as shown in Table 6-8. While the absolute share of Japan is less than that of West Germany or the United States, the speed of the change was rapid and unprecedented. Even if there had been an exactly offsetting growth of imports in Japan, the rapidity of its export growth would have strained the absorptive capacity of world markets. The adjustment problem was compounded by the fact that the Japanese concentrated their export efforts in a few markets, especially the United States and Asia.[22] The higher the rate of Japanese economic growth, the greater the strain in foreign markets imposed by Japanese export expansion. A very rapid growth rate in Japan also causes sharp increases in demand for imported raw materials, which can cause worldwide inflation in commodity prices if supplies cannot be increased as quickly as demand and the exchange rate does not adjust promptly.

21. "Economic Growth and the Balance of Payments: A Monetary Approach," *Journal of Political Economy*, vol. 77 (January–February 1969), pp. 35–48.
22. As is discussed below, the concentration of Japanese exports was due in part to discriminatory trade restraints imposed by many countries against Japanese goods.

Table 6-8. *Value of Exported Goods and Share of Exports of Industrial Countries, 1955–73*

Year	All industrial countries	Japan	West Germany	Italy	United States
	Value (millions of dollars)				
1955	54,589	2,011	6,120	1,856	15,558
1960	78,510	4,055	11,418	3,648	20,584
1965	118,520	8,459	17,893	7,200	27,530
1970	208,110	19,318	34,192	13,206	43,224
1972	275,698	28,591	46,695	18,606	49,788
1973	376,013	36,840	66,703	22,245	71,339
	Share (percent)				
1955	100.0	3.68	11.21	3.40	28.50
1960	100.0	5.16	14.54	4.65	26.22
1965	100.0	7.14	15.10	6.07	23.23
1970	100.0	9.28	16.43	6.35	20.77
1972	100.0	10.37	16.94	6.75	18.06
1973	100.0	9.80	17.74	5.92	18.97

Source: International Monetary Fund, *International Financial Statistics* (July 1956), p. 30; (July 1966), pp. 34, 138, 176, 184, 298; (March 1975), pp. 40, 154, 222, 392,

Evolution of Japan's Comparative Advantage

The rapid economic growth of Japan relative to other countries should be reflected in a changing structure of the goods that Japan imports and exports. This is because international comparative advantage flows from relative costs, costs reflect factor prices and productivities, and growth affects both factor prices and productivities. As noted in Chapters 7 and 9, Japan has two distinct industrial structures: a modern sector of large firms paying high wages for labor and low interest rates for borrowed capital, and a traditional sector paying low wages and high interest rates. This situation—called dualism—has permitted Japan to be competitive in the export both of such traditional products as toys and textiles and of modern capital and technologically advanced products.[23] Because of a lack of competition from local producers, one would expect Japan to be somewhat more successful in selling traditional products to advanced countries and modern products to less developed countries.[24] Rapid economic growth, however, has had the effect of eroding

23. Masahiro Tatemoto and Shin'ichi Ichimura, "Factor Proportions and Foreign Trade: The Case of Japan," *Review of Economics and Statistics,* vol. 61 (November 1959), pp. 442–46.
24. William V. Rapp, "A Theory of Changing Trade Patterns under Economic Growth: Tested for Japan," *Yale Economic Essays,* vol. 7 (Fall 1967), pp. 69–135.

the economic dualism that should be reflected in changes in the structure of Japanese exports.[25]

As a first approximation, goods can be classified as being either labor intensive or capital intensive, depending on which is the dominant factor in their production. Traditional Japanese products correspond closely to the labor-intensive classification and modern products to the capital-intensive one. In a study by the General Agreement on Tariffs and Trade (GATT), it was found that traditional products made up 56 percent of Japanese exports in 1955 and only 22 percent in 1970, and that the share of modern products rose from 44 percent to 78 percent in that period.[26] This drastic change in the structure of Japanese exports was attributed to increasing tightness in the labor market, rising wages, and massive expansion of capital stock, all of which are a reflection of rapid Japanese growth.

A two-part classification of goods becomes increasingly inadequate as higher levels of economic development are reached. (It is also inadequate at low levels of development when natural resources provide a basis for international comparative advantage, but this is not relevant for Japan.) For instance, goods that require a great deal of highly skilled labor in production need to be distinguished from traditional labor-intensive goods. Some products are the result of rapid technological change; these goods might best be described as research-and-development intensive and must be distinguished from capital-intensive goods. Thus four elements of production—unskilled labor, skilled labor, R&D, and capital—can be used to form a classification scheme that might require more than four categories, since some products might best be described as intensive with respect to two or more inputs. In another study, the GATT developed a five-part classification of goods: R&D intensive and high wage (skilled labor); R&D intensive, high wage, and capital intensive; high wage and capital intensive; other capital intensive; and residual (predominantly) labor intensive.[27] This scheme is used to classify Japanese exports in Table 6-9.[28]

25. In the absence of barriers to trade, both exports and imports would be affected. Since Japanese import restrictions were quite important until recent years, attention will be directed here to exports only.

26. General Agreement on Tariffs and Trade, *Japan's Economic Expansion and Foreign Trade 1955 to 1970,* GATT Studies in International Trade, no. 2 (July 1971).

27. GATT, *Trends in United States Merchandise Trade 1953–1970,* GATT Studies in International Trade, no. 3 (July 1972).

28. With adequate data econometric techniques could be utilized to measure the partial contribution of individual variables in the determination of comparative advantage. A study along these lines was undertaken by Peter S. Heller with some encouraging results ("Factor Endowment Change and the Structure of Comparative Advantage: The Case of Japan, 1956–1969" [December 1974; processed]).

Table 6-9. *Structure of Japanese Exports, 1955–73*

Classification of goods	Value (tens of millions of U.S. dollars)			Percent of total[a]		
	1955	1965	1973	1955	1965	1973
R&D intensive and high wage	6	34	214	3.0	4.0	5.8
Advanced electrical equipment	1	15	114	0.5	1.8	3.1
Optical and precision instruments	2	9	47	1.0	1.1	1.3
Special nonelectrical machinery	3	10	53	1.5	1.2	1.4
R&D and capital intensive and high wage	11	76	348	5.5	9.0	9.4
Chemicals and synthetic rubber	9	55	225	4.5	6.5	6.1
Power generating and office machines	1	7	106	0.5	0.8	2.9
Photographic equipment	1	14	17	0.5	1.7	0.5
Capital intensive and high wage	37	174	1,062	18.5	20.6	28.8
Mineral manufactures	3	4	11	1.5	0.5	0.3
Iron and steel	23	105	440	11.5	12.4	11.9
Nonferrous metals	6	9	23	3.0	1.1	0.6
Tractors, construction, and similar machines	1	4	66	0.5	0.5	1.8
Automobiles and trucks	1	27	395	0.5	3.2	10.7
Paper, synthetic fibers, and similar manufactures	3	25	127	1.5	3.0	3.4
Other capital intensive	6	67	309	3.0	7.9	8.4
Artificial yarns and thread	2	10	10	1.0	1.2	0.3
Consumer electronics and equipment	0	38	223	...	4.5	6.0
Other nonelectrical machinery and others	4	19	76	2.0	2.2	2.1
Labor intensive	130	446	1,608	65.0	52.8	43.5
Textiles and clothing	72	133	232	36.0	15.7	6.3
Building materials and others	5	15	46	2.5	1.8	1.2
Other metal manufactures	4	23	101	2.0	2.7	2.7
Metalworking and certain electrical equipment	8	43	259	4.0	5.1	7.0
Motorcycles, ships, and others	10	95	516	5.0	11.2	14.0
Food, beverages, and tobacco	14	34	82	7.0	4.0	2.2
Miscellaneous	17	103	372	8.5	12.2	10.1
Unallocated	10	48	152	5.0	5.7	4.1
Total exports	200	845	3,693	100.0	100.0	100.0

Sources: Classification, General Agreement on Tariffs and Trade, *Trends in United States Merchandise Trade 1953–1970*, GATT Studies in International Trade, no. 3 (July 1972), table E; 1955 data, United Nations, Secretariat Statistical Office, *Yearbook of International Trade Statistics, 1958*, vol. 1 (1959), pp. 326–27; 1965 data, ibid., *1968* (1970), pp. 455–58; 1973 data, ibid., *1972–73* (1974), pp. 439–42.

a. Figures may not add to totals because of rounding.

The most striking change in the structure of Japanese exports is the steady decline in the share of labor-intensive products, particularly of traditional goods, revealed in the GATT study. Even the inclusion of some modern labor-intensive products such as motorcycles and ships that have had expanding shares has been insufficient to offset the overall decline. The decline can be attributed to the rise in Japanese labor costs, which is expected to continue. If the classification scheme is correct, even the modern products in this group will not be making much of a contribution in the future to the growth of Japanese exports since their comparative advantage rests on relatively cheap labor costs.

Furthermore, from 1965 to 1973, the share of exports of goods whose comparative advantage rests only on capital availability has stagnated. Such modern products as consumer electronics, artificial fibers, and paper products come under this classification. This suggests that in a world in which capital is internationally mobile, the high savings rate of Japan and the resulting availability of capital will be insufficient by itself as a basis for Japan's comparative advantage.

The category of products whose share of Japanese exports has grown the most includes those goods characterized as capital intensive and high wage (implying skilled labor). This classification is dominated by automobiles, which have been a particularly dynamic Japanese export. Most steel mill products also fall within this group, and although these exports have done well in the past, the future is less certain because of the lack of suitable land sites for expansion. Nevertheless the combination of skilled labor and capital would appear to constitute a stable basis for comparative advantage, and Japan is likely to continue to have these inputs in relative abundance in the future.

A growing share of Japanese exports is also related to research and development advances. When the two classifications with R&D inputs are combined, a continuing trend toward expansion emerges. These classifications include products such as advanced electronics and chemicals. Given the expectation that R&D expenditures will retain a high priority in Japan (as indicated in Chapter 8), Japan should have a solid basis for expanding comparative advantage in this area.

Over the whole period 1955 to 1973, it is clear that traditional exports have receded in importance as new products have entered the Japanese export basket. The role of these new products in generating the rapid growth of Japanese exports is examined in the next section.

Japan's Balance of Payments

Because so much has been published by government agencies and academic economists about Japan's balance of payments, particularly about the balance of trade, a number of significant developments are treated only summarily below. The focus of attention here is on the interaction of the balance of payments and the domestic economy. The postwar era can be divided into five periods: (1) the preindependence period up to 1951; (2) the 1952–60 period of rationalization of industry; (3) the 1961–68 period of increasing participation in the international society; (4) the 1969–73 period of balance-of-payments surpluses and corrective measures; and (5) the period since 1973 of the new adjustment.

Preindependence

During the preindependence period, many government policies that were to be long lived were introduced. It was a period when providing the minimum essentials of life for the Japanese people, including the millions of persons repatriated from abroad, was the top priority. Imports provided for some essential goods, but they had to be held to a minimum because exports to pay for them were limited.[29]

In relation to the balance of payments, the most significant developments of the period were:

1. The promulgation of laws and regulations for the control of trade and payments.[30]

2. The establishment of the Ministry of International Trade and Industry (MITI) in 1949.

3. The fixing of the exchange rate at $1 = ¥360 in 1949.

4. The introduction of a foreign exchange budget system and import deposit scheme in recognition of the shortage of foreign exchange.[31]

5. The drafting of the first government economic plan.[32]

The regulations governing trade and payments were the result of three basic laws. Under the "standard method of payment," export transactions were treated more generously than imports. In combination with financial preferences that stimulated foreign trade in general, resource allocation was directed toward tradable goods and, therefore, away from purely domestic transactions. It is noteworthy that financial preferences for foreign trade in the form of lower interest rates were not completely eliminated until August 1971.

The intricate regulations on foreign trade gave the Ministry of International Trade and Industry significant powers. The MITI had to approve, on a case-by-case basis, any foreign trade transaction that was not to be based on the standard method. Thus the MITI became intimately involved in business decisions from its beginning and was able to evolve into a very powerful ministry.

The setting of the exchange rate in April 1949 marked a return to more normal operations of the Japanese economy. It came on the heels of the adoption of a disinflationary budget and replaced the previous multiple ex-

29. MITI, *Nihon bōeki no tenkai* [Evolution of Japan's Foreign Trade] (Shoko Shuppan, 1956).

30. See the appendix to this chapter, items 4, 5, 6, and 7.

31. Appendix items 10 and 11.

32. Appendix item 15.

change rate system.[33] Control of foreign exchange was turned over to the Foreign Exchange Control Board (replaced by the Ministry of Finance in 1952). The significance of these acts arose from the fact that the exchange rate, once set, became a fixed element of policy; in fact, the ¥360 rate survived until the end of 1971.

The foreign exchange budget and the import deposit scheme were utilized together to bridge the shortage of foreign exchange existing at the ¥360 rate by controlling imports. The budget classified importable goods into three categories: fund allocation (which became import quotas after 1964), automatic fund allocation (which became automatic import quotas), and automatic approval. The import deposit scheme, which was in operation until 1969, required deposit of collateral for imports at the time permission to import was requested; the collateral was forfeited if the importation was not executed. The rates of collateral were differentiated by category of goods (raw materials, consumption goods, capital equipment, and so forth). In addition to the prime objective of limiting imports to the availability of foreign exchange, these policies restrained speculation in imported commodities and discriminated against the importation of consumption goods. The import deposit scheme acting through the credit system also reinforced an anticyclical monetary policy.

The first government economic plan provided an analytical framework for the many policies then in effect, which in their totality set the primary goal of the economy—industrialization and export promotion. Among the measures utilized to promote this goal were preferential access to credit for foreign trade, and at favorable interest rates, customs exemptions for specified imported machinery, accelerated depreciation for investments in products for export and other tax advantages for exporters, and even subsidies for some products not internationally competitive.[34] In addition, a number of government institutions were formed during this period to help promote the economic goal.[35]

Thus a policy direction was set for the economy that lasted for over twenty years. Though subsequently criticized as leading to pollution and congestion as well as balance-of-payments surpluses, this policy did in fact achieve its primary goal of rapid industrialization and the generation of ample foreign exchange to buy required imports. In a real sense, the postwar policy was not a new one, but merely an extension of the Meiji Restoration's goal of

33. Bank of Japan, *Manual of Foreign Exchange and Foreign Trade System in Japan* (May 1972).
34. Appendix items 1, 2, 3, 12, 13, and 16.
35. Appendix items 17, 18, 19, and 20.

catching up with advanced Western nations. As is now clear, the postwar policy was carried to an extreme and overshot its mark, but given that the essence of that policy had been in existence for a century, some recognition lag was probably to be expected.

Rationalizing Japanese Industry, 1952–60

During the 1950s, the Japanese economy made rapid strides. The Korean War triggered considerable, if temporary, expansion through the direct and indirect expenditures of the U.S. forces, and by 1953–54 the economy finally reached its prewar level of per capita production. Some important refinements were also added to the policy measures already enacted.

It was recognized that simply promoting industrialization was not enough; higher standards of living required in particular heavy manufacturing and chemical industries, and these had to be able to export at competitive prices if economies of scale were to be obtained. Accordingly, plans were formulated by the MITI to modernize and rationalize the steel industry, to create a petrochemical industry (1955), to promote and rationalize the heavy machinery and automobile industries (1955), to promote the electronics and synthetic rubber industries (1957), and to revive the airplane industry (1958).

The MITI method contained four basic ingredients:

1. Setting numerical goals for output and reduction of unit costs.

2. Giving financal aid in the form of low-interest-rate government loans and preferred access to loans of private financial institutions.

3. Giving tax allowances primarily through accelerated depreciation and tax-free reserves.

4. The creation of advisory councils that included representatives of the government, the industry, and outside experts. With the help of these councils, a consensus on an industry plan was reached through persuasion, not coercion.

The rationalizing of domestic industry was accompanied by complete protection from import competition through the quota system—unnecessary imports were simply not permitted. In addition, more refined methods of export promotion were developed. They included more extensive financing aids, tax subsidies, and limited exemptions from antitrust laws.[36] Since a license to import scarce raw materials was very valuable, these licenses were at times granted to encourage exports that would otherwise be unprofitable

36. Appendix items 22, 24, 25, 26, 27, 28, 31, 34, and 36.

for firms, as provided for by the "Link Trade" system. Textile producers, for example, were authorized to import cotton and wool if their export performance had been satisfactory in the previous year. Until 1955, shipbuilders were given the windfall gains from the importation of sugar in order to subsidize their export of ships. Further, a new institution was created by the government called the Export Conference, whose task was to promote exports by setting targets every six months and monitoring the results closely.

It should be remembered that it was not easy for Japanese exports to enter many new markets. Although Japan joined the GATT in 1955, fourteen countries (including the United Kingdom, France, and Australia) and their dependent territories did not extend most-favored-nation treatment to Japan, as they were permitted to do under Article 35 of the GATT. Furthermore, individual products such as cotton textiles and stainless steel flatware were restricted by so-called voluntary agreements in the United States and other countries.

During this period Japan began to utilize foreign borrowing to foster even greater capital investment and faster growth. While private investment by foreigners in Japan was strictly controlled to protect domestic firms, selective foreign borrowing by or through the government was undertaken. Thus credits from the U. S. Export-Import Bank were taken, and, starting in 1955, Japan borrowed intermittently from the International Bank for Reconstruction and Development, having joined the IBRD and the International Monetary Fund in 1952. The IBRD loans were used primarily to equip the steel industry. This type of borrowing was tightly constrained by guidelines for fear of creating a difficult repayment burden and also because of concerns about inflation. These loans, along with short-term credits obtained through Japanese agency banks operating in the United States, also helped to ease the balance-of-payments constraints plaguing the economy.

By the end of the 1950s, the economy had reached what could be described as full employment for the first time since the war. Import liberalization could then be contemplated as an aid in redirecting the utilization of the labor force—a new problem for the economy. Furthermore, Europe had completed the liberalization of its temporary quantitative restrictions on imports by then, and the Japanese government felt that it also had to make a start in this direction. Thus the government adopted a three-year plan to liberalize 80 percent of its imports; as a first step, 257 commodities (four-digit items covered by the Brussels Tariff Nomenclature [BTN] system) were freed, representing 44 percent of the value of imports at that time.[37]

37. Appendix item 37.

Furthermore, Japan made a start at assisting less developed countries by lending India $50 million in 1958. This was in addition to the reparations payments that were being made to many of the less developed countries in Asia since the end of World War II.

It is hard to evaluate the consequences of governmental policy during this period as neither the benefits nor the costs can be calculated. Clearly one of the major beneficial functions of the government was the provision and dissemination of valuable information for the business community. The MITI and other government bodies, such as the Japan External Trade Organization (JETRO), studied industrial trends and market developments abroad so that Japanese firms could direct their investments to making products with an expanding world demand. Their investigation of foreign production costs exposed the "possibilities frontier" and became a target for individual company efforts. Firms were also encouraged to license or buy technology from abroad. Since foreign firms could neither export manufactured goods to Japan nor make direct investments there, they were frequently prepared to license their processes and products as the only way to share in the market. Through its regulating power over these technology agreements, the MITI made sure that Japanese firms did not overpay for technology and on occasion refused to approve agreements previously entered into by Japanese and foreign firms on the ground that the price was too high—often suggesting at what price the parties might agree.

Nevertheless one may well question the wisdom of the governmental policy of forgoing the exchange rate as a policy instrument. At the end of the Korean War, the yen from all appearances was overvalued, yet it was not devalued, nor was devaluation even given serious consideration. This is surprising since many European countries in similar circumstances were devaluing at this time, France more than once. Many Japanese policies were designed essentially to overcome currency overvaluation on an item-by-item basis, possibly involving great inefficiencies that could have been avoided through market allocation of foreign exchange. No doubt the bureaucracies of the MITI, the Ministry of Finance, and the Bank of Japan gained considerable leverage over the private economy by maintaining the overvaluation of the currency. Furthermore, almost any policy could gain public approval in the name of promoting exports, even if the major motivation was helping an industry at public expense.

The motivation of the government no doubt lies deeper, however, than mere bureaucratic politics. Maintaining the ¥360 rate had become a matter of honor. Japan had been "given" its exchange rate by Joseph Dodge and it was felt in Japan that the United States wanted the rate maintained. Also,

Table 6-10. *Japan's Balance of Payments, 1961–73*
Millions of dollars

Year	Exports	Imports	Trade balance[a]	Services	Net transfers	Current account	Long-term capital flows	Basic balance	Short-term capital flows	Errors and omissions	Official settlements
1961	4,149	4,707	−558	−383	−41	−982	−11	−993	21	20	−952
1962	4,861	4,460	401	−420	−29	−48	172	124	107	6	237
1963	5,391	5,557	−166	−569	−45	−780	467	−313	107	45	−161
1964	6,704	6,327	377	−784	−73	−480	107	−373	234	10	−129
1965	8,332	6,431	1,901	−884	−85	932	−415	517	−61	−51	405
1966	9,641	7,366	2,275	−886	−135	1,254	−808	446	−64	−45	337
1967	10,231	9,071	1,160	−1,172	−178	−190	−812	−1,002	506	−75	−571
1968	12,751	10,222	2,529	−1,306	−175	1,048	−239	809	209	84	1,102
1969	15,679	11,980	3,699	−1,399	−181	2,119	−155	1,964	178	141	2,283
1970	18,969	15,006	3,963	−1,785	−208	1,970	−1,591	379	724	271	1,374
1971	23,566	15,779	7,787	−1,738	−252	5,797	−1,082	4,715	2,435	527	7,677
1972	28,032	19,061	8,971	−1,883	−464	6,624	−4,487	2,137	1,966	638	4,741
1973	36,264	32,576	3,688	−3,510	−314	−136	−9,750	−9,886	2,407	−2,595	−10,074

Source: Bank of Japan, *Balance of Payments Monthly* (March 1970) pp. 1–2; (May 1973), pp. 1–2; (March 1974), pp. 1–2.
a. Exports and imports valued free on board (f.o.b.).

there was some fear of undermining foreign confidence in the currency just when foreign borrowing was beginning. The government would have lost face at home and abroad if it had permitted the exchange rate to fall, just as it would if it had permitted a high rate of interest on government bonds and thereby exposed their lack of popularity with the people.

In this regard it is instructive to recall the 1931 devaluation of the yen. After the collapse of the silk market, the yen was devalued from 49.0 cents to 29.4 cents. The devaluation was remarkably effective, permitting Japanese exports of manufactures to grow rapidly during the 1930s and cushioning the consequences of the Great Depression. Nevertheless, the experience is not recalled with approval in Japan. Rather the devaluation, along with deficit spending, is associated with militarism and preparations for war and thus is not an experience to be repeated. Clearly, maintaining a fixed exchange rate was more a matter of ideology than economic reality in Japan.

Participation in the International Society, 1961–68

During the 1960s, the Japanese economy made its greatest strides foward, with an increasingly rapid rate of growth and improvement in the balance of payments. The balance of payments was extremely sensitive to domestic growth. When domestic growth was very rapid—as in 1961 when 15 percent real growth was achieved—a deficit was recorded in the basic balance of payments, as shown in Table 6-10. But when growth fell below 7 percent in the following year, 1962, the basic balance moved into surplus. Taking the average of the years 1962–64, real growth was about 10 percent a year and the basic balance was near zero, so a balance-of-payments equilibrium can be said to have existed.[38] Basic equilibrium in the balance of payments does not prevent an actual deficit from occurring in a particular year when the economy is growing faster than its potential, as happened in Japan in 1967. Indeed, failure to record a deficit in such circumstances is a sign of an underlying surplus in the balance of payments. Japanese growth in 1967 might have been even greater, for instance, if policymakers had not worried about the balance of payments—which did not in fact indicate an underlying disequilibrium—and had used owned or borrowed reserves to cover the recorded deficit.[39] It must be remembered, of course, that the degree of commercial policy liberalization in Japan was quite low at this time compared to that of other advanced countries, so a particular type of equilibrium was

38. Namiki dated the turnaround at 1965, but his analysis relates only to the current account balance ("Growth of Japanese Exports," p. 478).
39. See Chapter 3.

involved. The equilibrium was not long maintained, however, and a growing surplus soon appeared.

The shift in Japan's balance of payments appears most dramatically in the balance of goods and services. This account recorded a deficit of nearly $1 billion in 1961, yet by 1971 it was in surplus by $6 billion. This turnaround of $7 billion over a ten-year period is of great interest because it is at the center of the adjustment difficulties that Japan experienced with other countries, principally the United States. The change occurred exclusively in the trade balance, which recorded an increase of exports over imports of $8.3 billion, while the service accounts deteriorated by $1.3 billion.

What needs chiefly to be examined here is the increase of Japanese exports from $4.1 billion in 1961 to $23.6 billion in 1971 and the import increase from $4.7 billion f.o.b. (free on board) in 1961 to only $15.8 billion in 1971. The factors that have contributed to this conversion of the Japanese trade balance from deficit to surplus are discussed below. For greater clarity, exports and imports are considered separately, but some of the causative elements such as price developments are obviously similar and are related in the two accounts.

EXPORTS. Four factors determined the $19.5 billion increase in Japanese exports during the decade 1961–71: the growth of world incomes and international trade; the prices of Japanese exports relative to those of other industrial countries; structural changes in Japanese manufactured output; and foreign commercial policies.

The growth of world incomes and trade can be separated into two elements: one relates to the normal growth of incomes, while the other relates to the Vietnam War. The major force in the world economy was the growth of money incomes, which in turn led to the growth of world trade from $117.4 billion in 1961 to $314.4 billion in 1971, with industrial countries being the major exporters. Japan's share of the world exports of industrial countries was 5.11 percent in 1961. If Japan had simply maintained that share of world trade, the value of Japanese exports would have grown from $4.1 billion to $11.9 billion during the decade. Thus $7.8 billion of Japanese export growth can be attributed to the regular growth of world trade.[40]

40. This procedure assumes that in a completely specified econometric model the foreign income (or import) elasticity of demand for Japanese exports would be exactly unity. This requires the slightly favorable commodity composition of Japanese exports at the start of the period to be offset by the slightly unfavorable distribution of Japanese markets. Actual econometric results such as those obtained by the Denken model show this elasticity to be much above unity (3.07 with respect to U.S. output and 1.85 with respect to other world trade). These estimates can be considered as picking up the consequences of excluded variables.

The Vietnam conflict also had an effect upon Japanese exports (though less of one than the Korean War) because all the countries involved—Vietnam, Laos, and Cambodia (Khmer), plus Thailand, South Korea, and Taiwan—are located near Japan and were important customers for Japanese goods. It is assumed that had the conflict not escalated in 1965, the rate of growth of imports of these countries from 1961 to 1965 would have continued through 1971 and that Japan's share of the market would have been maintained. Under this assumption, total imports of these countries would have been about $4.0 billion in 1971 instead of the $6.2 billion actually recorded. Actual Japanese exports to these countries rose from less than $0.4 billion in 1961 to $2.4 billion in 1971, with most of the gain occurring after 1965. Of the estimated $2.2 billion of unusual imports of these countries, $1.2 billion is estimated to have come from Japan under the constant-share assumption. Thus it is estimated that the Indochina conflict added over a billion dollars to Japanese exports in 1971.

The second major factor explaining the rise of Japanese exports is the price competitiveness of Japanese manufactured goods relative to those of other industrial countries.[41] Table 6-11 shows the substantial improvement in price competitiveness registered by Japanese exports in the 1960s. During the first part of the decade, the improvement came from the absolute decline in Japanese export prices at the same time as other countries' prices were slowly rising. The improvement later in the decade was due to the fact that Japanese prices rose less rapidly than those of other producers.

From 1960 to 1962, the Japanese export price index declined by 7.1 percent, mainly as a result of a decline in export prices of 14 percent for metals, 13 percent for machinery, and 15 percent for chemicals. These were the industries that had benefited from government-encouraged rationalization programs in the previous five years, which led in some cases to temporary periods of excess capacity. Thus, even though unit labor cost rose for manufacturing as a whole, the wholesale prices of manufactured goods declined. It is noteworthy that import prices of raw materials were also declining, which helped Japanese producers lower their selling prices. Since Japan depends more heavily on imported raw materials than other countries, a decline of raw material prices in international trade tends to improve Japan's competitiveness, while the reverse effect occurs with rising raw material prices. It is also noteworthy that the export prices of these critical industries declined more than their domestic wholesale prices, indicating that the government

41. It should be noted that more recently Japan has faced competition in labor-intensive products from newly industrializing countries, but this was not the case during the sixties.

Table 6-11. *Indexes of Manufacturing Costs and Export Prices Relative to Competitors, 1960–73*

1967 = 100

Year	Labor produc- tivity (1)	Cash earnings (2)	Unit labor costs (3)	Japan Yen (4)	Japan Dollars[a] (5)	Other indus- trial coun- tries[b] (6)	Japanese relative export prices (4) ÷ (6) (7)	(5) ÷ (6) (8)[a]
1960	52.7	48.7	92.4	103.7	n.a.	92.2	112.5	n.a.
1961	58.1	54.4	93.6	99.5	n.a.	93.3	106.6	n.a.
1962	59.7	59.6	99.8	96.3	n.a.	93.1	103.4	n.a.
1963	65.4	65.9	100.8	98.7	n.a.	94.1	104.9	n.a.
1964	73.4	72.8	99.2	100.1	n.a.	95.7	104.6	n.a.
1965	75.9	79.1	104.2	99.5	n.a.	97.4	102.2	n.a.
1966	85.8	88.4	103.0	99.6	n.a.	99.8	99.8	n.a.
1967	100.0	100.0	100.0	100.0	n.a.	100.0	100.0	n.a.
1968	119.5	114.9	96.1	100.4	n.a.	98.7	101.7	n.a.
1969	135.6	133.6	98.5	103.1	n.a.	103.6	99.5	n.a.
1970	149.7	157.2	105.0	108.1	108.2	108.2	99.9	100.0
1971	156.3	179.1	114.6	108.9	112.2	113.5	95.9	98.9
1972	173.7	207.1	119.2	105.7	121.2	122.7	86.1	98.8
1973	208.1	256.0	123.0	115.2	128.9	147.8	77.9	87.2

Sources: Statistics Department, Bank of Japan, *Economic Statistics of Japan, 1965* (March 1966); idem, *Economic Statistics Annual*, various issues; International Monetary Fund, *International Financial Statistics*, various issues.

n.a. Not available.

a. Since the yen was fixed to the dollar until the 1970s, no adjustment was necessary in making a comparison between the yen-based index and the dollar index. From 1970 on, the dollar index of Japanese export prices adjusts for the appreciation of the yen relative to the dollar, using average monthly exchange rates from the *Federal Reserve Bulletin*.

b. Weighted index of dollar export prices of industrial Europe, the United States, and the United Kingdom.

incentives for exports were effective or that profit margins on export sales were being shaved. Thus the gain in Japanese price competitiveness in the early 1960s can be attributed to domestic factors and had amounted to 9.2 percent improvement by 1965 (that is, the competitive export price index declined from 112.5 to 102.2).

In contrast, the improvement in Japanese competitiveness in the late sixties can be attributed mainly to inflationary developments abroad. Led by the 16.3 percent increase in U.S. export prices, the composite price index of Japan's competitors rose by 11.1 percent between 1965 and 1970. Japanese export prices also rose, but by a lesser amount—8.6 percent. In this instance the export price index and the wholesale price index for manufacturing in Japan showed almost identical movements. The Japanese price rise was concentrated at the end of the period, as it was for many other countries. As a result, Japanese competitiveness improved by a further 2.3 percent (the competitive index declined from 102.2 to 99.9).

The consequences of these price developments for Japanese exports were evaluated by using the export equations of the Denken model.[42] Because of domestic Japanese developments that were responsible for improved competitiveness between 1960 and 1964, it is estimated that Japanese exports were $740 million higher in 1965, an amount that, because of the subsequent rise of incomes, was worth $1.1 billion in 1971. For the 1964–70 period, in which foreign inflation was the principal cause of improved Japanese competitiveness, it is estimated that Japanese exports were increased an additional $1.3 billion. Thus price developments led to a total $2.4 billion expansion of Japanese exports over the decade.

The third major factor explaining increased Japanese exports relates to structural changes in Japan's manufacturing output. Through a combination of importing foreign technology, domestic efforts in research and develop-

---

42. These calculations indicate only rough orders of magnitude, and care should be exercised in using them for any purpose for which refined measurements are required. While the Denken model is a short-run model, our ten-year time span falls within the sample period. Nevertheless, the measured price elasticities may underestimate the responsiveness of trade to price change over such a long period. The Denken model separates Japanese exports to the United States from those to other countries. The price elasticities in the model are as follows: for exports to the United States, the ratio of Japanese export prices to U.S. wholesale prices is the appropriate variable with an elasticity of −4.3930; for exports to other areas, the ratio of Japanese export prices to prices of world manufactures is used with an elasticity of −2.0335. The price variables were applied with a one-year lag. The calculation proceeded as follows: Japanese price competitiveness relative to the United States improved by 4 percent between 1960 and 1964, which led to an 18 percent increase in exports (0.04 × 4.3930) amounting to $200 million in 1965 (0.18 times the 1961 trade level of $1.1 billion), which increased further to $350 million by 1971 because of the general increase in U.S. imports ($200 million times the growth in U.S. imports of 73 percent between 1965 and 1971). Japanese export prices relative to prices of world manufactures improved by 9 percent between 1960 and 1964, which led to an 18 percent rise in Japanese exports (0.09 × 2.0335) amounting to $540 million in 1965 (0.18 times the 1961 trade level of $3.0 billion), which increased further to $760 million by 1971 because of world trade growth ($540 million times the world trade growth of 41 percent between 1965 and 1971). Between 1964 and 1970, Japanese prices relative to U.S. prices improved by 9 percent, which led to a 39 percent rise in exports amounting to a $710 million rise in exports to the United States in 1971 (0.39 times the 1965 base of $1.8 billion). Japanese price competitiveness relative to prices of world manufactures improved by 6 percent between 1964 and 1970, which led to a 12 percent increase in exports amounting to $590 million in exports in 1971 (0.12 times the 1965 base of $4.9 billion).

ment, and heavy investment in business plant and equipment, supply capabilities were created during the 1960s for many products that previously did not exist or were only in the early stages of development. This process is well documented by Watanabe and Egaizu.[43]

New products were a very important element in Japanese export growth.[44] Kiyoshi Kojima has described this process as the "catching-up product cycle," which he has investigated for Japan.[45] In 1961 less than $400 million of Japanese exports of new products was recorded, and they accounted for only 9.0 percent of total Japanese exports in that year. If the export of these products had increased only because of the income and price variables previously analyzed, they would have amounted to $1.0 billion in 1971. In fact, $7.8 billion in exports of these products was recorded in 1971, making up 32.6 percent of total Japanese foreign sales. Thus it is estimated that new product development during the 1960s was responsible for $6.8 billion of Japanese exports in 1971.[46]

The final factor that helps explain Japanese export growth relates to developments in commercial policy. During the 1960s, the Kennedy Round of trade negotiations under the GATT was completed and implemented. The Kennedy Round was particularly successful in reducing tariffs on manufactured products exported by developed countries. Since these are the products exported by Japan, Japanese trade reaped substantial benefits. It is true that barriers to such traditional Japanese exports as cotton textiles were not liberalized, but these products were not of great importance to Japan's export growth. Similarly some of the previous discriminations against Japanese trade were liberalized or became less important during the 1960s as the

43. Tsunehiko Watanabe and F. Egaizu, "Gijutsu shinpo to keizai seichō" [Technical Progress and Economic Growth], in Motoo Kaji (ed.), *Keizai seichō to shigen bunpai* [Economic Growth and Resource Allocation] (Iwanami Shoten, 1967).

44. The products involved were synthetic fibers, yarns, and fabrics, plastics, power generating machinery, office machinery, electric generators, television receivers, motor vehicles, motorcycles, watches, tape recorders, and optical equipment. Some of these products had received MITI attention for their export potential, but many others developed without government encouragement.

45. Kiyoshi Kojima (ed.), *Structure and Development of Japanese Trade* (Tokyo: Shiseidō, 1972).

46. Roughly similar results were obtained in a study by Kanamori, Sekiguchi, and Shōda. Utilizing a finer product classification of traded items, they identified twenty-six products as new to the Japanese export basket. These products accounted for 25.5 percent of total exports in 1969 and only 0.7 percent in 1953, an increase of 24.8 percentage points, as compared to the increase from 9.0 percent to 32.6 percent, or 23.6 percentage points noted above. H. Kanamori, S. Sekiguchi, and Y. Shōda, "Nihon no bōeki no hatten keitai to shōrai" [Development of Japanese Foreign Trade and Its Prospects], *Keizai hyōron* (October 1970), pp. 59–75.

structure of Japanese manufacturing shifted away from labor-intensive products. Of course not all commercial policy developments were favorable. The list of so-called voluntary export quotas was expanded, and from time to time various countries levied temporary import surcharges, the United States among them. But it is instructive to note that such actions were taken only after explosive growth in trade had occurred, and in most cases the restraints still permitted further moderate growth.

The results of the Kennedy Round were analyzed for Japanese trade by Kojima.[47] Industrial tariffs were reduced by an average of 35 percent in most of Japan's principal markets. Taking into account the previous level of tariffs and the Kennedy Round reductions, Kojima examined sixty-nine export and sixty-six import items (those covered by the Standard Industrial Trade Classification three-digit system) that registered at least $1 million in trade before the reductions were initiated. Export and import increases were calculated using a plausible price elasticity for each category of commodities. On this basis Kojima estimated that Japanese exports were stimulated by 24.1 percent and imports by only 8.5 percent. By applying such percentage changes to the totality of Japanese trade, one can estimate that exports were increased by $1.3 billion and imports by less than $0.5 billion.

To summarize, the four factors determining the $19.5 billion increase in Japanese exports from 1961 to 1971 had the following relative weights: growth of world incomes and trade, 46.4 percent; improved Japanese price competitiveness, 12.4 percent; structural developments in Japanese manufacturing, 35.0 percent; and foreign commercial policy liberalization, 6.2 percent.

IMPORTS. A similar group of four factors explains the rise of Japanese imports: the growth of income in Japan; changes in the prices of imports; structural shifts in Japanese manufacturing; and Japanese commercial policies and their changes. Japanese imports (as shown in Table 6-10) rose from $4.7 billion in 1961 to $15.8 billion in 1971 (f.o.b.).[48] These imports can be classified into three end-use categories: industrial supplies (71 percent of the total in 1961), consumer goods including food (19 percent), and capital equipment (10 percent). The distribution had changed only moderately by

47. Kiyoshi Kojima, *Taiheiyō keizaiken to Nippon* (Kunimoto Shobo, 1969); published in English as *Japan and a Pacific Free Trade Area* (University of California Press, 1969).

48. Most Japanese detailed import statistics are reported on a customs clearance basis (c.i.f.—cost, insurance, and freight). Total imports on this basis were 23.4 percent higher than on an f.o.b. basis in 1961 and 24.8 percent higher in 1971. Since the aggregate mark-up did not change appreciably, it is assumed that freight charges and the like on individual items will not bias the analysis based on c.i.f. data.

1971, with industrial supplies declining by 4 percentage points, and each of the others rising by 2 points.

The main factor determining the behavior of imports has been the rise of Japanese incomes. In this connection, the three categories of imports responded to different components of national income—industrial supplies to changes in industrial output, consumer goods to changes in consumption expenditures, and capital equipment to changes in gross domestic fixed capital expenditures. Under the assumption that imports would maintain the same share of the corresponding real expenditure (measured in 1961 prices), Japanese imports should have risen from $4.7 billion in 1961 to $13.7 billion in 1971.

The second factor concerns developments in import prices. As noted above, Japanese commercial policy did not permit entry of competitive imports until well into the 1960s. For simplicity it is assumed, therefore, that during the 1960s Japanese import demand was perfectly inelastic with respect to price, although it is recognized that this somewhat exaggerates reality.[49] This implies that the value of imports rises and falls in direct proportion to import price changes. Total import prices rose by 6.2 percent between 1961 and 1971, with food and consumer items rising 15.6 percent, capital equipment 6.4 percent, and industrial supplies only 5.5 percent. Under the assumption of perfectly inelastic demand, the value of imports was $1.0 billion higher in 1971 because of the price rise.

By way of contrast, the overall GNP deflator for Japan rose 57.2 percent from 1961 to 1971, with the personal consumption deflator rising 79.1 percent, the deflator for gross fixed capital increasing 30.7 percent, and industrial prices rising 7.4 percent. If import prices followed the corresponding domestic sector price, imports would have increased by an additional $1.9 billion (total price rise equal to $2.9 billion in imports in 1971). Alternatively, if import prices had risen at the same rate as Japanese export prices between 1961 and 1971, import values would still have been $300 million more than they actually were ($1.3 billion total increase). Thus it can be concluded that Japan's trade accounts benefited from the very moderate pace of import price increases during this period—a moderate pace even by the standard of Japanese export prices.

The third factor affecting imports relates to the structural shift in Japanese manufacturing. In each industry, Japanese value added has been rising rela-

49. Japanese import liberalization has accelerated since 1968. Of the four import equations in the Denken model, only one of the product classes (manufactured imports other than food) has a price variable, and its measured elasticity is less than one-half. The Denken model was not utilized here because it would have required a different end-use classification than desirable for present purposes.

tive to purchased imported inputs. In part this has been due to the substitution of synthetic materials for natural ones (such as rubber), and in part due to the upgrading of the goods being produced (such as more cold rolled sheets in the output mix of the steel industry). Another element involved has been the shift in the composition of industrial output away from industries such as textiles, which depend heavily on imported raw material, to industries such as electronics, which are much less dependent.

These trends were present even before the war, as recognized by Lockwood.[50] Namiki has investigated more recent developments through the use of the 1960 and 1965 input-output tables.[51] He found that reduced import requirements per unit of output and the compositional shifts noted above accounted for savings of between $0.6 billion and $1.0 billion in imports between 1960 and 1965. From this he concludes that the import saving trend is worth about 1.5 percent a year. Namiki also found some countering tendencies. He noted that imported petroleum tended to replace domestic coal in energy production and that there was also some rise in imported consumer goods because of the growing labor shortage.

There is little evidence of import saving for the economy as a whole for the decade 1961 to 1971. While recorded imports constituted a smaller share of GNP in 1971 than in 1961, the decline is due entirely to the differential trend in prices—that is, domestic prices rising more than import prices. As noted above, if imports had maintained their share in each of the three end-use categories, imports would have been $13.7 billion in 1971 (in 1961 prices). Actual imports, however, were $14.7 billion in 1971 (in 1961 prices), so the import dependence of the economy actually increased rather than decreased when price changes are taken into account. Kanamori came to the same conclusion using aggregate data.[52] The increase of imports was greatest for food and consumer items, and there is a slight trend toward growth of imports of industrial supplies. It may well be that the forces causing increased imports, as discussed by Namiki, are stronger than those causing reduced ones. Following Namiki, the factors reducing imports are estimated as accounting for $2.5 billion for the decade 1961–71, but the forces increasing them are estimated to have generated $3.5 billion for the same period.

The final factor explaining the rise in Japanese imports lies in the changes in Japanese commercial policy. As noted previously, Japan began to liberalize its import quota system in 1961. In recognition of its economic

50. William W. Lockwood, *The Economic Development of Japan: Growth and Structural Change* (Princeton University Press, 1968).

51. Namiki, "Growth of Japanese Exports."

52. Hisao Kanamori, "Structure of Foreign Trade," *The Developing Economies*, vol. 10 (December 1972), pp. 359–84.

Table 6-12. *Japanese Import Quota Restrictions, 1962–73*[a]

Date	Number of items under quota restriction	Number of items under residual restrictions under the GATT[b]
April 1962	490	...
April 1963	229	n.a.
April 1964	174	136
October 1965	161	122
May 1966[c]	168	126
October 1968	164	121
October 1969	161	118
September 1970	133	90
April 1972	79	33
April 1973	83	32
October 1973	82	31

Source: MITI, *Annual Survey of Foreign Trade*, various issues.
n.a. Not available.
a. Includes items covered by the four-digit Brussels Tariff Nomenclature (BTN) system, out of a total of 603 classifications.
b. GATT = General Agreement on Tariffs and Trade.
c. Increases are due to the revision of the classifications as a result of Japan's participation in the BTN treaty.

strength and improving international competitiveness, Japan accepted Article 11 of the GATT in 1963 and Article 8 of the IMF in 1964; it also joined the Organisation for Economic Co-operation and Development (OECD) in that year. Nevertheless, few further steps toward liberalizing the treatment of imports were taken, while measures to promote exports were still being initiated until late in the decade.[53] After 1965, the Japanese balance of payments was moving into a surplus position, yet the government was slow to recognize this development. The small deficit recorded in 1967, despite the extraordinary 14 percent real growth rate of the economy in that year, should have been taken as a sign of fundamental surplus in the balance of payments, but was instead treated like the deficits of the 1950s. Although some dissenting views were developing within the government and some academic economists made public statements indicating that the yen was undervalued, no significant action was taken.

While not of great significance in the aggregate, some steps toward liberalization were taken during the 1960s. The quota system was transformed in 1962–63 and the number of items subject to quotas gradually reduced, as shown in Table 6-12. But it was not until December 1968 that a political decision was made really to open the economy to foreign competition, and

53. Appendix items 49 through 55.

even then the change was to take place over a three-year period rather than immediately.

The reason that the previous liberalization had had little impact on imports was that the weakening or removal of the quota restrictions (QRs) only exposed a tariff barrier that was itself very limiting, and possibly also other barriers of a more amorphous character.[54] As investigated by Ippei Yamazawa,[55] the effective tariff rate on competitive manufactured goods was extremely high because of the sharp escalation of Japanese tariffs from the raw material through higher processing stages. As shown in Table 6-13, the effective tariff rate on such manufactured consumer goods as cotton clothing was above 45 percent before the Kennedy Round; even after partial implementation of the reductions, consumer goods carried a tariff of 35 percent. This helps to explain how the Kojima estimate of the effect of the Kennedy Round could be so small—less than $500 million.[56]

In summary, the relative weight of the factors determining the $11.1 billion increase in Japanese imports is as follows: Japanese economic growth, 81.1 percent; the rise of import prices, 9.0 percent; structural shifts in production, 7.2 percent; and Japanese import liberalization, 2.7 percent.

SURPLUS IN THE BALANCE OF TRADE. Some judgment is now possible concerning the development of the Japanese trade surplus. Table 6-14 summarizes how the various factors discussed above affected Japanese export and import growth. The trade balance improved by $8.4 billion from 1961 to 1971. Of this amount $1.2 billion can be attributed to the direct trade consequences of the Indochina conflict. The unbalancing results of the Kennedy Round can be credited with $0.8 billion. The favorable development of prices for Japanese trade can be assigned $2.7 billion. (This estimate was arrived at by comparing the estimate of the actual price changes with a hypothetical situation in which world export and import prices moved in the same way as Japan's export prices, in which case Japanese exports would have been $2.4 billion lower and Japanese imports $0.3 billion higher.) The remaining $3.6 billion improvement came from rapid growth and structural changes in Japan's economy, the combined result of the development of new export products, the adoption of import-saving technology, compositional shifts, and the import-raising consequences of declining sectors and rapid growth itself. Thus it can be concluded that about half the turnaround in trade in

54. Kiyoshi Kojima, *Nontariff Barriers to Japan's Trade* (Japan Economic Research Center, December 1971).
55. "Tariff Structure and Protection for Industry" [in Japanese], *Sekai keizai hyōron* (June 1957).
56. In this analysis, some double counting exists between the stimulation of imports through import liberalization and the estimate of increasing food and consumer goods imports because of structural shifts.

Table 6-13. *Estimates of Effect of Kennedy Round Reductions on Effective Tariffs in Japan*
Percent

Product	Nominal rate	Effective rate
Before Kennedy Round reductions (1967)		
Cotton	free	...
Cotton yarn	5.0	9.9
Cotton textiles	16.0	36.2
Clothing	27.8	48.8
Pulp woods	free	...
Pulp	5.0	3.0
Paper and paper board	13.6	30.2
Manufactured paper and paper board	15.0	16.7
Iron ore and scrap	free	...
Pig iron	10.0	24.4
Steel ingot	12.5	47.0
Rolled steel	15.0	35.1
Automobiles	36.0	66.5
After partial Kennedy Round reductions (1968)		
Raw materials	3.9	0.9
Capital goods	15.2	22.3
Intermediate goods	14.1	21.7
Finished capital goods	16.9	23.2
Consumer goods	23.6	35.8
After completion of Kennedy Round reductions (1972)		
Raw materials	2.3	0.8
Capital goods	9.3	13.7
Intermediate goods	8.9	14.7
Finished capital goods	9.9	11.9
Consumer goods	11.2	13.9

Sources: For 1967, estimates by Ippei Yamazawa, "Tariff Structure and Protection for Industry" [in Japanese], *Sekai keizai hyōron* (June 1967); for 1968, estimates by Watanabe and Mutō, in Ministry of Finance, *Kanzei chōsa geppō*, vol. 24 (April–June 1971), p. 71; for 1972, estimates in ibid., vol. 26 (January–March 1973).

the sixties occurred because of factors unique to the period, while the other half resulted from factors seemingly deepseated in the Japanese economy.

Balance-of-Payments Surpluses and Adjustment, 1969–72

By 1969 it was becoming increasingly evident that the Japanese balance of payments would be continually in surplus. Despite rates of economic growth in 1968–69 that were among the highest in the postwar period (14.4

Table 6-14. *Factors Affecting the Growth of Japanese Exports and Imports, 1961–71*

Billions of dollars

Item	Amount
Exports	
Foreign economic growth and expansion of world trade	9.0
Usual	7.8
Vietnam-connected	1.2
Improved price competitiveness	2.4
From domestic factors	1.1
From foreign inflation	1.3
Structural changes	6.8
Liberalization of commercial policies of other countries	1.3
Total	19.5
Imports	
Growth of Japanese economy	9.0
Import price increases	1.0
Structural changes	1.0
Import-saving	2.5
Import-raising	3.5
Liberalization of Japanese commercial policy	0.8
Less double counting	−0.4
Total	11.1

Source: See text.

percent and 11.9 percent), the Japanese trade balance and current account were recording rising surpluses. There was no instant consensus on what if anything to do about them. Since Japanese official reserves were quite low, further increases were still desirable, which suggested that an immediate reversal of the surplus was not necessary. Furthermore, the Japanese government was quite prepared to follow the European lead and blame the world's disequilibrium on the United States, and it suggested that the United States had an obligation to take corrective action.

A body of opinion was developing, however, that suggested that a Japanese initiative was required. As a result of a forecast of the economy in 1975 published in 1969, which predicted massive balance-of-payments surpluses, the Japan Economic Research Center (JERC) concluded that Japan would have to promote commodity imports, capital exports, and foreign aid beyond what governmental policies then in existence dictated if balance-of-payments disequilibria were to be avoided.[57] It suggested that Japan should consider a yen revaluation in the first half of the 1970s to increase real consumption in order to avoid an export-led inflation.

In general, there were four possible approaches to correcting the surplus problem: product-specific measures (including both imports and exports), capital outflows, domestic inflation, and yen revaluation. The alternatives were discussed during the spring and summer of 1971 and again in 1972 after the first revaluation of the yen appeared inadequate. The four approaches are not mutually exclusive, so combinations of them are possible and were indeed proposed.

PRODUCT-SPECIFIC MEASURES. Because of decisions already taken in 1968, Japan was committed to a three-year program of liberalizing residual import restrictions, and it first proceeded to reduce the number of items under quota restrictions (see Table 6-12). Neither the speed of the dismantling of the controls nor their quantitative importance, however, seemed adequate to solve the balance-of-payments surplus. Thus in June 1971, the government developed an eight-point plan to attack the problem and thereby avoid the necessity of revaluing the yen. The plan included tariff cuts, enlarging the General Scheme of Preferential Tariffs for the manufactured exports of less developed countries, further reductions of QRs, reducing other nontariff barriers, and the orderly marketing of exports.[58]

The measures aimed at liberalizing imports were desirable in themselves and long overdue. There is some evidence that up to 1969 one particular class of imports, consumer manufactured products (excluding processed foodstuffs), was being held to a level of imports below what could have been expected for a country at Japan's stage of development. Table 6-15 shows cross-country comparisons on this dimension. One would expect that a country like Japan, with high relative wages and per capita incomes, would import a considerable amount of manufactured consumer products because these goods tend to be labor intensive in production. Thus, as incomes rise, the amount of consumer goods imported (except for agricultural products) would be expected to increase more than proportionally. Japan's per capita income in 1969 was approximately equal to that achieved by France, West Germany, and the United Kingdom in 1963—countries somewhat similar to Japan in industrial structure. The ratio of imported manufactured consumer products to total personal consumption for France and the United Kingdom

57. Japan Economic Research Center, *Shōwa 50-nen no Nihon keizai* [The Japanese Economy in 1975] (December 1969).
58. Appendix item 75.

Table 6-15. *Imports of Manufactured Consumer Goods, Japan and Western European Countries,*[a] *Selected Years*

	Japan		West Germany		France		United Kingdom	
Item	1969	1972	1963	1969	1963	1969	1963	1971
Per capita income (dollars)	1,647	2,786	1,670	2,537	1,760	2,816	1,600	2,477
Total imports of manufactured consumer goods (millions of dollars)[b]	413	1,185	868.3	2,640.9	569.6	1,833.3	645.3	2,326.5
Total consumer expenditures (millions of dollars)	87,535	155,614	54,550	84,760	51,957	84,625	56,392	84,545
Ratio of imports to expenditures	0.0047	0.0076	0.0159	0.0312	0.0110	0.0217	0.0114	0.0275

Sources: 1969–72 income and expenditure figures, International Monetary Fund, *International Financial Statistics*, various issues. Import totals, Organisation for Economic Co-operation and Development, *National Accounts of OECD Countries, 1953–69* (Paris, 1971); OECD, *Trade by Commodities: Imports*, series C, January–December 1971, vols. 1, 2 (Paris, 1973); United Nations, *Yearbook of International Trade Statistics*, various issues; Ministry of Finance, *Japan Exports and Imports, 1972.*
a. Exchange rates are average annual rates, as follows: Japan—¥358 = $1, ¥303 = $1; West Germany—4DM = $1, 3.92DM = $1; France—4.9FF = $1, 5.18FF = $1; United Kingdom—$2.80 = £1, $2.44 = £1.
b. Consumer goods imports classified according to Ministry of Finance, *The Summary Report: Trade of Japan*, no. 3 (1973), p. 187.

was twice as large as for Japan, and Germany's was three times as great. It would, of course, be a mere coincidence if these ratios were identical, but the size of the discrepancy demands an explanation.

Two factors seem to be of great importance in explaining the low level of Japan's imports of manufactured consumer products—undervaluation of the yen and import barriers. The undervaluation is discussed below, but it should be noted here that it was particularly effective in restraining imports of those products for which domestic substitutes were available—and this category includes consumer manufactures. The second element, import barriers, is reflected in the escalation of tariff rates shown in Table 6-13. Even after partial Kennedy Round reductions had taken place, consumer goods carried an effective tariff rate of over 35 percent, a level that is high in itself and much above the Japanese average tariff, although the full Kennedy Round reductions moderated the protection greatly. The import deposit system also discriminated against consumption goods until 1969. Furthermore, the fact that the large general trading companies handled the importation of some of the consumer goods suggests that an ambiguous situation existed: imports could compete with certain domestic producers who were clients of the trading companies, and under these circumstances it is unlikely that competitive imports were sought or promoted very aggressively. Foreign producers also were not making great efforts to enter the Japanese market. Foreign exporters tended to market their products in Japan through exclusive distributorships, which in some well-known cases such as scotch whiskey tended to mark up prices excessively and thereby limited sales (though this changed in the later 1960s as it was recognized that such arrangements were not in the interests of either foreign producers or Japanese consumers). Thus formidable barriers existed to limit consumer imports.

While some further general tariff reductions served to liberalize consumer trade, and the Japanese also initiated tariff preferences for less developed countries (the General Scheme of Preferential Tariffs), the most important change was one of attitude toward competing imports. Since many less developed countries have some comparative advantage in the production of labor-intensive consumer products, the Japanese program of giving preferential access to these countries can be credited with some of the increase in consumer imports shown in Table 6-15, and it will be even more important in the future. Between 1969 and 1972, the share of imported manufactured consumer products in total consumption increased sharply in Japan, and much of that increase came from less developed countries. While the ratios of the other developed countries shown in the table also increased, Japan's increase was accomplished in a very few years—a significant difference.

Other Japanese actions regarding specific products were less effective and, from a social point of view, less desirable. There was some speeding up of the importation of such commodities as nuclear materials, particularly those from the United States; but since these commodities were not available from domestic sources, it is hard to see how such a policy could have any long-run effect on the balance-of-payments surplus. In addition, Japan put further restraints on the exports of certain manufactures such as steel and automobiles aimed primarily, though not exclusively, at the U.S. market. This circumvention of the market mechanism probably increased inefficiency and can be defended only on the grounds of temporary expediency, the Japanese being threatened by permanent quotas on the part of importing countries. The fact that these restraints could be relaxed following the second revaluation of the yen suggests that there was wisdom in the Japanese decision to control exports themselves; however, little credit can be given to these product-specific measures in solving the fundamental problem.

CAPITAL OUTFLOWS. International capital flows had been under rigorous controls during the entire postwar period. With the onset of the balance-of-payments surplus, steps were taken to ease restrictions on capital outflows; indeed, promoting long-term capital outflows became a major instrument in correcting the surplus. As shown in Table 6-10, the policy was effective: net long-term capital outflows rose from $155 million in 1969 to $4.5 billion in 1972. The outflow has taken many forms, including direct investment, long-term trade credits, participation in long-term Eurodollar loans, and flotations of IBRD, Asian Development Bank, and foreign government bonds of various sorts.[59]

Despite the apparent success of this policy, its usefulness as the primary long-run mechanism for adjusting the balance of payments is questionable. Japanese asset holders, liberated from restrictions, were presumably buying foreign assets for purposes of portfolio balance. Once the portfolio adjustment is completed, however, there is no reason to believe that continuing outflows would match expected trade surpluses. Furthermore, investment abroad soon yields a growing stream of returned interest, dividends, and profits (plus royalties and fees from controlled foreign enterprises). Thus a credit surplus in services would soon follow, requiring even larger new capital outflows. It is hard to believe that world capital markets would long support a movement of that magnitude. The removal of capital controls and the resulting increase in Japanese foreign investment are desirable developments for a liberal international economic system, but they do not replace the healthy functioning of a balance-of-payments adjustment mechanism.

DOMESTIC INFLATION. Some Japanese recognized that the imbalance of trade was due to the low level of Japanese prices relative to other countries at existing exchange rates. If the yen was not to be revalued, the imbalance could still be corrected through an increase in Japan's domestic prices, a so-called adjustment inflation. This view was espoused by the economist Osamu Shimomura;[60] he argued that such an inflation would promote economic growth. Also the Japanese Communist party advocated raising wages rather than revaluing the yen. It was argued that exchange parities should remain fixed even if that required a substantial increase in domestic prices.

While domestic inflation was considered by many Japanese to be an unavoidable part of the adjustment process, few supported a policy of actually creating an inflation for this purpose. The difficulties engendered by inflation are great because of the uncertain nature of the dynamic process, the misallocation of resources involved, and the social and political problems resulting from the inequity in the distribution of rewards and penalties among different groups. The undesirability of inflation also lies in the inability of governments to control it so as not to over- or undercorrect the surplus. Thus it is hard to believe that inflation was the best, or even a good, remedy for

59. Wilbur F. Monroe, *Japan: Financial Markets and the World Economy* (Praeger, 1973), pp. 153–64.

60. Shimomura is generally credited with being the father of the income-doubling plan during the Ikeda administration. He responded at that time to fears of rising prices by denying that consumer price increases constituted inflation if wholesale prices were stable.

the surplus problem, but it became the major consequence of the delay in revaluing the yen.

REVALUATION OF THE YEN. Having successfully resisted a devaluation of the yen when faced with a balance-of-payments deficit in the 1950s, the Japanese had some reason to believe that they could similarly resist a revaluation to correct a surplus. Nevertheless, there was growing evidence that the yen was seriously undervalued. As seen in Table 6-11, Japanese export prices had risen much less than those of competing industrial countries. Furthermore, the Canadian dollar had risen in value after being floated during the summer of 1970; the German D-mark and Dutch guilder had risen since they began to float in the spring of 1971; and even the Swiss franc, a currency whose gold value had not been altered since the 1930s, had been revalued in May 1971. These actions of other countries increased the undervaluation of the yen, which by the summer of 1971 was being described as the most undervalued major currency in the world.

In addition to its natural reluctance to change the parity in either direction, the Japanese government had a number of reasons for not wanting to revalue the yen in 1971.[61] The Japanese economy had hit a cyclical peak at the end of 1969 and had been in a slowdown throughout 1970 and into 1971. The government was concerned that a revaluation of the yen would postpone the recovery through its inhibiting effect on export prospects and business sentiment. Furthermore, some observers thought the balance of payments would return to equilibrium once economic recovery was under way, thus obviating the need for a revaluation. There was also much support for the belief that Japan should liberalize its trade restrictions as a first step to restoring equilibrium. Such a strategy would put competitive pressures only on import-competing industries, which would enhance gains in productivity, whereas revaluation would also place a heavy adjustment burden on export industries, some of which had substantial currency exposure through fixed-price contracts in dollars.[62] Finally, it was thought that satisfying the unmet needs of the Japanese economy, such as greater personal consumption, more and better housing, social services, and pollution abatement, would drain domestic resources to the extent that the surplus balance of payments would soon disappear without revaluation.

61. Summarized in the *Mitsubishi Bank Review,* vol. 2 (July 1971).
62. Japanese shipbuilders, for example, had many fixed-price export contracts in dollars for deliveries a number of years in the future. Because of exchange control, these contracts could not be hedged in the forward market. Yen revaluation, therefore, reduced the yen receipts from export sales and, without a reduction in yen costs of production, cut directly into profits.

The discussion of revaluation was not one-sided, however, and influential voices were suggesting that revaluation would not have the dire consequences being claimed and, in fact, would even be desirable from a Japanese perspective. Masahiro Tatemoto, for example, published an econometric study that simulated a 10 percent revaluation to take place in January–March 1970.[63] He concluded that the current overseas surplus would be decreased by 11 percent during the first year (fiscal 1970), that the real growth rate of GNP would not be seriously affected (11 percent in fiscal 1970 versus 11.4 percent without revaluation), that the rise in the consumer price index would be moderated (from a 5.5 percent rise to 4.7 percent) and the expected rise in wholesale prices converted to a decline (2.1 percent to −1.9 percent). Tatemoto also found that a complementary fiscal policy to increase government investment by ¥200 billion at the time of revaluation would decrease the current surplus by 40 percent, while keeping price changes almost the same and maintaining the growth rate at 11.4 percent. Another simulation utilizing a sliding parity with a revaluation of 3 percent per quarter for four quarters suggested greater effectiveness in recovering external equilibrium as well as domestic price stabilization.

In June 1971, a group of academic economists led by Akihiro Amano and Ryūtarō Komiya publicly endorsed the concept of a yen revaluation through a crawling peg system of exchange rates, whereby rates were revalued gradually rather than abruptly or than being allowed to float.[64] The group concluded that a crawling peg system would permit Japan to recover both external and internal equilibrium, based on the recognition that external equilibrium could not be attained at bearable costs without a revaluation and that the crawling peg method would reduce the adjustment costs for domestic industries and decrease possible disturbances from short-term capital movements.

Whether a consensus would ever develop on revaluing the yen became a moot question when on August 15, 1971, President Nixon announced the "new economic policy" of the United States, including the suspension of convertibility of the dollar into gold or other reserve assets and a temporary 10 percent import surcharge. The United States made known its intention of

63. Reported in *Nihon keizai shinbun* [Japan Economic Journal] (March 1970). He utilized a short-term econometric model of the Japan Economic Research Center. The analysis compared two projections, one similar to the standard short-term JERC forecast without revaluation and the other with the same conditions and exogenous variables but with revaluation.

64. Kawase Seisaku Kenkyūkai, "Yen rate no kokizami chōsei ni tsuite" [A Proposal for Yen Revaluation through a Crawling Peg System], reprinted in *Gendai keizai*, vol. 2 (September 1971).

wanting the dollar to float downward in value, and the surcharge was widely interpreted as an attempt to exert leverage on countries such as Japan that might be tempted to support their old dollar parities by buying dollars, even though they would not be convertible into gold. In fact the Bank of Japan did continue to buy dollars at the old rate for a number of days following the "Nixon shock." The bank bought $4.5 billion during the month of August alone, an amount equal to the entire reserve holdings of Japan before 1971. Even after the yen was permitted to float, the bank intervened frequently and thereby accumulated another $3.0 billion by the end of the year, when reserves reached a total of $15.4 billion.

It is still somewhat difficult to explain the behavior of the Bank of Japan during this period. It could be argued that the government still wanted to avoid revaluation of the yen at any cost, but this thesis is hard to support. With all other major currencies appreciating against the dollar, Japan would surely have faced increasingly discriminatory trade restrictions if it had attempted to maintain an undervalued currency, and this must have been realized in the government. A more plausible hypothesis is that the Ministry of Finance recognized the foreign currency exposure of Japanese firms, particularly the large trading firms, and wanted to give them a chance to cover their positions before changing the rate. Since Japanese exchange controls were quite strict, the resulting windfalls would be distributed only to Japanese and not to foreigners. Japanese firms, as might be expected, responded by selling all the dollars they owned or could borrow, with a resulting increase in Japanese reserves and a huge capital loss to the central bank.[65]

As part of the Smithsonian Agreement of December 18, 1971, the Japanese revalued the yen by 16.88 percent against the dollar. Since other countries also changed their parities, the effective revaluation of the yen on a trade-weighted basis was 12.5 percent. According to a purchasing-power-parity type of analysis based on comparative unit labor costs in manufacturing, the Smithsonian revaluation more than offset Japan's competitive gains since 1963 and thus could have been expected in time to restore equilibrium.[66] Nevertheless, actual developments during the course of 1972 did not seem to bear out this expectation. The surplus on current account rose quarter by quarter, despite the fact that the real growth of the economy was accelerating. While some perverse movements might be expected in the current

65. According to U.S. figures, Japanese parent firms withdrew $531 million from their U.S. subsidiaries during 1971, so that by the end of the year the parent firms owed more to their subsidiaries than they had invested in them.

66. Morgan Guaranty Trust Company of New York, *World Financial Markets*, May 18, 1972, pp. 4–9.

account immediately after a revaluation (the inverted J-curve), their contin-uation under adverse cyclical conditions seemed abnormal and indicated that a further revaluation was required. This underestimate of the required re-valuation can occur because a comparative unit labor cost analysis fails to pick up those competitive gains that come from the new industries or new products that were of great importance for Japan during the 1960s, and it also fails to reflect capital movements.

By the late fall of 1972, many observers were expecting another revalua-tion of the yen to take place after the elections for the Lower House of the Diet, which were held in early December and confirmed Kakuei Tanaka as prime minister. Surprisingly, however, Prime Minister Tanaka insisted that the yen would not be revalued further. Japanese companies once again began to sell dollars, which the Bank of Japan was forced to buy to maintain the ¥308 rate; the resulting inflow raised Japanese reserves to over $18 billion.[67] By mid-February 1973, the run from the dollar had become so widespread that the United States took the initiative to devalue the dollar a second time. As part of the arrangement, Japan agreed to let the yen float and a new rela-tionship of about 265 yen per dollar was soon established in the market, representing a further 15 percent revaluation against the dollar. On March 2, 1973, most other countries joined Japan in letting their currencies float against the dollar. Based on a trade-weighted calculation, the yen had gained a further 11.1 percent on average, and thus a full 24.7 percent appreciation against its pre-May 1971 value.

Two econometric studies estimated the expected consequences of the yen revaluation—one by the Japan Economic Research Center under the direc-tion of Tadao Uchida, the other by Akihiro Amano as a result of a compre-hensive study of the Japanese balance of payments.[68] Uchida's study is an attempt actually to forecast the consequences of revaluation, although in a simplified manner. His results indicated a rather rapid correction of the cur-rent overseas surplus—a $4 billion reduction in the $8 billion surplus in fiscal 1971, with slight modifications in the following two years. The Amano study is much more comprehensive and analytical, but difficult to apply to the actual situation. Nonetheless, an approximate application of his findings

67. Since the Bank of Japan does not count as part of its reserves certain long-term foreign assets it owns, effective reserve assets were even higher. Also the Ministry of Finance placed dollar deposits with commercial banks to forestall their further borrow-ing from abroad and to encourage repayment of previous short-term dollar borrowings. These deposits are also not counted in official reserves.

68. Tadao Uchida, in *Nihon keizai shinbun*, Feb. 11, 1973; Akihiro Amano, *An Econometric Model of the Japanese Balance of Payments and Its Policy Implications*, JERC Paper no. 22 (August 1973).

would suggest that the reduction in the current overseas surplus would be 40 percent in the first year following the revaluation and would rise to 60 percent by the third year.[69]

Having learned from actual experience with revaluation, as well as the various academic studies and intensive public discussion of the subject, the Japanese government is showing much greater willingness to utilize foreign exchange rate policy. In the 1973 economic whitepaper, the government recognized the contribution that a more flexible exchange rate can make in achieving economic goals.[70] It accepted the idea that monetary and fiscal policy can be more effective in achieving internal and external balance when combined with foreign exchange rate policy. This was a substantial change from the time only a few years ago when a rigid exchange rate was accepted as a matter of dogma and moral imperative.

The New Adjustment of 1973–74

Each of the four approaches to correcting the balance-of-payments surplus outlined above seems to have made some impact in 1973, though it is not possible to distinguish clearly among the effects of yen revaluation, domestic inflation, and trade liberalization measures; capital outflows, however, can to some extent be separately discussed. In combination, these approaches cut the trade surplus in half in 1973, thus seemingly confirming the econometric forecasts. The current account surplus was eliminated and a deficit was recorded in the basic balance and the official settlements balances. The oil crisis late in 1973 helped to create a new deficit problem for Japan, as it did for most other oil-importing countries.

The delay until February in revaluing the yen had the unintended and undesirable consequence of generating tremendous growth in domestic monetary liquidities and created substantial inflationary pressures within the economy. Even though the Ministry of Finance subsequently shifted to a policy of monetary restraint, the damage could not easily be corrected. Thus domestic inflation and yen revaluation combined to raise imports and restrain exports.

Total imports into Japan in 1973 expanded by a remarkable 71 percent in current dollar value; close to half the increase resulted from higher volume

69. This result is calculated from his table 5.14 (p. 109), which is based on a 10 percent revaluation. The trade consequences were multiplied by 2.47 to correspond to the actual revaluation.

70. Economic Planning Agency, *Annual Survey on the Japanese Economy, 1972* (August 1973), pp. 38–64.

and the remainder from price increases. Japanese exports expanded by 29 percent in 1973, but almost all the increase was due to higher dollar prices. Raw materials accounted for $7.6 billion of the $13.5 billion increase in imports, but their gain was only 60 percent, or less than the average for all imports. Thus manufactured products, which are expected to show greater import demand elasticities, seemed in fact to do so. In particular, imports of clothing and other consumer goods showed a sharp increase, reflecting both price developments and import liberalization. The monetary inflation was noticeable in the import of such luxury items as diamonds, art objects, and race horses, and also certain raw materials such as wool, which more than doubled in value.

Some important shifts in trade patterns were also visible in 1973. Japanese trade with less developed countries and with some communist countries expanded faster than trade with developed countries. For instance, Japanese exports to the United States increased by less than 7 percent in value, while imports increased by 58 percent. U.S.–Japanese trade was thus asymmetric because the change in the dollar/yen exchange rate was larger than the change in the yen exchange rate with most other currencies. Japanese exports to Europe, where the yen revaluation was smaller, did better, expanding by 38 percent; imports also grew sharply, by 64 percent, but from a smaller base. Exports and imports with the less developed countries, especially in South and East Asia and the Middle East, expanded very rapidly and constituted a rising fraction of Japanese trade. Finally, imports from both China and the Soviet Union almost doubled and exports to China increased by 70 percent, but there was little export gain to the U.S.S.R. Thus, while a rough trade balance was created between China and Japan, Japan ran a sizable bilateral trade deficit with the Soviet Union.

The effects of inflation and yen revaluation also appeared in the service accounts. Service payments expanded by $3.9 billion and receipts by only $2.3 billion, raising the overall service deficit from $1.9 billion in 1972 to $3.5 billion in 1973. Inflation, in particular, raised the cost of ocean transportation as time charters and freight rates advanced. Both inflation and revaluation affected personal travel: receipts remained constant, but payments went up by almost $500 million. Many Japanese tourists took advantage of their higher valued currency to visit foreign countries, and groups of Japanese visitors became an increasingly common sight at most tourist meccas of the world. Significantly, Japanese investment income expanded faster than payments to foreigners, reflecting developments in capital flows. As discussed in the next section, in 1973 outflows of Japanese long-term investment expanded rapidly while foreigners reduced their long-term investments in

Japan; this caused the large deficit in the basic balance and official settlements.

Further deterioration in Japan's balance of payments resulted from the oil embargo and subsequent increases in oil prices. Most imports of crude petroleum come from the Persian Gulf, but the source of the import hardly matters for the balance of payments, since all oil exporters raised their prices in a coordinated fashion. Japan imported $4 billion of crude oil in 1972 and $6 billion in 1973. In 1974, after the rise in prices, oil imports rose to above $20 billion. The Japanese adjustment burden is part of the worldwide problem and cannot be considered independently of developments in the rest of the world. Elements in the adjustment process will include increased prices of other products, possibly somewhat lower real prices for oil, more efficient use of energy by all users, tapping new sources of energy, and larger real exports to the oil-producing nations. It is notable that Japanese exports to the Middle East had already increased by over 50 percent in 1973, and great efforts are being made to continue the expansion.

From the beginning of 1974, Japan's exchange rate policy underwent further modification. The Ministry of Finance had already shown its willingness to change the rate through the two revaluations and, in the latter part of 1973, through a series of small devaluations; but all these moves represented the government dictating to the market what the rate should be. As of 1974, however, the government seemed to be accepting less responsibility for setting spot rates and let the market fluctuate more from day to day. Of course, exchange controls were operated to limit overall participation in the market, but allowing greater freedom in the spot market is a significant development.

International Investment and Japan

The caution with which Japan reestablished contacts with the international capital market after World War II stands in sharp contrast to the speed with which trade ties were forged and flows promoted. The balance of payments was considered primarily in trade terms until the surplus emerged in the 1970s. In recent years, however, capital flows have become more important to the balance of payments, and direct investment, both inward and outward, has begun to have an impact on the evolution of the entire Japanese economy.

Japan's Asset-Liability Position

During the years when the government feared a balance-of-payments deficit, rigorous exchange controls were maintained to prevent capital outflows.

Capital inflows, however, were also controlled, lest a burdensome repayment problem develop from private-sector borrowing; furthermore, the government was financing its own expenditures out of current tax receipts and thus had no need to place debt abroad. Fundamentally, Japan did not borrow much abroad because of the adequacy of domestic saving. Nevertheless, some capital flows did take place, as the balance-of-payments accounts show (see Table 6-10). The resulting long-term asset-and-liability position is shown in Table 6-16.

As would be expected, Japan was a net debtor country in the early 1960s, but by relatively small amounts. In 1962, Japanese liabilities exceeded assets by less than $1 billion, and in the trough year of 1964 the excess was less than $2 billion. The major form of borrowing was in loans to help finance domestic industrial investment. Japanese foreign lending in these years was primarily in trade credits and was undertaken to encourage exports. When the shift to surplus in the balance of payments occurred in 1965, the tempo of foreign lending picked up and Japan reached net creditor status in 1967. The forms of borrowing and lending stayed much the same, though foreign interest in Japanese securities became greater and Japanese lending in loan form expanded in the latter half of the 1960s.

With a lag of a few years, Japanese net earnings on foreign investment reflected the shift from debtor to creditor status. As pictured in Figure 6-1, the largest net outflow of earnings was about $300 million, recorded in 1969. Net inflows began in the fourth quarter of 1971 and reached almost $500 million in 1973. Returned earnings reflect many different factors, including such items as the composition of portfolios and the portion of concessionary finance in total loans, and they are subject to a variable time lag. Though exact measurements are not possible because of the limited experience, approximate calculations of rates of return seem to indicate that Japan received a somewhat lower rate of return on its foreign investment (between 7 and 9 percent) than it paid to foreigners on their investment in Japan. The difference, however, is not great and may not reflect real factors. It is likely that net foreign earnings will be making a major contribution to Japan's balance of payments in the future and will obviate the need for a trade surplus.

Despite steps to liberalize capital movements within recent years, they are still the most controlled segment of Japanese international commerce. Unlike trade, the government has apparently not endorsed, even in principle, the idea of freedom of capital movements of all types. It has used controls as an instrument to offset other developments in the balance of payments; and there have been many changes—some liberalizing and some restricting, some dealing with inflows and others with outflows. When the large current account surplus developed in 1971–72, restrictions against capital outflows were

Table 6-16. *Japanese Long-Term Foreign Assets and Liabilities Outstanding, 1962–73*[a]
Millions of dollars

Item	1962	1963	1964	1965	1966	1967	1968	1969	1970	1971	1972	1973
Long-term assets	1,478	1,760	2,041	2,503	3,209	4,082	5,181	6,689	8,745	11,270	16,185	24,623
Direct investments	395	515	562	639	746	866	1,089	1,295	1,647	1,851	2,574	4,460
Trade credits	633	737	1,072	1,315	1,716	2,200	2,783	3,457	4,270	5,125	5,412	6,493
Loans	64	124	173	287	436	655	894	1,230	1,859	2,806	4,546	7,626
Other	386	384	234	262	311	361	415	707	969	1,488	3,653	6,044
Long-term liabilities	2,428	3,243	3,898	3,932	3,825	3,880	4,538	5,891	6,326	9,554	13,147	14,427
Direct investments	274	376	477	522	552	598	673	745	837	1,337	1,645	1,687
Trade credits	37	95	176	167	133	94	90	93	103	97	141	149
Loans	1,144	1,557	1,894	1,915	1,896	1,925	2,192	2,577	2,654	2,617	2,388	2,704
Security investments	156	276	291	231	206	275	505	1,235	1,485	3,838	7,351	7,941
External bonds	327	481	635	708	683	669	789	989	1,033	235	217	415
Other	490	458	425	389	355	319	289	252	214	1,430	1,405	1,531
Net asset-liability position												
Total long-term position	−950	−1,483	−1,857	−1,429	−616	202	643	798	2,419	1,716	3,038	10,196
Direct investments	121	139	85	117	194	268	416	550	810	514	929	2,773
Trade credits	596	642	896	1,148	1,583	2,106	2,693	3,364	4,167	5,028	5,271	6,344
Loans	−1,080	−1,433	−1,721	−1,628	−1,460	−1,270	−1,298	−1,347	−795	189	2,158	4,922
Other	−587	−831	−1,117	−1,066	−933	−902	−1,168	−1,769	−1,763	−4,015	−5,320	−3,843

Sources: For 1962–70, estimates made by an anonymous leading commercial bank and collected by Akihiro Amano; for 1971–73, *Nihon keizai shinbun*, July 25, 1969, Jan. 4, 1970, Jan. 4, 1971, Oct. 3, 1971, April 17, 1974. Figures for recent years have also been published by the Ministry of Finance. Estimates should correspond to the sum of the annual flows from the balance-of-payments accounts (with an appropriate change of sign) plus a correction for price changes of market securities, bad debts, and the like.

a. End of years.

Figure 6-1. *Japan's Long-Term Net Foreign Assets-Liability Position
and Net Return on Foreign Investments, 1961–73*

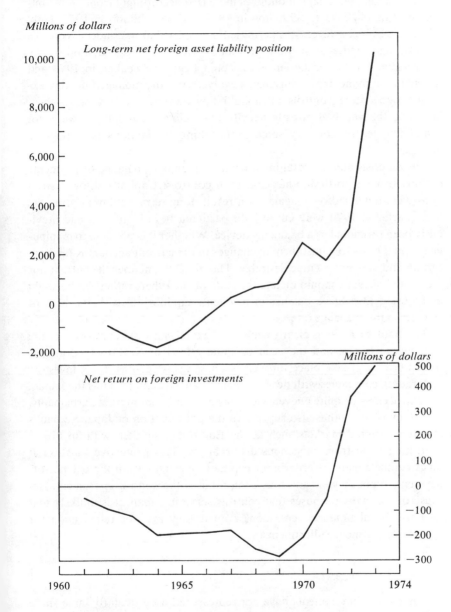

Millions of dollars

Long-term net foreign asset liability position

10,000

8,000

6,000

4,000

2,000

0

−2,000

Millions of dollars

500

Net return on foreign investments

400

300

200

100

0

−100

−200

−300

1960   1965   1970   1974

Sources: Asset-liability position, Table 6-16; return on investments, Bank of Japan, *Balance
of Payments Monthly* (March 1970 and March 1974).

eased, and long-term capital outflows increased accordingly from the $2 billion level of 1970–71 to $5 billion in 1972 and $8.5 billion in 1973. Only selective easing, however, was permitted on capital inflows; indeed, controls were strengthened against short-term inflows to prevent speculation on the yen revaluation. When the current account began to weaken in 1973 and international monetary arrangements evolved into the managed floating exchange rate system, controls on capital inflows were eased further. By then, however, the yen had already heavily appreciated and inflows were not stimulated; to the contrary some profit-taking liquidations by foreigners occurred.

The oil crisis and the resulting downturn in Japan's balance-of-payments outlook brought forth another change in controls. Capital outflow restrictions were tightened once again; as a result, long-term outflows during the first quarter of 1974 were cut in half, particularly in loans that had previously been promoted as a balancing device. Whether it is possible to manipulate capital flows to adjust them to changes in the current account is far from certain and may not even be desirable. Theoretically, neither the current nor the capital account should dictate the state of the other; rather, both should be adjusted to achieve balance-of-payments equilibrium with the help of changes in the exchange rate.

The Bank of Japan is clearly capable of exercising strict controls over the commercial banks, and they can be quite effective. Nevertheless, uncontrolled flows can take place through business firms such as direct investors and trading companies with ties to foreign financial centers. Thus the impact of controls may be quite uneven with respect to different market participants. The Bank of Japan has also supervised the participation of Japanese banks in foreign capital markets such as the Eurodollar market, with an eye to protecting them from exogenous disturbances. This protective function at times conflicts with the criteria for capital movements from the balance-of-payments point of view and thus compromises the control instrument. Because of the many purposes that controls serve in Japan, it is unlikely that they will be abandoned very soon, even if they are not relied upon for balance-of-payments adjustments.

Direct Investments

While direct investments have not represented a particularly large share of Japanese overseas assets or liabilities, they have been the most controversial form of financial involvement with the rest of the world and, for much of the postwar period, the most drastically controlled.[71] The reason that direct investment has received so much attention is that it involves the total transplanting of a foreign enterprise, including its entrepreneurs, technology, and marketing skills, as well as capital. Japanese distrust of foreigners, with its deep historical roots, was undoubtedly a crucial element in setting the restrictive tone of Japan's attitudes toward foreign enterprises in Japan.

The control of foreign investment was laid down in 1950 through the Law Concerning Foreign Investment.[72] The law was intended to protect Japanese-owned firms from foreign competition. Foreign investment was permitted only when it helped achieve Japanese self-sufficiency and thereby contributed to overcoming the balance-of-payments deficit. Foreign firms were permitted at most only 49 percent ownership of Japanese enterprises. Over time a number of changes were introduced into the controls, which culminated in a series of five rounds of liberalization.[73] Under the fifth round of liberalization of May 1, 1973, foreigners could obtain 100 percent ownership of Japanese enterprises, subject to certain exceptions. Investment in five industries was restricted in various ways, and for seventeen other industries, full liberalization was delayed according to a specified schedule.[74]

Some foreign investors took advantage of the opportunities provided and

71. For other work of the present authors on this subject, see Lawrence B. Krause, "Evolution of Foreign Direct Investment: The United States and Japan," in Jerome B. Cohen, (ed.), *Pacific Partnership: United States–Japan Trade, Prospects and Recommendations for the Seventies* (Japan Society, 1973), pp. 149–76; idem, "The International Economic System and the Multinational Enterprise," *The Annals,* vol. 403 (September 1972), pp. 93–103; Sueo Sekiguchi and K. Matsuba, *Nihon no chokasetsu tōshi* [Japan's Direct Investments] (Nihon Keizai Shinbunsha, 1974).

72. Appendix item 14.

73. Appendix items 32a, 62, 69, and 80.

74. The restricted industries where foreign investment is subject to case-by-case screening include the primary industries (agriculture, forestry, and fishing), the oil industry, and leather or leather products manufacturing. In the mining industry, foreign investment is permitted up to 50 percent participation, and in retail trade operations foreign participation is permitted up to 50 percent of ownershp, but only in companies with eleven stores or fewer. The dates of full liberalization of the seventeen other restricted industries are as follows: fruit juice or fruit materials manufacturing and photosensitized material manufacturing, May 1, 1976; information processing, April 1, 1976; manufacturing, sales, or leasing of electronic computers, December 1, 1975; meat products manufacturing, tomato products manufacturing, precooked foods for distribution to restaurants, manufacturing of or wholesale trade in apparel, drugs and agricultural chemicals manufacturing, ferroalloy products manufacturing, hydraulic equipment manufacturing, packaging- or packing-machinery manufacturing, electronic precision instruments for medical or electric measurement manufacturing, phonographic records manufacturing, and real estate business, May 1, 1975; integrated circuits manufacturing, December 1, 1974.

Table 6-17. *Estimates of the Cumulative Value of Foreign Direct Investment in Japan, 1960–73*

Millions of dollars

End of Year	Source of estimate			
	Table 6-16 (1)	Balance of payments (2)	Special survey (3)	Book value of U.S. direct investment in Japan (4)
1960	n.a.	185	91	254
1961	n.a.	229	n.a.	302
1962	274	274	n.a.	373
1963	376	362	n.a.	472
1964	477	445	n.a.	598
1965	522	492	272	675
1966	552	522	313	756
1967	598	567	345	870
1968	673	643	412	1,050
1969	745	715	482	1,244
1970	837	809	596	1,483
1971	1,337	1,019	851	1,821
1972	1,645	1,188	1,011	2,222
1973	1,687	1,146	n.a.	2,733

Sources: Col. (1), same as Table 6-16; col. (2), benchmarked in 1962 from Table 6-6 and cumulated from annual figures from Bank of Japan, *Balance of Payments Monthly*; col. (3), Keizai Chōsa Kyōkai, "Kigyōbetsu gaishi dōnyū sōran" [Survey on Capital Importation by Enterprises], *Setting Up in Japan* (Tokyo), p. 5; col. (4), U.S. Department of Commerce, *Survey of Current Business*, and *Balance of Payments: Statistical Supplement*.
n.a. Not available.

made rather modest investments in Japan, as shown in Table 6-17. The value of direct foreign investment is not easily calculated, and estimates made from various sources differ somewhat. The differences relate to the definition of what constitutes a direct investment as distinct from a portfolio investment or a loan to a controlled enterprise, timing differences, and inclusion of retained earnings. All Japanese estimates for 1972 fall within a range of $1.0 billion to $1.6 billion. According to these sources, 66 percent of foreign investment in Japan is owned by Americans. From U. S. data, the book value of U. S. direct investment in Japan is given as $2.2 billion in 1972, which implies $3.4 billion for total foreign investment (as defined by the U.S. Department of Commerce). Despite the ambiguity, it is clear that total foreign investment is quite small in relation to the size of the Japanese economy. Foreign investment is concentrated in machinery manufacturing, petroleum, and chemicals; only in the case of petroleum is the percentage of foreign ownership of the domestic industry very large.

The slow process of the liberalization of controls, which came about only after great pressure from abroad, indicates that the government did not believe that the benefits to Japan of inward foreign investment were very great relative to the costs. The Japanese have not been short of domestic entrepreneurs or of domestic capital for business investment, and while foreign technology was coveted, it was obtainable through license or purchase (as discussed in Chapter 8). Nevertheless, liberalization was finally recognized by the government as a necessity, particularly in view of the intention of Japanese firms to invest abroad heavily themselves. Foreign firms have sought entry into Japan for the usual business reasons: the Japanese market is large and growing rapidly, Japanese firms have achieved major technological advancements, and direct investment in Japan is considered the best way of sharing in the market and maintaining competitiveness vis-à-vis Japanese enterprises.

Outward direct investment by Japanese firms was also strictly controlled for balance-of-payments reasons. As the fear of deficits receded in the 1960s, more investment was permitted, and foreign investment was subsequently encouraged in order to correct the surplus when that condition was recognized.[75] By 1971 the Japanese government was encouraging direct investment to develop natural resources abroad through special tax provisions aimed principally at the production of oil, coal, uranium, iron ore, and nonferrous ores.[76]

Despite the controls on outflows, Japanese direct investment abroad was greater than inward foreign direct investment, even in the early 1960s. Once the constraints were lifted, Japanese firms responded aggressively to the opportunities to invest abroad. As shown in Table 6-18, annual increases in investment rose dramatically after 1969;[77] by 1972, the Japanese were among the largest direct investors in the world.

The distribution of Japanese foreign direct investment by industry is shown in Table 6-19. Investment in manufacturing constitutes only about

75. Appendix items 70, 73, and 74.
76. Appendix item 76.
77. Japanese data are of two sorts: approval data as reported by the Ministry of Finance and the MITI, and balance-of-payments data as reported by the Bank of Japan. They differ considerably, with figures on approvals being much larger and reported in greater detail; this is because approvals precede expenditures leading to a timing difference. Approvals are more broadly defined to include all management ties, while the data for payments have a minimum cutoff of 25 percent ownership. Approval data also recognize currency adjustments and the like and thus come close to the U.S. concept of book value. Approval data indicate different forms of direct investment, all of which would appear as direct investment under U.S. definitions. Most of the subsequent analysis is based on approval data.

448 LAWRENCE KRAUSE AND SUEO SEKIGUCHI

Table 6-18. *Capital and Income Flows of Japanese Direct Investment Abroad, 1951–73*

Millions of dollars

Fiscal year	Direct investments, approval basis[a]	Balance-of-payments basis	
		Direct investments	Income
1951–60	289	n.a.	n.a.
1961	166	104	9
1962	99	62	11
1963	126	125	12
1964	120	44	12
1965	160	105	15
1966	228	101	21
1967	278	137	27
1968	559	228	37
1969	667	230	48
1970	912	397	90
1971	876	417	118
1972	2,338	852	184
1973	3,600[b]	2,199	240
Total	10,418	5,001	824

Sources: United States–Japan Trade Council, *Council Report*, no. 56 (Sept. 21, 1973); Bank of Japan, *Balance of Payments Monthly* (August 1971, May 1973, and March 1974).

n.a. Not available.

a. Includes acquisition of shares of and loans to companies controlled by Japanese interests, direct foreign operations, and overseas branches.

b. Based on nine-month data.

one-quarter of the total, with textiles the largest single industry concentration. This distribution differs from that of other advanced countries both in the small share of manufacturing in the total and in the large share of textiles. The textile industry is generally characterized by rather small firms, and a unique feature of Japanese direct investment has been the participation of smaller firms aided by the general trading companies. The major investment activities of the Japanese have been in mining (including crude petroleum), and this concentration has been increasing in recent years. In fiscal 1972, close to one-half of new investment was in mining. No doubt this reflects Japan's need for imported raw materials, and possibly also the tax incentive noted above.

The motivation of Japanese firms to invest abroad stems from the usual business desire to stay competitive with foreign enterprises and also from the particular resource endowment of Japan. Japan has a plentiful supply of entrepreneurs and management skills and thus can export these resources to others through direct investment. Japan has shortages in other areas, how-

Table 6-19. *Japan's Overseas Investment, by Industry,*
through Fiscal 1972[a]

Industry	Fiscal 1972		Cumulative total, through fiscal 1972	
	Amount (millions of dollars)	Percent of total	Amount (millions of dollars)	Percent of total
Manufacturing	524	22.4	1,777	26.2
Food	29	1.2	109	1.6
Textiles	163	7.0	417	6.2
Lumber and pulp	35	1.5	296	4.4
Chemicals	67	2.9	143	2.1
Iron and nonferrous metals	53	2.3	241	3.6
Nonelectric machinery	37	1.6	128	1.9
Electric machinery	69	3.0	167	2.5
Transportation machinery	42	1.8	157	2.3
Other	31	1.3	119	1.8
Nonmanufacturing	1,814	77.6	4,996	73.8
Agriculture and forestry	16	0.7	85	1.3
Fishery	12	0.5	51	0.8
Mining (including crude oil)	1,136	48.6	2,491	36.8
Construction	7	0.3	47	0.7
Commerce	230	9.8	754	11.1
Finance and insurance	189	8.1	565	8.3
Other	224	9.6	1,003	14.8
Total	2,338	100.0	6,773	100.0

Source: Ministry of International Trade and Industry data of August 7, 1973, cited in United States–Japan Trade Council, *Council Report*, no. 56 (Sept. 21, 1973).
a. All figures for fiscal 1972 are preliminary.

ever, which can be made up through direct investment. In recent years the Japanese labor market has been tightening and wages have been rising rapidly. Whether or not this situation should be described as a labor short-age, it is clear that Japanese producers of labor-intensive products such as textiles and consumer electronics have been losing their competitiveness in domestic plants; they have sought to recoup their losses in such places as Korea and Taiwan, where wages are lower. In addition, Japan has what might be described as a natural endowment shortage. New plants sites, par-ticularly tidewater locations, are hard to find because of a shortage of land and also because previous experience with industrial pollution has made many communities cautious about permitting more development. New anti-pollution laws further reinforce the difficulty of engaging in pollution-causing industry in Japan. Thus Japanese firms are seeking foreign locations with the requisite physical characteristics and a permissive political environment.

Moreover, Japanese firms continually seek new sources of raw materials to provide for their ever-increasing needs. Direct investment can make a contribution by helping discover and exploit promising resources in countries lacking the capital or technical knowledge to do it themselves. Furthermore, in a world subject to supply interruptions, some control over raw material production adds marginally to Japan's economic security, although the oil crisis proved that mere ownership of foreign resources does not guarantee continuity of supplies. Since all the factors promoting outward direct investment are likely to continue to exist, the Japanese desire for large investments abroad is likely to be maintained for some time.

Conclusions

One must conclude any study of Japan's economic involvement with the rest of the world by recalling its lack of domestic raw materials and the consequent dependence on other countries, a dependence that colors all economic relations with foreigners. This dependence is so overriding that one can be misled into exaggerating the importance of foreign trade for the growth of the Japanese economy. As this chapter has shown, foreign trade has been of strategic importance, but by no means the critical force driving Japan's economy.

Part of the Japanese economic miracle, however, may be the result of inherent weakness—the Japanese learned to make the best of adversity. Because of Japan's isolation and its ignorance of the outside world, the general trading company was developed, which proved tremendously efficient in conducting international commerce. Because of the lack of domestic raw materials and the consequent need to import, Japan pioneered the development of bulk carriers, which reduced the cost of water transportation, and created the most advanced shipbuilding industry in the world. Japan also developed tidewater sites for processing plants to make the best use of these carriers. Because these sites required large investments, they could be justified only by large plants, which in turn permitted the capturing of economies of scale in manufacturing. In the case of agriculture, where small-scale farms persisted, a small-scale agricultural implements industry developed to serve their needs. The lesson the world might learn from the Japanese example is not, of course, to seek adversity, but to recognize that most difficulties can be transformed in such a way as to advance society.

While Japanese policy has been responsive to balance-of-payments needs, it has not been crowned with infinite wisdom. In particular, the rigidity that has characterized exchange rate policy until recent years was unfortunate. While understandable within the historical setting, the failure of Japan to correct the overvaluation of the yen during the 1950s and the undervaluation in the late 1960s led to some unnecessary economic costs. Most of these costs were borne by the Japanese themselves, but part of the burden fell on other countries when Japan resisted revaluation. The exchange rate lesson has been learned, but whether Japan will be fully mindful of its impact on other countries in different contexts remains to be seen.

It should not be concluded that Japan has solved all its economic problems or properly worked out all its international relations. Many problems remain to be addressed. With respect to international economic relations, the root of many problems lies in the difficulty the Japanese have in communicating with other countries and understanding the world around them. The language and culture of Japan are isolating in themselves, and constant efforts are required to overcome this barrier. Furthermore, since Japan's natural resource deficiency can only become more acute, continuing efforts will be required to obtain sufficient economic security.

Appendix: Chronology of Japan's Trade and Balance-of-Payments Policies

The policies that had a direct impact on Japanese international trade and payments are listed below. Other policies, such as the 1947 Law of Prohibition of Private Monopoly and Maintenance of Fair Trade, had indirect effects on trade, but are excluded for the sake of brevity; every economic policy affects trade in some manner and it would neither be possible nor useful to be that inclusive.

1. "Discount Preference for Foreign Trade Bills" [Bōeki tegata seido], 1946. A policy to promote exports by encouraging banks to grant export trade credits in preference to other types of loans.

2. "Certificate of the Fund Demand for Exportation" [Yushutsu shikin juyō shōmei seido], 1947. A policy to direct lending to firms in such a way as to promote exports. The certificates created by the program were made eligible for rediscounting by the central bank in 1950.

3. "Exemption of the Custom Duty for the Importation of Specified Imported Machinery" [Jūyō kikai yunyūzei menzei seido], 1949. Industrial firms were encouraged through duty rebates to import machinery not available in Japan for the purpose of replacing imported products or expanding exports.

4. "Law of Management of Foreign Exchange and Foreign Trade" [Gaikoku kawase oyobi gaikoku bōeki kanri hō], 1949, and "System of Centralization of Foreign Exchange" [Gaikoku kawase shuchu seido], 1949–72.

5. "Ordinance for the Management of Export Trade" [Yushutsu bōeki kanrirei], 1949.

6. "Ordinance for the Management of Import Trade" [Yunyū bōeki kanrirei], 1949.

7. "Rules of the Standard Method of Payments" [Hyōjun kessai hōhō ni kansuru kisoku], 1949. Items 4, 5, and 6 were the basic laws and this was the basic ministerial ordinance that regulated trade and payments.

8. Fixing of the foreign exchange rate at ¥360 = $1, 1949.

9. Creation of the Ministry of International Trade and Industry, 1949.

10. "Budget of Foreign Exchange" [Gaika yosan seido], 1949–63. Set up an allocation mechanism of scarce foreign exchange.

11. "Import Deposit" [Yunyu tanpokin seido], 1949. Required import deposits at the time import licenses were requested.

12. "Import Bill Rediscount" [Yunyū bōeki tegata seido]. 1950.

13. "Usance by the Bank of Japan" [Nichigin usance], 1950. Together with item 12, this gave a preference to approved imports over purely domestic projects in competition for finance.

14. "Law Concerning Foreign Investment," 1950. An elaboration of item 4 dealing specifically with capital investment in Japan by foreigners.

15. "Three Year Plan for Economic Independence" [Keizai jiritsu 3-nen keikaku], 1950. Government's first economic plan in which priority was given to industrialization and export promotion.

16. "System of Pre-Export Financing" [Yushutsu maegashi seido], 1950. A financial preference system to facilitate exports by easing financial terms during the production process.

17. Creation of a new institution for "Export Insurance," 1950.

18. Creation of Japan Export Bank to supply long-term loans for exports, 1951. Reorganized in 1952 as the Japan Export and Import Bank.

19. Creation of the Japan External Trade Organization, 1951, to supply marketing information for Japanese exporters.

20. Creation of Japan Development Bank, 1951, to supply long-term financing for industrialization.

21. Revision of tariff schedules, 1951. A temporary revision of the prewar tariff system to adapt it to postwar circumstances.

22. Creation of the "Link Trade" System, 1952. An arrangement whereby import licenses were allocated based on export performance.

23. Japan joined the IMF and the IBRD, 1952.

24. "Law of Export and Import Transactions" [Yushutsunyū torihiki ho], 1953. Permitted exemptions from antitrust laws for the purpose of allowing exporters and importers to cartelize trade under certain circumstances.

25. "Preferential Finance for the Period Preceding Exportation" [Yushutsu maegashi tegata seido], 1953–71. An elaboration of item 16. It also integrated into one system the various financial preferences extended by the Bank of Japan.

26. "Tax Credit for Export Income" [Yushutsu shotoku kōjo], 1953–64. Tax credits were provided in relation to sales: 1 percent for trading companies, 3 percent for export producers, and 5 percent for plant makers, or 50 percent of income from exporting, whichever was the smaller. For the period 1961–63, the credit was allowed only for firms that exceeded their performance of the previous year.

27. "Extra Depreciation Allowance for the Fixed Assets of Overseas Branches"

[Kaigai shiten kotei shisan no tokubetsu shōkyaku], 1953–58. This tax deduction was given to exporters to create or expand foreign sales facilities.

28. Establishment of the "Export Conference" [Yushutsu kaigi], 1954–69. It was given legal status only in 1962. This was a superior council formed to discuss export-promoting devices and consisted of the prime minister, relevant ministers, governors of the Bank of Japan, head of the Export-Import Bank of Japan, and business leaders. It published an export target for the coming half year and in 1964 started a system of rewarding those firms contributing to increases in Japanese exports by granting them tax credits.

29. Revision of the Law of Tariff Rates and Customs Duty, 1954. In order to prepare for participation in the GATT, the tariff system was revised to shift to ad valorem tariffs, to reduce extremely high rates of tariffs on consumer goods, to reduce tariffs on raw materials to negligible dimensions, and to unify protective tariffs at rates between 30 percent and 40 percent while introducing tariff escalation.

30. Japan joined the GATT, 1955.

31. Creation of the "Japan Association for Plant Exportation" [Nippon plant kyōkai], 1955. This was a nonprofit organization to assist export contractors of heavy machinery and plants by providing consulting services and market research.

32. Japan for the first time borrowed from the IBRD in the amount of $350 million to be used by the Yawata Iron and Steel Company, 1955.

32a. In 1956 an exception was permitted to the Law Concerning Foreign Investment (item 14) that allowed foreign firms to obtain full ownership of Japanese firms if they would forgo the explicit right to repatriate profits and principal. These enterprises were known as "yen-based" companies.

33. Japan started voluntary restraints on exports of cotton textiles to the United States under the legal authority of item 24, 1957.

34. "Extra Tax Credit for Exports" [Yushutsu warimashi kōjo seido], 1957–61. The maximum tax credit on export income noted in item 26 was raised from 50 percent to 80 percent. In addition, for those exporters whose growth in export sales exceeded the previous year by 50 percent, a further tax credit was granted equal to 100 percent of export income, 1.5 percent of export sales of trading firms, 4.5 percent of export sales for export producers, or 7.5 percent of export sales for plant makers, whichever was smaller.

35. Creation of the Southeast Asia Development Fund, 1958. A fund to make loans to less developed countries. The first yen-loan was made in 1958 to India in the amount of $50 million.

36. "Tax Credit for Technology Exportation" [Gijutsu yushutsu shotoku kōjo seido], 1959. A tax credit was granted in the amount of 50 percent of the value of exports of technology or 50 percent of related costs in all factories of the firm, whichever was smaller.

37. "Fundamental Policy to Liberalize Foreign Trade and Exchanges" [Bōeki kawase jiyūka keikaku taibō], June 1960. Liberalized 257 four-digit Brussels Nomenclature for Tariffs (BTN) items of import trade. Permitted foreigners to purchase Japanese equity shares within certain limits.

38. Financial preference for import bills under item 12 was abolished to prevent a drastic increase in imports following import liberalization, 1960.

39. Reorganization of the Southeast Asia Development Fund (item 35) into

the Overseas Economic Cooperation Fund, 1961. Increased the geographical coverage of countries eligible for loans. The government also began to subsidize the losses of Japanese firms from the importing of primary goods from certain developing countries.

40. Revision of the law of the Export-Import Bank, 1961. Allowed the bank to extend finance for deferred payments with softer conditions (see item 18).

41. The Bank of Japan reduced the rediscount rate for export bills from 5.48 percent to 5.11 percent, while at the same time raising the rediscount rate on other bills from 6.57 percent to 6.94 percent, July 1961.

42. The reporting system for quota restrictions on imports was switched from a positive list of items that could be imported to a negative list of items that could be imported only with explicit authorization, April 1962.

43. Japan accepted the GATT declaration and agreed to phase out or abolish export subsidies, November 1962.

44. The MITI published a ministerial ordinance entitled "The Management of Invisible Trade Induced by Commodity Trade" [Bōeki kankei bōekigai torihiki no kanri ni kansuru shorei], March 1963. Permitted Japanese firms to import technology without approval of the MITI as long as the price was below $30,000 and there was no foreign participation in management.

45. Japan declared Article 11 status in the GATT, 1963. Japan agreed to end direct export subsidization through tax credits (item 26) and to end the foreign exchange budget allocations (item 10), but preferential access to credit for exporting was continued. See also items 49 through 55 below.

46. Japan declared Article 8 status in the IMF, 1964.

47. Japan became a member of the OECD, 1964.

48. The OECD decided to allow Japan to maintain its restrictions on capital movements, July 1964.

49. "Special Depreciation Allowance for Exporting Companies" [Yushutsu warimashi shōkyaku seido], 1964–72. A new indirect subsidy for exporting via accelerated depreciation rules. Viewed as a partial replacement for direct tax credits for exporting.

50. "Extra Depreciation Allowance for Exporting Companies" [Kaigai torihiki ga aru baai no warimashi seido], 1964–72. For companies exporting commodities or technologies extra depreciation was allowed equal to ordinary depreciation times the percentage share of exports in total sales.

51. "Special Reserve for the Exploitation of Foreign Markets" [Kaigaishijō kaitaku junbikin seido], 1964–69, renewed in 1969. A firm was permitted to set up a reserve fund for the cost of exploiting new foreign markets that could be currently expended for tax calculations. The reserve would have to be used up in five equal annual installments and could amount to 0.5 percent of sales of large trading firms (more than ¥100 million), 1.0 percent of sales of other trading firms, and 1.5 percent of sales of manufacturers.

52. "Special Reserve for the Losses from Foreign Investment" [Kaigai tōshi sonshitsu junbikin seido], 1964–69, renewed in 1969. A firm was permitted to create a reserve fund for foreign investment that could be expended currently for tax calculations. The reserve would have to be used up in five annual installments after a five-year grace period and amounted to one-half of the foreign investment.

53. The tax credit for technology exports (item 36) was renewed in 1964–69 and again in 1969.

54. "Special Treatment of Export Promotion Expenses [Yushutsu kōsaihi ni kansuru kazei no tokurei], 1964. A firm was permitted to claim all the costs paid for traveling and living expenses of foreign buyers as a legitimate tax deduction.

55. "Special Extra Depreciation for the Exporting Companies Authorized by the Minister of the MITI" [Yushutsu kōken kigyo seido], 1964–69. Created a concept of an "export-contributing" company, defined as a firm that (1) increased its exports by 1 percent over the previous year, or (2) maintained the same ratio of exports to total sales as the previous year or increased its exports over the previous year by at least two-thirds of the national average. Companies under (1) were granted depreciation of 1.3 times the normal amount and companies under (2) 1.6 times the normal.

56. The MITI raised import collateral authorized under item 11 from 5 percent to 35 percent for consumption goods and from 1 percent to 5 percent for production goods, March 1964, but original rates were reestablished in April 1965.

57. Imports of completed cars were liberalized, 1965.

58. Japan took an active role in creating the Asian Development Bank, 1966. Also JETRO began to supply special financing for imports from developing countries.

59. Japan joined the treaty establishing the BTN, 1966.

60. Japan relaxed the restrictions on the amount of foreign exchange each Japanese citizen could purchase for the purpose of traveling abroad. Business travelers were allowed $2,000 and tourists $1,000.

61. The Bank of Japan relaxed the regulation on importing Eurodollars to avoid a so-called yen shift caused by the discrepancies between foreign and domestic levels of interest rates, July 1966.

62. First liberalization of the Law Concerning Foreign Investment (items 14 and 32a) for inward direct investment, June 1967. The liberalization made explicit the characteristics of desired investment: it should be noninjurious to related domestic industries and contribute to improvement in the balance of payments. Three categories were created that permitted 100 percent foreign ownership for thirty-three industries and 50 percent foreign ownership for seventeen others. All other industries fall into a third category in which foreign investment is allowed on a case-by-case basis.

63. Japan participated in the Kennedy Round of GATT negotiations completed in 1967.

64. The Bank of Japan implemented controls on the principal foreign exchange dealings of commercial banks to prevent drastic shifts between domestic and foreign markets, February 1968.

65. Importation of technology both with and without foreign management was liberalized by the MITI (except for seven specific manufacturing industries), June 1968.

66. The Japanese began to limit exports of steel to the United States, January 1969.

67. The Export Conference (item 28) was reorganized into the "Trade Council" [Bōeki Kaigi], 1969. The declaration of export targets was discontinued, the

preferential rate of interest on export bills was repealed (item 1), and the super-extra and extra depreciation for exporting companies was stopped (items 49, 50, and 55).

68. The Import Deposit System (item 11) stopped discriminating against consumer products by reducing all collateral to 1 percent, October 1969.

69. The second step in the liberalization of inward direct investment (items 14, 32a, and 62) was taken, March 1969. The first category of industries permitting 100 percent foreign ownership was increased to 160 industries and the second category of 50 percent ownership was set at 44 industries.

70. The Bank of Japan granted automatic approval for all outward direct investment of $200,000 or less, October 1969.

71. Japan pledged to reduce its import quota restraints from 120 to 60 items within two years. The plan was completely implemented by June 1971 after being proposed in the fall of 1969.

72. The Import Deposit System (items 11 and 68) ceased to operate, but the system was not abolished as such, May 1970.

73. The Bank of Japan increased to $1 million the amount of outward direct investment given automatic approval (item 70), May 1970.

74. The Bank of Japan ceased limiting outward direct investment and allowed the purchase of foreign common stock by trust funds with automatic approval up to $100 million (items 70 and 73), July 1971.

75. Government adopted a plan entitled "Eight Items of Urgent Policy Measures to Avoid Yen Revaluation," June 1971. These included: (1) reduction of quantitative restraints, (2) promotion of capital exportation, (3) tariff cuts, (4) increase of government expenditures, (5) creation and enlargement of a General Scheme of Preferential Tariffs for imports of manufactures from less developed countries, (6) reduction of nontariff barriers, (7) promotion of economic cooperation, and (8) arrangements for the orderly marketing of exports.

76. "Reserve Fund for the Losses from Natural Resource Exploitation Investment Abroad" [Shigen kaihatsu tōshi sonshitsu junbikin], 1971. A reserve fund equal to 100 percent of investment was permitted to be currently expended for tax purposes. After a five-year grace period, the fund must be used up in five equal annual installments. Qualified investments include natural resource exploitation such as oil, nonferrous metals, uranium, iron ore, and coal.

77. Japan implemented a General Scheme of Preferential Tariffs, August 1971. It is a general preference for imports from less developed countries with quite limited ceilings for each item. Certain items were excluded for various reasons.

78. "Accelerated Depreciation for the Companies in the Industries Related to GSP (General Scheme of Preference) to Adjust" [Tokkei jigyō tenken kuriage shōkyaku seido], 1971. Accelerated depreciation was permitted for companies competing with less developed countries that would be unfavorably affected by the GSP.

79. Japan agreed to restrain noncotton textile exports to the United States, October 1971.

80. Third and fourth steps were taken to liberalize inward direct investment (items 14, 32a, 62, and 69), April 1971 and August 1971. The first category was

expanded to 453 industries and the second category to 77 industries. Automobiles were included at this time. Furthermore, the system was switched from a positive to a negative listing. In August 1971, seven industries were listed that required case-by-case approval and 228 industries were listed in which automatic approval was applicable only up to 50 percent foreign ownership.

81. The Bank of Japan further liberalized the restrictions for travelers abroad (item 60), June 1971. Business travelers and tourists were allowed $3,000.

82. Some liberalizations were announced by the Bank of Japan with respect to foreign exchanges, June 1971. Residents were permitted to hold foreign exchange for one month rather than ten days; trading companies could hold foreign exchanges in a deposit account for six months rather than twenty days; and the limit of fifteen kinds of foreign currency that an exporter could receive was abolished.

83. The Bank of Japan freed the yen from its ¥360 = $1 parity, August 1971. The bank continued to intervene in the exchange market during this period. It also strengthened its control on foreign exchange to prevent speculative transactions.

84. As part of the Smithsonian Agreement, the yen was revalued by 16.88 percent against the dollar to ¥308 = $1 (item 8), December 1971.

85. Government adopted a seven-point "International Economic Countermeasures Emergency Program," May 1972. This included: (1) increased fiscal expenditures for domestic purposes plus easing of monetary policy; (2) promotion of imports through enlargement of quotas and surveys of import prices to ensure yen revaluation effects; (3) promotion of orderly exports through the MITI; (4) expansion of capital exports through liberalization of restrictions on Japanese purchase of foreign equities and facilitation of issuance of yen bonds by international organizations and governments; (5) redepositing official reserves in foreign exchange banks to help repay foreign liabilities and in the Export-Import Bank of Japan to encourage direct investment of natural resources abroad, plus easing import financing; (6) promotion of cooperation with developing countries through greater economic assistance, including ending of tied aid in the future; and (7) revision of certain laws to implement policy changes.

86. The MITI created an "Orderly Marketing Maintenance Committee," July 1972. Committee was to work out administrative guidance to promote orderly export marketing. In the event that voluntary cooperation was lacking, the MITI announced its intention to invoke the Export Trade Control Order. Voluntary export controls were imposed on twenty groups of products in September 1972.

87. Cabinet decision to take measures to improve international cooperation, September 1972. Measures included: (1) intention to liberalize foreign capital investment to 100 percent in principle; (2) expansion of permitted imports of restricted items; (3) lowering tariff rates in advance of international negotiations; (4) expanding duty-free exemption for returning travelers and lowering duties on luxury goods; (5) enlarging stockpiles of petroleum and rare metals; (6) expanding preferential tariff privileges; (7) ending government's "Japan-only" purchase policy; (8) ending the Bank of Japan's financing system for promoting exports; and (9) simplifying import procedures. In October a 20 percent across-the-board cut in tariffs on industrial and processed agricultural products was an-

nounced, as well as a 30 percent (or more) increase in permitted imports of items under quota, the consolidation of the import licensing system, abolition of the overseas market exploration deposit system, reduction in the number of export items covered by the export cargo material rebate system, and other measures.

88. Japan announced contribution of $15 million to the new "African Development Fund," November 1972.

89. The Bank of Japan no longer attempted to peg the exchange rate, although active intervention was indicated. The rate quickly rose from ¥308 = $1 to about ¥265 = $1, February 1973.

90. Fifth round of capital liberalization announced (items 14, 32a, 62, 69, and 80), May 1973. Number of excluded industries was reduced to five (agriculture, mining, oil refining, leather manufactures, and retailing) and the schedule was advanced for liberalizing seventeen other industries.

91. Japan pledged to provide one-third of funding—$175 million—of the Asian Development Bank, April 1973. Japan also announced its intention to raise its share of IDA funding from 6 percent to 9 percent—the same as West Germany.

92. The GATT Council of Ministers met in Tokyo to begin a new round of trade negotiations, September 1973.

93. Listing of foreign issues on Tokyo Stock Exchange scheduled to begin on December 15, 1973.

94. Voluntary export controls instituted under item 86 were rescinded, September 1973.

CHAPTER SEVEN

Industrial Organization

Richard E. Caves, Harvard University
with the collaboration of
Masu Uekusa, Keiō University

AN AMERICAN studying Japan's industrial organization cannot avoid comparing it with that of the United States, a comparison that immediately sets certain institutional features into sharp relief. Rooted in Japan's culture and its recent and rapid development as an industrial nation, these features seem to promise economic behavior far removed from that of the Western model. Do they make the economy work differently, or does its operation, despite these novel trappings, fundamentally reflect Western modes?

General Characteristics of Business and Industry

The speed of Japan's modernization has brought the various sectors of the nation's economy to uneven levels of development. Coexisting with steel mills as large and efficient as any in the world are industries manufacturing important consumer goods by handicraft methods only modestly touched by the Industrial Revolution. Important features of the economy, from the general trading companies to the complex and relatively inefficient distribution sector, resist explanation until their foundations predating the twentieth century are noted. The role of government in Japanese industrial organization in part reflects the rapid modernization. The active if selective hand taken by government in promoting economic development during the Meiji restoration of 1868–1912 resembles the contemporary pattern of close and informal relations between the government and those sectors of the economy with which public policy is concerned.

Such cultural traits as Japan's relative lack of individualism and legalism also have imprinted themselves on business and industrial organization. The employment practices and thus the cost structure of firms reflect the Japanese tendency to regard the individual as part of a group, which makes it natural for the worker to attach himself to a large company as a permanent employee and for the company to assume a pervasive and paternalistic attitude toward his well-being. Relations between businesses as customers or competitors and the process whereby government agencies supply guidance on business behavior are affected by the absence of a tradition of legalism in contractual

Note. This chapter summarizes our book *Industrial Organization in Japan* (Brookings Institution, forthcoming). The book contains more detail—of particular interest to the specialist in industrial organization—on most points. It also presents the data sources and procedures that underlie our own statistical research, whereas this chapter merely summarizes the results.

461

arrangements. Consequently, disputes tend to be settled not by resort to legal precedents or the language of valid contracts, but by a balancing of equities as perceived by the parties in the situation at hand.

Special Features of the Environment

Certain features of Japan's social and economic organization are significant in its industrial organization. These will receive more detailed attention in the course of this chapter, but to provide a background their principal characteristics should be sketched in briefly.

ENTERPRISE GROUPS. Groups of large enterprises are based in different industries but bound together by ties of fractional ownership and a variety of continuing lender-borrower and buyer-seller relations. Some of these are direct successors of the *zaibatsu,* large collections of industrial, trading, and financial corporations controlled by wealthy families and representing yet another persistent legacy of the Meiji period. They reached the height of their power and coherence during the 1930s and World War II, at the end of which the four largest *zaibatsu* controlled about one-fourth of the paid-in capital of Japanese incorporated business.[1] They were dissolved by direction of the occupation powers after the war, but a decade later they pulled themselves together in somewhat looser form. These successors represent merely the most conspicuous kind of interfirm grouping in Japan.

THE SMALL- AND MEDIUM-SIZE ENTERPRISE PROBLEM. No feature of industrial organization is more studied in Japan than the persistence of a large number of relatively small manufacturing and services enterprises with low productivity. In 1967 only 3 percent of U.S. manufacturing employment was in establishments with fewer than ten workers; the figure for Japan was 16 percent, and it had been 23 percent in 1954. Value added per worker in these small plants was about 25 percent of that in Japan's largest manufacturing establishments, whereas in the United States the proportion was 70 percent.[2]

PRICE DISCRIMINATION IN FACTOR MARKETS. Both capital and labor markets in Japan show imperfections that are closely tied to the economy's historical development. These affect the cost structure of firms, their market

---

1. See Eleanor M. Hadley, *Antitrust in Japan* (Princeton University Press, 1970), especially chap. 3; and T. A. Bisson, *Zaibatsu Dissolution in Japan* (University of California Press, 1954).

2. (Japan) Ministry of International Trade and Industry, *Census of Manufactures, 1967;* and (U.S.) Bureau of the Census, *Census of Manufactures, 1967.* These data are analyzed by Ron W. Napier, "The Labor Market and Structural Change in Postwar Japanese Development" (senior honors thesis, Harvard College, 1972; processed), chap. 1.

behavior, and the allocative efficiency of the economy. In the labor market the substantial wage gap between small and large enterprises is closing only slowly as Japan loses its dual economy traits and competitive pressure gnaws at the labor supply of the small enterprises. A reverse discrimination appears in the capital market, in which corporations with equity capital of less than ¥10 million incur 50 percent higher borrowing costs than firms with capital of more than ¥1 billion. Banking enterprises have generally not been independent of nonfinancial firms; although the direction of dependence is a complex matter, it bears some relation to capital-market discrimination in favor of large firms. The lack of a mature market for debentures and other long-term debt instruments makes loans from banks and other financial intermediaries critical in company finance. As Shinohara has noted, the ratio of interest rate to average wages paid can easily be four times as high for small as for large firms.[3]

RAPIDITY OF ECONOMIC GROWTH. Grinding as it does against the economy's legacies from the past, the phenomenon of rapid growth has itself become an important factor in business decisionmaking and market competition. The significance of rapid growth for the behavior of firms and industries depends on the principal sources of growth and thus the nature of the adjustment problems seen by firms. It also depends on how fully growth is anticipated and adjusted to: what matters is often not an absolute rate of change, but rather the actual rate relative to the expectation that businessmen have built into their plans.

ECONOMIC POLICY. The public policy environment surrounding Japanese industrial organization is far removed in both substance and procedure from that of the United States. Antitrust legislation following the American model was impressed upon Japan's statute books during the postwar occupation, but thereafter it was weakened by amendments and received only weak and partial enforcement. The Fair Trade Commission (FTCJ), charged with enforcement, has played a role subordinate to other governmental agencies, notably the Ministry of International Trade and Industry (MITI), which have held sharply differing views on the means and ends of industrial policy.

Business Structure and Administration

No feature of an economy relates more closely to its social and historical context than the organization and management of its business enterprises.

---

3. Miyohei Shinohara, "A Survey of the Japanese Literature on Small Industry," in Bert F. Hoselitz (ed.), *The Role of Small Industry in the Process of Economic Growth* (Paris and The Hague: Mouton, 1968), pp. 51–54. For a discussion of financial markets, see Chapter 4 in this volume.

Out of this context arise the motivation of business decisions and the ability of firms to perceive opportunities and threats and to carry out plans, factors that are central to the behavior of industries and the performance of the economy. Economists accustomed to thinking in terms of well-defined production functions and determinate relations may find it difficult to contemplate such subjects as quality of entrepreneurial talent and effectiveness of a nation's business practices and business organization. Yet the evidence points persistently to the importance of these issues in determining national levels of productivity and rates of growth.[4]

We shall concentrate on four aspects of contemporary business organization in Japan: the development of entrepreneurial attitudes, the supply and quality of entrepreneurial talent, the divorce of ownership from control in large firms, and the trends in business organization and managerial practice.

ENTREPRENEURSHIP AND BUSINESS MOTIVATION. The literature on Japanese entrepreneurship identifies several historical patterns of development linked to continuing traits of entrepreneurship and business organization.[5] The motivation and objectives of business organizations have deep historical roots. The pursuit of profit, like selling, has never been held in high esteem in Japan. Some entrepreneurs and enterprise groups have formulated business goals that seem to substitute another motive for that of profit. Others have constructed a rationalization for business activity that does not appear to be maximization of profit but resembles it rather closely. Before the Meiji era the largest and most advanced sector of the economy was apparently wholesaling and distribution, activities carried on by low-status but sometimes very wealthy families. Ensuring the continuity and growth of the commercial house, as well as its honor, became an important objective of business activity for owner and employee alike; the "family" comprising members of the business was looked on as an entity closely akin to the biological family. In economic theory, the long-run growth-maximizing firm differs from the profit maximizer only in the rate of reinvestment in the business, not in its short-run deployment of the resources at hand.[6] The strong emphasis in the historical record on the frugality of entrepreneurial families, the high rate of reinvestment, and their concern with maintaining the quality

4. Richard E. Caves and others, *Britain's Economic Prospects* (Brookings Institution, 1968), especially chaps. 6–8.

5. See, for example, Johannes Hirschmeier and Tsunehiko Yui, *The Development of Japanese Business, 1600–1973* (Harvard University Press, 1975), chaps. 1, 2; and Michael Y. Yoshino, *Japan's Managerial System: Tradition and Innovation* (M.I.T. Press, 1968), chaps. 1–3.

6. John D. Williamson, "Profit, Growth and Sales Maximization," *Economica*, vol. 33 (February 1966), pp. 1–16.

of family managerial talent all suggest that the goal of growth maximization carried some weight in determining business behavior.[7]

An inconclusive debate continues over the relative role of the aristocratic samurai and other classes as a source of entrepreneurial talent in the Meiji period.[8] We shall not be concerned with the balance of evidence, because it is clear that both samurai and lower classes were important as founders of the new industrial enterprises. The samurai role is distinctive, however, in that the traditions of the class inclined it heavily toward public service, rationality, and a faith in education. Just as the latter two traits suited them well to serve as importers of foreign technology, so their zeal for public service may have brought about some submersion of private business goals to the public welfare and the officially voiced interests of the state.

The close and informal relations between business and government that characterize contemporary Japan thus have their echoes in the earliest days of industrialization. One result of samurai influence is the long-established tradition of high levels of education for Japanese business executives. As early as 1924 a survey of the 181 largest operating companies showed that 64 percent of executives held college degrees or the equivalent—a level that surely could not have been matched in the United States at that time.[9]

PREVALENCE OF ENTREPRENEURIAL SKILLS. The quantity and level of entrepreneurial ability in a society and the degree to which social values and convention give it free play are important determinants of how rapidly an economy can grow and how readily it will adapt to change. To most observers, the overall growth rate of industrial production since World War II, the great shifts in the composition of national output, and the increased quality of many products alone would provide sufficient evidence that Japanese entrepreneurs are both abundant and active.

But there is evidence beyond these striking phenomena. After the war, 2,210 officers from 632 *zaibatsu* corporations and some 2,500 high-ranking officers and large stockholders of other large companies were purged for wartime activities. Such a purge might have crippled an economy with limited entrepreneurial resources, but in fact it contributed heavily to the postwar revival and growth. The purged *zaibatsu* executives had been caught in two highly dysfunctional traditions. First, they were accustomed to serving in-

7. See Yasuzo Horie, "The Role of the *Ie* in the Economic Modernization of Japan," *Kyoto University Economic Review*, vol. 36 (April 1966), pp. 1–16, especially pp. 9–10.

8. Yoshino, *Japan's Managerial System*, chap. 3; and Yasuzō Horie, "Modern Entrepreneurship in Meiji Japan," in William W. Lockwood (ed.), *The State and Economic Enterprise in Japan* (Princeton University Press, 1965), chap. 4.

9. Hirschmeier and Yui, *Development of Japanese Business*, pp. 164–65.

dustrial buyers, especially the government, and had little feeling for adapting the product to emergent needs of the market in other areas. Second, they were selected for their loyalty to the *zaibatsu* families, not their independent decisionmaking ability. Third, they were on average quite elderly, their formative experience having been gained in the 1920s and 1930s. Their replacements, generally subordinates who stood next in line, were younger men who showed a marked ability to adapt to their own and their companies' new-found independence.[10]

Additional testimony to Japanese entrepreneurial talent lies in the many giant and successful companies that have been built from scratch since the war. The ripeness of conditions must be given some of the credit, but the pervasiveness of entrepreneurial success stories, in small as well as large enterprises, suggests that favorable circumstances were not all.[11] Top university graduates today look with greater favor on business careers and take employment not only with large companies but in some cases strike out on their own.

DIVORCE OF OWNERSHIP AND CONTROL. In the process of economic growth, large corporations tend to slip from the control of their founders or the heirs of the founders. Stockholdings become widely dispersed, and management in large measure controls its own fate. This shift is economically important, because the evidence for the United States suggests (somewhat weakly) that ownership structure and management compensation do influence company performance.[12]

In Japan the divorce of ownership from control has proceeded rapidly, especially as a result of the *zaibatsu* dissolution and dispersion of families' shareholdings. In 1959, 33 of the 200 largest companies remained owner controlled; 60 others were *zaibatsu* affiliates, substantial proportions of whose shares were held by their corporate affiliates but in individually modest blocks. If control of these companies eludes their managers, it is because of the influence of other affiliated companies and not ultimate personal or institutional shareholders. The remaining 107 (95 nonfinancial, 12 financial) are controlled by their managers. The 95 nonfinancial concerns include 85 that are affiliated with important financial institutions and thus may be sub-

10. See Kazuo Noda, "Postwar Japanese Executives," in Ryūtarō Komiya (ed.), *Postwar Economic Growth in Japan* (University of California Press, 1966), pp. 231–35; Hirschmeier and Yui, *Development of Japanese Business,* chap. 4; and Yoshino, *Japan's Managerial System,* pp. 86–87.

11. See Noda, "Postwar Japanese Executives," pp. 243–44; and Hirschmeier and Yui, *Development of Japanese Business,* chap. 4.

12. See, for example, Robert T. Masson, "Executive Motivations, Earnings, and Consequent Equity Performance," *Journal of Political Economy,* vol. 79 (November–December 1971), pp. 1278–92.

ject to some extramanagerial control.[13] In 1963 only 13 of the 200 largest nonfinancial corporations in the United States were under owner control and 8 more were under cohesive control through a legal device; managers controlled 169.[14]

Thus, the divorce of control from ownership has not proceeded as far in Japan as in the United States. On the contrary, recent data show a rapid shift of shareholding toward companies and financial intermediaries that may be restoring cohesive minority-owner control over some Japanese firms. Individuals held 61.3 percent of the shares of listed companies in 1950 but only 37.2 percent in 1971, whereas monetary institutions climbed from a position of 12.6 to 32.6 percent.[15] Japanese financial intermediaries seem much less passive than their American counterparts in voicing their views on the operation of companies in which they hold shares.

Managers of Japanese companies with widely dispersed shareholdings still find themselves in positions of great independence. A change in Japan's commercial code in 1950 boosted the position of professional managers by means of reducing the power of shareholders relative to boards of directors and allowing nonshareholders to become directors.[16] Individual shareholders are notably passive, and there are no corporate raiders who buy up corporate interests to oust managements that are failing to maximize profits. Even boards of directors often consist mostly of employees subordinate to top management and thus unlikely to play an independent critical role. In 1964, 44.1 percent of 397 large companies had no outside directors, and another 33 percent had only one or two.

What influence the divorce of ownership from control has on company behavior depends not only on the locus of control but also on the terms of managerial compensation. What evidence is available for Japan suggests a shift away from executive compensation geared to profit. Noda argues that since the war corporate managers have held company stocks in much smaller proportion than before the war and receive conspicuously smaller bonuses, a component of pay at least partly dependent on profits.[17] We conclude that management in large Japanese companies enjoys a rather broad scope for

13. Yūichi Hirose, *Kabushiki kaisha shihai no kōzō* [Structure of Corporate Management] (Nihon Hyōron-Shin Sha, 1963), summarized by Noda, "Postwar Japanese Executives," pp. 236–37.

14. Robert J. Larner, "Ownership and Control in the 200 Largest Nonfinancial Corporations, 1929 and 1963," *American Economic Review,* vol. 56 (September 1966), pp. 777–87.

15. "Stockholdings by Corporations," *The Oriental Economist,* vol. 41 (May 1973), pp. 18–22.

16. Noda, "Postwar Japanese Executives," p. 235.

17. Ibid. Before the war high-paid *zaibatsu* executives tended to buy heavily into their companies and become relatively substantial owners.

acting on motives other than profit maximization, although it is impossible to measure the weight of competing motives.

MANAGEMENT TECHNIQUES AND EMPLOYMENT PRACTICES. Little need be said about business organization in its literal organization chart sense, if only because the same forms are generally employed as in the United States, and the movement toward decentralized profit centers continues actively.[18] More interesting questions surround the practice of permanent employment and the roles of merit and seniority in determining promotion.

Japan emerged from World War II lagging in managerial techniques as well as industrial technology. About 1955 there occurred a "management science boom," a great wave of interest in absorbing managerial techniques used in the West, particularly the United States. As part of this widely recognized phenomenon, many organized efforts were mounted to spread the gospel of scientific management.[19] Some observers have interpreted the resulting inflow of managerial techniques as a necessary ingredient for Japan's greatly accelerated growth.[20] Evidence testifies to the rapidly spreading use of certain managerial techniques, whether imported or not. A large majority of executives came to feel, for example, that long-run planning should be a staff function that systematically explores alternatives, as against a consensus process devolving from the chief executive,[21] and the development of information relating to cost control was given high priority.[22]

Japanese industry continues its tradition of seeking employees with high levels of general rather than specialized business education and then giving them a great deal of training within the company.[23] Contemporary surveys continue to document the high level of education of top management. In 1966, 94 percent of the top managers of twenty-five large companies were college or university graduates, as were 74 percent of middle managers.[24]

A major issue in Japanese business organization is the retention of certain

18. They were employed by 34 percent of a group of large firms surveyed in 1963. See Ryōichi Iwauchi, "Adaptation to Technological Change," *The Developing Economies,* vol. 7 (December 1969), pp. 446–47.

19. Noda, "Postwar Japanese Executives," pp. 237–40.

20. Ibid, p. 239; cf. p. 249.

21. See Yasuo Kotaka, "Survey of Top Executives' Views on Business Organization," *Keio Business Review,* no. 3 (1964), pp. 14–17; and Economic Planning Agency, *Economic Survey of Japan, 1968–69* (1969), table 116.

22. In a survey, 84 percent of executives favored a statement lauding its value, and only 13 percent a statement suggesting that cost control is overrated. See Kotaka, "Survey," pp. 22–26.

23. Iwauchi, "Adaptation," pp. 428–34, 442.

24. James C. Abegglen (ed.), *Business Strategies for Japan* (Tokyo: Sophia University, 1970), p. 44.

business practices that accord with traits of the national culture but have obvious drawbacks for organizational effectiveness. The practice of permanent employment—whereby regular employees of large companies continue to receive seniority raises and are dismissed only if the business is in dire straits—continues unchanged, despite some predictions of its demise.[25] But some mobility among top executives is now evident. A 1965 study of 1,410 professional managers found that 46 percent had spent their entire careers with a single company; of the others, 19 percent had moved from financial institutions, 9 percent from government.[26] There is also evidence of greater emphasis in promotions being placed on merit rather than on seniority;[27] and furthermore, seniority does not control the staffing of a company's top jobs.

Persons interviewed about Japanese management practice stressed that permanent employment often means putting up with less than satisfactory competence in significant positions, and Abegglen in his study of the Japanese factory blamed it for much of the evident overstaffing.[28] On the positive side permanent employment, in addition to its consistency with Japanese desires for secure and ordered personal affiliations, has some direct benefits, notably in reducing both recruitment costs and resistance to technological change and job reassignment. It also makes it easier for firms to realize the rents from the on-the-job training that they provide.

Another feature of business organization rooted in Japan's culture is an emphasis on the group rather than the individual as the acting unit. Some observers have placed great emphasis on the need of business management to consult widely within the company and develop a consensus before any decision is made. Harmony, they insist, must be maintained among the ranks, and responsibility cannot be firmly placed. In view of the dynamism and bold maneuvers widely noted in Japanese business, we are somewhat skeptical about whether executive decisions are really preceded by great amounts of multilateral communing and soul-searching—at least when there is pressure of time. Surveys seem to suggest a prevalent feeling that although consideration of the views and interests of subordinate employees is important for successful management in Japan, top executives must act with a firm and responsible hand.

25. See the evidence on employee turnover rates in ibid., pp. 48–51, and a survey cited by Iwauchi, "Adaptation," p. 450.

26. Cited in Yoshino, "Japan's Managerial System," pp. 88–89.

27. See Iwauchi, "Adaptation," p. 449; and Abegglen (ed.), *Business Strategies*, p. 48.

28. James C. Abegglen, *The Japanese Factory: Aspects of Its Social Organization* (Free Press, 1958), especially chap. 2.

Structure of Japanese Industry

In Japan, as in other countries, most of the available information on the principal elements of market structure pertains to the manufacturing sector. Thus, we shall be restricted to only casual references to other sectors of industry.

Seller Concentration

The common casual view of Japanese industry, we would venture, holds that it is monopolistic in the extreme. This view draws heavily on the role of cartels and other collusive arrangements—a matter distinct from seller concentration—and on the presence of organized groups of large enterprises. Important as these phenomena are in Japan's economy, theory tells us that they represent responses to conditions in individual product and factor markets. The concentration of sellers in the typical product market is an important filter through which the influence of these more dramatic economic institutions can be observed. Therefore, we shall first examine concentration in Japanese manufacturing in comparison with that of the United States.

COMPARATIVE JAPANESE–U.S. CONCENTRATION. Although concentration in particular product markets will be emphasized, the overall concentration of corporate assets in Japan is worth noting. In fiscal 1963 the 100 largest nonfinancial corporations controlled 53.2 percent of all paid-in corporate capital, 39.4 percent directly and another 13.8 percent through affiliates. Apparently the share of this category has been increasing since at least 1958, especially in the manufacturing sector. The concentration of paid-in capital (that is, preferred and common shares issued, not including surplus or debt capital) is much greater than the concentration of operating profit or value added.

The data available on overall concentration in the United States are not strictly comparable, because they bear on total assets rather than paid-in capital. For what it is worth, Kaplan found that in 1960 the 100 largest U.S. industrial corporations controlled 30.8 percent of total corporate assets, as reported in taxation statistics.[29] Thus, Japanese concentration appears to exceed American unless Japan's concentration of paid-in capital greatly exceeds its concentration of total assets. Another qualification is that small enterprise may take the corporate form more often in the United States than

29. A. D. H. Kaplan, *Big Enterprise in a Competitive System* (rev. ed., Brookings Institution, 1964), pp. 120, 124.

in Japan, thereby deflating the share of U.S. corporate assets held by the giants.

But ultimately more important than overall concentration is the concentration of sellers in particular markets. Table 7-1 compares the distribution of concentration ratios for individual Japanese and American manufacturing industries. The two countries' concentration ratios are constructed on the same principles for the same year (1963) and use the same definition: the concentration ratio is the proportion of an industry's shipments accounted for by its four largest firms, expressed as a percentage. The industrial classifications of the two countries also are constructed along similar lines. At the level of disaggregation shown in Table 7-1, however, Japanese manufacturing is divided into 512 sectors, whereas U.S. manufacturing is divided into 417 sectors—19 percent fewer. Assuming that each manufacturing sector contains the same number and distribution of true economic industries (groups of competing sellers of homogeneous products) to which the standard industrial classification scheme is an approximation, the somewhat more aggregated U.S. classification implies that slightly lower American concentration ratios could signal the same level of effective concentration in the underlying true markets.

Table 7-1. *Number of Industries and Value of Shipments,*
by Concentration Ratio, for the Four Largest Firms, United States
and Japan, 1963

	By number of industries				By value of shipments			
	United States		Japan		United States		Japan	
Concentration ratio	Number	Cumulative percent	Number	Cumulative percent	Billions of dollars	Cumulative percent	Billions of dollars^a	Cumulative percent
80–100	27	6.5	46	9.0	50.9	12.2	3.7	5.6
70–79	18	10.8	21	13.1	14.3	15.6	3.5	10.8
60–69	29	17.8	29	18.8	23.8	21.3	1.8	13.4
50–59	43	28.1	61	30.7	49.3	33.2	10.6	28.9
40–49	49	39.8	56	41.6	31.9	40.9	8.5	41.3
30–39	80	59.0	63	53.9	72.8	58.4	7.6	52.5
20–29	81	78.4	79	69.3	90.5	80.2	9.7	66.7
0–19	90	100.0	157	100.0	82.4	100.0	22.7	100.0
Total	417	...	512	...	415.7	...	68.2	...

Sources: Subcommittee on Antitrust and Monopoly of the Senate Committee on the Judiciary, *Concentration Ratios in Manufacturing Industry, 1963* (1966), table 2; and Ministry of International Trade and Industry, *Seisan shūchūdo chōsa hōkoku* [Report of Survey of Concentration Ratios of Production] (1966).

a. Converted to dollars at ¥360 = $1.

According to the data of Table 7-1, the weighted average concentration ratio is 40.9 for U.S. manufacturing, 35.4 for Japanese; unweighted figures are 38.3 and 37.5 percent, respectively. If anything, concentration in Japan appears lower. The columns showing the cumulative distribution of unweighted concentration ratios suggest that the Japanese distribution is more dispersed than the American. Of Japanese industries, 40 percent have concentration ratios over 80 or under 20 percent, whereas only 28 percent of U.S. industries lie in the tails of the distribution. This difference may reflect the surviving dual structure of the Japanese manufacturing sector: the traditional sector comprising extremely small-scale enterprise and the modern sectors in which public policy and private interest have concurred on the choice of very large scales for both plants and firms. This suggestion is tentative, however, because the same pattern does not appear in the shipments-weighted figures.

Research by Pryor and others on the industrial structures of Western countries suggests that concentration ratios tend to be highly correlated between countries, and Japan appears to be no exception.[30] We undertook a statistical study of the relation between concentration in ninety-nine comparable Japanese and U.S. industries. Concentration in a Japanese industry is closely related to that in the comparable U.S. industry even after accounting for variations in the size of Japanese plants and markets and the capital intensity of production in Japan. Furthermore, the close relation holds not just for the conventional four-firm concentration ratio but for marginal concentration—the combined share of firms ranking fifth through eighth—as well. Those Japanese industries whose concentration appears highly deviant after accounting for these influences include sectors producing differentiated consumer goods that are relatively new to Japan and high-technology industries in which governmental policies favoring concentration have been influential.

Only casual evidence is available on concentration in nonmanufacturing sectors of Japan's economy. Concentration patterns in other sectors differ little from those in the United States. Agriculture, the services, and distributive trades are unconcentrated. The important public utilities and transportation sector is highly concentrated in Japan; part is under public ownership, part is privately held but regulated.

In conclusion, we concur with previous investigators in finding no great

30. Frederic L. Pryor, "An International Comparison of Concentration Ratios," *Review of Economics and Statistics,* vol. 54 (May 1972), pp. 130–40; and Y. Higuchi, "Shūchūdo no kokusai hikaku: Nihon to Amerika" [International Comparison of the Degree of Concentration: the United States and Japan], *Kōsei torihiki* (June 1968).

difference in concentration between Japan and the United States. Bain found that industrial concentration is "about the same or slightly higher in Japan than it is in the United States," while Rotwein held that "even with the incomparabilities removed it is unlikely, conservatively speaking, that the results would reveal a substantially higher level of concentration in Japan than in the United States."[31]

TRENDS IN CONCENTRATION. In Western countries the average level of seller concentration in industrial markets has been quite stable over time, showing visible trends in certain periods but little cumulative movement in the long run. Is Japan's pattern similar, despite the rapid growth and the shocks of World War II and its aftermath? The limited available evidence points to a decline during the period 1937–50.[32] For later years we have an annual index covering the more concentrated industries, prepared by the Fair Trade Commission of Japan (FTCJ). Commission data indicate a continued decline in most sectors from 1950 at least into the 1960s, except for food and related products. The index is ambiguous about the change between 1960 and 1965, but it points to a definite increase between 1965 and 1970.[33] The FTCJ cites horizontal mergers among large firms as an important component in the increase after 1965. We conclude that the trend over the period for which data are available is if anything one of declining concentration, though with most of the reduction accomplished by the early 1960s. But there is no basis for believing that the recent upturn will be only temporary.

Just as these indicators show no strongly sustained long-term trend in average concentration, the concentration of individual industries has tended to hold rather steady. Nishikawa found a (Kendall) rank correlation of 0.53 among five-firm concentration ratios for twenty-eight commodities between 1937 and 1962.[34]

MERGERS. Most industrial countries have experienced numerous corporate mergers in the past two decades and a rising trend throughout the 1960s. In the United States the merger wave was directed into the conglomerate

31. Joe S. Bain, *International Differences in Industrial Structure* (Yale University Press, 1966), p. 83; and Eugene Rotwein, "Economic Concentration and Monopoly in Japan," *Journal of Political Economy*, vol. 72 (June 1964), p. 276.

32. Rotwein, "Economic Concentration," pp. 264–65. Also see Hadley, *Antitrust in Japan*, pp. 330–37.

33. Fair Trade Commission, *Shuyō sangyō ni okeru seisan shūchūdo: 1955–1970* [Concentration Ratios of Production in the Main Industries: 1955–1970] (Fair Trade Institute, 1973), p. 2.

34. Shunsaku Nishikawa, "Concentration under Rapid Economic Growth: Japanese Manufacturing, 1956 to 1962," Discussion Paper no. 7, Economic Research Institute (EPA, 1969; processed), pp. 3–5.

channel during the 1950s, when horizontal and vertical mergers were branded illegal where even a modest possibility existed that they might reduce competition. Mergers in America surely contributed to the increasing share of assets held by the 100 largest corporations, but their role in elevating seller concentration in individual product markets is at most indirect.

Japan, like the European countries, experienced a similar ballooning of mergers: the annual average number more than doubled from the 1950s to the 1960s.[35] Public policy, however, imposed no strong check on horizontal or vertical combinations. Most of the combinations have been among relatively small companies, but mergers among very large companies became increasingly common during the 1960s. For the last few years data are available on large mergers classified by type: horizontal, vertical, and conglomerate, as well as their subcategories. The figures in Table 7-2 show that about half of the large mergers have been horizontal, tending thereby to confirm the suggestion that such mergers were a major force in reversing the trend toward declining seller concentration in Japanese manufacturing. The same impression emerges from the distribution of assets acquired in all mergers that took place in 1970: 50.3 percent were absorbed in horizontal combination, 9.2 percent in vertical mergers, and 38.0 percent in conglomerate acquisitions (13.7 percent were market extension mergers); 2.5 percent were unclassified.

The FTCJ explanation for the upswing in number of mergers in the 1960s echoes one often heard in Western Europe. A liberalization of international trade in 1962 prompted Japanese corporations to adopt a defensive expansion policy that doubled the annual number of mergers over that period. The further increase in 1967–69 is due partially to the expansion policy of larger firms faced with the liberalization of controls over foreign investment in Japan, and partly to the rationalization and modernization policies designed to improve the productive technique and capital facilities of smaller firms.[36] The influence of public policy is surely also significant. Many measures have been designed to encourage rationalization in smaller companies through merger (among other means), although it is difficult to link such policies to the timing of the merger wave. Among large companies public policy was important at least in its permissive attitude, and some combinations received active public encouragement.

35. The series shows some tendency to move inversely with the business cycle. See Jirō Ono, "The Characteristics of Recent Corporate Mergers in Japan," *Kōbe Economic and Business Review,* vol. 17 (1970), pp. 53–67.

36. Fair Trade Commission, *Nihon no kigyō shūchū* [Corporate Mergers in Japan] (Printing Office of the Ministry of Finance, 1971), p. 49. Data on the distribution of acquired assets, cited above, are given on pp. 68–71 of this document. See also Ono, "Characteristics of Recent Corporate Mergers," pp. 61–67.

Table 7-2. *Number and Type of Mergers Involving Large Firms,*[a] *1967–70*

Type of merger	1967	1968	1969	1970
Horizontal	21	17	24	31
Vertical	6	5	4	4
Backward	2	3	2	3
Forward	4	2	2	1
Conglomerate	12	12	27	24
Market extension	2	7	14	11
Product extension	8	4	8	4
Other	2	1	5	9
Total	39	34	55	59

Source: Fair Trade Commission, *Nihon no kigyō shūchū* [Corporate Mergers in Japan] (Printing Office of the Ministry of Finance, 1971), p. 66.
a. Defined as mergers in which the assets of the combined companies exceed ¥1 billion.

But seller concentration is only one trait of market structure that affects economic performance, and arguably not the most important one. In looking at several others, we shall emphasize the ways in which Japanese conditions differ from those in the United States and other industrial countries.

Product Differentiation

The ability of producers to differentiate their products through advertising and related techniques has been a potent influence on market competition in the United States. It not only insulates sellers from competitors' actions but also tends to raise barriers to the entry of new sellers. In the abstract, one might expect a country whose social patterns and values differ from Western norms to exhibit a different level and kind of product differentiation, both overall and in individual industries. Yet the most casual traveler in Japan quickly finds the promotional gimmicks quite similar to those of the West. Promotional techniques—whether for cosmetics, pharmaceuticals, or convenience foods—seem to be exploited with a relentless thoroughness.

Product differentiation in Japan, however, cannot be marked down as simply a close match to its American counterpart. Rebates and premiums, for example, are more important sales promotion devices in Japan than in the United States. Another distinction lies in timing. The rise of large-scale manufacturing enterprises in the differentiated consumer-goods industries has occurred only since World War II, and the structural consequences of mass advertising surely are still working themselves out. The data suggest that general and nationwide media—television and newspapers—claim proportionally larger advertising outlays in Japan than in the United States. The firm trying to break into the circle of successfully differentiated producers thus may face a problem of scale economies in nationwide sales promotion at least as great as its U.S. counterpart. Inspection of advertising-to-sales ratios for leading firms in similar Japanese and American industries prompts the suggestion, however, that overall spending by the Japanese may be lower on average.

It may be fair to associate the extent and character of product differentiation in Japan with certain traits of the society, notably a lack of individualism and a strong susceptibility to demonstration effects. To producers, these traits suggest a potential large gain for the seller who can successfully market the in-vogue variety of the product. In the absence of oligopolistic collusion on product characteristics, this prospective reward would tempt individual sellers into heavy outlays on sales promotion either to defend a market position already achieved or to attempt to enter the charmed circle. It would also imply relatively little product variety and an absence of the proliferation of product varieties said to occur in highly stratified societies such as that of Great Britain.

Another important feature of product differentiation in Japan lies in the extensive control exercised in many industries over the channels of distribution. The full story is complicated and involves the efforts of large consumer-goods manufacturers to overcome the complexities and inefficiencies of Japan's fragmented distribution system. In some industries the cooperation of the channels of distribution is important in differentiating individual brands. Direct control of distribution assures the manufacturer of the best possible display, promotional, pricing, and servicing policies for the product by the retailer. Indirectly, this control may yield the further advantage of forcing the potential entrant to incur heavy fixed costs to set up exclusive distribution channels of his own.

Distribution in Japan before World War II was dominated by wholesalers and large-scale trading companies whose market information guided the production of the small manufacturers who supplied them. Since the war vertically integrated control by the manufacturers has become quite common in oligopolistic and fast-growing consumer-goods sectors.[37] The extent and variety of this control appears to exceed what is found in the United States. In a few industries (for example, sewing machines and Western-style beds) it takes the form of fully owned means of wholesale and retail distribution. Other manufacturers (gasoline, automobiles, and some confectionery) exercise control through exclusive or nonexclusive franchises. Still others have organized existing outlets into affiliated groups of wholesalers and retailers.

37. Much of this and the following paragraph is drawn from M. Y. Yoshino, *The Japanese Marketing System: Adaptations and Innovations* (M.I.T. Press, 1971), chap. 3; and Distribution Economics Institute of Japan, *Outline of Japanese Distribution Structures* (1971).

Although many of these developments reflect the efforts of producers to rationalize Japan's distribution sector, the effect, intentional or unintentional, is to reduce competition among sellers and raise barriers to the entry of newcomers. Organizing the traditionally independent distributors entails heavy fixed costs in managerial effort, costs that impose great burdens on small manufacturing firms.

Barriers to New Competition

The structural trait of barriers to entry depends also in part on technological factors, and to that extent should vary little from country to country. The dependence is incomplete, however, because a country's institutions can raise or lower the fences that protect the market power of going sellers. Japan's institutions seem to lower these barriers.

In the United States product differentiation through advertising and related promotional activities appears to be the most potent inhibitor of new entry. Patterns of product differentiation in Japan are converging on those in the West, but their development only in recent decades suggests the likelihood that many Japanese firms are less well entrenched. The turbulence of the economy since World War II has favored new entrants by increasing the vulnerability of the positions of going firms.[38] The economy is relatively large, and thus entry is not severely taxed by scale economies to the plant or firm. Absolute-cost advantages of going firms are not a major source of entry barriers in Japan. Raw materials are bought on the world market; access to them is seldom under the control of established processors. Groups of firms often pool their capital to finance entry into an industry, thereby reducing the incidence of capital-cost entry barriers. Miyazaki has argued that bank rivalries have led to the development by the leading city banks of parallel and complete families of affiliated industrial firms.[39] It is often asserted in Japan that this behavior leads to cutthroat competition and excess capacity in many industries. Our judgment is that the hypothesis may explain some developments during the period of rapid industrial development in the late 1950s, but that probably it remains relevant only for new and fast-growing industries.

Rates of Macroeconomic Growth

The extraordinary rates of growth of Japanese industrial output since 1950 are important in the environment of business decisionmaking and mar-

---

38. Yoshino, *Japan's Managerial System,* chap. 6, especially p. 166.
39. Y. Miyazaki, *Sengo Nihon no keizai kikō* [Economic Organization of Postwar Japan] (Shinhyōronsha, 1966).

ket competition. We suggest, tentatively, the following interpretation. During some parts of the last two decades, such as the latter 1950s and latter 1960s, profitable expansions of output were limited in many industries only by short-term constraints in supply and planning. This was the result, in macro-economic terms, of a combination of forces, especially the favorable exchange rate of the yen, a large labor supply that could be shifted from agriculture and other sectors with low productivity, and a high rate of saving. At the exchange rate, yen selling prices for many internationally traded goods were high enough to make profitable a seemingly unlimited expansion of output at the going supply prices of capital and labor.[40]

The microeconomic effect of such conditions is at least to dampen the concern of producers about their mutual interdependence, since each anticipates the sale of all he can produce at the going world price—whether on foreign or domestic markets. Market strategies to improve one's position at the expense of rivals thus assume a low priority. The concentration of sellers in the market then would be expected to have little influence on their profit. In such circumstances fluctuations in profit are likely to result mostly from varying short-run windfalls. In an industry in which producers can adapt their actual plant capacities only slowly to the levels they would desire in a rapidly growing market, profits will be inflated by short-run windfalls whatever their normal level over the long run. Where expansion to desired capacity comes quickly, these windfalls will not accrue.

But fast growth can also affect the rivalry among oligopolistic sellers directly. Suppose that, because of various intertemporal factors in the determinants of the demand for his product—experience and goodwill, cumulative effects of advertising, and the like—the share a seller can command in a market today depends on the share he held yesterday. The more rapidly the market is growing, the more it will pay the seller to invest in market share for tomorrow by selling more today than short-run profit maximization would indicate. Learning-curve phenomena on the production side also promote such behavior. With Japan's abundant entrepreneurial capacity, conditions

40. This mechanism depends on output expansion being profitable at international prices, not necessarily on its actually being sold on international markets. This is, export of an increasing proportion of manufactured output would strongly support the argument but is not necessary to it. Between 1960 and 1968, thirteen of seventeen broadly defined manufacturing industries did increase their (direct and indirect) dependence on exports, but the evidence suggests that this shift came primarily toward the end of the period, and one is not inclined to brand this growth "export led." See Economic Planning Agency, *Economic Survey of Japan, 1969–70* (1970), p. 78; and Tuvia Blumenthal, "Exports and Economic Growth: The Case of Postwar Japan," *Quarterly Journal of Economics,* vol. 86 (November 1972), pp. 617–31.

of rapid growth thus are likely to support the entry of new firms and the diversification of established ones into the more rapidly growing sectors. Market shares should be rendered less stable by these same forces.

Company Finance and Capital Markets

Early in this chapter some of the unusual general features of factor markets in Japan, as well as their implication for the allocation of resources, were noted. Relevant here is the way in which market structure is affected by the capital market's discrimination in favor of large firms and the high leverage found in the capital structures of Japanese corporations.

LEVERAGE AND RISK. Ministry of Finance data on effective interest rates (allowing for compensating balances and other terms of transaction) show that small firms pay at least 50 percent more than medium-size ones. Data assembled from company records show a weak tendency for this discrimination to continue in favor of the large relative to the medium sized. Capital markets also have low and declining ratios of corporate owners' equity to total capital, as shown below:[41]

Year	Manufacturing	All industries
1950	31.4	26.9
1955	34.0	29.0
1960	27.6	22.6
1965	23.1	19.0
1970	19.9	16.1

The decline, which may be partly an accounting phenomenon, has been greater among large firms than small ones. Little difference now exists among firms by size of paid-in capital, but formerly the financial structures of the smaller corporations were more highly leveraged. The end of this trend to increasing leverage has been predicted as Japanese growth slows somewhat and the self-financing capability of businesses increases.[42] The data, however, do not yet show such a turnaround.

The effect of this high financial leverage depends on how Japanese holders of debt instruments view their risk-bearing function. There is evidence that financial institutions have adapted their behavior extensively to the prevailing high leverage of their corporate debtors. (By "financial institutions" we really mean banks, because debentures comprise only a few percent of new corporate funds—4 percent in 1966[43]—so that the bank loans must be

41. Ministry of Finance, *Hōjin kigyō tōkei nenpō* [Annual Statistics on Corporations] (annual issues).
42. EPA, *Economic Survey of Japan, 1968–69*, pp. 116–21.
43. Abegglen (ed.), *Business Strategies*, p. 58.

counted actually as long term.) The banks hedge themselves in several important ways on the risk exposure of their business loans. A given corporation borrows from many different banks; the largest lender—a company's leading bank—is said usually to account for 30 percent of the company's borrowings, but the data suggest that even this figure is high. The risks of a given large firms' default are spread widely among lenders—more so than in other countries. Furthermore, several observers suggest that loans to large companies are in effect guaranteed by the Bank of Japan, which will assist in a rescue if a large company gets in trouble.[44] Finally, one wonders whether banks do not manage somehow to share in the riches when their principal borrowers do particularly well. One study of the city banks found their profits fairly closely related to the growth rate of their client enterprises.[45] It is possible, of course, that this seeming equity relation runs solely through shares owned by the banks rather than through the proceeds of loans.

MARKET CONSEQUENCES. What effects on market performance should result from these traits of company finance? The interest-rate differences that favor large firms cause artificial (that is, private but not social) economies for large-scale enterprise and tend to make firms larger and markets more concentrated than they need be. (Labor costs, as noted earlier, cut the other way, but information is not sufficient to determine how they balance out—especially since industries vary in their opportunities to substitute capital for labor.)

The high nominal leverage of the financial structures of Japanese companies should tend to increase their preference for safe, conservative conduct: for example, making collusive arrangements that remove uncertainties as well as opportunities to improve one's own position at the expense of the rivals. But this proposition has its limitations: for example, some types of collusive arrangements can actually destabilize profits. Nonetheless, industry studies in the United States suggest that high leverage (and other heavy fixed costs) raise the desires of firms to collude, whether or not structural conditions are such as to make collusion effective.[46] High leverage also tends to discourage innovative risk taking, even by the firm unconcerned with competitors. These predictions from the high leverage observed in corporate financial structures are the more important because of the relative fixity of the labor costs of large firms caused by permanent employment.

44. Hadley, *Antitrust in Japan,* pp. 234–35; Abegglen (ed.), *Business Strategies,* p. 62.

45. EPA, *Economic Survey of Japan, 1968–69,* pp. 121–22.

46. Roger Sherman and Robert Tollison, "Technology, Profit Risk, and Assessments of Market Performance," *Quarterly Journal of Economics,* vol. 86 (August 1972), pp. 448–62.

International Linkages

Elements of structure that often are neglected in studies of industrial organization are the international linkages associated with international trade, foreign direct investment, international technology agreements, and the like. These linkages, though they are largely favorable to competitive behavior within a national market, are no guarantee of it, and their impact varies from market to market.[47]

TRADE. Evident among Japan's successful exporters is a trend away from light industry and competitive sectors populated by small firms and toward the heavy and chemical industries dominated by large firms. The proportion of output exported by small businesses dropped from 10 percent in 1960 to 7 percent in 1971, and their share of exports by a considerable amount. The share of output exported by large companies rose from 7 to 12 percent.[48] Exports are now associated positively with an industry's research intensity, a phenomenon not evident in figures gathered a decade ago.[49] Surveys of the effects of import competition seem to indicate that the small-business sector is increasingly exposed to rivalry from lower-wage Asian countries undergoing rapid industrialization.[50]

Under certain assumptions the effects of import competition and export opportunities are symmetrical in restraining an industry from exploiting its monopoly power in the domestic market. This symmetry tends to break down, however, when the export industries are concentrated enough—and protected by high enough tariffs—to charge different prices in the home and export markets. Thus, the shift of Japan's comparative advantage bringing the concentrated industries into export status is probably adverse to effective competition in the domestic market. They can dump abroad and collude in the home market, although the liberalization of trade controls on imports puts some limits on their ability to dump.

FOREIGN DIRECT INVESTMENT. Foreign direct investment also can make

47. R. E. Caves, *International Trade, International Investment, and Imperfect Markets,* Special Papers in International Economics, no. 10 (International Finance Section, Princeton University, 1974).

48. EPA, *Economic Survey of Japan, 1971–72,* p. 76. This source puts the small-business share of exports in 1971 at 40 percent, but there is evidence that this figure is an overestimate. On the long-run trend, see William V. Rapp, "Firm Size and Japan's Export Structure: A Micro-view of Japan's Changing Export Competitiveness since Meiji," in Hugh Patrick (ed.), *Japanese Industrialization and Its Social Consequences* (University of California Press, forthcoming).

49. EPA, *Economic Survey of Japan, 1967–68,* p. 93.

50. Ibid., pp. 120–22.

up a significant element of market structure. In an industry with substantial barriers to entry, multinational companies are important potential entrants, and the foreign subsidiary (especially in its early days) may provide a significant competitive force.

Foreign investment in Japan reveals patterns quite different from that in Western industrial countries, chiefly if not solely because of Japanese governmental restrictions. Foreign-affiliated firms are found principally in the producer-goods sector and consist largely of joint ventures, often with complex parentage. Their shares of the market are relatively small. Evidence from a detailed survey of their behavior suggests that they are less potent sources of entrepreneurial initiative than an independent company might be.[51]

IMPORT OF TECHNOLOGY. Agreements to import foreign technology into Japan represent a major feature of the growth in productivity since World War II. Such an agreement allows the Japanese firm either to enter a new product market or to produce with some combination of higher quality and lower cost. Access to foreign technology therefore is a significant factor in competition, since control over technology is a standard source of absolute cost barriers to entry. Statistical evidence shows that technology imports have become more numerous but probably individually less important over the postwar years. The degree to which technology imports are concentrated in large companies has dropped sharply, as has the average amount of investment associated with each introduction.[52] The drop is probably associated more with a shift in the relative importance of industries as importers of technology than with changes in the pattern of the typical industry's imports.

Public Policy toward Industry

Public policy wields a structural influence on Japanese business much more direct and continuous than that of American antitrust and related policies on U.S. industries. Some accounts imply that the structures of markets and the forces of competition, displaced by an intimate and informal government-business relation, carry little weight in the behavior of the Japanese economy. Subsequent sections of this chapter present evidence that contradicts that view. Nonetheless, the influence of public policy does weigh heavily on the conduct and performance of industries in Japan.

51. Ministry of International Trade and Industry, *Foreign-Affiliated Enterprises in Japan* (Trade Bulletin Corp., 1969); and Robert J. Ballon (ed.), *Joint Ventures and Japan* (Tokyo: Sophia University, 1967), chaps. 1, 6.

52. EPA, *Economic Survey of Japan, 1966–67*, pp. 66–67. For more detail, see Chapter 8 in this volume.

Antimonopoly Legislation

Antimonopoly legislation in Japan is a legacy of the U.S. occupation following World War II.[53] The chief statute, the Antimonopoly Law, was imposed on the country in 1947 by the Supreme Commander for the Allied Powers. Based largely on U.S. statutes, it employed concepts such as "public interest," "substantial," and "competition" that had appeared in no previous Japanese legislation and thus conveyed no clear meaning to the public who would have to comply with it. The quasi-judicial Fair Trade Commission of Japan, created to enforce the act, was likewise without precedent.

PROVISIONS OF THE ANTIMONOPOLY LAW. The law absolutely prohibits private monopolization, defined as individual or collective actions to exclude or control the activities of others and thereby to cause a substantial restraint of trade contrary to the public interest. The law is thus clear on a point long ambiguous in the Sherman Act of the United States: in Japan it is illegal to seek a monopoly or bolster a monopoly position, but not to have a monopoly. In parallel with this emphasis on conduct, the law of mergers and other combinations sounds fairly strict. The formation of a holding company is prohibited: a reflection of their role in cementing the old *zaibatsu* structures. Financial institutions cannot hold more than 10 percent of the total outstanding shares of the issuing company without special permission from the FTCJ. Any merger or acquisition must be reported to the FTCJ thirty days in advance and is prohibited where the effect may be substantially to restrain competition in any particular field of trade or where unfair business practices have been employed.

Unreasonable restraints of trade are prohibited, meaning those which substantially restrain competition in any particular field of trade by fixing or raising prices, limiting production, technology, or facilities, or dividing the market. The effect of this provision is to prohibit cartels and related horizontal agreements. Certain practices of trade associations are proscribed: those substantially restricting competition, limiting entry, unduly restricting the activities of members, or promoting unfair business practices.

The act prohibits six categories of unfair business practices. As elaborated in a 1953 notification by the FTCJ, they include boycotts and refusals to deal; discrimination in prices, terms, or access to concerted activities; unreasonably high or low prices intended to injure a competitor or as a coercive

53. We sketch only the major facts about the background of antimonopoly legislation, because detailed analyses in English are readily available. See Hadley, *Antitrust in Japan;* Kōzō Yamamura, *Economic Policy in Postwar Japan: Growth versus Economic Democracy* (University of California Press, 1967); and Hiroshi Iyori, *Antimonopoly Legislation in Japan* (Federal Legal Publications, 1969).

inducement of customers; exclusive dealing; vertical restrictive agreements including tying and (generally) resale price maintenance; and "abuse of a dominant bargaining position," or interference with the business activities of competitors. In addition, the FTCJ can designate certain business practices as unfair within particular industries; designations of this kind have been made in thirteen industries.

In September 1974 the FTCJ proposed a series of amendments that would greatly strengthen the scope of the law and the commission's enforcement power. Companies with extremely high market shares could be divided into smaller units, and cost data on near-monopoly products could be published. Prices charged by cartels could be rolled back and unfair profits surcharged. Fines would be raised, and shareholding by both banks and large nonfinancial companies limited.

ENFORCEMENT. The Fair Trade Commission's enforcement has gone through historical phases and has concentrated on certain provisions of the act. Antimonopoly policy was largely inoperative while the economy remained under comprehensive economic controls, but in 1949–51 a series of cases was brought concerning trade associations (under a stronger separate law then in force) and exclusive dealing arrangements built into international technology agreements. During the following decade, 1952–62, pressures were continually applied to weaken or eliminate features of the Antimonopoly Law. Enforcement was correspondingly reticent and passive, with the FTCJ bringing only a few cases against cartels. The legislation did attract support and withstand determined efforts to weaken it, especially during 1958–62, and this vitality ultimately gave heart to the commission. Price-fixing cartels, especially in consumer goods, came under extensive attack in the 1960s, and cases dealing with unfair business practices became more numerous.[54]

The FTCJ's most numerous cases have been brought against cartels and trade associations for price fixing (see Table 7-3). Unfair trade practices, especially boycotts and refusals to deal, also have drawn many enforcements. But the FTCJ has made little headway in enforcing the merger and monopoly provisions of the act. Critical tests of the merger provisions came in 1968 when plans were announced for mergers of the three largest paper companies, with a combined share of newsprint production of 60 percent, and of the two largest steel makers, with a combined share of crude steel of 35.6 percent. Both mergers exceeded the standard of a 30 percent market share that the FTCJ had established as a criterion for evaluating mergers. The steel merger, backed by the Ministry of International Trade and Industry,

54. Iyori, *Antimonopoly Legislation*, pp. 22–23, 26, 124–31.

Table 7-3. *Violations Found by the Fair Trade Commission of Japan, by Fiscal Year and Type of Offense, 1947–71*

Offense	1967	1968	1969	1970	1971	Total 1947–71
Price-fixing agreements	11	27	20	43	32	} 420
Other collusive agreements[a]	0	0	3	1	4	
Unfair trade practices	7	7	2	0	1	61
Resale price maintenance	2	4	0	0	0	
Tying arrangements	0	0	0	0	1	
Refusal to deal	0	3	2	0	0	
Other	5	0	0	0	0	
Mergers and intercorporate shareholding	0	0	2	0	0	} 31
Other	0	0	0	1	0	
Total	18	34	27	45	37	512

Source: Fair Trade Commission, *Annual Report* (1969), pp. 156–57; (1970), pp. 211–12; (1971), pp. 222–23; and History of Twenty Years of Antimonopoly Policy (1972), pp. 732–33.
a. Distribution-channel agreements and quantity restrictions.

went to a formal hearing and was finally approved by the FTCJ under pressure. The paper merger was dropped, however, in anticipation of the FTCJ's rejection.[55] The first significant case concerning monopolization, against Tōyō Seikan (Tōyō Can Manufacturing Company) for controlling competitors in the metal container industry, was decided in 1972.[56]

The FTCJ's approvals of depression cartels, an exemption contained in the Antimonopoly Law, have been quite generous at times. Depression cartels have sometimes been sought by industries having trouble working out clandestine arrangements, and it seems likely that illegal secret cartels have sometimes continued after legally authorized cartels reached their expiration dates. The FTCJ's approval of depression cartels has sometimes contained an important tactical element, the commission preferring formal but temporary cartel arrangements to the alternative of administrative curtailments of output managed by the MITI.[57]

Exemptions from Antimonopoly Policy

The Antimonopoly Law has been weakened by both general amendment and specific statutory exemptions or administrative intervention by the MITI and other ministries. The statutory exemptions are singular and political by their nature but fall into certain patterns: favoring small enterprises, sectors

55. Iyori, *Antimonopoly Legislation*, pp. 31–32, 58, 67–68, 72–73, 125; and Eugene J. Kaplan, *Japan: The Government-Business Relationship* (U.S. Department of Commerce, 1972), pp. 149–51.
56. FTCJ decision of Sept. 18, 1972, 1972(R), no. 11.
57. Iyori, *Antimonopoly Legislation*, p. 30.

subject to other government regulations, and sectors exposed to foreign trade. In many cases the cartel arrangements require approval by a ministry and notice to, or consultation with, the FTCJ.[58]

The Antimonopoly Law itself contains general exemptions for natural monopolies (public utilities), regulated industries, and industrial property rights. Agreements with individual dealers to maintain resale prices are exempted by the act for copyrighted works and for other products designated under certain rules by the FTCJ; as of 1973 the designated list included cosmetics, toothpastes, soaps, detergents, and drugs.

Two types of cartels are permitted. "Depression cartels" can be approved in advance by the FTCJ, under certain conditions, if supply exceeds demand, prices fall below average costs, and a number of producers are likely to go out of business. Approval usually covers no more than one year, and membership is voluntary. Rationalization cartels also can be formed with prior approval to carry out concerted efforts to exchange or restrict technology, standardize goods produced, work out specializations by product line, or make common use of transport or storage facilities.

The importance of these exemptions is seen in the prevalence of officially sanctioned cartels in Japanese industry. In 1963 the FTCJ tabulated the incidence of statutory and administrative cartels in manufacturing industries at the six-digit level of disaggregation. Of 1,748 commodity groups, 336, or 19.2 percent, were subject to cartelization of the domestic market, either directly or as an adjunct to an export agreement. Weighted by value of shipments (from the 1960 census), these items accounted for 28 percent of the total. If we remove those agreements ancillary to a joint restriction of exports, these percentages fall to 12.0 percent (number of commodities) and 19.7 percent (value of shipments). Cartels seem more common, as one would expect, in the less concentrated and less differentiated manufacturing sectors.[59] As Table 7-4 shows, the total number of exempted cartels rose from 248 in 1956 to 595 in 1960, then to its peak in 1966. From that time the number has not changed greatly.[60]

Industrial Policy and Administrative Control of Competition

Japan's policies toward competition must be put into the larger setting of the nation's industrial policy. Competition policy has been applied only as

58. Ibid., pp. 104–07.
59. Figures quoted by Hiroshi Iyori, "Cartel and Concentration Trend in Japan," *International Asienforum,* vol. 4 (1973), p. 423.
60. Iyori, *Antimonopoly Legislation,* pp. 24–25, 131–34; and idem, "Cartel and Concentration Trend," pp. 420–21.

Table 7-4. *Cartel Agreements Exempted from the Antimonopoly Law by the Fair Trade Commission of Japan, by Year and Exempting Statute, 1964–73*[a]

Statutory basis for exemption	1964	1965	1966	1967	1968	1969	1970	1971	1972	1973
Depression cartels	2	2	16	1	0	0	0	0	9	2
Rationalization cartels	14	14	14	13	13	12	10	13	10	10
Export cartels	201	208	211	206	213	217	214	192	175	180
Import cartels	1	2	3	4	3	4	4	3	2	2
Cartels under Medium and Small Enterprises Organization Act	588	587	652	634	582	522	469	439	604	607
Cartels under Environment Sanitation Act	106	122	123	123	123	123	123	123	123	123
Cartels under Coastal Shipping Association Act	15	14	16	15	22	22	22	21	19	19
Cartels under other statutes	43	50	44	44	47	48	56	53	34	42
Total	970	999	1,079	1,040	1,003	948	898	844	976	985

Source: FTCJ, Staff Office, *The Antimonopoly Act of Japan* (1973), p. 27.
a. Number in force in March of each year.

one tool—and not a major one—of a broader set of industrial policies. Yet those broader policies have evolved not as an integrated whole—logically plotted to achieve coherent long-run objectives—but as the outgrowth of political interaction, a pushing and hauling between the business and government sectors and the ad hoc measures and compromises that such interaction casts up.[61]

POLICY FORMATION. Industrial policy results from an intense and continuing interaction between business interest groups and the government bureaucratic apparatus. Each has its objectives: the former, a straightforward pursuit of self-interest; the latter, the achievement of policy objectives that may change over time and wax and wane in importance.

Each sector of the Japanese economy has a cliental relation to a ministry or agency of the government. The ministry by statute can wield various sticks and carrots in its dealings with the economic sector, but it also holds a general implied administrative responsibility and authority that goes well beyond what is customary in the United States, though it may come close to French practice. The Ministry of International Trade and Industry plays the most prominent role, but its operations are not otherwise distinctive. In Lockwood's oft-quoted words: "The industrial bureaus of MITI proliferate sectoral targets and plans; they confer, they tinker, they exhort. This is the 'economics by admonition' to a degree inconceivable in Washington or Lon-

61. Information on this policy system is contained in Kaplan, *Japan: The Government-Business Relationship;* Organisation for Economic Co-operation and Development, *The Industrial Policy of Japan* (Paris: OECD, 1972); Chitoshi Yanaga, *Big Business in Japanese Politics,* Yale Studies in Political Science, no. 22 (Yale University Press, 1968); William W. Lockwood, "Japan's 'New Capitalism'," in Lockwood (ed.), *State and Economic Enterprise,* chap. 10.

don. Business makes few major decisions without consulting the appropriate governmental authority; the same is true in reverse."[62]

The MITI's goals have varied over time in weight and composition, but some have recurred regularly since its founding in 1949. One has been to promote the movement of resources toward certain favored industries—first to the heavy and chemical industries, later to a group of industries in which Japan seemed to enjoy a comparative advantage in international markets. Another goal has been to enlarge the scales of plant and firm in certain industries—larger plants from an abiding faith in economies of scale, larger firms from a belief that, as controls on foreign trade and investment were lifted, Japanese firms must be as large as their American competitors in order to compete with them effectively. This goal has led at times to a considerable enthusiasm for mergers and the restriction of new entry into industries of interest to the MITI. The ministry has encouraged the importation and dissemination of new technology, promoting industrywide cooperation in its use. And it has sought to protect Japanese markets from the intrusion of foreign competition through imports or foreign investment.

IMPLEMENTATION. The means for pursuing these policies have been various. A major sanction until the mid-1960s was the MITI's authority over the allocation of foreign exchange for the purchase of essential inputs.[63] Other controls over foreign transactions also received heavy use. Licenses to import foreign technology were used to restrict entry into various industries and keep individual oligopolists form gaining excessive leads over their rivals. As a positive inducement the ministry has influenced access to generous lending facilities of the public Japan Development Bank. And public control over access to capital does not stop with public sources of funds: it may include some prodding of private lenders. "The government's support for the project at hand . . . is most helpful in obtaining loans from the commercial banks. Japan's . . . 'city banks' with their numerous branches are closely supervised by the Bank of Japan and the Ministry of Finance."[64]

The MITI's control over industrial structure and behavior has also proceeded through informal "administrative guidance," applied via trade associations and industrywide coordinating groups, and now depends mainly on this technique. The concern of these groups has included deciding on the rate of expansion of capacity and dividing the increments among actual and

62. Lockwood, "Japan's 'New Capitalism'," p. 503.

63. Kaplan, *Japan: The Government-Business Relationship,* pp. 146–48; and Lockwood, "Japan's 'New Capitalism'," pp. 501–03.

64. Kaplan, *Japan: The Government-Business Relationship,* chap. 4, especially p. 37; and OECD, *Industrial Policy,* chap. 2.

would-be competing firms. Harmony does not always come easily. Controls over international transactions have often served as a club when gentle persuasion failed. The dividing up of increments to capacity among rival producers is not easy when large-scale plants are involved.[65]

Various case studies show that the MITI's ability to get its way is limited when its goals clash with the interests of business firms or other government agencies. For example, the MITI's desire to consolidate the auto industry around Toyota and Nissan served the interests of those firms and of struggling smaller firms that they might absorb, but not the stronger medium-size firms that carried on independently; the alliances made by the latter with U.S. auto producers hardly served MITI preferences. Sometimes the MITI is blocked by clashes with other government agencies, as in the quarrel with Japan Telephone and Telegraph over the use of telephone lines for time-sharing systems.[66] Conflict with the FTCJ has, of course, been endemic.

POLICY TOWARD SMALL BUSINESS. Not all significant industrial policies lie in the MITI's hands. The Ministry of Finance and other ministries have regulatory powers over economic sectors under their general charge. An area that cannot be neglected is policy toward small business. Although a quantitative appraisal is impossible, at least the principal types of measures now in use can be noted.

First, financing assistance involves long-term loans at low rates of interest. These loans are passed through various public financial intermediaries, and modernization loans are provided through prefectural governments. Organizations have been formed to lease equipment and to guarantee loans for small business. Small business investment companies provide equity capital.

Second, guidance is provided from local public offices on managerial practice and technology. Management training is offered, along with various aids to technical development.

Third, cooperative organizations are authorized, either to reduce excessive competition or to handle insurance and other cooperative activities or facilities. The government can order the participation of nonmember enterprises in these arrangements.

Fourth, modernization schemes are promoted by various means such as advice, loans and tax concessions, and regional planning operations. Various inducements to environmental improvement also are slanted toward small enterprises.[67]

65. Kaplan, *Japan: The Government-Business Relationship*, pp. 144–48.
66. See the case studies in ibid., pp. 77–158.
67. See Ministry of International Trade and Industry, Small and Medium Enterprise Agency, *Outline of Major Measures for Small and Medium Enterprises in Japan* (1972).

Patterns of Competition

The price charged and the character of the product sold by an industry result from interaction among the competing sellers—that is, their market conduct. When sellers are few or when they are numerous but can collude formally, interaction differs from that in the theoretical model of pure competition. What patterns of market conduct can be expected in an economy outside of Western cultural and legal traditions is uncertain, so giving equal consideration to market conduct can easily be justified. Patterns of business behavior reflect the conventions of social behavior and the constraints and opportunities created by public policy, so a given market structure in Japan cannot be expected—with confidence—to cast up the same patterns of conduct as in the United States.

Thus, this section examines the historical origins and characteristics of market conduct in Japanese industry and relates them to the guiding hand of Japanese industrial policy. Collusive practices might be expected to be more widespread in Japan than in comparably structured U.S. industries, if only because of the greater leniency of Japanese public policy. But how effective are these collusive arrangements and how great an impact do they have on the overall performance of the economy?

Cultural and Historical Background

The roots of collusive and parallel behavior in Japanese business predate the Meiji era. Associations resembling medieval guilds anticipated the modern trade association in their arrangements for members' common welfare—for example, quality standards, joint insurance, training and welfare programs, and price-fixing arrangements. These were particularly important in sectors such as textiles, paper, sugar, milling, and coal mining.[68]

Because the large enterprises that spearheaded the development of new industries during the Meiji period had few if any domestic rivals, only later did the formation of collusive arrangements among them suit their self-interest. Cartels developed during the 1920s (with earlier precedents) and spread rapidly during the 1930s through a combination of economic and political events: the price collapse of the depression following World War I, the financial crisis of 1927, and later the Great Depression on the economic

68. Hirschmeier and Yui, *Development of Japanese Business*, chaps. 1, 3.

side—as well as the beginning of military engagements and preparation for the larger one to come. Legislation in 1925 authorized cartels and provided for compulsory adherence by members, and a 1931 act authorized the government to compel membership of all firms in an industry when more than two-thirds requested it. Wartime controls in operation from 1938 dictated compulsory cartels under government supervision. A review after World War II discovered 1,538 of these control organizations. Although the wartime controls in effect expropriated many small firms, two decades of a cartelized economy convinced large enterprises of the virtues of collusion. As Hadley puts it: "Japan's business leaders had come to like the cartel way of doing business; certainly it was enthusiastically subscribed to by a number of the ministries. . . ."[69] The weakly enforced antimonopoly legislation of the postwar years has evidently left ample scope for the operation of cartels, both legal and illegal. Nonetheless, not all collusive coordination of sellers takes place through formal cartels. And the terms of these agreements, however formal, enjoy less than perfect adherence.

Patterns of Seller Coordination

Any description of contemporary patterns of conduct in Japanese industry must be impressionistic. These patterns can be observed accurately only through close study of an industry—and then may be subject to frequent change. What follows necessarily generalizes from examples and does not attempt to supply a comprehensive picture.

Many Japanese industries use the same informal, tacit devices that are known in the United States. Price leadership by the dominant firm is or has been common in such highly concentrated sectors as the production of beer, film, flat glass, aluminum ingot, synthetic fibers, metal cans, newsprint, wire and cable, and many steel products. The stability of these leadership patterns has varied, and has not been great in certain industries subject to fast technological change. Maintenance of resale prices, now losing its legal status, has been important in blocking the erosion of price structures at retail in goods such as soap and detergents, drugs, cameras, cosmetics, books, and phonograph records. Trade associations assist coordination through the exchange of information among sellers in those producer-goods industries which are only moderately concentrated and sell homogeneous products.

69. Hadley, *Antitrust in Japan,* p. 372; for fuller detail, see pp. 357–72. For the complex history of the legal status of Japanese cartels, see ibid., chaps. 6, 9; Yamamura, *Economic Policy in Postwar Japan,* chaps. 3–5; and Iyori, "Cartel and Concentration Trend," pp. 416–32.

Common practices among those in Japan include open-price reporting (especially chemicals and steel), the publication of common price lists, and the maintenance of statistics on inventories and production.

The significance of these arrangements is best understood by observing situations in which sellers are responding to some disturbance or breakdown in consensus. In the pharmaceutical industry a ban on competition through means other than price—namely, through the donation of goods to hospitals and physicians who purchased other products—led to an outbreak of active price rivalry and increased promotional outlays. Rivalry for market shares among the electrical appliance manufacturers prompted them to increase their control over distribution channels and retail prices.[70]

Other devices, although they fall short of full cartel arrangements, allow for more forceful restrictions on competition than those mentioned above. Some industries create joint selling or distribution agencies, such as the one handling rental installations for computer manufacturers.[71] Cooperation among oligopolists is also furthered when the leading firms acquire fractional shareholdings in their competitors. These shareholdings could tip the balance when a firm must choose between an action expected to increase profits on an industrywide basis and one designed to raise its own net revenues at the expense of its rivals. Such shareholding rewards a firm's stockholders with a weighted average of its own profits plus those of its fractionally owned competitors.[72]

A critical question about all collusive devices, formal or informal, is the degree to which firms adhere to them. The greater the success in raising the profitability of marginal sales, the greater the private temptation to cheat and perhaps undermine the agreement. There is only impressionistic evidence to support any view on the adherence to collusive arrangements in Japanese manufacturing. It does seem that members have adhered to the terms of legally sanctioned cartels with moderate regularity, but much less is known about clandestine and invisible arrangements. There are certainly many cases of collusive arrangements being shaken or even demolished by inconsistent market-share goals of large firms. Also observed is a tendency for terms of collusive arrangements to be expanded: rivalry suppressed in one dimension transfers itself to some other variable and impels further efforts to suppress it.

70. See *The Oriental Economist,* vol. 41 (August 1973); and Yoshino, *The Japanese Marketing System,* pp. 113–19.

71. *The Oriental Economist,* vol. 41 (June 1973), pp. 14–17, 43–44.

72. The case of the Japanese metal can industry, which illustrates the importance of shareholding among competitors, is documented in a decision of the Fair Trade Commission concerning Tōyō Seikan Kaisha, Ltd. (FTCJ decision of Sept. 18, 1972, 1972 [R] no. 11).

Coordination and Administrative Guidance

An important if fluid role in coordinating the actions of rival sellers has been played by agencies of the Japanese government, particularly the Ministry of International Trade and Industry. It has acted not only to secure legislation favorable to collusive practices but also has actively promoted coordination in a number of industries through direct administrative guidance. This practice, which lacks explicit statutory authority or legalistic procedure, reflects a recognized common interest between the MITI and the leading firms in certain oligopolistic industries, the latter recognizing that guidance may occasionally impair their profits but in the long run will promote joint net revenues across the industry.[73]

The MITI's guidance deals in particular with the construction of new capacity and the entry of new firms into an industry, and rests on concern for the construction of plants of efficient scale, as well as a fear of excess capacity and ensuing price competition. Because discussion among economists of collusive practices so often turns on fixing minimum prices, the fundamental role of control over investment must be stressed. When an oligopoly sells in a growing market, maintenance of an excess of price over long-run marginal cost ultimately turns on parallel action among rival firms in, first, controlling the rate at which the industry's capacity is expanded and, second, finding an acceptable way to dole out the increments of capacity among themselves. The maintenance of prices yielding excess profit is a short-run matter, managed in the context of production capacity already determined by these investment decisions. Price collusion without the recognition of mutual dependence relative to expanding capacity can lead to deficient social performance, such as chronic excess capacity, but is unlikely to generate much monopoly profit. Agreement on capacity, furthermore, can allow each seller occasionally to construct a new plant of efficient scale or, alternatively, to lock the rivals into simultaneous, continual investment in inefficiently small units.

The MITI's policies have had complex and devious effects. At certain times they have probably supplied an artificial incentive to enter certain industries. When it seems that the MITI will shortly slam the door on further entry, thus brightening the profits picture for established firms, wise firms are likely to seize the chance to enter while it lasts.[74] The MITI's fears of

---

73. For general discussions, see Yamamura, *Economic Policy*, chap. 5; Hadley, *Antitrust in Japan*, pp. 380–86; and Thomas F. M. Adams and N. Kobayashi, *The World of Japanese Business* (Kōdansha International, 1969), p. 177.

74. Hadley, *Antitrust in Japan*, pp. 286–87.

cutthroat competition have been strongly self-validating. When the ministry considers allowing a few firms to enter an industry, a large crowd of would-be entrants, each anticipating substantial profits if it is chosen, collects at the door. MITI officials observe the queue and become convinced that, but for their resolute efforts, all the applicants actually would enter and the market would collapse into just such cutthroat competition.

Effect of Collusive Practices

Collusive arrangements in an industry can affect its performance in two principal ways. First, they can alter its allocative efficiency by changing the actual level of output relative to the competitive ideal. Second, they can affect technical efficiency in various ways, increasing or decreasing the real cost of producing whatever level of output actually prevails.

Measuring the net misallocation of resources caused by collusive arrangements is never easy, and in this case we have only bits of evidence. Some data suggest that prices may have risen in the cartelized small-business industries relative to other small-business industries. A study of actual reductions in monthly outputs as against those ordered under official depression cartels showed that some contraction in output did occur, but usually less than the officially designated amount.[75]

The effect of collusion on technical efficiency is in some cases more apparent. Efforts to reduce market-share rivalry have led to extended controls by manufacturers over their distribution channels. These controls divert more resources toward sales promotion of various sorts and, in the long run, encourage manufacturing enterprises of inefficient scale by speeding the differentiation of the product. On the other hand, the MITI's contention that intervention has been necessary to guarantee construction of efficient-scale plants cannot simply be ruled out. In certain oligopolistic market structures, firms may choose to build inefficiently small plants or add product lines made in inefficiently small volumes.

Zaibatsu and Other Intermarket Group Relations

Does a market's performance depend only on the sales and capacity shares held by the rival sellers? Or does it matter as well that some sellers may be very large firms in absolute size, or that they may face each other as rivals in several other markets? The competitive significance of a firm's extra-

75. Rotwein, "Economic Concentration," pp. 274–75.

market assets and activities is a controversial question in industrial organization—and nowhere more so than in Japan, where *zaibatsu* and other affiliations link industrial, commercial, and financial firms in a thick and complex skein of relations matched in no other industrial country.

Japan is a group-oriented society, and its economy exhibits a startling variety of groupings of firms that extend beyond well-defined commodity markets. These groups in turn are cemented by a variety of commercial linkages: between buyer and seller of goods, lender and borrower, shareholder and issuer of equity. The structure of these relations is not simple to describe, but their importance is illustrated by evidence on the concentration of ownership of large joint-stock companies. In 1966 one-fourth of them reported significant blocks of their shares (3 percent or more) to be held by other companies, and for another one-third significant blocks were held by groups of companies.[76] To demonstrate the possible significance of these links through ownership and otherwise, we concentrate on the *zaibatsu* and groups clustering around the major banks.

Character of the Zaibatsu

The *zaibatsu* organizations are collections of manufacturing, trading, and financial corporations, with a group generally including oligopolistic firms from a number of industries but few rivals in individual product markets.

GENERAL FORM. The long and complex histories of the *zaibatsu* groups date from the Meiji period or before.[77] At the end of World War II the Big Four—Mitsui, Mitsubishi, Sumitomo, and Yasuda—controlled about one-quarter of the paid-in capital of incorporated business in Japan. Besides these four, consensus identifies six others that were generally smaller and less complete in their galaxy of financial institutions.

Control of the *zaibatsu* firms generally reposed in wealthy families. Their personal wealth, vast though it was, stretched to control much larger amounts of corporate assets by means of holding companies and other pyramid-type devices. Direction of each *zaibatsu* centered in a "top holding company" under family control, with the top holding company controlling the principal operating companies of the group and those firms in turn controlling many others through subsidiaries and fractional shareholdings. The manufacturing firms of the organizations were mostly in the producer-goods sectors, includ-

76. Yoshikazu Miyazaki, *Kasen* [Oligopoly] (Iwanamishinsho, 1972), p. 42.

77. See Hadley, *Antitrust in Japan*, chaps. 1–10; Bisson, *Zaibatsu Dissolution in Japan*. Whether the term *zaibatsu* should be applied to the present-day groups, which are much altered from the earlier model, is questionable. Here, it is applied purely for expository convenience to the three direct successors: Mitsui, Mitsubishi, and Sumitomo.

ing mining and primary industrial materials. They had become important suppliers to the Japanese military during the 1930s and 1940s, and for this and other reasons were relatively unconcerned with distributing and selling consumer goods. The organizations included large banks and other financial intermediaries, such as insurance companies. They also included giant general trading firms, that unique Japanese commercial institution that deals as buyer and seller with a wide variety of raw materials, as well as semifinished and some finished goods.

Holding-company relations were only one linkage that knitted the *zaibatsu* together. Family ownership reached into the operating companies directly, as well as through the top holding companies. The banks and financial intermediaries were principal suppliers of capital to the operating companies. The trading companies procured many of the inputs required by group firms and sold many of their outputs. The manufacturing firms themselves, being dominant makers of producer goods, bought from and sold to each other extensively. Decisionmaking was coordinated not just through the formal equity and financial links of the groups, but also more personally through the families' control of key personnel in the operating companies and the absolute loyalty owed to the families by the operating executives.

SIGNIFICANCE IN THE MARKET. Granted that the *zaibatsu* evidently represented vast concentrations of wealth under centralized control and played a far from benign role in public policy, what was their significance as market phenomena? The members of a given *zaibatsu* were seldom the individual or joint monopolists of product markets, but rather oligopolists with shares of various markets that might run from modest to dominant. The members' market relations with one another were generally vertical within the complex network of input-output relations that can readily arise among major sellers of producer goods. Thus, conglomerate relations and business reciprocity are concepts much closer to their market linkages than single-market monopoly.

The formal interpretation that we propose has indeed been advanced to explain the nature of profit-maximizing reciprocity—two-way trading relations among a subgroup of diversified transactors.[78] Consider a general-equilibrium situation in which n traders barter m commodities among themselves. Markets are not assumed free from monopoly power, and so equilibrium price ratios are in general not equal to ratios of marginal opportunity costs of production. Suppose that some of the traders band together and

---

78. The model, which has its roots in the theory of customs unions, is set forth in R. E. Caves, "The Economics of Reciprocity: Theory and Evidence on Bilateral Trading Arrangements," in W. Sellekaerts (ed.), *International Trade and Finance: Essays in Honour of Jan Tinbergen* (Macmillan, 1974), pp. 17–54.

explore the possibility of changing their trading arrangements so as to maximize their joint profits. They can do so by trading among themselves at competitive shadow prices computed to align price ratios to the relevant opportunity-cost ratios among members of the group. And they would trade jointly with the outside world at prices that would make profit-maximizing use of their joint monopoly-monopsony power.

Putting these arrangements into force would leave several telltale marks on the group's commercial relations. First, the prices charged on transactions among members would in general not be the same as those offered or demanded in transactions of members with the outside world. Second, the group's transactions with the outside world must pass through a single set of hands, if the joint monopoly-monopsony power is to be efficiently exploited. Third, because the optimal pricing arrangements would tend to lower the commercial profits of some members while raising those of others (and the group as a whole), lump-sum profit transfers must take place among the members or their individual profits must flow into a central treasury.

The descriptive evidence that we have seen suggests a close match between the institutional structures of the old *zaibatsu* and the operational predictions of the model. Internal transfer prices among members were not always the same as the prices attached to transactions with outsiders. The general trading companies provided the hands that manipulated transactions with the outside world to maximize monopoly power of the group. And the common ownership links stretching up to the top holding company secured the requisite indifference to the distribution of commercial profits among the member companies (although the interests of outside minority shareholders at various stages of the pyramid could potentially provide some check on the jointly optimal arrangements). Although we have not attempted the elaborate job of economic archaeology that would be necessary for a formal test of this model, we are impressed with the casual evidence that is consistent with it.[79]

Dissolution and Reassembly of the Zaibatsu

The *zaibatsu* were a major target of the economic reforms imposed on Japan during the postwar occupation. Although these organizations pulled themselves together once more in the decade after the peace treaty in 1952, both form and substance have undergone major changes. The top holding

79. It also seems consistent with the evidence and interpretations put forth by Hadley, *Antitrust in Japan*, especially chaps, 2, 3, and 8; and Rotwein, "Economic Concentration."

companies of the four major and six lesser *zaibatsu* were dissolved during the occupation, as were all other holding companies. The owning families were deprived of their shares in the holding companies and some proportion of their direct equity holdings in the operating companies; these shares were dispersed in relatively small personal stockholdings. Banks were forbidden to hold more than 5 (later 10) percent of the stock of a given operating company. Cross-ties of ownership among the operating companies, however, were in the end left unaffected. The two largest general trading companies, Mitsui and Mitsubishi, were dissolved. The banks and financial intermediaries escaped serious restraint from the deconcentration measures, however, despite the fact that they had clearly discriminated in favor of member firms in extending credit. A purge of top executives from the *zaibatsu* and other companies removed key officers who were thought to have played a major part in the war effort; they were replaced by subordinates promoted from within the companies. Finally, further use of the old *zaibatsu* trademarks was forbidden.[80]

NEW GROUPINGS. After the occupation ended, three leading *zaibatsu*—Mitsui, Mitsubishi, and Sumitomo—began to reassemble themselves, and they are once more a major and conspicuous force in the Japanese economy. The restoration is only partial, however, and lacks the coordinated muscle that the groups displayed in the 1930s and 1940s. The prohibition on the *zaibatsu* trademarks was quickly rescinded. The two major trading companies were put back together, as were some of the manufacturing firms that had been dissolved—notably Mitsubishi Heavy Industries. The top holding companies and the controlling family equities were gone forever, and the purged top executives did not return. Nonetheless, loyalties among the group operating firms survived, and mechanisms for coordination were restored in the form of presidents' clubs. The smaller and less complete of the *zaibatsu* did not reappear in their previous form, but groups have emerged centered on giant banks—especially Fuji (successor to the Yasuda *zaibatsu*), Dai-ichi, and Sanwa—that reunite some former *zaibatsu* brethren.

Some perspective on these groupings in contemporary Japan can be gained from Table 7-5, which classifies the larger corporations—those with more than ¥5 billion in tangible assets—according to what is considered to be their group affiliations. The public sector's predominance in the capital-intensive transportation and public utilities sectors makes it bulk large in the total, but it is growing more slowly and its share is dropping. Independent private corporations outside the affiliate system have expanded the most

80. Hadley, *Antitrust in Japan*, especially chaps. 2, 4, 5, 8, 10.

Table 7-5. *Distribution of Assets of Large Corporations, by Group Affiliation, 1955, 1962, and 1970*[a]
Percent

Affiliate group	Distribution of assets		
	1955	1962	1970
State enterprise groups[b]	62.2	50.1	38.3
Long-term credit bank groups[c]	2.1	3.3	4.3
Private financial institution groups[d]	23.3	28.4	29.2
Mitsui	6.1	3.8[e]	5.0
Mitsubishi	5.0	6.4	7.2
Sumitomo	3.2	5.9	5.4
Fuji Bank (Yasuda)	2.9	3.6	3.8
Dai-ichi Bank	3.1	3.5	3.2
Sanwa Bank	1.4	2.2	2.6
Giant industrial corporations[f]	5.6	9.5[e]	8.8
Foreign-owned enterprises	1.0	1.4	1.4
Companies outside the affiliate system	5.8	7.3	18.0

Sources: Y. Miyazaki, *Sengo Nihon no keizai kikō* [Economic Organization of Postwar Japan] (Shinhyōronsha, 1966), p. 208; and idem, "Shōwa 40 nendo kigyō shūdan hyō ni tsuite" [On Corporate Group Tabulations in 1965], in Shigeto Tsuru (ed.), *Atarashii seiji keizaigaku o motomete III* [For a New Political Economics III] (Keisō Shobō, 1970), table 2, p. 381.

a. Large corporations defined as those with tangible assets of more than ¥5 billion.
b. Public corporations whose capital is wholly or partly government owned.
c. Affiliates of long-term credit banks whose capital is partly government owned.
d. Affiliates of *zaibatsu* and large banks. The total includes smaller bank groups not shown separately.
e. If Toshiba Electric is transferred to Mitsui, these figures increase and decrease, respectively, by 1.6.
f. Corporations with vertical and conglomerate structures of subsidiaries and affiliates.

rapidly, although each private-sector group has picked up part of the state enterprises' declining share.

LINKAGES. Hadley's careful study assesses the internal linkages of the three revived *zaibatsu*. Only small minorities of the common shares of group firms are now held by fellow group members—between 10 and 20 percent on average—and these fractions are in turn divided among many holders. *Zaibatsu* firms, like others in Japan, are heavily dependent on bank loans for finance, but do only part of their borrowing from fraternal banks—the weighted average is apparently about half for Mitsubishi and Sumitomo firms, less for Mitsui. The evidence does not suggest to Hadley "in the *usual* situation that banks are the inheritors of the former top-holding company role."[81] The presidents' clubs and interlocking directorates provide no effective means of continuing coordination, and contemporary accounts of the groups' behavior suggest no more than sporadic mutual aid and collaboration

81. Hadley, *Antitrust in Japan,* chap. 11 (quotation from p. 244).

in joint ventures. Fraternal battles over shares in specific product markets even break out occasionally.[82]

MARKET INTERACTION. Finally, the extent of current transactions among the *zaibatsu* members may supply some index of their internal coordination. The trading companies provide a possible vehicle, for reasons outlined in the theoretical analysis set forth above. They are active in securing economies of joint advertising using group trademarks, and they have extensive personnel interlocks with the other members of the groups. The core manufacturing companies use the trading companies sometimes, but sometimes buy and sell on their own.[83] The model suggested that direct buyer-seller relations among group firms would be necessary for joint maximization and thus an indicator of the extent of internal coordination. Rotwein's evidence suggests that firms of the three groups do business with each other more extensively than if buyer-seller pairings occurred on a random basis.[84] Although all firms transact extensively with independent firms or members of other *zaibatsu,* their relative dependence on group associates is unmistakable.

Does this evidence of business reciprocity suggest extensive group coordination? Probably not. Suppose that producer goods are generally subject to some monopolization, so that posted prices exceed marginal costs. When firm A chooses between B and C as its supplier, paying the list price for its purchases, it confers a rent on the chosen supplier. If A happens to own a fractional equity share in B, part of that rent returns to A in incremental dividend payments as trading stamps for its patronage. Hence, given intragroup minority shareholdings, intragroup reciprocity in current transactions is a rational procedure individually and jointly, and a partial substitute for the price discrimination that would be needed (according to the model set forth above) to attain full joint maximization for a *zaibatsu*'s members.

Other Conglomerate Groupings

If the other conglomerate groupings identified in Japanese industry are at all significant economically, it is for the same reasons as the *zaibatsu* successors. Hence, we can apply the same tests for their internal coherence. The most widely recognized groups are the firms for which three large banks are the principal lenders: Fuji, Dai-ichi Kangyō, and Sanwa, The Fuji group is a direct successor of the Yasuda *zaibatsu,* and the others contain subgroups

---

82. See the articles appearing periodically in *The Oriental Economist,* especially in issues from August to November 1972.

83. Hadley, *Antitrust in Japan,* pp. 247–49.

84. Rotwein, "Economic Concentration," p. 267.

of firms that were affiliated in the earlier *zaibatsu*. Hadley's study convinces her that the level and stability of ownership and transactions relations within these groups are relatively weak and their potential significance thus quite modest. ". . . Controls are not sufficient to compel unity of behavior. . . . Corporate decisions may be influenced by member companies, but hardly compelled."[85]

Beyond the *zaibatsu* and principal bank groups, some commentators claim to find a ring of lesser but still significant groupings of nominally independent enterprises. One is the sets of firms for which each of the larger banks is the principal lender—an extension of the three recognized bank groups described above. Attention centers on eleven large banks: nine city banks and two long-term credit banks. The view is advanced that a firm's borrowings from its principal bank usually represent about 30 percent of its external debt, and that it possesses an unspecified but close and continuing relation to this bank. Hadley's statistical analysis, covering a sample of firms that are dominant in their chief product lines, reveals little strength in these relations.[86]

A more direct ownership link binds the cluster of subsidiaries that surrounds the typical large nonfinancial corporation. A 1965 study by the Fair Trade Commission defined a subsidiary as a company in which the firm has an ownership interest of 30 percent or more or in which it possesses 10 to 29 percent ownership plus other control linkages such as loans or interlocking directorates. On this basis, the 100 top nonfinancial corporations had 4,270 firms dependent on them, with ownership interest of 50 percent or more in 58.8 percent of the cases, 30 percent or more in 82.4 percent. Interlocking officerships are present in 75 percent of the cases, loans from the senior partner in 36 percent.[87]

The product-market relation between parent and subsidiary can be anything—vertical, horizontal, conglomerate—and there is little aggregate information on the relative importance of the various types. For many large firms engaged in assembly-type manufacturing operations, subsidiaries function chiefly as suppliers of parts and components. Their separate existence is explained in part by peculiarities of Japan's factor markets. Being much smaller than their parents, the subsidiaries apparently pay wages appropriate to firms of their own size rather than that of their parents. They also appear to be less locked into the system of permanent employment, and provide among other things a place to locate the parent's retired but still useful supervisory or middle-management employees. Thus, looked at from the view-

85. Hadley, *Antitrust in Japan*, pp. 268–69; for more details, see pp. 257–69.
86. Ibid., pp. 269–84.
87. Information summarized in ibid., pp. 291–92.

point of the parent firm, the subsidiary provides both a route of access to lower labor costs and a source of flexibility in dealing with fluctuations in the parent's level of productive activity. The prevalence of subsidiaries is thus related to the general phenomenon of subcontracting, discussed later in the context of small-scale enterprise.

Intercorporate shareholding is very common in Japan, and not just among group affiliates. Miyazaki's figures (given in Table 7-6) show the prevalence of minority participations large enough to qualify the interpretation of conventional data on concentration and to encourage a considerable amount of business reciprocity. Data on the scale and forms of these shareholdings appear in Table 7-6. All forms of intercorporation shareholding have been increasing apace: in 1960, 53.2 percent of the shares of companies listed on Japanese stock exchanges were owned by corporations. This figure had increased to 62.4 percent in 1971, with the increase concentrated in monetary institutions and business and industrial firms. The continued concentration of stock in corporate hands is ascribed both to the tightening of intragroup relations and the cementing of control by firms over their subsidiaries or supplying affiliates.[88]

Effects of Group Behavior

The evidence that we found on the economic effects of conglomerate groups in Japanese industry was all circumstantial and based on their organizational arrangements, not on the consequences of their behavior. Therefore we undertook statistical studies of the profitability of group membership and the interaction of the zaibatsu groups in Japan's product markets.

If group membership generates either monopoly or efficiency rents for member firms, their profits on the average should be higher than those of independent firms. To test this hypothesis we employed data on the average profit rates of 243 large companies over a ten-year period. To explain the variance of profit rates among these firms we included variables reflecting the market power that firms share in their chief product markets (for example, seller concentration and advertising outlays), power adhering in their own assets and positions (absolute size and diversification), the risk to which they are exposed (variance of sales), and any windfalls due to unusual growth of markets. In addition, dummy variables indicated membership in a zaibatsu or bank group.

We found that group membership in general lowers profit rates on equity,

88. "Stockholdings by Corporations," *The Oriental Economist*, vol. 41 (May 1973), p. 18.

Table 7-6. *Ownership and Immediate Control of Joint-Stock Corporations with Tangible Assets of More than Five Billion Yen, Fiscal Year 1966*

	Number of companies							
	By percentage of shareholding							
	Majority control		Minority control					Percent of total
Ownership	Over 90 percent	50–90 percent	30–50 percent	10–30 percent	Under 10 percent	Management controlled	Total	
Family owned	1	4	6	18	12	...	41	8.8
Corporate affiliates	0	3	6	22	9	...	40	8.6
Single companies	12	15	19	36	24	...	106	22.8
Domestic nonfinancial	9	13	17	28	4	...	71	15.2
Banks	0	0	0	4	20	...	24	5.2
Insurance companies	0	0	0	4	0	...	4	0.9
Foreign companies	3	2	2	0	0	...	7	1.5
Multicompany groups	12	26	17	68	31	...	154	32.9
Domestic nonfinancial	4	12	3	5	1	...	25	5.4
Domestic, including financial	0	7	7	57	29	...	100	21.5
Foreign companies	0	2	0	0	0	...	2	0.4
Foreign and domestic	8	5	7	6	1	...	27	5.6
Management controlled	...	...	...	...	...	117	117	25.2
Central and local government	1	4	1	2	0	...	8	1.7
Total	26	52	49	146	76	117	466	100.0
Percent of total	5.6	11.2	10.5	31.2	16.3	25.2	100.0	...

Source: Yoshikazu Miyazaki, *Kasen* [Oligopoly] (Iwanamishinsho, 1972), p. 42. Figures may not add to totals because of rounding.

rather than raising them, and to a lesser extent also lowers profits plus interest on total assets. Our results thus confirm the observation that the independent firms without group affiliation include many innovative, fast-growing, and profitable ones in the consumer-goods sector. We cannot say whether group membership would appear profitable if our sample more successfully controlled for differences in firms' market environments.

Because group membership reduces profit rates plus interest on total assets by a smaller percentage (and with less statistical certainty) than profits on equity, we also investigated the financial structures and average interest paid by the firms in our sample. Financial leverage does not differ significantly between group members and other firms. Nonetheless, average interest paid by group firms is significantly higher. We thus find our evidence consistent with the following interpretation. The banks, generally credited with a leadership role in the groups, collect interest charges from group firms that include rents of 0.2 to 0.3 percent on their borrowed capital. These come partly from exploitation of group firms' equity shareholders, who receive a lower return than shareholders in independent companies. They may also come from efficiency rents or monopoly power in product markets, but that conjecture is not supported by our statistical analysis. Unfortunately we cannot tell how these rents are divided between the principal bank and other lenders.

504

Another statistical test concerned market relations among the three leading *zaibatsu*. In the 1930s they appeared to respect each other's industrial spheres of influence. But recent observers have suggested a behavior pattern in which the groups are in rivalry with one another and seek parallel representation in the chief industrial markets. These two opposed hypotheses imply different patterns of changes over time in market shares held by group members. In pursuit of these patterns we analyzed data on market-share changes for various short periods during the years 1937–66. No regular patterns were found. We conclude that either no systematic patterns of economic relations exist among the groups, or the data available to us were too aggregated—covering industries defined too broadly—to be revealing.

Allocative Efficiency and Its Determinants

Several studies have been undertaken of the determinants of allocative efficiency in Japanese industry, primarily in the manufacturing sector. We summarize previous research and present an interpretation of the pattern of results, then report our own statistical analyses.

Findings of Previous Studies

Several statistical studies have sought to explain the variation in rates of profit on equity among Japanese manufacturing industries. Their results seem to clash, yet we believe that overall they fall into a consistent and revealing pattern. Two major phenomena emerge from these studies.

The first involves the significant influence wielded by seller concentration on profits in periods when Japan's economy has grown with normal rapidity, but not when it has proceeded at an explosive pace. Earlier we set forth reasoning and evidence about why periods of very fast macroeconomic growth should translate themselves into microeconomic disequilibria. When it appears profitable at the margin to expand production in practically every industry, an industry's profit rate may depend primarily on how fast it can enlarge its capacity. In industries that can expand capacity only with long lags for planning and construction, substantial short-run windfalls may accrue, even if the industry is potentially competitive enough that they will be eliminated in the long run. Industries that adjust more quickly will reap smaller windfalls, even if concentration is high enough to keep profits above the competitive norm in the long run. Thus, concentration may fail to register a significant influence on profits in periods of explosive growth, at least unless account is taken of differences in short-run constraints on the expansion of industries' outputs. And it is logical that growth should be a more potent determinant of profit rates in periods when it is very rapid than when it is normal.

The other striking finding is the strong performance of concentration as a determinant of profits in Japan, except when growth is explosive, along with the relatively weak performance of statistical variables that represent the barriers to the entry of new firms. Studies done in the United States generally have pointed to just the opposite result. The significance of entry-barrier variables and the insignificance of concentration have been rationalized, when they are included, on the ground that in the long run entry barriers determine concentration; when industries are observed in or near long-run equilibrium, concentration will be determined by, and thus collinear with, the entry-barrier variables. How, then, do we explain the reversed results for Japan? Two sets of forces may be at work.

The first relates to entry into Japanese industries, which is clearly impeded by forces omitted from Bain's model[89] and thus from the statistical specifications. The most obvious of these is governmental intervention to deter or (occasionally) promote entry. The evidence cited above in discussing patterns of competition made it clear that the Ministry of International Trade and Industry has used various formal and informal powers not only to regulate competition within industries but also to control the flow of new entrants. With public authority standing at the gate, the ability of a would-be entrant to clamber over the economic barriers to entry is a necessary but no longer sufficient condition for his entry. The statistical performance of the entry-barrier variables should thus become less significant. By the same token, with entry impeded by the MITI as well as natural forces, actual concentration should become more important in determining the ability of going firms to capture monopoly rents within an industry.

The second set of forces intertwines with the rate of growth, discussed above. Cross-industry statistical investigations in industrial organization generally assume that industries are observed in long-run equilibrium, or at least in an equilibrium disturbed only by separable fluctuations in the growth rate and profit windfalls. We have already argued that these windfalls could obscure the influence of seller concentration. We now suggest that they could obscure even more readily the influences of the condition of entry. A new firm's entry into an industry is subject to a longer lag of perception, planning, and execution than is the decision of a going firm to change its level of out-

89. Joe S. Bain, *Barriers to New Competition* (Harvard University Press, 1956).

put or capacity. Thus, whatever the tendency of fast growth to obscure the influence of concentration, it would obscure even more the influence of the long-run structural barriers to entry. If going firms take account of the entry lag in their planning, concentration could in fact be elevated in its significance, because firms in highly concentrated industries are in a position to seize short-run windfalls, knowing that entry in any case is apt to occur in the future. Hence, this line of reasoning is consistent with a significant role for concentration in all but periods of explosive growth, as well as with the lessened influence of the structural barriers to entry.

Statistical Tests of Allocative Performance

We employed two interrelated series of tests to secure further evidence on the determinants of market power in Japan. In one we analyzed the determinants of profit rates over the years 1961–70 for 243 large manufacturing companies. This inquiry, designed primarily to test the effect of group affiliation, was reported briefly in the preceding section of this paper. We also identified the leading firms in thirty-five manufacturing industries, computed industry profit rates that were weighted-average profit rates for the firms classified to each industry, and related these profit rates to various independent variables measuring structural conditions in the industries.

The profits after taxes but before interest on total assets are significantly related to seller concentration and to advertising rates (as an indicator of the leading source of barriers to entry) in both the firm and industry analyses. Concentration is always a significant influence on profits on equity in the industry analysis, but advertising is only irregularly significant. In general we can explain gross profits on total assets much better than profits on equity. This result is logical enough when we consider the peculiar relations between Japanese firms and their lenders. It is not only for the *zaibatsu* firms that these carry a definite connotation of equity participation for the lender.

Both analyses included variables to remove components of profit not related to market power. The variance of sales, a measure of risk exposure, is positively related to the profit rates of firms. Growth, which can influence profits through short-run windfalls as well as in other ways, is a positive influence on the profits of both firms and industries.

We tested several other hypotheses about the determinants of market power. The profits of firms increase with their total size, though only up to a point. This relation may be due to capital-cost barriers to entry or the discrimination in favor of large firms observed in the Japanese capital market. These profits are not increased by diversification—indeed, there is a significant negative relation between profit and diversity. It probably means that some firms have diversified in order to escape from slow-growing and relatively unprofitable industries, whereas others have strained to keep up with highly profitable demand in their base industry and thus emerged with higher profits.[90]

As an independent variable in the industry-level analysis we included exports as a percentage of total shipments. Theory is somewhat ambiguous about the sign of this relation, and in fact it is insignificant. We also tried to test the influence of cost fixity on profits, considering the large burdens on Japanese companies of unavoidable cost due to permanent employees and debt capital. It is not easy to devise a straightforward and conceptually correct measure of the proportional burden of fixed costs, and perhaps for that reason the variables we tried were unsuccessful.

We also confirmed the result of previous studies in finding that scale economies or capital requirements as a source of entry barriers had no influence on profits in Japanese industries. Advertising is also a less robust determinant of industries' profits than in similar studies using data for Western countries. Therefore, we find our results consistent with our previous interpretation of entry barriers in Japan, to which the intrusion of government, the special institutions that for some entrants lessen the problems of large capital requirements, and the unsettled state of product differentiation are contributory factors.

In short, we conclude that market power tends to garner excess profits in Japan as elsewhere, but the sources of market power are somewhat altered because the barriers to entry are different. And the distinctive macroeconomic environment of Japanese industry has played its part in molding the determinants of profitability.

Market Structure and Wage-Price Movements

Positions of market power can produce short-run distortions in price movements as well as long-run distortions in the allocation of resources. Despite Japan's long-sustained price stability, observers did come to suggest that market power was influencing the movement of the price level. Some studies provide evidence on two hypotheses about this relation.

1. Inflexibility of oligopolistic prices. Kobayashi examined the price movements that occurred in successive recessions between 1957 and 1971

---

90. Specialization and concentration interact positively in contributing to profit. That is, the profitability of the specialized firm in a concentrated industry is greater than we predict by summing the statistical influences of concentration and specialization.

and found that a steadily growing proportion of products failed to show any decline. He also showed that the average rate of price decline has been greater the less the seller concentration—at least in comparing industries near the upper and lower limits of seller concentration. He also compared measures of the variability of prices to measures of the year-to-year variability of seller concentration, finding a close relation between the instability of concentration and the flexibility of prices.[91] A study by the Economic Planning Agency suggests that in the more concentrated sectors wages are more sensitive to the firm's profit rate in larger firms, more sensitive to excess demand in the labor market for smaller firms.[92]

2. Oligopolistic sectors as sources of inflationary disturbances. The Economic Planning Agency found a relation between changes in concentration and changes in sectoral wholesale prices over a five-year period. Largely negative results have emerged from studies that relate movements in sectoral prices over a run of years to the level of concentration after controlling for input-price movements.[93] It appears that structural disturbances in concentrated industries can influence their inflation rates, but concentration has not been a source of inflationary disturbance in any long-run sense.

Technical Efficiency and Small Business

Despite the overriding concern of neoclassical economics with allocative efficiency, it is widely acknowledged that the potential social gains from improvements in allocative efficiency are probably small relative to those attainable by improvements in technical efficiency. Technical efficiency is associated with use of the minimum-cost bundle of resources to produce a given bill of output. Costs might not be minimized because firms use more resources than are necessary, the wrong bundle of resources (at going factor prices), or produce at scales that do not minimize long-run average costs. Research on these defects is difficult for theoretical and empirical reasons: theoretically, because we lack satisfying explanations why technical inefficiency should persist; empirically, because the data needed to determine who is or is not technically efficient are seldom readily at hand.

The aspect of technical inefficiency most tractable for research is ineffi-

91. Yoshihiro Kobayashi, "Market Structure and Inflexibility of Wholesale Price" (working paper, Hokkaido University, 1974; processed).

92. EPA, *Economic Survey of Japan, 1970–71*, pp. 106–07.

93. Yoshihiro Kobayashi, "The Determination of Wholesale Price in Japanese Economy," *Hokudai Economic Papers*, vol. 3 (1972–73), pp. 77–91.

ciently small scales of operation in the plant or enterprise. We concentrate on that problem for the reason stated and also because of the preoccupation in Japan with the "small- and medium-enterprise problem."[94]

Small Enterprise in Manufacturing

Japan's vast small-business population is clearly a diverse and multidimensional phenomenon, one related to many features of the economy. Some small manufacturing activities are carried on part time in the household by family workers primarily engaged in seasonal occupations, especially agriculture. The persistence of such enterprise reflects the underuse of labor in the family's primary activity, and thus is directly associated with the dualeconomy aspects of Japan's system. Other small manufacturers are essentially the direct descendants of the traditional handicraft industries that existed in the Meiji period, although their technology may have changed greatly in the interim. One survey of ninety-five small-business industries found that eighty-one of them had existed in the Meiji period, and of these fifty-eight, or 72 percent, were than predominantly handicraft; as of 1958–59, however, only 16 percent were still classed as handicraft.[95]

Another survival of an earlier stage of Japan's development is small manufacturing done on the putting-out system, in which wholesalers or assemblers supply working capital and distribution services to household enterprise. The origins of this relation lie in the relatively large size and abundance of capital attained by some merchant organizations in pre-Meiji Japan. Finally, a large proportion of small manufacturers are subcontractors of larger—often very large—manufacturing firms. Many subcontractors are wholly dependent on a single buyer and may well have been set up in business by him, but nonexclusive relations are increasingly common.

FACTOR-MARKET IMPERFECTIONS. The factor-market imperfections described earlier are the most important feature of the Japanese economy contributing to the scope of the small-business sector. Capital-cost differences of at least 50 percent exist between large and small enterprises. Further, because supplies of funds to the small-business sector tend to be sensitive to business cycles, that sector is first to feel any squeeze on availability. This discrimination in the capital market is not easy to explain. During the first

94. Following Japanese practice, we shall switch freely between talking about small plants and small firms. The problems they create could be quite different—for example, for large enterprises to maintain some inefficiently small plants—but in practice the distinction does not seem important.
95. Shinohara, "Survey," pp. 58–61.

half of the Meiji period there occurred a broad institutional development of small-scale moneylenders, merchant banks, and mutual loan associations. The smaller financial institutions have undergone squeezes—as from 1919 to 1932, during which period the total number of banks declined greatly— but the present structure again seems to contain a wide array of lenders by size, function, and locality. Why, then, has arbitrage not tended to reduce, if not eliminate, this great difference? The market power and abundant tangible property of the large industrial borrower entail a potentially lower level of risk, of course, but it is hard to write off a 50-percent difference as merely a risk premium.[96] Loans to small business are well collateralized by land, and rates of loss to lenders appear very low. Interest differences in the United States between large- and small-business borrowers, which are much smaller than those in Japan, appear to result mostly from differences in transactions costs,[97] but it seems unlikely that transactions costs could explain this large difference in Japan.

Discrimination in the labor market of course runs the other way—in favor of small enterprises. The rapid absorption of surplus labor from Japanese agriculture has led to much concern about how rapidly the disequilibrium of the dual economy would be eliminated and how painful a squeeze its termination would put on the small-business sector. Wages for young workers with middle-school or less education are now about the same in small and large establishments, although the seniority gradient remains much steeper in the larger establishments and hence their average labor costs remain higher. The same general pattern holds for women (but with flatter seniority gradients) and for office workers (steeper seniority gradients). Less than one-fifth of the average wage difference between large (more than 1,000 employees) and small (10–99 employees) establishments in 1959 could be explained by quality-of-labor factors: age (as a proxy for experience), sex, and education.[98] If the quality-adjusted wage difference between large and small establishments disappears and the capital-cost discrimination remains, market pressures will be artificially loaded against small enterprises.

TRENDS IN SMALL ENTERPRISE. How has the small-enterprise sector fared

96. Shinohara, "Survey," pp. 51–57; and Taikichi Itoh, *Structural Analysis of the Problem of Medium and Small Enterprises in Contemporary Japan,* Management and Labor Studies, English Series, no. 21 (Institute of Management and Labor Studies, Keio University, 1972), pp. 16–17.

97. Albert M. Levenson, "Interest Rate and Cost Differentials in Bank Lending to Small and Large Business," *Review of Economics and Statistics,* vol. 44 (May 1962), pp. 190–97; and Stephen H. Archer and LeRoy G. Faerber, "Firm Size and the Cost of Externally Secured Equity Capital," *Journal of Finance,* vol. 21 (March 1966), pp. 69–83.

98. Napier, "The Labor Market and Structural Change," chap. 2.

in the face of these pressures? Census data can be analyzed to establish three sets of propositions:

First, when we subdivide firms by two-digit industry and by size class, we find that those industry–size-class groups which pay initially high wages increase their shares of the labor force faster (or lose position more slowly) than low-wage groups. The interindustry variance of the ratio of small-firm to large-firm wages has declined steadily over the last two decades. Putting together these and other data, we conclude that distortions due to imperfections in the labor market have been reduced both among industries and among size classes within industries.

Second, the fate of the small-enterprise sector as these imperfections erode depends partly on its ability to increase technical efficiency. In 1967 the ratio of value added per worker in the largest to the smallest class of Japanese manufacturing establishments was 1.71 (for the United States it was 1.16). Until about 1963 small-business productivity grew at least as rapidly as that of big business and thereby limited the pressure on relative factor costs. After 1963 productivity in the small-enterprise sector faltered in the race, despite a more rapid increase of capital per worker than in large enterprises. The growth of small-business employment slowed, and over the period 1955–67 was one-third less rapid than in establishments employing 1,000 or more.[99]

Third, the displacement of the small-enterprise sector will be constrained by its own low capital intensity and the considerable amount of capital formation needed to shift the labor force toward larger plants while maintaining the present capital-labor ratios in those large plants. But the elimination of factor-price distortions will also put the greatest cost pressure on firms in those industries in which opportunities to substitute capital for labor are rich. Thus, we expect that small enterprises will retain their shares more readily in the assembly industries, which have limited possibilities of capital-labor substitution, than in process industries, in which such possibilities tend to be greater.[100] This prediction rather closely matches official evaluations of the sectors in which small firms continue to enjoy relative success.[101]

SUBCONTRACTING. Many small- and medium-size manufacturing firms produce under subcontract to other firms. Traditionally this has been a highly dependent relation, long-lived although based on annual contracts. The firm offering the contract takes complete charge of design, specification,

99. Based on calculations by Napier, chaps. 1, 3.
100. See EPA, *Economic Survey of Japan, 1967–68*, pp. 91–92; and Shinohara, "Survey," p. 45.
101. Small and Medium Enterprises Agency, "White Paper on Small and Medium Enterprises," in *White Papers of Japan, 1969–70: Annual Abstract of Official Reports and Statistics of the Japanese Government* (Japan Institute of International Affairs, 1971), pp. 295–96.

and approval of quality, generally paying the subcontractor cost (with 5 percent leeway) plus a processing fee and expecting continual cost-reducing productivity gains. Most subcontractors are very small, although some have as many as 1,000 employees.[102] More than three-fourths of manufacturing firms employing more than 100 use subcontractors. The number of subcontractors rises steadily with the size of the parent. A large company may subcontract more than 50 percent of the direct labor going into its product. The industries in which subcontracting is especially common engage in assembly or discrete processing operations—those in which the final output can feasibly pass in stages under multiple factory roofs.

Why is subcontracting so prevalent? We already argued that, given the distortions in Japan's factor markets, subcontracting allows the contracting enterprise to reduce its labor costs. Also, where it produces part of its input requirements and subcontracts the balance, it can shift part of the risk of fluctuations in demand and keep its own permanent labor force busy. It also provides a selective way to reward (and retain the use of) able employees after they are retired at fifty-five, when they are often shifted to, or set up in business as, subcontractors. Because consolidated financial statements are not required by Japanese commercial law, subcontracts can conceal the parent firm's unprofitable activities.[103]

Does the subcontractor derive any market power or other benefits from his status? Much has been written in Japan on the question of exploitation in the subcontracting relation. The subcontractor tied to a single large company with no alternative is clearly vulnerable to an all-or-nothing offer. Probably the typical subcontractor does have alternatives, though, and is better described as a pure competitor who in the long run must be paid his opportunity cost to keep him at work. A good deal of evidence supports this view. There are many examples of cyclical sensitivities in the processing fees paid to subcontractors; their relation to the contracting company neither denies them profit from excess demand nor protects them from dark days of excess supply.[104] Yoshino suggests that, as rapid growth set in during the 1950s, the need to encourage expansion of the subcontractors' capacities (along with those of the contracting firm) significantly improved the treatment of subcontractors.[105] The same incentive forces the contracting firm to be concerned about technological change and the ability of their subcontractors

102. Abegglen (ed.), *Business Strategies*, pp. 162–63.
103. See Yoshino, *Japan's Managerial System*, pp. 150–55.
104. Shinohara, "Survey," p. 65; idem, *Structural Changes in Japan's Economic Development* (Tokyo: Kinokuniya, 1970), pp. 327–28.
105. Yoshino, *Japan's Managerial System*, p. 156.

to finance investment. The increasing tendency for subcontractors to secure business from more than one firm[106] clearly affords a potential improvement in their bargaining power.

Is subcontracting an efficient practice? There is no doubting its private rationality, but much of that turns on advantages that may not translate into social costs. Wage differences by plant size could make subcontracting profitable even where the subcontractor is less efficient in real terms. The use of retired employees merely reflects the perversity of the retirement system and the practice of permanent employment. Critics have held that subcontracting can impair the flexibility of the contracting firm, precludes an arm's-length make-or-buy decision, and delays the development of independent large-scale component producers who might enjoy greater economies of scale.[107] It is difficult to think of any social advantages of subcontracting on so broad a scale save as a palliative to distortions in the economy's factor prices and retirement system. Still, to remedy a distortion is to earn a welcome.

Small Enterprise in the Distribution Sector

It is widely agreed that Japan's distribution system represents a major problem of technical efficiency. For instance, with half the population, Japan has 2.2 times as many grocery outlets as the United States. Typically specialized by product line, they had average daily sales in 1968 of less than $60. Abegglen calculated that the net income of the average owner was surely less than half of what a worker in a large factory could earn.[108] The pattern prevails throughout retailing: 64 percent of establishments had only one or two employees in 1970, only 3.7 percent had ten or more. Productivity in retailing varies markedly with scale. The wholesalers are also relatively small —averaging 10.8 employees in 1968—as well as numerous, and transactions wind through long chains of wholesalers. In 1965–66, 40 percent of sales by wholesalers were to other wholesalers, whereas a comparable figure for the United States was only 23 percent as far back as 1947.[109]

Students of marketing in Japan blame the manifest inefficiency and low productivity of distribution on several causes. Congestion in the large cities and high land costs discourage increases in the size of establishments. The practice of retiring employees at fifty-five with inadequate pensions gen-

106. Shinohara, "Survey," pp. 76–77.
107. See Yoshino, *Japan's Managerial System*, pp. 158–60.
108. Abegglen (ed.), *Business Strategies*, pp. 141–45. See also Yoshino, *The Japanese Marketing System*, chap. 1.
109. EPA, *Economic Survey of Japan, 1967–68*, pp. 131–33.

erates a supply of "cannon fodder" entrepreneurs who have few alternatives to opening a small shop as an income supplement.The heavy use of resale price maintenance has deterred growth through aggressive pricing. And in Japan as elsewhere the organization of the distribution sector reflects traditional household shopping patterns. The low mobility of housewives has resulted in a proliferation of neighborhood stores that are necessarily small. Low household income and, until recently, a lack of consumer durables, especially refrigerators, has meant frequent shopping and small-scale transactions—hostile to scale economies in store operation. Affluence is relaxing these constraints, but the shopping habits they bred linger on.

These forces keeping the retail outlets small make wholesale transactions small as well and thus tend to frustrate the pursuit of scale economies farther upstream. The subnormal returns to many enterprises tend to discourage investment in improvements that would raise productivity. The only long-standing distribution enterprises on a large scale are the department stores, which have been content with maintaining a traditional image of high quality and personal service.

The absence of large-scale manufacturing of consumer goods in Japan until after World War II probably helped to sustain the complex and inefficient distribution system. Since then some manufacturers have tried to seize the initiative in improving the organization of the distribution channels simply to serve their self-interest.[110] It is generally not rational, though, for one manufacturer to pioneer in reorganizing distribution, because the administrative costs are sure to be heavy, and the rents he can collect for his efforts will be much less than the total productivity gain if he succeeds.[111]

As Yoshino's study shows, change is beginning to come to the distributive sector.[112] A shift toward larger retail establishments is apparent: those with fifty or more employees raised their share of sales from 13.1 percent in 1960 to 17.8 percent in 1966. In addition to the conventional chain-store organizations, most of which are associations of existing stores, innovative mass merchandisers are starting to appear: supermarkets that handle high-volume foodstuffs, household goods, and kitchen utensils on a discount basis, as well as department stores that specialize in installment sales. The 112 retailing firms with annual volumes exceeding ¥5 billion in 1969 (there were 31 in

110. For an example, see Yoshino, *The Japanese Marketing System*, p. 96.
111. Abegglen (ed.), *Business Strategies*, pp. 139–41.
112. Most information in this paragraph is taken from Yoshino, *The Japanese Marketing System*, chap. 4; and Distribution Economics Institute, *Outline of Japanese Distribution Structures* (1971), chaps. 3, 4.

1960) included 46 department stores, 52 supermarkets, 5 installment credit stores, and 9 specialty stores. Supermarkets have appealed successfully to persons at the lower end of the income distribution, and self-service sales in large cities account for over half of total sales of some popular food products.

This innovative beachhead may well have increasingly wide impact. Manufacturers of major brands are taking a warmer view of mass distributors rather than sticking tightly with their traditional channels. So are the general trading firms, which otherwise have been a passive force. In many classes of products, mass-merchandising firms are attempting to bypass the labyrinthine wholesale sector and deal directly with the manufacturer, and some have gone into private branding.[113] The prospect is for improvement in the relative productivity of the distribution system, but it is coming later and slower than would have seemed desirable. Government policy has long actively discouraged change and intersectoral competition in distribution, and only recently has it begun to support changes that improve productivity.[114]

Other Aspects of Technical Efficiency

Our information on other possible sources of technical inefficiency in the Japanese economy is sharply limited, but one deserves mention. Oligopolistic price fixing and other collusive practices are often held to nurture inefficiency because they allow the inefficient firm to muddle on, earning at least normal profits. Observers hold that the price collusion commonly found in Japanese manufacturing has had this effect.[115] It sometimes generates efficiency costs of excess capacity. Because production curtailments—as under the MITI's guidance—often are devised to leave all firms using the same percentage of their capacity, an incentive is created for building in excess capacity when the opportunity arises. While increasing total cost, this practice also increases the firm's expected volume of sales at prices in excess of marginal cost.

A close study of technical efficiency in Japan's big-business sector would be welcome. Its rapid growth of productivity and conspicuous success on international markets suggest that its technical efficiency must be awesome. Yet we have found many structural traits of industry and the economy that could shelter inefficiency. We explored the possibility of identifying sources of technical inefficiency statistically in the determinants of firms' administra-

---

113. Yoshino, *The Japanese Marketing System*, pp. 158–59, 170–71.
114. Ibid., chap. 7.
115. Yoshino, *Japan's Managerial System*, p. 118.

tive costs as a percentage of total costs. We found seller concentration un-related to administrative costs, but barriers to entry because of sales pro-motion may influence them substantially (data difficulties precluding a sharper judgment). There is no evidence that scale economies in administra-tion accrue endlessly as firms are enlarged. Uncertainty, measured by the variability of sales, inflates administrative costs, but fast growth does not. Finally, there is some indication that membership in a *zaibatsu* or bank group significantly inflates administrative costs.

Market Structure, Transfer of Technology, and Technical Performance

A key element in the postwar growth of Japan has been the rapid import of foreign technology, ending a period of near isolation from developments in international technology that ran through World War II and the prewar period of military preparation. That story has been told elsewhere.[116] But the nation's manifest ability to import and adapt foreign technology overall leaves unsettled some vital issues about the efficacy of the process from sector to sector. How have the structures of various Japanese industries af-fected their rates of innovation and productivity growth? Has growth in pro-ductivity depended relatively more on technology imported from abroad or on research carried out in Japan? Has public policy been designed to further the strength and productivity of Japanese industry?

Market Structure and Research Activity

The technical performance of a nation's industries has two dimensions. First, the economy should invest in research and development at an optimal rate—that is, one that equalizes the marginal value product of this activity with those resulting from other uses of resources—and put the results of re-search promptly to use. Second, it should absorb new technology from abroad promptly and efficiently, maintaining effective listening posts to discover what is available and making prompt arrangements to import useful knowl-edge. The two dimensions are clearly interdependent: there is no point in expending one's own resources to rediscover what is already available abroad —unless, of course, the asking price exceeds the expected cost of local discovery.

116. See Chapters 2 and 8 in this volume.

Economists have presumed the amount of spending for domestic research and development to be suboptimal because the individual discoverer generally cannot capture all the quasi-rents due to his innovation. Because the leakage is apt to be less in more concentrated markets, as well as for other reasons having to do with the availability of funds for speculative investments, some have hypothesized that the more monopolistic the market structure and the larger the firms, the more nearly optimal would be the industry's research performance. Others have found this reasoning to support only a preference for somewhat concentrated as against completely atomistic market structures. In any case, the factual point at issue is simply the relation, other things being equal, between R&D activity and both concentration and firm size.

Two studies have been undertaken of this relation in Japan. Imai found no clear-cut relation between firm size and various measures of research and development input and output for firms in fifteen two-digit manufacturing and construction industries in 1967, and his study gives no general support to a policy of enlarging the size of firms as a method of raising total R&D activity.[117] Uekusa examined the relation between firm size and R&D expenditures for a sample of nearly 300 large companies in manufacturing and construction. For the whole sample, R&D expenditures rise more or less proportionally with size up to a point and then decline. But the pattern varies with the innovative potential of the firms' base industries. In highly innovative industries R&D expenditures indeed increase more than proportionally with sales; in less innovative industry groups R&D expenditures rise less than proportionally with size in the size range of the larger firms.[118] Size thus may contribute to increasing research inputs in the economy's more innovative sectors. Uekusa found the statistical relation between R&D and seller concentration to be negative (although not significant). Size may help, but concentration in itself does not.

These results should probably be interpreted as describing the relation between research activity and scale for those firms that are fairly large and undertake some research. It is unclear whether they apply to all larger firms, including those that do no research: that is, the samples may be biased to-

117. K. Imai, "Jōhō gijutsu kigyō kibō" [Information, Technology, and Firm Size], in K. Imai, Y. Murakami, and J. Tsukui (eds.), *Jōhō to gijutsu no keizazi bunseki* [Economic Analysis of Information and Technology], Research Paper no. 24 (Japan Economic Research Center, 1970), chap. 10.

118. Masu Uekusa, "Sangyō soshiki to inobeshon" [Industrial Organization and Innovation], in B. Hijikata and T. Miyazawa (eds.), *Kigyō kōdō to inobeshon* [Firm Behavior and Innovation] (Nihon Keizai Shinbunsha, 1973), chap. 3.

ward firms that carry out some research. The results probably do not apply to the fringe of smaller firms that do no formal research aside from some tinkering with their production processes.

Market Structure and Transfer of Technology

Although Japan is now becoming a significant producer of research discoveries, its industrial success since World War II clearly has depended on a massive import of technology from abroad. Proportionally, its dependence on foreign technology will continue to be high, simply because there is no reason for any country—the United States included—to be either self-sufficient in technology or the sole world producer. Thus, the efficiency with which technology is imported and put to work represents a vital dimension of economic performance.

SOURCES. We have at hand only a small amount of information about the determinants of the import of technology. Uekusa found no relation between seller concentration in Japanese industries and the volume of payments for technology imports; rather, the level of a firm's payments was related to the size of its sales.[119] Certain information is available from surveys of small businesses to show what channels they use in acquiring new scientific and technical information, whether from domestic or foreign sources. The percentage of firms replying that they use each of the following channels is:[120]

Source of information	Percent of firms using
Machinery manufacturers	47.7
People in the same trade	36.5
Domestic newspapers and periodicals	35.7
Material makers	33.5
Information from cooperatives and trade associations	33.3
Products of other firms	33.3
Training courses and workshops	32.5
Exhibitions	29.5
Parent companies	22.6
Scholarly sources (universities, learned societies)	22.2
Overseas periodicals	17.0
Public guidance institutions	16.6

119. Uekusa, "Industrial Organization."
120. Kazuhiko Otsuka, *Balanced Industrial Structure and Transfer of Technology: A Study of Technology Transfer in Small-Scale Industries* (Ministry of International Trade and Industry, 1972), chart IV.

The role of self-interested sales promotion by makers of producer goods appears quite important, as does that of industry associations. Because about half of these firms are subcontractors, it is perhaps surprising that the percentage of respondents listing parent companies is no larger than it is. The small dependence on scholarly sources of new basic science confirms that this information must be converted into directly usable forms elsewhere. The unimportance of foreign relative to domestic information channels is noteworthy, though probably not unique to Japan.

DETERMINANTS OF PRODUCTIVITY GROWTH. To assess the relative importance of innovation and diffusion, as well as of domestic and foreign sources of new knowledge, we undertook a statistical analysis of the determinants of productivity growth in ninety-nine manufacturing industries over the years 1958–67. These industries, as defined in Japan's census of manufactures, could be matched to their counterparts in the United States' standard industrial classification. We hypothesized that the rate of productivity growth, measured by growth of value added per worker, could be explained by three sets of determinants.

—An industry's access to technological progress from abroad, measured by the rate of productivity growth in the comparable U.S. industry and the volume of foreign technology licensing agreements made by the Japanese industry.

—Domestic forces influencing innovation and productivity growth, including rates of expenditure on research and development, level of seller concentration, and rate of change in the average size of the industry's manufacturing establishments.

—Factors that adjust for the deficiencies of growth of value added per worker as a measure of productivity change.[121]

We concluded that the productivity growth of a Japanese industry is indeed related to the expansion of its production possibilities on a worldwide scale, proxied by productivity growth experienced by its U.S. counterpart. There was no relation between productivity growth and the number of technology agreements coming into force, probably because our measure of this inflow of technology is very crude: however, the absence of a relation may confirm the success of the MITI's efforts to keep the rents from passing into foreign hands.

---

121. The statistical procedure makes the strong assumption that all industries operate on the same Cobb-Douglas production function. Therefore, the rate of growth of capital per worker is included as an independent variable.

Ample room remains to explain productivity growth by structural determinants within the Japanese economy. By far the most potent of these is change in the size of an industry's establishments. We used two measures, one reflecting changes in the size of the industry's larger plants, the other heavily weighted by changes in the number of relatively small establishments. Both are statistically significant when entered separately, but the measure weighted toward change in small establishments is more significant and has a larger coefficient, and the difference between the two measures when entered as an independent variable is quite insignificant. We conclude that the consolidation or enlargement of small establishments generally has made a greater contribution to the growth of industrial productivity than has the promotion of large-scale enterprises. We thus question the policy preference of the MITI for promoting very large plants. Of course, the cross-industry statistical evidence does not preclude the possibility that this policy can raise productivity in a small number of situations.

SUMMARY INDICATIONS. The results of our examination of the influence of research and development in Japan on productivity growth rates are somewhat negative. Productivity growth does bear a strong relation to the stock of patents held by an industry, a crude measure of its stock of intangible knowledge useful for raising net output. But the regression coefficient of expenditure rates for research and development—or of R&D employees as a percentage of total employment—is negative and significant. This may be because of collinearity with other variables, but the zero-order correlation coefficients between these measures of R&D input and productivity growth are negative (though insignificant). Industry R&D and productivity growth are positively related among U.S. industries. U.S. evidence also supplies a possible explanation for our result in showing that productivity gains from R&D often occur primarily in an industry other than the one that does the research: for example, through embodiment in capital goods. At most, our statistical results call in question the effectiveness of general incentives to raise R&D expenditure as a means of speeding productivity growth.

High seller concentration does not have a favorable influence on productivity growth. The statistical results are somewhat irregular, but in general they show no relation between productivity growth and the share of sales controlled by the four or eight largest firms in each industry. The relation to productivity growth is negative and significant in the case of the marginal concentration ratios. Roughly speaking, this means that an industry dominated by a group of oligopolists fairly equal in size is likely to display relatively slow growth in productivity.

Concluding Reflections

Does industrial market competition work the same way in Japan as in Western industrial countries such as the United States? Do Japan's distinctive institutions leave a sharp imprint on the economy's performance? Are there lessons about policymaking or institution building to be studied by the United States?

The outsider who studies the Japanese economy must pass through three stages of analysis and interpretation to gain the full value of his cross-cultural quest. First, do his analytical tools appear to work in a recognizable and familiar way when applied to Japan's markets? Second, do they reveal the influence of Japan's distinctive institutions by showing their net effect on the operation of the economic system? Third, does Japan offer lessons for other countries to emulate—or avoid—in the institutions it has built or the policies it has chosen?

Our studies provide an affirmative answer to the first question. The framework of analysis that explains industrial structures and their effects in other industrial countries illuminates the Japanese economy as well. Concentrated industries do earn excess profits. High rates of outlay on advertising do sustain market power. Concentration in Japanese manufacturing industries differs little overall from that in U.S. industries and varies from market to market in response to similar forces.

But this same framework also reveals the effect of Japanese institutions and conditions that diverge from Western norms. In periods of extremely rapid growth the conventional patterns of behavior of rival sellers are displaced, and the market structures of individual industries have little effect on their performance. The imprint of rapid growth also appears in the relatively strong position of nondiversified large companies, which evidently have kept busy enough exploiting the opportunities available in their base markets.

We also found that entry barriers into Japanese industries differ from those in the United States. Commercial barriers are lowered by sources of collaborative financing of new ventures, the less solidified state of product differentiation in consumer goods industries, and the well-organized access to the technology held by firms abroad. But barriers also have been elevated in some industries by governmental actions aimed at enlarging the size of Japanese firms or ensuring the construction of large plants.

Economic theory has also proved helpful in understanding the role of groups in Japanese industry—the bank-centered alliances and successors to the *zaibatsu* organizations. Their potential mutual benefit seems to lie not only in risk sharing or use of joint monopoly-monopsony power but also in internal pricing that could rationalize the price structures prevailing in imperfectly competitive ambient markets. But institutional evidence creates doubt that the coordination of the contemporary group is tight enough to annex many of these gains—and our statistical analysis fails to reveal any gains at all. That is, group firms appear if anything less profitable than large independent companies, after controlling for differences in the market opportunities that they face, and we detect only a diversion of profits from equity shareholders into the financial institutions, which rightly enjoy status as the central agencies of today's groups.

Our attempts to discern the effects of Japan's distinctive institutions have had little success on some fronts; on others, the distinctiveness of the institutions has been called into question. We found much descriptive evidence suggesting that the nation's cultural traits place their stamp on the management of business enterprises. Yet there is little evidence further connecting the form of business organization and the style of management to the external behavior of Japanese businesses. Neither the incidence of allegedly cumbersome internal decisionmaking processes nor the effects of heavy burdens of fixed costs can be isolated in the actions of business firms. An area in which we question the distinctiveness of a Japanese institution, if not the importance of its consequences, is the role of small enterprise. Our analysis of Japan in comparison with other countries shows that the prominence of small enterprise is not abnormal considering the country's size, income level, and speed of recent growth. Nonetheless, the size of the small-business sector and its choice of production techniques clearly reflects the factor-price distortions prevailing in the Japanese economy, and its fate depends on the changes taking place in those distortions. And we found interindustry differences in the prominence of these small enterprises to be an important factor explaining differences in productivity growth.

On the basis of these results, what can be said about the service of Japanese industrial policy to the nation's economic interests and the lessons it conveys for other industrial countries? Japan's antimonopoly policy has been a hobbled and limited copy of that long used in the United States. Its enforcement has fallen far short of the U.S. model, which itself hardly enjoys total adherence. The Japanese economy has borne significant costs in the form of allocative inefficiency and diversion of rivalry into costly nonprice forms. We can detect no corresponding gains. The obvious industrial success stories rest on new-product ventures not dependent on collusion for either encouragement or protection or on a penetration of world markets that ultimately is the result of favorable real-cost conditions.

Policy toward small enterprise has been a mixed bag of many measures. Most of those affecting the manufacturing sector have been sensible in their conception, but we have not tried to evaluate their net effects. Policy toward the distributive sector has been protective and inappropriate until recently. Industrial policy aimed at encouraging the development of large firms has been more opportunistic in practice than its public image would suggest. In some instances it may have speeded the development of large-scale and efficient ventures by reducing uncertainties surrounding them and assisting access to the necessary finance. But we find no evidence that the shift of production toward large-scale units has been critical to the success of industries in productivity growth. We conclude that little of Japan's industrial policy will transplant readily and effectively to other countries.

CHAPTER EIGHT

Technology

Merton J. Peck, Yale University
with the collaboration of
Shūji Tamura, Ministry of International Trade and Industry

Tables

IN THEIR CHAPTER IN THIS VOLUME, Laurence B. Krause and Sueo Sekiguchi state that the Japanese "have shown an extraordinary ability to organize and adopt modern technology." Japan is often characterized— sometimes in tones of envy, more often in tones of admiration—as the best of all nations in technological borrowing. The borrowing of technology is not itself unusual; even the research-rich United States imports technology. Nor is a sizable gap between the best production practice possible with current knowledge and the practice in actual use, a gap that underlies extensive borrowing, distinctively Japanese. All countries have such gaps, and the term "technology gap" achieved its popularity in the early 1960s to describe Western Europe relative to the United States.

Rather than any such gap, the distinctive features of Japan in relation to technological development are the following:

—High returns from importing technology in terms of exports and productivity.

—Extensive government controls over the importation of technology and the use of these controls to shape the structure of some industries and possibly to shape the overall growth process itself.

—The adroit and extensive use of management, investment, and domestic research and development to capitalize upon imported technology.

These three features are not solely postwar phenomena: a major theme of Japanese economic history is the gradual development of the capability to borrow technology and to absorb more advanced production methods, along with an activitist role for the government in the process.[1] Some of the postwar success may be derived from this historical legacy. But the economy and its technological components had special characteristics during the 1950s and 1960s. These characteristics are the subjects of this chapter, with emphasis given to the role of government policy and with an overview of the organization of Japanese research and development. Speculations on the future of technology in the Japanese economy are offered in the conclusion.

Note. The authors wish to thank the Japanese businessmen, government officials, and scholars who were most helpful in discussions. They also wish to thank Robert Wilson, Lee Collier, and Joe Altonji, all Yale students, for their excellent research assistance, and Virginia Casey, who provided able secretarial assistance.

1. See, for example, Kazushi Ohkawa and Henry Rosovsky, *Japanese Economic Growth Trend Acceleration in the Twentieth Century* (Stanford University Press, 1973).

Table 8-1. *Exports, Imports, and Production of Japanese Industry, by Research and Technological Intensity of Industry Groups, Selected Years*

Percent

Industry group	Share of total Japanese exports		Share of total Japanese imports		Share of Japanese exports in total OECD exports			Share in value added in Japanese manufacturing		
	1963	1970	1963	1970	1963	1966	1970	1953	1960	1968
Group A										
Chemical elements and products, pharmaceuticals, plastics, machinery, aircraft, road motor vehicles, ships and boats, instruments, synthetic fibers, and petroleum products (including some unrefined petroleum products)	34.3	50.1	32.0	31.3	4.6	7.3	9.4	34.7	42.4	47.1
Group B										
Rubber, ferrous metal, nonferrous metal, metal products, stone, clay, glass, and paper	23.6	23.7	4.3	7.9	8.2	10.0	12.1	33.0	30.0	29.4
Group C										
Food, lumber, textile fibers, iron ores and scrap, coal, textiles, clothing, furniture, and fixtures	28.3	15.3	46.9	42.4	6.0	6.6	6.7	29.5	23.5	21.7
Other[a]	13.8	10.9	16.8	18.4	...	...	...	2.8	4.1	1.8
Total	100.0	100.0	100.0	100.0	5.6	7.4	9.0	100.0	100.0	100.0

Sources: Trade statistics, computed from Organisation for Economic Co-operation and Development, *Trade Statistics*, series B (January–December 1964, 1966, and 1970). Value-added statistics, computed from United Nations, Department of Economic and Social Affairs, *The Growth of World Industry*, vol. I, *General Industrial Statistics* (1970 edition), p. 260, (1967 edition), p. 121.

a. Includes nonmanufactured products and miscellaneous manufactures for imports and exports and miscellaneous manufactures for the value-added percentages. Shares not computed for total OECD exports.

Technical Change and Economic Change

This section examines the growing role of the technically more advanced industries in Japanese manufacturing and trade, as well as of the levels and trends of spending for imported technology and of domestic research and development.

Technology, Industrial Structure, and Exports

Industries using more complex technology have become of increasing importance in Japan. Organized around a classification of industries into groups—A, B, and C, according to their research intensity and the technological complexity of their product—the data in Table 8-1 show that the more research-intensive industries, those in group A, have expanded their share in value added in Japanese manufacturing at the expense of less technologically intensive industries, those in group C—a shift that also has occurred in the United States.[2] The same pattern occurs in the relative growth in exports. Between 1963 and 1970 products of the A industries rose from about a third to a half of Japanese exports, matched by a relative decline in the exports of the products of the C industries, a shift that did not occur in other countries belonging to the Organisation for Economic Co-operation and Development (OECD).[3]

The export growth of the A industries in Japan reflects not only the rising proportion of A industry products in international trade but also Japan's increasing share of the total trade in these products. Japan's share of all OECD exports of the A industries rose from 4.6 percent in 1963 to 9.4 percent in 1970, gains made at the expense of the shares of the United States

2. The United Kingdom opened the 1950s with a high proportion of its production in the group A industries, but that group's share increased only slightly during the decade. France had a relatively low proportion of its production in the group A industries during the 1960s, but the data do not allow determination of the trend. The results for the United Kingdom and France are derived from United Nations, Department of Economic and Social Affairs, *The Growth of World Industry*, vol. I, *General Industrial Statistics* (1970), pp. 164, 178, 260, 505; (1969), pp. 143, 446; (1967), pp. 73, 121, 240; idem, *The Growth of World Industry: National Tables: 1953–1965*, pp. 458–59.

3. Group A exports in the United States showed a small shift from slightly less than half of exports to just over a half from 1963 to 1970; in the United Kingdom they remained relatively constant at just over a half of exports; and in France they shifted slightly from just over a third to about four-tenths of exports. The proportions were computed from OECD, *Trade Statistics*, series B (January–December 1964, 1966, and 1970).

and the United Kingdom.[4] A further indication of the association of research intensity and exports is the statistically significant positive rank correlation between Japanese industries ranked by research spending as a percent of sales and by the increase in export share for products of these industries from 1963 to 1970.[5] A statistically significant positive rank correlation also exists for the same period between the increase in the OECD export share of each Japanese industry and the number of technology import agreements between Japanese and foreign companies in the same industry.[6] Technology-intensive industries in Japan therefore are seen to have become a larger fraction of manufacturing and to have accounted for a major part of the country's trade success during the 1960s.

Payments for Technology

The entry for imports of technology in the balance-of-payments statistics—the sum of payments by Japanese companies to foreign companies for patent licenses, know-how, and associated expenses—provides an aggregate measure of flow of technology. In the 1950s such payments grew at an annual rate of 31.5 percent from 1951 to 1955 and 34.0 percent from 1955 to 1961.[7] Payments grew at a slower yet still impressive rate during the 1960s. Table 8-2 records the trade in technology and Table 8-3 shows the average annual rate of growth of technology payments for Japan, the United States, the United Kingdom, France, and West Germany. The average annual rate of growth as adjusted for changes in royalty rates for new contracts is also shown for Japan. In both the adjusted and unadjusted rates of growth an upsurge is evident in Japan's rate after 1964, which suggests that a considerable amount of technology importation continues to characterize the country's economy.

This upsurge since the mid-1960s is puzzling. The puzzle is not new.

4. The United States went from 25.9 percent of total OECD exports in group A industries in 1963 to 22.2 percent in 1970; the United Kingdom dropped from 15.4 to 10.1 percent over the same period (proportions computed from ibid.).
5. The rank correlation coefficients were as follows: Kendall's $T = 0.54$; Spearman $\rho = 0.75$, significant at 0.01; calculated from ibid. and Bureau of Statistics, Office of the Prime Minister, *Kagaku gijutsu kenkyū chōsa hōkoku* [Report on the Survey of Research and Development in Japan] (1970), pp. 64–65.
6. The correlation coefficients were as follows: Kendall's $T = 0.51$; Spearman $\rho = 0.66$, significant at 0.01. Calculated from OECD, *Trade Statistics,* series B (January–December 1963 and 1970), and Science and Technology Agency, Office of the Prime Minister, *Gaikoku gijutsu dōnyū nenji hōkoku* [Annual Report of the Import of Foreign Technology] (1961), pp. 24–27.
7. Ohkawa and Rosovsky, *Japanese Economic Growth,* pp. 93–94.

Table 8-2. *Payments and Receipts for Technology, Japan and Other Industrialized Countries, and Number of New Technical Agreements Made by Japan, Selected Years, 1961–70*

Millions of dollars at official exchange rates

Country	Year				
	1961	1964	1967	1970	1971
Japan					
Payments	112	156	239	433	488
Receipts	3	14	27	59	60
New technical agreements (number)[a]	320	500	638	1,330	1,546
France					
Payments	105	191	230	350	450
Receipts	56	144	195	214	264
United Kingdom					
Payments	n.a.	115	165	239	265
Receipts	n.a.	123	176	264	283
United States					
Payments	80	127	171	227	218
Receipts	711	1,057	1,567	2,158	2,465
West Germany					
Payments	n.a.	153	192	307	405
Receipts	n.a.	62	90	119	149

Source: Science and Technology Agency, *Gaikoku gijutsu dōnyū nenji hōkoku* [Annual Report of the Import of Foreign Technology] (1972), table 21, p. 53, and table 2, pp. 30–33.

n.a. Not available.

a. Number of agreements are for category A only. Category A (*kōshu*) agreements are for more than one year, with the payment of royalties guaranteed to be made in foreign currency. Category B (*otsushu*) agreements are for less than one year or call for royalty payments in Japanese yen.

Ohkawa and Rosovsky say about the longer sweep of Japanese economic history: "This initial gap can go a long way toward explaining nineteenth century growth. But the real challenge is to explain accelerated growth in the twentieth century while economic backwardness was *decreasing*."[8] For the late 1960s two factors must be stressed. First, a worldwide increase occurred in rate of growth of trade in technology, as shown in Tables 8-2 and 8-3. The increase may be more marked in Japan because its institutions and practices appear to be better suited than those of other countries to capitalize on increasing trade in technology. Second, importation of technology into Japan was government controlled, and a liberalization of technology import policy in successive steps after 1965 opened the door to the technology that had previously been restricted. Evidence is insufficient to permit a sorting out of the relative influence of these two and other factors, though the impact of

8. Ibid., p. 213.

Table 8-3. *Average Annual Growth Rates in Payments for Technology, Japan and Other Industrialized Countries, by Four-Year Periods, 1961–70*
Percent

Country	1961–64	1964–67	1967–70
Japan[a]	11.2	15.4	21.9
	(12.3)	(16.7)	(17.1)
France	22.1	6.4	15.0
United Kingdom	n.a.	12.7	13.3
United States	16.7	10.4	9.9
West Germany	n.a.	7.8	16.9

Source: Table 8-2.
n.a. Not available.
a. Figures in parentheses represent an adjustment for changes in royalty rates, in an attempt to estimate those payments in constant prices—that is, to factor out the effect of changing royalty rates. The estimate was obtained by a procedure that reflected the long-term character of technology agreements and the fact that royalty rate changes affect only new contracts. Contracts have a median life of about 10 years; outstanding contracts for any given year were assumed to be composed of the contracts signed during that year and each of the nine preceding years. Average royalty rates for each year were obtained from Table 8-8. Contracts were assigned the average royalty rate of the year in which they were signed. A weighted average royalty rate was calculated for each year and used to convert total payments into constant prices, with 1960 as the base year. This assumes that the composition of technology bought was not reflected in the change in royalty rate.

the relaxation of government controls will be examined in more detail subsequently.[9]

Research and Development Effort

The usual emphasis on importing technology tends to obscure the fact that the Japanese economy is research intensive. It is true that Japan ranks behind the United States, the United Kingdom, West Germany, and France by the commonly used indicator of research intensity—the proportion of GNP devoted to research and development expenditures (see Table 8-4). But a

9. Another factor was that real gross domestic product (GDP) grew faster in Japan (11.6 percent annually in 1967–70) than in other countries, and such growth is accompanied by increased opportunities for utilization of imported technology. Ozawa has shown a relation between investment and technology imports for 1950–60, and investment in turn is related to growth in GNP. See Terutomo Ozawa, *Japan's Technological Challenge to the West, 1950–1974, Motivation and Accomplishment* (M.I.T. Press, 1974), pp. 38–39. Both France and Germany, which had high average annual rates of growth in real GDP during 1967 to 1970 (5.9 and 6.6 percent, respectively), also had high growth rates in payments for technology. The United States, with slowing GDP rise (the average annual growth rate of real GDP in 1961–64 was 5.1 percent and in 1967–70 2.2 percent), had a slowing rate of growth in its payments for technology. Growth rates of real GDP calculated from OECD, *National Accounts of OECD Countries, 1960–1970* (Paris: OECD, 1971). There is also a built-in relation between GNP growth and growth in payments for technology in that royalty agreements are stated in terms of a percentage of sales. Increases in real GDP imply increases in sales and thus increasing royalty payments.

Table 8-4. *Total and Nonmilitary Research and Development Expenditure as a Percentage of Gross National Product, Japan and Other Industrialized Countries, Selected Years, 1962–71*

Country	1962	1965	1967	1969	1971
		Total			
Japan	1.3	1.3	1.3	1.5	1.7
France	1.4	2.1	2.2	1.9	1.8
United Kingdom	n.a.	2.3[a]	2.4	2.2	2.1[b]
United States	2.8	3.0	3.0	2.8	2.6
West Germany	1.6	1.8	2.0	2.0	2.1
		Nonmilitary			
Japan	1.3	1.3	1.3	1.5	1.6
France	1.1	1.6	1.8	1.6	1.5
United Kingdom	n.a.	1.6[a]	1.7	1.7	1.7[b]
United States	1.6	2.0	2.0	1.9	1.9
West Germany	1.5	1.6	1.8	1.8	1.9[b]

Source: Science and Technology Agency, *Kagaku gijutsu hakusho* [White Paper on Science and Technology] (1974), pp. 462–67.
n.a. Not available.
a. 1964.
b. 1970.

significant portion of research and development (R&D) expenditures in some countries is for the military, largely for weapons systems that add little to economic growth.[10] The argument that there are economic benefits from military R&D, apart from the value of the weapons themselves, rests on the potential spillover of knowledge into the commercial sector. Military R&D in the United States during the 1950s, for example, had immediate benefits for commercial aviation and electronics. Over the last decade, however, military products have become extremely advanced technologically and increasingly divergent from commercial products, so even spillovers for these industries have become smaller. Military R&D may be better than no R&D, but it is of less economic value than commercially oriented R&D and perhaps even basic research.[11] Thus, comparisons of nonmilitary R&D expenditures may

10. In terms of measured economic growth, a weapons system adds the amount of its value added to GNP, just as any other final product does, though whether there is any addition to consumer satisfaction is a philosophical issue. New products, to the extent to which they are intermediate goods that lower costs, such as new machinery, add to productivity, as do new processes that lower costs. Increased productivity is the essence of measured economic growth.

11. One crude measure of commercial significance is the proportion of patents yielded by military and nonmilitary R&D. From 1951 to 1956 patents from military R&D accounted for 4 percent of all applications in the United States, even though in those years defense-financed R&D represented more than half of all corporate R&D activity. Merton J. Peck and Frederic M. Scherer, *The Weapons Acquisition Process: An Economic Analysis* (Harvard University, Graduate School of Business Administration, Division of Research, 1962), pp. 215–16.

be more relevant with respect to economic growth. In this, Japan ranks not far behind the United States, the United Kingdom, and West Germany, as the figures in Table 8-4 indicate.

The percentage of GNP spent on research and development is only one measure of research effort. Another is the number of researchers per unit of population, by which measure Japan ranks with the United States and ahead of Western European countries.[12] Another measure—comparisons of absolute levels of research spending—is plagued with problems of exchange rate adjustments. At official exchange rates, Japan ranked in 1969 with Germany and France and well behind the United States and the Soviet Union in aggregate R&D expenditures. Japanese R&D expenditures were about 10 percent of those of the United States, but exclusion of military R&D raises the proportion to almost a third.[13] If a rough allowance is made for relative costs of research, the Japanese nonmilitary R&D effort is perhaps a half to two-thirds that of the United States, and the percentage of GNP devoted to nonmilitary R&D is comparable in the two countries.[14]

Japanese R&D expenditures are increasing faster than GNP, as is shown in Table 8-4. Further, the annual rate of increase is high compared to that of other countries: in money terms, the annual rate was 33 percent from 1967 to 1969 as compared with a 5 percent rate of increase in the United States.[15]

The upward trend in research spending has government blessing: the 1971 report of the Council for Science and Technology set a target for R&D spending of "2.5 percent [of GNP] at the earliest possible date in the present decade with the ultimate objective of attaining 3 percent."[16]

12. National Science Foundation, *Science Indicators, 1972*, Report of the National Science Board (1973), p. 103. Researchers are defined as professional scientists and engineers engaged primarily in research and development. Japan had twenty-five researchers per 10,000 population in 1971, as did the United States; France had twelve and Germany fifteen.

13. Science and Technology Agency, *Fiscal Year 1972 White Paper on Science and Technology: Science and Technology Aiming at Society Hopeful* (English summary), p. 44.

14. Calculated from data in NSF, *Science Indicators*.

15. National Science Foundation, *National Patterns of R&D Resources, 1953–1972*, p. 3. Japan's increase is not due to change in industry mix since chemicals, electrical machinery, transportation equipment and machinery industries accounted for more than two-thirds of industrial R&D in both 1967 and 1970. See Bureau of Statistics, *Report on the Survey of Research and Development in Japan* (1973), p. 56.

16. Council for Science and Technology, *1970 nendai ni okeru sōgōteki kagaku gijutsu seisaku no kihon ni tsuite* [The Fundamentals of Comprehensive Science and Technology Policy for the 1970s], p. 18. Even the initial goal would result in a Japanese research intensity exceeding that of the United States for nonmilitary research and development; the longer-run goal would make Japan nearly 50 percent more research

Importation of Technology

Economists sometimes write as though Japan's postwar importation of technology were a unified process, whereas in fact, it falls into three periods distinguished by differences in governmental policy, terms of purchases, kinds of technology imported, and effects on the industrial structure and the economy. These shifts may explain why the importation of technology has remained a feature of the Japanese economy through the 1960s.

From 1952 to 1960 extensive government controls, prompted by concern with the balance of payments, were administered by the Ministry of International Trade and Industry (MITI). The structure of the controls reflected the government's preoccupation with making Japan more self-sufficient in such intermediate material inputs as chemicals and iron and steel. Technology of prewar and wartime vintage was brought in, and often it represented the first application of the particular technology in the country. Imports of technology usually required large-scale, capital-intensive production processes. Royalty rates reflected limited competition on the sellers' side, with the initiative for transactions often coming from Japanese firms working with the MITI.

During 1960–65 imports of technology became more oriented toward consumer goods and potential exports. The vintage of this technology was more current and often represented improvements on previously imported technology. There was also the beginning of duplicate imports: that is, agreements covering the import of technology previously brought into Japan under earlier agreements. Competition on the sellers' side increased as sellers of technology perceived the possibilities of substantial royalty payments and as Japanese firms sought technology in Western Europe and from smaller American firms. The price of technology declined. Increasing interest developed on the part of sellers in joint ventures and direct investment—both of which, however, were subject to government controls. Controls on technology importation by the MITI also continued, though they were administered in a more liberal fashion.

Imports of technology in 1966–72 were increasingly for improvements of technology previously imported; again, they were more oriented toward consumer products and required less investment for their application. The export orientation continued. Duplicate imports accounted for most technology

---

intensive than the United States in nonmilitary R&D, and, in fact, would exceed the overall 2.8 percent of GNP that the United States spent for R&D in 1969.

imports. Large American corporations, major sellers of technology, became
more concerned with direct investment in Japan than with selling technology.
The price of technology increased and governmental controls on technology
importation were further liberalized, particularly after 1968.

This periodization will serve as a background for understanding the role
of imported technology as a significant factor in postwar Japanese economic
growth. Throughout, Japanese firms purchased their technology in a highly
elaborate market and expended significant sums; firms also invested substantially in capital equipment and domestic R&D to utilize, adapt, and improve imported technology, and an active set of government policies not
only influenced the importation of technology but also shaped the structure
of Japanese industry through that control.

Trade in Technology

Economists like to think of trade in technology as analogous to the importing and exporting of commodities. But what is exchanged is information, that
most subtle of intangibles. Thus, issues of importance are how such purchases began, the manner in which the transfers took place, and the kinds of
technology involved. In addition, Japan's growing sales of technology represent a major development in this area.

INITIAL YEARS AND THE TECHNOLOGY PACKAGE. Buying technology requires, first, information about what to buy. Such information was acquired
by Japanese firms and government agencies by all the means which any one
society uses to learn about another: textbooks, journals, travel, and foreign
education. Another source was trade itself and, particularly in the early
years, the feedback from Japanese trading companies about the technology
of foreign products and production.[17] These informal efforts were supplemented after 1955 by the organized programs of the Japanese Productivity
Center.

The center was founded with the financial support of Japanese companies
and the government. From 1955 to 1961 the center sent parties of from ten
to twenty people each to the United States, with the U.S. government paying
for the foreign exchange cost of these trips under its economic assistance
program. About 2,500 persons participated in trips of this kind during those
six years.

The function of these productivity missions is partly indicated by their

17. For a description of trading companies, see Chapter 6.

diverse composition: businessmen, engineers, union officials, journalists, academics, and government officials. This diversity reflected a concern with promotion of productivity consciousness throughout the society. Members of the missions wrote reports that were widely circulated, and they lectured in the principal cities of Japan. The missions also were intended to obtain background information about business practices and the use of technology in the United States.

From the beginning, however, the missions provided only background information. Specific product design and process know-how almost always was obtained by company-to-company technology agreements between Japanese and foreign firms.

The productivity missions continued on a smaller scale after 1961, with financial support from only the Japanese government and industry. By the 1960s, however, the extensive technology agreements held by Japanese companies and their extensive export operations made the missions, along with the trading companies, a relatively less important source of background information about new technology and its use. The larger Japanese firms, particularly those in technologically advanced industries, established ongoing relations with foreign firms that involved continued access to technology and often a cross licensing of patents between the Japanese and foreign firm.

Although the relations were often continuing ones, the formal agreements on technology followed a common pattern, usually providing for patent rights; detailed drawings, operating instructions, and manuals; and interchange of personnel between the Japanese buyer and the foreign seller.[18] A substantial number of such agreements also covered marketing data.

Renewals and new agreements in the 1970s continue to provide far more than patent licensing, despite the rising technological sophistication of Japanese industry.[19] In 1972 only 17.2 percent of the technical agreements pro-

18. A detailed published description of technology importation in one area is provided by George R. Hall and Robert E. Johnson, "Transfers of United States Aerospace Technology to Japan," in Raymond Vernon (ed.), *The Technology Factor in International Trade* (National Bureau of Economic Research, 1970), pp. 305–58. They conclude that "transfer [of technology] entails not only a movement of ideas in the form of blueprints, drawings and other data, but a movement of material and men. Put differently, a transfer of manufacturing technology for a sophisticated product involves a transfer of rights and data, a technical assistance program and material support" (p. 355).

19. Some general idea of the technology gap is apparent from a survey of 1,000 firms that imported technology from 1950 to 1966. They were asked to characterize the

vided patent rights alone; the remainder included know-how and other forms of technical assistance.[20]

Economists have often treated technical knowledge, once discovered, as a free good, available to all without charge. In fact, the Japanese experience adds to the evidence that such knowledge can be appropriated by those who possess it and can be bought and sold. Patents and the information so disclosed are often insufficient to permit utilization of an invention; additional know-how embodied in working drawings and technical advice is also required.

CHANGING COMPOSITION OF IMPORTED TECHNOLOGY. Though the scope of the information purchased remained constant, the particular kinds of technology bought shifted from the 1950s to the 1960s. The same technology-intensive industries—nonelectrical machinery, chemicals, and electrical machinery—remained the major importers of technology (see Table 8-5). Within each industry, however, greater emphasis was placed, first, on technology for consumer goods rather than producer goods; second, on more importation of improvement technology and less of major products or processes; and, third, on more importation of duplicate technology and less of technology not already in use in Japan.

The first shift is illustrated by changes within the electrical equipment category, for which more of the imported technology was for consumer goods such as room air conditioners and color television sets, and less for manufacturers' machinery.[21] Another demonstration of this shift is the increase in the number of consumer goods agreements. From 1963 to 1971 the number of long-term technology agreements signed for local consumer-oriented industries—packaging, leisure products, furniture, cosmetics, and dress designs—rose from 58 to 216, a greater percentage increase than for

---

technological level of their own firms relative to those abroad. The results, expressed in percentages, are as follows:

Characterization	At time of import	In June 1968
Overwhelmingly backward	32.7	3.5
Lagging considerably behind	46.0	21.8
Roughly the same level	15.5	56.1
Other	5.9	18.6

See Science and Technology Agency, *1972 White Paper on Science and Technology* (English summary), p. 229.

20. Science and Technology Agency, *Annual Report of the Import of Foreign Technology* (1972), pp. 15, 47. Data are limited to technology agreements for more than one year. Similar percentages prevailed in other postwar years.

21. Ibid. (1967), pp. 40–41.

Table 8-5. *Distribution of Japanese Technology Import Agreements,*
by Type of Industry, 1949–65 and 1965–72
Percent

Industry	1949–65	1965–72
Nonelectrical machinery	26.3	25.5
Electrical machinery	22.2	15.7
Chemicals	15.4	15.3
Iron and steel	6.0	3.4
Transport machinery	5.7	5.0
Textiles and fabrics	4.4	6.5
Metal products	3.1	3.1
Precision instruments	2.4	2.9
Ceramics	2.0	2.4
Petroleum and coal	1.6	2.5
Construction	1.2	1.0
Food processing	0.7	2.3
Other	9.0	14.4

Sources: 1949–65 data, Science and Technology Agency, *Gaikoku gijutsu dōnyū nenji hōkoku* [Annual Report of the Import of Foreign Technology] (1970); 1965–72 data, Science and Technology Agency, *Kagaku gijutsu hakusho* [White Paper on Science and Technology] (1974), p. 288.

all agreements.[22] The second shift—toward greater improvement in technology—was recorded in the discussions published in the Science Board Report and in interviews conducted by the present authors.[23] For electrical machinery, most of the technology imported in 1968 was an improvement of existing technology; for nonelectrical machinery most of the technology was characterized as an improvement of the speed, automation, or capacity of existing technology.[24]

The third shift—toward the importation of duplicate technology—is more measurable, with duplications accounting for 36 percent of the agreements

22. Long-term, or category A, agreements, are for more than one year. Such agreements for consumer goods increased by 356 percent, all category A agreements by 272 percent, from 1963 to 1971. It should also be noted that unless otherwise specified, the number of agreements cited in this chapter refers to the long-term category A agreements. Category B agreements—for less than one year—are more important, however, in consumer goods, and these increased from 21 in 1963 to 111 in 1971, while the number of all category B agreements decreased from 573 to 461. See Ozawa, *Japan's Technological Challenge,* fig. 2.1, p. 19 (all agreements) and table 8.2, p. 122 (consumer agreements); and, for an excellent discussion of the changing pattern of technology importation, chap. 8.

23. See discussion in Science and Technology Board, *Foreign Technology Introduction White Paper* (1967).

24. Science and Technology Agency, *Annual Report of the Import of Foreign Technology* (1968), p. 11.

Table 8-6. *Duplicate Technology and Total Technology Imported by Japan, Selected Years, 1963–70*

Year	Agreements for technology import, total[a]	Duplicate agreements	
		Number	Percent of total
1963	564	201	35.6
1965	460	251	54.6
1966	526	297	56.4
1967	554	356	63.5
1968	952	670	70.4
1969	1,018	742	72.9
1970	1,157	852	73.6

Sources: 1963 data, Science and Technology Agency, *Gaikoku gijutsu dōnyū nenji hōkoku* [Annual Report of the Import of Foreign Technology] (1967 and 1970 eds.); and data from subsequent reports of the same agency, as cited by Ozawa, *Japan's Technological Challenge*, p. 119, for subsequent years.
a. Category A agreements only.

in 1963 and 74 percent in 1971, as Table 8-6 indicates. As indicated earlier, duplicate technology imports refers to agreements covering products and processes already brought into Japan by other Japanese firms through previous technology agreements; as such, they represent a diffusion of technology.[25] Such duplication occurs in part because the patent license terms of the initial agreement do not permit sublicensing and thus force new Japanese users to sign new agreements.

Another reason for imports of duplicate technology is that foreign sellers will supply more know-how and offer more reasonable terms than would Japanese sellers. In addition, Japanese buyers are reluctant to deal with other Japanese firms, since such aid may disclose their own technical and management practices.[26] This reluctance is intensified by the fact that the

25. Ozawa notes: "Surprisingly, Japan has been importing Western technology even when its counterpart is available domestically." *Japan's Technical Challenge*, p. 119. He also reports that the ratio of domestically substitutable technology to total technology imported rose from 49.2 percent in 1965 to 68.8 percent in 1970 (ibid., table 8.1, p. 119), a pattern consistent with more duplications, though he does not give a precise definition of this term.
26. These reasons for the preference of Japanese firms to purchase and sell technology abroad are discussed in The Oriental Economist, *Japan Economic Yearbook, 1972* (Tokyo, 1972), p. 127, and were confirmed by the authors' interviews with Japanese research and development executives. Expenditures on the purchase of domestic technology by Japanese were about 4 percent of those on foreign technology in 1972. See Agency of Industrial Science and Technology, Ministry of International Trade and Industry, *Kenkyu kaihatsu oyobi gijutsu kōryu ni kansuru chōsa hōkokusho* [Report on the Survey Concerning Research and Development and the Exchange of Technology] (1974), table 27, p. 94.

terms of technology exchange are often long range and would present difficulties with either another Japanese firm's foreign partner or a domestic competitor. The reason for preferring technology from abroad can be summed up
as a reluctance to seek or to give aid to actual or potential competitors or to
the domestic competitor's present source of foreign technology. The same
phenomenon exists in the United States, in which firms will license patents
for use abroad that they will not license domestically.

These changes in the composition of technology imports proceed then, in
part, from a purely technological logic: once the basic processes are imported, the demand will shift to importing improved technology. And once
the import of technology for the basic processes has made such materials as
plastics available, a demand is created for importation of fabricating techniques using those materials. Furthermore, rising incomes create demand
for consumer goods, thus calling for more technology imports for those
goods. And, finally, the extensive importation of duplicate technology proceeds from the competitive logic of the private sale and purchase of technology.

JAPAN AS A SELLER OF TECHNOLOGY. As a percentage of its technology
payments, Japan's receipts for selling technology increased from 2.7 percent
in 1961 to 12.3 percent in 1971.[27] These aggregate statistics are determined,
however, largely by royalty payments under technology agreements signed
in previous years, and so they change slowly.[28] A more sensitive indicator of
Japan's standing is the ratio of receipts to payments for new programs (those
agreements signed in the calendar year). By this index Japan emerges as a net
seller in 1973, when the ratio was 1.26; in 1972 it had been 0.71.[29]

It is too early to tell whether this change reflects a long-term trend, particularly since 37 percent of the technology exports were in one industry, chemicals, to one region, Southeast Asia. Technology sales to Europe by a wide
range of industries ranked second, accounting for 28.1 percent of 1973 new
program sales, but here receipts were only 58.4 percent of payments. Sales
to North America ranked third, accounting for 20.2 percent of the 1973 new
programs, with the receipts being 37.7 percent of payments. Two industries
stand out as net sellers. In chemical products Japan is a net seller of technology on new programs to both North America (the ratio is 1.71) and

27. Calculated from data in Table 8-2.
28. Technology agreements have a median life of ten years. See note to Table 8-3.
29. Bureau of Statistics, *Report on the Survey of Research and Development in
Japan* (1972), pp. 146–49; and ibid. (1973), pp. 150–54. All the data cited in this and
the following paragraph are calculated from the latter source; no comparable data are
available for years before 1972.

Europe (2.25) and in iron and steel to Europe (1.27). In these two industries, Japan is considered to have been at a high technical level since 1970, and in iron and steel it is considered to be a world leader. Overall, the gap is still large between sales and purchases to industrialized regions, from which Japan is likely to remain a net importer of technology for some time, even though a growing number of particular industries may become net exporters.

A substantial proportion of technology exports to the less industrialized countries is related to direct Japanese investment in those countries. Technology is often transferred along with capital, making it difficult to separate the payments for technology from the earnings on capital. A certain fraction of technology payments is probably included in the returns to direct investment, and so the technology payments are likely to be underestimates of the actual export of technology. This seems to be the case for technology exports to Southeast Asia.[30] The relation between technology exports and direct investment means that Japan's technology exports depend on the international activities of large Japanese firms, as well as on the level of Japanese technology relative to other countries.

Adaptive Research and the Investment Requirements of Technology Imports

As indicated earlier, efforts were made to modify and improve imported technology through extensive research and development. As the data in Table 8-7 indicate, one-third of R&D expenditures by respondents to a 1962 MITI survey were for modifying or improving imported technology. Expenditures per imported product or process were higher than for those of domestic origin, reflecting their greater technical complexity. Engineering services for plant layout and production are several times the direct research expenditures.

Such expenditures have often been viewed as adaptive research, implying that the objective is to modify the technology for Japanese conditions. Interviews with Japanese executives suggest, however, that "improvement engineering" may be the better description. The emphasis was, first of all, on quality control, with the goal being to exceed the product quality of the for-

---

30. In an early 1960s sample of 961 firms abroad in which there was some significant Japanese direct investment, 673 firms (70.1 percent) used technology supplied by Japanese investors, 20 (2.1 percent) used technology from other sources, and 179 firms (18.1 percent) were involved in marketing or service activities. Enterprise Bureau, Ministry of International Trade and Industry, *Nihon kigyō no kokusaiteki tenkai: Wagakuni kigyō no kaigai jigyō katsudo chōsa hōkokusho* [International Activity of Japanese Firms: A Report of Overseas Activity of Japanese Firms] (1963), p. 76.

Table 8-7. *Ratios of Expenditures for Research and Development and Plant Layout and Production Engineering to New Products and Processes, for Indigenous and Imported Technology, Japan, 1957–62*

Item	Research and development	Plant layout and production engineering
Indigenous technology		
Expenditure (millions of yen)	24.9	126.6
Number of new products and processes	1,061	819
Expenditure/number of new products and processes	0.023	0.154
Imported technology		
Expenditure (millions of yen)	12.8	175.0
Number of new products and processes	257	279
Expenditure/number of new products and processes	0.049	0.627

Source: MITI, *Gijutsu dōkō chōsa hōkokusho* [Report on the Trend of Technology] (1963), as reported in Ozawa, *Japan's Technological Challenge*, p. 69. The statistics came from a survey made by the Ministry of International Trade and Industry in November 1962. 1,937 companies were selected for the survey. All the companies with capital assets worth more than ¥100 million were included. The remainder of the sample comprised half of the total number of companies with assets of ¥50–100 million. The rate of response was about 54 percent.

eign manufacturer. There was an explicit view that sales in both the domestic and export markets would be sensitive to quality defects, including reliability; that the label "Made in Japan," as well as individual company trademarks, should stand for quality production. The result, according to Ozawa, was "that Japan has succeeded in casting off the old stigma of being an exporter of shoddy manufactures and is now gaining a reputation as an exporter of high quality products."[31] A second and lower priority was to improve the product in terms of operating simplicity, attractiveness, and technical performance. Export and domestic sales were also considered to be highly responsive to such improvements, particularly those that would make Japanese products distinctive and superior to competing foreign products. Cost reduction, in the authors' interviews, was given a lower priority.

Survey data provide a more systematic measure of the major goal of company research efforts in Japan compared with those in the United States. Cost reduction was chosen as the major goal of company R&D by 49 percent of Japanese manufacturing companies, with improvement of present products chosen by 34 percent. In the United States, development of entirely new products was ranked first, with 47 percent of the companies listing this as the main objective, compared with only 17 percent in Japan. About the same number in each country chose improvement of present products as the

31. Terutomo Ozawa, "Japan Technology Now Challenges the West," *Columbia Journal of World Business* (March–April 1973) p. 41.

major goal. These results are consistent with the authors' findings, in that development of new products consumes much less company R&D efforts in Japan than in the United States. We are unable to reconcile the lower priority assigned to cost reductions by our Japanese interviewees than by the survey results.[32]

The volume of capital investment required to use imported technology was substantial: MITI surveys during the 1950s show more than 25 percent of the total investment in producer's equipment represented the purchase of equipment directly associated with importation of technology. This is only the direct effect; a substantial amount of the remaining investment in the firms that imported technology was also associated with technology imports —and these firms accounted for as much as 40 percent of Japan's equipment investment in the late 1950s.[33]

Comparable surveys unfortunately are lacking for the 1960s. The two surveys in that decade show a trend toward less capital investment: the proportion of technology imports requiring no investment increased from 42 percent in 1961 to 60 percent in 1966 and the proportion requiring substantial investment declined from 31 to 14 percent.[34] Identified as technology imports requiring no investment are improvements on already imported technology, supplements to domestic technology, sales and management technology, and patent licensing to permit export of existing products.

Governmental Controls

One of the most distinctive features of Japan's import of technology was the application of extensive governmental controls, and as of early 1968, Japan was the only OECD country that retained controls on technology imports.[35] The Foreign Investment Act of 1950 required governmental

32. The surveys were for 1962 for the United States and 1963 for Japan. There were differences in the questions in the two surveys. Those pertaining to improvement in present products and the development of new products were worded about the same, but the third choice was cost reduction in the Japanese survey and new processes in the U.S. survey, a difference that may have colored the results. For the data, see McGraw-Hill Department of Economics, *15th Annual McGraw-Hill Survey, Business Plans for New Plant and Equipment* (April 1962), table xv; and Ministry of International Trade and Industry, *Report on Current State of Technologies* (May 1963), as quoted in Yoshiro Tsurumi, "Technology Transfer and Foreign Trade: The Case of Japan, 1950–1966" (Ph.D. thesis, Harvard University Business School, 1968).

33. See data in MITI, *Current Status and Problems of Foreign Technology Absorption* (1962), as cited in Ozawa, *Japan's Technological Challenge*, p. 40.

34. Science and Technology Agency, *Annual Report of the Import of Foreign Technology* (1967), p. 37.

35. Robert S. Ozaki, *The Control of Imports and Foreign Capital in Japan* (Praeger, 1972), p. 94.

approval of all transactions involving remittances in a foreign currency. Because almost all technology imports involved such remittances, this legislation provided the basis for extensive control by the MITI.[36] Applications were screened individually in some detail and were usually preceded by discussions between the Japanese company and MITI officials, with the foreign sellers sometimes included. Careful review was facilitated by the fact that the number of agreements was relatively small, averaging about 100 annually in the 1950s and about 500 in the 1960s.[37] The approval rate for formal applications was high. From 1962 to 1966, 90.4 percent of the applications were approved and 4.6 percent were rejected; 4.7 percent were still pending in 1966.[38] The high approval rate, however, is an inadequate measure of the impact of the review process, since applications usually were not submitted unless the preliminary discussions indicated that approval would be forthcoming.[39]

Although the formal rationale for the controls lay in concern for balance of payments, it would be difficult to argue that they have made much difference in Japan's overall balance-of-payments situation. Royalty payments represented only 0.5 percent of all foreign exchange payments in 1953 and 1.8 percent in 1960. Even if liberalization had tripled these payments, Japan's overall balance-of-payments position would have changed little.[40] In applying for OECD membership in 1963, the Japanese government justified its controls as a safeguard against sudden disruptions in the small-business sector, but as Ozaki states: "In actuality there have been few reported cases of notable disruptions among small businesses in Japan on account of the induction of foreign technology, and practically all applications for technical assistance to the small business sectors have been validated."[41]

More important than any stated rationale for controls is their impact on the price of technology, the composition of the imported technology, and

36. The MITI had a role only with respect to industrial technology, which was, however, the major category. Approvals from the Ministry of Finance and the Science and Technology Agency were also required for industrial technology, and applications were formally submitted through the Bank of Japan. Other ministries had jurisdiction over technologies relevant to them: the Ministry of Agriculture, for example, reviewed the import of agricultural technology. See Ozaki, *The Control of Imports*, pp. 92–95.

37. Data, for class A agreements only, from Ozawa, *Japan's Technological Challenge,* table 2.2, p. 23.

38. Ryūtarō Komiya, "Direct Foreign Investment in Japan," in Peter Drysdale (ed.), *Direct Foreign Investment in Asia and the Pacific* (Australia National University Press, 1972), p. 137.

39. From 1962 to 1966, years in which direct foreign investment in Japan was regarded as highly restricted, 83.6 percent of the formal direct investment applications were approved. Ibid., p. 153.

40. See Ozaki, *The Control of Imports*, p. 98.

41. Ibid., p. 94.

the industrial structure—all areas in which the evidence suggests that governmental controls did make a difference.

The several changes in royalty rates and the level of technology imports following successive liberalizations provide a rough measure of the impact of the controls prior to liberalization. The first important changes occurred in 1959, when the government expanded its list of desired technologies and adopted a conditional approval system with easier standards; and in early 1961, when it shifted from a positive to a negative criterion for approval— from requiring that the applicant show that the agreement would make a positive contribution to the balance of payments or the economic growth of important industries to a position under which "technology imports became free in principle except for those cases which were believed detrimental to the Japanese economy."[42] This change in standard was considered to represent a significant liberalization in the administration of the controls. It is difficult to date this liberalization precisely, for although the two orders were effective July 21, 1959, and May 21, 1961, in administration of controls the government apparently shifted toward a less restrictive stance beginning in 1960.

Other procedural changes were made in April 1964 and August and November 1966 that further liberalized the administration, but these appear to have been minor actions.[43]

Ozawa reports that in 1968 "a full scale of technology import liberalization took place."[44] The actual steps do not quite support so broad a conclusion,[45] but most observers agree that beginning in 1968 technology imports became in fact freer of governmental controls. The government has reserved its authority to apply controls, and it is unclear how active the MITI remains, on an informal basis, in the review process.

THE MITI AND THE PRICE OF TECHNOLOGY. One of the most often cited activities of the MITI has been its participation in royalty negotiations. The series of royalty rates shown in Table 8-8 indicates a decline in rates until 1965, then a sharp jump with the major liberalization in 1968. This series must be viewed with caution, however. The percentages shown are for run-

---

42. Ibid., p. 95.
43. Ibid.
44. Ozawa, *Japan's Technological Challenge*, p. 22.
45. The provision limited automatic approval to agreements involving compensations of less than $50,000 and excluded aircraft weapons, explosives, nuclear energy, space explorations, computers, and petrochemicals (see ibid.). Ozaki reports that in 1968 and 1969 the Japanese government withdrew most of its previous reservations with respect to the provisions of the OECD Code of Liberalization of Current Non-Trade Transactions. See *The Control of Imports*, p. 95.

Table 8-8. *Japanese Class A Technology Agreements at Various Running Royalty Rates, by Fiscal Year, 1963–71*[a]

Item	1963	1964	1965	1966	1967	1968	1969	1970	1971
Total number of agreements	442	349	306	344	340	567	693	763	893
Royalties less than 5 percent									
Number	319	295	245	264	255	281	312	347	412
Percent of total	72.2	84.5	80.1	76.7	75.0	49.6	45.0	45.5	46.1
Royalties 5 to 8 percent									
Number	110	51	55	71	77	246	328	337	375
Percent of total	24.9	14.6	18.0	20.6	22.6	43.4	47.3	44.2	42.0
Royalties 8 percent or more									
Number	13	3	6	9	8	40	53	79	106
Percent of total	2.9	.9	2.0	2.6	2.4	7.1	7.6	10.4	11.9
Average royalty (percent)[b]	4.1	3.5	3.5	4.2	4.0	5.1	5.2	5.2	5.3
Median royalty (percent)[c]	3.9	3.4	3.6	3.7	3.8	5.0	5.3	5.3	5.3

Source: Science and Technology Agency, *Gaikoku gijutsu dōnyū nenji hōkoku* [Annual Report of the Import of Foreign Technology], various editions. Data for 1963–67 are taken from the 1967 edition, pp. 50–51; data for 1968–70 from the 1972 edition, p. 21. Data for earlier years are unavailable.

a. Agreements are for new contracts of more than one year's duration signed by Japanese firms during the year for the purchase of technology from foreign suppliers. Some renewals are also included. Running royalty rates are the rates paid by Japanese firms over the life of the contract. Rates are usually calculated as a percentage of sales of the products covered by the agreement, but in some cases as a percent of the cost of production.

b. Calculated by using the midpoints of the finer intervals published for 1968–71. For other years published data are used. The average royalty rate from 1949 to 1960 was 4.6 percent.

c. Calculated by using the finer intervals published in the 1967–1971 editions.

ning royalties paid by Japanese firms to foreign suppliers of technology. They represent payments due over the period of the agreement and are stated in percentages, usually of sales but sometimes of the direct costs of production. There are also often annual minimums and an initial payment, but these are typically a small proportion of the total. The royalty rates shown in the table are primarily for new agreements for the specified fiscal year; as noted earlier, technical agreements have a median life of ten years, and running royalty rates are usually unchanged for the life of the agreement. Hence, the royalty rate changes apply to only a small proportion of the current payments: in 1973, for example, 8.3 percent of all technology payments were for new agreements. Because the government data do not report averages after 1967 and the averages for 1968 and subsequent years were computed from frequency distributions, the sharpness of the 1968 jump shown in the table should be partially discounted. Nonetheless, the rates clearly increased after 1967, since the fraction of agreements in the 5 to 8 percent rate interval doubled.

The mid-1960s, with the lowest royalty rates, represented the period of most intensive MITI intervention. The requirement of MITI approval served to reduce competition among Japanese firms, especially since there was sometimes informal designation by the MITI of a particular Japanese firm to negotiate with a specific foreign company. Beyond this, the MITI would delay its approval or make it conditional upon revisions that would lower rates. Such interventions provoked criticisms abroad. An OECD study, for instance, took a sharp view of MITI intervention in technological purchases:

Apart from the application of general principles of "exceptional adjustment," it happens that, after the Japanese and the foreign partner have agreed on the terms of a contract, the authorities make approval conditional on amendments, usually in favor of the former. The scope of the technology is frequently changed; the royalties and initial payments are reduced; minimum royalties and back royalties are eliminated; arrangements must be made for the Japanese partner to get privileged access to certain foreign markets; provisions are disallowed under which the Japanese partner renounces manufacture after the expiry of the contract or to make certain competitive products; sub-licensing is made subject to further governmental approval; undertakings are deleted under which the Japanese partner would hand over a list of his customers at the end of the contract; the duration of the contract is reduced; automatic renewal is excluded; etc. All these changes of the terms of his contract are imposed upon the resident (as well as the non-resident) whether he wishes it or not, although as long as they are in favour, he would be unlikely to object to this form of official guardianship over his interests. Government action is generally supposed to be for the good of its nationals, but in this case it takes an unusually direct form of interference with bona fide private contracts.[46]

In 1966, the MITI announced that it would limit its revisions to agreements with royalty rates of less than 3 percent, a figure well below the prevailing average rate and one that allowed the MITI to continue playing an active role in most agreements.[47]

    46. OECD, *Liberalization of International Capital Movements: Japan* (Paris: OECD, 1968), pp. 57–58, quoted in Ozawa, *Japan's Technological Challenge,* pp. 53–54.
    47. The guidelines also involved a fixed fee not exceeding $50,000 and a term of less than seven years. Machinery agreements were allowed rates of 5 percent. See Ozaki, *The Control of Imports,* p. 95. No suitable data are available for other countries to make comparisons of royalty rates. In a survey of 27 British companies in chemical, electrical, and mechanical engineering conducted in 1969, the mean royalty on licenses to other British and foreign firms was 4.2 percent. C. T. Taylor and Z. A. Silberston, *The Economic Impact of the Patent System* (Cambridge University Press, 1973), p. 123. This suggests that Japanese firms, even during the high point of MITI intervention, did not obtain unusually low rates. (The average payment was 3.5 percent in 1964.) But given the limited size of the British sample, the comparison should be regarded with caution. The more critical point is that the unique controls on direct investment in Japan led to the licensing of valuable technology that in other countries could be exploited by

The MITI also objected to technological agreements that limited exports. Again, this may have reflected a divergence of interest between the Japanese buyer of technology and the MITI's general economic goals. The Japanese firm may have been willing to trade off export markets for lower royalty rates, but given the government's interest in exports, such a tradeoff would have been unacceptable to the MITI. Yet despite the MITI's dislike of such restrictions, they were common. In 1971 three-quarters of the technology agreements had export restrictions, the most common being those limiting sales to Japan and Southeast Asia.[48] In 1962, when the MITI was more active, export restrictions were somewhat less common; about half the agreements had such restrictions.[49]

One reason for export restrictions was the holding of exclusive patent licenses for specific geographical areas by non-Japanese firms. In addition, the MITI's limited success with respect to geographical restrictions reflects their high value to the sellers of technology. If an agreement restricts the Japanese firm to markets otherwise inaccessible to the seller because of trade barriers, marketing disadvantages, or manufacturing costs, then all the royalty income becomes a clear gain for the seller. Market limitations are common in technology agreements; there are no data that indicate whether agreements with Japanese firms have had fewer such provisions than is the case in other countries. The effect of these restrictions on Japanese exports should not be exaggerated because the limitations usually applied only to direct sales; restrictions on a synthetic fabric or a plastic, for example, usually precluded the export of only the material itself, not finished products made from it.

In addition, the MITI favored the use of class B technology agreements— agreements that are for less than one year or that allow royalty payments only in yen. The short term served to depress the payments of Japanese buyers while the payments in yen conserved foreign currency. The number of class B agreements actually declined after the liberalization in 1968.[50]

Thus, the overall effect of MITI intervention in the mid-1960s was to provide Japanese firms with technology on more favorable terms than they

---

direct investment by foreign firms. These phenomena are apparent in the data on foreign patent license receipts of U.S. firms. Less than a third of patent license receipts from Japan were from operations related to direct investment, whereas about 60 percent from Western Europe were so related. Robert Wilson, "Sale of Technology through Licensing" (Ph.D. thesis, Yale University, in progress). Data from U.S. Department of Commerce, *Survey of Current Business* (December 1973), pp. 16–17.

48. Ozawa, *Japan's Technological Challenge*, p. 125.
49. OECD, *Review of National Science Policy: Japan* (Paris: OECD, 1967), p. 144.
50. Ozawa, *Japan's Technological Challenge*, p. 19.

would have been able to obtain in the more open economies of the United States or Western Europe. It is clearly a mistake, though, to think of Japanese governmental policy as imposing restrictions on an otherwise perfect market. To the extent that inventions are patented, technology becomes a legal monopoly, and much of the unpatented technology is available only from a few sellers and of interest only to a limited number of buyers. MITI controls thus were applied to a situation of oligopolistic bargaining.

A lessening of government intervention, however, is only part of the story behind rising royalty rates after 1968. The British journalist P. B. Stone reported that American firms began in the mid-1960s to press for higher royalty rates, and even that "some foreign companies are refusing to sell, especially now that Japan is a dangerous competitor in the world markets."[51] This stiffening position reflected a general perception by sellers that their technology may have been underpriced in the early 1960s because of poor forecasts of both the growth of the Japanese market and the eventual loss of export sales in third markets to Japanese firms.

Reluctance to sell technology also reflects increasing interest by multinational corporations in direct investment as an alternative way of capitalizing on their technology in the Japanese market. According to M. Y. Yoshino:

International corporations began to use their advanced technology as a wedge to demand equity participation and a less restrictive investment climate. Thus, no longer able to rely predominantly on licensing, an increasing number of Japanese corporations were compelled to form joint ventures in order to obtain coveted foreign technology. Having enjoyed a partial success with this strategy, international corporations further pressed for less restrictive investment climate. Thus, the Japanese came under increasing pressure for capital policy liberalization in order to assure continued access to advanced technology.[52]

If foreign technology has become increasingly valuable to Japanese firms with the passage of time, a simple increase in price might be expected rather than outright refusals to sell and pressures for investment liberalization. To be sure, some of the statements can be viewed as part of the bargaining process, but the drive for investment participation also reflects a view held by sellers of technology that licensing activities may not extract the full value of technology. Licensing inherently is—as compared with direct investment, with its greater control and flow of information—a clumsy way to extract the maximum gains from a foreign market. A survey of large American companies reports that "companies generally are reluctant to license technology

51. P. B. Stone, *Japan Surges Ahead: The Story of an Economic Miracle* (Praeger, 1969), p. 137.

52. M. Y. Yoshino, "Japan as Host to the International Corporation," in Charles P. Kindleberger (ed.), *The International Corporation* (M.I.T. Press, 1970), pp. 351–52.

which they believe has significant commercial potential. . . . By directly entering foreign markets, companies normally anticipate earning larger profits than by licensing others to use it."[53]

Direct investment was successively liberalized by Japan beginning in 1967, with further actions in 1971 and again in 1973—although the extent to which the liberalization in fact means full freedom for direct investment is a matter of debate.[54] Access to technology was not the prime reason for the change; rather, these moves were part of Japan's response to its growing surplus in its balance of payments.

Such moves meant, however, that direct investment became for foreign firms a more feasible alternative to technology agreements as a means of exploiting their technology in Japan. This would have the effect of raising sellers' prices for such agreements. Even so, the overall burden of technology payments for Japanese firms seems to be lessening: each of the six large Japanese firms interviewed by the authors in the summer of 1973 was paying proportionally less for imported technology than in the past. The 1973 burden is indicated by payments for imported technology of 5.2 percent of the operating profits of manufacturing companies that imported technology.[55] Factors offsetting the rate rise include a decline in the proportion of sales covered by technology agreements and the fact that renewals of existing agreements (not included in the rates reported in Table 8-8) have had lower royalty rates than new agreements. These lower rates reflect an increasing ability by Japanese firms to offer cross licenses on their own patents and a decline in their need for unpatented know-how.[56]

53. D. B. Zenoff, "Licensing as a Means of Penetrating Foreign Markets," *Idea: Patent, Trademark, and Copyright Journal of Education and Research,* vol. 14 (Summer 1970), p. 300. An examination of the history of invention suggests that inventors taking their rewards on a royalty basis seldom capture more than a small fraction of their potential gains. Major technological innovations—cellophane or aluminum, for example—often become the basis for a dominant market share in a major industry, and the usual range of royalty fees is totally inadequate to capture the long-run value of such market shares. Of course, achieving a significant market position in a foreign country may involve high risks and require more than simply technological knowledge, but large multinational corporations also have the production, marketing, and financing resources needed to achieve significant market shares.

54. A number of activities, primarily relating to agriculture, forestry, fisheries, and retailing remain tightly restricted, but lesser restrictions on seventeen manufacturing industries are to be relaxed by May 1976.

55. Bureau of Statistics, *Report on the Survey of Research and Development* (1973), p. 153. The highest payments were in industrial chemicals, in which payments were 14.0 percent of operating profits.

56. The number of new cross-licensing agreements was eight in 1966, forty in 1968, and fifty-four in 1971. See Ozawa, *Japan's Technological Challenge,* p. 127.

Averages nonetheless are deceptive, and in rare cases high rates have precluded the use of imported technology—though, as interviews suggested, substitutes usually were available from domestic R&D or from other companies abroad. Among exceptions, the Texas Instruments case is the best known. P. B. Stone reported: "Texas Instruments which owns much of the integrated circuit know-how is severely hampering the latest desk calculator boom by insisting on permission to establish a wholly-owned subsidiary in Japan before releasing licenses."[57] Texas Instruments applied for permission for a wholly owned subsidiary in 1964. Negotiations followed, and in 1966 the MITI required that the venture be 50–50 with a Japanese firm and involve licensing to other Japanese producers and output limitations for the first three years (presumably to allow the other Japanese producers to achieve significant market shares). The matter was resolved in 1968, when Texas Instruments announced a joint venture and licenses to four Japanese companies.[58]

Although there may be similar cases, the rising price of technology seems unlikely to be a major constraint on Japanese importation of technology, though it may lead to somewhat more direct foreign investment than the Japanese would desire. On the margin, of course, a higher price for imported technology tips the balance toward reliance on domestic R&D—which, by providing Japanese firms with an alternative technology of their own for cross licensing, improves their bargaining position and so serves to keep the price of imported technology down.

MITI CONTROLS OVER THE COMPOSITION OF TECHNOLOGY IMPORTS. In 1950 the MITI issued a list of thirty-three desired technologies, of which most were technologies for heavy industries such as chemicals or for manufacturing processes such as continuous wire drawing.[59] The only three technologies for consumer products were in pharmaceuticals. Additions to the list in 1959 were electronic and jet aircraft items and for techniques making processes continuous, more efficient, or automated in any industry. Although the list of desired technologies was used to review applications, each import proposal was required to show positive benefits to the economy. The list was only a guide: agreements for technologies not on the MITI's list also were approved. Still, controls apparently did suppress the demand for foreign technology. With the first liberalization, the number of agreements rose from

57. *Japan Surges Ahead*, p. 137.
58. Komiya, "Direct Foreign Investment," pp. 155–56.
59. Article 7-1 of the Foreign Investment Law, quoted in Ozawa, *Japan's Technological Challenge*, p. 138; the lists are reproduced in table 2-1, p. 21. This section is based in large part on Ozawa, pp. 20–24, but the interpretations are the authors'.

153 in 1959 to 327 in 1960, and the liberalization of 1968 produced a rise in the number of technology agreements from 638 in 1967 to 1,061 in 1968.[60]

That controls would be imposed apparently to reduce the amounts of technology imported is puzzling. Economic growth, then Japan's principal priority, required a maximum of technology imports, which promised high gains in productivity and represented only a small item in the balance of payments. But the controls gave priority to technology for intermediate goods such as various chemicals and for producers' equipment such as machine tools, and they suppressed the demand for consumer-goods technology. Access to imported technology was a major source of profit, and to deny such access to some industries served to tilt the pattern of investment and output toward what were regarded as basic industries. Although the control of technology was viewed as a major instrument in growth policy and access to it was a major source of profits, there are no quantitative measures of the difference the controls made for the postwar pattern of growth, particularly since the kinds of changes in the composition of technology imports discussed earlier can be explained as the result of market forces. Working with rather than against market forces seems characteristic of many Japanese government policies. But this does not point to the conclusion that controls therefore did not matter; in a fast-growing economy it can be of importance whether government policy delays or speeds up the use of a particular technology by only three or four years.

TECHNOLOGY IMPORTATION AND THE STRUCTURE OF INDUSTRY. MITI controls served also to shape the structure of new industries—it can be argued that in this dimension the controls had their most discernible effect. The increase in duplicate imports of technology, many of which represent additional entrants into new industries, was the most visible consequence of liberalization. The announced objective in controlling duplicate technology imports was effective utilization of imported technology, meaning that approval of a technology agreement was conditional upon its meeting the MITI's interests, first, in the construction of plants of efficient scale and, second, in avoiding excess capacity and the ensuing price competition.[61] But to protect the economy from the dominance of a few sellers the MITI sought at the same time to bring new firms into industries. The hoped-for result of the interplay between these two sets of objectives—one restrictive and the other expansive—was an increasing number of sellers, but never at the expense of unused capacity or excessive competition.

60. Ibid., table 2-2, p. 23.
61. For a detailed discussion of these objectives, see Chapter 7.

This policy required an ample supply of potential entrants. The first entrant sometimes was given governmental encouragement in the form of loans and an informal assurance that government aid would be forthcoming if financial difficulties were encountered. But beyond that, Japan's high rate of growth, together with MITI policies restricting entry, made entry appear to be profitable, so a choice usually was possible among several eager candidates.[62] One important rule for the MITI's decisionmaking process seems to have been that opportunities were to be distributed among all the major groups.[63] Entry patterns have been generally consistent with the one-set hypothesis discussed in Chapter 7: that is, that each group would have a firm in each major new industry. And although the companies in a group might help form the new company, the latter was not viewed as a subsidiary, but rather as a new group member. In the early years a group's bank was the major source of capital. A second source of entrants was through diversification by an existing large company, usually by establishing a subsidiary.

Each situation had its individual peculiarities, but the process of entry into an industry, importation of duplicate technology, and market growth can be illustrated by a case involving production of low-density, high-pressure process polyethylene, a raw material for plastics used in such items as containers, furniture, and electric insulation. This particular product was singled out by the MITI for domestic production in the 1950s, and the first two entries occurred in 1955 and 1957 (see Table 8-9). In 1955 the MITI approved a petrochemical development program that included this product. The program had three stated objectives: to provide a stable supply of intermediate raw materials to the growing synthetic fiber and plastics industries, to save foreign exchange by substituting domestic production, and to reduce

62. The higher politics of this choice is illustrated by the following account, drawn to our attention by Professor Ozawa:

For some years, Toray had a virtual monopoly on nylon manufacture in Japan and waxed exceeding profitable. The Japanese government finally granted four other producers permission to license nylon know-how from Western firms and enter nylon production. When these producers came onstream, prices collapsed calamitously to the considerable disadvantage of Toray's profitability, and left Toray, it may be assumed, with a certain call on the government for future favor. It is not entirely surprising that when Toray applied for permission to license patents and know-how to enter the fast-growing field of silicones, despite two other domestic producers already in the field the application received the fastest approval in post-war history.

James C. Abegglen (ed.), *Business Strategies for Japan* (Tokyo: Sophia University, 1970), p. 125.

63. A group is a collection of major firms in several industries that have some interlocking ownership and a practice of consultation between the managements of group members. Groups are the descendants of the prewar *zaibatsu*.

Table 8-9. *Process of Development and Diversification of the Low-Density, High-Pressure Process Polyethylene Industry in Japan, 1955–67*

Year of licensing contract	Company	Origins	Foreign source of technology
1955	Sumitomo Chemical	Chemical company member of the well established and large Sumitomo group	Imperial Chemical, United Kingdom
1957	Mitsubishi Petrochemical	Created two years earlier as a new company by members of the large Mitsubishi group and Shell Petroleum	BASF, West Germany
1960	Mitsui Polychemical	Created as a new company by members of the large Mitsui group	DuPont, United States
1961	Nippon Unicar	Joint venture of a Japanese chemical and synthetic fiber company with Union Carbide	Union Carbide, United States
1962	Asahi Dow	Joint venture of Japanese chemical company with Dow	Dow Chemical, United States
1963	Ube Industries	Japanese coal and chemical company	Dart Industries, United States
1964	Toyo Soda	Japanese chemical company	National Distillers, United Kingdom
1965	Nippon Petro-chemical	New petrochemical company established by a Japanese petroleum refining company	Dart Industries, United States
1966	Showa Denko	Chemical company member of the medium-size Showa group	Ethylene Plastique, France
1967	Mitsubishi Chemical	Chemical company member of the well-established and large Mitsubishi group	Gulf Oil, United States

Source: Adapted from data in Association of Petrochemical Industries in Japan, *Sekiyukagaku kōgyō jyunen shi* [Ten Year History of the Petrochemical Industry] (1971).

the price of petrochemical products.[64] Entrants were to be selected from petroleum or chemical firms with the proven managerial ability and technical competence to produce these new products.

At the end of 1964 the Cooperative Consultation Committee of the Association of Petrochemical Industries was established to provide guidance to the MITI and the industry; it comprised government officials, industrialists, and public members. The committee first established a criterion for minimum economic scale for each company's production of ethylene (a primary intermediate material for petrochemical products), and then set standards for companies that would produce secondary products, such as polyethylene, having smaller economies of scale. The criterion for minimum economic scale of ethylene production was set at 300,000 tons annually, about 17 percent of the 1968 industry capacity for that product. The scale for production of polyethylene was set at 30,000 tons annually, about 5 percent of the 1968 capacity and 3.4 percent of 1970 capacity.[65]

The pattern of entry in the 1950s and 1960s is shown in Table 8-9. From 1960 to 1970 capacity increased over thirtyfold and the number of producers increased from two to ten. Three features about the entry pattern are worth noting. First, three initial entrants came from Japan's three largest groups, but as the process continued smaller groups and other companies entered. Second, with one exception, Japanese companies chose different foreign companies as a source of technology, reflecting the reluctance of Japanese companies to share technological sources with competitors. Third, each entrant has its origins in either a group or firm in an allied industry; in no case did entrants into this technically complex and capital-intensive industry come from a totally new venture. New entrants appear at regular intervals, paralleling growth in demand. The last three entrants had a capacity of about 30,000 tons annually, the minimum economic scale determined by the MITI. Existing firms expanded, but the share of capacity held by the four firms that entered before 1962 declined to 63 percent by 1970, as Table 8-10 indicates.

Low-density polyethylene is a case in which an entire new industry was created. Control of technology imports takes a somewhat different form, of course, in the case of a process applicable to an established industry, where the MITI's concern was with maintaining competitive parity among existing firms. When a technique was introduced for one firm, an effort was made to

64. Association of Petrochemical Industries in Japan, *Sekiyukagaku kōgyō jyunen shi* [Ten Year History of the Petrochemical Industry] (1971), pp. 68–69.
65. Ibid., pp. 197–99.

Table 8-10. *New Entry of Low-Density Polyethylene Production in Japan and Distribution of Industry Capacity, 1958–70*

Company	Percent of industry capacity						
	1958	*1960*	*1962*	*1964*	*1966*	*1968*	*1970*
Sumitomo Chemical	100.0	58.3	33.0	35.0	23.5	22.5	17.9
Mitsubishi Petrochemical	...	41.7	33.0	21.8	25.2	18.3	17.9
Mitsui Polychemical	...	...	16.1	21.4	11.5	13.7	13.9
Nippon Unicar	...	...	17.8	17.2	12.7	15.3	12.1
Asahi Dow	...	...	...	4.3	5.9	5.1	8.6
Ube Industries	...	...	...	...	12.9	14.6	11.5
Toya Soda	...	...	...	...	8.0	4.9	7.4
Nippon Petrochemical	...	...	...	...	...	4.3	3.4
Showa Denko	...	...	...	...	...	...	3.4
Mitsubishi Chemical	...	...	...	...	...	...	3.4
Total capacity (thousands of tons a year)	11	24	151	228	424	683	863

Source: Association of Petrochemical Industries in Japan, *Sekiyukagaku kōgyō jyunen shi* [Ten Year History of the Petrochemical Industry] (1971), p. 198, supplemented and recomputed by Shūji Tamura using data provided by the MITI.

see that it was available to others. One example involves the liquid oxygen process in steel making. All Japanese steel companies had at least two liquid oxygen furnaces by 1961, only four years after the first use of the process in Japan. This quick diffusion was prompted by MITI policies.

The oxygen process was developed by a steel company in Austria, where it was in use by 1952. Two leading Japanese steel companies began research and development on the process in 1952 based on European academic information. Experimentation on a relatively large scale used existing furnaces, and the technical data thus acquired provided the basis for a decision to launch a commercial operation. A third Japanese steel company began a development project at this time. In 1953 one of the three contacted the Austrian company to explore the possibility of acquiring the technology and sent a mission for detailed negotiation in 1955. Another of the three had similar negotiations with the German company that had supplied the equipment to the Austrian firm.

The MITI—whose policy was to ensure widespread use of this technology throughout the steel industry—asked the industry to select a single firm to diffuse the technology most effectively. One company was selected as an exclusive licensee of the European technology in Japan, with the provision that it would sublicense and provide without charge the necessary technical assistance to any Japanese companies.[66]

These two examples hardly do justice to use of the control of technology for shaping an industry's structure. Rosovsky writes that "Japan must be the only capitalistic country in the world in which the government decides how many firms there should be in a given industry and then sets about to arrange the desired number."[67] The unqualified statement applies only to a few industries and hardly accounts for the complexities of bargaining and other interaction between business and government in Japan. Nonetheless, the tendency toward an active governmental policy that shapes the structure of industry is clear, and control of technology imports was a major policy instrument. With the goals of avoiding excessive competition and realizing economies of scale and at the same time establishing several competitors in each industry, the MITI, it is widely believed, showed more concern about the risks of too much rather than too little competition.[68]

Organization of Research and Development

The importation of technology is the most striking feature of postwar Japan, but gains from that activity resulted in part from Japan's considerable domestic R&D capability. This section examines the organization and the allocation of Japan's R&D among industry, government, and the universities.[69]

---

66. See "The Story of the Introduction of the Liquid Oxygen Process in Steel Making," *Steel Life Weekly*, vol. 1 (Tokyo: Steel Life Company, September 1973), pp. 48–53.

67. Henry Rosovsky, "What Are the Lessons of Japanese Economic History," in A. J. Youngson (ed.), *Economic Development in the Long Run* (London: George Allen and Unwin, 1972), p. 244.

68. See the discussion in Chapter 7.

69. Throughout this discussion international comparisons of R&D spending will be used. These comparisons have been greatly facilitated by OECD's standardization of procedures for the reporting of research spending in member countries. Visits by the authors to Japanese statistical organizations confirmed that Japanese data compare favorably in quality with those of other OECD countries, except in making distinctions between spending for basic and applied research. Published government data indicate that 23.3 percent of all Japanese R&D expenditures in 1970 were for basic research, an exceptionally high ratio that is explained by the inclusion of faculty salaries in Japanese universities as R&D expenditures because teaching and research are considered highly interrelated. (The Oriental Economist, *Japan Economic Yearbook, 1972* [Tokyo, 1972], p. 125.) Basic research also is overstated in the industrial sector because of errors in reporting the expenditures by the central research laboratories of Japanese firms. Given these problems, no reliance in this analysis will be placed on the distinction between

Table 8-11. *Distribution of Research Performance and Funding in Japan and Other Principal Industrialized Countries, 1969*
Percent

	Performed by				Funded by		
Country	Industry	Govern- ment	Nonprofit organiza- tions	Univer- sities	Industry	Govern- ment	Other
Japan	67.3	12.1	1.6	19.0	66.8	26.3	6.9
France	55.5	29.2	1.0	14.2	32.5	62.3	5.2
United Kingdom	64.7	24.5	2.5	8.3	43.5	50.6	5.9
United States	70.0	13.4	3.6	13.0	38.3	57.0	4.7
West Germany	68.2	4.7	9.7	17.5	60.0	39.1	2.8

Source: Science and Technology Agency, *Fiscal Year 1972 White Paper on Science and Technology* [English summary] (Tokyo, 1973), p. 48.

Industrial Research and Development

Private industry pays for a larger share of the nation's research effort in Japan than in other major industrialized countries, as the data in Table 8-11 indicate, and carries out more than in some others. Both aspects deserve emphasis, for although an even greater proportion of research is carried out by industrial firms in the United States, much of it is financed by government defense contracts.

basic and applied research—which in the best of circumstances has ambiguities. An inspection of R&D data suggests that the inclusion of faculty salaries may overstate total Japanese R&D by about 10 percent.

The differing costs of research, another problem in international comparisons of R&D, are usually offset by stating research expenditure as a percent of GNP. The use of official exchange rates to compare R&D spending, however, can be misleading because the official exchange rates may fail to reflect relative research costs. R&D exchange rates have been calculated based on research costs comparisons, and these differ from official exchange rates. Japan in 1963–64 had a high discrepancy between the R&D and the official exchange rates. For example, a British pound converted into yen at official exchange rates would have bought 1.7 times as much research in Japan as in England; whereas converted into dollars it would have bought 0.6 times as much research in the United States—only a third the research input it would have commanded in Japan. A. S. McDonald, "Exchange Rates for National Expenditures on Research and Development," *Economic Journal,* vol. 83 (June 1973), p. 481. But since these calculations were made, both official exchange rates and wage rates have undergone changes that have brought Japanese research exchange rates closer to the official rate: a dollar in 1973 bought less than twice as much research in Japan, rather than the triple quantity that prevailed in 1963–64.

In this section the focus is on the distribution of Japanese research and development among sectors, which allows bypassing of the difficult problem of research exchange rates that plagues comparisons between countries.

INDUSTRY AND FIRM CONCENTRATION OF RESEARCH EXPENDITURES. The industry-by-industry distribution of company-financed research is roughly the same in Japan and the United States. In 1970 about 80 percent of Japanese R&D in manufacturing was accounted for by the technology-intensive "group A" industries (see Table 8-1); the corresponding figure was 88 percent in the United States.[70] Similarities are also apparent in the pattern of research spending by industry, as shown in relation to sales and employment in Table 8-12. The same industries are research intensive in both countries, but the overall Japanese level of research intensity is about two-thirds that of the United States, even when the comparison is limited to company-financed research.

Japanese R&D expenditures are less concentrated among the larger firms than are those in the United States, as Table 8-13 indicates.[71] This comparison is limited to company-financed research, and so the greater U.S. concentration is explained not by defense contracts but rather largely by the greater concentration of sales among the larger American firms.[72] The lower level of sales concentration in Japan reflects a continuation of the prewar pattern in which the zaibatsu—a combine of interlocking ownership and management of major firms—were represented in several industries rather than dominant in any one.[73]

Another indication of the concentration of research activity in each

70. Computed from data in Bureau of Statistics, Report on the Survey of Research and Development in Japan (1970), pp. 101–11; and National Science Foundation, Research and Development in Industry 1970 (1972), pp. 41–42.

71. Adams found that R&D expenditures also are less concentrated in France than in the United States. William J. Adams, "Firm Size and Research Activity: France and the United States," Quarterly Journal of Economics, vol. 84 (August 1970), pp. 386–404.

72. Statistical tests suggest that the hypothesis that the differences in R&D concentration are attributable solely to differences in sales concentration cannot be rejected. When a linear regression is fitted separately to the U.S. and Japanese data for the largest twenty companies in each industry in Table 8-13, with R&D concentration used as the dependent variable and sales concentration as the independent variable, the Fisher-Chow test for the equality of sets of regression coefficients indicates that there is no significant difference between the relations in the two sets of data.

73. See William W. Lockwood, "Japan's New Capitalism," in Lockwood (ed.), The State and Economic Enterprise (Princeton University Press, 1965), pp. 494–95. The group itself is not an important element in research activities, even though some groups have their own research institutes. These are engaged primarily in studies of Japan's future and its implications for long-range business planning and in other social science research rather than in the development of specific products and processes. Trade associations also engage in some research activities. The small role of these two activities is indicated by the fact that only 3.2 percent of 1970 company R&D spending was external: that is, to other companies, universities, research institutes, and trade associations. See Bureau of Statistics, Report on the Survey of Research and Development in Japan (1970), pp. 83–91.

Table 8-12. *Research Intensity of Major Industries in Japan and the United States, in Relation to Sales and Employment, 1970*[a]

Technology and industry group	Research and development expenditure (percent of sales)			Research workers per 1,000 employees	
		United States			
	Japan	Total	Company funded only	Japan	United States
Group A					
Aircraft and missiles	n.a.	18.3	3.9	n.a.	74
Chemicals	2.1	4.1	3.7	35	38
Electrical equipment	3.0	7.5	3.6	28	39
Instruments	2.0	5.9	4.3	18	31
Motor vehicles	1.7	3.5	2.9	15	20
Nonelectrical machinery	1.4	4.2	3.5	15	28
Petroleum	0.3	1.1	1.0	14	18
Group B					
Ferrous metals	0.6	0.7	0.7	8	4
Metal products	0.8	1.2	1.1	12	10
Nonferrous metals	0.9	1.0	1.0	13	9
Paper	0.4	0.7	0.7[b]	11	6
Rubber	1.2	2.1	1.7	13	18
Stone, clay, and glass	1.0	1.9	1.9	11	14
Group C					
Food processing	0.5	0.4	0.4	14	6
Lumber and wood products	n.a.	0.4	0.4	n.a.	4
Textiles and clothing	0.6	0.5	0.4[b]	8	4
Total	1.2	3.8	2.2	15	24

Sources: Bureau of Statistics, *Kagaku gijutsu kenkyū chōsa hōkoku* [Report on the Survey of Research and Development in Japan] (1972), summary tables 5, 10; National Science Foundation, *Research and Development in Industry 1970* (1972), tables 32, 40, 42.

n.a. Not available.

a. The data for both countries are only for companies that actually carry out research and development. For example, the high ratio of research employees in Japanese food industries reflects not any greater research and development intensity for the industry but rather the fact that Japan has more small food processors without research programs that are omitted from the survey.

b. 1965.

country is the proportion of total industrial research activity carried out by firms having 10,000 or more employees. The data in Table 8-14 show that such firms accounted for less than half of Japan's company-funded industrial research in 1970 but more than three-quarters of American industrial research in 1967.[74] The ratio of R&D spending to sales by size of firm shows

74. There were, of course, only 76 such firms in Japan in 1970 as against some 300 in the United States. Bureau of Statistics, *Report on the Survey of Research and Development in Japan* (1970), p. 82; and National Science Foundation, *Research and Development in Industry 1970* (1972), p. 11.

Table 8-13. *Concentration of Industrywide Research and Development Funds and Net Sales in Major Industries, Japan and the United States, 1970*
Percent

Industry	Top twenty companies		Top four or five companies[a]	
	Japan	United States	Japan	United States
	Share of total industrywide research and development			
Chemicals	45	69	20	29
Electrical equipment	79	74	53	45
Instruments	64	85	30	61
Motor vehicles	93	99	71	91
Nonelectrical machinery	52	79	37	52
Petroleum	89	96	73	62
	Share of sales[b]			
Chemicals	35	49	16	22
Electrical equipment	63	65	37	33
Instruments	56	72	16	35
Motor vehicles	85	93	61	77
Nonelectrical machinery	43	48	29	19
Petroleum	84	92	62	35

Sources: Bureau of Statistics, *Kagaku gijutsu kenkyū chōsa hōkoku* [Report on the Survey of Research and Development in Japan] (1970), table 12; National Science Foundation, *Research and Development in Industry 1970* (1972), tables 4, 8, 10, 17 in app. B for research and development concentration and table B-17 for sales concentration.
a. Top five in Japan; top four in the United States.
b. Net sales of all companies industrywide performing research and development.

similar patterns in the two countries, with the 10,000-or-more-employee firms spending about 50 percent more than smaller firms. The comparable ratios are, of course, lower in Japan. The greater portion of R&D carried out by large firms in the United States reflects their greater share of total manufacturing activity rather than a great discrepancy in research intensity between large and small firms.

Government officials and industrialists in both Japan and Europe express fear of the competitive threat posed by these large research expenditures by American firms. This concern often has led to suggestions for mergers to create larger firms in Japan, but economists in the United States and, to a lesser extent, elsewhere are skeptical about whether such a step would increase research activity. The greater research intensity prevails in both the small and large firms in the United States, which suggests that American research intensity arises out of forces that are economywide rather than related to size.[75]

75. F. M. Scherer reports that "increases in size beyond an employment level of roughly 5,000 are not in general accompanied by more than a proportional rise in in-

Table 8-14. *Distribution of Industrial Research Activity in Manufacturing, by Firm Size, Japan (1970) and the United States (1967)*

Size of firm by number of employees	Percent of firms performing research and development	Company-funded research and development as a percent of sales[a]	Percent of total industrial research and development
Japan			
All firms	7.1	1.27	100.0
Less than 1,000	6.5	1.16	19.3
1,000–2,999	69.6	0.96	14.3
3,000–9,999	84.0	1.06	20.6
10,000 or more	97.4	1.67	45.7
United States			
All firms	3.4–20.3[b]	2.1	100.0
Less than 1,000	3.0–20.0	1.6	5.7
1,000–4,999	56.0	1.4	8.0
5,000–9,999	} 93.0	1.6	8.0
10,000 or more		2.3	78.0

Sources: Bureau of Statistics, *Kagaku gijutsu kenkyū chōsa hōkoku* [Report on the Survey of Research and Development in Japan] (1970), pp. 82–85; National Science Foundation, *Research and Development in Industry 1970* (1972), pp. 42, 80; and National Science Foundation statistics quoted in F. M. Scherer, *Industrial Market Structure and Economic Performance* (Rand McNally, 1970), p. 359.

a. For firms that have research expenditures. Companies with less than 1,000 employees are much less likely to conduct R&D, but those which do generally specialize in activities requiring much R&D. Hence the somewhat surprising result of the smallest companies being more R&D intensive than the larger companies.

b. Percentages of U.S. manufacturing firms carrying out R&D are for 1958, with the higher number for small firms coming from a more extensive 1953 survey.

CONSTRAINTS ON JAPAN'S TECHNOLOGICAL LEADERSHIP. Japanese executives, however, regard the smaller average size of Japanese firms as a deterrent to their matching the product-development capability of American firms. Another major constraint mentioned during the authors' interviews was the comparatively low level of spending on high-risk, long-term research in Japan. Research managers regard their present resources as fully committed to the modification and improvement of existing products. Funds for R&D were increasing in the 1960s, but not fast enough to provide a surplus above the demands from operating divisions for projects yielding immediate improvements. Such improvement R&D, often beginning from imported technology, is given priority because the returns are regarded as

novative inputs or outputs." He lists and summarizes the various studies in the United States on this issue. See his *Industrial Market Structure and Economic Performance* (Rand McNally, 1970), pp. 352–62; quotation, page 360. The greater research intensity of firms with 10,000 or more employees as compared with those with 5,000 (see Table 8-14) is partly a reflection of industry composition.

more certain. Japanese companies often define a technical objective for each project and compile a success rate for various classes of projects. In one company the success rate for projects that improved on imported technology was one in five, whereas on projects drawn from their own research the rate was less than one in ten. Other companies reported even higher success ratios for projects on improving technology, but they had so little experience in other kinds of research that own-research comparisons were not possible.

Allocation for low-risk and short-term projects also reflects the preferences of Japanese engineers for the esteem which is to be gained within the company from immediate technical success. A Japanese research executive with experience in the United States reported that American researchers on the long-term projects were motivated by the prospect of publication and scientific reputation, quite apart from the commercial success, perhaps because many American researchers had academic aspirations and because scientific achievement itself brought greater prestige within the company. Neither of these factors was said to be as important in Japanese companies. Another and related constraint on major projects may be that Japanese training and personnel practices are better suited to applied, short-term projects than to long-term, scientifically advanced ones, a possibility discussed later in this chapter.

For the economy as a whole, another constraint on major innovation may be the difficulties in founding new research-oriented companies. A distinctive feature of the American economy in the 1950s and 1960s was the creation of such companies, particularly in electronics. Japanese equivalents, called "brain companies," have some success stories comparable to those of analogous American firms.[76] But such companies play a small role in the Japanese economy, particularly in comparison with the United States, and they encounter perhaps greater difficulty in raising capital and recruiting personnel.

The importance of all these constraints is difficult to evaluate. Japanese research managers are optimistic for the long run; they regard the 1950s as a decade in which it was a necessity to undertake improvement research. Similarly, they regard the 1970s as a decade in which it is a necessity at least partly to match the research activities of large American firms.

DIFFUSION OF TECHNOLOGY AND SMALL BUSINESS. The Japanese economy has often been characterized as having a dual structure, in which large enterprises exist side by side with small ones, with large differences in wage levels, capital, and technology. About 51 percent of the value added in Japanese

76. Four of these companies are described in Hideichiro Nakamura, "Small and Medium Enterprise" (Tokyo, 1971; processed).

manufacturing originates in small- and medium-size enterprises—those with fewer than 300 employees.[77] Most studies of imported technology and domestic research and development focus on the large Japanese enterprises, and yet one of Japan's continuing problems is the inflationary pressure from the slow growth in productivity of small enterprises, combined with a labor shortage that is reducing the traditional wage difference between large and small enterprises. Although these tendencies are most clear in the behavior of prices in the service sector, they are also apparent in manufacturing. The prices of large enterprise products in the manufacturing sector increased by a total of less than 1 percent from 1967 to 1972, whereas the price of small enterprise products rose by 19 percent.[78]

Japan has three distinctive institutions that facilitate the diffusion of new technology to small enterprises. The first and best known of these is the subcontractor system discussed in Chapter 7. Subcontractors make parts for large companies and receive assistance in technology, management, and finance from their large customers, which facilitates diffusion of new technology.[79]

Small business associations also play a role in diffusion; they are organized by locality, by industry, by principal customer, or by further combinations of these categories such as the subcontractors of a large firm for one product line in a given locality. Most small businessmen belong to several such associations. A sample survey showed that the most frequently listed function was mutual friendship, but 9.9 percent carry on joint research and development activities.[80] In aggregate, however, the research executed by business associations is minimal: among the 10,527 companies with R&D spending in the two smallest size classes in 1972, only 1,366 disbursed research funds

77. About 35 percent of value added in American manufacturing originates in establishments with fewer than 250 employees. The difference is more marked for firms with fewer than 100 employees. In the United States such firms account for 20 percent of value added; in Japan, for 35 percent. (Computed from U.S. Bureau of the Census, *Census of Manufactures* [1971], vol. 1, p. 2.6 [MC 67]; and Bureau of Statistics, *Japan Statistical Year Book, 1971*, pp. 186–87.)

78. Large enterprise products represent those items in which 50 percent or more of the value of shipments is produced by firms capitalized at ¥50 million or more. These products account for about three-quarters of manufacturing output. Small enterprise products are the remainder. Statistics Department, Bank of Japan, *Economic Statistics Annual, 1972* (Tokyo, 1972), p. 268.

79. Masaru Saitō, "Diffusion Mechanism of Technology and Industrial Transformation: Case of Small Scale Industries in Japan," *Keizaigaku ronsan*, vol. 13 (September 1972), p. 180.

80. Masaru Saitō, "Diffusion Mechanism of Technology and Industrial Transformation" (paper presented at a seminar on the role of small-scale industries in transfer of technology, sponsored by OECD, Paris, 1973; processed), p. 9.

to nongovernmental agencies, mainly research associations, which amounted to about 2 percent of their R&D spending.[81] The major contribution of these associations to the spread of new technology occurs through their seminars and other information services.

A third distinctive institution that facilitates diffusion of technology to small firms is the local government research institution, of which there were 558 funded by local tax revenues in 1972.[82] Some, such as the Osaka and Nagoya city institutes of industry, are substantial in size, with about 100 researchers and a budget of between $1 million and $2 million. They have allied associations of local companies and it is estimated that about 80 percent of their research activities are in behalf of small enterprises.[83] Although their R&D expenditures are only about 2 percent of all industrial R&D, their expenditures are still sizable relative to R&D spending by firms with fewer than 300 employees.[84] The activities of the local research institutes are shaped by the kind of industry prevalent in the locality, and they provide consulting services and seminars as well as carrying on R&D. Finally, in Japan, as elsewhere, equipment manufacturers, newspapers, competitors, and so forth, play a key role in diffusion of technology, but the focus here has been on three institutions distinctive to Japan.

These institutions provide the Japanese economy with more extensive formal arrangements for making technology available to small business than exist in the United States and most other industrial countries. Improving productivity among small manufacturing firms is one of Japan's critical economic problems, but as the preceding chapter points out, solutions require a much wider set of policies than those relating to the diffusion of technology alone.

Government-Sponsored Research and Development

Research spending by the Japanese government not only stands at a lower level than in other major countries, but also has a different pattern of distribution, as the data in Table 8-15 indicate. Other governments, particularly that of the United States, spend most money on defense, space, and

81. Bureau of Statistics, *Report on the Survey of Research and Development in Japan* (1972), pp. 122–23.
82. Saitō, "Diffusion Mechanism," p. 11.
83. Ibid.
84. Bureau of Statistics, *Report on the Survey of Research and Development in Japan* (1972), pp. 76, 150. R&D spending by these institutes is a third that of the small firms. This comparison includes local government research institute expenditures on science and engineering only, since they make their largest expenditures in agricultural research.

Table 8-15. *Distribution of Government Research and Development Expenditures among National Objectives, Japan and Other Industrialized Countries, 1969*

Percent

	Japan[a]					
	Including national universities	Excluding national universities		United	United	West
Objective			France	Kingdom	States	Germany
National defense	2	4	31	40	49	19
Space	1	2	7	4	24	6
Community services	4	7	3	4	12	2
Economic development (including agriculture)	23	42	16	26	7	2
Nuclear energy	8	15	18	12	6	17
Advancement of science	61	30	24	13	2	39

Source: Organisation for Economic Co-operation and Development, *Research and Development in OECD Member Countries: Trends and Objectives* (OECD, 1971), pp. 48, 74, 95, 120.

a. Most expenditures for national universities are for instruction rather than research and development.

community services (especially health); the Japanese government spends most money on economic development, the advancement of science, and nuclear energy. (The second column for Japan in Table 8-15 does not include expenditures on national universities, most of which are for instruction rather than research.) Therefore, the following discussion focuses primarily on the expenditures for industrial technology, an area dominated by activities of the Ministry of International Trade and Industry.

THE AGENCY OF INDUSTRIAL SCIENCE AND TECHNOLOGY. Three-fifths of the expenditures on economic development are by the MITI's Agency of Industrial Science and Technology,[85] with the Ministry of Agriculture ranking next. In relative size, however, the agency had a budget of about $75 million in fiscal 1972, about 2 percent of industrial R&D.[86] Nonetheless, in certain industrial areas the agency's activities do make a difference, most notably the national research and development program, which consisted of the projects listed below:[87]

85. This agency should not be confused with the Science and Technology Agency in the prime minister's office, which is discussed below.

86. Bureau of Statistics, *Report on the Survey of Research and Development in Japan* (1973), p. 67; and MITI, *Agency of Industrial Science and Technology* (1973; processed), p. 6. The dollar figure is based on an exchange rate of ¥308 = $1.

87. From MITI, *Agency of Industrial Science and Technology*, pp. 10–11. The dollar figures are based on an exchange rate of ¥308 = $1.

Project title	Period of project	Cost (millions of dollars)	Status
Magneto-hydrodynamic generator	1966–72	18.0	Completed
Super-high-performance electronic computer systems	1966–71	32.0	Completed
Desulfurization process (sulfur removal from stock gas and fuel oil)	1966–71	8.0	Completed
New process for olefin products	1967–73	13.0	Suspended
Seawater desalting and by-products recovery	1969–75	16.0	Ongoing
Remotely controlled undersea oil-drilling rig, first phase	1970–74	17.0	Ongoing
Electric automobile	1971–75	16.0	Ongoing
Pattern information processing system	1971–78	114.0	Ongoing
Turbofan engine for aircraft, first phase	1971–75	22.0	Ongoing
Direct steelmaking process using high-temperature deoxidized gas	1973–79	24.0	Ongoing
Comprehensive motor vehicle traffic control technology	1973–78	16.0	Ongoing

The selection of the projects is guided by the following criteria:[88]

—Projects should have a prospect for providing technical advances for a wide sector of the economy—what economists call "high social returns."

—Projects should be unable to be undertaken by private firms because of the requirements of large investment, long-term gestation period, absence of profit motives, high risk, and so on—situations economists call "market failure."

—Projects should utilize technologies that can be clearly specified; extensive basic research should not be required.

—Projects should be carried out cooperatively by universities, government laboratories, and industry; projects involving only one firm are usually rejected.

Selection of projects begins with suggestions from companies, universities,

88. Ibid., p. 10.

and government laboratories; further modifications are made by the agency and the MITI. Final approval is given by an agency advisory council comprising representatives from the universities, industry, and public. Projects are managed by an agency development officer, with various tasks assigned to companies, government laboratories, and universities. Each is reimbursed its full costs, with companies often further benefiting from a three-year, non-exclusive, royalty discounted or reduced license of patents resulting from the project. (Eventually the patents are made available to all Japanese firms.) The success of these projects cannot be evaluated, since only a few have been completed. None has developed commercial products, and development is being continued by the industrial contractors with their own funds.

A second, separate agency program provides subsidies for other industrial research that is considered important to the economy but unlikely to be carried out without such help. Proposals originate with companies, who pay half the development cost. This is a relatively small program; in 1972 it involved fifty-three projects but a government expenditure of only about $7.7 million.[89] Patents, designs, and research results belong exclusively to the developing company.

More widespread use is made of several tax concessions: accelerated depreciation is provided for pilot plant construction for new technology; accelerated depreciation is also provided for the construction of research facilities and for the initial expenses of research associations; and a partial tax exemption is given to corporate profits originating in receipts from the sale of technology abroad. A quantitative estimate of the importance of these tax subsidies is unavailable, but the general impression given during interviews was that such tax incentives were not a major factor in Japanese industrial research and development spending.

Activities of the national research laboratories represent a third program of the agency. In general, laboratories emphasize applied science: that is, research that falls between that directed at scientific publication and that directed toward specific patentable products or processes.[90] Research results from those laboratories are useful mostly to large firms, in contrast to those from the local government research institutes described earlier. Four of the sixteen agency laboratories, however, work on the research needs of their region rather than a specific engineering field.[91]

Another significant agency activity is administration of national standards. Governments set standards in most industrial nations but these appear to

89. Ibid., pp. 11–12, supplemented by interviews with Japanese government officials.
90. For a description of these laboratories as of 1972, see ibid., pp. 18–44.
91. Ibid., pp. 18–44, supplemented by interviews with Japanese government officials.

play a larger role in Japan, which has standards for about 8,000 items. Standards in their present form were instituted about fifteen years ago to raise export quality; initially they were applied largely to exports but are now commonly used domestically. The standards are not compulsory, but they are often specified in purchases by government agencies, companies, wholesalers, and exporters. Standards are held to have several benefits for technical change:

—By emphasizing best practice, they tend to promote diffusion of technology among laggards by providing a strong incentive to conform. Government publications are often available to show how to produce products that will meet standards.

—Standards facilitate subcontracting by providing a clear definition of what is wanted for purchase.

—Standards reduce spare parts inventory by providing interchangeability of parts. This has proved helpful in foreign markets. An example cited was the marketing of Japanese bicycles in Southeast Asia, where the local repairman could serve most Japanese-made bicycles with a small inventory of parts.

Standards could have adverse effects on innovation by discouraging the introduction of nonstandard products, particularly those offering tradeoffs between quality and price different from those contemplated in the standards, and criticism of this kind has been made in Japan, as it has in other countries. Japanese officials point out, however, that the standards are voluntary and most innovations involve radically different products, such as a new alloy, for which no standards will as yet exist.[92]

OTHER AGENCIES AND INDUSTRIAL TECHNOLOGY. The Science and Technology Agency in the Office of the Prime Minister also administers major programs having an impact on industrial technology. The distinguishing characteristic of its programs is a greater emphasis on basic science than on industrial application. Three-quarters of the agency's budget in 1972 was allocated for two projects: promotion of atomic energy as a source of power and promotion of space development. The first has an obvious economic potential, but in contrast to the MITI's projects the economic gains are farther in the future.[93]

Almost all other government ministries sponsor research programs and

92. Standards are not set for new products until they have been on the market for some time so that design and production technology can become stabilized. See ibid., p. 13, which was supplemented by interviews with Japanese government officials.

93. Science and Technology Agency, *Science and Technology Agency: An Outline* (1972).

laboratories to serve their particular needs. The Ministry of Agriculture and Forestry carries on a large-scale program of agricultural research; the Ministry of Health and Welfare carries out medical research; the Defense Agency supports military research; and the Ministries of Transport, Communication, and Construction support research related to their functions. Examples of smaller-scale research activities are the National Research Institute of Police in the National Public Safety Commission, the Radio Research Institute in the Ministry of Post and Telecommunications, and the Printing Research Institute of the Printing Bureau in the Ministry of Finance.[94]

GOVERNMENT AND THE COMPUTER INDUSTRY. The most entensive government involvement in a particular industry involves computers. The statutory basis for these measures is the 1971 law concerning "Temporary Measures for the Promotion of Specified Electronic Industries and Specified Machinery Industries."[95] That statute authorizes the government to formulate an improvement plan for individual industries. The improvement plan for computers announced in November 1971 represented a program of government support unmatched for any other Japanese industry. The Japanese computer industry, under firm government guidance, was to be reorganized from six manufacturing firms into three groups. The government was to fund (about $100 million) development of a high-performance computer, to be completed by 1978, as well as development of several smaller computers and peripheral equipment (another $100 million) on a matching basis. Japan's quasi-government computer rental company would continue its large loan program so manufacturers could refinance rentals and receive an immediate return; the Japanese Development Bank would also make loans available for improving the efficiency of computer manufacturing. Special tax-free reserves were established against which the return of leased computers could be charged by manufacturers, and tax benefits were also provided for users of computers to encourage purchase. Measures had been taken in 1970 in the software area, to encourage the development of computer programs, to purchase existing programs to make them widely available, and to guarantee loans to software firms.[96]

These measures reflect concern about American—and particularly IBM —dominance of the computer industry,[97] intensified by the prospective lib-

94. Ibid., especially the organization chart following p. 36.

95. For a discussion, see Japanese Computer Usage Development Institute, *Computer White Paper, 1972: A Summary of Highlights Compiled from the Japanese Original* (1972), p. 33.

96. Ibid., pp. 34–36.

97. The Computer White Paper states: "The structure of the computer industry is, on a ·world-wide basis, overwhelmingly dominated by American firms as is seen from

eralization of trade and investment in computers that could expose the Japanese computer industry to direct competition from American firms in the Japanese market.[98]

The computer industry is often cited as an example of "Japan Incorporated," the close cooperation of government and business to promote Japanese industry at the expense of foreign firms. The computer industry, however, is an exception: no other major industry has a share of the world market comparable to that held by one American firm, nor do foreign firms in other industries approach IBM's share of the Japanese market. Further, the Japanese government believes that improved computer technology holds vast implications for productivity in other industries. Perhaps these two factors have made this the major Japanese industry with extensive government support.

University-Based Research

Japanese universities accounted for 16 percent of the nation's R&D expenditures in 1972, divided between externally and self-financed research. Externally financed research, about 8 percent of all university R&D expenditures, represents grants made for specific projects. (About six-sevenths of the external funds come from the government and the remainder from industry.)[99] The remaining 92 percent is part of the regular university budget financed from government appropriations (in the case of public universities) and tuition income (in the case of private universities). The amounts are for both teaching and research. Such intermingling of the two functions is most obvious in the chair system found in the national universities, by which the professor holding the chair receives a regular research allowance along with funds for research assistants. The intent—followed through with much less

---

the fact that they control 94% of the world's markets. IBM alone controls 70% of the U.S. market and 66% of the world market and thus has unrivaled hegemony. No other firm has attained a size one-tenth that of IBM and there results a Gulliver-type economic structure consisting of one giant and a number of Lilliputians. As the Japanese computer industry controls a mere 2% of the world's markets, the influence of IBM and other large foreign manufacturers is very great." Ibid., p. 20.

98. The manufacturing, sale, and rental of computers is to be completely liberalized by May 1, 1976, at which time American firms would have no restriction on their investments in Japan. Until then investment requires government approval unless the amount of foreign investment per investor is less than 10 percent of the total equity of a Japanese computer firm and the total amount of foreign ownership is less than 15 percent of the firm. See Ozawa, *Japan's Technological Challenge*, p. 61.

99. These figures include research in the social sciences and humanities, but the major part is for the natural sciences. See Bureau of Statistics, *Report on the Survey of Research and Development in Japan* (1973), pp. 50–51.

success in other Japanese universities—is to guarantee resources for research. The Japanese system is similar to that in continental Europe but in contrast to the system of financing research by short-term projects found in the United States. The more institutionalized chair system avoids the exhausting hunt for contracts and grants, but since chair allocations and budgets are seldom changed, the system is also more rigid in allocations between individuals and fields.[100]

Another feature of Japanese universities is the existence of the research institutes attached to them. These account for about 6 percent of the reported R&D expenditures included in the 92 percent of self-financed expenditures.[101] The institutes are found in most national, public (or local), and private universities, but 93 percent of the institute expenditures are made by the seventy-three institutes affiliated with the national universities.[102]

The smaller institutes tend to be closely linked with the senior faculty of the university, who have joint faculty-institute appointments. The junior personnel are full-time researchers who often move after a few years into teaching appointments at the affiliated university or elsewhere. The larger institutes are more independent of their universities and draw some of their researchers on leaves of absence or a part-time basis from other universities. Several large institutes have been specifically designated as "common use facilities," and some of these, such as the world famous Institute of Plasma Physics at Nagoya, are not affiliated with a university. Funding for these common use institutes comes from the Science and Technology Agency as well as the Ministry of Education.

Scientists who have worked at the large institutes in Japan and in large American universities report that both institutions have ample research budgets and adequate equipment, though the American universities enjoy a higher level of equipment maintenance and secretarial support. American programs suffer more from fluctuations and uncertainties in funding, reflecting the project system, whereas once a research institute has been established in Japan, its budget tends to be renewed annually, with major questions arising only following requests for expansion. A sharper difference in the level of research support can be seen when a comparison is made between the smaller Japanese institutes and the smaller American universities, in which case support for second-level research is more generous in the United States.

100. For a discussion of the two systems, see the Organisation for Economic Cooperation and Development, *The Research System* (Paris: OECD, 1972), pp. 79–81.
101. Bureau of Statistics, *Report on the Survey of Research and Development in Japan* (1973), p. 174.
102. Ibid., p. 172.

Japanese companies often have long-standing relationships with individual professors in science and engineering. Such professors tend to be associated with several companies, serving as their research advisers and sending
them their best students. The companies in turn often provide research funds
and stipends for promising research students. But the process of interaction
between universities and industry is limited by the lack of large staffs of
basic researchers in Japanese firms. Large American chemical and electronic
companies in particular have sizable basic research staffs carrying on work
that is science-oriented and publicized in scientific journals and academic
conferences. Such U.S. scientists also tend to be mobile between universities,
the government, and industrial research laboratories.

It is unclear, however, what role the most advanced science plays in the
technological change necessary for economic growth—and thus how much
Japanese industrial progress is hindered by the comparatively low level of
support for basic research in Japanese universities. Basic science is likely to
be published extensively and to be freely available worldwide, and a long
gestation period is likely to be necessary before its industrial application.
Still, there are suggestions that the lag between scientific discovery and economic application is growing shorter, so in developing new products it may
become increasingly important to have the latest research easily obtainable.
And in a more general relation between technology and science, the quality
of basic research often determines the general quality of both scientific and
engineering training in a country.[103] Either way, the level of university science could be a constraint upon a country's achievement of technological
leadership.

It is impossible to say whether the present level of Japanese academic science constitutes such a constraint. Japanese academic science is of high
quality and suffers by comparison only with the United States—and then
not in the general quality but only with respect to being at the frontiers. Some
Japanese industrial research executives are becoming concerned about the
level and quality of domestic basic research, and these concerns are apparent
in a report of the government's Council for Science and Technology.[104] The
American experience suggests that a parallel expansion of basic research in
industry may also be necessary to capitalize effectively on an increase in
academic research.

103. See OECD, *The Research System*, vol. 1, p. 204.
104. Council for Science and Technology, *The Fundamentals of Comprehensive
Science Policy for the 1970s*, p. 31.

Manpower for Science and Technology

Two propositions can be used to consider issues relevant to Japan's supply of engineers and scientists. The first holds that Japan's postwar economic growth was greatly facilitated by an ample and increasing supply of professionals. The second, more tentative and certainly more controversial, holds that the qualitative characteristics of Japan's engineers and scientists are better suited to a kind of catch-up technology than to pioneering in the most advanced fields.

The Supply of Professional Manpower

The Japanese people entered the postwar era with a relatively high level of education: literacy was almost universal and secondary and university education almost as widespread as in Western Europe. From this starting point there occurred an increase in professional manpower during the 1950s and 1960s such that by 1971 Japan ranked high in the international comparisons of engineers and scientists per 1,000 population—ahead of West Germany, France, and the United Kingdom, though still well behind the United States.[105]

The total stock of engineers and scientists, however, is only the crudest measure of the availability of technical manpower and indicates little about the relation of supply and demand. The wages of engineers and scientists relative to the general wage level provide a better indicator, although only very gross data are available. The increased supply of university graduates in Japan in the last decade is reflected in the decline in the ratio of starting salaries of all university graduates to the starting salary of graduates of middle school (the end of compulsory education). This ratio—for male graduates only—was 2.63 in 1954 and 1.54 in 1971, a dramatic shift that is explained at least in part by university enrollments that have more than doubled.[106] In 1973, however, engineers and scientists continued to com-

105. Science and Technology Agency, *White Paper on Science and Technology* (1974), table 2-5-1, p. 327. Japan had 1.9 qualified scientists and engineers per 1,000 population in 1971, as compared with 2.6 for United States, 0.8 for the United Kingdom (1970), 1.4 for West Germany, and 1.1 for France.

106. Ministry of Education, *Basic Guidelines for the Reform of Education* (1972), p. 106; and Bureau of Statistics, *Japanese Statistical Yearbook, 1972,* p. 408. The decline in salary differences was a general trend in postwar Japan; the factors involved are discussed in Chapter 9.

mand a salary premium above that paid other university graduates: in several large companies their starting salaries were said to be about 10 percent above those of business and economics graduates.

Relative wages are an imperfect indicator of trends in this market, given the sluggishness of adjustments. Another measure of the relative availability is the proportion of professionals among total R&D personnel, which includes technicians, research assistants, and others without university training. With a plentiful supply of professional manpower the ratio would be high; scarcity forces the substitution of paraprofessionals for professionals. By this measure Japan appears to have a plentiful supply, ranking only behind the United States in the proportion of its R&D labor force that is professional.[107]

Although market forces were largely responsible for the increase in the number of scientists and engineers, governmental planning also contributed. Beginning in 1955 the Ministry of Education became concerned that the number of scientists and engineers would be inadequate for the achievement of the economic growth projected by the government. The ministry set forth a plan to increase the number of science and engineering graduates by 1962, the final year of the new long-term economic plan. It estimated a demand in 1962 for about 27,500 graduates, whereas the existing educational capacity was 19,500 graduates. The plan to increase capacity by about 8,000 graduates was accomplished by 1960, two years earlier than the target year,[108] but with little direct government spending or explicit direction of the educational system. A system of entrance quotas was established annually for each school and faculty within a school. These quotas were fairly decisive in determining actual enrollment in the national and local public universities. For private universities, however, they played almost no role, for private universities exceeded their quotas by almost 100 percent in some years.[109]

After fulfillment of the first plan, the Ministry of Education launched another plan based on estimated requirements during the 1960s for science

107. The percentage of professionals in total R&D personnel in 1962 was as follows: Japan, 33.7 percent; United States, 37.6; United Kingdom, 27.8; France, 25.2; West Germany, 28.1. See OECD, *Review of National Science Policy: Japan*, pp. 72–73; and Christopher Freeman and A. Young, *The R&D Effort in Western Europe, North America, and the Soviet Union* (Paris: OECD, 1965), p. 72.

108. Ministry of Education, *Wagakuni no kōtō kyōiku: Sengo ni okeru kōtō kyōiku no ayumi* [Higher Education in Japan: Progress of Higher Education in the Post War Period] (1964), pp. 100–01.

109. Henry Birnbaum, "Japanese Educational Patterns in Science and Engineering," *Science*, vol. 181, Sept. 28, 1973, pp. 1224–25.

and engineering graduates. The number of new enrollments for science and engineering increased from 30,694 in 1960 to 89,661 in 1970, an increase in excess of government targets.[110] The increase in technical enrollment, however, was not achieved by a redirection of higher education toward engineering and science; the proportion of enrollment in those two fields increased only slightly. Rather, the major source of the increase in the number of engineers and scientists was the massive overall increase in university enrollment.[111]

This expansion was not without its drawbacks. The student-teacher ratio in higher education increased from 19.6 in 1959 to 25.6 in 1969; it is now significantly higher than in the United States (15.4) and the United Kingdom (7.9), but comparable to that of France (22.6) and West Germany (28.3).[112] These ratios and lower relative faculty salaries have resulted in a low cost per student: expressed as a percent of per capita national income to reflect relative wage rates, the Japanese cost per university student is about half that of Britain and Germany and comparable to that of the United States.[113] There is a wide discrepancy in Japan between the cost per student in the private sector and the public sector, with cost per student in private universities only a third of that in public universities.[114] Engineering and science enrollment, however, tends to be concentrated in the better financed national universities, with proportionally fewer in the private institutions.[115]

Japan's treatment of its universities has been much criticized by scholars

110. For 1960 data, see Ministry of Education, *Higher Education in Japan,* p. 101; for 1970 data, see Ministry of Education, *Gakkō kihon chōsa hōkokusho* [Basic Report on Educational Institutions] (1970), pp. 102, 107.

111. See data in Ministry of Education, *Educational Standards in Japan* (1970), pp. 207–08.

112. The figures reported for the United States, United Kingdom, France, and West Germany are for the years 1968, 1967, and 1966, respectively. Ibid., pp. 100, 223. The national universities have a student-faculty ratio of 8.1, comparable to that of the United Kingdom. Birnbaum, "Japanese Educational Patterns," p. 1225.

113. The comparisons reflect both private and public expenditure on higher education. Ministry of Education, *Educational Standards in Japan,* pp. 109, 243. Based on 1967 data; the low U.S. ratio reflects a higher level of national income per capita.

114. Calculated from data in ibid., p. 247.

115. In 1971 the national universities had about 40 percent of the science undergraduate enrollment and about 25 percent of the engineering enrollment, whereas these universities had about 20 percent of overall enrollment. Two-thirds of the national universities, but only a quarter of the private universities, have engineering or science programs. Birnbaum, "Educational Patterns," pp. 1224–26. In some of Japan's leading universities engineering students account for a large share of the enrollment: 55 percent of the students at Osaka University and 41 percent at Kyoto were in engineering in 1967. William K. Cummings, "The Japanese Private University," *Minerva,* vol. 11, (July 1973), p. 358.

of higher education. Economizing on university resources is said to result in faculty and student unrest and, in the longer run, alienation of faculty and many students from the rest of society.[116] The alternative of restricting enrollment and utilizing more resources per student, a policy followed in the United Kingdom, would create a different set of problems—greater scarcity of university-educated manpower and a denial of educational opportunity. It is as difficult to evaluate these two policies for higher education as it is a third, one much favored by professional educators—that is, simply to increase the resources devoted to higher education.

Qualitative Aspects of Technical Manpower

Engineering education in Japan is similar in form to that in the United States. Both are four-year programs of similar courses, and American textbooks often are used.[117] This close correspondence reflects the general reorganization of Japanese education to match American practices during the occupation. The major differences are that Japan has a higher faculty-student ratio and a smaller provision for such other resources as laboratory facilities.

But the principal point is that Japan provided its industry with a large and growing supply of technical manpower. For these professionals two features of Japanese society may have mitigated the effect of educating large numbers at low cost in the universities: the rigor of high school instruction in mathematics and the post-university training provided by large companies to their engineers. The quality of Japanese mathematical instruction is reflected in Japan's high ranks in international mathematics tests administered to a sample of thirteen- and eighteen-year-olds in twelve countries.[118]

The elaborate character of post-university training can be illustrated by the practices of one internationally known company.[119] This company treats

116. For an analysis of the problems of the Japanese universities and attempts at reform, see Kazuyuki Kitamura and William K. Cummings, "The 'Big Bang' Theory and Japanese University Reform," *Comparative Education Review,* vol. 16 (June 1972), pp. 303–24.

117. A comparison of courses in mechanical and chemical engineering in the two countries shows only one major difference: that the Japanese curriculum allocates time to foreign languages (mainly English), whereas the American curriculum does not. See Ministry of Education, *Japan's Growth and Education* (1963), p. 85.

118. See Chapter 12, as well as Ministry of Education, *Educational Standards in Japan,* pp. 68–69.

119. This section is based on the authors' interviews. Other large companies have similar programs, although some make a distinction at the outset between those hired for R&D and those for production. The third-year thesis is a distinctive feature of this company.

its newly hired engineers as trainees for the first three years and rotates them through a variety of assignments, including both production and research. The trainees are also given occasional two-week courses at the company's educational center. In the third year each trainee is assigned a thesis, an individual paper to be written on a technical topic. At the end of the third year the trainees are given permanent assignments, to either R&D or production.

Training is continued even after the third year. Each engineering section has monthly seminars, featuring presentations by its members, engineers and managers from elsewhere in the company, and occasionally faculty from nearby universities. These are supplemented by one- and two-week full-time courses at the educational center. Quite apart from their technical content, the seminars and the short courses appear to have the function of solidifying morale and promoting company policies. A few engineers are sent abroad or, less occasionally, to a Japanese university for graduate training.[120] Another training technique, also used selectively, is the temporary assignment of senior engineers to different functions—as, for example, the shift of a development engineer to a manufacturing operation.

American and British firms, of course, also have training programs for their technical personnel, but these are typically not as elaborate as those in Japan. An obvious explanation of the difference is that Japanese engineers are considered to be committed to a lifetime career in a particular firm. Therefore, it pays the Japanese firm to make such an extensive investment in training.[121]

In interviews with Japanese R&D executives, particularly those with American experience, an effort was made to assess the value of this kind of training in the context of a pattern of lifetime career in one organization. The Japanese engineer was said to be more familiar than the American engineer with the capabilities and problems of his own company but less familiar with practices in other companies and university research in his

120. The phenomenon of lifetime employment raises the question of how the Japanese firms shift the mix between different engineering specialties—between, say, electrical and mechanical engineers. This is done largely in the new hiring, although instances were cited of sending individual employees to master's degree programs to provide more senior personnel in a specialty in short supply. There was also some hiring away of experienced personnel in scarce specialties, largely from university faculties and government laboratories rather than other firms.

121. The lifetime commitment is, of course, not universal even in Japan. Instances were cited of engineers moving to smaller companies or to engineering teaching positions, as well as funding their own companies. Movement among large firms, except among those in the same group, seems to be rare.

specialty.[122] A few executives ventured the opinion that the Japanese career pattern is better suited for applying and improving technology, which often involves close working relations with production engineers, whereas the American pattern is better suited to major technological innovation.

Another distinctive feature is that the Japanese mix of technical manpower is heavily weighted toward a large number of engineers relative to the number of scientists. In 1963 Japan had a ratio of seven engineers to one scientist, whereas the United States, the United Kingdom, and France had, respectively, three, one, and three engineers for each scientist.[123] A smaller proportion of Japanese technical manpower also is trained at the graduate level. Thus, the annual number of doctors' degrees awarded in science and engineering has been only half that of the United Kingdom and of France and a tenth that of the United States, whereas the undergraduate enrollment in engineering and science has been significantly larger in Japan than in the United Kingdom and France and two-thirds that of the United States.[124]

The training represented by the bachelor's degree in engineering appears to be well suited to the widespread diffusion of technical innovations. In the initial development of the technically advanced products, however, a significant number of scientists with graduate training may be required. Here, again, Japan's education system appears more in line with the catch-up phase than with research leadership, particularly in fields producing technically advanced products.

Other characteristics of Japan's technical manpower pool also seem best suited to adaptation and improvement: the strong identification with the firm rather than the profession, the emphasis on training within the company rather than at a university graduate school, and the lifelong career in one company rather than mobility across companies. But it is unclear how immutable these differences would be if Japanese industry should shift its de-

122. The Japanese interviewees may overestimate the mobility of American engineers, since their experience was with American electronic firms, which, particularly in the 1950s and 1960s, experienced considerable movement of engineers between companies.

123. For Japan, see OECD, *Review of National Science Policy: Japan,* pp. 188–89; for the United Kingdom, France, and the United States, OECD, *Resources of Scientific and Technical Personnel in the OECD Area* (Paris: OECD, 1963), p. 130. (The low ratio for the United Kingdom reflects the fact that many British engineers are trained outside universities and as nongraduates are not counted in the computations.) These ratios are also reflected in university entrance quotas in Japan, as set by the Minister of Education. Those quotas in 1971 provided for about five engineers for each scientist. Birnbaum, "Japanese Educational Patterns," p. 1224.

124. Ministry of Education, *Educational Standards,* pp. 211, 214.

mand for researchers toward the science-oriented style of some large American corporations.

Japanese R&D executives point out that at present there is no shortage of able scientists who could be hired by industry. There is, however, a shortage of individuals to serve as project leaders, a position that requires both executive ability and an extensive scientific background. The United States and Great Britain were held by Japanese executives to have more such individuals, largely as the result of government-funded R&D for military purposes. Yet if the demand for such professionals were to become extensive in Japanese industry, it may well be that, with some time lags, the scientific community could provide them.

Overview of the Japanese Experience

This section draws together some factors in the Japanese success and examines some future problems Japan may encounter.

Factors in Japanese Success in Applying Technology

Japan stands out in the postwar period as an example of purposive national effort to apply technology to achieve economic growth. Most nations have undergone the rhetoric of such an effort. Thus, British Prime Minister Harold Wilson established the Ministry of Science and Technology in 1966 and promised a "white hot technical revolution."[125] Senior governmental officials in the United States have spoken repeatedly through the 1960s and 1970s of relying on American technology for growth and improved trade performance. Only in Japan do the achievements appear to have matched the words.

Japan did not apply its technology resources to purposes remote from economic growth. In contrast, the academic basic science establishments in the United Kingdom and the United States have obtained significant shares of the R&D resources of the two countries. Both countries have supported large defense establishments that consumed even greater shares of the R&D resources. The United States had its space effort and Britain its Concorde project, both of which could improve research capabilities but inherently had little immediate impact on measured economic growth. Their returns were in prestige rather than increases in gross national product.

125. *The Economist,* March 19, 1966, p. 1147.

A second factor that distinguishes Japan is the range of policies in applying technology. The British and American approaches appear rather timid, limited for the most part to modest attempts to encourage commercial application—by, for example, increasing the supply of scientists and engineers, some tax concessions, occasional direct government financing of commercial R&D, and some industry-oriented work in government laboratories. There has been great reluctance in these two countries to interfere with decision-making within firms, to carry on any large amount of industrial R&D with public funds, or to alter the structure of industry.

Japanese policy has been bolder. To be sure, research and development has been privately financed and privately executed to an even greater extent than in Britain or the United States, though most of this difference actually stems from the absence of extensive defense R&D. The basic mechanism of Japanese allocation of R&D has been the market, and the guiding incentive, private profitability. But as has been observed, the market system is overlaid with extensive government intervention, particularly in the control of import of technology. This intervention has become less comprehensive as foreign exchange transactions have been liberalized, but there still remains some informal guidance and intervention by the MITI, the extent and character of which are difficult to discern.

There are also three further characteristics to consider in evaluating the MITI's role. First, Japanese government intervention is imposed primarily on those concentrated industries—steel, petroleum, chemicals, computers —which in the United States and Britain are subject to antitrust action, price-wage guidelines, government procurement actions, import quotas, and the like. Thus, the comparison is not simply between Japanese activism and Western laissez-faire but between two sets of governmental policies. Second, Japanese industry is more export oriented than industry in the United States (but not more so than that in the United Kingdom) and hence more subject to the pressures of international competition for efficiency and growth. Third, Japan's general economic setting—characterized by rapid growth, high profits, and high rates of investment—has been one which would tend to make the economic gains for new technology impressive, with or without MITI controls.

Yet to ascribe Japan's successful application of technology to economic growth solely to the general economic setting or to MITI policy ignores those Japanese institutions which encouraged rapid diffusion and those extensive research and development activities which modified imported technology.

These same institutions could give Japan a comparative advantage in the application of technology. Japan might continue to import technology, but its speed of application could exceed that of other industrial countries. Given more efficient diffusion, the impetus for growth from technology could still be greater than in other countries. Japan might consistently be first in being second—that is, the most successful follower. The reasons would be a variant of those factors that make a country a technological leader: possession of resources for improvement R&D and of institutions that make this kind of R&D highly productive.

Relying on imported technology, however, does raise problems in the application of the latest technology. Here, the dividing line between application of technology and initial research is blurred. Further, the problems of reasonable payment for imported technology become more acute. This suggests that Japan will find a need to rely more on domestic research and development. The Japanese economy can be viewed as having two margins for the application of its R&D resources—one for adapting technology and one for initial development. The returns from adaptation may be smaller in the future and require some reallocation of R&D efforts toward initial development. Yet if Japan has the comparative advantage in followership suggested above, the shifts required for the most advantageous use of technology in the next decade may be relatively minor.

Changing Priorities in the Application of Technology

The major issues of the late 1970s may lie not in the application of technology to economic growth but rather in attempting to use technology to achieve other social goals—particularly those concerning the environment.[126] In recent reports the Japanese government has adopted this emphasis for

126. See Council for Science and Technology, *The Fundamentals of Comprehensive Science and Technology Policy for the 1970s.* A poetic expression of this change in view is found on page 13 of "Industrial Policy and MITI's Role," released by the MITI Information Office in June 1973: "The Blue Bird the Japanese had been in quest of has been the strengthening of Japan's materialistic production capacity. The Blue Bird of today, however, is taking on various different tinges of color. They are a beautiful land, a life worth living, or a decent life." A more explicit statement of this change in priorities is the following: "If science and technology are to meet the diversified needs of modern society and solve the problems now facing us, it will be necessary to introduce a change in the direction of scientific and technological development. Science and technology must function not merely as a means of producing 'good' but as a factor for balanced progress of society, closely related to other equally important factors for development—namely, nature and man." Science and Technology Agency, *White Paper on Science and Technology: New Demands and Responses to Them* (English summary) (1972), p. 15. See also Science and Technology Agency, *1972 White Paper on Science and Technology: Science and Technology Aiming at Society Hopeful* (English summary) (1973), especially pt. 1.

science and technology. The shift in emphasis was accompanied by a recognition that the technology Japan needs for solving such problems is difficult to obtain abroad, simply because other industrial societies also have only begun to recognize such needs.[127] There was also recognition that research expenditures for social objectives cannot depend primarily on private market incentives, since the possibility of profits from research on pollution are modest compared with those from research on improved products or processes.

The actual measures to implement this shift in priorities have been threefold. First, there was an increase in R&D in pollution control by central government research institutes. From 1971 to 1972 these expenditures almost doubled, but still reached only about $8 million.[128] Second, from 1971 to 1972 there was also a 62 percent increase in private corporate spending for pollution R&D, to a level of $152 million.[129] Nearly half of these expenditures were by the motor vehicle industry. Third, local government research institutes (financed largely through local government budgets) had a smaller increase in pollution R&D—only 14 percent from 1971 to 1972—but their 1972 level was $13.9 million, more than that of the central government.[130]

As the absolute sums suggest, R&D in pollution control remained only a small part of the total R&D effort: in 1972, about 3.1 percent of the R&D expenditures of government research institutes and about 4.4 percent of corporate R&D expenditures.[131]

Given the massive transition problems of redirecting R&D, the small proportions are not surprising. Plans for the future call for further sharp increases in pollution research. A sizable redirection of R&D resources toward such social objectives would require more pioneering R&D and more public spending than has been customary, requirements that are recognized in Japanese government reports. Japan, however, is not without sectors in which publicly financed R&D expenditures dominate: nuclear energy and the space program have been mentioned.[132] Thus, there are both precedents and experience for organizing public R&D. What remains uncertain is how great a

127. Science and Technology Agency, *White Paper on Science and Technology: New Demands and Responses to Them,* p. 18.
128. Dollar values were obtained by using an exchange rate of ¥280 = $1. Bureau of Statistics, *Report on the Survey of Research and Development in Japan* (1972), p. 157; (1973), p. 163.
129. Ibid. (1972), p. 133; (1973), p. 137.
130. Ibid. (1972), p. 157; (1973), p. 163.
131. Calculated from data in ibid. (1973), pp. 136–37, 163.
132. See Science and Technology Agency, *Science and Technology Agency: An Outline* (1972), pp. 12 ff.; and Roy Lockheimer, "Science and Technology," in *Area Handbook on Japan* (American University, 1974), pp. 246–61.

sacrifice will be made in the use of R&D for economic growth to achieve the new quality-of-life goals.

In the fall of 1973 Japan was badly rocked by the sharp rise in the cost of oil, which may lead to a still different set of research priorities involving reduction in energy costs. Like pollution research, such priorities could require significant increases in public spending on R&D. The effect of concern about both pollution and energy may well be that Japan's R&D sector will move to a greater reliance on public financing, and that neither moderating the pollution problem nor offsetting the rising cost of energy will produce the direct gains for economic growth that technology was able to provide for Japan in the 1950s and 1960s.

CHAPTER NINE

The Japanese Labor Market

Walter Galenson, Cornell University
with the collaboration of
Konosuke Odaka, Hitotsubashi University

Conclusions   669

Tables

THE GREAT Japanese economic drive of the past two decades has been fueled by a relatively abundant supply of labor. Some tightening in the labor market occurred as the 1960s progressed, but it would be difficult to demonstrate that a higher rate of growth might have obtained had there been a continuing abundance in the labor supply. This situation has had a profound effect upon the major institutions of the labor market: the wage system, tenure of employment, the structure and power of the labor movement, and the system of collective bargaining.

Labor Supply and Demand

There are differences of opinion in Japan on the outlook for the 1970s. Some observers maintain that, despite a sharply reduced rate of growth in the labor force, the supply will continue to be adequate to permit a high rate of economic expansion. Others argue that the labor factor may become a real constraint, and that labor shortages not only will retard growth but also may impair the viability of existing labor market institutions.

Statistical Indicators

The data in Table 9-1 show that Japan was relatively well endowed with manpower during the 1960s. In terms of population of working age and total labor force, the annual percentage growth rate exceeded that of the major member nations of the Organisation for Economic Co-operation and Development (OECD), except for the United States, by a wide margin.

Note. During our visits to Japan, many individuals in government, management, labor unions, and universities interrupted busy schedules to give us the benefit of their advice. Since they are too numerous to name individually, we would like to thank them collectively for their many courtesies. Several experts on Japanese labor problems were kind enough to let us have their detailed comments on a preliminary version of the manuscript: Professor Robert E. Cole of the University of Michigan, Professor Ronald Dore of the University of Sussex, Professor Robert Evans, Jr., of Brandeis University, and Professor Solomon B. Levine of the University of Wisconsin. Discussions with staff members of the Japanese Institute of Labor in Tokyo were of great value, and we are also indebted to the institute for scheduling interviews. Dr. Haruo Shimada of Keiō University helped make our stay in Tokyo more profitable. Our colleagues on the project did not spare the rod, for which we are grateful, at least in retrospect. None of the foregoing persons should be implicated in any of the views expressed in this paper; however misguided, they are our own.

Table 9-1. *Average Annual Change in Manpower, Major OECD Countries, 1960–70*

Percent

Country	Population aged 15–64	Total labor force	Wage earners and salaried employees
Japan	1.9	1.3	3.4
France	1.1	0.8	2.0
West Germany	0.3	0.3	0.9
Italy	0.7	−0.7	0.9
United Kingdom	0.3	0.2	0.2
United States	1.6	1.8	2.5

Source: Organisation for Economic Co-operation and Development, *Labour Force Statistics 1959–1970* (Paris: OECD, 1972).

The rate of growth in number of wage earners and salaried employees was particularly high, indicating that the relatively large number of self-employed workers in Japan was being drawn down to satisfy the manpower demands of the rapidly expanding large enterprises.[1]

Table 9-2 contains comparative data on the distribution of the labor force among three broad economic sectors for 1960 and 1970. Among the major OECD countries only Italy's labor force reserve in agriculture was as large as Japan's in 1960. This reserve was substantially reduced in both countries by the end of the decade, but because of demographic differences, changing labor force participation rates, or (in the case of Italy) emigration, the growth of the industrial and service sector labor force in Italy lagged far behind that of Japan. The remarkable increase in the Japanese industrial labor force reflected—and made possible—the country's rapid economic growth. This did not take place, however, at the expense of the service sector, which itself showed a labor force increase greater than all other countries except the United States.

The Japanese labor force bonanza of the 1960s was due essentially to a baby boom from 1947 to 1949 plus a sharp decline in the death rate. But "before ten years had passed after the start of the baby boom, the annual birth count was cut in half—a rate of decline without precedent in world demographic history."[2]

1. Even in 1970, Japan still had only 65 percent of its labor force in wage and salaried positions, compared with 78 percent for France, 82 percent for Germany, 68 percent for Italy, 93 percent for the United Kingdom, and 90 percent for the United States. Organisation for Economic Co-operation and Development, *Labour Force Statistics 1959–1970* (Paris: OECD, 1972).

2. Minoru Tachi and Yōichi Okazaki, "Japan's Postwar Population and Labor Force," *The Developing Economies*, vol. 7 (June 1969), p. 173.

Table 9-2. *Distribution of the Labor Force in Major OECD Countries,
by Major Sector, 1960 and 1970*

Percent

Country	Agriculture, forestry, and fishing		Industry		Service and other	
	1960	1970	1960	1970	1960	1970
Japan	30.2	17.4	28.5	35.7	41.3	46.9
France	22.4	14.0	37.8	38.8	39.8	47.1
West Germany	14.0	9.0	48.8	50.3	37.3	40.7
Italy	32.8	19.6	36.9	43.7	30.2	36.7
United Kingdom	4.1	2.9	48.8	46.6	47.0	50.6
United States	8.3	4.4	33.6	32.3	58.1	63.3

Source: Same as Table 9-1. Figures are rounded.

These dramatic demographic changes produced a marked decline in
the availability of new recruits to the labor force, an effect reinforced by an
extension in years of schooling. The principal source of new blue-collar
workers for large enterprises had been middle school graduates aged fifteen,
but the number of these entering employment fell from a peak of 764,000
in 1963 to 324,000 in 1969. The number of secondary school graduates
who went into the labor market rose from 626,000 to 882,000 between
these two years, but many of these traditionally sought white-collar work.
The number of secondary school graduates who entered higher institutions
increased from 199,000 to 334,000, and thus the possibility of recruiting
them for blue-collar employment was lost.[3]

Along with a sharp reduction in supply there occurred a great increase in
demand. The ratio of new vacancies to new applications from middle school
graduates recorded by the public employment system rose from 1.2 in 1959
to 5.5 in 1972; the corresponding change for high school graduates was
from 1.1 to 3.2.[4] This growing imbalance led Japanese employers, particularly those who did most of their hiring directly out of schools, to talk of
manpower shortages.

Japan has had a relatively high labor force participation rate, particularly for women. In 1960 the rate for women was higher than that in the
other major OECD nations. Among the reasons were the relatively large
proportion of the Japanese labor force engaged in agriculture, the loss of

3. Japan Institute of Labor, *Japan Labor Statistics* (1970), p. 48.
4. Ibid., p. 47, and Bank of Japan, *Economic Statistics Annual, 1973* (March
1974), p. 263. Preliminary figures for 1973 indicate even higher ratios: 8.0 and 4.0,
respectively. *Japan Labor Bulletin*, Sept. 1, 1974.

males in World War II, low family income when there was only one wage earner, and late age of marriage. As these conditions changed, the overall rate of female participation fell, from 54.8 percent in fiscal 1960 to 48.1 percent in fiscal 1972,[5] although it still remained relatively high in the OECD ranks. There was a particularly severe drop in the propensity of younger women to work as more of them went on to secondary and higher education. Because of the increasing pressure on the labor market, the percentage of women over forty who reentered the labor market tended to rise as incomes became more attractive; this was particularly true of small enterprises, since the large firms preferred to hire directly from school.[6] But the recent employment trend for women overall has been a minus rather than a plus for labor supply.

The ability of the growth sectors of the economy to secure sufficient supplies of labor was due to mobility both among and within sectors. The big loser has been agriculture. Not only have the younger people in rural areas (including the eldest sons, who traditionally inherited the farms) taken nonagricultural jobs in pursuit of higher incomes, but many farm owners themselves have obtained industrial employment on a seasonal basis.[7]

During the 1950s, industry was attracting labor at the expense of the service sector, but in recent years the flow has been in the other direction.[8] The earlier flow reflected the typical pattern for a less developed economy, from low-productivity service trades to better paying industrial jobs. The relatively large service sector in 1960 (see Table 9-2), given Japan's level of economic development at the time, tends to substantiate this statement.[9] As the pool of low-paid service workers dried up and the normal trend toward service orientation in the modern sector set in, new entrants to the labor force, as well as persons employed in low-productivity manufacturing, provided a slowly increasing flow into service occupations, a process facilitated by rising educational standards.

The internal flow of manpower within manufacturing tends to support the conclusion that, although the supply of manpower is diminishing, crucial

5. Bureau of Statistics, Office of the Prime Minister, *Annual Report on the Labor Force Survey, 1972*, p. 157. The figures represent the ratio of the female labor force to the female population aged fifteen and over.

6. Shōjirō Ujihara, "The Labor Market," in Kazuo Ōkōchi, Bernard Karsh, and Solomon B. Levine (eds.), *Workers and Employers in Japan: The Japanese Employment Relations System* (Princeton University Press and University of Tokyo Press, 1974), p. 157.

7. Ibid., pp. 144–45.

8. Yoshio Kaneko, "Employment and Wages," *The Developing Economies*, vol. 8 (December 1970), pp. 454–55.

9. See Kōichi Emi, "Employment Structure in the Service Industries," *The Developing Economies*, vol. 7 (June 1969), passim.

shortages are not yet in evidence. Of 1.7 million employees newly hired by manufacturing enterprises in 1972, some 43 percent came from other manufacturing firms. The large firms, those with more than 1,000 employees, secured 24 percent of their intrasector hires from small firms (fewer than 30 employees). Because of the substantial wage difference between large and small firms, a tight labor market situation would have led to an even stronger movement of workers. But the percentage has been rising: it had been only 22 percent in 1971.[10]

Some reverse flow of manpower occurred: the small firms secured 7 percent of their intrasector hires from the large firms, but this probably consisted mainly of fifty-five-year-old retirees from the large firms and some young workers who could not adjust to working conditions in the large enterprises.

Contributing to the favorable labor market situation was a remarkable increase in labor productivity. From 1960 to 1970 industrial productivity rose by an average (compounded) annual rate of 11 percent; for manufacturing alone the figure was 10.7 percent. The rate fell somewhat in 1971, to 4.5 and 4.4 percent, respectively, because of the recession in that year; returned in 1972 to the trend rates, 11 and 11.1 percent; and increased in 1973 to astonishing levels, 19.8 percent for all industry, 20.1 percent for manufacturing—rates of productivity growth that are probably unmatched in the modern history of advanced nations.[11]

A full explanation of the Japanese productivity record is beyond the scope of this study. One element, however—the improved quality of the labor force—might be mentioned briefly. In 1965, 38.6 percent of newly graduated employees came from the middle schools, 50.6 percent from secondary schools, and 10.8 percent from higher schools. By 1972 there had been a drastic change in the ratios: to 16.0 percent, 57.6 percent, and 26.4 percent, respectively.[12] Although there is no precise relation between educational inputs and increases in labor productivity, the importance of this major change can hardly be doubted.

Future Need and Supply

In tandem with the widely held view that labor is already in short supply is the belief that once recovery from the oil shock of 1973 and the sub-

10. Ministry of Labor, *Year Book of Labor Statistics, 1972*, p. 29; and *1971*, p. 39.

11. Calculated from Japan Institute of Labor, *Japan Labor Statistics* (1970), pp. 122–23; and Japan Productivity Center, *Quarterly Journal of Productivity Statistics*, no. 63 (1974), pp. 8–9.

12. Calculated from Ministry of Labor, *Year Book of Labor Statistics, 1965*, p. 30; and *1972*, p. 16.

Table 9-3. *Estimated Rate of Change of Labor Inputs in Japan, 1960–80*

Percent

	Rate of change during period				
Input item	*1960–65*	*1965–70*	*1970–75*	*1975–80*	*1980–85*
Size of labor force	1.2	1.7	0.8	0.5	0.4
Adjustment factors					
Working hours	−1.0	−0.1	−1.0	−0.7	−0.4
Improvement in quality of education	0.2	0.4	0.4	0.3	0.3
Improvement in quality by changes in age and sex ratios	0.3	0.3	0.3	0.2	0.1
Labor input adjusted for quality	0.7	2.3	0.5	0.3	0.4

Source: Japan Economic Research Center, *The Outlook for a Trillion Dollar Economy* (1971), p. 2.

sequent economic downturn sets in, labor may become a critical constraint to economic growth. The demographic picture indicates some foundation for these fears. The labor force, which grew at the annual rate of 1.2 percent a year from fiscal 1965 to fiscal 1971, will increase at the much reduced annual rate of 0.75 percent a year for the period 1971–77—because of not only a declining rate of population growth in the relevant age groups but also an anticipated decline in the labor force participation rate of women, from 48.5 percent in 1971 to 46.2 percent in 1977.[13]

QUALITY ADJUSTMENT FACTORS. Estimates of labor inputs adjusted for educational improvement, a more experienced labor force, and a lower female-male ratio, are shown in Table 9-3. The move to the five-day week, which has been going on apace, leads to the sharp drop in inputs of working hours shown in the table. As for age, there is expected to be a decline in the proportion of fifteen- to twenty-four-year-olds in the labor force (21.6 percent in 1970 to 13.1 percent in 1980) and a compensating increase in the forty-five- to sixty-four-year-old group (26.2 percent to 33.2 percent). Of particular significance for the larger enterprises, with their strong preference for hiring new employees directly out of school, is the projected decline in the rate of entry of new school graduates, shown in Table 9-4. It is this phenomenon, more than anything else, that is causing concern among large enterprises, which have been accustomed to skimming the cream off each year's graduating class.

The quality adjustment for education is a positive one, reflecting a continuing increase in years of schooling. But there is a negative side to more

13. Economic Planning Agency, *Basic Economic and Social Plan: Toward a Vigorous Welfare Society, 1973–1977* (1973), p. 147.

Table 9-4. *Estimated Employment of New School Graduates in Japan, by School Level, Selected Years, 1970–85*

	Thousands of employed new graduates			
School level	1970	1975	1980	1985
Middle school	268	204	175	142
High school and junior college	928	775	769	876
College	203	221	226	270
Total	1,399	1,199	1,170	1,289

Source: Japan Economic Research Center, *The Outlook for a Trillion Dollar Economy* (1971), p. 22. Figures are rounded.

schooling as well. The declining number of those who terminate their education at the middle school level means a reduced supply of semiskilled factory hands, which Japan cannot replenish as Germany and France have done by importing guest workers—except in the unlikely event that citizens of neighboring countries are invited into Japan. Some senior high school graduates may be obliged by economic circumstances to accept semiskilled jobs.

The high proportion of older women employed in agriculture, together with the increasing urbanization of the economy, is the foundation for the projected decline in the overall rate of participation of women in the labor force, a decline that runs counter to the trend elsewhere. But because Japan currently has a relatively high participation rate of women, the adjustment is in the direction of countries with comparable income levels.

NEW SOURCES OF LABOR. All of this suggests that for the coming decade the labor supply will grow at a lower rate than over the past decade (particularly during the cornucopia years 1965–70). Is there, however, an internal reserve of low-productivity workers who can be upgraded should the demand arise? The traditional locus of the reserve was agriculture and related pursuits, and it is apparent from Table 9-2 that a substantial number of Japanese are still engaged in these activities.

The projections of labor force distribution by sector shown in Table 9-5 suggest that a continuing decline in primary sector employment is likely during the next decade.[14] In absolute terms, instead of the 9 million persons who were working in primary industries in 1970, there will be 7.3 million in 1975, 5.8 million in 1980, and 4.5 million in 1985.[15]

14. The small discrepancies between the 1970 figures shown in Tables 9-2 and 9-5 may be due to definitional differences, or possibly to rounding. The data come from different sources.

15. Japan Economic Research Center, *The Outlook for a Trillion Dollar Economy* (1971), p. 78.

Table 9-5. *Projected Distribution of the Japanese Labor Force, by Major Sector of the Economy, Selected Years, 1970–85*
Percent

Sector	Distribution			
	1970	1975	1980	1985
Primary (agriculture, forestry, and fishing)	18	14	11	8
Secondary (manufacturing, mining, and construction)	35	38	39	40
Tertiary (service and other industries)	48	49	50	52

Source: Japan Economic Research Center, *The Outlook for a Trillion Dollar Economy* (1971), p. 4.

If the age distribution of the agricultural (primary sector) labor force were the same as that for nonagriculture, it could be assumed that some 4.5 million people from agriculture would be available to the rest of the economy between 1970 and 1985, either through direct transfer or through the movement of rural youths to nonagricultural jobs on completion of school. But the age distribution among the three sectors is quite different. The agricultural labor force is considerably older than that of the other sectors. About 31 percent of the agricultural labor in 1972 consisted of people over fifty, most of whom will be retired by 1985. Of the 7.05 million people who worked in agriculture in 1972, at least 2.2 million will have died or retired by 1985, leaving 4.85 million in 1985, which is not too far from the estimated agricultural labor force given in the previous paragraph.[16]

The net manpower contribution of the rural sector to the rest of the economy during the coming decade will be roughly equal, therefore, to the number of young people from farm families who complete school and enter employment. If we apply the projected primary sectoral labor force ratios in Table 9-5 to the estimated number of new labor market entrants in Table 9-4, the contribution from this source, other things being equal, would be on the order of 170,000 in 1975, 130,000 in 1980, and 100,000 in 1985—roughly 1.3 million for the decade. This is not a negligible contribution, but it is best seen in perspective against a projected labor force of over 51 million in 1985. As a manpower expert in the Japanese Ministry of Labor put it in the course of an interview: "Agriculture has completed its historic role as a large supplier of labor to other sectors."

INTERSECTORAL MOVEMENT. More difficult to assess is the supply of labor that can be drawn from low-productivity tasks in both the manufac-

16. Bureau of Statistics, *Annual Report on the Labor Force Survey, 1972*, p. 104.

turing and service sectors. There appears to be a fairly substantial potential supply from this source. In 1972, 22 percent of all those employed in the nonagricultural sector were either self-employed or family workers.[17] Not all of these are necessarily in low-productivity occupations, but lower average incomes and a consistent downward trend in the percentage of non-employees in the labor force ratio suggests that many of them are.[18]

A partly related factor is the continued existence of many small firms in Japan. In manufacturing, firms with fewer than thirty employees accounted for 26.5 percent of total employment in 1972 and paid average monthly earnings that were 73 percent of those in the large firms.[19] There is a much larger proportion of small-firm employment in some branches of the services: some 46 percent of those engaged in wholesale and retail trade, insurance, and real estate in 1972 were in enterprises employing fewer than thirty persons.[20] Wages also are lower in the small service enterprises: the ratio of small- to large-firm earnings was 77 percent for wholesale and retail trade and 79 percent for finance and insurance (1972).[21]

The share of tertiary (service) sector employment as a whole is expected to increase at about the same rate as that of manufacturing during the next decade (Table 9-5). This implies some reshuffling within the service sector itself. Government employment in Japan is remarkably low, which appears to be due in good measure to the poor development of the social welfare system. If there is movement toward a welfare state, government employment will rise substantially.[22]

Trends and Modeling Projections

To summarize the argument thus far:

—The rate of growth of the labor force will decline during the next decade.

—Labor inputs also will decline because of a reduction in working hours.

17. Ministry of Labor, *Year Book of Labor Statistics, 1972*, p. 7.

18. See Bureau of Statistics, *Annual Report on the Labor Force Survey, 1972*, pp. 135–36.

19. Ibid., p. 75; and Ministry of Labor, *Year Book of Labor Statistics, 1972*, p. 77. The wage figure for the small firms is actually for firms with between five and twenty-nine employees, since firms with from one to four employees are not covered in the regular monthly wage survey. The percentage would undoubtedly be lower if the latter group was included. In this context, the large firms are those with more than twenty-nine employees.

20. Bureau of Statistics, *Annual Report on the Labor Force Survey, 1972*, p. 76.

21. Ministry of Labor, *Year Book of Labor Statistics, 1972*, p. 82. The wage data for the smaller firms exclude those with fewer than five employees.

22. See Emi, "Employment Structure," p. 140, and passim.

—The quality of the labor force will rise as a result of higher average levels of education in the work force.

—There will be some contribution from a declining agricultural labor force to the nonagricultural sector, but the contribution will be much lower than in the past.

—There is still a pool of workers in low-productivity jobs, both in manufacturing and in service trades, who can be shifted to high-productivity tasks if the demand warrants it.

Whether this adds up to a labor shortage that would impose constraints upon economic growth can only be estimated with the aid of a macromodel of the economy that incorporates demand. A preliminary study of this nature has been made for the years up to 1977; the results are instructive.[23] There were several basic assumptions behind the model: among them, that the average rate of growth of the gross national product (GNP) for the years 1970–77 will be 9 percent a year,[24] and that a significant shift will occur in the structure of demand from private investment and export goods to consumption and public investment.[25]

Results were obtained in two principal areas. First, the rate of increase in the demand for labor will drop from 1.8 percent a year for the period 1965–70 to 1.4 percent a year for 1970–77. But the increase in the labor supply will also fall, to an average of approximately 0.7 percent a year for 1970–77. Using the labor force survey data for 1970 as a base, application of these rates yields a total labor demand of 57.3 million by 1977 against a supply of 54.2 million, or a "deficit" of 3.1 million persons.

23. We are greatly indebted to Shōzō Ichino and his coworkers in the Bureau of Systems Analysis, Ministry of Labor, for their courtesy in explaining their work to us and for their permission to quote it. They have emphasized that the work is experimental rather than definitive, and that the computations were made in December 1972, with data available at that time. Inflation since 1972 may particularly affect final demand by changing price ratios, leading to substitution and in turn to changes in input-output ratios.

24. This is roughly the same as the rate of growth (9.4 percent for fiscal 1972–77) assumed in the medium-term macromodel developed by the Economic Planning Agency. See EPA, *Basic Economic and Social Plan, 1973–1977*, p. 138. In a more recent program covering the period 1973–85, the EPA has scaled the average annual growth rate down to 7.1 percent. See *Japan Labor Bulletin*, Aug. 1, 1974.

25. Final demand was estimated, by industry, through the use of a 68-square input-output matrix, and manpower requirements were obtained through the use of historical coefficients, modified appropriately for changes in labor productivity. Essentially, the elasticities of labor demand with respect to output were assumed to be the same as those prevailing during the period 1965–70. Adjustment was made for the degree of dependence on imported goods and for the rate of increase of the capital stock.

Second, in individual sectors for the periods 1965–70 and 1970–77, respectively:

—The annual rate of decline in primary employment—agriculture, forestry, and fishing—will increase from 2.8 to 4.1 percent.

—Employment in manufacturing will increase at a slower rate, from 3.1 annually to 1.9 percent.

—The annual rate of increase in service sector employment will fall from 3.0 to 2.2 percent. Employment in retail trade, corporate services, and personal services, however, will increase at a higher rate than the average.

Further, with respect to occupational categories, for the same periods:

—Professional and administrative occupations will increase at a comparatively high rate, 7.7 and 6.6 percent, respectively.

—There will be a sharp decline in the increase in employment of skilled production workers, from 3.4 to 2.4 percent. Diminishing rates of increase will also apply to the employment of office workers (from 3.3 to 2.2 percent) and sales personnel (from 2.3 to 1.8 percent).

These conclusions are only as good as the assumptions on which they are based. A rate of GNP growth higher than the 9 percent assumed would lead to a tighter labor market; a lower rate of growth, which appears very probable at this writing, would have the opposite effect. A sharper turn toward a welfare state than is anticipated or greater emphasis on consumption would mean a smaller increase in labor productivity and greater pressure on labor supply. Finally, it is difficult to make appropriate adjustments for the vagaries of foreign trade.

Nevertheless, the results seem reasonable in the light of the data cited earlier. Manpower will be in shorter supply, at least for the remainder of the 1970s. Unless the recession of 1974 continues, the demand for labor should be adequate to sustain full employment. On the other hand, the magnitude of a possible manpower "deficit" is not so great as to impose substantial constraints on any reasonable level of economic growth. It has been observed, with justification, that "the labor shortage now confronting Japan is of a different nature from that endemic to Western European industry. It by no means indicates an over-taxing of available manpower reserves, but derives rather from the continuation, under increasingly inappropriate conditions, of the kind of labor-intensive production that had characterized the 1950s, when labor was cheap and plentiful."[26]

This is not to say that particular labor market practices will be unaffected by portending changes in the labor balance. For example, the gradual

26. Tachi and Okazaki, "Japan's Postwar Population and Labor Force," p. 184.

aging of the labor force may affect the prevailing systems of employment and wages. The decline in the number of younger workers available will reduce the proclivity of the large firms to rely so heavily on new school graduates for labor force expansion; it may result also in greater mobility of older workers. The practice of relating wages to seniority will become more expensive as the labor force grows older. These and related matters are considered below. But a sharp break with the past should not be necessitated by pure manpower considerations. Gradual modification, rather than abrupt change, is more likely—unless other forces intervene.

Wages

In Japan wages are paid on a monthly basis, and therefore income usually is conceptualized in monthly cash earnings. Piecework systems are not customary, and hourly rate payment is rare except for part-time employees.[27] It is important, however, to take into account changes in hours worked, since overtime is common.[28] Moreover, special payments such as semiannual bonuses, which are paid in addition to monthly contract wages, constitute an integral part of annual income. For examining wage trends it is thus appropriate to select total hourly earnings as the unit of observation.

Wage Trends

Table 9-6 shows the average hourly money wages for selected industries, including monthly contract cash earnings, bonuses, and other types of special earnings. The data are for firms with five or more employees and exclude nonmoney earnings. The inclusion of enterprises with less than five employees would probably not change the conclusions that can be drawn from the table. It is interesting to observe, first, that the industrial ranking of hourly earnings has changed little over the years, except for occasional reversals of the order between manufacturing and construction; and, second, that the rate of increase in money wages has been in favor of such relatively low-paying industries as trade and manufacturing as against

27. Before World War II the daily wage was the basic unit of earnings calculation for blue-collar workers, though wages might be distributed monthly, and piecework was also practiced.

28. The labor standards law stipulates that the overtime premium be at least 25 percent higher than regular wage rates, and most companies pay only this minimum.

Table 9-6. *Average Total Hourly Earnings of Workers in Selected Japanese Industries, Selected Years, 1958–73*[a]

Yen

Industry	Average hourly earnings[b]					
	1958	*1961*	*1964*	*1967*	*1970*	*1973*
All industries	92	118	169	232	365	602
Mining	120	144	185	247	389	594
Construction	83	108	165	223	343	538
Manufacturing	83	110	157	219	355	590
Wholesale and retail trade	72	96	147	203	320	555
Finance and insurance	129	182	245	333	481	791
Real estate	122	155	212	323	473	751
Transportation and communication	121	149	208	284	429	690
Electricity, gas, and water supply	174	212	298	399	589	918

Source: Calculated from Ministry of Labor, *Year Book of Labor Statistics*, various issues, 1961–72; and idem, *Monthly Labor Survey* (monthly reports, 1973).

a. As of January in the years listed (April in the case of 1973) new samples were chosen as the bases of observation; these years have been selected in order to minimize sampling errors.

b. Inclusive of special earnings such as bonuses but excluding nonmoney earnings. The data exclude enterprises with fewer than five employees.

the higher-paid sectors in the last four rows. Mining is an exception, but it is a declining industry. The overall implication is that interindustrial wage differentials have narrowed during this fifteen-year period.

When the money earnings data are corrected for price change, the magnitude of the relative advance in Japanese wages during the past decade becomes clear. Table 9-7 contains a comparison of money and real wage earnings in manufacturing for the decade 1962–72, for Japan and the major industrial nations of the West, from which it is apparent that Japanese employees have done relatively well: their real earnings have been rising considerably faster than those in the West.

Wage Structure

A closer examination of the trend toward wage equalization, noted in the comments on Table 9-6, is in order. Occupational wage differentials are fundamental. Because Japanese wage differentials by size of firm have attracted so much attention, it is also appropriate to examine them. Finally, the trend over time in the industrial wage structure—which reflects a combination of occupational, firm-size, and geographical factors—also must be considered.

Table 9-7. *Changes in Money and Real Hourly Earnings in Manufacturing, Japan and Major Western Industrialized Countries, 1962–72*

| | Index of change[a] | | | Average annual increase in real earnings (percent) |
Country	Money earnings	Consumer prices	Real earnings	
Japan	384	172	223	8.4
France	238	154	155	4.5
West Germany	224	138	162	4.9
Italy	263	153	172	5.6
United Kingdom	232	162	143	3.6
United States	159	138	115	1.4

Sources: Calculated from data in Ministry of Labor, *Year Book of Labor Statistics, 1972* pp. 346, 348; and International Labour Office, *Year Book of Labour Statistics, 1973* (Geneva, 1974), tables 19A, 25A.
a. 1962 = 100.

OCCUPATION AND WAGE. Table 9-8, designed to illustrate the nature of the Japanese wage structure, contains a number of comparisons of occupational wage differences. The concept of skill is not clear-cut. A specifically required skill constantly changes for technological reasons. Moreover, Japanese workers are not so much occupation conscious as company oriented; the Western concept of occupation does not pertain. Therefore three examples of skill differences have been selected, mainly on the basis of ease of observation, and their trends are followed over time: (a) sex differences as a specific form of occupational differences for office workers in manufacturing; (b) differences between the earnings of a truck driver and an average industrial worker; and (c) skill margins in the construction industry between a carpenter and a manual laborer engaged in light work.

The first comparison is made on the basis of monthly contract cash earnings, the other two, by average hourly rates. That female-male differentials have been slowly diminishing since 1960 is particularly noteworthy. Apart from construction wages, there was a gradual narrowing of occupational differences throughout the 1960s, although the narrowing subsided late in the decade.

RELATION OF EMPLOYER SIZE TO WAGES. Duality in the Japanese labor market has been a popular subject in the literature, and pay differentials by size of enterprise have often been cited as evidence of dualism.[29] There is no theoretical reason to expect that such differentials should persist, but

29. See, for example, Kazushi Ohkawa and Henry Rosovsky, *Japanese Economic Growth: Trend Acceleration in the Twentieth Century* (Stanford University Press, 1973), chap. 5.

Table 9-8. *Wage Differentials in Japan for Selected Occupational Variables, 1952–72*

Percent

	Occupational variable			
Year	Female/male office workers[a] in manufacturing	Light-duty laborer/ carpenter[b]	Truck driver/ average male industrial worker[c]	Small firm employee/ large firm employee[d]
1952	43.0	...	71.1	58.8
1953	42.4	...	62.3	59.8
1954	42.3	68.3	61.0	60.0
1955	41.4	65.6	62.9	58.8
1956	40.5	67.0	58.4	56.1
1957	39.7	67.8	56.9	56.0
1958	39.5	65.6	61.1	54.7
1959	39.3	66.7	59.3	56.1
1960	39.4	68.3	62.7	58.9
1961	40.0	65.1	65.0	61.7
1962	41.8	64.0	67.1	66.7
1963	43.1	61.6	71.3	68.8
1964	43.6	61.6	71.9	69.5
1965	44.9	60.9	71.3	71.0
1966	45.1	61.2	71.4	69.8
1967	44.3	62.4	72.8	67.7
1968	45.2	62.3	74.1	68.9
1969	45.8	61.4	73.9	69.6
1970	46.5	65.2	74.2	69.6
1971	47.8	65.4	74.1	69.9
1972	48.7	66.8	72.6	69.8

Sources: First column: 1952–61, from Ministry of Labor, *1962 Labor White Paper*, p. 355; 1962–72, from *1973 Labor White Paper*, p. 391. Second and third columns: calculated from Ministry of Labor, *Year Book of Labor Statistics*, various issues, 1952–72. Fourth column: 1952–59, from Japan Institute of Labor, *Japan Labor Statistics* (1970), p. 79; 1960–72, from Ministry of Labor, *1973 Labor White Paper*, p, 390.

a. Comparison of monthly contractual cash earnings.

b. Both series are taken from the survey of construction workers. Comparison is on hourly basis.

c. Driver of large trucks versus average male worker in the nonprimary sector, on an hourly basis. The latter series is based on the monthly labor survey (covering enterprises with thirty or more employees) and includes all special earnings.

d. Small firms are those with from thirty to ninety-nine employees; large firms, those with five hundred or more employees. Wages are on a monthly basis and include all cash earnings. The data have been adjusted for variations caused by sample changes.

in fact they do. Blumenthal has shown the existence of substantial differentials in monthly earnings in 1964 for manufacturing production workers aged thirty to thirty-nine with middle school education, between firms with 1,000 or more employees and those with from ten to ninety-nine employees, with other factors held constant.[30] Similar computations made by others have led to the same conclusion, although some dispute remains about the relative importance of enterprise size differentials as against other possible causes.[31]

On the assumption that duality is genuine, the statistics can be examined. It is sufficient for present purposes to follow the unadjusted trend of the inter-firm-scale differentials over time, encompassing various factors such as changes in industrial structure, age composition of the workers, and the skill mix. We take relative total cash earnings in manufacturing of two firm-size groups as the measure of the differential, where five hundred or more workers stand for large and thirty to ninety-nine workers for small firms. The computations indicate clearly that an equalizing tendency prevailed from 1952 to 1972, though the trend was not monotonic (see Table 9-8). It should be added that this observation is confirmed by examining fixed-weight wage series for respective size groups, where sex, industrial composition, and other factors are held constant.[32]

Other sets of data yield the same conclusion. For example, Napier has made use of the Census of Manufactures for 1955, 1963, and 1967 to cal-culate interscale wage dispersions. The unit of observation was the absolute difference of the average wage in each subsector from the average for the entire sector, each difference being weighted by the proportion of workers in the corresponding sector. He found that the interscale dispersion ratios for manufacturing as a whole "declined from 0.348 in 1955 to 0.248 in 1963 and 0.231 in 1967."[33] Blumenthal, on the basis of an analysis of variance using 1958, 1961, and 1964 issues of the Basic Wage Survey, concluded that "during the whole period there has taken place a process of reduction in differentials (except for a few cases). In most of the groups

30. Tuvia Blumenthal, "Scarcity of Labor and Wage Differentials in the Japanese Economy, 1958–64," *Economic Development and Cultural Change*, vol. 17 (October 1968), app. table 3.

31. See, for example, Ron W. Napier, "The Labor Market and Structural Change in Postwar Japanese Development" (honors thesis, Harvard College, 1972; processed), pp. 27–42. It is possible, however, that the statistical adjustments do not exhaust all the quality differences in manpower. For example, workers in larger companies may have higher IQs, may have graduated with honors, or may be more highly motivated.

32. Akira Ono, *Sengo Nihon no chingin kettei* [Wage Determination in Postwar Japan] (Tōyō Keizai Shinpo Sha, 1973), p. 207.

33. "The Labor Market," pp. 54–57 (quotation is from p. 55). Napier notes that "in 1967 the highest interscale dispersions were found in . . . industries [which] are characterized by the existence of a large traditional sector," and vice versa in indus-tries with a proportionately larger share of modern elements. He concludes that the dual structure was on the decline but still "prospered in the 1955–67 period." (Ibid., pp. 55–57.)

up to age 29, there has actually been a reversal of the differentials, as the workers in the smaller-scale firms get higher wages than in larger firms."[34]

Tightening of the labor market appears to be a major factor underlying the narrowing of interscale differentials. An examination of wage differentials for new school graduates may help illustrate the point. Graduates seek work in a fairly competitive, open labor market, whereas the markets for older workers are relatively segmented, with less mobility.

If the ratio of placements to the number of openings for new graduates is taken as an index of labor market tightness, and is compared with wage differentials by size of enterprise, there is a clear relation over time between the two, as shown in Table 9-9.[35] Here the wage differentials are measured between firms with five hundred or more employees and those with from thirty to ninety-nine. There are inconsistencies in the data, for the wages of males are compared with an excess-supply index that covers both sexes. Nonetheless, it is clear that in the 1960s the small firms paid starting wages comparable with those of the large ones in order to attract new entrants. Interscale wage differentials had already disappeared from this segment of the market.

There has also been a recent decline in industrial wage differentials. Napier found, on the basis of Census of Manufactures data, that inter-industry wage dispersion, weighted by employment, diminished from 0.316 in 1955 to 0.246 in 1963 and 0.236 in 1967.[36] For a more recent period, the same results emerge from statistics compiled from an annual company survey conducted by the Oriental Economist. Inquiries were made of some 470 firms about their standard expected earnings for certain specific types of employees (model wages). For example, for male office workers aged thirty, with twelve to thirteen years of service and two dependents, the coefficient of dispersion, calculated over twenty industries (unweighted), was 0.097 for 1962 and fell to 0.052 for 1971.[37]

In sum, it seems safe to conclude that almost all types of Japanese wage differentials have been declining during the past decade.[38] In all probability,

34. "Scarcity of Labor and Wage Differentials," p. 22.
35. A lower number of placements in relation to new openings means a tight labor market, and vice versa.
36. "The Labor Market," p. 55.
37. The dispersion coefficient is defined here as (third quartile − first quartile)/ median, and calculated from data available from the Oriental Economist, *Japan Economic Yearbook* (1963), p. 204, and (1973), p. 302.
38. An exception may be noted for the behavior of differentials between day versus regular employees: they have shown, after a brief period of narrowing between

Table 9-9. *Labor Market Conditions and Wage Differentials for New Graduates of Middle Schools, 1956–72*
Percent

Year	Ratio of placements to new openings[a]	Ratio of starting wages for males in firms with 500 or more employees to their starting wages in firms with 30–99 employees[b]
1956	73.7	133.8
1957	65.0	127.2
1958	60.8	119.7
1959	63.5	114.5
1960	43.7	113.7
1961	31.4	102.2
1962	29.6	96.8
1963	32.9	98.8
1964	25.3	93.7
1965	24.7	98.3
1966	31.8	96.9
1967	26.7	100.3
1968	21.0	101.0
1969	19.3	100.1
1970	17.2	97.9
1971	14.6	99.3
1972	18.2	96.4

Sources: Japan Institute of Labor, *Japan Labor Statistics* (1967), pp. 42–43, 82–83; ibid. (1970), pp. 46–47, 90–91; and Ministry of Labor, *1973 Labor White Paper*, pp. 378, 411–12.
a. All industries. Both sexes; separate figures for the sexes are available only after 1960.
b. Manufacturing only.

the rapid rate of economic growth has been largely responsible for this phenomenon: by tightening the labor market and pulling up earnings of underprivileged workers such as those in small firms, the unskilled, and females. Another factor has been the tendency of union settlements for wage increases to be couched in absolute amounts rather than percentages, a practice that also helps produce wage equalization.

On the basis of what has been happening in other countries, a further compression of the Japanese wage structure can be anticipated.[39] The

1959 and 1962, a tendency to widen regardless of firm size (see the 1962 and 1973 editions of Ministry of Labor, *Labor White Paper,* pp. 355 and 391, respectively). This may reflect in part a deterioration in the quality of day laborers, since employers have lately been attempting to transfer better-quality temporary workers to the regular payrolls.
39. There may be some exceptions. For example, by 1973 starting salaries for male junior high school graduates had already reached 88 percent of those for senior high school graduates, and further compression is unlikely. *Japan Labor Bulletin,* July 1, 1974.

Table 9-10. *Ratio of Special Payments to Average Annual Total Cash Earnings of Japanese Workers, Selected Years, 1958–73*
Percent

	Workers in all industries		Workers in manufacturing	
Year[a]	Firms with 5 or more employees	Firms with 5–29 employees only	Firms with 5 or more employees	Firms with 5–29 employees only
1958	15.5	10.5	14.4	5.9
1961	19.5	13.6	18.9	10.1
1964	19.8	14.6	18.9	11.9
1967	20.9	15.3	20.1	12.7
1970	23.3	17.4	23.4	15.7
1973	25.3	20.0	25.6	18.0

Source: Ministry of Labor, *Year Book of Labor Statistics*, various issues, 1958–73.
a. For the basis for selection of these years, see note b to Table 9-6.

growing shortage of unskilled labor caused by increased length of schooling will intensify this trend. Duality in the market will tend to disappear and such differentials as those related to firm size will diminish.

Supplements to Basic Wage Rates

In addition to regular monthly contract earnings, most Japanese employees receive fairly large bonuses both at the middle and at the end of each calendar year.[40] This arrangement has become particularly widespread since World War II. Bonuses before World War II were quite insignificant compared with those of the postwar decades. The proportion of special cash payments, which include bonuses, is consistently higher for large enterprises, and has increased over the past decade (see Table 9-10).[41]

The system of bonuses is important in many ways. First, it provides the employer with a means of reducing the pressure of labor costs during recessions through adjusting the amount of the bonus, though it was pointed

40. The bonuses apply to government employees as well, but they may receive their bonuses in three installments.
41. The definition of "special cash payments" given in the official statistics is as follows: the amount actually paid to the employee for extraordinary or emergency cases, and without any previous agreement, contract, or rule. Retroactive payment of wages for past months as a result of a new agreement is also included. Though their terms and amount are established by collective agreements, payments such as summer and year-end bonuses, which are paid for each period longer than three months, and allowances such as marriage allowances, which are paid for unforeseen events, are included. Ministry of Labor, *Year Book of Labor Statistics, 1973*, p. 363.

out to us during interviews that the degree of flexibility is not as great as is commonly supposed.[42] The bonus is an important subject of collective bargaining, and it is by no means determined unilaterally by the employer. Nonetheless, its potential adjustability remains valuable to management.

Second, the bonus system significantly influences the consumption pattern of workers. Because the semiannual payments are expected regularly, they can hardly be called transitory in the Friedmanesque sense. Nevertheless, active sales promotion in July and December suggests that workers are prepared to purchase expensive commodities, such as major consumer durables, at bonus time. They have a quite compelling reason to behave in this manner: consumer credit is relatively underdeveloped in Japan.

In addition to the substantial bonus payments, to which families eagerly look forward each year, Japanese workers normally receive various forms of fringe benefits, pecuniary or in kind. Living and other allowances have always been an important component of monthly cash earnings. Essentially, they are supplementary forms of compensation that originated during periods when wages could not keep up with rapid inflation. The experience of the war years is perhaps an inappropriate example because strict control of wages and prices was in effect. Many allowances, however, were invented and persisted for some time even after the war.

As the economy stabilized and well-structured personnel and wage systems developed, the relative weight of supplementary allowances diminished. In 1972 basic wages in industry constituted 75.9 percent of earnings, with overtime contributing an additional 10.6 percent. The remaining portion consisted of incentive payments (3.0 percent), remuneration for special job conditions (3.4 percent), allowances for good attendance (1.0 percent), and cost-of-living and miscellaneous allowances (6.1 percent).[43]

Apart from these regular monthly allowances, employees receive three major nonwage benefits: severance pay, various types of payments in kind, and welfare services. In 1972 severance pay, which goes mostly to retirees, added 3.8 percent to cash earnings in manufacturing plants. Another 10.5 percent went for welfare benefits, about half of which were obligatory employer contributions to social insurance, while the rest went for the main-

42. For example, although the financial outlook for the automobile industry was rather bleak for 1974, the auto unions indicated that they were willing neither to forgo the bonus altogether nor to accept anything less than the 1973 settlement.
43. Ministry of Labor, *Year Book of Labor Statistics, 1972*, pp. 186–87. These figures relate to industrial firms with thirty or more employees. The amounts, types, and proportions of fringe benefits vary with size of firm. The cost-of-living allowance comprises payments for commuting, housing, and high local costs, as well as family allowances.

tenance of recreational facilities, company housing, and vacation resorts.[44] Employer-subsidized recreational facilities suggest the existence of a social demand for a better environment and a political insensitivity to it—a theme to which we shall return.

The Internal Wage Structure: The Seniority Wage System

The seniority wage, or *nenkō*, system, in its purest form, is one of wage payment whereby earnings are related solely to length of service with a company regardless of such qualifications as skill, past experience, position, and degree of responsibility. The system is widely practiced in determining the level of compensation in both private or public employment, and it is more common in the larger organizations. Because there is no necessary relation between seniority and work performance, the rationale of the system has often been attributed to sociocultural factors.

Two things should be pointed out with respect to the *nenkō* system. First, age is a basic factor in determining the standard wage profile, but accumulated merit credits for length of service can be crucial in determining the order of promotion between two persons with otherwise equal qualifications. Under permanent tenure, seniority is closely associated with age, so that the former may appear to be the controlling factor in wage determination.

Second, the pure *nenkō* system is only an abstraction. Despite the commonly held notion that noneconomic, cultural factors are the decisive element in wage determination, in practice high efficiency is rewarded in one way or another.

But there is no denying the fact that the main features of the Japanese internal wage system have been geared more toward personal attributes than to pure economic efficiency. A good illustration of the working of the system may be found in governmental offices, in which the seniority wage is strictly observed. In a strategically important public service, exceptions might be made through the existence of separate elite tracks and accelerated promotion. But breaking tradition is very difficult in a stagnant and less strategic sector of the government bureaucracy. In government-financed universities, for example, extreme egalitarianism prevails, and there are almost no incentives for superior performance.

How the *nenkō* system evolved has been a matter of speculation, but the following two points may be noted. First, a fundamental idea of Japanese

44. Ibid., p. 205. Housing subsidies are discussed in greater detail below. The percentages in the text represent ratios to total wage earnings.

personnel management, developed since World War II, has been that workers should be guaranteed sufficient income to maintain adequate standards of living. A factor in the determination of earnings therefore should be family need, which starts low and increases with the age of the family head. When unions demanded in the late 1940s that wages should be closely related to family living costs, the idea was not foreign to management thinking.

Second, the ideal *nenkō* system assumes the homogeneity of the work force. All employees, once hired, are entitled equally to all the rights and privileges of the organization to which they belong. There may be variations in individual talent, but it is assumed that everyone is doing his best to serve the company in his own way; no one should be discriminated against. Given this assumption, the only objective and fair criterion of wages would be the age of the employee.

The seniority wage system can function smoothly as long as homogeneity in the quality of employees is more or less maintained. Once heterogeneity develops, however, the system encounters difficulties, since it is not suited to deal with inefficient, inferior members of the organization. Furthermore, the pressure of labor cost builds up when the firm's rate of growth slackens and the average age of its employees increases.

Whatever the merits of *nenkō*, there have been attempts to remedy the deficiencies by introducing modifications. Nikkeiren, the Japan Federation of Employers' Associations, has long argued for the adoption of ability-related wage systems. One of the first attempts to introduce a Western-type wage system was made by the Jūjō Paper Manufacturing Company in 1949, but it failed. Perhaps the time was not yet ripe; workers showed little enthusiasm for the experiment. More recently, however, young employees have been voicing their dissatisfaction with *nenkō*. Frequent complaints are heard, particularly among young engineers, who feel that they are not being compensated adequately. In a seller's market, such employees can simply quit or be hired away by competitiors.

As a result, more job-oriented wage systems are gradually being implemented by management. They are usually called job ability payment, or *shokunō-kyū*, schemes, and are not as precise as American systems; for one thing, the concept of job is much broader in Japan. Moreover, elements of *nenkō* are never totally eliminated. The result is a rather complex system of remuneration, integrating two distinct principles: payments according to ability and payments according to family needs.

It is difficult to document this transformation in statistical terms. There are clear indications, however, that work-related elements weigh increasingly heavily in compensation; according to the annual wage survey of the Ministry of Labor, the proportion of job-related wages in total monthly cash earnings increased from 8.9 percent in 1966 to 30.6 percent in 1972.[45]

Some examples, based on interviews conducted in 1973 and 1974, may help to clarify what these concepts mean in practice. In large manufacturing concerns, the personnel department usually develops a system of compensation based upon some or all of four factors: base pay, performance, ability, and allowances. The labor force is divided into several broad categories, such as production workers, office clerks, technicians, and managerial staff, each of which has its own promotion ladder. (There is a separate remuneration system for top management.) Each of the job categories is structured into several skill grades, often on the basis of job evaluation.

Example 1. In a leading steel cable manufacturing company, monthly earnings for both production and white-collar workers, including middle management, are determined as follows:

—Base pay: starting wage, fixed by age and sex; annual pay raise, on the basis of an overall performance review.

—Payment for the job: job rate, fixed by job evaluation; increase in job rate, on the basis of either efficiency or transfer to a new job.

—Family allowance: allowance for spouse; allowance for children.

Consequently, workers of the same age might receive wages of substantially different amounts depending upon personal characteristics and evaluations. As of May 1972 the proportions of these three components were 81, 15, and 4 percent, respectively. The job rate was introduced relatively recently, in 1965. In addition to these, the company offered a 30 percent premium for overtime and holiday work.[46] The personnel administrator expressed his personal view that ideally the wage should be based half on job and half on age.

Example 2. In a shipyard building supertankers, individual variance of base pay was roughly ±4 percent. All jobs were slotted into five broad skill groups, each group with a number of grades. An employee moved up this ability-skill table based on personal ability. The rates in the table moved up as a whole during the annual spring wage adjustment. Performance was evaluated every two months, and base pay multiplied by a

45. Ministry of Labor, *1972 Labor White Paper,* p. 213; and idem, *Year Book of Labor Statistics, 1972,* pp. 186–87.

46. Members of the technical staff were included and were treated differently in only one respect: the determination of their starting salaries also took into account specific educational attainments and previous experience.

performance coefficient. The semiannual bonus was in part affected by performance, resulting in overall earnings variance of ±9 percent for individuals with about the same seniority.

For the entire yard, 1972 wages averaged ¥69,000 per month, broken down into three elements:

—Base pay and family allowance: ¥31,000 (45 percent).
—Job rate (ability): ¥24,000 (35 percent).
—Performance: ¥14,000 (20 percent).

Example 3. The wage system of a leading textile firm was based upon two factors: (a) age and ability and (b) job rates. Ability was measured by physical efficiency. About 45 percent of the wage was determined by the first factor, and of this, 70 percent was based on age (length of service). Four major job classifications, three subdivided further, pertained to job rates:

—Administrative.
—Professional A: three grades.
 Professional B: three grades.
—Technicians: four grades.
—Operatives: five grades.

Grades were determined by the nature of the work. The piece rates in effect until 1950 were abolished because of adjustment difficulties during a period of technological change.

Example 4. In a large steel mill there were three components of earnings:

—Base pay (47 percent) of total.
—Job rates (30 percent).
—Incentive pay (23 percent).

The base wage was determined by experience, age, and other personal factors, such as level of education. The more than 200 occupational categories were grouped into six skill levels by job evaluation. Each level had three grades, determined by physical conditions (50 percent) and the degree of experience and knowledge required (50 percent). Ratings were made three times a year by immediate supervisors. There was a definite promotion ladder, and better workers were moved up faster. If it were necessary to move a man to a lower-skill job, his previous rate was guaranteed for six months.

The current wage systems reflect the ingenuity of Japanese management. Under the principle of job-ability payment, hard work is rewarded. Combined with *nenkō* wages, the system shields the employee from fear of income insecurity arising from the introduction of new technology. This has been instrumental in enabling management to introduce new methods of production while maintaining complete power over job allocation. In fact, Japanese management has virtually unquestioned authority in determining the wage structure, including the administration of job evaluation. Although all the factors entering into earnings are appropriate subjects of collective bargaining, unions apparently have been concerned mainly with general increases in the average wage level rather than with detailed wage structure.[47]

What of the future of the *nenkō* system? It has functioned smoothly with an abundant supply of labor; young, highly motivated workers could be recruited with relative ease, and they were content with meager starting wages because they expected a rising income stream in the future. With the tightening of the market and an increasing proportion of older workers in the labor force, management finds it difficult to maintain as sharp an age-income profile as before. Management will probably find it increasingly desirable to restructure the wage system to reflect individual efficiency in production, with heavier reliance on job-ability criteria and gradual abolition of the *nenkō* element.[48]

The Employment System

One of the most widely publicized features of the Japanese labor market is the system of what has been called permanent commitment.[49] This is often interpreted to mean that once an employee, white- and blue-collar alike, achieves a regular status with a firm, he is guaranteed employment with the same firm for the duration of his working life, regardless of his performance or the firm's need for his services. The system, however, is far from being that simple.

47. Unions could challenge management authority, but their enterprise-oriented structure (see below) makes it difficult for them to touch this complicated system for internal political reasons, if nothing else.

48. Robert Evans, Jr., dissents from this prediction. It is his view that "there is little evidence to date that *nenkō* is evolving into something else." He anticipates that, given the advantages of the present system, "the expectation should really be that American practices will move in the direction of the Japanese pattern, rather than the other way." "Japan's Labor Economy: Prospect for the Future," *Monthly Labor Review*, vol. 95 (October 1972), pp. 5, 8.

49. For an excellent recent review of this subject, see Robert E. Cole, "Permanent Employment in Japan: Facts and Fantasies," *Industrial and Labor Relations Review*, vol. 26 (October 1972), pp. 615–30.

Permanent Commitment

In the ideal system, all employees are hired by the enterprise directly from school: blue-collar workers from junior and senior high school, clerical employees from senior high school, and managerial personnel from college. After a probationary period, which, depending on the degree of skill involved, may last as long as a year, the employee achieves tenured status, under which he can be discharged only for specified reasons, such as lengthy unexcused absenteeism, behavior detrimental to the company's reputation, involvement in fights, or the commission of crimes. Such discharges are rare and come only after lengthy consultation with the enterprise union. The employee is not subject to discharge or even to temporary layoff because a decline in business renders his services superfluous to the firm or because his work is not up to standard. He may, of course, resign, but this is highly unusual. Tenure continues until the age of fifty-five, when retirement is compulsory.

ORIGINS AND INCIDENCE. The origins of the system are in some dispute. Some regard it as a feudal carryover from pre-Meiji times. Odaka feels that this is a misinterpretation, at least for blue-collar workers, and argues that "it was not until a shortage of skilled workers developed in the 1920s that length of service generally grew longer and longer and turnover declined. Previous to this period, labor mobility was fairly high even in large enterprises."[50] Taira argues convincingly that lifetime commitment was not general between the two world wars, and only after World War II was the system established in its present form.[51] The system certainly received great impetus from the large excess of labor that existed in Japan after World War II. At that time it was the blue-collar workers and their unions who were pushing hard for this form of job security.

From the mid-1950s to the present, permanent commitment has been practiced formally by a substantial number of firms, but the system is by no means universal. Apart from the civil service, it is limited primarily to large- and medium-size enterprises. About 51 percent of all male employees covered in a survey of the nonagricultural private sector conducted in 1972 were in firms employing fewer than 100 employees, which are not likely to practice permanent commitment. Another 21 percent were in firms employing between 100 and 1,000 employees, where there is only partial use of

50. Kunio Odaka, *Toward Industrial Democracy: Management and the Workers in Modern Japan* (in press).

51. Kōji Taira, *Economic Development and the Labor Market in Japan* (Columbia University Press, 1970), p. 156.

the system. It is primarily in the remaining 28 percent that permanency of employment would be the rule.[52]

EXCLUSION OF WOMEN EMPLOYEES. By no means all of the employees of even the large firms conform to the ideal in terms of their lifetime career patterns. In the first place, female employees generally are excluded from the system. It is customary for women to quit at the average age of marriage (about twenty-five)—even those who do not get married. Until recently, at least, this was encouraged by employers, who prefer younger women for routine, monotonous jobs. Of the females employed in 1972 by manufacturing firms with more than 1,000 employees, some 70 percent were under twenty-five, and an additional 10 percent were between twenty-five and thirty.[53]

When women leave firms that practice permanent employment, their tenure is broken; if they return to the same firm later in their careers—not a common practice—they are not credited with their previous service in either wages or job responsibility. During a visit to a large textile mill we were told that older women are willing to do the dirty jobs that their younger colleagues will not do. Women who are hired as regular employees by larger firms when they return to working life may share the permanent employment guarantee with men, but in almost every other respect they are very much second-class citizens: many firms, for example, retire women at fifty whereas men stay on until fifty-five (although the constitutionality of this form of discrimination is now being litigated in the courts).

Some firms are beginning to change their treatment of women workers. Matsushita Electric Company (maker of Panasonic products), to cite one, now accords women who leave for marriage after three or more years of service the right of return within ten years, with reinstatement to the same kind of job they left and with credit for previous service in determining retirement allowances.[54] This trend undoubtedly will be reinforced by the increasing tightness of the labor market, but for the present—for one rea-

52. Bureau of Statistics, *Annual Report on the Labor Force Survey, 1972*, p. 126. For manufacturing, the figures were 40 percent, 25 percent, and 35 percent, respectively. Also note the following observations about the 1950s: "[Permanent commitment] applies only to the employees in the largest firms and government agencies, probably to no more than one-third of the workers in the medium-size firm category, and in all likelihood not at all, or in very rare cases, in small companies with fewer than 100 workers." Solomon B. Levine, "Labor Markets and Collective Bargaining in Japan," in William W. Lockwood (ed.), *The State and Economic Enterprise in Japan: Essays in the Political Economy of Growth* (Princeton University Press, 1965), p. 661.

53. Ministry of Labor, *Year Book of Labor Statistics, 1972*, p. 141.

54. *Japan Labor Bulletin*, Nov. 1, 1970.

son or another—the great majority of women workers do not enjoy the benefits of permanent employment.

TURNOVER AMONG MALES. There are departures from the ideal lifetime employment pattern for regular male employees as well. A good many young men leave their jobs voluntarily. There are no aggregate data covering only those firms which practice permanent commitment, but the matter often came up in interviews. In one of the largest steel mills in Japan, 5 percent of the regular employees quit each year—particularly young men, who found night-shift work restrictive. About 17.5 percent of the men in an electrical manufacturing plant were reported to leave each year because of monotonous or demanding work, and the company was experimenting with production of complete units by a single individual to replace the assembly line as a means of reducing turnover. An average of 8 percent of employees of a large shipyard were said to leave each year. There is a general feeling that voluntary quitting by young men is likely to increase, but as yet there are no firm data to support this conclusion.

It is not always easy to draw the line between voluntary and involuntary separation. Japanese managers are very skillful in easing out undesirable employees. Transfer to a job or to a new location that may not be acceptable to an employee is a method not uncommonly used to induce resignations.[55]

As employees grow older, it becomes more difficult for them to leave their jobs. This is a universal phenomenon, but in Japan there has been an added obstacle in the reluctance of many firms to hire midcareer workers. Several firms interviewed indicated that it was against their policy to hire employees away from competitors; it was not a question of formal anti-pirating agreements, just an informal policy. The report of an OECD investigating team substantiates this impression: "There has been little inter-firm labor mobility in most of the modern sector, at least in big firms. This arrangement seems to have been rather effectively policed by employer understandings not to poach regular employees of another firm, or hire such former employees."[56]

The growing shortage of school graduates is forcing a change in this policy. Even the large firms have been hiring on the open market for certain categories of labor. Although they tend to find these midcareer workers

---

55. Rodney Clark, "Social Relations in a Japanese Company" (Ph.D. dissertation, University of London, 1972), p. 144.

56. OECD, "Manpower Policy in Japan" (Oct. 14, 1971; processed), p. II-2. It is interesting to note that the second sentence was omitted from the version of the report printed. Cf. OECD, *Manpower Policy in Japan* (Paris: OECD, 1973), p. 98.

in smaller firms, there is some labor mobility as well among the large firms.[57] This is a last resort, however: the large firms still prefer to hire directly out of school. A firm's management will derive a good deal of pride from being able to say that it can fulfill all its permanent personnel needs by hiring only from among recent school graduates; this kind of elitist recruitment guarantees them the cream of the crop.

LAYOFFS. A major purpose of mergers has been to rationalize employment, and substantial numbers of workers occasionally have been made redundant. Although efforts are made to transfer surplus workers to other activities, either outright discharge or pressure for voluntary retirement is not uncommon.[58]

The system was tested by the recession of 1971, the Nixon shock, and the oil shock of 1973. In 1971 a number of large firms in the electrical machinery, textile, and chemical industries laid workers off but guaranteed between 80 and 100 percent of wages during the layoff.[59] Teijin, a firm with 14,800 employees, laid off 264 employees for three months under the following conditions: each was given one month's salary, and transportation to his home town was paid. It was reported that 800 persons volunteered for the layoff.[60] The Komatsu Manufacturing Company, a machine manufacturing firm with 17,000 employees, laid off 1,125 workers for five months at 65 percent of earnings. When the workers were called back, however, 168 were informed that their layoff was to be extended by another four months. The company was taken to court, but before final adjudication it agreed to reinstate all 168 with back pay.[61]

The severe economic recession that began in late 1974 provided the first major challenge to the viability of the permanent employment commitment. A number of large enterprises—Toshiba Electric, Hitachi, Sanyo, and Nissan Motors among them—furloughed workers at 90 percent of their regular salaries. The Tōyōbō Textile Company reached agreement with its enterprise union to reduce the labor force by 10 percent through early retirement. The chairman of the enterprise union at a major camera

57. In 1972, industrial firms with more than 1,000 employees hired 23 percent of experienced men from firms of similar size and 25 percent from firms with fewer than 30 employees. Ministry of Labor, *Year Book of Labor Statistics, 1972*, p. 29.

58. *Japan Labor Bulletin*, Aug. 1, 1969.

59. Ibid., Dec. 1, 1971.

60. Ibid., July 1, 1972. Japanese employers do not consider seniority in layoffs and rehiring.

61. Ibid., Dec. 1, 1972, and April 1, 1973. The case drew considerable public attention because it was among the first involving temporary layoffs to be brought before the courts.

company attempted suicide after a company decision to dismiss 900 employees following a plant closure.[62] But it is far too soon to predict the demise of a system that has become so deeply imbedded in Japanese industrial practice.

INTERNATIONAL COMPARISON. To what extent is permanent commitment reflected in aggregate labor turnover data in comparison with other countries? Because of the limited application of the system in Japan, results of comparisons are not unambiguous. The OECD noted that "measured as the rate of separations and hirings (around or above 30% per year among regular workers during the 1960's in the Japanese labour market as a whole) [turnover] is not so much lower than that of Europe or America."[63] But a comparison of Japan and the United States in the ratio of employed persons changing jobs during 1965–66 revealed that although the ratios for women were very close, the U.S. ratio for men was more than twice as high as the Japanese: "the greatest gap among males is in the twenty to twenty-four age category where the ratio in the United States is almost four times higher than in Japan."[64] American turnover rates tend to be somewhat higher than those of Western Europe, so that the OECD observation might be more accurate if restricted to the European nations.

Economic Rationale of the System

Is the Japanese system unique? After all, seniority systems in large American corporations confer almost the equivalent of a lifetime guarantee of employment on workers who have acquired substantial seniority. There may be occasional layoffs, but state unemployment compensation plus the supplementary benefits paid in such industries as steel and automobiles bridge the financial gap for some without great discomfort. In the absence of a severe depression or major technological change, men with seniority can count on staying with the same employer. Nor do large and expanding European firms normally lay off employees with long service—even in the absence of seniority agreements. More voluntary quitting undoubtedly occurs in the West than in Japan, perhaps in part because of the unwillingness of Japanese firms to hire midcareer people—but this is hardly an advantage of the system from the point of view of the individual worker, who presumably leaves a job only when he can find a better one.

62. *New York Times*, Oct. 24, 1974.
63. OECD, *Manpower Policy in Japan* (1973), pp. 103–04.
64. Cole, "Permanent Employment," p. 626. See also Robert Evans, Jr., *The Labor Economies of Japan and the United States* (Praeger, 1971), pp. 84–87.

Why, then, has the system of lifetime commitment come to be regarded as the basis of the Japanese system of industrial relations? We suggest that, for a number of reasons, it has been a completely rational policy in terms of costs and benefits for large Japanese employers, and that although workers welcomed the job security that it brought, particularly in the decade after World War II, the main reason for its survival has been economic efficiency. The rest of this section is devoted to arguing this thesis.

RESPONSIVENESS TO FLUCTUATION IN DEMAND. The system by no means implies that large Japanese firms are unable to adjust their staffs during periods of economic fluctuation. As indicated earlier, reduction of overtime, bonuses, and allowances are among the other means available to employers to cut labor costs. And because the permanent commitment is limited to regular workers, two categories of workers bear the brunt of cyclical needs for change: temporary employees and employees of subcontractors.

Temporary employees are taken on for specific, relatively short periods of time, though they may be rehired. They may be doing the same work as regular employees or special work, but until the early 1960s they received lower wages and were not entitled to welfare fringe benefits. Nor are they members of the enterprise unions, a status normally reserved for regular workers. Estimates of the number of temporary workers vary greatly, but there is general agreement that there has been a decline. The official statistics put the number of temporary workers in manufacturing—defined as those employed for a specified period of between one month and one year—at 5.3 percent of all employees in 1972, with an additional 2 percent of day laborers employed for a specified period of less than a month.[65] But this is undoubtedly an underestimate, as Taira argues; he cites an independent survey in 1961 in which the ratio of temporary to regular workers was almost two and a half times the official estimate.[66] Some industries, such as primary metals, machinery, electrical equipment, and shipbuilding, make substantially greater use of temporary employees to meet peak demands.

Much work is subcontracted out. In many cases, subcontractors work exclusively for a single company. Much of the work involved is other than regular production—construction, repair, loading, cleaning up—but peak load extras are also supplied in this manner.

For example, in a large steel mill we visited, 12,000 regular employees

65. Ministry of Labor, *Year Book of Labor Statistics, 1972*, p. 11.
66. Taira, *Economic Development and the Labor Market*, pp. 180–81.

were at work. Four subsidiary companies located at the same site provided power and performed other auxiliary functions; they employed an additional 1,500 workers who were not considered employees of the parent company. About 150 subcontracting companies employing an additional 8,000 men—3,000 in construction—also worked at the site. The nonregular employees were easily identifiable by hard hats of a different color from those of the regular men. The company acknowledged that there were some problems in keeping the subcontractors up to scratch, but it was unwilling to increase the numbers of its regular employees. In the event of a slowdown, marginal subcontractors would be eliminated before any other personnel adjustments were made.

A shipyard employing 3,400 men reported that an additional 570 were in the employ of subcontractors, engaged mainly in cleaning and painting. All skilled welding and fitting was done by regular employees. The basis for subcontracting was said to be historical: until a few years ago, subcontract workers received lower wages, and although this is no longer true, the practice persists.

A third example illustrates the ingenuity with which Japanese firms maintain a fair degree of labor force flexibility within the system of permanent employment. Every large firm faces the problem of providing work for employees who because of illness or age are no longer able to perform arduous physical labor. In the United States this is normally handled by reserving lighter jobs for these employees, who are paid a lower wage commensurate with their new duties. In Japan, however, because the wage system implies an increasing personal rate until retirement, this is not possible.

A large Japanese steel mill had on its payroll about 350 employees who had contracted various occupational diseases and were unable to engage in primary production. Put to work at such tasks as sweeping, cleaning up waste oil, and planting and watering trees, flowers, and shrubs, they were looked upon by other workers as second-class citizens, and were unhappy despite the fact that their wages were maintained. To solve the problem, a subsidiary enterprise was created, to which they were transferred. They accepted a wage reduction of 20 percent. A market survey of independent contractors engaged in similar work in the vicinity had indicated that the competitive cut should have been 40 percent, so this represented a compromise.

At first the plan was opposed by the employees concerned, who did not want to lose their regular status, and by the enterprise union, which objected in principle to this quasi-discharge. But the new arrangement has worked well, not only because what the employees are doing is the main business of the new company, but also because its major work is pollution control and beautification, fashionable activities in Japan at present. If the subsidiary has not become financially independent within five years, it will be closed down and its remaining employees taken back by the parent company. It is attempting to diversify, but is hampered by its relatively high wage level. The employees, however, have transferred their loyalty to the new firm and are attempting through intensive study programs to become specialists in their trades in order to justify the higher wages and keep the enterprise afloat.

There are no aggregate data on the number of subcontract employees in Japan working at the same site as regular workers. In most Western countries such workers would be direct employees of the major firm and members of the same union as the regular workers.[67] These examples imply that the numbers must be considerable, and the phenomenon helps explain the economics of lifetime commitment.

Viewed broadly, the dual industrial structure characteristic of much of Japanese industry contributes to the same end. Many large enterprises depend upon small subcontractors for off-site production as well as for on-site auxiliary operations. Subcontractors are often financed and supervised by large firms, and one of their functions is to bear the initial shock of fluctuation in demand, reducing the burden of the employment commitment borne by the major producers.

THE RETIREMENT SYSTEM. Another cost-reducing element is provided by the retirement system. The normal retirement age for men is fifty-five, except members of boards of directors. Unions currently are demanding delay in retirement, and whether as the result of their pressure or the growing labor stringency, the age of compulsory retirement is slowly moving upward toward sixty.

Most retirees continue to work, either at their old firms or elsewhere. A 1970 survey of retirees during the previous six years indicated that 75 percent were still employees, 12 percent were self-employed, and 13 percent were not working. Of the latter group, 80 percent indicated that they were involuntarily unemployed. There was a substantial decline in earnings: 20 percent for managerial personnel, 25 percent for professionals, 33 percent for clerical workers, 23 percent for handicraftsmen, and 29 percent for sales personnel. Work status changed as well: the managerial contingent among the retirees fell from 26 percent before retirement to 9 percent

67. A flurry of attempts some years ago by American manufacturing companies to subcontract maintenance and repair to construction contractors met with much hostility from the production unions.

after, whereas the clerical employee percentage rose from 15 to 20 percent. There was a large increase in salesmen, from 0.7 to 9 percent. Former managers were being shifted into clerical, sales, and service work.[68]

Compulsory early retirement is a legacy of the past, when life expectancy was short and labor in abundant supply. Its persistence in Japan results in no small measure from the manpower flexibility that it affords large enterprises. Most retirees cannot afford not to work, since their pensions are inadequate. They constitute a reservoir of relatively cheap labor prepared to accept short-term employment. Many of them are taken on by subsidiaries or subcontractors of the main enterprise. This is particularly true of management personnel: "The managerial and supervisory staff in most subsidiaries of major corporations is made up largely of employees retired from the parent concern."[69] Above all, early retirement reduces the potential cost of the employment guarantee by simply curtailing the regular working lifetime to a stage well below that common to nations at Japan's level of development.

With all the cost-reducing elements—limitation mainly to male employees, exclusion of substantial numbers of temporary workers, subcontracting, and early retirement—there have undoubtedly been occasions when Japanese firms would have preferred to discharge regular employees, either as a rationalization measure in the face of technological change or during cyclical downswings, or simply to get rid of incompetents. The extra cost of refraining from doing so (no one, to our knowledge, has attempted to measure it, although it would be a useful exercise) is borne, in our view, not so much because of any tradition of paternalism, but simply because the compensating benefits are substantial.

THE ROLE OF THE UNIONS. Among the most important of the benefits is the enterprise form of unionism that is considered below. Union members have been prepared to forgo the advantages of full-time professional representation and such outside assistance as strike benefits in times of crisis for the presumed advantages of permanent employment. They have been willing to work alongside nonunion, nonregular employees to maintain their favored position. Their interest is in keeping the bargaining unit small, since this provides maximum insulation against employment insecurity. The issue most likely to create union militancy is discharge.

68. Economic Planning Agency, *Whitepaper on National Life, 1973: The Life and Its Quality in Japan* (1973), pp. 64–74.

69. M. Y. Yoshino, *Japan's Managerial System: Tradition and Innovation* (M.I.T. Press, 1968), p. 152. Yoshino notes also that incompetent managerial staff who cannot be discharged are often transferred to subsidiaries.

The basic ideology of Japanese unionism rests squarely on the prevailing employment system. If the commitment should weaken, profound changes could occur in union structure and function, all in the direction of a greater aggressiveness. Corporate management in many countries probably would grasp the opportunity of trading off a guarantee of lifetime employment to a portion of their labor force in return for docile unions.

ALLOCATION OF LABOR. Other advantages flow from the system. Japanese employers have a virtually free hand in allocating labor within the enterprise, authority that American employers prize highly but hold to a much more limited extent. There are no intrafirm craft jurisdictional boundaries or promotion ladders to block assignment of labor where it can be most productive. And Japan has some very large firms, so that intraenterprise mobility can encompass geographical or even interindustrial mobility.

A survey made in 1972 by the Japan Institute of Labor indicated that the principal cause of intracompany transfer was the establishment of new factories; the foundation of new subsidiaries followed close behind. Closing factories, curtailment of operations, and mergers ranked next. Union influence was exerted primarily through informal discussion rather than collective bargaining. In most cases, the plant manager made the selection of individuals to be transferred, and personal factors such as health, employment of other family members, and schooling of children were taken into account.[70] Housing assistance generally is provided at the new place of work, as well as a salary incentive.[71] Reluctance to accept transfer is not uncommon, but in most cases it appears to be overcome by appeal to company loyalty.[72] But outright refusal to make a move that involved a change of residence normally would not be cause for discharge.

There is no tradition of craft unionism, and unions have nothing to do with skill training. Companies have virtually unlimited freedom to define job boundaries, which makes it easier to adapt to new technology. The other side of the coin is that workers have no guarantee that they can continue to ply their skills. To the extent that their earnings depend upon

70. See *Japan Labor Bulletin*, April 1, 1973. The survey covered eighty-four companies employing an average of 5,700 employees each. The transfer affected an average of 18 percent of all employees, and it was estimated that transferred personnel filled 44 percent of job openings at new facilities.

71. Companies expanding into new areas commonly provide housing at rents as low as one-quarter of the market rate. Tax authorities examine rent and other payments in kind company by company and work out an agreement on a permissible average nontaxable maximum for the entire company. This permits tax-free items to be concentrated in new factories, thus providing an additional incentive to move.

72. On this point, see Robert E. Cole, *Japanese Blue Collar: The Changing Tradition* (University of California Press, 1971), pp. 256–57.

seniority, they are protected against loss of income. They may not suffer a wage cut, but earnings on the new job may rise more slowly than at the previous job. Some would argue that the transfer system results in underuse of employee skills.

Another negative aspect of employer freedom to transfer employees is summarized in the following passage:

In the U.S. factory, competition among workers over promotion, overtime, job assignments, etc., is decided to a high degree by relatively objective criteria such as skill or seniority. Favoritism, though not unimportant, plays a limited role; one of the major achievements of American unions is the strong plant organizations which diminish such treatment. In Japan, once minimum standards of seniority and skill are met, worker competition often is decided by a worker's vertical relationship to his superiors. Great emphasis is placed on impressing superiors, on flattery, and behind-the-door deals. It increases friction among workers and makes it difficult to develop deep horizontal friendships and worker solidarity.[73]

TRAINING. A concept that has received considerable attention in the United States in connection with human-capital theory—the distinction between general and specific training—might be thought to constitute another significant employer benefit in the Japanese context. American employers are said to be reluctant to invest in training that imparts general skills, transferable to other employers, and more willing to train for jobs unique to the individual firm, leaving the general training to vocational schools.

It is generally recognized that Japan's state-run vocational school system is modest.[74] But neither does there appear to be a lavish expenditure on training within the individual enterprise. An OECD manpower team pointed out that despite a considerable volume of internal training, most of it was brief. In attempting to explain the Japanese success in skill formation, the team came up with the following comment: "Maybe the conclusion can be drawn that the special features of the Japanese employment relationship—the whole system of consultation, social participation, informal training, incentives and motivations which exist in the individual enterprises—make an *ad hoc* process of skill acquisition highly effective."[75]

To have precise comparisons of the resources allocated to industrial

73. Ibid., pp. 165–66.
74. See Beatrice G. Reubens, "Manpower Training in Japan," *Monthly Labor Review,* vol. 96 (September 1973), p. 18. Reubens points out that 250,000 public trainees a year for a labor force of 50 million is not impressive. Sweden, with a labor force of 4 million, had 94,000 students enrolled in government training programs in 1971.
75. OECD, *Manpower Policy in Japan* (1973), p. 138.

training in Japan and other industrialized nations would be of interest. In their absence, it can only be pointed out that Japanese enterprises obviously have managed—in one way or another—to create the skills necessary to maintain their rapid rate of expansion. And it is scarcely necessary to add that in times of labor stringency, permanent employment guarantees, buttressed by informal antipirating pacts among employers, represent an excellent means for large enterprises to ensure a core of experienced employees.

EMPLOYEE LOYALTY. There is an additional benefit that cannot be estimated quantitatively but that is undoubtedly of great value: the extra productivity deriving from individual employee loyalty to the enterprise. Regardless of dissatisfaction with specific attributes of work—wages, equipment, or working conditions—a worker must have a strong concern for the viability of an institution in which he plans to spend his entire working life.

An anecdote may serve to point up the intensity of this enterprise loyalty in Japan. Some time ago, a top management official in one of the major steel companies was hired away by a competitor—a rare event. The explanation was that the competitor was installing processes with which the official was familiar and badly needed his expertise. After five years on the new job, the official became seriously ill and had to be hospitalized. He insisted that he wanted to die in a hospital run by his old company—and he did.

The kind of company loyalty that exists in Japan is a direct function of permanent commitment on both sides of the employment bargain. It carries with it a willingness to remain after hours to finish up work, without extra compensation; to improve skills as much for company as for personal advancement. It leads to some peculiar results as well, as evidenced by what we were told by a leading trade unionist: "The degree to which Japanese unions collaborate with employers is beyond the American imagination. Companies will often line up in back of union-supported political candidates. Even all the subcontractors join in. The company figures it will benefit from having a loyal enterprise union man in the Diet; for example, if it were accused of pollution."

The same theme emerged repeatedly in the course of interviews. The director of the Employers' Federation noted that "when a man is asked his occupation, he will answer 'I work for Company X,' and this is considered a perfectly adequate reply." A company official who had once worked for Inland Steel in Chicago and belonged to the steelworkers' union there felt that American workers were far less company conscious than the Japanese; in particular, the many black and Mexican workers in the Inland plant had virtually no feeling of identification with the company. The chairman of the enterprise union in a medium-size clothing company remarked: "There is a gentleman's agreement that the union will cooperate to raise labor productivity. The rate of production is not a subject for bargaining. Products are of high quality, and profitability depends on morale. But it is company philosophy that business is not just for profit." The president of a medium-size paper-products company said: "Our basic managerial principle is to provide a good life in work, so that workers can look back upon their productive life with satisfaction."

There is some evidence that enterprise loyalty is weakening, particularly among the large number of younger people who have entered industry.[76] But there is near unanimity of opinion that it remains the dominant ideology of Japanese employees, from top management to unskilled production workers, particularly in large enterprises; and that it has been and remains a potent source for the achievement of high productivity.

Summary

The Japanese system of lifetime employment guarantee, as practiced by virtually all large corporations and many medium-size ones as well, is a noteworthy aspect of the country's labor market organization. Although limited in scope to a minority of the labor force, where it applies it has provided firms with major benefits at relatively small cost. In our view, its economic rationality is beyond question. Japanese customs and traditions may have contributed a great deal to its adoption and to its continuing ideological strength, but the profitability criterion alone would be sufficient to sustain its popularity in business circles. Whether it has served the worker equally well is a different question, which is considered below.

Would a slowing down in the rate of economic growth threaten the viability of the permanent commitment system? In our judgment, it would not, particularly in view of a diminishing supply of new labor. A deep depression might make it impossible for some firms to honor the employment guarantee, but the system has so many safeguards that anything short of a major economic catastrophe is unlikely to shake it.

Nor does there appear to be any serious challenge from the employee side. Although there seems to be a greater propensity than in the past for younger men to change jobs, once a satisfactory regular employment niche is found, the great majority seem satisfied to continue with the same organization for the rest of their working lives. Japan has had two decades of

76. See particularly Odaka, *Toward Industrial Democracy*, especially chap. 4.

phenomenal growth and low unemployment, but the psychological environment created by a labor surplus economy persists. By 1982, however, more than half of all Japanese employees will have been born after 1945,[77] and it may be that this will be a turning point, for they will have no memory at all of the period of turmoil and hardship that followed World War II. The prospect of a lifetime in the service of a single organization, determined at the time of graduation from school, may come to seem less enticing.

Trade Unions and Management

Several characteristics of Japanese trade unionism differentiate it from Western European or American models. Among them are the following:
—The locus of power and money at the local or enterprise union level.
—A concomitant weakness of national and federation union bodies.
—The concentration of collective bargaining at the local level and of political action at the federation level.
—A high degree of organization of white-collar employees and their inclusion in the same unions as blue-collar workers.
—Worker loyalty to the enterprise union rather than to class, craft, or occupational groupings.

These features of labor organization have sometimes been ascribed to psychological motivations of the Japanese people or to the nation's sociological structure. How else can one account for apparently gross deviations from what are customarily regarded as trade union norms when nations emerge into industrial maturity? In the following pages, we shall attempt to explain the logic of Japanese unionism largely in terms of the country's course of development; we do not think it necessary to fall back on well-worn generalizations about family structure and the hierarchical, traditionalist nature of Japanese society.

Patterns of Representation and Affiliation

Japan has a long history of trade unionism, but the movement achieved no substantial organization or economic power before World War II. But prewar trade unionism had considerable influence on such postwar developments as enterprise unionism and political factionalism, and it was im-

77. Unofficial estimate of the Japanese Ministry of Labor, made available by Mr. S. Ichino.

portant in preserving memories of employer resistance and government repression. For all practical purposes, trade unionism ceased to exist in Japan in 1938, when a government-dominated labor front was installed.

GROWTH AND COVERAGE. As part of the policy of imposing democratic institutions on Japan, the U.S. military authorities encouraged trade unionism from the start of the occupation. Despite efforts to guide the nascent movement along purely economic lines, the first organizing drives were directed to a considerable extent by communist and other leaders concerned more with the political than the economic aspects of unionism. Operating at first with little resistance from employers and none from government, they achieved quick success: within four years of the end of hostilities, trade union membership reached 6.65 million, a rate of growth unequaled before or since.[78] As Sumiya has written:

In the economic confusion caused by Japan's military defeat and the rapidly progressing inflation that followed, all workers faced difficulties in making a living; therefore, in an effort to protect their livelihood and to oppose employers who were unable or unwilling to conform to reconstruction policies, they organized labor unions. . . . With the destruction of the value system that supported the old social order and because of the critical living conditions—lack of food, clothing, and housing—most union members became sympathetic toward radical union policies, although it is questionable to what extent they agreed with the political ideologies of the union movement.[79]

Despite a purge of communists ordered by occupation authorities in 1950, membership growth continued, though at a more moderate rate, reaching a total of 12.1 million in 1973.[80] This meant that 33 percent of all employees were unionized, a rate comparable to that of the United States and West Germany and exceeded among major industrial nations only by that of Great Britain.

Civil servants and employees of government-owned enterprises constitute 27 percent of Japanese union membership. Although government employees are well organized—to a considerably greater extent than in the United States, for example—they enjoy only limited rights of collective bargaining. Moreover, the strength of a labor movement rarely lies in the public sector; unions of government workers may be militant enough, as they are in a number of countries, but they are up against a formidable adversary. And so it is in Japan: 63.5 percent of the members of Sōhyō,

78. See Solomon B. Levine, *Industrial Relations in Postwar Japan* (University of Illinois Press, 1958), chap. 1.

79. Mikio Sumiya, "Contemporary Arrangements: An Overview," in Ōkōchi, Karsh, and Levine (eds.), *Workers and Employers in Japan*, p. 57.

80. *Japan Labor Bulletin*, March 1, 1974.

the largest federation, were in the public sector in 1973, yet their legal right to strike had been withdrawn from them in 1947 by an occupation order.

In the private sector, unionism is confined primarily to the larger companies. Almost 65 percent of the employees of firms employing 500 or more workers were organized in 1972, but the percentage dropped to 31.5 percent for firms with between 100 and 500 employees; 9 percent for those employing from 30 to 100; and 3.4 percent for firms with fewer than 30 employees.[81] In most countries, small firms are more difficult to organize than large ones, and the dual industrial structure of Japan creates a special problem for the unions.

FRAGMENTATION AND POLITICIZATION. Unity on a national level generally is a source of strength to a labor movement, whereas division into competing federations tends to reduce its effectiveness. The United States, West Germany, and Great Britain have single national federations (though not all industrial or craft unions are affiliated with them), whereas in France and Italy the unions are split among competing federations. It would be a great oversimplification to attribute the relative strength of the first group, compared with the second, to this factor alone, but undoubtedly it is an important element. A leader who speaks "in the name of all organized labor" need not shout to be heard above the voices of his rivals.

To explain how Japanese unionism has reached its present splintered state would require a volume in itself.[82] Suffice it to say that the initial hothouse growth of unionism under the American occupation, the immediate factionalism along prewar lines, and the purge of communists in 1950 imparted an internal instability that has proved impossible to overcome. The preoccupation of labor federations with political issues, in part a function of their impotence in economic matters, led inevitably to interunion rivalries that reflected political divisions. The particular tendencies that prevail in Japan are not identical with those in France and Italy—there is, for example, no labor federation in Japan dominated by the Communist party—but there is some parallel in the causes of division.

NATIONAL FEDERATIONS. The largest of the Japanese labor federations is Sōhyō (an acronym for General Council of Trade Unions of Japan), which had 36 percent of union membership in 1973; a substantial majority of its membership is in the public sector. Of the ten largest national unions in

---

81. Ibid., March 1, 1973.

82. For more detailed coverage of this issue, see Levine, *Industrial Relations;* Alice H. Cook, *An Introduction to Japanese Trade Unionism* (Cornell University Press, 1966); and Ōkōchi, Karsh, and Levine (eds.), *Workers and Employers in Japan.*

the private sector, only three are affiliated with it, and one of these is the union of private railway workers. Its industrial base includes only the steelworkers' union and the smaller of two unions of metalworkers.[83] Its 1972 share of organized workers in manufacturing was only 19 percent. Moreover, over the period 1963–73, Sōhyō's total membership rose only from 4.2 to 4.3 million despite a substantially larger growth for the union movement as a whole and the tremendous advance of Japanese industry.

The second largest federation is Dōmei (Japanese Confederation of Labor). Its share of union membership was almost 19 percent in 1973, and it had an increase in membership from 1.3 million to 2.3 million over the previous decade. More than 90 percent of its members are in the private sector, and it numbers among its affiliates four of the ten largest unions in the private sector: in textiles, the metal trades, shipbuilding, and automobiles, the last three of which have grown rapidly in recent years.

A third federation, Chūritsuroren (Federation of Independent Unions), with 11 percent of union membership, is confined almost entirely to the private sector. Three of the ten largest national unions in the private sector are affiliated with it: in electrical machinery, life insurance, and construction, all growth industries. Chūritsuroren membership rose from 868,000 in 1962 to 1.4 million in 1972. Chūritsuroren works closely with Sōhyō during the spring wage bargaining, though not politically. Together, they are significantly larger than Dōmei in the private sector, and their combined growth for the decade was not much below Dōmei's. A fourth federation, Shinsanbetsu (National Federation of Industrial Organizations), had less than 1 percent of union membership in 1972.

ENTERPRISE UNIONS. More than a third of all union members, however, are not affiliated with any federation. These include several large national unions—bank employees, a second union of automobile workers, and transport workers—as well as a large number of organizations confined to a single enterprise without any national affiliation.

Nonaffiliated national unions are not unknown in the West—the powerful teamsters' and automobile workers' unions of the United States are good examples—but nowhere else among the developed nations is there as large a bloc of unions limited to a single enterprise as in Japan. Enterprise unions often exist in less developed countries, representing a more primitive type of union structure, a transitional stage between loose, preunion associations within the single factory and multiemployer unions proper.

83. Relations between Sōhyō and the steelworkers have become strained; the latter's delegates to the 1973 Sōhyō convention were suspended because of the steelworkers' refusal to pay a special levy to Sōhyō.

Vulnerable to employer pressure, the single-enterprise unions eventually band together not only for mutual aid and protection, but also to regulate wage competition within the industry or craft. Perhaps the most notable features of Japanese labor history have been, first, the failure of many of the single-enterprise unions that sprang up during the immediate postwar years to participate in the final consolidating step; and, second, the imperfect degree of integration that characterizes the process of union structural development for most of the rest.

The early history of unionism in the U.S. automobile industry offers an analogy. In 1933, when the advent of the Roosevelt administration made possible the existence of unions in the mass production industries, small independent organizations developed simultaneously in several automobile plants: Hudson, General Motors Truck, Oldsmobile, and Chrysler, among others. Within three years they had combined into the United Automobile Workers of America. Unionism in the Japanese automobile industry, by comparison, remains divided despite attempts to bring about unity.

POLITICAL ACTIVITY. To understand what separates the federations, it is necessary to consider briefly the pattern of trade union political action that prevails in Japan. Sōhyō backs the Japanese Socialist party (JSP), the largest of the opposition parties in the Japanese Diet, which won 118 seats in the House of Representatives to 271 for the governing Liberal Democratic party in the 1972 elections. Pursuant to a resolution adopted at its convention in August 1972, a resolution that was opposed by sixteen national affiliates, Sōhyō supported all JSP candidates in the 1972 elections and raised almost $2 million to help finance their campaigns. Special endorsement was given to seventy-seven candidates who were members of Sōhyō unions; fifty-eight of them were elected. The considerable success of the JSP in this election convinced Sōhyō of the wisdom of its political activities, and it can be anticipated that this policy will be continued, at least into the immediate future. The main threat may come from the Japanese Communist party (JCP), which is critical of exclusive Sōhyō support of the socialists and may soon be in a position to take effective action.[84]

The JSP represents relatively radical socialism in the international political spectrum. Its closest counterpart in the West would be the left-wing socialist parties of Italy; it is more radical than parties advocating social

84. A straw in the wind was a statement by the secretary general of Sōhyō in July 1974, to the effect that within one or two years Sōhyō probably would be supporting all "progressive" parties, including the JCP. *Japan Labor Bulletin*, Sept. 1, 1974. The great success of the JCP in the 1974 elections to the upper house of the Diet undoubtedly contributed to Sōhyō's movement in this direction.

democracy in Northern Europe. The several diverse doctrinal currents within the JSP make it difficult to predict its positions on specific issues.[85] At times there have been strong tendencies toward close cooperation with the JCP, but the recent electoral success of the latter (its Diet strength increased from fourteen to thirty-eight seats in the 1972 elections), posing a threat to the hegemony of the socialists, has cooled this desire.

Dōmei is committed to the support of the Japanese Democratic Socialist party (JDSP), which is close in ideology to the mainstream of European social democracy. Dōmei leaders argue that although they favor moves toward a socialist organization of industry through democratic means, they reject the concept of the class struggle and any resort to revolutionary force. Dōmei has representation on the central executive committee of the JDSP, and funds its election campaigns.

The elections of 1972 marked a sharp setback for the JDSP: its strength in the House of Representatives fell from twenty-nine to nineteen. It lost one seat in the upper house in the 1974 elections, whereas the socialists gained three and the communists nine. Although Dōmei is more heavily committed than Sōhyō to collective bargaining because of the greater concentration of its constituency in the private sector, there appears to be little prospect of its abandoning its formal political commitment toward the democratic socialists.

Chūritsuroren is politically neutral (mainly because of a fear of ideological division within individual affiliates if it were not), as are most of the nonaffiliated enterprise unions. Leaders of independent unions often say that they have not joined Sōhyō or Dōmei because their members want to be free to support the political party of their own choice, including the Liberal Democrats.

Unity negotiations have been held between Sōhyō and Dōmei, but the chances for success, which would do much to strengthen the Japanese labor movement, are not great. Dōmei has been advocating unification of the unions in the private sector as a first step, but Sōhyō, concerned lest it be subject to an internal split, has insisted on a formula for joint private–public–sector unification. There appears to be too great an ideological gulf between the leadership of the two organizations to be easily bridged. Dōmei is firmly dedicated to collective bargaining and labor-management cooperation as the basic means of improving the life of the Japanese worker,

85. For a full account, which is already somewhat dated because of the fast pace of events, see Allan B. Cole, George O. Totten, and Cecil H. Uyehara, *Socialist Parties in Postwar Japan* (Yale University Press, 1966).

whereas Sōhyō regards political action through government as the more productive means. With mounting concern among all elements of the Japanese people, workers included, about such issues as pollution, inflation, and problems of housing and commuting, the political winds appear to be veering toward the Sōhyō position. Unless collective bargaining becomes more effective than it is now, Dōmei may find itself obliged to alter its course.

Internal Structure of Trade Unions

The internal structure of Japanese trade unionism differs in a number of respects from that of Western unions. Perhaps the most important is the relatively greater power in Japan of the local or branch union, which normally is coterminous with the enterprise. Enterprise unionism contains elements of strength stemming from its closeness to its constituency, but also serious drawbacks in economic power. A number of factors contribute to the weakness of the labor movement in Japan, but none more fundamentally than this structural feature.

MEMBERSHIP AND DUES. The general rule in unionized firms is that all permanent employees, white collar as well as blue collar, including several echelons of supervisors below the rank of section chief, belong to a single union—regardless of craft or occupation. The union shop by agreement with the employer is quite common, though by no means universal. The checkoff of union dues is quite general in the public service, but only about half the unions in the private sector enjoy it. These, however, tend to be the larger unions.

Lack of funds appears not to be an inhibiting factor for the enterprise unions. Dues are fixed by the union, often as a percentage of the wage, which protects the union against inflation. Amounts collected vary widely, but 1 percent of income, plus an additional contribution to a strike fund, seems to be a target figure. These figures compare favorably with the dues in the West; in many countries, amounts are stated in absolute terms, which allow the level of dues to erode in periods of inflation.

But there is a major difference in the amounts allotted to the various echelons of trade union organization. The lion's share is retained by the enterprise union in Japan, whereas local unions in the West normally transmit a major portion of dues received to the parent national organization. An official of Dōmei reported in an interview (1974) that the average union member paid about ¥2,000 monthly, 80 percent of which remained with the local. Locals, however, bear some of the costs normally borne by the national bodies in the West: for example, they finance the annual Dōmei conventions. Nevertheless, the bulk of union assets are held locally in Japan.

OFFICIALS. The larger enterprise unions have full-time officers and clerical staff; several unions surveyed reported a ratio of one full-time person (officers and staff) for each 600 to 1,000 members, whereas earlier surveys suggested ratios of from 250 to 300 members.[86] Part-time officials are reimbursed for wages lost during time spent on union work. But virtually all small unions, and many large ones as well, are given office space by the employer, and use company facilities for membership meetings. Litigation of grievances, a costly activity in the West, is not practiced in Japan. Some unions prepare educational literature, but this appears to be modest in format and cost.

The internal organization of the enterprise union depends largely on the size of the enterprise. In large firms, plant locals send representatives to companywide bodies, which in turn select the top officials. Local officers normally are elected at annual general membership meetings, but rival slates seem to be the exception rather than the rule. There is no general practice with respect to turnover in union office. One gets the impression that in small enterprises there is considerable rotation, since people are not anxious to hold jobs that require considerable extra work with little compensation in money or status. In large enterprises, successive terms of office are more common. A crucial point is that in both cases all enterprise union officials retain their status as company employees. Except for a few, the career ladder for an ambitious young man is not through the union or its allied political party, but with the company. The most able union officials, particularly among white-collar employees, can look forward to promotion to section chief, which often (though not necessarily) takes them out of the bargaining unit. For the most part, however, enterprise union officers expect to resume their regular jobs when they finish their terms of office (though in public enterprises there is no guarantee of reappointment for union officials who complete their terms of office).

INTERPOSITION OF MANAGEMENT. The lack of a cadre of professional officers at the local level must be regarded as a major source of weakness in the Japanese labor movement. Worker representatives at this level can scarcely be expected to withstand management pressures when they are subordinates rather than equals. To compound the problem, there is a tendency for the unions to be run by first and second line supervisors, who

86. Cook, *An Introduction to Japanese Trade Unionism*, p. 58.

would be outside the bargaining unit in the United States. Many of these are just on the verge of promotion into middle management and are not likely to do anything that might jeopardize their future prospects. A study of the operation of a local union at the Kawasaki plant of Nihon Kōkan, one of the largest steel companies in Japan, concluded that "the proportion of company group and crew chiefs . . . among the elected union officers is very high. . . . The labor union is operated by the company's key employees. As a result, the union is not free to function separately and independently of company policy but rather might be described as 'cohesive' with the company."[87] A detailed and careful study of labor relations in a corrugated paper box enterprise came to very similar conclusions.[88]

It does not follow, of course, that all Japanese enterprise union officials are under the thumb of management. Some of them take refuge in Marxist ideology as "moral armour to confront management and sustain them in their opposition."[89] In the course of interviews, we encountered others who appeared to differ little in their independence of attitude from their Western counterparts. But in principle, the Japanese system affords the opportunity for management intervention in union affairs to a degree that would not be tolerated in the West.

This is regarded as a major problem by national union leaders with whom we talked, but they indicated that there was little they could do about it. Revocation of a local's charter is a remedy not consistent with either the theory or the reality of Japanese union structure. Charges of unfair labor practices by an employer can be brought to governmental labor relations commissions, but until recently, at least against large enterprises, this was not common.[90] Managerial personnel who are not members of the union almost never explicitly threaten or persuade. The lower level super-

87. Masumi Tsuda, "Personnel Administration at the Industrial Plant Level," in Ōkōchi, Karsh, and Levine (eds.), *Workers and Employers in Japan*, pp. 423–24.

88. Clark, "Social Relations in a Japanese Company," chap. 7.

89. Cole, *Japanese Blue Collar*, p. 266.

90. A few years ago, a Japanese expert reported that no unfair labor practice charges were brought against large enterprises. Toru Ariizumi, "The Legal Framework: Past and Present," in Ōkōchi, Karsh, and Levine (eds.), *Workers and Employers in Japan*, pp. 129–30. A recent survey of unfair labor practice charges submitted to the labor relations commissions revealed, however, that from 1968 to 1972, the number of such charges varied from a low of 569 in 1971 to a high of 1,483 in 1970, 30 to 50 percent of them involving firms with more than 1,000 employees. See *Japan Labor Bulletin*, July 1, 1974. By comparison, 26,487 unfair labor practice charges were filed with the National Labor Relations Board in the United States during fiscal 1973. See U.S. National Labor Relations Board, *Thirty-Eighth Annual Report* (1973), p. 10.

visory personnel are union members, and they are within their legal rights in discussing union affairs with subordinates. Some employer tactics occasionally used are transfer of militants to shops with poor working conditions, placement of union voting booths near supervisors' desks, giving the slate favored by the company (if there is more than one slate) top billing on the ballot, and the carrot of more rapid promotion that has been possible through greater use of pay-by-ability wage systems.

WHITE-COLLAR–BLUE-COLLAR PARTNERSHIP. The phenomenon of a common organization for blue- and white-collar employees is not usual in the West. White-collar employees working in close contiguity to manual workers are sometimes included in the same unit, but employees in a head office are almost never included. Among Western countries, Sweden has the highest degree of organization among white-collar employees, but they belong to a federation that is completely independent of the traditional manualist body. It has been estimated that almost a quarter of unionized workers in Japanese manufacturing are engaged in white-collar tasks; if government employment and the services are included, the proportion rises to 35 percent or more.[91]

The unionization of Japanese white-collar employees has been attributed to the relative decline in their earnings during and immediately after World War II and to their identification with blue-collar workers in the quest for political democracy.[92] During the early postwar years white-collar employees provided a substantial proportion of enterprise union leadership. In 1950 half of the elected union officers came from this group. The percentage has been declining, and manual workers are much more reluctant now to entrust their interests to office or sales personnel, whose aspirations may be quite different from their own. In the large firms, all but the eldest management officials were union members at one stage of their careers, and it is not unusual to meet a personnel manager who had once been chairman of the enterprise union.[93]

In the late 1950s and the early 1960s it was not uncommon, where the leadership of a union had fallen into the hands of militants, for white-collar employees to lead the formation of second, or breakaway, unions with management encouragement. But these divisions rarely persisted, and in

91. Solomon B. Levine, "Unionization of White-Collar Employees in Japan," in Adolf Sturmthal (ed.), *White-Collar Trade Unions* (University of Illinois Press, 1966), pp. 224–26.

92. Sumiya, "Contemporary Arrangements," in Ōkōchi, Karsh, and Levine (eds.), *Workers and Employers in Japan*, p. 59.

93. The effect of this exposure on the attitude of the personnel department to unionism is an interesting question to which we have not found any good answers.

the course of interviews we encountered only two dual-union situations: one in a shipyard, where the greatly outnumbered staff personnel had seceded because they felt that the enterprise union was not sympathetic to the preservation of their wage advantage, and one in a medium-size textile plant.

There is no discernible trend toward white-collar separatism, a fact often attributed to equality of status between blue- and white-collar employees and to the lack of class consciousness in Japan. Cited in support of this view are the facts that all employees in the large firms work under the same wage systems and that their employment is equally secure. There is an opposing view that substantial differences in status do exist, and that in reality "the social prestige of white-collar workers has continued to be higher than that of the blue-collar, and their opportunities for promotion have been relatively open."[94] The concept of class is a slippery one, and attempts to measure it have not been successful. What can be said of Japan is that employees of the large firms, white- and blue-collar alike, are overwhelmingly company conscious, and as long as this continues, unified enterprise unions are likely to persist.[95]

The national union in Japan, with a few notable exceptions, is a loose association of enterprise local unions without either constitutional or customary authority over their policies. Many national union leaders return to their companies when their terms of office run out, although others go into politics. They often owe their power to their identification with large enterprise unions rather than to any constitutional authority at the national union level. National unions also suffer from the fact that many enterprise unions in their industries do not affiliate with them, thus limiting their capacity to act as coordinating bodies.

It would be quite inaccurate to say that national unions are of little importance in Japan. They are playing an increasingly significant role in annual wage movements, helping to set the patterns that serve as benchmarks for the enterprise unions. They are the focus of support for political parties and seek to raise funds for election campaigns. At times, locals use the threat of following their more radical national bodies if the employer

94. Hideaki Okamoto, "Management and Their Organizations," in Ōkōchi, Karsh, and Levine (eds.), *Workers and Employers in Japan*, p. 182. To the same effect, see Masumi Tsuda, "Personnel Administration," in ibid., p. 400.

95. Walter Reuther once asked the enterprise union leaders of a large Japanese automobile concern why they did not adopt the United Automobile Workers' tactic of selecting one company as an initial strike target in order to set a pattern for others to follow. He was told that this could not be done because the workers would not be willing to jeopardize their company's market share.

does not give in to their demands. On the other hand, they do little or no collective bargaining, which in most countries is the principal function of the national union.

The top federations, particularly Sōhyō and Dōmei, represent the national interests of labor through lobbying, public pronouncements, and representation on national committees—like their counterparts elsewhere. In September 1972, for example, Sōhyō and Dōmei joined the Japanese Federation of Employers' Associations (Nikkeiren) in petitioning the government to raise the level of tax-exempt retirement pay. More recently they joined in recommending to their affiliates a later retirement age and movement toward the five-day week. Above all, Sōhyō, in cooperation with Chūritsuroren, pioneered and led the annual spring wage offensive that has become an integral part of the bargaining system.

In many ways, the federations set the tone of Japanese industrial relations. However, their influence falls short of that of corresponding bodies in most Western nations, not only because of the strength of the enterprise unions, but also because their allied political parties have not gained sufficient political power. Should the socialist and communist parties win a parliamentary majority, the status of Sōhyō and Dōmei relative to other echelons in the structure of the labor movement would undoubtedly be increased.

Ideological Bases of Labor-Management Relations

A major source of what we perceive as trade union weakness in Japan lies in the philosophy of industrial relations that is dominant not only in management circles but also among many employees. The following is a good summary of this ideology:

The relationship between employer and his employees is not only the relationship of providing labor and paying wages but also is a relationship of protection and family-like dependence. The employer is father of the enterprise family and the employees are his children. The relationship includes not only the economic relationship of give and take but also the relationship of sentiment, friendship and kindness. The relationship between employer and enterprise union is also of the same character. Japanese enterprise unions are expected to negotiate with the employer only within the limits of this amicable atmosphere created by the enterprise family.[96]

96. Tadashi Hanami, "The Characteristics of Labor Disputes and Their Settlements in Japan," in Japan Institute of Labor, *Social and Cultural Background of Labor-Management Relations in Asian Countries* (1971), p. 213. It might be noted that Hanami is merely describing this phenomenon and does not necessarily sub-

Ichirō Nakayama, the dean of Japanese labor economists, put it this way:

One of the facts that is frequently referred to as the most marked characteristic of labor-management relations in Japan is the relative absence of conflict between employer and worker in all phases of industrial relations, or, in other words, the extremely intimate relationship between employers and their workers or union members. This is manifest in various features of the trade union organization known as the enterprise-wide union. For example, the lack of a strong feeling of confrontation at the collective bargaining table, the lack of a serious feeling in labor disputes, the ambiguous distinction between union membership and employee's status, the lack of adequate grievance procedures and the importance attached to the system of life-long employment. When compared with those in Western countries, labor-management relations in Japan are conspicuous, in the last analysis, by the common characteristic of a close human relationship between employers and employees. We may even go so far as to say that it is doubtful if there is in Japan the basic prerequisite for constituting the special form of human interaction that is called "labor-management relations" in the West, that is, the antagonisms or conflict of interests between employers and employees.[97]

These features of Japanese industrial relations are variously attributed to the community ideal of village life, to the traditional pattern of family relationships, to the homogeneity of the Japanese population, to the vertical nature of Japanese society, and to the character of Japanese economic development. They have also been viewed as a conscious reaction by management to the challenge posed by trade unions in the early postwar period.[98]

An inquiry into the origins of this ideology is beyond the scope of the present study; suffice it to say that it is a source of considerable controversy in Japan. There can be little disagreement, however, about the proposition that the ideology has been of inestimable value to management in its drive for expansion and growth and that it is appreciated as such. Kunio Odaka, a leading Japanese sociologist, remarked that emphasis on the success and uniqueness of the Japanese experience may lead to the argument that "it does not matter even today how traditionalistic and undemocratic man-

---

scribe to it. Ronald P. Dore feels that the family metaphor has largely been dropped, or if retained, only as a loose symbol. He argues that for large corporations the employer no longer exists, merely salaried managers (letter to the authors, May 9, 1974). The metaphor did come up in conversations with company officials, however, and it still appears to have some currency.

97. Ichirō Nakayama, "The Modernization of Industrial Relations in Japan," in Japan Institute of Labor, *The Changing Patterns of Industrial Relations* (1965), pp. 86–87.

98. See Yoshino, *Japan's Managerial System*, chap. 4.

agerial practices may be, since the enterprise has progressed and Japanese industry has exhibited a steady growth; there is in fact no need to reform the methods of management." He continues: "This is precisely the view which has been taken by some Japanese businessmen. Abegglen's book, *The Japanese Factory*, seems to have a similar effect; it stresses the merits, rather than the demerits, of traditional practices. It is not farfetched to assume that it was for this reason that the book was enthusiastically welcomed in Japanese business circles."[99]

If the main tenets of the ideology are accepted, there is no rationale for strikes, for detailed collective agreements setting forth the rights and obligations of labor and management, for elaborate grievance machinery with final resolution through neutral parties, for organization of workers beyond the confines of the enterprise. Indeed, there would be little justification even for enterprise unions were it not for outside influences that cloud workers' understanding of their true relations with their employers. The personnel manager of a large corporation, when queried about his conception of the proper role of unions, replied that "unions improve morale, develop mutual respect and confidence, and prevent sabotage."

It might be easier to accept this stereotype of Japanese industrial relations were it not for the fact that other countries have gone through similar stages of ideological development. The present Japanese scene is strongly reminiscent of the United States in the 1920s—sometimes called the era of welfare capitalism. The period was one of substantial economic expansion, of rapid growth for large corporations, of new products and technologies. The reputation of the business community and its influence on national affairs were at a peak.

Largely under the inspiration of Rockefeller interests, company unionism developed into a consistent philosophy that had great appeal to a large segment of American management. As Irving Bernstein has pointed out: "The employer's acceptance of this theory was conditioned upon the employees' acceptance of the idea that the firm was an island, cut off from contact with other companies in the same labor market or the same industry. Rockefeller and his followers preached that 'the fundamental idea of Welfare Capitalism [is] that the only solidarity natural in industry is the solidarity which unites all those in the same business establishment'. The

99. Odaka, *Toward Industrial Democracy*, chap. 3. The book to which reference is made, originally published in 1958, has been reissued: James C. Abegglen, *Management and Worker: The Japanese Solution* (Sophia University in cooperation with Kodansha International Ltd., 1973).

great goal of industrial harmony could be achieved only within the insulated system of the firm."[100]

This philosophy implied a belief that there is a fundamental concord of interest between employer and employee, that the welfare of an individual is inextricably bound up with the progress of his company, that petty personal grievances should be subordinated to the common enterprise. The following remarks by a company union officer at the time epitomized this approach: "The final recourse we, as employees, have is to strike. Membership in the trade union or the company union does not change this. Certainly we want no strike, and I believe Mr. General Manager will play fair with us in the future as he has in the past. A strike would make us lose wages and the company lose production. It would put them in wrong with their customers and mean a loss of business, which would mean that when the difficulty is straightened out there would be less jobs and some of us would be out of luck."[101] Welfare capitalism in the United States did not originate in any particular social tradition; it was a conscious and, in some cases at least, sincere attempt by business leaders to find a solution to a vexing problem. Its span of existence was brief, and it never had more than a toehold among workers. The social revolution of the 1930s eliminated it as a meaningful force in American life.

The American experience is by no means the only one that can be cited. French employers have long had a strong predilection for dealing with their own employees to the exclusion of national unions,[102] and they were reinforced in their views by Gaullist conceptions of partnership in industry. A general strike in 1968, followed by legislation, finally established the primacy of the national unions in collective bargaining. The long history of the workers' council movement in Europe attests to the persistence of interest in enterprise particularism, and the Japanese experience provides a good example of why European trade unions have maintained a cautious attitude toward this institution.[103]

What is unique to Japan is not that management welcomed the enterprise union system as an alternative to the forms of industrial relations

100. Irving Bernstein, *The Lean Years: A History of the American Worker 1920–1933* (Houghton Mifflin, 1960), p. 170.

101. Quoted in U.S. Department of Labor, Bureau of Labor Statistics, *Characteristics of Company Unions 1935,* Bulletin 634 (June 1937), p. 160.

102. See Val R. Lorwin, *The French Labor Movement* (Harvard University Press, 1954), pp. 269–76.

103. See Adolf Sturmthal, *Workers Councils* (Harvard University Press, 1964), chap. 7.

customarily found in Western capitalist societies, but rather that what Ronald Dore has aptly termed "welfare corporatism"[104] has become so well established in its institutional framework. There are various explanations having to do with political power, the sociological aspects of industrial relations, and the course of the nation's economic development. The interested reader is urged to consult the burgeoning body of relevant literature.[105] In any event, there appears to be no current trend away from enterprise unionism; as a labor leader remarked to us, it is still true that the higher up you go in Japanese union structure, the weaker you get. The arguments raised against the national unions by management reflect deep distrust: they have neither the means nor the personnel to formulate sound policy; if they were to be established as strong bodies it is possible that they would be dominated by the Communist party; they might be used to bring direct pressure on the government through general strikes, thus eroding the democratic process based upon the Diet; even if Dōmei leaders understand the problems of the enterprise, they cannot be responsible in negotiation because of their rivalry with Sōhyō. Nor is there any optimism among national union leaders that this distrust can be overcome through negotiation or that opposition to change can be effectively challenged by direct worker action. A shift in the political balance of power appears to be their main hope, though their expectations are not high.

The Bargaining System

The system of collective bargaining in Japan, less than two decades old, represents an ingenious attempt to compensate in some measure for the weakness of trade union structure by providing a degree of centralized wage and standard setting.

Two principal types of disputes occur in an industrial relations system: over new agreements and over the interpretation of existing agreements. Although individual grievances arising under agreements may well have the greater impact on employee morale, most of the literature on Japan deals

104. Ronald Dore, *British Factory–Japanese Factory: The Origins of National Diversity in Industrial Relations* (University of California Press, 1973). The reader should consult this book for a different view of the importance and authority of the enterprise union from that expressed above.

105. Since 1971 three major books on Japanese labor have been published in English: Cole, *Japanese Blue Collar;* Dore, *British Factory–Japanese Factory;* and Ōkōchi, Karsh, and Levine (eds.), *Workers and Employers in Japan.* A fourth—Clark, "Social Relations in a Japanese Company"—fully merits publication.

with the former. It is precisely in the area of grievances that Japanese unionism is weakest, as seen from a Western point of view. Consultation between management and employees over a range of matters that are not strictly within the purview of labor relations is another characteristic of the Japanese scene. The line between this activity and collective bargaining is not always easy to draw, but its pervasiveness compels us to treat it under this rubric. Finally, we must cover one of the most controversial current issues in Japan: the right of government employees to bargain collectively and to strike. Because so large a proportion of Sōhyō members are in government service, national and local, this is a bread-and-butter issue for the unions.

Bargaining over New Agreements

The most striking aspect of Japanese bargaining is the spring offensive, or Shuntō, to use the Japanese acronym. The publicity accorded this annual campaign might suggest that it is the decisive bargaining forum. The Shuntō is important, but bargaining actually takes place at the company level. The bargaining unit is overwhelmingly the enterprise, whether it is a small firm with a single shop or a giant one with far-flung plants. With few exceptions (principally the maritime trades, the textile industry, and, to some extent, the steel industry), neither national unions nor employer groups engage in collective bargaining. The Japanese system diverges at this point most sharply from that of Western Europe, and even that of the United States, where most individual corporations prefer to bargain alone.

PATTERN OF MANAGEMENT BARGAINING. The spring offensive in its present form began in 1955, at the initiative of Sōhyō, to help develop a national pattern for the guidance of enterprise unions. The number of employees involved through participation of their unions has risen from 735,000 in the first year to 6.5 million at present. Initially, the committee that conducted the campaign comprised representatives of only Sōhyō and Chūritsuroren affiliates, but some Dōmei affiliates now participate as well.

Perhaps the best way to explain the operation of the annual Shuntō is to describe one—that of 1973. The first step was the issuance in December 1972 of a white paper on wages by the Spring Offensive Committee, composed of representatives of Sōhyō and Chūritsuroren; it called for an average wage increase of ¥20,000 a month. Dōmei had issued a similar document a few weeks earlier. In response, the board of directors of Nikkeiren, the Japanese Federation of Employers' Associations, offered to recommend wage increases proportionate to the rise in productivity.

The opening move came in April 1973, when the four major steel companies offered their enterprise unions an average wage increase of ¥10,600 a month on a take-it-or-leave-it basis, a practice that has been followed since 1957. But steel company negotiators are much concerned not to antagonize the incumbent enterprise union leadership: they are regarded as moderate in comparison with the radical leadership that was ousted at the end of the 1950s. Before making the offer, therefore, each company's management had talked with the leaders of its enterprise union and ascertained that the offer would be acceptable to the unions.

To no one's surprise, the steel unions, which had demanded ¥13,000, accepted the offer. Unions customarily call for strike votes before negotiations begin, more as a symbolic gesture than a reality, but from 1966 to 1971 at least one or two of the major enterprise unions in steel failed to get a majority vote for a strike. After 1971 the national steel labor union induced the enterprise unions to withhold a strike vote until after the companies had made their offer.

The private railway workers' union, which in 1973 was a pattern setter, called a one-day work stoppage, after which it accepted a relatively favorable settlement. By the end of May most unions had signed agreements; the average increase for the larger companies amounted to about 20 percent above the 1972 level of wages.

There are several things to be noted about this process. The most important is that the precise settlement was determined in every case by bargaining between the enterprise union and its employer. Even in steel, the original offer of ¥10,600 was adjusted company by company through various types of allowances so that the final settlement averaged ¥15,000, equivalent to the national average settlement. In the case of a sample of firms interviewed by us, the increases ranged from 24.5 percent (garment manufacturer) and 22 percent (electronics firm) to below-average figures for firms in less favorable economic circumstances.

The variance produced by this type of bargaining is sufficiently great to raise the question of whether the spring offensive does in fact tend to bring about some degree of wage standardization. Several econometric studies suggest that it does.[106] In particular, a study by the Economic Planning Agency found over eight wage rounds a substantial degree of correlation between increases gained by the pattern-setting national unions and each of fifteen follower nationals. An ability-to-pay variable, represented by increases in labor productivity, added little to the explanation. In a second

106. These are summarized in Makoto Ohtsu, "Unions and Wage Structure in Japan" (Ph.D. dissertation, University of Illinois, 1972), pp. 67–74.

exercise, wages obtained by the fifteen follower national unions were compared with wage changes for the economy as a whole, with additional variables representing unemployment, ability to pay, and cost of living. The wage leadership pattern and unemployment variables proved to be significant, more so in large than in small firms.[107]

The variability of Shuntō wage settlement increases has declined substantially over the past decade. This should not necessarily be ascribed to the Shuntō bargaining procedure; an increasingly tight labor market, obliging smaller firms to follow the national pattern in order to hold their labor, was undoubtedly a contributing factor. The Shuntō pattern provides a figure that serves as the starting point for wage calculations: in determining what wage concessions are necessary to maintain employee morale and to protect enterprise union leadership, in the case of large employers; to prevent loss of workers, in the case of small ones; or to recruit new employees, for both.[108] Every management official interviewed indicated that Shuntō-plus-or-minus was the basis of his company's settlement. Union officials measured success or failure with reference to Shuntō averages and explained deviations by special circumstances.

The bunching of wage adjustments has also contributed to reduction of variability. In 1971, 84 percent of organized enterprises and 50 percent of the unorganized ones raised wages during the Shuntō season. The annual adjustment cycle has become all but universal, reinforcing the pattern effect.

INTRAFIRM DISTRIBUTION OF BENEFITS. Another important aspect of the bargaining process is the manner in which average wage increases are distributed within the particular firm. The role of the enterprise union is even more important here than in determining the average; in the great majority of firms, unions participate in the allocative process. This is a tricky affair, since it involves competing equity claims within the bargaining unit. Portions of the total wage increase amount are given as flat sums to all employees, as a proportion of the base wage, as supplements to specific job classifications, for individual merit ratings, and for improvement in overtime rates and shift premiums. The annual wage round, particularly where the increment is large, provides a good opportunity to change the weight of the various elements that make up the individual wage packet.

There is a lack of specific information on the extent to which employers consult with one another prior to bargaining. In the case of the major steel

107. Cited in ibid., pp. 71–72.
108. See Japan Institute of Labor, *Wage Problems and Industrial Relations in Japan* (1971), p. 6.

companies, there is considerable discussion before the key Shuntō offer is made. Neither the national, regional, nor industrywide employer associations participate in the actual bargaining, although they do supply their members with relevant information. An important contribution of Nikkeiren is the computation of model wages for standard workers of various ages and seniority, which may contribute to uniformity in employer bargaining positions. But there are many informal contacts among management officials and conferences of personnel officers to exchange information and presumably to plan strategy. The essence of the system is that each company has complete freedom to determine its own wage policy within the constraints set by its reading of the labor market and the bargaining power of its own employees. The industrywide bargaining so common in Western Europe has no counterpart in Japan.

STRIKES. The essence of genuine bargaining of any kind is that either party can say no if its minimum demands are not met. Private sector employees in Japan have the full legal right to strike, but there the strike is more a demonstration than a prolonged test of economic strength. Japanese strikes rarely last beyond a day, and they come mainly during the spring offensive. They often take place before real bargaining has begun and are in the nature of a ritualistic fist-shaking to show employers how serious the workers are in their demands. Substitutes for strikes that are occasionally used include working to rule, reduction of overtime, and objection to transfer, but there is no way of estimating their incidence or effectiveness.

There are occasional longer strikes in Japan, but they are carried on mainly by the few strong national unions, the seamen's union in particular. Many national unions would like to mount more serious strike threats as a bargaining weapon, but they are faced not only with the reluctance of their locals to act against their companies but also with the fear of the consequences if strikes could be called. A strike led by the coal miners' union against Miike Mines in 1960, which lasted 282 days, led to the formation of a second union, mainly by white-collar workers, the discharge of most leaders of the striking union, and eventual dominance by the second union. Although this took place years ago, its freshness in the minds of Japanese union leaders suggests that they lack confidence in their ability to stand up against the opposition of employers.

Some obvious questions arise. Why should Japanese workers and their unions engage in strikes if they have been doing so well without them? Would not work interruptions, by reducing output, reduce the potential for improvement in living standards? Is there any necessary relation between strike activity and union strength? Is not the Japanese situation vastly superior to, say, that of Italy, in which there is a combination of constant short strikes and weak unions? Or even to that of the United States, in which strong unions must occasionally resort to lengthy strikes to achieve their objectives?

Different perceptions of history can produce different answers. It is our conviction, first, that strong, independent labor unions can exist only where there is a legal right to strike and where this right is exercised from time to time as a manifestation of bargaining power; and, second, that strong, independent unions bring about both levels and distributions of income more favorable to their members than would prevail in their absence. (We return to the second theme in the next section.) Moreover, in the long run they provide an outlet for the orderly expression of individual aspiration and concern that might otherwise find a destructive outlet, either in lower productive efforts or in outbursts of political irresponsibility.

Our perception of Japanese trade union status and power may be at fault. Perhaps they do accurately reflect the true aspirations of the Japanese worker; perhaps Japan is a unique case to which enterprise unionism represents an optimal adaptation. Dore goes so far as to assert that the Japanese model is an advanced one toward which other nations are moving, rather than the reverse.[109] We obviously do not agree with these propositions; we subscribe rather to Dore's own apt characterization of the Japanese enterprise union as "a Finland to the management's Russia."[110]

THE ROLE OF GOVERNMENT. To summarize the formal legal system does scant justice to the sublety and complexity of real government influence in Japanese labor relations. Legislation permits the prime minister to delay work stoppages in disputes that could create a national emergency, but the power has never been invoked. The government has authority to extend collective agreements to cover all workers in a locality engaged in occupations similar to those covered by agreements, but this is rarely done. On the other hand, tripartite labor relations commissions in which the neutrals are prominent private individuals rather than government officials often play an important conciliatory role in the bargaining process and at times have had a major impact on the annual wage settlement.

Recent events have led to increasing government concern with overall wage policy. The Sumiya Report, produced by a committee set up by the Economic Council and issued in May 1972, held that cost push did not contribute to the wage-price acceleration that began in the 1960s; it predicted that future inflationary tendencies might be caused by "difficulty in

109. See *British Factory–Japanese Factory,* especially chap. 12.
110. Ibid., p. 174.

securing manpower, inflation caused by differentials in the rate of productivity increase between sectors, demand shift inflation and imported inflation." An incomes policy was not regarded as a likely necessity in the near future.[111]

These conclusions were rapidly overtaken by events. Wages rose by 16 percent in 1972, 20 percent was added by the 1973 spring offensive, and 32.2 percent (for major corporations) in 1974. Views on the desirability of some form of incomes policy may be changing.

Adjustment of Grievances

It is in the area of determining rights under collective and individual agreements that the Japanese industrial relations system departs most sharply from that of the West. The Japanese system is so nebulous in this respect that it is difficult for a nonparticipant to gain any real understanding of it. An additional difficulty is that the relevant literature is sparse, perhaps because of a lack of standardization that makes generalization hazardous even for insiders.

Japanese collective agreements are functionally quite different from those of Western nations. The following description is a representative view of such documents:

Japanese agreements are couched in abstract and general terms open to widely divergent interpretations. The reason for this ambiguity goes back to the Japanese sociological context of any contractual relationship. It is deeply felt that the contract need not be specific and exact; its terms are not too important. Rather than depending on the written word, the parties rely on their relationship itself, the circumstances that brought them together, the background against which their relationship has evolved, the human *rapport* established between them. It is this harmony (*wa*) that counts; the contract is a mere formality! ... The gist of the so-called collective agreement is, therefore, a mere declaration of principles: the friendly relationship between labor and management, the recognition of the union's rights, and other general provisions already found in governmental labor legislation.[112]

In the West, the enforcement of individual and collective rights under written agreements has become one of the major purposes of unionism,

111. Economic Council, *Report of the Committee on Prices, Incomes, and Productivity* (May 1972).

112. Tadashi Hanami, "Labor Disputes and Their Settlement," in Robert J. Ballon (ed.), *The Japanese Employee* (Sophia University, 1969), pp. 242–43. See also Levine, *Industrial Relations*, pp. 123–27. In their business dealings with foreigners, Japanese firms are often much concerned with the precise wording and interpretation of contracts.

rivaling the wage function. In theory, this is true also of Japan, but in practice, a formal mechanism is virtually nonexistent in most enterprises. How, then, are labor-management differences resolved?

The question was posed to company and union officials, and their replies were not especially enlightening. The personnel manager of one of the largest enterprises in Japan proudly produced a lengthy document containing an elaborate four-step grievance procedure terminating in compulsory arbitration by a district labor relations commission or a mutually agreed-upon third party. Written filing of grievances was required, and a strict timetable of referral from step to step was stipulated. It turned out, however, that these provisions had been adopted in 1952 and remained unaltered since then. Moreover, not only had there never been an arbitration, but the formal procedure itself was never used. Individual grievances, of which there were a substantial number, particularly among younger workers, were handled by foremen, sometimes in consultation with union representatives. They were all somehow settled by informal discussion.

Similar replies were given elsewhere.

• A small drug manufacturer: "Any problems that arise in the plant are first handled by the first line supervisor, and if no agreement is reached, the union representative discusses it with the management. Agreement has always been reached by negotiation. The union does not support bad grievances."

• A large chemical engineering and construction firm: "There is in our collective agreement a formal four-step grievance procedure, ending in third-party arbitration. But in eleven years, there has been only one arbitration, involving an individual's complaint about his merit rating."

• One of the largest textile manufacturers in Japan: "There are about twenty grievances a year, concerning mainly heating, air conditioning, and welfare facilities. Union representatives discuss all grievances informally with management. There is no arbitration. There has never been a grievance strike. The system works satisfactorily."

• One of the largest steel mills in Japan: "The contract calls for an elaborate four-step grievance system over job ratings. This was set up in 1960 at the instigation of management. However, no grievance has ever gotten beyond the second step: namely, discussion between the factory supervisor and the union representative for the particular department concerned."

• The management of a major electronics firm: "There is no formal grievance machinery. Evaluation of performance rests with management, and anyone who is dissatisfied with his rating can take it up with management." The chairman of the union local disputed this assertion, declaring that in two-thirds of the disputed cases the union prevailed. He admitted, however, that "the union cannot strike over individual grievances; workers would not support it."

• The union chairman in a medium-size textile weaving mill: "Justified grievances are taken up by the unions with management. Serious matters are brought to the bargaining table. When a new system is introduced, the work load is discussed. Otherwise, the rate of production has not been an issue. When problems arise, the union representatives take them up immediately with the personnel manager. All disputes have been resolved by discussion."

• A major shipbuilding company: "If a man feels that he has been rated unfairly, he can appeal to his supervisor, and is entitled to an explanation. The union rarely takes up individual complaints. Foremen are union members, so they are not unsympathetic with the workers."

• The union secretary of a machine-tool plant: "There has never been a strike. There is no procedure for handling individual grievances. If an individual feels aggrieved, he can always take the matter up with his supervisor."

No student of industrial relations would dissent from the proposition that resolution of grievances by informal discussion is far superior to any other method. The problem is that no country has been able to achieve this ideal. If Japan is an exception, it is a large plus in the productivity column, since unresolved grievances contribute heavily to the lowering of employee morale. The key issue becomes whether virtually all Japanese grievances actually are settled satisfactorily by informal discussion.

Employers are obliged by law to draw up rules of employment and submit them to the union, if there is one, before filing with the local labor inspectorate. Only a minority of collective agreements contain specific criteria for disciplinary action; in most cases, these are covered by the general rules of employment.[113] Normally, disciplinary actions are a prolific source of grievances, but apparently this is not true in Japan. Nor do individuals press their rights under substantive clauses of collective agreements with the same vigor as in the West. As Cole concludes from an intensive study of two plants: "Individual workers seldom become identified with specific grievances being processed by the union. Workers in both firms showed a lack of consciousness of their rights and a reluctance to exercise them; this was especially notable among the young, inexperienced auto workers. The historic subordination of workers to management authority, although shaken

113. *Japan Labor Bulletin*, Nov. 1, 1969.

and weakened by the Occupation and subsequent developments, has not been dislodged and remains a persistent force."[114]

And there the matter rests. There are grievances in Japan, and they are settled in the main without formal adjustment machinery. There are no data on the outcome, and therefore it is not possible to judge whether individuals and unions are accorded adequate redress for their complaints. Japan's ability to avoid private arbitration (as in the United States), special labor courts (West Germany and Scandinavia), or instant strikes (Great Britain) as methods of resolving stubborn plant-level differences may indeed be a function of a unique social system. On the other hand, it may be due to the permanent employment system, to the rapid rate of economic growth, or simply to weak unions. This subject warrants more attention than it has received.

Joint Consultation

Frequent consultation between management and employees on a wide range of issues germane to the company is an important element in the Japanese industrial relations system.[115] For the most part such proceedings are limited to discussion, though decisions are sometimes taken. It is not always easy to determine precisely where bargaining leaves off and consultation begins.

Consultation takes place at every level. Periodic discussions are held by foremen and their working groups, and more highly structured meetings take place at the plant and at companywide levels. A survey of labor-management communication in 1972 revealed that 90 percent of large firms (those with more than 1,000 employees) had formal consultation systems.[116] Among the subjects discussed, in addition to working conditions, are production plans, projected technological change, and social welfare policy, including company housing. A particularly important issue in recent years has been the prospective transfer of personnel to new plants. On this there is generally early and full discussion with the union to facilitate labor mobility, particularly if a change of domicile is involved. Meetings are usually held once a month or somewhat less frequently, and on company time.[117]

Matters relating to wages and working conditions, which are properly

114. Cole, *Japanese Blue Collar*, p. 230.
115. Though plant consultation is not, of course, unique to Japan; it is widely practiced in Scandinavian countries as well as in other countries of Western Europe.
116. Ministry of Labor, *Year Book of Labor Statistics, 1972*, p. 332.
117. See Yoshio Keiya, "Some Aspects of Workers' Participation in Industry in Japan," in Japan Institute of Labor, *Social and Cultural Background of Labor-Management Relations*, pp. 246–54.

the subject of collective bargaining, are sometimes discussed at joint consultation sessions before going to the bargaining table, since the same people
are generally involved in both. The failure to maintain this distinction is a
peculiarly Japanese practice; most unions elsewhere would not countenance
it, since it tends to dilute the bargaining process. Western trade unions generally insist that bargainable issues, subject to contract, should be handled
exclusively by the official trade union representatives and not by plant committees. To permit such issues to be discussed by plant committees outside
the union framework would tend to subvert the authority of the union.

The rationale of the consultation system appears to be the raising of
productivity, not the furthering of employee participation in corporate decisionmaking. The most active protagonist of consultation has been the
Japan Productivity Center, which has surveyed existing practices and attempted to develop standard consultation techniques.[118]

The effectiveness of Japanese labor-management consultation in either
of these two objectives is difficult to determine, since the evidence is largely
anecdotal. Much depends on the quantity and quality of the information
that management makes available to labor representatives, as well as the
lead time that is allowed for employee input before proposed changes are
made. In a large electric cable company that we visited, the union chairman said that the company was supposed to notify the union well in advance of any technological change or new plant project—and actually did
so. Some workers in the plant felt that the union should have a voice in the
making of decisions, but this sentiment was not strong. The union chairman thought that it might be a good idea for the union to select a well-
qualified person to sit on the board of directors. Japanese unions are familiar with German codetermination, but we were told by a Dōmei official
that there have been no serious discussions within his organization about
the desirability of advocating this practice: Japanese unions, it is felt, have
not yet reached a sufficient level of maturity. Dōmei favors joint consultation in principle, but Sōhyō is concerned lest it impair union militancy, and
favors it only when actual decisions are involved.

Cole asserts that "with their strong emphasis on increasing production
and developing the enterprise, these [joint] committees often work against
the emergence of an autonomous union devoted to the protection of worker
rights and interests."[119] This may be a somewhat harsh judgment, but perhaps if there were stronger unions, Japanese management would be less

118. See Japan Productivity Center, *Economic Growth and the Productivity Movement in Japan* (1973).
119. *Japanese Blue Collar*, p. 255.

enthusiastic about consultation. In one way, enterprise unionism is ideal for consultation in that it guarantees that no outsiders will participate. It will be interesting to see how well the practice holds up when the economic news to be imparted is bad rather than good. As one enterprise union chairman put it, union participation is fine in boom times, but the union would not want to take any responsibility for retrenchment.

A number of joint councils have been established at the industrywide level to discuss industrial economic policy, pollution, foreign trade, and other matters of mutual interest. As yet this movement seems not to have gone far, and the emphasis upon the individual company will work against it. The assertion that there is a strong trend in this direction prompted by union realization "that collective bargaining and political action in a constant atmosphere of class warfare are insufficient to achieve their ends" certainly can be questioned.[120] We detected no such groundswell of sentiment.

There are individuals in government and academic life who would like to expand the representation of national trade union bodies on advisory commissions of various sorts, but the Liberal Democratic government does not appear to favor this policy. As a result, trade unions have less influence on the formulation of national economic policy in Japan than in any Western democracy.

Collective Bargaining by Public Employees

The single most controversial issue in Japanese industrial relations during the past five years has been the right of government employees to engage in collective bargaining,[121] both because of the size of the group involved and because of their concentration in Sōhyō unions.

Although most public sector employees were given the right to strike soon after World War II, it was withdrawn in 1947 by order of the American occupation authorities. All public employees have the right to join unions, but the bargaining system is not uniform for the various types of government employment.

About half of the 500,000 national civil servants in 1973 were organized. They have the right neither to bargain nor to strike. Their wages are set by the government on the advice of the National Personnel Authority. Recom-

---

120. Tadashi Mitsufuji and Kiyohiko Hagisawa, "Recent Trends in Collective Bargaining in Japan," *International Labour Review*, vol. 105 (February 1972), p. 151.

121. For a recent survey of this subject, see Alice H. Cook, Solomon B. Levine, and Tadashi Mitsufuji, *Public Employee Labor Relations in Japan: Three Aspects* (University of Michigan–Wayne State University Press, 1971).

mendations by the Authority are based upon comparative wage surveys but are not binding on the government. Since 1970, however, they have been accepted in full. The unions present their views to the Authority but do not participate in the wage surveys. They have complained for years that the surveys are biased against employees.

Of some 2 million employees of local governments in 1973, 1.7 million belonged to trade unions, almost all of them to two national unions: Nikkyōso, the teacher's union, with almost 600,000 members, and Jichirō, catering to the rest of the local government employees, whose membership of over 1 million makes it the largest union in the country. Like the national public service employees, local government employees do not have the right to strike. Although local personnel boards theoretically have the power to set wages, in fact wages follow the pattern recommended by the National Personnel Authority.

Finally, in 1973 there were 1.5 million employees in three public corporations (railway, telephone, and tobacco) and five national enterprises (postal service, forestry, alcohol monopoly, mint, and government printing office), of whom about 1 million were organized. This group cannot strike, but it can engage in collective bargaining. Eventual settlements are worked out through the Public Labor Relations Commission.

The Sōhyō unions have been attempting to win the right to strike through appeal to the International Labour Organization, alleging that the Japanese government is violating an international convention guaranteeing freedom of association, to which it is a signatory. Reliance on such ILO conventions has been a tactic practiced by weak unions the world over. Recourse to this slender reed is usually an index of the inability of a labor movement to marshal sufficient domestic support.

Japan is not alone in wrestling with the problem of bargaining rights for public employees. The solutions vary from country to country, but in the industrialized nations employees other than civil servants—particularly those in transportation, publicly owned utilities, and nationalized industries —generally have the same right to bargain and to strike as do employees in the private sector. Some countries extend this right even to civil servants, with appropriate safeguards, but normally provision is made for some form of neutral arbitration as a final step in resolving disputes.

By these standards, the Japanese government is backward—even by comparison with the United States, which is on the conservative side of the international spectrum in public sector bargaining. The issue will continue to remain in the forefront, if only because of its importance to Sōhyō. The right to strike could be a critical factor in public industrial relations because, unlike the situation in the private sector, there would not be the enterprise union concern with the profitability of the employer. It is not inconceivable that strikes of substantial length could occur in public enterprises if they were made legal. Nikkeiren, the Employers' Federation, took the position in 1971 that, except for railroad and postal workers, employees of government corporations and enterprises should be permitted to strike. Since Sōhyō has conceded the need for protecting the public from undue hardship, a consensus on a limited right to strike may put this troublesome issue to rest at some time not too far in the future.

Living Standards

The Japanese working people, we believe, do not enjoy a standard of living consonant with the nation's per capita income. Further, it is our hypothesis that to a considerable degree this has resulted from the inability of the labor movement to exercise any real influence on national economic policy.

Although we are concerned mainly with the living standards of wage earners and lower-salaried employees, standard international data do not lend themselves to separate treatment for these groups. The use of per capita data, however, does not seriously impair the value of the comparisons. In discussions of housing, pensions, recreational facilities, and consumer goods it can be assumed that the wealthy are not so numerous as to make the data unusable, and, further, that they are able to protect themselves against deficiencies in the availability of social goods.

Comparison of living standards across international boundaries involves extremely complex problems, both of theory and measurement. Even with necessities, differences in taste and patterns of consumption lead to variance in the price structure. Contradictory results are often obtained in aggregating identical market baskets using different sets of prices as weights. The difficulty is compounded when leisure, commuting time, job security, retirement support, and freedom from environmental pollution are entered into the equation. Until indicators of social welfare are developed, all that can be done is to cite some crude indexes that the Japanese themselves are using in the current controversy over welfare against growth of national product.

In principle, we are using the five large developed economies of the West for comparison with Japan: France, West Germany, Italy, the United Kingdom, and the United States. The list is curtailed only when we were unable

Table 9-11. *Per Capita Gross Domestic Product, 1971, and Gross Fixed Investment as a Percentage of GDP, 1967–71, Japan and Principal Western Industrialized Countries*

Country	Per capita GDP, 1971 (U.S. dollars)	Gross fixed investment as a percentage of GDP, 1967–71[a]
Japan	2,150	37.8
France	3,180	26.1
West Germany	3,550	25.4
Italy	1,880	19.9
United Kingdom	2,430	19.3
United States	5,130	16.6

Source: OECD Economic Surveys, *Norway* (Paris: OECD, 1974), app.
a. Annual average.

to find the necessary data. Perhaps chief interest should attach to comparisons with Italy and the United Kingdom, since the per capita national products of these countries are roughly equal to that of Japan at present (see Table 9-11). It might be well also to keep in mind that West Germany, the United Kingdom, and the United States have powerful trade union movements with considerable labor market bargaining power as well as great influence on national economic policy, whereas the French, Italian, and Japanese labor movements lag considerably behind.

There can be no doubt that over the past decade Japan has outpaced the industrial nations of the West by a considerable margin in the rate of growth of real wages (see Table 9-7, above). But it does not necessarily follow that the growth path chosen by those who directed the Japanese economy was optimal for all segments of society. For example, the allocation of a greater portion of investment to social capital instead of manufacturing capacity might have resulted in a more equitable access to a full range of consumer goods and services at this time, even though the rate of GNP growth probably would have been lower. The current debate over national welfare and the acknowledgment by the Economic Planning Agency, in formulating the 1973–77 plan, that "a good number of people are dissatisfied with the present state of social overhead capital and social security"[122] suggest that many Japanese would agree with this proposition.

Japan has maintained an exceedingly high rate of investment, a major cause of its rapid economic growth (see Table 9-11). The achievement of this level of investment in a democratic nation is remarkable. But that this

122. Economic Planning Agency, *Basic Economic and Social Plan, 1973–1977,* p. 5.

merely reflected market forces would be difficult to argue, since government facilitated the allocation of resources toward investment, both directly and indirectly. The government itself has been a heavy investor: in 1970, for example, the public sector accounted for 23 percent of gross capital formation (as well as one-third of net capital formation). But at least 70 percent of that was for business-related purposes and less than one-quarter for health, welfare, and education.[123]

The Economic Planning Agency has pointed out that the "phenomenal increase in consumption since 1955 has centered around the explosive spread of durable consumer goods."[124] But a low rate of investment in supporting consumer facilities has tended to limit the utility of the newly acquired goods. Household equipment reduces already inadequate amounts of living space; sports equipment cannot be used without appropriate physical facilities; automobiles have less value when parking space and roads are inadequate to handle them. And, the agency continues, because of these limitations, "people seek trivial changes by frequently buying durable consumer goods for replacement, seek to buy goods or services for insignificantly cheaper prices or larger usefulness."[125]

Housing

One aspect of living standards in which Japan lags behind its national income level relative to other developed nations is housing. There are some special problems in density of population (though this is true of other countries as well—Great Britain, the Netherlands, and Belgium, for example—that have good housing standards) and risk of earthquakes, but a nation that soon will have the largest steel industry in the world despite the lack of raw materials and fuel and is already planning million-ton ships undoubtedly has the technical knowledge to solve them. What has been lacking is the will, to which the absence of effective pressure groups among the poorly housed sections of the population has contributed.

Part of the story is told in Table 9-12.[126] At first glance, it would appear

123. OECD Economic Surveys, *Japan* (Paris: OECD, 1972), p. 47.
124. EPA, *Whitepaper on National Life, 1973*, p. 240.
125. Ibid., pp. 241–42.
126. This subject is dealt with more fully in Chapter 10 of this volume, in connection with a discussion of urban problems. The comparative indexes shown in Table 9-12 are the only ones available at the present writing. Nonetheless, the preliminary results of a more sophisticated study of comparative living standards being prepared for the United Nations suggest that the data in this table, crude though they may be, present a fair picture of housing standards in Japan relative to those of the major Western industrial nations.

Table 9-12. *Comparative Investment and Standards in Housing, Japan and Principal Western Industrialized Countries*

Country	Residential construction as a percentage of GDP, 1967–71[a] (1)	Residential construction as a percentage of gross fixed capital formation, 1970 (2)	Number of persons per room[b] (3)	Percent of dwellings with flush toilets[c] (4)
Japan	6.5	20	1.1	17.1
France	6.5	27	0.9	51.8
West Germany	5.3	20	0.7	87.4
Italy	6.1	33	1.1	40.5
United Kingdom	3.4	16	0.8	97.9
United States	3.3	19	0.6	96.0

Sources: Column (1), from OECD Economic Surveys, *Norway* (1974), app.; column (2), from United Nations, *Yearbook of National Accounts Statistics, 1971* (1973); columns (3) and (4), from United Nations, *Statistical Yearbook, 1973* (1974), table 198.

a. Annual average.

b. Data for Japan, France, and Germany are for 1968; for Italy, 1961; for the United Kingdom, 1971; for the United States, 1970.

c. Data for Japan, France, and Germany are for 1968; for Italy, 1951; for the United Kingdom, 1966; for the United States, 1970.

that investment in housing has been at a relatively high level in Japan, judging from the percentage of the national product devoted to residential construction. But it should be recalled that total Japanese investment has been extremely high, and in this perspective, the amount that has gone into housing is not impressive. Japanese housing standards in 1945 were well below those of the Western industrialized nations—as was the Japanese national product—and it might have been expected that if the nation were willing to invest so large a proportion of its national product, a substantial share would have gone to make up the housing deficit. As it was, only the United Kingdom and the United States, both of which had a large stock of housing, devoted a smaller proportion of total investment to this purpose.

Not only in quantity, but in quality as well, Japanese housing is low by international standards. Uniform international indicators are few, but the ones shown in Table 9-12 bear out this contention. A pamphlet published by an agency of the Japan Trade Promotion Office in the United States describes current Tokyo housing standards in the following terms:

One third of the inhabitants of Tokyo, the world's largest city, live in small wooden apartment houses, where the average size of an apartment is 124 square feet. In a space 11 feet by 11 feet, one, two, and three member families dine, sleep, watch TV, read newspapers, meet friends and raise a family. Half have their own bathrooms; the other half use public toilets in the building or go to a commercial bath house. Modern sewage facilities are still an exception to the rule. In 1970, only 22 percent of all Tokyo residents had access to flush toilets.[127]

Large firms often provide housing assistance to some of their employees. According to a 1968 survey, 9 percent of Tokyo households occupied company housing,[128] but this figure is lower for the country as a whole. Many companies maintain dormitories for young single men and women recruits from rural areas. After marriage, small flats may be provided for them, but there is a growing tendency to restrict the tenure of occupancy to encourage employees to buy their own homes. An incentive is provided by subsidizing the market rates of interest that prevail in Japan; several firms interviewed indicated that they were making up a portion of the difference between 5 percent and the average rate of 9 percent, the amount depending upon length of service. Senior executives do somewhat better: a number of firms have sold them the company houses they occupied at book value (which means a large capital gain because of the rapid recent price rise) and financed the purchase by loans against retirement allowances.[129] The cost of housing to industrial enterprises is not a major expense item: a 1972 survey revealed that for manufacturing enterprises as a whole, company housing contributed 1.7 percent to total labor cost.[130]

An analysis of why rising real wages have not been translated into commensurately improved housing standards would take us too far afield. It is our impression that not lack of demand but rather the lack of appropriate institutional arrangements for making housing available at reasonable cost is the main reason. Land costs have been high, but recent speculation has driven them to levels that are difficult for a worker to afford.[131] In 1972, a house and lot in the Tokyo metropolitan area would have cost a production worker in manufacturing 7.5 years of average annual earnings; corresponding figures for Nagoya and Osaka were 6.8 and 6.3 years, respectively. An American worker in the northeastern states could have purchased a new house for the equivalent of 4.1 years' earnings, on the average, in 1971.[132]

127. United States–Japan Trade Council, *Another Aspect of Japan* (July 1974), p. 4.
128. *Japan Labor Bulletin*, Jan. 1, 1973.
129. James C. Abegglen, "Organizational Change," in Ballon (ed.), *The Japanese Employee*, p. 111.
130. Ministry of Labor, *Year Book of Labor Statistics, 1972*, tables 83, 84.
131. For a full discussion of land costs, see Chapter 10.
132. The Japanese data on housing costs are from Economic Planning Agency, *Whitepaper on National Life, 1973*, p. 98; on wages, from Ministry of Labor, *Year Book of Labor Statistics, 1972*, p. 69 (monthly wage data in the source were multiplied by twelve to obtain annual earnings). The U.S. construction data are from

In terms of quality, the buyer in Tokyo and Osaka would have secured a house of 670 square feet, not necessarily new, built on 1,100 square feet of land, and probably without flush toilets. The American worker would get a new house with 1,430 square feet of interior space and with either one or two full bathrooms.[133]

The lack of an adequate mortgage market is one of the factors behind the high rate of household saving in Japan.[134] Despite high land costs, 57 percent of construction costs for privately owned housing in the Tokyo area were self-financed in 1971. Another 14 percent were provided by employers, 17 percent by private banking institutions, 5 percent from the government Housing Loan Corporation, and the rest from other sources.[135] Self-financing has become increasingly difficult with inflation.

The main elements of a solution would include subsidized public housing for low-wage workers and reasonable mortgage money for the more affluent; heavy capital-gains taxation to dampen land speculation; and a much more liberal use of eminent domain to acquire land suitable for housing purposes. Such measures are called for in general terms in the 1973–77 plan.[136]

Recreation

An insufficiency of many social goods detracts from the quality of life for those who cannot afford private substitutes. The lack of park areas in Japan's major cities is striking. The comparative data in Table 9-13 indicate the Japanese lag in this respect.[137] It can be argued that Japan's popu-

---

U.S. Department of Commerce, *Construction Review*, vol. 19 (February 1973), pp. 4–8; the wage data are from U.S. Department of Labor, Bureau of Labor Statistics, *Employment and Earnings 1939–72*, Bulletin 1370-10. The wage figure used to compute the annual multiple cited is an employment-weighted average of wages for nine northeastern states. Weekly wage data in the source were multiplied by fifty-two to obtain annual earnings.

133. Japanese data are from U.S.–Japan Trade Council, *Another Aspect of Japan*, p. 5; U.S. data are from Department of Commerce, *Construction Review*, vol. 19 (February 1973), pp. 4–5.

134. See Chapter 4 in this volume.

135. Economic Planning Agency, *Whitepaper on National Life, 1973*, p. 99.

136. EPA, *Basic Economic and Social Plan, 1973–1977*, p. 60.

137. These gross figures are borne out by data for individual cities. Tokyo's major parks—Ueno, Hibiya, and Shinjuku Gyoen—have areas of 53, 16, and 58 hectares, respectively. In New York City, the areas of Central and Pelham Bay parks are 308 and 700 hectares, respectively; in London, Hyde Park and Kensington Gardens have 142 and 106 hectares; the Sokolyniki Park in Moscow has 300 hectares; the Tiergarten in Berlin has 245; and the Bois de Boulogne and Bois de Vincennes in Paris have 860 and 930 hectares. EPA, *Whitepaper on National Life, 1973*, p. 229.

Table 9-13. *Selected Indicators of Social Welfare, Japan and Principal Western Industrialized Countries*

Country	Parks as a percentage of city land area, 1967 (1)	Population per hospital bed[a] (2)	Population per physician[b] (3)
Japan	0.9	79	871
France	5.8	95	721
West Germany	14.4	89	561
Italy	10.4	94	530
United Kingdom	10.0	110	787
United States	19.0	133	634

Sources: Column (1), from Japanese Confederation of Labor (Dōmei), *Welfare Indicators of Workers* (1972), p. 20; columns (2) and (3), from United Nations, *Statistical Yearbook, 1973*, table 197.

a. Data for Italy are for 1970; for the remaining countries, for 1971.

b. Data for Japan, France, and the United Kingdom are for 1971; for the United States and Germany, 1970; and for Italy, 1972.

lation density makes it difficult to provide open space. But it can also be noted that during the decade 1962–72 the number of golf courses increased from 263 to 620; the latter figure may be compared with 934 public baseball fields in 1972, which occupied 2 percent of the land area taken up by golf courses.[138] Golf is for the affluent, baseball for the lower-income groups.[139]

Retirement Security

Provision for his years of retirement is also a matter of considerable concern to the Japanese worker. The standard age of retirement remains fifty-five, although it is moving up slowly. On retiring, permanent workers normally receive lump sum severance pay in lieu of pensions. There is no uniform amount, but large firms tend to pay about four years' salary to those who have worked for them for thirty years, with less for employees with shorter service. In the medium- and small-size firms the retirement pay is about two years' finishing salary.[140] The lump sum settlement, which is vulnerable to inflation, is relied upon "to start a small business, to acquire a farm, to settle debts (including those contracted for their children's edu-

138. Ibid., p. 220. Many large companies, however, have their own baseball fields.

139. "Unless one is aware that the golfing habit is largely supported by generous company expense accounts, it is hard to understand why this sport is flourishing in a tiny, space-hungry country." U.S.–Japan Trade Council, *Another Aspect of Japan*, p. 10.

140. Economic Planning Agency, *Whitepaper on National Life, 1973*, p. 75.

Table 9-14. *Social Security Expenditures and Labor Force Participation of the Aged, Japan and Principal Western Industrialized Countries*

Country	Social security expenditures as a percentage of GNP, 1965–66 (1)	Labor force participation rate, males[a] (percent)	
		Aged 60–64 (2)	Aged 65 and over (3)
Japan	5.8	85.8	54.5
France	15.6	65.7	19.3
West Germany	16.8	...	...
Italy	15.2	53.6	23.6
United Kingdom	12.4	...	23.4
United States	7.2	73.0	24.8

Sources: Column (1), from International Labour Office, *The Cost of Social Security* (1972), table 2; columns (2) and (3), from idem, *Year Book of Labour Statistics, 1973*, table 1.

a. Data for Italy are for 1961; for the United Kingdom, 1966; for France, 1968; and for Japan and the United States, 1970.

cation or the marriage of a daughter), to purchase a house to replace company housing, to support children who may in turn provide a home for the retired worker. . . ."[141]

The lack of an adequate system of public pensions imposes great hardship on retired Japanese employees. Japan's international position in this respect is shown in Table 9-14. The average monthly pension in 1972 was about 22.5 percent of average wage income at the time, low by international standards.[142] The result is that male pensioners continue to work as long as possible, as suggested by the high participation rate for workers over sixty-five shown in the table. There has been some discussion of tying pensions to the cost-of-living index, but no action has yet been taken toward this end.

Working Days, Holidays, and Vacations

In 1973, when the five-day week had become standard in the West, only 49 percent of Japanese industrial employees in firms with more than 100 employees enjoyed a two-day break at least once a month, and only 6 percent a weekly two-day rest.[143] As for vacations, it is required by law that

141. Paul Fisher, "Major Social Security Issues: Japan, 1972," U.S. Department of Health, Education, and Welfare, *Social Security Bulletin*, vol. 36 (March 1973), pp. 30–81.

142. Ibid., p. 27. The economic plan for 1977 called for an increase of old age pensions and medical care to 8.8 percent of national income in that year. In 1969, this ratio was almost 18 percent in the nine Common Market countries. OECD Economic Surveys, *Japan* (1973), p. 56.

143. *Japan Labor Bulletin*, July 1, 1974.

workers employed continuously by the same employer for one year be given six paid holidays a year, plus one extra day for each additional year of continuous employment up to a maximum of twenty days. Most firms appear simply to follow the legal minimums. In 1972 the modal number of annual holidays was fifteen to nineteen days, with ten to fourteen days coming next. Some 12 percent of all employers and 20.2 percent of the large (and thus unionized) ones gave between twenty and twenty-four days.[144]

Japanese workers, however, do not normally take more than a few consecutive days off. In 1972 the modal class of summer holidays was two days (three days for large firms), with only 7 percent of all employers providing more than five days (15.3 percent of large firms). The customary practice is to shut the plant down for a few days rather than allowing vacations to be taken in shifts.[145]

Workers often appear reluctant to take the holidays to which they are entitled lest they be regarded as imposing an undue burden upon the enterprise and their fellow workers. As Cole remarks: "When workers choose not to take their allotted vacations, this is seen as demonstrating their loyalty to the company. Such practices, however, are increasingly limited to older workers, with younger workers more willing to take full advantage of their rights under the law."[146] But young workers do grow older.

There are no comparative international data on vacations, and even for individual countries the information is sparse. A 1970 survey of forty U.S. collective agreements selected at random showed that in thirty-one cases the maximum vacation period was four weeks, and this may be regarded as current practice in the United States as far as the union sector is concerned.[147] This is more liberal than the prevailing norm in Europe, where a three-week maximum generally prevails. The formal Japanese vacation provisions are thus not too far out of line with Western Europe; the difference lies in the fact that virtually all Western workers take the entire vacation to which they are entitled, whereas Japanese workers do not.

The upshot of all this is that the number of days off from work in Japan

144. Ministry of Labor, *Year Book of Labor Statistics, 1972*, p. 249.
145. Ibid., pp. 252–53.
146. Cole, *Japanese Blue Collar*, p. 36. Dore confirms that many workers do not take all their days off. (*British Factory–Japanese Factory*, p. 188.) Clark remarks: "Only the more junior people took off their full holiday allowance, or anything like it. . . . The moral pressure on someone in the standard ranks, and even an ordinary worker, to waive his holiday allowance was very great." "Social Relations in a Japanese Company," p. 214. There is no indication that there was any extra compensation for holidays that were waived.
147. American Association of Industrial Management, *Holiday and Vacation Clauses* (July 1970).

averaged about 70 annually in 1971, compared with about 130 in the United States and 120 in West Germany.[148] Why this disparity should exist has been the subject of speculation: the economist might argue that the marginal value of extra income exceeds that for leisure; the sociologist might cite the persistence of a tradition of the work ethic and the rejection of hedonism. The lack of adequate vacation facilities may also be a factor; the Belgians and Dutch leave their densely crowded countries in large numbers each summer, but the Japanese have a more difficult problem, though package air tours are increasingly available. Whatever the reason, Japan is getting a substantially greater effort out of its labor force than the West simply in terms of annual hours of input per man, and unless work is somehow to be regarded as a consumer good, living standards in Japan are correspondingly lower.

Health and Unemployment

The Japanese people do fairly well in their health services. There are two systems of national health, one related to employment and the other administered directly by the government, with universal coverage between them. By the indexes of longevity of its citizens and available medical facilities (though not by the availability of physicians), Japan shows up well in comparison with the West (see Table 9-13).

A system of unemployment insurance was adopted in 1947 under a socialist-conservative coalition. The duration and amount of benefits vary with length of coverage and earnings. The system is financed by a payroll tax to which the employer and employee contribute an equal amount. Because of the generally low level of unemployment, the system has had few financial problems. The lifetime employment commitment by the larger firms has meant that most of the beneficiaries have been either women or men employed by small enterprises. That the unemployment insurance system is not high on the trade union reform agenda indicates that it is operating satisfactorily.[149]

Pollution

There are two additional aspects of social welfare that have great impact on living standards: education and environmental cleanliness. Both are considered in some detail elsewhere in this volume.[150] The pollution issue in

148. *Japan Labor Bulletin*, Oct. 1, 1971.
149. See Takeshi Takahashi, "Social Security for Workers," in Ōkōchi, Karsh, and Levine (eds.), *Workers and Employers in Japan*, pp. 463–68.
150. See Chapters 10 and 12.

Table 9-15. *Private Final Consumption Expenditure, by Category,*
Japan and Principal Western Industrialized Countries, 1970
Percent of total expenditure[a]

Country	Food, beverages, tobacco	Clothing and footwear	Rent, fuel, and power	Furniture, furnishings, and household equipment	Medical care and health expenditures	Transportation and communication	Recreation, entertainment, education, and culture	Miscellaneous
Japan	35.1	8.2	16.3	9.3	8.6	4.3	8.4	9.9
France	32.9	10.2	13.3	10.1	9.1	9.7	9.8	4.8
West Germany	30.0	11.8	14.8	13.0	2.7	11.9	7.0	9.1
Italy	42.2	9.1	12.9	6.9	6.2	10.5	5.4	6.8
United Kingdom	33.1	8.5	17.4	8.6	0.4	12.2	5.6	14.2
United States	19.5	8.6	18.5	8.6	9.3	14.7	10.2	10.6

Sources: United Nations, *Yearbook of National Accounts Statistics, 1971;* Economic Planning Agency, *Annual Report on National Income Statistics, 1972,* pp. 220–21. Rows may not add to 100 because of rounding.

a. The total used here is for private final consumption in the domestic market; that is, it excludes purchases abroad by resident households, purchases in the domestic market by nonresident households, and gifts in kind sent abroad. For Japan, expenditures of private nonprofit institutions and of residents abroad are also excluded.

particular has aroused much trade union interest since 1970. The national federations have spoken out on the environment problem, but the decentralized structure of the labor movement has reduced the effectiveness of their protests. The union quandary has been well summarized thus: "The trade union movement has not always worked actively to improve pollution control since their own welfare has often been closely tied up with a given enterprise or industry. . . . In many cases, labor unions have been accused of actively colluding with the enterprise."[151]

Household Expenditures

When it comes to current household expenditures, as compared with housing and the social welfare system, the rising level of real wages in Japan has been amply reflected in living standards. The pattern of expenditure appears normal for a country in Japan's per capita income range (see Table 9-15). The proportion of income going for food is well below that of Italy, and the

151. Remarks of Kazutoshi Koshiro in *Japan Labor Bulletin,* Aug. 1, 1973.

Table 9-16. *Indicators of Food Consumption, Japan and Principal Western Industrialized Countries*

Country	Calories per day	Calories of animal origin (percent)	Daily proteins (grams)
Japan	2,470	15	77
France	3,270	41	103
West Germany	3,180	43	83
Italy	3,020	21	88
United Kingdom	3,170	43	87
United States	3,300	40	99

Source: United Nations, *Statistical Yearbook, 1972*, table 162. Data for France, West Germany, and Italy are for 1969–70; for Japan and the United States, 1970; and for the United Kingdom, 1970–71.

general pattern of private consumption follows most closely that of France. But, as the data in Table 9-16 suggest, the Japanese consumer is getting less for the food portion of his expenditures than his counterpart in the other OECD countries, and the lower-income groups are particularly affected.

The area of consumer durable goods is clearly the one in which Japanese consumers have done best. The Japanese lag in automobile ownership, shown in Table 9-17, is narrowing rapidly. Some 98 percent of Japanese households own washing machines; 95 percent, refrigerators; 86 percent, vacuum cleaners; 70 percent, television sets; 77 percent, cameras. Air conditioners are enjoyed by only 12 percent of households, though the proportion is rising rapidly. Less than 1 percent have central heating, however—a reflection of low housing standards.[152] The great industrial machine that has been built up during the last two decades is geared to the mass production of durable goods, and the Japanese consumer has been sharing its fruits with the rest of the world.

Expense Accounts

One form of expenditure raises the living standards of a few and the ire of many: the expense account. Expense account expenditures in 1971 almost equaled the total amount of dividends paid by Japanese companies in that year.[153] Japanese business executives enjoy tax-free meals at expensive restaurants, chauffeur-driven limousines, vacations at company resorts, and foreign travel to an extent that is reputedly high compared with other nations.[154]

152. *Japan Labor Bulletin*, Jan. 1, 1973.
153. U.S.–Japan Trade Council, *Another Aspect of Japan*, p. 10.
154. For a further discussion of expense accounts, see Chapter 5.

Table 9-17. *Consumption of Consumer Durables, Japan and Principal Western Industrialized Countries*

Number per 1,000 inhabitants

Country	Passenger cars, 1970	Television sets, 1971	Telephones in use, 1971
Japan	85	222	282
France	245	227	185
West Germany	237	299	249
Italy	187	191	188
United Kingdom	213	298	289
United States	432	449	604

Source: OECD Economic Surveys, *Norway* (1974), app.

Union Responsibility

Would the existence of powerful Japanese trade unions have made any substantial difference in the composition of investment and consumption? In particular, would the share of social goods have been greater? If the answers are in the affirmative, would not the Japanese working man now be worse off by virtue of the lower rate of economic growth that in all likelihood would have been the consequence of a reduced investment rate?

The opportunity to bring about a Japanese experience closer to the Western European labor union model existed from 1945 to 1950, but a number of circumstances, including the exercise of employer and governmental power, as well as ideological divisions within the labor movement itself, contributed to the evolution of the present Japanese system. If instead of fragmented and relatively impecunious labor federations there now existed a single national body capable of supporting an allied political movement, it is our belief that the investment decisions of the past two decades would have been quite different. The modern welfare state—the United States entered the club fairly recently—did not come into being through the beneficence of entrepreneurs or of their political representatives. The drive has always come from organizations of working people, expressed in both the economic and political spheres. Long before the advent of socialist governments in Western Europe or of the American New Deal, trade unions had established mutual aid societies to promote health care, unemployment compensation, pensions, and housing, and these functions have gradually been taken over by governments. The rise of welfarism in the United States clearly paralleled the growth of the labor movement, and unions have worked persistently for improvement of social services. The American labor movement actually provides the best example of the use of economic bargaining power, as against political action, to achieve welfare goals. Collectively bargained pension plans increased the interest of American employers in raising the level of government social security benefits; the spread of health insurance has occurred largely because of union effort; and government-subsidized housing owes much to the building trades.

National union leaders in Japan are well aware of the inability of their organizations to play a broader social role, and they have been attempting to broaden the spring offensive to encompass more than wages. In 1974, for example, union demands included higher minimum wages, more generous public assistance payments, indexing of pensions, freezing of public utility charges, and the expansion of low-interest loans for small firms.[155] This was little more than rhetoric, however, since the unions had neither the parliamentary strength nor the direct economic power to make these demands stick.[156]

Retrospect—Prospect

It is likely, in our view, that if the desires of Japanese wage earners had been given more effective organized expression during the past two decades, the nation's economy would look quite different than it does today. The rate of industrial investment would be lower, and that portion of consumption going into collective goods would have been greater. More effective mechanisms to facilitate the acquisition of individual homes where that was possible—or of flats where crowding made homeownership impossible— would probably have been created. Japan might well have had a more adequate system of pensions to help alleviate the anxieties of those approaching retirement. There would probably be a five-day working week, and employees would be taking in full the vacations to which they are entitled.

All of this would have had a price tag; it is scarcely likely that so rapid a rate of economic growth could have been sustained had there been a major diversion of resources to consumption and collective welfare goods and services. The stock of consumer durables owned by the average Japanese family might well have been smaller, although the family would probably be eating just as well. Corporate profits would certainly have been

155. *Japan Labor Bulletin*, March 1, 1974, and April 1, 1974.
156. Although Sōhyō would like to use the strike as a means of pushing its social demands—a tactic used successfully in recent years by the Italian unions, as the Sōhyō leadership is well aware—Dōmei rejects strikes for this purpose, seeing this course as a subversion of the Diet and inappropriate in a democratic society.

lower, reducing reinvestment potential. But as two students of the Japanese growth pattern remarked, "consumer sacrifice was a price willingly paid by those in charge."[157]

It will not be easy to change the direction of the Japanese economy, even if there is a firm determination to do it. As the Economic Planning Agency has pointed out, major changes will have to occur in industrial structure. Increasing profits and capital gains, together with inflation, tend to "enlarge inequities in income distribution and depreciate the value of private savings."[158] Disproportionate increases in the price of land further complicate the housing problem. And to cite the EPA again: "The more is the attainment of a welfare society delayed, the more serious difficulties would be faced by the Japanese economy. The Japanese economy of the future is no longer the linear extension of the postwar pattern of economic development. We must realize that the basic guiding idea for the new economy is the enhancement of social justice."[159]

Conclusions

The major findings that we derive from this survey of the Japanese labor market are these:

First, for the next decade, at least, the outlook is for a much less ample supply of labor than during the past decade. Manpower will not be a limiting factor, however, for any reasonable rate of economic growth.

Second, the present wage system, with its emphasis upon seniority, is already undergoing modification in the direction of efficiency-related compensation. This trend will continue, but seniority will retain substantial importance as a factor in determining wages for some time to come.

Third, the practice of permanent employment commitment followed by the larger enterprises will not be impaired by a reduction in the rate of economic growth to, say, Western European levels, although a prolonged major depression might seriously threaten it.

Fourth, because of economic and political weakness, the Japanese labor movement has been unable to secure for its members a level of social welfare or a degree of industrial democracy consistent with the nation's level of development.

It is our view—and we concede immediately that a great many think

157. Ohkawa and Rosovsky, *Japanese Economic Growth*, p. 225.
158. EPA, *Economic Survey of Japan, 1972–1973*, p. 153.
159. Ibid., p. 155.

otherwise—that movement toward a Western labor market model is optimal for the future social stability of Japan. In saying this, we are not unmindful of unique elements in Japanese culture that may make complete convergence impossible. Present circumstances must be viewed in the context of the historical legacy, which has endowed the social system with many traditional elements. Japanese workers have a relatively strong consciousness of enterprise loyalty and a weak consciousness of class, not only because of deliberate indoctrination but also because of genuine communal feelings of their own. The concept of contractual relations in industrial relations has never been strongly established; if anything, it is a borrowed concept for Japan. The following description of the nineteenth-century Japanese village may still have some relevance to current industrial relations: "Tensions were more quickly and intimately felt, but overt expression of them was more resolutely suppressed in favor of an appearance of community harmony—and they were the more explosive for that reason. Deep beneath the everyday appearance of propriety and friendliness there were in many Japanese villages suppressed hatreds that merely needed some shock, some momentary lapse of customary restraint to send them boiling to the surface."[160]

Nor are we unaware of the problems of the Western labor model: bureaucratization of trade unions, concentration of power, the damage that can be done by ideological extremists, and excessive work stoppages. Nevertheless, we feel that Western labor market organization has a good deal to offer in helping curb authoritarian tendencies in government and management and in providing consumption patterns that are more favorable to lower-income groups. In the long run it is also an economically efficient system in that those who have the less pleasant but nonetheless essential jobs in an industrial society have a ready means of expressing their discontent and of securing redress.

Historically, transition to a stable labor market system has rarely come about in the West without a great deal of industrial and political strife; Great Britain and the Scandinavian countries are among the few exceptions. It is difficult for employers who occupy a dominant position to yield power gracefully—and yielding power is essentially what is involved. Perhaps Japan will profit from the experience of other nations.

If there is to be a fundamental change in the Japanese system, the first requisite is the transformation of the labor movement from its enterprise base to a national structure. One way to do this would be to give tran-

160. Thomas C. Smith, *The Agrarian Origins of Modern Japan* (Stanford University Press, 1959), p. 172.

sitional government grants on a nondiscriminatory basis to the existing national unions and federations to permit them to acquire the expertise necessary to function as competent bargaining agencies.[161] Although in principle workers should finance their own organizations, help from the outside will probably be needed if an orderly change is to take place.

We are well aware that the Liberal Democratic government and employers are likely to look with deep suspicion on this or any suggestion that might strengthen national unionism. For one thing, wealthier national unions might be better able to support labor parties that could eventually attain governmental power. There is no answer if one anticipates an indefinite conservative political hegemony in Japan. If not, there are worse alternatives than labor governments that accept the constraints of parliamentary democracy.

The trade unions, of course, could move in the same direction autonomously by requiring that a larger share of dues income be allocated to national unions and by strengthening the constitutional authority of national unions over their locals. The labor relations commissions and the courts could aid in the process by stricter enforcement of the laws against employer influence in union affairs and by helping to turn off the flow of loyalty-to-the-company propaganda that is often inconsistent with genuine employer neutrality. Even under existing law, after all, employees are entitled to choose their bargaining representatives without employer restraint and coercion. The provision of company premises for union offices and the entertainment of union officials on company expense accounts are questionable practices. The involvement of supervisors in union government is hardly likely to foster independent unionism.

Whether there will in fact be a trend toward a more independent and socially influential labor movement is difficult to predict. Neither the large companies nor the Liberal Democratic government evidence any desire to alter the status quo in any major respect. It is possible that the labor movement, under the impact of inflation and a slowing down of the rate of economic growth, may overcome both its ideological differences and its parochial vision in the interest of more effective representation of its constituents. But the gulf between socialists to the left and right and communists, as well as between Sōhyō and Dōmei, remains wide. To judge by the experience of other countries that have had similar divisions in the ranks of labor, it will not be an easy gulf to bridge.

161. It is our understanding that a proposal of this nature has actually been made within the government bureaucracy but that it received no serious consideration.

CHAPTER TEN

Urbanization
and Urban Problems

Edwin S. Mills, Princeton University
and
Katsutoshi Ohta, Tokyo University

673

ECONOMIC DEVELOPMENT consists in part of the transfer of human and other resources from the extractive to the industrial and service sectors. Whereas extractive activities are mostly rural, industrial and service activities are concentrated in urban areas. Development of these sectors requires the growth of many large, highly specialized, and interactive economic institutions. Cities are basically places in which the requisite scale and interaction are achieved at low cost by proximate and dense locations of such activities.[1] Urbanization therefore is the inevitable handmaiden of economic development.

Throughout the nineteenth and twentieth centuries, the growth of the industrial and service sectors has everywhere been accompanied by the migration of a large part of the population from rural to urban areas. In every high-income country, a large majority of the population lives in urban areas.[2] People are attracted to cities by the income and employment opportunities found there and by the variety of consumer goods and services available. Incomes are higher in urban than rural areas in almost every country. Urbanization is among the most pervasive and dramatic events of modern history, and Japan is as dramatic an example as can be found.

Note. The authors are indebted to the many Japanese and U.S. scholars and public officials who contributed time and expertise to the education of the American author on Japanese urban problems. They wish especially to acknowledge the help of Professors Yukihide Ōkano, Kaoru Shimōsa, and Takashi Inouye, and Messrs. Tsuneto Yamagishi and Takashi Onishi, all of Tokyo University.

1. The exact relation between industrialization and urbanization has been the subject of extensive debate among urban specialists. Many studies have correlated measures of industrialization and urbanization among countries to test whether currently developing countries are more urbanized than seems to be justified by the extent of their industrialization. Roughly speaking, industrialization accounts for only about half the variance of urbanization among countries. But the basic point is that industrial production is by no means the only important function of urban areas and they are increasingly centers of service activities—in Japan, the United States, and elsewhere. See Edwin Mills, "City Sizes in Developing Economies," in Raanan Weitz (ed.), *Rehovot Conference on Urbanization and the Developing Countries* (Rehovot, Israel: Continuation Committee for the International Conference on Science in the Advancement of New States, 1971), for some data, a discussion of the issues, and references to the literature.

In this chapter, the term "urban area" will be used generically to refer to places in which people live and work in high densities. The term "urbanization" will refer to the process by which the urban population grows relative to the rural population. Terms such as "city," "standard metropolitan statistical areas" (SMSA), "major metropolitan area," and "urbanized area" will be used as defined by the census to which they refer. See Appendix A for census definitions of some terms.

2. Kingsley Davis, *World Urbanization, 1950–1970*, Population Monograph Series no. 4 (University of California Press, 1969).

Rapid urbanization is almost always accompanied by serious social problems and conflicts. Migrants are poorer, less educated, and less accustomed to the complexities of urban life than are longer-term urban residents. In many developing countries, extremely high unemployment rates have been reported among recent migrants. They may have no housing except what they have built with their own hands. They place great strain on already overloaded public services such as schools, transportation, health services, water supply, and waste disposal. They are the focus of political discontent and agitation, which leads public officials to attempt to limit urban growth, despite clear evidence that migration to urban areas is the principal way in which the rural poor can improve their lives and those of their children.

The United States faced most of these problems during the period of rapid influx of foreign and rural migrants to the cities in the nineteenth and early twentieth centuries. Since World War II, racial trauma has been added to other problems as poor blacks and whites have migrated to cities from small towns and rural areas.

Japan has had as rapid a rate of urbanization as any country in the postwar world. In comparison with the experience of any country in that period, and perhaps in the history of the world, Japan has escaped almost all of the most serious problems that have accompanied urbanization elsewhere. It is a racially and ethnically homogeneous country; it has had no substantial influx of foreigners with different languages, customs, and educations. Equally important, the high quality of Japanese education outside the cities has meant that migrants have been able to cope with city life and compete for city jobs. Above all, the rapid postwar economic growth and the great employment potential of the cities have meant that no significant pool of unemployed and desperate people has grown up in the cities. The production of housing and public services has more than kept pace with the rapid flow of migrants.

We do not imply that urban problems do not exist in Japan. They certainly do, and they deserve the most imaginative solutions the public and private sectors can provide. In fact, there is a strong and growing sense of dissatisfaction with the quality of urban life in Japan. Public opinion polls and the attention paid to the subject by the media indicate about the same degree of dissatisfaction with urban life as is found in the United States, and the term "urban crisis" is used with about equal frequency in the two countries. In both countries, this dissatisfaction reflects in part only the determination of people to improve their lives and the efforts of the media to mobilize and voice these feelings. But it also reflects feelings of discontent about specific aspects of urban life.

Although some urban problems are common to the two countries—inadequate housing, for example, especially for low-income residents, as well as environmental pollution—the general content of the urban crisis is quite different. In the United States, public opinion polls, the media, and the campaigns of aspirants to public office confirm that violent crime, drug abuse, racial antagonism, and the decline of central cities rank high on the list of urban problems. Yet none of these would be identified as a major urban problem in Japan, where the issues of urban land values and land use and of protection against natural disasters hold much higher priority as urban problems.

The plan of the chapter is as follows. The next section is an overview of Japanese urbanization. A detailed comparative study of urban structure in Japan and the United States follows. The remainder of the chapter focuses on four broad urban problems: housing, transportation, environmental quality, and land values and land uses. Any selection and classification of urban problems are to some extent subjective, and we recognize that others would classify problems differently. In the concluding section, we bring together some speculations about future directions for national urban policy in Japan.

Characteristics of Urbanization in Japan

Nearly everyone knows that Japan is a crowded country. It is smaller than California and has more than five times as many people. Its overall population density is nearly thirteen times that of the United States—287 people per square kilometer compared with 22 in the United States. Of the few countries that have densities as high as Japan's, Japan is by far the largest: among countries with at least 4 million inhabitants, only Belgium, the Netherlands, South Korea, and Taiwan had densities in excess of Japan's in 1972. In comparison with Japan's density of 287 people per square kilometer, China has a density of 83, India, 172, and the United Kingdom, 226.[3] And Japan is even more crowded than these figures suggest. It is a mountainous country, and only about 25 percent of its land has a slope of less than 10 percent; both farms and cities are thus concentrated on the small amount of relatively flat land. Both urban and rural population densities inevitably are greater in Japan than in the United States, but urban densities differ only modestly between the two countries, whereas rural densities in Japan are much greater.

3. The figures in the paragraph are from United Nations, *Statistical Yearbook, 1973* (1974), table 18, pp. 67–73.

Urban and Rural Population Densities

Japan is one of the world's most industrialized and urbanized countries. Table 10-1 shows the numbers, percent, and density of the urban and rural population for census years from 1920 to 1970, and for densely inhabited districts (DIDs) from 1960 to 1970.[4] The percentage of Japanese living in cities in 1970, 72.2, nearly matched that in the United States, 73.5, in the same year. These percentages are typical of industrialized, high-income countries throughout the world.[5]

America's urbanization has been rapid during the twentieth century, but that of Japan has been even faster during the second and third quarters of the century, paralleling its rapid economic growth. In 1920, slightly more than half the U.S. population, but less than one-fifth the Japanese population, was urban. The rapid urbanization of the 1920s and 1930s was reversed during the war, as people migrated to the countryside to escape the bombing of the cities. Since 1945, Japanese urbanization has been among the fastest in the world: the urban population more than tripled during the following twenty-five years.[6] The rate of urbanization may have slowed somewhat during the 1960s, but the figures do not suggest that the period of rapid urban migration has ended. The speed of Japanese postwar urbanization is illustrated by the 45 percent decline in the rural population between 1945 and 1970. This is in striking contrast to the United States, where the rural population has hardly changed despite urbanization.

In 1970, Japan's 579 cities occupied about one-fourth of the country's land area. Eight cities had populations in excess of 1 million and a total population of 20 million. In 1920, the same eight cities had a total population less than 6 million.

Urban density data are difficult to compare among countries. They are usually compiled for local government jurisdictions, and they depend much on where political boundaries are drawn—a principal justification for the study of density functions reported in the next section. The fairly steady decline in the population densities of Japanese cities from 1920 to 1970 shown

4. See Appendix A for definitions of terms. The definition of "urban" has changed since 1920, and the data in Table 10-1 may understate the urban population for the early years included.

5. United Nations, *Statistical Yearbook, 1972.*

6. Perhaps half the increase in urban population between 1950 and 1955 resulted from movement of city boundaries and from the formation of new cities from towns and villages. But the U.S. Census Bureau also broadened the definition of urban to much the same effect and at about the same time.

Table 10-1. *Urban and Rural Population and Population Density*[a]
in Japan, Census Years, 1920–70

	Total population		Urban population			Rural population		Densely inhabited district[b] population		
Census year	Number (thousands)	Density	Number (thousands)	Density	Percent of total	Number (thousands)	Density	Number (thousands)	Density	Percent of total
1920	55,391	146	10,020	7,326	18.1	45,371	120	...	...	...
1925	59,179	156	12,822	5,898	21.7	46,358	123	...	...	...
1930	63,872	168	15,364	5,220	24.1	48,509	129	...	...	...
1935	68,662	181	22,582	4,439	32.9	46,080	123	...	...	...
1940	72,540	191	27,494	3,109	37.9	45,045	121	...	...	...
1945	71,998	195	20,022	1,379	27.8	51,976	147	...	...	...
1950	83,200	226	31,203	1,575	37.5	51,996	149	...	...	...
1955	89,276	242	50,288	742	56.3	38,988	130	...	...	...
1960	93,419	253	59,333	719	63.5	34,084	119	40,830	10,563	43.7
1965	98,275	266	66,919	760	68.1	31,356	112	47,261	10,263	48.1
1970	103,720	280	74,353	791	72.2	28,867	105	55,535	8,688	53.5

Source: Bureau of Statistics, Office of the Prime Minister, *1970 Population Census of Japan* (1971), vol. 1, pp. 2, 4-6. See Appendix A for definitions of terms.
a. Density is in persons per square kilometer.
b. The densely inhabited district was first used as a census unit in the population census of 1960.

in Table 10-1 in part represents the process of urban decentralization that has been observed and studied in many countries[7] and is examined in more detail in the next section. The more than 50 percent decrease in urban density recorded between 1940 and 1945 is the result largely of the war, and the further 50 percent decrease between 1950 and 1955 is the result partly of enlargement of city boundaries and creation of new cities during that period. The gradual increases in city densities from 1960 to 1970 resulted from the growth of the urban population in the rural areas annexed to cities in the early 1950s. The decrease in densities of DIDs recorded from 1960 to 1970 shows that the process of urban decentralization is continuing.

The density data in Table 10-1 can be compared with density data for U.S. SMSAs and urbanized areas:[8] in 1970 the average population density of SMSAs was 140 people per square kilometer, and that of urbanized areas was 1,300. The large difference results from the fact that about 90 percent of the land in SMSAs was rural. Thus, the 1970 density of 791 for Japanese

7. See for example, Colin Clark, *Population Growth and Land Use* (St. Martin's Press, 1967); and Edwin Mills, *Studies in the Structure of the Urban Economy* (Johns Hopkins University Press, 1972).
8. A Japanese city normally contains at least 50,000 people, although there are many exceptions. A U.S. SMSA consists of a central city of at least 50,000 population and any contiguous counties that are substantially urban; a U.S. urbanized area consists of an SMSA central city and the urbanized parts of the surrounding area. The Japanese city and the U.S. SMSA are the most nearly comparable urban concepts reported by the Japanese and U.S. census. But comparability is not great, and neither one is a good urban concept.

cities is larger than that of U.S. SMSAs, but smaller than that of U.S. urbanized areas. This indicates that urban densities in Japan and the United States are of similar magnitudes. It follows that the much greater overall population density of Japan reflects mainly the much higher rural densities in Japan than in the United States.

Although overall urban densities are comparable in Japan and the United States, the most densely populated parts of Japanese cities have much higher densities than do U.S. cities. The last column of Table 10-1 shows that more than half the Japanese population lived in DIDs, in which the average density was 8,700 people per square kilometer in 1970. These extremely high densities can be matched in only a few places in the United States. By contrast, U.S. SMSA central cities had an average density of 1,750 in 1970.

As a rough summary, overall density in Japan is about ten times that in the United States. Urban density in Japan may be one and a half times that in the United States. Densities in the densest parts of large cities of Japan may be two or three times those in comparable census tracts in large U.S. cities.

Megalopolitan Population and Employment Densities

There is a remarkable analogy between the set of metropolitan areas stretched along the Pacific coast of Japan from Tokyo to Osaka, sometimes referred to as the Tokaido megalopolis, and the set of metropolitan areas stretched along the east coast of the United States from New York to Washington, sometimes referred to as the East Coast megalopolis. Each comprises an almost continuous set of densely populated metropolitan areas stretched along about 500 kilometers of coastline. Each contains the country's largest metropolitan area, which is its leading financial, headquarters, industrial, and port area. Each contains two additional leading ports. Each contains the national capital. In addition, large amounts of farmland remain between both New York and Washington and Tokyo and Osaka, which indicates that the term "megalopolis" is somewhat fanciful.

Table 10-2 contains recent population data for the two megalopolitan areas. By the measures used there, the Japanese megalopolis has about 40 percent greater population than its U.S. counterpart. Because the two cover about the same area, densities are considerably greater in the Japanese megalopolis. More than 40 percent of the Japanese population lives in the Tokaido region, whereas the U.S. East Coast region contains only about 11 percent of the country's population. Although the growth rate of the Tokyo area appears to have slackened somewhat in recent years, the data in Table 10-2 show that both it and the entire Tokaido region continued to grow rapidly

Table 10-2. *Population of the Tokaido and U.S. East Coast
Megalopolises, Two Most Recent Censuses*
Population in thousands

Tokaido[a]				U.S. East Coast[b]			
Area	1965	1970	Percent change	Area	1960	1970	Percent change
Tokyo	18,942	21,954	15.9	New York City	14,759	16,179	9.6
Nagoya	6,096	6,774	11.1	Philadelphia	6,999	7,818	11.7
Osaka	12,063	13,640	13.1	Baltimore-			
				Washington	3,881	4,932	27.1
Total	37,101	42,368	14.2	Total	25,639	28,929	12.8

Sources: Japanese data, Bureau of Statistics, *1970 Population Census of Japan* (1971), vol. 1, table 6; U.S. data, Bureau of the Census, *Census of Population, 1970* (1972), vol. 1, pt. A, sec. 1, tables 32, 33.
a. Includes people living within 50 kilometers of the named cities.
b. Includes people in the New York Standard Consolidated Area, the Philadelphia Region (Allentown-Bethlehem-Easton, Atlantic City, Harrisburg, Lancaster, Philadelphia, Reading, Trenton, Vineland-Millville-Bridgeton, Wilmington, and York SMSAs), and the Baltimore and Washington SMSAs.

between 1965 and 1970—a 14.2 percent five-year growth of Tokaido, compared with a 5.5 percent growth of the entire population during the same period. And Tokyo was the most rapidly growing of the three metropolitan areas in the region. By contrast, the U.S. East Coast megalopolis grew by only 12.8 percent during the entire decade of the 1960s, more slowly than the 13.3 percent growth of the U.S. population.

Tokyo and New York are frequently said to be the world's two largest metropolitan areas. Table 10-3 contains population and employment data for the two areas that are as nearly comparable as possible. The data in the table impute about 50 percent more people to the Tokyo than to the New York region and about the same land area. Thus, Tokyo's population density is nearly 50 percent greater than New York's. The striking characteristic of the data in Table 10-3 is the similarity between the two great metropolises. Within 20 kilometers of the center (an area somewhat larger than the twenty-three-wards area in Tokyo and somewhat larger than New York City excluding Staten Island), population density is nearly identical in the two areas. Employment density is about 25 percent greater in Tokyo than in New York. The land area is about 35 percent greater within 20 kilometers of the center of Tokyo than of New York because New York is more nearly surrounded by water than Tokyo. In the more distant rings, Tokyo's population and employment densities are between 50 and 100 percent greater than New York's. Tokyo's employment densities are larger than New York's relative to its

Table 10-3. *Population and Employment in the Tokyo and
New York City Regions*[a]

Item	Distance from center (kilometers)					Total
	0–20	*20–40*	*40–60*	*40–80*	*60–70*	*Total*
Tokyo						
Population						
Number (thousands)	11,694	7,733	3,887	...	1,161	24,475
Density (persons per						
square kilometer)	10,960	2,348	666	...	345	1,806
Percent of region	47.8	31.6	15.9	...	4.7	100.0
Employment						
Number (thousands)	7,028	2,840	1,687	...	567	12,122
Density (persons per						
square kilometer)	6,587	862	289	...	169	895
Percent of region	58.0	23.4	13.9	...	4.7	100.0
Area (square kilometers)	1,067	3,293	5,833	...	3,360	13,552
New York						
Population						
Number (thousands)	8,188	5,176	...	2,698	...	16,062
Density (persons per						
square kilometer)	10,351	1,390	...	335	...	1,279
Percent of region	51.0	32.2	...	16.8	...	100.0
Employment						
Number (thousands)	4,188	1,977	...	799	...	6,964
Density (persons per						
square kilometer)	5,295	531	...	99	...	555
Percent of region	60.1	28.4	...	11.5	...	100.0
Area (square kilometers)	791	3,725	...	8,042	...	12,558

Source: Katsutoshi Ohta, "Tokyo and New York: A Comparative Analysis of Their Urban
Structures and Living Environment," *Tōyō keizai tōkei geppō* [Tōyō Keizai's Statistics Monthly],
vol. 32 (August 1972).

a. Tokyo data are for 1970; New York data, for 1963.

population densities because the Japanese labor force participation rate exceeds the U.S. rate.

Table 10-4 provides more detailed data for the central parts of the Tokyo
and New York regions. The three sets of places—the core of the central business district (CBD), the CBD, and the central area—have been chosen to
have roughly the same areas in the two metropolitan areas. The largest percentage of CBD land is devoted to employment, and employment densities
therefore are much greater than population densities there. In the CBD core,
New York's employment density exceeds Tokyo's by 50 percent, and New
York's population density is 2.5 times that of Tokyo. In the entire CBD, employment densities are about the same in the two metropolises, but New

Table 10-4. *Population and Employment in Central Parts of the Tokyo and New York City Regions, 1970*[a]

	Core of central business district		Central business district		Central area	
	Tokyo two wards	Man-hattan CBD	Tokyo three wards	Man-hattan	Tokyo wards area	New York City ex-cluding Staten Island
Population (thousands)	178	518	402	1,539	8,840	7,600
Employment (thousands)	1,260	2,122	1,721	2,518	5,891	3,915
Population density (persons per square kilometer)	8,250	21,400	9,790	26,540	15,320	11,290
Employment density (persons per square kilometer)	58,410	88,420	41,930	43,410	10,210	5,820
Area (square kilometers)	22	24	41	58	577	673

Source: Same as Table 10-3.

a. New York employment data are for 1963. Manhattan CBD is the part of Manhattan south of Central Park. The Tokyo two-wards data refer to Chiyoda-ku and Chuō-ku. The three-wards data include Minato-ku.

York's population density is much greater than Tokyo's even in the larger area. Only in the largest of the three areas do Tokyo's densities exceed those of New York.

Tokyo and other large Japanese cities have achieved their high population and employment densities by using small interior spaces in buildings, leaving little uncovered land around structures, and devoting little land to such public purposes as streets and parks. Japanese cities have gone much further in these directions than U.S. cities. New York's extremely high densities are achieved by the use of very tall buildings for employment and housing, whereas Tokyo had few buildings more than ten stories high until a few years ago, when a surge of tall-building construction began in Tokyo. There are now several buildings of skyscraper height and many more of between ten and twenty-five stories. Tokyo's uncovered land prices exceed those in New York, with the highest prices being well over $50 million per acre. But then why have New Yorkers, by constructing tall buildings, gone so much further than Tokyoites in substituting capital for land? First, until recently Tokyo had stringent building-height controls based in part on the danger of earthquakes, and relaxation of controls accounts for the present boom in high-rise build-ing. Second, Tokyo has relatively poor subsoil foundations for tall buildings, which, given the safety standards that are required, make them expensive to

build. Third, the Japanese construction industry has grown more sophisticated only in recent years.

The data in Table 10-4 suggest strongly that the pressure to increase employment in Tokyo's CBD core, which has little more than half the employment of New York's, will continue. As the country's financial, business, and
government center, it has great advantages to employers engaged in international and domestic commerce. Technology is clearly no longer a barrier
to construction of tall buildings in central Tokyo, and its land values provide
incentive to build them. Thus, there is every reason to believe that employment will continue to increase in Tokyo's CBD core unless government prevents it.

Employment cannot expand in central Tokyo unless public transit facilities expand correspondingly. The excess carrying capacity of streets is small
and further road construction there is unlikely and undesirable. Some people
believe that central Tokyo already is saturated with rail and subway lines,
but that is clearly not so. If it is assumed that half the residents of the two
CBD cores work there, the data in Table 10-4 imply that about 1.9 million
workers commute to the New York CBD core and 1.2 million to Tokyo's two
wards—a tribute to the capacity of New York's public transit system. New
York has more rail and subway lines into its CBD core than Tokyo and many
more bus lines. It would clearly be possible to increase public transit into
central Tokyo if it were found desirable to do so.

Japanese and U.S. Urban Density Functions

That urban areas in the developed world tend to decentralize or sub-
urbanize as time passes is well known, and urban specialists have devoted
considerable effort to measuring and explaining the process.[9] In the previous
section, evidence of decentralization in Japanese urban areas was seen in the
data on declining urban densities. That the extent and speed of decentralization vary greatly among cities within and among countries also is well known.
There is disagreement among urban specialists about how to measure the
complex notion of urban decentralization, and even more disagreement
about its causes and consequences.

9. The pioneer in this work is Colin Clark, whose research is summarized in *Population Growth and Land Use*. U.S. studies include those by Mills, *Studies in the Structure
of the Urban Economy;* and Richard Muth, *Cities and Housing: The Spatial Pattern
of Urban Residential Land Use* (University of Chicago Press, 1969). Japanese studies
include those by Isao Orishima, "Land Use and Land Price," *Real Estate Appraisal*
(May 1973); and A. Otomo, "Population Density Models for Urban Areas," *Chiri*
(April 1974).

Urban business activity tends to concentrate at particular places, which become central business districts—to obtain efficient scale as well as access to port and rail terminal facilities, to other businesses, and to as many of the urban area's residents as possible. Housing and diverse businesses are located near the CBD; hence, as the previous section indicated, employment is more centralized than housing in urban areas. Land closest to the center is most valuable for almost all purposes. Its price is bid high, inducing substitution of capital and other nonland inputs for land and resulting in extremely high central densities. The value of land surrounding the CBD decreases with distance from the CBD. The rate of decrease is determined by transport costs to the center of the city, by the ability to substitute land for nonland inputs as land values fall, and by long lags in adjusting land use to changing circumstances.

The reasons for residential decentralization are fairly well understood. As transport improves, commutation becomes economical from residences farther from the center, which enables workers to obtain less expensive, larger, and lower-density housing. American observers sometimes attribute urban decentralization mainly to increased use of automobiles, but it is clear from U.S. and other experience that improvements in public transit have much the same effect. As incomes rise, two things happen. First, housing demand increases and it pays workers to move farther from the center, to where land, and therefore housing, is cheaper. Second, demand becomes great enough to support many urban activities at efficient scales with customers from only part of the urban area, and subcenters spring up away from the CBD. Subcenters also result from sheer growth of the urban area's population.

The growth of subcenters is one cause of employment decentralization in urban areas. A second important cause, especially of decentralization of manufacturing employment, is the substitution of trucks for trains and ships to transport material inputs to, and finished goods from, cities. Road haulage places less emphasis than rail or water on locations close to centralized terminal facilities. A third cause of employment decentralization is residential decentralization: other things equal, locating an employment facility near employees' residences is advantageous. Causation, of course, runs in the opposite direction as well: decentralization of employment causes residential decentralization.[10]

This section reports a study of comparative density and decentralization of population and employment in a sample of Japanese and U.S. cities. One justification for the study is that decentralization is a fundamental and per-

10. Theoretical models of the type surveyed in the last three paragraphs are surveyed in Edwin Mills, *Urban Economics* (Scott, Foresman, 1972), chaps. 3–5.

vasive urban phenomenon, and it is of intrinsic interest to compare two highly industrialized and urbanized countries. Another justification is as background for the analysis of specific urban problems in subsequent sections of the chapter. Solution of problems in housing, transport, pollution, and other areas of urban concern will be affected by the pattern of urban decentralization in Japan.

Density Function Estimates

This section consists of the estimation and analysis of density functions, showing how density varies with distance from city centers. There is considerable evidence that the negative-exponential function, which assumes a constant percentage decrease in density per mile of distance from the urban center, provides as good an approximation to urban population density patterns as any simple function.[11] The evidence is much less strong that employment densities fit the negative-exponential well, but there is no evidence that another form gives a better fit, and the simplicity and comparability provided by the negative-exponential justify its use. Although the negative-exponential can be derived from simplified theoretical models, its main value is as a simple and empirically accurate descriptive device. At best, the negative-exponential density function for population can hold only outside the CBD, in which there is relatively little housing. (In Japan, the near absence of housing in CBDs is sometimes referred to as the doughnut-ization of cities.) Likewise, it is likely that any monotonic or continuously falling density function is a more accurate descriptive tool for relatively small metropolitan areas than for large metropolises with many subcenters and satellite communities.

The negative-exponential function can be written:

$$(1) \qquad\qquad D(x) = D_0 e^{-gx},$$

where $D(x)$ is density at distance x from the center, D_0 and g are constants to be estimated from the data, and e is the base of the natural logarithm. D_0 is the density at the center and g is the percentage change in density per unit increase in distance from the center, referred to as the gradient of the density function. D_0 is positive since density is positive; g is positive if density decreases with distance from the center. The larger is g, the faster density falls with distance, which suggests that g can be used as a measure of decentralization. Specifically, among all cities that are circular (or semicircular with a pie slice of the same number of radians removed by a harbor or other natural barrier) and have exponential density functions, the percentage of total pop-

11. See Muth, *Cities and Housing.*

ulation or employment within a given distance of the center is uniquely related to g and does not depend on D_0. In these restrictive conditions, g is an unambiguous measure of the degree of decentralization. More realistic conditions introduce ambiguity into the measure.

We have estimated density functions for samples of twenty-two Japanese cities and twenty U.S. urbanized areas. The sample urban areas, as they will be referred to generically, were chosen purposively. First, the samples intentionally include New York and Tokyo. Second, cities with major natural barriers were avoided because of the ambiguity in the use of g as a measure of decentralization. This is especially important in Japan, where many cities are located in narrow valleys. Third, urban areas that touched other urban areas were avoided. Fourth, an attempt was made to include urban areas in a variety of regions and sizes.

An important purpose of the study is to trace and compare the patterns of decentralization through time, so each density function should be estimated for at least two dates. Ideally, the dates should be the same for the samples of sectors and cities in the two countries, but national censuses are the only sources of the required data, and the estimates therefore are constrained to be for census years. Density functions have been estimated for population, total employment, and manufacturing employment for the following years: population—Japan, 1965 and 1970, United States, 1960 and 1970; employment—Japan, 1969 and 1972, United States, 1960 and 1970; manufacturing employment—Japan, 1969 and 1972, United States, 1963 and 1967. Because there are forty-two cities, three sectors, and two years, there are about 250 density functions.[12]

Each density function was estimated by computing the appropriate density for a random sample of small areas within each urban area: the small areas are census tracts in the United States and clusters of enumeration districts in Japan. Distance from the center of the urban area to each small area in the sample was measured on census maps. This procedure provides a random sample of densities and distances for each urban area, sector, year, and country. Using these random samples, each density function can be estimated by linear regression since, from equation 1, the log of density is linear in distance. This procedure cannot be used to estimate U.S. employment and manufacturing employment density functions because the required employment data are not available by census tract. The procedure by which these density functions were estimated—as well as details about data sources, estimation procedures, and the density functions themselves—are described

12. The actual number is 248, since the required data for manufacturing employment are not available for two U.S. urban areas.

in Appendix B. All population data are numbers of people who live in sample places, and employment data are numbers of people who work in sample places.

The Japanese density functions have much larger values of D_0 (persons per square kilometer) than their U.S. analogs. For population, for example, most U.S. D_0s are between 1,000 and 10,000, whereas most Japanese D_0s are between 10,000 and 25,000. The estimated density functions imply that population densities are at least twice as great near the centers of Japanese cities as near centers of U.S. cities, but it should be remembered that D_0 greatly overstates actual population density at the city center. D_0 tends to be larger for larger cities in both countries. Similar statements can be made regarding the D_0s for total employment and for manufacturing employment.

Table 10-5 shows averages of the estimated gradients, g, for population, total employment, and manufacturing employment. The Japanese density functions are much steeper than their U.S. counterparts. For 1970, the average Japanese population gradient is more than three times as large as the average in the United States. The relative differences between average employment gradients are not quite as large, but they are substantial. Thus, Japanese urbanized areas are much more centralized than U.S. urban areas. To see what this means in practical terms, consider the 1970 population density functions for Sapporo and Atlanta, each of which had just over 1 million people.

<table>
<tr><td align="center">Sapporo</td><td align="center">Atlanta</td></tr>
<tr><td align="center">$D(x) = 22,652e^{-0.231x}$</td><td align="center">$D(x) = 5,985e^{-0.126x}$</td></tr>
</table>

Both urban areas are approximately circular. Sapporo's density function implies that the urban area's radius is about six kilometers, and its area is about 113 square kilometers; Atlanta's density function implies that its radius is about 12 kilometers, and its area is about 450 square kilometers.[13] The low densities of U.S. urban areas make them voracious users of land.

Average employment gradients are, of course, much steeper than average population gradients, indicating that employment is more centralized than population—or, equivalently, that more people commute inward than outward on the way to work. The relation between employment and population gradients has important implications for commuting. If the two were equal, it would mean that the same fraction of employment and population was located at each distance from the center. Thus, it would be possible for each worker to live and work at the same place. Even if that did not happen, the

13. These radii are obtained by calculating how big the urban area must be to hold its known population, given that residential densities are those indicated by the density function.

Table 10-5. *Average Density Gradients for Japanese and U.S. Urban Areas,*[a] *Various Years*

	Japan		United States	
Sector	Year	Average gradient	Year	Average gradient
Population	1965	0.457	1960	0.199
	1970	0.391	1970	0.123
Employment	1969	0.841	1960	0.303
	1972	0.641	1970	0.226
Manufacturing employment	1969	0.343	1963	0.082
	1972	0.393	1967	0.048

Source: Appendix B.
a. The unit distance is one kilometer.

amount of inward commuting would equal the amount of outward commuting at each distance from the center. The steeper the employment gradient relative to the population gradient, the greater the minimum of commuting necessary to get workers from place of residence to place of work. Interpolating between the average 1969 and 1972 employment gradients, the average Japanese population gradient in 1970 was 50.5 percent of the average employment gradient; the corresponding U.S. figure was 54.4 percent. These ratios are very close to one another and suggest strongly that any differences in commuting patterns between urban areas in the two countries are not to be explained by differences in relative centralization of employment and population.

In both countries, manufacturing employment is more decentralized than total employment. But the average U.S. manufacturing employment gradient is much smaller both absolutely and relative to that for total employment than the average Japanese manufacturing employment gradient. Furthermore, U.S. manufacturing employment is decentralizing rapidly. In 1967 a substantial minority of U.S. urban areas in the sample had higher densities of manufacturing employment in the suburbs than in central cities: that is, g was negative. The 1973 census of manufacturing probably will show approximately uniform manufacturing employment density within U.S. urban areas. On the other hand, the Japanese data show a slight but insignificant increase in the average centralization of manufacturing employment.

The data for both countries show extremely rapid decentralization of both population and total employment. The average Japanese population gradient decreased by 0.0132 point a year during the five years covered by the table, whereas the average U.S. population gradient decreased by 0.0076 point a year during the decade covered by the table. As a percentage of its initial value, the annual fall in the U.S. average gradient was somewhat faster than the Japanese. The Japanese average employment gradient fell much more rapidly per year, both absolutely and relatively, than the average population gradient. Thus, Japanese urban employment appears to be suburbanizing even more rapidly than urban population. Although Japanese urban areas are much more centralized than American ones, the speed of decentralization is such that the Japanese density functions resemble those of many U.S. urban areas as recently as the 1950s.[14]

Determinants of Density Gradients

Rapid urban decentralization in Japan, the United States, and elsewhere raises intriguing questions about future urban structure. Here, analysis is confined to the issue of whether Japanese urban areas are likely to continue to decentralize and, presumably, become more like U.S. urban areas. As was indicated above, the process of urban decentralization is complex, influenced by technical, cultural, and legal considerations, as well as economics. But the pervasiveness of urban decentralization in the developed world suggests that legal and cultural factors that are specific to particular countries are not among the important influences. It therefore seems worthwhile to investigate whether the observed pattern can be explained by a few important economic variables whose influence is common to the two countries and that are available for the entire set of urban areas.

The discussion at the beginning of this section indicated that income, the population of the urban area, and the cost and availability of transport are likely to be the major determinants of urban decentralization, and that population decentralization was likely to cause employment decentralization, and vice versa. Although income and urban population data are readily available, data cannot be found that would adequately characterize transportation systems in the sample urban areas. Furthermore, both dimensional considerations and some experimentation with the data indicate that logarithms of population and income provide better explanations of decentralization than the variables themselves. Therefore, the basic hypothesis is that within each country the value of the density gradient for one sector—say, population— should be determined by the logarithm of the urban area's population, the logarithm of per capita income, and the density gradient in the other sector.

Urban decentralization is inevitably a slow process, since it results from

---

14. For some U.S. density functions for the 1950s, see Mills, *Studies in the Structure of the Urban Economy*, and Muth, *Cities and Housing*.

the construction, demolition, and alteration of long-lived structures. Thus, long lags should be expected between the change in an independent variable such as income and the resulting change in the density gradient. A common assumption, used in many applications in economics, is that the adjustment process follows a distributed lag in which the dependent variable moves a fixed percentage of the distance between its initial and equilibrium values in each time period. The percentage adjustment per period can be estimated from the data.

It is shown in Appendix B that the assumptions in the two preceding paragraphs lead to the regression of each sector's density gradient on the logarithms of urban population and income and on the lagged values of the density gradients for both the population and employment sectors. Estimates of these regressions from the data in Appendix B are shown in Table 10-6.

In all four equations, the coefficients of the logarithms of population and income have the anticipated negative sign, indicating that both population and employment decentralize as the urban area's population and income increase. In three of the four equations, including both population equations, the coefficients of the lagged dependent variables have the anticipated positive sign, indicating partial adjustment of the dependent variable to its equilibrium value within the interval covered by the data. The exception is the

Table 10-6. *Regression Equations for Japanese and U.S. Density Gradients*[a]

Dependent variable	Con- stant	Log population	Log income	Lagged population density gradient	Lagged employment density gradient	R^2
Japan						
Population density gradient	0.785 (0.7)	−0.031 (0.8)	−0.078 (0.4)	0.340 (2.2)	0.114 (1.1)	0.583
Employment density gradient	2.910 (2.0)	−0.071 (1.4)	−0.320 (1.3)	0.295 (1.4)	−0.092 (0.7)	0.498
United States						
Population density gradient	2.945 (1.4)	−0.018 (0.9)	−0.292 (1.3)	0.074 (0.4)	−0.082 (0.9)	0.268
Employment density gradient	0.578 (0.1)	−0.031 (0.6)	−0.032 (0.1)	−0.150 (0.3)	0.534 (2.2)	0.413

Source: Appendix B.
a. Numbers in parentheses are *t*-values of the coefficient. In addition to those reported, regressions were estimated using population and income rather than their logs. They were marginally less satisfactory than those reported. Also included in the Japanese regressions were a variable equal to the number of decades since the urban area was officially designated a city and a dummy variable to designate prefectural capitals. Neither improved the regressions.

Japanese employment equation, in which the coefficient of the lagged dependent variable is negative. In two of the four equations, the coefficient of the lagged value of the other density gradient has the anticipated positive sign, indicating that decentralization in each sector causes decentralization in the other. The two wrong signs, in the two U.S. equations, have the implausible implication that decentralization in one sector causes centralization in the other.

The coefficients of the logarithm of population are about twice as large in the Japanese equations as in the corresponding U.S. equations. This means that a 1 percent increase in the population of an urban area causes the Japanese density gradients to decrease by about twice as many points as the corresponding U.S. gradients. The U.S. population gradient is much more responsive to increases in income than the Japanese, but the U.S. employment gradient is less responsive to income increases than is the Japanese gradient.

Care is needed in interpreting the magnitudes of the coefficients of the lagged dependent variables because the time intervals are not the same in all the equations. It is shown in Appendix B that the adjustment coefficients are 1 minus the coefficients of the lagged dependent variables in the table. If the estimated adjustment coefficients are divided by the number of years between observations, the results are:

	Japan	United States
Population	0.132	0.093
Employment	0.364	0.047

The figure for Japanese population means, for example, that about 13 percent of any disequilibrium in the Japanese population gradient is corrected each year. These calculations imply that Japanese urban areas adjust to disequilibrium considerably more rapidly than do U.S. urban areas. Why this is so would be fascinating to know. One reason almost certainly is that Japanese structures, especially dwellings, contain less capital per person than U.S. structures and therefore can be built more quickly. Other possibilities are that the Japanese have a relatively larger construction industry or fewer government regulations and less red tape to slow urban construction.

Implications for Urban Decentralization

Regression analysis of the kind reported above is of uncertain accuracy, and reliance on precision of estimates is unwise. But the individual density functions reported in Appendix B, the regression equations, and other evidence support the contention that urban areas decentralize as they become larger and wealthier. It is inconceivable that urban decentralization will not continue at a rapid pace in Japan—and, for the matter, in the United States. It could be prevented only by rigorous government prevention of land conversion from rural to urban uses at the existing urban fringes. In the absence of such a measure, Japanese urban areas will occupy more land per capita in the future than in the past. Given the present disagreeably high urban densities, about which the Japanese complain, this is certainly a desirable trend to increase social welfare. But it means that heated conflict and controversy about land conversion from agricultural to suburban uses and about development controls and planning will continue, especially about the effect of conversion on Japan's efforts to become self-sufficient in food production. The foregoing analysis suggests that this controversy will continue and intensify.

Although the analysis implies that Japanese urban areas will continue to decentralize rapidly, it does not imply that Japanese urban densities will eventually be as low as those in the United States. For one thing, U.S. urban areas are also decentralizing rapidly, and it is not clear whether Japanese cities are catching up. More important, the relative price of land is much higher in Japan than in the United States—a permanent inducement to urban users to economize on land. Even at U.S. income levels, half-acre suburban lots would be rare in a country in which, as in Japan, they cost $250,000. A better model of the future Japanese city undoubtedly is the northern European city, in which land values are higher than in the United States but probably well below Japanese levels. These European cities appear to have densities between those of Japanese and U.S. cities of comparable size. It is likely that Japanese urban densities will continue to fall, but probably not to the extremely low densities of U.S. urban areas.

The analysis also does not imply that commuting distances will increase in Japanese urban areas as they decentralize. Commuting distances depend mainly on the difference between the concentration of employment and population. The regression equations imply that employment density gradients are even more responsive to population and income growth than are population density gradients in Japan. Thus, the regression analysis suggests that employment may decentralize faster than population in coming years. If so, it could result in some shortening of commuting distances.

Further Results for Tokyo and New York

Before concluding this section, it is worthwhile to report more detailed analysis of population density patterns for the Tokyo and New York metropolitan areas. No monotonic density function can be an exact description of the density pattern in a large urban area because of the importance of large subcenters there. Furthermore, it was seen in the previous section that Tokyo and New York are exceptions to the pattern that central densities are greater in Japanese than in U.S. urban areas. For these reasons, it was decided to estimate from the Tokyo and New York data density functions that permit departures from the exponential pattern. The simplest such departure is to add a quadratic term to the exponent in equation 1. The density function then becomes:

$$(2) \qquad\qquad D(x) = D_0 e^{-gx + hx^2},$$

rather than equation 1. The quadratic term was given a plus sign on the expectation that h would be positive. Equation 2 was estimated for Tokyo for census years between 1950 and 1970 and for New York for 1960 and 1970, with the following results (the numbers in parentheses are t-statistics):

Metropolitan area	Year	D_0	g	h	R^2
Tokyo	1950	42,946	0.210	0.00248	0.522
		(13.1)	(3.5)	(2.5)	
Tokyo	1955	58,647	0.219	0.00254	0.526
		(12.6)	(3.4)	(2.4)	
Tokyo	1960	72,780	0.222	0.00250	0.536
		(12.3)	(3.3)	(2.2)	
Tokyo	1965	40,372	0.131	0.000825	0.612
		(12.8)	(2.1)	(0.8)	
Tokyo	1970	41,999	0.123	0.000708	0.597
		(12.7)	(2.0)	(0.7)	
New York	1960	68,590	0.149	0.00190	0.306
		(16.8)	(2.2)	(1.4)	
New York	1970	90,917	0.183	0.00169	0.657
		(23.1)	(3.9)	(2.2)	

The Tokyo density functions display one pattern during the 1950s, another during the 1960s. During the earlier decade, density near the center increased, reaching a very high level in 1960; but since 1960 it has fallen. The Tokyo density functions also became steeper near the center during the earlier decade and less steep during the more recent decade. The Tokyo metropolitan area grew rapidly during the twenty-year period. But during the 1960s rising incomes and improved transportation caused the rapid decentralization indicated by the density functions.

The density functions for the later years conform closely to those conjectured for the two metropolitan areas in the previous section. New York's central density is much greater in 1960 and 1970 than Tokyo's is in 1965 and 1970. And, close to the center, New York's density falls more rapidly than Tokyo's in the same years. According to the 1970 density functions,

New York's density falls below Tokyo's at about thirteen kilometers from the center. All the density functions show more curvature than those in Appendix B without the quadratic terms, since the sign of the quadratic terms is positive in all seven functions. The 1970 functions become practically flat in the distant suburbs, reaching their minimum values at eighty-seven kilometers for Tokyo and fifty-four kilometers for New York, about the distance of the furthest observations (at seventy and fifty-five kilometers, respectively). New York's 1970 function has more curvature than Tokyo's. Both Tokyo's and New York's density functions became more nearly negative-exponential after 1960, since the quadratic terms became smaller.

It is fascinating to speculate about why the Tokyo–New York comparison should provide such a strong exception to the predominant pattern of higher central densities in Japanese than in U.S. urban areas. The most likely reasons are that Manhattan is more nearly surrounded by important natural barriers than is central Tokyo, and that building height controls have placed much greater constraint on central densities in Tokyo than in other Japanese cities or in New York.

Land Use and Land Values

Pervading this chapter is the notion that land is a scarce and valuable resource in Japan. The statements that Japan's population density is ten times that of the United States or that its gross national product per acre is five times that in the United States, fail to convey the depth of concern and emotion of many Japanese, who feel that the way land is priced and used is the most important social problem facing the country.

At the heart of the land-use issue is controversy over the extent to which markets are to be allowed to determine land uses. All governments interfere with land markets in one way or another. For example, most governments own much land and use it for public purposes; most governments regulate the use of privately owned land in various ways; and most governments tax the ownership and transfer of land. All three functions are subject to great controversy in Japan.

Role of Land Values

From the extreme scarcity of land in Japan it follows, first, that land is expensive in the most fundamental sense—that the opportunity cost of using it for any purpose is to forgo valuable alternative uses. (This fact is independent of the extent to which markets are permitted to determine land uses. Government can obscure the high value of land by public ownership or vigorous price controls on land, but cannot change it.) Second, it is extremely important that land be used efficiently in Japan. Valued at market prices, land constitutes a much larger percentage of total wealth in Japan than in the United States, and misallocation of land is thus far more serious.

Because land is so valuable, the collection of data on land values is widespread, and the data are much better than those in the United States. It has been estimated that the market value of all the land in Japan (excluding Okinawa) was ￥306,000 trillion in January 1973, or about $12,000 per acre—3.32 times Japan's GNP in 1972. A comparable estimate for U.S. land is $523 billion, about $225 per acre or 69.7 percent of the nation's GNP in 1966.[15] Such estimates inevitably are subject to large margins of error, because most land is not sold in any given year and because it is difficult to separate the value of land from the value of structures on it. But no margin of error can erase the conclusion that, relative to incomes, land values are much higher in Japan than in the United States.

Land values are of course important in that they allocate land among alternative uses. But why is the comparison between overall land values and GNP significant? One reason is that land rents are a form of property income and a component of GNP. If land rents are a large share of GNP, earned incomes and other property incomes must be smaller shares. The rent of a parcel of land is the value of its marginal product, and the price of the parcel is the discounted value of the market's forecast of its future rents. Thus, the higher the interest rates, the higher rents will be relative to land prices; and the more rapidly the value of land's marginal product is expected to rise, the lower rents will be.

Data on land rents are relatively scarce, since most must be imputed. The best U.S. estimate[16] is that land rents fell from 7.7 percent of GNP in 1850 to 6.4 in 1956. The latter figure is almost identical with 10 percent—a plausible discount rate for the United States, since it is about the average rate of return on corporate assets—of the $269 billion estimate of land values in 1956.[17] There are no comprehensive Japanese data on land rents, but a com-

15. See N.F.B. Research Institute, Ltd., *Wagakuni ni okeru tochi sōkakaku to fudōsan torihikigaku no suisan ni tsuite* [Estimates of Total Land Value and Total Amount of Real Estate Transactions] (Tokyo, 1973); and National Commission on Urban Problems, *Three Land Research Studies* (U.S. Government Printing Office, 1968). Both estimates are of the total value of all land, urban and rural, public and private, but exclude the value of structures.

16. Joseph Keiper and others, *Theory and Measurement of Rent* (Chilton, 1961).

17. See National Commission on Urban Problems, *Three Land Research Studies*.

parable 10 percent of the estimated land values given above equals about one-third of Japan's GNP. Because this figure exceeds the estimate of the share of all property income in the Japanese national income accounts, land rents must be much less than 10 percent of land values. The explanation for this discrepancy undoubtedly lies in the fact that current land rents are capitalized into land values at a low rate in Japan because of the expectation of rapid growth in the productivity of land, a rapidity corresponding to that of total factor productivity. If, for example, the interest rate were 15 percent and the productivity (and therefore rent) of land were expected to grow at 10 percent (roughly the growth rate of real Japanese per capita GNP), the discount rate for capitalizing current land rents into land values would be 5 percent. This figure, when applied to the estimate of land values, gives a more reasonable result: that land rents were about 16 percent rather than one-third of Japan's GNP in 1973.

A second reason for interest in overall land values is that capital gains on land have an important and visible effect on income distribution in Japan. The national government publishes the names and incomes of taxpayers who report incomes in excess of ¥10 million (about $35,000) on their tax returns. In 1973, 97 of the 100 persons with the highest incomes made capital gains on land sales. The large fortunes made in land sales in Japan are probably the most important cause of demands for land price controls.

Price Changes

Japanese land values have risen rapidly during the period of postwar economic growth. Indexes of urban and rural land prices during the twenty-year period 1955–74 are shown in Table 10-7. Land prices rose at an average compound rate of 19.2 percent per year in a sample of 140 cities, and at a slightly higher rate in six large cities. The data in the table suggest that urban land values have risen more than twice as fast as rural land values during the period. The final column, containing indexes of construction costs of a traditional Japanese house, indicates that housing construction costs have risen less than half as fast as urban land values.

Land values of course are highest near the centers of large cities—in Tokyo, probably the highest of all. Land transactions in excess of $50 million an acre have been reported close to Tokyo's center, and private estimates[18] indicate that almost no land within ten kilometers was worth less than $1

18. See Tōkyu Fudōsan Kabushiki Kaisha, *Land Prices, 1972* (Tokyo Real Estate Co., 1973).

Table 10-7. Indexes of Urban and Rural Land Prices and of Housing Construction Costs in Japan, Selected Years, 1955–74[a]
1955 = 100

Year	Gross national product	Wholesale price index	Urban land				Rural land				Average of urban and rural lands	Construction cost of wooden houses
			Average of 140 cities			Average of 6 largest cities[b]	Rice paddy	Farm field	Timber forest	Fuel forest		
			Commercial areas	Residential areas	Industrial areas							
1955	100	100.0	100	100	100	100	100	100	100	100	100	100.0
1960	183	101.7	282	269	293	294	161	165	179	175	280	120.4
1965	370	103.6	712	707	911	1,082	176	182	231	219	768	192.3
1970	826	115.4	1,333	1,412	1,449	1,692	282	272	366	327	1,395	302.9
1974	1,326[c]	171.0	2,442	3,094	2,921	3,444	409[c]	427[c]	533[c]	466[c]	2,812	591.9
Average annual increase (percent)	15.4	2.9	18.3	19.8	19.4	20.5	8.1	8.4	9.7	8.9	19.2	9.8

Sources: Computed from data in Japan Real Estate Institute, Indices of Urban Land Prices and Construction Cost of Wooden Houses in Japan, 1974 (Tokyo: JREI, 1974); idem, Surveys of Paddy and Field Prices and Farm Rents (1974); and idem, Surveys of Forest Land Prices and Prices of Trees at Forests (1974).
a. Data are for March of each year.
b. The six largest cities are Tokyo, Yokohama, Nagoya, Kyoto, Osaka, and Kobe.
c. Figure is for 1973.

million an acre in 1972. To the south and west of the city much of the land within twenty kilometers of the center was worth at least that much.

Such high and rapidly rising land values affect both income distribution and land uses. The importance of capital gains from land sales has been noted, but in general, little is known about the distribution of landownership by income class—in either Japan or the United States. Although many people in Japan believe that rising land values increase the inequality of incomes, the opposite may actually be true. Widespread owner occupancy of housing and the predominance of small family-owned farms may mean that land-ownership in Japan is less concentrated among high-income groups than are other forms of wealth. If so, increases in land values somewhat reduce the concentration of wealth.

Comparative Land Uses: Japan and the United States

Table 10-8 contains land-use data for five Japanese and five U.S. urban areas for which comparable data are available.[19] The fact that much larger percentages of land are used for housing in Japanese urban areas is striking, especially in view of the Japanese concern that high land prices make it difficult for residents to bid against other potential users for land. The section on density functions pointed out that urban areas in Japan occupy much less land than those in the United States with similar populations, and the amount of residential land per capita clearly is much less. Nonetheless, high land prices have by no means impaired the competitiveness of housing in Japanese cities relative to other land uses.

Other characteristics of the data in Table 10-8 are more to be expected. Smaller shares of land are used for open spaces in Japanese than in U.S. urban areas. For example, Japanese cities have an average of less than three square meters of parkland per resident, whereas even New York has thirteen, and London has twenty-three.[20] Small shares of land also are devoted to schools, libraries, hospitals, and other public and semipublic institutions. The shares of land used for industrial and commercial purposes are similar in the two countries. The larger share used for transportation and utilities in U.S. urban areas probably is explained by the fact that parking lots are included in this category, and they undoubtedly use more land in U.S. than in Japanese cities.

19. The data supposedly pertain only to the urbanized parts of the cities or metropolitan areas. Both within and between the two countries, the data were collected by a variety of people for a variety of purposes. Therefore, definitions and criteria probably vary, and great reliance should not be placed on the precision of the estimates.
20. See Environment Agency, *Quality of the Environment in Japan, 1973* (1973).

Table 10-8. *Estimated Distribution of Land Uses in Various Urban Areas in Japan and the United States*[a]
Percent

Land use	Japan						United States					
	Nagoya	Sapporo	Sendai	Kuma-moto	Utsuno-miya	Average	Balti-more	Pitts-burgh	Nash-ville	Chatta-nooga	Tucson	Average
Residential	47.3	80.9	82.5	76.5	74.5	72.3	47.1	59.3	61.9	67.4	59.8	59.1
Open space[b]	6.6	2.7	4.0	4.8	[c]	3.6	13.5	15.2	[c]	2.6	6.1	7.5
Public and semipublic[d]	11.6	3.6	1.7	6.4	7.2	6.1	16.2	7.1	22.3	7.1	14.9	13.5
Industrial	18.1	2.7	3.5	2.8	11.4	7.7	19.8	6.0	4.1	17.7	3.3	10.2
Commercial	9.3	6.6	7.9	8.2	6.3	7.7	3.4	4.7	3.6	5.1	8.6	5.1
Transportation and utilities	7.0	3.5	0.4	1.2	0.5	2.5	[c]	7.7	8.0	[c]	7.1	4.6

Sources: Computed from data in Ministry of Construction, *Shōwa 43-nendo tōshi jidōsha kishūten chōsa hōkokusho* [Report on Urban Vehicular O-D Study of 1968] (1969); and Wilbur Smith and Associates, *Transportation and Parking for Tomorrow's Cities* (prepared for Automobile Manufacturers Association, 1966), pp. 305–07.

a. Japanese data are for years in the late 1960s; U.S. data for various years around 1960. Figures may not add to 100 because of rounding. Streets and highways are excluded. See also text note 19.
b. Parks, playgrounds, vacant lots, and the like.
c. Included in other categories.
d. Government offices, schools, libraries, museums, and the like.

Governmental Planning and Controls

Zoning and other government controls on private land use traditionally have been rather unimportant in Japan. As a result, Japanese cities have grown with relatively little segregation of residences by income level or of commercial and industrial use from residential. Both kinds of segregation have been carried to much greater extremes in U.S. urban areas, especially in suburbs. But the situation is changing in Japan. A city planning law passed in 1968 gives increased powers to control land uses to prefectural and local governments and provides for the drawing of master plans of the kind used as planning devices in Western cities. It prohibits land development without permission of the government except in certain listed circumstances and empowers governments to encourage or discourage the growth of urban areas.[21] Thus, the Japanese are now committed to government controls on the density and other characteristics of residential development and to controls to segregate commercial, industrial, and residential land uses. The idea of government controls on urban growth is about as controversial in Japan as in the United States.

In the United States controls on lot sizes and on multiple-family dwellings are used most extensively in metropolitan suburbs, where their rationale has been largely fiscal and racial. But except in the largest metropolitan areas, a single city government in Japan has jurisdiction over an entire metropolitan area, and the incentive to exclude people from residence in one part of the metropolitan area for fiscal reasons therefore is absent. In suburban jurisdictions around Tokyo, however, certain kinds of exclusionary practices familiar in American suburbs have emerged in recent years.

Few economists would deny that some controls on private land use are desirable. Most would agree that zoning is justified to separate to some extent residential from other land uses, although many doubt that such separation should be as extreme as is found in many American suburbs. Residents, for example, can shop on foot in Japanese cities, an activity generally not possible in most American suburbs because land-use controls segregate commercial activities. Economists are divided, however, about the desirability of giving controls over residential densities to small local governments, especially in metropolitan areas with multiple jurisdictions. In the United States, such controls permit suburban governments to exclude prospective residents who cannot or will not pay real estate taxes that cover their share of the cost of local government services. This may be desirable on grounds of efficiency,

---

21. For a brief description of the new law, see United Nations, *Urban Land Policies and Land-Use Control Measures,* vol. 7.

but it is almost certainly undesirable on grounds of equity. Most doubtful of all is the desirability of giving governments controls over the growth and sizes of urban areas. There is no reason to think that such controls provide efficient solutions to any urban problems, and they apply exclusionary practices at the scale of an entire urban area.

The trend toward greater government control over land use in Japan was accelerated by passage in May 1974 of the National Land Use Act, which established the National Land Agency. The law provides for formulation of national land-use plans and, perhaps most important, permits prefectural governments to establish control areas within which all land transactions require government permission and are subject to governmentally established price ceilings.

The effects of the 1974 act cannot yet be measured. It imposes a degree of government control and regulation of private activity that is unknown in recent Japanese history. If taken literally, it poses tremendous administrative burdens.

Whatever the detailed merits of the new law, it seems clear that passage was facilitated by widespread resentment at the 32.4 percent increase in land prices in 1973. Increases in land prices are widely blamed on speculators, whose considerable activity in recent years can hardly be denied. But excessive weight probably has been given to the role of the speculator, who cannot permanently affect the price of a traded commodity unless he holds substantial monopoly power, and who can make abnormal profits only to the extent that he helps stabilize the market.

Land and structures are subject to real estate taxes in Japan, but effective tax rates are much lower than in the United States. A modest capital gains tax on certain land sales by corporations was instituted in 1973.[22] It is surprising that so little attention has been paid to taxation of unearned increments in land values in a country that is so concerned about the equity of such gains. To tax away all capital gains in land would eliminate private incentives to find the most valuable use of land, but even very high taxes would not distort land uses, since land is a nonproduced input.

The national government tries to direct future urban development away from existing large cities and metropolitan areas in a variety of ways. Among them are improved road and rail linkages of all parts of the country, the development of port facilities away from established trade centers, and informal advice and guidance about industrial location. The recent planning and land-use and price control legislation undoubtedly will be used with increasing frequency to influence regional development in coming years.

22. See Chapter 5 for a full description of land taxes in Japan.

Urban Housing

Many Japanese regard inadequacy of housing as the country's most urgent social problem. Housing concerns focus on the size, quality, and safety (against fire, earthquake, and flooding) of Japanese housing.

Quantity and Quality of Housing

Number of rooms is an inadequate measure of house size: rooms vary in size, and in traditional Japanese houses they are not used in the way they are in Western houses (see Appendix A). Nevertheless, persons per room is the only measure of house size that is available for a large number of countries. In Japan, dwellings had an average of 1.0 occupant per room in 1970. Most countries of Western Europe and North America, with considerably higher incomes per capita than Japan, had less crowded dwellings; the U.S. figure, for example, is 0.6. Most low-income countries in Asia and elsewhere had much more crowded dwellings, with many countries exceeding two persons per room. The following are average occupancy figures for some countries that, in the year indicated, had per capita national incomes within $200 of Japan's 1970 figure of $1,658: Austria (1970), 0.9; Finland (1968), 1.1; France (1963), 1.1; Israel (1971), 1.5.[23] These data suggest that the Japanese have about half the dwelling space per capita of the world's highest-income countries and about twice that in many poor countries, and that Japanese dwelling sizes are about in line with those in other countries with comparable incomes. Table 10-9 contains more detailed data on trends in Japanese house size since World War II. The floor space data confirm the indication in the UN data that sizes of Japanese houses are somewhat more than half those in the United States. A typical U.S. dwelling with four residents might have 1,200–1,400 square feet (112–130 square meters) of floor space, whose midpoint is about 30.2 square meters per capita.[24] The figure in Table 10-9 for floor space per capita in Japan is 62 percent of this figure. The table also shows that rural dwellings are more spacious than urban dwellings in Japan. In addition, DID dwellings are more crowded than those

23. United Nations, *Statistical Yearbook, 1972* (1973). Occupancy was interpolated between census years for Finland and France.

24. There are no comprehensive data on floor space in U.S. dwellings. In recent years new single-family houses with Federal Housing Administration mortgages have averaged 1,500–1,600 square feet of floor space. Their floor space increases somewhat each year, and 1,300 square feet (131 square meters) is a reasonable guess as to the floor space per four residents in U.S. dwellings. See Department of Housing and Urban Development, *Annual Report* (various issues).

Table 10-9. *Size of Japanese Dwellings, Selected Years, 1948–68*

	All Japan		All cities		All densely inhabited districts		Wards area of Tokyo	
Year	Floor space	Tatami	Floor space	Tatami	Floor space	Tatami	Floor space	Tatami
1948	n.a.	3.50	n.a.	3.20	n.a.	n.a.	n.a.	2.73
1953	n.a.	n.a.	n.a.	3.30	n.a.	n.a.	n.a.	2.80
1958	n.a.	4.04	n.a.	3.73	n.a.	n.a.	n.a.	3.00
1963	16.4	4.91	15.2	4.57	14.3	4.27	13.7	3.87
1968	18.6	5.56	17.4	5.22	16.4	4.88	14.3	4.39

Source: Bureau of Statistics, *Census of Housing 1968* (1970). Floor space is in square meters per capita and includes all interior dwelling space. Tatami is in tatami per capita. A tatami is a floor covering of about 1.65 square meters. See also Appendix A.
n.a. Not available.

elsewhere in cities, and dwellings in the central city of Tokyo are most crowded of all. The explanation is, of course, that land values are higher in cities than in rural areas, in DIDs than elsewhere in cities, and in Tokyo than anywhere in Japan. People consume relatively little housing where one of its important inputs, land, is expensive. This pattern is observed in many countries, especially in those where, as in Japan, urban and rural incomes do not differ greatly. It is not, however, found in the United States, where urban dwellings are more spacious and of higher quality than rural dwellings.

The most striking characteristic of the data in Table 10-9 is the rapid rate of improvement they indicate. The tatami data indicate roughly a 60 percent increase in dwelling size per capita during the twenty-year period 1948–68, a compound annual growth rate of about 2.5 percent. Probably few countries in the world have increased their per capita housing stock so rapidly since the war. And the data for all cities and for Tokyo show even greater rates of improvement. All of the three series in the table that cover the entire twenty-year period show during the second decade a growth rate of tatami per capita at least twice as fast as during the first. Japanese urban housing was devastated by air raids during the war, and much of the early postwar construction was concentrated on rapid provision of at least small dwellings for people who might otherwise be homeless, whereas in more recent years it was concentrated on dwellings of a larger size. Overall, the data show no evidence of a slackening in the growth rate of the Japanese housing stock.

Despite the terrible devastation of urban housing during World War II, evidence indicates that Japanese housing has been more adequate throughout much of the postwar period than it was before the war. The best estimate is that the urban housing stock increased only from 8.3 to 9.0 square meters

Table 10-10. *Percent of Japanese Dwellings Not Needing Repairs,*
Five-Year Intervals, 1953–68

Year	All Japan	All cities	All densely inhabited districts	Wards area of Tokyo
1953	n.a.	68.9	n.a.	69.0
1958	51.9	56.4	n.a.	68.8
1963	67.7	73.1	n.a.	81.1
1968	80.7	82.6	83.0	85.7

Source: Bureau of Statistics, *Census of Housing 1968* (1970).
n.a. Not available.

per capita from 1890 to 1940.[25] The data in Table 10-9 suggest that the 9.0 square meter figure must have been surpassed in Japanese cities sometime in the late 1950s.

Measuring the quality of housing is harder than measuring its quantity, and few countries have usable data. All measures are subjective in some degree and depend on the judgment of the enumerator. Since 1953, the Japanese housing survey has classified housing by the extent and kinds of repair needed, with "no repairs needed" being a residual category for dwellings judged to be in adequate condition. Table 10-10 summarizes these data. The data indicate rapid and pervasive improvement in the quality of Japanese housing and that urban housing is in better condition than rural housing. Most striking is the indication that housing in DIDs, the densest parts of cities, is in better condition than housing in cities as a whole—and that Tokyo housing is in the best condition of all. One reason that urban housing is in better condition than rural undoubtedly is that on the average it is newer. But that can hardly explain why housing in DIDs or in the Tokyo wards area is in such good condition. In the United States, urban housing is of higher quality than rural: the incidence of substandard housing is more than twice as great in rural as in urban areas. But in U.S. metropolitan areas, the poorest quality housing is found in the parts of central cities with the greatest population densities.

As Japanese dwellings are much smaller than U.S. dwellings, they also are clearly of lower quality. In 1968 Japan had 22.2 million wooden dwellings out of a total of 24.2 million dwellings; the proportions were similar in cities and DIDs. Since then the proportion certainly has fallen, because new housing construction in Tokyo and other large cities is increasingly of other materials. Wood is the traditional housing material in Japan, and the Japa-

25. Kazushi Ohkawa and others, *Estimates of Long Term Economic Statistics of Japan since 1868*, vol. 3, *Capital Stock* (Tokyo: Tōyō Keizai Shinpōsha, 1966), pp. 224–25.

nese prefer single-family, wooden, owner-occupied houses. But wooden houses are a terrible fire hazard in densely populated areas. In addition, use of wood is not economical in the construction of large apartment houses. Although most wooden houses are owner occupied, in 1968 there were 5.7 million privately owned rental wooden dwellings, which generally are regarded as low-quality houses. Many wooden houses are drafty in winter and hot and stuffy in summer, and many have shared toilets and other facilities.

Another indication of low-quality housing is that 2.7 million Japanese lived in dormitories and boardinghouses in 1968, most of them young, single persons who had moved from their family homes, many of them coming to cities to work after leaving school. Lodgers were taken in by 0.6 million households, a practice that was more common in the early postwar period. In 1968 there were water supply, sink, and toilet facilities for the exclusive use of residents in 21.3 million of the 24.2 million dwellings. But sewage disposal is primitive in much of Japan, including large parts of many cities, and only 4.1 million dwellings had a flush toilet in 1968. Finally, many urban dwellings have no frontage on a public street, and have access only by narrow walkways. As land values have risen, many property owners have subdivided lots and built housing in the rear for rent or sale.[26]

Although data are of course incomplete, it is virtually certain that nearly every measure of Japanese housing quality and quantity shows rapid improvement in recent years. Many inadequacies in housing remain, and large amounts of resources should be devoted to housing improvement in coming years. Yet the level of discontent about housing—actually a pervasive sense of crisis—seems to be inconsonant with the facts. The media are filled with stories of inadequate housing. A 1972 Tokyo Metropolitan Government publication[27] painted a picture of housing crisis that is hard to square with the facts. Careful central government nationwide opinion polls[28] present a more balanced but nevertheless distressing picture of people's concern. In 1960, 35.8 percent of respondents to the poll felt they had a serious housing problem; the percent jumped to 43.9 in 1966 but fell gradually to 35.1 in 1973. Housing dissatisfaction is greater in Tokyo than elsewhere. Of those who report a serious housing problem, about half complain their dwellings are too small; about 13 percent complain of dilapidated housing; the rest complain of inadequate facilities, poor sanitary conditions, high rents, and inconvenient locations relative to places of work.

26. Data in this paragraph are from Bureau of Statistics, *Census of Housing 1969* (1970).

27. *Tokyo's Housing Problems* (TMG Municipal Library, no. 5, 1972).

28. Ministry of Construction, *Report of Housing Need Study* (1973).

Part of the sense of crisis results from an accurate perception of housing inadequacies in a rapidly growing economy. Another part results from the concentration of the media in Tokyo, where housing problems certainly are more severe than elsewhere. A third part results from the use of housing as a weapon in the political warfare between predominantly left-of-center local governments and a conservative national government. Whether these parts add up to a satisfactory explanation is difficult to say.

Investment in Housing

The rapid improvement in housing despite the massive urban migration of the population implies that the Japanese have devoted large amounts of resources to housing in recent years. In the early postwar years gross capital formation in housing was a very small share of Japanese gross national product: 1.5 percent in 1950, it grew to 4.3 percent in 1960. The Japanese share first exceeded the U.S. share in the early 1960s. Thus, up to about 1960 the Japanese were only slowly reducing their backlog of housing needs growing out of wartime devastation and postwar economic growth.

The data in Table 10-11 show that housing investment has been a substantially greater percentage of GNP in Japan than in the United States in recent years, and also that the Japanese share is still rising, whereas the U.S. share now shows little growth. Housing construction is, however, a smaller share of gross capital formation in Japan than in the United States, since gross capital formation is a much larger percentage of Japanese than of U.S. GNP. That the Japanese have an even larger relative share of nonresidential than of residential capital formation in GNP is an important fact, but consideration of it is beyond the scope of this paper.

People sometimes claim that the figures shown in Table 10-11 give an exaggerated impression of housing construction in Japan because land values represent such a large share of housing costs: that land values are much higher relative to housing costs and GNP in Japan than in the United States is undeniable. But land values are not part of gross capital formation. Construction of a dwelling on land previously used, say, for agriculture represents a transfer of the land asset from one use to another, but it does not enter saving or investment figures in the national income accounts.

That the Japanese build new houses at a rapid rate is confirmed by the data on housing starts in Table 10-12. In 1972, Japanese housing starts were four times as large as in 1960, whereas in the United States they were less than twice as large. In 1972, Japan, with half the U.S. population, had 78 percent as many housing starts.

Table 10-11. *Housing Investment as a Percent of Gross Capital Formation and Gross National Product, Japan and the United States, Selected Years, 1964–72*

| | Housing investment as a percent of | | | |
| | Gross capital formation | | Gross national product | |
Year	Japan	United States	Japan	United States
1964	16.1	28.8	5.7	4.3
1968	17.7	23.9	6.7	3.5
1971	19.2	28.0	7.0	4.1
1972	20.8	29.9	7.6	4.7

Sources: *Economic Report of the President, 1974*, pp. 249, 264; Economic Planning Agency, *Annual Report on National Income Statistics, 1972* (1972), pp. 6, 224; and ibid., *1974* (1974), pp. 3, 146–47. Japanese data are for fiscal years; U.S. data for calendar years.

Ownership and Rental of Housing

Housing tenure is not strikingly different in Japan than in the United States.

INCIDENCE. In contrast with the United States, the percentage of owner-occupied housing has fallen in recent years: after rising in the early postwar period, the share fell from 71.2 percent in 1958 to 58.2 percent in 1970, compared with 63 percent in the United States. Twenty-seven percent of Japanese dwellings were rented from private landlords, 7 percent were rented from employers, and 6 percent were government owned and, as in the United States, rented mostly to low-income households. Owner occupancy is less common in cities than elsewhere, but the percentage of owner-occupied housing also has fallen within cities: from 62.9 in 1958 to 50.7 in 1970. During this period the shares of company- and government-owned rental housing have increased slightly, but the big increase has occurred in the private rental market.

Several factors probably account for the recent falling share of owner-

Table 10-12. *Housing Starts in Japan and the United States, Selected Years, 1960–72*

Thousands

Country	1960	1965	1970	1971	1972
Japan	453	845	1,491	1,532	1,856
United States	1,296	1,510	1,469	2,085	2,379

Sources: *Economic Report of the President, 1974*, p. 294; and Ministry of Construction, *White Paper on Construction, 1972* (1972).

occupied housing. The first is urbanization. Apartments account for a larger fraction of urban than of rural dwellings, and owner occupancy is less common in apartments than in single-family houses. In recent years, however, there has been a surge in owner-occupied apartments in large cities, and future housing surveys may show a reversal of the trend away from owner occupancy.

In addition, the Japanese appear to have become much more mobile in recent years, even aside from the large urban migration. The 1970 census shows that 35 percent of the population changed their residences within the five years preceding the census and 12 percent within the year preceding, a figure about half the U.S. annual mobility figure of 20 percent. The 1960 census had reported that only 7.9 percent of the population had moved in the previous year, but the increase in mobility from 1960 to 1970 cannot be attributed to urban migration, since urban migration proceeded rapidly throughout the postwar period. It is unlikely that increased mobility reflects an increased rate of job change, since that is still rare in Japan. The most probable explanation is that it reflects a growing desire to shorten commuting times by living closer to the place of work. Many Japanese have long commuting times, and this is widely regarded as a serious national problem.

Finally, it is possible that rising house prices and interest rates have favored rental over ownership. The possibility is paradoxical, and the subject will be covered in greater detail later, after a discussion of housing finance. What is significant here is that there is little tax advantage in homeownership over rental in Japan. In contrast to the U.S. system, real estate taxes and interest are not deductible in computing income taxes, but, as in the United States, imputed income on owner-occupied houses is free of income tax. Tax status may account for a small share of owner-occupied dwellings, but it cannot account for the declining share. The absence of a significant tax advantage for owner occupancy may, however, make the share of owner-occupied dwellings sensitive to changes in financial markets. For example, deterioration of the terms on which individuals can borrow, relative to those available to companies, could cause a decrease in owner occupancy.

There can be no doubt that housing is expensive in Japan or that the main reason is high land values. A price of $1 million an acre was not uncommon for residential land in central parts of cities in 1973.[29] The average Japanese urban resident in 1973 lived in a dwelling on land probably worth at least $500,000 an acre, a figure that exceeds typical U.S. urban residential land values by at least ten times. Although exact data are not available, land values

29. Ministry of Construction, *Officially Posted Land Prices of 1973* (1973).

are probably not much less than half of total urban house values in Japan, whereas they are certainly less than 20 percent in the United States.

HOUSING COSTS. The Japanese housing census, like its U.S. counterpart, collects data on contract rents in rental dwellings, but it does not collect estimates of market value of owner-occupied dwellings. The rental data show an average annual increase of 13 percent in contract rent per tatami of floor space in Japanese cities during the decade 1958–68. That is consistent with a privately prepared index of urban land values that rose 17 percent a year and an index of construction costs that rose 8 percent a year during the same period;[30] it is also about equal to the average annual growth of money national income during the same period. During the rapid inflations of 1973 and 1974, land values and house rents rose more rapidly than before. As would be expected, house rents are higher in urban than rural areas, and those in Tokyo are about twice the level for all Japan.

Rents are heavily subsidized in government-owned, low-income housing, whose quality probably is at least as high as that of private rental dwellings but which are perhaps somewhat less advantageously located. The 1968 housing survey reported that rent per tatami in such housing was only about half that in private rental dwellings. Governments not only set initial rents below market levels but also find it difficult to raise rents once a tenant is in the dwelling. Thus, the subsidy to tenants in this housing almost certainly has increased during the recent years of rapid inflation. The fact that rent increases little for a sitting tenant in a government-owned dwelling obviously reduces the mobility of tenants and makes their commuting trips longer than they otherwise would be. Priority is given to low-income applicants for government-owned housing, but it is rare to evict a tenant whose income rises during his tenancy. Thus, as with many U.S. government housing and government-subsidized housing programs, Japanese government housing provides a large subsidy to a small group of relatively low-income tenants.

Despite its high costs, the Japanese do not spend a large fraction of their incomes on housing. The national income statistics indicate that rent (including imputed rent of owner-occupied houses) is less than 10 percent of personal income. The figure may be somewhat low because it fails to include subsidies for government- and employer-owned housing—but that could hardly raise the total more than a percentage point or two. The comparable figure in the United States is just over 11 percent. Careful studies of housing demand are only now being undertaken in Japan, but these observations are consistent with U.S. estimates of housing demand equations. The

30. See Japan Real Estate Institute, *Indices of Urban Land Prices and Construction Cost of Wooden Houses in Japan, 1974* (1974).

best U.S. studies indicate that the price elasticity of housing demand is close to 1 and the income elasticity is somewhat above 1, perhaps 1.2.[31] If those properties also characterized Japanese housing demand, it would mean that housing consumption would fall as price rose; total housing expenditure, though, would rise as a percentage of income as income rises, but would be a smaller fraction of income than in the United States, since Japanese incomes are lower. Likewise, Japanese would consume a smaller housing area than Americans at comparable incomes, because the relative price of housing is higher in Japan than in the United States.

Clearly, land prices are higher relative to construction costs in Japan than in the United States. Thus, Japanese housing would be expected to economize on land, which can be accomplished in two ways: houses can be built on small lots, and high-rise apartments can be built. Both methods have been used, and they help to account for the high residential densities noted earlier. But reduction of lot sizes seems to have been more important than high-rise apartments. Most Japanese urban houses have almost no uncovered land around them, but single-family houses of one or two stories are common even in large cities; until recent years residences of more than three stories were rare. Low structures have persisted partly as a result of public policy to protect against earthquakes, but such restrictions are being relaxed and high-rise apartments are going up rapidly, especially on expensive land near commuter railway and subway stops. It seems clear that housing output per unit of land occupied by housing is below market equilibrium in much of urban Japan, and most so near centers of larger cities. If public policy permits, it seems certain that the boom in high-rise apartments will continue.

Financing of Housing

The Japanese pattern of housing finance is different from that in the United States. Government- and employer-owned dwellings are 6 and 7 percent of the total, respectively; both considerably higher than corresponding U.S. figures. Most subsidies to government housing are financed by national government appropriations, although much of the housing is owned by local governments. Subsidies to employer-owned housing are financed from general business revenues. The rest of the housing stock is privately owned, built by large developers, speculative builders, or contractors.

But the major difference between the two countries in the financing of housing is in the financing of owner-occupied houses. A government survey

31. Frank d. Leeuw, "Demand for Housing: A Review of Cross Section Evidence," *Review of Economics and Statistics,* vol. 53 (February 1971), pp. 1–10.

of owner-occupied houses built in 1971 reveals the following percentage distribution of sources for the purchase price: liquidation of other assets of owner, 55.7; loans from employer, 15.2; loans from Housing Loan Corporation, 6.7; loans from relations, 5.1; loans from banks, 14.3; loans from construction and real estate companies, 1.6; other, 1.3.[32] The Housing Loan Corporation (HLC), a national government agency somewhat similar to the Federal Housing Administration in the United States, provides loans only for new and rehabilitated dwellings and finances only a small part of the cost of new housing. The striking characteristic of these data and of Japanese housing finance in general is the virtual absence of a mortgage market for new and, especially, used houses. There is no Japanese institution analogous to the savings and loan association. The Japanese have a high rate of personal saving and, as is suggested by the above data, much of it is invested in housing. Opinion surveys find homeownership to be a high priority of personal saving.

PRIVATE FINANCE AND PUBLIC POLICY. One conjecture about why a housing mortgage market has developed so slowly in Japan is that the country lacks an adequate legal foundation for savings and loan associations. If that were so, however, the situation would be easy to change—or, alternatively, the country's elaborate banking system could fulfill the function. The data above and other evidence indicate that the banking system is beginning to do so, at least for new homes. Another conjecture involves the frequent difficulty of obtaining clear title to property and of evicting people from dwellings in Japan, with the consequence that houses are not high-quality collateral in Japan. But those factors would militate also against rental housing, the market for which is large and growing. A third conjecture is that the profitability of loans to industry has drained off money that otherwise would have been available for mortgages. But, because housing would seem to have been among the most profitable of investments in all of Japan in recent years, this is unlikely unless loan rates are prevented from reaching equilibrium levels.

The most plausible conjecture is that informal government controls have kept mortgage rates below levels at which they could compete with loans to businesses and have otherwise discouraged loans to individuals. Although it is difficult to obtain evidence that would permit quantitative estimates of the effects of such controls, it is known that the Bank of Japan has pressed banks to keep down interest rates on loans to individuals. Government probably has looked with disfavor on bank loans to individuals, perhaps in line with the longstanding policy of encouraging industrial growth. Interest rates are high

32. See Economic Planning Agency, *Whitepaper on National Life, 1973: The Life and Its Quality in Japan* (1973).

in Japan and mortgage rates certainly would have to be correspondingly high to be competitive, but land and housing values have escalated so rapidly that owner occupancy would be profitable even at high mortgage rates. The wisdom of a government policy that keeps mortgage rates below levels at which mortgages can compete for funds can be seriously questioned—especially in a country in which the adequacy of housing is widely regarded as the principal social problem.

Whatever the specific reason, it is likely that the pattern of Japanese interest rates has made it more difficult for individual homebuyers to obtain loans than for businesses that might build or purchase dwellings for rent. In an increasingly mobile society, that might account for a falling share of owner-occupied dwellings. The same result would follow if, as interest rates have risen, government has pressured banks harder to keep down interest rates on loans to individuals than on those to companies.

FINANCE, HOUSING LOCATION, AND COMMUTING. The virtual absence of a mortgage market, especially for used homes, has a second, more serious, and longer-term consequence: it requires workers to commute longer distances. Many Japanese believe that excessive commuting is a serious urban problem, a belief consistent with available evidence (discussed in the following section) and related to the functioning of the housing market. In every urban society, the choice of residence is complex, depending on the location of housing of the desired price, size, quality, and style, as well as upon the major consideration, location of place of work. The absence of a lively market for used housing means that choice of residential locations must be made mainly on other criteria than location of place of work—for example, locations of vacant land on which to build, of housing inherited from relatives, or of housing owned by the employer. Even housing provided by employers is often far from the place of employment. Lacking a used-housing market, employers tend to buy large tracts of undeveloped land, much of it in distant suburbs, and build a complex of employee housing. Alternatively, housing must be rented on the open market, which forces the renter to forgo the capital gains accruing from ownership. The inevitable result is that, on the average, people live in housing that is far from their place of work. Place of work certainly receives some weight in choosing location of housing in urban Japan, but it receives less weight than it would if there were a lively market for used homes.

Alternatives for Housing Policy

What should government do to improve housing in Japan? First, it seems clear that the national government should take steps to enable private markets to mobilize mortgage funds better than in the past. This would enable relatively low-income families to buy into what probably will continue to be a profitable asset. It also would facilitate the choice of residences in reasonable proximity to places of work, thus reducing the extensive commuting now necessary in large cities. Specifically, the government should avoid any action that keeps interest rates on housing loans to individuals at uncompetitively low levels. If needed, legislative measures should be introduced to enable dwellings to be high-quality collateral.

Although a better mortgage market would enable the Japanese to obtain more satisfactory housing, to reduce commuting, and to invest savings profitably, it would be unlikely to reduce housing prices. Many Japanese feel that high housing prices are the basis of their housing crisis, and that high land prices are the principal cause of high housing prices. Urban land inevitably is a scarce and valuable commodity in a country as industrialized, densely populated, and urbanized as Japan. Government land price controls, as envisaged by the National Land Use Act of 1974, can obscure that fact and can prevent markets from allocating land to its most valuable use, but they cannot change it. Recent changes in tax laws that provide for much higher taxes on profits from land sales represent a better alternative to price controls for solving the equity problem resulting from concentrated land ownership.

In recent years trading companies and other speculators have been accused of buying up large tracts of undeveloped land around cities and holding them off the market to force up prices. Economists generally hold that speculators in competitive markets cannot permanently affect the price of the traded commodity and that they can make profits only by helping to stabilize the market. These conclusions could fail to hold only if speculators held large enough tracts of land to achieve monopoly power. How much land must be held to provide substantial monopoly power is difficult to estimate. We have been unable to collect evidence on this issue that is persuasive one way or the other. But if monopoly power in urban land ownership does exist, that situation is no less deserving of governmental remedy than other forms of monopoly.

Finally, government-owned housing represents only about 6 percent of Japan's housing stock. Of course, housing subsidization does not require that housing be government owned, but there may be reasons of both efficiency and equity for government ownership. It would be efficient if government were able to provide dwellings more cheaply than the private sector, but there is no evidence of this in either Japan or the United States. Regarding equity, subsidized housing may be a desirable way to redistribute income to low-income residents, but in both Japan and the United States government-owned housing tends to provide a relatively large subsidy to only a small fraction of low-income residents. The point to be emphasized here is that government housing in Japan undoubtedly contributes to the commuting problem. The large subsidy it entails induces people to accept government housing where it is available, with little regard to its proximity to place of work. And the fact that rents tend not to be raised in public housing makes tenants reluctant to move to other dwellings closer to places of work. A solution to this problem is either to design income-redistribution programs that do not involve housing ownership or subsidization by government or to design housing-subsidy programs that are not attached to residence in particular dwellings.

Urban Transportation

The subject of urban transportation is one of concern and controversy in almost all urbanized societies. The list of problems is similar, but by no means identical, in Japan and the United States. In the United States, a major concern is the decline in the quality of public transportation, as measured by routes covered, speed, frequency, and reliability. Americans perceive that public transportation has deteriorated during the postwar period, and are concerned about whether more resources should be devoted to it. Whatever else the Japanese feel about their public transit systems, they are likely to agree that they are technically efficient and have improved greatly since the war. The Japanese, however, are much concerned about crowding on public transit during rush hours and about the time and distance required for commuting in large cities. In both countries there is great concern about the proper role of public transit in small- and middle-size cities of up to about 2 million inhabitants. Although the role of the automobile is different in the two countries, there is great concern about its proper future role in both Japanese and U.S. cities—including emission of pollutants (to be discussed in the following section), noise and personal danger, and, most important, the extent to which the automobile is a socially efficient means of urban transportation. Even if the automobile is desirable as the dominant mode of urban passenger movement, it fails to solve the problem of providing transportation for disadvantaged groups who lack access to automobiles.

Statistical Measures

Urban transportation is unusually well documented in Japan: more commuting data are collected in the Japanese than in the U.S. census. The Ministry of Construction has undertaken vehicular origin-destination studies in large cities every three years since 1958. The first comprehensive urban transportation study based on a person-trip survey was done for Hiroshima in 1967, and these surveys have since been completed for Tokyo and other cities. Urban goods movement also is important in that much of the traffic on city streets moves goods rather than people, and there are fewer alternatives to moving goods than to moving people on streets. More is known about urban movement of people than of goods, but large-scale studies of urban goods movement have been undertaken in Hiroshima and Tokyo since 1970.

MODES OF COMMUTING. Although the place of work is neither the origin nor the destination of the majority of urban trips, commuting is by far the most studied and most important kind of urban travel. The data in Table 10-13 show the percent distribution of commuting trips by mode of travel in Japanese cities and U.S. SMSAs. The main difference between urban commuting modes obviously lies in the role of the automobile. Nearly 80 percent of U.S. urban commuters, but less than 15 percent of the Japanese, travel by car. Nearly half of Japanese urban commuters travel by the four main public transit vehicles, which carry only 12 percent of U.S. urban commuters. Another important difference is that a much larger proportion of Japanese than of U.S. urban workers walk to work. Most of the large "other" category in Japan comprises bicycle and motorcycle riders.

Table 10-14 provides more detailed data on modes of commuting in Japan's three largest cities. Not surprisingly, large cities rely more than small cities on public transit: 86 percent of those who work in the Tokyo CBD, and two-thirds of those who work in the central city commute by train or subway. (Streetcars have been superseded by subways and buses in Tokyo and are no longer important there.) These figures are higher than those for New York, where much larger percentages of commuters travel by car. Although all three cities have subways, Nagoya's was opened only in 1957, and is relatively small; only there do more than 10 percent of commuters travel by car.

Table 10-13. *Modes of Commuting in Japanese Cities and U.S. SMSAs, 1970*
Percent

Mode	Japan[a]	United States[b]
Automobile	14.5	78.3
Train, subway, bus, or streetcar	46.0	12.1
Foot	23.4	6.4
Other	16.1	3.2

Sources: U.S. Bureau of the Census, *Census of Population, 1970*, PC(1)-C1, summary table 109; and Bureau of Statistics, *1970 Population Census of Japan* (1971).
a. Includes student commuters.
b. Includes standard metropolitan statistical areas with at least 250,000 population.

Table 10-14. *Modes of Commuting, by Place of Work or Schooling, Large Japanese Cities, 1970*

		Percentage commuting by				
City	Number of commuters (thousands)	Foot	Rail, subway, or streetcar	Bus	Auto-mobile	Bicycle or motor-cycle	Other
Tokyo central business district	1,847	3.1	85.8	4.2	5.3	0.4	1.1
Tokyo ward area	5,599	15.1	66.5	7.2	7.2	3.1	0.9
Osaka city	2,137	16.0	60.2	8.5	9.7	4.9	0.8
Nagoya city	1,136	16.5	29.6	24.6	20.9	6.9	1.5

Source: Bureau of Statistics, *1970 Population Census of Japan* (1971).

(In addition to Tokyo, Osaka, and Nagoya, Yokohoma, Sapporo, and Kobe also have subways.)

RATES OF CHANGE. Table 10-15 contains data on growth in passengers for all trip purposes by important travel modes for Japan's three largest metropolitan areas from 1955 to 1972. Not surprisingly, total travel has grown rapidly in all three areas during the seventeen-year period. Tokyo's travel growth, which has been somewhat faster than that of Osaka but slower than that of Nagoya, has been at a compound rate of more than 6 percent per year.

Table 10-15. *Modes of Transportation in Three Japanese Metropolitan Areas, Indexes for Selected Years, 1955–72*[a]

Metropolitan area	Year	Japan National Railway	Private railway	Subway	Street-car	Bus	Auto-mobile	Taxi	Total
Tokyo	1955	100(36)	100(23)	100(3)	100(16)	100(15)	n.a.	100(7)	100(n.a.)
	1960	139(35)	150(23)	209(4)	100(11)	182(19)	n.a.	168(8)	146(n.a.)
	1965	186(33)	220(24)	497(7)	81(6)	278(21)	n.a.	288(9)	207(n.a.)
	1970	193(25)	273(22)	878(9)	21(1)	324(18)	149(18)	341(8)	233(100)
	1972	230(27)	285(21)	1057(10)	9(1)	340(17)	163(18)	277(6)	305(100)
Osaka	1955	100(15)	100(38)	100(5)	100(23)	100(13)	n.a.	100(5)	100(n.a.)
	1960	147(17)	112(32)	155(6)	119(21)	181(17)	n.a.	183(7)	134(n.a.)
	1965	224(18)	162(33)	250(7)	98(12)	314(21)	n.a.	342(10)	190(n.a.)
	1970	238(14)	217(32)	519(10)	30(3)	319(16)	181(17)	362(8)	211(100)
	1972	248(14)	224(32)	542(10)	20(2)	338(16)	219(20)	325(7)	270(100)
Nagoya	1955	100(8)	100(32)	...	100(36)	100(18)	n.a.	100(6)	100(n.a.)
	1960	141(8)	134(28)	100(2)	90(21)	276(33)	n.a.	198(8)	151(n.a.)
	1965	194(7)	181(26)	364(5)	73(12)	509(41)	n.a.	338(9)	223(n.a.)
	1970	249(7)	199(20)	637(6)	33(4)	431(24)	209(32)	416(8)	217(100)
	1972	275(6)	208(8)	1068(8)	16(1)	416(20)	307(41)	362(6)	375(100)

Source: Ministry of Transport, *Shōwa 49-nen-ban tōshi kōtsū nenpō* [Annual Report on Urban Transportation, 1974] (1974). Data are for the fifty-kilometer regions around Tokyo and Osaka and the forty-kilometer region around Nagoya.

n.a. Not available.

a. Indexes are based on 1955 volumes except for automobiles (base year 1968) and the Nagoya subway (base year 1960). Figures in parentheses are the percentages of persons moved. Percentages may not add to totals because of rounding.

Public transit has expanded dramatically in all three metropolitan areas. The most rapid increase has been in subway travel, which in 1972 was more than ten times its base-year level in Tokyo and Nagoya and more than five times that level in Osaka—reflecting an enormous program of subway construction in the three metropolitan areas since the war. Railways and buses are also important and have expanded rapidly in the three areas. Intercity railroads are owned by the Japan National Railway, an agency of the national government; private railroads, which also have expanded rapidly through new construction since the war, serve mainly suburbs, the most rapidly growing parts of urban areas. Despite their slower growth, railroads still carry several times more urban travelers than subways.

Despite a rapid expansion since 1955, bus travel has had a falling share of urban travel in all three metropolitan areas since 1965 because of the improvements in train and, especially, subway service and the growing congestion on streets, which increases surface travel time. In Tokyo, bus travel is now important mainly in suburbs in which rail and subway service are poorer and in which buses are used as feeder services between residential areas and suburban train and subway stations. Streetcars, which gradually are being phased out in Japanese, as in U.S., cities, are the only mode of public transit that is in decline in the three metropolitan areas. The expansion of public transit in Japan is in dramatic contrast with the situation in the United States. Passenger travel by public transit declined by about a third between the early 1950s and the early 1970s in U.S. urban areas. Even the largest metropolitan areas, including New York, have experienced both absolute and relative declines in public transit.

Factors in Choice of Mode

Choice between public and private travel modes is an important and controversial subject in many countries. It is a widespread popular belief in the United States that many people have an irrational preference for travel by private car. But careful research and experience in many countries support the belief that people make modal choices carefully, based on considerations of cost, travel time, comfort, and convenience.

AUTOMOBILE OWNERSHIP AND TRAVEL. The data in Tables 10-14 and 10-15 show that the car is a relatively minor mode of travel in large Japanese cities, but they fail adequately to characterize the growing importance of the car in Japan—which is now the world's second-largest producer of motor vehicles, with annual output about half the U.S. volume. Japan produced 7.1 million motor vehicles (4.5 million cars) in 1973, of which 2.1 million (1.5

Table 10-16. *Comparative Measures of Road Transportation, Japan and Selected Western Industrial Countries, 1972*[a]

Country	Vehicles (thousands)	Vehicles per 100 persons	Vehicles per 100 square kilometers of land	Vehicles per kilometer of paved road length
United States	109,300	52.8	11.7	41.0
West Germany	16,820	28.4	67.6	53.7
United Kingdom	13,790	24.8	60.0	40.9
France	15,020	29.3	27.3	24.0
Italy	12,340	22.8	41.0	46.7
Japan	20,430	19.5	55.2	90.0

Source: Ministry of Construction, *Shōwa 47-nen-ban kensetsū hakusho* [Whitepaper on Construction, 1972] (1972).
a. Four-wheeled motor vehicles only are included.

million cars) were exported. Motor vehicles in Japan increased from 1.45 (0.49 cars) per 100 persons in 1960 to 23.07 (13.36 cars) in 1973. These figures represent an extraordinary 25 percent compound annual growth rate in the total stock of cars. Table 10-16 contains some international comparisons of road transportation. Japan now has more motor vehicles than any other country in the world except the United States, and vehicles per capita are rapidly approaching the levels of Western Europe. In vehicles per thousand square kilometers of land area, Japan is exceeded only by West Germany and the United Kingdom; in vehicles per kilometer of paved road, no country is close to Japan.[33]

The early postwar production of motor vehicles in Japan was heavily weighted in favor of trucks and buses. Only in 1968 did the output of cars first exceed that of trucks and buses, and only in the early 1970s did the stock of cars exceed that of other vehicles. But car ownership is rapidly becoming widespread. In 1965, only six percent of households owned at least one car; in 1973, it was 38 percent, and 4 percent owned two or more cars. Corresponding U.S. figures for 1970 are about 80 percent and 30 percent.

There is a distinct pattern of car ownership and use according to place of residence in Japan. In the twelve largest cities, only 31 percent of families own cars. The proportion rises somewhat irregularly with decreasing size of community, reaching 42 percent in small towns and villages. These patterns reflect mainly the greater availability of public transit in large urban areas.

33. Data in this paragraph are from Environment Agency, *Quality of the Environment in Japan, 1972* (1972), and Ministry of Construction, *Shōwa 47-nen-ban kensetsū hakusho* [Whitepaper on Construction, 1972] (1972). The term "vehicles" refers only to four-wheeled motor vehicles.

The use of cars for commuting follows much the same pattern. Table 10-15 shows that few people commute by car in the largest cities. The percent rises in small cities and is quite high in villages. Automobile commuting within large cities appears to be most common among those who live and work in suburbs and least common among those who commute from suburb to the CBD. Many car-owning families in big cities use the car almost exclusively for nonwork-connected travel.

The future role of the automobile in Japan is intensely controversial. Choice of mode of urban travel depends on the relative costs, which consist of time costs (the subjective valuation of travel time) and vehicle costs (fares on public transit and the cost of owning and operating private cars). Time cost rises with income and is usually estimated to be more than half of total trip cost for commuting in high-income countries. Automobile trip time depends on distance, congestion, and the physical character of roads. Public transit trip time depends on walking, waiting, and time spent in the vehicle. The evidence surveyed above suggests that public transit in large Japanese cities is provided with sufficient speed and frequency over a large enough network and at low enough fares that relatively few persons are tempted to commute by car.

TRAFFIC CONGESTION. Almost all rush-hour travel is badly congested in the narrow streets of Japanese cities. Unlike the situation in most U.S. urban areas, some of the worst road congestion is found in suburbs, where automobile commuting is most common. Contributing to this problem is the small percentage of urban land that is used for streets: in Tokyo and other large cities, for example, it is little more than 10 percent, whereas the percentage is two or three times as large in New York and other large urban areas in the United States. Most urban streets in Japan have no separate pedestrian right-of-way, which results in hazards and inconvenience to pedestrians (as discussed in the next section). There can be no doubt that rush-hour congestion is a serious deterrent to automobile commuting for many urban Japanese workers.

Congestion is a serious problem for public as well as private transit in Japan. Several of Tokyo's busy subway lines carry more than 50,000 passengers an hour during peak morning and evening periods. Capacities are greater on railway lines, mainly because the cars are larger. The busiest of all is the Chuo line, operated by Japan National Railway from the western suburbs to Tokyo's central station. Its express line carries nearly 100,000 passengers in the busiest rush hour; the adjacent local line carries more than 50,000 passengers an hour. As a technical feat, this is probably unmatched anywhere in the world at the speed and safety provided by JNR. It is accomplished, however, only by averaging 300 passengers a car—and ten cars a train with two-minute headway on the express line—with a consequent tiring, uncomfortable ride. Passengers are fewer on other public transit lines, but all are extremely crowded. During recent years, however, rush-hour crowding appears to have lessened somewhat, and presumably it will lessen further as train and subway lines now planned and under construction come into operation.

COSTS. Public transit systems are heavily subsidized in both Japan and the United States. In both countries, it is difficult to compute the percentage of total cost that is paid by fares. Netzer has estimated it at 80 percent in the United States,[34] and it is difficult to imagine that it is higher in Japan. Japanese transit riders can purchase passes, which are good between places of work and residence and average about half the cost of regular fares. These passes are used mainly for commuting, with the result that peak-hour travel is cheaper than off-peak travel. Presumably, large commuting subsidies induce Japanese urban workers to commute more than they otherwise would, worsening peak-hour congestion on transit systems. The subject is complicated by the fact that most Japanese employers reimburse employees for commuting costs, which makes transit demand relatively unresponsive to fares. Although the economic case for higher peak-hour fares seems to be overwhelming, transit fares are a major political issue in Japan and can be changed only with great difficulty. In one way, however, the issue of transit fares is less complex in Japan than in the United States. Public transit is most used by relatively low-income residents in the United States, which means that fare increases redistribute income regressively. In Japan, however, public transit is used by a more representative cross section of income classes, so that fare increases have only minor distributional effects.

Automobile commuting is expensive in Japan. Gasoline is heavily taxed and since the onset of the energy crisis has sold for more than $1.30 a U.S. gallon. Off-street parking is scarce and expensive in central parts of cities. Furthermore, urban expressway and arterial road construction have met increasing opposition because of the noise, pollution, and disruption caused by their traffic. Some projects have been modified or abandoned as a result.

SUMMARY. Public transit is cheap, fast, frequent, and reliable in large Japanese cities and covers a large network of origins and destinations. Crowding, however, causes fatigue and discomfort, especially on long trips. Automobile commuting, expensive and slowed by congestion, is restricted mostly to places where high-quality public transit is unavailable. If Japan

34. Dick Netzer, *Economics and Urban Problems* (Basic Books, 1970).

continues to improve the quality and expand the routes covered by public transit and continues its policy of limited urban road construction, commuting by automobile probably will not become much more important in coming years than it is now.

Although we are broadly sympathetic with this policy, we do not underestimate the value of automobile use. Urban residents in many countries place great value on ownership and use of cars, and the amount of driving clearly will continue to increase rapidly in Japan. Public policy, we believe, should accommodate this growing demand for automobile use—as long as road construction and use are planned so that they do not impose large external costs on residents and as long as drivers pay the full social cost of that activity. This criterion should lead to continued and expanded use of public transit in large cities.

Commutation Time and Urban Density

In the earlier study of urban density functions, we concluded that Japanese cities almost certainly will continue to decentralize as incomes rise and cities grow. Extremely low urban densities reduce the efficiency of public transit relative to automobiles because traffic on particular routes is insufficient to exhaust scale economies of public transit, especially subways. But urban densities in Japan are unlikely to become so low as to pose that problem in the foreseeable future. The high land values probably will encourage sufficient urban densities to permit continued efficient operation of public transit systems.

Time spent commuting by workers in large cities is a subject of considerable concern in Japan. Many Japanese feel that they spend excessive and increasing amounts of time commuting. This issue is difficult to evaluate. Very few countries have comprehensive data on commuting times. Survey results are difficult to compare: surveys may or may not average in with other commuters those who walk to work or work at home, and some responses refer to line-haul time and some to door-to-door time, especially where the mode is a public transit vehicle. Japan is among the few countries whose census publishes data on commuting times. Summary data on one-way commuting times from 1968 are as follows: for all Japan, thirty-two minutes; for all DIDs, thirty-two minutes; for the Tokyo capital region, forty-four minutes; for the Tokyo metropolitan area, thirty-eight minutes; and for the Osaka metropolitan area, twenty-nine minutes.[35] Not surprisingly, travel

35. Bureau of Statistics, *Census of Housing 1968,* table 48, p. 584.

times tend to be longer the larger the metropolitan area. Scattered surveys suggest average U.S. urban commuting times of about thirty minutes, which seems consistent with the Japanese data.

But commuting times undoubtedly are lengthening in Japan. The growth from 1955 to 1970 in the numbers of persons who commute at least thirty minutes is shown below: [36]

Number of commuters (in thousands)

Year	City population 300,000–1,000,000	City population over 1,000,000
1955	705	4,151
1960	1,190	6,005
1965	2,040	7,654
1970	2,580	8,508

Of course, the numbers of workers in the cities in the size ranges shown have also grown, but the data imply increases in the fraction of workers commuting at least thirty minutes.

The most dramatic evidence of long commuting times in Japan comes from data on workers in Tokyo's CBD. In 1968, 20 percent of the 1.5 million people who worked there had one-way commuting times of more than sixty minutes. Comparable data do not seem to be available for New York, but the figure for Manhattan probably would be less than 20 percent.

These and other inadequate data suggest that Japanese urban workers probably spend somewhat more time commuting than U.S. workers in urban areas of comparable sizes. Commuting speeds also probably are somewhat greater in large urban areas of Japan. Japanese public transit certainly is faster and requires shorter waiting time than U.S. public transit, but these factors in themselves are inconclusive in any comparison of the two countries because the majority of U.S. workers commute by car, even in large urban areas. At least near urban centers, U.S. rush-hour car travel is mostly at ten to twenty miles an hour, which is considerably slower than Japanese subway and rail commuter travel.

If, as seems likely, the average commuter in large Japanese urban areas spends somewhat longer commuting and travels at somewhat greater speeds than comparable U.S. commuters, commuting distances in Japan must be substantially greater than in the United States. As was shown in the section on urban density functions, Japanese urban areas occupy considerably less space than U.S. urban areas of comparable population. And because employment is not more centralized relative to housing in Japan than in the

36. Economic Council of Japan, *Measuring Net National Welfare of Japan* (1973).

United States, the only possible explanation for longer Japanese than U.S. commuting distances is that housing is chosen with less regard to location of place of work in Japan than in the United States—an important part of the evidence for the claim in the section on housing that Japanese housing markets provide urban families with too few options on location of residence.

Travel in Small Urban Areas

The problem is quite different in small urban areas, in which there are too few passengers on particular routes to take advantage of the scale economies permitted by public transit. Considerable effort has been devoted to the study of transportation systems for small communities in Japan. Present plans call for subway construction in several cities below 1 million population, but subways become infeasible at population levels much below that, even at Japanese densities. Buses and streetcars are now used extensively in smaller urban areas. Some cities are seriously considering monorails, for which a recent law provides national construction subsidies similar to those available for subways. Monorails have the advantage of being relatively quiet and of operating above existing streets—but they require wide streets, of which there are few in Japanese cities. Their use on relatively narrow streets is aesthetically displeasing and entails annoyance to residents. The most promising alternatives in small urban areas seem to be exclusive bus lanes and elevated trains with rubber tires.

Interurban Travel

Most interurban passenger travel is by the efficient rail system of the Japan National Railway. Its service—fast, frequent, comfortable, and inexpensive—is most renowned for its bullet train that covers the 550 kilometers between Tokyo and Osaka in 190 minutes. Inaugurated in 1964, the line's sixteen-coach trains operate at more than 80 percent of their 1,400-passenger capacity and carried 270,000 passengers a day in 1971. Bullet trains leave Tokyo and Osaka every fifteen minutes during peak hours. In contrast to the situation that pertains among American railroads, JNR's interurban passenger service is relatively profitable compared with its freight service.

JNR has begun to extend high-speed rail passenger service to a network that will link all major Japanese cities; plans call for a 7,000-kilometer super-express network by 1985, by which time all prefectural capitals will be accessible from Tokyo or Osaka on one-day return trips. Now under construction as part of this network is a fifty-four-kilometer undersea tunnel to link the northern island, Hokkaido, with the main island, Honshu—a tunnel of about the same length as that once planned under the English Channel.

Japan's first interurban expressway opened in 1964 between Osaka and Nagoya. A 7,600-kilometer network of interurban expressways is under construction, with completion planned by 1983; 1,500 kilometers of the system are now in operation. The network is designed at expressway standards and is financed by tolls.

A primary goal of the interurban road and rail networks is to encourage greater regional development and thereby to lessen future growth within the Tokaido megalopolis.

Environmental Problems

The term "environment" has come to have broad implications in both Japan and the United States. This discussion, however, focuses on air and water pollution, with brief remarks on the incidence of urban traffic accidents and natural disasters.

Although pollution became a public issue somewhat later in Japan than in the United States, public debate in the two countries had reached remarkable similarity in 1973 and 1974: in both countries, pollution receives considerable attention in newspapers and magazines; debate and confrontation take place among government, business, and environmental groups; elaborate pollution control laws have been passed by national and local legislatures; and judgments differ about whether existing governmental programs will improve the environment significantly in the near future.

Environmental data have become more plentiful and accurate since about 1970. One result of a belated but serious attempt at data gathering has been a better appreciation of the complexities of environmental metering. The critical distinction, on which national policy floundered in the United States for many years, lies between the discharge of wastes or residuals into the environment and their concentration in the ambient environment. Discharges and ambient concentrations are related, but in complex ways. Discharge data are more plentiful, but ambient concentrations are more important to fish in the streams and to people on the streets. Ambient concentrations are difficult to measure for many reasons: for example, people and animals may be sensitive to extremely small concentrations of certain substances, and environmental quality may be extremely localized. Carbon monoxide levels vary greatly depending on whether they are recorded in the middle of a block or at an intersection 100 meters away. All environmental data must be regarded with a healthy skepticism.

But regardless of the inadequacies of the data, the Japanese are justified in their concern about environmental quality. That death and disability have resulted from special pollution problems is well documented, and long-term exposure to air pollution probably causes and aggravates respiratory diseases. Any perceptive observer can see that Tokyo has a problem of photochemical smog and that estuaries in the Pacific coastal region are badly polluted.

Goods production consists of the application of energy to materials to convert them from their natural states into products that are useful to man. An industrialized society extracts massive amounts of such materials from the environment. Because economic activity converts, but does not create or destroy, materials, everything extracted from the environment must eventually be returned to it. Furthermore, energy conversion also entails environmental discharges in the form of heat and unburned or partly burned components of fuels. All discharges are polluting in the broadest sense, although the harm they do depends heavily on the amount, form, time, and place of discharge. Every portion of the environment has a capacity to absorb limited amounts of discharges without being seriously degraded, and pollution becomes serious only when discharges occur at a rate that exceeds the capacity of the environment to absorb them. Pollution therefore depends—among other things—on the area over which discharges are spread. In Japan industrial activity and population are concentrated in a very small area, and in some parts of the country population and production per square kilometer are as great as anywhere in the world. Environmental discharges are correspondingly great, and there is a strong tendency for them to degrade the environment. The gross national product produced and the energy consumed per square kilometer in Japan are many times the levels of the United States and exceed the levels of the industrialized countries of Western Europe. In the absence of special measures to control them, discharges into the air and water of urbanized Japan therefore should be expected to be much greater than corresponding U.S. levels.

Discharges into the environment occur at all stages of economic activity: extraction, processing, and consumption. Because Japan imports more of its raw materials than most industrialized countries, environmental degradation caused by extraction is relatively minor there compared with the United States. Strip mining, for example, is hardly an issue in Japan. But the intensity of land use in Japan has meant that extractive industries, especially farming and fishing, are affected more by pollutants discharged by processing industries than in the United States; and the intensity of farming has meant that farms are the sources of large volumes of pollutants, such as nutrients from fertilizer.

Water Pollution

The kind of pollution that is best understood is from organic waste discharges to water bodies. Organic wastes come from human and other household wastes and from a variety of industrial processes, especially in the food processing, chemical, textile, and paper industries. Most organic materials can be removed from waste water by a variety of treatment processes, the most common of which is the ordinary municipal sewage treatment plant. When discharged to water bodies, organic material decays, removing dissolved oxygen (DO) from the water. Most fish require four to eight parts per million of DO, and the numbers and kinds of fish are a fairly accurate indication of the DO content of the water. If all DO is removed from a water body it is said to be anaerobic and the decay of organic material then causes the water to stink. Anaerobic water bodies can support no fish life and are useless for most purposes. Average DO levels are extremely low in the rivers and estuaries of Japan's large cities. Among twenty-one sampling stations in and around Tokyo, for example, only six recorded average DO levels in excess of four parts per million in 1969.[37] Many rivers are anaerobic in the late summer. Although many U.S. rivers are badly polluted, average DO levels are higher than in similarly developed areas in Japan. Japan's organic pollution results from the concentration of industry and its poor waste treatment, as well as from the fact that an average of only 35 percent of the urban population is sewered—even in Tokyo the proportion is less than half—and by no means all of sewered waste is treated.[38] These figures are in sharp contrast with those for the United States, where almost all of the urban population is sewered and most of its wastes receive at least primary treatment.

Organic pollution is annoying and greatly impairs fishing, an important food source in Japan. But most direct harm to humans is avoided by withdrawing drinking water from upstream reaches of rivers and by controlling discharges upstream from such withdrawals. Many inorganic substances that are known or suspected causes of grave injury to human beings are discharged into water bodies: for example, cyanides, chrome, arsenic, cadmium, lead, mercury, and phosphorus. Some are discharged inadvertently by

37. See Tokyo Metropolitan Government, *Tokyo Fights Pollution* (TMG Municipal Library, no. 4, 1971).
38. Ibid.

chemical industries, some are difficult to meter in water bodies, some affect people in complex and extremely harmful ways, and some have effects about which science remains substantially ignorant.

The Japanese mercury poisoning episode, recently summarized in a remarkably frank government publication,[39] is among the world's worst recent environmental tragedies. In 1956 a patient was admitted to a hospital in Minamata, a small city on the west coast of the southern island of Kyushu, with severe and peculiar neurological symptoms. It was soon discovered that others in the area had displayed similar symptoms for at least three years, but the disease was believed locally to be contagious and was concealed. In 1959, a medical research team announced that the malady was caused by ingestion of fish contaminated with mercury discharged into the Minamata Bay from a local chemical plant. Symptoms include numbness, ataxia, sensory disturbances, and, finally, death. The disease, known in Japan as Minamata disease, is incurable. There followed a decade of medical, scientific, legal, and political activity and maneuvering but, incredibly, only in 1968 did the national government institute severe controls on industrial discharges of mercury. By 1972, the government had confirmed 181 victims of the disease in the Minamata area, 52 of whom had died. In 1965, Minamata disease was detected among residents of the Agano River basin, on the Japan Sea side of Honshu. There the cause was again traced to mercury discharges of a local chemical plant. The government has identified 102 victims, including two deaths, of Minamata disease in the Agano area. Some private experts have speculated that there may be many subclinical victims of the Minamata disease in these and other areas.

Almost as tragic has been the Itai-Itai disease.[40] The term means "ouch-ouch" and characterizes the extremely painful nature of the disease. Ultimate symptoms are unbearable pain and such weakness of the bones that sufferers break them by ordinary movement. Reports of the symptoms among residents of the Jinzu River basin, also on the Japan Sea side of Honshu, go back to 1910, but the peculiar disease received attention in Japanese medical literature only during the mid-1950s. The disease was identified as cadmium poisoning in 1959. During the 1960s the diagnosis was confirmed and the source identified as a local mining and smelting company. Apparently, human ingestion resulted from pollution of rice paddies by irrigation water into which the plant's wastewater had been discharged. Ingestion may also have come from polluted groundwater. The disease attacks mainly postmeno-

39. See Environment Agency, *Pollution Related Diseases and Relief Measures in Japan* (1972).
40. See ibid.

pausal women who are long-time residents of the area. The government identified 123 victims, of whom 32 have died. National government controls on cadmium discharges were instituted in 1968.

Thus, in contrast to the United States, Japan has well-documented cases of peculiarly horrible and irreparable damages to people's health from water pollution. The situation is made worse by the facts that the offending substances are ones normally not metered in discharges or ambient water environments, that they are sometimes discharged inadvertently and unknowingly, that the causal linkages in health damage are not well understood, and that the worst damages have come through the food chain rather than by ingestion of polluted water. What region will be affected next? What other substances might produce similar or worse effects? The fear and uncertainty surrounding these questions have caused large and erratic changes in Japanese fish consumption, which has badly disrupted the large fishing industry.

Although no direct threat to human health has been posed, organic pollution reduces the availability of edible fish in Japanese waters. Organic and nutrient pollution also impair the use of waters for recreational purposes. Lakes, rivers, and estuaries are affected, but the most serious recreational disruption has been in the Seto Inland Sea, a saltwater body partly enclosed by the southwestern part of Honshu and by Shikoku and Kyushu islands. The sea receives large industrial, municipal, and agricultural discharges, and its flushing action is impaired by the surrounding islands. Once a beautiful recreational area, it is now badly polluted.

Air Pollution

Comprehensive estimates have been made of total discharges of various residuals into the air in both Japan and the United States. Most such estimates in both countries are made indirectly and are subject to substantial margins of error. Some discharges, for example, are estimated from data on amounts and components of fuels burned. Many substances are discharged into the air, but in terms of total quantity and availability of data the most important are carbon monoxide, sulfur oxides, particles, hydrocarbons, and nitrogen oxides. Practically all discharges result from the burning of fossil fuels or from industrial processes. The best data pertain to discharges from motor vehicles: public transit vehicles run by electricity also require combustion, but it takes place in a thermal electric plant and its emissions are recorded as products of the electricity-generating industry rather than the transportation sector.

STATISTICAL MEASUREMENTS. The data in Table 10-17 show total emis-

Table 10-17. *Estimated Emission of Principal Air Pollutants in Japan and the United States, 1968*

	Japan		United States	
Substance	Total emissions (thousands of tons)	Emissions per square kilometer (tons)	Total emissions (thousands of tons)	Emissions per square kilometer (tons)
Carbon monoxide	5,780	15.6	100,100	10.7
Sulfur oxides	3,600	9.7	33,200	3.5
Hydrocarbons	1,260	3.4	32,000	3.4
Nitrogen oxides	1,330	3.6	20,600	2.2
Particulates	250	0.7	28,300	3.0
Total	12,220	33.0	214,200	22.9

Source: Toshio Odaira and Mitsuru Udagawa, "Kōtsū kōgai no jittai" [Studies of Transportation Related Environmental Destruction], *Kōtsu kōgaku* [Traffic Engineering], vol. 7 (1972).

sions and emissions per square kilometer of the five major air pollutants for Japan and the United States in 1968. They indicate that emissions per square kilometer are about 50 percent greater in Japan than in the United States, showing vividly the effects of the geographical concentration of people and industry on Japan's small islands.

Table 10-18 contains estimates of emissions of major air pollutants from transportation in Japan and the United States and for various metropolitan areas in each country, as well as estimates of the percentage that the figures constitute of total emissions of the pollutant in the time and place indicated. Both total emissions and transportation emissions in Japan are only five or ten percent of their U.S. volumes for most pollutants. Emissions data for large cities are of more comparable magnitudes, but the Japanese quantities are smaller partly because of the smaller role of the automobile. The transportation sector emits about the same percentage of total air pollutants in Japan as in the United States.

The automobile is the source of most of the large volume of carbon monoxide and hydrocarbons emitted in both countries, and discharges of sulfur oxide come mainly from thermal electric plants and space heating rather than from vehicles. Most particulates come from the same sources and from industrial processes in the United States, but in Japan a much larger percentage comes from transportation. This probably reflects the greater importance in Japan of diesel trucks relative to cars.

As with water, ambient air concentrations rather than discharge volumes of pollutants affect human health and property. Ambient concentrations are related to discharge volumes in complex ways. Meteorological conditions vary from place to place and from time to time, and pollutants have a variety of complex and poorly understood chemical and physical fates in the at-

Table 10-18. *Emissions of Principal Air Pollutants from the Transportation Sector, Japan and the United States, Selected Years*

	Japan			United States		
Pollutant	Total, 1967	Tokyo-to, 1972	Osaka prefec- ture, 1970	Total, 1970	Los Angeles area, 1971	New York City, 1970
Carbon monoxide						
Tons a day	13,890	1,534	1,932	301,370	8,960	3,221
Percent of total emissions[a]	99.6	94.4	n.a.	75.4	98.4	92.3
Hydrocarbons						
Tons a day	2,957	400	207	53,425	1,620	597
Percent of total emissions[a]	94.7	66.5	n.a.	56.2	65.7	68.9
Nitrous oxides						
Tons a day	1,130	180	87	32,055	755	255
Percent of total emissions[a]	31.6	68.1	23.3	51.5	71.7	28.0
Sulfur oxides						
Tons a day	242	10	13	2,740	35	n.a.
Percent of total emissions[a]	2.3	4.4	1.5	2.9	14.0	...
Particulates						
Tons a day	348	3	42	1,918	55	n.a.
Percent of total emissions[a]	49.7	4.5	20.4	2.8	42.3	...
All transportation sector						
Tons a day	18,567	2,127	2,281	391,508	11,425	n.a.
Percent of total emissions[a]	58.3	76.6	n.a.	54.4	88.0	...

Source: Katsutoshi Ohta, "Automotive Air Pollution and Its Implications for Urban Transportation Planning," *Expressways and Automobiles*, vol. 17 (1974).
n.a. Not available.
a. Percent of total emissions of the pollutant that come from the transportation sector.

mosphere. International comparisons are especially treacherous because data depend heavily on the times, places, and frequencies of measurements and on the devices by which concentrations are measured. Both the Japanese and U.S. governments have had several years of experience with programs of intensive air-quality metering.

The data in Table 10-19 present comparisons of average annual concentrations of three pollutants in large cities in both countries. Nitrogen oxide concentrations are about twice as great in U.S. cities. Internal combustion engines generate large volumes of nitrogen dioxide, and data in the table reflect the preponderance of their use in U.S. urban transportation systems.

Table 10-19. *Average Annual Concentrations of Principal Air Pollutants in Large Japanese and U.S. Cities, 1970*

	Nitrogen dioxide (parts per million)	Sulfur oxides (parts per million)	Particulates (milligrams per cubic meter)
Japan			
Kawasaki	0.04	0.08	0.30
Kita-Kyushu	0.02	0.04	0.31
Osaka	0.03	0.06	0.21
Sapporo	0.03	0.02	0.24
Tokyo	0.04	0.03	0.18
United States			
Baltimore	0.09	0.02	0.11
Detroit	0.09	0.02	0.11
New York	0.08	0.03	0.12
Philadelphia	0.12	0.03	0.13
St. Louis	0.09	0.02	0.16

Source: Environment Agency, *Quality of the Environment in Japan, 1973* (1973).

Sulfur oxide concentrations, mainly from the burning of coal and oil, are higher in Japanese than in U.S. cities, in which the relatively low levels reflect widespread use of natural gas and the substitution, for environmental reasons, of oil with low sulfur content for oil with high content. Most petroleum used in Japan comes from the Middle East and contains relatively large amounts of sulfur. Particulate concentrations are two or three times as great in Japanese cities, perhaps reflecting high background concentrations and differences in metering devices. U.S. particulate concentrations have been declining for at least twenty years, reflecting decreased burning of soft coal and improved combustion systems. Data more fragmentary than those in Table 10-19 suggest that ambient carbon monoxide concentrations over U.S. cities are about 25 percent greater than those over Japanese cities, which also reflects the large-scale use of automobiles in U.S. cities.

The remarkable thing about the data summarized in the previous paragraph is the similarity they indicate between ambient air quality levels in the two countries. The data suggest that both countries have significant air pollution problems, but they do not suggest that the Japanese problem is much more serious than that in the United States—a remarkable phenomenon given the greater geographical concentrations of industry in Japan and the fact that the United States has had a national program for air pollution abatement since 1963, whereas the Japanese program was inaugurated only in the late 1960s.

TRENDS. More important than international comparisons is the issue of

Table 10-20. *Average Annual Concentrations of Air Pollutants in a Sample of Japanese Cities, 1965–72*

Pollutant	1965	1966	1967	1968	1969	1970	1971	1972
Sulfur oxides[a]	0.055	0.059	0.058	0.057	0.050	0.045	0.038	0.032
Carbon monoxide[a]	n.a.	n.a.	n.a.	4.9	3.5	2.3	2.4	2.3
Particulates[b]	n.a.	n.a.	0.237	0.233	0.169	0.110	0.087	n.a.
Nitrous oxides[a]	n.a.	n.a.	n.a.	0.023	0.023	0.025	0.025	0.028
Hydrocarbons[a]	n.a.	n.a.	n.a.	0.90	1.00	0.79	0.90	1.00

Source: Environment Agency, *White Paper on the Environment* (1974).
n.a. Not available.
a. Parts per million.
b. Milligrams per cubic meter.

whether air quality is becoming better or worse in Japanese cities. For several years the Japanese have monitored air quality at a small number of stations in a few large cities, and their time series on air quality are about as good as those available in the United States. Table 10-20 contains a summary of data from 1965 to 1972. The first three series show clear evidence of recent improvement, whereas the last two show deterioration over the corresponding period. Again, the similarity to U.S. experience is striking. U.S. government data show rising concentrations of most air pollutants until the mid-1960s, after which modest improvement has taken place.[41]

What harm is done by air pollution? All the substances discussed in the previous paragraphs are harmful or deadly in sufficiently high concentrations; some can damage structures, finishes, crops, and animals. But there is great disagreement about the effect of observed concentrations. Three kinds of evidence are available. The first is that derived from laboratory experiments, usually on small mammals, in which the health effects of high concentrations are recorded. The uncertainty of the results revolves around the appropriate extrapolations that can be made to human response, to overall and low as well as high concentrations.

A second kind of evidence comes from morbidity and mortality data on episodes of extremely high pollution levels accompanied by adverse meteorological conditions, which have occurred for a few days in certain cities. Morbidity and mortality rates have risen during such episodes, and the occasions—the most infamous in Donora (Pennsylvania), London, and New York—have been widely reported. Relatively mild episodes have been reported in Japan, especially when school children complain of eye and throat irritation during exercise.[42] These have been attributed to photochemical

41. See Council on Environmental Quality, *Environmental Quality, 1972.*
42. See Environment Agency, *Quality of the Environment in Japan, 1973* (1973).

smog and, less frequently, to acid rain comprising dilute sulfuric acid formed from sulfur oxides. Japan appears not to have had a serious episode of this kind, perhaps because it luckily has escaped the coincidence of meteorological conditions and sulfur oxide concentrations that would cause such an episode. Relatively modest discharge abatement programs seem to have avoided serious episodes elsewhere in recent years, and Japan may have escaped them permanently.

The third kind of evidence comes from statistical studies that relate data on air pollution and other variables to mortality and morbidity rates, usually by applying regression analysis to cross-sectional data. The best of these studies, using better data and more sophisticated techniques than were available in earlier years, concludes that halving the 1970 concentrations of sulfur oxides and particulates over a typical U.S. metropolitan area would add four or five years to the life expectancy of a newborn.[43] Little evidence has been turned up of the effects on health of observed levels of carbon monoxide, nitrogen oxides, or hydrocarbon concentrations in U.S. cities. Statistical studies in this area are inevitably somewhat gross, but they provide the best data available about chronic effects of low-level exposure. There is evidence that air pollution causes an unusually high incidence of respiratory disease in some areas of Japan, and if U.S. and European studies have any validity, serious consequences to health can hardly be avoided at the pollution levels observed in Kawasaki and elsewhere. It is a good guess that the potential for development of chronic health problems from air pollution is greater in Japan than in the United States, since the former has higher concentrations than the latter of sulfur oxides and particulates, the two pollutants subject to the strongest indictment. Careful studies of health effects of air pollutants are under way in areas of high pollution, and the Japanese government has designated twelve areas for special relief measures.

GOVERNMENTAL STANDARDS. The pollution abatement programs of the Japanese and U.S. governments are similar in many ways.[44] The first comprehensive pollution control law was passed in Japan in 1967, eleven years after passage of the first U.S. law. Like the U.S. program, the Japanese has three objectives: regulation of discharges, dispersal of funds for the construction of local waste treatment facilities, and research, development, monitor-

---

43. See Lester Lave and Eugene Seskin, *Air Pollution and Human Health* (Resources for the Future, forthcoming).

44. For a brief history of pollution control measures in the United States, see A. Myrick Freeman III, Robert H. Haveman, and Allen V. Kneese, *The Economics of Environmental Policy* (John Wiley, 1973).

ing, and data collection. A 1969 law provided for relief for victims of pollution, a program that the United States lacks. The entire control program was strengthened and broadened in 1970.

The law provides for national and prefectural governments to establish standards for ambient water quality covering a variety of pollutants and to formulate and enforce discharge standards to achieve the quality desired. This procedure is similar to the U.S. program that existed until 1972, when a law was passed requiring that discharge permits be issued by national and state governments. By 1974, standards had been issued for several water pollutants in Japan.

The U.S. regulatory program has been strongly criticized by government and private groups as being cumbersome, rigid, and excessively costly.[45] Many economists have claimed that the enforcement program should be replaced in part by effluent fees. As yet there has been little debate in Japan about the imposition of effluent fees or about whether the abatement program is workable, and it is too early to judge its results.

Japanese governments also began to establish both ambient and discharge standards for air quality in 1971. Japanese law restricted carbon monoxide emissions from cars starting in 1966—comparable U.S. standards became effective with 1968 cars—but hydrocarbons and nitrogen oxides have been controlled only since 1971. It is now stated national policy in Japan to require that Japanese cars meet the stringent standards that U.S. cars are required to meet in 1975 and later years. Emission test procedures are now almost identical in Japan and the United States, but Japanese auto manufacturers have been more imaginative than U.S. manufacturers in their approach to automobile emission control.[46] Japanese cars were the first to be certified by the U.S. government as meeting the 1975 federal emission standards. The stratified-charge engine developed by the Japanese appears to be a more cost-effective way of meeting the stringent emission standards scheduled for the late 1970s and early 1980s than the clumsy devices that U.S. manufacturers are planning to attach to conventional internal combustion engines. The Japanese government, however, may permit delays in meeting stringent nitrogen oxide standards, as did the U.S. government in 1973 and 1974.

The consensus among U.S. economists is that the federal program of discharge regulation has been clumsy, wasteful, and rigid and that recent changes

45. See ibid.
46. See National Academy of Sciences, *Report by the Committee on Motor Vehicle Emissions* (1973).

probably will worsen rather than improve the situation. Although the formal structure of the Japanese pollution control program is similar to that of the U.S. program, there is no guarantee that it will work as badly. Much depends on the flexibility and imaginativeness of its administrators.

Natural Disasters

Japan is subject to more frequent and more serious natural disasters than is most of the United States. It is situated on the earthquake-prone rim of the Pacific and is plagued with minor and major quakes. The worst damage was done by the earthquake of 1923, in which it is estimated that 100,000 people were killed. Most deaths and injuries in earthquakes result from burning and falling structures, and the latter hazard is made worse by the scarcity of open space away from buildings that might collapse. The Japanese tried in the past to limit such damage by controlling building heights. These controls have now been relaxed in Tokyo, however, and emphasis is being placed on modern earthquake-proof construction. The threat of fire has brought about controls on building materials in large cities. In Tokyo, most new structures are of nonflammable or fireproofed materials, which are gradually replacing the wood of traditional Japanese housing. But overall, despite deep concern, the Japanese seem not to have undertaken a careful quantitative study of the cost effectiveness of alternative strategies for limiting earthquake damage; and another earthquake of the magnitude of that of 1923 could cause many times the loss of life.

Damage from typhoons and flooding is also common in Japan. Many cities are located on low alluvial plains and most are on or near the coast. Parts of Tokyo and Osaka actually lie below sea level because of subsidence caused by the pumping of groundwater.

Traffic Safety

Japan shares with America a great concern over traffic safety. In addition to their congestion, most streets in large Japanese cities are narrow and lack separated pedestrian rights-of-way. Life, as a result, is hazardous for both drivers and pedestrians. The number of deaths in motor vehicle accidents in the United States is about three times that of Japan.[47] And because the U.S. population is about twice Japan's, U.S. traffic deaths per capita are 50 per-

47. The statistics in this and the following paragraph are from Tokyo Metropolitan Government, *Tokyo Fights Pollution,* and National Safety Council, *Accident Facts* (Chicago: NSC, 1972).

cent greater than the Japanese figure. But there are five times as many vehicles in the United States, and therefore the number of traffic deaths per motor vehicle in Japan is nearly twice that of the United States. This last statistic ranks Japan alongside the European countries with the highest traffic fatality records.

Compared with New York City, Tokyo does not have a high rate of traffic fatalities. Although Tokyo proper had a somewhat larger population than New York in 1970, it had somewhat fewer traffic fatalities—824 compared with 892. Tokyo is also somewhat safer than New York in terms of traffic fatalities per 10,000 vehicles—4.0 compared with 4.6. But New York is the most dangerous of large American cities by this measure, and Tokyo is more dangerous than Los Angeles, Chicago, Detroit, or Houston. Nonetheless, traffic fatalities per vehicle have fallen sharply in Tokyo since 1955.

Urban Prospects

Pervading much Japanese thought and writing on social problems in recent years is a recognition that although the nation has been extremely successful in raising its material standard of living during the last quarter century, its use of resources to maintain and improve the quality of life in other respects has been neglected. We are in broad sympathy with this viewpoint. There is a need in Japan for a substantial relative shift of resources from the production of private goods and services to what can be called public uses.

A high priority for the use of public resources should be environmental protection. Among the industrial nations, Japan probably has the worst record in the postwar world in pollution-inflicted damage to health and property —and there is a pervasive fear that the massive discharge of pollutants may have sown seeds of disaster on a far larger scale than so far has been experienced. The country is now in the process of diverting a much greater share of its resources for environmental protection. We are convinced that these expenditures are justified. Large reductions in air pollution from mobile and stationary sources, extreme measures to control discharges of heavy metals and persistent chemicals into inland and coastal waters, and a broad program to clean up Japan's rivers and estuaries are important public uses of resources.

Estimates of expenditures on pollution control are always uncertain. But Japanese and U.S. government data[48] indicate that public and private ex-

48. See Environment Agency, *Quality of the Environment in Japan, 1973*, and Council on Environmental Quality, *Environmental Quality, 1973*.

penditures on pollution control have risen to between 1 and 2 percent of each country's gross national product in the early 1970s. The latest data and forecasts point toward continuing growth of pollution control expenditures at rates in excess of GNP growth, but antipollution expenditures should not have to rise much above 3 percent of GNP to achieve national goals in either country—a cost unlikely to impose intolerable economic burdens. We are doubtful, based on U.S. experience, whether elaborate direct discharge controls, to the neglect of economic incentives, represent the most efficient possible program for achieving environmental protection, but the Japanese experience can be evaluated after a few years.

Much of the expenditure on environmental protection will be by private industry, but there is a need for government expenditures as well. Japanese cities are far behind those in other industrialized countries in their facilities for the collection, treatment, and disposal of both liquid and solid wastes. And, in a broader sense of the environment, there are other needs for resource uses for public purposes. We have referred to the inadequate protection of urban residents from the noise, vibration, and physical danger from motor vehicles. Japanese cities need more and better park and recreational areas, many of which can be provided only by governments.

The Japanese must continue to make large-scale investments in urban transportation systems. Urban areas will continue to grow and decentralize, and both phenomena will require additional transportation facilities. As we have indicated, the principal emphasis should continue to be on expansion of public transit in large cities rather than on increased use of motor vehicles.

Investment in housing will almost certainly continue on a large scale in Japan. Individual families have strong incentives to increase housing expenditures as incomes rise, and the private construction industry has been responsive and efficient in meeting these demands. Governments must ensure that additional land becomes available on which to increase the supply of urban housing. This will require first, that governments invest in infrastructure, and, second, that governments see to it that conversion of land to urban uses is not blocked either by private monopoly power in land or by excessive controls on land use.

Improving the quality of life in Japan requires two kinds of government policies: a shift of resources from the private to the public sector and government controls on the operation of the private sector. Controls may take the form of direct regulations or of economic incentives. It is important that controls on the private sector be carefully designed for specific purposes. For example, the abatement of polluting discharges unquestionably requires direct or indirect controls on the private sector, but governments are tempted to introduce broad controls for vague and diffuse purposes. Such controls rarely accomplish much and tend to interfere with the desirable functioning of the private sector. We are concerned that the National Land Use Act of 1974 may fall into this category. Overall controls on urban growth are incapable of solving specific urban problems. They cannot reduce congestion or increase the housing supply, but they impose far-reaching limitations on private decisionmaking and compromise the ability of the private sector to produce needed goods and services. Likewise, controls on land prices cannot make land less scarce; they can only interfere with the ability of the market to allocate land in ways that reflect its scarcity. Such controls inevitably create excess demand for land and force government to decide its uses in great detail. We are not convinced that this is the way in which Japan can best solve its urban problems.

More effective than controls on land prices would be high and broadly based taxes on capital gains from rising land values. Such taxes could eliminate the social dissension that inevitably arises when large fortunes are made with no socially useful effort on the part of the recipient. In addition, such taxes would yield revenues to help finance those kinds of public expenditures which have been suggested as necessary for continued improvement in the quality of life.

Appendix A: Population and Housing Censuses in Japan

The Japanese government publishes excellent censuses of population and housing (with Japanese and English text) every five years. The census of population has been published since 1920 for years ending with five and zero. The census of housing has been published for years ending with three and eight since 1948.

For census purposes, Japan is divided into enumeration districts, numbering about 580,000 in 1970, with an average population each of about 200 people. These enumeration districts differ from U.S. census tracts in two ways. First, census tracts contain about ten times as many people; and, second, they are designated only in metropolitan areas, whereas enumeration districts blanket the country. Beginning with the 1970 population census, the Japanese government defined permanent census tracts, with an average population of 10,000, for large cities.

All of Japan is covered by local government jurisdictions classified as *shi* (city), *machi* (town), and *mura* (village); the last two are known collectively as *gun*. Some census data are published for *shi* and *gun*, urban and rural. After 1953 the boundaries of the *shi* were expanded to take in substantial rural areas, and many new *shi* were formed. This requires that time series comparisons of *shi* populations be made with care. *Shi* now cover about 25 percent of the land area in Japan, and half their land area is rural in the generic sense. There are also forty-seven *ken,* or prefectures, analogous to states in the United States.

Since 1960 Japanese censuses have used a new concept in defining urban areas and populations—the densely inhabited district, or DID. A DID is a set of contiguous enumeration districts, each having a population density of at least 4,000 people per square kilometer and a total population of at least 5,000. DIDs are defined without regard to legal boundaries. The 1,141 DIDs existing in 1970 contained 53.5 percent of Japan's population, whereas the 579 *shi* contained 72.2 percent.

Like standard metropolitan statistical areas and urbanized areas in the United States, *shi* normally contain at least 50,000 people. But there is no close correspondence between any pair of urban concepts used in U.S. and Japanese censuses. SMSAs, with about 90 percent of their land rural, represent the most inclusive concept. The Japanese *shi* is next most inclusive, with a smaller percentage of its area rural. The *shi* is more inclusive than the U.S. urbanized area, which includes only the urbanized part of the SMSA. Likewise, the *shi* is more inclusive than U.S. central cities, which include only the central cores of SMSAs. The DID, the least inclusive, may be only a large, densely populated neighborhood. The average population density of the *shi,* 791 people per square kilometer, falls between that of U.S. urbanized areas (1,350) and SMSAs (142). But average urbanized area density is only one-third the minimum density for a DID.

Each population census beginning with that of 1960 has presented data for major metropolitan areas, the definition of which has changed somewhat with each census. In the 1970 census there were seven major metropolitan areas, each comprising one or more central cities with at least 500,000 inhabitants and those surrounding local jurisdictions from which at least 1.5 percent of the population commuted to the central city.

Data pertaining to Tokyo use two additional terms. The *ku*-area, or wards area, refers to the twenty-three wards of the central city, whose population was 8.8 million in 1970. Tokyo-*to* refers to the prefecture, which includes the *ku*-area and some surrounding area, including islands. The population of Tokyo-*to* in 1970 was 11.4 million.

Persons per room, used in U.S., UN, and other housing statistics, is a particularly inappropriate measure of housing space in Japan. Many traditional Japanese houses are not divided into rooms in the manner of Western houses.

Instead, floors in the living areas—usually all areas except halls, kitchens, and bathrooms—are covered with straw tatami mats; these areas are used for eating and other activities during the day and for sleeping at night. Many Japanese data measure house space by tatami, which measures about 90 by 180 centimeters, or about 3 by 6 feet, or 1.65 square meters. This measure is not entirely satisfactory because of traditional regional differences in tatami size and variations in floor space not covered by tatami. The most satisfactory measure of house space is square meters per person.[49]

Appendix B: Density Functions

This appendix presents details about the data, procedures, and results for the study of Japanese and U.S. density functions presented earlier in this chapter.

The basic hypothesis is that the equilibrium density gradients are related in linear fashion to the logarithm of the urban area's population, the logarithm of per capita income, and the other density gradient. The equations can be written:

(2) $$g_P^* = a_0^* + a_1^* \log P + a_2^* \log Y + a_3^* g_{E-1}$$

and

(3) $$g_E^* = b_0^* + b_1^* \log P + b_2^* \log Y + b_3^* g_{P-1},$$

where g_P^* and g_E^* are equilibrium values of population and employment density gradients, P is population of the urban area, Y is per capita income, and g_{E-1} and g_{P-1} are lagged values of the observed density gradients.

It was then assumed that observed density gradients adjust to their equilibrium values by a distributed lag process:

(4) $$g = g_{-1} + \lambda(g^* - g_{-1}) = \lambda g^* + (1 - \lambda)g_{-1},$$

where g and g_{-1} are observed current and lagged density gradients, g^* is the equilibrium value, and λ is the adjustment coefficient. The larger λ is, the faster adjustment is.

Substituting equations 2 and 3 for g^* in appropriate versions of equation 4 gives:

(5) $$g_P = a_0 + a_1 \log P + a_2 \log Y + a_3 g_{E-1} + (1 - \lambda_P)g_{P-1}$$

and

(6) $$g_E = b_0 + b_1 \log P + b_2 \log Y + b_3 g_{P-1} + (1 - \lambda_E)g_{E-1},$$

---

49. These issues are covered in more detail in Henry Rosovsky, *Capital Formation in Japan, 1868–1940* (Free Press, 1961).

Table 10-21. *Population Density Functions for Sample Japanese Cities, 1965 and 1970*[a]

City	1965			1970		
	D_0	g	R^2	D_0	g	R^2
Aomori	29,673	0.490	0.507	22,902	0.359	0.390
	(25.2)	(3.7)		(32.0)	(2.9)	
Asahikawa	29,466	0.568	0.948	22,159	0.483	0.772
	(67.6)	(15.3)		(38.7)	(6.6)	
Fukui	13,373	0.545	0.518	9,769	0.346	0.181
	(20.0)	(3.7)		(14.8)	(1.7)	
Fukushima	17,501	0.482	0.562	18,732	0.596	0.644
	(25.1)	(4.1)		(27.8)	(4.8)	
Hirosaki	19,149	0.523	0.704	15,931	0.517	0.704
	(35.8)	(5.6)		(34.6)	(5.6)	
Hiroshima	25,745	0.173	0.200	14,341	0.020	0.007
	(36.7)	(1.8)		(48.7)	(0.3)	
Kofu	24,909	0.712	0.852	22,159	0.581	0.719
	(44.9)	(8.6)		(37.7)	(5.8)	
Kumamoto	36,171	0.513	0.732	16,933	0.281	0.564
	(39.5)	(6.0)		(52.9)	(4.1)	
Matsumoto	15,979	0.550	0.771	6,721	0.363	0.241
	(35.2)	(6.6)		(14.6)	(2.0)	
Mito	11,556	0.387	0.380	13,630	0.382	0.476
	(16.9)	(2.8)		(22.8)	(3.4)	
Morioka	5,261	0.001	0.048	16,747	0.438	0.473
	(24.6)	(0.8)		(28.0)	(3.4)	
Niigata	31,603	0.365	0.786	22,359	0.187	0.561
	(44.6)	(6.9)		(35.1)	(4.1)	
Okayama	20,090	0.378	0.412	24,612	0.470	0.393
	(23.4)	(3.0)		(24.4)	(2.9)	
Okazaki	9,643	0.448	0.199	12,040	0.382	0.400
	(15.1)	(1.8)		(25.6)	(2.9)	
Saga	21,163	0.842	0.789	12,708	0.658	0.648
	(25.5)	(7.0)		(24.7)	(4.9)	
Sapporo	23,506	0.414	0.378	22,652	0.231	0.200
	(15.5)	(2.8)		(22.0)	(1.8)	
Sendai	22,880	0.355	0.755	14,501	0.246	0.201
	(40.1)	(6.3)		(24.5)	(1.8)	
Takamatsu	43,347	0.893	0.870	31,729	0.548	0.729
	(45.0)	(9.3)		(34.2)	(5.9)	

Table 10-21 (*continued*)

City	1965			1970		
	D_0	g	R^2	D_0	g	R^2
Tokyo	22,218	0.082	0.605	25,157	0.081	0.592
	(26.6)	(7.6)		(26.6)	(7.4)	
	11,956[b]	0.073[b]	0.473[b]			
	(21.5)	(5.8)				
	9,337[c]	0.068[c]	0.455[c]			
	(21.7)	(5.6)				
	7,143[d]	0.063[d]	0.444[d]			
	(22.4)	(5.5)				
Tottori	20,578	0.671	0.447	15,414	0.661	0.624
	(21.7)	(3.2)		(23.0)	(4.6)	
Tsu	10,436	0.297	0.225	8,111	0.232	0.158
	(18.9)	(1.9)		(25.0)	(1.6)	
Utsunomiya	12,939	0.373	0.730	20,620	0.543	0.694
	(30.7)	(5.9)		(35.9)	(5.4)	

Source: See text.
a. Figures in parentheses are *t*-statistics. For explanation of column headings, see text.
b. 1960.
c. 1955.
d. 1950.

where $a_i = a_i^* \lambda_P$ and $b_i = b_i^* \lambda_E$. Estimates of equations 5 and 6 are presented in Table 10-6 above.

The intent was to select a sample of twenty urban areas each from Japan and the United States. However, twenty-two Japanese areas were selected in case data were unavailable for one or two, but since data turned out to be available for all, the Japanese sample consists of twenty-two areas. The samples were purposively rather than randomly selected. New York and Tokyo were intentionally included. In so far as possible, we avoided urban areas constrained by natural barriers, such as harbors and mountains, and by manmade barriers, especially other urban areas. We tried to select urban areas in a variety of regions and size categories. Selection was from among urbanized areas in the United States and cities or major metropolitan areas in Japan, so that each has a population of at least 50,000.

In each urban area, we randomly sampled fifteen small areas, except in Tokyo and New York, where forty and thirty areas, respectively, were sampled. In the United States the small areas were census tracts, most of which have populations of between 2,000 and 10,000; in Japan they were clusters of enumeration districts, each with a population of about 200. To each enumeration district we added a set of contiguous districts to bring the population of

Table 10-22. Total Employment and Manufacturing Employment Density Functions for Sample Japanese Cities, 1969 and 1972[a]

City	Total employment						Manufacturing employment					
	1969			1972			1969			1972		
	D_0	g	R^2	D_0	g	R^2	D_0	g	R^2	D_0	g	R^2
Aomori	30,881 (20.5)	1.282 (5.3)	0.685	18,922 (28.9)	0.725 (6.1)	0.739	362 (5.3)	0.590 (1.1)	0.087	723 (10.0)	0.363 (1.6)	0.160
Asahikawa	38,207 (25.1)	1.136 (5.9)	0.725	6,786 (12.6)	0.543 (3.9)	0.538	356 (5.7)	0.009 (0.0)	0.000	490 (7.2)	0.506 (3.0)	0.402
Fukui	36,112 (32.4)	1.605 (8.7)	0.853	9,243 (21.6)	0.491 (4.9)	0.647	2,315 (17.8)	0.944 (3.8)	0.526	2,165 (18.8)	0.446 (4.6)	0.617
Fukushima	19,996 (37.5)	0.919 (10.3)	0.891	5,962 (14.1)	0.421 (3.2)	0.434	823 (7.3)	0.439 (1.4)	0.132	456 (8.9)	0.242 (1.6)	0.168
Hirosaki	10,505 (22.9)	1.243 (5.9)	0.729	10,374 (24.7)	0.694 (5.4)	0.689	391 (6.9)	0.749 (1.7)	0.175	940 (20.9)	0.498 (4.4)	0.503
Hiroshima	29,466 (22.1)	0.646 (3.5)	0.483	34,811 (31.6)	0.517 (4.9)	0.652	1,557 (11.5)	0.301 (1.2)	0.097	920 (10.0)	0.012 (0.1)	0.000
Kofu	10,366 (25.3)	0.788 (4.7)	0.632	24,445 (45.9)	1.036 (10.3)	0.890	511 (6.6)	0.165 (0.4)	0.011	4,564 (16.7)	0.877 (3.8)	0.526
Kumamoto	15,222 (17.4)	0.577 (2.7)	0.353	16,669 (17.3)	0.623 (3.6)	0.503	156 (5.0)	-0.234 (0.6)	0.026	463 (4.8)	0.431 (1.1)	0.085
Matsumoto	16,526 (32.2)	0.988 (9.4)	0.871	16,045 (35.9)	0.976 (7.4)	0.809	1,682 (20.9)	0.787 (6.4)	0.757	1,672 (17.1)	0.661 (3.1)	0.427
Mito	18,109 (18.3)	0.686 (3.5)	0.483	24,874 (20.9)	0.927 (5.5)	0.696	59 (3.6)	-0.511 (1.2)	0.105	1,658 (14.4)	0.740 (4.1)	0.565
Morioka	6,894 (10.2)	0.704 (1.5)	0.142	8,919 (11.6)	0.673 (2.3)	0.295	255 (5.6)	0.323 (0.6)	0.026	534 (6.4)	0.526 (1.4)	0.139
Niigata	21,228 (27.9)	0.494 (7.2)	0.799	16,363 (24.5)	0.486 (3.4)	0.478	566 (6.9)	0.202 (1.1)	0.091	921 (14.4)	0.143 (0.9)	0.053

Okayama	27,587 (25.9)	0.728 (6.2)	0.750	18,251 (34.4)	0.565 (5.7)	0.715	2,368 (12.6)	0.566 (3.1)	0.429	753 (8.8)	0.168 (0.6)	0.031
Okazaki	18,059 (37.9)	0.775 (10.0)	0.885	11,718 (34.9)	0.562 (5.9)	0.727	2,669 (15.5)	0.540 (3.5)	0.490	1,217 (16.3)	0.322 (2.1)	0.248
Saga	12,401 (32.6)	1.115 (8.2)	0.837	10,075 (28.7)	0.721 (4.8)	0.637	578 (7.5)	0.787 (2.0)	0.228	298 (10.9)	0.249 (1.0)	0.073
Sapporo	18,486 (27.4)	0.531 (5.5)	0.696	38,162 (17.2)	0.715 (4.1)	0.561	1,941 (12.9)	0.425 (2.7)	0.345	3,768 (7.2)	0.833 (2.5)	0.330
Sendai	18,194 (17.7)	0.517 (2.5)	0.333	17,708 (15.4)	0.701 (3.3)	0.451	23 (3.2)	0.894 (2.4)	0.316	690 (6.9)	0.445 (1.4)	0.130
Takamatsu	23,192 (33.8)	0.737 (6.8)	0.783	19,657 (39.9)	0.694 (9.3)	0.870	783 (16.0)	0.258 (1.7)	0.183	969 (16.9)	0.350 (2.9)	0.386
Tokyo	3,546 (16.4)	0.060 (4.5)	0.344	9,136 (20.8)	0.085 (6.8)	0.547	1,257 (12.8)	0.058 (3.8)	0.280	3,177 (16.3)	0.084 (6.0)	0.484
Tottori	12,007 (21.1)	1.506 (4.4)	0.603	15,958 (31.2)	0.929 (5.5)	0.697	117 (3.7)	−0.006 (0.0)	0.000	1,218 (20.0)	0.390 (2.0)	0.236
Tsu	5,753 (34.1)	0.375 (3.8)	0.529	7,724 (21.4)	0.449 (2.5)	0.318	139 (7.2)	−0.313 (1.2)	0.097	324 (16.8)	−0.065 (0.4)	0.014
Utsunomiya	18,241 (32.3)	1.079 (9.8)	0.880	11,998 (23.4)	0.571 (4.9)	0.645	594 (8.3)	0.576 (2.0)	0.244	842 (21.3)	0.394 (4.3)	0.582

Source: See text.
a. Figures in parentheses are t-statistics. For explanation of column headings, see text.

Table 10-23. *Population Density Functions for Sample U.S. Cities, 1960 and 1970*[a]

City	1960			1970		
	D_0	g	R^2	D_0	g	R^2
Atlanta	5,193	0.130	0.714	5,985	0.126	0.912
	(25.2)	(5.7)		(39.2)	(11.6)	
Baton Rouge	6,768	0.273	0.820	3,241	0.181	0.656
	(25.8)	(7.7)		(19.1)	(5.0)	
Binghamton, N.Y.	2,357	0.161	0.802	953	0.136	0.528
	(28.3)	(7.2)		(11.8)	(3.8)	
Charlotte, N.C.	3,511	0.250	0.838	1,691	0.124	0.857
	(29.4)	(8.2)		(30.3)	(8.8)	
Columbus, Ohio	24,248	0.324	0.909	2,463	0.069	0.379
	(35.9)	(11.4)		(18.5)	(2.8)	
Corpus Christi	1,598	0.043	0.102	1,795	0.111	0.309
	(12.6)	(1.2)		(9.8)	(2.4)	
Denver	10,625	0.220	0.700	1,283	0.013	0.013
	(20.7)	(5.5)		(11.0)	(0.4)	
Fresno	1,275	0.089	0.645	2,137	0.101	0.880
	(16.1)	(4.9)		(24.9)	(9.7)	
Grand Rapids	11,048	0.322	0.849	1,380	0.044	0.199
	(43.0)	(8.5)		(12.0)	(1.8)	
Indianapolis	14,045	0.336	0.643	1,558	−0.014	0.001
	(14.9)	(4.8)		(8.7)	(0.1)	
Kalamazoo	2,586	0.262	0.760	2,158	0.170	0.700
	(21.1)	(6.4)		(24.1)	(5.5)	
New York City	31,606	0.060	0.257	36,483	0.086	0.597
	(28.3)	(3.1)		(38.0)	(6.4)	
Oklahoma City	1,209	0.085	0.387	1,454	0.149	0.701
	(25.0)	(2.8)		(15.1)	(5.5)	
Omaha	8,357	0.254	0.908	2,577	0.115	0.542
	(32.7)	(11.3)		(19.8)	(3.9)	
Phoenix	3,159	0.135	0.641	5,012	0.174	0.489
	(11.9)	(4.8)		(11.9)	(3.5)	
Pittsburgh	4,746	0.064	0.459	1,712	0.032	0.091
	(18.1)	(3.3)		(13.0)	(1.1)	
Rockford, Ill.	4,861	0.328	0.807	3,858	0.218	0.793
	(22.6)	(7.4)		(22.0)	(7.1)	
San Antonio	8,086	0.226	0.809	12,472	0.286	0.841
	(22.6)	(7.4)		(23.4)	(8.3)	
Toledo	9,168	0.196	0.782	3,093	0.114	0.665
	(31.4)	(6.8)		(18.0)	(5.1)	
Wichita	3,823	0.208	0.872	4,652	0.222	0.905
	(30.3)	(9.4)		(40.3)	(11.1)	

Source: See text.
a. Figures in parentheses are *t*-statistics. For explanation of column headings, see text.

Table 10-24. *Total Employment and Manufacturing Employment Density Functions for Sample U.S. Cities, Selected Years*[a]

| | Total employment | | | | Manufacturing employment | | | |
| | 1960 | | 1970 | | 1963 | | 1967 | |
City	D_0	g	D_0	g	D_0	g	D_0	g
Atlanta	3,339	0.242	2,074	0.138	248	0.069	196	0.042
Baton Rouge	5,034	0.468	1,679	0.198	41	−0.112	274	0.177
Binghamton, N.Y.	3,379	0.478	3,286	0.541	223	−0.175	524	0.070
Charlotte, N.C.	6,550	0.676	12,535	0.801	40	−0.232	51	−0.184
Columbus, Ohio	2,915	0.239	1,209	0.095	888	0.228	624	0.178
Corpus Christi	1,214	0.186	277	0.022	2	−0.369	1	−0.413
Denver	4,263	0.267	3,340	0.202	n.a.	n.a.	n.a.	n.a.
Fresno	3,283	0.480	1,427	0.233	51	−0.101	18	−0.271
Grand Rapids	4,661	0.504	2,432	0.312	945	0.252	885	0.222
Indianapolis	5,483	0.345	52	−0.143	148	−0.047	31	−0.147
Kalamazoo	5,469	0.878	2,488	0.481	540	0.252	673	0.298
New York City	11,796	0.089	8,676	0.071	3,241	0.051	747	0.049
Oklahoma City	47	−0.121	741	0.096	257	0.232	1	−0.245
Omaha	3,720	0.348	2,083	0.221	588	0.276	822	0.352
Phoenix	285	−0.009	394	0.015	59	0.007	96	0.033
Pittsburgh	4,558	0.203	4,736	0.203	1,047	0.138	1,092	0.137
Rockford, Ill.	1,793	0.206	2,818	0.406	2,320	0.529	810	0.160
San Antonio	696	0.066	4,480	0.326	146	0.146	157	0.141
Toledo	3,742	0.359	3,112	0.297	1,413	0.332	1,150	0.276
Wichita	1,162	0.152	457	0.008	n.a.	n.a.	n.a.	n.a.

Source: See text.
n.a. Not available.
a. For explanation of column headings, see text.

the cluster to between 1,000 and 2,000. In both countries, small areas with small populations were avoided.

For each small area, we recorded population from census data.[50] For Japanese small areas, total employment (1969 data exclude government employment, which was not available by enumeration district until 1972) and manufacturing employment were recorded.[51] U.S. censuses do not present employment by census tract, so an entirely different procedure (described below) was used to estimate total and manufacturing employment density functions. For each small area, using census maps we measured straight line distance from the center of the central business district to the center of the small area and estimated the size of the small areas by mechanical integration devices. We then calculated population, total employment, and manufacturing employment densities for each small area. Densities are in people per square kilometer and distances are in kilometers.

The density functions were estimated by linear least squares regression of the logarithms of density of small areas on distance from the CBD's center. The estimated density functions are presented in Tables 10-21–10-24.

50. See Bureau of the Census, *Census of Population, 1970,* and Bureau of Statistics, *1970 Population Census of Japan* (1971).

51. See Bureau of Statistics, *Establishment Census of Japan* (1969, 1972).

Table 10-25. *Population and Income Data for Sample U.S. and Japanese Urban Areas, 1969 and 1970*

	United States			Japan		
Urbanized area	Population, 1970 (*thousands*)	Income per family, 1969 (*dollars*)		City	Population, 1970 (*thousands*)	Income per capita, 1969 (*hundreds of yen*)
Atlanta	1,173	10,698		Aomori	240	317
Baton Rouge	249	9,501		Asahikawa	288	408
Binghamton, N.Y.	167	10,527		Fukui	201	397
Charlotte, N.C.	280	10,069		Fukushima	227	356
Columbus, Ohio	790	10,536		Hirosaki	158	317
Corpus Christi	213	8,587		Hiroshima	542	487
Denver	1,047	10,734		Kofu	183	379
Fresno	263	9,172		Kumamoto	440	329
Grand Rapids	353	10,728		Matsumoto	163	401
Indianapolis	820	10,881		Mito	174	389
Kalamazoo	152	10,940		Morioka	196	318
New York City	16,207	11,142		Niigata	384	393
Oklahoma City	580	9,471		Okayama	375	462
Omaha	492	10,214		Okazaki	211	568
Phoenix	863	10,097		Saga	143	345
Pittsburgh	1,846	9,945		Sapporo	1,010	408
Rockford, Ill.	206	11,043		Sendai	545	387
San Antonio	773	8,016		Takamatsu	274	427
Toledo	488	10,926		Tokyo	24,113	763
Wichita	302	9,502		Tottori	113	344
				Tsu	125	440
				Utsunomiya	301	415

Source: See text.

To estimate equations 5 and 6, we also needed population and per capita income of the urban areas. Populations of U.S. urbanized areas and of Japanese cities were obtained from the respective population censuses. Per capita income by urbanized area was obtained from the U.S. census. The Japanese census gives no income data, but the national income statistics give income by prefecture, so the Japanese income variable is income per capita in the prefecture in which the city is located.[52] These data are presented in Table 10-25.

No small-area data on employment are available for U.S. urban areas, so the above procedure could not be used to estimate density functions for U.S. total and manufacturing employment.

The U.S. Census of Manufactures[53] presents data on manufacturing em-

52. See Bureau of Statistics, *1973 Statistics of Japan* (1973).
53. See Bureau of the Census, *Census of Manufactures, 1967*.

ployment in central cities and suburbs of SMSAs, but not in smaller areas. The population census presents employment by place of residence, but not by place of employment. But the 1960 and 1970 population censuses also present numbers of workers who commute between central city and suburb. Thus, one can compute employment by place of employment as between central city and suburb. For example, central city employment equals the number of workers resident in the central city plus the number who commute in from suburbs minus the number who commute out from central city. Thus, total employment and manufacturing employment are available by central city and suburb, but not for smaller areas.

The central city–suburb data provide two truncated integrals of the employment density function. Because the exponential density function is a two-parameter family, it is possible to estimate it from the two truncated integrals.[54] Suppose that either employment or manufacturing employment is given by the exponential density function

$$D(x) = D_0 e^{-gx},$$

where x is distance from the urban center, g and D_0 are constants determined by the data, e is the base of the natural logarithm, and $D(x)$ is density at distance x. Assume that the urban area is circular except that a pie slice of $(2\pi - \phi)$ radians has been removed by a natural barrier. Then the total employment or manufacturing employment within x' kilometers of the CBD's center is:

(7) $$N(x') = \int_0^{x'} \phi x D_0 e^{-gx} dx = \frac{\phi D_0}{g^2} [1 - (1 + gx')e^{-gx'}].$$

Let $\bar{x}$ be the radius of the urban area and $\underset{\sim}{x}$ be the radius of the central city. Then

(8) $$\frac{N(\bar{x})}{N(\underset{\sim}{x})} = \frac{1 - (1 + g\bar{x})e^{-g\bar{x}}}{1 - (1 + g\underset{\sim}{x})e^{-g\underset{\sim}{x}}}$$

is the ratio of urban area to central city employment. The values of ϕ, $\underset{\sim}{x}$ and $\bar{x}$ were estimated from census maps. $N(\underset{\sim}{x})$ and $N(\bar{x})$ were calculated as described above. Using these numbers, equation 8 contains only the unknown parameter g. It was solved for g using the Newton-Raphson method. Having estimated g from equation 8, D_0 can be calculated from equation 7 by making x' equal to $\underset{\sim}{x}$ or $\bar{x}$.

The U.S. employment and manufacturing employment density functions in Table 10-24 were calculated in this way.

54. The procedure described here is an improvement on that used in Mills, *Studies in the Structure of the Urban Economy*, in which advantages of the central city–suburban data are discussed in more detail.

CHAPTER ELEVEN

Politics, Government, and Economic Growth in Japan

Philip H. Trezise, Brookings Institution
with the collaboration of
Yukio Suzuki, Japan Economic Journal

754 PHILIP TREZISE AND YUKIO SUZUKI

Tables

IN A WORLD in which levels of national economic activity are considered to be closely responsive to public policies—with governments being rewarded or punished accordingly by their voters—a rapid and sustained increase in gross national product provides a presumption of good political judgment and sound execution. In the case of Japan, real output grew sevenfold in the twenty years of virtually uninterrupted expansion that followed the end of the Allied occupation in 1952. It is not surprising, then, that many observers came to conclude that Japan's political and administrative system had somehow been uniquely designed to prosecute the objective of rapid growth of output, and that the series of governments in Tokyo during this period have had special capacities for economic management.

In much of the popular commentary, this conclusion was stated in highly purposive terms. It was felt that not only had Japanese governments, like governments elsewhere, shaped their overall fiscal and monetary policies with economic growth as a basic objective—and even that postwar, like prewar, Japan had put growth very high among all national aims—but also that a wide range of governmental measures, including direct controls and subsidies as well as other means of direction and suasion, had been consciously and skillfully used to allocate the national resources to those economic or industrial sectors that would provide the greatest returns in terms of growth. In effect, Japan has been looked on as an instance in which central planning and control in a considerable degree of detail have been tried and have worked, in some respects worked spectacularly well. An editor of *The Economist,* in one of that periodical's surveys of Japan, put the case this way: "The ultimate responsibility for industrial planning, for deciding in which new directions Japan's burgeoning industrial effort should try to go, and for fostering and protecting business as it moves in those directions, lies with the government."[1] More free-swinging descriptions of Japan's governmental structure and economic policymaking are represented by Richard Halloran's statement that "Japan's economy today is probably the world's most deftly guided economy, governed by a set of controls more refined than Karl Marx, V. I. Lenin, or Josef Stalin ever dreamed of."[2]

1. Norman Macrae, "The Risen Sun," *The Economist,* May 27, 1967, p. xx. The same writer concludes in rather opposite fashion, however, that "the idea of entering some new [industrial] field does not come from the bureaucracy. . . . Japan does not plunge its technological resources into romantic Concordes, but into what a business thinks will pay." "Pacific Century, 1975–2075?" ibid., Jan. 4, 1975, p. 31.

2. *Japan: Images and Realities* (Tokyo: Charles E. Tuttle Co., 1970), p. 133. In

Because the Japanese economy, despite quite extensive governmental intervention, is based predominantly on private ownership and enterprise, the usual and probably necessary assumption was that the government had worked in intimate and harmonious alliance with business to make its growth policies successful. The phrase "Japan, Incorporated" has become the conventional shorthand for the proposition that economic growth policies have been jointly decided and jointly executed by politicians and appointed officials together with representatives of private business.[3] The hypothesis gained plausibility from two facts: first, that successive Japanese governments and Japanese business have had close links, and, second, that governments throughout the postwar period have been actively interventionist in the nation's economic life. When these considerations were taken together with observed growth rates of the nation's GNP, it was only a short step to picturing Japan as a prime example of planning without tears, of public controls finely tuned to assure private results, of a wise government guiding—and at the same time being guided by—an equally wise and also unfailingly responsive private sector. Here was a country, it could be said, that has long managed its economic affairs in highly particular ways and yet avoided those mistakes and rigidities which have marked centralized economic direction elsewhere. In this version of things the special genius of the Japanese became the ability to harness the energies and skills of private businessmen within a centrally planned and closely regulated system and thus to reach exceptionally ambitious economic goals.

The thesis of the present chapter is that this and like models of Japan's postwar economic development are subject to so substantial a discount as to make them largely valueless as guides to understanding. There is no question, of course, but that, as in all modern states, the political environ-

---

1971, Peter G. Peterson, then assistant to the President for international economic affairs, described the Japanese economy as "a type of informal conglomerate . . . a form of business organization which, through strong financial management, can channel cash flows rapidly from low-growth to high-growth sectors. The Bank of Japan is the financial center and, following guidelines of the Planning Agency, determines the nature and direction of growth." *The United States in the Changing World Economy*, vol. 2, *Background Material* (Government Printing Office, 1971), p. 58.

3. See, for example, James C. Abegglen (ed.), *Business Strategies for Japan* (Tokyo: Sophia University, 1970), pp. 8–13. A more or less standard political model has seen Japan as governed by a tripartite elite consisting of the conservative (Liberal Democratic) party leadership, senior bureaucrats, and big businessmen. See Haruhiro Fukui, *Party in Power: The Japanese Liberal Democrats and Policy-Making* (University of California Press, 1970), pp. 162–67; and idem, "Economic Planning in Postwar Japan: A Case Study in Policy Making," *Asian Survey*, vol. 12 (April 1972), pp. 327–48.

ment and the economic policies that were among its products have influenced economic events pervasively and in some respects crucially. To suppose, however, that politicians and officials in league with businessmen were able to plan and guide Japan's explosive economic growth in detail is neither credible in the abstract nor (as will be seen) supported by the realities.

Japan is, after all, a large and in the main an extremely open society. Its postwar political system has been a quite vigorously functioning democracy, which has had regularly to accommodate the disparate interests of the many groups making up a country of more than 100 million people. Only brief reflection is needed to grasp that in such a system a great many political and administrative decisions must have been determined by other than an unerringly accurate perception of what was good for the nation's economic growth. Neither officials nor politicians could have been immune to pressures from special interests other than business—and business itself has had its own divisions and differences of interest. The growth objective must often have been in conflict with perceived political necessity.

Nor could governmental responses to rapid economic change at home and abroad have failed from time to time to be tardy or wrongheaded, even as in other countries. The tendency to endow Japanese leaders and officials with unusual insight and skill is all too easily overdone. There is much that is different about Japan, but not everything.

Other chapters in this volume[4] touch at various points on the role of government, in specific or general terms. The purpose here will be to add detail and perhaps perspective to what is said elsewhere. The plan is to consider, first, postwar party politics and their evolution and, second, governmental administration based on the permanent civil service—both, of course, in relation to Japan's economic development. This is a convenient and customary division. The interaction between politics and administration will be taken into account in a concluding assessment.

The Political Scene

Japan's postwar political system on the face of it is anything but unusual, mysterious, or specially adapted to the performance of economic or other miracles. It is a parliamentary democracy, patterned generally after the Western European model, with a two-body legislature, the Diet, that is, in the words of the constitution, "the highest organ of state power." Its cabi-

---

4. In particular, Chapters 1, 3, 5, 6, 7, and 8.

net, the members of which are drawn almost invariably from among the elected legislators, is constitutionally and in fact accountable to the Diet. The Diet is chosen under a franchise that is universal for citizens aged twenty-one and over. The franchise is exercised about as widely as in Western Europe, more widely than in the United States.

National elections for the 491-member lower house, which has the legislative originating power, must by constitutional article be held at least every four years, but may be, and typically are, called at shorter intervals. The upper House of Councillors, which has a limited veto power over lower house actions, has 252 members elected for six years, with half of them up for election every third year. Unlike the lower house, all of whose members come from local electoral districts, the House of Councillors has 40 percent of its membership elected on a nationwide basis.

The Japanese constitution was written and imposed by the Allied occupation and it remains unchanged by so much as one word today. Its drafters' intention was to put sovereignty in the hands of the people, in contrast to the prewar constitution which gave ultimate power to the emperor. This principle of popular sovereignty has never been challenged in any serious way. Japanese democracy since the end of the occupation has been as disorderly as any, and also as successful.

It has spawned a lineup of political parties of a fairly familiar kind: a right-to-center conservative party, the Liberal Democrats; two socialist parties, the larger more or less standard Marxist in philosophy, the other reformist; a small but active communist party; and, a recent arrival, a political-religious party originating in a Buddhist sect and appealing to the small shopkeeper and other discontented but nonleftist groups. These have created a lively political scene, where elections are contested seriously (and expensively) and policies debated vigorously and now and then violently. The electorate is one of the most literate in the world. It is informed by a bewildering range of organs of communication and opinion that reach into literally every household. By most evidence, the country was thoroughly inoculated by painful experience against any tendencies toward totalitarianism. Representative rule, with its virtues and defects, seems to be a firmly based condition of Japanese political life.

If any feature of Japan's political life has been particularly relevant to rapid growth of the gross national product, it must have been the virtually unbroken dominance of a party or parties committed to an economic system based on private ownership.

In the unsettled situation after the surrender in 1945 party politics in Japan quickly polarized around groups philosophically attached to the goal of a socialist society and those predisposed to the traditional pattern of private business enterprise. This division between progressive and conservative political camps has persisted to the present. Control of the government gravitated early to the conservatives, and there it has remained.

An alliance between conservative politicians and business leaders did not need to be forged: it was an integral part of the political sorting out that took place in the confused years of defeat and recuperation. Business needed defenders against the threat supposedly presented by the socialist aspirants to political power, and the nonsocialist political personalities saw this as one of their parties' purposes.[5] Financial support from business for the conservative parties was as natural as it was indispensable.

Shared values and shared interests thus brought together businessmen and conservative politicians in a relationship that has endured throughout the entire postwar period. This association was accompanied by recovery and then by an extraordinary expansion of the nation's economy, to the benefit and satisfaction of both elements in the alliance. Whether these economic developments could have occurred under different political auspices can only be guessed at, but given the alternatives at hand in Japan, it must be considered quite doubtful.

This much having been said, the relationship between politics and growth becomes more ambiguous. The conservatives were not preoccupied uniquely with economic affairs or growth; big business was only one of the interest groups that exerted political influence, and political life was more discordant and countervailing pressures more important than the extended record of one-party rule might suggest.

The Liberal Democratic Party

Since November 1955 the standard-bearer of political conservatism (in the Japanese sense of the term) has been the Liberal Democratic party (LDP), a party created out of a merger of the Liberal and the Democratic parties that had vied for power with one another and with the left-wing parties throughout the occupation and the early postoccupation years.

EVOLUTION. The roots of the LDP go well back into Japanese history, to the Liberal and Progressive parties that emerged in embryo during the

5. Not that Japanese conservatives were of one mind as to the kind of private enterprise system they favored. There were advocates of modified and progressive capitalism based on cooperation between social classes, as against those—a majority— who opposed any compromise with the socialists and communists. See Shigeru Yoshida, *The Yoshida Memoirs: The Story of Japan in Crisis* (Greenwood Press, 1961), chap. 9; and Fukui, *Party in Power*, pp. 40–42.

second decade after the Meiji restoration in 1867–68. These parties, which
came in time to be the principal groupings in the imperial Diet, had their
origins in rural Japan, among the agrarian landowners who dominated
Meiji society.[6] Even as industrialization and urbanization gained momen-
tum and the two parties turned to the great *zaibatsu* houses for financial
support, their rural flavor persisted—as it has in the LDP to this day. Suppressed in 1940, the parties reappeared soon after the surrender in August
1945, their organizational structures and party traditions intact. Despite
large-scale purges by the occupation authorities, especially among members
of the resurrected Progressive (later Democratic) party, they became once
again the principal political forces in Japan. By the end of the occupation
they held almost 70 percent of the seats in the lower house of the Diet and
62 percent in the upper house.

Differences within and between the two conservative political parties—
mainly of personalities but to some degree of policy—cast a pall of uncertainty and instability on the years immediately following independence in
1952, years that many Japanese saw as critical for the country's future.
After three national elections and four governments in a little more than three
years and a rising number of votes for the Japanese Socialist party (JSP),
pressure for a conservative merger from the business community and from
senior political leaders became irresistible, and the new party was formally
created in late 1955.[7] The unified LDP has never again reached the 63 percent of the votes in the lower house that it garnered immediately after the
merger—rather, it has suffered a steady decline in its share of the popular
vote, to a low point of 47 percent—but neither has its control of the national government ever been seriously challenged by the opposition parties.
The "party which will rule half an eternity"[8] has some distance to go, but
by the standards of most democratic states it has been a notably durable
institution.

The image of political stability to be drawn from the record of an unbroken LDP majority in the Diet is made the sharper by party discipline in

6. Robert A. Scalapino and Junnosuke Masumi, *Parties and Politics in Contemporary Japan* (University of California Press, 1964), chap. 1. See also Fukui,
Party in Power, chaps. 1 and 2; and Nobutaka Ike, "Political Leadership and Political
Parties: Japan," in Robert E. Ward and Dankwart A. Rustow (eds.), *Political Modernization in Japan and Turkey* (Princeton University Press, 1964), pp. 389–410.
7. See Chitoshi Yanaga, *Big Business in Japanese Politics* (Yale University Press,
1968), chap. 5.
8. Quoted in Nathaniel B. Thayer, *How the Conservatives Rule Japan* (Princeton
University Press, 1969), p. 13.

the legislature. Although the party has always been afflicted by factionalism, its command of the Diet, once the necessary internal party decisions have been arrived at, has been secure. The opposition, to be sure, has been badly fragmented, but even against a coalition of other parties the disciplined LDP would have had ultimate control over legislative proceedings.

In its fundamental ideology, too, the LDP can be seen as being essentially agreed on central principles. The party as a whole certainly stands for an economic system based on private ownership of industry, in contrast to the position of the principal opposition party. Its foreign policy, though with occasional wavering in the ranks, has remained fixed on the alliance with the United States—again, in direct contradiction to the JSP. Its platform has been to modify occupation-imposed reforms, as in education or police powers. Like any party intending to stay in power, it has favored full employment and prosperity—in the Japanese case, rapid industrial expansion—and it has given less emphasis to welfare policies than have the ruling parties or coalitions in other industrial democracies.[9]

For all its stability, however, the LDP is far from being a monolith, and it has been anything but innovative or activist in policymaking. Its membership covers a spectrum of political thought from far right to moderate liberal. Its electoral base has been slowly eroding, and its efforts to develop a mass membership have been unsuccessful. Its leadership is aging. Its apparent cohesion is badly flawed. And one of its noteworthy features is the virtual institutionalization of factions within the party.

FACTIONALISM. Faction and division are an old story in Japanese politics, probably tracing back to patterns of personal leadership in feudal times; the LDP is well established in this traditional mold.[10] The two conservative parties from which it was formed were themselves faction ridden. Once unified, the party immediately divided into eight rival factions, each headed by an aspiring prime minister or power broker. A decade later the distinguishable factions in the Diet numbered a dozen, and today there are nine. They are now an integral element in the party structure, and despite

9. Between 1954–55 and 1968–69, real national output grew more than fivefold while transfer payments as a share of Japan's GNP declined, whereas they rose sharply in all other principal countries of the Organisation for Economic Co-operation and Development. See OECD, *Economic Surveys: Japan* (Paris: OECD, 1972), pp. 50–51.

10. For a discussion of LDP factionalism, see Thayer, *How the Conservatives Rule Japan*, and Thayer in James W. Morley (ed.), *Forecast for Japan: Security in the 1970's* (Princeton University Press, 1972), chap. 3. See also Robert E. Ward, *Japan's Political System* (Prentice-Hall, 1967); and Scalapino and Masumi, *Parties and Politics*, chap. 3.

constant complaint and wringing of hands about the evils of factionalism by many of the party's business supporters, there is no discernible prospect for an end to factions in the LDP.

Factionalism reflects the ambitions of the stronger political personalities for the posts of party president–prime minister and for the other ministerial or party positions that confer prestige, power, and (usually) political longevity on those selected. It also reflects the policy differences and the varied special interest groups that are found within the wide political range covered by the parent party—though to a lesser extent, because a faction cannot afford to have too narrow a base of supporters or be committed to a restricted range of issues if its leader hopes to exert maximum influence or to reach the party presidency.

Each faction leader in the LDP maintains his personal fund-raising association independent of the party organization. Because every leader's present strength and future prospects depend on keeping the loyalty of his following, his financial needs are constant and large and his sources of contributions are of great moment to him. He must provide money for election campaigning, and he is expected to help his Diet supporters meet expenses between elections. He can expect some financial support on the basis of personal and local ties, some because business contributors will look on donations to him as a form of insurance in the event of his rise to power, and some because his factional strength already gives him a voice in intraparty negotiation and bargaining on policy questions.[11] If his principal sources were to dry up, his prospects and power would fade rapidly.

Financing problems act to limit the size of the factions. In practice, no politician is likely ever to obtain enough funds to sustain a majority following among LDP members. Thus, the election of a party president—who automatically becomes the prime minister—requires agreement among a coalition of faction leaders. Although the choice usually is made from among the leaders of the largest factions, this need not follow. At the present writing, the prime minister, Takeo Miki, is a party veteran who has been able to hold together a relatively small faction—forty-odd members— over many years. He was in position to be the compromise choice when neither of the two largest factions could assemble enough votes after the fall of former Prime Minister Kakuei Tanaka.

11. It is of interest that major business contributors usually choose to distribute their funds among the factions rather than to concentrate them on one or a few leaders. See Thayer, *How the Conservatives Rule Japan*, pp. 73–75. Just as the factions must be able to demonstrate a reasonably broad base of support, a large company is unlikely to consider its interests adequately covered unless it spreads its funds among at least the principal factions.

Factional rivalries are hardly unknown in political parties elsewhere in the democratic world. If factionalism in Japan is different, it is in the degree to which it provides the locus for so much of the substance of politics. Factional membership is so taken for granted that it is recorded in the Diet directory. Changes in the size of the factions are taken as indicative of political trends, and shifts in factional alliances are signals of impending reshuffles of ministerial positions, including that of prime minister. Decisions on the main political issues of the day must command the assent of a coalition of factions before they can be taken.

In addition to its chronic and imbedded factionalism, the LDP is heir to other divisions traditional to Japan's conservative parties. At the prefectural and local levels a lively antipathy between former Liberal and Democratic party adherents persists.[12] This split coincides to some extent with an even more basic division between politicians who have come up through the local party ranks and the former officials who have come into politics after a bureaucratic career and who have tended to dominate LDP policymaking by virtue of their past associations with the government ministries and their grasp of the complexities of governmental administration. Differences between the local party politicians and the former bureaucrats may be partly only a matter of bickering over political styles; but there is also the more fundamental distinction between men whose chief concern is with local problems and particular interests—such as small businesses, farmers, or veterans—and Diet members who are more accustomed to taking a national viewpoint on issues.

These internal differences inevitably tend to blur and qualify the LDP's political power. The restraints imposed by the party's divisions are most noticeable in the position of the prime minister, whose election to the party presidency automatically is translated by the LDP Diet majority into the prime ministership. He must have the support of several factions other than his own not only to be chosen, but also to be reelected after his three-year term of office. Usually he is unable either to exercise strong leadership or to initiate long-range change in policy. Much of his energy and political skill must go to maintaining a balance among the principal factions, which means that he is required to choose his cabinet ministers as much for purposes of factional harmony as for ability. As the head of a faction uneasily and often temporarily aligned with other powerful factional leaders, he is not likely to be a man of action, even if he is temperamentally so inclined, for any important policy change will threaten the intraparty balance. Most

12. For a firsthand study of a Japanese election campaign, see Gerald L. Curtis, *Election Campaigning Japanese Style* (Columbia University Press, 1971), chap. 1.

LDP leaders, understandably, have been prudent public figures, careful that their ties with party rivals not be unduly strained by too high a personal profile.

A well-remembered prime minister, Nobushuke Kishi, departed from this standard of cautious behavior during his term in 1957–60. He first proposed a strengthening of national police powers to cope with labor and political violence; when this prompted widespread protests, his factional rivals promptly denounced his high-handedness and forced him to abandon the legislation. Then in 1960 he ended a raucous and sometimes violent Diet row with the socialists by insisting on a vote to ratify the U.S.–Japan mutual security treaty. This action and its aftermath of disorders made his party position untenable and ended his career as a national political leader. Ironically, the renegotiated treaty gave Japan the very concessions that had been sought for eight years and involved no new obligations, but diplomatic success was not enough to offset the prime minister's vulnerability to his party opponents.[13] Kishi's successor, Hayato Ikeda, made a low political posture his hallmark. Ikeda summarized a variety of economic policy proposals in his catchy and useful slogan "double national income," continued the economic policies of the past, and went on to be a noncontroversial and competent party chief until illness caused his resignation. Eisaku Sato, who succeeded Ikeda, was the very model of political caution; and his tenure of four terms as party president, and thereby prime minister, set a record.

The troubles of Kakuei Tanaka, Sato's successor, may also prove the rule. A successful businessman, he entered politics early and became a faithful worker in the party ranks. Lacking the customary bureaucratic and university background, not entirely trusted by big business, and relatively young, Tanaka took office not only as a new, charismatic kind of prime minister but also as a politician with a long-range vision of Japan's future, spelled out in some detail in a best-selling book titled *Building a New Japan*. Although his emphasis on the need to turn governmental attention to the questions of urbanization and environmental pollution surely reflected a main current of public concern in Japan, and in spite of the unprecedented popularity he gained initially, Tanaka saw his position erode quickly and his reputation as a strong man become a principal count against him. Far from rallying around a beleaguered party leader, other factional leaders (including some who had made his election possible) responded by

13. See Martin E. Weinstein, "Strategic Thought and the U.S.–Japan Alliance," in Morley (ed.), *Forecast for Japan*, pp. 67–68; and Scalapino and Masumi, *Parties and Politics*, chap. 5.

leaving his administration in preparation for his expected downfall—which came even before the next scheduled party election in the wake of an exposé of his personal and political finances.

POLICY AND POLICY PROCEDURE. The LDP is not so constructed as to allow it much capacity for innovation and decisionmaking. It is even less of a mass national organization than most Western political parties, and its electorate is less than representative of this heavily urbanized country. Diet members owe primary allegiance to their faction leaders. Cabinet ministers are shuffled frequently and seldom remain in power long enough to make a major imprint on policy. The party's record, unsurprisingly, is quite barren of notable departures in policy.

At its founding, the party took on two basic missions requiring specific legislative action: to revise the occupation-dictated constitution and to modify the occupation's educational reforms.[14] Neither has been accomplished, and constitutional revision has been permanently shelved. The party's mandate has in practice fallen well short of the support needed to override its opponents—including elements within the LDP—on these controversial matters.

In foreign policy, the LDP has been able to maintain its consensus on Japan's alliance with the United States in the face of consistent and sometimes violent opposition from the socialist and communist parties, most of the trade unions, and many of the country's intellectuals. After the near debacle caused by the security treaty revision in 1960 foreign policy initiatives were approached warily for fear of disrupting the party's fragile unity.[15] Thus, on so crucial a question as relations with Communist China, the party's internal divisions, going beyond factionalism, effectively foreclosed action until a decision was forced on Tokyo by the U.S. approach to Peking in 1972.[16]

Domestic economic policy has been similarly marked by caution and attachment to precedent. The much disliked antimonopoly statute imposed

14. See supplementary material in the Japanese version of Fukui, *Party in Power* (*Jiyu Minshutō to seisaku kettei* [The Liberal Democratic Pary and Policy-making] [Tokyo: Fukumura Shuppan, 1971], p. 242). We are indebted to Hideo Sato for this information. Other missions were the renovation of the political and bureaucratic system, the pursuit of peace diplomacy, the achievement of economic independence, and the establishment of a welfare society.

15. Among discussions of foreign policy decisionmaking in Japan, see Frank C. Langdon, *Japan's Foreign Policy* (Vancouver: University of British Columbia Press, 1973); Donald C. Hellmann, *Japanese Foreign Policy and Domestic Politics* (University of California Press, 1969); and Haruhiro Fukui, "Foreign Policy Making in Japan" (paper presented to the Association of Asian Studies, April 1974; processed).

16. Fukui, *Party in Power*, chap. 9; idem, "Foreign Policy Making in Japan."

by the occupation authorities[17] was weakened by amendment and administrative intervention after independence, but it was not repealed and current discussion is about strengthening it.[18]

The liberalization of imports and capital transactions as a consequence of international pressure was accomplished so gradually as to receive little approbation abroad—but also, as intended, only a manageable amount of opposition at home. Decisions to revalue the yen in 1971 and 1973 were made only after costly and agonized delay. Bold proposals—for example, the draft legislation from the Ministry of International Trade and Industry in 1962 to promote mergers and otherwise to foster specially designated industries—failed to achieve the necessary consensus and was dropped. And a prime minister's assent, as former President Richard Nixon learned during the rancorous 1969–71 dispute over the textile trade, does not ensure that the government will or can act to overrule the views of a moderately large domestic interest group.

The LDP's principal and warranted claim to accomplishment is that it presided over a period of unbroken economic growth from its establishment in 1956 through 1973. And the conclusion reached by Ackley and Ishi—that the "policy of all-out expansion in booms, followed by restraint only when it became clear that it was needed, was probably close to optimal"[19] in terms of the growth objective—is surely right. This was a matter, however, that in the main could be left to the technocrats in the Ministry of Finance, acting in response to well-marked, almost traditional guidelines —for example, the state of the balance of payments, the occupation's doctrinal legacy of a balanced budget, and the obviously popular attachment to an annual tax reduction.[20]

Had the party leadership been able to take a central role in economic policy, it is doubtful whether Japanese budgets could have been kept under control as they have been. Neither the prime minister's office nor the party leaders in the Diet decide in advance on the broad policy objectives and priorities to be expressed in the budget; these are left essentially to the Ministry of Finance. The party does issue a statement of Basic Policy for Budget Compilation that purports to establish objectives and priorities, but

17. Former Prime Minister Yoshida referred to it as one of the shackles impeding economic recovery. See *The Yoshida Memoirs*, p. 41.
18. See Chapter 7 in this volume. See also Masao Baba, "Industrial Concentration in Japan: The Economic Background to the Revision of the Anti-Monopoly Law" (paper prepared for the Japan–U.S. Assembly, American Enterprise Institute for Public Policy Research, April 7–8, 1975; processed).
19. Chapter 3.
20. For details of the last point, see Chapter 5.

it is vague in its terminology and all-inclusive in its coverage. In addition, it is made public just before the Ministry of Finance unveils its own draft, the particulars of which have been thoroughly negotiated over several months with the spending ministries and cannot be greatly changed thereafter.

During the budgetary process individual Diet members or groups of members exert pressure on behalf of items of interest to their constituencies, but only within a framework fixed by the ministry's budget experts. At the stage of final appeals, the LDP leaders negotiate with the ministry over issues of special party concern. Typically, these are directly connected with important interest groups—war-related pensions, health insurance subsidies promoted by the Japan Medical Association, public works, budget outlays for price supports for rice, and the like—and the adjustments are invariably upward.[21]

BIG BUSINESS AND THE LDP. These subjects of prime interest to the LDP obviously reflect the preoccupations of politicians who are concerned above all with staying in power. A major flaw in the proposition that the LDP is uniquely the party of Japan's big business is that it also must be the party of many other interest groups whose votes are necessary to winning elections. The LDP's political longevity, as well as some of its weaknesses, are the result of its ability to appeal successfully to this variety of interests—including but certainly not ending with big business.

The attachment of big business to the LDP follows as a matter of course from the socialist party's ideological stand against private ownership of the major industries. The party in turn finds its links to big business important, even indispensable. The affinity between the two is evident in political financing, in LDP membership, and in procedures designed to facilitate communication between spokesmen for big business and senior LDP politicians.

There can be no argument about the importance of the financial aid from business to the LDP. Japanese elections, and Japanese politics more generally, have become exceedingly costly activities. As of mid-1974, an LDP candidate for a national constituency seat in the House of Councillors could expect to spend from $1 million to $3 million or even more to win a place in a body that has quite limited powers.[22] Typically, a Diet member must get continuing donations to finance his office staff and the expenses of

21. The details of this discussion have been drawn from an exhaustive study of the Japanese budgetary process by John C. Campbell, "Contemporary Japanese Budget Politics" (Ph.D. dissertation, University of Michigan, 1973).

22. *Asahi Evening News*, July 10, 1974. The 250 seats in the House of Councillors are elected from prefectural districts (150) and the nation at large (100).

his local organization between elections; these expenses currently run to
¥1.5 million (about $5,000) a month for a relatively junior member of the
lower house.[23] Thus, the LDP politician generally looks to business—directly
as well as through his faction leader and the party—first, for the funds needed
to get elected and, second, for funds to conduct his political activities thereafter.

Because contributions flow through a variety of channels to the LDP, to
faction leaders, and to individual Diet members, there is no reliable figure
for total political spending in Japan. Since 1961, however, big business has
sought to direct its financing for the LDP organization proper through the
Kokumin Kyōkai, or People's Association.[24] This is not organizationally a
party agency, and its membership is open to the population at large. Although it has a propaganda mission, its central purpose has been to collect
funds for the LDP. Its principal sources have been large corporations and
trade associations, which have had the amounts of their contributions assigned to them by the officials of the Keidanren, or Federation of Business
Organizations.[25] In 1973, which was not an election year, the Kokumin
Kyōkai is reported to have raised nearly ¥20 billion, or $70 million, for
the LDP, a sum quite apart from donations by business to the LDP factions and to individual politicians.[26]

Businessmen are less conspicuous in the party's Diet membership than
in its financing. About half of the LDP membership of the House of Representatives is more or less equally divided between former career public
servants and former local politicians, but former businessmen—who may
range from a retail store owner to an executive of a major company—come
next in number, with somewhat more than 20 percent of the total, followed
by journalists and, well back, by lawyers.[27] At the senior levels of the LDP,
in the ministerial posts and the party's policymaking bodies, former bureaucrats are dominant, as befits their presumed greater familiarity with
the administrative process and with sources of information on national
issues. A prime minister with even a distant business background, such as

23. Interview, LDP Diet member Tetsuo Kondō, August 1974.

24. Fukui, *Party in Power*, pp. 146–48.

25. After the conspicuously costly upper house election in July 1974, the newly
installed Keidanren president, Toshio Dokō, announced that the organization would
no longer play this role for the LDP.

26. *Mainichi* (English edition), Aug. 18, 1974.

27. Fukui, *Party in Power*, p. 58; Yanaga, *Big Business in Japanese Politics*, pp.
27–28; Gerald Curtis, "Big Business and Political Influence in Japan," in Ezra F.
Vogel (ed.), *Modern Japanese Organization and Decision Making* (University of
California Press, 1975).

Kakuei Tanaka, was a distinct novelty, and it has been unusual to find other than former government officials at the head of such key ministries as Finance, International Trade and Industry, or Foreign Affairs. But a senior civil servant who opts for a political career is likely both to have had a long working acquaintance with business groups and to be dependent on business financing for his electoral progress. He may have a more sophisticated understanding of the political and governmental process than his former businessman colleague, but by ideology and interest he will normally be similarly minded toward the private business community.

One of Japan's inheritances from the American occupation is the institution of public committees and councils in an advisory capacity to the government. Businessmen customarily dominate the membership in these bodies. But big business has other and more direct communications channels to the LDP leadership, notably through the clubs that the prime minister and other top politicians have traditionally used to maintain contact with business groups. The clubs meet more or less regularly—Itsukakai, or "fifth-day-of-the-month club," is a well-known example—often in an informal setting such as a geisha restaurant. In these meetings senior businessmen are afforded opportunities to press their views on leading politicians, including the prime minister.[28] Such opportunities obviously are not available to other private citizens.

Furthermore, big business in Japan is elaborately organized to express its views on public policies. There is the Keidanren, which includes in its membership both trade or industry associations and the country's major corporations; it is usually considered to be the preeminent spokesman for big business. Keizai Dōyūkai, the Committee for Economic Development, was founded originally to give younger businessmen a forum for considering as individuals the problems of Japan's economic reconstruction. Over the years it has acquired the reputation for having a somewhat more progressive outlook than Keidanren, although the overlap of senior members between the two organizations tends to blur distinctions. Nikkeiren is the coordinator of big business' labor policies. The Japan Chamber of Commerce, or Nissho, is the oldest and most inclusive of the organized business groups, for it speaks for the interests of small- and medium-size business to a degree that the others do not. All of these bodies have professional staffs to conduct research, to organize a seemingly incessant round of conferences, many of them international in character, and to draft business

28. For the most extensive discussion in English of the club phenomenon, see Curtis, "Big Business and Political Influence," pp. 23–32.

positions and recommendations on subjects of current or long-range interest. Separately, they constitute a set of pressure groups analogous to those in Western countries. Together, they can claim to represent the majority of Japan's business community, but most especially big business.

The leading members of these organizations are sometimes considered to make up a special pressure group that wields extraordinary political power. This is the so-called *zaikai*—or, as the term is usually construed, an elite set of business leaders whose views are believed by some observers to be ultimately powerful in Japanese political life.[29]

A full judgment about the influence of big business on government will be deferred to a later section, since business manifestly is concerned with the numerous administrative decisions that have to be left to career civil service officials, as well as with policymaking at high political levels. That the influence is there is hardly in question, however. As a business-supported political party brought into being partly in response to pressure from big business groups, the LDP would be unlikely to take positions known to be unanimously and strongly opposed by the four major business organizations. Business views about, say, tax or competition policies or about foreign investment in Japan must necessarily weigh heavily with a conservative party in power. On any truly fundamental issue of domestic or foreign policy, business can expect to be consulted and listened to.

These statements are valid only to a point, after which the inescapable qualifications begin. The LDP had scarcely been established, with the approbation and at the instance of big business, when then Prime Minister Ichiro Hatoyama proceeded with peace negotiations with the Soviet Union despite opposition by the four major business organizations and outright demands from them that he resign.[30] Curtis observes that the *zaikai* not only was unable to force Hatoyama's resignation but also was unable to designate his successor when he retired, just as later it could not prevent Hideo Sato from running against Prime Minister Hayato Ikeda or Kakuei Tanaka from winning the party presidency in 1972 over its preferred can-

29. See Yanaga, *Big Business in Japanese Politics*, pp. 28–29. Curtis quotes a Japanese commentator as saying that "the greatest, most powerful pressure group is the *zaikai*, whose desires it is taboo for the political world and the bureaucracy to reject" ("Big Business and Political Influence," p. 7). A study group, the Sangyō Mondai Kenkyūkai (Council on Industrial Policy), or Sanken, formed in 1966 by a group of some twenty Keidanren and Keizai Dōyūkai members of undoubted *zaikai* stature, has been credited with having special influence. Hidetoshi Katō, "Sanken: A Power above Government," in *Shūkan Asahi* [Asahi Weekly], Nov. 28, 1969, trans. in *The Japan Interpreter*, vol. 7 (Winter 1971), pp. 36–42.

30. Hellmann, *Japanese Foreign Policy and Domestic Politics*, pp. 126–29.

didate, then Foreign Minister Takeo Fukuda.[31] And in what was perhaps the one great macroeconomic policy debate of the postwar period, over whether the Bank of Japan or the Ministry of Finance would control monetary policy, the views of big business and big banking in favor of the Bank of Japan did not carry the day.[32]

In all these instances big business was more or less unified on its political objectives. It is not unusual, of course, to find divisions within the business community. Thus, Japanese rearmament has long had an active proponent in the Keidanren's Defense Production Committee, which, however, has had no more than the most cautious support from its parent body and the outspoken opposition of the Keizai Dōyūkai.[33] Over the years the debate on China policy saw big business split between pro-Taiwan and pro-Peking groups, a split that had its counterpart within the senior ranks of the LDP as well. Conflicts of business interest are built into many issues. Industries subject to import competition could not be expected to take as relaxed a view of Japan's trade liberalization as those sectors heavily dependent on exports. The synthetic fiber industry's bitter struggle against the American demand for export restraints from 1969 to 1971 was looked on unenthusiastically by the big business organizations, which are always sensitive to the temper of Japan's relations with the United States.[34]

As for the connection between business contributions to the LDP and political influence, it either must exist or Japanese big business has been operating under an extraordinary delusion over the past two decades. Still, the argument has limits. For one thing, a threat to refuse essential campaign funds because the LDP did not faithfully follow business recommendations would have small credibility in the absence of an alternative conservative party. Although a spate of complaints about wasteful political spending occurred in the aftermath of the 1974 upper house election, many businessmen apparently considered the idea of withholding financial help to be a dangerous course.[35] For another, political contributions from business go to the factional leaders as well as to the party proper thereby diffusing the impact of the money among the chronic contenders for power. And al-

31. See "Big Business and Political Influence," pp. 11–12.
32. See Frank C. Langdon, "Big Business Lobbying in Japan: The Case of Central Bank Reform," *American Political Science Review*, vol. 55 (September 1961), pp. 527–38.
33. Frank C. Langdon, "The Attitudes of the Business Community," in Morley (ed.), *Forecast for Japan*, pp. 122–24.
34. *Asahi Shinbun*, Oct. 1, 971.
35. *Asahi Evening News*, Aug. 23, 1974, where an unidentified Keidanren member was quoted as asking: "Are we going to leave the Prime Minister in the lurch?"

though the LDP has not been free of scandal and corruption, the standard of government under its rule seems to have been generally an honest one.

In the end, the problem with the attribution of any unique political influence to big business is that the LDP must rely as well on other interest groups. The argument that the LDP is the party of big business in Japan, although valid enough, cannot be taken to mean that it is less the party of other interest groups, some of which indeed have, along with votes, points of view and economic demands contrary to the interests of big business.

AGRICULTURE, SMALL BUSINESS, AND OTHER INTEREST GROUPS. The LDP's base of electoral power is not Japan's great urban industrial-commercial centers but its small towns and farms. Historically, Japanese political parties sprang from the agrarian landowning families who dominated the political landscape. The core of conservative strength has continued to lie in rural and semirural Japan. An occupation-enforced land reform in 1946 that created a large number of new farmer-owners was profoundly in the interest of political conservatism. Most important, the electoral districts drawn then, when the agricultural population was swollen by an influx of demobilized soldiers, repatriates from the former colonies, and unemployed city dwellers (some 57 percent of the national working force was in agriculture in 1946–47), have been kept intact since. In a now urbanized Japan, this amounts to a huge gerrymander. Rural and small town districts account for more than 300 Diet seats out of a current total of 491. The number of voters per seat range from 400,000 in one electoral district of Osaka to 76,000 in a rural Hyogo Prefecture district. In the rural districts —in which the voting rate is significantly higher than in the big cities— the LDP has consistently held more than 60 percent of the popular vote, whereas its urban and metropolitan proportion has gradually slipped to less than 30 percent. Of the 271 LDP lower house Diet members elected in December 1972, 165, or 61 percent, represent rural or semirural districts[36] and only 10 percent the chief metropolitan centers—Tokyo, Nagoya, Osaka-Kobe, and Fukuoka. To this day, most of Japan's leading conservative politicians have their origins and constituencies in the rural prefectures. And the agricultural cooperatives and other agrarian groups are sources of political funds as well as organizations able to mobilize votes.

Because any serious voter disaffection in the countryside would pose a grave threat to the LDP, concern for the Japanese farmer—who today is most often only a part-time farmer—has been a continuing preoccupation

36. *Asahi Shinbun*, Dec. 12, 1972.

of conservative governments. Agriculture has been the most heavily protected of industries. Even the most modest liberalization of agricultural
imports has been the subject of prolonged and anguished debate, and even
now twenty farm products, including rice, wheat, meat, and dairy products,
remain under quantitative import controls. Domestic price supports for
major crops have been among the highest in the world, and consumer prices
have risen accordingly.[37] The Ministry of Agriculture and Forestry has
been getting approximately 10 to 12 percent of the national general account
budget year in and year out,[38] and in fiscal 1974 spent the equivalent of
$2.3 billion on farm price supports, principally for rice—a figure to be
compared with the $3.5 billion budgeted for national defense. With the
producer's price for rice having risen by more than 35 percent in 1974, the
fiscal 1975 budget calls for more than $3 billion in support for agricultural
prices.

The resources devoted to a subsidized agriculture have had their consequences, of course, in high food prices and restricted diets for Japanese
consumers. From the LDP's point of view, it has been an unavoidable
tradeoff. As long ago as 1961 the need for a new program for agriculture
was expressed in an agricultural act, which proposed to alter the basic
structure of Japanese farming by enlarging farms, adjusting output to changing consumption patterns, and raising labor productivity. In fact, the act's
injunction that farmers be assured a fair income has had priority over its
other provisions. Relative farm incomes were indeed raised, whereas structural reform has been slighted.[39] Because most farmers grow rice, agricultural policy has been centered on this crop. Rice subsidies have absorbed
as much as half of the total budget of the Ministry of Agriculture and Forestry, and in the face of falling consumption the existence of rice surpluses
has periodically been a costly embarrassment to the government. In short,
in agriculture the political system—far from exhibiting special capacities
for adapting economic activity to favor the high-growth sectors—has been

37. Thus, food prices led the steady inflation in consumer prices during the 1960s,
with the food index rising from 80.3 in 1960 (1963 = 100) to 150 in 1970, while the
nonfood index moved from 84.9 to 140.1 over the same period. OECD, *Main Economic Indicators*, various issues.
38. Kenzō Henmi, 'Structural Adjustment of Japanese Agriculture," Fifth Pacific
Trade and Development Conference (Tokyo: Japan Economic Research Center,
January 1973), pp. 8–10.
39. The budget for the "Development and Improvement of the Basic Structure of
Agriculture" actually fell as a proportion of the total agricultural budget after 1960.
Ibid., p. 10.

unable even to provide incentives for a shift of resources from rice growing
to those farm sectors such as livestock or dairy farming in which productivity gains promise to be greatest.[40]

Small business is the other broad interest group that inevitably com-
mends itself to most LDP politicians. For all the impressive expansion of
big business, the small enterprise sector has proved to be remarkably durable in Japan. During the years of high growth, from 1963 to 1969, enterprises employing fewer than thirty workers held their share of total nonagricultural employment at 50 percent; and in 1969, nearly 3.5 million
business establishments classified as sole proprietorships employed more
than 10 million persons.[41]

Although financial support from small-scale enterprises is of considerable importance to individual Diet members,[42] the political attractions of
small business lie even more in its voting power and in its potential volatility among the parties contending for power. Big business in the last analysis has no ready alternative to the LDP, whereas small business has traditionally had a place in the Japanese Socialist party,[43] and today it can and
apparently does shop around among all the parties, including even the
Japanese Communist party. The slow erosion of LDP voting strength in the
country as a whole makes it imperative that defections from this important
source of votes be kept to a minimum.

In Chapter 7 Caves and Uekusa discuss in some detail the disabilities
under which small business has labored in Japan. Whether the official prescriptions for treating the ills of small business have been altogether helpful or not, the government has been visibly active in legislating and appro-
priating on behalf of this sector. The 1974 white paper of the Small and
Medium Enterprises Agency,[44] a part of the Ministry of International Trade
and Industry, lists eighteen extant statutes aimed at fostering the well-being
of small firms. All these fall under an umbrella policy statement, the Fundamental Law for Small and Medium Enterprise, which asserts it to be the
government's policy to aid in rationalizing and modernizing small business

40. Yūjiro Hayami, "Rice Policy in Japan's Economic Development," *American Journal of Agricultural Economics*, vol. 54 (February 1972), p. 26 (Tokyo Center for Economic Research reprint, June 1972).

41. Bureau of Statistics, Office of the Prime Minister, *Japan Statistical Yearbook, 1970* (1971), pp. 88–89.

42. See Fukui, *Party in Power*, pp. 160–61; and Curtis, *Election Campaigning Japanese Style*, pp. 230–42.

43. Scalapino and Masumi, *Parties and Politics,* pp. 66–67.

44. Summarized in World Economic Information Services, *Economic Information File, Japan, 1974–75* (Tokyo, 1974), pp. 106–24.

and in protecting it from unfair treatment by large enterprises. There is a law to foster small enterprise cooperatives, another to promote managerial and technical improvement in small business, another to protect subcontractors against being victimized by prime contractors, and so on through the long list.

Within the swarm of public corporations found in Japan, seven are devoted to small business needs: the People's Finance Corporation (1949), the Small Business Finance Corporation (1953), the Bank for Commerce and Industrial Cooperatives (1955), the Small Business Credit Insurance Corporation (1958), the Small Business Investment Company (1963), the Small Business Promotion Corporation (1967), and the Environmental Sanitation Business Finance Corporation (1967). Over the years the combined lending of the Small Business Finance Corporation and the People's Finance Corporation, the two chief loan facilities for small business, has consistently exceeded by a wide margin the loans of the Japan Development Bank, which has been the principal public agency for domestic lending to large business (see Table 11-1).

This proliferation of legislation and agencies strikes a familiar chord for American observers, accustomed to similar accommodations to pressures from a large but not very coherent interest group. There being no easy or grand solution to the genuine economic problems of small business, a patchwork of assistance measures has been the natural response.

The impact of small business on Japanese politics tends to be diffused among the numerous Diet members who receive support from small local enterprises and political leaders whose home constituencies include a concentration of small firms in such industries as textiles and stainless steel tableware. But this influence can be important on specific issues. During

Table 11-1. *Fiscal Investment and Loan Program Expenditures in Japan, by Lending Agency, Fiscal Years 1966–73*[a]

Billions of yen

Lending agency	1966	1967	1968	1969	1970	1971	1972	1973
All agencies	1,412.7	1,817.4	2,252.3	2,643.2	3,209.6	3,945.3	4,910.7	6,444.6
People's Finance Corporation	127.9	185.9	195.0	233.5	284.4	372.1	412.7	418.9
Small Business Finance Corporation	106.0	132.2	169.9	221.0	256.1	345.5	354.4	394.6
Japan Development Bank	138.7	162.1	205.7	228.6	261.2	336.0	352.5	385.7
Other	1,040.1	1,337.2	1,681.7	1,960.1	2,407.9	2,890.7	3,791.1	5,245.4

Source: Bank of Japan, *Economic Statistics Annual, 1971*, p. 176; and *1973*, p. 184.

a. The Fiscal Loan and Investment Program in effect constitutes Japan's capital budget, separate from the general account budget. It includes allocations for the national railways, highways, public housing, and other public investments, as well as for the lending agencies listed here.

the textile trade dispute between the United States and Japan in 1969 the small textile firms helped to rally Diet support of the chemical fiber makers and the large textile fabric companies whose interests were principally engaged. According to a senior Ministry of Finance participant in the policy debate on yen revaluation in 1971, the opposition of Kakuei Tanaka, then MITI minister, was a result of pressures from his Niigata Prefecture electoral district, in which the tableware industry is centered.

During the mid-1950s a gifted organizer, Gisuke Aikawa, was able briefly to bring small enterprise into focus as a national political force. After two years of vigorous political agitation and electioneering, his federation of small and medium businesses, Chuseiren, succeeded over the opposition of big business (and big labor) in having enacted the Law on the Formation of Small and Medium Enterprise Organizations, which was intended to strengthen the bargaining position of small suppliers and subcontractors against big business.[45] But although Aikawa soon faded from the scene and organized small business failed to regain these heights of political power, the small enterprise organization remains, along with the agricultural cooperatives, one of the two economic interest groups accorded an honored place at the annual policy conference of the Liberal Democrats.

As in other democracies, more narrowly specialized interest groups are numerous and persistent.[46] Organized medicine has been active in exerting pressure for budgetary help for the deficit-ridden health insurance system; former landlords conducted a long campaign to get compensation for property taken during the postwar land reform; veterans and other persons with war-related claims have pressed for public relief; and hosts of craft and trade organizations have looked to Tokyo's politicians for special favors. The nationally organized groups have professional secretariats to document their demands and to direct the lobbying process.

All of this obviously dilutes and disperses the Japanese political process. The conservative party's many constituencies are sprawled across the country's economic and social landscape, their interests inevitably different from one another. And the divergent pressures they bring to bear on the ruling conservatives are given added significance because the political opposition is a more potent force in Japanese life than its nominal position would suggest.

45. Frank C. Langdon, "Organized Interests in Japan and Their Influence on Political Parties," *Pacific Affairs*, vol. 34 (1961), p. 277.

46. Fukuji Taguchi, "Pressure Groups in Japanese Politics," *The Developing Economies*, vol. 6 (December 1968), pp. 468–86; Thayer, *How the Conservatives Rule Japan*, chap. 8; Fukui, *Party in Power*, chaps. 6 and 7; Curtis, *Election Campaigning Japanese Style*, especially chap. 7.

The Political Opposition

Since its formation in 1955 the Liberal Democratic party has won six national elections for the lower house and has formed nineteen cabinets; it has never held fewer than 55 percent of the seats in the lower house, even without counting the usual scattering of independents who regularly vote with the Diet majority. The principal opposition parties—the Japanese Socialist party (JSP), the Democratic Socialist party (DSP), the Japanese Communist party (JCP), and the Kōmeito, or Clean Government party— reached a high-water mark in 1972 with a combined 41.5 percent of the seats. Because these four parties are united only in the narrow sense that all are formally opposed to the LDP, the picture of opposition futility and frustration is seemingly complete—all the more so if account is taken of the left-wing–right-wing divisions among the socialists, of the conspicuous failure of Komeito to maintain its early promise of becoming a dynamic political movement, and of the likelihood that the fastest-growing of the opposition parties, the communist, will peak still at a low percentage of the country's vote.

The appearance of an ineffectual opposition is not wholly misleading, but it requires qualification. In the popular vote the LDP's initial lopsided lower house majority—about 58 percent in its first contest as a merged party in 1958—had fallen to a minority of about 47 percent by 1972 (see Table 11-2). And in the 1974 upper house election the LDP's share in local constituency votes fell for the first time below 40 percent (see Table 11-3).

These indications of deterioration in the LDP's basic voting strength could not but enhance the impact and leverage of the other parties, notably the JSP, on policies and programs. Under Japan's electoral system, the LDP simply cannot afford continuing voter defections. Japan has 123 election districts, all but one of which chooses three to five members of the lower house; each voter casts his ballot for one candidate, and the candidates with the highest totals are the winners. The procedure of course puts a premium on limiting the number of candidates of each party in accordance with the solid party vote in the district.[47] It is not uncommon for the JSP, for example, to offer a single candidate in a district, in the reasonable expectation that he will win by gaining all of the socialist votes, whereas with two candidates dividing the socialist vote both would lose. The LDP, as the majority party, has always had the problem of restricting the number

47. Curtis, *Election Campaigning Japanese Style*, pp. 10–11.

Table 11-2. *Results of General Elections to the Lower House of the Japanese Diet, by Party, 1958–72*[a]

Year of election	Liberal Demo-cratic	Social-ist	Demo-cratic Social-ist[b]	Com-munist	Kō-meito[c]	Other	Inde-pen-dents
1958							
Seats held	287	166	...	1	...	1	12
	(61.5)	(35.5)		(0.2)		(0.2)	(2.6)
Votes won (thousands)	22,977	13,094	...	1,012	...	288	2,381
	(57.8)	(32.9)		(2.6)		(0.7)	(6.0)
1960							
Seats held	296	145	17	3	...	1	5
	(63.4)	(31.0)	(3.7)	(0.6)		(0.2)	(1.1)
Votes won (thousands)	22,740	10,887	3,464	1,157	...	142	1,119
	(57.56)	(27.56)	(8.77)	(2.93)		(0.35)	(2.83)
1963							
Seats held	283	144	23	5	...	0	12
	(60.6)	(30.8)	(4.9)	(1.1)		(0)	(2.6)
Votes won (thousands)	22,424	11,907	3,023	1,646	...	60	1,956
	(54.67)	(29.03)	(7.37)	(4.01)		(0.15)	(4.77)
1967							
Seats held	277	140	30	5	25	0	9
	(57.0)	(28.8)	(6.2)	(1.0)	(5.1)	(0)	(1.9)
Votes won (thousands)	22,448	12,826	3,404	2,191	2,472	101	2,554
	(48.80)	(27.89)	(7.40)	(4.76)	(5.38)	(0.22)	(5.55)
1969							
Seats held	288	90	31	14	47	0	16
	(59.2)	(18.5)	(6.4)	(2.9)	(9.7)	(0)	(3.3)
Votes won (thousands)	22,382	10,074	3,637	3,199	5,125	81	2,493
	(47.63)	(21.44)	(7.74)	(6.81)	(10.9)	(0.17)	(5.30)
1972							
Seats held	271	118	19	38	29	2	14
	(55.2)	(24.0)	(3.9)	(7.7)	(5.9)	(0.4)	(2.9)
Votes won (thousands)	24,563	11,479	3,661	5,479	4,437	143	2,646
	(46.85)	(21.90)	(6.98)	(10.49)	(8.46)	(0.27)	(5.05)

Source: *Asahi nenkan* [Asahi Yearbook], issues for 1959–74.

a. Figures in parentheses are percents of total.

b. The Democratic Socialist party was formed in 1960 by a dissident group from the Japan Socialist party.

c. Kōmeito, the political arm of the Sōka Gakkai, a Buddhist sect, first contested for the national constituency seats of the upper house in 1962, but did not enter candidates in the lower house election until 1967.

of party-endorsed candidates so as to get maximum electoral advantage from the conservative vote. But if the downward trend in the LDP's popular vote continues, even incumbent Diet members could find themselves in competition with one another for the available conservative votes; at this point losses would be inevitable, whether or not the districts concerned still had a conservative majority.

Thus, it was no accident that LDP Diet members were as vigorous in the 1974 public interrogations of business executives about allegations of hoarding and price gouging as were JSP representatives, for this was clearly a popular and potentially a vote-getting position that could not be left entirely for the opposition to exploit. More generally, decisions on all key national issues—as certainly was true of the revaluations of the yen in 1971 and 1973—must be considered in light of their likely effect on votes for the opposition.

At the national level, the socialists have been a good deal less than innovative or imaginative about presenting a domestic program competitive with the LDP's association with rapidly rising standards of living. They have chosen rather to devote what might be considered inordinate effort and energy to making an issue of the mutual security treaty with the United States and of questions related to it, to which the public response has only sporadically been other than apathetic. Locally, however, some of the progressive big city mayors and prefectural governors have shown quite notable initiative in pollution control and social welfare and in fostering citizen participation in government.[48] These developments, particularly as they take place in Tokyo Prefecture under an exceptionally popular governor, have had at least a limited influence on policies of the national government.

Given the Japanese social and political environment, moreover, the LDP's authority has never been anything like as absolute as its voting majority in the Diet. In the legislative process as elsewhere the habit of consensus is strong; to rule by majority on all questions and at all times simply would be unthinkable. Most legislative measures in fact are debated in orderly and civil fashion, and in their final form they usually represent compromises worked out to meet opposition objections.[49] Confrontation, when it occurs, is likely to be either on a foreign policy question or on edu-

48. Terry Edward MacDougall, "Local Politics and the Emergence of a Viable Political Opposition in Japan" (paper prepared for a seminar on Japan by 1980, New Haven, Conn., January 1973; processed).

49. Shigeo Misawa, "An Outline of the Policy-Making Process in Japan," in Hiroshi Itoh (ed. and trans.), *Japanese Politics: An Inside View* (Cornell University Press, 1973), pp. 33–34.

Table 11-3. *Results of General Elections to the Upper House of the Japanese Diet, by Party, 1956–74*[a]

Year of election	Party						
	LDP	Social-ist	Demo-cratic Social-ist[b]	Com-munist	Kō-meito[c]	Other	Inde-pen-dents
1956							
Seats held	61	49	...	2	...	6	9
	(48.0)	(38.6)		(1.6)		(4.7)	(7.1)
Votes won							
National constituencies	11,357	8,550	...	599	...	3,666	4,444
	(39.4)	(29.9)		(2.1)		(12.8)	(15.5)
Local constituencies	14,354	11,156	...	1,149	...	890	2,136
	(48.4)	(37.6)		(3.9)		(3.0)	(7.1)
1959							
Seats held	71	38	...	1	...	7	10
	(55.9)	(29.9)		(0.8)		(5.5)	(7.9)
Votes won							
National constituencies	12,121	7,795	...	552	...	3,136	5,817
	(41.2)	(26.5)		(1.9)		(10.6)	(19.8)
Local constituencies	15,667	10,265	...	999	...	886	2,311
	(52.0)	(34.1)		(3.3)		(2.9)	(7.7)
1962							
Seats held	69	37	4	3	9	2	3
	(54.3)	(29.2)	(3.2)	(2.2)	(7.3)	(3.8)	(2.2)
Votes won							
National constituencies	16,582	8,667	1,900	1,124	4,124	1,956	1,404
	(46.4)	(24.3)	(5.3)	(3.1)	(11.5)	(5.5)	(3.9)
Local constituencies	17,113	11,918	2,649	1,760	958	188	1,726
	(47.1)	(32.8)	(7.3)	(4.8)	(2.6)	(0.6)	(4.8)
1965							
Seats held	71	36	3	3	11	...	3
	(55.9)	(28.3)	(2.4)	(2.4)	(8.6)		(2.4)
Votes won							
National constituencies	17,583	8,730	2,124	1,652	5,098	298	1,701
	(47.2)	(23.4)	(5.9)	(4.4)	(13.7)	(0.8)	(4.6)
Local constituencies	16,651	12,347	2,304	1,609	1,911	186	1,665
	(44.2)	(32.8)	(6.1)	(6.9)	(5.1)	(0.5)	(4.4)
1968							
Seats held	69	28	7	4	13	...	5
	(54.7)	(22.2)	(5.6)	(3.2)	(10.3)		(4.0)
Votes won							
National constituencies	20,120	8,542	2,579	2,147	6,657	158	2,872
	(46.7)	(19.8)	(6.0)	(5.0)	(15.4)	(0.4)	(6.7)
Local constituencies	19,406	12,618	3,010	3,577	2,633	107	1,910
	(44.9)	(29.2)	(6.9)	(8.3)	(6.1)	(0.2)	(4.4)

Table 11-3 (*continued*)

Year of election	LDP	Social-ist	Demo-cratic Social-ist[b]	Com-munist	Kō-meito[c]	Other	Inde-pen-dents
				Party			
1971							
Seats held	62	39	6	6	10	...	2
	(49.6)	(31.2)	(4.8)	(4.8)	(8.0)		(1.6)
Votes won							
National constituencies	17,759	8,494	2,442	3,219	5,626	48	2,343
	(44.4)	(21.3)	(6.1)	(8.1)	(14.1)	(0.1)	(5.9)
Local constituencies	17,727	12,598	1,920	4,879	1,392	75	1,741
	(43.9)	(31.2)	(4.8)	(12.1)	(3.5)	(0.2)	(4.3)
1974							
Seats held	62	28	5	13	14	8	...
	(49.6)	(21.5)	(3.8)	(10)	(10.7)	(5.5)	
Votes won							
National constituencies	23,314	7,983	3,112	4,927	6,356	6,889	...
	(44.3)	(15.1)	(5.9)	(9.3)	(12.1)	(13.0)	
Local constituencies	21,115	13,892	2,353	6,425	6,727	2,941	...
	(39.5)	(25.9)	(4.4)	(12.0)	(12.6)	(5.5)	

Source: *Asahi nenkan*, issues for 1957–75.

a. Figures in parentheses are percents of total.

b. The Democratic Socialist party was formed in 1960 by a dissident group from the Japan Socialist party.

c. Kōmeito, the political arm of the Sōka Gakkai, a Buddhist sect, first contested for the national constituency seats of the upper house in 1962, but did not enter candidates in the lower house election until 1967.

cation: the former, because of the socialist attachment to the aim of a neutralist Japan; the latter, because of the fear—not wholly unfounded—that the LDP might attempt to reduce the power of the leftist teachers' organization. On other legislation, including most economic legislation, the socialist members of the Diet typically and amicably help the Liberal Democrats to shape the final statutes.

Finally, the political opposition can count on the trade unions, consumer groups, intellectuals, and the press to aid in checking any possible tendencies toward the exercise of unbridled political power. In particular, the role of the national press and other media in publicizing—and generating —debate and controversy cannot be underestimated. In Japan's media-saturated society, in which some 40 million newspapers are circulated daily (as of October 1973) and 99 percent of the households have television sets, few adult citizens can escape being exposed, in some measure at least, to political issues. The usual criticism of the press as a public watchdog is that the prevailing system of reporters' clubs in the government agencies and assignment of reporters to major politicians amounts to reliance on handouts and personal favors rather than on independent newsgathering.[50] But for all that, the coverage of Diet debate (the more raucous the arguments the better the coverage) and of the factions and their internecine struggles, as well as the incessant editorial preaching at the politicians, makes the press a vital part of the political scene.[51] Japanese cabinet meetings are said to begin with an exchange on press comments, and anyone who has dealt with officials and politicians in Japan will recognize that sensitivity to editorial criticism and press treatment is probably as acute and as inhibiting as it is in any other democracy.

Politics and Bureaucracy

Briefly summarized, the Japanese political scene is pluralist, competitive, and subject to inherent and effective checks and balances. In essentials, Japanese politics do not differ from politics in other democracies. A complex of pressures and interests and motivations operates constantly, and its results are predictable only in very general ways. A plausible argument can be made that, given the alternatives, the hegemony of the political conservatives has been good for economic growth. But there is little else about the Japanese political system that can be cited as having a peculiar and positive bearing on the country's economic success.

Governing, however, is more than a matter of what politicians do or fail to do. In Japan, as in other cabinet government systems (and perhaps more than in most), the career civil service, or bureaucracy, holds substantial responsibilities and authority. Cabinet ministers come and go with great frequency. Senior civil servants—administrative vice ministers and the directors of bureaus, with long experience and technical expertise—often can be the initiators as well as the executors of policy. As executors, moreover, their freedom to interpret or manipulate regulations has in theory given even lower-ranking members of the bureaucracy the power to improve the welfare or damage the interests of the private sector—or, for that mat-

50. Don Oberdorfer discusses this in relation to the failure of the daily press to expose former Prime Minister Tanaka's financial dealings (*Washington Post*, Jan. 4, 1975). Richard Halloran develops the general theme in detail (*Images and Realities*, chap. 7).

51. "Although the national press professes a strict neutrality with regard to parties, its general thrust has been against the party in power." Herbert Passin, "Intellectuals in the Decision-Making Process," in Vogel (ed.), *Modern Japanese Organization and Decision Making*, p. 260.

ter, of Diet members. The bureaucracy is also more truly an elite group in educational background and attitude than either the politicians or business leaders. Its role in Japan's economic life must now be considered in greater detail.

Bureaucratic Governance

One heading in an *Economist* survey of Japan is "The Most Intelligent Bureaucracy."[52] Because it was applied to the staff of one of the less influential economic affairs agencies, it could have been taken to suggest either that Japan was so blessed with excellent officials as to be able to assign the best of them to tasks of only modest importance or that at the time of the survey Japanese bureaucratic talent was being unaccountably misallocated. But as in many of the popularized Western discussions of Japan's economic success, the image presented to the reader was that of a bureaucratic superagency, manned by bureaucratic supermen and guiding Japan with consummate skill to ever higher levels of gross national product.[53] Another *Economist* comment was that "a word from the powerful Ministry of International Trade and Industry can redirect exports, lift import barriers, or establish new industries without reference to legislation or sanctions";[54] numerous like statements attributing exceptional authority to the civil service can readily be assembled.

These kinds of judgments suffer from liabilities similar to those applicable to the view that Japan's political life can be explained virtually wholly by the interaction between big business and conservative politicians. It takes nothing real away from past and present Japanese civil servants to recognize that their powers and capacities have been and are limited in a number of ways. Their role in Japan's economy of course has been significant. But a closer look fails to find support for the notion that since the war the bureaucracy concerned with economic affairs has directed its efforts exclusively and always wisely to the objective of economic growth. The story of bureaucratic intervention in Japan's economic life is more complicated and its lessons more ambiguous.

It is true that the career officials in such key economic ministries as Finance and International Trade and Industry are selected through a fairly

52. Macrae, "The Risen Sun," p. xxiii.
53. For an academician's view along the same lines, see Ezra F. Vogel, "The Social Base of Japan's Postwar Economic Growth," in *United States International Economic Policy in an Interdependent World*, vol. 2 (Government Printing Office, 1971), p. 129.
54. "Enter the Third Man," Sept. 29, 1973, pp. 15–16.

rigorous examination procedure and that a great majority are graduates of
the most prestigious and highly selective universities, led by Tokyo University. (The ties between fellow university graduates and especially university
classmates are generally believed also to be a signal factor promoting cohesion and cooperation within the official establishment and between the
establishment and other elements in Japanese society.) As in Europe, officials in Japan receive from the public and even from politicians a degree of
deference that is not usually accorded civil servants in the United States.
In a cabinet government, with ministers regularly moving in and out, these
officials by custom and necessity exercise substantial responsibility for forming and carrying out national policies.

The bureaucracy has also exercised wide administrative powers. As the
occupation ended, all foreign transactions were subject in principle—and
largely in practice as well—to regulation through import quotas and foreign exchange controls. These were gradually liberalized, but to this day
capital movements, inward and outward, remain under governmental controls. For a few private industries, special laws have allowed government
ministries directly to guide and determine investment and expansion plans.
In both petroleum refining and shipbuilding, for example, additions to
capacity have long been subject to specific official approval. Similarly, the
merchant fleet has been expanded under detailed governmental plans and
programs. Other industries have been the objects of temporary legislation
giving the government powers to rationalize production and structural arrangements. More generally, the economic affairs ministries (or sections of
these ministries) were given responsibility for guiding individual industries
in desired directions. The responsible agencies, *genkyoku*, not only possessed whatever legal authority might exist for day-to-day administrative
decisions but also could resort to the practice of administrative guidance,
under which an official or an agency, without having specific legal authority
to do so, might direct or induce private persons to take or refrain from
certain actions—such as, for example, buying a domestically produced
rather than an imported machine. This practice may not be unique to
Japan, but it has perhaps been a more widely accepted feature of governmental administration in that country than in other democracies.[55]

55. The first major challenge to administrative guidance arose in 1974 when the
Japan Petroleum Association and most of its member companies were indicted for
price fixing and other illegal acts allegedly taken in response to MITI direction. The
ministry did not deny having had a role, but instead defended administrative guidance
as justified by MITI's statutory mandate to promote economic development. *Asahi
Evening News*, April 16, 1974; and United States–Japan Trade Council, *Council
Report*, no. 45 (July 8, 1974).

In these circumstances it is not surprising that the bureaucracy and the private economic sector came to develop close ties. For example, the Heavy Industries Bureau of the MITI, as the *genkyoku* for iron and steel, machinery, and so on, has been intimately involved with the fortunes of these industries, as has the Ministry of Transport with shipping and shipbuilding, the Ministry of Finance with the banks, and so on. Systematic exchanges of information between officials and representatives of the particular industries have been greatly facilitated by the elaborate formal structure of the advisory councils, *shingikai*, inherited from the American occupation; since the ministries select the councils and serve as their secretariats, the councils are heavily influenced by the bureaucracy.[56] To some observers, the ultimate bureaucracy-industry link is found in the process of *amakudari* (literally, "descending from heaven"), the movement of retired officials to jobs in business, often to companies with which they or at least their ministries have had working relations.[57] This mobility from government to industry, which rarely works in reverse, is promoted by early retirement and low pensions for civil servants. It nourishes, of course, the supposition that working bureaucrats normally will so conduct themselves as to enhance their prospects for remunerative private employment, and that once retired to industry they will maintain and reinforce the connections between business and government.

Finally, and on a more abstract note, Japan's economic affairs bureaucracy undoubtedly shared fully in the broad consensus that after the occupation saw economic or industrial growth as the road to national revival and independence. Some of those who were senior officials in the 1950s and 1960s recall the period of rapid economic recovery and expansion as a

56. Kazuo Nukazawa, "Government-Business Relations in Japan" (Keidanren, 1971; processed). Toshio Shishido, a former official himself, comments: "These . . . councils are little more than window-dressing for the public. They initiate no recommendations. . . . No council would venture to change or throw out any proposal submitted to it [by officials]." "The Framework of Decision-Making in Japanese Economic Policies," in Allen Taylor (ed.), *Perspectives on U.S.–Japan Economic Relations* (Ballinger, 1973), p. 200.

57. "This connection is the lever by which the government operates its so far uniquely successful powers of guidance over the economy." Brian Beedham, "A Special Strength: A Survey of Japan," *The Economist,* March 31, 1973, supplement, p. 23. The practice of moving from government to industry on retirement is hardly unique to Japan, of course. In the United States the employment of retired military officers by defense contractors has been a matter of congressional concern. A Defense Department survey conducted in 1969 at the request of Wisconsin Senator William Proxmire showed more than 2,000 retired colonels or navy captains or higher ranks employed by the 100 largest defense contractors. Adam Yarmolinsky, *The Military Establishment: Its Impacts on American Society* (Harper and Row, 1971), pp. 60–68.

time when bureaucratic morale and sense of mission were exceptionally high. Not only was there scope for civil servants to act but the results of their endeavors were apparent and certainly satisfying and self-justifying.

All this granted, limitations on the scope and effectiveness of the bureaucracy are also evident. A first and major point is that responsibility and power among the Japanese operating agencies is by no means thoroughly centralized or easily coordinated.

Bureaucratic Sectionalism

The focus of much of the comment on economic direction and controls in Japan is on the Ministry of Finance and the MITI. Finance is the budget-making agency, it has extensive powers over macroeconomic policy, and it is the coordinating ministry for those other agencies with economic responsibility. It shares with the MITI numerous responsibilities for microeconomic policy. Many of the major instruments of economic decision-making are lodged, in part or whole, in the two ministries. When the large role of the government bureaucracy in Japan's economic life is cited, the far-reaching authority that was or still is delegated by law and custom to Finance and MITI is implicitly in mind.

Other ministries and agencies, however, are charged with administering economic policies. The sway of the Ministry of Transport extends from the merchant fleet and air and land transport to shipbuilding, which has been one of Japan's principal growth industries. The Ministry of Agriculture and Forestry has paramount responsibility for the farming sector and for the politically potent fisheries industry. The Ministries of Construction, Posts and Telecommunications, Health and Welfare, Education, and Labor all have economic portfolios. The Bank of Japan, the Economic Planning Agency, and the Fair Trade Commission are among the noncabinet economic agencies. A number of government lending institutions and a bewildering roster of public corporations have particular economic missions, some of them important, some less so.[58]

58. The larger ones administer the national railways, the telephone and telegraph services, and the tobacco and salt monopoly, but some sixty other areas are included, such as air transport, housing, highways, petroleum development, tourism, environment, space, livestock promotion, sugar beets, and regional development. See Japan Institute of International Affairs, *White Papers of Japan, 1970–71* (Tokyo: East West Publications, Inc., 1972), pp. 285–86, for the rather plaintive remarks of the Administrative Management Agency (in the Office of the Prime Minister) about the proliferation of public corporations and the problems they present: "Once government corporations are established they are apt to survive even after they have . . . lost [their] raison d'être. . . . [They often] are set up separately only for convenience to

To believe that all of these bodies could always work in close harmony toward single, well-understood objectives would be to believe in bureaucratic miracles. Chie Nakane's book[59] about the vertical structure of Japanese society has been found by some readers to go far toward explaining Japan. Whether Professor Nakane's explanation is adequate or not, the sense of "belonging" to a ministry—that is, to a vertically constructed organization—is observably a strong force for cohesion among groups in the bureaucracy, as is reputedly true also among workers in, say, the Matsushita electronics company. But loyalty, more or less fierce, to the Ministry of Agriculture or Construction is not conducive to the ready acceptance of guidance from the Ministry of Finance; rather, it leads to sectionalism of perhaps a more rigid kind than in other bureaucracies.[60]

Thus, coordination among agencies and ministries in Japan is not less difficult than it is elsewhere. Interagency rivalries, attempts at bureaucratic empire building, and diffusion of responsibility are at least as common as in the West. The need for clearances holds up action as in all governments.[61] The Ministry of Finance, with its mission of coordinating economic affairs, must call upon all of the skills that its elite officials are said to possess if it is to keep this complex and diffused system in any reasonable order.[62]

The dispersal of economic responsibility among agencies that are jealous of existing prerogatives and in many cases anxious to expand them tends to reflect competing claims and interests within the society as a whole. It means among other things that public resources as such have not typically

---

each competent ministry or pressure group, though their functions are closely related [to] each other. . . . [Some] budgets . . . have to be approved by the Diet, while . . . [others] are authorized by the competent ministers. . . . How to adjust . . . the public interest and the enterprise profitability in case of determination of the rate is a difficult problem."

59. *Japanese Society* (London: Weidenfeld and Nicolson, 1970).

60. "Partly as a result of sheer ambition for status and partly as a reflection of divergent interests within the society itself, there is intense rivalry and jealousy among the ruling agencies and their personnel. In competing for power, they tend to neutralize one another's authority." Leon Hollerman, *Japan's Dependence on the World Economy* (Princeton University Press, 1967), pp. 160–61.

61. Yanaga cites a document that required no fewer than fifty-one separate clearances before it could go to the relevant minister for approval. *Big Business in Japanese Politics*, p. 100.

62. The MOF is itself extremely careful to guard its prerogatives and has resisted all efforts by other agencies to encroach on its authority. Campbell concludes after his study of budgeting that the first objective of the ministry and its Budget Bureau has been to protect the MOF's status and autonomy; control on spending comes only second to bureaucratic interest. "Contemporary Japanese Budget Politics," chap. 4.

been concentrated on the putatively high-growth sectors of the economy. The general accounts budget—and for that matter the capital budget, that is, the Fiscal Investment and Loan Program (FILP)—have regularly been divided among a large number of claimants, with the actual distribution being heavily influenced by political pressures and by the tenacity and imaginativeness of the officials of the spending ministries and agencies.[63] The most successful demanders did not necessarily—or even often—represent the growth industries.

It is possible also to speculate whether the sheer volume of particular decisions left to the bureaucracy, especially during the years of full-scale foreign exchange and quantitative import controls, did not strain the capacities of officials to make best choices. The procedures governing imports of technology, for example, required intensive case-by-case screening until mid-1968.[64] During the period 1949–68 some 5,000 type A technology import agreements (those involving outlays of foreign exchange) were processed, all of them presumably calling for judgments as to their technical and economic merits and each subject to the joint approval of the Bank of Japan, the MITI, and, after 1956, the Science and Technology Agency.[65] In these matters, the guidelines had to be general in character, allowing room for good guesses as well as bad: that only good ones were made is not very plausible.

Considerations of this kind suggest a healthy skepticism toward assigning to Japan's civil service capabilities not visible in other bureaucracies. Most Japanese officials probably would agree, at least in regard to the staffs of agencies other than their own. But what about the policies of planning, guidance, assistance, and extensive intervention that were to some extent designed and to a preponderant extent applied by government officials during the decades when Japan made such extraordinary economic strides? Were the policies and their application a principal source of the country's

63. Campbell (ibid., chap. 3) documents various strategies employed by the spending ministries to maneuver the MOF into a position of being unable to reject their claims for additional funds.

64. Under liberalization measures in July 1968 and July 1972, contracts for technology imports with royalty payments not greater than $300,000 are automatically approved; others are automatically approved within one month of application unless the government determines during that period that they will "adversely affect" the Japanese economy. World Economic Information Services, *Economic Information File, Japan, 1974–75*, p. 102.

65. OECD, Committee for Invisible Transactions, *Liberalization of International Capital Movements: Japan* (Paris, 1967), pp. 56–58; OECD, *Review of National Science Policy: Japan* (Paris, 1967); "A White Paper on Science and Technology," in Japan Institute of International Affairs, *White Papers of Japan, 1969–70*, pp. 227–43.

growth, or did the broad sweep of the expansion make the policies seem more pertinent to the outcome than in fact they were? Without supposing that conclusive answers can be offered, it is of interest to look further at what did happen.

National Plans

As with many of the institutions and procedures in Japan's postwar economic policymaking, the elaboration of formal national economic plans had its origin in the American occupation. At the suggestion of the Supreme Commander, Allied Powers, an Economic Stabilization Board (ESB) was set up in 1946 with a planning mandate. In 1947 a memorandum was sent to Prime Minister Yoshida over General MacArthur's signature asking that the ESB be strengthened and that more effort be directed into overall economic planning.[66] By the next year the board had produced a "Draft Plan for Economic Rehabilitation, 1949–1953." Neither this nor a new plan that was offered in 1949 received cabinet approval, and a 1951 "Economic Self-Support Plan" was set aside as being invalid because the Korean War had radically changed Japan's economic situation and prospects. Their impact on economic recovery, which had proceeded more than satisfactorily anyway, lay if anywhere in their emphasis on the expansion of those industries considered critical to reconstruction: coal, steel, fertilizer, electric power, and shipbuilding. Nonetheless, the pattern of planning for a high level of industrialization had been set. After independence had been regained, the ESB was replaced by an Economic Council Board, which was to coordinate economic policy and formulate long-range plans.

In 1955 the Economic Council Board became the present Economic Planning Agency (EPA), which was created by statute as an agency in the prime minister's office; its director, although not a minister as such, was made a member of the cabinet. The EPA was specifically directed to draw up national plans for cabinet consideration and approval. These were to become the guidelines for government economic policy. The EPA, beginning with the 1955 "Five Year Plan for Economic Self-Support," has now prepared seven medium- or long-term plans. Each established a planned rate of real economic growth (with projections or targets for major variables) and proclaimed a set of qualitative economic goals to be attained

66. Aiichirō Fujiyama, *Keizai Kikakuchō nijū-nen no shōshi* [A Short Twenty-Year History of the Economic Planning Agency] (Economic Planning Agency, 1966). The sketch of planning history presented here is taken mainly from this work. We are indebted to Stephen Watt for a summary translation.

along the way. The projections in all of the plans since the 1965 "Medium-Term Economic Plan" have been based on an extensive use of econometric techniques.

Procedurally, the planning process depends mainly on the bureaucracy, despite an elaborate system of participation by representatives from the private sector. As a formal matter, the prime minister asks his Economic Council—an advisory committee of private citizens heavily weighted with business leaders—to prepare a new plan.[67] The council in turn is nominally responsible for guiding and directing the EPA staff in drawing up a document for submission to the cabinet, which in principle can revise or reject it.

Under the Economic Council, with thirty permanent members, fall a number of subcommittees made up of some two hundred distinguished persons from business, the universities, the press, and various organized private groups. The staff of the EPA and officials of the several ministries and agencies concerned act as the secretariat for the subcommittees and are responsible for providing documentation and technical materials and for the drafting of the plan itself. The private participants—for the most part busy individuals in their everyday capacities—have only a modest role in the substantive work of preparing the plan.[68] As for the cabinet, it has approved every draft national plan without modification. The Diet is excluded from the procedure, so that discussion looking to amendment or revision of the draft effectively ends when the Economic Council sends the plan to the prime minister.

Because cabinet approval makes the plan a guiding principle of economic policies during the period, economic planning would seem to confer on the EPA, as the principal agency involved, a large grant of authority over decisionmaking. In reality, it does nothing of the sort.

For one thing, the plans have no binding force on anyone.[69] Private investors may at times have responded to the announcement effect of the plans, but hardly according to the envisioned targets. After the plan to

67. On August 23, 1972, Prime Minister Tanaka wrote to Kazutaka Kikawada, chairman of the council, to ask: "What will be a long-term economic plan to seek the fulfillment of national welfare and the promotion of international collaboration in this time of rapid change both at home and abroad?" Economic Planning Agency, *Basic Economic and Social Plan: Toward a Vigorous Welfare Society, 1973–1977* (1973), p. 131.

68. Isamu Miyazaki, *Keizai kikaku* [Economic Planning] (Tokyo: Chikuma-Shobō, 1971), pp. 104–06 (summary translation provided by Stephen Watt); Ryūtarō Komiya, "Economic Planning in Japan" (paper delivered before a conference on "Economic Planning, East and West," Bellagio, Italy, September–October, 1973; processed).

69. See Chapter 3 in this volume.

double national income was unveiled in December 1960, private plant and equipment investment in the next year alone almost reached the level projected for 1970. In the subsequent plan, adopted in 1965, the planners withheld their sectoral output estimates in an attempt to dampen the investment response,[70] but the volume of private investment, excluding residential construction, rose by more than one-third over the next two years, helping to set off a boom that continued through 1970. Apart from any incentive to investment deriving from the announcement of the plans, the projections for broad sectors—for example, agriculture, basic metals, miscellaneous manufactured products (by far the largest single category), transportation equipment (which includes two of Japan's major industries, shipbuilding and automobiles), services, and so on—can have offered at most only a very general guide to private decisionmaking.

As for the public sector, the volume of government capital formation is decided in the annual budgetary process, which is influenced only remotely, if at all, by the plan. Every plan, beginning with that for doubling national income in 1960, has emphasized the need for greater relative emphasis on expenditures for social overhead capital. The public-private capital formation ratio nonetheless was roughly the same in 1973 as in 1961: about one to three.[71]

Professor Tsunehiko Watanabe of Osaka University has suggested that the plans have been drafted to understate deliberately the growth of national income as a part of the management of fiscal policy.[72] As he reconstructs the procedure, the low growth rates, relative to actual performance, that were projected in the plans allowed the Ministry of Finance regularly to propose budgets that understated revenues. The normal and intended result was a budget surplus and a subsequent income tax reduction. Spending on public facilities and social services thus was systematically held down.

Whether there was ever so carefully designed a strategy is not certain, but a tendency toward underestimation undoubtedly does inhere in the planning process.[73] In the drafting of national plans, the MOF experts usually will take a bearish view of the growth outlook, because to do otherwise might unduly encourage the budget expectations of the spending min-

70. Saburō Ōkita, *The Experience of Economic Planning in Japan* (Tokyo: Japan Economic Research Center, April 1974), p. 18.

71. OECD, *Economic Surveys: Japan* (1974), statistical annex, table B, p. 70. See also Chapter 3 in this volume.

72. See his "National Planning and Economic Development," *Economics of Planning* (Norway), vol. 10 (1970), pp. 46–47.

73. For a discussion of the policy aim of limiting public sector growth, see Chapter 5.

istries. In the negotiation of an eventual compromise growth figure, this view will tend to find support from the EPA's economists (some of whom will have been assigned temporarily to the EPA from the MOF) because of their concern for the inflationary implications of high growth forecasts and because prudence in forecasting is more becoming than exuberance. In any case, once the figure has been decided upon, the pertinence of the medium- or long-term estimate of growth rate becomes more questionable. Each year the EPA sends its economic forecast to the cabinet just before, or simultaneously with, the MOF's draft budget. But the budget draft is founded on revenue projections made by the MOF's Research and Planning Division, which has to have its own estimated growth rate. Although the latter cannot be wildly and embarrassingly different from the official EPA figure, it need not be the same.[74]

The description of the qualitative goals offered in the plans usually has been in quite general terms—for instance, "another requirement will be active promotion of science and technology"[75]—and the plans must have had much the same effect on action as have similar policy statements in other countries. The Basic Economic and Social Plan for 1973–77 found price stabilization to be a "fundamentally crucial issue," after a decade of increases in the consumer price index that had averaged almost 6 percent a year. The prescriptions offered for stabilization were themselves unexceptionable: import liberalization (subject to special consideration for "hard-hit" domestic industries), more vigorous enforcement of policies on competition, structural improvements in sectors of low productivity, a review of policy on public utility rates, and possible emergency measures. An alert official in any operating ministry could, however, find in the text of the plan the words needed to justify a qualified or even a negative position on these broad policy proposals.

Industrial Policy

Planning of an only slightly less comprehensive kind goes on in another agency, the Ministry of International Trade and Industry. This highly activist bureaucracy has not hesitated to assume for itself the responsibility for devising a new industrial policy[76] to replace the one it claims to have created and applied in the 1950s and 1960s, and the scope of the MITI's thinking

74. Campbell, "Contemporary Japanese Budget Politics," chap. 4.
75. EPA, *Basic Economic and Social Plan, 1973–1977*, p. 19.
76. See Industrial Structure Council, "Basic Direction for Japan's Industrial Structure" (Tokyo, Sept. 13, 1974; processed). See also *Japan Economic Journal*, Sept. 24, 1974, p. 12.

extends broadly across the economy. The announced intention is to reshape fundamentally Japan's industrial structure in the 1970s and 1980s just as was done, according to MITI doctrine, in the earlier period.

The OECD's Industry Committee has produced a comprehensive account of past Japanese industrial policy, as provided by the MITI itself in 1970, at the height of Japan's economic success.[77] Then Administrative Vice-Minister Yoshihisa Ojimi gave the OECD committee an authoritative retrospective statement of the MITI's accomplishments:

> The Ministry of International Trade and Industry [after the war] decided to establish in Japan industries which require extensive employment of capital and technology, industries that in consideration of comparative cost of production should be the most appropriate for Japan, industries such as steel, oil refining, petro-chemicals, automobiles, aircraft, industrial machinery of all sorts, and electronics, including electronic computers. From a short-run, static viewpoint, encouragement of such industries would seem to conflict with economic rationalism. But, from a long-range viewpoint, these are precisely the industries where income elasticity of demand is high, technological progress is rapid, and labour productivity rises fast. . . . According to Napoleon and Clausewitz, the secret of a successful strategy is the concentration of fighting power on the main battle grounds; fortunately . . . Japan has been able to concentrate its scant capital in strategic industries. . . .
>
> . . . MITI policies have succeeded in the quarter of a century since the war in overcoming an imbalance of surplus population and scarcity of natural resources, capital and technology by bringing about economic development, mainly through encouragement of industry and promotion of exports, and in building on a cramped land area a giant economy that ranks second in the free world.[78]

Obviously, official puffery is not lacking in these assertions. But the MITI did, of course, engage in an extraordinary amount of legal and extra-legal guidance, assistance, and intervention in the Japanese private sector during a period in which the economy's growth performance was exceptionally strong. The policies espoused by the MITI—import protection, controls on foreign investment and on purchases of foreign technology, financial aid to selected industries through government lending institutions, selective tax incentives, and administrative leadership to prevent excesses in investment and production—did not in any case prevent the economy from going forward at a rapid pace. It is a good deal less clear that these policies provided the consistent and positive—to say nothing of overwhelming—contribution to economic growth that has been attributed to them, and not only by spokesmen for the MITI.

---

77. OECD, *The Industrial Policy of Japan* (Paris: OECD, 1972).
78. Ibid., pp. 15–17. It is of interest that Ojimi did not so much as mention the national plans anywhere in his text.

At the heart of the question is the role of the MITI in the allocation of resources among Japanese industries. According to the official definition, "industrial policy" means a systematic selection of industries to be encouraged or (presumably) discouraged by government action or deliberate inaction. And if the main objective of policy is economic growth, the selection process presumably looks to relative productive efficiency (or the prospects therefor) as the principal criterion for assisting or hindering particular industries.

As has been indicated, the structure of Japanese politics and government did not leave the matter of choosing exclusively to the MITI. Agriculture, which became one of the largest claimants for governmental resources, was a domain unto itself under the watch of its ministry, which also supervises the food-processing and nonalcoholic beverage industries. The Ministry of Finance has been responsible not only for banking, insurance, and securities, but also for alcoholic beverages. Pharmaceuticals, the fastest growing sector of the chemical industry during 1960–69,[79] comes under the Ministry of Welfare. Similarly, transportation and construction have their home ministries.

In any event, the pattern of Japan's growth industries does not suggest that everything was decided at the center. In the early postwar period, the emphasis was naturally on the basic industries: coal, fertilizer, steel, and electric power—along with shipbuilding, many of whose facilities remained intact. Of these, steel and shipbuilding became spectacular successes. So did some others later singled out for special attention: petroleum refining, petrochemicals (including synthetic fibers), and automobiles. (Computers, an industry still the object of elaborate government concern, remains an incomplete story.) But many other industries of lesser or scant governmental interest also were growth industries. Established industries such as cement, paper, glass, and bicycles grew three- and fourfold between 1955 and 1970. The output (by volume) of aluminum and corrugated board rose faster than that of steel. Among the new growth industries not singled out by the MITI were radio, television, optical goods, and motorcycles. The reality, of course, was that economic expansion spread across the industrial spectrum, as could be expected.

There is a further difficulty, however. The industries selected for intensive governmental attention included, not surprisingly, the ailing industries as well as those with high growth potential. Agriculture and coal were chosen, for obvious political reasons. Interestingly, so was the merchant

79. Bureau of Statistics, *Japan Statistical Yearbook, 1970*, table 131, pp. 212–14.

shipping industry. A planned shipbuilding program for the merchant fleet was instituted during the occupation, in 1947, and is still being pursued essentially along the lines laid down at that time. Each year the government —that is to say, the Ministry of Transport in consultation with its industry advisers in the Shipping and Shipbuilding Rationalization Council—decides on the tonnage of ships to be built, by type (tankers, ore carriers, liners, and so on), and allocates production contracts and the ships among the applicant domestic shipbuilders and shipowners. The selected shipping lines receive preferential financing and in turn are subject to close government supervision.[80]

In the literature on government-business relations in Japan, the Japan Development Bank (JDB) is customarily cited as having a central role in assistance to the prospective growth industries.[81] As the instrument for direct government lending for "industrial development and [since 1972] economic and social progress," the JDB operates under a "basic policy for employing government funds for investment in industrial equipment and facilities" laid down at the beginning of each fiscal year by the cabinet. In the bank's words, it "was expected to . . . [supply] long-term funds from time to time to the areas considered important by the national policy standard."[82] Beyond its immediate role as a long-term lender, the JDB was seen by the MITI as a "catalyst encouraging the types of industrial development aimed at by government policy."[83] A JDB loan, that is, would be a signal to the commercial banks that the government favored the expansion of this or that industry.

Where did the JDB put its funds and what indicators did it give thereby

80. In the early 1960s, a Law Concerning Temporary Measures for Reorganization of Shipping Enterprises was enacted to create special incentives to encourage a consolidation of the ailing shipping industry into six core companies. One firm, the Sanko Steamship Company, declined to participate in the consolidation because of the close governmental supervision it entailed. Sanko was able to raise equity money to expand its fleet, and in spite of some minor harassment by the Ministry of Transport it seems to have maintained its place in the industry without difficulty. See the successive white papers on shipping; conversations with Yoshiya Ariyoshi, chairman, NYK Lines, August 1974; "Marine Transport in an Age of Transition," *The Oriental Economist,* July 1974, pp. 47–51; Komiya, "Economic Planning in Japan," pp. 27–28.

81. See, for example, OECD, *The Industrial Policy of Japan,* p. 16; Eugene J. Kaplan, *Japan: The Government-Business Relationship (A Guide for the American Businessman)* (U.S. Department of Commerce, February 1972), p. 37; Macrae, "The Risen Sun," *The Economist,* June 3, 1967, p. xviii.

82. Japan Development Bank, International Department, "Functions and Activities of the Japan Development Bank" (Tokyo, June 10, 1974; processed).

83. OECD, *The Industrial Policy of Japan,* p. 50. See also Kaplan, *Government-Business Relationship,* p. 38.

Table 11-4. *Loans Made by the Japan Development Bank, by Type of Project, 1951–72*[a]

Type of project	Percent of total amount lent
Marine transportation	31.5
Electric power development	21.3
Regional development	14.0
Urban development	9.6
Development of technology	6.6
National life	4.0
Machinery industries	4.1
Chemical industries	3.5
Hotels	1.7
Textiles	0.9
Iron and steel	0.9
Others	1.9

Source: Japan Development Bank, International Department.
a. Total lending was equivalent to approximately $13 billion over this period.

to the private banks? The loan breakdown by categories from the time of the bank's creation through 1972 is shown in Table 11-4.

During any year of the bank's operations prior to 1973, when a distinct shift to urban and regional development and pollution control took place, the owners of Japan's merchant fleet and the electric power industry were its principal customers. The persistent emphasis on the maritime industry certainly did not derive from its economic potential, for it has been a chronic weak sister, requiring not only annual infusions of public lending but interest-rate subsidies as well. Initially, building subsidies for the domestic shipowners could be related to the development of the shipbuilding industry. By 1955, however, Japan had become the world's largest shipbuilder, yet thereafter the subsidies were increased. A balance-of-payments case for expanding the fleet was also offered, of course, but in the four years of embarrassing payments surpluses, 1969–72, the tonnage built under planned shipbuilding exceeded the total of the previous nineteen years.[84] In the end the arguments came down, vaguely, to national security and, more pertinently, to political pressures. Now, in the face of steady increases in the wages of Japanese seamen[85] and of other costs, a trend has developed toward "arrangement building"—that is, toward flags of con-

84. *Zōsen* [Shipbuilding], vol. 18 (June 1973), p. 11.
85. The cost of a Japanese crew as of mid-1974 was said to be about three times that of a Philippine or Korean crew. *The Oriental Economist,* July 1974, p. 48.

venience that do not qualify for subsidies under planned shipbuilding. For this and other market-oriented reasons the official targets for new tonnage for the fleet for 1973 and 1974 had to be revised sharply downward—but not because the Ministry of Transport or anyone else in the government had decided that the time had come to scale down the resources going to the shipping industry.

Controls on Foreign Transactions

Import controls and related measures must be given a ranking position among the industrial policy techniques available to the MITI, and to the other ministries as well. Japan emerged from the occupation with a set of stringent controls on foreign trade and exchange transactions. Industrial raw materials and other imports were subject to quota allocation, foreign equipment purchases were under license, contracts for foreign technology were screened in detail by civil servants before approval could be obtained, and inward and outward investment was carefully monitored and restricted. There was no serious modification of the system during the 1950s, and many of its elements were retained until late into the 1960s. Infant industries were painstakingly protected well into adulthood, but so were all industries in which import competition might have been a factor—including one so conspicuously costly and unsustainable as coal mining, a MITI responsibility.

Inescapably, the rationing of imports (or, for that matter, of opportunities to travel abroad in pursuit of business, although this constraint was widely evaded even in the 1950s) had to affect Japan's industrial structure. The assignment of highest priority to imports of raw materials and advanced industrial equipment and the virtual prohibition of consumer manufactures ensured—in blunt-instrument fashion—that productivity in the industries covered by the rather elastic adjectives "heavy" and "chemical" would be fostered and that many consumer goods would be costly. It is not evident that the system went much beyond that, however. For example, preoccupation with exports and compelling political interests made it necessary that adequate supplies of raw cotton be provided to the otherwise nonstrategic textile industry. On the other hand, petroleum imports, and thus the petroleum refining industry, had to be held down out of concern for the coal mining industry—again, on both balance-of-payments and political grounds. The MITI's definitive statement on industrial policy says virtually nothing about this, perhaps because there was no consistent or clear-cut way to reconcile all of the objectives of the import controls with growth policy.

The case-by-case scrutiny of all technological imports, which was continued in force until mid-1968, has been cited as a special example of the effective interaction of the business community and the government.[86] There is no doubt, either, that government bureaus acted in consultation with interested business groups in determining what kinds of technology imports would be desirable, and that this was undertaken in a quite systematic way. The government authorities also were ready to insist on all kinds of adjustments in the terms of technology contracts as a condition of approval.[87] This led to the justifiable suspicion among foreign sellers that there was government-business collusion to improve the bargaining position of the Japanese purchasers.

The amount of net benefit contributed by this control over the import of technology to economic growth may be open to argument. The Sony Corporation, for example, had to wait almost two years after 1952 to get approval to import the transistor technology that it subsequently applied so successfully to radio manufacture—the delay caused by a minor MITI official who had concluded that this then small company lacked the skills to develop an untried technology.[88] Similar delays—and an occasional failure to complete a deal—were inevitable. There was, in other words, a price for the government's intervention, and it may have been a substantial offset to the gains derived from it.

A somewhat similar observation can be made about the long-continued and strict limitations on foreign direct investment in Japan. On a straightforward basis of promoting industrial growth, restrictions on investment surely would have been fewer and more selective, but there were other considerations. One was a balance-of-payments problem that it was feared would be caused by profit remittances; another was worry about the monopoly potential of giant foreign firms; and there was the political need to protect small business from the competition of foreign firms. But the overriding issue probably was the wish to prevent foreign control of strategic— that is, technologically advanced—industries. This latter consideration led, for instance, to the extended and difficult negotiation with Texas Instruments over the production of integrated circuits in Japan, one result of which may have been a serious delay in Japan's development of advanced

86. Abegglen (ed.), *Business Strategies for Japan*, pp. 121–22.
87. See Chapter 8.
88. Interviews with Sony officials, August 1974; Masaru Ibuka, "The Challenge of Qualitative Economic Growth" (1972; processed). (Ibuka is chairman of Sony Corporation.) The MITI's objections were eventually overcome by bringing to bear the influence of well-placed friends rather than by technical or economic arguments.

computer technology.[89] In any event, it is impossible to find in direct investment policy any definable concern for its impact on growth as such.

Industrial policy also had an important export component, for Japanese officials were preoccupied from the first with what the MITI has labeled "the nightmare choice of either exporting or perishing."[90] Most of the strategic industries were expected to—and did—become exporters on a large scale. Export credits and guarantees and special export tax incentives were elements of industrial policy; these may have been of particular significance in the early period during which the yen was probably overvalued. It is somewhat more than a quibble to remark that these export aids were applied without discrimination, so that products under voluntary export restraint were subsidized along with everything else, and were continued long after Japan's international competitiveness had been well established. This is only to say that in Japan, as in most countries, a policy course once embarked upon is likely to have a life of its own—or that adaptability has been no more a feature of bureaucratic decisionmaking in Japan than elsewhere.

In addition to the tax incentives for promoting exports, Japan has had a range of special tax measures intended to direct resources into particular sectors such as small business and into industries considered to be important, to hasten modernization in some industries, to foster corporate mergers, or (more recently) to increase investment abroad and research and development activity at home.[91] These measures must have worked in the sense that private business did respond to them. Some industries doubtless expanded faster than they otherwise might have, as was the design. But as Pechman and Kaizuka point out in Chapter 5, the tendency of the gov-

89. This was a famous instance of a foreign firm's refusal to make its technology available except through direct investment. According to Texas Instruments, the episode came at a strategic point: "By the mid-1960s the U.S. data processing industry was in the middle of the second or transistor generation [of computers] and initiating the beginnings of the third or integrated circuit generation. The Japanese computer industry was far enough behind so had it had access to TI's integrated circuits, it could have moved to the third or integrated circuit generation substantially at the same time as did the U.S. industry. It is entirely possible that by starting the third generation without the handicap of existing second-generation machines, the Japanese industry might even have achieved a technical lead instead of just parity. Because they did not have U.S. integrated circuit technology available, the Japanese repeated the full three generations and stayed behind the U.S. computer technology during the critical years of the middle and late 1960s." Letter to the authors from P. E. Haggerty, chairman of Texas Instruments, Nov. 25, 1974.

90. OECD, *The Industrial Policy of Japan*, p. 16.

91. See Chapter 5. See also Ken Bieda, *The Structure and Operation of the Japanese Economy* (Sydney: John Wiley, 1970), pp. 116–18.

ernment was to respond to the pressures that these measures evoked by extending special tax breaks to additional claimants, thus diffusing the impact of the incentives.

Industrial Readjustment

It was suggested earlier that the Japanese government, like others, was reluctant to abandon existing industries. Few things could be less accurate, in fact, than the proposition that Tokyo was ever prepared to have its older or weaker industries run down as a matter of deliberate planning.[92]

Agriculture, of course, was a prime case in which pure growth policy would have argued for a course sharply different from the one actually followed. (This is not to say that the policy of agricultural subsidies may not have had ample justification as a means of slowing down what might otherwise have been a socially and politically explosive exodus from the farms.) Coal was another. As in agriculture, employment in the coal mines dropped very abruptly over the 1950s and 1960s: from 413,000 in 1952 to 212,000 in 1961 and 34,000 in 1972;[93] a projection in 1973 estimated that only 10,000 miners would be at work by 1980.[94] The employment fall was not deliberately planned, however. Rather, the central theme of policy was to slow down the decline of coal output and employment by requiring both the electric power and the steel industries to use quotas of subsidized domestic coal.[95] Between 1956 and 1961, coal output in Japan was increased by 17 percent even though its competitive position as against oil was steadily weakening. The decline in production thereafter reflected workers leaving coal mining for other jobs or through retirement, rather than a policy decision by government. The 1960 and 1964 plan targets called for stabilized domestic production at about 50 million tons; but actual output by 1973 was down to 22 million tons.[96]

92. For a contrary view see, for example, Thomas Hout, "Sources of Japanese Economic Performance Relative to the United States," in Taylor (ed.), *Perspectives on U.S.–Japan Economic Relations*, pp. 103–04.

93. Bureau of Statistics, *Japan Statistical Yearbook, 1958*, table 77, p. 139; ibid., *1973–74*, table 116, p. 171; Nobuyoshi Namiki, "The Japanese Economy: An Introduction to Its Industrial Adjustment Problems," in Kiyoshi Kojima (ed.), *Structural Adjustments in Asian-Pacific Trade*, vol. 2 (Tokyo: Japan Economic Research Center, July 1973), pp. 256–57.

94. Namiki, "The Japanese Economy," p. 257.

95. "The Energy Policy of Japan," *OECD Observer*, no. 48 (October 1970), p. 18; Kiyoshi Kawahito, *The Japanese Steel Industry: With an Analysis of the U.S. Steel Import Problem* (Praeger, 1972), p. 83.

96. Bank of Japan, *Economic Statistics Annual, 1973*, p. 225.

The cotton textile and apparel industries perhaps can be considered as proxies for the low-productivity–low-wage manufacturing sectors that industrial policy presumably should have discouraged in Japan. Troubles with overcapacity and downward pressures on prices in cotton textiles date from the 1950s, even before competition from synthetics had become a factor. The MITI's prescription for a cure was the familiar one: a cartel to restrict output. Cartelization worked badly in this fragmented industry, and after 1956 excessive competition was attacked by a government-sponsored program to retire surplus spindles. In due course the reduction of spindles in operation was applied to chemical and synthetic fibers as well, even though synthetic textile production had been promoted by the government.[97] Legislation in 1964 was again directed to the surplus spindle problem, as well as to equipment modernization. In 1967 structural improvement, or the concentration of small firms, was added, but small-scale textile firms are scattered and difficult to manage. "By and large the . . . . rates for disposal of surplus equipment and the grouping of enterprises are low."[98] In all this there was no suggestion that cotton textiles was an industry that should be scaled down in favor of imported products. Textile tariffs were kept at high levels through and beyond the Kennedy Round of trade negotiations in 1967.[99] Japanese overseas investments in fibers and textiles, as has been the case with most other manufacturing industry investments abroad, have been overwhelmingly devoted to producing goods for sale in host countries or for export to third countries: a MITI survey published in 1974[100] found that less than 2 percent of the sales of the overseas fiber and textile plants was going to Japan. If it is possible to find in the textile ex-

97. William W. Lockwood states: "In 1959, this practice [restrictions on allowable spindles in use] was extended to chemical and synthetic fibers as well. . . . It has artificially maintained natural fibers against the inroads of synthetics and in various ways handicapped the Japanese textile industry." "Japan's New Capitalism," in Lockwood (ed.), *The State and Economic Enterprise in Japan* (Princeton University Press, 1965), p. 501.

98. Namiki, "The Japanese Economy," p. 260.

99. Post–Kennedy Round duties on cotton yarn and fabrics—and on woolen and synthetic yarns and fabrics as well—were in generally the same range as those of the European Economic Community: typically 7.5 to 20 percent. See General Agreement on Tariffs and Trade (GATT), *Study on Textiles: Report of the Working Party on Trade in Textiles*, GATT no. L/3797 (Geneva, Dec. 29, 1972), tables 58–60, pp. 89–106. In implementing the Generalized System of Preferences, beginning August 1, 1971, Japan granted tariff reductions of 50 percent on textiles and textile products, subject to individual ceilings on imports based on actual imports from beneficiary countries in 1968, not a year of large textile imports.

100. Summarized in *Japanese Companies' Overseas Investments* (Tokyo: Dodwell Marketing Consultants, 1974), p. 20.

perience a policy of "progressively giving away industries to other countries,"[101] the search must be thoroughgoing indeed.

It is not evident, either, that the structure of the textile industry as a whole was much changed during the rapid economic growth of the 1960s, despite the decline in cottons and the marked expansion of synthetic fabrics. Textiles' share of total manufacturing employment fell from 15.5 percent in 1960 to 10.5 percent in 1971, but small firms became smaller and relatively more numerous in the industry, and value added per worker remained above only that in the apparel industry (see Table 11-5).

The apparel industry is highly diversified and presumably would not have been suitable for a single and definitive restructuring program. It was and is, however, at the bottom of the manufacturing industry in value added per worker; it was and is an industry of small establishments. The data on the relatively unchanging structure of the industry between 1960 and 1971 (see Table 11-5) show that the industry's relative share of manufacturing employment increased substantially over this period of high economic growth. It remains, with textiles and wood products, the most fragmented of the manufacturing industries.[102] Trade policy might have been used to hasten adjustment, but it was not.[103]

Excessive Competition

Still another feature of Japan's industrial policy has been the MITI's chronic preoccupation with excessive competition as being a threat to economic order and well-being.[104] The antimonopoly law enacted by direction of the Allied Supreme Commander in 1947 was modified in 1949, before the occupation ended, and again in 1953, the second time to allow formation of recession and rationalization cartels, subject to Fair Trade Commission approval.

101. OECD, *The Industrial Policy of Japan*, p. 28.

102. For what the comparison is worth, the American apparel industry has been consolidating at a much faster rate. Between the Censuses of Manufactures for 1958 and 1972, the percentage of U.S. apparel establishments with twenty or more workers increased from 44 to 50 percent, and the average number of workers per establishment increased by 40 percent, from forty workers to fifty-six. U.S. Bureau of the Census, *1958 Census of Manufactures*, vol. 2, table 3, pp. 1–6; and *1972 Census of Manufactures*, preliminary report, summary series, p. 2.

103. GATT, *Study on Textiles*. It should be noted, however, that imports of textile products, including clothing, rose sharply after the yen's revaluation, reaching a total value of $1.7 billion in 1973, up 5.5 times from 1970. Japan Tariff Association, *The Summary Report: Trade of Japan* (January 1974), pp. 80–81.

104. Eleanor M. Hadley, *Antitrust in Japan* (Princeton University Press, 1970), pp. 397, 448; see also the discussion by Caves and Uekusa in Chapter 7.

Table 11-5. *Structural Characteristics of the Japanese Textile and Apparel Industries, 1960 and 1971*

Characteristic	1960	1971
Manufacturing establishments: size and employment		
Textile industry		
Establishments with nine or fewer employees		
Number	60,401	92,796
Percent of total	73	84
Number of employees	206,959	308,980
Average number per establishment	3.4	3.3
Establishments with ten or more employees		
Number	22,438	17,287
Percent of total	27	16
Number of employees	1,057,694	900,138
Average number per establishment	47	52
Apparel industry		
Establishments with nine or fewer employees		
Number	13,787	23,069
Percent of total	72	71.5
Number of employees	50,031	94,372
Average number per establishment	3.6	4.1
Establishments with ten or more employees		
Number	5,427	9,195
Percent of total	28	28.5
Number of employees	160,068	327,635
Average number per establishment	29	35.6
Employment in relation to all manufacturing industries		
All manufacturing industries		
Number of employees	8,169,484	11,463,756
Percent of all manufacturing	100.0	100.0
Textile industry		
Number of employees	1,264,263	1,209,118
Percent of all manufacturing	15.5	10.5
Apparel industry		
Number of employees	210,099	422,367
Percent of all manufacturing	2.57	3.68
Value added per worker in relation to size of establishment and other manufacturing industries (thousands of yen)		
All manufacturing industries		
Establishments with nine or fewer employees	253.7	1,089.9
Establishments with ten or more employees	668.0	2,469.3
Textile industry		
Establishments with nine or fewer employees	209.0	767.0
Establishments with ten or more employees	407.2	1,472.6
Apparel industry		
Establishments with nine or fewer employees	196.3	920.3
Establishments with ten or more employees	281.9	1,058.8
Wood and lumber products industries		
Establishments with nine or fewer employees	250.6	1,053.5
Establishments with ten or more employees	355.4	1,455.1

Source: Bureau of Statistics, *Japan Statistical Yearbook, 1973–74*, table 121, pp. 178–79.

The discontent of the MITI and some business figures with the law was not ended: apart from the addition of several specific statutory exemptions, unsuccessful attempts to add other and far-reaching amendments were made in 1958 and 1963. Meanwhile the MITI pursued industrial concentration and cartel policies with a persistence that could be accounted for only by true belief. A predictable MITI response—whether the problem was excessive capacity (as during one of Japan's brief and mild recessions), an ailing industry such as cotton textiles, a supposed inability to compete abroad, or the threat of takeovers by foreign multinational firms—was to sponsor some form of systematic limitation on excessive competition. For completeness, however, it should be observed that a large number of export cartels were formed to meet the demands of Japan's foreign customers for so-called orderly marketing measures.

Antitrust has not been a part of Japan's political heritage. The MITI's skeptical philosophy toward competition had fairly consistent support in high political circles and in the business world as well. Cartels naturally have often attracted individual companies and industries that are anxious for relief from competitive difficulties. Moreover, the dual structure of the Japanese economy—a vast number of small firms coexisting with big industry—seemed sensibly to call for mergers among the smaller companies.

It is not surprising, therefore, that the Fair Trade Commission could identify no fewer than 836 legally authorized cartels as of March 1971, or that more than 9,000 mergers occurred during the period 1960–70. These numbers are somewhat deflatable, to be sure: more than three-quarters of the cartels were formed under the Export-Import Trading Act (by whose terms most of the cartels had to be created for orderly marketing, as in textiles and sundries) and under a law applying to small- and medium-size industries (with many of the cartels organized for regional markets).[105] Similarly, the impressive number of mergers included relatively few in which the postmerger firms had become large; only 57 of the more than 9,000 merged enterprises were capitalized at more than $3 million. Moreover, the merger phenomenon came to be most marked in the area of distribution, an industry in which fragmentation had been extreme.[106]

The MITI also encountered resistance to its policies toward competition. The proposal in 1963 to amend further the antimonopoly law would have allowed the MITI to exempt specified industries from the application of the

105. K. Yamamura, "Structure Is Behavior: An Appraisal of Japanese Economic Policy: 1960–72" (paper prepared for Japan Subcommittee of the Committee for Economic Development, July 1972; processed).

106. Ibid. See also M. Y. Yoshino, *The Japanese Marketing System: Adaptations and Innovations* (M.I.T. Press, 1971), chap. 7.

law for a period of up to five years, during which time mergers would be promoted and other measures taken to enable Japanese companies to compete more successfully against their foreign rivals in Japan and in world markets. This time the MITI encountered opposition from organized industry and from the banks, and although a compromise bill was finally approved by the cabinet, it failed in the Diet.[107] Without this legal club, the MITI's strenuous efforts over a number of years to consolidate the motor vehicle industry came in practice to nothing.[108]

Japanese enterprises may decide to reject governmental consolidation and merger proposals for a variety of reasons, ranging from inability to agree on a redistribution of managerial positions to an absolute unwillingness to withdraw from a growth industry. Equally obvious reasons may facilitate a merger, as when the Prince Motor Company's financial difficulties forced it into a merger with Nissan.[109] Less obviously, the motivation in the merger of two giant steel firms, Yawata and Fuji, included the notion of reviving the prewar Japan Steel Company as the world's second-largest producer.

In any case, business concentration has been marked in Japan, as in other countries. Government policy has played an important affirmative role, through direct pressure from the MITI and other agencies as well as the Fair Trade Commission's relative bureaucratic and political weakness. What clearly has not been verified is the image of the MITI steamrolling Japanese business into a set of predetermined patterns. After two decades of determined MITI paternalism, Japanese industry remains a mixture of competitiveness and restrictionism in which, as Caves and Uekusa remark, "market structure and rivalrous market behavior seem to control market performance."[110]

Macroeconomic Policy

If industrial policy was in some respects contradictory to the objective of economic growth, or at least not unambiguously directed toward it, monetary and fiscal policies under the guidance of the Ministry of Finance

107. Yanaga, *Big Business*, pp. 168–71.

108. Kaplan, *Government-Business Relationship*, pp. 120–28. William C. Duncan deals at length with the MITI's attempt to reorganize the auto industry by means of administrative guidance. He concludes: "MITI must rely heavily on the cooperation of the industries concerned, a cooperation which is not always forthcoming. Indeed, it was partly due to excessive 'administrative guidance' that the smaller assembly firms began to look abroad for capital, technology, and marketing assistance." *U.S.–Japan Automobile Diplomacy* (Ballinger, 1973), chap. 7; quotation is from p. 100.

109. Kaplan, *Government-Business Relationship*, pp. 124–26.

110. Chapter 7.

were directed purposefully toward growth within what was in the main a consistent analytical framework. These policies are discussed in detail elsewhere in this volume,[111] and only a few comments need be made here. One is that the dual goals of "easy money with a surplus budget," which proved to be such powerful tools of economic management in the Japanese context, were as much adaptation to circumstances as they were preconceived policy.[112] The other is that the bureaucracy (and its political leaders) reacted, if anything, less flexibly than their counterparts elsewhere when the consequences of policy came into real doubt.

During the occupation the collapse of the domestic securities market and an extended delay in revaluing industrial assets cut off industry from its main prewar sources of funds and led to a heavy dependence on commercial bank loans. After independence, a policy of administered low interest rates and easy money (on the basis of the Bank of Japan's readiness to support commercial bank liquidity) seemed to be an obviously desirable policy on practical as well as theoretical grounds. Budgetary policy was an inheritance from the latter days of the American occupation and could have been scrapped after the peace treaty. But the balanced budget prescription, once adopted, gave the MOF's Budget Bureau a compelling argument to be used against the claims for expanded programs and more funds from other agencies and their political supporters.

It is true, however, that an expansionist policy was followed with considerable vigor in the face of some opposition. Throughout the 1950s and well into the 1960s Japan's balance of payments could always be described as precarious, and the MOF had constantly to consider the risks of payments crises arising out of growth-induced import requirements. The Bank of Japan, the private banking community, and spokesmen for big business were publicly hostile in the late 1950s to the MOF's allegedly inflationary policies, especially after the exceptionally severe balance-of-payments crisis of 1957,[113] but they failed to shake the ministry.

Whatever early doubts the city bankers and the industrial leaders may have had about Japan's monetary policy, their reaction to it could scarcely have been more unrestrained. The great boom in plant and equipment investment, which ran with only minor interruption through more than two decades, astonished almost everyone inside as well as outside of Japan. The actual investment level reached in 1962 exceeded the 1970 target of the then daring double national income plan of 1960 for private fixed invest-

111. See Chapter 3.
112. See Watanabe, "National Planning and Economic Development," pp. 44–48.
113. Langdon, "Big Business Lobbying in Japan," pp. 527–38.

ment. After a brief check in 1965, the investment surge was resumed with even greater vigor and continued well into 1970. So far as public policy was relevant, the government set the conditions for the investment boom and the associated rapid growth of national output. The hyperactive response of the city banks and their industrial customers was consistent with the intent and tone of governmental actions.

Although criticism of MOF policy on the grounds of its inflationary bias was effectively overwhelmed by the fact that incomes rose considerably faster than prices, a more pointed and politically potent objection was found in the accumulation of deficiencies in public facilities of all kinds—roads, sewers, parks, and so on—and in the nation's provisions for social welfare. These results were deliberately planned, in the sense, first, that fiscal policy was aimed at regular tax cuts and, second, that public investment was focused, so far as possible, on the facilities needed to complement industrial expansion in the Pacific coast industrial corridor between Tokyo and Osaka-Kobe. Typically, a growing volume of public complaint on this score was met by a laggard political-bureaucratic response. The national plans had identified the problem as early as 1965, yet it was not until fiscal 1973 that the government's loan and investment program provided more funds for water, sewage, and similar public works than for "key industries and export promotion."[114]

A similar attachment to established policy and doctrine was in evidence during the international monetary storms of 1969–73. In late 1969, in the face of an increasingly large external surplus, the MOF reacted to a modest rise in the wholesale price index by turning to domestic monetary restraint, with the expectable result that the surplus grew even larger. When dollar convertibility was suspended in August 1971, the first decision by Tokyo was to defend the established yen rate by unlimited purchases of dollars by the Bank of Japan. When intervention on this scale proved too expensive, the choice still was to try by periodic BOJ purchases in the exchange market to limit the extent of the revaluation that had become inescapable. In 1972, as the balance-of-payments surplus continued and pressure grew for another revaluation, the policy reply again was a stubborn, costly, and eventually losing struggle to maintain the exchange rate. Meanwhile both monetary and fiscal restraints were relaxed, in part as a means of reducing the troublesome balance-of-payments surplus, in part as a delayed recognition of the needs of the public sector. Thus, the government first generated a huge volume of liquidity in the private sector by its (fruitless) sales of

114. OECD, *Economic Surveys: Japan* (1974), statistical annex, table E-1, p. 73.

yen against privately held dollars and then further stimulated the economy with an easy money policy and an upsurge of public spending. In the end, the consequence of these policy choices was a disaster for price stability.

It is possible, of course, to read too much into these slow or ill-timed responses to changing circumstances. The popular and political pressures for investment in public facilities and for greater welfare spending were themselves generated rather slowly in a country in which incomes were rising rapidly, and so a quick turnaround in bureaucratic attitudes was inherently improbable. As for the decisions made in reaction to Japan's unexpectedly strong external position, no government anywhere responded as promptly or as assuredly to the evident strains on the international monetary system as might have been desired. Still and all, it is a fair comment that the Japanese decisionmaking machine performed with even less flexibility than most others. For all its undoubted capacities and power, the civil service elite in Tokyo showed that it could be hampered to an extreme degree by the constraints not only of political pressures but also of habit and established doctrine—and, no doubt, of fear of the unknown.

General Assessment

What can be said in the way of a general judgment about the role of politics and government in Japan's astonishing economic upsurge?

A warranted conclusion is that the durability of conservative political rule was a positive factor. If private business provided much of the motive force for growth, business also had the assurance at virtually every point that government would be safe and sane, partial to profits and dedicated to business growth, willing to listen to business views, devoted to trying to maintain a social order in which business could feel secure, and committed to the close relation with the United States that most of the business community considered to be essential on economic as well as security grounds. Moreover, the government's economic policymakers were ready to indulge the expansionary instincts of Japanese private enterprise. Once it had been determined that a rising level of private investment was to be the response to low interest rates and elastic credit lines, a succession of conservative Ministry of Finance officials and their equally conservative political superiors were prepared most of the time to resolve doubts in favor of allowing each boom to run its course and to restore the monetary conditions for a new one as promptly as possible.

And there were doubts to be overcome, too. Tokyo's official and business community regularly generates a bewildering variety of argument and advice, all magnified by an excitable press, about economic policy and the dangers just ahead. But whatever the hesitations may have been in the face of genuine problems of the external accounts and the consumer price index, the general direction of demand management was consistently expansionist.

Of more limited importance, national planning probably did contribute to the buoyancy of the economy. In a climate of extremely aggressive competition for shares of markets, periodic indications that the government expected the expansion to continue may well have worked to sustain and strengthen the propensity to build more plants and order more equipment. In this sense, it is possible that the plans themselves contributed to the growth psychology.

For the rest, the evidence is at best ambiguous. It is one thing to say that conservative leadership provided a political climate that was on the whole highly favorable to business investment and innovation; it is another to argue that big business had a determining voice in political choices and that this made growth possible. Like their counterparts in other democracies, Japanese politicians have been subject to competing demands and to fluctuating voter sentiments. Even if business in so large and complex a society could have spoken regularly with a single policy voice—and that voice expressing the optimal policy position for economic growth—no government could have equated its fortunes with the wishes of business alone. If Japan is accepted as being a pluralist society in which politics constantly require compromises among a variety of interests, the critical role of political leadership in economic growth can be put in perspective. The essence of that role was not to conspire with business, big or small, but rather to keep within bounds those social and political pressures which had to accompany rapid growth and urbanization. This role was acted out reasonably well, partly because the ruling party's rural electoral base made it necessary to moderate the decline of Japanese agriculture.

At the official level, Japan's civil service gave the country honest and competent administration. Its dedication to rather detailed guidance of the activities of the private sector was a part of the Japanese inheritance, and no amount of argument can show that the bureaucratic controls that it exercised so extensively could have been a net disservice to economic growth. But neither does the fact that the economy grew rapidly under the bureaucrats make the case that official planning and direction did it. Thus, among the nonagricultural industries on which much of the attention and resources were lavished were a number—such as cotton textiles, shipping, and coal—that would hardly have been selected on the basis of growth criteria alone. The small business sector had to be helped no matter what its potential. Some of the favored or strategic industries—steel, petroleum refining, petrochemicals, and electric power—had profit rates substantially below the manufacturing industry average during the 1960s,[115] and it could easily be argued that the national income objective would have been better served by a different allocation of investment. It is easy, moreover, to cite specific instances—officially sponsored cartels that did not restrict the entry of new firms into an industry, limits on the expansion of synthetic textiles that helped maintain a declining cotton textile industry, and export incentives applied to products under voluntary export restraints—to suggest that Japanese civil servants, like their counterparts elsewhere, often found themselves pulled in different directions by diverse forces. At the macroeconomic policy level, as has been noted, the Japanese system had its own rigidities, which it was notably slow to overcome.

In Chapter 7 Caves and Uekusa correctly emphasize the importance of entrepreneurship to postwar Japanese economic growth. Here, surely, was a crucial ingredient. If the general environment was favorable for enterprise, it was after all the enterprisers who seized the opportunities. Companies such as Sony, Honda, and Matsushita, founded by brilliant innovators and managers, are widely known outside Japan, but there were many others—in steel, textiles, cement, automobiles, tires, oil refining, shipbuilding, and advertising—whose executives acted as pathfinders and catalysts in the expansion of Japanese industry. It is not credible that these talented men really could have been closely guided and directed by a cadre of civil servants, however well educated, or that their vision and skills could have been adequately exploited within a tightly managed, essentially bureaucratic system.

So it is that the tidier the model of Japan's political economy, the less it conforms to reality. Clearly, all but a relatively few of the day-to-day economic decisions must be made in the private sector—within, to be sure, the bounds set by law and custom, but certainly not according to a blueprint made in Tokyo. The bureaucracy has indeed had an extensive and active part in economic life, but it has been constantly subject to conflicting pressures, ranging from narrow loyalty to individual ministries to the demands of competing special interest groups. And politics in Japan has hardly been more orderly a process of bargain and compromise than in any other democracy. Economic growth was a ranking objective in this society, but the

115. Komiya, "Economic Planning in Japan."

particulars of the process were not willed or foreseen by anyone, politician or civil servant.

Japan has also been a changing society. In the context being considered here, the 1950s can be seen as a period in which concern for the country's supposed economic vulnerabilities was used to justify numerous governmental constraints on the private economy. As the economy grew very fast through the 1960s, many of these constraints were modified or dropped: because they were seen to be unnecessary, because of international pressures, or because the private sector had simply become too large to be subject to particularistic intervention.

Since the end of the 1960s Japan has had to confront new issues, and heretofore latent problems have suddenly been projected to center stage. The exchange rate revaluations forced on an unwilling Japan in 1971 and 1973 were major shocks to the official Tokyo establishment. The subsequent inflationary surge has called into question the government's capacity to control economic events. Again, the oil, or energy, crisis has made vividly clear Japan's extreme dependence on the outside world for indispensable commodities. There are pending decisions, thus far mostly deferred, about the desirable allocation of resources between public and private uses in a heavily urbanized nation. Denison and Chung, in Chapter 2, suggest in plausible detail that basic sources of growth will be in total weaker than in the past, with the result that the nation's internal tensions will be less easily allayed by ever and dramatically rising incomes.

Whether and how the Japanese will deal with these and other challenges is unknowable, but there are reasons to expect that the country's political and social system will endure in its accustomed form for some time. No sharp break with conservative political domination can be considered imminent, given the basic divisions among the opposition parties and an electoral structure that greatly overweights rural votes but that no major group proposes to change. If the confidence of politicians and bureaucrats in their ability to manage affairs has been shaken, they can observe that their counterparts elsewhere face problems as difficult, often in situations more tenuous than that in Japan. If others can muddle through, so can Japan. There is less reason now than in the past to endow Japanese leaders and officials with either magical capabilities or superhuman qualities or to see Japan as a society fundamentally different from the other industrial democracies. But the genuine strengths of the country, noted throughout this book, remains. And it is on these rather than on fanciful constructions that Japan must make its future way.

CHAPTER TWELVE

Social and Cultural Factors in Japanese Economic Growth

Nathan Glazer, Harvard University

HOWEVER IMPRECISE and uncertain economists take their analyses and interpretations to be, they are based on the most rigorous of the social sciences, one which manipulates well-defined concepts, to which numbers can generally be attached and which can be grouped into well developed and frequently tested generalizations. However loose the realm of political science may be considered to be, it deals with one set of institutions, the political, which can be specifically delimited. There is no difficulty in perceiving the significance of the political system for the functioning of the economy, though disagreement may exist about which manipulates which, and how. But around both the economic complex and its particular political environment there is discernible another environment that is the concern of the sociologist, the anthropologist, and the social psychologist. It is a murky environment indeed, and despite the importance that men attribute to it, it has not been ordered—and apparently cannot be ordered—in any simple manner. Or, rather, it has been ordered in so many ways by so many different scholars that little guidance akin to science seems available. And yet this further realm—let it be called "the social and cultural factors in Japanese economic growth"—cannot be ignored.

Japan remains socially the most distinctive of the great industrial nations, and there is considerable argument over whether and to what extent its distinctiveness has diminished as its economy has developed. The question Japan has prompted, since about the last decade of the nineteenth century, is why its economic development has been so strikingly more successful than that of other non-Western countries. One would think that this question would have declined in significance as China and India, more or less adequately, also developed modern industrial sectors. But it has not, because the remarkable postwar economic growth of Japan—a growth whose rate

Note. I am indebted to Ezra F. Vogel, Herbert Passin, and William K. Cummings, who generously shared with me their deep knowledge of contemporary Japan and who, going far beyond any scholarly duty, gave two drafts of this manuscript careful and critical readings. I am also indebted to Daniel Bell, S. M. Lipset, and David Riesman for their extensive comments on drafts of this manuscript; unfortunately I could not make use of many of their suggestions here but hope to do so in an expanded version of this study. Kōkichi Shōji assisted me while I was in Japan in the summer of 1973, arranging interviews, summarizing material available only in Japanese, and discussing with me the approach I was developing. I appreciate his assistance. Isao Amagi, Ikao Arai, Haruo Matsubara, Hideaki Okamoto, and Hiroshi Mannari generously gave me helpful interviews and provided material. T. J. Pempel responded at length to an inquiry. Richard Dyck gave me assistance in Japan and in the United States. And many others too numerous to list also willingly gave me assistance.

has surpassed that of major Western nations, let alone Asian nations—has actually intensified the question. It is uncertain, though, whether the question is still the same one: whether whatever it was that explained Japan's uniqueness in entering the path of economic development also explains its postwar economic performance and suggests what its future economic development will be. Although economists carefully distinguish these and other questions related to the periodization of Japanese economic history, much of the discussion by sociologists and anthropologists has tended to collapse the periods and to find constant elements in the form of social structure, culture, and values.

Culture and Economy: The Japanese Paradox

Contributing in one way or another to economic growth, it is felt, is something more than falls into the sphere of the economy, more than falls into the sphere of the political system. There is, to use a term favored by economists, an "exogenous" reality. But what?—and of what significance? There are values that seem to permeate the economic system, values determined not simply by economic necessity and requirements: if they were, there would be no need for this chapter.

Two anthropologists, the American Ruth Benedict and the Japanese Chie Nakane, seem to agree on a common ethos that affects Japanese society and the individuals and institutions that make it up.[1] The pictures drawn by these scholars have been enormously influential, among Japanese as well as non-Japanese, in shaping the common view of Japanese society. Benedict did not know Japanese but gained her knowledge of Japanese society from interviews with informants in the United States during World War II who had been raised in prewar Japan. Nakane's knowledge comes from the application of her insight as an anthropologist to a Japan that had undergone twenty-five years of vigorous economic growth and remarkable social change. Yet whatever the differences in detail between them, both agree on the difference between Japan and the West: a difference exhibited in a net of obligations that binds individuals together and makes strong institutions of the family, principally, but by extension of the school and the workplace. Both pictures strike Westerners as "traditional": individual values and institutional needs are brought together in some kind of organic connection and with only moderate strains from individual psychological resistance.

1. Ruth Benedict, *The Chrysanthemum and the Sword: Patterns of Japanese Culture* (Houghton Mifflin, 1946); Chie Nakane, *Japanese Society* (University of California Press, 1970).

The books of these two anthropologists are in some respects classic. The first was to be found in the kit of every sophisticated postwar observer; the second has replaced it in the flight bags of more recent sophisticated travelers. And yet, however satisfying in some respects these books are in filling the American's insistent need to know what is Japanese about the Japanese, it is not easy to make a link between Japanese social and cultural characteristics and economic growth. It is not really clear why the traditional values of Japan were suited to economic growth, while not so dissimilar values of other societies were not.

Nakane has studied both India and Japan as an anthropologist—the one country an economic failure, at least to date, the other an economic success. In both cases, as in most traditional agricultural societies, there have been strong families, wealthy and dominant families, hierarchy. The caste system of India, it may be argued, found a parallel in the strict four-class system of Tokugawa Japan; in both countries there was a "vertical" society. Japan succeeded in transferring the "verticality" of the family and community into the school and workplace, modified to accommodate the specific objectives of those institutions; India did not. Can the specific differences in social structure and values explain the difference in economic outcome? The suspicion cannot be ignored that if it were India that had turned out an economic success and Japan an economic failure, the ingenious social scientist also could have explained these outcomes by the two different kinds of verticality in these two societies. After all, some of the differences seem on their face to have favored India in economic development.

Take one example. Nakane points out[2] that the Japanese cannot directly confront disagreement; they smile. The Indians, on the other hand, insist on a logical presentation of their point of view on any matter in conflict, regardless of what this does to the immediate web of personal relations. These different responses reflect both different values and different behavior patterns. And yet does not creativity in entrepreneurship and science require confrontation and conflict? Even Japan's remarkable homogeneity—and no other great industrial nation has so homogeneous a population, ethnically, culturally, even socially—might be considered a defect rather than an advantage in contrast to an India that is divided by religion, language, and caste. Diversity, after all, is considered a useful seedbed of economic growth. Early modern Europe was divided between Catholics, Protestants, and Jews, as well as many different nascent nations. Each of these religions has had its scholarly partisans asserting that *it* was the chief factor in the initiation of economic growth.

2. Chie Nakane, "Logic and the Smile: When Japanese Meet Indians," *Japan Quarterly*, vol. 11 (October–December 1964), pp. 434–38.

In other words, the web of values so elegantly drawn by Benedict and Nakane explains too much or too little. To get them to explain just what it is they do explain demands a subtlety and intuitive feeling that one respects in the hands of the most skilled practitioners of the science of culture—but that one despairs of being able to turn into an instrument for general use or understanding.

Social scientists feel they come closer to their objective of relating specific values to economic growth in the pattern variables that have been developed by Talcott Parsons. They are derived largely from the monumental researches of Max Weber and have been used by Parsons and others (such as Marion Levy and Bert Hoselitz) to explain economic growth.[3] A classic work by Robert N. Bellah[4] applied the pattern variables explicitly to the problem of early Japanese economic growth. This general approach is the most popular one now found among sociologists and political scientists to explain differences in achievement of societies in economic growth. It argues that some dissolution of traditionalism was necessary for economic growth to be sustained over a long period of time. The bonds of the family had to be somewhat dissolved; the power of traditional religion, village, and clan had to be weakened; government had to be rationalized. Human interactions had to become somewhat more broadly based on (1) "universalistic" rather than "particularistic" standards; human beings had to be judged in terms of (2) "achievement" rather than "ascription" (for example, what they do rather than their race or caste); human relations had to become (3) "specific" rather than "diffuse" (for example, relating to persons as a whole rather than in terms of their specific functions), (4) "affectively neutral" rather than "affective." Different sets of pattern variables, drawn from a number of formulations of Parsons, have been used by different analysts at different times, but the four sets of terms contrasted above do seem to describe the necessary movement of a society from traditionalism to modernity, from economic stagnation to economic growth.

There are problems in understanding just what the pattern variables are;

3. Talcott Parsons, *The Social System* (Free Press, 1951); Horace M. Miner, "Community-Society Continua," in David L. Sills (ed.), *International Encyclopedia of the Social Sciences*, vol. 3 (Macmillan and the Free Press, 1968), pp. 174–80, and references therein; Seymour M. Lipset, "Anglo-American Society," in ibid., vol. 1, pp. 289–302, and references therein; Bert F. Hoselitz, "Economic Growth: Noneconomic Aspects," in ibid., vol. 4, pp. 422–29, and references therein. For an extended and sophisticated application of the pattern variables for an understanding of problems of modernization and economic growth, see Seymour Martin Lipset, *The First New Nation* (Basic Books, 1963), chap. 6; and his *Revolution and Counterrevolution* (Basic Books, 1968), pt. 2.

4. *Tokugawa Religion: The Values of Pre-Industrial Japan* (Free Press, 1957).

they are used as explanations as well as classifications. It is also not clear whether the pattern variables that characterize modern societies and might be used to explain sustained economic growth depended on a historically unique combination of developments and circumstances that came together in sixteenth-century Europe and whose influence then spread by diffusion (this seemed to be Max Weber's view, for the combination required the specific history of two millennia that preceded it to make it possible) or whether some specific collection of circumstances elsewhere might quite regularly reproduce it. Nor is it clear whether, if it was a historically unique development, some of the peculiarities that characterized it in the West—for example, a religious revolution giving rise to new values with a rather complex relation to economic growth—might have to be reproduced to make spontaneous reinvention possible.

It would be convenient to lean on this fairly well-developed and widely used set of patterns to structure a consideration of the social and economic factors in Japanese economic growth. There are some operational definitions, even tests, for some of the variables involved, and in the mass of survey data that has been accumulated in Japan evidence could be found of the rise or fall of one or another of these variables. (Some of this survey data is analyzed below in the section "Values, Savings, and the Family.") But the pattern variables are part of the problem rather than part of the solution. Contemporary Japan can (with hesitation) be assigned to the "universalistic" instead of the "particularistic" pole, but the problem remains of how this universalistic society seems to have leapt almost full blown from a most particularistic one a mere hundred years ago. With equal uncertainty Japan may be assigned to the "achievement" rather than to the "ascription" pattern variable, but here again there is a problem: after a student experiences the pure achievement emphasis of the Japanese school and gets his first job, he is caught up, in a role henceforth determined to seniority and education, in a pattern that smacks of ascription. Early achievement seems to be the basis for later ascription. But then achievement takes over again as the more competent are advanced farthest. The same pattern can be found, of course, in other countries—in, for example, the attitude toward diplomas and degrees—but many argue that the use of early achievement for later ascription is more marked in Japan.

The third pair of pattern variables, diffuseness and specificity, presents the greatest difficulty, because Japan, quite unaccountably for a modern society, ends up in the wrong box—diffuseness—whether one looks at school, workplace, or even the bureaucratic institutions of government. And similarly with affective and affectively neutral: the Japanese insist on the significance of feeling in all social relations. Another pair of pattern variables related to modernization, self-orientation versus collectivity orientation (whether one values one's self or the collectivity in one's choices and decisions) is sometimes proposed. Japan ends up on the side of collectivity orientation, a position that also tends to be regarded as traditional and thereby unfavorable to economic growth.

When the second- or third-strongest economy in the world is found to be characterized by a society that more nearly approaches the traditional pole on two out of four pattern variables, what is to be made of this set of categories? Answers aside, the difficulty in itself helps to define the contradictions that Westerners sense between Japan's economic performance and its social and cultural characteristics; it also sets for social scientists the problem of whether these contradictions are real or illusory or whether their understanding of the necessary conditions for economic growth is not somewhat too limited and culture bound.[5]

Varied approaches are possible, of course, in considering the role of social and economic factors in Japanese economic growth. I have selected three topics for discussion: the Japanese educational system; changes in Japanese values, as investigated in opinion surveys and other empirical research; and practices of the Japanese factory and workplace.[6]

The selection of these topics is not arbitrary: all three clearly have a significant relation to economic growth. Further, they are the topics that sociologists, anthropologists, and social psychologists are best qualified to investigate and have investigated, and on all three there is substantial empirical material. Finally, it is hard to think of other topics related with equal significance to economic growth. One such candidate is Japanese management, on which there is some literature. Unfortunately, I have had to exclude this topic because a sufficient body of empirical material is not available to me. I do consider, however, some of the issues that have been taken up in discussions of Japanese management.

All three sections can be treated as paradoxes, as in some measure they are: from the point of view of a Western understanding of economic develop-

5. Other writers have recognized the distinctive mix of pattern variables displayed by Japan and the problems that this mix presents for modernization theory: see, for example, Ronald Dore, *British Factory–Japanese Factory: The Origins of National Diversity in Industrial Relations* (University of California Press, 1973), pp. 269–75; and Lipset, *Revolution and Counterrevolution*, pp. 109–11.

6. In each case I have drawn upon the existing empirical materials, Japanese and foreign, insofar as they are available in English or other Western languages. I also conducted interviews with Japanese scholars and experts and had summaries prepared of Japanese materials, but I have used both of these sources with caution.

ment, there is no reason why the educational system, the complex of prevailing values, or the characteristic patterns of the workplace should have been at least consistent with, and very likely contributory to, a pattern of rapid economic growth. The aim of this chapter is to explore these paradoxes.

"There Are No Dropouts in Japan": The Japanese Educational System

The basic paradox of Japanese education is that—underfunded (at least and most prominently at the college level), devoid of any marked evidence of innovation (at the elementary, secondary, or college and university level), sharply criticized for its enormous emphasis on examinations, under attack from business for the quality of its college graduates, with limited research facilities and a modest system of graduate education, torn by conflict between an alienated and radicalized teaching force in the elementary and secondary schools and a firmly conservative Ministry of Education, characterized by a college and university intelligentsia most of whom are opposed to the national government and unsympathetic to the emphasis on economic growth —it manages nevertheless to educate a labor force that serves the needs of Japanese business, industry, and government.

From the point of view of the foreign observer, the Japanese educational system seems to serve these needs well: it provides a highly literate work force, one as literate as any in the world, through a system of education that covers every child for nine years (the elementary and junior high school) and almost all children for an additional three (the senior high school) and that sends a higher proportion of young people on to higher education than any nation but the United States and (perhaps) the Soviet Union.[7] Whatever may be said of literacy where it depends on learning twenty-six letters and various combinations thereof, literacy in the complex written language of Japan can be the product only of an effective school system. The Japanese are also a highly numerate population—indeed, from comparative tests, perhaps the most numerate in the world. They are also—and here comparative measures are less helpful—as committed a work force in their behavior as any. It is not easy to say what is responsible for these qualities or to what extent the Japanese economy will be able to count on them in the future, but the educational system must be in large part responsible, at least for literacy and

7. Ministry of Education, *Educational Standards in Japan, 1970* (March 1971), p. 31.

822 NATHAN GLAZER

numeracy.[8] In view of the objective deficiencies of some elements of the educational system, and the massive criticism and dissatisfaction with many aspects evident in Japan, the question must be simply: why and how?

Higher Education[9]

The Japanese system of higher education consists of a small group of public universities that are maintained by the national government, prefectures,

8. In their studies of effects of education on economic growth, economists tend to look at gross features: at, for example, the number of years of schooling workers have had and how that affects their earnings. From this point of view, one probably can argue that in the past the Japanese labor force has been overeducated (and in view of the rapid expansion of higher education in recent years, may be even more overeducated in the future). See, for example Tsunehiko Watanabe, "Improvement of Labor Quality and Economic Growth: Japan's Postwar Experience," *Economic Development and Cultural Change,* vol. 21 (October 1972), pp. 33–53; and Kazushi Ohkawa and Henry Rosovsky, *Japanese Economic Growth: Trend Acceleration in the Twentieth Century* (Stanford University Press, 1973), pp. 54–55. Watanabe suggests that there has been "an excess supply of highly educated laborers... in Japan... [and] an underemployment of qualified laborers" (p. 48). The effects of the recent shortage of labor have been to reduce wage differences by education even further and thus, in this kind of analysis, to reduce further the contribution of education to economic growth (p. 51). This technique assumes an economically rational estimation by employers of the contribution of education, age, and other factors; but if, for example, for cultural or social reasons, age is overvalued (as there is good reason to believe is generally done in Japan), the actual contribution of education to labor quality inevitably will be reduced by this type of analysis.

9. On the background and development of Japanese education, see Herbert Passin, *Society and Education in Japan* (Teachers College Press, 1965). For other independent foreign assessments, see idem, "Japan," in James A. Perkins and Barbara B. Israel (eds.), *Higher Education: From Autonomy to Systems* (New York: International Council for Educational Development, 1972), pp. 219–27; William K. Cummings, "The Changing Academic Marketplace and University Reform in Japan" (Ph.D. dissertation, Harvard University, 1971); and Kazuyuki Kitamura and William Cummings, "The 'Big Bang' Theory and Japanese University Reform," *Comparative Education Review,* vol. 16 (June 1972), pp. 303–24; William Cummings, "The Crisis of Japanese Higher Education," *Minerva,* vol. 10 (October 1972), pp. 631–38; idem, "The Japanese Private University," ibid., vol. 11 (June 1973), pp. 348–71; T. J. Pempel, "The Politics of Enrollment Expansion in Japanese Universities," *Journal of Asian Studies,* vol. 33 (November 1973), pp. 67–86; Henry Birnbaum, "Japanese Educational Patterns in Science and Engineering," *Science,* Sept. 28, 1973, pp. 1222–27. For the opinion of a leading Japanese critic of the universities, see Michio Nagai, *Higher Education in Japan: Its Take-off and Crash* (Tokyo University Press, 1971) [NB: the author's name appears in this volume in the Japanese order, Nagai Michio]. For the work of a group of leading foreign experts (Joseph Ben-David, Roland P. Dore, Edgar Faure, Johan Galtung, and Edwin O. Reischauer), see Organisation for Economic Co-operation and Development, *Reviews of National Policies for Education: Japan* (Paris: OECD, 1971). For the view of an official Japanese commission, see Central Council for Education, *Basic Guidelines for the Reform of Education: On the Basic Guidelines for the Development of an Integrated Educational System Suited for Contemporary Society,* Report to the Ministry of Education (Tokyo, 1972).

and cities and a much larger group of private universities that are privately funded and maintained largely out of tuition. As in the United States and to a lesser degree in other developed nations, the universities form a hierarchy, with a clear and unambiguous ranking. In Japan, the hierarchy is even more marked and more significant for future prospects than in the United States.

In 1971 there were 389 colleges and universities in Japan, enrolling nearly 1,470,000 students and employing nearly 123,000 teachers; there were also 486 junior colleges, predominantly for women, enrolling more than 275,000 students and employing nearly 32,500 teachers.[10]

The system has grown rapidly. Postwar reforms under the occupation installed an American model, which upgraded a large number of teachers' colleges and other postsecondary institutions into colleges and universities. Then, during the 1960s there occurred an enormous increase in the number of private institutions, which grew rapidly to accommodate the increasing demand for higher education.[11] The number of national and local public universities grew hardly at all between 1952 and 1972 (from 105 to 108); while the number of private universities rose from 116 to 291. The proportion of students enrolled in private universities grew from 57 to almost 80 percent.[12] Thus, as against the experience of the United States, in which a large proportion of the postwar increase in university enrollment was accommodated in the better-funded public universities, in Japan it was the private sector that accommodated the increase.

In one important respect Japanese higher education is ahead of that in the European nations, but behind the United States: the size of the system in terms of the number of students enrolled and number graduating. A comparison for the years 1967–69 shows Japanese higher education enrolling 16.2 students per 1,000 population in 1969, against 34.7 for the United States in 1968, 18.9 for the Soviet Union in 1968, 10.6 for France in 1967, and lower figures for Great Britain and West Germany.[13] Pempel estimates that about 25 percent of each age cohort enters some institution of higher education in Japan, second only to the 35 percent in the United States.[14] Passin points out that 35 percent of men aged eighteen to twenty-one are in

10. Bureau of Statistics, Office of the Prime Minister, *Japan Statistical Yearbook, 1972*, p. 544.

11. Pempel points out that the apparent enormous growth of the system as a result of the occupation reforms—from 84,000 students in 84 institutions in 1944 to 502,000 students in 226 institutions in 1952—is only apparent: in all postsecondary institutions, including those that did not bear the title of "university," 400,000 students were enrolled in 1944. But the later growth, to 399 institutions in 1972, was not illusory. "The Politics of Enrollment," pp. 67–68, 73.

12. Ibid., pp. 73–74.

13. Ministry of Education, *Educational Standards in Japan, 1970*, p. 31.

14. "The Politics of Enrollment," p. 68.

universities (women form, compared to the United States, a much smaller percentage of college and university students), a figure almost as high as that for the United States.[15]

PRIVATE INSTITUTIONS. The first major issue raised by the internal and external critics of Japanese higher education involves the quality of the private sector, which has grown to encompass four-fifths of the students. This sector is considered on the whole to be inferior—considerably inferior—to the public sector, though a good number of individual private institutions are of high quality and retain a high reputation. With some exceptions, they are almost without endowment, and because they have received almost no public support until recent years, they depend almost entirely on student fees and loans.

15. "Japan," p. 220. Exact comparisons between nations are difficult because of the form of available statistics, and are somewhat contradictory, but it is possible that at present more Japansese than Americans complete senior high school and that proportionately almost as many males are graduating with four-year degrees from colleges and universities. A calculation for 1970 shows that 33.1 percent of the population aged fifteen and over in Japan has completed high school, against 29.7 percent in the United States (OECD, "Inequalities in the Distribution of Education Between Countries, Sexes, Generations and Individuals" [prepared for a seminar on Education, Inequality and Life Chances, Paris, Jan. 6–10, 1975], p. 31). My own effort at comparison suggests, however, that in 1970 slightly fewer members of the appropriate age grade were graduating from senior high school in Japan than in the United States. In 1970 it was reported that 76.1 percent of the relevant age grade (half of the seventeen- and eighteen-year-olds in the United States) graduated from high school (Office of Management and Budget, *Social Indicators, 1973* [1973], p. 99). In Japan, using the same calculation, I came to 73.8 percent of the age grade (Bureau of Statistics, *Japan Statistical Yearbook, 1972,* pp. 561, 24). But although the American percentage has been stable since 1967, the Japanese percentage has been rising rapidly and may well by now surpass the American.

In 1970, 26.4 percent of Japanese male graduates continued directly to college (ibid., pp. 544, 561), and another 20.3 percent who were not in school or at work were probably preparing for university entrance examinations, a typical pattern in Japan. In the United States, for about the same years, 52.7 percent of male high school graduates who were aged twenty and twenty-one in 1972 had completed at least one year of college (U.S. Bureau of the Census, *Current Population Reports,* series P-20, no. 274 [1974], p. 5). It has been estimated that fewer than 50 percent of entering students get a degree in four years in the United States (Alexander W. Astin, *College Dropouts: A National Profile* [American Council on Education Research Reports, vol. 17 (February 1972)], p. 10), while in Japan almost all do. Thus, the number of students receiving degrees from four-year institutions in 1969 was 94.5 percent of the number entering in 1965 (Bureau of Statistics, *Japan Statistical Yearbook, 1972,* p. 554).

If the higher concentration of Japanese male students in the sciences and engineering is taken into account, Japan was graduating proportionately as many male students in these areas in about 1970 as the United States. Figures for all students receiving degrees (four-year and graduate) for Japan and the United States show 178,000 degrees in 1969 in the United States for men in the natural sciences, engineering, medical sciences, and agriculture and 101,000 in Japan in 1970 (UNESCO, *Statistical Yearbook, 1972,* pp. 414–15, 420–21).

Charging students five times as much as the public universities, they neverthe-less spent only one-sixth as much per student—posing issues of equity as well.[16]

In 1969, student-faculty ratios were 39.5:1 in private universities (in public universities, 12.2:1), against 7.9:1 and 15.4:1 in Great Britain (1967) and the United States (1968), respectively. The ratio in the humanities and social sciences rises to 45:1 in the private universities.[17]

The floor area of university buildings per student varied from 19.5 square meters in national universities to 14.2 in local public universities and a mere 5.7 in private institutions in 1968.[18]

Japan's expenditures on higher education, public and private, are low by international standards. "Both in absolute terms and relative to national in-come per capita, Japanese investment is considerably lower for higher edu-cation than is that of other countries," the OECD examiners reported in 1971.[19]

The financial inadequacy in the private universities is reflected in small and overcrowded libraries, inadequate facilities for science, and underpaid faculty who are tempted to take on heavy loads of outside work. "Even at national universities 66 percent of those of professorial rank and 53 percent of the assistant professors hold some job outside their home institutions. . . . In private universities the situation is much more acute . . . [and] it is com-mon for the number of part-time faculty members at private universities to be

16. Passin, "Japan," p. 222.
17. Ministry of Education, *Educational Standards in Japan, 1970*, pp. 100–01.
18. Ibid., p. 230.
19. OECD, *Reviews of National Policies for Education*, p. 75. Mysteriously, the OECD report also asserts that Japan spends about the same percent of the gross national product (GNP) on education as other major OECD nations, about 7 percent, which sug-gests it spends a higher percentage of GNP on elementary and secondary education. More recently, OECD has reported on a special study comparing educational costs in France, Japan, and the United Kingdom, from which it appears that Japan spends much less per pupil in higher education than the United Kingdom, less than France, but more than either for primary education, as shown below (data supplied by OECD Department of Social Affairs):

Expenditure (dollars per pupil per year)

Educational level	France	Japan, average of public and private institutions	United Kingdom
Primary	276	326	257
Secondary, first cycle	504	365	496
Secondary, second cycle	874	426	804
Higher	1,011	824	2,507

nearly equal to that of full-time teachers."[20] Although the exact meaning of
these figures is not clear (what is an outside job? what proportion of faculty
members in other countries have outside sources of income? to what extent
are these outside sources of income complementary to the basic university
job?) and although certain advantages in the part-time employment pattern
are evident (access of poorly funded private universities to the large concentration of able people in Tokyo), for a leading Japanese critic this situation
nonetheless illustrates a basic deficiency: the inability of the private university (and, in some measure, the public) to provide a faculty adequately
committed to the task of education.

But most striking to an outside observer is the fact that private universities
are required to fund themselves through bank loans, and payment of interest
on these loans consumes a growing proportion of their income. Pempel, referring to a Japanese study, reports that 20 percent of the budgets of private
universities goes into debt service.[21] Again, as in the case of outside jobs, it
can be argued that this is not necessarily the worst way to expand higher education. Nonetheless, public opinion does consider it a very poor way, as contributing to what is seen as the injustice of heavy tuition fees in private universities and very low ones in public.

But the situation has not been left without redress. In 1970, the Private
School Promotion Foundation was established by the government, to provide
by the middle 1970s nearly half of the salaries of teachers in private institutions.[22] Even with this substantial improvement, however, the circumstances
of the universities responsible for 80 percent of the student population are
considered grave.

HIERARCHY AND SCHOLARSHIP IN HIGHER EDUCATION. A second major
focus of criticism of higher education—again, not unfamiliar in other countries—is the rigidity of its organization. From this criticism the great national
universities, Tokyo and Kyoto, are not exempt. Although systems of gover-
nance in Japanese universities vary, in the major universities the senior faculty is supreme, and a chair system has been dominant. One professor dominates a group of associates ranked hierarchically below him and has little
contact with fellow professors occupying related chairs—a system in which,
according to Nakane[23] and other observers, little communication takes
place between related disciplines or between workers in the same discipline in
the same university. Further, the national universities are considered the seat

20. Nagai, *Higher Education in Japan,* pp. 5, 127.
21. "The Politics of Enrollment," p. 80.
22. Passin, "Japan," p. 223.
23. *Japanese Society,* pp. 21, 34, 59, and elsewhere.

and center of a "boss" system in which younger scholars are held almost as feudal servitors of older scholars and are required to assist them in their research, to support their views publicly, to have nothing to do with their opponents, to consult them in all the crucial decisions of their lives, and in return to receive protection and placement in academic jobs—perhaps finally to move up to replace the full professor-patron who holds the chair. This picture is drawn from many sources, but even if it is somewhat exaggerated, even if it is undergoing changes, in its main dimensions it appears to be accepted as accurate.

This criticism is similar to criticisms of the type of organization in other institutions in Japan (business and government), and contradicts what Western social scientists consider to be necessary conditions for change, adaptation, growth, and creative achievement. Thus, if the Japanese tend to form vertical social organizations in which superior is linked to inferior and patron to client, and if these vertical organizations are insulated from other organizations in the society—both those with the same objectives and others—then interchange of personnel is rare, learning from others is rare, and a society of tight and impenetrable groupings is created.

An official committee, reflecting common opinion, reports that "both educational and research activities have stagnated as a result of the inbreeding and immobility of university scholars."[24] The degree of inbreeding is reported in a major study of an elite sample: only 24 percent of Japanese faculty members have taught at other universities, compared with 34 percent for England, 46 percent for the United States, 41 percent for France, and 32 percent for Germany. "Teaching positions at the two leading schools, the University of Tokyo . . . and Kyoto University . . . are almost completely monopolized by their own graduates (95.3 percent for Tokyo and 88.9 percent . . . [for] Kyoto)." The inbreeding goes further still, because universities and colleges lower in the hierarchy traditionally take their faculty from one university that stands higher in the hierarchy.[25]

Perhaps the common view of Japanese universities as being inbred and immobile has been exaggerated; similar inbreeding, after all, is found in other university systems. Cummings points out that the Japanese pattern is not that distinctive—compare the patterns of recruitment in the American university—and that apparently it does not lead to the promotion of the incompetent: "More than 90 percent of all Japanese university scholars have

24. "Final Recommendation of the Central Council for Education," translated in Cummings, "The Changing Academic Marketplace," p. 394.
25. Nagai, *Higher Education in Japan*, pp. 133–34, reporting data from a study by Michiya Shimbori.

published an article and over 60 percent have published a book whereas less than 75 percent of America's university scholars have published an article and less than 40 percent have published a book. . . . Despite beliefs to the contrary, most of the publications of Japanese scholars are serious academic works."[26]

ENTRANCE. The dominant charge in the criticism of Japanese education, higher and lower, is that the mechanism for entry into higher education, the examination system—often referred to in Japan as "examination hell"—distorts all education. Entrance into universities is universally through examinations, given independently by each college and university and given independently by each faculty of multifaculty universities. Almost the entire secondary school system is oriented toward succeeding in these examinations. Entrance to secondary schools is also by examination, with a similar desperate scramble to get into the upper secondary school that has the best record of getting students into good colleges. There have been some recent modifications, such that in some cities a student must attend the upper secondary school in his area of residence. This leads to further distortions. Employees will refuse to take new job assignments, commute long distances, or register their children with relatives so they may attend what are reputed to be the best secondary schools for university entrance examinations.[27]

The key examinations are those for the university and college, where only 70 to 80 percent of aspiring graduates from upper secondary school can be accommodated.[28] In 1968, 51 percent of students succeeded in getting into the institutions of their first choice; 29 percent failed to be admitted to any institution,[29] though they may have resisted taking examinations for an institution of lower status to which they might have been admitted. This leads to the notorious *rōnin* problem, in which great numbers of aspiring students stay out of school to try for a second or a third time. Of successful applicants for universities in 1967, 31 percent had been through a *rōnin* period. In medicine and dentistry, the percentage rose to almost 50 percent.[30]

The need to pass the examinations gives rise to a huge tutoring industry—and even getting into the better tutoring schools requires an examination. Entrance exams to the public upper secondary schools, given by the prefectures, are universal. Most prefectures examine in five subjects, three in

26. Cummings, "The Changing Academic Marketplace," p. 394. Others disagree with this assessment of the level of Japanese scholarship.
27. Birnbaum, "Japanese Educational Patterns in Science and Engineering," p. 1222.
28. Ministry of Education, *Educational Standards in Japan, 1970*, p. 90.
29. Ibid., p. 79.
30. Central Council for Education, *Basic Guidelines*, p. 89.

as many as nine, whereas four enlightened prefectures give examinations in only three subjects. An official report states: "The great impact that entrance examinations for upper secondary schools may have upon the lower secondary school system makes it necessary to appraise the appropriateness of conducting examinations."[31] Efforts have been made to reform both systems of examination, but the rate of change has been glacial. Change in the system of examinations for higher education has only come slowly. "In spite of [many proposals for reform], students are still admitted to universities exclusively on the basis of one time scholastic examinations."[32] Reform is now under way on coordinating the examinations for national and public universities.

The impact of the Japanese examination system has been reported in much of the popular media around the world, and in Japan the system is widely believed to be responsible for the unusually high rate of suicide among Japanese youth.[33]

Once again—as in the cases of the financing of private universities and of rigidities in higher education—I am not making an independent criticism of the examination system; I am presenting the almost universal opinion of Japanese writers on education. They think it is a very bad system, and that it should be made more flexible: it should take into account school grades, as well as examinations; it should reduce the pressure on young people (a common Japanese expression asserts that if a schoolchild sleeps more than four hours a night, failure will result); it should be reformed so as to reduce tension in family life, distortions in residential location, attempts to bribe teachers with gifts, and so forth.[34] The Japanese feel that the slow rate of change reflects a rigid system, one unsympathetic to change and unresponsive to human needs. Certainly a more rational system of examination—for example, one examination given for all institutions or a range of them—can be

31. Ministry of Education, *Educational Standards in Japan, 1970*, p. 89.

32. Ibid., pp. 90, 91.

33. Nagai, *Higher Education in Japan*, p. 88. The suicide rate among Japanese youth during the late 1950s was remarkably high, but it declined rapidly during the 1960s. Examination pressure clearly was only part of—and perhaps not an important part of—the explanation of youth suicide. See Hisao Naka, "Modernization and Anomie: Suicide in Japan" (paper prepared for delivery at the meeting of the Association for Asian Studies, March 27–29, 1972; processed), p. 20.

34. One of the best descriptions of some of these effects of the examination system is to be found in Ezra F. Vogel, "Entrance Examinations and Emotional Disturbances in Japan's 'New Middle Class'," in Robert Smith and Richard K. Beardsley (eds.), *Japanese Culture* (Aldine, 1962), pp. 140–52; and Vogel, *Japan's New Middle Class: The Salary Man and His Family in a Tokyo Suburb* (University of California Press, 1963), chap. 3.

imagined, even if a totally different alternative cannot. In some measure the criticisms do make sense.

GRADUATE EDUCATION AND RESEARCH. Conceivably the most relevant factor in considering the possible relations of higher education to economic growth is the relatively small scale of Japanese graduate education. Only 4.5 percent of Japanese university graduates go on to graduate education (12.1 from the national universities), a tiny proportion by American standards. The total graduate enrollment in 1971 was only 41,637.[35] The only slight development of graduate education is generally explained by the fact that there is little financial advantage to a graduate degree,[36] since business and government recruit first-degree graduates, expect to train them for specialized tasks, and reward them on the basis of length of employment rather than possession of graduate degrees. This makes sense, and whether it is a disadvantage in terms of the potential contribution of education to an economy is arguable. Americans seem to place much more faith in graduate education —as, increasingly, do Europeans. One likely explanation for the greater development of graduate education in the United States is the devaluation of the first higher degree because of the large numbers given it. In Japan, the hierarchy of institutions is more marked, and the rewards of graduation from an institution higher up in the hierarchy more automatic. Many companies, for example, recruit only from certain institutions; the management track in certain governmental agencies is staffed almost entirely by Tokyo University graduates. As a result there is little need to develop an additional system for differentiation through graduate education.

DISSATISFACTION WITH THE SYSTEM. The criticisms of higher education I have reported may be excessive, but the fact of dissatisfaction is undeniable, and on a scale even larger than is found in other developed countries. Cummings reports that in comparable periods two out of five Japanese students expressed discontent with their education, against one in ten in the United States; that one in four faculty wish they had chosen another occupation, against one in ten in the United States.[37] Nagai, who is extremely critical of

35. Birnbaum, "Japanese Educational Patterns in Science and Engineering," pp. 1223–24. In 1970, 13,000 graduate degrees were granted in Japan, against 238,000 in the United States in 1969. (UNESCO, *Statistical Yearbook, 1972*, p. 440. I have taken "third-level" degrees in the source as graduate degrees.) But other approaches to making the comparison would show a lesser distortion: since medical and law degrees, for example, are undergraduate degrees in Japan, a comparison of Ph.D.s would be more meaningful. The number of Ph.D.s granted per 100,000 population in 1967 or 1968 were: in Japan, 4.5; Great Britain, 8.2; United States, 13.1; France, 13.0; and West Germany, 13.5 (Ministry of Education, *Educational Standards in Japan*, p. 36).

36. Birnbaum, "Japanese Educational Patterns in Science and Engineering," p. 1226.

37. "The Changing Academic Marketplace," pp. 396, 403.

the research performance of the Japanese university, points out unhappily that Japan produced only two Nobel prize winners in science between 1901 and 1967, against seventy-three for the United States, fifty-one for Germany, forty-seven for Great Britain, and twenty for France. The Soviet Union had produced only nine, but seven of these had won since 1950.[38]

The dissatisfaction of university professors, social critics, government advisory bodies, newspapers, and students is paralleled by the dissatisfaction of businessmen, which discussion with Japanese businessmen confirms. The Central Council for Education, a government-appointed body that also has sounded business opinion and reviewed survey findings of business, reports criticism of both secondary school and college graduates: "Large enterprises feel that fundamental scholastic achievements are lacking: there are many people in technical fields who do not have the basic scientific background just as there are those in clerical fields who lack the ability to think and judge for themselves. . . . A considerable number of graduates employed by large-scale enterprises are thought to be unoriginal, uncreative, unspontaneous and unconstructive."[39]

FACULTY POLITICS. The foregoing paragraphs have explored a paradox: a much criticized system of higher education, poorly funded and with dissatisfied students and teachers, which nevertheless contributes a willing work force to Japanese business and government. The element that completes the paradox is that university faculties are found to stand predominantly on the political left; they tend to be sharp critics of their society and government and, in particular, of the role of economic considerations in the setting of government policy. Much larger proportions of the faculties than of the general public vote for the left-wing parties, socialist, democratic socialist, and communist; much smaller proportions vote for the conservative Liberal Democratic party.[40] Aside from the issue of how these attitudes affect their students—education is correlated with voting for leftist parties in Japan —a predominantly antigovernment viewpoint among faculty also inhibits university reform insofar as it would have to flow from proposals of a government that is viewed with suspicion. Thus, a central examination for college entrance would be suspect because the Ministry of Education would have to play a major role.[41]

38. *Higher Education in Japan*, pp. 125–26.
39. Central Council for Education, *Basic Guidelines,* p. 121.
40. Cummings, "The Changing Academic Marketplace," pp. 229, 233.
41. There is really no model in Japan for the establishment of a nongovernmental and yet widely accepted institution such as the Educational Testing Service. But examples of this kind of role for nongovernmental agencies exist in scarcely any nation but the United States, so in this respect Japan is not unique.

The tendency of groups to stick to themselves, to communicate only among themselves rather than to create a broad front, is another feature of Japanese society that seems to militate against reform through a cooperative attack on problems. This at least is Cummings' explanation of the almost uniform failure of efforts at reform begun at the level of the national government, even when these efforts have been formulated by representative consultative bodies:

> The principal consequence of lack of [movement between different levels of university government, and government and university] . . . appears to be that ideas developed at one level fail to gain legitimacy at another level. Each level, and for that matter, groups within each level refuse to allow outsiders to participate in their discussions and policy formation sessions. . . . The different groups formulate good ideas, but then they can not persuade outsiders to accept these ideas. Since the closed groups have not "coopted" outsiders in the course of their reform planning, they have no chance [for carrying] on healthy dialogue with other groups in ironing out differences. This problem is illustrated by the reception given to the Central Council for Education's Final Recommendation on educational reform [1971].[42]

These proposals, many of which had virtue, were almost universally criticized. But this seems in general to be the fate of government proposals in Japan: the government wins elections, but it is viewed with deep suspicion by intellectuals and social critics and ordinary publicists, as well as by faculty.

Primary and Secondary Education

Perhaps the paradox represented by the Japanese system of higher education can be explained by the remarkably effective system of compulsory primary and secondary education, which consists of six years in elementary school and three years in the lower secondary school. Almost all such schools are public. In 1973, 89.4 percent of students went on to the three-year upper secondary education, which is not compulsory. Here, there is a greater number of private schools.[43] In the more prosperous urban prefectures such as Tokyo almost all students go on to upper secondary school. Until a few years ago there were very high student-teacher ratios, and schools were old and of wooden construction and had poor facilities. In 1958 the standard class size was set by law at fifty (though many were larger) and in 1963 it was reduced

42. Ibid., pp. 460–62.
43. *Japan Times,* Nov. 18, 1973. Private schools at the elementary level enroll about 0.5 percent of students; 3 percent of students attend private lower secondary schools; 31 percent attend private upper secondary schools. Bureau of Statistics, *Japan Statistical Yearbook, 1972,* p. 544.

to forty-five. But actual class size in 1969 averaged thirty-three for public elementary and thirty-seven for lower secondary schools. In 1959, 90 percent of elementary schools and 89 percent of lower secondary were of wood; by 1969 these figures had fallen to 63 and 58 percent, respectively—and, even more surprising, 31 and 27 percent of elementary and lower secondary schools, respectively, had a swimming pool.[44]

TEACHER MILITANCY. Two elements in the criticism of higher education link the compulsory school system to higher education: first, the examination system, whose impact is greatest at the upper secondary level but reaches down to lower secondary school, elementary school, and even kindergarten; and, second, the political outlook that characterizes teachers and separates them from the regime. In the political area, the polarization is sharper among lower-level teachers than that which divides university teachers from the ruling Liberal Democratic government and the institutions of a capitalist society. Elementary and secondary school teachers are organized into a strong and radical union, Nikkyōso, which has at different times been under varying degrees of communist or socialist domination and has engaged in endless struggles with the Ministry of Education. The struggles that have repeatedly divided teachers from their employers—as well as teachers from teachers, teachers from principals, and teachers from parents—might be expected to have had severe effects on the education of Japanese children. In any case, they were clearly upsetting to parents.

Severe shocks to the school system began with the end of the war. The first was the reorganization, from its roots up, of the long-established and respected prewar school system to follow an American model that permitted no deviation. The second great postwar shock was the purge of right-wing teachers, part of the general postwar purge of right-wing elements: 22 percent of all teachers lost their jobs in 1946–47.[45] The third, in 1949, consisted of a purge of left-wing teachers, 1,000 of whom were dismissed. But the impact of this purge was traumatic, because by this time the teachers were solidly organized by left-wing unions, and they saw this action as a betrayal of what they had understood to be the new democracy of free unions, free speech, and open struggle.

From this point on, teachers were continuously embroiled with a Ministry of Education that tried to reduce their power. As the American occupation came to an end, a struggle began over the restoration of "morals education," which had been banned by the occupation because of its glorification of the

44. Ministry of Education, *Educational Standards in Japan, 1970,* pp. 95, 124, 229.
45. Benjamin C. Duke, *Japan's Militant Teachers: A History of the Left-Wing Teachers' Movement* (University Press of Hawaii, 1973), pp. 46–55.

emperor. Its restoration was resisted by the teachers, who feared its impact would inevitably be conservative, whatever its specific curricular content. There was also a struggle over the replacement of elected boards of education by appointed ones. The teachers eventually lost on both issues. In 1954 a national walkout, protesting laws that would limit teachers' political rights, affected 70 percent of all classes nationwide. In 1956 half a million teachers walked out, to protest other bills affecting school board elections and textbooks. In 1958, 35,000 of the 37,000 teachers in Tokyo struck over a government plan to rate teachers. This was part of a national struggle, in the course of which 80,000 teachers were transferred (according to the union) for opposing the government. In 1966, as a result of a strike that combined political with economic demands (which is illegal), scores of union leaders were arrested and 20,000 teachers were dismissed or suspended.[46] The struggle between the teachers' union and the Ministry of Education over many issues remains sustained and intense.[47]

Conceivably, the effects of this battling between the union and the government have not particularly been felt in the classroom. Strikes and walkouts in Japan are one-day or half-day affairs, and the impact on education that might be expected from a sustained teachers' strike in New York City would not necessarily be found in Japan. Yet the scale of conflict between state and teachers has undoubtedly been much greater in Japan than in the educational systems of other countries.

SCHOLASTIC ACHIEVEMENT. To demonstrate the other side of the paradox, that despite this turmoil the Japanese educational system is perhaps the most effective in the world, is not simple—what constitutes effectiveness in the educational milieu?—and yet there are some persuasive comparative international data.

Achievement in mathematics and science at the elementary and secondary levels has undergone extensive comparative study organized by the International Association for the Evaluation of Educational Achievement. In 1964 tests were conducted to establish relative national achievement in mathematics for thirteen-year-olds and for students in the grade immediately preceding university entrance. Japan scored second, next to Israel, among twelve na-

46. Ibid., pp. 90–91, 124, 133, 143, 184.
47. In another study of the teacher's union, Donald R. Thurston, *Teachers and Politics in Japan* (Princeton University Press, 1973), adds a great deal to Duke's account, particularly in the analysis of the structure of the union and of the specific issues on which it has opposed the Ministry of Education. He agrees with Duke, however, on the specific point I have been making: "The obstreperous conduct of the Japan Teachers' Union has kept the educational world of postwar Japan in an uproar" (p. 82).

tions for the thirteen-year-old group, sixth for mathematics majors in the preuniversity group, and third for students for whom mathematics was not a major. But when differences in enrollment ratios in the preuniversity group among nations were controlled for—that is, when comparisons were limited to the top 3 or 4 percent of the entire age group, whether in or out of school —Japan scored first for mathematics majors in the preuniversity grade and first by a remarkably wide margin for the nonuniversity majors.[48]

A major study of science education a few years later (the tests were conducted in 1970) gave evidence of the same success. Although this massive study in nineteen countries cautions against intercountry comparisons, the samples were drawn with a great deal of attention to intercountry comparability: tests used were the same in each country and the sampled schools in each country were based on those key social and educational variables which affect schools. The Japanese sample, for example, provided for proper sampling of rural and city schools, according to the main educational distinctions recognized by the Japanese, just as the American schools were sampled according to socioeconomic levels served. Tests were given to ten-year-olds and to fourteen-year-olds. The Japanese ten-year-olds scored first in subtests for earth sciences, chemistry, and biology. Among the fourteen-year-olds, the Japanese scored second to Hungary in biology, and first in physics, chemistry, and a practical test. Instruments were designed to test different objectives of science education: information, understanding, and application, as well as such supposed higher processes as synthesis and evaluation. If it is thought that the achievement of the Japanese students was based simply on memorization and rote learning, their actual achievement would rapidly disabuse the idea: the Japanese ten-year-olds ranked only fourth in information but first in understanding, application, and higher processes. The fourteen-year-olds also ranked only second in information but first in understanding, application, and higher processes.[49] The conclusion can only be that in tests of scientific understanding as Westerners understand it—the International Science Committee included one Japanese among nine members —the Japanese scored remarkably well.[50]

48. Ministry of Education, *Educational Standards in Japan, 1970,* pp. 68–70. See Torsten Husén (ed.), *International Study of Achievement in Mathematics: A Comparison of Twelve Countries* (Wiley, 1967), for a full report of this study.

49. It would be pointless to try to second-guess the researchers in this elaborate undertaking, to try to determine whether their subtests were indeed valid instruments for measuring some of these elusive qualities.

50. L. C. Comber and John P. Keeves, *Science Education in Nineteen Countries: An Empirical Study* (Wiley, 1973), pp. 119–24.

836   NATHAN GLAZER

Factors Contributing to Achievement

There can be little doubt that high achievement in mathematics and science in an educational system that covers virtually 100 percent of the population up to the age of fifteen and more than 80 percent up to the preuniversity year represents a positive value for an economic system. And it would seem that achievement in mathematics and science, as against reading ability, must in some substantial measure be attributed to the school system. Whatever the character of home background and exposure to the mass media, the direct contribution of these factors to achievement in mathematics and science must be relatively modest compared with the contribution of other factors inherent in formal schooling. The science study also provides comparative data on school systems that suggest which factors may lead to this effectiveness in education.

UNIFORMITY. The first factor that stands out as distinctive in Japanese schools is their uniformity. They are all the same, and the same everywhere throughout Japan. Thus, the Japanese schools in the study are all coeducational (only Sweden among the other participating countries has all-coed schools); 99 percent have a parent-teacher association (only communist Hungary reaches a 99 percent proportion, but the Federal Republic of Germany is close with 97 and the United States next with a ragged 79). For the schools attended by the fourteen-year-olds, 100 percent have parent-teacher associations; even Hungary, with 96 percent, falls short of this mark. Further, every Japanese school in the study provides only one curriculum for fourteen-year-olds (though there are different types of upper secondary schools); among the other countries only Sweden, with its recent school reforms, also provides a single curriculum for all fourteen-year-olds.[51]

The image that emerges is one in which the schools are very much the same everywhere, the parents are organized, and the teachers are organized. Perhaps the most striking example of one-hundred-percentism emerges from the report on the student samples: in every country, finding a sample of ten-year-olds and fourteen-year-olds required the sampling of a number of grades aside from the modal grade characteristic of students at this age. But in Japan 100 percent of both samples was drawn from a single grade, for in Japan no one is left back or advanced; all move along at the same rate.

Uniformity at a low level of quality obviously would not be a virtue in itself. But in Japan the uniformity apparently is combined with other features that suggest high quality. In the science study, the middle schools of Japan had the highest percentage of university-trained teachers (and also, for de-

51. Ibid., pp. 71–73.

veloped countries, of male teachers, which reflects at least the traditional seriousness with which education is undertaken in Japan and the high status accorded the teacher).[52] The uniformity extends to curriculum, teacher training, and teacher salaries, and is maintained by substantial central government efforts to attract teachers to isolated areas by higher salaries and to maintain the quality of schools there by special grants.

This uniformity also reflects the more or less general social homogeneity of the Japanese people. Thus, the ethnic minorities of Japan are the smallest of any developed nation. The Korean is the largest, but well under 1 percent; the *burakumin* (descendants of the former lower caste in Japan), the other large disadvantaged group in Japan, constitute 1 or 2 percent of the population. Effective measures for overcoming the traditionally lower levels of educational achievement of the *burakumin* are apparently in effect in some places. For example, in Kyoto only 32 percent of *burakumin* children advanced to senior high school in 1961, against 73 percent for the city as a whole; in 1969 these percentages were 72 and 87, respectively.[53]

EGALITARIANISM. Uniformity itself implies a high degree of egalitarianism, but other distinctive practices in Japanese schools emphasize the equal condition and equal treatment of the children and limit tendencies to introduce distinctions among them based on class, background, or intellectual capacity.

The most striking evidence of egalitarianism is the absence of tracking within schools on the basis of ability and the universality of automatic promotion. One might think these features derive from the social revolution that transformed Japanese education and society during the occupation, and in some measure they do. Tracking was common in prewar Japan. But then American reformers imposed on Japanese schools what they were not able to impose on their own, as a result of which the radical teachers' union became, ironically, the firmest supporter of an American-imposed practice —as the anti-American left in Japan is the firmest supporter of the American-imposed constitution.

There are perhaps native roots to the system of automatic promotion.[54]

52. Ibid., pp. 48, 82.

53. Eugene E. Ruyle, "Ghetto and Schools in Kyoto, Japan," *Integrated Education* (July–October 1973), pp. 29, 33. On the education of the *burakumin,* see also Theodore Brameld, *Japan: Culture, Education and Change in Two Communities* (Holt, Rinehart, and Winston, 1968); on the *burakumin* generally, George DeVos and Hiroshi Wagatsuma, *Japan's Invisible Race* (University of California Press, 1966). On the Korean population, see Richard Hanks Mitchell, *The Korean Minority in Japan* (University of California Press, 1967), p. 159.

54. Ronald Dore, "Talent and the Social Order in Tokugawa Japan," in John W. Hall and Marius B. Jansen (eds.), *Studies in the Institutional History of Early Modern Japan* (Princeton University Press, 1968), pp. 349–53.

These roots may go back to Tokugawa Japan, in which, when schools were introduced, the embarrassing consequences of lower-ranking samurai doing better in school than higher-ranking samurai had to be avoided. They were avoided by emphasizing virtue, attendance, and age. Whether or not it is necessary to go that far back, it is clear that the pattern is deeply rooted and considered not only democratic but necessary for the psychological well-being of the child. Two accounts of Japanese society, one prewar, one post-war, describe the motives behind automatic promotion as follows:

> Teachers feel that, if they left some child behind his class, he would feel very badly about it and that the resulting psychological effect and family chagrin would not be compensated for by any good the child might receive mentally by repeating a school grade.[55]

> Though the children undergo periodic tests, they almost invariably are promoted each year and so stay with the same groups of schoolmates, with whom they form friendships that endure through life. Teachers in lower (elementary) and middle school almost never inflict on a child the sense of failure, which would be reflected on the child's family and buraku [hamlet], so the slow children pass through school at the same rate as the bright ones.[56]

These descriptions of rural Japanese schools seemed so apt to John Singleton, studying a school in a small city near Tokyo in the 1960s, that he quotes them approvingly to explain the pattern. Automatic promotion contributes to enduring friendships among children. The common bond between classmates through life is a strong feature of Japanese society.

Once having entered a school, a Japanese student is guaranteed completion. One might extend the thought and suggest that the apparently complete absence of dropouts from school because of the mild rules determining progress may result in the absence of any large number of dropouts from work in later years and from established Japanese society generally. The scarcity of dropouts in these realms reflects some deeper tendency in the society and culture, one in which age and seniority have been emphasized as the proper basis of making distinctions, and in which individual accomplishment has been deemphasized. Perhaps even deeper is the need for a supportive and nurturant group, which would be disrupted if too much emphasis were placed on the accomplishment of an individual within the group.

Aside from the lack of tracking and automatic promotion, other aspects of Japanese education and society give evidence of egalitarianism. Thus, the

---

55. John F. Embree, *Suye Mura: A Japanese Village* (University of Chicago Press, 1939), p. 188, quoted in John C. Singleton, *Nichū: A Japanese School* (Holt, Rinehart, and Winston, 1967), p. 16.

56. Richard K. Beardsley, John W. Hall, and Robert E. Ward, *Village Japan* (University of Chicago Press, 1959), p. 302, quoted in Singleton, *Nichū*, p. 16.

fierce testing for admission to colleges and universities, the most marked break with the pattern of automatic promotion, has surprising results from an American or Western European perspective. It would be expected to become a means of transferring social differences from father to son, in which the best endowed not only in terms of intelligence but in family background (wealth, education, and occupation) would be successful. In the West, purely meritocratic processes of selection heavily overselect from the higher social strata. Yet in Japan, the objective tests for the fiercely sought tickets for admission to the national universities have in the past selected fairly equally proportions from each income class, though recently the first quintile has pulled ahead. In 1964, 26.9 percent were selected from the top income quintile, 19.8 percent from the bottom, but the most recent available statistics show 35.1 and 17.4 percent, respectively, with the bottom quintile still getting a higher representation than the second and fourth quintiles.

The point is not that income does not matter: the private universities, with their high fees, select very disproportionately from upper income groups: 52.8 percent from the top quintile, only 5.8 percent from the bottom. It is, rather, that the differential socializing of youth matters less than in other countries: on the crucial tests for national universities, youths from the lowest income group do as well as, or better than, those from the middle three.[57] This result, I believe, reflects not only the equal conditions in the schools but also the homogeneity of culture and the more nearly equal conditions of daily life.[58]

Other evidence of either more nearly equal conditions in the schools or

57. Statistics from Economic Planning Agency, *Whitepaper on National Life, 1973: The Life and Its Quality in Japan* (1973), p. 57; and Pempel, "The Politics of Enrollment," p. 82.

58. Whether income is distributed more evenly in Japan than in the United States is the subject of considerable debate. In the early postwar period, as a result of the destruction of prewar values through inflation and of land redistribution in return for bonds (which rapidly lost most of their value), a more even distribution is a distinct possibility. What is undoubtedly true, however, is that the lower stratum of society, the "underclass," in Gunnar Myrdal's term, the group in which a "culture of poverty" might be expected to flourish, is remarkably small. The minority groups from which it could be drawn are tiny. The farmers are no longer a depressed class—and in any case would not qualify as a group with deviant or anomic values because of the strong bonds of a common Japanese culture. The criminal class is small. On the other extreme, even the wealthy do not lead lives markedly different from those of middle-class Japanese. There is no substantial break in Japanese metropolitan areas between very wealthy and very poor areas, as in American cities: the residential distribution by income is more even, which again helps contribute to the egalitarian tone of the classroom. All these features would help reduce class and income differences in achievement, even were the distribution of income similar to that in the United States. On the question of inequality of income distribution in Japan, see Chapters 4 and 5.

more nearly equal conditions in life is to be found in a large comparative study of occupational aspirations in Japan and in the United States. In the Japanese study the students from the lowest group in social status had much higher occupational aspirations than students from the lowest social status group in the United States; Japanese students from the highest status group had slightly lower occupational aspirations than students from the highest status group in the United States. Aspirations thus were less closely correlated with social status in Japan.[59]

In general, there seems to be evidence of a lesser degree of determination of occupation by family background factors in Japan than in the United States.[60] Analysis of determinants of occupation in Japan is simply not able to explain as much of the variance as can be explained in the United States. Japanese believe that a great deal depends on individual will and effort—evidence the facts that students are traditionally exhorted to sleep no more than four hours a night, and that a student may take entrance examinations for universities as often as he wishes. A large proportion of Japanese youth, by becoming *rōnin*—taking a year out to study harder—is regularly involved in such an exercise of effort and will. If Japanese data indicate only a modest determining effect of parental background on school and occupational attainment, they indicate almost nothing about the effect of native intelligence—what might be measured by an intelligence quotient. Cummings ascribes the absence of I.Q. studies in Japan in part to political resistance from the socialist teachers' union, as well as from the right.[61] The fact that effort and will are popularly believed in Japan to be key determinants of educational and occupational outcomes may well indicate that in reality class background and native intelligence do count for less. In a reanalysis of the data on comparative science achievement, Cummings found that for the Japanese those variables which stood out most strongly in a regression analysis in explaining science achievement were interest and ambition.[62] This outcome is what would be expected in a fairly egalitarian society; and of course it is what

59. Yasumasa Tomoda, "Occupational Aspirations of Japanese High School Students," *Educational Sciences: An International Journal,* vol. 2 (September 1968), pp. 217–25.

60. William K. Cummings, "The Effects of Japanese Schools" (paper presented at the Eighth International Congress of Sociology, 1974; processed), pp. 17–23, and earlier unpublished work by Cummings cited there.

61. Ibid., pp. 9, 14–15. I noted with surprise that, although the Japanese translate almost everything, they had not translated recent work by Arthur Jensen and others on the significance of inherited intellectual abilities on school achievement and later occupational achievement. In a country as intellectually alive as Japan, the absence of such a line of research would suggest to me not that it had been overlooked but that it was simply considered unimportant.

62. Ibid., p. 12. The Japanese sample was not tested for I.Q.

would be expected in a society in which individuals were less sharply differ-entiated from each other by class and ethnicity.

EMPATHY AND RESPONSIBILITY. A third distinctive feature of the Japanese school is a pattern of empathy and responsibility that links teacher and stu-dent. Consider the following quotations from Japanese teachers observing American classrooms and what they imply about the prevailing attitudes in Japanese classrooms. The picture that emerges—of American schools and, by reflection, Japanese—is surprising. It should be pointed out that these teachers were visiting generally well-endowed, middle-class American schools; it was difficult to make arrangements to have them conduct their observations in American slum schools.

I cannot help feeling that American homeroom teachers [the teacher who has charge of a class independent of his or her subject-matter teaching] are more formalistic than Japanese. There are no opportunities to visit the homes, and the practice of many hours of individual discussion on a face-to-face basis seems to be rare. There is a rule permitting detention after classes, but it is a formal mea-sure for penal purposes completely different from the practice in Japan where it is used for very intimate personal contacts.[63]

There is a certain limitation to the amount of guidance of pupils' behavior given in public schools. Therefore, teachers do not go beyond the scope of keep-ing general order. . . . They do not care much about what their pupils do once outside the school campus. . . . Even when a pupil is taken to the police station, his teacher is not called to account. When I said that in some districts in Japan, school teachers assist the police by supervising the students within the community and, thereby, prevent delinquent behavior, American teachers were very much surprised and appeared to be unable to understand what I said.[64]

From what I saw in the United States, teachers generally leave school at 2:50 PM. In Japan the minimum working time is forty-four hours per week. Using this extra time, teachers give life guidance to children with special problems. They visit the homes of such children to find ways of solving their problems. When a child has particularly difficult problems, teachers meet several times to discuss the proper method of guidance.[65]

The scholars who organized this study sum up one finding:

The criticism of the lack of follow-up of pupils' homelife by the American teachers is one of the more striking findings of the entire project. Japanese teachers customarily take a total interest in the lives of their pupils and such totality demands that teachers be acquainted with the pupils' parents and that they view the home circumstances in which their pupils live.[66]

In the United States, in contrast, there is frequent recourse to legal action on the part of students, parents, teachers, administrators, and school boards,

63. George Z. F. Bereday and Shigeo Masui, *American Education through Japanese Eyes* (The University Press of Hawaii, 1973), p. 53.

64. Ibid., p. 59.

65. Ibid., p. 201.

66. Ibid., pp. 59–60.

all of which makes it difficult to use informal norms effectively—or, alternatively, the use of formal rules and litigation is a reflection of the weakness of accepted informal norms. A Japanese teacher asked why the children had to line up before entering the school (a common sight in the American public school). The answer was: "The most important reason is that the school starts at 8:25 AM. If we let the pupils into the school building prior to that and if any accident should happen to them, such an accident would be the responsibility of the school authorities." The Japanese teacher concluded his account with the surprising and revealing comment: "I was very much embarrassed at this answer."[67] One assumes the embarrassment was at seeing a teacher so reduced from his general (diffuse) role as a guide and protector to a specific role, hemmed in by legal requirements.

It is not surprising, then, that in the comparative science study described earlier it was found that Japanese students at the primary and secondary level like school more than students in other countries.[68]

Thus, there emerges a pattern of empathy and responsibility within an accepted hierarchy, a pattern that will be found again in the subsequent discussion of the Japanese factory. Other descriptions would fit, too. Clearly, what can be seen here are "diffuse" patterns in a situation (teacher-student) that might call for "specific" ones. The teachers and students dig fishponds together; they plant flowers together; teachers watch over the school at night instead of watchmen; and students sweep up and wash up—the most surprising sight one may see in a visit to a Japanese school—as a result of which "no janitors or maintenance men are employed."[69]

These characteristics of the Japanese school suggest a community—a sense that all are bound together by common feelings, common experience, and well-understood objectives, characteristics that seem to follow logically from the long historical experience of an isolated and homogeneous nation on a distant group of islands. (I use "distant" not only from an American perspective but also from a Japanese, for to the Japanese their islands are distant from everywhere.)

Why Japanese Education Works

Communities are of various types, and I suggest that the Japanese type combines empathy and responsibility within a hierarchy that is itself based on certain established principles: age and, within limits, achievement. Be-

67. Ibid., p. 62.
68. Comber and Keeves, *Science Education in Nineteen Countries*, pp. 107–08.
69. Singleton, *Nichū*, p. 33.

yond that one finds a uniform, nationwide system with strong egalitarian traditions and commitments. Other writers, such as Passin and Cummings, whom I follow with respect, have also emphasized the high position traditionally given in Japan to education and teachers. The word "teacher" in Japanese, *sensei*, is a term of respect. The Japanese teachers who visited American schools commented that "American teachers do not seem to have the same spirit of selfless devotion that Japanese teachers have."[70] And as has been seen, a higher proportion of teachers, particularly in high school, have traditionally been men—reflecting the high status of the teacher—though this is now changing. This, too, is certainly an aspect of Japanese educational success, but the most distinctive element to my mind is the complex of uniformity, egalitarianism, and empathy within hierarchy—the community that binds teachers and students, parents and school.

Two other striking features of Japanese education may be regarded as contradicting this picture: the fierce political conflicts and the examination system. Can the term "community" be applied to a situation characterized by such polarization of political attitudes? Clearly the conflict is real, though the elements of community are real, too. The conflict, to the outside observer, seems to have limited power to spill over to affect personal relations and the requirements of the individual's role as teacher. The same teachers who stand against the Ministry of Education and who with their strikes and walkouts agitate education-conscious parents seem very committed to their students. Singleton, who has studied one Japanese school, ponders the contradiction between the commitment of the teachers in the school to the union and their commitment to their daily tasks of education.[71] The teachers in Singleton's school—they are from farm homes and probably not as politicized as those in large cities—feel that as teachers they must join the union; again, Japanese one-hundred-percentism. They did not personally oppose the national achievement tests, yet as members of the union they felt they had to support its stand and as a group oppose the achievement tests.[72]

It is also possible that the conflicts between union and education ministry have not undermined commitment to the teaching role because they have been interpreted by the union and its active members as a struggle to prevent a rigid and conservative style of education, one opposed to children's inter-

70. Bereday and Masui, *American Education through Japanese Eyes*, p. 194.
71. It is indeed a contradiction, for in the United States trade union emphases on wages, hours, working conditions, class size, and the like would be expected to undermine a full commitment to the teaching task and to replace some of the diffuse character of teaching with specific, rather legalistically detailed obligations; and this is in fact what happens.
72. Singleton, *Nichū*, p. 107.

ests, from being imposed on the schools. On the whole, the conflicts between union and ministry have not been about wages and hours but rather about such issues as whether teachers should be rated for efficiency, whether there should be national achievement tests, whether morals instruction should be reintroduced into the classroom (and in what form), or whether the ministry should have the right to approve textbooks and limit the right of teachers and school districts to select textbooks freely.

And yet the conflict between teachers and state is real and undoubtedly has certain consequences. Perhaps it contributes to the rather more sour attitude of educated Japanese youth toward their society and government than generally is found among analogous groups in other countries.[73] George DeVos, a perceptive researcher on Japanese character and personality, has suggested in conversation that the high school teacher represents the greatest single source of social strain within Japan: radicalized and resentful, he passes on his criticism of Japanese society to his students and contributes to a weakening of those values on which Japanese society—and, to extend DeVos's thought, economic growth—are based. There is no easy way of resolving this paradox. The same question arises in studies of the Japanese factory: whether the elements of conflict, which are real, will overcome the elements of harmony and community, which are equally real. The answer will be given only by history.

The examination system, too, seems contradictory to the picture described: a group of students all treated alike, kept together, the more able with the less able, all under the guidance of the empathetic teacher. Through the examination system there is introduced an element of fierce competitiveness, on the basis of which an elite will be selected and set above the others.

But there are a number of points to be noted about the selection of this elite. First, in the thinking of the Japanese this elite is not selected on the basis of hereditary distinctions of wealth, education, occupation, status, or even inherited intelligence. The Japanese believe instead that it is selected on the basis of will or effort, which anyone can put forward. Thus, the examination system leads to much less resentment than would be expected. It is seen, I would argue, as fair—more fair than the system by which students are selected for the Ivy League. It is not an inherited status that is legitimated, but a new status that is created. The Ivy League is seen as selecting and adding to the advantages of a preexisting elite, one based on the wealth and status of parents; Tokyo and Kyoto universities are seen as selecting from

73. These are the findings of a study conducted for the Japanese government by the Gallup polling organization. See Cummings, "The Effects of Japanese Schools," p. 23.

the entire nation a group that, fairly and justly, through its own effort, will become an elite. Both pictures, of course, are great exaggerations: effort and will are rewarded in the United States, and background gives an "unfair" advantage in Japan, where the high-fee private university is always available for those from more affluent families. But I am reporting the bias of the two systems—as it is perceived and as in large measure it exists.

Second, remarkable measures are taken to maintain the empathetic and nurturant tone of the school throughout the examination hell. Thus, the teacher is seen as the supporter of the youth: he, after all, will not grade the examinations, or set them; he is not the impersonal judge, nor is any individual. There are no interviews, only the objective test, so the aspiring student cannot complain that "the interviewer didn't like my long hair" or that "he preferred tennis to baseball."

Third, measures are taken to eliminate the sense of face-to-face competition between students. Thus, their grades in school will not be a source of conflict among them. I was asked by an authority on American education whether Japanese students study together to prepare for these awesome examinations. I had not heard of such a practice: the student gets a private teacher, goes to a tutoring class, studies on his own; the image is of the student spending endless hours alone at his desk. This pattern of lonely struggle helps preserve the empathetic group. One may compare it with the study group of law students in the movie *The Paper Chase,* which is dissolved by conflict as its members prepare for first-year law examinations.

Fourth, and finally, there is the fascinating thesis of Christie W. Kiefer,[74] who studied the Japanese middle-class family some years after Vogel's classic study *Japan's New Middle Class,* and found the same overwhelming significance of the examination. Kiefer's argument is that the examination period serves the psychological function of transferring the strong ties that bind mother and son in Japan, and male teacher and male student, to that new organization of which he will become a member: the bureaucracy. The bureaucracy will replace the warm group ties of family and school with the new ties of a company group and of a relationship to a patron. But in between there occurs a testing period during which the student has the strong support of his mother, working and feeling with him, and of his teacher.

The final point to be made about the paradoxes of Japanese education—sustained criticism and the maintenance of those patterns which are criticized, a uniformity and egalitarianism designed to select out an elite, a strong

74. "The Psychological Interdependence of Family, School, and Bureaucracy in Japan," *American Anthropologist,* vol. 72 (February 1970), pp. 66–75.

sense of community challenged by political conflict and the rigors of the examination system—is that for the most part the educational system is seen as just and fair. And a system works when it is seen as fair and does not work when it is seen as unfair—whatever its objective characteristics.[75] The new form of social selection that swept aside traditional Japanese distinctions during the Meiji period in the late nineteenth century—and that whatever the changes within it and the incongruities with which it operates, has retained its unique overwhelming predominance—is seen as fair. The criticism of Japanese radicals somehow does not reach it to undermine its general acceptance. If a system that calls for effort and hard work and asserts that each person is capable of putting forth such effort and hard work then distributes —with rigid fairness by some standard (leaving aside questions of the validity of the selection system)—the choice roles within the society on the basis of a measure of the effort set forth, one has an institutional pattern that is well designed to sustain a high level of effort.

The System in Perspective

To sum up a lengthy discussion, the Japanese elementary and secondary schools work well. Part of this working well may be attributed simply to a good educational system—uniform, national, of high standards, with well-trained teachers.[76] The morale of the teachers as teachers is high, which certainly can be attributed to the high prestige accorded them in Japan. This educational system is embedded in a social system that accepts it as egalitarian and fair. And its rigors[77] are tempered by empathetic and supportive relations between teachers and students. This pattern extends to the family, in which there also is behavioral support for the student (quiet for his

75. See Irving Kristol, " 'When Virtue Loses All Her Loveliness': Some Reflections on Capitalism and 'The Free Society'," *The Public Interest,* no. 21 (Fall 1970), pp. 3–15.

76. In the international study of science education, only Japan and Sweden responded that their teachers were drawn from the top half of the distribution of students in higher education.

77. Perhaps in my concern to elucidate the less obvious features of the social organization of Japanese schooling I have underemphasized its rigors. I have pointed out that Japanese students are expected to—and do—work very hard. They work very hard at outside lessons as well as at those in school. A study of fifth-grade students reported that in 1972 80 percent of the boys and 86 percent of the girls were taking outside lessons, up from approximately 70 percent in 1968. Calligraphy was in the lead, with 36 percent, but 26 percent were engaged in outside academic studies, 30 percent were taking abacus lessons, and 13 percent were studying the piano or organ (Kondō Sumio, "Off We Go to Our Lessons," *The Japan Interpreter,* vol. 9 [Spring 1974], pp. 15–16). Many Japanese teachers and education writers are concerned that the pressure on children is excessive.

study, no pressure to participate in home duties) and encouragement to do well.[78]

These features do not operate at the university level. Although the entrance examinations to the public and private universities are considered fair, they are also considered too arbitrary and harsh. It is not considered fair that those who enter the public universities should pay almost nothing, comparatively, for a good education, while those who enter the private ones pay heavily for a poorer one. Yet these distinctions are being reduced: the fees for national universities are rising, and in the last few years substantial public funds have begun to flow to private universities. There is little positive feeling about the educational process within the universities, public or private. But in effect a good part of the educational task that is performed by colleges and universities in other countries is performed by other means in Japan: earlier, by an effective primary or secondary system; later, by business corporations and government agencies, recruiting their employees directly from among the graduates of the four-year colleges. For the most part, Japanese enterprises train their own specialists and conduct their own research. Only 1 percent of the research of Japanese industrial enterprises is contracted out to universities.[79]

Thus, a strong primary and secondary education system is supplemented by a system of education within the enterprise. Although the system of higher education relative to the number of youth is larger than that of any developed nation except the United States, less money is spent on it on a per student basis than in other developed nations, and it is subject to severe internal

78. This discussion has concentrated entirely on the male student. Universal education does, of course, include girls up through the required nine years. The noncompulsory upper secondary school has as high a percentage of girls, 49 percent, as the lower secondary. Almost as many female as male graduates of the upper secondary school go on to higher education: 24.9 percent of the females, 26.5 percent of the males. The majority of the girls, however, enter the two-year junior college, whereas almost all the boys go on to college and university. Junior colleges (1971 enrollment, 275,000) are 82.9 percent female; college and university enrollment (1971, 1,469,000) is only 19.4 percent female (Bureau of Statistics, *Japan Statistical Yearbook, 1972*, pp. 544, 561). Women's courses of study also differ from men's: very small proportions go into natural science and engineering (UNESCO, *Statistical Yearbook, 1972*, pp. 384–85). This pattern is similar to that of other nations but more marked (see, for example, the ratios of male to female students working in science in their first year at a university reported in Comber and Keeves, *Science Education in Nineteen Countries*, p. 141: the sex ratios diverge more for Japan than for any other major country). The pressure on doing well to pass examinations for a good university is primarily a pressure on male students; most female students are expected to take a different course in studies and in life. Females are also excluded from the pattern of lifetime employment, as is discussed later.

79. Cummings, "The Changing Academic Marketplace," p. 419. See also Chapter 8 in this volume.

criticism for lack of effectiveness. The level of expenditure for higher education is rapidly rising, however—and in any case, even if higher education
has lagged in certain respects in comparison with other developed nations,
it does not seem to have hurt Japanese economic growth.

Values, Savings, and the Family

The study of values feeds into economic growth in three ways: first, by
explaining or attempting to explain an orientation toward achievement,
which can take various forms, depending on one's status as student, worker,
entrepreneur, manager, or whatever; second, by explaining how the individual fits into economic organization, which will be taken up in the following section; and third, perhaps, by explaining the substantially different rates
of personal savings among developed countries, rates that help explain the
level of investment and the rate of economic growth.

Values are considered as a problem in economic growth because it is assumed that—aside from rational calculation or a simple adaptation to given
circumstances that determines actions—there is some distinctive bent or
tendency or disposition that affects actions in a given society. If individuals
save more in one society than another, this can be regarded as the result of
various conditions: for example, that their incomes are going up fast, that
parts of it come in large lump sums, that they are eager to replace stock
destroyed by war, that they are preparing to pay for the education of their
children or their security in old age, or are adapting to a poorly developed
system of installment purchasing or mortgage financing to acquire large-cost
items such as automobiles and houses. All these factors have been studied in
an effort to explain the unusually high rate of personal savings in Japan since
World War II. But in addition, it might be considered that the Japanese have
a bent or disposition for saving, that they value saving highly for itself—
independently of their given circumstances and of any rational adaptation to
them.

In the same way, it is conceivable that education may be valued highly;
that good and careful work may be valued highly; that loyalty to superiors
may be valued highly; that a helpful concern for inferiors may be valued
highly.

Approaches to Values

But the study of values, and in particular the estimation of their weight in
explaining action, is extremely difficult. Three possible approaches stand out.
The first, exemplified in the classic studies by Benedict and Nakane referred

to above, is the study of patterns of behavior and the abstraction from them of certain themes that seem to explain behavior in a variety of circumstances and in different institutional settings. Thus, for Benedict the dominant theme in Japanese society is the network of obligations; for Nakane it is the tendency to emphasize the vertical aspects of social relations rather than the horizontal. Both analyses have been found highly enlightening by many observers of Japanese society, both native and foreign. This patterns-of-culture approach, however, leaves many others dissatisfied. The research that produces this kind of insight cannot be replicated or its weight as against other factors in explaining action justly estimated. Because the sources or the causes of the patterns are obscure—historical residue? family structure? education, informal or formal?—it is hard to determine how deeply rooted or shallow these patterns are and thus to say anything about when or whether they will change. Both Benedict and Nakane consider the patterns to be so deeply rooted that they believe they persist even after profound social changes. Thus, Nakane finds in the modern university something like the structure of the village complex of linked farming families; and Benedict, speculating at the end of the war that it was possible that the Japanese could shift rapidly from an authoritarian to a democratic society and polity, seemed to think that the pattern of linking and dominating obligations would not change—the best that could be hoped for was that the pattern could be adapted to democracy. Further, and also related to the problem of estimating change, this approach to values, because it operates on a large scale, tends not to differentiate between social levels, classes, and regions, and it leads to the query, "*All Japanese?*"

A second approach to the study of values in principle permits an estimation of the possibility and scale of change: this is the study of values as they are exhibited in the individual and produced in the family setting, particularly the practices of child rearing. It is psychoanalytic in approach, or at least psychologically developmental.[80] In this approach the proximate source of

80. Practitioners of this approach include William A. Caudill, who devoted many years to a patient and detailed comparative study of Japanese and American child rearing; George DeVos, who has used the thematic apperception test to unveil basic psychological themes in Japanese villagers and urbanities; and Takeo Doi, who has developed the significance of the concept of *amae*—acting so as to induce nurturant behavior in others—for Japanese. For Caudill, see "The Influence of Social Structure and Culture on Human Behavior in Modern Japan," *The Journal of Nervous and Mental Disease,* vol. 157 (1973), pp. 240–57; Caudill and Carmi Schooler, "Child Behavior and Child Rearing in Japan and the United States: An Interim Report," ibid., pp. 323–38; and references to other articles by Caudill in the bibliographies of these articles. For DeVos, see *Socialization for Achievement: Essays on the Cultural Psychology of the Japanese* (University of California Press, 1973), with contributions by Hiroshi Wagatsuma, William Caudill, and Keiichi Mizushima; and DeVos and Wagatsuma, *Heritage of Endur-*

values is at least clear: it is in the family drama. But many of the same questions can be raised that come up with the patterns-of-culture approach. How do practices of child rearing come about, how are they related to the economic structure of the society, how do they change, are they simply adaptive to economic necessity (for example, the rearing of both docile workers and aggressive entrepreneurs as they are needed by the system), or do they serve as an independent input? But once again, as in the case of the patterns-of-culture approach, the valuable insights and understandings produced by this approach can hardly be ignored.

Finally, the positivist social scientist will perhaps be happiest with a social-survey approach to values. Samples can be drawn of a whole society—or of workers or entrepreneurs or bureaucrats—and questions in the same form can be asked of each. Precise answers can be given about the extent of a response, its variation by occupation, income, residence, age, and sex, its change over time, and the difference in response among samples drawn from different nations. Precision certainly is increased by this approach, but the meaning of responses remains almost always arguable. If the aim is to tap underlying and significant values—as against tapping an opinion picked up from the mass media, affected by changing events, easily presented to an interviewer and as easily abandoned—there is no assurance that this has truly been achieved.

There is no easy solution to the problem: depth and insight apparently are traded off against precision and comparability. My aim in this section is to summarize what seems to me valuable in this large literature.

Values and Achievement

The approach of Benedict and Nakane seems to me most valuable in explaining the patterns of Japanese organization, which do present a dilemma to the Western mind. The standard Western interpretation of modernization assumes that for development to occur and proceed the network of traditional obligations must be broken. It is assumed that the traditional network will, for example, inhibit the originality, energy, and independence of the young and enterprising that is considered to be necessary if new technological and organizational forms are to be developed and adopted. This network may reduce motivation to produce because of fixed obligations to kin and authorities, and because it limits the possibilities of individual recognition and gain.

ance (University of Chicago Press, forthcoming). For Doi, see his " 'Amae': A Key Concept for Understanding Japanese Personality Structure," in Robert J. Smith and Richard K. Beardsley (eds.), *Japanese Culture* (Aldine, 1962), pp. 132–39; and *The Anatomy of Dependence* (Tokyo: Kōdansha, 1973).

In the patterns-of-culture approach, this traditional network in Japan is looked on as not having been superseded as radically as in other developed nations; rather, it persists or has been reconstructed under the new conditions of modernization. The great cycles of growth in Japan—those following the Meiji period (late nineteenth century) and World War II—took place after a breaking up of some part of the traditional network of obligations and vertical organization, but the argument of the pattern analysts is that the network subsequently was reestablished.

drive to family, nation, school, firm

DeVos and Caudill explain how the strong obligational net nevertheless produces a strong drive to individual achievement and thus to economic growth. The net of obligations woven by the family is directed toward getting (male) children to achieve in school and beyond—the means by which the basic obligations to the family can be paid off. The sense of obligation was transferred in the prewar period to the nation and the productive group, in the postwar period to the productive group alone.[81] Through achievement the "debt" to those owed—family, nation, school, firm—is repaid. The mechanism is quite distinct from that of the psychological pattern and values that underlie achievement in Western understanding, as developed by David McClelland and his collaborators.[82] The most striking contrast is that the Westerner's achievement motive, according to McClelland, seems to involve an obligation to oneself, and is based on training in independence and autonomy, with the result that one of the main empirical hallmarks of an achieving society is the age at which children are taught to do things for themselves. In the Japanese emotional economy, achievement seems to be an outgrowth of interdependency rather than independence. In Caudill's work this is traced to the earliest interaction between mother and child:

American infants show greater amounts of gross bodily activity, play (with toys, hands and other objects), and happy vocalization; in contrast, Japanese infants seem passive, having only a greater amount of unhappy vocalization. . . .

In America, even the infant is encouraged in some ways to care for his own needs; whereas in Japan the infant has learned that his needs will be taken care of by others if he complains hard enough. . . .

At age 2½ American children are more likely to do housework than are Japanese, and at age 6 they are more likely to be involved in the preparation of food and care of younger children than are Japanese children.

The overall conclusion is this:

[The Japanese child] grows up in an atmosphere of interdependence and collateral relations so that one of the very real psychological struggles for the grow-

---

81. See the discussion of the Kiefer article above.

82. David C. McClelland and others, *The Achievement Motive* (Appleton-Century-Crofts, 1953); McClelland and others, *Talent and Society* (Von Nostrand, 1958); and McClelland, *The Achieving Society* (Von Nostrand, 1961).

ing individual is to separate his identity from what he is only in relation to others —at first in the family, later in school, and still later in his occupation and marriage. In almost any area of interpersonal relations in Japan today the emphasis is still upon the interdependency of people who stand in highly particularistic relations to one another....[83]

The embarrassing whiff of ethnocentrism cannot be avoided in this kind of work, and the samples on which these observations were based were small: thirty infants each in Japan and the United States. Yet observations were taken over a period of six years, thousands of observations were made, and the results are congruent with a host of other observations of Japanese children and adults. Vogel also found little training for independence.[84] DeVos, in the use of projective psychological tests with Japanese adults, "found a pervasive preoccupation with achievement and accomplishment, no matter what group of Japanese was tested, but the achievement imagery differs from that found in American samples. . . . The Japanese . . . show both very high need affiliation [that is, "the need to be affiliated or connected with others"] and concern with nurturance and dependence, conflicting with American data, which usually suggest a negative correspondence between . . . [the need for] achievement and [the] need [for] affiliation."[85]

Finally, the concept of *amae* (a term introduced by Takeo Doi) is prominent in discussions of Japanese personality by writers of this school, and is described by DeVos as "the manipulation . . . of a potential giver by one who is dependent. This type of manipulation is explicitly recognized by the culture in the well-used words *amae* (noun) or *amaeru* (verb). . . . *Amaeru* . . . is an active verb in Japanese, designating a passive induction of nurturance towards one's self from others. . . . To *amaeru* is to produce passively the state of being loved or indulged or appreciated by another, a form of emotional judo." DeVos argues that in Japan "passivity and dependence [are] without the sense of shame or personal discomfort that a Westerner would feel if, as an adult, he gave himself over to a passive, dependent, yet manipulative role in social relationships. . . . [They run] counter to the Western ideal of personal autonomy."[86]

Analysts of this school trace this pleasure in interdependency and the induction of nurturance into later stages of life: into, for example, the common family and communal bath, the widespread practice of an entire family's sleeping in the same room (according to Caudill's studies, this is not differ-

83. Caudill and Schooler, "Child Behavior and Child Rearing," pp. 324, 334, 326, and 332, respectively.

84. *Japan's New Middle Class,* chap. 12.

85. DeVos, *Socialization for Achievement,* p. 180.

86. Ibid., p. 49.

entiated by class or occupation), and the style of entertainment of men by geisha.[87]

These psychological mechanisms should be seen as normative rather than pathological or aberrant—though undoubtedly they may take such forms, just as Western individualism may. From a Western point of view it can be asked how such a developmental pattern can be the basis of a drive for achievement; from a Japanese point of view, it can be, and is: the guilt induced by the nurturing parent is used to fuel the drive to achievement. Thus, an emphasis on interdependency, a yearning for nurturance and security within a group, may be as substantial a basis for achievement as Western emphases on personal autonomy and early independence.

Traditional and Modern Values

This kind of work has laid the basis for the positivistic approach to the study of values, the approach based on the questionnaire survey of given samples, statistically analyzed. The volume of such material is enormous. Perhaps most substantial and most interesting are repeated surveys of the Institute of Statistical Mathematics at five-year intervals since 1953.[88] These surveys were designed to determine whether changes were occurring in Japanese character, from what might be considered traditionalism to modernism. There is a problem, however, in using this work in an effort to project the future of the Japanese economy: if Japanese achievement is based on a distinctively Japanese pattern of personality and values and social structure, will the change to a "modern" (Western) form presage a decline in the strength of the sociopsychological basis of achievement, or its strengthening? The Japanese writer referred to by Dore[89] thought that democracy would

87. Caudill, "Influence of Social Structure and Culture," p. 254. R. P. Dore, commenting on this preference for a family's sleeping together in the same room, writes: "There is much to be said for the theory that this low evaluation of individual privacy is linked with the general preference for group, over individual, action and responsibility which characterizes Japanese society if compared with the 'individualistic' West. A Japanese newspaper writer once remarked that Japan will never be democratized or the principle of individual responsibility established until Japanese are brought up in separate bedrooms with solid sound-proof walls and locks on the doors." *City Life in Japan* (University of California Press, 1958), p. 49. Westerners may wonder how this affects sexual development, but in Japan sleeping together, just as bathing together, apparently implies coziness rather than sexuality. In any case, I have found no reference to the harmful effects of this practice on children.

88. My analysis is based on the English language summary published at the conclusion of Chikio Hayashi and others, *Nihonjin no kokuminsei* [A Study of Japanese National Character], vol. 2 (Tokyo: Shiseidō, 1970), pp. 507–52.

89. See note 87.

never be safe in Japan until each person had his own room. Similarly, it can be asked whether growth—which has soared while the Japanese family slept together, nurturing interdependency—is threatened or secured by a shift to Western patterns? The difficulty of answering this question undermines any substantial effort to use sociopsychological materials in a projection of economic developments in Japan.

Nevertheless, some trends have emerged from the Japanese surveys, although their meaning is in doubt. The decline of some Japanese traditional values—or traditional forms of stating them—is clear: there has been a regular increase over the fifteen years covered by the four surveys (1953 to 1968) in the preference stated for a life that "suits one's own taste" (from 21 to 32 percent) and a decline in the number of those who choose a "pure and just life" (from 29 to 17 percent). One key question testing traditional attitudes asks whether "it [is] necessary to adopt a child in order to continue the family line, even if there is no blood relationship." The proportion of persons responding affirmatively has declined from 73 to 43 percent. Another question, which shows a more modest decline in traditionalism, asks whether a parent should maintain denial of the fact if a child asks whether it is true that a teacher "had done something to get himself in trouble"; those voting for "deny" drop from 38 to 29 percent. The number believing "man must conquer nature to be happy" rose from 23 to 34 percent, and the number who thought it was best for a new prime minister to make a visit to the shrine at Ise dropped from 57 to 31 percent.

And yet among the questions that have elicited the least change to a more modern response are some that seem most closely related to economic behavior. One question asks whether the respondent prefers a department chief who "always sticks to the work rules and never demands any unreasonable work, but on the other hand, never does anything for you personally in matters not connected with the work"; or one "who sometimes demands extra work in spite of rules against it, but on the other hand, looks after you personally in matters not connected with the work." Those preferring the non-paternalistic supervisor have remained at a scarcely varying 12 percent; those preferring the paternalistic one have remained at an equally steady 84 percent. This high preference is not affected by age, sex, or occupation. Clearly, the preference for what may be considered a nurturant work setting has remained high.

The results of another intriguing—and characteristically Japanese—question are more difficult to interpret. The respondent is asked to imagine a situation in which an orphan boy was adopted and given a good education and rose to become president of a company. "One day he gets a telegram saying that Mr. A., who brought him up, is seriously ill and asking if he would come at once. This telegram arrives just at the moment when he is going to an important meeting which will decide whether his firm is to go bankrupt or to survive." What should he do? The proportion of those saying "leave everything and go home" has declined slightly but regularly over the years, from 54 to 46 percent, and those urging that he go to the meeting risen regularly but slightly, from 41 to 47 percent. But which response is the more "modern"? Both deal with obligations, and the question actually raises more the issue of the clash between two traditional obligations[90] than that of conflicts between traditionalism and modernism.

What explains this somewhat erratic shift to more modern responses? A multivariate analysis of the 1963 survey shows that the strongest factors in more modern responses are those of age and education, with more modest regional, occupational, and rural-urban–residence effects.[91]

In general, Japanese surveys suggest—as might be expected in a homogeneous society in which class differences are modest and the impact of World War II and the occupation were enormous in changing society—that the largest differences in responses on a host of questions are by age rather than by occupation or income. If one takes the clearly and most obviously traditional responses (adopting a child to maintain the family line, traditional Japanese formulations of the good life as conforming to nature and aiding the nation, the prime minister visiting Ise, and the like), there is no question that the young are the more "modern." But if the concern is with understanding the deeper values that underlie a modern orientation, it is arguable how much change has occurred in Japanese youth.

Lewis Austin has studied two generations of Japanese administrators—of middle and high level, in public and private enterprise, from universities of high prestige, of one generation that completed its education before the end of World War II and one after—and compared them with two generations of Yale alumni. His aim was to determine whether the younger Japanese and American generations were becoming more alike on measures of

90. This survey has been repeated with Japanese Americans in Honolulu. Its results give some help in determining which is the more "modern" or less "traditional" response to these questions. Only 58 percent of the Japanese Americans prefer the paternalistic supervisor; only 8 percent would deny to their child a rumor to the discredit of the child's schoolteacher if it were true; but the split on loyalty to one's benefactor versus business obligation is similar to that in Japan. Tatsuzo Suzuki and others, "A Study of Japanese Americans in Honolulu, Hawaii," *Annals of the Institute of Statistical Mathematics,* suppl. 7 (1972), pp. 19, 21, 23.

91. William K. Cummings and Michael J. Barnas, "Variability in Japanese National Character: A Test of the Modernization Perspective" (June 1974; processed).

authoritarianism and in their attitudes toward hierarchy and dogmatism, trust and suspicion, autonomy and dependence on the group, conflict and harmony. No clear evidence emerged of a convergence of Japanese and American values, and only mixed evidence of a shift in the younger Japanese generation to what are considered by contemporary social scientists to be the more modern values. Among the findings are these: "Dogmatic and hierarchical values declined in Japan, but not enough to keep pace with a greater decline in the United States. . . . We find a marked increase in individualistic attitudes in the United States but no change in Japan."[92]

The conclusion from even these unsatisfactory data—and all data on deep-seated values seem to be so—is clear: Japan is changing, but it remains substantially different in basic values from Western societies.[93]

Values and Saving

It would seem that the strongest link between values and economic growth could be demonstrated by showing some link between values and saving, yet the evidence as to what distinctive Japanese values contribute in explaining the extraordinarily high postwar rate of personal savings is ambiguous.

There are numerous studies investigating what in translation come out as "way of life preferred" and "goals in life." These record a very sharp shift, perhaps a continuing one, from a prewar emphasis (still to be seen in the older generations) on service to society and selflessness to a postwar emphasis on following one's own desires and tastes (somewhat stronger in the younger generations). Thus, the same question about "way of life" was put to military recruits before the war, in 1931 and 1940, and to the national samples surveyed by the Institute for Statistical Mathematics. One of the alternative responses is "resist all evils in the world and live a pure and just life." Before the war 30 or 40 percent chose this response; 29 percent chose it in the first postwar survey (1953), and the proportion has declined steadily to 17 percent in 1968. The shift downward is more marked among

92. Lewis Austin, "The Political Culture of Two Generations: Evolution and Divergence in Japanese and American Values" (paper prepared for delivery at a seminar on Japan by 1980, Yale University, March 15, 1973; processed), pp. 24–25.

93. Ezra Vogel has pointed out in correspondence that one value that emerges clearly from the literature on Japanese values is the long-range perspective that is accepted: the willingness to work for a distant future. Japanese stories emphasize years of preparation and training, in contrast to those of Communist China, which emphasize quick results. Undoubtedly many separate themes in the present study are illuminated by such an emphasis: the long struggle to get into the correct and best university, beginning in kindergarten, and (to be discussed below) the willingness of young employees to work for low wages, looking ahead to the rewards that become significant after long service.

young people. An almost equally severe drop from the prewar period is recorded for the response "never think of yourself; give everything in service to society." A sharp rise is recorded for the nontraditional "don't think about money or fame; just live a life that suits your own tastes," which has risen steadily in the postwar surveys from 21 to 32 percent, with a rather sharper rise for youth; and for "live each day as it comes, cheerfully and without worrying," which shows a postwar rise from 11 to 20 percent. A strong shift to nontraditional values—to those which deemphasize service to society (and in other surveys, to the nation) and to higher impersonal values, and which emphasize a life devoted to oneself and one's pleasures—is clear.

But it would be a mistake to conclude that these newer statements of goals in life reflect a rampant hedonism. The concrete meaning of these responses seems to imply an emphasis on work and study, the family, the children's development, and, for the young in particular, leisure. There is some evidence that the shift toward these newer, "this-worldly" values is more marked in the younger than older age groups. Yet the most thorough effort to analyze this matter seems to suggest that goals in life, after undergoing a marked postwar shift, have remained fairly stable, changing only with the ongoing stages in the individual's life cycle. Dominant are such goals in life as work and study, the home, and the children; for the young, leisure and friends replace children and family, but work and study maintain their primacy.[94]

If the consequences for savings were to be projected from these surveys, they would be ambiguous: the new emphasis on following one's own way and on leisure might suggest a lower rate of saving; the overwhelming emphasis on home and children might suggest a higher. If, further, the overwhelming Tokugawa and Meiji and pre–World War II official emphasis on frugality for both the lower and the upper classes were taken into account,[95] the savings rate might have been expected to fall. The fact is, of course, that the rate of household saving increased in the late 1950s and 1960s to considerably higher levels than in the Meiji or pre–World War II periods—indeed, to rates

94. The sources for the above are Hayashi and others, "A Study of the Japanese National Character," p. 522; Munesuke Mita, *Gendai no ikigai: kawaru nihonjin no jinseikan* [The Goals of Life in Our Time: Changing Life Philosophy in Japanese People] (Tokyo: Nihon Keizai Shinbunsha, 1970), pp. 38, 44–45, 49. One survey and analysis—Munesuke Mita, *Gendai no seinenzō* [Contemporary Young People] (Tokyo: Kōdansha, 1968)—suggests a smaller role for work, but in general the picture is as presented in the text. For the two sources in Japanese I follow a summary prepared by Professor Kōkichi Shōji.

95. This emphasis declined suddenly after World War II. Although it has been replaced by a continuous prosavings campaign by the Bank of Japan and other banks, the latter probably has little of the power of the prewar emphasis which was supported by political, military, and educational authorities.

higher than ever seen before in developed nations. Thus, it is difficult to perceive any direct relation between the Japanese value pattern, at least as it is accessible to surveys and questionnaires, and the intense proclivity to save. Econometric analyses of the relevance of specific economic factors, as well as of factors of social and occupational structure, to the proclivity to save seem to explain the phenomenon much better.[96]

Various analysts agree to one degree or another on the following as significant:

—The rapid increase in income of all groups after the war, which certainly made possible more savings, which could be further explained by a lag in consumption habits. (This would fit in with the general post-Meiji experience in Japan, when the shift to consumption of different and more expensive items of clothing, housing, and food developed only slowly.)

—The important role of the bonus system, which gives large chunks of income to wage earners twice a year, permitting them to adapt to living on their regular income and to consider the bonus as something extra that can be saved.

—The prominant role in the Japanese economy of the self-employed, who cannot look forward to company or government pensions and thus must save for their old age and for maintenance of their small farms or businesses.

—The very small government contribution to higher education and to social security, which makes savings for the education of one's children and for one's old age important.

—The pattern by which wage earners in large companies, blue-collar and white-collar, are required to retire early but are given a large lump-sum retirement benefit, which also can be saved for the future.

—The underdevelopment of mortgage financing, personal loans, and installment buying, which requires savings for acquisition of a plot to build on, a house, an automobile, or other expensive items.

96. I have drawn on the following, among others, for the summary in the text: Ryūtarō Komiya, "The Supply of Personal Savings," in Komiya (ed.), *Postwar Economic Growth in Japan* (University of California Press, 1966), pp. 155–81, and comment on same by Miyohei Shinohara, pp. 182–86; Toshiyuki Mizoguchi, *Personal Savings and Consumption in Postwar Japan* (Tokyo: Kinokuniya, 1970), and "High Personal Savings Rate and Change in the Consumption Pattern in Postwar Japan," *The Developing Economies,* vol. 8 (December 1970), pp. 407–26; Tuvia Blumenthal, *Savings in Postwar Japan* (Harvard University Press, 1970); K. Tominaga and M. Naoi, "Kakei chochiku kōdō no kettei yōin" [Determinants of Household Savings Behavior], *Chochiku jihō* [Savings Journal], no. 97 (September 1973), using a summary prepared by Konosuke Odaka; and Ohkawa and Rosovsky, *Japanese Economic Growth,* pp. 167–72. See also Chapter 4 in this volume.

Results from econometric analyses are supported by direct survey answers about reasons for saving. In order, the reasons given in multiple-answer responses in 1972 are: in preparation for illness or untimely accidents, 76.6 percent; for children's education and weddings, 49.7 percent; for purchase of land or house or for construction or repair of house, 33.7 percent; for life after retirement, 37.3 percent; for purchase of commodities of considerable value, 10.3 percent; to travel or enjoy leisure activities, 7.7 percent; for no special reason, 28.7 percent. These responses remained fairly stable between 1966 and 1972.[97]

With improvements in the Japanese system of social security for illness and old age, which are constantly under consideration and to some extent are being made, and with a greater government contribution to the costs of university education, which also is taking place, some of the major reasons for saving will be reduced in importance. There is also a good deal of pressure from government to raise the age of formal retirement (now still widely set at fifty-five, but in fact often higher) to reduce the gap in the period between forced retirement and the availability of pensions.[98] But considerable room for improvement remains: Japanese taxes and social insurance contributions are apparently the lowest of developed countries.[99] Other analyses, outside the scope of this paper, may show a slackening in the rate of income growth, a decline in the self-employed sector, and changes in the system of mortgage financing, personal finance, and installment buying, all of which may serve to depress the rate of savings. But there seems to be little inclination to change the pattern whereby substantial parts of income are received as bonuses. While economic factors explain the savings rate, distinctive Japanese values—for example, the long-range perspective mentioned above—must also play some role.[100]

The Family

No discussion of values can conclude without some comment on the Japanese family, which has been a principal focus of sociological and anthropological study, in part because of its strong role in law and fixed custom in

97. Economic Planning Agency, *Whitepaper on National Life, 1973,* p. 250.

98. Developments in the field of health insurance and old age pensions are inevitably complex. For a recent summary of the situation and proposed changes, see Paul Fisher, "Major Social Security Issues: Japan, 1972," *Social Security Bulletin,* vol. 36 (March 1973), pp. 26–38; and Chapter 1 of this volume.

99. EPA, *Whitepaper on National Life, 1973,* p. 249.

100. See note 93. For example, David Riesman asks (in correspondence) whether American wage earners would bank the same proportion of their bonuses, particularly if they faced the high inflation and low interest rates on savings of Japan.

Japanese society before the war and the radical legal changes imposed by the occupation. The family before the war was something like a small state: decisions affecting the lives of children, such as education, marriage, and occupation, were made in large measure by the father as "ruler," and his power passed to the first son. Continuance of the family was given great importance, and if there were no son one would be adopted, either as a daughter's husband who took the family name or directly as a child or adult without marriage into the family. The family was Japanese society, headed by the emperor, writ small. It was rooted in an agricultural past, even if it was an urban family. The family register was kept in the rural hamlet that was the wellspring of most Japanese families, and this was regularly visited by the city members of the family. The aged parents were accommodated with respect in the household of the eldest son, who inherited the family property.

But in 1947 equal inheritance, equal responsibility to support parents, marriage based on the desires of the contracting partners rather than the families, and similar Western customs were imposed as legal norms. The family ideology that had been so prominent a part of prewar Japanese education and culture disappeared from the school curriculum and official announcements. These changes in law and ideology were accompanied by the rapid decline of the large agricultural sector, which weakened the strong patriarchal family.

Startling changes occurred as a result in the family. Household size, which had remained steady at about 5.0 persons since 1920, began to decline suddenly in 1955; by 1968 it had fallen to 4.08. The proportion of nuclear families—those containing only parents and children—rose rapidly, from 46.4 percent of all families in 1954 to 65.4 percent in 1967. The proportion of single families—those in which one of the parents was missing and households consisting of a single person—rose from 9.0 to 19.6 percent. As a result, those households holding three generations of a family fell from 44.6 to 15.0 percent. The birthrate dropped rapidly immediately after the war and has remained quite low.[101]

Amidst all this revolutionary change, however, there remain signs of substantial stability—at least compared with other countries. The divorce rate has been rising for the past ten years, but quite slowly—from 0.75 per 1,000 persons in 1962 to 0.99 in 1971, or about one divorce to every 10.5 marriages. In the United States there is more than one divorce for every three marriages. The number of persons receiving public assistance is extremely low and falling, from 1.7 million in 1962 to 1.3 million in 1971, only slightly more than 1 percent of the population. The comparable American

101. Haruo Matsubara, "The Family and Japanese Society after World War II," *The Developing Economies,* vol. 7 (December 1969), pp. 499–508.

statistic in 1972 was about 7 percent. Only 10 percent of the assisted house-holds in Japan in 1971 consisted of only mother and children, while the rest were mainly aged and invalids; the American case load is predominantly the fatherless family. The percentage of aged accommodated in residential or nursing homes in Japan, as against those living with their children or in their own homes, is low: 1 percent, compared to 2.7 percent in the United States. This kind of statistic may simply reflect the lack of accommodation, but other evidence suggests that although this may in part be the case, the problem of the homeless aged is much less severe in Japan than in the United States or other developed nations—another sign of how in Japan traditionalism in some respects may accompany rapid modernization.

A stable and unbroken family certainly is not the sole factor lowering the incidence of juvenile delinquency, though it seems to be a major one. Rates of juvenile delinquency in Japan are remarkably low, as are rates of crime generally; and for the most part they have been falling for the past ten years. Compare the following sets of statistics on numbers of crimes in Japan and the United States (the latter having about twice the population):[102]

Country and year	Homicide	Robbery	Rape
Japan			
1963	2,281	4,021	6,239
1972	2,060	2,500	4,677
United States			
1960	9,000	107,000	17,000
1972	19,000	375,000	46,000

The Japanese family is undoubtedly changing; but for a developed country it still maintains a remarkable stability, which underlies the stability of the value pattern and, to my mind, contributes to the pattern of achievement in school and work.

The Sociology of the Workplace[103]

The subject of the workplace and its character in Japan lies at the heart of discussions about the possible contribution of social and cultural features to Japanese economic performance. Whether and to what extent the Japa-

102. The sources for data on family, welfare, and crime are Bureau of Statistics, *Monthly Statistics of Japan* (May 1973), pp. 4, 125, 128; Economic Planning Agency, *Whitepaper on National Life, 1973,* pp. 17, 19, 36; and U.S. Bureau of the Census, *Statistical Abstract of the United States, 1973,* pp. 65, 146, 308.

103. This section inevitably overlaps considerably with Chapter 9, and only modest efforts have been made to eliminate such overlap. My approach, contrasting with that of

nese workplace—factory, office, or any other enterprise—is affected by Japanese society and culture has been a much disputed and much researched question. The lines of the argument were drawn by an early and classic statement by James Abegglen,[104] which has had as great an effect on thinking about Japan (by Westerners and Japanese, whether they accepted it or disputed it) as Benedict's *The Chrysanthemum and the Sword*. It was Abegglen who first brought to the attention of many Westerners certain peculiarities of Japanese industrial organization.

As he described it, the first peculiarity was the existence of a lifetime employment system: the employee was hired for life, the company expected to keep him for life, the worker expected to stay for life and felt committed to do so.

The second, directly related to the first, dealt with the process of recruitment. If the employee was to be hired for life, he (the permanent employment system was limited to men) of course would have to be examined more closely, and thus such factors as his moral character, his education, and the character of his family and references might all be relevant to the choice. He should if at all possible be recruited directly from school.

Third, the process of advancement in the system of employment for life was on the basis of seniority rather than of merit or achievement.

Fourth, the whole system worked. To Western thinking, a system that guaranteed lifetime employment and advanced its members on the basis of age and length of service had to be a guarantor of sloth and incompetence rather than a spur to harder work and greater efficiency. But the system worked because the Japanese company was a community, with a moral commitment by the worker to the welfare of the company of which he felt himself to be a part. And this aspect of the company—a community, with members ranked in a hierarchy, each of them accepting his obligations rather than insisting on his rights—represented a heritage of Japanese feudalism that had persisted into the modern corporation.

Fifth, the peculiar character of the Japanese labor movement reinforced this community aspect of the company. Springing into existence under the benign influence of the American occupation, the movement rapidly went through a radical phase, but its form of organization was that of the enterprise union—that is, the union encompassing all the workers, white collar and blue collar, of a single company. Although the enterprise unions were

---

Galenson and Odaka in orientation and intention, concentrates on studies of the workplace and factory, and my concern is to trace the impact on, and implications for, the workplace of themes in Japanese culture and society raised in the first two sections.

104. *The Japanese Factory: Aspects of Its Social Organization* (Free Press, 1958).

linked in national unions, the seat of power and of collective bargaining remained for the most part at the enterprise rather than the national level.[105]

A great many questions could be—and were—raised about this picture. First, could it possibly be true? Second, if it was true, how could it possibly motivate workers to give their best to the firm and how could it be compatible with the most rapidly growing economy in the world? Third, if it was true, and if for some reason it was compatible with economic growth, how could it possibly last? A fourth question deals with the origins of this system but perhaps is relevant to its future: what was its origin and what sustained it?

A great deal more is known now about the sociology of the Japanese workplace than when Abegglen first brought its peculiarities to the attention of the West, and some brief answers to these questions can be given.

Lifetime Employment

Was it true? In considering the permanent employment feature, several important qualifications crop up. First, Abegglen admitted that he described the employment system of only the large Japanese companies, which made up only a small part of the Japanese economy.

Second, the employment contract comes to an end at age fifty-five in that part of the economy in which lifetime employment was best established. At that age, workers receive a substantial lump-sum retirement benefit (in recent years, three and a half to four years of pay);[106] they are either reemployed by the same company at a lower wage or go to a smaller company (possibly one linked with the larger company), open a small business, or actually retire. But typically they continue work at reduced wages.

Third, lifetime employment does not apply to women. Although they form a higher proportion of the Japanese labor force than in the United States, they are generally considered part of the regular body of employees only until they get married. Only up to that point do they get regular increases, and the great majority leave the firm long before they have achieved a substantial wage. Married women do work, but for the most part not as regular employees of large firms. They may be part-time employees there or they may work in smaller firms, but in any case the female part of the labor force is not generally included in the system of lifetime employment.

---

105. Abegglen actually had little to say about the Japanese union; the view of the union summarized here is based on Solomon B. Levine, *Industrial Relations in Postwar Japan* (University of Illinois Press, 1958).

106. Shun'ichiro Umetani, "Life of the Worker," *Japan Labor Bulletin* (January 1973), p. 5.

Fourth, because the large companies make such a commitment, they are careful not to increase the number of permanent employees beyond what they may need in a recession. They protect themselves from the vagaries of the market by hiring temporary employees, by surrounding themselves with a host of smaller companies, contractors, and subcontractors, and by having many of their services (trucking, janitorial, waste handling, and so on) done by subordinate companies. Presumably it is these satellites that bear the burden of unemployment as a result of downturns in the economic cycle.

Finally, there are two significant limitations on the extent to which permanent employment could be considered to be a permanent feature of the Japanese economy. First, what would happen if the system were to be severely tested by recession and unemployment? Second, could it be maintained in view of the changing attitudes and increasing education of youth? Permanent employment involves not only the commitment of the worker to the firm, but also his acceptance of a lifetime pattern in which he achieves the full benefit of long-term commitment only after long service. Will contemporary youth accept that?

In the years since Abegglen wrote, various developments have extended the reach of permanent employment. Large companies have grown: whereas in 1956 only 25.5 percent of workers in the private sector were employed by companies with more than 500 workers, by 1968 this had risen to 31.8 percent. In the manufacturing sector the rise was from 30.6 to 37.5 percent, in the services sector, from 53.0 to 61.9 percent, in retail and wholesale and financial and real estate services, from 16.8 to 25.9 percent.[107] The proportion of temporary employees has declined because of the labor shortages that have been recurrent in the last fifteen years.[108]

Since Abegglen wrote, the system of lifetime employment also has been tested in a number of recessions, and it did not seem to moderate the effects of recession on employment.[109] The most severe test of the system began with the deep recession of 1974–75, and it is too early to make any definitive statements about the results.

HOW MUCH JOB MOBILITY? One general test of the strength of the system of lifetime employment is to be found in the actual numbers of workers changing jobs in any given period and in the seniority built up by workers. The percentage of employees leaving manufacturing firms of all sizes was 28.1 in 1963 and 28.3 in 1967, and no trend was discernible in the years between. Monthly separation rates for the manufacturing sector in Japan were 2.0 per-

107. Yoshio Kaneko, "Employment and Wages," *The Developing Economies,* vol. 8 (December 1970), pp. 454–55.
108. This matter is explored in greater detail in Chapter 9.
109. OECD, *Manpower Policy in Japan* (Paris: OECD, 1973), pp. 104–05.

cent in 1959 and 2.3 percent in 1968. Again, no marked trend could be discerned. Comparable American figures for this period moved upward from 4.1 to 4.6 percent. Interfirm moves have a curvilinear relation to size: in 1967, the separation rate was 30.0 percent in firms of from 5 to 29 employees, 35.6 percent for from 30 to 99, 30.5 percent for from 100 to 499, and 21.1 percent for firms with more than 500.[110]

A comparison in 1966 showed that 56 percent of males aged thirty-five to thirty-nine had more than ten years' seniority in Japan, against only 34 percent of the same group in the United States; 12 percent of the Japanese high seniority group had more than twenty years' seniority, as against 2 percent of the American.[111] More recent statistics suggest that the pattern of low overall mobility is being maintained. Between 1966 and 1970, the total separation rate showed no significant trend: 20.1 percent at the beginning, 21.3 percent at the end.[112] And the most recent figures for rate of turnover suggest actually something of a decline.[113]

Thus, in a crude sense the pattern of lifetime employment—with all the limitations already mentioned, and others to come—has maintained its dominance. It is the pattern of public employment and of employment in the large firms, and it is the ideal to which smaller firms aspire. Although it does not include the majority of nonagricultural workers in Japan, it remains the central distinguishing feature of the Japanese employment system.

HOW MUCH RECRUITMENT FROM THE SCHOOLS? Lifetime employment is linked to distinctive systems of recruiting workers and of compensating labor. Much of the post-Abegglen dispute has centered on the extent to which Japanese employers can still draw their work force fresh from the schools and expect to keep them. In the past, the graduate of the middle school, the equivalent of the American junior high school, expected to go into manual work, the graduate of the high school (senior high school) into white-collar work, and

110. Robert M. Marsh and Hiroshi Mannari, "Lifetime Commitment in Japan: Roles, Norms, and Values," *American Journal of Sociology,* vol. 76 (March 1971), pp. 798–99. I have not examined the original sources for these data.

111. Robert E. Cole, "Permanent Employment in Japan: Facts and Fantasies," *Industrial and Labor Relations Review,* vol. 26 (October 1972), p. 618. Cole (p. 619), using the statistic of employed males changing jobs in one year in nonagricultural industries, shows an upward trend of job-changing in Japan: from 2.7 percent in 1959 to 4.4 percent in 1968. But he also writes: "The extent of recent changes should not be exaggerated.... Many of the changes have been a response to timing in the business cycle rather than part of a clearly discernible upward trend in labor mobility" (p. 623).

112. Umetani, "Life of the Worker," p. 5.

113. Ministry of Labor, *Year Book of Labor Statistics, 1972,* p. 18. For industries (excluding services) the separation rate dropped from 2.8 percent in 1968 to 2.2 percent in 1972 (monthly averages), for manufacturing alone from 2.5 to 1.8 percent.

the university graduate into junior management and higher technical positions. Employees of all education levels could be part of the permanent employment work force. Before the war and when Abegglen wrote, different terms were used to refer to white-collar workers (staff) and manual workers, and there were different systems of compensation and benefits, but increasingly the term used for all workers in the firm, the system of compensation, and the system of benefits, have become the same. (Both white-collar workers and manual workers are typically members of the same enterprise union.)

The first significant strain on the system, developing in the 1960s, was a growing shortage of middle school graduates that resulted from the rapid increase in the number of students going on to high school, as well as the ending of the effects of the baby boom in the early 1950s. In 1955, 69 percent of those entering the labor force from schools and universities (700,000 out of 1,020,000) were middle school graduates, but by 1968 the figure was only 27 percent (390,000 out of 1,430,000), and by 1972, only 16 percent (147,000 out of 915,000). In 1973, only 109,000 middle school graduates entered the labor market. Meanwhile, senior high school graduates entering the labor force climbed steadily, from 260,000 (25 percent) in 1955 to 526,500 (57.5 percent) in 1972. University and junior college graduates entering the labor force also rose markedly, from 70,000 (7 percent) in 1955 to 242,000 (26 percent) in 1972. Throughout this entire period middle school graduates were in greater demand than high school or college and university graduates: official figures reported almost six openings for every middle school graduate in 1973 and only a little more than three openings for each high school graduate.[114]

There are three observable effects of this rising educational level of the work force. First, differences in earnings among employees by educational level have been reduced as the number of available workers who could be brought into the firm directly from middle school, the desired pattern, has been reduced.[115]

Second, young Japanese workers, greatly in demand, have become more mobile. A 1969 survey of the Ministry of Labor examined 950,000 graduates of middle schools over a three-year period from 1965 and discovered

114. Economic Planning Agency, *New Economic and Social Development Plan, 1970–75*, p. 142; Ministry of Labor, *Year Book of Labor Statistics, 1972*, pp. 24–25; and *Japan Labor Bulletin* (November 1973).

115. See data in Robert M. Marsh and Hiroshi Mannari, "A New Look at 'Lifetime Commitment' in Japanese Industry," *Economic Development and Cultural Change*, vol. 20 (July 1972), p. 625.

that 20 percent had left their jobs within one year of employment and 52.5 percent within three years.[116] Even with this increasing flightiness of the young, they are far less mobile than young American workers.[117]

Cole points out that comparisons with the United States are with a very mobile society: Japanese rates are only slightly lower than those in England and West Germany, according to the Organisation for Economic Co-operation and Development.[118]

A change in the young is always difficult to explain. It is a generational change, with long-term consequences for this generation's behavior as it becomes older? Or an age effect, which will pass as workers become older, get married, assume more obligations, and build up seniority in a firm, all of which make it increasingly difficult to leave? Or the effect of an increase in outside opportunities? Rodney Clark, an anthropologist studying one Japanese company intensively, concluded: "My own view . . . is that the opinions of the young people of Japan are engendered as much by their age as by their generation; especially so in industry where the promotion by age system and the nature of the labour market create very different conditions for young and old."[119]

The third effect of the shortage of the middle school workers is interesting but unfortunately the least studied: more and more senior high school graduates must now accept blue-collar jobs, and more and more students with higher education will in the future find it difficult to get the jobs they expect. From the point of view of social stress, the failure of the system to fulfill traditional expectations would seem to be its most vulnerable point. According to Cole: "In 1964 high school graduates made up 16.7 percent of all blue-collar workers, as compared to 13.4 percent in 1958,"[120] and the percentage is rising. It is perhaps revealing that among the group of Japanese factories that have been intensively studied, one, a die-casting plant in

116. For this survey, see Robert E. Cole, "The Theory of Institutionalization: Permanent Employment and Tradition in Japan," *Economic Development and Cultural Change,* vol. 20 (October 1971), p. 66.

117. In 1965–66 the percentage of eighteen- to thirty-four-year-olds changing jobs in the United States was more than three times as high as in Japan (Cole, "Permanent Employment in Japan," p. 627).

118. OECD, *Wage and Labour Mobility* (Paris: OECD, 1965), p. 50, as given in Cole, "Permanent Employment in Japan," p. 626.

119. Rodney Clark, "Social Relations in a Japanese Company" (Ph.D. dissertation, University of London, 1972), p. 45.

120. Robert E. Cole, *Japanese Blue Collar: The Changing Tradition* (University of California Press, 1971), p. 83. I calculate that about 34 percent of high school graduates had to take jobs as manual workers in 1971 (Ministry of Labor, *Year Book of Labor Statistics, 1972,* pp. 24–25, 33).

Tokyo in which Robert E. Cole worked, stands out for the militancy of its workers, their cynicism, and their refusal to accept a subordinate and docile position to management except insofar as it is forced on them. This plant also stands out because of the high proportion of high school graduates in its labor force (80 percent of the blue-collar workers). There were many factors that could explain why the workers in this plant were more militant than others who have been studied: it was in the middle of Tokyo, and its workers reflected big-city skepticism and cynicism; its management had recently changed, and in trying to save a failing company it ran into much conflict with workers. But surely a major factor was that its workers were high school graduates doing blue-collar jobs and discontented for that reason.

MIDCAREER EMPLOYEES. Thus, changes have occurred in the pattern of recruitment of labor into Japanese firms. The direct and accepted passage from school to permanent employment has been in some measure broken by the increasing mobility of young workers and by labor shortages that lead to a continual search for more employees. (Aside from hiring directly from school, there is also still a large flow of employees for the modern sector directly from the traditional sectors of agriculture and family employment, which helps maintain the strength of traditional patterns.) But the effect of these newer patterns of recruitment on the overall lifetime employment pattern is not yet clear. The number of employees hired in midcareer from other companies is increasing. Traditionally, the worker brought up by a firm—that is, taken directly from school—has been considered more loyal, immobile, and dependable, whereas the worker hired in midcareer has been looked on with suspicion, has had to begin at a lower wage and work himself up to the level of his age-mates who began in the firm. But it seems clear that with labor shortages he is increasingly being treated better, more like the employees who have been with the firm from the beginning of their careers.[121] If the new midcareer employee is treated as well as the brought-up employee, this presumably will encourage mobility. Another inference that can be drawn is that the midcareer changer may also be facing his last chance to connect with the lifetime employment system and thus is eager to make good and to make up the deficiency of not having been with the firm from the beginning.

In the Marumaru corrugated board plant studied by Rodney Clark, a growing firm that was approaching 1,000 employees, the midcareer employee is stabler and more dependable than the new school employee. Although the

---

121. Marsh and Mannari, "A New Look at 'Lifetime Commitment'," pp. 617–21.

midcareer recruits were no more likely to leave than those recruited from school (who were rather casual about what Marumaru had to offer them in a booming labor market), the company invested great effort in recruiting the new school graduates and inducting them as members of the company through elaborate training programs and public ceremonies. Here it was reflecting the bias of the Japanese company for the brought-up worker—as well as the pragmatic consideration that as young workers they were cheaper. At the time Clark was conducting his study in 1970 the company was spending ¥500,000 each to recruit school graduates, but almost nothing to recruit midcareer workers. "It was considered quite impossible to attract workers with experience of corrugated board manufacture; and advertising for them would only have the effect of antagonizing rival companies." Clark believes, however, that this attitude reflected a cultural bias, and that real opportunities existed in the labor market that the company failed to exploit.[122]

In the large Hitachi plants studied by Dore, located in and near the town of Hitachi, there seemed to be few midcareer recruits—or, at any rate, Dore devotes little space to them. These plants are in a rural setting, dominate the area, and are in a prefecture in which the proportions of students going on to high school and college are much smaller than in Tokyo and other large cities. For these reasons, Hitachi apparently is able to meet most of its needs by recruiting directly from school, and is able to get the guarantees of character from teachers and family[123] that are the ideal of the Japanese employment system:

Among the younger third of the Hitachi sample 32% said in answer to a question asking how they came to find their job, that they had been recommended by the school or by a particular teacher (. . . less than 1% of the [comparable] British engineering sample). Mostly the rest were introduced by relatives and friends; only 6% came (like 50% of the British sample) in response to an advertisement or by direct application unmediated by any personal connection. . . .

Hitachi still has means—and uses them—of checking to make sure that the family of prospective employees had no criminal record. . . .

Recruitment can be seen as the "handing over" by school and by family, of one of its members to the firm.[124]

There remains something distinctive about the recruitment of workers in Japan.

122. Clark, "Social Relations in a Japanese Company," pp. 40, 86, and chap. 3.

123. These are more than references: the person who recommends a new employee guarantees his good behavior. For example, he may argue with the young worker should he wish to leave the firm and urge him to fulfill his obligations—to his guarantors as well as his employer.

124. Dore, *British Factory–Japanese Factory*, p. 61.

Are Rewards Based on Age and Seniority?

A wage system based principally on age and length of service, rather than on how well the worker is doing his job, produced until the very recent past striking disparities between the wages of young and old workers. Thus, in 1958 and 1967, the ratios of monthly pay of retiring male employees to new male employees in Japanese manufacturing were:[125]

Educational level	1958	1967
College graduates (clerical, white collar)	5.7	4.7
High school graduates (clerical, white collar)	6.5	5.2
High school graduates (manual, blue collar)	5.1 (1963)	4.3
Middle school graduates (manual, blue collar)	6.4	4.7

Calculating comparable American ratios is complicated by the fact that there is no uniform retiring age of fifty-five. However, Marsh and Mannari take, for 1959, mean annual earnings for the male experienced labor force, and find that the earnings of workers with high school and elementary school education, whether in clerical or manual work, do not increase with age. Only for college graduates do we find any significant progression of earnings by age: the wages of college graduate managers, officials, and proprietors (except farm), aged fifty-five to sixty-four, are 2.3 times those of college graduates in this occupational category aged twenty-five to thirty-four. The wages of college graduate clerical and kindred workers aged forty-five to fifty-four are 1.3 times those of the same category aged twenty-five to thirty-four.[126] Despite its steady retreat, payment related to age and seniority still maintains a much stronger place in Japanese practice than in American.

For at least ten years Japanese management has sought to modify a wage system based on age and education by introducing more elements related to the specific job and individual ability and achievement, but detailed accounts of these efforts reflect the pervasive, conservative influence of the *nenkō* pattern.

The study of these matters is complicated by the inclusion of many discrete elements in the Japanese system of wage determination: base pay, work and ability allowance, grade and rank payment, family allowance, travel allowance, incentive payments, and the like. The situation is further complicated by the determination of base pay itself on different bases: age, seniority, and education are most common, but it may also be affected by estimates of ability and job held. Further complications are introduced by the

125. Marsh and Mannari, "A New Look at 'Lifetime Commitment'," pp. 615, 625.
126. Ibid.

bonus system, which is itself calculated on various bases that may include merit judgments. Thus, to attempt to determine the degree to which earnings in Japanese industry are determined by age and seniority as against job and ability is a task of herculean difficulties. I have found detailed studies of individual firms more enlightening than attempts at overall analysis, which are inevitably ambiguous. A reader may be informed that 7.4 percent of Japanese firms with thirty or more regular employees use a seniority system of pay, 41.0 percent an ability system, 44.3 percent a mixture of seniority and ability, 7.3 percent a nonidentifiable system—but what this means is hard to understand outside the individual and concrete context of each enterprise.[127]

AN AUTO-PARTS PLANT. Robert Cole has described the characteristics of the incentive system that prevailed in an auto-parts plant, one of those in which he worked. This system had a long history at this plant and reflected an earlier wave of influence from the West—the theories of Frederick Taylor —but it had recently been modernized. "The 25 percent of the wage accounted for by the group incentive system is calculated," Cole reports, "as a percentage of a worker's basic wage. This means that each worker's share is graded according to his length of service and age," because this determines the basic wage. So, just as elements of payment by ability and job may be used to moderate basic pay, payments by seniority are used to moderate incentive payments.

Did it work as an incentive?

Cole reports that the quotas set as part of the system were used not as an incentive to be surpassed, but simply as a production norm to be met. This was all the easier because raw materials were allocated precisely according to the quota, making it impossible to exceed the production norm. In addition, because wages were paid monthly, the incentive feature was quite distant from the immediate work setting. The production units that were rewarded as a group were large. Thus, differences between sections tended to cancel each other out. "Workers simply thought of the premium wage as a fixed amount within the wage. They often did not know how it was calculated. There was not the constant preoccupation whether or by how much

127. These figures are as reported from Ministry of Labor, *Year Book of Labor Statistics, 1971,* tables 43, 46, in Beatrice G. Reubens, "Manpower Training in Japan," *Monthly Labor Review,* vol. 96 (September 1973), p. 17. The *Year Book of Labor Statistics, 1972,* table 37, reports that the decisive factor in job promotion is "occupational ability" in 90.1 percent of enterprises, and "duration of service, educational attainment and age" in only 39.9 percent (2.6 percent reported "others"), with multiple responses allowed, but the weight and meaning of "ability" versus other factors is still to be determined.

they should exceed the production norm . . . as is often the case among American workers on individual piece-rate systems."

Many of the explanations for restricting production, Cole reports, are similar to those American workers would give: the company will simply increase the quota, and one does not want to interfere with good social relations on the line. There are three differences from the American case: no fear of unemployment if one works too hard, lack of understanding of the purpose and operation of the group incentive system, and the conspicuous absence of the union in the entire process.[128]

AN ELECTRIC APPLIANCE COMPANY. Marsh and Mannari have studied the effects of a shift in the basis of pay at an electric applicance company. Previous to 1967, the criteria used to determine pay were education, length of service, age, sex, and the superior's evaluation of performance. In 1965 the company announced that this system was "opposed to modern rationality," developed a new system, and received union agreement to put it into effect. Jobs were evaluated and classified on the basis of the knowledge, education, and experience they required, the degree of mental or physical burden imposed, and the leadership and supervision required. The new components of pay were now to be monthly base pay (presumably based on the job), position or rank allowance (Japanese companies typically give ranks to each employee), allowance for specially dangerous or unpleasant jobs, allowance for those who did not get overtime pay, and family allowance. The most significant change in the system was that it permitted university graduates with little seniority to receive more pay than the lesser educated with much greater seniority—not because of the education in itself, but because the jobs held by university graduates were classified as "creative." The system retained the traditional ranks by name as well as the new level of job classifications; these might coincide, but not necessarily. Marsh and Mannari conducted a multiple regression analysis after the new system was introduced to uncover the determinants of pay. They reported:

Pay has a high zero-order correlation with seniority (.77), job classification (.68), rank (.64), and sex (.63). However, these independent variables are themselves highly correlated, especially seniority and job classification (.79). This multicollinearity clouds our interpretation of the correlations of each independent variable with pay when the other independent variables are held constant.

Looked at in terms of the per cent of variance in pay explained, seniority alone accounts for 60 per cent . . . [and] seniority and rank, together, explain 76 percent of the variance in pay.

Two interpretations are possible: "[The] new job classification wage system is only the older seniority wage system in another guise. . . . Provisions

128. Cole, *Japanese Blue Collar*, pp. 93–98.

that make a certain minimum number of years in a given job classification or rank a precondition for advancement . . . are retained in the new wage system." There is also a less cynical interpretation: "Over time, the influence of seniority on pay will in fact decline, and that of job classification will increase." But, the authors conclude, "we cannot at present empirically reject either of these two interpretations. . . ."[129]

MARUMARU. In Clark's corrugated board factory, Marumaru, which had been established largely through the efforts of one man and had grown rapidly during the postwar boom, the ideology of the management emphasized that it—distinct from Japanese companies in general—was meritocratic. But as it approached 1,000 employees in size, it became set ever firmer in a mode characteristic of Japanese enterprises.

Marumaru had a system of standard ranks for employees to which increases of base pay and allowances were keyed. These ranks were not necessarily closely related to job function, which created confusion, and Marumaru, as other large companies were doing, set up a new system of grades in 1964. As in Marsh and Mannari's electric appliance company, there were now two systems of ranking. Status and pay were now to be determined entirely by the new grade, and the old ranks would now be used truly to denote function. In this way, the conflict of two men of equal ability in a section, one of whom only could become the head, could be dealt with: the disappointed man's ability could be recognized by a rise in grade. The grades were expected to indicate clearly the difficulty of a job (at the lower levels) or the ability of a man (at the higher levels). But once again there seemed to be some reservation about wholehearted adoption of a system that would indicate ability or merit without mixing in some element that recognized seniority. "In practice, however," writes Clark, "there was only a poor correspondence between step and ability or even reputation for ability. At the end of each year every employee automatically moved up one step within his grade. A man who had been doing a grade 5 job for six years would therefore be in the sixth step at least, regardless of whether he was better at his job than a colleague who was only in the third step." And similarly, when a man was moved from a job that was rated higher to a job that was rated lower, he would not be asked to take a wage cut; rather, a complex maneuver was performed within the steps and grades to maintain or actually increase his earnings. "Even if he knew nothing at all of the new work he would still be put into a step which was supposed to indicate great skill at it."[130]

"The labor department director and other senior managers, in adopting

129. Robert M. Marsh and Hiroshi Mannari, "Pay and Social Structure in a Japanese Firm," *Industrial Relations,* vol. 12 (February 1973), pp. 17–25.

130. Clark, "Social Relations in a Japanese Company," pp. 172–73.

new forms of organization . . . saw themselves as pioneers bringing in modern methods in spite of the hostile conservatism of the employees. . . . It seemed to be fashion, more than reason, that was the motive for the change."[131]

In any case, although the new system did help to distinguish more able from less able employees, the differences in pay it produced were small. After six years of the system, "the highest paid married graduate only earned a salary of 9.3% larger than the lowest paid. . . . The reward for ability was, at this level . . . rather smaller than the marriage allowance. . . . The high and middle school intakes of the same year [the first year of the new system] showed even less variation with pay."[132]

Clark's conclusion:

> Just as Marumaru was promoting all but a handful of men through the standard ranks by age, so it was in effect also paying its employees by age. It was enabled to do so by the flexibility of the work and ability ratings, which allowed the company to give the impression that merit was being carefully measured and generously rewarded—and which no doubt actually were used, in one or two instances, to increase the pay of an outstanding worker—while at the same time allowing the company to continue to provide very similar wages for all the members of an intake long after their different capabilities had become known.[133]

HITACHI. The story is very similar in a major Japanese corporation, Hitachi, as described by Dore. Salary is made up of four elements: basic salary (41.8 percent), merit supplement (23.3 percent), job-level supplement (31.0 percent), and various allowances (3.9 percent). The basic salary is itself a function of seniority and merit, determined in ways too complex to report here but, according to Dore, "based on the exponential principle that the higher you go the faster you rise, designed to give recognition to both seniority and assessed merit. The seniority principle requires that everybody goes up a notch every year of some minimal proportions. The merit assessment is two-fold—first in determining how quickly a man shall be promoted to the next highest grade, secondly in determining whether his annual rise shall be higher, lower, or the same as, the average for workers in his grade."

The merit supplement gives an additional push to the merit element of the basic salary; it "does, however, operate in practice to accelerate the effect of the seniority element of the wage since the *average* percentage merit rating which individuals shall receive, and also the minimum rating, are subject to annual contract with the union. . . . Thus, by agreement, workers in the lowest and youngest grade will on average receive a 59% rating and never less than 48%."

131. Ibid., p. 175.
132. Ibid., p. 221.
133. Ibid., p. 224.

The job-level supplement, dating from 1966, is part of the revolution in wage setting of the mid-1960s. "It is the only part of the wage which is 'function-related' rather than 'person-related'." All jobs were graded, and earnings were now to be affected by what one actually did:

The introduction of "western-style" job-related wages has been hailed as a great advance, the final breakthrough out of a transitional adolescent stage of repressive feudalism into a state of full maturity in which workers are paid "properly"—as economists would say, according to market principles, or as sociologists would say, according to achievement rather than ascriptive norms.

To say the least this is an exaggeration. . . . First, although the relative weight of the job related element has been gradually increased . . . no one is proposing to take it *beyond* 50% [of the wage bill].

Secondly, despite rapid increases in the *total amount* of the wage being paid on this scale, the floor remains high, and the differentials relatively small. . . .

Thirdly, the assertion that this scale is "function-related rather than person-related" is itself open to question.

As against broad and simple job descriptions, each job description was divided into a number of grades related to the overall ladder of job descriptions. Lathe mechanics, for example, stretch from the third step of the job-related scale to the eighth, which permitted many adjustments in pay, regardless of job description. The union contract does not permit a worker to lose his job-related payment if he is moved to a lower-grade job and specifies a minimum job-related grade for workers over forty: "If . . . the introduction of this complex system of job-related payments produced very little change in individual pay packets, why was it embarked on? One part of the answer probably lies in . . . the scientism, intellectuality and fashion proneness of Japanese managers, their exaggerated respect for American management consultants, and their willingness to believe that their wage system left workers 'without incentives.' " But in addition, it did flatten the age-wage gradient, to the benefit of the younger workers.[134]

MERIT? What emerges from all the trees can be reduced, I believe, to three large patches of forest. First, the various changes in methods of determining earnings have served to compress the wage structure, to give more to younger workers, and to promise them that the great differences in compensation between younger workers and older workers will be reduced. This, one would think, is a clear response to the situation in the labor market.

Second, they have also served to maintain a system of compensation by age and seniority, even if compressed, and even if modified somewhat more than in the past by judgments (themselves very complex, and which I have not bothered to report) of merit or ability.

Third, they have maintained and made more complex a system of grades

134. Dore, *British Factory–Japanese Factory,* pp. 98–106.

or levels. No Japanese wage system described in the literature has fewer than two such gradings—one more traditional, in which the same terms are commonly used throughout Japanese industry, and one a newer set of grades related to the job description. The function of this system, it appears, is to maintain motivation in a lifetime employment system and in a seniority and age-based wage system by providing a series of small rewards over a long stretch of time.[135]

The Workplace Community and Union

Two final aspects distinguish the Japanese workplace—the community formed by its members and the linking of the union to the specific enterprise. The individual Japanese enterprise is markedly distinguished from both its American and British counterparts by the degree to which company and workers, company and union, and different levels of management and workers are bound together by the sense of a common enterprise marked off from its competitors and the surrounding society.

Robert Cole, the foreign observer of the Japanese factory most sensitive to signs of conflict and the observer who found the most, nevertheless writes, "The extent of worker acceptance of company goals in Japan is seldom seen in an American factory. . . ." He points out that the Japanese word generally used to refer to the company is *uchi,* which he translates as "we within," and which is also used to refer to one's own home. Whether or not the paternalism and sense of community of the Japanese factory can be shown to be derived from the *ie,* the traditional farm household continuous through the ages, or from the *han,* the feudal clan, the sense of familism is nevertheless communicated by the very language used for it. Cole points out that a person doing research on American factories usually is warned not to get too close to the personnel men, or he will damage his relations with the workers; quite the contrary situation prevailed in the Japanese factories in which he worked. The workers in the militant Takei plant maintain close relations with each other, even with their ideological enemies, in a way that he believes could not be found in an American factory. Westerners would consider such behavior to be insincere and would want to maintain a unified front: enemies in politics, coolness in personal relations. Not so in Takei, where the workplace relation dominates, even in a declining firm with a good

135. In Chapter 9, Galenson and Odaka also discuss the *nenkō* system and come to similar conclusions. Their treatment, however, gives slightly more weight to the changes in the system than mine, which is based on accounts of anthropologists and sociologists. This may be the result of the greater readiness of sociologists and anthropologists to find constraints within the social system.

deal of turnover. Relations between foremen and workers even here are close, "affective." Besides their union, Takei workers maintained a labor bank, travel club, camera club, youth section, mutual financing association, and friendship associations within each section—this in a plant with 185 workers. The workers in the plants he studied used informal language (Japanese has levels of formality) in talking with each other but formal language in talking with the workers across the street.[136]

Marsh and Mannari, in a number of studies, have been at great pains to demonstrate that lifetime commitment is not a moral norm, as argued by Abegglen, but rather a pragmatic adaptation of workers to their best interests: they stick with their job when their position in terms of seniority and age makes it unwise to move, not because they feel loyal to the company.[137] But they do not dispute the findings of Whitehill and Takezawa,[138] which they sum up as follows: "In contrast to Americans, Japanese are in fact more in favor of company paternalism, more identified with their company, more likely to think employees should participate in its recreational activities, higher in the level of support for lifetime commitment norms and values, less bureaucratic, and more likely to prefer a reward system that emphasizes collective rather than individual criteria and that gives wage allowances for family dependents."[139]

And in their study of a factory of 1,200 workers they found that there was no relation between employee beliefs as to how employees should be compensated and the employee's own status as highly skilled or unskilled, of high seniority or low seniority, of high rank or low rank (in the company ranking system), and having dependents or not. Even more striking, there were no differences of view by age or sex and only minor differences between managerial-supervisory and rank-and-file personnel. It is hard to imagine a more convincing demonstration that a common value system binds together old and young, educated and less educated, managers and workers, men and women among the labor force of a large Japanese factory.

It is true that the values that were so strikingly held in common are modern, achievement-oriented values, as has been found in most surveys of Japanese employees' attitudes: that is, the employees asserted that ability should

136. Cole, *Japanese Blue Collar,* pp. 172, 177, 136–42, 184–88.

137. Marsh and Mannari, "Lifetime Commitment in Japan," pp. 795–812.

138. Arthur M. Whitehill and Shin'ichi Takezawa, *The Other Worker: A Comparative Study of Industrial Relations in the United States and Japan* (East-West Center Press, 1968).

139. Robert M. Marsh and Hiroshi Mannari, "The 'Japanese Factory' Revisited" (paper prepared for delivery at the annual meeting of the American Sociological Association, 1973; processed), p. 3.

be the most important factor affecting pay, with skill- and job-classification second and seniority only third. (Contribution to company profits was fourth, education fifth, and number of dependents sixth.) Undoubtedly these beliefs will support further attenuation of the age and seniority bases of payment, but they also suggest that these changes will reflect a common commitment, which is changing from traditional to modern values, and will be accompanied by only modest conflict between union and company and between the different categories of workers who will have different degrees of loss and gain as the changeover takes place.[140] In the same company, there were strong differences among employees in responses to a program of automation;[141] clearly, the members of the company will not agree on everything.

Clark gives the most striking picture of the company as a community, though he emphasizes the negative features of the closed-in company. There is an absence of outside corporate directors in his company, as in just about all others in Japan; each director has come up through the company; there is no movement of employees between the corrugated board company and its competitors; the enterprise union emphasizes the isolation; great effort is still exercised to recruit new workers from the prefecture of its origins to its plant in Yokohama; half the employees live in company houses or hostels, which accentuates social relations among employees; the company makes great efforts to maintain its community image by emphasizing its history, its common aims (growth), its common style and culture (the company flower, badge, uniform, songs, outings). "Above all, the people of Marumaru were agreed that there should be a community, that relations between company members should not be superficial and simple, but intense and multifarious."[142]

140. Marsh and Mannari, "Pay and Social Structure," pp. 29–31.

141. Robert M. Marsh and Hiroshi Mannari, "Japanese Workers' Responses to Mechanization and Automation," *Human Organization,* vol. 32 (Spring 1973), pp. 85–93. Even so, the evidence that managers and workers have clearly differentiated responses is mixed, as can be seen by the percent of workers approving automation by level (responses other than "approval" were almost entirely "mixed" rather than "disapproval," as shown in the following table (p. 90):

Level	Approval (percent)
Kachō, Creative-5, Operative-6	73.0
Creative-4, Operative-4, 5	51.6
Routine-3	22.2
Routine-2, 1	40.9
Trainee-3	67.7
Trainee-2	31.3
Trainee-1	37.0

142. Clark, "Social Relations in a Japanese Company," p. 105.

Among the negative features that Clark notes is the virtual absence of learning from other firms in the industry, with which relations were distant and formal. Marumaru people knew more about European and American factories in the same field than Japanese ones. (When they encountered competitors at a meeting, they addressed one another by the name of the company: "Marumaru-san.") Above all, personal relations were seriously affected by the fact that all were bound together; each was inevitably in competition for advancement, and yet the loser was obliged to maintain good relations.

In so confined a space, quarrels and jealousies could arouse unhappiness out of all proportion to their causes. It was in order to avoid the bitterness invidious appointments might arouse that the directors, despite their attachment to the rule of merit, promoted men by age. And it was the need to maintain harmony in a closed community that required the management to yield to a union which could not strike. . . .

By the time I left Marumaru departments that once seemed to me models of "good human relations" had been revealed to be full of animosities and spites. . . . The strain of dissembling, self-effacement, and ingratiation required in Marumaru life was eased by two processes: transfers and going to bars.[143]

In Cole's more mobile Takei plant, such feelings were eased by leaving.

One concludes from Clark that the emphasis on "good human relations" in the Japanese firm is not only a cause of the strong community, but also made necessary by the very existence of a strong community.

The distinctive tendency of the Japanese enterprise to form a community is best known in such giant firms as Hitachi. A few elements from Dore's masterful treatment of British and Japanese factories indicate the scope of Japanese community-making efforts. When a worker leaves work at English Electric, he leaves on his own, alone, as a citizen. At Hitachi, for each queue of bus or train commuters a uniformed communications committee member is present to see that all goes well and perhaps to make sure that everybody is aboard. At English Electric, membership in welfare and recreational clubs is voluntary. At Hitachi, this may also be true in theory, but 100 percent membership is the norm. If there are troubles, at English Electric one's workmates help out spontaneously, and there is a specialized welfare department for visiting the sick and the like. At Hitachi, the foreman organizes it: "If a man dies, the foreman tells a couple of the work team to take two or three days off to help the widow with the funeral arrangements." Hitachi is much more concerned with character training. Hitachi is also much more concerned with a man's family than English Electric: there are educational loans

143. Ibid., pp. 90, 265.

for children, a dormitory in Tokyo for employees' children attending university or tutoring school, and regular gifts for such important family events as births and marriages. The family is expected to assist the worker in meeting the demands of the firm—the wife and children would be regarded as selfish, for example, if they expected him to take the family on an outing rather than do overtime work. The threats to this expectation that the family will assist the firm come from new values emphasizing privacy and home life. These values are so "un-Japanese" that English words are used to denote them. The desire for privacy, if Japanse words were used, would have overtones of "selfishness" or "loneliness." *Puraibashii* has had to be borrowed to overcome this: "It remains, still, somewhat an intellectual's word, symbolic of a value which only those most influenced by Western individualistic ideas have come to attach importance to." More popular as expressing the desires for a private life is the term *mai-hōmu-shugi,* "my-home-ism." "The articulate business leader sees it as a threat to social progress and national economic development." The threat is undoubtedly spreading, with shorter hours, the five-day week, more time for leisure, and more money to indulge it.[144]

Finally, Japanese society has always downplayed an individual's specific "occupation" and emphasized his firm. Evans points out the different biases of the statistics on wages available in Japan and the United States: the Japanese report age, length of service, education, and size of firm. The United States, in contrast, reports occupational wage differences (and, one might add, racial differences, too), and has few systematic data on wage differences by size of firm.[145] Cole and Tominaga point out it was not until 1920 that occupational statistics were systematically collected in Japan, and even thereafter the occupational categories were not well fixed and the system of classification changed frequently. Meaningful comparisons can be made only beginning with the census of 1950.[146] Dore notes that the words "technician" and "craftsman" cannot be easily translated into Japanese. The national professional organizations of engineers and the like are rather weak in Japan: the professional is typically tied to his firm, where he has received his training, and is less of an independent agent.

144. Dore, *British Factory–Japanese Factory,* p. 212.
145. Robert Evans, Jr., *The Labor Economies of Japan and the United States* (Praeger, 1971), pp. 154, 191.
146. Robert E. Cole and Kenichi Tominaga, "Japan's Changing Occupational Structure and Its Significance" (paper prepared for the Conference on Industrialization and Its Consequences for Modern Japan, 1973, sponsored by the Joint Committee on Japanese Studies of the Social Science Research Council and the American Council of Learned Societies; processed), p. 4.

The Japanese bodies are dominated by university professors and are centered in university departments, whereas the British institutions are dominated by professional practicing engineers. . . . [N]one of the Japanese bodies is concerned with what has always been a major function of the British institutions—maintaining professional standards by testing and certifying the competence of individuals. . . .

Skills belong, at English Electric, to individuals. A man's craft "papers," his Institution membership, are guarantees of his level of competence, a certified indication to possible buyers of what he has to sell in the market. At Hitachi whether the skill of a man "belongs to" him or to the firm is a question which would be likely, one suspects, to receive a different answer.[147]

After all, he was brought up in the company, and it has trained him.

All these details are reflections of a generalization that has been made again and again: compared to Westerners, the Japanese are less individualistic, more attached to, and comfortable in, organizations—and organizations of a vertical character. When these generalizations are seen to be reflected in distinctive statistical practices and linguistic usage, they become meaningful.[148]

Finally, a few words about the Japanese unions. As to the facts, there is

147. Dore, *British Factory–Japanese Factory*, pp. 60, 47, 72.
148. The emphasis on community and common values, the expectation of inferiors in a hierarchy that superiors will be concerned with their welfare, and the capacity to combine hierarchical relations with empathy are discussed in a number of papers in Ezra F. Vogel (ed.), *Modern Japanese Organization and Decision-Making* (University of California Press, 1975), particularly in Thomas P. Rohlen, "The Work Group in Japanese Company Organization." When harmony is found in the modern world, however, the finder should always be suspicious, and I have tried to be. Thus, in Chapter 9 Galenson and Odaka see in many characteristics of Japanese management-worker relations a large measure of management self-interest and manipulation operating against the best interests of workers; parallels also can be seen to the exhortation to work in a communal spirit for common goals so characteristic of Communist China and Cuba. I would insist that there are differences: in contrast to communist countries, Japan does not impose force as the ultimate sanction requiring communal behavior. In contrast to the United States, there is the reality still of a common culture drawing together the different ranks in an enterprise in a way that would be difficult outside of small family enterprises or enterprises limited to a single ethnic group in the United States.

There is, of course, tension and competition: workers leave Cole's Tokyo automobile factory if they feel they have been given an insufficient increase in wages and status; there is misery in Clark's company when a worker loses out in competition and, unable to express open disappointment and anger, the feeling comes out in spite and back biting. Vogel, in correspondence, expresses the belief that my treatment underplays the amount of competition within the group and the emphasis on relative status both in company and in school (where parents know the rank in class of their children). The pressure is undoubtedly enormous, and certainly it can be sensed again and again in Japan. But this pressure must be placed within a framework in which there is an agreed-upon level of security. It is not, I feel, an ultimate pressure: "succeed or else." And much of the competitiveness, Vogel points out, is over who will be seen as conforming best.

little disagreement. The enterprise union works far more closely with the firm than do the unions of the United States and England. Their officials show less concern about being identified with the company, about being wined and dined by company officials; and the company officials show less concern about sharing information with the union leaders, whom they regard as good company men. For the most part, union officials do not form a distinct occupational group: they have come out of the enterprise, and will return to it. Tenure in leadership is short, and service as an officer is often considered a task taken on for the benefit of the entire enterprise. Many who run for election to union office take it on as an act of noblesse oblige. They are the natural factory leaders who at an earlier time were often the white-collar workers and since the war have been part of the same unions as blue-collar workers; in more recent accounts, they are often foremen or older workers. The strike tends to be a formality in the process of collective bargaining rather than an all-out struggle. The political objectives of the national federations seem generally not to influence relations at the enterprise and factory level. Contracts are simpler than in the United States and lead to few formal grievance procedures. Basically, the American and British trade unions present themselves as fighting organizations in a two-party, zero-sum conflict; in Japan, although the national unions act that way, the enterprise unions, even though they defend and represent worker interests, do so in a perspective in which they see themselves as junior partners in a team enterprise. There are substantial exceptions to this picture, particularly among unions of public service employees, but the foregoing characterization applies generally to the enterprise unions of large firms.

Whether this situation is seen as a sign of the backwardness of the Japanese labor relations system and a lack of manly independence on the part of Japanese workers, and one that must be succeeded by more combative unions if the Japanese worker is to gain his proper rights and if Japan is to become a true example of industrial democracy—or as a model that other nations with a more adversary type of union-management relations might aspire to—depends on the perspective of the viewer. Perhaps, too, it depends on whether the viewer regards nations as isolated cockpits for union-management struggles or as involved in desperate international competition. In either case, there is little argument about the character of Japanese trade unionism, in which area there is perhaps the least amount of evidence of a convergence with the Western type.[149]

149. This brief characterization is drawn from Solomon B. Levine, *Industrial Relations in Postwar Japan;* idem, "Labor Markets and Collective Bargaining in Japan," in William W. Lockwood (ed.), *The State and Economic Enterprise in Japan* (Princeton

The scale of labor disputes in Japan and the United States is an index to some of these differences (U.S. data for 1972 not available):[150]

	Millions of man-days lost in labor disputes	
Year	Japan	United States
1968	2.8	49.0
1969	3.6	42.9
1970	3.9	66.4
1971	6.0	47.6
1972	5.1	n.a.

Why the System Works

It is hard to communicate the reality of such elements as "a feeling of community" without the personal background of those who have experienced it, which is why the testimony of the anthropologists and sociologists who have worked in Japanese factories is to my mind so revealing. As more and more such studies are published, the simple picture inevitably becomes more complicated: the large enterprise is seen as different from the small one, the factory using a rural labor force different from the one using an urban labor force, the plant with a complex modern technology different from the one with a simple or traditional one, the factory with a large complement of machinists different from the one with unskilled female operatives, and so on. Nevertheless, there remains the overall impression that Abegglen was right: there is a significantly distinctive quality to Japanese industry, and such themes as lifetime employment, direct recruiting from schools, advancement by seniority and age, and a sense of community all help to characterize it— even if they are by no means universal, even if they all suffer decline in significance with time, and even if they are not rooted in age-old Japanese practices. And it all makes sense because these characteristics harmonize with other characteristics of the society.

University Press, 1965), pp. 633–67; idem, "Postwar Trade Unionism, Collective Bargaining, and Japanese Social Structure," in R. P. Dore (ed.), *Aspects of Social Change in Modern Japan* (Princeton University Press, 1967), pp. 245–85; Kazuo Ōkōchi, Bernard B. Karsh, and Solomon B. Levine (eds.), *Workers and Employers in Japan* (Princeton University Press, 1973); Dore, *British Factory–Japanese Factory;* and Cole, *Japanese Blue Collar.* See also Walter Galenson's interesting review of books by Abegglen, Dore, and Cole in "The Japanese Worker," *Science,* May 10, 1974, pp. 697–98; and the full treatment of unions in Chapter 9 of this volume.

150. Data from Ministry of Labor, *Year Book of Labor Statistics, 1972,* p. 326; and *Statistical Abstract of the United States, 1973,* p. 251.

Some of them can even be given statistical form. For example, by American standards there are almost no lawyers in Japan: 1 for every 13,000 people in 1964, as against 1 for every 950 in the United States. The number of lawyers in Japan has remained stable since 1964, whereas Americans can look back to that year as almost a halcyon age of nonlitigiousness, as the number of lawyers leaps upward annually. In Japan, people bring their disputes to the police for settlement: in 1958 there were 21,596 such cases in Tokyo (of which 39 percent were settled), but only 6,815 were brought to district courts for settlement. Over 90 percent of divorces in Japan are by agreement, arranged apparently by go-betweens, relatives, or others. It is understandable that the foreman would expect to be, and would be expected to be, a fatherly figure, guiding younger workers and settling their disputes. These differences cannot to my mind be summed up by any simplistic comparison such as "one society is traditional and the other modern, one paternalistic and the other democratic." Perhaps more to the point is to say that the Japanese have lived together on their islands for a long time without the physical intrusion of great numbers of people of different race and customs, whereas Americans— and in lesser measure citizens of other Western industrialized societies—are more mixed in composition and values and need more in the way of impersonal and formal institutions to arrange their lives.[151]

But why should it work? Why should this pattern have been compatible with very rapid economic growth? Why should it have led to effort, ingenuity, innovation, and adaptation rather than to sloth, conservatism, and hostility to change? Why should it be the case that in the West—and in the developing world—it was necessary and remains continually necessary to "break the cake of custom" for change and growth to occur, whereas in Japan so much of the cake was retained or reconstructed? Certainly Japan has taught many analysts to note the advantages for growth of what appeared at first to be such a backward system as lifetime employment and progression by age and seniority. For example, it has been pointed out that in such a system there is less resistance to technical innovation, both because of the commitment of the company to retain workers if it can, and because the weakness of occupational identification (consistent with the system) makes it easier to move workers from one job to another. If pay is related to personal status rather

151. On the specifics of the Japanese legal system, see Dan Fenno Henderson, "Law and Political Modernization in Japan," in Robert E. Ward (ed.), *Political Development in Modern Japan* (Princeton University Press, 1968), pp. 452–53; for a general characterization and historical background, see Richard W. Rabinowitz, "Law and the Social Process in Japan," *Transactions of the Asiatic Society of Japan,* 3rd series, vol. 10 (August 1968), pp. 5–96.

than what a worker is doing, he is (or may be) willing to do almost anything as long as it serves the needs of the enterprise: in Clark's corrugated board factory, university graduates worked the machines for long periods when labor was not available. We have pointed out that even when jobs are rated by skill and level, when a worker is moved from a higher-level job to a lower-level job, his level of earnings is retained. Thus, economic analysis alone can suggest certain advantages as well as certain disadvantages for growth in the Japanese system.

Perhaps the more strictly social considerations are more important. If the company is a community, tries to become a community, tries to induct young people so as to think of it as a community—in competition with others both for the company's greater glory and the welfare of each of the participants—then motivation can be expected to remain high even if a greater measure of security has been assured.

But more than this can be said about the system of motivation. One of the most intriguing aspects of the Japanese company is the system of ranks. These have been compared by Dore and Clark and others to something like a civil service or an army. Just as in a civil service or an army, the ranks do not coincide with any given function—and indeed may not coincide with a function considered appropriate to the rank, as when a GS-15 or a colonel is shunted off to a job he considers beneath his dignity. One reason why he continues to do it in the civil service or the army is that he is still working for his pension or retirement. The same motivations can be expected to prevail in the Japanese company, but even more striking is the fact that the system does permit advancement. Everyone has something to look forward to: an increase in the traditional rank or an increase in the job-related grade (for even if the job-related grades are supposed to reflect individual ability and merit, one is always guaranteed some rate of increase up the scale). Both Cole and Dore, divergent in so many respects, agree on this aspect of the situation: motivation is high and maintained by the system of ranks and grades: "Differences in annual increments may seem small to outside observers and unlikely to serve as incentives, but they are important. Takei workers discussed and compared their annual increments with great intensity. The annual increments are a reflection of daily competition among workers in terms of production and winning the favor of superiors. Workers have quit in both the diecast and auto parts company when they learned that other workers of the same age and with the same length of service received slightly higher increments."[152]

152. Cole, *Japanese Blue Collar*, p. 77.

The desire for advancement within the firm is strong among Cole's Japanese blue-collar workers, stronger than among American workers. This, he believes, is the result not of cultural differences but of institutional ones. First, advancement to such positions as foreman comes in Japan to *older* workers with long service, and this motivates them. In the American automobile plants studied by Eli Chinoy, workers over age thirty-five no longer could hope to be advanced. Thus, the fact that advancement comes late and with age maintains ambition. Second, the differences among blue-collar workers in Japanese firms are exaggerated: many grades are created, depending on age, seniority, education, ability, and the like, and the worker hopes to advance through these levels. In the American firm, the number and type of levels is fewer, and the opportunities for promotion consequently rarer.

The sense of community is maintained, despite the variety of grades, by certain institutional features. The annual recruiting assures an age spread of workers, competition for higher positions is thus limited to a certain age grade, and the advancement of an older worker is less often seen as a cause for resentment by younger workers.

Of course, many workers are left behind: they may weed themselves out through their behavior and may see the advancement of one of their number as just. Further, the needs of efficiency and in particular the introduction of new machinery often demands that younger workers be advanced before older ones and have older workers under them; and when this is done, a delicate situation ensues.

But most workers believe that effort and talent are necessary to get ahead, and accept this as just: Cole suggests they view age and seniority only as a precondition.[153]

If this is the level of motivation in Cole's conflict-ridden Takei plant, it is stronger in Dore's Hitachi. The system of ranks there permits "faithful service by men of mediocre ability to be rewarded by an increase in rank without the disadvantage of dysfunctionally promoting them to positions of greater authority. . . . Only 13% of the Japanese sample, compared with 46% of the British samples said they had no chance at all [for advancement]. And of those who said that they had little or no chance at all, 28% in Britain . . . [and] 16% in Hitachi gave as their reason the injustice of the firm's method of selection rather than their own lack of qualifications or personal deficiencies."[154]

153. Ibid., pp. 104–09.
154. Dore, *British Factory–Japanese Factory*, pp. 67–68.

The Egalitarian Factory

But is not a system of petty grades and minor advantages designed to maintain motivation a recipe for small-mindedness and stagnation rather than for progress? To this characterization must be added one other feature, however, perhaps the most important: the Japanese factory or company is at present perhaps the most egalitarian in the world, outside China. In a society marked by endless bowing this is hard to believe, but it is the uniform report. In all the plants studied, for example, there is no distinction of dress between white-collar and manual workers: all go to work in the same clothes. There is an effort to minimize distinction in dress at work: all put on the same smock or working dress. The level of speech used in factories, among the employees of different levels is the informal speech of familiars and members of a family; the formal levels of address are used with those on the outside. And most significant, there is no distinction between annual salaries and hourly pay, payment by the month or by the week: everybody is paid the same way, and the term used for earnings is the same for all levels. Hours of work for white-collar and blue-collar workers are the same. Even the terms that used to distinguish white-collar staff from blue-collar operatives, both of whom are in the same union, have fallen into disuse. Many benefits are the same: sick pay, use of the company cafeteria (the same one for all), access to the sports clubs and vacation resorts, and vacations themselves (except that the managers do not take them and workers are encouraged not to—it would be against the community spirit). Many exceptions can be found to each of these statements, but in general it is true that the sense of class distinction within the factory is remarkably muted.[155]

It is not playing with words to say that rank and level are important and class is not. Class, after all, refers not to a number or a grade and the specific rewards attached to it; rather, it refers to a complex of key elements in life that serve to mark off one stratum from another. Obviously distinctions of rank can also be distinctions of class—as when, to reach a certain rank, a person must be of a certain social class, or when certain ranks form a new privileged class. In general this is not the situation that prevails in the Japanese factory. The class-conscious rhetoric of the socialist and communist parties and the unions that follow their lead seems surprisingly to be just

155. These remarks obtain mainly at the factory level. There are indeed privileges for rank in a company—the graded expense account, the company car, and the like—but these are generally features of the higher levels of a company, among its staff, management elite, and directors.

that—rhetoric. At the factory level, the report goes, no sense of class privilege or sense of class resentment is to be found. Nor, to my mind, is the sense of classlessness an illusion or a case of false consciousness, as is demonstrated by the reality of the similarity of benefits, and by the probability that age remains the most significant factor in inequalities in pay. And one thing can be said for structuring the inequalities of a society according to age rather than class: if there is to be privilege, let it be the old who are privileged and the young who are resentful. The young, after all, constitute the one social category to whose members society can promise with absolute sureness that they, too, will in turn become privileged, for they are bound to get older.

The Japanese company emerges in these studies as something like the Israeli army. Of course there are ranks, for neither an army nor a factory could operate without them, but both are democratic in that the ranks are not firmly linked to class, and the association between ranks encourages social equality rather than class distinction and distance. Both institutions are also remarkably effective, but, whatever their internal effectiveness, both remain susceptible to outside developments that they cannot control.

To say that there is an absence of class in a Japanese factory would be to go too far. The issue is its relative weight and presence, as indicated by a complex of dress, accent, educational background, amount and type of pay, by who orders whom—and with the whole complex coalescing along the same lines of social origin. Clearly, class is relatively less evident than in England, and even relatively less evident than in the United States.

Education, however, is beginning to play a larger and larger role in determining status and level in the factory. The distinction is now not so much between the middle school and the high school graduate but between the high school and the university graduate. There are tensions there, and as a higher and higher proportion of the formerly high school educated go on to college, there are signs of a certain hardening of lines. In Clark's small meritocratic firm, it was becoming more difficult for a worker who was not a university graduate to rise into a white-collar job—it had earlier been more likely. The desperate struggle to get a university education and to get into the best possible university reflects the significance of this new precondition for a better life. Thus, it seems crucial for the stability of the society that higher education extend its reputation for being fair and meritocratic, that it not become regarded as being linked to a fixed social class. Statistics from the past ten years that show that the once relatively even distribution of students by income background in the national universities is becoming less even—that show that students whose families are economically and professionally more advantaged are doing better in the race—are troubling. Yet in contrast to other countries with relatively free societies and economies, the egalitarianism of Japan stands out: the ranks of the factory are justified in some measure by their relation to age and seniority, a traditionally accepted basis of distinction; in some measure by their relation to ability and merit, which are increasingly recognized as being the proper basis on which distinctions in work should be made; and, finally, in some measure by their increasing base in education and a system of education that is itself seen as open to talent.

A delicate structure, but it has been working. In the end I come to the same conclusion made earlier about the education system. If it is seen as fair, it will work; and it *is* seen as fair.[156]

The Future

Can it go on? I exclude the two major things that may be happening to make all the parameters different: a radical change in the world economic environment and a radical change in the domestic political situation in Japan —that is, the coming to power in Japan of a government that in some measure reflects the left-wing opposition. These possibilities are considered in other chapters. It *is* possible for Japan to undergo revolutionary change: it did so after the Meiji restoration and again during the occupation. In both periods the basis of power of the previously privileged classes was wiped out, although without the violence Westerners seem to consider a necessary concomitant of a real revolution.[157] Conceivably such revolutionary changes will occur again, either because of a world economic crisis or because the generation-long rule by the Liberal Democratic party will come to an end.

The issue I limit myself to is whether there are long-term forces in Japanese society that must bring this distinctive system of organizing work to an end, and bring it into greater conformity with the practice of Western industrial states. The distinctive social practices surrounding the Japanese workplace are changing, and changing in the direction of those common in the West. Education and tested ability replace age and seniority, recruitment

156. "What happens to those workers who do not benefit from the Japanese life employment system? There does not appear to be much influential complaint in Japan that there is anything unfair or unjust in this exclusion." OECD, *Manpower Policy in Japan* (1973), p. 104.

157. Just as some German intellectuals believe that because Germany did not undergo a real bourgeois or proletarian revolution it must forever lack some key elements of democracy, so many Japanese intellectuals hold that feudal and backward classes must dominate the society, and true democracy cannot exist until a violent civil war takes place. This point of view is sometimes expressed in rather more sophisticated forms, but it has never convinced me.

from the school is increasingly supplemented with recruitment from the marketplace, mobility increases and lifetime commitment declines, the sense of community within the firm apparently also declines, but more slowly, and even the labor movement may be convinced to replace its odd mixture of radical rhetoric at the top and cooperation below with the perhaps rather more effective nonideological combat stance of American unions. As these things come to pass, what will be the effect on Japanese economic growth? Certainly, "modern" attitudes and institutions must lead to greater productivity, must they not? In Japan, they need not, and in my judgment they would not.

There are two principal reasons why the decline of distinctively Japanese values and practices and their replacement by more characteristically "modern" values should be expected to moderate Japan's economic growth. First, to my mind industrialization everywhere has been based on some reservoir of values that can be called traditional in the sense that they were deeply ingrained, unquestioned, passed down in the family, sustained by the authority of society, and sustaining of a commitment to work. The source of these values in different societies was different,[158] and there were many routes to the creation of such values. They were to be found in Protestant Europe, in the peasant societies of Catholic Europe, in the peasant family of China, among urbanized Jews, and elsewhere. There are many different kinds of traditional values that in varying degrees are compatible with industrialization.

In Japan their distinctive sources were the agricultural household, the *ie*, and the culture developed by the hereditary military and bureaucratic class of samurai. It would be naive to say that these values were transmitted directly to the factory. Rather, a complicated history ensued, and many different routes were taken to industrialization: there were the state factory run as a bureaucracy, the small textile factory drawing on the daughters of the samurai and then farmers for a labor force, the construction projects that utilized the traditional Japanese form of boss to whom workers were committed (the so-called *oyabun-kobun* pattern) in a quasi-familial way, the incorporation of some of these bosses as foremen so as to create a stable labor force, the continuing influence of the great number of small artisans, the industrial enterprises with their recruitment of workers who were incorporated into a familylike pattern.[159] In the course of this complex process of industrializa-

158. For an analysis of the contrast between Protestant Europe and Japan, see Robert Bellah, *Tokugawa Religion* (Free Press, 1957).

159. See Kōji Taira, *Economic Development and the Labor Market in Japan* (Columbia University Press, 1970); John W. Bennett and Iwao Ishino, *Paternalism in the Japanese Economy: Anthropological Studies of Oyabun-Kobun Patterns* (University of Minnesota Press, 1963); and Dore, *British Factory–Japanse Factory,* chap. 14.

tion, the traditional values supporting work and commitment to a community were passed on and remained active.

Until quite recently there stood behind these values the agricultural household, or the urban household based on an economic enterprise, the store, or artisan's shop, or small manufacturing enterprise. This household is the *ie*, whose distinctive feature was that it was a family that was eternal, that was permanently bound to a specific enterprise, that could renew itself through adoption so as to maintain its permanence and its capacity to carry out its economic function, and that was linked to other families in hierarchical relations. The process by which the younger sons of the *ie* were recruited into the industrial labor force has been analyzed in an enlightening article by Ezra Vogel:[160] it was a process controlled by these predominantly rural households, and it ensured a relatively easy transition from the primary to the secondary sector.

One of the most striking aspects of Japanese urbanization and industrialization, as Vogel points out, is that it did not result in the kind or degree of social disorganization that was common in the cities of Western Europe and the United States. There never existed in Japan anything like an urban mob; nor did an urban underclass ever emerge. The Japanese day laborers at the bottom of the social ladder, who occupy what are considered the lowest-status and worst areas of Tokyo and Osaka, live in sections that to the visitor's eye are not much different from other working-class areas. They live in inns, drink cheaper whiskey, and make more trouble for the police than the residents of other sections; but few men are to be seen on the street idle or drunk. Instead, they line up for work early in the morning, and, symbolically to the Western eye, their shoes are neatly lined up outside the doors of their inns. Statistics support the generalizations from history and the impressions of observers about the relatively nontraumatic transition from village to city: the divorce rate, for example, went down with urbanization.[161] Vogel explains this by the control the rural family was able to exercise on the process of migration to the city. It was second and third sons, who would not inherit the family property, who migrated, and control over them was exercised by the fact that their placement in jobs (and later their marriage) was arranged in part through family connections, which provided to employer and bride's family the expected guarantee of good character.

160. "Kinship Structure, Migration to the City, and Modernization," in Dore (ed.), *Aspects of Social Change in Modern Japan*, pp. 91–111.

161. Takeyoshi Kawashima and Kurt Steiner, "Modernization and Divorce Rate Trends in Japan," *Economic Development and Cultural Change*, vol. 9 (1960), pp. 213–39, as quoted in Vogel, "Kinship Structure, Migration to the City, and Modernization," p. 105. It should be pointed out, however, that divorce was common in the traditional society.

Recruitment of an industrial labor supply from among the excess sons and daughters of the traditional sector is a common feature of industrialization. Vogel contrasts the Japanese pattern with one in which the worker was not committed to the new setting, but hoped only to make enough to return: for example, many of the Chinese or Italian migrants to American cities. In such cases the hold of the traditional pattern and family was strong. But the parents of the Japanese *ie* "told their migrating children that they should make good in the city so they would not have to come back. . . . Because the *ie* removed the migrant from its membership and did not expect him to return once he had gone to the city, it played an important role in motivating the migrant to acquire these skills that would give him sufficient security to remain."[162] The Japanese industrial employer had the best of both worlds: a worker reared under traditional controls, committed nevertheless to his new social setting.

Social analysts often overrate the rate of change. This pattern—the feeding of its younger sons into the industrial labor force by the *ie*—did not disappear overnight. One of the most striking of Japanese statistics is the remarkable stability of the absolute number of those rural households which provided these members of the labor force until quite recently. This was for decades fixed at about 5.5 million, so that the pattern of stable rural families' sending out excess sons to work in the city and establish branch households remainded dominant until perhaps twenty years ago.

A second source of industrial employees was the reservoir of second and third sons of traditional city families based on small retail and wholesale and craft enterprises. These are placed by the Japanese census in the category of the self-employed, which includes more than the traditional elements of farmers and urban craft and retail and wholesale proprietors, although these make up the bulk of it. Once extremely large, this census category has declined slowly as a proportion of the total labor force: 25.6 percent in 1950, it was still 19.0 percent in 1970.[163]

As in the case of the farm household, these urban families based on the small-family enterprise could be expected to show a strong element of traditionalism in child rearing and a substantial degree of parental control over education and first job—further elements that made the labor force of Japan more traditional than its degree of industrialization might suggest. Many

162. Vogel, "Kinship Structure, Migration to the City, and Modernization, p. 106.
163. Cole and Tominaga, "Japan's Changing Occupational Structure and Its Significance," table 14. This figure is larger than that for the United States (8 percent in 1970), the United Kingdom (6 percent in 1966), or West Germany (10 percent in 1970), but smaller than that for France (21 percent in 1970).

workers in industry have come directly from family employment, either on farms or in small-scale urban enterprises.[164]

The factories that have been studied by Cole, Clark, and Dore, which I have referred to often, are not atypical in their continued closeness to the background of the agricultural household. Of the male workers at the main Hitachi plant, 45 percent were sons of farmers. One of the two factories studied by Cole drew its working force entirely from the rural hinterland in which it was located. The firm studied by Rodney Clark still draws many of its new workers from the agricultural prefecture in which it originated.

But this entire process was of course transitional, even if the transition is still going on 100 years after it began. The labor force is drawn increasingly from urban families now remote from *ie* influences, highly educated, strongly affected by a modern society in which the joys of consumption, leisure, and recreation are advertised by mass media that provide a denser coverage of the population than anywhere else in the world; and an increasing proportion of rural families live in the same world as the urban ones. It is easy enough to document the steady erosion of the traditional values. Kunio Odaka and his students have studied the attitudes of Japanese workers since World War II. He has defined an attitude that he calls "pro-pro": positive toward both management and the union—and, as has been seen, they are often closely linked in Japan. This kind of orientation maintains the basic cleavages of Japanese society, which, as Vogel has described them, "have not been between different social classes but between one corporate group (composed of people at different social positions) and other corporate groups. The strong commitment of an individual to his group and the lack of cross-cutting membership to other groups has not been conducive to the smooth integration of groups in the wider society, but it has been conducive to a very high degree of solidarity and conformity within any single group."[165]

Marxist-oriented analysts of the Japanese working class have hoped to see "pro-management and con-union" sentiment drop, which has happened, and "con-management and pro-union" sentiment rise, which has not. Instead, a point of view that Odaka calls "con-con"—against both management and union—has risen, reflecting the privatizing values that are now emerging in the society, overcoming the group- and organization-oriented values of the past. The pro-pro attitudes remain strongest, of course, among the older and less-educated workers, the con-con attitudes, among the

. The proportion of family workers in Japan remains remarkably high: 16 percent of the labor force, against 7 percent in Germany, 3 percent in France, 8 percent in Italy, and 1 percent in the United Kingdom and the United States. Ibid.
165. Vogel, "Kinship Structure, Migration to the City, and Modernization," p. 109.

younger and better-educated workers. Although some modification of these attitudes can be expected with age, the general direction of change is clear.[166]

The second reason for an expectation that the decline of distinctive Japanese values and social practices would moderate economic growth is that Japan, like other highly developed capitalist societies, seems to be subject to the process first described by Joseph Schumpeter, and which has recently been given effective contemporary formulations by Irving Kristol and Daniel Bell:[167] a society must be seen as good and noble, as well as productive, to enlist the loyalty of its intellectuals. Bourgeois capitalist society was never seen as good and noble by its intellectuals. Today its intellectuals—the "adversary culture"—are in the saddle as far as the formulation of prevailing ideas toward the society and the culture go. Progress toward a more productive economy and a fairer distribution of its products can scarcely mollify those who shape the prevailing ideas of society and who are inveterately opposed to a society that does not make an effective claim to enhancing virtue among men and within the society in which they live. Capitalism gave up any such claim a long time ago.

Japan, distinctively, did not follow the course of early bourgeois capitalist society, which asserted its claim to virtue and loyalty by the fact that it provided freedom to individuals to fulfill themselves as they uniquely wished: Japan's claim to virtue and to loyalty was based instead on the fact that it was an orderly society, properly organized under the emperor, who embodied and maintained traditional social relations in a just hierarchy. This claim was abandoned with the defeat of 1945, and Japan became a bourgeois, capitalist, democratic society. As such, it became heir to all the spiritual ills of such societies, as well as to those of its own. Its intellectuals had never fully accepted traditional Japan and for the most part were not ready to accept the American model of liberal bourgeois capitalism and democracy that was presented to them as a suitable ideal. This model was established remarkably successfully on the ruins of the emperor system, but it seems never to have gained full legitimacy, never to have received the love and loyalty and affection of the intellectuals and of substantial bodies of the Japanese citizenry.

The Japanese intellectuals—and by this I mean leading social scientists,

166. Kunio Odaka, *Toward Industrial Democracy: Management and the Workers in Japan* (Harvard University Press, forthcoming). Kokichi Shōji, in "Studies on Social Consciousness in Modern Japan" (1974; processed), pp. 15–22, has summarized a number of surveys available only in Japanese, and their prevailing direction is the same.

167. Joseph Schumpeter, *Capitalism, Socialism and Democracy* (Harper, 1942); Kristol, " 'When Virtue Loses All Her Loveliness'," pp. 3–15; idem, *On the Democratic Idea in America* (Harper and Row, 1972), chap. 6; and Daniel Bell, "The Cultural Contradictions of Capitalism," *The Public Interest*, no. 21 (Fall 1970), pp. 16–43.

college professors, social critics, high school teachers, journalists, and all those who shape Japanese thinking on any subject—are remarkably critical of their society. No intelligentsia is so uniformly in opposition, and it is hard to find any substantial body of thinkers who support the existing arrangements in Japan, rewarding though they have been for the overwhelming majority of its people. It is hard to find even a flourishing conservative intelligentsia that accepts the status quo, for conservatism in Japan seems rapidly to become right wing, mystical, feudal. It is perhaps for this reason that foreign conservative intellectuals who see something positive in Japan as it exists—for example, Herman Kahn and Peter Drucker—are taken up by the Japanese with such enthusiasm; there are apparently no native Japanese equivalents of the same stature.[168]

If the intellectuals are in opposition, those whom they influence—the modern sector, which includes educated management, white-collar workers, and blue-collar workers—must also be in opposition; they have come through the high schools and universities that are dominated by the ideas of the intellectuals, and are influenced by the mass media that these intellectuals dominate. The political configuration of Japan is therefore striking: it is divided generally between traditional sectors who support the Liberal Democrats and modern sectors who oppose them on the basis of some vague commitment to Marxism and socialism. The country is split politically in a unique manner, between professionals and white-collar and blue-collar employees who support the left opposition parties (democratic socialists, socialists, and communists) and farmers, proprietors, and the self-employed, who support the Liberal Democrats.[169] This represents at the same time a division between

168. It is not easy to document or support such a general characterization of intellectuals' attitudes toward contemporary Japanese economy and polity: it is drawn from reading and conversation. For background on Japanese intellectuals, see the subtle and deeply informed papers of Herbert Passin: "Writer and Journalist in the Transitional Society," in Lucian W. Pye (ed.), *Communication and Political Development* (Princeton University Press, 1963); "Modernization and the Japanese Intellectual: Some Comparative Observations," in Marius B. Jansen (ed.), *Changing Japanese Attitudes Toward Modernization* (Princeton University Press, 1965); and "Intellectuals in the Policy-Making Process," in Vogel (ed.), *Modern Japanese Organization and Decision-Making.* See also the perceptive article by David Riesman, "Japanese Intellectuals and Americans," *The American Scholar,* vol. 34 (Winter 1964–65), pp. 51–66; and the insightful report by David and Evelyn Thompson Riesman on their meetings with Japanese intellectuals, *Conversations in Japan* (Basic Books, 1967).

169. See, for example, Sigeki Nisihira and Tatsuso Susuki, "Le Vote des Ouvriers au Japon," Research Memorandum no. 57 (The Institute of Statistical Mathematics, June 1973, for the Congrès mondial, l'Association internationale de science politique), graph 4; and Jōji Watanuki, "Japanese Politics in Flux," in James William Morley (ed.), *Prologue to the Future: The United States and Japan in the Postindustrial Age* (D. C. Heath, 1974), pp. 72–74. See also Chapter 11 in this volume.

the more educated and the less educated, between the younger and the older.
(One modern sector, the managers of large enterprises, does support the
Liberal Democrats.)

In summary, the direction of change seems clear; the rate of change is
unclear; and even more unclear is the relative rate of change as between
Japan and the industrially developed nations of the West. It is this difference
in rates that has allowed Japan, despite the enormous changes it has undergone since World War II, to retain some part of its traditional "Japanese"
character. This difference in rates may well help to sustain a markedly superior economic performance for some time to come.

CHAPTER THIRTEEN

Prospects for the Future and Some Other Implications

Hugh Patrick, Yale University
and
Henry Rosovsky, Harvard University

To SUMMARIZE the main findings of this volume would be a nearly impossible task: each chapter was written as a self-contained entity, the authors do not always agree with one another, and a few generalizations could not do justice to the individual contributions. Instead, we shall briefly discuss three subjects emanating from the main concerns of this study: suggested reformulations of stereotypes about Japan; the prospective growth of the economy; and the lessons to be drawn from the Japanese experience. What follows are our own conclusions and opinions, as the editors; they were greatly enriched by criticisms and suggestions offered by all the authors, but they are our views rather than a consensual statement.

Reformulation of Stereotypes

The literature concerning the economic development of postwar Japan is no longer small, especially if one adds to the expanding scholarly output the work of popular writers, pundits, and the press. Most of this work is American or Japanese—although some has come from Europe and Asia—and from it has emerged a series of easily recognizable stereotypes. One intriguing and valuable aspect of this study is its challenge to many aspects of received wisdom, evident in the findings or interpretations of every one of the authors.

These findings fall into two broad categories: those related specifically to the economic framework and those related more broadly to the political economy and the socioeconomic framework. In each case we will attempt to state the stereotype and then indicate how it may have to be revised.

The Economy

Considerable attention and praise have been lavished on the Japanese tax system. Many believe that their particularly good tax formula has helped the Japanese achieve a high rate of growth. Special tax measures—accelerated depreciation, extraordinary deductions for income from exports, and others—are frequently held up as models of a system designed to support growth. Taking a much more agnostic attitude, Pechman and Kaizuka point out in Chapter 5 that the Japanese have no secret tax formula that can be related directly to the high growth rate, and that the highly elastic increase in tax revenues is due primarily to fast growth, not to any peculiarities in the tax structure. Special tax measures are seen as overused gimmicks; indeed, these

authors are quite critical of the entire tax structure. (Gimmickry and the
inefficiency of special measures are also noted by Krause and Sekiguchi in
Chapter 6.) Unlike most other observers, these authors are skeptical about
the role import restrictions have played in restricting imports, and about the
contribution of direct promotion of exports to the expansion of that sector.
Pechman and Kaizuka's conclusions are that the low burden of the tax system—the lowest among the developed countries—has been its greatest stimulus to postwar growth. These low effective rates have reflected Japan's small
expenditures on defense and on social security and general social welfare,
and are unlikely to remain intact; but a combination of low tax burden and
rapid growth of demand has obviously worked very well in the past.

While the tax system has gained general approval, the financial system of
Japan has been subject to suspicion. Western observers have seen numerous
deficiencies: tight control of interest rates, absence of a bond market, discriminatory allocation of resources in favor of large firms in selected industries, and others. "Overloan" and "overborrowing" have also made potential
foreign investors nervous. Studying the financial system in detail in Chapter 4,
the Wallichs, however, take a much more positive view. They see it as a
disequilibrium system in which institutional controls, including rationing,
have deprived interest rates of much of their function in allocating resources,
though usually directing the economy toward faster growth. Disadvantaged
credit seekers and household savers bear the costs of disequilibrium, but receive some compensation as faster growth enhances their incomes. The Wallichs also conclude that the structure of financial markets and institutions is
strongly influenced by positive public policy, which often, though not always,
pushes the system in the same direction as market forces would have done,
but more rapidly.

In Chapter 3, Ackley and Ishi make a revisionist observation of a somewhat more technical nature. Japanese demand-management policy has
generally been perceived as aiming toward stable and rapid growth. Occasionally, the economy threatened to grow too rapidly or to slow down unnecessarily. However, flexible monetary and fiscal policies succeeded in
minimizing the resulting fluctuations. Ackley and Ishi suggest this is an inadequate interpretation. Demand management in Japan was basically aimed
not toward stable growth but toward maximum feasible growth. From time
to time, however, problems of balance-of-payments disequilibrium, or (less
often) the threat of faster inflation, required a slowdown in economic activity in order to correct these difficulties. The resulting recessions were therefore not unfortunate or accidental occurrences, which contracyclical policy
was (or should have been) used to combat, but deliberate interruptions to
growth designed to deal with specific problem situations.

Krause and Sekiguchi undermine the stereotype of Japanese manufacturers as producers exclusively or even primarily for export. Although foreign markets were not neglected, expansion of productive capacity in manufacturing was undertaken mainly with domestic sales in mind. Compared to other industrial countries, Japan exports a relatively small share of its output. This share has tended to rise over the postwar period, but all industrial countries have experienced this trend and the Japanese share has yet to reach its accustomed prewar level. Only during the late 1960s and early 1970s was there strong evidence that foreign demand lent more fuel to Japanese industrial expansion than did domestic forces. This short period of disequilibrium was corrected with the revaluation of the yen.

Stereotypes are especially prevalent in the area of industrial organization. Japanese industries often have been depicted as highly concentrated, with unusual monopoly power. The financial-industrial groups are said to be particularly profitable; entry is difficult; and collusion among the major producers is thought to be commonplace. Caves and Uekusa, in Chapter 7, redraw this picture almost entirely. Manufacturing industries are no more concentrated than in the United States, although the dominance of large enterprises in the nonfinancial sector may be greater. Entry barriers from "commercial" sources—that is, apart from direct actions by the Ministry of International Trade and Industry (MITI)—are lower. Affiliation with bank groups does not appear to increase the profits of manufacturing firms. In Japanese industry, effective collusion varies with market structure much in the way it does in the United States. Where collusive practices were permitted or encouraged in Japan—that is, in areas of weak antimonopoly policy—no particular benefits to growth accrued. The authors found no evidence that Japanese entrepreneurs lacked fortitude and hence required protection by public policy, or that public policy preferred enlarging firm and plant sizes where they were already sizable. One additional point should be mentioned The "small and medium enterprise problem" has often been noted as a Japanese peculiarity. It is distinctive among industrial countries, although the chapter by Caves and Uekusa shows that it is closely related to Japan's level and speed of development. In that sense it is not "abnormal."

One of the stereotypical explanations of the rapid industrial growth of Japan, and of its potential slowing, is the famed "catching-up thesis" about development that rests on the importation of technology. According to this view, over the past twenty years Japan has benefited from a wide gap between its own and the best Western technologies. Since this gap has substantially narrowed, however, opportunities for further easy growth by this route are limited, and Japan will have to depend more on its native inventiveness. By contrast, Peck and Tamura suggest in Chapter 8 that Japan could continue to do very well for some years by maintaining a strategy of "number two": continually searching the world for the best new ideas and inventions, and using their own skills to embody them rapidly in commercially and economically attractive goods and services.

While the Denison and Chung study of the sources of growth in Chapter 2 does not make a frontal assault on any of the stereotypes, perhaps its findings are the most damaging of all to simple, single-factor explanations. The measures these authors offer demonstrate that Japan's extraordinary economic success cannot be ascribed to any factor, such as capital formation, technical progress, or education, taken alone, but results rather from a combination of many factors, none of which predominates.

The Socioeconomic Context

Of the socioeconomic stereotypes that have been called into question by the authors, perhaps the most obvious is that concerning Japan's cities, traditionally pictured in the West, and by many Japanese themselves, as containing all the elements of an urban horror story: crowding; small, ill-equipped, and antiquated housing; and air polluted to the danger point. Mills and Ohta, in Chapter 10, find, however, that Japanese urban densities are similar to those in Western Europe and not much greater than those in the United States. (In fact, it is the rural areas that have dramatically higher densities than are found in the West.) Housing space per capita is meager, but large amounts of resources are devoted to its improvement, and progress over the past decade has been dramatic. Pollution issues may be particularly upsetting to Americans: the quality of Japanese water is undoubtedly somewhat worse than ours, but available data suggest that the quality of the air is about the same.

If Japan's urban ills have been exaggerated, the traditional view of labor relations may have erred in the opposite direction in its idyllic descriptions of permanent employment, paternalism, low rates of turnover and unemployment, and happy workers laboring energetically on behalf of their companies. In a bleaker and more controversial version of reality, Galenson and Odaka argue in Chapter 9 that labor harmony was achieved at the expense of the worker, that labor relations are less serene than their surface suggests, and that good chances exist for severe conflict in the future. These authors feel that labor has not received its fair share of the epic economic achievements of the postwar era, certainly not when compared with the social democracies of Western Europe. If unions had not been emasculated in the fifties, industrial investment and GNP growth would have been lower and social investment higher. All this raises an intriguing and unanswered question: Why did the Japanese sustain a government that allowed more than a third of the national income to be plowed back into investment, most of it in private business plant and equipment? Or, to put it another way, why were the workers seemingly willing to make an income shift to a relatively distant future?

The champion destroyers of graven images among the authors are Trezise and Suzuki (Chapter 11). Discarding the usual view of the Japanese government as the wise and powerful leader of the economic miracle, these authors suggest that it usually just managed to muddle through. They reject the notion of a monolithic "Japan, Inc.," in which big business dominates the design of economic policy; they see it sharing power with small business and agriculture. Furthermore, government bureaucrats, in their view, adopt pluralist and competitively oriented approaches, goals, and methods. Policy often has been contradictory and poorly defined, and the MITI has had far less influence on the pattern of industrial growth than have the forces of Japanese entrepreneurship and competition. Even trade policy has exhibited the traditional preoccupation with protecting labor-intensive and inefficient sectors. How else can one explain the government's long-term concerns for cotton textiles and coal mining? The Japanese government—like all governments—is pleased to take credit for any successes of the system, and blithely ignores its mistakes.

In Chapter 12, Glazer supports some of Trezise and Suzuki's findings. He, too, describes Japanese companies as discrete and exclusive communities vis-à-vis their competitors and, indeed, the rest of the world. There is very little cooperation among companies, and this is not in line with the usual presentation of "Japan, Inc."

The revisions proposed for these stereotypes do not, we believe, warrant their total discard. Many of them retain some validity, as will be evident in the discussion of the lessons of the Japanese experience. However, all too frequently these generalizations have been excessively sweeping, lacking in comparative perspective, and sometimes self-serving. The results of this study provide a healthy and necessary sense of balance.

Prospects for Japanese Economic Growth

While the essays in this study were in preparation, the Japanese economy shifted from very rapid growth into a period marked by the oil crisis, intolerable inflation, and the worst slowdown in production of the postwar period. Japan thus has not been immune to the plagues of all industrialized countries in the mid-1970s: inflation, balance-of-payments deficits, and recession. The lesson of Japan's great vulnerability in an unstable world economic environment—due to its overwhelming dependence on imports of oil, food, and industrial raw materials—has been brought home once again by the events of 1973 and 1974. It is not surprising that the Cassandras in Japan and elsewhere have predicted, if not doom, at least the cessation of growth and prosperity. To them, the bubble of the Japanese miracle has burst.

We do not share such pessimism. We recognize Japan's great difficulties, and can visualize a tricky path of adjustment in 1975 and perhaps 1976 as policymakers attempt both to end rapid inflation and to restore full employment of resources in a growth context. However, we are confident that the Japanese economy will resume its successful performance.

But what do we mean by a successful economic performance? More important, what do the Japanese themselves have in mind? This has been the subject of intense debate, crystallizing around the issue of the economic growth rate. The debate proceeds at two different, though interrelated and often confused, levels: First, what *should* the long-run growth rate be? Or, put another way, what is an optimal rate in the light of changing economic and social goals? Second, what growth rates are possible and feasible, given the constraints? Japanese perspectives and objective conditions bearing on both questions have altered substantially.

Growth for What?

Beginning in the late 1960s many have remarked that the Japanese people are becoming "disillusioned with economic growth." While this is a vague proposition, hard to test empirically, a recent change of popular mood concerning the economy is readily apparent.

In the fifties and throughout most of the sixties, many Japanese appeared to consider the rate of growth of aggregate output an end in itself: the higher it went, the greater the national merit. Ordinary people were remarkably well informed about the facts of economic success (often to the second decimal place); few—whether in Japan or elsewhere—had the foresight to question a policy that maximized the speed of GNP growth. By the sixties, "two-digit growth" had become an article of faith, and to many the heroes of Japan were the businessmen and bureaucrats who could take credit for its achievement.

This attitude was not irrational. Rapid economic growth enabled Japan to recover from the devastation of World War II, and allowed its people to achieve the highest standard of living they have ever known. The full measure of this achievement has been substantially documented in this book. However, it can be fully appreciated only by those of us who first saw Japan shortly after World War II—devastated and occupied, its people underfed and in tatters—and who now see not only the glitter and opulence of Tokyo but the solid prosperity throughout Japan's other cities, towns, and countryside.

What, if anything, has happened in the recent past to temper this exuberance? To some extent, the Japanese have mirrored changes in world opinion, especially in the United States and Western Europe. In Japan, too, people have become concerned with the quality of life, with zero population growth, ecology, ebbing world resources, monotonous assembly lines, and the like. No doubt, foreign ideas (and fads) have a considerable impact in Japan, especially when they project a melancholy future. At the same time, worsening urban congestion, pollution, and unrequited demands for government services—at a time when private consumption demands were ever better met—increasingly came to shape Japanese views. In a major shift of emphasis, an emerging consensus in Japan held that two-digit growth not only *could* not but *should* not be maintained, and that policy should stabilize growth at a slower rate and develop methods to keep it there.

The Environment

A detailed discussion of these issues must start with the deterioration of the environment and its direct relation to the rapid growth of GNP. As the introductory chapter and the chapters by Mills and Ohta and Galenson and Odaka have demonstrated, the quality of the air, water, and natural environment have all suffered. In most cases a direct connection between a worsening environment and industry is readily made, and the famous pollution trials that have made Itai-Itai, Minamata, and Yokkaichi familiar names have left a strong imprint on the national conscience. However, the indirect consequences, such as the rise of "leisure pollution" due to higher per capita income, are also highly deleterious.

These problems are at least as serious in Japan as in other advanced countries. One exacerbating factor is that Japan has the highest GNP in the world *per square mile,* whether of total land, flat land, or land devoted to industrial uses; in other words, compared with other countries, Japan's economic activity is concentrated in less space. This situation is only partially offset by proximity to the sea, which is Japan's substitute for the hinterland that other countries use as a dumping ground for pollutants. Environmental deterioration has taken another, broader, form in Japan: everything has become more crowded. Houses are expensive, and their location requires ever-longer commuting on trains inadequate to rush-hour demands. The legendary beauty of the country has been degraded in many places as rising income has made tourism a mass-consumption activity. Of course, the golden age existed only for a few, and the benefits to the many of rapid growth have been enormous. But no wonder so many Japanese feel that life has deteriorated in the last ten years, and that the present situation is "unacceptable,"[1] when—to take one instance—the government in 1972 had to set guidelines for fish consumption because of its rising mercury content.

Thus, the spreading perception of these problems has been as important in raising issues about the quality of life as have the objective facts of environmental deterioration. Many of these difficulties began to disturb not just the few and powerless who lived next to factories, but government bureaucrats, middle management, and journalists who also suffered the discomforts of air pollution, long commuting, and lack of public amenities. Why did these issues not surface sooner in Japan—or in other countries, for that matter? One significant reason surely is that for most people, tackling them is a luxury, to be indulged in only after income has reached fairly high levels. Moreover, especially in Japan, high income is achievable only with intense industrial activity, and the consequent creation—perhaps exponential rather than linear—of pollution, congestion, and other external diseconomies. Besides, many such disamenities have distinct thresholds: below them, discomfort and damage are mild enough to be ignored; but once the threshold is crossed, they attract sharply increased attention.

Income Distribution

Another seed of doubt about the benefits of rapid growth has been planted by critics concerned with income distribution. They question who the principal heirs of the economic miracle have been and whether the division of proceeds has been equitable. These queries are at once simple and complicated. The formula for Japanese economic development from the early 1950s to the present undoubtedly was highly favorable to private business (and agriculture). The governmental draft on resources has remained consistently low—well below that in the United States—and thus the private sector has kept for its own uses the increments attained through rapid expansion. Until recently, Japan could be fairly described as a businessman's economic and political paradise. As is amply documented in this book, the economic suc-

1. According to a national public opinion poll, the percentage who regarded environmental pollution emanating from industrial development as unacceptable rose from 27 percent in 1966 to 49 percent in 1971; see Environment Agency, *Quality of the Environment in Japan, 1973* (1973), p. 39.

cess of the last twenty years was closely related to these policies. Business was able to finance gigantic investment programs, which have been a basic feature of the 10 percent growth Japan has experienced and which in turn has promoted the rapid increases in output and personal income from which everyone benefited—if not equally.

A policy that favored the private business sector has placed a special burden on those segments of society normally catered to by government: the aged and those who depend on such public services as transportation or on some form of public welfare or aid for education. In Japan welfare—in the broadest sense—was until very recently considered a private matter, the responsibility of family and relations. Aged people were supposed to be absorbed by extended families; yet this is becoming less true in urban, nuclear-family Japan, while the proportion of older people has sharply climbed. Social security is inadequate. Retirement programs come early—usually between the ages of fifty-five and sixty—and are quite scanty, forcing retirees back into the labor force (as is discussed in Chapter 9). Urban transportation systems do move people from one place to another, but all too often in very crowded circumstances and at a slow pace.

The same reasons underlie all these problems. Of all advanced nations in the world, Japan is furthest from a European-style welfare state. The extra resources that policy has directed toward entrepreneurs have not been available to the government for social purposes. Critics argue that such needs should have had a high priority, even at the expense of lower measured growth. For them, it is quality, not quantity, that counts.

Problems of income distribution have been exacerbated by the severe inflation since early 1973. It is premature to analyze the burdens brought by rapidly rising prices, but some of their effects are clear even now. The real standard of living of the population has not risen much since 1973, and groups whose incomes are not somehow indexed have suffered. In 1974, for the first time since World War II, real wages of labor did not rise.

The Answer?

For all these reasons the chorus of detractors has grown louder. The voices are strong among social critics (largely academics and journalists) and those politicians and bureaucrats who must satisfy their urban working-class constituencies. Even a number of business leaders have joined in. Significantly, the most recent five-year plan (1973–77) bears the subtitle, "Towards a Vigorous Welfare Society."

The "growth for what?" debate embraces two schools: those who believe that the improvement in the quality of life can best be achieved by slow growth, and those who argue that it can come only through the allocation of new resources made possible by relatively rapid growth itself. Proponents of slow growth argue that growth itself caused environmental deterioration and human degradation, and that the only effective way to reverse the process is first to slow growth drastically and then to attack the problems at their existing, rather than worsening, levels. They propose diverting to welfare purposes the investible (saved) resources that would otherwise serve to expand potential GNP supply capacity.

For what it is worth, our own view is that within the Japanese social and political context—as in other industrial democracies—far-reaching new welfare expenditures and social overhead investment by government probably can come only from incremental resources accruing from relatively rapid growth. Raising tax rates, or borrowing, within existing resources appears an unlikely way for the government to increase its expenditure share in GNP to meet these welfare needs. Some of the growth will have to be diverted to cleaning up the additional pollution it creates, but that share is relatively small. Given Pechman and Kaizuka's analysis of the tax structure, obtaining incremental resources will not require higher tax rates; the government simply must refrain from reductions in tax rates, or minimize those they do make. We regard this as the politically easier path. Thus, we do not subscribe to the school that urges slow growth.

Economic Growth: 1975–85

"Rapid growth" and "slow growth" are vague phrases. In Japan, where judgments concerning the future tend to run to extremes, they can be especially misleading. Between the extreme optimism of Herman Kahn (The Japanese Century!) and the gloom of the 1973 oil crisis (It's All Over!) there has been plenty of room for erroneous predictions. No one expects the coming decade to see a repetition of Japan's 11 to 12 percent annual growth of the late 1960s. Nor does anyone expect the growth rate to subside to the postwar level in the United Kingdom or the United States. But a wide range of possibilities remains. The advocates of slow growth seem to focus on the 4 to 6 percent range, while proponents of fast growth deal in the 8 to 10 percent range.

We are inclined to be relatively optimistic. Our optimism is based on the belief that both the basic institutions of Japan and its economy are fundamentally sound—*not* the house of cards that some suggest. Moreover, Japan's people possess organizational ability, education, and skills, combined with a tradition of hard work, none of which is apt soon to evaporate. An optimistic forecast to us means an average annual rate of GNP growth in the neighborhood of 6 to 8 percent until, say, 1985—well below the record of the previous twenty years but still ahead of the likely American or European performance.

"Forecast" is much too pretentious a word for this judgment and for the discussion that follows. Indeed, looking at recent history, we are skeptical of any single-number ten-year projection. Technically, economists do not understand the evolving structure of an economy well enough to make precise long-run projections; the range of alternative projections consistent with the basic data embedded in a good model widens dramatically as the time horizon lengthens. Moreover, the fundamental changes in values, institutions, and politics that are at work in any society, though they significantly affect the course of events, are insufficiently understood to be incorporated into economic models. And Japan, like other economies, can be buffeted by exogenous or random shocks. Particularly in the interdependent world of which Japan is now such an important part, what occurs in the rest of the world can deeply affect Japanese economic performance.

The Japanese frequently use the English word "vision" for their ten-year projections, and that is probably preferable to "forecasts." Their visions and ours are, at present, rather close to one another. Among the long-term projections that have been released within the last year by the Economic Planning Agency, the MITI, and the Japan Economic Research Center and some other private organizations, long-term GNP growth of about 6.5 percent seems to be the modal guess. The range of estimates is wider than has previously been true,[2] but reflects the greater uncertainty concerning both domestic and international circumstances. The precise number itself is without great meaning. As a symbol, however, it stresses the expectation of some slowdown, but, compared to other advanced countries, the continuation of relatively rapid growth.

Many of the factors behind this expected pattern have already been analyzed in other chapters. Here, we merely summarize that discussion and incorporate other broad factors—solely from our own point of view.

2. The Economic Council of the Economic Planning Agency recently projected a 5.5 percent growth rate or a 7 percent rate for 1975–84, depending on the oil supply; *New York Times,* Dec. 27, 1974. The October projection of the MITI's equally prestigious Industrial Structure Council embodies growth-rate assumptions of 7 percent annually for 1975–80 and 6.5 percent for 1980–85; MITI, *Sangyō kōzō no chōki bijion* [Vision of the Long-Term Industrial Structure] (November 1974), p. 28. A recent Japan Economic Research Center forecast suggests a real average growth rate of GNP of 7 percent for the period 1975–85; see *Japan Economic Journal,* Feb. 18, 1975.

Domestic Factors

Basically, the unusually favorable secular conditions required for two-digit growth seem to be disappearing. While still quite ample by some Western standards, labor supplies have tightened perceptibly. "Cheap labor" is a thing of the past; only U.S. and West German wages are higher than the Japanese. The large reservoirs of underutilized, well-educated workers have dropped, while shorter working hours and longer vacations have become more common. Both importing technology and developing it domestically are becoming more expensive, although, as Peck and Tamura suggest in Chapter 8, broad opportunities for borrowing may exist for some years. The very large productivity gains associated with the introduction of new products and new methods may shrink to more marginal accretions as the technological base becomes ever more sophisticated.[3] In adversely affecting the rate of return on capital, these factors could lower the growth of private investment. A change in the composition of investment toward housing and social-overhead capital is also a strong possibility. This may lower the contribution of capital to the growth of GNP, while perhaps raising its contribution to net national welfare. A further concern is the declining availability of prime industrial sites—with a welcoming or at least acquiescent local populace, adequate industrial water supplies and transport facilities, and other requisites.

The restructuring of priorities implicit in the question, "growth for what?" involves important tradeoffs. Not even the Japanese are exempt from this constraint: they cannot have two-digit growth, relatively stable prices, greater social amenities, better welfare, and eradication of pollution all at once. Marginal choices will have to be made, and some will tend to depress the rate of growth during the next decade. Broadly speaking, much of "the vigorous welfare society" that is perceived as desirable in Japan today will divert saving from private production to public social needs. Quite plainly, building a hospital or even a road does not contribute as much to measured output as does installing new petrochemical machinery. Furthermore, and fundamentally, how valid is the current political rhetoric? Do they—the government, the bureaucrats, the leaders of opinion—really mean it? We tend to think that they do. If not, we foresee political realignments that will bring about more socially oriented policies.

3. Denison and Chung reach very similar conclusions in their decomposition of the aggregate growth rate during the 1960s. They suggest that approximately two-thirds of the sources of rapid growth are "transitional," and that many of these will lose their positive effect in the late 1970s and early 1980s. They also realize that unanticipated positive "transitional" factors may arise in the coming decade.

In the face of these factors making for slow domestic growth, our optimistic expectation for expansion rests on our belief that economies tend to exhibit the conditions for rapid growth before they attain maturity. In essence, we accept (empirically) an "S"-shaped path. In these terms, Japan's transformation from a semideveloped economy—a description apt for the early 1950s— to a fully developed one has not yet been completed. Agricultural workers still compose about 15 percent of the total, even though most of these are women and older people. Concomitantly, much flat land suitable for industrial sites is still in agrarian use. Traditional small-scale enterprises, frequently based on nonwage family labor, still account for a large share of employment and of output. The entire distributive sector has only barely begun to modernize. Even today, one can describe Japan as a dualistic economy in which the productivity gaps remain unusually wide. So long as they do, opportunities for rationalization and technological progress will be great, opening the way for relatively rapid growth.

International Constraints

Since the end of the occupation in 1952, major changes have occurred in the world economic environment and, along with them, in Japan's position in it and in Japan's international image. On the one hand, Japan's economic achievements have been much admired: many less developed countries would like to use Japan as a model. On the other hand, the very rapidity of economic growth, combined sometimes with Japanese insensitivity, has stirred friction with other nations. If this is the price for achieving the most rapidly expanding economy in the world, is the achievement worth it? What constraints on future Japanese economic growth may these frictions portend?

This book has focused mainly upon Japan's domestic economy, and properly so since that is where almost nine-tenths of the available goods and services are produced and consumed. To shift the focus, a brief review of the postwar history of Japan's international relations may therefore be useful.

Right after the war nearly everyone believed that the Japanese were condemned to a long period of national poverty, and—aside from reparations— the world community had little interest in them. As the domestic economy recovered in the 1950s, during and after the Korean War, and as the country grew economically more powerful every year, the Japanese exhibited a so-called low posture in international affairs, hoping thereby to avoid conflicts and confrontation. Indeed, Japan's foreign policy during the postwar years appeared to have no object other than support for national economic development. Japan obtained membership in the United Nations, concluded a mutual security pact with the United States, and provided economic aid to developing nations. However, it played no major role in world affairs until the late 1960s.

To have both a low posture and the most rapidly growing large economy in the world is to be in a paradoxical and, in the long run, probably an untenable position. Beginning in the middle sixties, the strains became plain. The conflict with the United States was largely economic, as discussed in our introductory chapter and in Chapter 6. Problems also arose with the less developed world, particularly in Southeast and South Asia. In that part of the globe, Japan's presence spread with its search for cheap labor, markets, and resources. While referring to the Japanese as "economic animals" (as a foreign minister of Pakistan was the first to do) is unfair, and the epithet is equally applicable to other nations, it well articulates the prevailing feelings. More recently, Prime Minister Tanaka was met with extensive anti-Japanese rioting in Bangkok and Jakarta; though both Thailand and Indonesia had domestic difficulties that were exploited on this occasion, the hostility was a sign of the times. A word should be added about the attitude of the Europeans. They had little interest in Japan until the late sixties, when exports became a potentially serious issue. Since then they have apparently focused on one thing: keeping Japan at bay.

Little wonder that the Japanese felt beleaguered and unloved. At the same time that they were viewed as selfish and excessively oriented toward exports, they worsened their image by closing their own markets to foreign competition. The facts did not matter too much: few abroad were disposed to see events from the Japanese point of view. A growing number also understood that one source of the problem was the imbalance of economic growth among countries: Japan's rate of expansion was approximately twice as rapid as that of the rest of the world.

Mo of the world economic tensions of the early 1970s were not the fault of Japan alone, nor was ts growth a major cause of the fundamental problems of the international economic system. Nonetheless, rapid growth, tardy liberalization of imports and capital flows, and burgeoning balance-of-payments surpluses all were catalysts for the major changes in the world economy between 1971 and 1973. By mid-1973 the Bretton Woods system of fixed exchange rates had been discarded, and was replaced by a more flexible set of ad hoc arrangements involving exchange-rate adjustments under controlled floats and cooperation to prevent competitive depreciations of currencies. At the same time, awareness of the world food problem and rampant world-wide inflation emerged. Japan, too, came to behave much more responsibly. It substantially liberalized trade and capital flows, and moved to the forefront of the nations urging further liberalization. It gave up its rigid

adherence to fixed exchange rates, and cooperated in subsequent rate adjustments. By mid-1973, through a variety of measures, Japan was eliminating
the balance-of-payments surplus that put so much pressure on the United
States and the rest of the world.

Then, in October 1973, the Japanese suffered—briefly, to be sure—a national nervous breakdown. The war between the Arabs and Israel, and the
consequent short-term disruption of oil flows accompanied by longer-term
major price increases, forcefully underlined Japan's vulnerability in raw materials. While all this was part of a longer-run problem, the immediate reaction
both in Japan and elsewhere was grossly exaggerated. Some foreign experts
were ready to bury Japan because the price of oil had tripled or quadrupled;
the Japanese themselves appeared ready to approach the Arabs on their
knees. These immediate reactions were, in retrospect, absurd, but the long-
term problem remains serious.[4]

As is frequently and correctly emphasized, the Japanese have virtually no
natural resources of their own, except some relatively expensive coal. Their
major resource is human: a large educated population. Such a large and
expanding economy has an enormous appetite for imported materials: for
many vital industrial raw materials, the import ratio stands at over 90 percent. Their continual acquisition and stockpiling at reasonable prices is thus
a major economic and political problem. These difficulties loom largest in
petroleum and food. Petroleum is an overwhelmingly important energy resource for Japan; it accounts for the largest monetary value of any single
commodity in world trade; its exporting producers have succeeded in creating a cartel, something less likely to occur in other raw materials. Japan now
imports half of its calorie consumption; possible world food shortages and
embargoes by exporters (the specter raised by the U.S. export embargo on
soybeans in the summer of 1973) understandably cause great anxiety among
thoughtful Japanese. Obviously, a reduction in Japan's rate of growth, or
certain changes in the nature of economic activity, would lighten the resource
burden as well as lower the temperature of certain foreign conflicts. Not surprisingly, then, this theme has entered the debate over the optimal rate of
growth. After all, an important objective, valued in its own right, is Japan's
good relations with *all* of the rest of the world.

These new international factors figure as potential constraints on Japan's
growth. A whole host of new problems has emerged, symbolized by oil.
Will Japan be able to obtain as much oil, food, and other natural resources as

4. Perhaps it is worth mentioning that most of the individual chapters were in first
draft before the oil crisis of 1973. That event, however, did not require any major change
either in the separate analyses or in our conclusions.

it desires, or will new embargoes or quantitative restrictions be imposed by exporters? Will the terms of trade move so much against Japan that domestic incentives to invest will be seriously eroded or growth retarded in some other way? How will Japan pay for its imports without disrupting economic relations with the rest of the industrial world?

Many Japanese now take the first problem very seriously. Indeed, the recent growth projections by the Economic Planning Agency and the MITI are based on the explicit assumption that Japan will *not* be able to increase its imports of oil much more than 5 to 6 percent annually.[5] Otherwise, Japan's share of world oil imports would soon exceed 18 percent—and some assert that somehow the rest of the world would find this intolerable. We are somewhat more sanguine on this issue: quota restrictions on Japanese oil imports do not appear likely, and we believe that Japan could increase its share in world oil imports more than government planners currently assume.

Nor do we see a dramatic slowdown in the growth rate caused by worsened terms of trade. The more complex problem is paying for needed imports. Japan will be more dependent than ever on imports—not only of energy, food, and industrial raw materials, but also of a rising share of intermediate products: the expansion of domestic production of iron and steel, nonferrous metals, paper pulp, and certain chemical products is limited by pollution, water supply, and other constraints. In the now-lost world in which Japan could ignore its own economic effects on major countries, it could have readily reallocated resources to export production and adjusted the exchange rate to finance the higher import bill by increased export earnings. Since Japan is simply too large a force in the world economy, such actions are not politically feasible. Clearly, the members of the Organization of Petroleum Exporting Countries (OPEC) cannot spend all their export earnings on imports of goods and services, at least in the relatively near future. Their annual combined current-account surplus over the next five years will be very large indeed,[6] and the current account of the rest of the world will be in deficit in equal amount. An attempt by any major industrial country to achieve current-account balance can succeed only at the expense of the other major coun-

---

5. See MITI, *Vision of the Long-Term Industrial Structure*, pp. 162–63. The clear implication is that if more oil were available, Japan's growth rate would be higher.

6. One estimate of $30 billion to $40 billion is presented in Hollis B. Chenery, "Restructuring the World Economy," *Foreign Affairs*, vol. 53 (January 1975), p. 254. A much higher estimate of $80 billion to $90 billion appears in Khodadad Farmanfarmaian and others, "How Can the World Afford OPEC Oil?" ibid., p. 203. Both articles provide good discussions of the oil-recycling problem and suggest feasible policy solutions. Chenery points out that the best way to repay these borrowings is by the supply capacity and export creation of more rapid growth.

tries. Japan, Europe, and the United States are constrained to cooperate with each other on policies relating to exchange rates, trade, and the recycling of oil funds if a trade war and restrictive protectionism by all are to be avoided.[7]

Of all the industrial countries, Japan finds the payments problem most difficult because it is the largest oil importer and because it may not be a major first-line recipient of OPEC surplus funds. The Japanese fear that too few oil dollars will be recycled to them to meet their balance-of-payments requirements. This concern is exacerbated by their desire to engage in direct investment abroad, especially in natural resources and heavy and chemical industries.[8] To pay for these capital outflows Japan will have either to borrow more abroad or increase its trade surplus. The latter seems politically difficult, and indeed the magnitude of the currently projected foreign investment outflow may be unrealistic.

One further, frankly speculative, matter is the Japanese sense that, despite all its economic success, the country is not a fully accredited member of the major-power club. Admittedly, this is an intangible matter, difficult to define or document. Nevertheless, it cannot be ignored as a cause of disillusionment with the past twenty years and of fear for the future. In support of this feeling, modern Japanese history can plausibly be viewed as a series of rejections by the Western powers. In the 1890s the Japanese were prevented from grabbing parts of China by European imperialist powers. At Versailles they were denied a racial-equality clause. In the 1930s the United States strongly opposed expansion by Japan—a position it did not always take with respect to other countries—and eventually resorted to an economic blockade. Would history repeat itself in the 1970s? Would the achievements of the last twenty years result in another blackballing by a "whites only" club?

We are not suggesting that this is an accurate interpretation of history, but it is a tenable view in Japan, where all Western opposition seems to be directed at the one country in Asia that has succeeded in industrializing. In recent years Japanese exports have encountered special resistance in other countries, and protectionist talk has rumbled close to the surface. Anti-Japanese articles have been easy to find in newspapers and magazines, especially amid the tension of 1971–72; often these featured sinister descriptions of "Japan, Inc.," that mythical, all-powerful instrument of the national will. If it really existed, presumably no one could compete with it according to

7. See Robert Solomon, "The Allocation of 'Oil Deficits'," *Brookings Papers on Economic Activity, 1:1975*, pp. 61–79.

8. The MITI projection for the outstanding amount of Japanese direct foreign investment is $10 billion in 1973, to rise to $45 billion in 1980 and $93.5 billion in 1985; MITI, *Vision of the Long-Term Industrial Structure*, pp. 180–81.

gentlemanly rules of the game, and therefore special rules might be permissible and desirable. These feelings were seldom found in print, but they certainly existed among some Americans and perhaps more Europeans, and were communicated to the Japanese. The anxieties they aroused were exacerbated by the failure to consult with Japan over major international decisions: Nixon shocks, China relations, soybean embargoes, and the like. While in no way lending credence to these allegations, or implying that the fears they arouse are widely held in informed Japanese circles, we would suggest that they deepen Japan's nagging doubts about its relationship with other industrial powers.

In our view, these various difficulties—availability of natural resources, recycling of oil dollars, and so on—are not likely severely to constrain Japanese domestic economic performance. Part of our optimism reflects our belief that the industrial world will muddle through—and in a cooperative fashion —so that in due course the dual scourge of inflation and recession will end. Part of it reflects our sense that Japan will continue to accord a relatively high priority to economic goals, and will attempt to achieve them in the sensible and orderly manner that has characterized national decisionmaking over the past two decades.

Possible Adverse Circumstances

Suppose, however, that our optimism is not warranted. What are the potential problems?

First, a serious confrontation could develop between labor and management, a difficulty that Japan has managed to avoid thus far. Unions have not been strong, prolonged strikes are virtually unknown, and in general the voice of management has prevailed both in the factory and with the government. In the past, workers have been relatively content: real wages rose rapidly, a good job was a prized possession, and working conditions were improving. But as productivity growth declines and the pace of real wage increases therefore slows—in the face of continuing inflation and a realization by labor of its power to disrupt the economy—might there not take place costly confrontations that would, in the English fashion, impede rapid growth? Galenson and Odaka's observation that Japanese labor relations are reminiscent of the United States in the 1920s suggests the likelihood of a future filled with conflict. Any answer we give can be no more than an educated guess, and we do not even claim much education in these matters. But if relatively rapid growth continues, a sharp deterioration in labor relations before 1985 seems to us a low probability. This belief hinges on the likely demand and supply conditions for labor. As long as the supply remains *relatively* ample (though tighter than in the fifties and sixties)—that is, as long as workers actively compete for better jobs—prolonged conflict can probably be avoided. To put it slightly differently, given its less than fully developed status—characterized by a relatively large portion of the labor force in agriculture, small-scale enterprises, and services, and by persisting underemployment—the Japanese economy still has effective protection against militant unionism and all its consequences. Slower growth will reinforce this protection. One safeguard should be the persistence of enterprise unions that tie the welfare of the workers to the firm rather than to the industry, together with the bonus system that bears some relation to the profitability of the company. We believe that as the economy slows and productivity growth declines, tensions will rise if inflation is not controlled. But because organized labor is too weak, we do not see this phenomenon as a major threat.

What if the Japanese lose their love of work and put a much higher premium on leisure? To some extent, in fact, the Japanese have exhibited an enhanced desire for leisure during the entire postwar period. For example, in the fifties most shops closed only twice a month and Saturday was a full workday in nearly every office and factory. Very recently, the five-and-a-half-day week has been gaining acceptance, as are Sunday store closings; and movement toward a five-day week is steady. Such changes could affect the level and growth of productivity, but they come about only gradually, and in ten years are unlikely to change the scene radically.

Furthermore, Japanese consumers are still highly acquisitive. In many respects, they strike us as at least as materialistic as Americans. In the largest cities they are extremely brand- and fashion-conscious, and especially eager to consume luxury foreign products. Per capita income is high—though not very high—and the list of unsatisfied wants remains long. It seems to us that the prevailing strong desire for a high and continually rising standard of living is the best guarantee of a continued commitment to hard work and to large inflows into savings. After all, the individual himself will have to provide for his own rising standard of living; no one else will do it for him. That is a crucial point in Japan. Certainly, more social services will be provided, and perhaps certain types of goods and services, such as housing and education, will become easier to obtain. However, Japan cannot possibly transform itself into a Scandinavian-type welfare state in a decade. How the individual Japanese lives will, as before, depend—other things equal—on his own hard work, and, therefore, every consideration suggests a continued high level of effort.

Another scenario turns on the economic effects of political instability.

After all, the Liberal Democratic party (LDP) did poorly in the Upper House elections in the summer of 1974, and Prime Minister Tanaka had, unprecedentedly, to resign in December following heightened intraparty dissension and disclosures of his possible financial improprieties. Could a likely outcome of political developments affect growth adversely? Discounting this possibility, Trezise and Suzuki point out that the role of government policy has been exaggerated, and that the main contribution of the public sector has been its low draft on national resources. A change of government thus should stir no alarm, unless opposition parties with a very different philosophy should succeed in forming an administration. Because those parties are in even greater disarray than the LDP, that is a most unlikely outcome; and, say, a Socialist victory with a strong nationalization mandate is hard to imagine. The most likely change would be a coalition government formed by some factions of the LDP and some moderate elements now in opposition. None of this signals major shifts in governmental attitudes toward the private sector or toward the economy in general.

In the international sphere, Japan is vulnerable not so much to the usual economic forces—price changes, new competitors, altered market conditions—as to political retaliation. The economy can undoubtedly adjust to higher import or lower export prices of any number of commodities. It can also adjust to deterioration in certain markets, as the sequel to the OPEC crisis demonstrated—the national nervous breakdown notwithstanding. An event like the quadrupling of the price of oil can raise production costs and perhaps reduce the aggregate rate of growth, but it need not cause an irreversible disaster.

Nonetheless, because of Japan's nearly total lack of natural resources and its long lines of communications, its political vulnerability is unique among the major world economies. The issue is not price or conditions of sale or long-term credits, but expropriation, blockade, refusal to deliver, and the like. A pessimistic scenario requires the belief that the resource-exporting countries will attempt a prolonged boycott of Japan and that they will succeed. We regard this as highly improbable. Japan is unlikely to be singled out for unfavorable treatment by the producers; indeed, it is just as likely to receive favorable treatment. Any effects on other major economies would surely mobilize political pressures that would force a relatively rapid solution (in, say, three to six months).

On a broader level, could the economic isolation of Japan become real because a world that cannot cope with an ever-growing economic giant discriminates specifically against her? In the early 1970s, when the international

economic system was under severe pressure and Japan appeared a dis-
rupter seemingly unaware of its own influence, this type of foreign reaction
might have been credible. Influential business and governmental quarters
abroad found Japan uncooperative, bent on pushing its own exports, not
above dumping, and acting only in its own narrow interest. Attempted isolation of Japan would have been poor policy and would certainly have failed,
yet to some it seemed an option. Today, the atmosphere has vastly improved.
International economic problems remain serious, but it is generally accepted
in the United States, in Europe, and in Japan that all three regions must be
partners to any solution. The threat of enforced isolation, and of the counter-
punch of Japanese-sponsored blocs in Asia and possibly elsewhere, has very
much diminished.

These possibilities could still become an unfortunate reality if the world
trade system breaks down into competing blocs—say, an inward-looking
European Community, an isolationist United States, a Japan virtually invited
to form its own sphere of influence. There is always the danger that, in the
throes of recession, unemployment, and balance-of-payments deficits, the
United States or Europe might succumb to protectionist temptations. No
nation desires such an outcome, Japan least of all. While it is one of our
greatest concerns, on balance we think it will not occur.

We end this section by noting some of the implications of a growth rate for
Japan that outstrips that of Europe or the United States. Inevitably, this
disparity means that the economic power of Japan relative to the United
States will continue to rise. However, this rise will be less rapid than in the
past, and presumably will take place in a more flexible world economic system, making the adjustment process easier for all. Moreover, Japan will probably no longer be the most rapidly growing nation. A number of economically
successful developing countries—some of them large, such as Brazil—may
well maintain sustained rapid rates of growth. And the relative position of
OPEC nations will probably expand. Thus, economic power will be more
widely distributed among a large number of nations.

Lessons?

Nearly all the authors felt that a section bearing this title—without the
question mark—was of considerable importance. However, when we asked
them what lessons their own chapters taught, most remained silent or resorted
to the narrowly technical. These responses are not surprising: lessons are a

well-known intellectual quagmire, and most of us would rather be angels than fools. We studied Japan not to derive directly useful prescriptions for ourselves or anyone else, but to learn about an important economy and to widen our own horizons. Furthermore, Japan is an especially difficult country and economy to use as an example. Aside from its specific culture and history, only Japan among the major industrial nations is so totally dependent on imported natural resources. Furthermore, our study deals only with the relatively recent past, and therefore we may well have focused on those aspects of the Japanese experience least relevant to less developed countries. Japan was certainly not an undeveloped country at the end of World War II. In addition, lessons learned from a single country may be especially suspect: what may strike Americans as noteworthy in Japan could well turn out to be commonplace—even invalid—when set against a broader background.

Despite these difficulties, we still think it valuable to attempt a few brief statements concerning the findings that seem directly relevant to America. Perhaps "the obvious is better than the obvious avoidance of it."

• What happened to Japan's economy after World War II cannot be described as miraculous. The Japanese are not a nation of supermen who can do everything in the economic sphere better than anyone else. No single factor can explain the success of recent years; the explanation lies, rather, in a variety of factors that were unusually favorable up to the early 1970s. As these factors become less favorable, we expect the rate of growth of aggregate output to decline somewhat. Thus, rapid economic growth is the consequence not of some mysterious oriental secret, but of a combination of favorable internal and external circumstances and supportive public policy. What is the lesson? We need not live in awe or fear of Japan; given the right circumstances, we (and others) could do as well relative to our own potential.

• Nonetheless, the Japanese economy is today the world's third largest and will continue to grow both absolutely and relatively. Consequently, the world view of the United States—indeed, of every nation or individual—can afford to ignore neither the legitimate interests of Japan nor the opportunities afforded by the Japanese presence. This makes it ever more important that we enhance our knowledge and understanding of Japan. Clearly, over the next decade at least, Japan will remain far more important to American interests than China or any other Asian nation.

• Rapid economic growth hides many blemishes and makes nearly everything and everyone look good—for a while. But this study has shown that, amidst all the success, the Japanese government frequently merely muddled through, labor relations were far from ideal, and the tax structure was not especially efficient. More important, the growth pattern imposed rising social costs in pollution, urban congestion, and inadequate attention to housing and related amenities. The lesson here is subtle and subject to debate. In Japan, rapid growth has been a powerful political factor that built consensus and weakened opposition, but prevented the timely consideration of some social problems. Everyone benefits from rapid growth, if not necessarily in equal measure. Still, the widespread evidence of improvements in the national standard of living promotes an atmosphere of patience and hope that is of great help to any government.

• Japan has learned to make the best of adversity. For one example, its isolation, ignorance of the outside world, and a severe language barrier spurred the development of the general trading company, which has proved tremendously efficient in conducting international commerce. Lacking a domestic raw-material base, Japan pioneered in bulk carriers, which reduced the cost of water transportation, and also developed the most advanced shipbuilding industry in the world. Furthermore, to make best use of these carriers, they built tidewater sites, the heavy investments for which could be justified only by large plants which in turn permitted capturing economies of scale in manufacturing. To serve the needs of the small-scale farms that persistently characterize the nation's agriculture, an industry supplying implements of the appropriate size arose. The lesson here is not to seek adversity, but to recognize that meeting it can serve to advance society—a timely reminder to the United States in the 1970s!

• Many of the chapters have already demonstrated that "Japan, Inc." is a meaningless simplification or at best a misleading caricature. Nevertheless, relations between the public and private sectors in Japan are unusual by U.S. standards, and may contain the seeds of at least three alternative approaches to these relations for the United States and other countries.

First, no one can study the Japanese experience without being struck by the close cooperation between government and business—especially big business. Major economic decisions are made only after extensive discussions, negotiations, and compromises in what is a formally and informally institutionalized, highly effective process. Of course, this does not mean that business and government always agree, that the government ignores other constituencies, or that the favoring of big business has not entailed certain social costs. On balance, however, the alliance was supportive of national economic growth. Great efficiency was achieved in marshaling and using economic information as private and government efforts complemented rather than duplicated one another and economies of scale obtained. Through this cooperation, the planning horizon of both the government and private business was lengthened, to the benefit of economic performance. Some governmental agencies—for example, the Economic Planning Agency, the MITI, and the Japan External Trade Organization—achieved particularly high professional standards in providing services for business, just as business reinforced and strengthened the agencies. The lesson appears to be indirect: we should earnestly consider the advantages of negotiation and compromise in establishing the social compact, rather than relying so heavily on confrontation and adversary approaches to social decisions.

Second, the Japanese government has demonstrated an impressive capacity to maintain a *relatively* clear hierarchy of goals. One result is that both the government and the private sector have directed their efforts to solving the most serious problems facing the economy, particularly in the area of industrial growth and exports. While single-minded pursuit of these goals for two decades aggravated pollution and inflation, the evidence, especially in the early 1970s, indicates that the overall capacity of the Japanese government for economic goalsetting and implementation is still to be envied. Trade liberalization has progressed remarkably, the country has adjusted to two sizable currency revaluations, and the excessive rate of inflation seems to have been curbed. What message this sends to Americans is unclear, except that once again it reminds us to be aware of our own inadequacies.

Third, the Japanese experience has also shown the value and dynamism of private enterprise when it is encouraged by government. With the risks of unbridled competition and the imperfections of markets long recognized, no society seems willing to endorse free enterprise without qualification. However, in postwar Japan private enterprise did succeed in revolutionizing the living standards of the population; and to some extent the government— especially the bureaucracy—exercised a useful countervailing role *without* stifling private initiative. Japanese bureaucrats had a soft touch that their American counterparts might well emulate.

• Finally, the Japanese have shown a tremendous willingness to learn from the experience of foreigners. They are quick to adopt new ideas from abroad and integrate them into the domestic economy. This procedure saves resources that would otherwise have to be devoted to original development, and permits concentration on improvement and perfection of ideas. Since the Meiji period, the Japanese have seen that it is easier to follow than to lead. The risks are the possible undervaluing of originality, but as yet this does not appear to be a serious problem. Can the United States learn anything from this phenomenon? Since World War II, the United States has been the leader in nearly the entire economic sphere and experience elsewhere has seemed of small interest. Compared to the Japanese, we have become rather insular, secure in the belief that our own practices are the best, or at any rate uniquely suited to our own situation. This posture may well turn out to be a poor one for the last quarter of this century. Many practices in other countries—in labor relations, technology, health care, education, social welfare, and other spheres—are worth our study and, where appropriate, imitation. In the future, leadership is likely to be shared by many countries, each at the frontier in some particular set of activities. In such a world the capacity to learn from others, which the Japanese have so strikingly demonstrated, will be especially useful for Americans—indeed, for all peoples.

Index of Names

Abegglen, James C., 49n, 468n, 469n, 479n, 512n, 513n, 514n, 554n, 640, 659n, 756n, 798n, 862, 863, 866, 877, 883
Ackley, Gardner, 67n, 116n, 123, 174n, 245n, 256, 319n, 365n, 766n, 900
Adams, T. F. M., 278n, 493n
Adams, William J., 560n
Ahluwalia, Montek S., 369n
Aikawa, Gisuke, 776
Akabane, Takao, 239n
Alterman, Jack, 67n
Amagi, Isao, 815n
Amano, Akihiro, 435, 437
Arai, Ikao, 815n
Archer, Stephen H., 510n
Ariizumi, Toru, 635n
Ariyoshi, Yoshiya, 795n
Astin, Alexander W., 824n
Austin, Lewis, 855, 856n

Baba, Keinosuke, 177n
Baba, Masao, 233n, 766n
Bain, Joe S., 473n, 505
Ballon, Robert J., 482n
Barnas, Michael J., 855n
Barrett, M. Edgar, 304n
Beardsley, Richard K., 829n, 838n, 850n
Bellah, Robert, 890n
Bell, Daniel, 815n, 894
Ben-David, Joseph, 822n
Benedict, Ruth, 816, 818, 848, 849, 850, 862
Bennett, John W., 29n, 890n
Bereday, George Z. F., 841n, 843n
Bergson, Abram, 70
Bernstein, Irving, 640
Bhagwati, Jagdish N., 399n
Bieda, Ken, 799n
Bird, Richard M., 319n
Birnbaum, Henry, 576n, 577n, 822n, 828n, 830n

Bisson, T. A., 462n, 495n
Blumenthal, Tuvia, 258n, 401n, 478n, 603, 604, 858n
Bronfenbrenner, Martin, 180n, 321n, 332n

Campbell, John C., 767n, 787n, 788n, 792n
Caudill, William A., 849n, 851, 852, 853n
Caves, Richard E., 197n, 297n, 399n, 400, 402n, 464n, 481n, 496n, 774, 802n, 805, 810, 901
Chenery, Hollis, 369n, 914n
Chinoy, Eli, 886
Chūbachi, Masao, 40n
Chung, William K., 15, 83n, 90n, 811, 902, 910n
Clark, Colin, 681n, 686n
Clark, Rodney, 616n, 635n, 642n, 663n, 867, 868, 869, 873, 874, 878, 879, 885, 888, 893
Cohen, Jerome B., 59n, 445n
Cohen, Jerry S., 48n
Cole, Allan B., 632n
Cole, Robert E., 589n, 613n, 618n, 623n, 635n, 642n, 650, 651n, 652, 663, 865n, 867, 868, 871, 872, 876, 880, 883n, 885, 886, 892n, 893
Comber, L. C., 835n, 842n, 847n
Cook, Alice H., 629n, 634n, 653n
Crowley, James B., 6n, 72n
Cummings, William K., 577n, 578n, 815n, 822n, 827, 828n, 830, 831n, 832, 840, 843, 844n, 847, 855n
Curtis, Gerald L., 50n, 763n, 768n, 769n, 774n, 776n, 777n

Daly, D. J., 70
Davis, Kingsley, 667n
Denison, Edward F., 15, 83n, 89n, 90n, 91n, 811, 902, 910n
DeVos, George, 42n, 837n, 844, 849n, 851, 852
d. Leeuw, Frank, 713n

General Index

931

DATE DUE